THE CORE TEAM

THE ECONOMY

ECONOMICS FOR A CHANGING WORLD

THE CORE TEAM

THE ECONOMY

OXFORD
UNIVERSITY PRESS

OXFORD

UNIVERSITY PRESS

Great Clarendon Street, Oxford, OX2 6DP,
United Kingdom

Oxford University Press is a department of the University of Oxford.
It furthers the University's objective of excellence in research, scholarship,
and education by publishing worldwide. Oxford is a registered trade mark of
Oxford University Press in the UK and in certain other countries

© CORE Economics Education 2017

Published in the United States of America by Oxford University Press
198 Madison Avenue, New York, NY 10016, United States of America

British Library Cataloguing in Publication Data
Data available

Library of Congress Control Number: 2017952076

ISBN (print) 978-0-19-881024-7
ISBN (ebook) 978-1-5272-1209-1

Design and layout by Fire and Lion
Printed in Great Britain by Ashford Colour Press Ltd, Gosport, Hampshire

CONTENTS

MACRO
202

MACRO
202

PREFACE

In 2014, when we published the first beta of *The Economy* online, Camila Cea provided a preface. At the time, she was a recent economics graduate, but already a veteran of a successful protest movement in Chile that was advocating policies to advance economic justice. She and her fellow students at the University of Chile had been shocked to discover their economics courses addressed none of their concerns about the problems of Chile's economy. They demanded changes in the curriculum. The director of the School of Economics and Business at the time, Oscar Landerretche, responded to their demands. Camila and Oscar are both now Trustees of CORE Economics Education.

Since then, courses based on CORE's text have been taught as the standard introduction to economics at University College London, Sciences Po (Paris), the Toulouse School of Economics, Azim Premji University (Bangalore), Humboldt University (Berlin), the Lahore University of Management Sciences and many other universities throughout the world. In July 2017, as we write this, 3,000 economics teachers from 89 countries have registered for access to our supplementary teaching materials.

Camila's perspective on The CORE Project at the beginning of our journey captures the motivation that continues to inspire us. She wrote:

> We want to change the way economics is taught. Students and teachers tell us this is long overdue. When the *Financial Times* in the UK wrote about CORE in November 2013, it sparked an online debate about teaching and learning economics that attracted 1,214 posts in 48 hours. Students in economics all over the world were asking, just as I had asked a few years previously: 'Why has the

Camila Cea

> subject of economics become detached from our experience of real life?'
>
> Nataly Grisales, like me an economics student from Latin America, recently wrote about learning economics on her blog: 'Before I chose economics a professor mentioned that economics would give me a way to describe and predict human behaviour through mathematical tools. That possibility still seems fantastic to me. However, after semesters of study I had many mathematical tools, but all the people whose behaviour I wanted to study had disappeared from the scene.'
>
> Like Nataly, I remember asking myself if my economics classes would ever get around to

addressing the questions that motivated me to take up economics in the first place.

And that's why my colleagues in the CORE team have created this material. It has made me believe again that studying economics can help you to understand the economic challenges of the real world, and prepare you to confront them.

Please join us.

Camila and Nataly did not get the best that economics has to offer. CORE's mission is to introduce students to what economists do now, and what we know. Today, economics is an empirical subject that uses models to make sense of data. These models guide government, business, and many other organizations on the trade-offs they face in designing policies.

Economics can provide tools, concepts and ways to understand the world that address the challenges that drive students like Nataly and Camila to the subject. Sadly, they are often not a big part of the courses that thousands of students take.

In the four years that The CORE Project has been running we have tried an experiment in classrooms around the world. We ask students: 'What is the most pressing problem that economists should address?' The word cloud below shows the response that students at Humboldt University gave to us on the first day of their first class in economics. The size of the word is proportional to the frequency with which they mentioned the word or phrase.

Word clouds from students in Sydney and Bogota are barely distinguishable from this one (you can see them on our website at www.core-econ.org). Even more remarkable, when in 2016 we asked new recruits—mostly but not entirely recent economics

graduates—at the Bank of England, and then professional economists and other staff at the New Zealand Treasury and Reserve Bank, both responded the same way: inequality was the most common word in their minds.

Local and global social problems are always on the minds of new students. In France, when we tried the same experiment, unemployment showed up more often. Climate change and environmental problems, automation, and financial instability were frequently mentioned around the world.

Our focus on these real-world problems explains why we called this book *The Economy* rather than *Economics*, which is the standard title for introductory texts. The economy is something in the real world. It governs how we interact with each other and with our natural environments in producing the goods and services on which we live. In contrast, economics is a way of understanding that economy, based on facts, concepts and models.

The Economy is a course in economics. Throughout, we start with a question or a problem about the economy—why the advent of capitalism is associated with a sharp increase in average living standards, for example—and then teach the tools of economics that contribute to an answer.

For each question, the material is in the same sequence. We begin with a historical or current problem, even if it is a complex one, and then we use models to illuminate it. CORE's pedagogy thus flips the convention in economics texts on its head. Traditionally, the models are derived first. Perhaps the introduction to the models includes a simple application such as shopping, and a promise that the model will be applied to economic problems in the real

The most pressing problems that economists should address, according to students at Humboldt University.

world either later in the course, or more likely in later courses.

Because CORE starts with big problems and questions from history and current affairs, the models and explanations we use need to take account of real-world phenomena. For example, actors never have complete information about everything relevant to the decisions they are making, motives other than self-interest are also important, and the exercise of power in strategic behaviour often has to be part of the explanation for the outcome we see.

Recent advances in economics have given us the tools to do this. And because we apply economic models to important, complex and difficult problems, CORE students learn immediately both the insights gained from modelling, and the unavoidable shortcomings of models.

A GLOBAL COMMITMENT

CORE is a truly global project in two ways. Its development spans the world, and it is open to anyone, anywhere, who wants to use it.

Much of our design and interactive features were initiated in Bangalore. The open-source platform for our text and online materials was produced in Cape Town. The printed book version of the material is published by Oxford University Press. Translations and localizations of *The Economy* are being prepared in French, Italian, Farsi, Spanish, Hindi, Kannada, Russian, and other languages. CORE is now also developing materials for secondary school courses.

Our online materials use a Creative Commons license that allows for non-commercial free use throughout the world. Material has been contributed, edited and reviewed by literally hundreds of scholars. The major authors of our units—all of them contributing their expertise for free—are from 13 countries.

We are a cooperative of knowledge producers committed to free digital access to *The Economy* to help build a global citizenry empowered by the language, facts and concepts of economics. We want as many people as possible to be able to reason about, and act to

address, the challenges of the twenty-first century economy, society, and biosphere. Our hope is that the best of economics can become part of how all citizens understand and seek to address the problems that we confront.

Currently economics has a reputation among the public, the media and potential students as an abstract subject that is unengaged with the real world. But for most of its history, economics has been about understanding and changing the way the world works, and we want to continue that tradition. Early economists—the Mercantilists in the sixteenth and seventeenth centuries, for example, or the Physiocrats in the years leading up to the French Revolution—were advisors to the rulers of their time. The same is true of important precursors of economics such as Ibn Khaldun in the fourteenth century. Today, macroeconomic policy-makers, private sector economists who create platforms for the online economy, economic development advisors, and think-tank experts continue this commitment to making the real world a better place. All economists can hope that their subject will help to alleviate poverty and secure the conditions in which people might flourish. This is both the most inspiring calling and the greatest challenge of the discipline.

If you are a student or an instructor, and you are curious about our approach to economics, and its inspiration in recent developments in the discipline, you can find more in the article called 'Looking forward to economics after CORE', that you will find at the end of the book.

The launch of our completed online text, and the publication of the same material as a printed book in a partnership with Oxford University Press, are two satisfying milestones for us. But they are just the beginning. CORE is not just a book or a course. It is a growing global community of teachers and learners, and we welcome your curiosity, comments, suggestions and improvements at www.core-econ.org.

As Camila said four years ago: join us!

The CORE team
July 2017

A NOTE TO INSTRUCTORS

The many ways to teach and learn from *The Economy*

The Economy has been classroom-tested in a variety of settings ranging from secondary schools to postgraduate courses. You can find out more about the many uses of the CORE material at www.core-econ.org.

STRUCTURED FOR FLEXIBILITY
Several features make our text particularly flexible and adaptable.

Capstone units
Units 17 to 22 can be taught as standalone units at the end of a course, allowing a schedule that devotes additional time to topics of special student interest or instructor expertise. The topics of the capstone units have been addressed in earlier passages of the text, in most cases beginning with Unit 1. The capstone units make use of conceptual and empirical tools that have been developed in earlier units, so although they are modular with respect to each other, they cannot be taught unless the earlier material has been covered.

Cumulative learning of basic concepts
Units 1 to 16 provide cumulative learning of concepts and tools.

Colour-coded themes
The topics of the capstone units appear throughout the entire 22 units so that instructors wishing to focus on the topics of one or more of the capstone topics can easily identify from the table of contents the sections that will be of special relevance to their students.

THEMES AND CAPSTONE UNITS
- 17: History, instability, and growth
- 18: Global economy
- 19: Inequality
- 20: Environment
- 21: Innovation
- 22: Politics and policy

UNDERSTANDING HOW CORE'S *THE ECONOMY* IS DIFFERENT
The text focuses throughout on evidence on the economy, from around the world, and from history. It is motivated by questions—how can we explain what we see? The method is to ask interesting questions first and then to introduce models that help to answer them. Standard tools such as constrained optimization are taught by showing how they give insight into real-world problems. Economics as a discipline is set in a social, political, and ethical context in which institutions matter.

CORE teaches students to be economists:

- Start with a question, and look at the evidence.
- Build a model that helps you understand what you see.
- Critically evaluate the model: does it provide insight into the question, and explain the evidence?

Figure A provides a way to understand the structure of the text by comparing it with standard principles textbooks.

Looking more closely at the eight parts in the right hand side of Figure A, we summarize the central concepts in each unit.

- *The economy*
  Unit 1 *The big picture* about how the global economy came to look as it does today.
- *Economic decision making (a single actor)*
  Unit 2 *Choosing a technology, given factor prices:* Doing the best you can: incentives, innovation rents. Equilibrium.
  Unit 3 *Working hours:* Doing the best you can within a feasible set: indifference curves, feasible frontier, MRS = MRT
- *Economic relationships and interactions*
  Unit 4 *Strategic interactions:* Doing the best you can, given what others do: social dilemmas, self-interest, social interest, altruism, public goods, external effects
  Unit 5 *Bilateral trade:* Doing the best you can, given what others do, and given the rules of the game: institutions, bargaining power, Pareto efficiency, fairness
  Unit 6 *Employment relationship:* Doing the best you can, given what others do and the rules of the game, when contracts are incomplete
- *Markets*
  Unit 7 *Firm producing a differentiated good, setting the price:* Profit maximization (demand plus isoprofit curves); costs, competition, market failure
  Unit 8 *Supply and demand; price-taking and competitive markets:* Prices as messages. Competitive equilibrium; price-taking firms and Pareto efficiency.
  Unit 9 *Labour market:* From wage-setting (Unit 6) and price-setting (Unit 7) to the whole economy
  Unit 10 *Credit market:* Consumption smoothing; borrowing and lending; incomplete contracts; money and banks
- *Market dynamics, how markets work, or may not work*
  Unit 11 *Rent-seeking, price-setting, and market dynamics:* Rents and the achievement of short- and long-run equilibrium. Prices as messages. Bubbles. Non-clearing markets.
  Unit 12 *Markets, efficiency, and public policy:* Property rights, incomplete contracts, externalities
- *The aggregate economy in the short and medium run*
  Unit 13 *Economic fluctuations and aggregate demand:* Consumption-smoothing and its limits, investment volatility as a coordination problem, measuring the aggregate economy
  Unit 14 *Fiscal policy and employment:* Components of aggregate demand, multiplier, demand shocks, government finance, fiscal policy
  Unit 15 *Monetary policy, unemployment, and inflation:* Phillips curve, expectations and supply shocks, inflation targeting, transmission mechanisms, including exchange rate
- *The aggregate economy in the long run*
  Unit 16 *Technological change and employment:* Aggregate production function and productivity growth. Job destruction and creation. Institutions and comparative economic performance.
- *CORE's capstone units: topic-focused applications of models*
  Unit 17 *One hundred years of economic history from*

Standard principles text	CORE's *The Economy*
Part 1. What is economics?	Unit 1. The big questions about the economy
Part 2. Supply and demand	Units 2–3. Economic decision making
Part 3. The production decision and factor markets	Units 4–6. Economic relationships and interactions
Part 4. Beyond perfect competition	Units 7–10. Markets
Part 5. Microeconomics and public policy	Units 11–12. Market dynamics, how markets work and don't work
Part 6. Long-run growth	Units 13–15. The aggregate economy in the short and medium run
Part 7. Short-run fluctuations and stabilization policy	Unit 16. The aggregate economy in the long run
Part 8. Macroeconomic applications	Capstone units 17–22

Figure A Standard principles textbooks compared with *The Economy*.

the Great Depression to the global financial crisis
Unit 18 *Globalization—trade, migration and investment*
Unit 19 *Inequality*
Unit 20 *Environmental sustainability and collapse*
Unit 21 *Innovation, intellectual property, and the networked economy*
Unit 22 *Politics, economics, and public policy*

OPTIONS FOR COURSE STRUCTURE

This book has been the basis of many different types of course. On our website, you can find case studies from instructors who have adapted *The Economy* to specific needs.

A first course (one year)

The Economy can be taught as a year-long first course in economics, as has been done with earlier versions of this material at University College London (UCL), Birkbeck, University of London, Azim Premji University (Bangalore), and elsewhere. A typical year-long course would teach the first 16 units and conclude with anything from one to all of the capstone units (devoting two or more weeks to each, if time allows). Spending three or four weeks on one of the capstones is an opportunity to bring in additional materials, student research or reports.

An introduction to microeconomics (one semester)

The Toulouse School of Economics and the Lahore University of Management Sciences use *The Economy* as its introduction to microeconomics. This course might teach Unit 1 and Units 3 to 12, with the remaining weeks of the course devoted to a combination of Unit 2 with capstone Unit 21, or capstone Units 17 to 20.

An introduction to macroeconomics (one semester)

A one-semester introduction to macroeconomics based on the CORE text has been taught at Sciences Po, Paris and Middlebury College, Vermont, US. A possible configuration of such a course is Units 1 and 2; review of feasible set and indifference curves from Unit 3; 6 (wage-setting); 7 (price-setting); 9 and 10, and 13 to 17, plus a selection of capstone Units 18–22, possibly including the material on disequilibrium dynamics from Unit 11.

Introduction to economics (one semester)

A course along these lines has been taught at Humboldt University (Berlin), University of Sydney, and University of Bristol. Providing the basic concepts of the discipline in a single semester is a challenge but it can be done (in 14 weeks) using Units 1, 3 to 10, plus 12 to 16, ending the course with Unit 17 (an application of macroeconomics) or one of the other capstone units, stressing microeconomic applications.

Masters courses in public policy

This text has been used at the School of International and Public Affairs at Columbia University, the School of Public Policy at the Central European University, and the Sol Price School of Public Policy at the University of Southern California, among others. The courses have implemented variants of the above course structures, making use of the depth of coverage of policy problems in the capstone units.

Secondary school courses

Schools including St Paul's School, London and Melville Senior High School, Western Australia have used parts of the text for extension activities for upper-level students.

OPTIONS FOR PEDAGOGY

The Economy also facilitates a range of teaching approaches, in line with recent developments in pedagogic methods.

Traditional teaching

The material can be taught in a traditional way, with the substantive theory in each unit delivered through lectures, and reinforced and elaborated in classes with problems and exercises.

Classroom games and experiments

The empirical emphasis of much of the material in *The Economy*, and the extensive embedding of game theory, encourage a more active approach to student learning through the use of classroom games and experiments, and problem-oriented learning using real data. Datasets and ideas for classroom games are provided on the Instructors' part of our website, to help teachers incorporate these methods in their teaching.

Flipping the classroom

Active classroom learning can be encouraged by the selective use of 'flipped' or 'inverted' approaches, in which traditional lectures are replaced by interactive sessions based on problems, games or discussions. In these teaching approaches, students are assigned material (readings, quizzes, or videos, for example) before class, which is then used as a basis for discussion and activity in the classes. Classroom polling software (or student response systems) can be used to test students' engagement with the assigned tasks through quizzes, and games and data work can then be used to deepen understanding and reinforce this understanding. *The Economy* lends itself well to this approach, because units progress from real case studies and narratives to the selection and use of appropriate theoretical tools for understanding these case studies, and then to the detailed underlying theory.

One approach to flipping the classroom is to encourage students to read the narratives and historical case studies outside class, and to think about the eco-nomic tools that can help explain these cases. The detailed use and understanding of the theory can then be developed within the class by the use of problem-oriented data work and classroom games. Experience in many classrooms with the beta versions of *The Economy* suggests that students engage more readily in pre-class reading of the interactive ebook than in previous introductory courses. The habit of reading ahead of class can be kick-started with a multimedia group project used in several CORE pilot universities (http://tinyco.re/6576000).

PRODUCING *THE ECONOMY*

The Economy was produced by a group of authors—the CORE team—together with teaching and learning experts, researchers, reviewers, instructors, students in the pilot universities, and editors, designers, and web developers.

THE CORE TEAM
The contents were produced by the CORE team of authors coordinated by Samuel Bowles, Wendy Carlin and Margaret Stevens; primary writers of each unit are listed below.

Unit 1 Samuel Bowles, Wendy Carlin, Arjun Jayadev, Margaret Stevens; **Unit 2** Kevin O'Rourke, Samuel Bowles, Wendy Carlin, Margaret Stevens; **Unit 3** Margaret Stevens, Samuel Bowles, Robin Naylor, David Hope; **Unit 4** Antonio Cabrales, Daniel Hojman, Samuel Bowles, Wendy Carlin, Margaret Stevens; **Unit 5** Samuel Bowles, Wendy Carlin, Margaret Stevens; **Unit 6** Samuel Bowles, Wendy Carlin, Margaret Stevens; **Unit 7** Margaret Stevens, Samuel Bowles, Wendy Carlin; **Unit 8** Margaret Stevens, Samuel Bowles, Wendy Carlin; **Unit 9** Samuel Bowles, Wendy Carlin, Margaret Stevens; **Unit 10** Wendy Carlin, Paul Segal, Samuel Bowles; **Unit 11** Rajiv Sethi, Samuel Bowles, Wendy Carlin, Margaret Stevens; **Unit 12** Margaret Stevens, Samuel Bowles, Rajiv Sethi; **Unit 13** Yann Algan, Wendy Carlin, Paul Segal; **Unit 14** Yann Algan, Wendy Carlin, Paul Segal; **Unit 15** Yann Algan, Wendy Carlin, Paul Segal; **Unit 16** Yann Algan, Wendy Carlin, Samuel Bowles, Paul Segal; **Unit 17** Wendy Carlin, Samuel Bowles, Paul Segal; **Unit 18** Kevin O'Rourke, Samuel Bowles, Wendy Carlin, David Hope, Paul Segal; **Unit 19** Suresh Naidu, Samuel Bowles, Wendy Carlin, Paul Segal; **Unit 20** Juan Camilo Cárdenas, Marion Dumas, Cameron Hepburn, Begüm Özkaynak, Alexander Teytelboym, Samuel Bowles, Wendy Carlin; **Unit 21** Diane Coyle, Georg von Graevenitz, Samuel Bowles, Wendy Carlin; **Unit 22** Suresh Naidu, Samuel Bowles, Wendy Carlin, Timothy Besley. The Leibniz supplements were provided by Malcolm Pemberton and Nicholas Rau. Rajiv Sethi is editor of CORE's 'Great economists' features.

THE TEACHING AND LEARNING COMMITTEE
Yann Algan (Sciences Po, Paris), Alvin Birdi (Chair of CORE's Teaching and Learning Committee, University of Bristol), Parama Chaudhury (UCL), Kenjiro Hori (Birkbeck University of London), Peter Howells (University of the West of England), Arjun Jayadev (Azim Premji University), Ashley Lait (The Economics Network), Christian Spielmann (UCL), Margaret Stevens (University of Oxford), Andrew Sykes (St Paul's School, London).

CORE RESEARCHERS AND INTERNS
Maria Balgova (University of Oxford), Jack Blundell (Stanford University and University of Oxford), Clemens Blab (UCL), Stefan Gitman (UCL), David Goll (UCL), Zoe Helding (University of Oxford), Stanislas Lalanne (University of Oxford), Becky McCann (University of Oxford), Ali Merali (UCL), Victoria Monro (UCL), Adam Nadzri (UCL), Karl Overdick (UCL), Valeria Rueda (University of Oxford), Alvaro Salamanca (University of Oxford), Shiva Sethi (University of North Carolina), Shreya Singh (UCL).

Yann Algan
Sciences Po, Paris

Timothy Besley
LSE

Samuel Bowles
Santa Fe Institute

Antonio Cabrales
UCL

Juan Camilo Cárdenas
Universidad de los Andes

Wendy Carlin
UCL

Diane Coyle
University of Manchester

Marion Dumas
Santa Fe Institute; LSE

Cameron Hepburn
University of Oxford

Daniel Hojman
University of Chile; Harvard University

David Hope
King's College London

Arjun Jayadev
Azim Premji University

Suresh Naidu
Columbia University

Robin Naylor
University of Warwick

Kevin O'Rourke
University of Oxford

Begüm Özkaynak
Boğaziçi University

Malcolm Pemberton
UCL

Nicholas Rau
UCL

Paul Segal
King's College London

Rajiv Sethi
Barnard College, Columbia University

Margaret Stevens
University of Oxford

Alexander Teytelboym
University of Oxford

Georg von Graevenitz
Queen Mary University of London

PRODUCTION TEAM FOR
THE ECONOMY 1.0
Luka Crnjakovic (project manager), Aashika Doshi (executive assistant), Davide Melcangi (economist), Tim Phillips (editor), Eileen Tipoe (economist)
Editorial, design and software-development: Arthur Attwell, Steve Barnett, Jennifer Jacobs, David Le Page, Karen Lilje, Craig Mason-Jones, Dione Mentis, Christina Tromp, Derika van Biljon

CORE 'ECONOMIST IN ACTION' VIDEOS
Anat Admati (Stanford University), Robert Allen (University of Oxford), Juan Camilo Cardenas (Universidad de los Andes), Arin Dube (University of Massachusetts Amherst), Esther Duflo (MIT), Barry Eichengreen (University of California Berkeley), Richard Freeman (Harvard University), Kathryn Graddy (Brandeis University), James Heckman (University of Chicago), Petra Moser (New York University), Suresh Naidu (Columbia

University), Thomas Piketty (Paris School of Economics), Dani Rodrik (Harvard University), Alvin Roth (Stanford University), F. M. Scherer (Harvard University), Juliet Schor (Boston College), John Van Reenen (MIT), Joseph Stiglitz (Columbia University). Directed by Bob Denham (Econ Films)

CONTRIBUTORS

Philippe Aghion, Manuel Agosin, Karishma Ajmera, David Alary, Philippe Alby, Gerhard Altmann, Alberto Andrade, Simon Angus, Hannes Ansorg, Rhys Ap Gwilym, Belinda Archibong, Janine Aron, the late Kenneth Arrow, the late Tony Atkinson, Orazio Attanasio, Rob Axtell, Peter Backus, Dani Ball, Faisal Bari, Abigail Barr, Kaushik Basu, Ralf Becker, Wilfred Beckerman, Anurag Behar, Eric Beinhocker, Alan Bennett, Richard Berg, Christoph Berger, Erik Berglof, V. Bhaskar, Rhian Bilclough, Neal Bobba, Olivier Blanchard, Jo Blanden, Nick Bloom, Richard Blundell, Eric Bottorff, Danielle Boudville, Sinéad Boultwood, Clara Bowyer, James Boyce, Andrei Bremzen, Stephen Broadberry, Clair Brown, Claudia Buch, Michael Burda, Gabriel Burdin, Aisha Burke, Esther Carlin, Sarah Caro, Andrea Carvallo, Jennifer Case, John Cassidy, Allan Castro, Camila Cea, Oscar Cervantes, Jagjit Chadha, Kah Kit Chan, Bruce Chapman, Axelle Charpentier, Ali Cheema, Syngjoo Choi, Adam Cockburn, Mihai Codreanu, Maeve Cohen, Chris Colvin, Ed Conway, Ian Corrick, Nicolas Courdacier, Nicholas Crafts, Kenneth Creamer, Martin Cripps, Edward Crutchley, Martha Curtis, Reza Daniels, Massimo D'Antoni, Richard Davies, Rahul De, David de Meza, Simon DeDeo, Marc Defosse, Richard Dietz, Andrew Dilnot, Ngan Dinh, Edgaras Dockus, Manfred Doll, Michael Dorsch, Peter Dougherty, Mirco Draca, Arnaud Dyevre, Ben Dyson, Joe Earle, Fabian Eckert, The Economics Network, Pinar Ertor, Husnain Fateh, Rana Fayez, Raphael Fischer, Stuart Foster, Matthew Furnell, David Garber, Nicolas Garrido, Maximilian Gerstenkorn, Bunt Ghosh, Abigail Gibson, Daniele Girardi, Jonathan Glyn, Ian Goldin, Christian Gollier, Mariusz Górski, Andrew Graham, Liam Graham, John Greenwood, Joe Grice, Arthur Grimes, Florian Grosset, Caterina Guidi, Marco Gundermann, Bishnupriya Gupta, Sergei Guriev, Andrew Gurney, Andrew Haldane, Simon Halliday, Gill Hammond, Emily Hanchett, Matthew Harding, Tim Harford, Colm Harmon, Pippa Harries, Roby Harrington, Ben Hartridge, Jerry Hausman, Teresa Healy, David Hendry, Frederic Henwood, Josh Hillman, William Hines, Carinna Hockham, Richard Holcroft, Sam Huby, Jimena Hurtado, Will Hutton, Zoulfikar Issop, David James, Cloda Jenkins, Colin Jennings, Sajaad Jetha, Rob Johnson, Noah Johnson, Anatole

Kaletsky, Girol Karacaoglu, Alexei Karas, John Kay, Jeong Hoon Keem, Lyyla Khalid, Bilal Khan, Julie Kilcoyne, Alan Kirman, Paul Klemperer, Amairisa Kouki, Pradeep Kumar, Oscar Landerretche, Philip Lane, Manfred Laubichler, Samuel Law, Jonathan Leape, Valerie Lechene, Howon Lee, Margaret Meyer, Murray Leibbrandt, Rob Levy, Peter Lindert, Bao Linh Le, Jose Lobo, Philipp Lohan, Deborah Mabbett, Stephen Machin, Rod Maddock, Lisa Magnani, Kamil Majczak, Alan Manning, Cecile Markarian, Jaime Marshall, Peter Matthews, Patrick McKenna, John McLaughlin, Hugh McLean, Rashid Memon, Atif Mian, Tom Michl, Branko Milanovic, Jennifer Miller, Catherine Mole, Bruno Momont, Alejandro Moyano, John Muellbauer, Anand Murugesan, Houda Nait El Barj, Venu Narayan, Andy Norman, Paul Novosad, Thomas O'Sullivan, Martha Olney, Jeremy Oppenheim, Andrew Oswald, Emily Pal, Stefania Paredes Fuentes, Jung Hoon Park, Marii Paskov, Bhavin Patel, Sean Payne, PEPS-Economie, Jonathan Pincus, Ashby Plant, Laura Povoledo, Ian Preston, Stefan Pricopie, Tim Prizeman, Stefan Prochnow, Louis Putterman, John Raiss, Ranjita Rajan, Wolfgang Reinicke, Derek Rice, Rebecca Riley, Federico Rocchi, Max Roser, Andy Ross, Alessandra Rossi, Jannie Rossouw, Robert Rowthorn, Phil Ruder, Tripti Rungta, Steve Russell, Michael Rybarczyk, Cristina Santos, Mark Schaffer, Philipp Schmidt, Monika Schnitzer, Paul Seabright, Anil Shamdasani, Eddie Shore, Gordon Shukwit, Jason Shure, Adrian Slack, Beatrice Smith, Stephen Smith, Neil Smith, Dennis Snower, Robert Solow, Daniel Sonnenstuhl, George Soros, David Soskice, Teresa Steininger, Nicholas Stern, Lucy Stewart, Joseph Stiglitz, Bob Sutcliffe, Peter Temin, Stefan Thewissen, Caroline Thomas, Sarah Thomas, Leith Thompson, Keith Thomson, Ahmet Tonak, Kautuk Trivedi, David Tuckett, Adair Turner, Burak Unveren, Romesh Vaitilingam, Imran Valodia, Philippe Van Parijs, Samo Varsik, Julia Veglesi, Andres Velasco, Paul Vertier, Nirusha Vigi, Charles Vincent, David Vines, Snjezana Voloscuk, Victoria Waldersee, Ian Walker, Danielle Walker Palmour, James Watson, Christopher Webb, Jorgen Weibull, Stephen Whelan, Ryan Wilson, Glenn Withers, Martin Wittenberg, Martin Wolf, Nikolaus Wolf, Cornelia Woll, Renbin Woo, Meredith Woo, Elisabeth Wood, Chris Wood, Ingrid Woolard, Stephen Wright, Kiichiro Yagi, Peyton Young, Homa Zarghamee.

The CORE team wishes to thank Jon Crowe, John Challice, Amber Stone-Galilee and Jen Crawley of Oxford University Press for being part of this pioneering collaboration.

UNIT 1
THE CAPITALIST REVOLUTION

HOW CAPITALISM REVOLUTIONIZED THE WAY WE LIVE, AND HOW ECONOMICS ATTEMPTS TO UNDERSTAND THIS AND OTHER ECONOMIC SYSTEMS

THEMES AND CAPSTONE UNITS

- 17: History, instability, and growth
- 18: Global economy
- 19: Inequality
- 20: Environment
- 21: Innovation
- 22: Politics and policy

- Since the 1700s, increases in average living standards became a permanent feature of economic life in many countries.
- This was associated with the emergence of a new economic system called capitalism, in which private property, markets and firms play a major role.
- Under this new way of organizing the economy, advances in technology and specialization in products and tasks raised the amount that could be produced in a day's work.
- This process, which we call the capitalist revolution, has been accompanied by growing threats to our natural environment, and by unprecedented global economic inequalities.
- Economics is the study of how people interact with each other, and with the natural environment, in producing their livelihoods.

Define capitalist revolution

Define Economics

In the fourteenth century, the Moroccan scholar Ibn Battuta described Bengal in India as 'A country of great extent, and one in which rice is extremely abundant. Indeed, I have seen no region of the earth in which provisions are so plentiful.'

And he had seen much of the world, having travelled to China, west Africa, the Middle East and Europe. Three centuries later, the same sentiment was expressed by the seventeenth century French diamond merchant Jean Baptiste Tavernier who wrote of the country:

> Even in the smallest villages, rice, flour, butter, milk, beans and other vegetables, sugar and sweetmeats, dry and liquid, can be procured in abundance.

Jean Baptiste Tavernier, *Travels in India* (1676).

At the time of Ibn Battuta's travels, India was not richer than the other parts of the world. But India was not much poorer, either. An observer at the time would have noticed that people, on average, were better off in Italy, China and England than in Japan or India. But the vast differences between the rich and the poor, which the traveller would have noted wherever he went, were much more striking than these differences across regions. Rich and poor would often have different titles: in some places they would be feudal lords and serfs, in others royalty and their subjects, slave owners and slaves, or merchants and the sailors who transported their goods. Then—as now—your prospects depended on where your parents were on the economic ladder and whether you were male or female. The difference in the fourteenth century, compared with today, was that back then the part of the world in which you were born mattered much less.

Fast forward to today. The people of India are far better off than they were seven centuries ago if we think about their access to food, medical care, shelter and the necessities of life, but by world standards today most are poor.

Figure 1.1a tells some of the story. To compare living standards in each country, we use a measure called GDP per capita. People obtain their incomes by producing and selling goods and services. GDP (gross domestic product) is the total value of everything produced in a given period such as a year, so GDP per capita corresponds here to average annual income. GDP is also referred to as gross domestic income. In Figure 1.1a the height of each line is an estimate of average income at the date on the horizontal axis.

On average, people are six times better off in Britain than in India by this measure. Japanese people are as rich as the British, just as they were in the fourteenth century, but now Americans are even better off than the Japanese, and Norwegians are better off still.

Ibn Battuta (1304–1368) was a Moroccan traveller and merchant. His travels, which lasted 30 years, took him across north and west Africa, eastern Europe, the Middle East, south and central Asia and China.

Jutta Bolt and Jan Juiten van Zanden. 2013. 'The First Update of the Maddison Project Re-Estimating Growth Before 1820'. Maddison-Project Working Paper WP-4 (January). Stephen Broadberry. 2013. Accounting for the great divergence. 1 November. Conference Board, The. 2015. Total Economy Database.

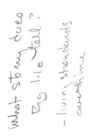

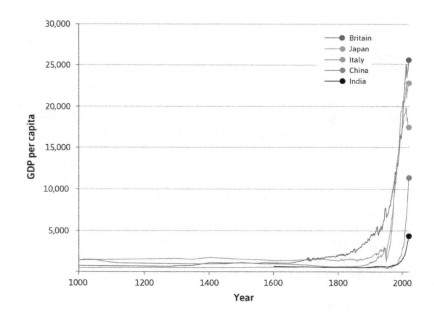

Figure 1.1a History's hockey stick: Gross domestic product per capita in five countries (1000–2015).

We can draw the graph in Figure 1.1a because of the work of Angus Maddison who dedicated his working life to finding the scarce data needed to make useful comparisons of how people lived across more than 1,000 years (his work is continuing in the Maddison Project). In this course you will see that data like this about regions of the world, and the people in it, is the starting point of all economics. In our video, the economists James Heckman and Thomas Piketty explain how collecting data has been fundamental to their work on inequality and the policies to reduce it.

1.1 INCOME INEQUALITY

A thousand years ago the world was flat, economically speaking. There were differences in income between the regions of the world; but as you can see from Figure 1.1a, the differences were small compared to what was to follow.

Nobody thinks the world is flat today, when it comes to income.

Figure 1.2 shows the distribution of income across and within countries. Countries are arranged according to GDP per capita from the poorest on the left of the diagram (Liberia), to the richest on the right (Singapore). The width of each country's bars represents its population.

For every country there are ten bars, corresponding to the ten deciles of income. The height of each bar is the average income of 10% of the population, ranging from the poorest 10% of people at the front of the diagram to the richest 10% at the back, measured in 2005 US dollars. Note that this doesn't mean 'the richest 10% of income earners'. It is the richest 10% of people, where each person in a household, including children, is assumed to have an equal share of the household's income.

The skyscrapers (the highest columns) at the back of the right-hand side of the figure represent the income of the richest 10% in the richest countries. The tallest skyscraper is the richest 10% of people in Singapore. In 2014, this exclusive group had an income per capita of more than $67,000. Norway, the country with the second highest GDP per capita, does not have a particularly tall skyscraper (it is hidden between the skyscrapers for Singapore and the third richest country, the US) because income is more evenly distributed in Norway than in some other rich countries.

The analysis in Figure 1.2 shows how the distribution of income has changed since 1980.

Two things are clear from the 2014 distribution. First, in every country, the rich have much more than the poor. A handy measure of inequality in a country is called the 90/10 ratio, which we define here as the average income of the richest 10% divided by the average income of the poorest 10%. It is more commonly defined as the income of the 90th percentile divided by that of the 10th percentile. Even in a relatively equal country such as Norway, the 90/10 ratio is 5.4; in the US it is 16 and in Botswana in southern Africa it is 145. Inequality within the very poorest countries is difficult to see in the graph, but it is definitely there: the 90/10 ratio is 22 in Nigeria, and 20 in India.

The second thing that jumps out from Figure 1.2 is the huge difference in income between countries. Average income in Norway is 19 times the average income in Nigeria. And the poorest 10% in Norway receive almost twice the income of the richest 10% in Nigeria.

Imagine the traveller Ibn Battuta's journey across regions of the world in the fourteenth century and think of how this would have looked in a

Maddison Project (data)

Thomas Piketty and James Heckman explain why data is fundamental to their work
http://tinyco.re/6056324

define: 90/10 ratio

GCIP 2015. Global Consumption and Income Project. Bob Sutcliffe designed the representation of global inequality in Figure 1.2. A first version was published in: Robert, B Sutcliffe. 2001. *100 Ways of Seeing an Unequal World.* London: Zed Books. See the interactive version of this graph on the Globalinc website (http://tinyco.re/7434364).

what story(s) does Fig 1.2 tell ?

· differences in distribution of income 'across nations' · differences within nations

Scale is doubling

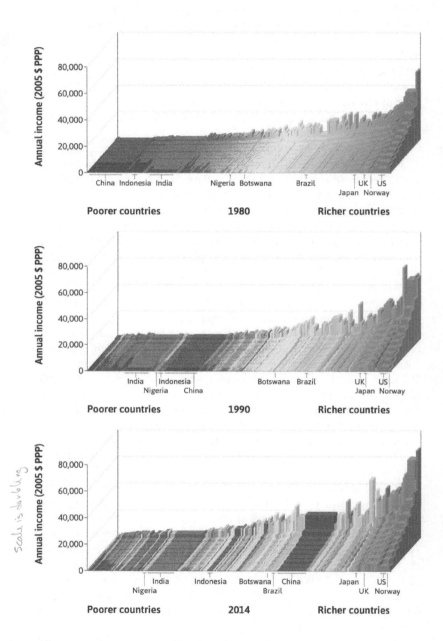

Figure 1.2 Countries are ranked by GDP per capita from left to right. For each country the heights of the bars show average income for deciles of the population, from the poorest 10% at the front to the richest 10% at the back. The width of the bar indicates the country's population.

diagram like Figure 1.2. He would of course notice that everywhere he went there were differences between the richest and poorest groups in the population of each region. He would report back that the differences in income between the countries of the world were relatively minor by comparison.

The vast differences in income between the countries of the world today take us back to Figure 1.1a, where we can begin to understand how this came about. The countries that took off economically before 1900—UK, Japan, Italy—are now rich. They (and countries like them) are in the skyscraper part of Figure 1.2. The countries that took off only recently, or not at all, are in the flatlands.

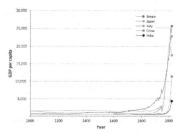

Countries that took off economically before 1900 (Figure 1.1a) are in the 'skyscraper' part of Figure 1.2.

EXERCISE 1.1 INEQUALITY IN THE FOURTEENTH CENTURY
What do you think a 'skyscraper' figure like Figure 1.2 (page 4) would have looked like at the time of Ibn Battuta (early to mid-fourteenth century)?

EXERCISE 1.2 WORKING WITH INCOME DATA
You can see the interactive graph (http://tinyco.re/7434364) and download the spreadsheet data (http://tinyco.re/7444763) that we used to create Figure 1.2. Choose five countries that you are interested in.

1. For each one calculate the 90/10 ratio in 1980, 1990 and 2014.
2. Describe the differences between countries and the changes over time that you find.
3. Can you think of any explanations for them?

Data Activity #1

our world in Data

1. The richest and poorest
In Singapore, the richest country on the furthest right, the average incomes of the richest and poorest 10% are $67,436 and $3,652 respectively. In Liberia, the furthest left, the corresponding incomes are $994 and $17.

2. Skyscrapers
The skyscraper bars in the back right of the figure are the richest 10% in some of the richest countries.

3. World income distribution in 1980
In 1980 the ranking of countries by GDP was different. The poorest countries, coloured darkest red, were Lesotho and China. The richest (darkest green) were Switzerland, Finland and then the US. At that time the skyscrapers were not as tall: the differences between the richest 10% and the rest of a country's population were not as pronounced.

4. World income distribution in 1990
You can see from the colours that some countries changed their ranking between 1980 and 1990. China (dark red) is now richer; Uganda, also red, is in the middle of the distribution amongst countries coloured yellow. Some taller skyscrapers have appeared: inequality increased in many countries during the 1980s.

5. World income distribution in 2014
By 2014, many countries have changed their ranking. China has grown rapidly since 1990. But the countries that were richest in 1980 (darkest green) are still near the top in 2014.

6. Inequality within countries has risen
Income distributions have become more unequal in many of the richer countries: some very tall skyscrapers have appeared. In the middle-income countries, too, there is a big step up at the back of the figure: the incomes of the richest 10% are now high relative to the rest of the population.

1.2 MEASURING INCOME AND LIVING STANDARDS

The estimate of living standards that we used in Figure 1.1a (GDP per capita) is a measure of the total goods and services produced in a country (called **gross domestic product**, or **GDP**), which is then divided by the country's population.

GDP measures the output of the economy in a given period, such as a year. Diane Coyle, an economist, says it 'adds up everything from nails to toothbrushes, tractors, shoes, haircuts, management consultancy, street cleaning, yoga teaching, plates, bandages, books, and the millions of other services and products in the economy'.

Adding up these millions of services and products requires finding some measure of how much a yoga class is worth compared to a toothbrush. Economists must first decide what should be included, but also how to give a value to each of these things. In practice, the easiest way to do this is by using their prices. When we do this, the value of GDP corresponds to the total income of everyone in the country.

Dividing by the population gives GDP per capita—the average income of people in a country. But is that the right way to measure their living standards, or wellbeing?

Disposable income

GDP per capita measures average income, but that is not the same as the **disposable income** of a typical person.

Disposable income is the amount of wages or salaries, profit, rent, interest and transfer payments from the government (such as unemployment or disability benefits) or from others (for example, gifts) received over a given period such as a year, minus any transfers the individual made to others (including taxes paid to the government). Disposable income is thought to be a good measure of living standards because it is the maximum amount of food, housing, clothing and other goods and services that the person can buy without having to borrow—that is, without going into debt or selling possessions.

Is our disposable income a good measure of our wellbeing?

Income is a major influence on wellbeing because it allows us to buy the goods and services that we need or enjoy. But it is insufficient, because many aspects of our wellbeing are not related to what we can buy.

For example, disposable income leaves out:

- The quality of our social and physical environment such as friendships and clean air.
- The amount of free time we have to relax or spend time with friends and family.
- Goods and services that we do not buy, such as healthcare and education, if they are provided by a government.
- Goods and services that are produced within the household, such as meals or childcare (predominantly provided by women).

Average disposable income and average wellbeing

When we're part of a group of people (a nation for example, or an ethnic group) is the average disposable income a good measure of how well off the group is? Consider a group in which each person initially has a disposable income of $5,000 a month, and imagine that, with no change in prices,

---

gross domestic product (GDP) A measure of the market value of the output of the economy in a given period.

Diane Coyle. 2014. *GDP: A Brief but Affectionate History*. Princeton, NJ: Princeton University Press.

Listen to Diane Coyle talking about the benefits and limitations of measuring GDP (http://tinyco.re/1216717).

disposable income Income available after paying taxes and receiving transfers from the government.

Jennifer Robison. 2011. 'Happiness Is Love – and $75,000' (http://tinyco.re/6313076). *Gallup Business Journal*. Updated 17 November 2011.

income has risen for every individual in the group. Then we would say that average or typical wellbeing had risen.

But now think about a different comparison. In a second group, the monthly disposable income of half the people is $10,000. The other half has just $500 to spend every month. The average income in the second group ($5,250) is higher than in the first (which was $5,000 before incomes rose). But would we say that the second group's wellbeing is greater than that of the first group, in which everyone has $5,000 a month? The additional income in the second group is unlikely to matter much to the rich people, but the poor half would think their poverty was a serious deprivation.

Absolute income matters for wellbeing, but we also know from research that people care about their relative position in the income distribution. They report lower wellbeing if they find they earn less than others in their group.

Since income distribution affects wellbeing, and because the same average income may result from very different distributions of income between rich and poor within a group, average income may fail to reflect how well off a group of people is by comparison to some other group.

Valuing government goods and services

GDP includes the goods and services produced by the government, such as schooling, national defence, and law enforcement. They contribute to wellbeing but are not included in disposable income. In this respect, GDP per capita is a better measure of living standards than disposable income.

But government services are difficult to value, even more so than services such as haircuts and yoga lessons. For goods and services that people buy we take their price as a rough measure of their value (if you valued the haircut less than its price, you would have just let your hair grow). But the goods and services produced by government are typically not sold, and the only measure of their value to us is how much it cost to produce them.

The gaps between what we mean by wellbeing, and what GDP per capita measures, should make us cautious about the literal use of GDP per capita to measure how well off people are.

But when the changes over time or differences among countries in this indicator are as great as those in Figure 1.1a (and in Figures 1.1b, 1.8 and 1.9 later in this unit), GDP per capita is undoubtedly telling us something about the differences in the availability of goods and services.

In the Einstein at the end of this section, we look in more detail at how GDP is calculated so that we can compare it through time and make comparisons between countries. (Many of the units have Einsteins. You don't have to use them, but they will show you how to calculate and under-stand many of the statistics that we employ.) Using these methods, we can use GDP per capita to unambiguously communicate ideas such as 'people in Japan are on average a lot richer than they were 200 years ago, and a lot richer than the people of India today.'

why might average income fail to reflect how well off a group of people is?

are well-being and GDP per capita equally good measures of how well off you are?

'Quality of Life Indicators— Measuring Quality of Life' (http://tinyco.re/8771109). Eurostat. Updated 5 November 2015.

*

Activity

EXERCISE 1.3 WHAT SHOULD WE MEASURE?
While campaigning for the US presidency on 18 March 1968, Senator Robert Kennedy gave a famous speech questioning 'the mere accumulation of material things' in American society, and why, among other things, air pollution, cigarette advertising and jails were counted when the US measured its living standards, but health, education or devotion to your country were not. He argued that 'it measures everything, in short, except that which makes life worthwhile.'

Read his speech in full (http://tinyco.re/9533853) or listen to a sound recording (http://tinyco.re/6486668) of it.

1. In the full text, which goods does he list as being included in a measure of GDP?
2. Do you think these should be included in such a measure, and why?
3. Which goods does he list in the full text as missing from the measure?
4. Do you think they should be included, and why?

QUESTION 1.1 CHOOSE THE CORRECT ANSWER(S)
What does UK GDP per capita measure?

☐ the total output of London's economy
☐ the average disposable income of a UK resident
☐ the total output of the UK residents, divided by the number of the residents
☐ the total output of the UK's economy, divided by the country's population

EINSTEIN

Comparing income at different times, and across different countries

The United Nations collects and publishes estimates of GDP from statistical agencies around the world. These estimates, along with those made by economic historians, allow us to construct charts like Figure 1.1a, comparing living standards across countries and at different time periods, and looking at whether the gap between rich and poor countries has narrowed or widened over time. Before we can make a statement like: 'On average, people in Italy are richer than people in China, but the gap between them is narrowing,' statisticians and economists must try to solve three problems:

- We need to separate the thing we want to measure—changes or differences in amounts of goods and services—from things that are not relevant to the comparison, especially changes or differences in the prices of the goods and services.
- When comparing output in one country at two points in time, it is necessary to take into account differences in prices between the two points in time.

- When comparing output between two countries at a point in time, it is necessary to take into account differences in prices between the two countries.

Notice how similar the last two statements are. Measuring changes in output at different points in time presents the same challenges as we face when we try to compare countries by measuring differences in their output at the same time. The challenge is to find a set of prices to use in this calculation that will allow us to identify changes or differences in outputs, without making the mistake of assuming that if the price of something rises in a country, but not in another, then the amount of output has increased in the country.

The starting point: Nominal GDP

When estimating the market value of output in the economy as a whole for a given period, such as a year, statisticians use the prices at which goods and services are sold in the market. By multiplying the quantities of the vast array of different goods and services by their prices, they can be converted into money, or nominal, terms. With everything in the common unit of nominal (or money) terms, they can be added together. Nominal GDP is written like this:

> **(price of a yoga lesson)× (number of yoga lessons)**
> **+ (price of a book) × (number of books) + …**
> **+ (price) × (quantity) for all other goods and services**

In general, we write that:

$$\textbf{nominal GDP} = \sum_i p_i q_i$$

Where p_i is the price of good i, q_i is the quantity of good i, and Σ indicates the sum of price times quantity for all the goods and services that we count.

Taking account of price changes over time: Real GDP

To gauge whether the economy is growing or shrinking, we need a measure of the quantity of goods and services purchased. This is called real GDP. If we compare the economy in two different years, and if all the quantities stay the same but the prices increase by, say, 2% from one year to the next, then nominal GDP rises by 2%, but real GDP is unchanged. The economy has not grown.

Because we cannot add together the number of computers, shoes, restaurant meals, flights, fork-lift trucks, and so on, it is not possible to measure real GDP directly. Instead, to get an estimate of real GDP, we have to begin with nominal GDP as defined above.

On the right-hand side of the equation for nominal GDP are the prices of each item of final sales multiplied by the quantity.

To track what is happening to real GDP, we begin by selecting a base year: for example, the year 2010. We then define real GDP using 2010 prices as equal to nominal GDP that year. The following year, nominal GDP for 2011 is calculated as usual using the prices prevailing in 2011.

constant prices Prices corrected for increases in prices (inflation) or decreases in prices (deflation) so that a unit of currency represents the same buying power in different periods of time. *See also: purchasing power parity.*

If you want the up-to-date statistic a website called Numbeo (http://tinyco.re/6386280) shows cost-of-living comparisons.

purchasing power parity (PPP) A statistical correction allowing comparisons of the amount of goods people can buy in different countries that have different currencies. *See also: constant prices.*

Next, we can see what has happened to real GDP by multiplying the 2011 quantities by the 2010 prices. If, using the base year prices, GDP has gone up, we can infer that real GDP has increased.

If this method produces the result that, when computed using 2010 prices, GDP in 2011 is the same as in 2010, we can infer that although there might have been a change in the composition of output (fewer flights taken but more computers sold, for example), the overall quantity of output of goods and services has not changed. The conclusion would be that real GDP, which is also called GDP at **constant prices**, is unchanged. The growth rate of the economy in real terms is zero.

Taking account of price differences among countries: International prices and purchasing power

To compare countries, we need to choose a set of prices and apply it to both countries.

To begin with, imagine a simple economy which produces only one product. As an example, we choose a regular cappuccino because we can easily find out the price of this standard product in different parts of the world. And we choose two economies that are very different in their level of development: Sweden and Indonesia.

At the time we wrote this, when prices are converted into US dollars using current exchange rates, a regular cappuccino costs $3.90 in Stockholm and $2.63 in Jakarta.

But simply expressing the two cappuccinos in a common currency is not enough, because the international current exchange rate that we used to get these numbers is not a very good measure of how much a rupiah will buy in Jakarta and how much a krona will get you in Stockholm.

This is why when comparing living standards across countries, we use estimates of GDP per capita in a common set of prices known as **purchasing power parity (PPP)** prices. As the name suggests, the idea is to achieve parity (equality) in the real purchasing power.

Prices are typically higher in richer countries—as in our example. One reason for this is that wages are higher, which translates into higher prices. Because prices of cappuccinos, restaurant meals, haircuts, most types of food, transport, rents and most other goods and services are more expensive in Sweden than in Indonesia, once a common set of prices is applied, the difference between GDP per capita in Sweden and Indonesia measured at PPP is smaller than it is if the comparison is made at current exchange rates.

At current exchange rates, GDP per capita in Indonesia is only 6% of the level of Sweden; at PPP where the comparison uses international prices, GDP per capita in Indonesia is 21% of the level of Sweden.

What this comparison shows is that the buying power of the Indonesian rupiah compared to the Swedish krona is more than three times greater than would be indicated by the current exchange rate between the two currencies.

We will examine the measurement of GDP (and other measures of the whole economy) in more detail in Unit 13.

●●●●

1.3 HISTORY'S HOCKEY STICK: GROWTH IN INCOME

A different way of looking at the data in Figure 1.1a is to use a scale that shows GDP per capita doubling as we move up the vertical axis (from $250 per capita per year to $500, then to $1,000, and so on). This is called a ratio scale and is shown in Figure 1.1b. The ratio scale is used for comparing growth rates.

By the growth rate of income or of any other quantity, for example population, we mean the rate of change:

$$\text{growth rate} = \frac{\text{change in income}}{\text{original level of income}}$$

If the level of GDP per capita in the year 2000 is $21,046, as it was in Britain in the data shown in Figure 1.1a, and $21,567 in 2001, then we can calculate the growth rate:

$$\text{growth rate} = \frac{\text{change in income}}{\text{original level of income}}$$
$$= \frac{y_{2001} - y_{2000}}{y_{2000}}$$
$$= \frac{21,567 - 21,046}{21,046}$$
$$= 0.025$$
$$= 2.5\%$$

Whether we want to compare levels or growth rates depends on the question we are asking. Figure 1.1a makes it easy to compare the levels of GDP per capita across countries, and at different times in history. Figure 1.1b uses a ratio scale, which makes it possible to compare growth rates across countries and at different periods. When a ratio scale is used, a series that grows at a constant rate looks like a straight line. This is because the percentage (or proportional growth rate) is constant. A steeper line in the ratio scale chart means a faster growth rate.

To see this, think of a growth rate of 100%: that means the level doubles. In Figure 1.1b, with the ratio scale, you can check that if GDP per capita doubled over 100 years from a level of $500 to $1,000, the line would have the same slope as a doubling from $2,000 to $4,000 dollars, or from $16,000 to $32,000 over 100 years. If, instead of doubling, the level quadrupled (from say, $500 to $2,000 over 100 years), the line would be twice as steep, reflecting a growth rate that was twice as high.

In some economies, substantial improvements in people's living standards did not occur until they gained independence from colonial rule or interference by European nations:

- *India*: According to Angus Deaton, an economist who specializes in the analysis of poverty, when 300 years of British rule of India ended in 1947: 'It is possible that the deprivation in childhood of Indians … was as severe as that of any large group in history'. In the closing years of British rule, a child born in India could expect to live for 27 years. Fifty years on, life expectancy at birth in India had risen to 65 years.
- *China*: It had once been richer than Britain, but by the middle of the twentieth century GDP per capita in China was one-fifteenth that of Britain.

If you have never have seen an ice-hockey stick (or experienced ice hockey) this shape is why we call these figures 'hockey-stick curves'.

Growth Rate Formula
= value in current year — value in previous year
————————————
value in previous year

fraction
percentage

11

- *Latin America*: Neither Spanish colonial rule, nor its aftermath following the independence of most Latin American nations early in the nineteenth century, saw anything resembling the hockey-stick upturn in living standards experienced by the countries in Figures 1.1a and 1.1b.

We learn two things from Figures 1.1a and 1.1b:

- For a very long time, living standards did not grow in any sustained way.
- When sustained growth occurred, it began at different times in different countries, leading to vast differences in living standards around the world.

Jutta Bolt and Jan Juiten van Zanden. 2013. 'The First Update of the Maddison Project Re-Estimating Growth Before 1820'. Maddison-Project Working Paper WP-4 (January). Stephen Broadberry. 2013. Accounting for the great divergence. 1 November. Conference Board, The. 2015. Total Economy Database.

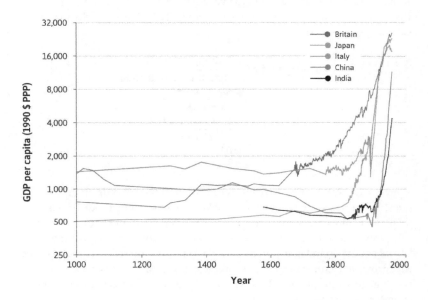

Figure 1.1b History's hockey stick: Living standards in five countries (1000–2015) using the ratio scale.

1. Before 1800 we have fewer data points
For the period before 1800 we have less information about GDP per capita, which is why there are fewer data points in that part of the figure.

2. A line is drawn through the data points
For each country the data points shown at the previous step have been joined with straight lines. Before 1800 we can't see how living standards fluctuated from year to year.

3. Britain
The hockey-stick kink is less abrupt in Britain, where growth began around 1650.

4. Japan
In Japan the kink is more defined, occurring around 1870.

5. China and India
The kink for China and India happened in the second half of the twentieth century. GDP per capita actually fell in India during British colonial rule. You can see that this is also true of China during the same period, when European nations dominated China's politics and economics.

6. Compare growth rates in China and Japan
The ratio scale makes it possible to see that recent growth rates in Japan and China were higher than elsewhere.

Understanding how this occurred has been one of the most important questions that economists have asked, starting with a founder of the field, Adam Smith, who gave his most important book the title *An Inquiry into the Nature and Causes of the Wealth of Nations*.

GREAT ECONOMISTS

Adam Smith

Adam Smith (1723–1790) is considered by many to be the founder of modern economics. Raised by a widowed mother in Scotland, he went on to study philosophy at the University of Glasgow and later at Oxford, where he wrote: 'the greater part of the ... professors have ... given up altogether even the pretence of teaching.'

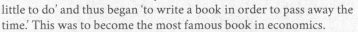

He travelled throughout Europe, visiting Toulouse, France where he claimed to have 'very little to do' and thus began 'to write a book in order to pass away the time.' This was to become the most famous book in economics.

In *An Inquiry into the Nature and Causes of the Wealth of Nations*, published in 1776, Smith asked: how can society coordinate the independent activities of large numbers of economic actors—producers, transporters, sellers, consumers—often unknown to each other and widely scattered across the world? His radical claim was that coordination among all of these actors might spontaneously arise, without any person or institution consciously attempting to create or maintain it. This challenged previous notions of political and economic organization, in which rulers imposed order on their subjects.

Even more radical was his idea that this could take place as a result of individuals pursuing their self-interest: 'It is not from the benevolence of the butcher, the brewer, or the baker that we expect our dinner, but from their regard to their own interest,' he wrote.

Elsewhere in the *Wealth of Nations*, Smith introduced one of the most enduring metaphors in the history of economics, that of the invisible hand. The businessman, he wrote: 'intends only his own gain, and he is in this, as in many other cases, led by an invisible hand to promote an end which was no part of his intention. Nor is it always the worse for the society that it was no part of it. By pursuing his own interest he frequently promotes that of the society more effectually than when he really intends to promote it.'

Among Smith's insights is the idea that a significant source of prosperity is the division of labour or specialization, and that this in turn is constrained by the 'extent of the market.' Smith illustrated this idea in a famous passage on the pin factory by observing that ten men, each fully specialized in one or two of 18 distinct operations, could produce close to 50,000 pins a day. But 'if they had all wrought [pins] separately and independently ... they certainly could not each of them have made twenty, perhaps not one pin in a day.'

An entertaining video (http://tinyco.re/3761488) by Hans Rosling, a statistician, shows how some countries got richer and healthier much earlier than others.

Adam Smith. (1776) 2003. *An Inquiry into the Nature and Causes of the Wealth of Nations*. New York, NY: Random House Publishing Group.

Smith, Adam. 1759. *The Theory of Moral Sentiments* (http://tinyco.re/6582039). London: Printed for A. Millar, and A. Kincaid and J. Bell.

But such an enormous number of pins could only find buyers if they were sold far from their point of production. Hence specialization was fostered by the construction of navigable canals and the expansion of foreign trade. And the resulting prosperity itself expanded the 'extent of the market', in a virtuous cycle of economic expansion.

Smith did not think that people were guided entirely by self-interest. Seventeen years before *The Wealth of Nations*, he had published a book about ethical behaviour called *The Theory of Moral Sentiments*.

He also understood that the market system had some failings, especially if sellers banded together so as to avoid competing with each other. 'People in the same trade seldom meet together,' he wrote, 'even for merriment and diversion, but the conversation ends in a conspiracy against the public; or in some contrivance to raise prices.'

He specifically targeted monopolies that were protected by governments, such as the British East India Company that not only controlled trade between India and Britain, but also administered much of the British colony there.

He agreed with his contemporaries that a government should protect its nation from external enemies, and ensure justice through the police and the court system. He also advocated government investment in education, and in public works such as bridges, roads, and canals.

Smith is often associated with the idea that prosperity arises from the pursuit of self-interest under free market conditions. However, his thinking on these issues was far more nuanced than he is given credit for.

EXERCISE 1.4 THE ADVANTAGES OF RATIO SCALES

Figure 1.1a (page 2) used a conventional scale for the vertical axis, and Figure 1.1b (page 12) used a ratio scale.

1. For Britain, identify a period of time when its growth rate was increasing and another period in which its growth rate was roughly constant. Which figure did you use, and why?
2. Identify a period during which GDP per capita was shrinking (a negative growth rate) faster than in India. Which figure did you use and why?

QUESTION 1.2 CHOOSE THE CORRECT ANSWER(S)

The GDP per capita of Greece was $22,494 in 2012 and $21,966 in 2013. Based on these figures, the growth rate of GDP between 2012 and 2013 (to two decimal places) was:

☐ −2.40%
☐ 2.35%
☐ −2.35%
☐ −0.24%

QUESTION 1.3 CHOOSE THE CORRECT ANSWER(S)

Imagine that the GDP per capita of a country had doubled every 100 years. You are asked to draw both linear and ratio scale graphs that plot GDP on the vertical axis, and the year on the horizontal axis. What will be the shapes of the curves?

Linear scale graph	Ratio scale graph
☐ An upward-sloping curve with increasing slope (called convex shape)	An upward-sloping straight line
☐ An upward-sloping straight line	A straight horizontal line
☐ An upward-sloping straight line	An upward-sloping curve with decreasing slope (called concave shape)
☐ An upward-sloping convex curve	An upward-sloping convex curve

Note: Linear scale graphs are 'normal' graphs in which the difference in height between 1 and 2, and the difference between 2 and 3, would be the same on the vertical axis.

1.4 THE PERMANENT TECHNOLOGICAL REVOLUTION

The science fiction show *Star Trek* is set in the year 2264, when humans travel the galaxy with friendly aliens aided by intelligent computers, faster-than-light propulsion, and replicators that create food and medicine on demand. Whether we find the stories silly or inspiring, most of us, in optimistic moods, can entertain the idea that the future will be transformed morally, socially, and materially by technological progress.

No *Star Trek* future awaited the peasant's grandchildren of 1250. The next 500 years would pass without any measurable change in the standard of living of an ordinary working person. While science fiction began to appear in the seventeenth century (Francis Bacon's *New Atlantis* being one of the first, in 1627), it was not until the eighteenth century that each new generation could look forward to a different life that was shaped by new technology.

Remarkable scientific and technological advances occurred more or less at the same time as the upward kink in the hockey stick in Britain in the middle of the eighteenth century.

Important new technologies were introduced in textiles, energy and transportation. Its cumulative character led to it being called the **Industrial Revolution**. As late as 1800, traditional craft-based techniques, using skills that had been handed down from one generation to the next, were still used in most production processes. The new era brought new ideas, new discoveries, new methods and new machines, making old ideas and old tools obsolete. These new ways were, in turn, made obsolete by even newer ones.

Industrial Revolution [handwritten note]

Industrial Revolution A wave of technological advances and organizational changes starting in Britain in the eighteenth century, which transformed an agrarian and craft-based economy into a commercial and industrial economy.

technology A process taking a set of materials and other inputs, including the work of people and machines, to produce an output.

In everyday usage, 'technology' refers to machinery, equipment and devices developed using scientific knowledge. In economics, **technology** is a process that takes a set of materials and other inputs—including the work of people and machines—and creates an output. For example, a technology for making a cake can be described by the recipe that specifies the combination of inputs (ingredients such as flour, and labour activities such as stirring) needed to create the output (the cake). Another technology for making cakes uses large-scale machinery, ingredients and labour (machine operators).

technological progress A change in technology that reduces the amount of resources (labour, machines, land, energy, time) required to produce a given amount of the output.

Until the Industrial Revolution, the economy's technology, like the skills needed to follow its recipes, was updated only slowly and passed from generation to generation. As **technological progress** revolutionized production, the time required to make a pair of shoes fell by half in only a few decades; the same was true of spinning and weaving, and of making cakes in a factory. This marked the beginning of a permanent technological revolution because the amount of time required for producing most products fell generation after generation.

Technological change in lighting

To get some idea of the unprecedented pace of change, consider the way we produce light. For most of human history technological progress in lighting was slow. Our distant ancestors typically had nothing brighter than a campfire at night. The recipe for producing light (had it existed) would have said: gather lots of firewood, borrow a lighting stick from some other place where a fire is maintained, and start and maintain a fire.

The first great technological breakthrough in lighting came 40,000 years ago, with the use of lamps that burned animal or vegetable oils. We measure technological progress in lighting by how many units of brightness called lumens could be generated by an hour of work. One lumen is approximately the amount of brightness in a square metre of moonlight. One lumen-hour (lm-hr) is this amount of brightness lasting an hour. For example, creating light by a campfire took about 1 hour of labour to produce 17 lm-hr, but animal fat lamps produced 20 lm-hr for the same amount of work. In Babylonian times (1750 BC) the invention of an improved lamp using sesame oil meant that an hour of labour produced 24 lm-hr. Technological progress was slow: this modest improvement took 7,000 years.

Three thousand years later, in the early 1800s, the most efficient forms of lighting (using tallow candles) provided about nine times as much light for an hour of labour as had the animal fat lamps of the past. Since then lighting has become more and more efficient with the development of town gas lamps, kerosene lamps, filament bulbs, fluorescent bulbs and other forms of lighting. Compact fluorescent bulbs introduced in 1992 are about 45,000 times more efficient, in terms of labour time expended, than lights were 200 years ago. Today the productivity of labour in producing light is half a million times greater than it was among our ancestors around their campfire.

Figure 1.3 charts this remarkable hockey-stick growth in efficiency in lighting using the ratio scale we introduced in Figure 1.1b.

The process of innovation did not end with the Industrial Revolution, as the case of labour productivity in lighting shows. It has continued with the application of new technologies in many industries, such as the steam engine, electricity, transportation (canals, railroads, automobiles), and most recently, the revolution in information processing and communication. These broadly applicable technological innovations give a particularly strong impetus to growth in living standards because they change the way that large parts of the economy work.

By reducing the amount of work-time it takes to produce the things we need, technological changes allowed significant increases in living standards. David Landes, an economic historian, wrote that the Industrial Revolution was 'an interrelated succession of technological changes' that transformed the societies in which these changes took place.

A connected world

In July 2012, the Korean hit 'Gangnam Style' was released. By the end of 2012 it had become the best-selling song in 33 countries, including Australia, Russia, Canada, France, Spain and the UK. With 2 billion views by the middle of 2014, 'Gangnam Style' also became the most watched video on YouTube. The permanent technological revolution has produced a connected world.

Everyone is part of it. The materials making up this introduction to economics were written by teams of economists, designers, programmers and editors, working together—often simultaneously—at computers in the UK, India, the US, Russia, Colombia, South Africa, Chile, Turkey, France and many other countries. If you are online, some of the transmission of information occurs at close to the speed of light. While most of the commodities traded around the globe still move at the pace of an ocean freighter, about 21 miles (33 km) per hour, international financial transactions are implemented in less time than it took you to read this sentence.

Transformational technological change is still occurring. Hans Rosling claims (http://tinyco.re/7334115) that we should say 'thank you industrialization' for creating the washing machine, a device that transformed the wellbeing of millions of women.

David S. Landes. 2003. *The Unbound Prometheus: Technological Change and Industrial Development in Western Europe from 1750 to the Present.* Cambridge: Cambridge University Press.

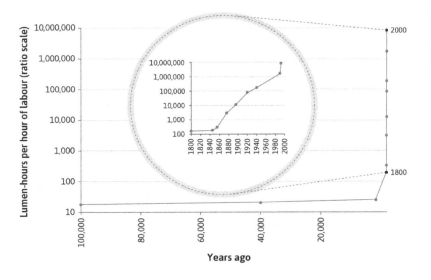

William Nordhaus. 1998. 'Do Real Output and Real Wage Measures Capture Reality? The History of Lighting Suggests Not'. Cowles Foundation For Research in Economics Paper 1078.

Figure 1.3 The productivity of labour in producing light.

The speed at which information travels provides more evidence of the novelty of the permanent technological revolution. By comparing the known date of a historical event with the date at which the event was first noted in other locations (in diaries, journals or newspapers) we can determine the speed at which news travelled. When Abraham Lincoln was elected US president in 1860, for example, the word was spread by telegraph from Washington to Fort Kearny, which was at the western end of the telegraph line. From there the news was carried by a relay of riders on horseback called the Pony Express, covering 1,260 miles (2,030 km) to Fort Churchill in Nevada, from where it was transmitted to California by telegraph. The process took seven days and 17 hours. Over the Pony Express segment of the route, the news travelled at 7 miles (11 km) per hour. A half-ounce (14 gram) letter carried over this route cost $5, or the equivalent of five days' wages.

From similar calculations we know that news travelled between ancient Rome and Egypt at about 1 mile (1.6 km) per hour, and 1,500 years later between Venice and other cities around the Mediterranean it was, if anything, slightly slower. But, a few centuries later, as Figure 1.4 shows, the pace began to quicken. It took 'only' 46 days for the news of a mutiny of Indian troops against British rule in 1857 to reach London, and readers of the *Times* of London knew of Lincoln's assassination only 13 days after the event. One year after Lincoln's death a transatlantic cable cut the time for news to travel between New York and London to a matter of minutes.

1.5 THE ECONOMY AND THE ENVIRONMENT

Humans have always relied on their environment for the resources they need to live and produce their livelihoods: the physical environment and the biosphere, which is the collection of all forms of life on earth, provide essentials for life such as air, water and food. The environment also provides the raw materials that we use in the production of other goods—such as wood, metals, and oil.

Tables 15.2 and 15.3 from Gregory Clark. 2007. *A Farewell to Alms: A Brief Economic History of the World.* Princeton, NJ: Princeton University Press.

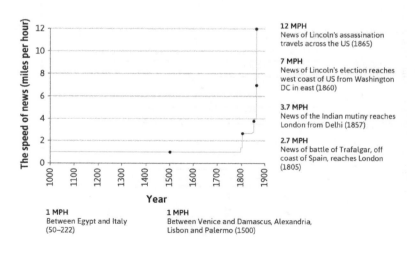

Figure 1.4 The speed at which information travelled (1000–1865).

Figure 1.5 shows one way of thinking about the economy: it is part of a larger social system, which is itself part of the biosphere. People interact with each other, and also with nature, in producing their livelihood.

Through most of their history, humans have regarded natural resources as freely available in unlimited quantities (except for the costs of extracting them). But as production has soared (see Figures 1.1a and 1.1b), so too have the use of our natural resources and degradation of our natural environment. Elements of the ecological system such as air, water, soil, and weather have been altered by humans more radically than ever before.

The most striking effect is climate change. Figures 1.6a and 1.6b present evidence that our use of fossil fuels—coal, oil, and natural gas—have profoundly affected the natural environment. After having remained relatively unchanged for many centuries, increasing emissions of carbon dioxide (CO_2) into the air during the twentieth century have resulted in measurably larger amounts of CO_2 in the earth's atmosphere (Figure 1.6a) and brought about perceptible increases in the northern hemisphere's average temperatures (Figure 1.6b). Figure 1.6a also shows that CO_2 emissions from fossil fuel consumption have risen dramatically since 1800.

EXERCISE 1.5 HOW MUCH DIFFERENCE DOES A COUPLE OF DEGREES WARMER OR COLDER MAKE?

Between 1300 and 1850 there were a number of exceptionally cold periods as you can see from Figure 1.6b (page 20). Research this so-called 'little ice age' in Europe and answer the following.

1. Describe the effects of these exceptionally cold periods on the economies of these countries.
2. Within a country or region, some groups of people were exceptionally hard hit by the climate change while others were less affected. Provide examples.
3. How 'extreme' were these cold periods compared to the temperature increases since the mid-twentieth century and those projected for the future?

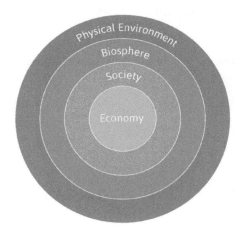

what Story does Figure tell?

Figure 1.5 The economy is part of society, which is part of the biosphere.

Figure 1.6b shows that the average temperature of the earth fluctuates from decade to decade. Many factors cause these fluctuations, including volcanic events such as the 1815 Mount Tambora eruption in Indonesia. Mount Tambora spewed so much ash that the earth's temperature was reduced by the cooling effect of these fine particles in the atmosphere, and 1816 became known as the 'year without a summer'.

Since 1900, average temperatures have risen in response to increasingly high levels of greenhouse gas concentrations. These have mostly resulted from the CO_2 emissions associated with the burning of fossil fuels.

The human causes and the reality of climate change are no longer widely disputed in the scientific community. The likely consequences of global warming are far-reaching: melting of the polar ice caps, rising sea levels that may put large coastal areas under water, and potential changes in climate and rain patterns that may destroy the world's food-growing areas. The long-term physical and economic consequences of these changes, and the appropriate policies that governments could adopt as a result, are discussed in detail in Unit 20 (Economics of the environment).

The authoritative source for research and data about climate change is the Intergovernmental Panel on Climate Change (http://tinyco.re/8844088).

Climate change is a global change. But many of the environmental impacts of burning fossil fuels are local, as residents of cities suffer respiratory and other illnesses as a result of high levels of harmful emissions from power plants, vehicles, and other sources. Rural communities, too, are impacted by deforestation (another cause of climate change) and the depletion of the supply of clean water and fishing stocks.

From global climate change to local resource exhaustion, these effects are results of both the expansion of the economy (illustrated by the growth

Years 1010–1975: David M. Etheridge, L. Paul Steele, Roger J. Francey, and Ray L. Langenfelds. 2012. 'Historical Record from the Law Dome DE08, DE08-2, and DSS Ice Cores'. Division of Atmospheric Research, CSIRO, Aspendale, Victoria, Australia. Years 1976–2010: Data from Mauna Loa observatory. T. A. Boden, G. Marland, and Robert J. Andres. 2010. 'Global, Regional and National Fossil-Fuel CO_2 Emissions'. Carbon Dioxide Information Analysis Center (CDIAC) Datasets.

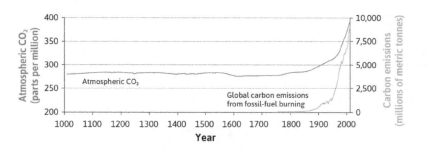

Figure 1.6a Carbon dioxide in the atmosphere (1010–2010) and global carbon emissions from burning fossil fuels (1750–2010).

Michael E. Mann, Zhihua Zhang, Malcolm K. Hughes, Raymond S. Bradley, Sonya K. Miller, Scott Rutherford, and Fenbiao Ni. 2008. 'Proxy-based reconstructions of hemispheric and global surface temperature variations over the past two millennia'. *Proceedings of the National Academy of Sciences* 105 (36): pp. 13252–13257.

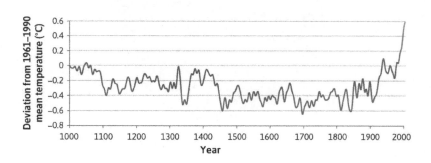

Figure 1.6b Northern hemisphere temperatures over the long run (1000–2006).

in total output) and the way the economy is organized (what kinds of things are valued and conserved, for example). The relationship between the economy and the environment shown in Figure 1.5 is two-way: we use natural resources in production, which may in turn affect the environment we live in and its capacity to support future production.

But the permanent technological revolution—which brought about dependence on fossil fuels—may also be part of the solution to today's environmental problems.

Look back at Figure 1.3, which showed the productivity of labour in producing light. The vast increases shown over the course of history and especially since the mid-nineteenth century occurred largely because the amount of light produced per unit of heat (for example from a campfire, candle, or light bulb) increased dramatically.

In lighting, the permanent technological revolution brought us more light for less heat, which conserved natural resources—from firewood to fossil fuels—used in generating the heat. Advances in technology today may allow greater reliance on wind, solar and other renewable sources of energy.

QUESTION 1.4 CHOOSE THE CORRECT ANSWER(S)

Which of the following variables have followed the so-called 'hockey-stick' trajectory—that is, little to no growth for most of history followed by a sudden and sharp change to a positive growth rate?

☐ GDP per capita
☐ labour productivity
☐ inequality
☐ atmospheric CO_2

1.6 CAPITALISM DEFINED: PRIVATE PROPERTY, MARKETS, AND FIRMS

Looking back over the data in Figures 1.1a (page 2), 1.1b (page 12), 1.3 (page 17), 1.4 (page 18) and 1.6 (page 20) we see an upward turn, like the kink in our hockey stick, repeated for:

- gross domestic product per capita
- productivity of labour (light per hour of work)
- connectivity of the various parts of the world (the speed at which news travels)
- impact of the economy on the global environment (carbon emissions and climate change)

How can we explain the change from a world in which living conditions changed little unless there was an epidemic or a war, to one in which each generation is noticeably, and predictably, better off than the previous one?

An important part of our answer will be what we call the capitalist revolution: the emergence in the eighteenth century and eventual global spread of a way of organizing the economy that we now call capitalism. The term 'capitalism'—which we will define shortly—was barely heard of a century ago, but as you can see from Figure 1.7, its use has skyrocketed since then. The figure shows the fraction of all articles in the *New York Times* (excluding the sports section) that include the term 'capitalism.'

Capitalism is an **economic system** characterized by a particular combination of **institutions**. An economic system is a way of organizing the production and distribution of goods and services in an entire economy. And by institutions, we mean the different sets of laws and social customs regulating production and distribution in different ways in families, private businesses, and government bodies.

In some economies in the past, the key economic institutions were **private property** (people owning things), markets (where goods could be bought and sold) and families. Goods were usually produced by families working together, rather than by firms with owners and employees.

In other societies, the government has been the institution controlling production, and deciding how goods should be distributed, and to whom. This is called a centrally planned economic system. It existed, for example, in the Soviet Union, East Germany and many other eastern European countries prior to the end of Communist Party rule in the early 1990s.

Though governments and families are essential parts of the workings of every economy, most economies today are capitalist. Since most of us live in capitalist economies, it is easy to overlook the importance of institutions that are fundamental for capitalism to work well. They are so familiar, we hardly ever notice them. Before seeing how private property, markets and firms combine in the capitalist economic system, we need to define them.

Over the course of human history, the extent of private property has varied. In some societies, such as the hunters and gatherers who are our distant ancestors, almost nothing except personal ornaments and clothing was owned by individuals. In others, crops and animals were private property, but land was not. The right to use the land was granted to families by consensus among members of a group, or by a chief, without allowing the family to sell the plot.

In other economic systems some human beings—slaves—were private property.

capitalism An economic system in which private property, markets, and firms play an important role.
economic system The institutions that organize the production and distribution of goods and services in an entire economy.
institution The laws and social customs governing the way people interact in society.

PRIVATE PROPERTY

This means that you can:

- enjoy your possessions in a way that you choose
- exclude others from their use if you wish
- dispose of them by gift or sale to someone else ...
- ... who becomes their owner

Calculations by Simon DeDeo, Santa Fe Institute, from *New York Times*. 2016. 'NYT article archive'.

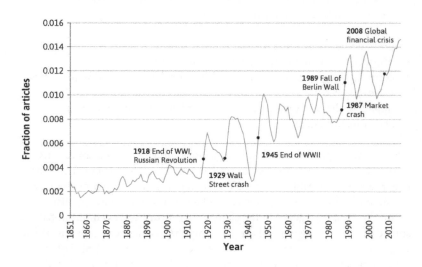

Figure 1.7 Mention of the word 'capitalism' in *New York Times* articles (1851–2015).

In a capitalist economy, an important type of private property is the equipment, buildings, raw materials, and other inputs used in producing goods and services. These are called **capital goods**.

Private property may be owned by an individual, a family, a business, or some entity other than the government. Some things that we value are not private property: for example, the air we breathe and most of the knowledge we use cannot be owned or bought and sold.

> **capital goods** The equipment, buildings, raw materials, and other inputs used in producing goods and services, including where applicable any patents or other intellectual property that is used.

QUESTION 1.5 CHOOSE THE CORRECT ANSWER(S)
Which of the following are examples of private property?

☐ computers belonging to your college
☐ a farmer's land in Soviet Russia
☐ shares in a company
☐ a worker's skills

Markets are a means of transferring goods or services from one person to another. There are other ways, such as by theft, a gift, or a government order. **Markets** differ from these in three respects:

They are reciprocated: unlike gifts and theft, one person's transfer of a good or service to another is directly reciprocated by a transfer in the other direction (either of another good or service as in barter exchange, or money, or a promise of a later transfer when one buys on credit). They are voluntary: Both transfers—by the buyer and the seller—are voluntary because the things being exchanged are private property. So the exchange must be beneficial in the opinion of both parties. In this, markets differ from theft, and also from the transfers of goods and services in a centrally planned economy.

In most markets there is competition. A seller charging a high price, for example, will find that buyers prefer to buy from other competing sellers.

> **MARKETS**
> Markets are:
> * a way of connecting people who may mutually benefit
> * by exchanging goods and services
> * through a process of buying and selling

EXERCISE 1.6 THE POOREST MAN'S COTTAGE
'The poorest man may in his cottage bid defiance to all the forces of the Crown. It may be frail, its roof may shake; the wind may blow through it; the storms may enter, the rain may enter—but the King of England cannot enter; all his forces dare not cross the threshold of the ruined tenement.' – William Pitt, 1st Earl of Chatham, speech in the British Parliament (1763).

1. What does this tell us about the meaning of private property?
2. Does it apply to people's homes in your country?

EXERCISE 1.7 MARKETS AND SOCIAL NETWORKS
Think about a social networking site that you use, for example Facebook. Now look at our definition of a market.

What are the similarities and differences between that social networking site and a market?

QUESTION 1.6 CHOOSE THE CORRECT ANSWER(S)
Which of the following are examples of markets?

☐ wartime food rationing
☐ auction websites such as eBay
☐ touts selling tickets outside concert halls
☐ sale of illegal arms

FIRM
A firm is a way of organizing production with the following characteristics:

- One or more individuals own a set of capital goods that are used in production.
- They pay wages and salaries to employees.
- They direct the employees (through the managers they also employ) in the production of goods and services.
- The goods and services are the property of the owners.
- The owners sell the goods and services on markets with the intention of making a profit.

labour market In this market, employers offer wages to individuals who may agree to work under their direction. Economists say that employers are on the demand side of this market, while employees are on the supply side. *See also: labour force.*

demand side The side of a market on which those participating are offering money in return for some other good or service (for example, those purchasing bread). *See also: supply side.*

supply side The side of a market on which those participating are offering something in return for money (for example, those selling bread). *See also: demand side.*

But private property and markets alone do not define capitalism. In many places they were important institutions long before capitalism. The most recent of the three components making up the capitalist economy is the **firm**.

The kinds of firms that make up a capitalist economy include restaurants, banks, large farms that pay others to work there, industrial establishments, supermarkets, and internet service providers. Other productive organizations that are not firms and which play a lesser role in a capitalist economy include family businesses, in which most or all of the people working are family members, non-profit organizations, employee-owned cooperatives, and government-owned entities (such as railways and power or water companies). These are not firms, either because they do not make a profit, or because the owners are not private individuals who own the assets of the firm and employ others to work there. Note: a firm pays wages or salaries to employees but, if it takes on unpaid student interns, it is still a firm.

Firms existed, playing a minor role, in many economies long before they became the predominant organizations for the production of goods and services, as in a capitalist economy. The expanded role of firms created a boom in another kind of market that had played a limited role in earlier economic systems: the **labour market**. Firm owners (or their managers) offer jobs at wages or salaries that are high enough to attract people who are looking for work.

In economic language, the employers are the **demand side** of the labour market (they 'demand' employees), while the workers are the **supply side**, offering to work under the direction of the owners and managers who hire them.

A striking characteristic of firms, distinguishing them from families and governments, is how quickly they can be born, expand, contract and die. A successful firm can grow from just a few employees to a global company with hundreds of thousands of customers, employing thousands of people, in a few years. Firms can do this because they are able to hire additional employees on the labour market, and attract funds to finance the purchase of the capital goods they need to expand production.

Firms can die in a few years too. This is because a firm that does not make profits will not have enough money (and will not be able to borrow money) to continue employing and producing. The firm shrinks, and some of the people who work there lose their jobs.

Contrast this with a successful family farm. The family will be better off than its neighbours; but unless it turns the family farm into a firm, and employs other people to work on it, expansion will be limited. If, instead, the family is not very good at farming, then it will simply be less well off than its neighbours. The family head cannot dismiss the children as a firm might get rid of unproductive workers. As long as the family can feed itself there is no equivalent mechanism to a firm's failure that will automatically put it out of business.

Government bodies also tend to be more limited in their capacity to expand if successful, and are usually protected from failure if they perform poorly.

Defining capitalism precisely

In everyday language, the word 'capitalism' is used in different ways, in part because people have strong feelings about it. In the language of economics, we use the term in a precise way because that helps us to communicate: we define capitalism as an economic system combining three institutions, each of which we need in turn to define.

'Capitalism' refers not to a specific economic system, but to a class of systems sharing these characteristics. How the institutions of capitalism—private property, markets, and firms—combine with each other and with families, governments, and other institutions differs greatly across countries. Just as ice and steam are both 'water' (defined chemically as a compound of two hydrogen atoms bonded with one oxygen atom), China and the US are both capitalist economies. But they differ in the extent to which the government influences economic affairs, and in many other ways. As this demonstrates, definitions in the social sciences often cannot be as precise as they are in the natural sciences.

Some people might say that 'ice is not really water', and object that the definition is not the 'true meaning' of the word. But debates about the 'true' meaning (especially when referring to complex abstract ideas like capitalism, or democracy) forget why definitions are valuable. Think of the definition of water, or of capitalism, not as capturing some true meaning—but rather as a device that is valuable because it makes it easier to communicate.

Definitions in the social sciences often cannot be as precise as they are in the natural sciences. Unlike water, we cannot identify a capitalist economic system using easy-to-measure physical characteristics.

1.7 CAPITALISM AS AN ECONOMIC SYSTEM

Figure 1.8 shows that the three parts of the definition of a capitalist economic system are nested concepts. The left-hand circle describes an economy of isolated families who own their capital goods and the goods they produce, but have little or no exchange with others.

In a capitalist system, production takes place in firms. Markets and private property are essential parts of how firms function for two reasons:

- *Inputs and outputs are private property*: The firm's buildings, equipment, patents, and other inputs into production, as well as the resulting outputs, belong to the owners.
- *Firms use markets to sell outputs*: The owners' profits depend on markets in which customers may willingly purchase the products at a price that will more than cover production costs.

Historically, economies like the left-hand circle have existed, but have been much less important than a system in which markets and private property are combined (the middle circle). Private property is an essential condition for the operation of markets: buyers will not want to pay for goods unless

---

EXERCISE 1.8 CAPITALISM

Look again at Figure 1.7 (page 22).

1. Can you suggest an explanation for why the usage of the term capitalism spikes when it does?
2. Why do you think it has remained so high since the late 1980s?

Paul Seabright. 2010. *The Company of Strangers: A Natural History of Economic Life* (Revised Edition). Princeton, NJ: Princeton University Press.

they can have the right to own them. In the middle circle most production is done either by individuals (shoemakers or blacksmiths, for example) or in families (for example, on a farm). Prior to 1600 a great many of the economies of the world were like this.

ownership The right to use and exclude others from the use of something, and the right to sell the thing that is owned.

The distinctive hallmark of the capitalist economic system is the private **ownership** of **capital goods** that are organized for use in firms. Other economic systems are distinctive because of the importance of privately owned land, the presence of slaves, because the government owns capital goods, or because of the limited role of firms. Capitalist economies differ, too, from earlier economies in the magnitude of the capital goods used in production. Massive power looms have replaced spinning wheels; a tractor now pulls a plough to do a job once done by a farmer using a hoe.

Capitalism is an economic system that combines centralization with decentralization. It concentrates power in the hands of owners and managers of firms who are then able to secure the cooperation of large numbers of employees in the production process. But it limits the powers of owners and of other individuals, because they face competition to buy and sell in markets.

So when the owner of a firm interacts with an employee, he or she is 'the boss'. But when the same owner interacts with a potential customer he or she is simply another person trying to make a sale, in competition with other firms. It is this unusual combination of competition among firms, and concentration of power and cooperation within them, that accounts for capitalism's success as an economic system.

How could capitalism lead to growth in living standards?

Two major changes accompanied the emergence of capitalism, both of which enhanced the productivity of individual workers:

Technology

As we have seen, the permanent technological revolution coincided with the transition to firms as the predominant means of organizing production. This does not mean that firms necessarily caused technological change. But firms competing with each other in markets had strong incentives to adopt and develop new and more productive technologies, and to invest in capital goods that would have been beyond the reach of small-scale family enterprises.

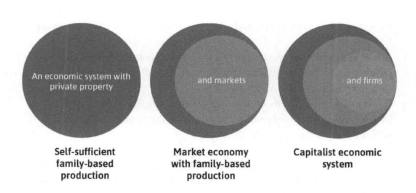

Self-sufficient family-based production — An economic system with private property

Market economy with family-based production — and markets

Capitalist economic system — and firms

Figure 1.8 Capitalism: Private property, markets and firms.

Specialization

The growth of firms employing large numbers of workers—and the expansion of markets linking the entire world in a process of exchange—allowed historically unprecedented specialization in the tasks and products on which people worked. In the next section, we will see how this specialization can raise labour productivity and living standards.

EXERCISE 1.9 FIRM OR NOT?

Using our definition, explain whether each of the following entities is a firm by investigating if it satisfies the characteristics that define a firm. Research the entity online if you are stuck.

1. John Lewis Partnership (UK)
2. a family farm in Vietnam
3. your current family doctor's office or practice
4. Walmart (US)
5. an eighteenth-century pirate ship (see our description of *The Royal Rover* in Unit 5)
6. Google (US)
7. Manchester United plc (UK)
8. Wikipedia

1.8 THE GAINS FROM SPECIALIZATION

Capitalism and specialization

Look around at the objects in your workspace. Do you know the person who made them? What about your clothing? Or anything else in sight from where you are sitting?

Now imagine that it is 1776, the year that Adam Smith wrote *The Wealth of Nations*. The same questions, asked anywhere in the world, would have had a different answer.

At that time many families produced a wide array of goods for their own use, including crops, meat, clothing, even tools. Many of the things that you might have spotted in Adam Smith's day would have been made by a member of the family, or of the village. You would have made some objects yourself; others would have been made locally and purchased from the village market.

One of the changes that was underway during Adam Smith's life, but has greatly accelerated since, is specialization in the production of goods and services. As Smith explained, we become better at producing things when we each focus on a limited range of activities. This is true for three reasons:

- *Learning by doing*: We acquire skills as we produce things.
- *Difference in ability*: For reasons of skill, or natural surroundings such as the quality of the soil, some people are better at producing some things than others.
- ***economies of scale***: Producing a large number of units of some good is often more cost-effective than producing a smaller number. We investigate this in more detail in Unit 7.

economies of scale These occur when doubling all of the inputs to a production process more than doubles the output. The shape of a firm's long-run average cost curve depends both on returns to scale in production and the effect of scale on the prices it pays for its inputs. *Also known as: increasing returns to scale. See also: diseconomies of scale.*

These are the advantages of working on a limited number of tasks or products. People do not typically produce the full range of goods and services that they use or consume in their daily life. Instead we specialize, some producing one good, others producing other goods, some working as welders, others as teachers or farmers.

But people will not specialize unless they have a way to acquire the other goods they need.

For this reason, specialization—called the division of labour—poses a problem for society: how are the goods and services to be distributed from the producer to the final user? In the course of history, this has happened in a number of distinct ways, from direct government requisitioning and distribution as was done in the US and many economies during the Second World War, to gifts and voluntary sharing as we do in families today and as practiced among even unrelated members of a community by our hunting and gathering ancestors. Capitalism enhanced our opportunities for specialization by expanding the economic importance of both markets and firms.

Specialization exists within governments and also in families, where who does which household chore is often associated with age and gender. Here we look at the division of labour in firms and in markets.

The division of labour in firms

Adam Smith begins *The Wealth of Nations* with the following sentence:

> The greatest improvement in the productive powers of labour, and the greater part of the skill, dexterity, and judgment with which it is anywhere directed, or applied, seem to have been the effects of the division of labour.

He went on to describe a pin factory in which the specialization of tasks among the working men allowed a level of productivity—pins produced per day—that seemed to him extraordinary. Firms may employ thousands or even hundreds of thousands of individuals, most of them working at specialized tasks under the direction of the owners or manager of the firm.

This description of the firm stresses its hierarchical nature from top to bottom. But you can also think of the firm as a means by which large numbers of people, each with distinct skills and capacities, contribute to a common outcome, the product. The firm thus facilitates a kind of cooperation among specialized producers that increases productivity.

We return to the question of who does what within the firm and why in Unit 6.

Markets, specialization, and comparative advantage

Chapter 3 in *The Wealth of Nations* is titled: 'That the Division of Labour is Limited by the Extent of the Market', in which Smith explains:

> When the market is very small, no person can have any encouragement to dedicate himself entirely to one employment, for want of the power to exchange all that surplus part of the produce of his own labour, which is over and above his own consumption, for such parts of the produce of other men's labour as he has occasion for.

When you hear the word 'market' what word do you think of? 'Competition' probably is what came to mind. And you would be right to associate the two words.

But you might have also come up with 'cooperation'. Why? Because markets allow each of us pursuing our private objectives to work together, producing and distributing goods and services in a way that, while far from perfect, is in many cases better than the alternatives.

Markets accomplish an extraordinary result: unintended cooperation on a global scale. The people who produced the phone on your desk did not know or care about you; they produced it rather than you because they are better at producing phones than you are, and you ended up with it because you paid them, allowing them to buy goods that they need, also produced by total strangers to them.

A simple example illustrates how, when people differ in their ability to produce different goods, markets allow them to specialize. It shows something surprising: <u>all</u> producers <u>can benefit by specializing and trading goods</u>, even when this means that one producer specializes in a good that another could produce at lower cost.

Imagine a world of just two individuals (Greta and Carlos) who each need both of two goods, apples and wheat, to survive. They differ in how productive they are in growing apples and wheat. If Greta spent all her time, say, 2,000 hours in a year, producing apples, she would produce 1,250. If she only produced wheat, she would produce 50 tonnes per annum. Carlos has less fertile land than Greta for producing both crops: if he devoted all his time (the same amount as Greta) to apple growing, he would produce 1,000 per year, and if he produced only wheat he would produce 20 tonnes. See Figure 1.9a for a summary.

Although Carlos' land is worse for producing both crops, his disadvantage is less, relative to Greta, in apples than in wheat. Greta can produce two and a half times more wheat as he can but only 25% more apples.

Economists distinguish who is better at producing what in two ways: absolute advantage and comparative advantage.

Greta has an **absolute advantage** in both crops. Carlos has an absolute disadvantage. She can produce more of either crop than he can.

Greta has a comparative advantage in wheat; Carlos has a **comparative advantage** in apples. Although she is better, Carlos is least disadvantaged in producing apples. Greta has a comparative advantage in producing wheat.

Initially, Carlos and Greta are not able to trade with each other. Both must be self-sufficient, consuming exactly what they produce, so they will each produce both goods in order to survive.

> **absolute advantage** A person or country has this in the production of a good if the inputs it uses to produce this good are less than in some other person or country. *See also: comparative advantage.*

> **comparative advantage** A person or country has comparative advantage in the production of a particular good, if the cost of producing an additional unit of that good relative to the cost of producing another good is lower than another person or country's cost to produce the same two goods. *See also: absolute advantage.*

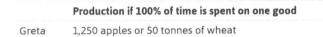

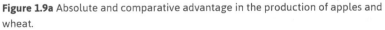

	Production if 100% of time is spent on one good
Greta	1,250 apples or 50 tonnes of wheat
Carlos	1,000 apples or 20 tonnes of wheat

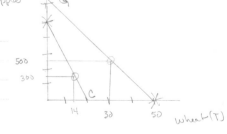

Figure 1.9a Absolute and comparative advantage in the production of apples and wheat.

Greta chooses to use 40% of her time in apple production, and the rest producing wheat. Column 1 of Figure 1.9b shows that she produces and consumes 500 apples and 30 tonnes of wheat. Carlos' consumption is also shown: he spends 30% of his time producing apples, and 70% producing wheat.

Now suppose that there are markets where apples and wheat may be bought and sold, and that 40 apples can be bought for the price of 1 tonne of wheat. If Greta specializes in growing wheat only, producing 50 tonnes of wheat and no apples, while Carlos specializes in apples, total production of both crops will be higher than it was under self-sufficiency (column 2). Then they can each sell some of their own crop in the market, and buy some of the good that the other produced.

For example, if Greta sells 15 tonnes of wheat (column 3) in order to buy 600 apples, she can now consume more apples and more wheat than before (column 4). And the table shows that buying the 15 tonnes of wheat produced by Greta, in return for 600 apples, similarly enables Carlos to consume more of both goods than was possible in the absence of specialization and trade.

In constructing this example we assumed market prices are such that a tonne of wheat could be exchanged for 40 apples. We will return to how markets work in Units 7 to 12, but Exercise 1.10 shows that this assumption was not critical. There are other prices at which both Greta and Carlos would benefit from trading with each other.

The opportunity to trade—that is, the existence of an apple market and a wheat market—has benefited both Greta and Carlos. This was possible because specializing in the production of a single good increased the total amount of each good produced, from 800 to 1,000 apples and from 44 to 50 tonnes of wheat. The surprising thing mentioned above is that Greta ended up buying 600 apples from Carlos even though she could have produced those apples at a lower cost herself (in terms of labour time). This was a better way to spend their time because while Greta had an absolute advantage in producing both goods, Carlos had a comparative advantage in producing apples.

		Self-sufficiency	Complete specialization and trade		
			Production	Trade	Consumption
		1	2	3	4
Greta	Apples	500	0		600
	Wheat	30	50 =	15 +	35
Carlos	Apples	300	1,000 =	600 +	400
	Wheat	14	0		15
Total	Apples	800	1,000	600	1,000
	Wheat	44	50	15	50

Figure 1.9b Comparing self-sufficiency and specialization. Under self-sufficiency, both consume exactly what they produce. Under complete specialization, Greta produces only wheat; Carlos produces only apples; and they trade the surplus of their production above what they consume.

Markets contribute to increasing the productivity of labour—and can therefore help to explain the hockey stick of history—by allowing people to specialize in the production of goods for which they have a comparative advantage, that is the things at which they are—relatively speaking—least bad!

EXERCISE 1.10 APPLES AND WHEAT

Suppose that market prices were such that 35 apples could be bought for 1 tonne of wheat.

1. If Greta sold 16 tonnes of wheat, would both she and Carlos still be better off?
2. What would happen if only 20 apples could be bought for the price of a tonne of wheat?

1.9 CAPITALISM, CAUSATION AND HISTORY'S HOCKEY STICK

We have seen that the institutions associated with capitalism have the potential to make people better off, through opportunities for both specialization and the introduction of new technologies, and that the permanent technological revolution coincided with the emergence of capitalism. But can we conclude that capitalism caused the upward kink in the hockey stick?

We should be sceptical when anyone claims that something complex (capitalism) 'causes' something else (increased living standards, technological improvement, a networked world, or environmental challenges).

In science, we support the statement that X causes Y by understanding the relationship between cause (X) and effect (Y) and performing experiments to gather evidence by measuring X and Y.

We want to make **causal** statements in economics—to understand why things happen, or to devise ways of changing something so that the economy works better. This means making a causal statement that policy X is likely to cause change Y. For example, an economist might claim that: 'If the central bank lowers the interest rate, more people will buy homes and cars.'

But an economy is made up of the interactions of millions of people. We cannot measure and understand them all, and it is rarely possible to gather evidence by conducting experiments (though in Unit 4 we will give examples of the use of conventional experiments in one area of economics). So how can economists do science? This example shows how the things we observe in the world can help us investigate causes and effects.

causality A direction from cause to effect, establishing that a change in one variable produces a change in another. While a correlation is simply an assessment that two things have moved together, causation implies a mechanism accounting for the association, and is therefore a more restrictive concept. *See also: natural experiment, correlation.*

HOW ECONOMISTS LEARN FROM FACTS

Do institutions matter for growth in income?

We can observe that capitalism emerged at the same time as, or just before, both the Industrial Revolution and the upward turn in our hockey sticks. This would be consistent with the hypothesis that capitalist institutions were among the causes of the era of continuous productivity growth. But the emergence of a free-thinking cultural environment known as 'The Enlightenment' also predated or coincided with the upturn in the hockey sticks. So was it institutions, or culture, both, or some other set of causes? Economists and historians disagree, as you will see in Unit 2, when we ask 'What were the causes of the Industrial Revolution?'

Scholars in all fields try to narrow the range of things on which they disagree by using facts. For complicated economic questions, like 'Do institutions matter economically?', facts may provide enough information to reach a conclusion.

A method for doing this is called a **natural experiment**. It is a situation in which there are differences in something of interest—a change in institutions for example—that are not associated with differences in other possible causes.

The division of Germany at the end of the Second World War into two separate economic systems—centrally planned in the east, capitalist in the west—provided a natural experiment. During this time a political 'Iron Curtain', as the British Prime Minister Winston Churchill described it, divided the country. It separated two populations that until then had shared the same language, culture, and capitalist economy.

In 1936, before the Second World War, living standards in what later became East and West Germany were the same. This is a suitable setting for using the natural experiment method. Before the war, firms in Saxony and Thuringia were world leaders in automobile and aircraft production, chemicals, optical equipment and precision engineering.

With the introduction of centralized planning in East Germany, private property, markets and firms virtually disappeared. Decisions about what to produce, how much and in which plants, offices, mines and farms were taken not by private individuals, but by government officials. The officials managing these economic organizations did not need to follow the principle of capitalism and produce goods and services that customers would buy at a price above their cost of manufacture.

West Germany remained a capitalist economy.

The East German Communist Party forecast in 1958 that material wellbeing would exceed the level of West Germany by 1961. The failure of this prediction was one of the reasons the Berlin Wall separating East from West Germany was built in 1961. By the time the Berlin Wall fell in 1989, and East Germany abandoned central planning, its GDP per capita was less than half of that of capitalist West Germany. Figure 1.10 shows the different paths taken by these and two other economies from 1950. It uses the ratio scale.

natural experiment An empirical study exploiting naturally occurring statistical controls in which researchers do not have the ability to assign participants to treatment and control groups, as is the case in conventional experiments. Instead, differences in law, policy, weather, or other events can offer the opportunity to analyse populations as if they had been part of an experiment. The validity of such studies depends on the premise that the assignment of subjects to the naturally occurring treatment and control groups can be plausibly argued to be random.

More detail about Winston Churchill's 'Iron Curtain' speech (http://tinyco.re/6053919).

Because we cannot change the past, even if it were practical to conduct experiments on entire populations, we rely on natural experiments. In this interview, Jared Diamond, a biologist, and James Robinson, a professor of government, explain (http://tinyco.re/8903951).

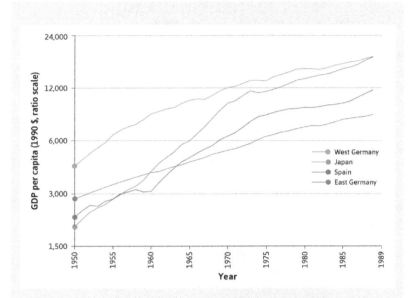

Conference Board, The. 2015. *Total Economy Database*. Angus Maddison. 2001. 'The World Economy: A Millennial Perspective'. Development Centre Studies. Paris: OECD.

Figure 1.10 The two Germanies: Planning and capitalism (1950–89).

Notice from Figure 1.10 that West Germany started from a more favourable position in 1950 than East Germany. Yet in 1936, before the war began, the two parts of Germany had virtually identical living standards. Both regions had achieved successful industrialization. East Germany's relative weakness in 1950 was not mainly because of differences in the amount of capital equipment or skills available per head of the population, but because the structure of industries in East Germany was more disrupted by splitting the country than was the case in West Germany.

Unlike some capitalist economies that had even lower per capita incomes in 1950, East Germany's planned economy did not catch up to the world leaders, which included West Germany. By 1989, the Japanese economy (which had also suffered war damage) had, with its own particular combination of private property, markets, and firms, along with a strong government coordinating role, caught up to West Germany, and Spain had closed part of the gap.

We cannot conclude from the German natural experiment that capitalism always promotes rapid economic growth while central planning is a recipe for relative stagnation. Instead what we can infer is more limited: during the second half of the twentieth century, the divergence of economic institutions mattered for the livelihoods of the German people.

Hartmut Berghoff and Uta Andrea Balbier. 2013. 'From Centrally Planned Economy to Capitalist Avant-Garde? The Creation, Collapse, and Transformation of a Socialist Economy'. In *The East German Economy, 1945–2010: Falling behind or Catching Up?* Cambridge: Cambridge University Press.

●●●
1.10 VARIETIES OF CAPITALISM: INSTITUTIONS, GOVERNMENT, AND THE ECONOMY

Not every capitalist country is the kind of economic success story exemplified in Figure 1.1a by Britain, later Japan, and the other countries that caught up. Figure 1.11 tracks the fortunes of a selection of countries across the world during the twentieth century. It shows for example that in Africa the success of Botswana in achieving sustained growth contrasts sharply with Nigeria's relative failure. Both are rich in natural resources (diamonds in Botswana, oil in Nigeria), but differences in the quality of their institutions—the extent of corruption and misdirection of government funds, for example—may help explain their contrasting trajectories.

The star performer in Figure 1.11 is South Korea. In 1950 its GDP per capita was the same as Nigeria's. By 2013 it was ten times richer by this measure.

South Korea's take-off occurred under institutions and policies sharply different from those prevailing in Britain in the eighteenth and nineteenth centuries. The most important difference is that the government of South Korea (along with a few very large corporations) played a leading role in directing the process of development, explicitly promoting some industries, requiring firms to compete in foreign markets and also providing high quality education for its workforce. The term **developmental state** has been applied to the leading role of the South Korean government in its economic take-off and now refers to any government playing this part in the economy. Japan and China are other examples of developmental states.

From Figure 1.11 we also see that in 1928, when the Soviet Union's first five-year economic plan was introduced, GDP per capita was one-tenth of the level in Argentina, similar to Brazil, and considerably higher than in South Korea. Central planning in the Soviet Union produced steady but unspectacular growth for nearly 50 years. GDP per capita in the Soviet

Doing Business

developmental state A government that takes a leading role in promoting the process of economic development through its public investments, subsidies of particular industries, education and other public policies.

World Bank, The. 1993. *The East Asian miracle: Economic growth and public policy.* New York, NY: Oxford University Press.

Jutta Bolt, and Jan Juiten van Zanden. 2013. 'The First Update of the Maddison Project Re-Estimating Growth Before 1820'. Maddison-Project Working Paper WP-4 (January).

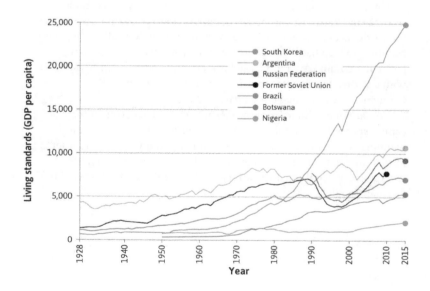

Figure 1.11 Divergence of GDP per capita among latecomers to the capitalist revolution (1928–2015).

Union outstripped Brazil by a wide margin and even overtook Argentina briefly just before Communist Party rule there ended in 1990.

The contrast between West and East Germany demonstrates that one reason central planning was abandoned as an economic system was its failure, in the last quarter of the twentieth century, to deliver the improvements in living standards achieved by some capitalist economies. Yet the varieties of capitalism that replaced central planning in the countries that had once made up the Soviet Union did not work so well either. This is evident from the pronounced dip in GDP per capita for the former Soviet Union after 1990.

When is capitalism dynamic?

The lagging performances of some of the economies in Figure 1.11 demonstrate that the existence of capitalist institutions is not enough, in itself, to create a dynamic economy—that is, an economy bringing sustained growth in living standards. Two sets of conditions contribute to the dynamism of the capitalist economic system. One set is economic; the other is political, and it concerns the government and the way it functions.

Economic conditions

Where capitalism is less dynamic, the explanation might be that:

- *Private property is not secure*: There is weak enforcement of the rule of law and of contracts, or expropriation either by criminal elements or by government bodies.
- *Markets are not competitive*: They fail to offer the carrots and wield the sticks that make a capitalist economy dynamic.
- *Firms are owned and managed by people who survive because of their connections to government or their privileged birth*: They did not become owners or managers because they were good at delivering high-quality goods and services at a competitive price. The other two failures would make this more likely to occur.

Combinations of failures of the three basic institutions of capitalism mean that individuals and groups often have more to gain by spending time and resources in lobbying, criminal activity, and other ways of shifting the distribution of income in their favour. They have less to gain from the direct creation of economic value.

Capitalism is the first economic system in human history in which membership of the elite often depends on a high level of economic performance. As a firm owner, if you fail, you are no longer part of the club. Nobody kicks you out, because that is not necessary: you simply go bankrupt. An important feature of the discipline of the market—produce good products profitably or fail—is that where it works well it is automatic, because having a friend in power is no guarantee that you could remain in business. The same discipline applies to firms and to individuals in firms: losers lose. Market competition provides a mechanism for weeding out those who underperform.

Think of how different this is from other economic systems. A feudal lord who managed his estate poorly was just a shabby lord. But the owner of a firm that could not produce goods that people would buy, at prices that more than covered the cost, is bankrupt—and a bankrupt owner is an ex-owner.

Some researchers question the validity of historical GDP estimates such as this outside of Europe, because the economies of these countries were so different in structure.

János Kornai. 2013. *Dynamism, Rivalry, and the Surplus Economy: Two Essays on the Nature of Capitalism*. Oxford: Oxford University Press.

Dolores Augustine. 2013. 'Innovation and Ideology: Werner Hartmann and the Failure of the East German Electronics Industry'. In *The East German Economy, 1945–2010: Falling behind or Catching Up?* Cambridge: Cambridge University Press.

Daron Acemoglu and James A. Robinson. 2012. *Why Nations Fail: The Origins of Power, Prosperity, and Poverty*. New York, NY: Crown Publishing Group.

Of course, if they are initially very wealthy or very well connected politically, owners and managers of capitalist firms survive, and firms may stay in business despite their failures, sometimes for long periods or even over generations. Losers sometimes survive. But there are no guarantees: staying ahead of the competition means constantly innovating.

Political conditions

Government is also important. We have seen that in some economies— South Korea, for example—governments have played a leading role in the capitalist revolution. And in virtually every modern capitalist economy, governments are a large part of the economy, accounting in some for more than half of GDP. But even where government's role is more limited, as in Britain at the time of its take-off, governments still establish, enforce and change the laws and regulations that influence how the economy works. Markets, private property and firms are all regulated by laws and policies.

For innovators to take the risk of introducing a new product or production process, their ownership of the resulting profits must be protected from theft by a well-functioning legal system. Governments also adjudicate disputes over ownership and enforce the property rights necessary for markets to work.

As Adam Smith warned, by creating or allowing **monopolies** such as the East India Company, governments may also take the teeth out of competition. If a large firm is able to establish a monopoly by excluding all competitors, or a group of firms is able to collude to keep the price high, the incentives for innovation and the discipline of prospective failure will be dulled. The same is true in modern economies when some banks or other firms are considered to be **too big to fail** and instead are bailed out by governments when they might otherwise have failed.

In addition to supporting the institutions of the capitalist economic system, the government provides essential goods and services such as physical infrastructure, education and national defence. In subsequent units we investigate why government policies in such areas as sustaining competition, taxing and subsidizing to protect the environment, influencing the distribution of income, the creation of wealth, and the level of employment and inflation may also make good economic sense.

In a nutshell, capitalism can be a dynamic economic system when it combines:

- *Private incentives for cost-reducing innovation*: These are derived from market competition and secure private property.
- *Firms led by those with proven ability to produce goods at low cost.*
- *Public policy supporting these conditions*: Public policy also supplies essential goods and services that would not be provided by private firms.
- *A stable society, biophysical environment and resource base*: As in Figures 1.5 and 1.12.

These are the conditions that together make up what we term the **capitalist revolution** that, first in Britain and then in some other economies, transformed the way that people interact with each other and with nature in producing their livelihoods.

monopoly A firm that is the only seller of a product without close substitutes. Also refers to a market with only one seller. *See also: monopoly power, natural monopoly.*

too big to fail Said to be a characteristic of large banks, whose central importance in the economy ensures they will be saved by the government if they are in financial difficulty. The bank thus does not bear all the costs of its activities and is therefore likely to take bigger risks. *See also: moral hazard.*

capitalist revolution Rapid improvements in technology combined with the emergence of a new economic system.

Political systems

One of the reasons why capitalism comes in so many forms is that over the course of history and today, capitalist economies have coexisted with many political systems. A **political system**, such as **democracy** or dictatorship, determines how governments will be selected, and how those governments will make and implement decisions that affect the population.

Capitalism emerged in Britain, the Netherlands, and in most of today's high-income countries long before democracy. In no country were most adults eligible to vote prior to the end of the nineteenth century (New Zealand was the first). Even in the recent past, capitalism has coexisted with undemocratic forms of rule, as in Chile from 1973 to 1990, in Brazil from 1964 to 1985, and in Japan until 1945. Contemporary China has a variant of the capitalist economic system, but its system of government is not a democracy by our definition. In most countries today, however, capitalism and democracy coexist, each system influencing how the other works.

Like capitalism, democracy comes in many forms. In some, the head of state is elected directly by the voters; in others it is an elected body, such as a parliament, that elects the head of state. In some democracies there are strict limits on the ways in which individuals can influence elections or public policy through their financial contributions; in others private money has great influence through contributions to electoral campaigns, lobbying, and even illicit contributions such as bribery.

These differences even among democracies are part of the explanation of why the government's importance in the capitalist economy differs so much among nations. In Japan and South Korea, for example, governments play an important role in setting the direction of their economies. But the total amount of taxes collected by government (both local and national) is low compared with some rich countries in northern Europe, where it is almost half of GDP. We shall see in Unit 19 that in Sweden and Denmark, inequality in disposable income (by one of the most commonly used measures) is just half of the level of income inequality before the payment of taxes and receipt of transfers. In Japan and South Korea, government taxes and transfers also reduce inequality in disposable income, but to a far lesser degree.

> **political system** A political system determines how governments will be selected, and how those governments will make and implement decisions that affect all or most members of a population.
>
> **democracy** A political system, that ideally gives equal political power to all citizens, defined by individual rights such as freedom of speech, assembly, and the press; fair elections in which virtually all adults are eligible to vote; and in which the government leaves office if it loses.

QUESTION 1.7 CHOOSE THE CORRECT ANSWER(S)

Look again at Figure 1.10 (page 33), which shows a graph of GDP per capita for West and East Germany, Japan and Spain between 1950 and 1990. Which of the following statements is correct?

☐ Having a much lower starting point in 1950 was the main reason for East Germany's poor performance compared to West Germany.

☐ The fact that Japan and West Germany have the highest GDP per capita in 1990 implies that they found the optimal economic system.

☐ Spain was able to grow at a higher growth rate than Germany between 1950 and 1990.

☐ The difference in East and West Germany's performance proves that capitalism always promotes rapid economic growth while central planning is a recipe for stagnation.

QUESTION 1.8 CHOOSE THE CORRECT ANSWER(S)
Look again at Figure 1.11 (page 34). Which of these conclusions is suggested by the graph?

☐ The Communist Party rule in the former Soviet Union before 1990 was a complete failure.
☐ The contrasting performances of Botswana and Nigeria illustrate that rich natural resources alone do not guarantee higher economic growth, but that higher quality institutions (government, markets and firms) may also be necessary.
☐ The impressive performance of South Korea's economy implies that other countries should copy their economic system.
☐ The evidence from the Russian Federation and the former Soviet Union after 1990 shows that the replacement of central planning by capitalism led to immediate economic growth.

1.11 ECONOMICS AND THE ECONOMY

economics The study of how people interact with each other and with their natural surroundings in providing their livelihoods, and how this changes over time.

Economics is the study of how people interact with each other and with their natural surroundings in producing their livelihoods, and how this changes over time. Therefore it is about:

* *How we come to acquire the things that make up our livelihood*: Things like food, clothing, shelter, or free time.
* *How we interact with each other*: Either as buyers and sellers, employees or employers, citizens and public officials, parents, children and other family members.
* *How we interact with our natural environment*: From breathing, to extracting raw materials from the earth.
* *How each of these changes over time.*

In Figure 1.5 we showed that the economy is part of society, which in turn is part of the biosphere. Figure 1.12 shows the position of firms and families in the economy, and the flows that occur within the economy and between the economy and the biosphere. Firms combine labour with structures and equipment, and produce goods and services that are used by households and other firms.

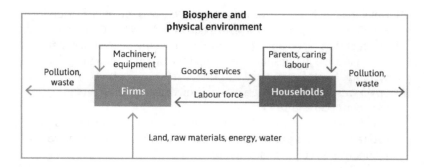

Figure 1.12 A model of the economy: Households and firms.

Production of goods and services also takes place within households, although unlike firms, households may not sell their outputs in the market.

In addition to producing goods and services, households are also producing people—the next generation of the labour force. The labour of parents, caregivers and others is combined with structures (for example, your home) and equipment (for example, the oven in that home) to reproduce and raise the future labour force working in firms, and the people who will work and reproduce in the households of the future.

All of this takes place as part of a biological and physical system in which firms and households make use of our natural surroundings and resources, ranging from fossil-fuel or renewable energy to the air we breathe. In the process, households and firms transform nature by using its resources, but also by producing inputs to nature. Currently, some of the most important of these inputs are the greenhouse gases, which contribute to the climate change problems that we saw in Section 1.5.

EXERCISE 1.11 WHERE AND WHEN WOULD YOU CHOOSE TO HAVE BEEN BORN?

Suppose you can choose to be born in any time period in any of the countries in Figure 1.1a (page 2), 1.10 (page 33) or 1.11 (page 34), but you know that you would be among the poorest 10% in the population.

1. In which country would you choose to be born?
2. Now suppose, instead, you know you would initially be among the poorest 10% in the population, but you would have a fifty-fifty chance of moving to the top 10% of the population if you work hard. In which country would you now choose to be born?
3. Now suppose that you can only decide on the country and time period of your birth. You cannot be sure if you would be born in the city or the countryside, would be male or female, rich or poor. In which time and country would you choose to be born?
4. For the scenario in (3), in which time and country you would least want to be born?

Use what you have learned from this unit to explain your choices.

1.12 CONCLUSION

Throughout most of history, living standards were similar around the world and changed little from century to century. Since 1700 they have risen rapidly in some countries. This upturn coincided with rapid technological progress, and with the advent of a new economic system, capitalism, in which private property, markets and firms play a major role. The capitalist economy provided incentives and opportunities for technological innovation, and gains from specialization.

Countries differ in the effectiveness of their institutions and government policy: not all capitalist economies have experienced sustained growth. Today, there are huge income inequalities between countries, and between the richest and poorest within countries. And the rise in production has been accompanied by depletion of natural resources and environmental damage, including climate change.

Concepts introduced in Unit 1
Before you move on, review these definitions:

- Economics
- Industrial Revolution
- Technology
- Economic system
- Capitalism
- Institutions
- Private property
- Markets
- Firms
- Capitalist revolution
- Democracy

Definitions

1.13 REFERENCES

Acemoglu, Daron, and James A. Robinson. 2012. *Why Nations Fail: The Origins of Power, Prosperity and Poverty*, 1st ed. New York, NY: Crown Publishers.

Augustine, Dolores. 2013. 'Innovation and Ideology: Werner Hartmann and the Failure of the East German Electronics Industry'. In *The East German Economy, 1945–2010: Falling behind or Catching Up?* by German Historical Institute, eds. Hartmut Berghoff and Uta Andrea Balbier. Cambridge: Cambridge University Press.

Berghoff, Hartmut, and Uta Andrea Balbier. 2013. 'From Centrally Planned Economy to Capitalist Avant-Garde? The Creation, Collapse, and Transformation of a Socialist Economy'. In *The East German Economy, 1945–2010 Falling behind or Catching Up?* by German Historical Institute, eds. Hartmut Berghoff and Uta Andrea Balbier. Cambridge: Cambridge University Press.

Coyle, Diane. 2014. *GDP: A Brief but Affectionate History*. Princeton, NJ: Princeton University Press.

Diamond, Jared, and James Robinson. 2014. *Natural Experiments of History*. Cambridge, MA: Belknap Press of Harvard University Press.

Eurostat. 2015. 'Quality of Life Indicators—Measuring Quality of Life' (http://tinyco.re/8771109). Updated 5 November 2015.

Kornai, János. 2013. *Dynamism, Rivalry, and the Surplus Economy: Two Essays on the Nature of Capitalism*. Oxford: Oxford University Press.

Landes, David S. 2003. *The Unbound Prometheus: Technological Change and Industrial Development in Western Europe from 1750 to the Present*. Cambridge, UK: Cambridge University Press.

Robison, Jennifer. 2011. 'Happiness Is Love – and $75,000' (http://tinyco.re/6313076). *Gallup Business Journal*. Updated 17 November 2011.

Seabright, Paul. 2010. *The Company of Strangers: A Natural History of Economic Life* (Revised Edition). Princeton, NJ: Princeton University Press.

Smith, Adam. 1759. *The Theory of Moral Sentiments* (http://tinyco.re/6582039). London: Printed for A. Millar, and A. Kincaid and J. Bell.

Smith, Adam. (1776) 2003. *An Inquiry into the Nature and Causes of the Wealth of Nations* (http://tinyco.re/9804148). New York, NY: Random House Publishing Group.

Sutcliffe, Robert B. 2001. *100 Ways of Seeing an Unequal World*. London: Zed Books.

World Bank, The. 1993. *The East Asian miracle: Economic growth and public policy* (http://tinyco.re/3040506). New York, NY: Oxford University Press.

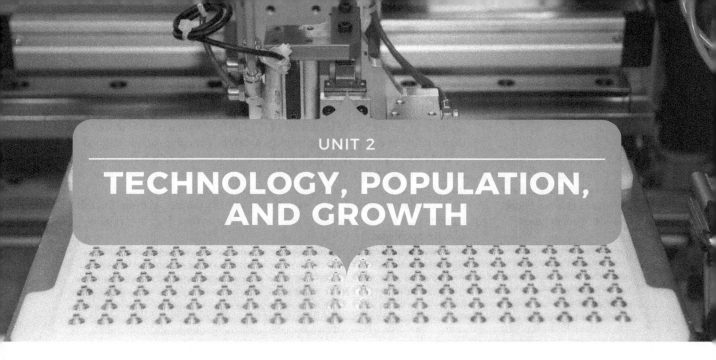

UNIT 2

TECHNOLOGY, POPULATION, AND GROWTH

HOW IMPROVEMENTS IN TECHNOLOGY HAPPEN, AND HOW THEY SUSTAIN GROWTH IN LIVING STANDARDS

- Economic models help explain the Industrial Revolution, and why it started in Britain.
- Wages, the cost of machinery, and other prices all matter when people make economic decisions.
- In a capitalist economy, innovation creates temporary rewards for the innovator, which provide incentives for improvements in technology that reduce costs.
- These rewards are destroyed by competition once the innovation diffuses throughout the economy.
- Population, the productivity of labour, and living standards may interact to produce a vicious circle of economic stagnation.
- The permanent technological revolution associated with capitalism allowed some countries to make a transition to sustained growth in living standards.

THEMES AND CAPSTONE UNITS
- 17: History, instability, and growth
- 18: Global economy
- 19: Inequality
- 21: Innovation

In 1845, a mysterious disease appeared for the first time in Ireland. It caused potatoes to rot in the ground, but by the time it became clear that a plant was infected, it was too late. The 'potato blight', as it became known, devastated Irish food supplies for the rest of the decade. Starvation spread. By the time the Irish famine ended, about a million people out of an initial total of 8.5 million had died, which in percentage terms is equivalent to the mortality suffered by Germany through defeat in the Second World War.

The Irish famine sparked a worldwide relief effort. Former slaves in the Caribbean, convicts in Sing Sing prison in New York, Bengalis both rich and poor, and Choctaw Native Americans all donated money, as did celebrities such as the Ottoman Sultan Abdulmecid and Pope Pius IX. Then, as now, ordinary people felt empathy for others who were suffering, and acted accordingly.

But many economists were much more hard-hearted. One of the best-known, Nassau Senior, consistently opposed British government famine relief, and was reported by a horrified Oxford University colleague as saying that 'he feared the famine of 1848 in Ireland would not kill more than a million people, and that would scarcely be enough to do much good.'

Senior's views are morally repulsive, but they did not reflect a genocidal desire to see Irish men and women die. Instead, they were a consequence of one of the most influential economic doctrines of the early nineteenth century, Malthusianism. This was a body of theory developed by an English clergyman, Thomas Robert Malthus, in *An Essay on the Principle of Population*, first published in 1798.

Malthus held that a sustained increase in income per capita would be impossible.

His logic was that, even if technology improved and raised the productivity of labour, people would still have more children as soon as they were somewhat better off. This population growth would continue until living standards fell to subsistence level, halting the population increase. Malthus' vicious circle of poverty was widely accepted as inevitable.

There is evidence that Victorian colonial administrators thought that famine was nature's response to overbreeding. Mike Davis argues that their attitudes caused an avoidable and unprecedented mass extinction, which he calls a 'cultural genocide'.

It provided an explanation of the world in which Malthus lived, in which incomes might fluctuate from year to year or even century to century, but not trend upwards. This had been the case in many countries for at least 700 years before Malthus published his essay, as we saw in Figure 1.1a.

Unlike Adam Smith, whose book *The Wealth of Nations* had appeared just 22 years earlier, Malthus did not offer an optimistic vision of economic progress—at least as far as ordinary farmers or workers were concerned. Even if people succeeded in improving technology, in the long run the vast majority would earn enough from their jobs or their farms to keep them alive, and no more.

But in Malthus' lifetime something big was happening all around him, changes that would soon allow Britain to escape from the vicious circle of population growth and income stagnation that he described. The change that had sprung Britain from the Malthusian trap, and would do the same for many countries in the 100 years that followed, is known as the **Industrial Revolution**—an extraordinary flowering of radical invention that allowed the same output to be produced with less labour.

In textiles, the most famous inventions involved spinning (traditionally carried out by women known as spinsters, meaning female spinner, a term which has come to mean an older unmarried woman), and weaving (traditionally carried out by men). In 1733, John Kay invented the flying shuttle, which greatly increased the amount a weaver could produce in an hour. This increased the demand for the yarn that was used in weaving to the point where it became difficult for spinsters to produce sufficient quantities using the spinning wheel technology of the day. James Hargreaves' spinning jenny, introduced in 1764, was a response to this problem.

Thomas R. Malthus. 1798. *An Essay on the Principle of Population* (http://tinyco.re/8473883). Library of Economics and Liberty. London: J. Johnson, in St. Paul's Church-yard.

Mike Davis. 2000. *Late Victorian holocausts: El Niño famines and the making of the Third world.* London: Verso Books.

Industrial Revolution A wave of technological advances and organizational changes starting in Britain in the eighteenth century, which transformed an agrarian and craft-based economy into a commercial and industrial economy.

Technological improvements in other areas were equally dramatic. James Watt's steam engine, introduced at the same time as Adam Smith published *The Wealth of Nations*, was a typical example. These engines were gradually improved over a long period of time and were eventually used across the economy: not just in mining, where the first steam engine powered water pumps, but also in textiles, manufacturing, railways and steamships. They are an example of what is termed a **general-purpose innovation** or **technology**. In recent decades the most obvious equivalent is the computer.

Coal played a central role in the Industrial Revolution, and Great Britain had a lot of it. Prior to the Industrial Revolution, most of the energy used in the economy was ultimately produced by edible plants, which converted sunlight into food for both animals and people, or by trees whose wood could be burned or transformed into charcoal. By switching to coal, humans were able to exploit a vast reserve of what is effectively stored sunlight. The cost has been the environmental impact of burning fossil fuels, as we saw in Unit 1 and will return to in Unit 20.

These inventions, alongside other innovations of the Industrial Revolution, broke Malthus' vicious circle. Advances in technology and the increased use of non-renewable resources raised the amount that a person could produce in a given amount of time (productivity), allowing incomes to rise even as the population was increasing. And as long as technology continued improving quickly enough, it could outpace the population growth that resulted from the increased income. Living standards could then rise. Much later, people would prefer smaller families, even when they earned enough to afford to have a lot of children. This is what happened in Britain, and later in many parts of the world.

Figure 2.1 shows an **index** of the average **real wage** (the money wage in each year, adjusted for changes in prices) of skilled craftsmen in London from 1264 to 2001, plotted together with the population of Britain over the same period. There is a long period in which living standards were trapped

> **general-purpose technologies**
> Technological advances that can be applied to many sectors, and spawn further innovations. Information and communications technology (ICT), and electricity are two common examples.

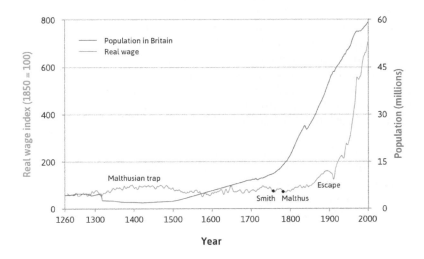

Robert C. Allen. 2001. 'The Great Divergence in European Wages and Prices from the Middle Ages to the First World War'. *Explorations in Economic History* 38 (4): pp. 411–447; Stephen Broadberry, Bruce Campbell, Alexander Klein, Mark Overton and Bas van Leeuwen. 2015. *British Economic Growth, 1270–1870*, Cambridge University Press.

Figure 2.1 Real wages over seven centuries: Wages of craftsmen (skilled workers) in London (1264–2001), and the population of Britain.

according to Malthusian logic, followed by a dramatic increase after 1830. You can see that at the time both were increasing.

INDEX OF REAL WAGES
The term 'index' means the value of some quantitative amount relative to its value at some other time (the reference period) which is usually normalized to 100.

The term 'real' means that the money wage (say, six shillings per hour at the time) in each year has been adjusted to take account of changes in prices over time. The result represents the real buying power of the money the workers earned.

The reference year is 1850 in this case, but the curve would have the same shape if any other year had been selected. It would be positioned higher or lower, but would still look like our familiar hockey stick.

QUESTION 2.1 CHOOSE THE CORRECT ANWER(S)
Figure 2.1 (page 45) shows an index of average real wages of skilled workers in London between 1264 and 2001. What can we conclude from this graph?

☐ Skilled workers were paid about £100 in 1408.
☐ The average wage in 1850 was about the same as that in 1408 in nominal terms (pounds).
☐ The average real wage was more or less constant between 1264 and 1850.
☐ The average real wage increased by around 600% between 1850 and 2001.

Why did the spinning jenny, the steam engine, and a cluster of other inventions emerge and spread across the economy in Britain at this time? This is one of the most important questions in economic history, and historians continue to argue about it.

In this unit we examine one explanation of how these improvements in technology came about, and why they first occurred in Britain only, and during the eighteenth century. We will also explore why the long flat part of Figure 2.1's hockey stick proved so hard to escape not only in Britain, but also throughout the world in the 200 years that followed. We will do this by building models: simplified representations that help us to understand what is going on by focusing attention on what is important. Models will help us understand both the kink in the hockey stick and the long flat handle.

●●●
2.1 ECONOMISTS, HISTORIANS, AND THE INDUSTRIAL REVOLUTION

Why did the Industrial Revolution happen first in the eighteenth century, on an island off the coast of Europe?

Robert C. Allen. 2011. *Global Economic History: A Very Short Introduction*. New York, NY: Oxford University Press.

The following sections of this unit present one model for the sudden and dramatic rise in living standards that began in eighteenth century Britain. Based on arguments from Robert Allen, an economic historian, this model gives a central role to two features of Britain's economy at the time. In this account, the relatively high cost of labour, coupled with the low cost of local energy sources, drove the structural changes of the Industrial Revolution.

What we call the Industrial Revolution was more than just the breaking of the Malthusian cycle: it was a complex combination of inter-related intellectual, technological, social, economic and moral changes. Historians and economists disagree about the relative importance of each of these elements, and have wrestled with explanations for the primacy of Britain, and Europe more generally, ever since their revolutions began. Allen's explanation is far from the only one.

- Joel Mokyr, who has worked extensively on the history of technology, claims that the real sources of technological change are to be found in Europe's scientific revolution and its Enlightenment of the century before. For Mokyr, this period brought the development of new ways to transfer and transform elite scientific knowledge into practical advice and tools for the engineers and skilled artisans, who used it to build the machines of that time. He claims that, while wages and energy prices might tilt the direction of invention in one direction or another, they are more like a steering wheel than the motor of technological progress.

Joel Mokyr. 2004. *The gifts of Athena: Historical origins of the knowledge economy*, 5th ed. Princeton, NJ: Princeton University Press.

- David Landes, a historian, emphasizes the political and cultural characteristics of nations as a whole (Mokyr, in contrast, focuses on artisans and entrepreneurs). He suggests European countries pulled ahead of China because the Chinese state was too powerful and stifled innovation, and because Chinese culture at the time favoured stability over change.

David S. Landes. 2006. 'Why Europe and the west? Why not China?' *Journal of Economic Perspectives* 20 (2) (June): pp. 3–22.

- Gregory Clark, an economic historian, also attributes Britain's take-off to culture. But for Clark, the keys to success were cultural attributes such as hard work and savings, which were passed on to future generations. Clark's argument follows a long tradition that includes the sociologist Max Weber, who saw the Protestant countries of northern Europe, where the Industrial Revolution began, as the particular home of virtues associated with the 'spirit of capitalism'.

Gregory Clark. 2007. *A farewell to alms: A brief economic history of the world*. Princeton, NJ: Princeton University Press.

- Kenneth Pomeranz, a historian, claims that superior European growth after 1800 was more due to the abundance of coal in Britain than to any cultural or institutional differences with other countries. Pomeranz also argues that Britain's access to agricultural production in its New World colonies (especially sugar and its by-products) fed the expanding class of industrial workers, thus helping them to escape the Malthusian trap.

Kenneth L. Pomeranz. 2000. *The great divergence: Europe, China, and the making of the modern world economy*. Princeton, NJ: Princeton University Press.

Scholars will probably never completely agree about what caused the Industrial Revolution. One problem is that this change happened only once, which makes it more difficult for social scientists to explain. Also, the European take-off was probably the result of a combination of scientific, demographic, political, geographic and military factors. Several scholars argue that it was partly due to interactions between Europe and the rest of the world too, not just due to changes within Europe.

Historians like Pomeranz tend to focus on peculiarities of time and place. They are more likely to conclude that the Industrial Revolution happened because of a unique combination of favourable circumstances (they may disagree about which ones).

Economists like Allen are more likely to look for general mechanisms that can explain success or failure across both time and space.

Economists have much to learn from historians, but often a historian's argument is not precise enough to be testable using a model (the approach we will use in this unit). On the other hand, historians may regard economists' models as simplistic, ignoring important historical facts. This creative tension is what makes economic history so fascinating.

Recently, economic historians have made progress in quantifying economic growth over the very long run. Their work helps clarify what happened, which makes it easier for us to think about why it happened. Some of their work involves comparing real wages in countries over the long run. This has involved collecting both wages and the prices of goods

If you want to know what these researchers think of each other's work, try searching for 'Gregory Clark review Joel Mokyr' or 'Robert Allen review Gregory Clark'.

that workers consumed. An even more ambitious series of projects has calculated GDP per capita back to the Middle Ages.

We will focus on the economic conditions that contributed to Britain's take-off, but each economy that broke out of the Malthusian trap took a different escape route. The national trajectories of the early followers were influenced in part by the dominant role that Britain had come to play in the world economy. Germany, for example, could not compete with Britain in textiles, but the government and large banks played a major role in building steel and other heavy industries. Japan outcompeted even Britain in some Asian textile markets, benefiting from the isolation it enjoyed by the sheer distance from the earlier starters (which in those days was weeks of travel).

Japan selectively copied both technology and institutions, introducing the capitalist economic system while retaining many traditional Japanese institutions including rule by an emperor, which would last until the Japanese defeat in the Second World War.

India and China provide even greater contrasts. China experienced the capitalist revolution when the Communist Party led a transition away from the centrally planned economy, the antithesis of capitalism that the Party itself had implemented. India, by contrast, is the first major economy in history to have adopted democracy, including universal voting rights, prior to its capitalist revolution.

David S. Landes. 1990. 'Why are We So Rich and They So Poor?'. *The American Economic Review* 80 (May): pp. 1–13.

As we saw in Unit 1, the Industrial Revolution did not lead to economic growth everywhere. Because it originated in Britain, and spread only slowly to the rest of the world, it also implied a huge increase in income inequality between countries. Looking at economic growth around the world in the nineteenth and twentieth centuries, David Landes once asked: 'Why are we so rich and they so poor?'

By 'we', he meant the rich societies of Europe and North America. By 'they' he meant the poorer societies of Africa, Asia and Latin America. Landes suggested, a little mischievously, that there were basically two answers to this question:

> One says that we are so rich and they so poor because we are so good and they so bad; that is, we are hardworking, knowledgeable, educated, well governed, efficacious, and productive, and they are the reverse. The other says that we are so rich and they so poor because we are so bad and they so good: we are greedy, ruthless, exploitative, aggressive, while they are weak, innocent, virtuous, abused, and vulnerable.

If you think that the Industrial Revolution happened in Europe because of the Protestant Reformation, or the Renaissance, or the scientific revolution, or the development of superior private property rights, or favourable government policies, then you are in the first camp. If you think that it happened because of colonialism, or slavery, or the demands of constant warfare, then you are in the second.

You will notice that these are all non-economic forces that, according to some scholars, had important economic consequences. You can probably also see how the question of which of Landes's two answers is right might become ideologically charged although, as Landes points out, 'It is not clear … that one line of argument necessarily precludes the other.'

2.2 ECONOMIC MODELS: HOW TO SEE MORE BY LOOKING AT LESS

What happens in the economy depends on what millions of people do, and how their decisions affect the behaviour of others. It would be impossible to understand the economy by describing every detail of how they act and interact. We need to be able to stand back and look at the big picture. To do this, we use models.

To create an effective model we need to distinguish between the essential features of the economy that are relevant to the question we want to answer, which should be included in the model, and unimportant details that can be ignored.

Models come in many forms—and you have seen three of them already in Figures 1.5, 1.8 and 1.12 in Unit 1. For example, Figure 1.12 illustrated that economic interactions involve **flows** of goods (for example when you buy a washing machine), services (when you purchase haircuts or bus rides), and also people (when you spend a day working for an employer).

Figure 1.12 was a diagrammatic model illustrating the flows that occur within the economy, and between the economy and the biosphere. The model is not 'realistic'—the economy and the biosphere don't look anything like it—but it nevertheless illustrates the relationships among them. The fact that the model omits many details—and in this sense is unrealistic—is a feature of the model, not a bug.

Malthus' explanation of why improvements in technology could not raise living standards was also based on a model: a simple description of the relationships between income and population.

Some economists have used physical models to illustrate and explore how the economy works. For his 1891 PhD thesis at Yale University, Irving Fisher designed a hydraulic apparatus (Figure 2.2) to represent flows in the economy. It consisted of interlinked levers and floating cisterns of water to show how the prices of goods depend on the amount of each good supplied, the incomes of consumers, and how much they value each good. The whole apparatus stops moving when the water levels in the cisterns are the same as the level in the surrounding tank. When it comes to rest, the position of a partition in each cistern corresponds to the price of each good. For the next 25 years he would use the contraption to teach students how markets work.

How models are used in economics

Fisher's study of the economy illustrates how all models are used:

1. First he built a model to capture the elements of the economy that he thought mattered for the determination of prices.
2. Then he used the model to show how interactions between these elements could result in a set of prices that did not change.
3. Finally he conducted experiments with the model to discover the effects of changes in economic conditions: for example, if the supply of one of the goods increased, what would happen to its price? What would happen to the prices of all of the other goods?

Irving Fisher's doctoral dissertation represented the economy as a big tank of water, but he wasn't an eccentric inventor. On the contrary, his machine was described by Paul Samuelson, himself one of the greatest economists of the twentieth century, as the 'greatest doctoral dissertation in economics

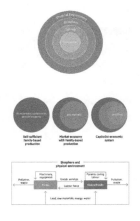

Models come in many forms. You have seen three of them already in Figures 1.5, 1.8 and 1.12 in Unit 1.

flow A quantity measured per unit of time, such as annual income or hourly wage.

ever written'. Fisher went on to become one of the most highly regarded economists of the twentieth century, and his contributions formed the basis of modern theories of borrowing and lending that we will describe in Unit 10.

Fisher's machine illustrates an important concept in economics. An **equilibrium** is a situation that is self-perpetuating, meaning that something of interest does not change unless an outside or external force for change is introduced that alters the model's description of the situation. Fisher's hydraulic apparatus represented equilibrium in his model economy by equalizing water levels, which represented constant prices.

We will use the concept of equilibrium to explain prices in later units, but we will also apply it to the Malthusian model. An income at **subsistence level** is an equilibrium because, just like differences in the water levels in the various cisterns in Fisher's machine, movements away from subsistence income are self-correcting: they automatically lead back to subsistence income as population rises.

Note that equilibrium means that one or more things in the model are constant. It does not need to mean that nothing changes. For example, we might see an equilibrium in which GDP or prices are increasing, but at a constant rate.

Although it is unlikely that you will build a hydraulic model for yourself, you will work with many existing models on paper or on a screen, and sometimes create your own models of the economy.

When we build a model, the process follows these steps:

1. We construct a simplified description of the conditions under which people take actions.
2. Then we describe in simple terms what determines the actions that people take.

> **equilibrium** A model outcome that is self-perpetuating. In this case, something of interest does not change unless an outside or external force is introduced that alters the model's description of the situation.

> **subsistence level** The level of living standards (measured by consumption or income) such that the population will not grow or decline.

William C. Brainard and Herbert E. Scarf. 2005. 'How to Compute Equilibrium Prices in 1891'. *American Journal of Economics and Sociology* 64 (1): pp. 57–83

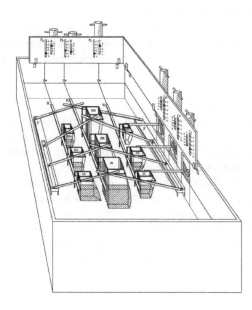

Figure 2.2 Irving Fisher's sketch of his hydraulic model of economic equilibrium (1891).

3. We determine how each of their actions affects each other.
4. We determine the outcome of these actions. This is often an equilibrium (something is constant).
5. Finally, we try to get more insight by studying what happens to certain variables when conditions change.

Economic models often use mathematical equations and graphs as well as words and pictures.

Mathematics is part of the language of economics, and can help us to communicate our statements about models precisely to others. Much of the knowledge of economics, however, cannot be expressed by using mathematics alone. It requires clear descriptions, using standard definitions of terms.

We will use mathematics as well as words to describe models, usually in the form of graphs. If you want, you will also be able to look at some of the equations behind the graphs. Just look for the references to our Leibniz features in the margins.

A model starts with some assumptions or hypotheses about how people behave, and often gives us predictions about what we will observe in the economy. Gathering data on the economy, and comparing it with what a model predicts, helps us to decide whether the assumptions we made when we built the model—what to include, and what to leave out—were justified.

Governments, central banks, corporations, trade unions, and anyone else who makes policies or forecasts use some type of simplified model.

Bad models can result in disastrous policies, as we will see later. To have confidence in a model, we need to see whether it is consistent with evidence.

We will see that our economic models of the vicious circle of Malthusian subsistence living standards and the permanent technological revolution pass this test—even though they leave many questions unanswered.

> **ECONOMIC MODELS**
> A good model has four attributes:
> - It is clear: It helps us better understand something important.
> - It predicts accurately: Its predictions are consistent with evidence.
> - It improves communication: It helps us to understand what we agree (and disagree) about.
> - It is useful: We can use it to find ways to improve how the economy works.

Introducing the Leibnizes
(http://tinyco.re/L020201)

> **EXERCISE 2.1 DESIGNING A MODEL**
> For a country (or city) of your choice, look up a map of the railway or public transport network.
>
> Much like economic models, maps are simplified representations of reality. They include relevant information, while abstracting from irrelevant details.
>
> 1. How do you think the designer selected which features of reality to include in the map you have selected?
> 2. In what way is a map not like an economic model?

2.3 BASIC CONCEPTS: PRICES, COSTS, AND INNOVATION RENTS

In this unit, we are going to build an economic model to help explain the circumstances under which new technologies are chosen, both in the past and in contemporary economies. We use four key ideas of economic modelling:

- *Ceteris paribus* and other simplifications help us focus on the variables of interest. We see more by looking at less.
- **Incentives** matter, because they affect the benefits and costs of taking one action as opposed to another.
- **Relative prices** help us compare alternatives.
- **Economic rent** is the basis of how people make choices.

Part of the process of learning to do economics involves learning a new language. The terms below will recur frequently in the units that follow, and it is important to learn how to use them precisely and with confidence.

Ceteris paribus and simplification

As is common in scientific inquiry, economists often simplify an analysis by setting aside things that are thought to be of less importance to the question of interest, by using the phrase 'holding other things constant' or, more often, the Latin expression *ceteris paribus*, meaning 'other things equal'. For example, later in the course we simplify an analysis of what people would choose to buy by looking at the effect of changing a price—ignoring other influences on our behaviour like brand loyalty, or what others would think of our choices. We ask: what would happen if the price changed, but everything else that might influence the decision was the same. These *ceteris paribus* assumptions, when used well, can clarify the picture without distorting the key facts.

When we study the way that a capitalist economic system promotes technological improvements, we will look at how changes in wages affect firms' choice of technology. For the simplest possible model we 'hold constant' other factors affecting firms. So we assume:

- Prices of all inputs are the same for all firms.
- All firms know the technologies used by other firms.
- Attitudes towards risk are similar among firm owners.

ceteris paribus Economists often simplify analysis by setting aside things that are thought to be of less importance to the question of interest. The literal meaning of the expression is 'other things equal'. In an economic model it means an analysis 'holds other things constant'.

incentive Economic reward or punishment, which influences the benefits and costs of alternative courses of action.

relative price The price of one good or service compared to another (usually expressed as a ratio).

economic rent A payment or other benefit received above and beyond what the individual would have received in his or her next best alternative (or reservation option). *See also: reservation option.*

EXERCISE 2.2 USING *CETERIS PARIBUS*

Suppose you build a model of the market for umbrellas, in which the predicted number of umbrellas sold by a shop depends on their colour and price, *ceteris paribus*.

1. The colour and the price are variables used to predict sales. Which other variables are being held constant?

Which of the following questions do you think this model might be able to answer? In each case, suggest improvements to the model that might help you to answer the question.

2. Why are annual umbrella sales higher in the capital city than in other towns?
3. Why are annual umbrella sales higher in some shops in the capital city than others?
4. Why have weekly umbrella sales in the capital city risen over the last six months?

Incentives matter

Why did the water in Fisher's hydraulic economy machine move when he changed the quantity of 'supply' or 'demand' for one or more of the goods, so that the prices were no longer in equilibrium?

- Gravity acts on the water so it finds the lowest level.
- Channels allow the water to seek out the lowest level, but restrict the ways in which it can flow.

All economic models have something equivalent to gravity, and a description of the kinds of movements that are possible. The equivalent of gravity is the assumption that, by taking one course of action over another, people are attempting to do as well as they can (according to some standard).

The analogy to the free movement of water in Fisher's machine is that people are free to select different courses of action, rather than simply being told what to do. This is where economic incentives affect the choices we make. But we can't do everything we want to do: not every channel is open to us.

Like many economic models, the one we use to explain the permanent technological revolution is based on the idea that people or firms respond to economic incentives. As we will see in Unit 4, people are motivated not only by the desire for material gain but also by love, hate, sense of duty, and desire for approval. But material comfort is an important motive, and economic incentives appeal to this motive.

When owners or managers of firms decide how many workers to hire, or when shoppers decide what and how much to buy, prices are going to be an important factor determining their decision. If prices are a lot lower in the discount supermarket than in the corner shop, and it is not too far away, then this will be a good argument for shopping in the supermarket rather than in the shop.

Relative prices

A third characteristic of many economic models is that we are often interested in ratios of things, rather than their absolute level. Economics focuses attention on alternatives and choices. If you are deciding where to shop, it is not the corner shop prices alone that matter, but rather the prices relative to those in the supermarket and relative to the costs of reaching the supermarket. If all of these were to rise by 5%, your decision probably wouldn't change.

Relative prices are simply the price of one option relative to another. We often express relative price as the ratio of two prices. We will see that they matter a lot in explaining not just what shoppers (or consumers, as we usually call them) decide to buy, but why firms make the choices that they do. When we study the Industrial Revolution, you will see that the ratio of energy prices (the price of coal, for example, to power a steam engine), to the wage rate (the price of an hour of a worker's time) plays an important part in the story.

Reservation positions and rents

Imagine that you have figured out a new way of reproducing sound in high quality. Your invention is much cheaper to use than anyone else's method. Your competitors cannot copy you, either because they cannot figure out how to do it or because you have a patent on the process (making it illegal for them to copy you). So they continue offering their services at a price that is much higher than your costs.

If you match their price, or undercut them by just a bit, you will be able to sell as much as you can produce, so you can charge the same price but make profits that greatly exceed those of your competitors. In this case, we say that you are making an innovation rent. Innovation rents are a form of economic rent—and economic rents occur throughout the economy. They are one of the reasons why capitalism can be such a dynamic system.

We will use the idea of innovation rents to explain some of the factors contributing to the Industrial Revolution. But **economic rent** is a general concept that will help explain many other features of the economy.

When taking some action (call it action A) results in a greater benefit to yourself than the next best action, we say that you have received an economic rent.

economic rent = benefit from option taken − benefit from next best option

The term is easily confused with everyday uses of the word, such as the rent for temporary use of a car, apartment, or piece of land. To avoid this confusion, when we mean economic rent, we emphasize the word 'economic'. Remember, an economic rent is something you would like to get, not something you have to pay.

The alternative action with the next greatest net benefit (action B), is often called the 'next best alternative', your 'reservation position', or the term we use: **reservation option**. It is 'in reserve' in case you do not choose A. Or, if you are enjoying A but then someone excludes you from doing it, your reservation option is your Plan B. This is why it is also called a 'fallback option'.

Economic rent gives us a simple decision rule:

- *If action A would give you an economic rent (and nobody else would suffer)*: Do it!
- *If you are already doing action A, and it earns you an economic rent*: Carry on doing it!

This decision rule motivates our explanation of why a firm may innovate by switching from one technology to another. We start in the next section by comparing technologies.

> **reservation option** A person's next best alternative among all options in a particular transaction. *Also known as: fallback option. See also: reservation price.*

QUESTION 2.2 CHOOSE THE CORRECT ANSWER(S)
Which of the following is an economic rent?

- ☐ The amount you pay your landlord for the use of an apartment.
- ☐ The amount you pay to hire a car for a weekend.
- ☐ The extra profit that a successful innovator makes on bringing a new product to the market before its competitors.
- ☐ The extra profit that a firm makes when it doubles in size and there are no changes to costs or the price for each unit of its output.

2.4 MODELLING A DYNAMIC ECONOMY: TECHNOLOGY AND COSTS

We now apply these modelling ideas to explain technological progress. In this section we consider:

- What is a technology?
- How does a firm evaluate the cost of different technologies?

What is a technology?

Suppose we ask an engineer to report on the technologies that are available to produce 100 metres of cloth, where the inputs are labour (number of workers, each working for a standard eight-hour day) and energy (tonnes of coal). The answer is represented in the diagram and table in Figure 2.3. The five points in the table represent five different technologies. For example, technology E uses 10 workers and 1 tonne of coal to produce 100 metres of cloth.

Follow the steps in Figure 2.3 (page 56) so you can understand the five technologies.

We describe the E-technology as relatively labour-intensive and the A-technology as relatively energy-intensive. If an economy were using technology E and shifted to using technology A or B we would say that they had adopted a labour-saving technology, because the amount of labour used to produce 100 metres of cloth with these two technologies is less than with technology E. This is what happened during the Industrial Revolution.

Which technology will the firm choose? The first step is to rule out technologies that are obviously inferior. We begin in Figure 2.4 with the A-technology and look to see whether any of the alternative technologies use at least as much labour and coal. The C-technology is inferior to A: to produce 100 metres of cloth, it uses more workers (three rather than one) and more coal (7 tonnes rather than 6 tonnes). We say the C-technology is **dominated** by the A-technology: assuming all inputs must be paid for, no firm will use technology C when A is available. The steps in Figure 2.4 show you how to see which of the technologies are dominated, and which technologies dominate.

Using only the engineering information about inputs, we have narrowed down the choices: the C- and D-technologies would never be chosen. But how does the firm choose between A, B and E? This requires an assumption about what the firm is trying to do. We assume its goal is to make as much profit as possible, which means producing cloth at the least possible cost.

Making a decision about technology also requires economic information about relative prices—the cost of hiring a worker relative to that of purchasing a tonne of coal. Intuitively, the labour-intensive E-technology would be chosen if labour was very cheap relative to the cost of coal; the energy-intensive A-technology would be preferable in a situation where coal is relatively cheap. An economic model helps us be more precise than this.

How does a firm evaluate the cost of production using different technologies?

The firm can calculate the cost of any combination of inputs that it might use by multiplying the number of workers by the wage and the tonnes of

> **dominated** We describe an outcome in this way if more of something that is positively valued can be attained without less of anything else that is positively valued. In short: an outcome is dominated if there is a win-win alternative.

coal by the price of coal. We use the symbol w for the wage, L for the number of workers, p for the price of coal and R for the tonnes of coal:

$$\text{cost} = (\text{wage} \times \text{workers}) + (\text{price of a tonne of coal} \times \text{number of tonnes})$$
$$= (w \times L) + (p \times R)$$

Suppose that the wage is £10 and the price of coal is £20 per tonne. In the table in Figure 2.5, we have calculated the cost of employing two workers and three tonnes of coal, which is £80. This corresponds to combination P_1 in the diagram. If the firm were to employ more workers—say, six—but reduce the input of coal to one tonne (point P_2), that would also cost £80.

isocost line A line that represents all combinations that cost a given total amount.

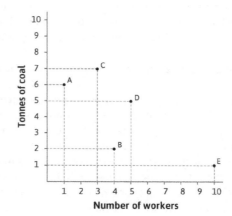

Technology	Number of workers	Coal required (tonnes)
A	1	6
B	4	2
C	3	7
D	5	5
E	10	1

Figure 2.3 Different technologies for producing 100 metres of cloth.

1. Five technologies for producing 100 metres of cloth compared
The table describes five different technologies that we refer to in the rest of this section. They use different quantities of labour and coal as inputs for producing 100 metres of cloth.

2. Technology A: energy-intensive
The A-technology is the most energy-intensive, using 1 worker and 6 tonnes of coal.

3. Technology B
The B-technology uses 4 workers and 2 tonnes of coal: it is a more labour-intensive technology than A.

4. Technology C
The C-technology uses 3 workers and 7 tonnes of coal.

5. Technology D
The D-technology uses 5 workers and 5 tonnes of coal.

6. Technology E: Labour-intensive
Finally, the E-technology uses 10 workers and 1 tonne of coal. This is the most labour-intensive of the five technologies.

Follow the steps in Figure 2.5 to see how we construct **isocost lines** to compare the costs of all combinations of inputs.

Isocost lines join all the combinations of workers and coal that cost the same amount. We can use them to help us compare the costs of the three technologies A, B, and E that remain in play (that is, are not dominated).

The table in Figure 2.6 shows the cost of producing 100 metres of cloth with each technology when the wage is £10 and the price of coal is £20. Clearly the B-technology allows the firm to produce cloth at lower cost.

In the diagram, we have drawn the isocost line through the point representing technology B. This shows immediately that, at these input prices (remember that the wage is the 'price' of labour), the other two technologies are more costly.

We can see from Figure 2.6 that B is the least-cost technology when $w = 10$ and $p = 20$. The other available technologies will not be chosen at these input prices. Notice that it is the relative price that matters and not the absolute price: if both prices doubled, the diagram would look almost

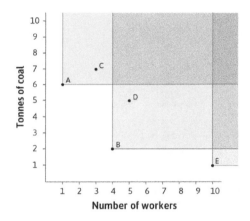

Figure 2.4 Technology A dominates C; technology B dominates D.

1. Which technologies dominate others?
The five technologies for producing 100 metres of cloth are represented by the points A to E. We can use this figure to show which technologies dominate others.

2. A dominates C
Clearly, technology A dominates the C-technology: the same amount of cloth can be produced using A with fewer inputs of labour and energy. This means that, whenever A is available, you would never use C.

3. B dominates D
Technology B dominates the D-technology: the same amount of cloth can be produced using B with fewer inputs of labour and energy. Note that B would dominate any other technology that is in the shaded area above and to the right of point B.

4. E does not dominate
Technology A dominates C; technology B dominates D. The E-technology does not dominate any of the other available technologies. We know this because none of the other four technologies are in the area above and to the right of E.

the same: the isocost line through B would have the same slope, although the cost would be £160.

We can now represent the isocost lines for any wage w and coal price p as equations. To do this, we write c for the cost of production. We begin with the cost of production equation:

$$c = (w \times L) + (p \times R)$$

that is:

$$c = wL + pR$$

This is one way to write the equation of the isocost line for any value of c.

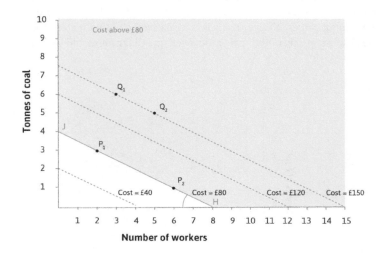

Figure 2.5 Isocost lines when the wage is £10 and the price of coal is £20.

1. The total cost at P_1
The total cost of employing 2 workers with 3 tonnes of coal is $(2 \times 10) + (3 \times 20) = £80$.

2. P_2 also costs £80
If the number of workers is increased to 6, costing £60, and the input of coal is reduced to 1 tonne, the total cost will still be £80.

3. The isocost line for £80
The straight line through P_1 and P_2 joins together all the points where the total cost is £80. We call this an **isocost line**: iso is the Greek for 'same'. When drawing the line, we simplify by assuming that fractions of workers and of coal can be purchased.

4. A higher isocost line
At point Q_1 (3 workers, 6 tonnes of coal) the total cost is £150. To find the £150 isocost line, look for another point costing £150: if 2 more workers are employed, the input of coal should be reduced by 1 tonne to keep the cost at £150. This is point Q_2.

5. More isocost lines
We could draw isocost lines through any other set of points in the diagram. If prices of inputs are fixed, the isocost lines are parallel. A simple way to draw any line is to find the end points: for example, the £80 line joins the points J (4 tonnes of coal and no workers) and H (8 workers, no coal).

6. The slope of every isocost line is:
$-(w/p)$
The slope of the isocost lines is negative (they slope downward). In this case the slope is -0.5, because at each point, if you hired one more worker, costing £10, and reduced the amount of coal by 0.5 tonnes, saving £10, the total cost would remain unchanged. The slope is equal to $-(w/p)$, the wage divided by the price of coal.

7. Points above an isocost line cost more
If we look at one isocost line—the £80 one—we can see that all points above the line cost more than £80, and all points below cost less.

To draw an isocost line, it can help to express it in the form:

$$y = a + bx$$

where a, which is a constant, is the vertical axis intercept and b is the slope of the line. In our model, tonnes of coal, R, are on the vertical axis, the number of workers, L, is on the horizontal axis and we shall see that the slope of the line is the wage relative to the price of coal, $-(w/p)$. The isocost line slopes downward so the slope term in the equation $-(w/p)$ is negative.

The equation:

$$c = wL + pR$$

can be rewritten as:

$$pR = c - wL$$

and further rearranged as:

$$R = \frac{c}{p} - \frac{w}{p}L$$

So when $w = 10$ and $p = 20$, the isocost line for $c = 80$ has a vertical axis intercept of $80/20 = 4$ and a negative slope equal to $-(w/p) = -1/2$. The slope is the relative price of labour.

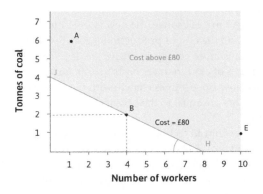

Technology	Number of workers	Coal required (tonnes)	Total cost (£)
B	4	2	80
A	1	6	130
E	10	1	120

Wage £10, cost of coal £20 per tonne

Figure 2.6 The cost of using different technologies to produce 100 metres of cloth: Low relative cost of labour.

EXERCISE 2.3 ISOCOST LINES

Suppose the wage is £10 but the price of coal is only £5.

1. What is the relative price of labour?
2. Using the method in the text, write down the equation of the isocost line for c = £60, and rewrite it in the standard form y = a + bx.
3. Write the equations for the £30 and £90 isocost lines in the standard form too, and draw all three lines on a diagram. How does the set of isocost lines for these input prices compare to the ones for w = 10 and p = 20?

2.5 MODELLING A DYNAMIC ECONOMY: INNOVATION AND PROFIT

We have seen that when the wage is £10 and the price of coal is £20, B is the least-cost technology.

Any change in the relative price of these two inputs will change the slope of the isocost lines. Looking at the positions of the three technologies in Figure 2.7, we can imagine that if the isocost line becomes sufficiently steep (with the wage rising relative to the cost of coal), B will no longer be the least-cost technology: the firm will switch to A. This is what happened in England in the eighteenth century.

Let's look at how a change in relative prices could cause this to happen. Suppose that the price of coal falls to £5 while the wage remains at £10.

Looking at the table in Figure 2.7, with the new prices, the A-technology allows the firm to produce 100 metres of cloth at least cost. Cheaper coal makes each method of production cheaper, but the energy-intensive technology is now cheapest.

Remember that to draw the isocost line through any point, such as A, we calculate the cost at A (£40) then look for another point with the same cost. The easiest way is to find one of the end points F or G. For example, if no coal was used, four workers could be hired for £40. This is point F.

You can see from Figure 2.7 that with the new relative price the A-technology lies on the £40 isocost line, and the other two available technologies lie above it. They will not be chosen if the A-technology is available.

How does a cost-reducing innovation raise the profits of the firm?
The next step is to calculate the gains to the first firm to adopt the least-cost technology (A) when the relative price of labour to coal rises. Like all its competitors, the firm is initially using the B-technology and minimizing its costs: this is shown in Figure 2.8 by the dashed isocost line through B (with end points H and J).

Once the relative prices change, the new isocost line through the B-technology is steeper and the cost of production is £50. Switching to the A-technology (which is more energy-intensive and less labour-intensive) to produce 100 metres of cloth reduces costs to £40. Follow the steps in Figure 2.8 to see how isocost lines change with the new relative prices.

The firm's profits are equal to the revenue it gets from selling output minus its costs.

Whether the new or old technology is used, the same prices have to be paid for labour and coal, and the same price is received for selling 100 metres of cloth. The change in profit is thus equal to the fall in costs associated with adopting the new technology, and profits rise by £10 per 100 metres of cloth:

$$\text{profit} = \text{revenue} - \text{costs}$$
$$\text{change in profit from switching to B} = \text{change in revenue} - \text{change in costs}$$
$$= 0 - (40 - 50)$$
$$= 10$$

In this case, the economic rent for a firm switching from B to A is £10 per 100 metres of cloth, which is the cost reduction made possible by the new technology. The decision rule (if the economic rent is positive, do it!) tells the firm to innovate.

In our example, the A-technology was available, but not in use until a first-adopter firm responded to the incentive created by the increase in the relative price of labour. The first adopter is called an **entrepreneur**. When we describe a person or firm as entrepreneurial, it refers to a willingness to try out new technologies and to start new businesses.

The economist Joseph Schumpeter (see below) made the adoption of technological improvements by entrepreneurs a key part of his explanation for the dynamism of capitalism. This is why innovation rents are often called Schumpeterian rents.

Innovation rents will not last forever. Other firms, noticing that entrepreneurs are making economic rents, will eventually adopt the new technology. They will also reduce their costs and their profits will increase.

> **entrepreneur** A person who creates or is an early adopter of new technologies, organizational forms, and other opportunities.

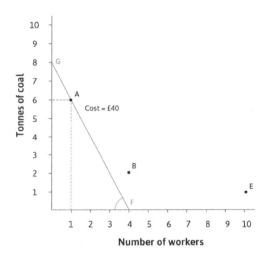

Technology	Number of workers	Coal required (tonnes)	Total cost (£)
B	4	2	50
A	1	6	40
E	10	1	105

Wage £10, cost of coal £5 per tonne

Figure 2.7 The cost of using different technologies to produce 100 metres of cloth: high relative cost of labour.

1. Technology A costs the least when coal is relatively cheap
When the wage is £10 and the price of coal is £5, the table shows that the A-technology, which is more energy-intensive than the others, can produce 100 metres of cloth at a lower cost than B or E.

2. The £40 isocost curve when w = 10 and p = 5
The A-technology is on the isocost line FG. At any point on this line, the total cost of inputs is £40. Technologies B and E are above this line, with higher costs.

3. The slope of the isocost line
The slope of the isocost line can be found by calculating the relative price of labour. It is equal to $-(10/5) = -2$. If you spent £10 on labour by hiring an extra worker, you could reduce coal by 2 tonnes and keep the total cost at £40.

> **creative destruction** Joseph Schumpeter's name for the process by which old technologies and the firms that do not adapt are swept away by the new, because they cannot compete in the market. In his view, the failure of unprofitable firms is creative because it releases labour and capital goods for use in new combinations.

In this case, with higher profits per 100 metres of cloth, the lower-cost firms will thrive. They will increase their output of cloth. As more firms introduce the new technology, the supply of cloth to the market increases and the price will start to fall. This process will continue until everyone is using the new technology, at which stage prices will have declined to the point where no one is earning innovation rents. The firms that stuck to the old B-technology will be unable to cover their costs at the new lower price for cloth, and they will go bankrupt. Joseph Schumpeter called this **creative destruction**.

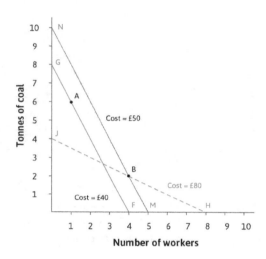

Technology	Number of workers	Coal required (tonnes)	Total cost (£)
Wage £10, Cost of coal £20 per tonne			
B	4	2	80
Wage £10, Cost of coal £5 per tonne			
B	4	2	50
A	1	6	40

Figure 2.8 The cost of using different technologies to produce 100 metres of cloth.

1. At the original relative price, B is the lower cost technology
When the wage is £10 and the price of coal is relatively high at £20, the cost of producing 100 metres of cloth using technology B is £80: choosing the B-technology puts the firm on the HJ isocost curve.

2. The price of coal falls to £5
If the price of coal falls relative to the wage as shown by the isocost curve FG, then using the A-technology, which is more energy-intensive than B, costs £40. From the table, we see that with these relative prices, A is now the least-cost technology.

3. B now costs more than A
At the new relative prices, the B-technology is on the isocost line MN, where the cost is £50. Switching to technology A will be cheaper.

QUESTION 2.3 CHOOSE THE CORRECT ANSWER(S)

Figure 2.3 (page 56) shows different technologies for producing 100 metres of cloth.

From the graph, what can we conclude?

- ☐ Technology D is more energy-intensive than technology C.
- ☐ Technology B dominates technology D.
- ☐ Technology A is the cost-minimizing technology at all prices of coal and wages.
- ☐ Technology C can sometimes be a cheaper technology than A.

QUESTION 2.4 CHOOSE THE CORRECT ANSWER(S)

Look at the three isocost lines in Figure 2.8 (page 62).

Based on this information, what can we conclude?

- ☐ When the wage is £10 and the price of coal is £5, the combination of inputs at point N is more costly than the inputs at point B.
- ☐ Isocosts MN and FG represent the same price ratio (wage/price of coal) but different total costs of production.
- ☐ Isocost HJ represents a higher (wage/price of coal) ratio than isocost FG.
- ☐ Isocost HJ represents all points that can produce 100 metres of cloth at a particular price ratio.

GREAT ECONOMISTS

Joseph Schumpeter

Joseph Schumpeter (1883–1950) developed one of the most important concepts of modern economics: **creative destruction**.

Schumpeter brought to economics the idea of the entrepreneur as the central actor in the capitalist economic system. The entrepreneur is the agent of change who introduces new products, new methods of production, and opens up new markets. Imitators follow, and the innovation is diffused through the economy. A new entrepreneur and innovation launch the next upswing.

For Schumpeter, creative destruction was the essential fact about capitalism: old technologies and the firms that do not adapt are swept away by the new, because they cannot compete in the market by selling goods at a price that covers the cost of production. The failure of unprofitable firms releases labour and capital goods for use in new combinations.

Lynne Kiesling, a historian of economic thought, discusses Joseph Schumpeter. http://tinyco.re/
1519059

evolutionary economics An approach that studies the process of economic change, including technological innovation, the diffusion of new social norms, and the development of novel institutions.

Joseph A. Schumpeter. 1949. 'Science and Ideology' (http://tinyco.re/4561610). *The American Economic Review* 39 (March): pp. 345–59.

Joseph A. Schumpeter. 1997. *Ten Great Economists*. London: Routledge.

Joseph A. Schumpeter. 1962. *Capitalism, Socialism, and Democracy*. New York: Harper & Brothers.

Robert Skidelsky. 2012. 'Robert Skidelsky—portrait: Joseph Schumpeter' (http://tinyco.re/8488199).

This decentralized process generates a continued improvement in productivity, which leads to growth, so Schumpeter argued it is virtuous. Both the destruction of old firms and the creation of new ones take time. The slowness of this process creates upswings and downswings in the economy. The branch of economic thought known as **evolutionary economics** (you can read articles on the subject in the *Journal of Evolutionary Economics* (http://tinyco.re/0746014)) can clearly trace its origins to Schumpeter's work, as well as most modern economic modelling that deals with entrepreneurship and innovation. Read Schumpeter's ideas and opinions in his own words, and an online essay about his work by Robert Skidelsky, a historian of economic thought.

Schumpeter was born in Austro-Hungary, but migrated to the US after the Nazis won the election in 1932 that led to the formation of the Third Reich in 1933. He had also experienced the First World War and the Great Depression of the 1930s, and died while writing an essay called 'The march into socialism', recording his concerns about the increasing role of government in the economy and the resulting 'migration of people's economic affairs from the private into the public sphere'. As a young professor in Austria he had fought and won a duel with the university librarian to ensure that students had access to books. He also claimed that as a young man he had three ambitions in life: to become the world's greatest economist, the world's greatest lover, and the world's greatest horseman. He added that only the decline of the cavalry had stopped him from succeeding in all three.

●●●

2.6 THE BRITISH INDUSTRIAL REVOLUTION AND INCENTIVES FOR NEW TECHNOLOGIES

Before the Industrial Revolution, weaving, spinning, and making clothes for the household were time-consuming tasks for most women. Single women were known as 'spinsters' because spinning was their primary occupation.

What did inventions such as the spinning jenny do? The first spinning jennies had eight spindles. One machine operated by just one adult therefore replaced eight spinsters working on eight spinning wheels. By the late nineteenth century, a single spinning mule operated by a very small number of people could replace more than 1,000 spinsters. These machines did not rely on human energy, but were powered first by water wheels, and later by coal-powered steam engines. Figure 2.9 summarizes these changes that happened in the Industrial Revolution.

Eve Fisher, a historian, calculated that making a shirt at this time required 500 hours of spinning, and 579 hours of work in total—costing $4,197.25 at today's minimum wage in the US.

The model in the previous section provides a hypothesis (potential explanation) for why someone would bother to invent such a technology, and why someone would want to use it. In this model, producers of cloth chose between technologies using just two inputs—energy and labour. This is a simplification, but it shows the importance of the relative costs of inputs for the choice of technology. When the cost of labour increased relative to the cost of energy, there were innovation rents to be earned from a switch to the energy-intensive technology.

This is just a hypothesis. Is it actually what happened? Looking at how relative prices differed among countries, and how they changed over time, can help us understand why technologies such as the spinning jenny were invented in Britain rather than elsewhere, and in the eighteenth century rather than at an earlier time.

Figure 2.10 shows the price of labour relative to the price of energy in various cities in the early 1700s—specifically, the wages of building labourers divided by the price of 1 million BTU (British Thermal Units, a unit of energy equivalent to slightly more than 1,000 joules). You can see that labour was more expensive relative to the cost of energy in England and the Netherlands than in France (Paris and Strasbourg), and much more so than in China.

Wages relative to the cost of energy were high in England, both because English wages were higher than wages elsewhere, and because coal was cheaper in coal-rich Britain than in the other countries in Figure 2.10.

Figure 2.11 shows trends in the cost of labour relative to the cost of capital goods in England and France, from the late sixteenth to the early nineteenth century. It shows the wages of building labourers divided by the cost of using capital goods. This cost is calculated from the prices of metal, wood, and brick, the cost of borrowing, and takes account of the rate at which the capital goods wear out, or depreciate.

As you can see, wages relative to the cost of capital goods were similar in England and France in the mid-seventeenth century but from then on, in England but not in France, workers became steadily more expensive relative to capital goods. In other words, the incentive to replace workers

Old technology	New technology
Lots of workers	Few workers
Little machinery (spinning wheels)	Lots of capital goods (spinning mules, factory buildings, water wheels or steam engines)
… requiring only human energy	… requiring energy (coal)
Labour-intensive	Labour-saving
Capital-saving	Capital-intensive
Energy-saving	Energy-intensive

Figure 2.9 The change in spinning technology during the Industrial Revolution.

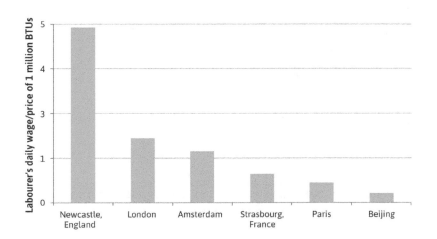

Page 140 of Robert C. Allen. 2008. *The British Industrial Revolution in Global Perspective*. Cambridge: Cambridge University Press.

Figure 2.10 Wages relative to the price of energy (early 1700s).

with machines was increasing in England during this time, but this was not true in France. In France, the incentive to save labour by innovating had been stronger during the late sixteenth century than it was 200 years later, at the time the Industrial Revolution began to transform Britain.

From the model in the previous section we learned that the technology chosen depends on relative input prices. Combining the predictions of the model with the historical data, we have one explanation for the timing and location of the Industrial Revolution:

- Wages relative to the cost of energy and capital goods rose in the eighteenth century in Britain compared with earlier historical periods.
- Wages relative to the cost of energy and capital goods were higher in Britain during the eighteenth century than elsewhere.

No doubt it helped, too, that Britain was such an inventive country. There were many skilled workmen, engineers and machine makers who could build the machines that inventors designed.

Why Britain industrialized when others did not http://tinyco.re/7830352

> **EXERCISE 2.4 BRITAIN BUT NOT FRANCE**
> Watch our video in which Bob Allen, an economic historian, explains his theory of why the Industrial Revolution occurred when and where it did.
>
> 1. Summarize Allen's claim using the concept of economic rents. Which *ceteris paribus* assumptions are you making?
> 2. What other important factors may explain the rise of energy-intensive technologies in Britain in the eighteenth century?

Page 138 in Robert C. Allen. 2008. *The British Industrial Revolution in Global Perspective*. Cambridge: Cambridge University Press.

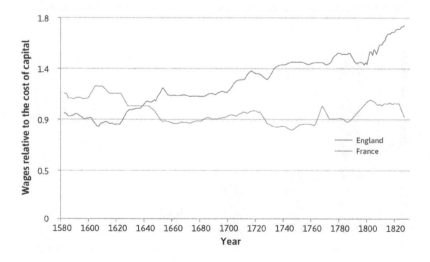

Figure 2.11 Wages relative to the cost of capital goods (late sixteenth to the early nineteenth century).

The relative prices of labour, energy and capital can help to explain why the labour-saving technologies of the Industrial Revolution were first adopted in England, and why at that time technology advanced more rapidly there than on the continent of Europe, and even more rapidly compared with Asia.

What explains the eventual adoption of these new technologies in countries like France and Germany, and ultimately China and India? One answer is further technological progress, where a new technology is developed that dominates the existing one in use. Technological progress would mean that it would take smaller quantities of inputs to produce 100 metres of cloth. We can use the model to illustrate this. In Figure 2.13, technological progress leads to the invention of a superior energy-intensive technology, labelled A'. The analysis in Figure 2.13 shows that once the A'-technology is available, it would be chosen both in countries using A, and in those using B.

A second factor that promoted the diffusion across the world of the new technologies was wage growth and falling energy costs (due, for example, to cheaper transportation, allowing countries to import energy cheaply from abroad). This made isocost lines steeper in poor countries, again providing an incentive to switch to a labour-saving technology.

Robert C. Allen. 2009. 'The industrial revolution in miniature: The spinning Jenny in Britain, France, and India'. *The Journal of Economic History* 69 (04) (November): p. 901.

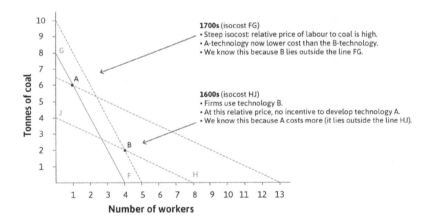

Figure 2.12 The cost of using different technologies to produce 100 metres of cloth in Britain in the seventeenth and eighteenth centuries.

1. Technology in the 1600s
In the 1600s, the relative prices are shown by isocost line HJ. The B-technology was used. At those relative prices, there was no incentive to develop a technology like A, which is outside the isocost line HJ.

2. Technology in the 1700s
In the 1700s, the isocost lines such as FG were much steeper, because the relative price of labour to coal was higher. The relative cost was sufficiently high to make the A-technology lower cost than the B-technology.

3. Why is technology A lower cost?
We know that when the relative price of labour is high, technology A is lower cost because the B-technology lies outside the isocost line FG.

David S. Landes. 2003. *The unbound Prometheus: Technological change and industrial development in western Europe from 1750 to the present.* Cambridge, UK: Cambridge University Press.

Either way, the new technologies spread, and the divergence in technologies and living standards was eventually replaced by convergence—at least among those countries where the capitalist revolution had taken off.

Nevertheless, in some countries we still observe the use of technologies that were replaced in Britain during the Industrial Revolution. The model predicts that the relative price of labour must be very low in such situations, making the isocost line very flat. The B-technology could be preferred in Figure 2.13 even when the A'-technology is available if the isocost line is flatter than HJ, so that it goes through B but below A'.

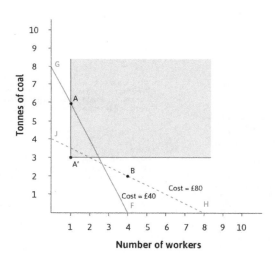

Figure 2.13 The cost of using different technologies to produce 100 metres of cloth.

1. Energy- or labour-intensive?

Where the relative price of labour is high, the energy-intensive technology, A, is chosen. Where the relative price of labour is low, the labour-intensive technology, B, is chosen.

2. An improvement in technology

Improvements in cloth-making technology occur, resulting in a new technology, labelled A'. This technology uses only half as much energy per worker to produce 100 metres of cloth. The new technology dominates the A-technology.

3. A' is least-cost

The A' technology is cheaper than both A and B, both in countries where wages are relatively high (isocost line FG) and in low-wage, expensive-energy economies (isocost line HJ). The new labour- and energy-saving technology, A', is inside FG and HJ, so it will be adopted in both economies.

QUESTION 2.5 CHOOSE THE CORRECT ANSWER(S)

Look again at Figure 2.12 (page 67) which depicts iso-cost lines for the 1600s and the 1700s in Britain.

Which of the following is true?

☐ The flatter isocost line HJ for 1600s Britain indicates higher wages relative to the price of coal.
☐ The increase in wages relative to the cost of energy in the 1700s is represented by the outward shift of the isocost line from HJ to the parallel iso-cost line going through A.
☐ Had the wage level fallen together with the falling energy costs (due for example to cheaper transportation), then 1700s Britain would definitely have stayed with technology B.
☐ The comparison between isocost line FG and the parallel isocost going through B suggests that an innovation rent was earned in 1700s Britain when firms moved from technology B to A.

EXERCISE 2.5 WHY DID THE INDUSTRIAL REVOLUTION NOT HAPPEN IN ASIA?

Read David Landes' answer to this question (http://tinyco.re/5958995), and this summary of research on the great divergence (http://tinyco.re/6223568) to discuss why the Industrial Revolution happened in Europe rather than in Asia, and in Britain rather than in Continental Europe.

1. Which arguments do you find most persuasive, and why?
2. Which arguments do you find least persuasive, and why?

2.7 MALTHUSIAN ECONOMICS: DIMINISHING AVERAGE PRODUCT OF LABOUR

The historical evidence supports our model that uses relative prices and innovation rents to provide a simple account of the timing and the geographical spread of the permanent technological revolution.

This is part of the explanation of the upward kink in the hockey stick. Explaining the long flat part of the stick is another story, requiring a different model.

Malthus provided a model of the economy that predicts a pattern of economic development consistent with the flat part of the GDP per capita hockey stick from Figure 1.1a in Unit 1. His model introduces concepts that are used widely in economics. One of the most important concepts is the idea of diminishing average product of a factor of production.

Diminishing average product of labour

To understand what this means, imagine an agricultural economy that produces just one good, grain. Suppose that grain production is very simple—it involves only farm labour, working on the land. In other words, ignore the fact that grain production also requires spades, combine harvesters, grain elevators, silos, and other types of buildings and equipment.

Labour and land (and the other inputs that we are ignoring) are called **factors of production**, meaning inputs into the production process. In the model of technological change above, the factors of production are energy and labour.

Gregory Clark, an economic historian, argues that the whole world was Malthusian from prehistory until the eighteenth century. Gregory Clark. 2007. *A farewell to alms: A brief economic history of the world.* Princeton, NJ: Princeton University Press. James Lee and Wang Feng discuss ways in which China's demographic system differed from Europe's, and question the Malthusian hypothesis that Chinese poverty was due to population growth. James Lee and Wang Feng. 1999. 'Malthusian models and Chinese realities: The Chinese demographic system 1700–2000'. *Population and Development Review* 25 (1) (March): pp. 33–65.

factors of production The labour, machinery and equipment (usually referred to as capital), land, and other inputs to a production process.

average product Total output divided by a particular input, for example per worker (divided by the number of workers) or per worker per hour (total output divided by the total number of hours of labour put in).

We will use a further simplifying *ceteris paribus* assumption: that the amount of land is fixed and all of the same quality. Imagine that the land is divided into 800 farms, each worked by a single farmer. Each farmer works the same total hours during a year. Together, these 800 farmers produce a total of 500,000 kg of grain. The **average product** of a farmer's labour is:

$$\text{average product of labour} = \frac{\text{total output}}{\text{total number of farmers}}$$

$$= \frac{500,000 \text{ kg}}{800 \text{ farmers}}$$

$$= 625 \text{ kg per farmer}$$

PRODUCTION FUNCTION
This describes the relationship between the amount of output produced and the amounts of inputs used to produce it.

To understand what will happen when the population grows and there are more farmers on the same limited space of farmland, we need something that economists call the **production function** for farming. This indicates the amount of output produced by any given number of farmers working on a given amount of land. In this case, we are holding constant all of the other inputs, including land, so we only consider how output varies with the amount of labour.

In the previous sections, you have already seen very simple production functions that specified the amounts of labour and energy necessary to produce 100 metres of cloth. For example, in Figure 2.3, the production function for technology B says that if 4 workers and 2 tonnes of coal are put into production, 100 metres of cloth will be the output. The production function for technology A gives us another 'if-then' statement: if 1 worker and 6 tonnes of coal are put into production using this technology, then 100 metres of cloth will be the output. The grain production function is a similar 'if-then' statement, indicating that if there are X farmers, then they will harvest Y grain.

Figure 2.14a lists some values of labour input and the corresponding grain production. In the third column we have calculated the average product of labour. In Figure 2.14b, we draw the function, assuming that the relationship holds for all farmers and grain production amounts in between those shown in the table.

Leibniz: Malthusian Economics: Diminishing Average Product of Labour (http://tinyco.re/L020701)

We call this a production function because a function is a relationship between two quantities (inputs and outputs in this case), expressed mathematically as:

$$Y = f(X)$$

We say that 'Y is a function of X'. X in this case is the amount of labour devoted to farming. Y is the output in grain that results from this input. The function f(X) describes the relationship between X and Y, represented by the curve in the figure.

EXERCISE 2.6 THE FARMERS' PRODUCTION FUNCTION

In Unit 1 we explained that the economy is part of the biosphere. Think of farming biologically.

1. Find out how many calories a farmer burns, and how many calories are contained in 1 kg of grain.
2. Does farming produce a surplus of calories—more calories in the output than used up in the work input—using the production function in Figure 2.14b?

Our grain production function is hypothetical, but it has two features that are plausible assumptions about how output depends on the number of farmers:

Labour combined with land is productive. No surprises there. The more farmers there are, the more grain is produced; at least up to a certain point (3,000 farmers, in this case).

As more farmers work on a fixed amount of land, the average product of labour falls. This **diminishing average product of labour** is one of the two foundations of Malthus' model.

Remember that the average product of labour is the grain output divided by the amount of labour input. From the production function in Figure 2.14b, or the table in Figure 2.14a (both show the same information) we see that an annual input of 800 farmers working the land brings an average per-farmer output of 625 kg of grain, while increasing the labour input to 1,600 farmers produces an average output per farmer of 458 kg.

The average product of labour falls as more labour is expended on production. This worried Malthus.

> **diminishing average product of labour** A situation in which, as more labour is used in a given production process, the average product of labour typically falls.

Labour input (number of workers)	Grain output (kg)	Average product of labour (kg/worker)
200	200,000	1,000
400	330,000	825
600	420,000	700
800	500,000	625
1,000	570,000	570
1,200	630,000	525
1,400	684,000	490
1,600	732,000	458
1,800	774,000	430
2,000	810,000	405
2,200	840,000	382
2,400	864,000	360
2,600	882,000	340
2,800	894,000	319
3,000	900,000	300

Figure 2.14a Recorded values of a farmer's production function: Diminishing average product of labour.

To see why he was worried, imagine that, a generation later, each farmer has had many children, so that instead of a single farmer working each farm, there are now two farmers working. The total labour input into farming was 800, but is now 1,600. Instead of a harvest of 625 kg of grain per farmer, the average harvest is now only 458 kg.

You might argue that in the real world, as the population grows, more land can be used for farming. But Malthus pointed out that earlier generations of farmers would have picked the best land, so any new land would be worse. This also reduces the average product of labour.

So diminishing average product of labour can be caused by:

- more labour devoted to a fixed quantity of land
- more (inferior) land brought into cultivation

Because the average product of labour diminishes as more labour is devoted to farming, their incomes inevitably fall.

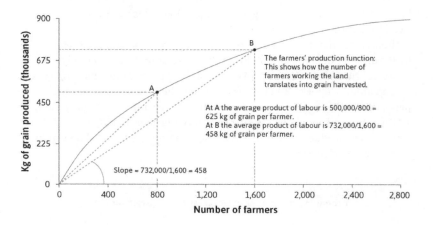

Figure 2.14b The farmers' production function: Diminishing average product of labour.

1. The farmers' production function
The production function shows how the number of farmers working the land translates into grain produced at the end of the growing season.

2. Output when there are 800 farmers
Point A on the production function shows the output of grain produced by 800 farmers.

3. Output when there are 1,600 farmers
Point B on the production function shows the amount of grain produced by 1,600 farmers.

4. The average product diminishes
At A, the average product of labour is 500,000 ÷ 800 = 625 kg of grain per farmer. At B, the average product of labour is 732,000 ÷ 1,600 = 458 kg of grain per farmer.

5. The slope of the ray is the average product
The slope of the ray from the origin to point B on the production function shows the average product of labour at point B. The slope is 458, meaning an average product of 458 kg per farmer when 1,600 farmers work the land.

6. The ray to A is steeper than the ray to B
The slope of the ray to point A is steeper than to point B. When only 800 farmers work the land there is a higher average product of labour. The slope is 625, the average product of 625 kg per farmer that we calculated previously.

QUESTION 2.6 CHOOSE THE CORRECT ANSWER(S)
Look again at Figure 2.14b (page 72) which depicts the production
function of grain for farmers under average growing conditions with
the currently available technology.

We can ascertain that:

☐ In a year with exceptionally good weather conditions, the production function curve will be higher and parallel to the curve above.
☐ A discovery of new high-yielding crop seeds would tilt the production function curve higher, pivoted anti-clockwise at the origin.
☐ In a year of bad drought, the production curve can slope downwards for large numbers of farmers.
☐ If there is an upper limit on the amount of grain that can be produced, then the curve will end up horizontal for large numbers of farmers.

2.8 MALTHUSIAN ECONOMICS: POPULATION GROWS WHEN LIVING STANDARDS RISE

On its own, the diminishing average product of labour does not explain the long, flat portion of the hockey stick. It just means that living standards depend on the size of the population. It doesn't say anything about why, over long periods, living standards and population didn't change much. For this we need the other part of Malthus's model: his argument that increased living standards create a population increase.

Malthus was not the first person to have this idea. Years before Malthus developed his theories, Richard Cantillon, an Irish economist, had stated that, 'Men multiply like mice in a barn if they have unlimited means of subsistence.'

Malthusian theory essentially regarded people as being not that different from other animals:

> Elevated as man is above all other animals by his intellectual facilities, it is not to be supposed that the physical laws to which he is subjected should be essentially different from those which are observed to prevail in other parts of the animated nature.

Thomas Robert Malthus, 1830. *A Summary View on the Principle of Population*. London: J. Murray.

So the two key ideas in Malthus' model are:

* the law of diminishing average product of labour
* population expands if living standards increase

Imagine a herd of antelopes on a vast and otherwise empty plain. Imagine also that there are no predators to complicate their lives (or our analysis). When the antelopes are better fed, they live longer and have more offspring. When the herd is small, the antelopes can eat all they want, and the herd gets larger.

Eventually the herd will get so large relative to the size of the plain that the antelopes can no longer eat all they want. As the amount of land per animal declines, their living standards will start to fall. This reduction in living standards will continue as long as the herd continues to increase in size.

Since each animal has less food to eat, the antelopes will have fewer offspring and die younger so population growth will slow down. Eventually, living standards will fall to the point where the herd is no longer increasing in size. The antelopes have filled up the plain. At this point, each animal will be eating an amount of food that we will define as the **subsistence level**. When the animals' living standards have been forced down to subsistence level as a result of population growth, the herd is no longer getting bigger.

If antelopes eat less than the subsistence level, the herd starts to get smaller. And when consumption exceeds the subsistence level, the herd grows.

Much of the same logic would apply, Malthus reasoned, to a human population living in a country with a fixed supply of agricultural land. While people are well-fed they would multiply like Cantillon's mice in a barn; but eventually they would fill the country, and further population growth would push down the incomes of most people as a result of diminishing average product of labour. Falling living standards would slow population growth as death rates increased and birth rates fell; ultimately incomes would settle at the subsistence level.

Malthus's model results in an **equilibrium** in which there is an income level just sufficient to allow a subsistence level of consumption. The variables that stay constant in this equilibrium are:

- the size of the population
- the income level of the people

If conditions change, then population and incomes may change too, but eventually the economy will return to an equilibrium with income at subsistence level.

EXERCISE 2.7 ARE PEOPLE REALLY LIKE OTHER ANIMALS?
Malthus wrote: '[I]t is not to be supposed that the physical laws to which [mankind] is subjected should be essentially different from those which are observed to prevail in other parts of the animated nature.'
    Do you agree? Explain your reasoning.

Malthusian economics: The effect of technological improvement
We know that over the centuries before the Industrial Revolution, improvements in technology occurred in many regions of the world, including Britain, and yet living standards remained constant. Can Malthus' model explain this?

Figure 2.15 illustrates how the combination of diminishing average product of labour and the effect of higher incomes on population growth mean that in the very long run, technological improvements will not result in higher income for farmers. In the figure, things on the left are causes of things to the right.

Beginning from equilibrium, with income at subsistence level, a new technology such as an improved seed raises income per person on the existing fixed quantity of land. Higher living standards lead to an increase

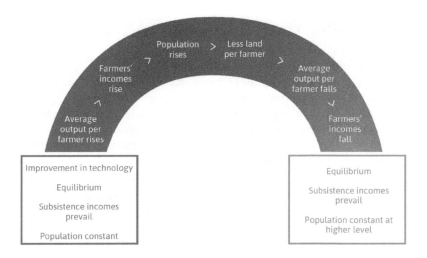

Figure 2.15 Malthus' model: The effect of an improvement in technology.

in population. As more people are added to the land, diminishing average product of labour means average income per person falls. Eventually incomes return to subsistence level, with a higher population.

Why is the population higher at the new equilibrium? Output per farmer is now higher for each number of farmers. Population does not fall back to the original level, because income would be above subsistence. A better technology can provide subsistence income for a larger population.

The Einstein at the end of this section shows how to represent Malthus' model graphically, and how to use it to investigate the effect of a new technology.

The Malthusian model predicts that improvements in technology will not raise living standards if:

- the average product of labour diminishes as more labour is applied to a fixed amount of land
- population grows in response to increases in real wages

Then in the long run, an increase in productivity will result in a larger population but not higher wages. This depressing conclusion was once regarded as so universal and inescapable that it was called Malthus' Law.

EINSTEIN

Modelling Malthus

Malthus's argument is summarized in Figure 2.16, using two diagrams.

The downward-sloping line in the left-hand figure shows that the higher the population, the lower the level of wages, due to the diminishing average product of labour. The upward-sloping line on the right shows the relationship between wages and population growth. When wages are high, population grows, because higher living standards lead to more births and fewer deaths.

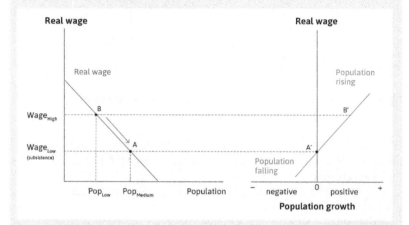

Figure 2.16 A Malthusian economy.

1. Left-hand diagram: How wages depend on the population level
At a medium population level, the wage of people who work the land is at subsistence level (point A). The wage is higher at point B, where the population is smaller, because the average product of labour is higher.

2. Right-hand diagram: How population growth depends on living standards
The line in the right-hand diagram slopes upward, showing that when wages (on the vertical axis) are high, population growth (on the horizontal axis) is positive (so the population will rise). When wages are low, population growth is negative (population falls).

3. Linking the two diagrams
At point A, on the left, population is medium-sized and the wage is at subsistence level. Tracing across to point A′ on the right shows that population growth is equal to zero. So if the economy is at point A, it is in equilibrium: population stays constant and wages remain at subsistence level.

4. A lower population
Suppose the economy is at B, with a higher wage and lower population. Point B′, on the right, shows that the population will be rising.

5. The economy returns to equilibrium
As the population rises, the economy moves down the line in the left diagram: wages fall until they reach equilibrium at A.

The two diagrams together explain the Malthusian population trap. Population will be constant when the wage is at subsistence level, it will rise when the wage is above subsistence level, and it will fall when the wage is below subsistence level.

Figure 2.17 shows how the Malthusian model predicts that even if productivity increases, living standards in the long run do not.

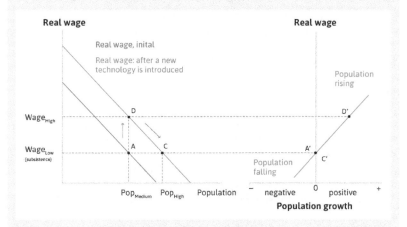

Figure 2.17 The introduction of a new technology in a Malthusian economy.

1. Initially the economy is in equilibrium
The economy starts at point A, with a medium-sized population and wage at subsistence level.

2. An advance in technology—wages rise
A technological improvement (for example, better seeds) raises the average product of labour, and the wage is higher for any level of population. The real wage line shifts upward. At the initial population level, the wage increases and the economy moves to point D.

3. Population begins to rise
At point D, the wage has risen above subsistence level and therefore the population starts to grow (point D′).

4. Population increases
As population rises, the wage falls, due to the diminishing average product of labour. The economy moves down the real-wage curve from D.

5. C is the equilibrium with the new technology
At C, the wage has reached subsistence level again. The population remains constant (point C′). The population is higher at equilibrium C than it was at equilibrium A.

EXERCISE 2.8 LIVING STANDARDS IN THE MALTHUSIAN WORLD
Imagine that the population growth curve in the right panel of Figure 2.16 (page 76) shifted to the left (with fewer people being born, or more people dying, at any level of wages). Explain what would happen to living standards describing the transition to the new equilibrium.

2.9 THE MALTHUSIAN TRAP AND LONG-TERM ECONOMIC STAGNATION

The major long-run impact of better technology in this Malthusian world was therefore more people. The writer H. G. Wells, author of *War of the Worlds*, wrote in 1905 that humanity 'spent the great gifts of science as rapidly as it got them in a mere insensate multiplication of the common life'.

So we now have a possible explanation of the long, flat portion of the hockey stick. Human beings periodically invented better ways of making things, both in agriculture and in industry, and this periodically raised the incomes of farmers and employees above subsistence. The Malthusian interpretation was that higher real wages led young couples to marry earlier and have more children, and they also led to lower death rates. Population growth eventually forced real wages back to subsistence levels, which might explain why China and India, with relatively sophisticated economies at the time, ended up with large populations but—until recently—very low incomes.

As with our model of innovation rents, relative prices and technological improvements, we need to ask: can we find evidence to support the central prediction of the Malthusian model, that incomes will return to subsistence level?

Figure 2.18 is consistent with what Malthus predicted. From the end of the thirteenth century to the beginning of the seventeenth century, Britain oscillated between periods of higher wages, leading to larger populations, leading to lower wages, leading to smaller populations, leading to … and so on, a vicious circle.

We get a different view of the vicious circle by taking Figure 2.18 and focusing on the period between 1340 and 1600, shown in Figure 2.19. As a result of the outbreak of bubonic plague known as the Black Death, from 1349 to 1351 between a quarter and a third of Europe's population died. The lower part of the figure shows the causal linkages that led to the effects we see in the top part.

Robert C. Allen. 2001. 'The Great Divergence in European Wages and Prices from the Middle Ages to the First World War'. *Explorations in Economic History* 38 (4): pp. 411–447.

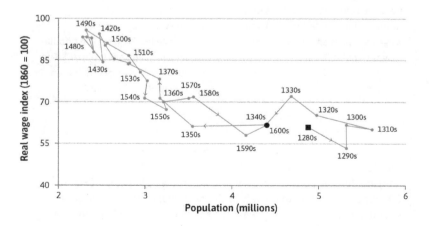

Figure 2.18 The Malthusian trap: Wages and population (1280–1600).

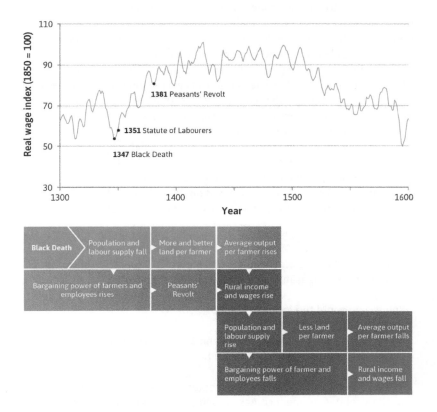

Robert C. Allen. 2001. 'The Great Divergence in European Wages and Prices from the Middle Ages to the First World War'. *Explorations in Economic History* 38 (4): pp. 411–447.

Figure 2.19 The Black Death, labour supply, politics, and the wage: A Malthusian economy.

1. A Malthusian economy in England (1300–1600)

In this figure, we examine the Malthusian economy that existed in England between the years 1300 and 1600, highlighted above.

2. The Black Death (1348–50)

The bubonic plague of 1348–50 was known as the Black Death. It killed 1.5 million people out of an estimated English population of 4 million, leading to a dramatic fall in labour supply.

3. Wages rose following the plague

This decline in the population had an economic benefit for the farmers and workers who survived: it meant that farmers had more and better land, and workers could demand higher wages. Incomes rose as the plague abated.

4. Farmers and workers used their power

In 1351, King Edward III of England tried to limit wage rises by law, helping to cause a period of rebellions against authority, notably the Peasants' Revolt of 1381. Despite the King's actions, incomes continued to increase.

5. Population increased in the sixteenth century

By the middle of the fifteenth century, the real wages of English building workers had doubled. Increased wages helped the population to recover in the sixteenth century, but Malthus' law asserted itself: as the population increased, incomes fell.

6. Malthusian stagnation (1350–1600)

By 1600, real wages had fallen to the level they were 300 years previously.

7. Cause and effect in Malthusian economics

Our model of Malthusian economics helps to explain the rise and fall of incomes between 1300 and 1600 in England.

The decline of the number of people working on farms during the Black Death raised agricultural productivity according to the principle of diminishing average product of labour. Farmers were better off, whether they owned their land or paid a fixed rent to a landlord. Employers in cities had to offer higher wages too, to attract workers from rural areas.

The causal links in Figure 2.19 combine the two features of the Malthusian model with the role of political developments as responses to, and causes of changes in, the economy. When, in 1349 and 1351, King Edward passed laws to try to restrain wage increases, economics (the reduced labour supply) won out over politics: wages continued to rise, and peasants began to exercise their increased power, notably by demanding more freedom and lower taxes in the Peasants' Revolt of 1381.

But when the population recovered in the sixteenth century, labour supply increased, lowering wages. Based on this evidence, the Malthusian explanation is consistent with the history of England at this time.

EXERCISE 2.9 WHAT WOULD YOU ADD?

The cause-and-effect diagram that we created in Figure 2.19 (page 79) made use of many *ceteris paribus* assumptions.

1. How does this model simplify reality?
2. What has been left out?
3. Try redrawing the figure to include other factors that you think are important.

QUESTION 2.7 CHOOSE THE CORRECT ANSWER(S)

Look again at Figure 2.1 (page 45) and Figure 2.19 (page 79) showing graphs of real wages in England between 1300 and 2000.

You are also told the following facts:

During the bubonic plague of 1348 and 1351, between one-quarter and one-third of Europe's population died.

In the seventeenth and eighteenth centuries, the wages of unskilled workers relative to the incomes of land owners were only one-fifth of what they had been in the sixteenth century.

What can we conclude from this information?

☐ According to the Malthusian model, the fall in the population due to the bubonic plague would have led to an increase in the average productivity of workers, causing the observed rise in the real wage post-plague.

☐ The doubling and halving of the real wage index over 250 years from around 1350 is contrary to the Malthusian model.

☐ The fall in the unskilled workers' share of total output in the seventeenth and eighteenth centuries was due to the fall in their average product of labour.

☐ The fall in the relative wages of the unskilled workers in the seventeenth and eighteenth centuries was one of the factors that led to the eventual shooting up of the real wage in the nineteenth century, seen in the graph.

William H. McNeill. 1976. *Plagues and peoples*. Garden City, NY: Anchor Press.

EXERCISE 2.10 DEFINING ECONOMIC PROGRESS

Real wages also rose sharply following the Black Death in other places for which we have evidence, such as Spain, Italy, Egypt, the Balkans, and Constantinople (present-day Istanbul).

1. How does the growth of real wages compare with the growth of real GDP per capita as a measure of economic progress?
2. Try out your arguments on others. Do you agree or not? If you disagree, are there any facts that could resolve your disagreement, and what are they? If there are not, why do you disagree?

We have focused on farmers and wage earners, but not everyone in the economy would be caught in a Malthusian trap. As population continues to grow, the demand for food also grows. Therefore the limited amount of land used to produce the food should become more valuable. In a Malthusian world, a rising population should therefore lead to an improvement in the relative economic position of landowners.

This occurred in England: Figure 2.19 shows that real wages did not increase in the very long run (they were no higher in 1800 than in 1450). And the income gap between landowners and workers increased. In the seventeenth and eighteenth centuries, the wages of unskilled English workers, relative to the incomes of landowners, were only one-fifth of what they had been in the sixteenth century.

But while wages were low compared to the rents of landlords, a different comparison of relative prices was the key to England's escape from the Malthusian trap: wages remained high compared to the price of coal (Figure 2.10) and even increased compared to the cost of using capital goods (Figure 2.11), as we have seen.

2.10 ESCAPING FROM MALTHUSIAN STAGNATION

Nassau Senior, the economist who lamented that the numbers perishing in the Irish famine would scarcely be enough to do much good, does not appear compassionate. But he and Malthus were right to think that population growth and a diminishing average product of labour could create a vicious circle of economic stagnation and poverty. However, the hockey-stick graphs of living standards show they were wrong to believe that this could never change.

They did not consider the possibility that improvements in technology could happen at a faster rate than population growth, offsetting the diminishing average product of labour.

The permanent technological revolution, it turns out, means that the Malthusian model is no longer a reasonable description of the world. Average living standards increased rapidly and permanently after the capitalist revolution.

Figure 2.20 shows the real wage and population data from the 1280s to the 1860s. As we saw in Figure 2.18, from the thirteenth to the sixteenth century there was a clear negative relationship between population and real wages: when one went up the other went down, just as Malthusian theory suggests.

Between the end of the sixteenth and the beginning of the eighteenth century, although wages rose there was relatively little population growth. Around 1740, we can see the Malthusian relationship again, labelled '18th century'. Then, around 1800, the economy moved to what appears to be an entirely new regime, with both population and real wages simultaneously increasing. This is labelled 'Escape'.

Figure 2.21 zooms in on this 'great escape' portion of the wage data.

The story of the permanent technological revolution demonstrates that there are two influences on wages.

- *How much is produced*: we can think of this as the size of the pie to be divided between workers and the owners of other inputs (land or machines).
- *The share going to workers*: This depends on their bargaining power, which in turn depends on how wages are determined (individually, or through bargaining with trade unions, for example) and the supply and demand for workers. If many workers are competing for the same job, wages are likely to be low.

After 1830, the pie continued growing, and the workers' share grew along with it.

Britain had escaped from the Malthusian trap. This process would soon be repeated in other countries, as Figures 1.1a and 1.1b showed.

Robert C. Allen. 2001. The Great Divergence in European Wages and Prices from the Middle Ages to the First World War. *Explorations in Economic History* 38 (4): pp. 411–447.

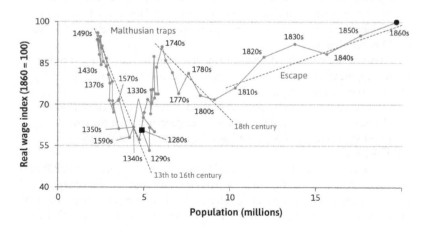

Figure 2.20 Escaping the Malthusian trap. Note: Labour productivity and real wages are five-year centred moving averages.

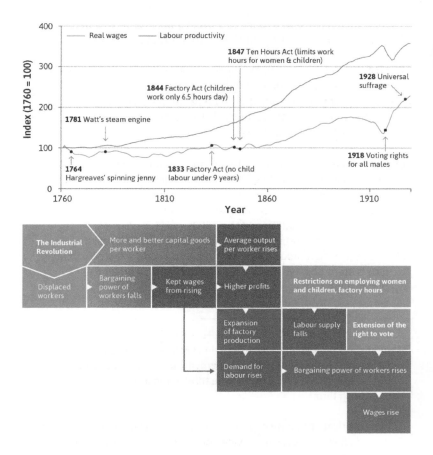

Robert C. Allen. 2001. 'The Great Divergence in European Wages and Prices from the Middle Ages to the First World War'. *Explorations in Economic History* 38 (4): pp. 411–447.

Figure 2.21 Escaping the Malthusian trap. Note: Labour productivity and real wages are five-year centred moving averages.

1. Escaping the Malthusian trap
In the eighteenth century, the Malthusian relationship persisted. In the nineteenth century, the economy appears to become a non-Malthusian regime, with real wages rising while population was increasing.

2. The permanent technological revolution
The story begins with technological improvements, such as the spinning jenny and the steam engine, that increased output per worker. Innovation continued as the technological revolution became permanent, displacing thousands of spinsters, weavers and farmers.

3. Urban unemployment
The loss of employment reduced workers' bargaining power, keeping wages low, seen in the flat line between 1750 and 1830. The size of the pie was increasing, but the workers' slice was not.

4. New opportunities
In the 1830s, higher productivity and low wages led to a surge in profits. Profits, competition, and technology drove businesses to expand. The demand for labour went up. People left farming for jobs in the new factories.

5. Workers' bargaining power
The supply of labour fell when business owners were stopped from employing children. The combination of higher labour demand and lower supply enhanced workers' bargaining power.

6. The escape from Malthusianism
The power of working people increased as they gained the right to vote and formed trade unions. These workers were able to claim a constant or rising share of the increases in productivity generated by the permanent technological revolution.

In our 'Economist in action' video, Suresh Naidu, an economic historian, explains how population growth, technological development and political events interacted to produce the real wage hockey stick.
http://tinyco.re/4539763

QUESTION 2.8 CHOOSE THE CORRECT ANSWER(S)
Look again at Figure 2.20 (page 82), which plots real wages against population in England from the 1280s to the 1860s.

According to Malthus, with diminishing average product of labour in production and population growth in response to increases in real wages, an increase in productivity will result in a larger population but not higher real wages in the long run. Based on the information above, which of the following statements is correct?

☐ Between the 1800s and the 1860s, population grows as real wages rise. This is entirely in line with Malthus's description of the economy's growth.
☐ There is a clear evidence of a persistent and continuous Malthusian trap between the 1280s and the 1800s.
☐ The Malthusian traps seem to occur in a cycle of 60 years.
☐ The Malthusian model does not take into account the possibility of a persistent positive technology shock that may offset the diminishing average product of labour.

EXERCISE 2.11 THE BASIC INSTITUTIONS OF CAPITALISM
The escape from the Malthusian trap, in which technological progress outstripped the effects of population growth, took place following the emergence of capitalism. Consider the three basic institutions of capitalism in turn:

1. Why is private property important for technological progress to occur?
2. Explain how markets can provide both carrots and sticks to encourage innovation.
3. How can production in firms, rather than families, contribute to the growth of living standards?

2.11 CONCLUSION

We have introduced an economic model in which firms' choice of production technologies depends on the relative prices of inputs, and the economic rent from adopting a new technology provides an incentive for firms to innovate. Testing this model against historical evidence shows that it could help to explain why the Industrial Revolution occurred in Britain in the eighteenth century.

We showed how the Malthusian model of a vicious circle, in which population growth offset temporary gains in income, could explain stagnation in living standards for centuries before the Industrial Revolution, until the permanent technological revolution allowed an escape due to improvements in technology.

> *Concepts introduced in Unit 2*
> Before you move on, review these definitions:
>
> • Equilibrium
> • *Ceteris paribus*
> • Relative prices
> • Incentives
> • Diminishing average product of labour
> • Reservation option
> • Economic rent
> • Isocost line
> • Innovation rent

2.12 REFERENCES

Allen, Robert C. 2009. 'The Industrial Revolution in Miniature: The Spinning Jenny in Britain, France, and India'. *The Journal of Economic History* 69 (04) (November): p. 901.

Allen, Robert C. 2011. *Global Economic History: A Very Short Introduction*. New York, NY: Oxford University Press.

Clark, Gregory. 2007. *A Farewell to Alms: A Brief Economic History of the World*. Princeton, NJ: Princeton University Press.

Davis, Mike. 2000. *Late Victorian holocausts: El Niño famines and the Making of the Third World*. London: Verso Books.

Landes, David S. 1990. 'Why are We So Rich and They So Poor?' (http://tinyco.re/5958995). *American Economic Review* 80 (May): pp. 1–13.

Landes, David S. 2003. *The Unbound Prometheus: Technological Change and Industrial Development in Western Europe from 1750 to the Present*. Cambridge, UK: Cambridge University Press.

Landes, David S. 2006. 'Why Europe and the West? Why not China?'. *Journal of Economic Perspectives* 20 (2) (June): pp. 3–22.

Lee, James, and Wang Feng. 1999. 'Malthusian models and Chinese realities: The Chinese demographic system 1700–2000'. *Population and Development Review* 25 (1) (March): pp. 33–65.

Malthus, Thomas R. 1798. *An Essay on the Principle of Population*. London: J. Johnson, in St. Paul's Church-yard. Library of Economics and Liberty (http://tinyco.re/8473883).

Malthus, Thomas R. 1830. *A Summary View on the Principle of Population*. London: J. Murray

McNeill, William Hardy H. 1976. *Plagues and Peoples*. Garden City, NY: Anchor Press.

Mokyr, Joel. 2004. *The Gifts of Athena: Historical Origins of the Knowledge Economy*, 5th ed. Princeton, NJ: Princeton University Press.

Pomeranz, Kenneth L. 2000. *The Great Divergence: Europe, China, and the Making of the Modern World Economy*. Princeton, NJ: Princeton University Press.

Schumpeter, Joseph A. 1949. 'Science and Ideology' (http://tinyco.re/4561610). *The American Economic Review* 39 (March): pp. 345–59.

Schumpeter, Joseph A. 1962. *Capitalism, Socialism, and Democracy*. New York: Harper & Brothers.

Schumpeter, Joseph A. 1997. *Ten Great Economists*. London: Routledge.
Skidelsky, Robert. 2012. 'Robert Skidelsky—portrait: Joseph Schumpeter' (http://tinyco.re/8488199). Updated 1 December 2007.

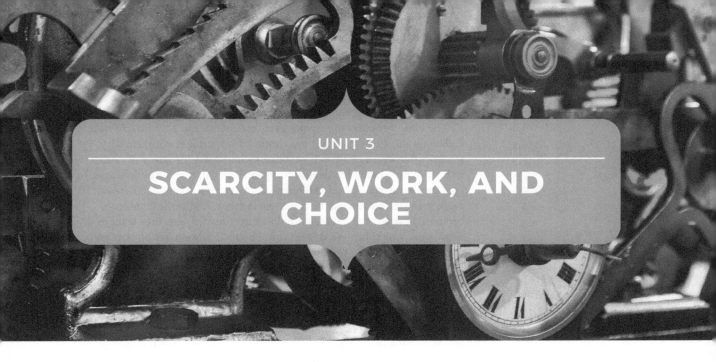

UNIT 3
SCARCITY, WORK, AND CHOICE

HOW INDIVIDUALS DO THE BEST THEY CAN, AND HOW THEY RESOLVE THE TRADE-OFF BETWEEN EARNINGS AND FREE TIME

- Decision making under scarcity is a common problem because we usually have limited means available to meet our objectives.
- Economists model these situations, first by defining all of the feasible actions, then evaluating which of these actions is best, given the objectives.
- Opportunity costs describe the unavoidable trade-offs in the presence of scarcity: satisfying one objective more means satisfying other objectives less.
- A model of decision making under scarcity can be applied to the question of how much time to spend working, when facing a trade-off between more free time and more income.
- This model also helps to explain differences in the hours that people work in different countries, and the changes in our hours of work throughout history.

THEMES AND CAPSTONE UNITS
- 17: History, instability, and growth
- 18: Global economy
- 21: Innovation
- 22: Politics and policy

Imagine that you are working in New York, in a job that is paying you $15 an hour for a 40-hour working week, which gives you earnings of $600 per week. There are 168 hours in a week, so after 40 hours of work, you are left with 128 hours of free time for all your non-work activities, including leisure and sleep.

Suppose, by some happy stroke of luck, you are offered a job at a much higher wage—six times higher. Your new hourly wage is $90. Not only that, your prospective employer lets you choose how many hours you work each week.

Will you carry on working 40 hours per week? If you do, your weekly pay will be six times higher than before: $3,600. Or will you decide that you are satisfied with the goods you can buy with your weekly earnings of $600? You can now earn this by cutting your weekly hours to just 6 hours and 40 minutes (a six-day weekend!), and enjoy about 26% more free time than before. Or would you use this higher hourly wage rate to raise both your weekly earnings and your free time by some intermediate amount?

The idea of suddenly receiving a six-fold increase in your hourly wage and being able to choose your own hours of work might not seem very realistic. But we know from Unit 2 that technological progress since the Industrial Revolution has been accompanied by a dramatic rise in wages. In fact, the average real hourly earnings of American workers did increase more than six-fold during the twentieth century. And while employees ordinarily cannot just tell their employer how many hours they want to work, over long time periods the typical hours that we work do change. In part, this is a response to how much we prefer to work. As individuals, we can choose part-time work, although this may restrict our job options. Political parties also respond to the preferences of voters, so changes in typical working hours have occurred in many countries as a result of legislation that imposes maximum working hours.

So have people used economic progress as a way to consume more goods, enjoy more free time, or both? The answer is both, but in different proportions in different countries. While hourly earnings increased by more than six-fold for twentieth century Americans, their average annual work time fell by a little more than one-third. So people at the end of this century enjoyed a four-fold increase in annual earnings with which they could buy goods and services, but a much smaller increase of slightly less than one-fifth in their free time. (The percentage increase in free time would be higher if you did not count time spent asleep as free time, but it is still small relative to the increase in earnings.) How does this compare with the choice you made when our hypothetical employer offered you a six-fold increase in your wage?

Figure 3.1 shows trends in income and working hours since 1870 in three countries.

As in Unit 1, income is measured as per-capita GDP in US dollars. This is not the same as average earnings, but gives us a useful indication of average income for the purposes of comparison across countries and through time. In the late nineteenth and early twentieth century, average income approximately trebled, and hours of work fell substantially. During the rest of the twentieth century, income per head rose four-fold.

Hours of work continued to fall in the Netherlands and France (albeit more slowly) but levelled off in the US, where there has been little change since 1960.

While many countries have experienced similar trends, there are still differences in outcomes. Figure 3.2 illustrates the wide disparities in free time and income between countries in 2013. Here we have calculated free time by subtracting average annual working hours from the number of hours in a year. You can see that the higher-income countries seem to have lower working hours and more free time, but there are also some striking differences between them. For example, the Netherlands and the US have similar levels of income, but Dutch workers have much more free time. And the US and Turkey have similar amounts of free time but a large difference in income.

In many countries there has been a huge increase in living standards since 1870. But in some places people have carried on working just as hard as before but consumed more, while in other countries people now have much more free time. Why has this happened? We will provide some answers to this question by studying a basic problem of economics—scarcity—and how we make choices when we cannot have all of everything that we want, such as goods and free time.

Study the model of decision making that we use carefully! It will be used repeatedly throughout the course, because it provides insight into a wide range of economic problems.

Elements of Model
Preferences (values
Constraints (limited
Objectives
  Constraints impose
    Opportunity cost
  ⇒ unavoidable trade-off
due to scarcity ⇒
  Limited means vs
  unlimited desires

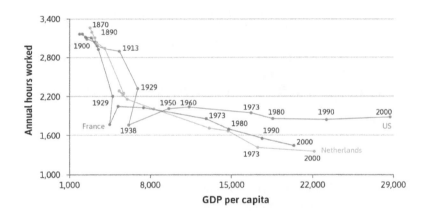

Maddison Project. 2013. 2013 edition. Michael Huberman and Chris Minns. 2007. 'The times they are not changin': Days and hours of work in Old and New Worlds, 1870–2000'. *Explorations in Economic History* 44 (4): pp. 538–567. GDP is measured at PPP in 1990 international Geary-Khamis dollars.

Figure 3.1 Annual hours of work and income (1870–2000).

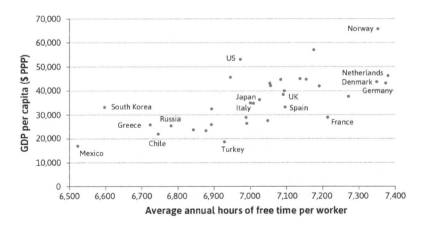

OECD. Average annual hours actually worked per worker (http://tinyco.re/6892498). OECD. Level of GDP per capita and productivity (http://tinyco.re/1840501). Accessed June 2016. Data for South Korea refers to 2012.

Figure 3.2 Annual hours of free time per worker and income (2013).

QUESTION 3.1 CHOOSE THE CORRECT ANSWER(S)
Currently you work for 40 hours per week at the wage rate of £20 an hour. Your free hours are defined as the number of hours not spent in work per week, which in this case is 24 hours × 7 days − 40 hours = 128 hours per week. Suppose now that your wage rate has increased by 25%. If you are happy to keep your total weekly income constant, then:

☐ Your total number of working hours per week will fall by 25%.
☐ Your total number of working hours per week will be 30 hours.
☐ Your total number of free hours per week will increase by 25%.
☐ Your total number of free hours per week will increase by 6.25%.

QUESTION 3.2 CHOOSE THE CORRECT ANSWER(S)
Look again at Figure 3.1 (page 89), which depicts the annual number of hours worked against GDP per capita in the US, France and the Netherlands, between 1870 and 2000. Which of the following is true?

☐ An increase in GDP per capita causes a reduction in the number of hours worked.
☐ The GDP per capita in the Netherlands is lower than that in the US because Dutch people work fewer hours.
☐ Between 1870 and 2000, French people have managed to increase their GDP per capita more than ten-fold while more than halving the number of hours worked.
☐ On the basis of the evidence in the graph, one day French people will be able to produce a GDP per capita of over $30,000 with less than 1,000 hours of work.

3.1 LABOUR AND PRODUCTION

In Unit 2 we saw that labour can be thought of as an input in the production of goods and services. Labour is work; for example the welding, assembling, and testing required to make a car. Work activity is often difficult to measure, which is an important point in later units because employers find it difficult to determine the exact amount of work that their employees are doing. We also cannot measure the effort required by different activities in a comparable way (for example, baking a cake versus building a car), so economists often measure labour simply as the number of hours worked by individuals engaged in production, and assume that as the number of hours worked increases, the amount of goods produced also increases.

As a student, you make a choice every day: how many hours to spend studying. There may be many factors influencing your choice: how much you enjoy your work, how difficult you find it, how much work your friends do, and so on. Perhaps part of the motivation to devote time to studying comes from your belief that the more time you spend studying, the higher the grade you will be able to obtain at the end of the course. In this unit, we will construct a simple model of a student's choice of how many hours to work, based on the assumption that the more time spent working, the better the final grade will be.

Assumption: positive relationship between the two variables

We assume a positive relationship between hours worked and final grade, but is there any evidence to back this up? A group of educational psychologists looked at the study behaviour of 84 students at Florida State University to identify the factors that affected their performance.

At first sight there seems to be only a weak relationship between the average number of hours per week the students spent studying and their Grade Point Average (GPA) at the end of the semester. This is in Figure 3.3.

The 84 students have been split into two groups according to their hours of study. The average GPA for those with high study time is 3.43—only just above the GPA of those with low study time.

Looking more closely, we discover this study is an interesting illustration of why we should be careful when we make *ceteris paribus* assumptions (remember from Unit 2 that this means 'holding other things constant'). Within each group of 42 students there are many potentially important differences. The conditions in which they study would be an obvious difference to consider: an hour working in a busy, noisy room may not be as useful as an hour spent in the library.

In Figure 3.4, we see that students studying in poor environments are more likely to study longer hours. Of these 42 students, 31 of them have high study time, compared with only 11 of the students with good environments. Perhaps they are distracted by other people around them, so it takes them longer to complete their assignments than students who work in the library.

Now look at the average GPAs in the top row: if the environment is good, students who study longer do better—and you can see in the bottom row that high study time pays off for those who work in poor environments too. This relationship was not as clear when we didn't consider the effect of the study environment.

So, after taking into account environment and other relevant factors (including the students' past GPAs, and the hours they spent in paid work or partying), the psychologists estimated that an additional hour of study time per week raised a student's GPA at the end of the semester by 0.24 points on average. If we take two students who are the same in all respects except for study time, we predict that the one who studies for longer will

Elizabeth Ashby Plant, Karl Anders Ericsson, Len Hill, and Kia Asberg. 2005. 'Why study time does not predict grade point average across college students: Implications of deliberate practice for academic performance.' *Contemporary Educational Psychology* 30 (1): pp. 96–116.

	High study time (42 students)	Low study time (42 students)
Average GPA	3.43	3.36

Figure 3.3 Study time and grades.

Elizabeth Ashby Plant, Karl Anders Ericsson, Len Hill, and Kia Asberg. 2005. 'Why study time does not predict grade point average across college students: Implications of deliberate practice for academic performance.' *Contemporary Educational Psychology* 30 (1): pp. 96–116. Additional calculations were conducted by Ashby Plant, Florida State University, in June 2015.

	High study time	Low study time
Good environment	3.63 (11 students)	3.43 (31 students)
Poor environment	3.36 (31 students)	3.17 (11 students)

Plant *et al.* 'Why study time does not predict grade point average across college students', ibid.

Figure 3.4 Average GPA in good and poor study environments.

have a GPA that is 0.24 points higher for each extra hour: study time raises GPA by 0.24 per hour, *ceteris paribus*.

EXERCISE 3.1 *CETERIS PARIBUS* ASSUMPTIONS

You have been asked to conduct a research study at your university, just like the one at Florida State University.

1. In addition to study environment, which factors do you think should ideally be held constant in a model of the relationship between study hours and final grade?
2. What information about the students would you want to collect beyond GPA, hours of study, and study environment?

Now imagine a student, whom we will call Alexei. He can vary the number of hours he spends studying. We will assume that, as in the Florida study, the hours he spends studying over the semester will increase the percentage grade that he will receive at the end, *ceteris paribus*. This relationship between study time and final grade is represented in the table in Figure 3.5. In this model, study time refers to all of the time that Alexei spends learning, whether in class or individually, measured per day (not per week, as for the Florida students). The table shows how his grade will vary if he changes his study hours, if all other factors—his social life, for example—are held constant.

> **production function** A graphical or mathematical expression describing the amount of output that can be produced by any given amount or combination of input(s). The function describes differing technologies capable of producing the same thing.

This is Alexei's **production function**: it translates the number of hours per day spent studying (his input of labour) into a percentage grade (his output). In reality, the final grade might also be affected by unpredictable events (in everyday life, we normally lump the effect of these things together and call it 'luck'). You can think of the production function as telling us what Alexei will get under normal conditions (if he is neither lucky nor unlucky).

If we plot this relationship on a graph, we get the curve in Figure 3.5. Alexei can achieve a higher grade by studying more, so the curve slopes upward. At 15 hours of work per day he gets the highest grade he is capable of, which is 90%. Any time spent studying beyond that does not affect his exam result (he will be so tired that studying more each day will not achieve anything), and the curve becomes flat.

> **average product** Total output divided by a particular input, for example per worker (divided by the number of workers) or per worker per hour (total output divided by the total number of hours of labour put in).

We can calculate Alexei's average product of labour, as we did for the farmers in Unit 2. If he works for 4 hours per day, he achieves a grade of 50. The **average product**—the average number of percentage points per hour of study—is 50 / 4 = 12.5. In Figure 3.5 it is the slope of a ray from the origin to the curve at 4 hours per day:

$$\text{slope} = \frac{\text{vertical distance}}{\text{horizontal distance}} = \frac{50}{4} = 12.5$$

> **marginal product** The additional amount of output that is produced if a particular input was increased by one unit, while holding all other inputs constant.

Alexei's **marginal product** is the increase in his grade from increasing study time by one hour. Follow the steps in Figure 3.5 to see how to calculate the marginal product, and compare it with the average product.

At each point on the production function, the marginal product is the increase in the grade from studying one more hour. The marginal product corresponds to the slope of the production function.

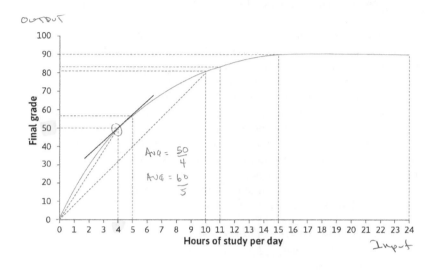

Study hours	0	1	2	3	4	5	6	7	8	9	10	11	12	13	14	15 or more
Grade	0	20	33	42	50	57	63	69	73	78	81	84	86	88	89	90

Figure 3.5 How does the amount of time spent studying affect Alexei's grade?

1. Alexei's production function
The curve is Alexei's production function. It shows how an input of study hours produces an output, the final grade.

2. Four hours of study per day
If Alexei studies for four hours his grade will be 50.

3. Ten hours of study per day
... and if he studies for 10 hours he will achieve a grade of 81.

4. Alexei's maximum grade
At 15 hours of study per day Alexei achieves his maximum possible grade, 90. After that, further hours will make no difference to his result: the curve is flat.

5. Increasing study time from 4 to 5 hours
Increasing study time from 4 to 5 hours raises Alexei's grade from 50 to 57. Therefore, at 4 hours of study, the marginal product of an additional hour is 7.

6. Increasing study time from 10 to 11 hours
Increasing study time from 10 to 11 hours raises Alexei's grade from 81 to 84. At 10 hours of study, the marginal product of an additional hour is 3. As we move along the curve, the slope of the curve falls, so the marginal product of an extra hour falls. The marginal product is diminishing.

7. The average product of an hour spent studying
When Alexei studies for four hours per day his average product is 50/4 = 12.5 percentage points, which is the slope of the ray from that point to the origin.

8. The marginal product is lower than the average product
At 4 hours per day the average product is 12.5. At 10 hours per day it is lower (81/10 = 8.1). The average product falls as we move along the curve. At each point the marginal product (the slope of the curve) is lower than the average product (the slope of the ray).

9. The marginal product is the slope of the tangent
The marginal product at four hours of study is approximately 7, which is the increase in the grade from one more hour of study. More precisely, the marginal product is the slope of the tangent at that point, which is slightly higher than 7.

Leibniz: Average and marginal productivity (http://tinyco.re/L030101)

diminishing returns A situation in which the use of an additional unit of a factor of production results in a smaller increase in output than the previous increase. *Also known as: diminishing marginal returns in production*

Leibniz: Diminishing marginal productivity (http://tinyco.re/L030102)

concave function A function of two variables for which the line segment between any two points on the function lies entirely below the curve representing the function (the function is convex when the line segment lies above the function).

Leibniz: Concave and convex functions (http://tinyco.re/L030103)

tangency When two curves share one point in common but do not cross. The tangent to a curve at a given point is a straight line that touches the curve at that point but does not cross it.

Alexei's production function in Figure 3.5 gets flatter the more hours he studies, so the marginal product of an additional hour falls as we move along the curve. The marginal product is **diminishing**. The model captures the idea that an extra hour of study helps a lot if you are not studying much, but if you are already studying a lot, then studying even more does not help very much.

In Figure 3.5, output increases as the input increases, but the marginal product falls—the function becomes gradually flatter. A production function with this shape is described as **concave**.

If we compare the marginal and average products at any point on Alexei's production function, we find that the marginal product is below the average product. For example, when he works for four hours his average product is 50/4 = 12.5 points per hour, but an extra hour's work raises his grade from 50 to 57, so the marginal product is 7. This happens because the marginal product is diminishing: each hour is less productive than the ones that came before. And it implies that the average product is also diminishing: each additional hour of study per day lowers the average product of all his study time, taken as a whole.

This is another example of the diminishing average product of labour that we saw in Unit 2. In that case, the average product of labour in food production (the food produced per worker) fell as more workers cultivated a fixed area of land.

Lastly, notice that if Alexei was already studying for 15 hours a day, the marginal product of an additional hour would be zero. Studying more would not improve his grade. As you might know from experience, a lack of either sleep or time to relax could even lower Alexei's grade if he worked more than 15 hours a day. If this were the case, then his production function would start to slope downward, and Alexei's marginal product would become negative.

Marginal change is an important and common concept in economics. You will often see it marked as a slope on a diagram. With a production function like the one in Figure 3.5, the slope changes continuously as we move along the curve. We have said that when Alexei studies for 4 hours a day the marginal product is 7, the increase in the grade from one more hour of study. Because the slope of the curve changes between 4 and 5 hours on the horizontal axis, this is only an approximation to the actual marginal product. More precisely, the marginal product is the rate at which the grade increases, per hour of additional study. In Figure 3.5 the true marginal product is the slope of the **tangent** to the curve at 4 hours. In this unit, we will use approximations so that we can work in whole numbers, but you may notice that sometimes these numbers are not quite the same as the slopes.

EXERCISE 3.2 PRODUCTION FUNCTIONS

1. Draw a graph to show a production function that, unlike Alexei's, becomes steeper as the input increases.
2. Can you think of an example of a production process that might have this shape? Why would the slope get steeper?
3. What can you say about the marginal and average products in this case?

QUESTION 3.3 CHOOSE THE CORRECT ANSWER(S)
Figure 3.5 (page 93) shows Alexei's production function, with the final grade (the output) related to the number of hours spent studying (the input).

Which of the following is true?

☐ The marginal product and average product are approximately the same for the initial hour.
☐ The marginal product and the average product are both constant beyond 15 hours.
☐ The horizontal production function beyond 15 hours means that studying for more than 15 hours is detrimental to Alexei's performance.
☐ The marginal product and the average product at 20 hours are both 4.5.

MARGINAL PRODUCT
The marginal product is the rate of change of the grade at 4 hours of study. Suppose Alexei has been studying for 4 hours a day, and studies for 1 minute longer each day (a total of 4.016667 hours). Then, according to the graph, his grade will rise by a very small amount—about 0.124. A more precise estimate of the marginal product (the rate of change) would be:

$$\frac{0.124}{0.016667} = 7.44$$

If we looked at smaller changes in study time even further (the rise in grade for each additional second of study per day, for example) we would get closer to the true marginal product, which is the slope of the tangent to the curve at 4 hours of study.

3.2 PREFERENCES

If Alexei has the production function shown in Figure 3.5, how many hours per day will he choose to study? The decision depends on his **preferences**—the things that he cares about. If he cared only about grades, he should study for 15 hours a day. But, like other people, Alexei also cares about his free time—he likes to sleep, go out or watch TV. So he faces a trade-off: how many percentage points is he willing to give up in order to spend time on things other than study?

We illustrate his preferences using Figure 3.6, with free time on the horizontal axis and final grade on the vertical axis. Free time is defined as all the time that he does not spend studying. Every point in the diagram represents a different combination of free time and final grade. Given his production function, not every combination that Alexei would want will be possible, but for the moment we will only consider the combinations that he would prefer.

We can assume:

- For a given grade, he prefers a combination with more free time to one with less free time. Therefore, even though both A and B in Figure 3.6 correspond to a grade of 84, Alexei prefers A because it gives him more free time.
- Similarly, if two combinations both have 20 hours of free time, he prefers the one with a higher grade.
- But compare points A and D in the table. Would Alexei prefer D (low grade, plenty of time) or A (higher grade, less time)? One way to find out would be to ask him.

Suppose he says he is indifferent between A and D, meaning he would feel equally satisfied with either outcome. We say that these two outcomes would give Alexei the same **utility**. And we know that he prefers A to B, so B provides lower utility than A or D.

A systematic way to graph Alexei's preferences would be to start by looking for all of the combinations that give him the same utility as A and D. We could ask Alexei another question: 'Imagine that you could have the combination at A (15 hours of free time, 84 points). How many points

preferences A description of the benefit or cost we associate with each possible outcome.

utility A numerical indicator of the value that one places on an outcome, such that higher valued outcomes will be chosen over lower valued ones when both are feasible.

would you be willing to sacrifice for an extra hour of free time?' Suppose that after due consideration, he answers 'nine'. Then we know that he is indifferent between A and E (16 hours, 75 points). Then we could ask the same question about combination E, and so on until point D. Eventually we could draw up a table like the one in Figure 3.6. Alexei is indifferent between A and E, between E and F, and so on, which means he is indifferent between all of the combinations from A to D.

The combinations in the table are plotted in Figure 3.6, and joined together to form a downward-sloping curve, called an **indifference curve**, which joins together all of the combinations that provide equal utility or 'satisfaction'.

> **indifference curve** A curve of the points which indicate the combinations of goods that provide a given level of utility to the individual.

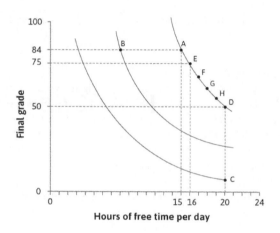

	A	E	F	G	H	D
Hours of free time	15	16	17	18	19	20
Final grade	84	75	67	60	54	50

Figure 3.6 Mapping Alexei's preferences.

1. Alexei prefers more free time to less free time
Combinations A and B both deliver a grade of 84, but Alexei will prefer A because it has more free time.

2. Alexei prefers a high grade to a low grade
At combinations C and D Alexei has 20 hours of free time per day, but he prefers D because it gives him a higher grade.

3. Indifference
... but we don't know whether Alexei prefers A or E, so we ask him: he says he is indifferent.

4. More combinations giving the same utility
Alexei says that F is another combination that would give him the same utility as A and E.

5. Constructing the indifference curve
By asking more questions, we discover that Alexei is indifferent between all of the combinations between A and D.

6. Constructing the indifference curve
These points are joined together to form an indifference curve.

7. Other indifference curves
Indifference curves can be drawn through any point in the diagram, to show other points giving the same utility. We can construct other curves starting from B or C in the same way as before, by finding out which combinations give the same amount of utility.

If you look at the three curves drawn in Figure 3.6, you can see that the one through A gives higher utility than the one through B. The curve through C gives the lowest utility of the three. To describe preferences we don't need to know the exact utility of each option; we only need to know which combinations provide more or less utility than others.

The curves we have drawn capture our typical assumptions about people's preferences between two goods. In other models, these will often be **consumption goods** such as food or clothing, and we refer to the person as a consumer. In our model of a student's preferences, the goods are 'final grade' and 'free time'. Notice that:

- *Indifference curves slope downward due to trade-offs*: If you are indifferent between two combinations, the combination that has more of one good must have less of the other good.
- *Higher indifference curves correspond to higher utility levels*: As we move up and to the right in the diagram, further away from the origin, we move to combinations with more of both goods.
- *Indifference curves are usually smooth*: Small changes in the amounts of goods don't cause big jumps in utility.
- *Indifference curves do not cross*: Why? See Exercise 3.3.
- *As you move to the right along an indifference curve, it becomes flatter.*

To understand the last property in the list, look at Alexei's indifference curves, which are plotted again in Figure 3.7. If he is at A, with 15 hours of free time and a grade of 84, he would be willing to sacrifice 9 percentage points for an extra hour of free time, taking him to E (remember that he is indifferent between A and E). We say that his **marginal rate of substitution (MRS)** between grade points and free time at A is nine; it is the reduction in his grade that would keep Alexei's utility constant following a one-hour increase of free time.

We have drawn the indifference curves as becoming gradually flatter because it seems reasonable to assume that the more free time and the lower the grade he has, the less willing he will be to sacrifice further percentage points in return for free time, so his MRS will be lower. In Figure 3.7 we have calculated the MRS at each combination along the indifference curve. You can see that, when Alexei has more free time and a lower grade, the MRS—the number of percentage points he would give up to get an extra hour of free time—gradually falls.

The MRS is just the slope of the indifference curve, and it falls as we move to the right along the curve. If you think about moving from one point to another in Figure 3.7, you can see that the indifference curves get flatter if you increase the amount of free time, and steeper if you increase the grade. When free time is scarce relative to grade points, Alexei is less willing to sacrifice an hour for a higher grade: his MRS is high and his indifference curve is steep.

As the analysis in Figure 3.7 shows, if you move up the vertical line through 15 hours, the indifference curves get steeper: the MRS increases. For a given amount of free time, Alexei is willing to give up more grade points for an additional hour when he has a lot of points compared to when he has few (for example, if he was in danger of failing the course). By the time you reach A, where his grade is 84, the MRS is high; grade points are so plentiful here that he is willing to give up 9 percentage points for an extra hour of free time.

consumption good A good or service that satisfies the needs of consumers over a short period.

marginal rate of substitution (MRS) The trade-off that a person is willing to make between two goods. At any point, this is the slope of the indifference curve. *See also: marginal rate of transformation.*

Leibniz: Indifference curves and the marginal rate of substitution (http://tinyco.re/L030201)

You can see the same effect if you fix the grade and vary the amount of free time. If you move to the right along the horizontal line for a grade of 54, the MRS becomes lower at each indifference curve. As free time becomes more plentiful, Alexei becomes less and less willing to give up grade points for more time.

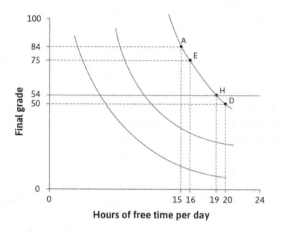

			A	E	F	G	H	D
Hours of free time			15	16	17	18	19	20
Final grade			84	75	67	60	54	50
Marginal rate of substitution between grade and free time			9	8	7	6	4	

Figure 3.7 The marginal rate of substitution.

1. Alexei's indifference curves
The diagram shows three indifference curves for Alexei. The curve furthest to the left offers the lowest satisfaction.

2. Point A
At A, he has 15 hours of free time and his grade is 84.

3. Alexei is indifferent between A and E
He would be willing to move from A to E, giving up 9 percentage points for an extra hour of free time. His marginal rate of substitution is 9. The indifference curve is steep at A.

4. Alexei is indifferent between H and D
At H he is only willing to give up 4 points for an extra hour of free time. His MRS is 4. As we move down the indifference curve, the MRS diminishes, because points become scarce relative to free time. The indifference curve becomes flatter.

5. All combinations with 15 hours of free time
Look at the combinations with 15 hours of free time. On the lowest curve the grade is low, and the MRS is small. Alexei would be willing to give up only a few points for an hour of free time. As we move up the vertical line the indifference curves are steeper: the MRS increases.

6. All combinations with a grade of 54
Now look at all the combinations with a grade of 54. On the curve furthest to the left, free time is scarce, and the MRS is high. As we move to the right along the red line he is less willing to give up points for free time. The MRS decreases–the indifference curves get flatter.

EXERCISE 3.3 WHY INDIFFERENCE CURVES NEVER CROSS

In the diagram below, IC_1 is an indifference curve joining all the combinations that give the same level of utility as A. Combination B is not on IC_1.

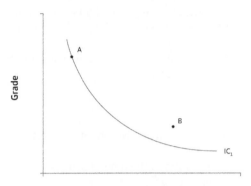

Hours of free time per day

1. Does combination B give higher or lower utility than combination A? How do you know?
2. Draw a sketch of the diagram, and add another indifference curve, IC_2, that goes through B and crosses IC_1. Label the point at which they cross as C.
3. Combinations B and C are both on IC_2. What does that imply about their levels of utility?
4. Combinations C and A are both on IC_1. What does that imply about their levels of utility?
5. According to your answers to (3) and (4), how do the levels of utility at combinations A and B compare?
6. Now compare your answers to (1) and (5), and explain how you know that indifference curves can never cross.

EXERCISE 3.4 YOUR MARGINAL RATE OF SUBSTITUTION

Imagine that you are offered a job at the end of your university course with a salary per hour (after taxes) of £12.50. Your future employer then says that you will work for 40 hours per week leaving you with 128 hours of free time per week. You tell a friend: 'at that wage, 40 hours is exactly what I would like.'

1. Draw a diagram with free time on the horizontal axis and weekly pay on the vertical axis, and plot the combination of hours and the wage corresponding to your job offer, calling it A. Assume you need about 10 hours a day for sleeping and eating, so you may want to draw the horizontal axis with 70 hours at the origin.
2. Now draw an indifference curve so that A represents the hours you would have chosen yourself.
3. Now imagine you were offered another job requiring 45 hours of work per week. Use the indifference curve you have drawn to estimate the level of weekly pay that would make you indifferent between this and the original offer.
4. Do the same for another job requiring 35 hours of work per week. What level of weekly pay would make you indifferent between this and the original offer?
5. Use your diagram to estimate your marginal rate of substitution between pay and free time at A.

QUESTION 3.4 CHOOSE THE CORRECT ANSWER(S)
Figure 3.6 (page 96) shows Alexei's indifference curves for free time and final grade. Which of the following is true?

☐ Alexei prefers C to B because at C he has more free time.
☐ Alexei is indifferent between the grade of 84 with 15 hours of free time, and the grade of 50 with 20 hours of free time.
☐ Alexei prefers D to C, because at D he has the same grade and more free time.
☐ At G, Alexei is willing to give up 2 hours of free time for 10 extra grade points.

QUESTION 3.5 CHOOSE THE CORRECT ANSWER(S)
What is the marginal rate of substitution (MRS)?

☐ The ratio of the amounts of the two goods at a point on the indifference curve.
☐ The amount of one good that the consumer is willing to trade for one unit of the other.
☐ The change in the consumer's utility when one good is substituted for another.
☐ The slope of the indifference curve.

3.3 OPPORTUNITY COSTS

opportunity cost When taking an action implies forgoing the next best alternative action, this is the net benefit of the foregone alternative.

Alexei faces a dilemma: we know from looking at his preferences that he wants both his grade and his free time to be as high as possible. But given his production function, he cannot increase his free time without getting a lower grade in the exam. Another way of expressing this is to say that free time has an **opportunity cost**: to get more free time, Alexei has to forgo the opportunity of getting a higher grade.

In economics, opportunity costs are relevant whenever we study individuals choosing between alternative and mutually exclusive courses of action. When we consider the cost of taking action A we include the fact that if we do A, we cannot do B. So 'not doing B' becomes part of the cost of doing A. This is called an opportunity cost because doing A means forgoing the opportunity to do B.

Imagine that an accountant and an economist have been asked to report the cost of going to a concert, A, in a theatre, which has a $25 admission cost. In a nearby park there is concert B, which is free but happens at the same time.

ACCOUNTANT: The cost of concert A is your 'out-of-pocket' cost: you paid $25 for a ticket, so the cost is $25.
ECONOMIST: But what do you have to give up to go to concert A? You give up $25, plus the enjoyment of the free concert in the park. So the cost of concert A for you is the out-of-pocket cost plus the opportunity cost.

Suppose that the most you would have been willing to pay to attend the free concert in the park (if it wasn't free) was $15. The benefit of your next best alternative to concert A would be $15 of enjoyment in the park. This is the opportunity cost of going to concert A.

So the total **economic cost** of concert A is $25 + $15 = $40. If the pleasure you anticipate from being at concert A is greater than the economic cost, say $50, then you will forego concert B and buy a ticket to the theatre. On the other hand, if you anticipate $35 worth of pleasure from concert A, then the economic cost of $40 means you will not choose to go to the theatre. In simple terms, given that you have to pay $25 for the ticket, you will instead opt for concert B, pocketing the $25 to spend on other things and enjoying $15 worth of benefit from the free park concert.

Why don't accountants think this way? Because it is not their job. Accountants are paid to keep track of money, not to provide decision rules on how to choose among alternatives, some of which do not have a stated price. But making sensible decisions and predicting how sensible people will make decisions involve more than keeping track of money. An accountant might argue that the park concert is irrelevant:

ACCOUNTANT: Whether or not there is a free park concert does not affect the cost of going to the concert A. The cost to you is always $25.

ECONOMIST: But whether or not there is a free park concert can affect whether you go to concert A or not, because it changes your available options. If your enjoyment from A is $35 and your next best alternative is staying at home, with enjoyment of $0, you will choose concert A. However, if concert B is available, you will choose it over A.

In Unit 2, we said that if an action brings greater net benefits than the next best alternative, it yields an **economic rent** and you will do it. Another way of saying this is that you receive an economic rent from taking an action when it results in a benefit greater than its economic cost (the sum of out-of-pocket and opportunity costs).

The table in Figure 3.8 summarizes the example of your choice of which concert to attend.

> **economic cost** The out-of-pocket cost of an action, plus the opportunity cost.

> **economic rent** A payment or other benefit received above and beyond what the individual would have received in his or her next best alternative (or reservation option). *See also: reservation option.*

	A high value on the theatre choice (A)	A low value on the theatre choice (A)
Out-of-pocket cost (price of ticket for A)	$25	$25
Opportunity cost (foregone pleasure of B, park concert)	$15	$15
Economic cost (sum of out-of-pocket and opportunity cost)	$40	$40
Enjoyment of theatre concert (A)	$50	$35
Economic rent (enjoyment minus economic cost)	$10	−$5
Decision	A: Go to the theatre concert.	B: Go to the park concert.

Figure 3.8 Opportunity costs and economic rent: Which concert will you choose?

You are a taxi driver in Melbourne who earns A$50 for a day's work. You have been offered a one-day ticket to the Australian Open for A$40. As a tennis fan, you value the experience at A$100. With this information, what can we say?

☐ The opportunity cost of the day at the Open is A$40.
☐ The economic cost of the day at the Open is A$40.
☐ The economic rent of the day at the Open is A$10.
☐ You would have paid up to A$100 for the ticket.

EXERCISE 3.5 OPPORTUNITY COSTS
The British government introduced legislation in 2012 that gave universities the option to raise their tuition fees. Most chose to increase annual tuition fees for students from £3,000 to £9,000.

Does this mean that the cost of going to university has tripled? (Think about how an accountant and an economist might answer this question. To simplify, assume that the tuition fee is an 'out of pocket' cost. Ignore student loans.)

3.4 THE FEASIBLE SET

Now we return to Alexei's problem of how to choose between grades and free time. Free time has an opportunity cost in the form of lost percentage points in his grade (equivalently, we might say that percentage points have an opportunity cost in the form of the free time Alexei has to give up to obtain them). But before we can describe how Alexei resolves his dilemma, we need to work out precisely which alternatives are available to him.

To answer this question, we look again at the production function. This time we will show how the final grade depends on the amount of free time, rather than study time. There are 24 hours in a day. Alexei must divide this time between studying (all the hours devoted to learning) and free time (all the rest of his time). Figure 3.9 shows the relationship between his final grade and hours of free time per day—the mirror image of Figure 3.5. If Alexei studies solidly for 24 hours, that means zero hours of free time and a final grade of 90. If he chooses 24 hours of free time per day, we assume he will get a grade of zero.

In Figure 3.9, the axes are final grade and free time, the two goods that give Alexei utility. If we think of him choosing to consume a combination of these two goods, the curved line in Figure 3.9 shows what is feasible. It represents his **feasible frontier**: the highest grade he can achieve given the amount of free time he takes. Follow the steps in Figure 3.9 to see which combinations of grade and free time are feasible, and which are not, and how the slope of the frontier represents the opportunity cost of free time.

feasible frontier The curve made of points that defines the maximum feasible quantity of one good for a given quantity of the other. *See also: feasible set.*

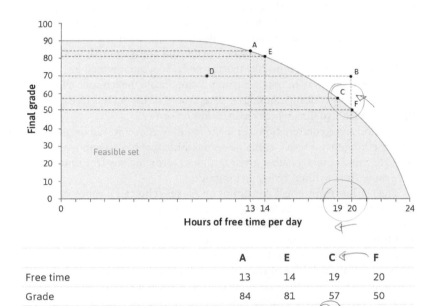

	A	**E**	**C**	**F**
Free time	13	14	19	20
Grade	84	81	57	50
Opportunity cost	3		7	

Figure 3.9 How does Alexei's choice of free time affect his grade?

1. The feasible frontier
This curve is called the feasible frontier. It shows the highest final grade Alexei can achieve given the amount of free time he takes. With 24 hours of free time, his grade would be zero. By having less free time, Alexei can achieve a higher grade.

2. A feasible combination
If Alexei chooses 13 hours of free time per day, he can achieve a grade of 84.

3. Infeasible combinations
Given Alexei's abilities and conditions of study, under normal conditions he cannot take 20 hours of free time and expect to get a grade of 70 (remember, we are assuming that luck plays no part). Therefore B is an infeasible combination of hours of free time and final grade.

4. A feasible combination
The maximum grade Alexei can achieve with 19 hours of free time per day is 57.

5. Inside the frontier
Combination D is feasible, but Alexei is wasting time or points in the exam. He could get a higher grade with the same hours of study per day, or have more free time and still get a grade of 70.

6. The feasible set
The area inside the frontier, together with the frontier itself, is called the **feasible set**. (A set is a collection of things–in this case all the feasible combinations of free time and grade.)

7. The opportunity cost of free time
At combination A Alexei could get an extra hour of free time by giving up 3 points in the exam. The opportunity cost of an hour of free time at A is 3 points.

8. The opportunity cost varies
The more free time he takes, the higher the marginal product of studying, so the opportunity cost of free time increases. At C the opportunity cost of an hour of free time is higher than at A: Alexei would have to give up 7 points.

9. The slope of the feasible frontier
The opportunity cost of free time at C is 7 points, corresponding to the slope of the feasible frontier. At C, Alexei would have to give up 7 percentage points (the vertical change is –7) to increase his free time by 1 hour (the horizontal change is 1). The slope is –7.

feasible set All of the combinations of the things under consideration that a decision-maker could choose given the economic, physical or other constraints that he faces. *See also: feasible frontier.*

Any combination of free time and final grade that is on or inside the frontier is feasible. Combinations outside the feasible frontier are said to be infeasible given Alexei's abilities and conditions of study. On the other hand, even though a combination lying inside the frontier is feasible, choosing it would imply Alexei has effectively thrown away something that he values. If he studied for 14 hours a day, then according to our model, he could guarantee himself a grade of 89. But he could obtain a lower grade (70, say), if he just stopped writing before the end of the exam. It would be foolish to throw away points like this for no reason, but it would be possible. Another way to obtain a combination inside the frontier might be to sit in the library doing nothing—Alexei would be taking less free time than is available to him, which again makes no sense.

By choosing a combination inside the frontier, Alexei would be giving up something that is freely available—something that has no opportunity cost. He could obtain a higher grade without sacrificing any free time, or have more time without reducing his grade.

The feasible frontier is a constraint on Alexei's choices. It represents the trade-off he must make between grade and free time. At any point on the frontier, taking more free time has an opportunity cost in terms of grade points foregone, corresponding to the slope of the frontier.

Another way to express the same idea is to say that the feasible frontier shows the **marginal rate of transformation**: the rate at which Alexei can transform free time into grade points. Look at the slope of the frontier between points A and E in Figure 3.9.

marginal rate of transformation (MRT) The quantity of some good that must be sacrificed to acquire one additional unit of another good. At any point, it is the slope of the feasible frontier. *See also: marginal rate of substitution.*

- The slope of AE (vertical distance divided by horizontal distance) is −3.
- At point A, Alexei could get one more unit of free time by giving up 3 grade points. The opportunity cost of a unit of free time is 3.
- At point E, Alexei could transform one unit of time into 3 grade points. The marginal rate at which he can transform free time into grade points is 3.

Note that the slope of AE is only an approximation to the slope of the frontier. More precisely, the slope at any point is the slope of the tangent, and this represents both the MRT and the opportunity cost at that point.

Note that we have now identified two trade-offs:

- *The marginal rate of substitution (MRS)*: In the previous section, we saw that it measures the trade-off that Alexei is willing to make between final grade and free time.
- *The marginal rate of transformation (MRT)*: In contrast, this measures the trade-off that Alexei is constrained to make by the feasible frontier.

As we shall see in the next section, the choice Alexei makes between his grade and his free time will strike a balance between these two trade-offs.

Leibniz: Marginal rates of transformation and substitution (http://tinyco.re/L030401)

Look at Figure 3.5 (page 93) which shows Alexei's production function: how the final grade (the output) depends on the number of hours spent studying (the input).

Free time per day is given by 24 hours minus the hours of study per day. Consider Alexei's feasible set of combinations of final grade and hours of free time per day. What can we conclude?

☐ To find the feasible set one needs to know the number of hours that Alexei sleeps per day.
☐ The feasible frontier is a mirror image of the production function above.
☐ The feasible frontier is horizontal between 0 and 10 hours of free time per day.
☐ The marginal product of labour at 10 hours of study equals the marginal rate of transformation at 14 hours of free time.

3.5 DECISION MAKING AND SCARCITY

The final step in this decision-making process is to determine the combination of final grade and free time that Alexei will choose. Figure 3.10a brings together his feasible frontier (Figure 3.9) and indifference curves (Figure 3.6). Recall that the indifference curves indicate what Alexei prefers, and their slopes shows the trade-offs that he is willing to make; the feasible frontier is the constraint on his choice, and its slope shows the trade-off he is constrained to make.

Figure 3.10a shows four indifference curves, labelled IC_1 to IC_4. IC_4 represents the highest level of utility because it is the furthest away from the origin. No combination of grade and free time on IC_4 is feasible, however, because the whole indifference curve lies outside the feasible set. Suppose that Alexei considers choosing a combination somewhere in the feasible set, on IC_1. By working through the steps in Figure 3.10a, you will see that he can increase his utility by moving to points on higher indifference curves until he reaches a feasible choice that maximizes his utility.

Alexei maximizes his utility at point E, at which his indifference curve is tangent to the feasible frontier. The model predicts that Alexei will:

- choose to spend 5 hours each day studying, and 19 hours on other activities
- obtain a grade of 57 as a result

We can see from Figure 3.10a that at E, the feasible frontier and the highest attainable indifference curve IC_3 are tangent to each other (they touch but do not cross). At E, the slope of the indifference curve is the same as the slope of the feasible frontier. Now, remember that the slopes represent the two trade-offs facing Alexei:

- *The slope of the indifference curve is the MRS*: It is the trade-off he is willing to make between free time and percentage points.
- *The slope of the frontier is the MRT*: It is the trade-off that he is constrained to make between free time and percentage points because it is not possible to go beyond the feasible frontier.

Alexei achieves the highest possible utility where the two trade-offs just balance (E). His optimal combination of grade and free time is at the point where the marginal rate of transformation is equal to the marginal rate of substitution.

Figure 3.10b shows the MRS (slope of indifference curve) and MRT (slope of feasible frontier) at the points shown in Figure 3.10a. At B and D, the number of points Alexei is willing to trade for an hour of free time (MRS) is greater than the opportunity cost of that hour (MRT), so he prefers to increase his free time. At A, the MRT is greater than the MRS so he prefers to decrease his free time. And, as expected, at E the MRS and MRT are equal.

Leibniz: Optimal allocation of free time: MRT meets MRS (http://tinyco.re/L030501)

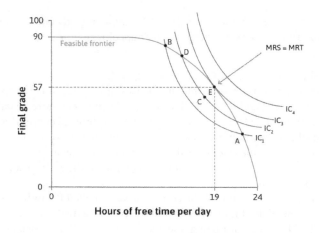

Figure 3.10a How many hours does Alexei decide to study?

1. Which point will Alexei choose?
The diagram brings together Alexei's indifference curves and his feasible frontier.

2. Feasible combinations
On the indifference curve IC$_1$, all combinations between A and B are feasible because they lie in the feasible set. Suppose Alexei chooses one of these points.

3. Could do better
All combinations in the lens-shaped area between IC$_1$ and the feasible frontier are feasible, and give higher utility than combinations on IC$_1$. For example, a movement to C would increase Alexei's utility.

4. Could do better
Moving from IC$_1$ to point C on IC$_2$ increases Alexei's utility. Switching from B to D would raise his utility by an equivalent amount.

5. The best feasible trade-off
But again, Alexei can raise his utility by moving into the lens-shaped area above IC$_2$. He can continue to find feasible combinations on higher indifference curves, until he reaches E.

6. The best feasible trade-off
At E, he has 19 hours of free time per day and a grade of 57. Alexei maximizes his utility: he is on the highest indifference curve obtainable, given the feasible frontier.

7. MRS = MRT
At E the indifference curve is tangent to the feasible frontier. The marginal rate of substitution (the slope of the indifference curve) is equal to the marginal rate of transformation (the slope of the frontier).

We have modelled the student's decision on study hours as what we call a **constrained choice problem**: a decision-maker (Alexei) pursues an objective (utility maximization in this case) subject to a constraint (his feasible frontier).

In our example, both free time and points in the exam are scarce for Alexei because:

- *Free time and grades are goods*: Alexei values both of them.
- *Each has an opportunity cost*: More of one good means less of the other.

In constrained choice problems, the solution is the individual's optimal choice. If we assume that utility maximization is Alexei's goal, the optimal combination of grade and free time is a point on the feasible frontier at which:

$$MRS = MRT$$

The table in Figure 3.11 summarizes Alexei's trade-offs.

> **constrained choice problem** This problem is about how we can do the best for ourselves, given our preferences and constraints, and when the things we value are scarce. *See also: constrained optimization problem.*

> **EXERCISE 3.6 EXPLORING SCARCITY**
> Describe a situation in which Alexei's grade points and free time would not be scarce. Remember, scarcity depends on both his preferences and the production function.

	B	D	E	A
Free time	13	15	19	22
Grade	84	78	57	33
MRT	2	4	7	9
MRS	20	15	7	3

Figure 3.10b How many hours does Alexei decide to study?

	The trade-off	Where it is on the diagram	It is equal to …
MRS	*Marginal rate of substitution*: The number of percentage points Alexei is willing to trade for an hour of free time	The slope of the indifference curve	
MRT, or opportunity cost of free time	*Marginal rate of transformation*: The number of percentage points Alexei would gain (or lose) by giving up (or taking) another hour of free time	The slope of the feasible frontier	The marginal product of labour

Figure 3.11 Alexei's trade-offs.

QUESTION 3.8 CHOOSE THE CORRECT ANSWER(S)

Figure 3.10a (page 106) shows Alexei's feasible frontier and his indifference curves for final grade and hours of free time per day. Suppose that all students have the same feasible frontier, but their indifference curves may differ in shape and slope depending on their preferences.

Use the diagram to decide which of the following is (are) correct.

☐ Alexei will choose a point where the marginal rate of substitution equals the marginal rate of transformation.

☐ C is below the feasible frontier but D is on the feasible frontier. Therefore, Alexei may select point D as his optimal choice.

☐ All students with downward-sloping indifference curves, whatever the slope, would choose point E.

☐ At E, Alexei has the highest ratio of final grade per hour of free time per day.

3.6 HOURS OF WORK AND ECONOMIC GROWTH

John Maynard Keynes. 1963. 'Economic Possibilities for our Grandchildren'. In *Essays in Persuasion*, New York, NY: W. W. Norton & Co.

Tim Harford. 2015. 'The rewards for working hard are too big for Keynes's vision'. *The Undercover Economist*. First published by *The Financial Times*. Updated 3 August 2015.

In 1930, John Maynard Keynes, a British economist, published an essay entitled 'Economic Possibilities for our Grandchildren', in which he suggested that in the 100 years that would follow, technological improvement would make us, on average, about eight times better off. What he called 'the economic problem, the struggle for subsistence' would be solved, and we would not have to work more than, say, 15 hours per week to satisfy our economic needs. The question he raised was: how would we cope with all of the additional leisure time?

Keynes' prediction for the rate of technological progress in countries such as the UK and the US has been approximately right, and working hours have indeed fallen, although much less than he expected—it seems unlikely that average working hours will be 15 hours per week by 2030. An article by Tim Harford in the Undercover Economist column of the *Financial Times* examines why Keynes' prediction was wrong.

As we saw in Unit 2, new technologies raise the productivity of labour. We now have the tools to analyse the effects of increased productivity on living standards, specifically on incomes and the free time of workers.

So far, we have considered Alexei's choice between studying and free time. We now apply our model of constrained choice to Angela, a self-sufficient farmer who chooses how many hours to work. We assume that Angela produces grain to eat and does not sell it to anyone else. If she produces too little grain, she will starve.

What is stopping her producing the most grain possible? Like the student, Angela also values free time—she gets utility from both free time and consuming grain.

But her choice is constrained: producing grain takes labour time, and each hour of labour means Angela foregoes an hour of free time. The hour of free time sacrificed is the opportunity cost of the grain produced. Like Alexei, Angela faces a problem of scarcity: she has to make a choice between her consumption of grain and her consumption of free time.

To understand her choice, and how it is affected by technological change, we need to model her production function, and her preferences.

Figure 3.12 shows the initial production function before the change occurs: the relationship between the number of hours worked and the amount of grain produced. Notice that the graph has a similar concave shape to Alexei's production function: the marginal product of an additional hour's work, shown by the slope, diminishes as the number of hours increases.

A technological improvement such as seeds with a higher yield, or better equipment that makes harvesting quicker, will increase the amount of grain produced in a given number of hours. The analysis in Figure 3.12 demonstrates the effect on the production function.

Notice that the new production function is steeper than the original one for every given number of hours. The new technology has increased Angela's marginal product of labour: at every point, an additional hour of work produces more grain than under the old technology.

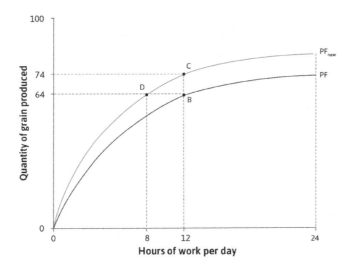

Working hours	0	1	2	3	4	5	6	7	8	9	10	11	12	13	18	24
Grain	0	9	18	26	33	40	46	51	55	58	60	62	64	66	69	72

Figure 3.12 How technological change affects the production function.

1. The initial technology
The table shows how the amount of grain produced depends on the number of hours worked per day. For example, if Angela works for 12 hours a day she will produce 64 units of grain. This is point B on the graph.

2. A technological improvement
An improvement in technology means that more grain is produced for a given number of working hours. The production function shifts upward, from PF to PF_{new}.

3. More grain for the same amount of work
Now if Angela works for 12 hours per day, she can produce 74 units of grain (point C).

4. Or same grain, less work
Alternatively, by working 8 hours a day she can produce 64 units of grain (point D), which previously took 12 hours.

Leibniz: Modelling technological change (http://tinyco.re/L030601)

Figure 3.13 shows Angela's feasible frontier, which is just the mirror image of the production function, for the original technology (FF), and the new one (FF$_{new}$).

As before, what we call free time is all of the time that is not spent working to produce grain—it includes time for eating, sleeping, and everything else that we don't count as farm work, as well as her leisure time. The feasible frontier shows how much grain can be consumed for each possible amount of free time. Points B, C, and D represent the same combinations of free time and grain as in Figure 3.12. The slope of the frontier represents the MRT (the marginal rate at which free time can be transformed into grain) or equivalently the opportunity cost of free time. You can see that technological progress expands the feasible set: it gives her a wider choice of combinations of grain and free time.

Now we add Angela's indifference curves to the diagram, representing her preferences for free time and grain consumption, to find which combination in the feasible set is best for her. Figure 3.14 shows that her optimal choice under the original technology is to work for 8 hours a day, giving her 16 hours of free time and 55 units of grain. This is the point of tangency, where her two trade-offs balance out: her marginal rate of substitution (MRS) between grain and free time (the slope of the indifference curve) is equal to the MRT (the slope of the feasible frontier). We can think of the combination of free time and grain at point A as a measure of her standard of living.

Follow the steps in Figure 3.14 to see how her choice changes as a result of technological progress.

Technological change raises Angela's standard of living: it enables her to achieve higher utility. Note that in Figure 3.14 she increases both her consumption of grain and her free time.

It is important to realize that this is just one possible result. Had we drawn the indifference curves or the frontier differently, the trade-offs Angela faces would have been different. We can say that the improvement in technology definitely makes it feasible to both consume more grain and

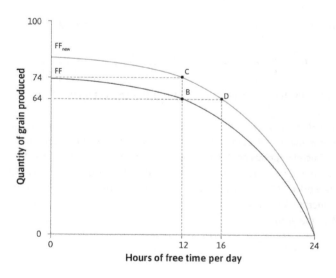

Figure 3.13 An improvement in technology expands Angela's feasible set.

have more free time, but whether Angela will choose to have more of both depends on her preferences between these two goods, and her willingness to substitute one for the other.

To understand why, remember that technological change makes the production function steeper: it increases Angela's marginal product of labour. This means that the opportunity cost of free time is higher, giving her a greater incentive to work. But also, now that she can have more grain for each amount of free time, she may be more willing to give up some grain for more free time: that is, reduce her hours of work.

These two effects of technological progress work in opposite directions. In Figure 3.14, the second effect dominates and she chooses point E, with more free time as well as more grain. In the next section, we look more carefully at these two opposing effects, using a different example to disentangle them.

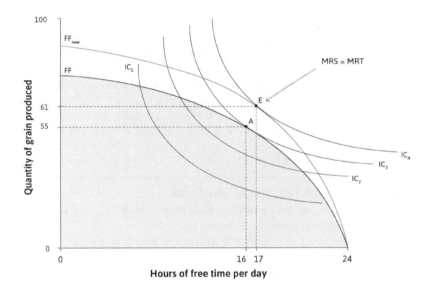

Figure 3.14 Angela's choice between free time and grain.

1. Maximizing utility with the original technology
The diagram shows the feasible set with the original production function, and Angela's indifference curves for combinations of grain and free time. The highest indifference curve she can attain is IC_3, at point A.

2. MRS = MRT for maximum utility
Her optimal choice is point A on the feasible frontier. She enjoys 16 hours of free time per day and consumes 55 units of grain. At A, her MRS is equal to the MRT.

3. Technological progress
An improvement in technology expands the feasible set. Now she can do better than at A.

4. Angela's new optimal choice
When the technology of farming has improved, Angela's optimal choice is point E, where FF_{new} is tangent to indifference curve IC_4. She has more free time and more grain than before.

QUESTION 3.9 CHOOSE THE CORRECT ANSWER(S)

The figures show Alexei's production function and his corresponding feasible frontier for final grade and hours of work or free time per day. They show the effect of an improvement in his studying technique, represented by the tilting up of the two curves.

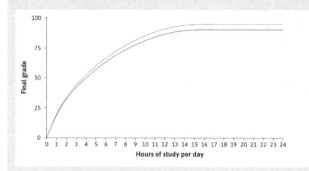

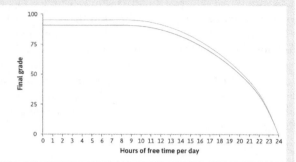

Consider now two cases of further changes in Alexei's study environment:

Case A. He suddenly finds himself needing to spend 4 hours a day caring for a family member. (You may assume that his marginal product of labour is unaffected for the hours that he studies.)

Case B. For health reasons his marginal product of labour for all hours is reduced by 10%.

Then:

☐ For case A, Alexei's production function shifts to the right.

☐ For case A, Alexei's feasible frontier shifts to the left.

☐ For case B, Alexei's production function shifts down in a parallel manner.

☐ For case B, Alexei's feasible frontier rotates downwards, pivoted at the intercept with the horizontal axis.

EXERCISE 3.7 YOUR PRODUCTION FUNCTION

1. What could bring about a technological improvement in your production function and those of your fellow students?
2. Draw a diagram to illustrate how this improvement would affect your feasible set of grades and study hours.
3. Analyse what might happen to your choice of study hours, and the choices that your peers might make.

3.7 INCOME AND SUBSTITUTION EFFECTS ON HOURS OF WORK AND FREE TIME

Imagine that you are looking for a job after you leave college. You expect to be able to earn a wage of $15 per hour. Jobs differ according to the number of hours you have to work—so what would be your ideal number of hours? Together, the wage and the hours of work will determine how much free time you will have, and your total earnings.

We will work in terms of daily average free time and consumption, as we did for Angela. We will assume that your spending—that is, your average consumption of food, accommodation, and other goods and services—cannot exceed your earnings (for example, you cannot borrow to increase your consumption). If we write w for the wage, and you have t hours of free time per day, then you work for (24 − t) hours, and your maximum level of consumption, c, is given by:

$$c = w(24 - t)$$

We will call this your **budget constraint**, because it shows what you can afford to buy.

In the table in Figure 3.15 we have calculated your free time for hours of work varying between 0 and 16 hours per day, and your maximum consumption, when your wage is w = $15.

Figure 3.15 shows the two goods in this problem: hours of free time (t) on the horizontal axis, and consumption (c) on the vertical axis. When we plot the points shown in the table, we get a downward-sloping straight line: this is the graph of the budget constraint. The equation of the budget constraint is:

$$c = 15(24 - t)$$

The slope of the budget constraint corresponds to the wage: for each additional hour of free time, consumption must decrease by $15. The area under the budget constraint is your feasible set. Your problem is quite similar to Angela's problem, except that your feasible frontier is a straight line. Remember that for Angela the slope of the feasible frontier is both the MRT (the rate at which free time could be transformed into grain) and the opportunity cost of an hour of free time (the grain foregone). These vary because Angela's marginal product changes with her hours of work. For you, the marginal rate at which you can transform free time into consumption, and the opportunity cost of free time, is constant and is equal to your wage (in absolute value): it is $15 for your first hour of work, and still $15 for every hour after that.

What would be your ideal job? Your preferred choice of free time and consumption will be the combination on the feasible frontier that is on the highest possible indifference curve. Work through Figure 3.15 to find the optimal choice.

If your indifference curves look like the ones in Figure 3.15, then you would choose point A, with 18 hours of free time. At this point your MRS— the rate at which you are willing to swap consumption for time—is equal to the wage ($15, the opportunity cost of time). You would like to find a job in which you can work for 6 hours per day, and your daily earnings would be $90.

Like the student, you are balancing two trade-offs:

Your optimal combination of consumption and free time is the point on the budget constraint where:

$$MRS = MRT = w$$

budget constraint An equation that represents all combinations of goods and services that one could acquire that exactly exhaust one's budgetary resources.

While considering this decision, you receive an email. A mysterious benefactor would like to give you an income of $50 a day—for life (all you have to do is provide your banking details.) You realize at once that this will affect your choice of job. The new situation is shown in Figure 3.17: for each level of free time, your total income (earnings plus the mystery gift) is $50 higher than before. So the budget constraint is shifted upwards by $50—the feasible set has expanded. Your budget constraint is now:

$$c = 15(24 - t) + 50$$

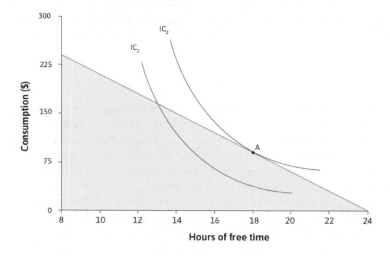

Hours of work	0	2	4	6	8	10	12	14	16
Free time, t	24	22	20	18	16	14	12	10	8
Consumption, c	0	$30	$60	$90	$120	$150	$180	$210	$240

The equation of the budget constraint is $c = w(24 - t)$
The wage is $w = 15, so the budget constraint is $c = 15(24 - t)$

Figure 3.15 Your preferred choice of free time and consumption.

1. The budget constraint
The straight line is your budget constraint: it shows the maximum amount of consumption you can have for each level of free time.

2. The slope of the budget constraint
The slope of the budget constraint is equal to the wage, $15 (in absolute value). This is your MRT (the rate at which you can transform time into consumption), and it is also the opportunity cost of free time.

3. The feasible set
The budget constraint is your feasible frontier, and the area below it is the feasible set.

4. Your ideal job
Your indifference curves show that your ideal job would be at point A, with 18 hours of free time and daily earnings of $90. At this point your MRS is equal to the slope of the budget constraint, which is the wage ($15).

Notice that the extra income of $50 does not change your opportunity cost of time: each hour of free time still reduces your consumption by $15 (the wage). Your new ideal job is at B, with 19.5 hours of free time. B is the point on IC_3 where the MRS is equal to $15. With the indifference curves shown in this diagram, your response to the extra income is not simply to spend $50 more; you increase consumption by less than $50, and you take some extra free time. Someone with different preferences might not choose to increase their free time: Figure 3.18 shows a case in which the MRS at each value of free time is the same on both IC_2 and the higher indifference curve IC_3. This person chooses to keep their free time the same, and consume $50 more.

The effect of additional (unearned) income on the choice of free time is called the **income effect**. Your income effect, shown in Figure 3.17, is positive—extra income raises your choice of free time. For the person in Figure 3.18, the income effect is zero. We assume that for most goods the income effect will be either positive or zero, but not negative: if your income increased, you would not choose to have less of something that you valued.

> **income effect** The effect that the additional income would have if there were no change in the price or opportunity cost.

	The trade-off	Where it is on the diagram
MRS	*Marginal rate of substitution*: The amount of consumption you are willing to trade for an hour of free time.	The slope of the indifference curve.
MRT	*Marginal rate of transformation*: The amount of consumption you can gain from giving up an hour of free time, which is equal to the wage, *w*.	The slope of the budget constraint (the feasible frontier) which is equal to the wage.

Figure 3.16 Your two trade-offs.

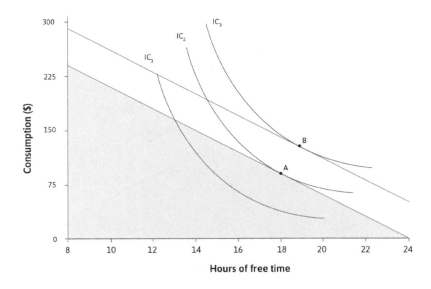

Figure 3.17 The effect of additional income on your choice of free time and consumption.

You suddenly realize that it might not be wise to give the mysterious stranger your bank account details (perhaps it is a hoax). With regret you return to the original plan, and find a job requiring 6 hours of work per day. A year later, your fortunes improve: your employer offers you a pay rise of $10 per hour and the chance to renegotiate your hours. Now your budget constraint is:

$$c = 25(24 - t)$$

In Figure 3.19a you can see how the budget constraint changes when the wage rises. With 24 hours of free time (and no work), your consumption would be 0 whatever the wage. But for each hour of free time you give up, your consumption can now rise by $25 rather than $15. So your new budget constraint is a steeper straight line through (24, 0), with a slope equal to $25. Your feasible set has expanded. And now you achieve the highest possible utility at point D, with only 17 hours of free time. So you ask your employer if you can work longer hours—a 7-hour day.

Compare the outcomes in Figure 3.17 and 3.19a. With an increase in unearned income you want to work fewer hours, while the wage increase in Figure 3.19a makes you decide to increase your working hours. Why does this happen? Because there are two effects of a wage increase:

- *More income for every hour worked*: For each level of free time you can have more consumption, and your MRS is higher: you are now more willing to sacrifice consumption for extra free time. This is the income effect we saw in Figure 3.17—you respond to additional income by taking more free time as well as increasing consumption.

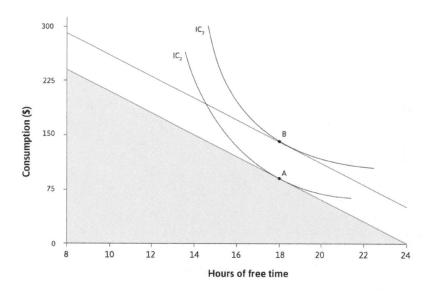

Figure 3.18 The effect of additional income for someone whose MRS doesn't change when consumption rises.

- *The budget constraint is steeper*: The opportunity cost of free time is now higher. In other words, the marginal rate at which you can transform time into income (the MRT) has increased. And that means you have an incentive to work more—to decrease your free time. This is called the **substitution effect**.

The substitution effect captures the idea that when a good becomes more expensive relative to another good, you choose to substitute some of the other good for it. It is the effect that a change in the opportunity cost would have on its own, for a given utility level.

We can show both of these effects in the diagram. Before the wage rise you are at A on IC_2. The higher wage enables you to reach point D on IC_4. Figure 3.19b shows how we can decompose the change from A to D into two parts that correspond to these two effects.

You can see in Figure 3.19b that with indifference curves of this typical shape a substitution effect will always be negative: with a higher opportunity cost of free time you choose a point on the indifference curve with a higher MRS, which is a point with less free time (and more consumption). The overall effect of a wage rise depends on the sum of the income and substitution effects. In Figure 3.19b the negative substitution effect is bigger than the positive income effect, so free time falls.

substitution effect The effect that is only due to changes in the price or opportunity cost, given the new level of utility.

Leibniz: Mathematics of income and substitution effects (http://tinyco.re/L030701)

INCOME AND SUBSTITUTION EFFECTS

A wage rise:

- raises your income for each level of free time, increasing the level of utility you can achieve
- increases the opportunity cost of free time

So it has two effects on your choice of free time:

- *The income effect* (because the budget constraint shifts outwards): the effect that the additional income would have if there were no change in the opportunity cost.
- *The substitution effect* (because the slope of the budget constraint, the MRT, rises): the effect of the change in the opportunity cost, given the new level of utility.

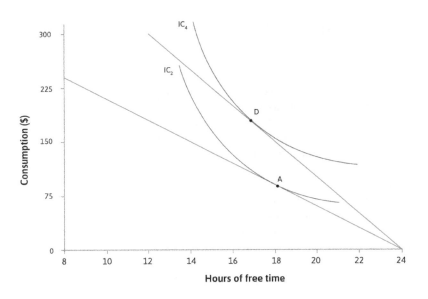

Figure 3.19a The effect of a wage rise on your choice of free time and consumption.

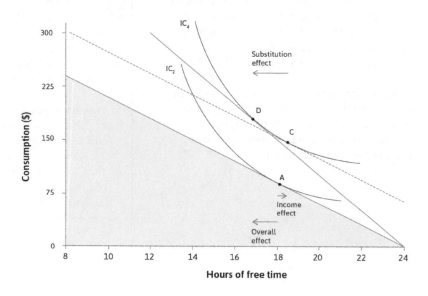

Figure 3.19b The effect of a wage rise on your choice of free time and consumption.

1. A rise in wages
When the wage is $15 your best choice of hours and consumption is at point A. The steeper line shows your new budget constraint when the wage rises to $25. Your feasible set has expanded.

2. Now you can reach a higher indifference curve
Point D on IC₄ gives you the highest utility. At point D, your MRS is equal to the new wage, $25. You have only 17 hours of free time, but your consumption has risen to $175.

3. If there was no change in opportunity cost of free time
The dotted line shows what would happen if you had enough income to reach IC₄ without a change in the opportunity cost of free time. You would choose C, with more free time.

4. The income effect
The shift from A to C is called the income effect of the wage rise; on its own it would cause you to take more free time.

5. The substitution effect
The rise in the opportunity cost of free time makes the budget constraint steeper. This causes you to choose D rather than C, with less free time. This is called the substitution effect of the wage rise.

6. The sum of the income and substitution effects
The overall effect of the wage rise depends on the sum of the income and substitution effects. In this case the substitution effect is bigger, so with the higher wage you take less free time.

Technological progress

If you look back at Section 3.6, you will see that Angela's response to a rise in productivity was also determined by these two opposing effects: an increased incentive to work produced by the rise in the opportunity cost of free time, and an increased desire for free time when her income rises.

We used the model of the self-sufficient farmer to see how technological change can affect working hours. Angela can respond directly to the increase in her productivity brought about by the introduction of a new technology. Employees also become more productive as a result of technological change, and if they have sufficient bargaining power, their wages will rise. The model in this section suggests that, if that happens, technological progress will also bring about a change in the amount of time employees wish to spend working.

The income effect of a higher wage makes workers want more free time, while the substitution effect provides an incentive to work longer hours. If the income effect dominates the substitution effect, workers will prefer fewer hours of work.

QUESTION 3.10 CHOOSE THE CORRECT ANSWER(S)

Figure 3.15 (page 114) depicts your budget constraint when the hourly wage is $15.

Which of the following is (are) true?

☐ The slope of the budget constraint is the negative of the wage rate (–15).
☐ The budget constraint is a feasible frontier with a constant marginal rate of transformation.
☐ An increase in the wage rate would cause a parallel upward shift in the budget constraint.
☐ A gift of $60 would make the budget constraint steeper, with the intercept on the vertical axis increasing to $300.

3.8 IS THIS A GOOD MODEL?

We have looked at three different contexts in which people decide how long to spend working—a student (Alexei), a farmer (Angela), and a wage earner. In each case we have modelled their preferences and feasible set, and the model tells us that their best (utility-maximizing) choice is the level of working hours at which the slope of the feasible frontier is equal to the slope of the indifference curve.

You may have been thinking: this is not what people do!

Billions of people organize their working lives without knowing anything about MRS and MRT (if they did make decisions that way, perhaps we would have to subtract the hours they would spend making calculations). And even if they did make their choice using mathematics, most of us can't just leave work whenever we want. So how can this model be useful?

Remember from Unit 2 that models help us 'see more by looking at less'. Lack of realism is an intentional feature of this model, not a shortcoming.

Trial and error replaces calculations

Can a model that ignores how we think possibly be a good model of how we choose?

Milton Friedman, an economist, explained that when economists use models in this way they do not claim that we actually think through these calculations (such as equating MRS to MRT) each time we make a decision. Instead we each try various choices (sometimes not even intentionally) and we tend to adopt habits, or rules of thumb that make us feel satisfied and not regret our decisions.

In his book *Essays in positive economics*, he described it as similar to playing billiards (pool):

> Consider the problem of predicting the shots made by an expert billiard player. It seems not at all unreasonable that excellent predictions would be yielded by the hypothesis that the billiard player made his shots as if he knew the complicated mathematical formulas that would give the optimum directions of travel, could estimate accurately by eye the angles, etc., describing the location of the balls, could make lightning calculations from the formulas, and could then make the balls travel in the direction indicated by the formulas.
>
> Our confidence in this hypothesis is not based on the belief that billiard players, even expert ones, can or do go through the process described. It derives rather from the belief that, unless in some way or other they were capable of reaching essentially the same result, they would not in fact be expert billiard players.

Milton Friedman. 1953. *Essays in positive economics*, 7th ed. Chicago: University of Chicago Press.

Similarly, if we see a person regularly choosing to go to the library after lectures instead of going out, or not putting in much work on their farm, or asking for longer shifts after a pay rise, we do not need to suppose that this person has done the calculations we set out. If that person later regretted the choice, next time they might go out a bit more, work harder on the farm, or cut their hours back. Eventually we could speculate they might end up with a decision on work time that is close to the result of our calculations.

That is why economic theory can help to explain, and sometimes even predict, what people do—even though those people are not performing the mathematical calculations that economists make in their models.

The influence of culture and politics

A second unrealistic aspect of the model: employers typically choose working hours, not individual workers, and employers often impose a longer working day than workers prefer. As a result, the hours that many people work are regulated by law, so that beyond some maximum amount neither the employee nor the employer can choose to work. In this case the government has limited the feasible set of hours and goods.

Although individual workers often have little freedom to choose their hours, it may nevertheless be the case that changes in working hours over time, and differences between countries, partly reflect the preferences of workers. If many individual workers in a democracy wish to lower their hours, they may 'choose' this indirectly as voters, if not individually as workers. Or they may bargain as members of a trade union for contracts requiring employers to pay higher overtime rates for longer hours.

This explanation stresses culture (meaning changes in preferences or differences in preferences among countries) and politics (meaning differences in laws, or trade union strength and objectives). They certainly help to explain differences in working hours between countries:

Cultures seem to differ. Some northern European cultures highly value their vacation times, while South Korea is famous for the long hours that employees put in. Legal limits on working time differ. In Belgium and France the normal work week is limited to 35–39 hours, while in Mexico the limit is 48 hours and in Kenya even longer.

But, even on an individual level, we may influence the hours we work. For example, employers who advertise jobs with the working hours that most people prefer may find they have more applicants than other employers offering too many (or too few) hours.

Remember, we also judge the quality of a model by whether it provides insight into something that we want to understand. In the next section, we will look at whether our model of the choice of hours of work can help us understand why working hours differ so much between countries and why, as we saw in the introduction, they have changed over time.

EXERCISE 3.8 ANOTHER DEFINITION OF ECONOMICS

Lionel Robbins, an economist, wrote in 1932 that: 'Economics is the science that studies human behaviour as a relationship between given ends and scarce means which have alternative uses.'

1. Give an example from this unit to illustrate the way that economics studies human behaviour as a relationship between 'given ends and scarce means with alternative uses'.
2. Are the 'ends' of economic activity, that is, the things we desire, fixed? Use examples from this unit (study time and grades, or working time and consumption) to illustrate your answer.
3. The subject matter that Robbins refers to—doing the best you can in a given situation—is an essential part of economics. But is economics limited to the study of 'scarce means which have alternative uses'? In answering this question, include a contrast between Robbins' definition and the one given in Unit 1, and note that Robbins wrote this passage at a time when 15% of the British workforce was unemployed.

Lionel Robbins. 1984. *An essay on the nature and significance of economic science*, 3rd ed. New York: New York University Press.

3.9 EXPLAINING OUR WORKING HOURS: CHANGES OVER TIME

During the year 1600, the average British worker was at work for 266 days. This statistic did not change much until the Industrial Revolution. Then, as we know from the previous unit, wages began to rise, and working time rose too: to 318 days in 1870.

Meanwhile, in the US, hours of work increased for many workers who shifted from farming to industrial jobs. In 1865 the US abolished slavery, and former slaves used their freedom to work much less. From the late nineteenth century until the middle of the twentieth century, working time in many countries gradually fell. Figure 3.1 at the beginning of this unit showed how annual working hours have fallen since 1870 in the Netherlands, the US and France.

Robert Whaples. 2001. 'Hours of work in U.S. History' EH.Net Encyclopedia.

The simple models we have constructed cannot tell the whole story. Remember that the *ceteris paribus* assumption can omit important details: things that we have held constant in models may vary in real life.

As we explained in the previous section, our model omitted two important explanations, which we called culture and politics. Our model provides another explanation: economics.

Look at the two points in Figure 3.20, giving estimates of average amounts of daily free time and goods per day for employees in the US in 1900 and in 2013. The slopes of the budget constraints through points A and D are the real wage (goods per hour) in 1900 and in 2013. This shows us the feasible sets of free time and goods that would have made these points possible. Then we consider the indifference curves of workers that would have led workers to choose the hours they did. We cannot measure indifference curves directly: we must use our best guess of what the preferences of workers would have been, given the actions that they took.

How does our model explain how we got from point A to point D? You know from Figure 3.19b that the increase in wages would lead to both an income effect and a substitution effect. In this case, the income effect outweighs the substitution effect, so both free time and goods consumed per day go up. Figure 3.20 is thus simply an application to history of the model illustrated in Figure 3.19b. Work through the steps to see the income and substitution effects.

How could reasoning in this way explain the other historical data that we have?

First, consider the period before 1870 in Britain, when both working hours and wages rose:

- *Income effect*: At the relatively low level of consumption in the period before 1870, workers' willingness to substitute free time for goods did not increase much when rising wages made higher consumption possible.
- *Substitution effect*: But they were more productive and paid more, so each hour of work brought more rewards than before in the form of goods, increasing the incentive to work longer hours.
- *Substitution effect dominated*: Therefore before 1870 the negative substitution effect (free time falls) was bigger than the positive income effect (free time rises), so work hours rose.

During the twentieth century we saw rising wages and falling working hours. Our model accounts for this change as follows:

- *Income effect*: By the late nineteenth century workers had a higher level of consumption and valued free time relatively more—their marginal rate of substitution was higher—so the income effect of a wage rise was larger.
- *Substitution effect*: This was consistent with the period before 1870.
- *Income effect now dominates*: When the income effect began to outweigh the substitution effect, working time fell.

We should also consider the possibility that preferences change over time. If you look carefully at Figure 3.1 you can see that in the last part of the twentieth century hours of work rose in the US, even though wages hardly increased. Hours of work also rose in Sweden during this period.

Why? Perhaps Swedes and Americans came to value consumption more over these years. In other words, their preferences changed so that their MRS fell (they became more like today's South Korean workers). This may have occurred because in both the US and Sweden the share of income gained by the very rich increased considerably, and the lavish consumption habits of the rich set a higher standard for everyone else. According to this explanation, Swedes and Americans were 'keeping up with the Joneses' and the Joneses got richer, leading everyone else to change their preferences.

The combined political, cultural and economic influences on our choices may produce some surprising trends. In our 'Economist in action' video, Juliet Schor, a sociologist and economist who has written about the paradox that many of the world's wealthiest people are working more despite gains in technology, asks what this means for our quality of life, and for the environment.

The economist Thorsten Veblen (1857–1929) coined the term **'conspicuous consumption'** in his explanation of why people of lesser means try to mimic the consumption habits of the rich.

Thorstein Veblen. 2007. *Theory of the leisure class.* Oxford: Oxford University Press.

conspicuous consumption The purchase of goods or services to publicly display one's social and economic status.

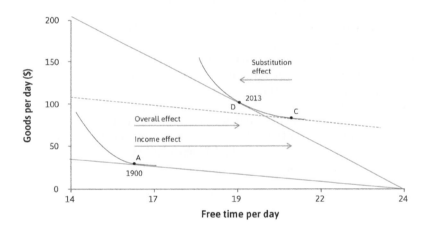

OECD. Average annual hours actually worked per worker (http://tinyco.re/6892498). Accessed June 2016. Michael Huberman and Chris Minns. 2007. 'The times they are not changin': Days and hours of work in Old and New Worlds, 1870–2000'. *Explorations in Economic History* 44 (4): pp. 538–567.

Figure 3.20 Applying the model to history: Increased goods and free time in the US (1900–2013).

1. Using the model to explain historical change
We can interpret the change between 1900 and 2013 in daily free time and goods per day for employees in the US using our model. The solid lines show the feasible sets for free time and goods in 1900 and 2013, where the slope of each budget constraint is the real wage.

2. The indifference curves
Assuming that workers chose the hours they worked, we can infer the approximate shape of their indifference curves.

3. The income effect
The shift from A to C is the income effect of the wage rise, which on its own would cause US workers to take more free time.

4. The substitution effect
The rise in the opportunity cost of free time caused US workers to choose D rather than C, with less free time.

5. Income and substitution effects
The overall effect of the wage rise depends on the sum of the income and substitution effects. In this case the income effect is bigger, so with the higher wage US workers took more free time as well as more goods.

Juliet Schor: Why do we work so hard? http://tinyco.re/8362335

QUESTION 3.11 CHOOSE THE CORRECT ANSWER(S)

Figure 3.20 (page 123) depicts a model of labour supply and consumption for the US in 1900 and 2013. The wage rate is shown to have increased between the two years.

Which of the following are true?

☐ The substitution effect corresponds to the steepening of the budget constraint. This is represented by the move from point A to point D.
☐ The income effect corresponds to the parallel shift in the budget constraint outwards due to the higher income. This is represented by the move from point A to C.
☐ As shown, the income effect dominates the substitution effect, leading to a reduction in the hours of work.
☐ If Americans had had different preferences, they might have responded to this wage rise by reducing their free time.

Robert William Fogel. 2000. *The fourth great awakening and the future of egalitarianism: The political realignment of the 1990s and the fate of egalitarianism*. Chicago: University of Chicago Press.

What about the future? The high-income economies will continue to experience a major transformation: the declining role of work in the course of our lifetimes. We go to work at a later age, stop working at an earlier age of our longer lives, and spend fewer hours at work during our working years. Robert Fogel, an economic historian, estimated the total working time, including travel to and from work and housework, in the past. He made projections for the year 2040, defining what he called discretionary time as 24 hours a day minus the amount we all need for biological maintenance (sleeping, eating and personal hygiene). Fogel calculated leisure time as discretionary time minus working time.

In 1880 he estimated that lifetime leisure time was just a quarter of lifetime work hours. In 1995 leisure time exceeded working time over a person's entire life. He predicted that lifetime leisure would be three times of lifetime working hours by the year 2040. His estimates are in Figure 3.21.

Robert William Fogel. 2000. *The Fourth Great Awakening and the Future of Egalitarianism*. Chicago: University of Chicago Press.

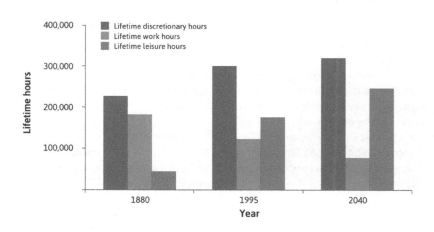

Figure 3.21 Estimated lifetime hours of work and leisure (1880, 1995, 2040).

We do not yet know if Fogel has overstated the future decline in working time, as Keynes once did. But he certainly is right that one of the great changes brought about by the technological revolution is the vastly reduced role of work in the life of an average person.

EXERCISE 3.9 SCARCITY AND CHOICE

1. Do our models of scarcity and choice provide a plausible explanation for the observed trends in working hours during the twentieth century?
2. What other factors, not included in the model, might be important in explaining what has happened?
3. Remember Keynes' prediction that working hours would fall to 15 hours per week in the century after 1930. Why do you think working hours have not changed as he expected? Have people's preferences changed? The model focuses on the number of hours workers would choose, so do you think that many employees are now working longer than they would like?
4. In his essay, Keynes said that people have two types of economic needs or wants: absolute needs that do not depend on the situation of other fellow humans, and relative needs—which he called 'the desire for superiority'. The phrase 'keeping up with the Joneses' captures a similar idea that our preferences could be affected by observing the consumption of others. Could relative needs help to explain why Keynes was so wrong about working hours?

3.10 EXPLAINING OUR WORKING HOURS: DIFFERENCES BETWEEN COUNTRIES

Figure 3.2 showed that in countries with higher income (GDP per capita) workers tend to have more free time, but also that there are big differences in annual hours of free time between countries with similar income levels. To analyse these differences using our model, we need a different measure of income that corresponds more closely to earnings from employment. The table in Figure 3.22 shows working hours for five countries, together with the disposable income of an average employee (based on the taxes and benefits for a single person without children).

From these figures we have calculated annual free time, and the average wage (by dividing annual income by annual hours worked). Finally, free time per day and daily consumption are calculated by dividing annual free time and earnings by 365.

Figure 3.23 shows how we might use this data, with the model of Section 3.7, to understand the differences between the countries. From the data in Figure 3.22, we have plotted daily consumption and free time for a typical worker in each country, with the corresponding budget constraint constructed as before, using a line through (24, 0) with slope equal to the wage. We have no information about the preferences of workers in each country, and we don't know whether the combinations in the diagram can be interpreted as a choice made by the workers. But, if we assume that they do reflect the workers' choices, we can consider what the data tells us about the preferences of workers in different countries.

From Figure 3.23, we see that average free time in Mexico and South Korea were virtually the same, although the wage was much higher in South

Korea than in Mexico. South Koreans, Americans and Dutch people have about as much to spend per day, but South Koreans have three hours less of free time. Could it be that South Koreans have the same preferences as Americans, so that if the wage increased in South Korea they would make the same choice? This seems unlikely: the substitution effect would lead them to consume more goods and take less free time, and it is implausible to suppose that the income effect of a wage rise would lead them to consume fewer goods. More plausible is the hypothesis that South Koreans and Americans (on average) have different preferences. Follow the steps in Figure 3.23 to see some hypothetical indifference curves that could explain the differences among countries. Notice that the indifference curves for the US and for South Korea cross. This means that South Koreans and Americans must have different preferences.

Point Q in the last step of the figure is the point of intersection of the two indifference curves shown for South Korea and the US. At that point the US indifference curve is steeper than the South Korean one. This means that the average American is willing to give up more units of daily goods for an hour of free time (this is the MRS) than the average South Korean, which is consistent with the idea that South Koreans work exceptionally hard. So it may be important to take account of differences in preferences among countries, or among individuals.

EXERCISE 3.10 PREFERENCES AND CULTURE

Suppose that the points plotted in Figure 3.23 (page 127) reflect the choices of free time and consumption made by workers in these five countries according to our model.

1. Is it possible that people in Turkey and the US have the same preferences? If so, how will a wage rise in Turkey affect consumption and free time? What does this imply about the income and substitution effects?
2. Suppose that people in Turkey and South Korea have the same preferences. In that case, what can you say about the income and substitution effects of a wage increase?
3. If wages in South Korea increased, would you expect consumption there to be higher or lower than in the Netherlands? Why?

Country	Average annual hours worked per employee	Average annual disposable income (single person, no children)	Average annual free time	Wage (disposable income per hour worked)	Freetime per day	Consumption per day
US	1,789	36,737	6,971	20.54	19.10	100.65
South Korea	2,163	39,686	6,597	18.35	18.07	108.73
Netherlands	1,383	40,171	7,377	29.05	20.21	110.06
Turkey	1,855	17,118	6,905	9.23	18.92	46.90
Mexico	2,226	11,046	6,534	4.96	17.90	30.26

Figure 3.22 Free time and consumption per day across countries (2013).
OECD. Average annual hours actually worked per worker (http://tinyco.re/6892498). Accessed June 2016. Net income after taxes calculated in US dollars using PPP exchange rates.

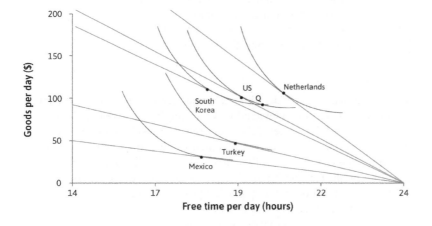

OECD. Average annual hours actually worked per worker (http://tinyco.re/6892498). Accessed June 2016. Net income after taxes calculated in US dollars using PPP exchange rates.

Figure 3.23 Using the model to explain free time and consumption per day across countries (2013).

1. Differences between countries
We can use our model and data from Figure 3.22 to understand the differences between the countries. The solid lines show the feasible sets of free time and goods for the five countries in Figure 3.22.

2. Indifference curves of workers
Using the model to explain free time and consumption per day across countries (2013).

3. The US and South Korea
Point Q is at the intersection of the indifference curves for the US and South Korea. At this point Americans are willing to give up more units of daily goods for an hour of free time than South Koreans.

Michael Huberman and Chris Minns. 2007. 'The times they are not changin': Days and hours of work in Old and New Worlds, 1870–2000' (http://tinyco.re/ 2758271). *Explorations in Economic History* 44 (4): pp. 538–567.

EXERCISE 3.11 WORKING HOURS ACROSS COUNTRIES AND TIME
The figure below illustrates what has happened to working hours in many countries during the twentieth century (the UK is in both charts to aid comparison).

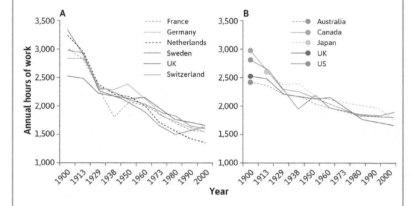

1. How would you describe what happened?
2. How are the countries in Panel A of the figure different from those in Panel B?
3. What possible explanations can you suggest for why the decline in working hours was greater in some countries than in others?
4. Why do you think that the decline in working hours is faster in most countries in the first half of the century?
5. In recent years, is there any country in which working hours have increased? Why do you think this happened?

3.11 CONCLUSION

We have used a model of decision making under scarcity to analyse choices of hours of work, and understand why working hours have fallen over the last century. People's preferences with respect to goods and free time are described by indifference curves, and their production function (or budget constraint) determines their feasible set. The choice that maximizes utility is a point on the feasible frontier where the marginal rate of substitution (MRS) between goods and free time is equal to the marginal rate of transformation (MRT).

An increase in productivity or wages alters the MRT, raising the opportunity cost of free time. This provides an incentive to work longer hours (the substitution effect). But higher income may increase the desire for free time (the income effect). The overall change in hours of work depends on which of these effects is bigger.

Concepts introduced in Unit 3
Before you move on, review these definitions:

- Constrained choice problem
- Scarcity
- Opportunity cost
- Marginal product
- Indifference curve
- Marginal rate of substitution (MRS)
- Marginal rate of transformation (MRT)
- Feasible set
- Budget constraint
- Income effect
- Substitution effect

3.12 REFERENCES

Fogel, Robert William. 2000. *The Fourth Great Awakening and the Future of Egalitarianism*. Chicago: University of Chicago Press.

Friedman, Milton. 1953. *Essays in Positive Economics*. Chicago: University of Chicago Press.

Harford, Tim. 2015. 'The rewards for working hard are too big for Keynes's vision' (http://tinyco.re/5829245). *The Undercover Economist*. First published by *The Financial Times*. Updated 3 August 2015.

Keynes, John Maynard. 1963. 'Economic Possibilities for our Grandchildren'. In *Essays in Persuasion*, New York, NY: W. W. Norton & Co.

Plant, E. Ashby, K. Anders Ericsson, Len Hill, and Kia Asberg. 2005. 'Why study time does not predict grade point average across college students: Implications of deliberate practice for academic performance'. *Contemporary Educational Psychology* 30 (1): pp. 96–116.

Robbins, Lionel. 1984. *An Essay on the Nature and Significance of Economic Science*. New York: New York University Press.

Schor, Juliet B. 1992. *The Overworked American: The Unexpected Decline Of Leisure*. New York, NY: Basic Books.

Veblen, Thorstein. 2007. *The Theory of the Leisure Class*. Oxford: Oxford University Press.

Whaples, Robert. 2001. 'Hours of work in U.S. History' (http://tinyco.re/1660378). EH.Net Encyclopedia.

UNIT 4
SOCIAL INTERACTIONS

A COMBINATION OF SELF-INTEREST, A REGARD FOR THE WELLBEING OF OTHERS, AND APPROPRIATE INSTITUTIONS CAN YIELD DESIRABLE SOCIAL OUTCOMES WHEN PEOPLE INTERACT

- Game theory is a way of understanding how people interact based on the constraints that limit their actions, their motives, and their beliefs about what others will do.
- Experiments and other evidence show that self-interest, a concern for others, and a preference for fairness are all important motives that explain how people interact.
- In most interactions there is some conflict of interest between people, but also some opportunity for mutual gain.
- The pursuit of self-interest can sometimes lead to results that are considered good by all participants, or outcomes that none of the participants would prefer.
- Self-interest can be harnessed for the general good in markets, by governments limiting the actions that people are free to take, and by one's peers imposing punishments on actions that lead to bad outcomes.
- A concern for others and for fairness allows us to internalize the effects of our actions on others, and so can contribute to good social outcomes.

THEMES AND CAPSTONE UNITS
- 18: Global economy
- 19: Inequality
- 20: Environment
- 21: Innovation
- 22: Politics and policy

> The scientific evidence is now overwhelming: climate change presents very serious global risks, and it demands an urgent global response.

This is the blunt beginning of the executive summary of the Stern Review, published in 2006. The British Chancellor of the Exchequer (finance minister) commissioned a group of economists, led by former World Bank chief economist Sir Nicholas (now Lord) Stern, to assess the evidence for climate change, and to try to understand its economic implications. The

Nicholas Stern. 2007. *The Economics of Climate Change: The Stern Review*. Cambridge: Cambridge University Press. Read the executive summary (http://tinyco.re/5785938).

IPCC. 2014. 'Climate Change 2014: Synthesis Report'. Contribution of Working Groups I, II and III to the Fifth Assessment Report of the Intergovernmental Panel on Climate Change. Geneva, Switzerland: IPCC.

Stern Review predicts that the benefits of early action to slow climate change will outweigh the costs of neglecting the issue.

The Fifth Assessment Report by the Intergovernmental Panel on Climate Change (IPCC) agrees. Early action would mean a significant cut in greenhouse gas emissions, by reducing our consumption of energy-intensive goods, a switch to different energy technologies, reducing the impacts of agriculture and land-use change, and an improvement in the efficiency of current technologies.

But none of this will happen if we pursue what Stern referred to as 'business as usual': a scenario in which people, governments and businesses are free to pursue their own pleasures, politics, and profits without taking adequate account of the effect of their actions on others, including future generations.

National governments disagree on the policies that should be adopted. Many nations in the developed world are pressing for strict global controls on carbon emissions, while others, whose economic catch-up has until recently been dependent on coal-burning technologies, have resisted these measures.

The problem of climate change is far from unique. It is an example of what is called a **social dilemma**. Social dilemmas—like climate change—occur when people do not take adequate account of the effects of their decisions on others, whether these are positive or negative.

social dilemma A situation in which actions taken independently by individuals in pursuit of their own private objectives result in an outcome which is inferior to some other feasible outcome that could have occurred if people had acted together, rather than as individuals.

Social dilemmas occur frequently in our lives. Traffic jams happen when our choice of a way to get around—for example driving alone to work rather than car-pooling—does not take account of the contribution to congestion that we make. Similarly, overusing antibiotics for minor illnesses may help the sick person who takes them recover more quickly, but creates antibiotic-resistant bacteria that have a much more harmful effect on many others.

The Tragedy of the Commons

Garrett Hardin. 1968. 'The Tragedy of the Commons'. Science 162 (3859): pp. 1243–1248.

In 1968, Garrett Hardin, a biologist, published an article about social dilemmas in the journal *Science*, called 'The Tragedy of the Commons'. He argued that resources that are not owned by anyone (sometimes called 'common property' or 'common-pool resources') such as the earth's atmosphere or fish stocks, are easily overexploited unless we control access in some way. Fishermen as a group would be better off not catching as much tuna, and consumers as a whole would be better off not eating too much of it. Humanity would be better off by emitting less pollutants, but if you, as an individual, decide to cut your consumption, your carbon footprint or the number of tuna you catch will hardly affect the global levels.

free ride Benefiting from the contributions of others to some cooperative project without contributing oneself.

Examples of Hardin's tragedies and other social dilemmas are all around us: if you live with roommates, or in a family, you know just how difficult it is to keep a clean kitchen or bathroom. When one person cleans, everyone benefits, but it is hard work. Whoever cleans up bears this cost. The others are sometimes called **free riders**. If as a student you have ever done a group assignment, you understand that the cost of effort (to study the problem, gather evidence, or write up the results) is individual, yet the benefits (a better grade, higher class standing, or simply the admiration of classmates) go to the whole group.

Elinor Ostrom. 2008. 'The Challenge of Common-Pool Resources'. *Environment: Science and Policy for Sustainable Development* 50 (4): pp. 8–21.

Resolving social dilemmas

There is nothing new about social dilemmas; we have been facing them since prehistory.

More than 2,500 years ago, the Greek storyteller Aesop wrote about a social dilemma in his fable *Belling the Cat*. A group of mice needs one of its members to place a bell around a cat's neck. Once the bell is on, the cat cannot catch and eat the other mice. But the outcome may not be so good for the mouse that takes the job. There are countless examples during wars or natural catastrophes in which individuals sacrifice their lives for others who are not family members, and may even be total strangers. These actions are termed **altruistic**.

Altruistic self-sacrifice is not the most important way that societies resolve social dilemmas and reduce free riding. Sometimes the problems can be resolved by government policies. For example, governments have successfully imposed quotas to prevent the over-exploitation of stocks of cod in the North Atlantic. In the UK, the amount of waste that is dumped in landfills, rather than being recycled, has been dramatically reduced by a landfill tax.

Local communities also create institutions to regulate behaviour. Irrigation communities need people to work to maintain the canals that benefit the whole community. Individuals also need to use scarce water sparingly so that other crops will flourish, although this will lead to smaller crops for themselves. In Valencia, Spain, communities of farmers have used a set of customary rules for centuries to regulate communal tasks and to avoid using too much water. Since the middle ages they have had an arbitration court called the *Tribunal de las Aguas* (Water Court) that resolves conflicts between farmers about the application of the rules. The ruling of the *Tribunal* is not legally enforceable. Its power comes only from the respect of the community, yet its decisions are almost universally followed.

Even present-day global environmental problems have sometimes been tackled effectively. The Montreal Protocol has been remarkably successful. It was created to phase out and eventually ban the chlorofluorocarbons (CFCs) that threatened to destroy the ozone layer that protects us against harmful ultraviolet radiation.

In this unit, we will use the tools of **game theory** to model **social interactions**, in which the decisions of individuals affect other people as well as themselves. We will look at situations that result in social dilemmas and how people can sometimes solve them—but sometimes not (or not yet), as in the case of climate change.

But not all social interactions lead to social dilemmas, even if individuals act in pursuit of their own interests. We will start in the next section with an example where the 'invisible hand' of the market, as described by Adam Smith, channels self-interest so that individuals acting independently do reach a mutually beneficial outcome.

altruism The willingness to bear a cost in order to benefit somebody else.

Aesop. 'Belling the Cat'. In *Fables*, retold by Joseph Jacobs. XVII, (1). The Harvard Classics. New York: P. F. Collier & Son, 1909–14; Bartleby.com, 2001.

game theory A branch of mathematics that studies strategic interactions, meaning situations in which each actor knows that the benefits they receive depend on the actions taken by all. *See also: game*.

social interactions Situations in which the actions taken by each person affect other people's outcomes as well as their own.

EXERCISE 4.1 SOCIAL DILEMMAS

Using the news headlines from last week:

1. Identify two social dilemmas that have been reported (try to use examples not discussed above).
2. For each, specify how it satisfies the definition of a **social dilemma**.

4.1 SOCIAL INTERACTIONS: GAME THEORY

On which side of the road should you drive? If you live in Japan, the UK, or Indonesia, you drive on the left. If you live in South Korea, France, or the US, you drive on the right. If you grew up in Sweden, you drove on the left until 5 p.m. on 3 September 1967, and at 5.01 p.m. you started driving on the right. The government sets a rule, and we follow it.

But suppose we just left the choice to drivers to pursue their self-interest and to select one side of the road or the other. If everyone else was already driving on the right, self-interest (avoiding a collision) would be sufficient to motivate a driver to drive on the right as well. Concern for other drivers, or a desire to obey the law, would not be necessary.

Devising policies to promote people's wellbeing requires an under-standing of the difference between situations in which self-interest can promote general wellbeing, and cases in which it leads to undesirable results. To analyse this, we will introduce game theory, a way of modelling how people interact.

In Unit 3 we saw how a student deciding how much to study and a farmer choosing how hard to work both faced a set of feasible options, determined by a production function. This person then makes decisions to obtain the best possible outcome. But in the models we have studied so far, the outcome did not depend on what anyone else did. Neither the student nor the farmer was engaged in a social interaction.

Social and strategic interactions

In this unit, we consider social interactions, meaning situations in which there are two or more people, and the actions taken by each person affects both their own outcome and other people's outcomes. For example, one person's choice of how much to heat his or her home will affect everyone's experience of global climate change.

We use four terms:

- When people are engaged in a social interaction and are aware of the ways that their actions affect others, and vice versa, we call this a **strategic interaction**.
- A **strategy** is defined as an action (or a course of action) that a person may take when that person is aware of the mutual dependence of the results for herself and for others. The outcomes depend not only on that person's actions, but also on the actions of others.
- Models of strategic interactions are described as **games**.
- Game theory is a set of models of strategic interactions. It is widely used in economics and elsewhere in the social sciences.

To see how game theory can clarify strategic interactions, imagine two farmers, who we will call Anil and Bala. They face a problem: should they grow rice or cassava? We assume that they have the ability to grow both types of crop, but can only grow one type at a time.

Anil's land is better suited for growing cassava, while Bala's is better suited for rice. The two farmers have to determine the **division of labour**, that is, who will specialize in which crop. They decide this independently, which means they do not meet together to discuss a course of action.

(Assuming independence may seem odd in this model of just two farm-ers, but later we apply the same logic to situations like climate change, in which hundreds or even millions of people interact, most of them total

strategic interaction A social interaction in which the participants are aware of the ways that their actions affect others (and the ways that the actions of others affect them).

strategy An action (or a course of action) that a person may take when that person is aware of the mutual dependence of the results for herself and for others. The outcomes depend not only on that person's actions, but also on the actions of others.

game A model of strategic interaction that describes the players, the feasible strategies, the information that the players have, and their payoffs. *See also: game theory.*

division of labour The specialization of producers to carry out different tasks in the produc-tion process. *Also known as: specialization.*

strangers to one another. So assuming that Anil and Bala do not come to some common agreement before taking action is useful for us.)

They both sell whatever crop they produce in a nearby village market. On market day, if they bring less rice to the market, the price will be higher. The same goes for cassava. Figure 4.1 describes their interaction, which is what we call a game. Let's explain what Figure 4.1 means, because you will be seeing this a lot.

Anil's choices are the rows of the table and Bala's are the columns. We call Anil the 'row player' and Bala the 'column player'.

When an interaction is represented in a table like Figure 4.1, each entry describes the outcome of a hypothetical situation. For example, the upper-left cell should be interpreted as:

> Suppose (for whatever reason) Anil planted rice and Bala planted rice too. What would we see?

There are four possible hypothetical situations. Figure 4.1 describes what would happen in each case.

To simplify the model, we assume that:

- There are no other people involved or affected in any way.
- The selection of which crop to grow is the only decision that Anil and Bala need to make.

> **GAME**
> A description of a social interaction, which specifies:
> - *The players*: Who is interacting with whom
> - *The feasible strategies*: Which actions are open to the players
> - *The information*: What each player knows when making their decision
> - *The payoffs*: What the outcomes will be for each of the possible combinations of actions

		Bala	
		Rice	Cassava
Anil	**Rice**	Both produce rice: there is a glut of rice (low price) There is a shortage of cassava Anil not producing cassava, which he is better able to produce	No market glut High prices for both crops Both farmers producing the crop for which they are less suited
	Cassava	No market glut High prices for both crops Both farmers producing the crop for which they are better suited	Both produce cassava: there is a glut of cassava (low price) There is a shortage of rice Bala not producing rice, which he is better able to produce

Figure 4.1 Social interactions in the invisible hand game.

- Anil and Bala will interact just once (this is called a 'one-shot game').
- They decide simultaneously. When a player makes a decision, that player doesn't know what the other person has decided to do.

Figure 4.2a shows the **payoffs** for Anil and Bala in each of the four hypothetical situations—the incomes they would receive if the hypothetical row and column actions were taken. Since their incomes depend on the market prices, which in turn depend on their decisions, we have called this an 'invisible hand' game.

payoff The benefit to each player associated with the joint actions of all the players.

- Because the market price falls when it is flooded with one crop, they can do better if they specialize compared to when they both produce the same good.
- When they produce different goods they would both do better if each person specialized in the crop that was most suitable for their land.

	Bala	
	Rice	Cassava
Anil Rice	Anil gets 1 Bala gets 3	Both get 2
Anil Cassava	Both get 4	Anil gets 3 Bala gets 1

Figure 4.2a The payoffs in the invisible hand game.

QUESTION 4.1 CHOOSE THE CORRECT ANSWER(S)
In a simultaneous one-shot game:

☐ A player observes what others do before deciding how to act.
☐ A player takes into account what other players may do in the future to decide his or her action today.
☐ Players coordinate to find the actions that lead to the optimal outcome for society.
☐ A player chooses an action taking into account the possible actions that other players can take.

4.2 EQUILIBRIUM IN THE INVISIBLE HAND GAME

Game theory describes social interactions, but it may also provide predictions about what will happen. To predict the outcome of a game, we need another concept: **best response**. This is the strategy that will give a player the highest payoff, given the strategies the other players select.

In Figure 4.2b we represent the payoffs for Anil and Bala in the invisible hand game using a standard format called a payoff matrix. A matrix is just any rectangular (in this case square) array of numbers. The first number in each box is the reward received by the row player (whose name begins with A as a reminder that his payoff is first). The second number is the column player's payoff.

Think about best responses in this game. Suppose you are Anil, and you consider the hypothetical case in which Bala has chosen to grow rice. Which response yields you the higher payoff? You would grow cassava (in this case, you—Anil—would get a payoff of 4, but you would get a payoff of only 1 if you grew rice instead).

Work through the steps in Figure 4.2b to see that choosing Cassava is also Anil's best response if Bala chooses Cassava. So Cassava is Anil's **dominant strategy**: it will give him the highest payoff, whatever Bala does. And you will see that in this game Bala also has a dominant strategy. The analysis also gives you a handy method for keeping track of best responses by placing dots and circles in the payoff matrix.

Because both players have a dominant strategy, we have a simple prediction about what each will do: play their dominant strategy. Anil will grow cassava, and Bala will grow rice.

This pair of strategies is a **dominant strategy equilibrium** of the game.

Remember from Unit 2 that an equilibrium is a self-perpetuating situation. Something of interest does not change. In this case, Anil choosing Cassava and Bala choosing Rice is an equilibrium because neither of them would want to change their decision after seeing what the other player chose.

If we find that both players in a two-player game have dominant strategies, the game has a dominant strategy equilibrium. As we will see later, this does not always happen. But when it does, we predict that these are the strategies that will be played.

Because both Anil and Bala have a dominant strategy, their choice of crop is not affected by what they expect the other person to do. This is similar to the models in Unit 3 in which Alexei's choice of hours of study, or Angela's working hours, did not depend on what others did. But here, even though the decision does not depend on what the others do, the payoff

best response In game theory, the strategy that will give a player the highest payoff, given the strategies that the other players select.

dominant strategy Action that yields the highest payoff for a player, no matter what the other players do.

dominant strategy equilibrium An outcome of a game in which every player plays his or her dominant strategy.

does. For example, if Anil is playing his dominant strategy (Cassava) he is better off if Bala plays Rice than if Bala plays Cassava as well.

In the dominant strategy equilibrium Anil and Bala have specialized in producing the good for which their land is better suited. Simply pursuing their self-interest—choosing the strategy for which they got the highest payoff—resulted in an outcome that was:

- the best of the four possible outcomes for each player
- the strategy that yielded the largest total payoffs for the two farmers combined

In this example, the dominant strategy equilibrium is the outcome that each would have chosen if they had a way of coordinating their decisions. Although they independently pursued their self-interest, they were guided

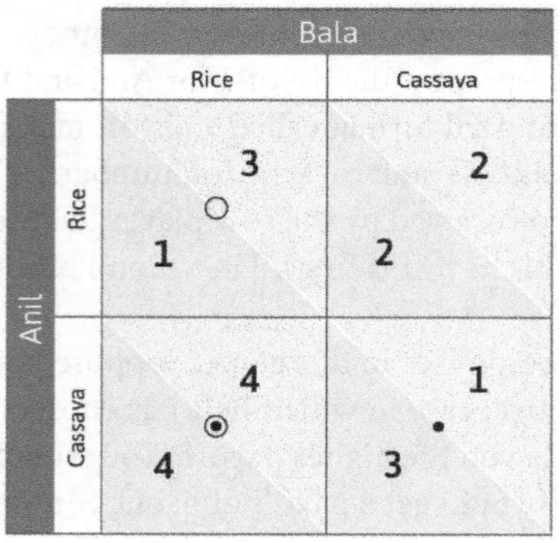

Figure 4.2b The payoff matrix in the invisible hand game.

1. Finding best responses
Begin with the row player (Anil) and ask: 'What would be his best response to the column player's (Bala's) decision to play Rice?'

2. Anil's best response if Bala grows rice
If Bala chooses Rice, Anil's best response is to choose Cassava—that gives him 4, rather than 1. Place a dot in the bottom left-hand cell. A dot in a cell means that this is the row player's best response.

3. Anil's best response if Bala grows cassava
If Bala chooses Cassava, Anil's best response is to choose Cassava too— giving him 3, rather than 2. Place a dot in the bottom right-hand cell.

4. Anil has a dominant strategy
Both dots are on the bottom row. Whatever Bala's choice, Anil's best response is to choose Cassava. Cassava is a dominant strategy for Anil.

5. Now find the column player's best responses
If Anil chooses Rice, Bala's best response is to choose Rice (3 rather than 2). Circles represent the column player's best responses. Place a circle in the upper left-hand cell.

6. Bala has a dominant strategy too
If Anil chooses Cassava, Bala's best response is again to choose Rice (he gets 4 rather than 3). Place a circle in the lower left-hand cell. Rice is Bala's dominant strategy (both circles are in the same column).

7. Both players will play their dominant strategies
We predict that Anil will choose Cassava and Bala will choose Rice because that is their dominant strategy. Where the dot and circle coincide, the players are both playing best responses to each other.

'as if by an invisible hand' to an outcome that was in both of their best interests.

Real economic problems are never this simple, but the basic logic is the same. The pursuit of self-interest without regard for others is sometimes considered to be morally bad, but the study of economics has identified cases in which it can lead to outcomes that are socially desirable. There are other cases, however, in which the pursuit of self-interest leads to results that are not in the self-interest of any of the players. The prisoners' dilemma game, which we study next, describes one of these situations.

QUESTION 4.2 CHOOSE THE CORRECT ANSWER(S)

Brian likes going to the cinema more than watching football. Anna, on the other hand, prefers watching football to going to the cinema. Either way, they both prefer to be together rather than spending an afternoon apart. The following table represents the happiness levels (payoffs) of Anna and Brian, depending on their choice of activity (the first number is Brian's happiness level while the second number is Anna's):

		Anna	
		Football	Cinema
Brian	Football	3 5	1 1
	Cinema	4 3	6 2

Based on the information above, we can conclude that:

☐ The dominant strategy for both players is Football.
☐ There is no dominant strategy equilibrium.
☐ The dominant strategy equilibrium yields the highest possible happiness for both.
☐ Neither player would want to deviate from the dominant strategy equilibrium.

WHEN ECONOMISTS DISAGREE

Homo economicus in question: Are people entirely selfish?

For centuries, economists and just about everyone else have debated whether people are entirely self-interested or are sometimes happy to help others even when it costs them something to do so. *Homo economicus* (economic man) is the nickname given to the selfish and calculating character that you find in economics textbooks. Have economists been right to imagine *homo economicus* as the only actor on the economic stage?

In the same book in which he first used the phrase 'invisible hand', Adam Smith also made it clear that he thought we were not *homo economicus*: 'How selfish soever man may be supposed, there are evidently some principles in his nature which interest him in the fortunes of others, and render their happiness necessary to him, though he derives nothing from it except the pleasure of seeing it.' (*The Theory of Moral Sentiments*, 1759)

But most economists since Smith have disagreed. In 1881, Francis Edgeworth, a founder of modern economics, made this perfectly clear in his book *Mathematical Psychics*: 'The first principle of economics is that every agent is actuated only by self-interest.'

Yet everyone has experienced, and sometimes even performed, great acts of kindness or bravery on behalf of others in situations in which there was little chance of a reward. The question for economists is: should the unselfishness evident in these acts be part of how we reason about behaviour?

Some say 'no': many seemingly generous acts are better understood as attempts to gain a favourable reputation among others that will benefit the actor in the future.

Maybe helping others and observing social norms is just self-interest with a long time horizon. This is what the essayist H. L. Mencken thought: 'conscience is the inner voice which warns that somebody may be looking.'

Since the 1990s, in an attempt to resolve the debate on empirical grounds, economists have performed hundreds of experiments all over the world in which the behaviour of individuals (students, farmers, whale hunters, warehouse workers, and CEOs) can be observed as they make real choices about sharing, using economic games.

In these experiments, we almost always see some self-interested behaviour. But we also observe **altruism**, **reciprocity**, **aversion to inequality**, and other preferences that are different from self-interest. In many experiments *homo economicus* is the minority. This is true even when the amounts being shared (or kept for oneself) amount to many days' wages.

Is the debate resolved? Many economists think so and now consider people who are sometimes altruistic, sometimes inequality averse, and sometimes reciprocal, in addition to *homo economicus*. They point out that the assumption of self-interest is appropriate for many economic settings, like shopping or the way that firms use technology to maximize profits. But it's not as appropriate in other settings, such as how we pay taxes, or why we work hard for our employer.

Francis Ysidro Edgeworth. 2003. *Mathematical Psychics and Further Papers on Political Economy.* Oxford: Oxford University Press.

H. L. Mencken. 2006. *A Little Book in C Major.* New York, NY: Kessinger Publishing.

reciprocity A preference to be kind or to help others who are kind and helpful, and to withhold help and kindness from people who are not helpful or kind.

inequality aversion A dislike of outcomes in which some individuals receive more than others.

4.3 THE PRISONERS' DILEMMA

Imagine that Anil and Bala are now facing a different problem. Each is deciding how to deal with pest insects that destroy the crops they cultivate in their adjacent fields. Each has two feasible strategies:

- The first is to use an inexpensive chemical called Terminator. It kills every insect for miles around. Terminator also leaks into the water supply that they both use.
- The second is to use integrated pest control (IPC) instead of a chemical. A farmer using IPC introduces beneficial insects to the farm. The beneficial insects eat the pest insects.

If just one of them chooses Terminator, the damage is quite limited. If they both choose it, water contamination becomes a serious problem, and they need to buy a costly filtering system. Figures 4.3a and 4.3b describe their interaction.

Both Anil and Bala are aware of these outcomes. As a result, they know that their payoff (the amount of money they will make at harvest time, minus the costs of their pest control strategy and the installation of water filtration if that becomes necessary), will depend not only on what choice they make, but also on the other's choice. This is a strategic interaction.

How will they play the game? To figure this out, we can use the same method as in the previous section (draw the dots and circles in the payoff matrix for yourself).

		Bala	
		IPC	Terminator
Anil	**IPC**	Beneficial insects spread over both fields, eliminating pests No water contamination	Bala's chemicals spread to Anil's field and kill his beneficial insects Limited water contamination
	Terminator	Anil's chemicals spread to Bala's field and kill his beneficial insects Limited water contamination	Eliminates all pests Heavy water contamination Requires costly filtration system

Figure 4.3a Social interactions in the pest control game.

Anil's best responses:

- *If Bala chooses IPC*: Terminator (cheap eradication of pests, with little water contamination).
- *If Bala chooses Terminator*: Terminator (IPC costs more and cannot work since Bala's chemicals will kill beneficial pests).

So Terminator is Anil's dominant strategy.

You can check, similarly, that Terminator is also a dominant strategy for Bala.

Because Terminator is the dominant strategy for both, we predict that both will use it. Both players using insecticide is the dominant strategy equilibrium of the game.

Anil and Bala each receive payoffs of 2. But both would be better off if they both used IPC instead. So the predicted outcome is not the best feasible outcome. The pest control game is a particular example of a game called the **prisoners' dilemma**.

The contrast between the invisible hand game and the prisoners' dilemma shows that self-interest can lead to favourable outcomes, but can also lead to outcomes that nobody would endorse. Such examples can help us understand more precisely how markets can harness self-interest to improve the workings of the economy, but also the limitations of markets.

Three aspects of the interaction between Anil and Bala caused us to predict an unfortunate outcome in their prisoners' dilemma game:

- They did not place any value on the payoffs of the other person, and so did not internalize (take account of) the costs that their actions inflicted on the other.
- There was no way that Anil, Bala or anyone else could make the farmer who used the insecticide pay for the harm that it caused.
- They were not able to make an agreement beforehand about what each would do. Had they been able to do so, they could have simply agreed to use IPC, or banned the use of Terminator.

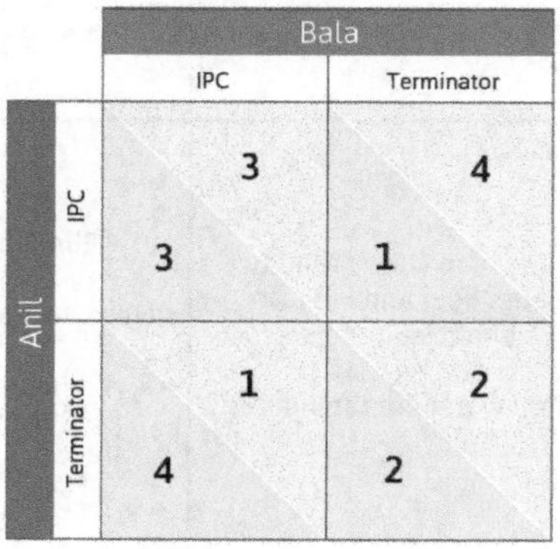

> **prisoners' dilemma** A game in which the payoffs in the dominant strategy equilibrium are lower for each player, and also lower in total, than if neither player played the dominant strategy.

	Bala	
	IPC	Terminator
Anil — IPC	3 / 3	4 / 1
Anil — Terminator	1 / 4	2 / 2

Figure 4.3b Payoff matrix for the pest control game.

The prisoners' dilemma

The name of this game comes from a story about two prisoners (we call them Thelma and Louise) whose strategies are either to Accuse (implicate) the other in a crime that the prisoners may have committed together, or Deny that the other prisoner was involved.

If both Thelma and Louise deny it, they are freed after a few days of questioning.

If one person accusing the other person, while the other person denies, the accuser will be freed immediately (a sentence of zero years), whereas the other person gets a long jail sentence (10 years).

Lastly, if both Thelma and Louise choose Accuse (meaning each implicates the other), they both get a jail sentence. This sentence is reduced from 10 years to 5 years because of their cooperation with the police. The payoffs of the game are shown in Figure 4.4.

		Louise	
		Deny	Accuse
Thelma	Deny	1 / 1	0 / 10
	Accuse	10 / 0	5 / 5

Figure 4.4 Prisoners' dilemma (payoffs are years in prison).

(The payoffs are written in terms of years of prison—so Louise and Thelma prefer lower numbers.)

In a prisoners' dilemma, both players have a dominant strategy (in this example, Accuse) which, when played by both, results in an outcome that is worse for both than if they had both adopted a different strategy (in this example, Deny).

Our story about Thelma and Louise is hypothetical, but this game applies to many real problems. For example, watch the clip from a TV quiz show called *Golden Balls* (http://tinyco.re/7018789), and you will see how one ordinary person ingeniously resolves the prisoners' dilemma.

In economic examples, the mutually beneficial strategy (Deny) is generally termed Cooperate, while the dominant strategy (Accuse) is called Defect. Cooperate does not mean that players get together and discuss what to do. The rules of the game are always that each player decides independently on a strategy.

A solution to the prisoners' dilemma on the show *Golden Balls*
http://tinyco.re/7018789

If we can overcome one or more of these problems, the outcome preferred by both of them would sometimes result. So, in the rest of this unit, we will examine ways to do this.

QUESTION 4.3 CHOOSE THE CORRECT ANSWER(S)

Dimitrios and Ameera work for an international investment bank as foreign exchange traders. They are being questioned by the police on their suspected involvement in a series of market manipulation trades. The table below shows the cost of each strategy (in terms of the length in years of jail sentences they will receive), depending on whether they accuse each other or deny the crime. The first number is the payoff to Dimitrios, while the second number is the payoff to Ameera (the negative numbers signify losses). Assume that the game is a simultaneous one-shot game.

		Ameera	
		Deny	Accuse
Dimitrios	Deny	−2, −2	0, −15
	Accuse	−15, 0	−8, −8

Based on this information, we can conclude that:

☐ Both traders will hold out and deny their involvement.
☐ Both traders will accuse each other, even though they will end up being in jail for eight years.
☐ Ameera will accuse, whatever she expects Dimitrios to do.
☐ There is a small possibility that both traders will get away with two years each.

EXERCISE 4.2 POLITICAL ADVERTISING

Many people consider political advertising (campaign advertisements) to be a classic example of a prisoners' dilemma.

1. Using examples from a recent political campaign with which you are familiar, explain whether this is the case.
2. Write down an example payoff matrix for this case.

4.4 SOCIAL PREFERENCES: ALTRUISM

When students play one-shot prisoners' dilemma games in classroom or laboratory experiments—sometimes for substantial sums of real money—it is common to observe half or more of the participants playing the Cooperate rather than Defect strategy, despite mutual defection being the dominant strategy for players who care only about their own monetary payoffs. One interpretation of these results is that players are altruistic.

For example, if Anil had cared sufficiently about the harm that he would inflict on Bala by using Terminator when Bala was using IPC, then IPC would have been Anil's best response to Bala's IPC. And if Bala had felt the same way, then IPC would have been a mutual best response, and the two would no longer have been in a prisoners' dilemma.

A person who is willing to bear a cost in order to help another person is said to have altruistic preferences. In the example just given, Anil was willing to give up 1 payoff unit because that would have imposed a loss of 2 on Bala. His opportunity cost of choosing IPC when Bala had chosen IPC was 1, and it conferred a benefit of 2 on Bala, meaning that he had acted altruistically.

The economic models we used in Unit 3 assumed self-interested preferences: Alexei, the student, and Angela, the farmer, cared about their own free time and their own grades or consumption. People generally do not care only about what happens to themselves, but also what happens to others. Then we say that the individual has **social preferences**. Altruism is an example of a social preference. Spite and envy are also social preferences.

> **social preferences** Preferences that place a value on what happens to other people, and on acting morally, even if it results in lower payoffs for the individual.

Altruistic preferences as indifference curves

In previous units, we used indifference curves and feasible sets to model Alexei's and Angela's behaviour. We can do the same to study how people interact when social preferences are part of their motivation.

Imagine the following situation. Anil was given some tickets for the national lottery, and one of them won a prize of 10,000 rupees. He can, of course, keep all the money for himself, but he can also share some of it with his neighbour Bala. Figure 4.5 represents the situation graphically. The horizontal axis represents the amount of money (in thousands of rupees) that Anil keeps for himself, and the vertical one the amount that he gives to Bala. Each point (x, y) represents a combination of amounts of money for Anil (x) and Bala (y) in thousands of rupees. The shaded triangle depicts the feasible choices for Anil. At the corner $(10, 0)$ on the horizontal axis, Anil keeps it all. At the other corner $(0, 10)$ on the vertical axis, Anil gives it all to Bala. Anil's feasible set is the shaded area.

The boundary of the shaded area is the feasible frontier. If Anil is dividing up his prize money between himself and Bala, he chooses a point on that frontier (being inside the frontier would mean throwing away some of the money). The choice among points on the feasible frontier is called a **zero sum game** because, when choosing point B rather than point A as in Figure 4.5, the sum of Anil's losses and Bala's gains is zero (for example, Anil has 3,000 fewer rupees at B than at A, and Bala has 3,000 rupees at B and nothing at A).

> **zero sum game** A game in which the payoff gains and losses of the individuals sum to zero, for all combinations of strategies they might pursue.

Anil's preferences can be represented by indifference curves, showing combinations of the amounts for Anil and Bala that are all equally preferred by Anil. Figure 4.5 illustrates two cases. In the first, Anil has self-interested preferences so his indifference curves are straight vertical lines; in the second he is somewhat altruistic—he cares about Bala—so his indifference curves are downward-sloping.

If Anil is self-interested, the best option given his feasible set is A, where he keeps all the money. If he derives utility from Bala's consumption, he has downward-sloping indifference curves so he may prefer an outcome where Bala gets some of the money.

Leibniz: Finding the optimal distribution with altruistic preferences (http://tinyco.re/L040401)

With the specific indifference curves shown in Figure 4.5, the best feasible option for Anil is point B (7, 3) where Anil keeps 7,000 rupees and gives 3,000 to Bala. Anil prefers to give 3,000 rupees to Bala, even at a cost of 3,000 rupees to him. This is an example of altruism: Anil is willing to bear a cost to benefit somebody else.

EXERCISE 4.3 ALTRUISM AND SELFLESSNESS
Using the same axes as in Figure 4.5:

1. What would Anil's indifference curves look like if he cared just as much about Bala's consumption as his own?
2. What would they look like if he derived utility only from the total of his and Bala's consumption?
3. What would they look like if he derived utility only from Bala's consumption?
4. For each of these cases, provide a real world situation in which Anil might have these preferences, making sure to specify how Anil and Bala derive their payoffs.

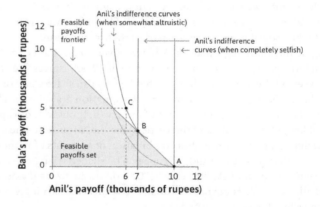

Figure 4.5 How Anil chooses to distribute his lottery winnings depends on whether he is selfish or altruistic.

1. Feasible payoffs
Each point (x, y) in the figure represents a combination of amounts of money for Anil (x) and Bala (y), in thousands of rupees. The shaded triangle depicts the feasible choices for Anil.

2. Indifference curves when Anil is self-interested
If Anil does not care at all about what Bala gets, his indifference curves are straight vertical lines. He is indifferent to whether Bala gets a lot or nothing. He prefers curves further to the right, since he gets more money.

3. Anil's best option
Given his feasible set, Anil's best option is A, where he keeps all the money.

4. What if Anil cares about Bala?
But Anil may care about his neighbour Bala, in which case he is happier if Bala is richer: that is, he derives utility from Bala's consumption. In this case he has downward-sloping indifference curves.

5. Anil's indifference curves when he is somewhat altruistic
Points B and C are equally preferred by Anil, so Anil keeping 7 and Bala getting 3 is just as good in Anil's eyes as Anil getting 6 and Bala getting 5. His best feasible option is point B.

QUESTION 4.4 CHOOSE THE CORRECT ANSWER(S)

In Figure 4.5 (page 146) Anil has just won the lottery and has received 10,000 rupees. He is considering how much (if at all) he would like to share this sum with his friend Bala. Before he manages to share his winnings, Anil receives a tax bill for these winnings of 3,000 rupees. Based on this information, which of the following statements is true?

☐ Bala will receive 3,000 rupees if Anil is somewhat altruistic.
☐ If Anil was somewhat altruistic and kept 7,000 rupees before the tax bill, he will still keep 7,000 rupees after the tax bill by turning completely selfish.
☐ Anil will be on a lower indifference curve after the tax bill.
☐ Had Anil been completely altruistic and only cared about Bala's share, then Bala would have received the same income before and after the tax bill.

4.5 ALTRUISTIC PREFERENCES IN THE PRISONERS' DILEMMA

When Anil and Bala wanted to get rid of pests (Section 4.3), they found themselves in a prisoners' dilemma. One reason for the unfortunate outcome was that they did not account for the costs that their actions inflicted on the other. The choice of pest control regime using the insecticide implied a **free ride** on the other farmer's contribution to ensuring clean water.

If Anil cares about Bala's wellbeing as well as his own, the outcome can be different.

In Figure 4.6 (page 148) the two axes now represent Anil and Bala's payoffs. Just as with the example of the lottery, the diagram shows the feasible outcomes. However, in this case the feasible set has only four points. We have shortened the names of the strategies for convenience: Terminator is T, IPC is I. Notice that movements upward and to the right from (T, T) to (I, I) are win-win: both get higher payoffs. On the other hand, moving up, and to the left, or down, and to the right—from (I, T) to (T, I) or the reverse—are win-lose changes. Win-lose means that Bala gets a higher payoff at the expense of Anil, or Anil benefits at the expense of Bala.

As in the case of dividing lottery winnings, we look at two cases. If Anil does not care about Bala's wellbeing, his indifference curves are vertical lines. If he does care, he has downward-sloping indifference curves. Work through Figure 4.6 to see what will happen in each case.

Figure 4.6 demonstrates that when Anil is completely self-interested, his dominant strategy is Terminator (as we saw before). But if Anil cares sufficiently about Bala, his dominant strategy is IPC. If Bala feels the same way, then the two would both choose IPC, resulting in the outcome that both of them prefer the most.

The main lesson is that if people care about one another, social dilemmas are easier to resolve. This helps us understand the historical examples in which people mutually cooperate for irrigation or enforce the Montreal Protocol to protect the ozone layer, rather than free riding on the cooperation of others.

QUESTION 4.5 CHOOSE THE CORRECT ANSWER(S)

Figure 4.6 shows Anil's preferences when he is completely selfish, and also when he is somewhat altruistic, when he and Bala participate in the prisoners' dilemma game.

Based on the graph, we can say that:

☐ When Anil is completely selfish, using Terminator is his dominant strategy.
☐ When Anil is somewhat altruistic, using Terminator is his dominant strategy.
☐ When Anil is completely selfish, (T, T) is the dominant strategy equilibrium even though it is on a lower indifference curve for him than (T, I).
☐ If Anil is somewhat altruistic, and Bala's preferences are the same as Anil's, (I, I) is attained as the dominant strategy equilibrium.

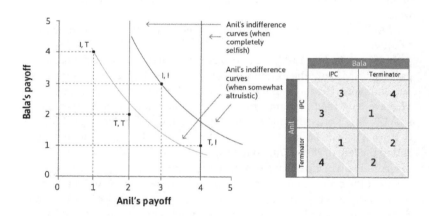

Figure 4.6 Anil's decision to use IPC (I) or Terminator (T) as his crop management strategy depends on whether he is completely selfish or somewhat altruistic.

1. Anil and Bala's payoffs

The two axes in the figure represent Anil and Bala's payoffs. The four points are the feasible outcomes associated to the strategies.

2. Anil's indifference curves if he doesn't care about Bala

If Anil does not care about Bala's wellbeing, his indifference curves are vertical, so (T, I) is his most preferred outcome. He prefers (T, I) to (I, I), so should choose T if Bala chooses I. If Anil is completely selfish, T is unambiguously his best choice.

3. Anil's indifference curves when he cares about Bala

When Anil cares about Bala's wellbeing, indifference curves are downward-sloping and (I, I) is his most preferred outcome. If Bala chooses I, Anil should choose I. Anil should also choose I if Bala chooses T, since he prefers (I, T) to (T, T).

4.6 PUBLIC GOODS, FREE RIDING, AND REPEATED INTERACTION

Now let's look at the second reason for an unfortunate outcome in the prisoners' dilemma game. There was no way that either Anil or Bala (or anyone else) could make whoever used the insecticide pay for the harm that it caused.

The problems of Anil and Bala are hypothetical, but they capture the real dilemmas of free riding that many people around the world face. For example, as in Spain, many farmers in southeast Asia rely on a shared irrigation facility to produce their crops. The system requires constant maintenance and new investment. Each farmer faces the decision of how much to contribute to these activities. These activities benefit the entire community and if the farmer does not volunteer to contribute, others may do the work anyway.

Imagine there are four farmers who are deciding whether to contribute to the maintenance of an irrigation project.

For each farmer, the cost of contributing to the project is $10. But when one farmer contributes, all four of them will benefit from an increase in their crop yields made possible by irrigation, so they will each gain $8. Contributing to the irrigation project is called a **public good**: when one individual bears a cost to provide the good, everyone receives a benefit.

Now, consider the decision facing Kim, one of the four farmers. Figure 4.7 shows how her decision depends on her total earnings, but also on the number of other farmers who decide to contribute to the irrigation project.

For example, if two of the others contribute, Kim will receive a benefit of $8 from each of their contributions. So if she makes no contribution herself, her total payoff, shown in red, is $16. If she decides to contribute, she will receive an additional benefit of $8 (and so will the other three farmers). But she will incur a cost of $10, so her total payoff is $14, as in Figure 4.7, and as calculated in Figure 4.8.

Figures 4.7 and 4.8 illustrate the social dilemma. Whatever the other farmers decide to do, Kim makes more money if she doesn't contribute than if she does. Not contributing is a dominant strategy. She can free ride on the contributions of the others.

This public goods game is a prisoners' dilemma in which there are more than two players. If the farmers care only about their own monetary payoff, there is a dominant strategy equilibrium in which no one contributes and their payoffs are all zero. On the other hand, if all contributed, each would

public good A good for which use by one person does not reduce its availability to others. *Also known as: non-rival good. See also: non-excludable public good, artificially scarce good.*

get $22. Everyone would benefit if everyone cooperated, but irrespective of what others do, each farmer does better by free riding on the others.

Altruism could help to solve the free rider problem: if Kim cared about the other farmers, she might be willing to contribute to the irrigation project. But if large numbers of people are involved in a public goods game, it is less likely that altruism will be sufficient to sustain a mutually beneficial outcome.

Elinor Ostrom. 2000. 'Collective Action and the Evolution of Social Norms'. *Journal of Economic Perspectives* 14 (3): pp. 137–58.

Yet around the world, real farmers and fishing people have faced public goods situations in many cases with great success. The evidence gathered by Elinor Ostrom, a political scientist, and other researchers on common irrigation projects in India, Nepal, and other countries, shows that the degree of cooperation varies. In some communities a history of trust encourages cooperation. In others, cooperation does not happen. In south India, for example, villages with extreme inequalities in land and caste status had more conflicts over water usage. Less unequal villages maintained irrigation systems better: it was easier to sustain cooperation.

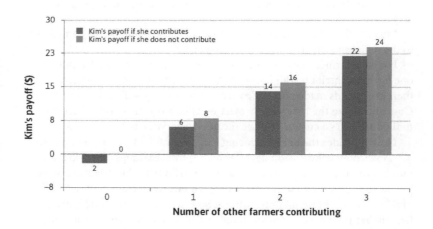

Figure 4.7 Kim's payoffs in the public goods game.

Benefit from the contribution of others	16
Plus benefit from her own contribution	+ 8
Minus cost of her contribution	− 10
Total	**$14**

Figure 4.8 Example: When two others contribute, Kim's payoff is lower if she contributes too.

GREAT ECONOMISTS

Elinor Ostrom

The choice of Elinor Ostrom (1933–2012), a political scientist, as a co-recipient of the 2009 Nobel Prize surprised most economists. For example, Steven Levitt, a professor at the University of Chicago, admitted he knew nothing about her work, and had 'no recollection of ever seeing or hearing her name mentioned by an economist'.

Some, however, vigorously defended the decision. Vernon Smith, an experimental economist who had previously been awarded the Prize, congratulated the Nobel committee for recognizing her originality, 'scientific common sense' and willingness to listen 'carefully to data'.

Ostrom's entire academic career was focused on a concept that plays a central role in economics but is seldom examined in much detail: property. Ronald Coase had established the importance of clearly delineated property rights when one person's actions affected the welfare of others. But Coase's main concern was the boundary between the individual and the state in regulating such actions. Ostrom explored the middle ground where communities, rather than individuals or formal governments, held property rights.

The conventional wisdom at the time was that informal collective ownership of resources would lead to a 'tragedy of the commons'. That is, economists believed that resources could not be used efficiently and sustainably under a common property regime. Thanks to Elinor Ostrom this is no longer a dominant view.

First, she made a distinction between resources held as common property and those subject to open access:

- *Common property* involves a well-defined community of users who are able in practice, if not under the law, to prevent outsiders from exploiting the resource. Inshore fisheries, grazing lands, or forest areas are examples.
- *Open-access resources* such as ocean fisheries or the atmosphere as a carbon sink, can be exploited without restrictions, other than those imposed by states acting alone or through international agreements.

Ostrom was not alone in stressing this distinction, but she drew on a unique combination of case studies, statistical methods, game theoretic models with unorthodox ingredients, and laboratory experiments to try to understand how tragedies of the commons could be averted.

She discovered great diversity in how common property is managed. Some communities were able to devise rules and draw on **social norms** to enforce sustainable resource use, while others failed to do so. Much of her career was devoted to identifying the criteria for success, and using

social norm An understanding that is common to most members of a society about what people should do in a given situation when their actions affect others.

theory to understand why some arrangements worked well while others did not.

Many economists believed that the diversity of outcomes could be understood using the theory of repeated games, which predicts that even when all individuals care only for themselves, if interactions are repeated with sufficiently high likelihood and individuals are patient enough, then cooperative outcomes can be sustained indefinitely.

But this was not a satisfying explanation for Ostrom, partly because the same theory predicted that any outcome, including rapid depletion, could also arise.

More importantly, Ostrom knew that sustainable use was enforced by actions that clearly deviated from the hypothesis of material self-interest. In particular, individuals would willingly bear considerable costs to punish violators of rules or norms. As the economist Paul Romer put it, she recognized the need to 'expand models of human preferences to include a contingent taste for punishing others'.

Ostrom developed simple game theoretic models in which individuals have unorthodox preferences, caring directly about trust and reciprocity. And she looked for the ways in which people faced with a social dilemma avoided tragedy by changing the rules so that the strategic nature of the interaction was transformed.

She worked with economists to run a pioneering series of experiments, confirming the widespread use of costly punishment in response to excessive resource extraction, and also demonstrated the power of communication and the critical role of informal agreements in supporting cooperation. Thomas Hobbes, a seventeenth-century philosopher, had asserted that agreements had to be enforced by governments, since 'covenants, without the sword, are but words and of no strength to secure a man at all'. Ostrom disagreed. As she wrote in the title of an influential article, covenants—even without a sword—make self-governance possible.

Elinor Ostrom, James Walker, and Roy Gardner. 1992. 'Covenants With and Without a Sword: Self-Governance is Possible'. *The American Political Science Review* 86 (2).

Social preferences partly explain why these communities avoid Garrett Hardin's tragedy of the commons. But they may also find ways of deterring free-riding behaviour.

Repeated games

Free riding today on the contributions of other members of one's community may have unpleasant consequences tomorrow or years from now. Ongoing relationships are an important feature of social interactions that was not captured in the models we have used so far: life is not a one-shot game.

The interaction between Anil and Bala in our model was a one-shot game. But as owners of neighbouring fields, Anil and Bala are more realistically portrayed as interacting repeatedly.

Imagine how differently things would work out if we represented their interaction as a game to be repeated each season. Suppose that Bala has adopted IPC. What is Anil's best response? He would reason like this:

ANIL: If I play IPC, then maybe Bala will continue to do so, but if I use Terminator—which would raise my profits this season—Bala would use Terminator next year. So unless I am extremely impatient for income now, I'd better stick with IPC.

Bala could reason in exactly the same way. The result might be that they would then continue playing IPC forever.

In the next section, we will look at experimental evidence of how people behave when a public goods game is repeated.

QUESTION 4.6 CHOOSE THE CORRECT ANSWER(S)

Four farmers are deciding whether to contribute to the maintenance of an irrigation project. For each farmer, the cost of contributing to the project is $10. But when one farmer contributes, all four of them will benefit from an increase in their crop yields, so they will each gain $8.

Which of the following statements is correct?

☐ If all the farmers are selfish, none of them will contribute.
☐ If one of the farmers, Kim, cares about her neighbour Jim just as much as herself, she will contribute $10.
☐ If Kim is altruistic and contributes $10, the others might contribute too, even if they are selfish.
☐ If the farmers have to reconsider this decision every year, they might choose to contribute to the project even if they are selfish.

4.7 PUBLIC GOOD CONTRIBUTIONS AND PEER PUNISHMENT

An experiment demonstrates that people can sustain high levels of cooperation in a public goods game, as long as they have opportunities to target free riders once it becomes clear who is contributing less than the norm.

Figure 4.9a shows the results of laboratory experiments that mimic the costs and benefits from contribution to a public good in the real world. The experiments were conducted in cities around the world. In each experiment participants play 10 rounds of a public goods game, similar to the one involving Kim and the other farmers that we just described. In each round, the people in the experiment (we call them subjects) are given $20. They are randomly sorted into small groups, typically of four people, who don't know each other. They are asked to decide on a contribution from their $20 to a common pool of money. The pool is a public good. For every dollar contributed, each person in the group receives $0.40, including the contributor.

Imagine that you are playing the game, and you expect the other three members of your group each to contribute $10. Then if you don't contribute, you will get $32 (three returns of $4 from their contributions, plus the initial $20 that you keep). The others have paid $10, so they only get $32 − $10 = $22 each. On the other hand, if you also contribute $10, then everyone, including you, will get $22 + $4 = $26. Unfortunately for the group, you do better by not contributing—that is, because the reward for free riding ($32) is greater than for contributing ($26). And, unfortunately for you, the same applies to each of the other members.

After each round, the participants are told the contributions of other members of their group. In Figure 4.9a, each line represents the evolution over time of average contributions in a different location around the world. Just as in the prisoners' dilemma, people are definitely not solely self-interested.

As you can see, players in Chengdu contributed $10 in the first round, just as we described above. In every population where the game was played, contributions to the public good were high in the first period, although much more so in some cities (Copenhagen) than in others (Melbourne). This is remarkable: if you care only about your own payoff, contributing nothing at all is the dominant strategy. The high initial contributions could have occurred because the participants in the experiment valued their contribution to the payoffs that others received (they were altruistic). But the difficulty (or, as Hardin would have described it, the tragedy) is obvious. Everywhere, the contributions to the public good decreased over time.

Nevertheless, the results also show that despite a large variation across societies, most of them still have high contribution levels at the end of the experiment.

The most plausible explanation of the pattern is not altruism. It is likely that contributors decreased their level of cooperation if they observed that others were contributing less than expected and were therefore free riding on them. It seems as if those people who contributed more than the average liked to punish the low contributors for their unfairness, or for violating a social norm of contributing. Since the payoffs of free riders depend on the total contribution to the public good, the only way to punish free riders in this experiment was to stop contributing. This is the tragedy of the commons.

Many people are happy to contribute as long as others reciprocate. A disappointed expectation of reciprocity is the most convincing reason that contributions fell so regularly in later rounds of this game.

To test this, the experimenters took the public goods game experiment shown in Figure 4.9a and introduced a punishment option. After observing the contributions of their group, individual players could pay to punish other players by making them pay a $3 fine. The punisher remained anonymous, but had to pay $1 per player punished. The effect is shown in Figure 4.9b. For the majority of subjects, including those in China, South Korea, northern Europe and the English-speaking countries, contributions increased when they had the opportunity to punish free riders.

Benedikt Herrmann, Christian Thoni, and Simon Gachter. 2008. 'Antisocial Punishment Across Societies'. *Science* 319 (5868): pp. 1362–67.

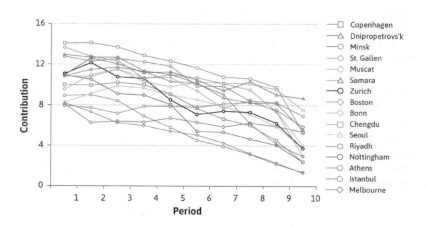

Figure 4.9a Worldwide public goods experiments: Contributions over 10 periods.

People who think that others have been unfair or have violated a social norm may retaliate, even if the cost to themselves is high. Their punishment of others is a form of altruism, because it costs them something to help deter free riding behaviour that is detrimental to the wellbeing of most members of the group.

This experiment illustrates the way that, even in large groups of people, a combination of repeated interactions and social preferences can support high levels of contribution to the public good.

The public goods game, like the prisoners' dilemma, is a situation in which there is something to gain for everyone by engaging with others in a common project such as pest control, maintaining an irrigation system, or controlling carbon emissions. But there is also something to lose when others free ride.

4.8 BEHAVIOURAL EXPERIMENTS IN THE LAB AND IN THE FIELD

To understand economic behaviour, we need to know about people's preferences. In the previous unit, for example, students and farmers valued free time. How much they valued it was part of the information we needed to predict how much time they spend studying and farming.

In the past, economists have learned about our preferences from:

- *Survey questions*: To determine political preferences, brand loyalty, degree of trust of others, or religious orientation.
- *Statistical studies of economic behaviour*: For example, purchases of one or more goods when the relative price varies—to determine preferences for the goods in question. One strategy is to reverse-engineer what the preferences must have been, as revealed by purchases. This is called **revealed preference**.

Surveys have a problem. Asking someone if they like ice cream will probably get an honest answer. But the answer to the question: 'How altruistic are you?' may be a mixture of truth, self-advertising, and wishful thinking. Statistical studies cannot control the decision-making environ-

revealed preference A way of studying preferences by reverse engineering the motives of an individual (her preferences) from observations about her or his actions.

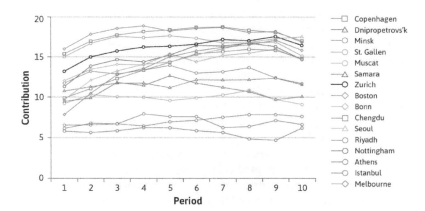

Figure 4.9b Worldwide public goods experiments with opportunities for peer punishment.

Benedikt Herrmann, Christian Thoni, and Simon Gachter. 2008. 'Antisocial Punishment Across Societies'. *Science* 319 (5868): pp. 1362–67.

ment in which the preferences were revealed, so it is difficult to compare the choices of different groups.

This is why economists sometimes use experiments, so that people's behaviour can be observed under controlled conditions.

HOW ECONOMISTS LEARN FROM FACTS

Laboratory experiments

Behavioural experiments have become important in the empirical study of preferences. Part of the motivation for experiments is that understanding someone's motivations (altruism, reciprocity, inequality aversion as well as self-interest) is essential to being able to predict how they will behave as employees, family members, custodians of the environment, and citizens.

Experiments measure what people do rather than what they say. Experiments are designed to be as realistic as possible, while controlling the situation:

- *Decisions have consequences*: The decisions in the experiment may decide how much money the subjects earn by taking part. Sometimes the stakes can be as high as a month's income.
- *Instructions, incentives and rules are common to all subjects*: There is also a common treatment. This means that if we want to compare two groups, the only difference between the control and treatment groups is the treatment itself, so that its effects can be identified.
- *Experiments can be replicated*: They are designed to be implementable with other groups of participants.
- *Experimenters attempt to control for other possible explanations*: Other variables are kept constant wherever possible, because they may affect the behaviour we want to measure.

This means that when people behave differently in the experiment, it is likely due to differences in their preferences, not in the situation that each person faces.

Economists have studied public goods extensively using laboratory experiments in which the subjects are asked to make decisions about how much to contribute to a public good. In some cases, economists have designed experiments that closely mimic real-world social dilemmas. The work of Juan Camilo Cárdenas, an economist at the Universidad de los Andes in Bogotá, Colombia is an example. He performs experiments about social dilemmas with people who are facing similar problems in their real life, such as overexploitation of a forest or a fish stock. In our 'Economist in action' video he describes his use of experimental economics in real-life situations, and how it helps us understand why people cooperate even when there are apparent incentives not to do so.

Economists have discovered that the way people behave in experiments can be used to predict how they react in real-life situations. For example, fishermen in Brazil who acted more cooperatively in an experimental game also practiced fishing in a more sustainable manner than the fishermen who were less cooperative in the experiment.

Colin Camerer and Ernst Fehr. 2004. 'Measuring Social Norms and Preferences Using Experimental Games: A Guide for Social Scientists'. In *Foundations of Human Sociality: Economic Experiments and Ethnographic Evidence from Fifteen Small-Scale Societies*, edited by Joseph Henrich, Robert Boyd, Samuel Bowles, Colin Camerer, and Herbert Gintis, Oxford: Oxford University Press.

In our 'Economist in action' video, Juan Camilo Cárdenas talks about his innovative use of experimental economics in real-life situations.
http://tinyco.re/8347533

For a summary of the kinds of experiments that have been run, the main results, and whether behaviour in the experimental lab predicts real-life behaviour, read the research done by some of the economists who specialize in experimental economics. For example, Colin Camerer and Ernst Fehr, Armin Falk and James Heckman, or the experiments done by Joseph Heinrich and a large team of collaborators around the world.

In Exercise 4.5, however, Stephen Levitt and John List ask whether people would behave the same way in the street as they do in the laboratory.

Colin Camerer and Ernst Fehr. 2004. 'Measuring Social Norms and Preferences Using Experimental Games: A Guide for Social Scientists'. In *Foundations of Human Sociality: Economic Experiments and Ethnographic Evidence from Fifteen Small-Scale Societies*, edited by Joseph Henrich, Robert Boyd, Samuel Bowles, Colin Camerer, and Herbert Gintis, Oxford: Oxford University Press.

Armin Falk and James J. Heckman. 2009. 'Lab Experiments Are a Major Source of Knowledge in the Social Sciences'. *Science* 326 (5952): pp. 535–538.

Joseph Henrich, Richard McElreath, Abigail Barr, Jean Ensminger, Clark Barrett, Alexander Bolyanatz, Juan Camilo Cardenas, Michael Gurven, Edwins Gwako, Natalie Henrich, Carolyn Lesorogol, Frank Marlowe, David Tracer, and John Ziker. 2006. 'Costly Punishment Across Human Societies'. *Science* 312 (5781): pp. 1767–1770.

QUESTION 4.7 CHOOSE THE CORRECT ANSWER(S)

According to the 'Economist in action' video of Juan Camilo Cárdenas (page 156), which of the following have economists discovered using experiments simulating public goods scenarios?

- ☐ The imposition of external regulation sometimes erodes the willingness of participants to cooperate.
- ☐ Populations with greater inequality exhibit a greater tendency to cooperate.
- ☐ Once real cash is used instead of tokens of hypothetical sums of money, people cease to act cooperatively.
- ☐ People are often willing to cooperate rather than free ride.

EXERCISE 4.5 ARE LAB EXPERIMENTS ALWAYS VALID?

In 2007, Steven Levitt and John List published a paper called 'What Do Laboratory Experiments Measuring Social Preferences Reveal about the Real World?' (http://tinyco.re/9601240). Read the paper to answer these two questions.

1. According to their paper, why and how might people's behaviour in real life vary from what has been observed in laboratory experiments?
2. Using the example of the public goods experiment in this section, explain why you might observe systematic differences between the observations recorded in Figures 4.9a (page 154) and 4.9b (page 155), and what might happen in real life.

Steven D. Levitt, and John A. List. 2007. 'What Do Laboratory Experiments Measuring Social Preferences Reveal About the Real World?' *Journal of Economic Perspectives* 21 (2): pp. 153–174.

Sometimes it is possible to conduct experiments 'in the field': that is, to deliberately change the economic conditions under which people make decisions, and observe how their behaviour changes. An experiment conducted in Israel in 1998 demonstrated that social preferences may be very sensitive to the context in which decisions are made.

It is common for parents to rush to pick up their children from daycare. Sometimes a few parents are late, making teachers stay extra time. What would you do to deter parents from being late? Two economists ran an experiment introducing fines in some daycare centres but not others (these were used as controls). The 'price of lateness' went from zero to ten Israeli shekels (about $3 at the time). Surprisingly, after the fine was introduced, the frequency of late pickups doubled. The top line in Figure 4.10 illustrates this.

Why did putting a price on lateness backfire?

One possible explanation is that before the fine was introduced, most parents were on time because they felt that it was the right thing to do. In other words, they came on time because of a moral obligation to avoid inconveniencing the daycare staff. Perhaps they felt an altruistic concern for the staff, or regarded a timely pick-up as a reciprocal responsibility in the joint care of the child. But the imposition of the fine signalled that the situation was really more like shopping. Lateness had a price and so could be purchased, like vegetables or ice-cream.

The use of a market-like incentive—the price of lateness—had provided what psychologists call a new 'frame' for the decision, making it one in which self-interest rather than concern for others was acceptable. When fines and prices have these unintended effects, we say that incentives have **crowded out** social preferences. Even worse, you can also see from Figure 4.10 that when the fine was removed, parents continued to pick up their children late.

Samuel Bowles. 2016. *The Moral Economy: Why Good Incentives Are No Substitute for Good Citizens*. New Haven, CT: Yale University Press.

crowding out There are two quite distinct uses of the term. One is the observed negative effect when economic incentives displace people's ethical or other-regarding motivations. In studies of individual behaviour, incentives may have a crowding out effect on social preferences. A second use of the term is to refer to the effect of an increase in government spending in reducing private spending, as would be expected for example in an economy working at full capacity utilization, or when a fiscal expansion is associated with a rise in the interest rate.

Uri Gneezy and Aldo Rustichini. 2000. 'A Fine Is a Price'. *The Journal of Legal Studies* 29 (January): pp. 1–17.

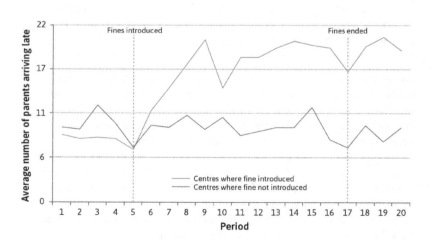

Figure 4.10 Average number of late-coming parents, per week.

QUESTION 4.8 CHOOSE THE CORRECT ANSWER(S)
Figure 4.10 (page 158) depicts the average number of late-coming parents per week in day-care centres, where a fine was introduced in some centres and not in others. The fines were eventually abolished, as indicated on the graph.

Based on this information, which of the following statements is correct?

☐ The introduction of the fine successfully reduced the number of late-coming parents.
☐ The fine can be considered as the 'price' for collecting a child.
☐ The graph suggests that the experiment may have permanently increased the parents' tendency to be late.
☐ The crowding out of the social preference did not occur until the fines ended.

EXERCISE 4.6 CROWDING OUT
Imagine you are the mayor of a small town and wish to motivate your citizens to get involved in 'City Beautiful Day', in which people spend one day to help cleaning parks and roads.
How would you design the day to motivate citizens to take part?

4.9 COOPERATION, NEGOTIATION, CONFLICTS OF INTEREST, AND SOCIAL NORMS

Cooperation means participating in a common project in such a way that mutual benefits occur. Cooperation need not be based on an agreement. We have seen examples in which players acting independently can still achieve a cooperative outcome:

> **cooperation** Participating in a common project that is intended to produce mutual benefits.

- *The invisible hand*: Anil and Bala chose their crops in pursuit of their own interests. Their engagement in the village market resulted in a mutually beneficial division of labour.
- *The repeated prisoners' dilemma*: They may refrain from using Terminator for pest control because they recognize the future losses they would suffer as a result of abandoning IPC.
- *The public goods game*: Players' willingness to punish others sustained high levels of cooperation in many countries, without the need for agreements.

In other cases, such as the one-shot prisoners' dilemma, independent actions led to an unfortunate outcome. Then, the players could do better if they could reach an agreement.

People commonly resort to negotiation to solve their economic and social problems. For example, international negotiation resulted in the Montreal Protocol, through which countries agreed to eliminate the use of chlorofluorocarbons (CFCs), in order to avoid a harmful outcome (the destruction of the ozone layer).

But negotiation does not always succeed, sometimes because of conflicts of interest over how the mutual gains to cooperation will be shared. The success of the Montreal Protocol contrasts with the relative failure of the Kyoto Protocol in reducing carbon emissions responsible for global warming. The reasons are partly scientific. The alternative technologies to CFCs were well-developed and the benefits relative to costs for large industrial countries, such as the US, were much clearer and larger than in the case of greenhouse gas emissions. But one of the obstacles to agreement at the Copenhagen climate change summit in 2009 was over how to share the costs and benefits of limiting emissions between developed and developing countries.

As a simpler example of a conflict of interest, consider a professor who might be willing to hire a student as a research assistant for the summer. In principle, both have something to gain from the relationship, because this might also be a good opportunity for the student to earn some money and learn. In spite of the potential for mutual benefit, there is also some room for conflict. The professor may want to pay less and have more of his research grant left over to buy a new computer, or he may need the work to be done quickly, meaning the student can't take time off. After negotiating, they may reach a compromise and agree that the student can earn a small salary while working from the beach. Or, perhaps, the negotiation will fail.

There are many situations like this in economics. A negotiation (sometimes called bargaining) is also an integral part of politics, foreign affairs, law, social life and even family dynamics. A parent may give a child a smartphone to play with in exchange for a quiet evening, a country might consider giving up land in exchange for peace, or a government might be willing to negotiate a deal with student protesters to avoid political instability. As with the student and the professor, each of these bargains might not actually happen if either side is not willing to do these things.

Negotiation: Sharing mutual gains

To help think about what makes a deal work, consider the following situation. You and a friend are walking down an empty street and you see a $100 note on the ground. How would you decide how to split your lucky find? If you split the amount equally, perhaps this reflects a social norm in your community that says that something you get by luck should be split 50–50.

Dividing something of value in equal shares (the 50–50 rule) is a social norm in many communities, as is giving gifts on birthdays to close family members and friends. Social norms are common to an entire group of people (almost all follow them) and tell a person what they should do in the eyes of most people in the community.

In economics we think of people as making decisions according to their preferences, by which we mean all of the likes, dislikes, attitudes, feelings, and beliefs that motivate them. So everyone's preferences are individual. They may be influenced by social norms, but they reflect what people want to do as well as what they think they ought to do.

We would expect that, even if there were a 50–50 norm in a community, some individuals might not respect the norm exactly. Some people may act more selfishly than the norm requires and others more generously. What happens next will depend both on the social norm (a fact about the world, which reflects attitudes to fairness that have evolved over long periods), but also on the specific preferences of the individuals concerned.

Suppose the person who saw the money first has picked it up. There are at least three reasons why that person might give some of it to a friend:

- **Altruism**: We have already considered this reason, in the case of Anil and Bala. This person might be altruistic and care about the other being happy, or about another aspect of the other's wellbeing.
- **Fairness**: Or, the person holding the money might think that 50–50 is fair. In this case, the person is motivated by fairness, or what economists term **inequality aversion**.
- **Reciprocity**: The friend may have been kind to the lucky money-finder in the past, or kind to others, and deserves to be treated generously because of this. In this case we say that our money-finder has reciprocal preferences.

These social preferences all influence our behaviour, sometimes working in opposite directions. For example, if the money-finder has strong fairness preferences but knows that the friend is entirely selfish, the fairness preferences tempt the finder to share but the reciprocity preferences push the finder to keep the money.

> **fairness** A way to evaluate an allocation based on one's conception of justice.

> **QUESTION 4.9 CHOOSE THE CORRECT ANSWER(S)**
> Anastasia and Belinda's favourite hobby is to go metal detecting. On one occasion Anastasia finds four Roman coins while Belinda is unsuccessful. Both women have reciprocal preferences. From this, can we say that:
>
> ☐ If both women are altruistic, then they will definitely share the find 50–50.
> ☐ If Anastasia is altruistic and Belinda is selfish, then Anastasia may not share the find.
> ☐ If Anastasia is selfish and Belinda is altruistic, then Anastasia will definitely not share the find.
> ☐ If Anastasia is altruistic and Belinda believes in fairness, then they may or may not share the find 50–50.

4.10 DIVIDING A PIE (OR LEAVING IT ON THE TABLE)

One of the most common tools to study social preferences is a two-person one-shot game known as the ultimatum game. It has been used around the world with experimental subjects including students, farmers, warehouse workers, and hunter-gatherers. By observing their choices we investigate the subjects' preferences and motives, such as pure self-interest, altruism, inequality aversion, or reciprocity.

The subjects of the experiment are invited to play a game in which they will win some money. How much they win will depend on how they and the others in the game play. Real money is at stake in experimental games like these, otherwise we could not be sure the subjects' answers to a hypothetical question would reflect their actions in real life.

The rules of the game are explained to the players. They are randomly matched in pairs, then one player is randomly assigned as the Proposer, and the other the Responder. The subjects do not know each other, but they know the other player was recruited to the experiment in the same way. Subjects remain anonymous.

The Proposer is provisionally given an amount of money, say $100, by the experimenter, and instructed to offer the Responder part of it. Any split is permitted, including keeping it all, or giving it all away. We will call this amount the 'pie' because the point of the experiment is how it will be divided up.

The split takes the form: 'x for me, y for you' where $x + y = \$100$. The Responder knows that the Proposer has $100 to split. After observing the offer, the Responder accepts or rejects it. If the offer is rejected, both individuals get nothing. If it is accepted, the split is implemented: the Proposer gets x and the Responder y. For example, if the Proposer offers $35 and the Responder accepts, the Proposer gets $65 and the Responder gets $35. If the Responder rejects the offer, they both get nothing.

This is called a take-it-or-leave-it offer. It is the ultimatum in the game's name. The Responder is faced with a choice: accept $35, or get nothing.

This is a game about sharing the **economic rents** that arise in an interaction. An entrepreneur wanting to introduce a new technology could share the rent—the higher profit than is available from the current technology—with employees if they cooperate in its introduction. Here, the rent arises because the experimenter provisionally gives the Proposer the pie to divide. If the negotiation succeeds (the Responder accepts), both players receive a rent (a slice of the pie); their next best alternative is to get nothing (the pie is thrown away).

In the example above, if the Responder accepts the Proposer's offer, then the Proposer gets a rent of $65, and the Responder gets $35. For the Responder there is a cost to saying no. He loses the rent that he would have received. Therefore $35 is the opportunity cost of rejecting the offer.

We start by thinking about a simplified case of the ultimatum game, represented in Figure 4.11 in a diagram called a 'game tree'. The Proposer's choices are either the 'fair offer' of an equal split, or the 'unfair offer' of 20 (keeping 80 for herself). Then the respondent has the choice to accept or reject. The payoffs are shown in the last row.

> **economic rent** A payment or other benefit received above and beyond what the individual would have received in his or her next best alternative (or reservation option). *See also: reservation option.*

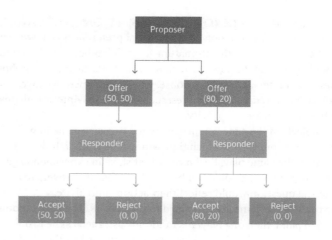

Figure 4.11 Game tree for the ultimatum game.

The game tree is a useful way to represent social interactions because it clarifies who does what, when they choose, and what are the results. We see that in the ultimatum game one player (the Proposer) chooses her strategy first, followed by the Responder. It is called a **sequential game**; previously we looked at **simultaneous games**, in which players chose strategies simultaneously.

What the Proposer will get depends on what the Responder does, so the Proposer has to think about the likely response of the other player. That is why this is called a strategic interaction. If you're the Proposer you can't try out a low offer to see what happens: you have only one chance to make an offer.

Put yourself in the place of the Responder in this game. Would you accept (50, 50)? Would you accept (80, 20)? Now switch roles. Suppose that you are the Proposer. What split would you offer to the Responder? Would your answer depend on whether the other person was a friend, a stranger, a person in need, or a competitor? A Responder who thinks that the Proposer's offer has violated a social norm of fairness, or that the offer is insultingly low for some other reason, might be willing to sacrifice the payoff to punish the Proposer.

Now return to the general case, in which the Proposer can offer any amount between $0 and $100. If you were the Responder, what is the minimum amount you would be willing to accept? If you were the Proposer, what would you offer?

If you work through the Einstein below, and Exercise 4.7 that follows it, you will see how to work out the **minimum acceptable offer**, taking account of the social norm and of the individual's own attitude to reciprocity. The minimal acceptable offer is the offer at which the pleasure of getting the money is equal to the satisfaction the person would get from refusing the offer and getting no money, but being able to punish the Proposer for violating the social norm of 50–50. If you are the Responder and your minimum acceptable offer is $35 (of the total pie of $100) then, if the Proposer offered you $36, you might not like the Proposer much, but you would still accept the offer instead of punishing the Proposer by rejecting the offer. If you rejected the offer, you would go home with satisfaction worth $35 and no money, when you could have had $36 in cash.

> **sequential game** A game in which all players do not choose their strategies at the same time, and players that choose later can see the strategies already chosen by the other players, for example the ultimatum game. *See also: simultaneous game.*

> **simultaneous game** A game in which players choose strategies simultaneously, for example the prisoners' dilemma. *See also: sequential game.*

> **minimum acceptable offer** In the ultimatum game, the smallest offer by the Proposer that will not be rejected by the Responder. Generally applied in bargaining situations to mean the least favourable offer that would be accepted.

EINSTEIN

When will an offer in the ultimatum game be accepted?
Suppose $100 is to be split, and there is a fairness norm of 50–50. When the proposal is $50 or above, ($y \geq 50$), the Responder feels positively disposed towards the Proposer and would naturally accept the proposal, as rejecting it would hurt both herself and the Proposer whom she appreciates because they conform to, or were even more generous than, the social norm. But if the offer is below $50 then she feels that the 50–50 norm is not being respected, and she may want to punish the Proposer for this breach. If she does reject the offer, this will come at a cost to her, because rejection means that both receive nothing.

Suppose the Responder's anger at the breach of the social norm depends on the size of the breach: if the Proposer offers nothing she will be furious, but she's more likely to be puzzled than angry at an offer of

$49.50 rather than the $50 offer she might have expected based on the social norm. So how much satisfaction she would derive from punishing a Proposer's low offer depends on two things: her private reciprocity motive (R), and the gain from accepting the offer (y). R is a number that indicates the strength of the Responder's private reciprocity motive: if R is a large number, then she cares a lot about whether the Proposer is acting generously and fairly or not, but if $R = 0$ she does not care about the Proposer's motives at all. So the satisfaction at rejecting a low offer is $R(50 - y)$. The gain from accepting the offer is the offer itself, or y.

The decision to accept or reject just depends on which of these two quantities is larger. We can write this as 'reject an offer if $y < R(50 - y)$'. This equation says that she will reject an offer of less than $50 according to how much lower than $50 the offer is (as measured by $(50 - y)$), multiplied by her private attitude to reciprocity (R).

To calculate her minimum acceptable offer we can rearrange this rejection equation like this:

$$y < R(50 - y)$$
$$y < 50R - Ry$$
$$y + Ry < 50R$$
$$y(1 + R) < 50R$$
$$y < \frac{50R}{1 + R}$$

$R = 1$ means that the Responder places equal importance on reciprocity and the social norm. When $R = 1$, then $y < 25$ and she will reject any offer less than $25. The cutoff point of $25 is where her two motivations of monetary gain and punishing the Proposer exactly balance out: if she rejects the offer of $25, she loses $25 but receives $25 worth of satisfaction from punishing the Proposer so her total payoff is $0.

The more the Responder cares about reciprocity, the higher the Proposer's offers have to be. For example, if $R = 0.5$, the Responder will reject offers below $16.67 ($y < 16.67$), but if $R = 2$, then the Responder will reject any offer less than $33.33.

EXERCISE 4.7 ACCEPTABLE OFFERS

1. How might the minimum acceptable offer depend on the method by which the Proposer acquired the $100 (for example, did she find it on the street, win it in the lottery, receive it as an inheritance, and so on)?
2. Suppose that the fairness norm in this society is 50–50. Can you imagine anyone offering more than 50% in such a society? If so, why?

4.11 FAIR FARMERS, SELF-INTERESTED STUDENTS?

If you are a Responder in the ultimatum game who cares only about your own payoffs, you should accept any positive offer because something, no matter how small, is always better than nothing. Therefore, in a world composed only of self-interested individuals, the Proposer would anticipate that the Responder would accept any offer and, for that reason, would offer the minimum possible amount—one cent—knowing it would be accepted.

Does this prediction match the experimental data? No, it does not. As in the prisoners' dilemma, we don't see the outcome we would predict if people were entirely self-interested. One-cent offers get rejected.

To see how farmers in Kenya and students in the US played this game, look at Figure 4.12. The height of each bar indicates the fraction of Responders who were willing to accept the offer indicated on the horizontal axis. Offers of more than half of the pie were acceptable to all of the subjects in both countries, as you would expect.

Notice that the Kenyan farmers are very unwilling to accept low offers, presumably regarding them as unfair, while the US students are much more willing to do so. For example, virtually all (90%) of the farmers would say no to an offer of one-fifth of the pie (the Proposer keeping 80%), while 63% of the students would accept such a low offer. More than half of the students would accept just 10% of the pie, but almost none of the farmers would.

Although the results in Figure 4.12 indicate that attitudes differ towards what is fair, and how important fairness is, nobody in the Kenyan and US experiments was willing to accept an offer of zero, even though by rejecting it they would also receive zero.

This is not always the case. In experiments in Papua New Guinea offers of more than half of the pie were commonly rejected by Responders who preferred to receive nothing than to participate in a very unequal outcome even if it was in the Responder's favour, or to incur the social debt of having received a large gift that might be difficult to reciprocate. The subjects were inequity averse, even if the inequality in question benefited them.

Joseph Henrich, Robert Boyd, Samuel Bowles, Colin Camerer, and Herbert Gintis (editors). 2004. *Foundations of Human Sociality: Economic Experiments and Ethnographic Evidence from Fifteen Small-Scale Societies.* Oxford: Oxford University Press.

EXERCISE 4.8 SOCIAL PREFERENCES

Consider the experiment described in Figure 4.12:

1. Which of the social preferences discussed above do you think motivated the subjects' willingness to reject low offers, even though by doing so they would receive nothing at all?
2. Why do you think that the results differed between the Kenyan farmers and the US students?
3. What responses would you expect if you played this game with two different sets of players—your classmates and your family? Explain whether or not you expect the results to differ across these groups. If possible, play the game with your classmates and your family and comment on whether the results are consistent with your predictions.

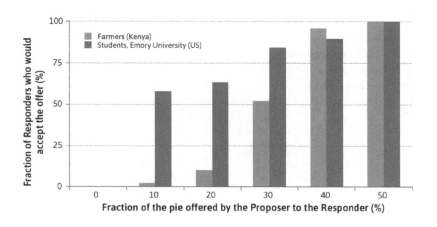

Figure 4.12 Acceptable offers in the ultimatum game.

Adapted from Joseph Henrich, Richard McElreath, Abigail Barr, Jean Ensminger, Clark Barrett, Alexander Bolyanatz, Juan Camilo Cardenas, Michael Gurven, Edwins Gwako, Natalie Henrich, Carolyn Lesorogol, Frank Marlowe, David Tracer, and John Ziker. 2006. 'Costly Punishment Across Human Societies'. *Science* 312 (5781): pp. 1767–1770.

The full height of each bar in Figure 4.13 indicates the percentage of the Kenyan and American Proposers who made the offer shown on the horizontal axis. For example, half of the farmers made proposals of 40%. Another 10% offered an even split. Only 11% of the students made such generous offers.

But were the farmers really generous? To answer, you have to think not only about how much they were offering, but also what they must have reasoned when considering whether the Respondent would accept the offer. If you look at Figure 4.13 and concentrate on the Kenyan farmers, you will see that very few proposed to keep the entire pie by offering zero (4% of them as shown in the far left-hand bar) and all of those offers would have been rejected (the entire bar is dark).

On the other hand, looking at the far right of the figure, we see that for the farmers, making an offer of half the pie ensured an acceptance rate of 100% (the entire bar is light). Those who offered 30% were about equally likely to see their offer rejected as accepted (the dark part of the bar is nearly as big as the light part).

A Proposer who wanted to earn as much as possible would choose something between the extreme of trying to take it all or dividing it equally. The farmers who offered 40% were very likely to see their offer accepted and receive 60% of the pie. In the experiment, half of the farmers chose an

Adapted from Joseph Henrich, Richard McElreath, Abigail Barr, Jean Ensminger, Clark Barrett, Alexander Bolyanatz, Juan Camilo Cardenas, Michael Gurven, Edwins Gwako, Natalie Henrich, Carolyn Lesorogol, Frank Marlowe, David Tracer, and John Ziker. 2006. 'Costly Punishment Across Human Societies'. *Science* 312 (5781): pp. 1767–1770.

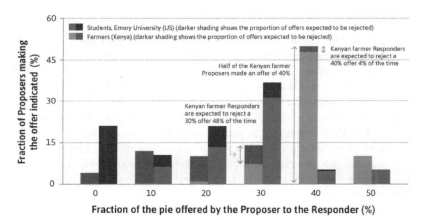

Figure 4.13 Actual offers and expected rejections in the ultimatum game.

1. What do the bars show?

The full height of each bar in the figure indicates the percentage of the Kenyan and American Proposers who made the offer shown on the horizontal axis.

2. Reading the figure

For example: for Kenyan farmers, 50% on the vertical axis and 40% on the horizontal axis means half of the Kenyan Proposers made an offer of 40%.

3. The dark-shaded area shows rejections

If Kenyan farmers made an offer of 30%, almost half of Responders would reject it. (The dark part of the bar is almost as big as the light part.)

4. Better offers, fewer rejections

The relative size of the dark area is smaller for better offers: for example Kenyan farmer Responders rejected a 40% offer only 4% of the time.

offer of 40%. We would expect the offer to be rejected only 4% of the time, as can be seen from the dark-shaded part of the bar at the 40% offer in Figure 4.13.

Now suppose you are a Kenyan farmer and all you care about is your own payoff.

Offering to give the Responder nothing is out of the question because that will ensure that you get nothing when they reject your offer. Offering half will get you half for sure—because the respondent will surely accept.

But you suspect that you can do better.

A Proposer who cares only about his own payoffs will compare what is called the expected payoffs of the two offers: that is, the payoff that one may expect, given what the other person is likely to do (accept or reject) in case this offer is made. Your expected payoff is the payoff you get if the offer is accepted, multiplied by the probability that it will be accepted (remember that if the offer is rejected, the Proposer gets nothing). Here is how the Proposer would calculate the expected payoffs of offering 40% or 30%:

Expected payoff of offering 40%:
 = 96% chance of keeping 60% of the pie
 = 0.96×0.60
 = 58

Expected payoff of offering 30%:
 = 52% chance of keeping 70% of the pie
 = 0.52×0.70
 = 36

We cannot know if the farmers actually made these calculations, of course. But if they did, they would have discovered that offering 40% maximized their expected payoff. This motivation contrasts with the case of the acceptable offers in which considerations of inequality aversion, reciprocity, or the desire to uphold a social norm were apparently at work. Unlike the Responders, many of the Proposers may have been trying to make as much money as possible in the experiment and had guessed correctly what the Responders would do.

Similar calculations indicate that, among the students, the expected payoff-maximizing offer was 30%, and this was the most common offer among them. The students' lower offers could be because they correctly anticipated that lowball offers (even as low as 10%) would sometimes be accepted. They may have been trying to maximize their payoffs and hoping that they could get away with making low offers.

EXERCISE 4.9 OFFERS IN THE ULTIMATUM GAME

1. Why do you think that some of the farmers offered more than 40%? Why did some of the students offer more than 30%?
2. Why did some offer less than 40% (farmers) and 30% (students)?
3. Which of the social preferences that you have studied might help to explain the results shown?

How do the two populations differ? Although many of the farmers and the students offered an amount that would maximize their expected payoffs, the similarity ends there. The Kenyan farmers were more likely to reject low offers. Is this a difference between Kenyans and Americans, or between farmers and students? Or is it something related to local social norms, rather than nationality and occupation? Experiments alone cannot answer these interesting questions, but before you jump to the conclusion that Kenyans are more averse to unfairness than Americans, when the same experiment was run with rural Missourians in the US, they were even more likely to reject low offers than the Kenyan farmers. Almost every Missourian Proposer offered half the pie.

QUESTION 4.10 CHOOSE THE CORRECT ANSWER(S)

Consider an ultimatum game where the Proposer offers a proportion of $100 to the Responder, who can either accept or reject the offer. If the Responder accepts, both the Proposer and the Responder keep the agreed share, while if the Responder rejects, then both receive nothing. Figure 4.12 (page 165) shows the results of a study that compares the responses of US university students and Kenyan farmers.

From this information, we can conclude that:

☐ Kenyans are more likely to reject low offers than Americans.
☐ Just over 50% of Kenyan farmers rejected the offer of the Proposer keeping 30%.
☐ Both groups of Responders are indifferent between accepting and rejecting an offer of receiving nothing.
☐ Kenyan farmers place higher importance on fairness than US students.

QUESTION 4.11 CHOOSE THE CORRECT ANSWER(S)

The following table shows the percentage of the Responders who rejected the amount offered by the Proposers in the ultimatum game played by Kenyan farmers and US university students. The pie is $100.

Amount offered		$0	$10	$20	$30	$40	$50
Proportion rejected	Kenyan farmers	100%	100%	90%	48%	4%	0%
	US students	100%	40%	35%	15%	10%	0%

From this information, we can say that:

☐ The expected payoff of offering $30 is $4.50 for the US students.
☐ The expected payoff of offering $40 is $6 for the US students.
☐ The expected payoff of offering $20 is $8 for the Kenyan farmers.
☐ The expected payoff of offering $10 is higher for the Kenyan farmers than for the US students.

4.12 COMPETITION IN THE ULTIMATUM GAME

Ultimatum game experiments with two players suggest how people may choose to share the rent arising from an economic interaction. But the outcome of a negotiation may be different if it is affected by competition. For example, the professor looking for a research assistant could consider several applicants rather than just one.

Imagine a new version of the ultimatum game in which a Proposer offers a two-way split of $100 to two respondents, instead of just one. If either of the Responders accepts but not the other, that Responder and the Proposer get the split, and the other Responder gets nothing. If no one accepts, no one gets anything, including the Proposer. If both Responders accept, one is chosen at random to receive the split.

If you are one of the Responders, what is the minimum offer you would accept? Are your answers any different, compared to the original ultimatum game with a single Responder? Perhaps. If I knew that my fellow competitor is strongly driven by 50–50 split norms, my answer would not be too different. But what if I suspect that my competitor wants the reward very much, or does not care too much about how fair the offer is?

And now suppose you are the Proposer. What split would you offer?

Figure 4.14 shows some laboratory evidence for a large group of subjects playing multiple rounds. Proposers and Responders were randomly and anonymously matched in each round.

The red bars show the fraction of offers that are rejected when there is a single Responder. The blue bars show what happens with two Responders. When there is competition, Responders are less likely to reject low offers. Their behaviour is more similar to what we would expect of self-interested individuals concerned mostly about their own monetary payoffs.

To explain this phenomenon to yourself, think about what happens when a Responder rejects a low offer. This means getting a zero payoff. Unlike the situation in which there is a sole Responder, the Responder in a competitive situation cannot be sure the Proposer will be punished, because the other Responder may accept the low offer (not everyone has the same norms about proposals, or is in the same state of need).

Consequently, even fair-minded people will accept low offers to avoid having the worst of both worlds. Of course, the Proposers also know this, so they will make lower offers, which Responders still accept. Notice how a small change in the rules or the situation can have a big effect on the outcome. As in the public goods game where the addition of an option to punish free riders greatly increased the levels of contribution, changes in the rules of the game matter.

EXERCISE 4.11 A SEQUENTIAL PRISONERS' DILEMMA

Return to the prisoners' dilemma pest control game that Anil and Bala played in Figure 4.3b (page 142), but now suppose that the game is played sequentially, like the ultimatum game. One player (chosen randomly) chooses a strategy first (the first mover), and then the second moves (the second mover).

1. Suppose you are the first mover and you know that the second mover has strong reciprocal preferences, meaning the second mover will act kindly towards someone who upholds social norms not to pollute and will act unkindly to someone who violates the norm. What would you do?
2. Suppose the reciprocal person is now the first mover interacting with the person she knows to be entirely self-interested. What do you think would be the outcome of the game?

●●●●
4.13 SOCIAL INTERACTIONS: CONFLICTS IN THE CHOICE AMONG NASH EQUILIBRIA

In the invisible hand game, the prisoners' dilemma, and the public goods game, the action that gave a player the highest payoffs did not depend on what the other player did. There was a dominant strategy for each player, and hence a single dominant strategy equilibrium.

But this is often not the case.

We have already mentioned a situation in which it is definitely untrue. Driving on the right or on the left. If others drive on the right, your best response is to drive on the right too. If they drive on the left, your best response is to drive on the left.

Adapted from Figure 6 in Urs Fischbacher, Christina M. Fong, and Ernst Fehr. 2009. 'Fairness, Errors and the Power of Competition'. *Journal of Economic Behavior & Organization* 72 (1): pp. 527–45.

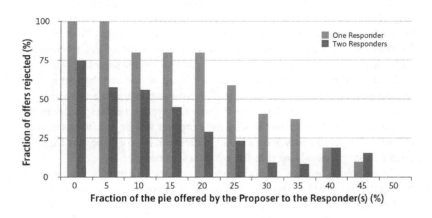

Figure 4.14 Fraction of offers rejected in the ultimatum game, according to offer size and the number of Responders.

In the US, everyone driving on the right is an equilibrium, in the sense that no one would want to change their strategy given what others are doing. In game theory, if everyone is playing their best response to the strategies of everyone else, these strategies are termed a **Nash equilibrium**.

In Japan, though, Drive on the Left is a Nash equilibrium. The driving 'game' has two Nash equilibria.

Many economic interactions do not have dominant strategy equilibria, but if we can find a Nash equilibrium, it gives us a prediction of what we should observe. We should expect to see all players doing the best they can, given what others are doing.

But even in simple economic problems there may be more than one Nash equilibrium (as in the driving game). Suppose that when Bala and Anil choose their crops the payoffs are as shown in Figure 4.15. This is different from the invisible hand game. If the two farmers produce the same crop, there is now such a large fall in price that it is better for each to specialize, even in the crop they are less suited to grow. Follow the steps in Figure 4.15 to find the two equilibria.

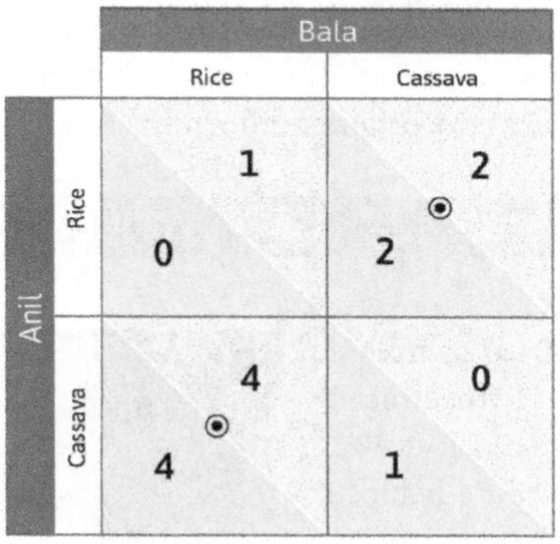

> **Nash equilibrium** A set of strategies, one for each player in the game, such that each player's strategy is a best response to the strategies chosen by everyone else.

Figure 4.15 A division of labour problem with more than one Nash equilibrium.

1. Anil's best response to Rice
If Bala is going to choose Rice, Anil's best response is to choose Cassava. We place a dot in the bottom left-hand cell.

2. Anil's best response to Cassava
If Bala is going to choose Cassava, Anil's best response is to choose Rice. Place a dot in the top right-hand cell. Notice that Anil does not have a dominant strategy.

3. Bala's best responses
If Anil chooses Rice, Bala's best response is to choose Cassava, and if Anil chooses Cassava he should choose Rice. The circles show Bala's best responses. He doesn't have a dominant strategy either.

4. (Cassava, Rice) is a Nash equilibrium
If Anil chooses Cassava and Bala chooses Rice, both of them are playing best responses (a dot and a circle coincide). So this is a Nash equilibrium.

5. (Rice, Cassava) is also a Nash equilibrium
If Anil chooses Rice and Bala chooses Cassava then both of them are playing best responses, so this is also a Nash equilibrium, but the payoffs are higher in the other equilibrium.

Situations with two Nash equilibria prompt us to ask two questions:

- Which equilibrium would we expect to observe in the world?
- Is there a conflict of interest because one equilibrium is preferable to some players, but not to others?

Whether you drive on the right or the left is not a matter of conflict in itself, as long as everyone you are driving towards has made the same decision as you. We can't say that driving on the left is better than driving on the right.

But in the division of labour game, it is clear that the Nash equilibrium with Anil choosing Cassava and Bala choosing Rice (where they specialize in the crop they produce best) is preferred to the other Nash equilibrium by both farmers.

Could we say, then, that we would expect to see Anil and Bala engaged in the 'correct' division of labour? Not necessarily. Remember, we are assuming that they take their decisions independently, without coordinating. Imagine that Bala's father had been especially good at growing cassava (unlike his son) and so the land remained dedicated to cassava even though it was better suited to producing rice. In response to this, Anil knows that Rice is his best response to Bala's Cassava, and so would have then chosen to grow rice. Bala would have no incentive to switch to what he is good at: growing rice.

The example makes an important point. If there is more than one Nash equilibrium, and if people choose their actions independently, then an economy can get 'stuck' in a Nash equilibrium in which all players are worse off than they would be at the other equilibrium.

GREAT ECONOMISTS

John Nash

John Nash (1928–2015) completed his doctoral thesis at Princeton University at the age of 21. It was just 27 pages long, yet it advanced game theory (which was a little-known branch of mathematics back then) in ways that led to a dramatic transformation of economics. He provided an answer to the question: when people interact strategically, what would one expect them to do? His answer, now known as a **Nash equilibrium**, is a collection of strategies, one for each player, such that if these strategies were to be publicly revealed, no player would regret his or her own choice. That is, if all players choose strategies that are consistent with a Nash equilibrium, then nobody can gain by unilaterally switching to a different strategy.

Nash did much more than simply introduce the concept of an equilibrium, he proved that such an equilibrium exists under very general conditions, provided that players are allowed to randomize over their available set of strategies. To see the importance of this, consider the two-player children's game rock-paper-scissors. If each of the players picks one of the three strategies with certainty, then at least one of the players would be sure to lose and would therefore have been better off choosing a different strategy. But if both players choose each available strategy with equal probability, then neither can do better by randomizing over strategies in a different way. This is accordingly a Nash equilibrium.

What Nash was able to prove is that any game with a finite number of players, each of whom has a finite number of strategies, must have at least one equilibrium, provided that players can randomize freely. This result is useful because strategies can be very complicated objects, specifying a complete plan that determines what action is to be taken in any situation that could possibly arise. The number of distinct strategies in chess, for instance, is greater than the number of atoms in the known universe. Yet we know that chess has a Nash equilibrium, although it remains unknown whether the equilibrium involves a win for white, a win for black, or a guaranteed draw.

What was remarkable about Nash's existence proof is that some of the most distinguished mathematicians of the twentieth century, including Emile Borel and John von Neumann, had tackled the problem without getting very far. They were able to show the existence of equilibrium only for certain zero-sum games; those in which the gain for one player equals the loss to the others. This clearly limited the scope of their theory for economic applications. Nash allowed for a much more general class of games, where players could have any goals whatsoever. They could be selfish, altruistic, spiteful, or fair-minded, for instance.

There is hardly a field in economics that the development of game theory has not completely transformed, and this development would have been impossible without Nash's equilibrium concept and existence proof. Remarkably, this was not Nash's only path-breaking contribution to economics—he also made a brilliantly original contribution to the theory of bargaining. In addition, he made pioneering contributions to other areas of mathematics, for which he was awarded the prestigious Abel Prize.

Nash would go on to share the Nobel Prize for his work. Roger Myerson, an economist who also won the prize, described the Nash equilibrium as 'one of the most important contributions in the history of economic thought.'

Nash originally wanted to be an electrical engineer like his father, and studied mathematics as an undergraduate at Carnegie Tech (now Carnegie-Mellon University). An elective course in International Economics stirred his interest in strategic interactions, which eventually led to his breakthrough.

For much of his life Nash suffered from mental illness that required hospitalization. He experienced hallucinations caused by schizophrenia that began in 1959, though after what he described as '25 years of partially deluded thinking' he continued his teaching and research at Princeton. The story of his insights and illness are told in the book (made into a film starring Russell Crowe) *A Beautiful Mind*.

Sylvia Nasar. 2011. *A Beautiful Mind: The Life of Mathematical Genius and Nobel Laureate John Nash*. New York, NY: Simon & Schuster.

Resolving conflict

A conflict of interest occurs if players in a game would prefer different Nash equilibria.

To see this, consider the case of Astrid and Bettina, two software engineers who are working on a project for which they will be paid. Their first decision is whether the code should be written in Java or C++ (imagine that either programming language is equally suitable, and that the project can be written partly in one language and partly in the other). They each have to choose one program or the other, but Astrid wants to write in Java because she is better at writing Java code. While this is a joint project with Bettina, her pay will be partly based on how many lines of code were written by her. Unfortunately Bettina prefers C++ for just the same reason. So the two strategies are called Java and C++.

Their interaction is described in Figure 4.16a, and their payoffs are in Figure 4.16b.

From Figure 4.16a, you can work out three things:

- They both do better if they work in the same language.
- Astrid does better if that language is Java, while the reverse is true for Bettina.
- Their total payoff is higher if they choose C++.

How would we predict the outcome of this game?

If you use the dot-and-circle method, you will find that each player's best responses are to choose the same language as the other player. So there are

		Bettina	
		Java	C++
Astrid	**Java**	Both work in the same language Astrid benefits more: she is better at Java coding	Each is working in the language they are better at But working in different languages is less productive than if both work in the same language
	C++	Each is working in the language they are less good at, and so neither works fast Working in different languages is less productive	Both work in the same language Bettina benefits more: she is better at C++ coding

Figure 4.16a Interactions in the choice of programming language.

two Nash equilibria. In one, both choose Java. In the other, both choose C++.

Can we say which of these two equilibria is more likely to occur? Astrid obviously prefers that they both play Java while Bettina prefers that they both play C++. With the information we have about how the two might interact, we can't yet predict what would happen. Exercise 4.9 gives some examples of the type of information that would help to clarify what we would observe.

EXERCISE 4.12 CONFLICT BETWEEN ASTRID AND BETTINA
What is the likely result of the game in Figure 4.16b if:

1. Astrid can choose which language she will use first, and commit to it (just as the Proposer in the ultimatum game commits to an offer, before the Responder responds)?
2. The two can make an agreement, including which language they use, and how much cash can be transferred from one to the other?
3. They have been working together for many years, and in the past they used Java on joint projects?

EXERCISE 4.13 CONFLICT IN BUSINESS
In the 1990s, Microsoft battled Netscape over market share for their web browsers, called Internet Explorer and Navigator. In the 2000s, Google and Yahoo fought over which company's search engine would be more popular. In the entertainment industry, a battle called the 'format wars' played out between Blu-Ray and HD-DVD.

Use one of these examples to analyse whether there are multiple equilibria and, if so, why one equilibrium might emerge in preference to the others.

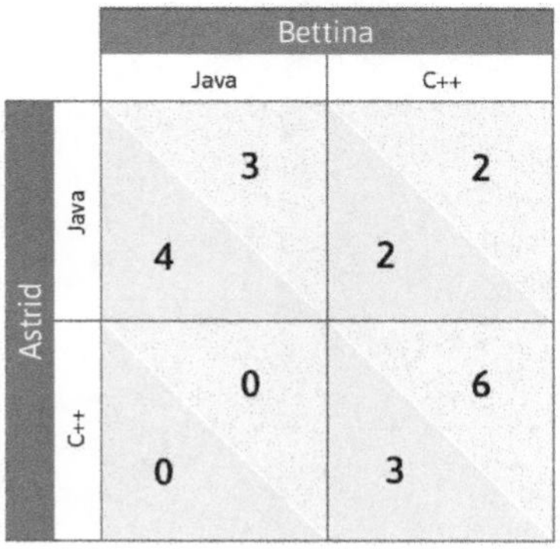

Figure 4.16b Payoffs (thousands of dollars to complete the project) according to the choice of programming language.

QUESTION 4.12 CHOOSE THE CORRECT ANSWER(S)

This table shows the payoff matrix for a simultaneous one-shot game in which Anil and Bala choose their crops.

		Bala	
		Rice	Cassava
Anil	Rice	0 1	2 2
	Cassava	4 4	1 0

We can conclude that:

☐ There are two Nash equilibria: (Cassava, Rice) and (Rice, Cassava).
☐ The choice of Cassava is a dominant strategy for Anil.
☐ The choice of Rice is a dominant strategy for Bala.
☐ There are two dominant strategy equilibria: (Cassava, Rice) and (Rice, Cassava).

EXERCISE 4.14 NASH EQUILIBRIA AND CLIMATE CHANGE

Think of the problem of climate change as a game between two countries called China and the US, considered as if each were a single individual. Each country has two possible strategies for addressing global carbon emissions: Restrict (taking measures to reduce emissions, for example by taxing the use of fossil fuels)

and BAU (the Stern report's business as usual scenario). Figure 4.17 describes the outcomes (top) and hypothetical payoffs (bottom), on a scale from best, through good and bad, to worst. This is called an ordinal scale (because all that matters is the order: whether one outcome is better than the other, and not by how much it is better).

	US	
	Restrict	BAU
China Restrict	Reduction in emissions sufficient to moderate climate change	US free rides on Chinese emissions cutbacks
China BAU	China free rides on US emissions cutbacks	No reduction in emissions

	US	
	Restrict	BAU
China Restrict	GOOD / GOOD	BEST / WORST
China BAU	WORST / BEST	BAD / BAD

	US	
	Restrict	BAU
China Restrict	BEST / BEST	GOOD / WORST
China BAU	WORST / GOOD	BAD / BAD

Figure 4.17 Climate change policy as a prisoners' dilemma (top). Payoffs for a climate change policy as a prisoners' dilemma (bottom left), and payoffs with inequality aversion and reciprocity (bottom right).

1. Show that both countries have a dominant strategy. What is the dominant strategy equilibrium?
2. The outcome would be better for both countries if they could negotiate a binding treaty to restrict emissions. Why might it be difficult to achieve this?
3. Explain how the payoffs in the bottom right of Figure 4.17 could represent the situation if both countries were inequality averse and motivated by reciprocity.

Show that there are two Nash equilibria. Would it be easier to negotiate a treaty in this case?

4. Describe the changes in preferences or in some other aspect of the problem that would convert the game to one in which (like the invisible hand game) both countries choosing Restrict is a dominant strategy equilibrium.

4.14 CONCLUSION

We have used game theory to model social interactions. The invisible hand game illustrates how markets may channel individual self-interest to achieve mutual benefits, but the dominant strategy equilibrium of the prisoners' dilemma game shows how individuals acting independently may be faced with a social dilemma.

Evidence suggests that individuals are not solely motivated by self-interest. Altruism, peer punishment, and negotiated agreements all contribute to the resolution of social dilemmas. There may be conflicts of interest over the sharing of the mutual gains from agreement, or because individuals prefer different equilibria, but social preferences and norms such as fairness can facilitate agreement.

Concepts introduced in Unit 4
Before you move on, review these definitions:

- Game
- Best response
- Dominant strategy equilibrium
- Social dilemma
- Altruism
- Reciprocity
- Inequality aversion
- Nash equilibrium
- Public good
- Prisoners' dilemma

4.15 REFERENCES

Aesop. 'Belling the Cat'. In *Fables*, retold by Joseph Jacobs. XVII, (1). The Harvard Classics. New York: P. F. Collier & Son, 1909–14; Bartleby.com (http://tinyco.re/6827567), 2001.

Bowles, Samuel. 2016. *The Moral Economy: Why Good Incentives Are No Substitute for Good Citizens*. New Haven, CT: Yale University Press.

Camerer, Colin, and Ernst Fehr. 2004. 'Measuring Social Norms and Preferences Using Experimental Games: A Guide for Social Scientists'. In *Foundations of Human Sociality: Economic Experiments and Ethnographic Evidence from Fifteen Small-Scale Societies*, eds. Joseph Henrich, Robert Boyd, Samuel Bowles, Colin Camerer, and Herbert Gintis. Oxford: Oxford University Press.

Edgeworth, Francis Ysidro. 2003. *Mathematical Psychics and Further Papers on Political Economy*. Oxford: Oxford University Press.

Falk, Armin, and James J. Heckman. 2009. 'Lab Experiments Are a Major Source of Knowledge in the Social Sciences'. *Science* 326 (5952): pp. 535–538.

Hardin, Garrett. 1968. 'The Tragedy of the Commons' (http://tinyco.re/4834967). *Science* 162 (3859): pp. 1243–1248.

Henrich, Joseph, Richard McElreath, Abigail Barr, Jean Ensminger, Clark Barrett, Alexander Bolyanatz, Juan Camilo Cardenas, Michael Gurven, Edwins Gwako, Natalie Henrich, Carolyn Lesorogol, Frank Marlowe, David Tracer, and John Ziker. 2006. 'Costly Punishment

Across Human Societies' (http://tinyco.re/2043845). *Science* 312 (5781): pp. 1767–1770.

Henrich, Joseph, Robert Boyd, Samuel Bowles, Colin Camerer, and Herbert Gintis (editors). 2004. *Foundations of Human Sociality: Economic Experiments and Ethnographic Evidence from Fifteen Small-Scale Societies*. Oxford: Oxford University Press.

IPCC. 2014. 'Climate Change 2014: Synthesis Report'. Contribution of Working Groups I, II and III to the Fifth Assessment Report of the Intergovernmental Panel on Climate Change. Geneva, Switzerland: IPCC.

Levitt, Steven D., and John A. List. 2007. 'What Do Laboratory Experiments Measuring Social Preferences Reveal About the Real World?' (http://tinyco.re/9601240). *Journal of Economic Perspectives* 21 (2): pp. 153–174.

Mencken, H. L. 2006. *A Little Book in C Major*. New York, NY: Kessinger Publishing.

Nasar, Sylvia. 2011. *A Beautiful Mind: The Life of Mathematical Genius and Novel Laureate John Nash*. New York, NY: Simon & Schuster.

Ostrom, Elinor. 2000. 'Collective Action and the Evolution of Social Norms' (http://tinyco.re/0059239). *Journal of Economic Perspectives* 14 (3): pp. 137–58.

Ostrom, Elinor. 2008. 'The Challenge of Common-Pool Resources' (http://tinyco.re/0296632). *Environment: Science and Policy for Sustainable Development* 50 (4): pp. 8–21.

Ostrom, Elinor, James Walker, and Roy Gardner. 1992. 'Covenants With and Without a Sword: Self-Governance is Possible' (http://tinyco.re/3121233). *The American Political Science Review* 86 (2).

Stern, Nicholas. 2007. *The Economics of Climate Change: The Stern Review* (http://tinyco.re/5785938). Cambridge: Cambridge University Press.

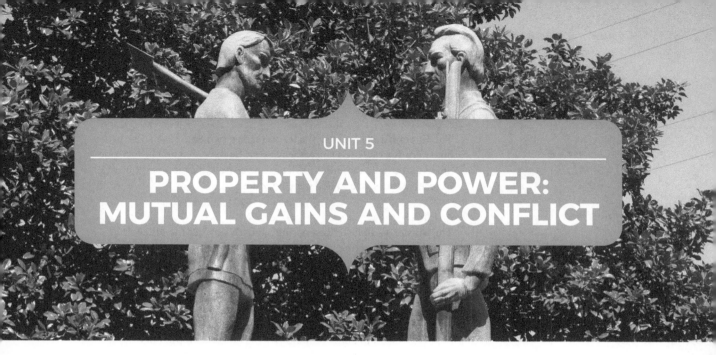

PROPERTY AND POWER: MUTUAL GAINS AND CONFLICT

HOW INSTITUTIONS INFLUENCE THE BALANCE OF POWER IN ECONOMIC INTERACTIONS, AND AFFECT THE FAIRNESS AND EFFICIENCY OF THE ALLOCATIONS THAT RESULT

- Technology, biology, economic institutions, and people's preferences are all important determinants of economic outcomes.
- Power is the ability to do and get the things we want in opposition to the intentions of others.
- Interactions between economic actors can result in mutual gains, but also in conflicts over how the gains are distributed.
- Institutions influence the power and other bargaining advantages of actors.
- The criteria of efficiency and fairness can help evaluate economic institutions and the outcomes of economic interactions.

THEMES AND CAPSTONE UNITS

- 17: History, instability, and growth
- 19: Inequality
- 22: Politics and policy

Perhaps one of your distant ancestors considered that the best way to get money was by shipping out with a pirate like Blackbeard or Captain Kidd. If he had settled on Captain Bartholomew Roberts' pirate ship the *Royal Rover*, he and the other members of the crew would have been required to consent to the ship's written constitution. This document (called *The Royal Rover's Articles*) guaranteed, among other things, that:

Peter T. Leeson. 2007. 'An–arrgh–chy: The Law and Economics of Pirate Organization'. *Journal of Political Economy* 115 (6): pp. 1049–94.

Article I
Every Man has a Vote in the Affairs on the Moment; has equal title to fresh Provisions …

Article III
No person to Game at Cards or Dice for Money.

Article IV
The Lights and Candles to be put out at eight a-Clock at Night; If any

of the Crew after that Hour still remained enclined for drinking, they are to do so on the open Deck …

Article X
The Captain and Quarter Master to receive two Shares of a Prize (the booty from a captured ship); the Master, Boatswain, and Gunner one Share and a half, and other Officers one and a Quarter (everyone else to receive one share, called his Dividend.)

Article XI
The Musicians to have Rest on the Sabbath Day but the other six Days and Nights none without special Favour.

The *Royal Rover* and its *Articles* were not unusual. During the heyday of European piracy in the late seventeenth and early eighteenth centuries, most pirate ships had written constitutions that guaranteed even more powers to the crew members. Their captains were democratically elected ('the Rank of Captain being obtained by the Suffrage of the Majority'). Many captains were also voted out, at least one for cowardice in battle. Crews also elected one of their number as the quartermaster who, when the ship was not in a battle, could countermand the captain's orders.

If your ancestor had served as a lookout and had been the first to spot a ship that was later taken as a prize, he would have received as a reward 'the best Pair of Pistols on board, over and above his Dividend'. Were he to have been seriously wounded in battle, the articles guaranteed him compensation for the injury (more for the loss of a right arm or leg than for the left). He would have worked as part of a multiracial, multi-ethnic crew of which probably about a quarter were of African origin, and the rest primarily of European descent, including Americans.

The result was that a pirate crew was often a close-knit group. A contemporary observer lamented that the pirates were 'wickedly united, and articled together'. Sailors of captured merchant ships often happily joined the 'roguish Commonwealth' of their pirate captors.

Another unhappy commentator remarked: 'These Men whom we term … the Scandal of human Nature, who were abandoned to all Vice … were strictly just among themselves.' If they were Responders in the ultimatum game (explained in Unit 4, Section 4.10), by this description they would have rejected any offer less than half of the pie!

5.1 INSTITUTIONS AND POWER

Nowhere else in the world during the late seventeenth and early eighteenth century did ordinary workers have the right to vote, to receive compensation for occupational injuries, or to be protected from the kinds of checks on arbitrary authority that were taken for granted on the *Royal Rover*. The *Royal Rover's* articles laid down in black and white the understandings among the pirates about their working conditions. They determined who did what aboard the ship and what each person would get. For example, the size of the helmsman's dividend compared to that of the gunner. There were also unwritten informal rules of appropriate behaviour that the pirates followed by custom, or to avoid condemnation by their crewmates.

These rules, both written and unwritten, were the **institutions** that governed the interactions among the crew members of the *Royal Rover*.

The institutions provided both the constraints (no drinking after 8 p.m. unless on deck) and the **incentives** (the best pair of pistols for the lookout who spotted a ship that was later taken). In the terminology of game theory from the previous unit, we could say that they were the 'rules of the game', specifying, as in the ultimatum game in Section 4.10, who can do what, when they can do it, and how the players' actions determine their payoffs.

In this unit, we use the terms 'institutions' and 'rules of the game' interchangeably.

Experiments in Unit 4 showed us that the rules of the game affect:

- how the game is played
- the size of the total payoff available to those participating
- how this total is divided

For example, in the ultimatum game the rules (institutions) specify the size of the pie, who gets to be the Proposer, what the Proposer can do (offer any fraction of the pie), what the Responder can do (accept or refuse), and who gets what as a result.

We also saw that changing the rules of the game changes the outcome. In particular, when there are two Responders in the ultimatum game, they are more likely to accept lower offers because each is not sure what the other will do. And this means that the Proposer can make a lower offer, and obtain a higher payoff.

Since institutions determine who can do what, and how payoffs are distributed, they determine the power individuals have to get what they want in interactions with others.

Power in economics takes two main forms:

- *It may set the terms of an exchange*: By making a take-it-or-leave-it offer (as in the ultimatum game).
- *It may impose or threaten to impose heavy costs*: Unless the other party acts in a way that benefits the person with power.

INSTITUTIONS
Institutions are written and unwritten rules that govern:
- what people do when they interact in a joint project
- the distribution of the products of their joint effort

incentive Economic reward or punishment, which influences the benefits and costs of alternative courses of action.

POWER
The ability to do and get the things we want in opposition to the intentions of others.

bargaining power The extent of a person's advantage in securing a larger share of the economic rents made possible by an interaction.

The rules of the ultimatum game determine the ability that the players have to obtain a high payoff—the extent of their advantage when dividing the pie—which is a form of power called **bargaining power**. The power to make a take-it-or-leave-it offer gives the Proposer more bargaining power than the Responder, and usually results in the Proposer getting more than half of the pie. Still, the Proposer's bargaining power is limited because the Responder has the power to refuse. If there are two Responders, the power to refuse is weaker, so the Proposer's bargaining power is increased.

In experiments the assignment of the role Proposer or Responder, and hence the assignment of bargaining power, is usually done by chance. In real economies, the assignment of power is definitely not random.

In the labour market, the power to set the terms of the exchange typically lies with those who own the factory or business: they are the ones proposing the wage and other terms of employment. Those seeking employment are like Responders, and since usually more than one person is applying for the same job, their bargaining power may be low, just as in the ultimatum game with more than one Responder. Also, because the place of employment is the employer's private property, the employer may be able to exclude the worker by firing her unless her work is up to the specifications of the employer.

Remember from Units 1 and 2 that the productivity of labour started to increase in Britain around the middle of the seventeenth century. But it was not until the middle of the nineteenth century that a combination of shifts in the supply and demand for labour, and new institutions such as trade unions and the right to vote for workers, gave wage earners the bargaining power to raise wages substantially.

We will see in the next unit how the labour market, along with other institutions, gives both kinds of power to employers. In Unit 7 we explain how some firms have the power to set high prices for their products, and in Unit 10, how the credit market gives power to banks and other lenders over people seeking mortgages and loans.

The power to say no

Suppose we allow a Proposer simply to divide up a pie in any way, without any role for the Responder other than to take whatever he gets (if anything). Under these rules, the Proposer has all the bargaining power and the Responder none. There is an experimental game like this, and it is called (you guessed it) the dictator game.

There are many past and present examples of economic institutions that are like the dictator game, in which there is no option to say no. Examples include today's remaining political dictatorships, such as The Democratic People's Republic of Korea (North Korea), and slavery, as it existed in the US prior to the end of the American Civil War in 1865. Criminal organizations involved in drugs and human trafficking would be another modern example, in which power may take the form of physical coercion or threats of violence.

In a capitalist economy in a democratic society, institutions exist to protect people against violence and coercion, and to ensure that most economic interactions are conducted voluntarily. Later in this unit we study the outcome of an interaction involving coercion, and how it changes with the power to say no.

5.2 EVALUATING INSTITUTIONS AND OUTCOMES: THE PARETO CRITERION

Whether it is fishermen seeking to make a living while not depleting the fish stocks, or farmers maintaining the channels of an irrigation system, or two people dividing up a pie, we want to be able to both describe what happens and to evaluate it—is it better or worse than other potential outcomes? The first involves facts; the second involves values.

We call the outcome of an economic interaction an **allocation**.

In the ultimatum game, for example, the allocation describes the proposed division of the pie by the Proposer, whether it was rejected or accepted, and the resulting payoffs to the two players.

Now suppose that we want to compare two possible allocations, A and B, that may result from an economic interaction. Can we say which is better? Suppose we find that everyone involved in the interaction would prefer allocation A. Then most people would agree that A is a better allocation than B. This criterion for judging between A and B is called the **Pareto criterion**, after Vilfredo Pareto, an Italian economist and sociologist.

Note that when we say an allocation makes someone 'better off' we mean that they prefer it, which does not necessarily mean they get more money.

> **allocation** A description of who does what, the consequences of their actions, and who gets what as a result.

> **THE PARETO CRITERION**
> According to the Pareto criterion, allocation A dominates allocation B if at least one party would be better off with A than B, and nobody would be worse off.
>
> We say that A **Pareto-dominates** B.

> **Pareto dominant** Allocation A Pareto-dominates allocation B if at least one party would be better off with A than B, and nobody would be worse off. *See also: Pareto efficient.*

GREAT ECONOMISTS

Vilfredo Pareto

Vilfredo Pareto (1848–1923), an Italian economist and sociologist, earned a degree in engineering for his research on the concept of equilibrium in physics. He is mostly remembered for the concept of efficiency that bears his name. He wanted economics and sociology to be fact-based sciences, similar to the physical sciences that he had studied when he was younger.

His empirical investigations led him to question the idea that the distribution of wealth resembles the familiar bell curve, with a few rich and a few poor in the tails of the distribution and a large middle-income class. In its place he proposed what came to be called Pareto's law, according to which, across the ages and differing types of economy, there were very few rich people and a lot of poor people.

His 80–20 rule—derived from Pareto's law—asserted that the richest 20% of a population typically held 80% of the wealth. Were he living in the US in 2015, he would have to revise that to 90% of the wealth held by the richest 20%, suggesting that his law might not be as universal as he had thought.

Vilfredo Pareto. (1906) 2014. *Manual of Political Economy: A Variorum Translation and Critical Edition*. Oxford, New York, NY: Oxford University Press.

In Pareto's view, the economic game was played for high stakes, with big winners and losers. Not surprisingly, then, he urged economists to study conflicts over the division of goods, and he thought the time and resources devoted to these conflicts were part of what economics should be about. In his most famous book, the *Manual of Political Economy* (1906), he wrote that: 'The efforts of men are utilized in two different ways: they are directed to the production or transformation of economic goods, or else to the appropriation of goods produced by others.'

Figure 5.1 compares the four allocations in the pest control game from Unit 4 by the Pareto criterion (using a similar method to the comparison of technologies in Unit 2). We assume that Anil and Bala are self-interested, so they prefer allocations with a higher payoff for themselves.

The blue rectangle with its corner at allocation (T, T) shows that (I, I) Pareto dominates (T, T). Follow the steps in Figure 5.1 to see more comparisons.

You can see from this example that the Pareto criterion may be of limited help in comparing allocations. Here, it tells us only that (I, I) is better than (T, T).

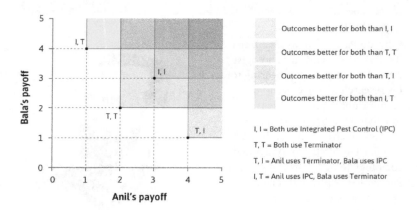

Figure 5.1 Pareto-efficient allocations. All of the allocations except mutual use of the pesticide (T, T) are Pareto efficient.

1. Anil and Bala's prisoners' dilemma
The diagram shows the allocations of the prisoners' dilemma game played by Anil and Bala.

2. A Pareto comparison
(I, I) lies in the rectangle to the north-east of (T, T), so an outcome where both Anil and Bala use IPC Pareto-dominates one where both use Terminator.

3. Compare (T, T) and (T, I)
If Anil uses Terminator and Bala IPC, then he is better off but Bala is worse off than when both use Terminator. The Pareto criterion cannot say which of these allocations is better.

4. No allocation Pareto-dominates (I, I)
None of the other allocations lie to the north-east of (I, I), so it is not Pareto-dominated.

5. What can we say about (I, T) and (T, I)?
Neither of these allocations are Pareto-dominated, but they do not dominate any other allocations either.

The diagram also shows that three of the four allocations are not Pareto-dominated by any other. An allocation with this property is called **Pareto efficient**.

If an allocation is Pareto efficient, then there is no alternative allocation in which at least one party would be better off and nobody worse off. The concept of Pareto efficiency is very widely used in economics and sounds like a good thing, but we need to be careful with it:

- *There is often more than one Pareto-efficient allocation*: In the pest-control game there are three.
- *The **Pareto criterion** does not tell us which of the Pareto-efficient allocations is better*: It does not give us any ranking of (I, I), (I, T) and (T, I).
- *If an allocation is Pareto efficient, this does not mean we should approve of it*: Anil playing IPC and Bala free riding by playing Terminator is Pareto efficient, but we (and Anil) may think this is unfair. Pareto efficiency has nothing to do with fairness.
- *Allocation (T, I) is Pareto efficient and (T, T) is not (it is Pareto inefficient)*: But the Pareto criterion does NOT tell us which is better.

There are many Pareto-efficient allocations that we would not evaluate favourably. If you look back at Figure 4.5 you can see that any split of Anil's lottery winnings (including giving Bala nothing) would be Pareto efficient (choose any point on the boundary of the feasible set of outcomes, and draw the rectangle with its corner at that point: there are no feasible points above and to the right). But some of these splits would seem very unfair. Similarly, in the ultimatum game an allocation of one cent to the Responder and $99.99 to the Proposer is also Pareto efficient, because there is no way to make the Responder better off without making the Proposer worse off.

The same is true of problems such as the allocation of food. If some people are more than satisfied while others are starving, we might say in everyday language: 'This is not a sensible way to provide nutrition. It is clearly inefficient.' But Pareto efficiency means something different. A very unequal distribution of food can be Pareto efficient as long as all the food is eaten by someone who enjoys it even a little.

Pareto efficient An allocation with the property that there is no alternative technically feasible allocation in which at least one person would be better off, and nobody worse off.

PARETO EFFICIENCY
An allocation that is not Pareto-dominated by any other allocation is described as Pareto efficient.

Pareto criterion According to the Pareto criterion, a desirable attribute of an allocation is that it be Pareto-efficient. *See also: Pareto dominant.*

QUESTION 5.1 CHOOSE THE CORRECT ANSWER(S)
Which of the following statements about the outcome of an economic interaction is correct?

- ☐ If the allocation is Pareto efficient, then you cannot make anyone better off without making someone else worse off.
- ☐ All participants are happy with what they get if the allocation is Pareto efficient.
- ☐ There cannot be more than one Pareto-efficient outcome.
- ☐ According to the Pareto criterion, a Pareto-efficient outcome is always better than an inefficient one.

5.3 EVALUATING INSTITUTIONS AND OUTCOMES: FAIRNESS

Although the Pareto criterion can help us to evaluate allocations, we will also want to use another criterion: justice. We will ask, is it fair?

Suppose, in the ultimatum game, the Proposer offered one cent from a total of $100. As we saw in Unit 4, Responders in experiments around the world typically reject such an offer, apparently judging it to be unfair. Many of us would have a similar reaction if we witnessed two friends, An and Bai, walking down the street. They spot a $100 bill, which An picks up. She offers one cent to her friend Bai, and says she wants to keep the rest.

We might be outraged. But we might think differently if we discovered that, though both An and Bai had worked hard all their lives, An had just lost her job and was homeless while Bai was well off. Letting An keep $99.99 might then seem fair. Thus we might apply a different standard of justice to the outcome when we know all of the facts.

We could also apply a standard of fairness not to the *outcome* of the game, but to the *rules of the game*. Suppose we had observed An proposing an even split, allocating $50 to Bai. Good for An, you say, that seems like a fair outcome. But if this occurred because Bai pulled a gun on An, and threatened that unless she offered an even split she would shoot her, we would probably judge the outcome to be unfair.

The example makes a basic point about fairness. Allocations can be judged unfair because of:

- *How unequal they are*: In terms of income, for example, or subjective wellbeing. These are **substantive judgments of fairness**.
- *How they came about*: For example by force, or by competition on a level playing field. These are **procedural judgements of fairness**.

Substantive and procedural judgements

To make a substantive judgement about fairness, all you need to know is the allocation itself. However, for procedural evaluations we also need to know the rules of the game and other factors that explain why this allocation occurred.

Two people making substantive evaluations of fairness about the same situation need not agree, of course. For example, they may disagree about whether fairness should be evaluated in terms of income or happiness. If we measure fairness using happiness as the criterion, a person with a serious physical or mental handicap may need much more income than a person without such disabilities to be equally satisfied with his or her life.

Substantive judgements

These are based on inequality in some aspect of the allocation such as:

- *Income*: The reward in money (or some equivalent measure) of the individual's command over valued goods and services.
- *Happiness*: Economists have developed indicators by which subjective wellbeing can be measured.
- *Freedom*: The extent that one can do (or be) what one chooses without socially imposed limits.

---

substantive judgements of fairness
Judgements based on the characteristics of the allocation itself, not how it was determined. *See also: procedural judgements of fairness.*
procedural judgements of fairness
An evaluation of an outcome based on how the allocation came about, and not on the characteristics of the outcome itself, (for example, how unequal it is). *See also: substantive judgements of fairness.*

Andrew Clark and Andrew Oswald. 2002. 'A Simple Statistical Method for Measuring How Life Events Affect Happiness'. *International Journal of Epidemiology* 31 (6): pp. 1139–1144.

> **EXERCISE 5.1 SUBSTANTIVE FAIRNESS**
> Consider the society you live in, or another society with which you are familiar.
>
> 1. To make society fairer, would you want greater equality of income, happiness, or freedom? Why? Would there be a trade-off between these aspects?
> 2. Are there other things that should be more equal to achieve greater fairness in this society?

Procedural judgements

The rules of the game that brought about the allocation may be evaluated according to aspects such as:

- *Voluntary exchange of private property acquired by legitimate means*: Were the actions resulting in the allocation the result of freely chosen actions by the individuals involved, for example each person buying or selling things that they had come to own through inheritance, purchase, or their own labour? Or was fraud or force involved?
- *Equal opportunity for economic advantage*: Did people have an equal opportunity to acquire a large share of the total to be divided up, or were they subjected to some kind of discrimination or other disadvantage because of their race, sexual preference, gender, or who their parents were?
- *Deservingness*: Did the rules of the game that determined the allocation take account of the extent to which an individual worked hard, or otherwise upheld social norms?

We can use these differing judgements to evaluate an outcome in the ultimatum game. The experimental rules of the game will appear to most people's minds as procedurally fair:

- Proposers are chosen randomly.
- The game is played anonymously.
- Discrimination is not possible.
- All actions are voluntary. The Responder can refuse to accept the offer, and the Proposer is typically free to propose any amount.

> **EXERCISE 5.2 PROCEDURAL FAIRNESS**
> Consider the society in which you live, or another society with which you are familiar. How fair is this society, according to the procedural judgements of fairness listed above?

Substantive judgements are evaluations of the allocation itself: how the pie is shared. We know from the behaviour of experimental subjects that many people would judge an allocation in which the Proposer took 90% of the pie to be unfair.

Evaluating fairness

The rules of the game in the real economy are a long way from the fair procedures of the ultimatum game, and procedural judgements of unfairness are very important to many people, as we will see in Unit 19 (Economic inequality).

People's values about what is fair differ. Some, for example, regard any amount of inequality as fair, as long as the rules of the game are fair. Others judge an allocation to be unfair if some people are seriously deprived of basic needs, while others consume luxuries.

The American philosopher John Rawls (1921–2002) devised a way to clarify these arguments, which can sometimes help us to find common ground on questions of values. We follow three steps:

1. *We adopt the principle that fairness applies to all people*: For example, if we swapped the positions of An and Bai, so that it was Bai instead of An who picked up $100, we would still apply exactly the same standard of justice to evaluate the outcome.
2. *Imagine a veil of ignorance*: Since fairness applies to everyone, including ourselves, Rawls asks us to imagine ourselves behind what he called a veil of ignorance, not knowing the position that we would occupy in the society we are considering. We could be male or female, healthy or ill, rich or poor (or with rich or poor parents), in a dominant or an ethnic minority group, and so on. In the $100 on the street game, we would not know if we would be the person picking up the money, or the person responding to the offer.
3. *From behind the veil of ignorance, we can make a judgement*: For example, the choice of a set of institutions—imagining as we do so that we will then become part of the society we have endorsed, with an equal chance of having any of the positions occupied by individuals in that society.

The veil of ignorance invites you, in making a judgement about fairness, to put yourself in the shoes of others quite different from yourself. You would then, Rawls argued, be able to evaluate the constitutions, laws, inheritance practices, and other institutions of a society as an impartial outsider.

EXERCISE 5.3 SPLITTING THE PROFITS IN A PARTNERSHIP

Suppose you and a partner are starting a business involving each of you selling a new app to the public. You are deciding how to divide the profits and are considering four alternatives. The profits could be split:

- equally
- in proportion to how many apps each of you sells
- in inverse proportion to how much income each of you has from other sources (for example, if one of you has twice the income of the other, the profits could be split one-third to the former and two-thirds to the latter)
- in proportion to how many hours each of you has spent selling.

Order these alternatives according to your preference and give arguments based on the concepts of fairness introduced in this section. If the order depends on other facts about this joint project, say what other facts you would need.

Neither philosophy, nor economics, nor any other science, can eliminate disagreements about questions of value. But economics can clarify:

- *How the dimensions of unfairness may be connected*: For example, how the rules of the game that give special advantages to one or another group may affect the degree of inequality.
- *The trade-offs between the dimensions of fairness*: For example, do we have to compromise on the equality of income if we also want equality of opportunity?
- *Public policies to address concerns about unfairness*: Also, whether these policies compromise other objectives.

5.4 A MODEL OF CHOICE AND CONFLICT

In the remainder of this unit we explore some economic interactions and evaluate the resulting allocations. As in the experiments in Unit 4, we will see that both cooperation and conflict occur. As in the experiments, and in history, we will find that the rules matter.

Recall the model in Unit 3 of the farmer, Angela, who produces a crop. We will develop the model into a sequence of scenarios involving two characters:

1. Initially, Angela works the land on her own, and gets everything she produces.
2. Next, we introduce a second person, who does not farm, but would also like some of the harvest. He is called Bruno.
3. At first, Bruno can force Angela to work for him. In order to survive, she has to do what he says.
4. Later, the rules change: the rule of law replaces the rule of force. Bruno can no longer coerce Angela to work. But he owns the land and if she wants to farm his land, she must agree, for example, to pay him some part of the harvest.
5. Eventually, the rules of the game change again in Angela's favour. She and her fellow farmers achieve the right to vote and legislation is passed that increases Angela's claim on the harvest.

For each of these steps we will analyse the changes in terms of both Pareto efficiency and the distribution of income between Angela and Bruno. Remember that:

- We can determine objectively whether an outcome is Pareto efficient or not.
- But whether the outcome is fair depends on your own analysis of the problem, using the concepts of substantive and procedural fairness.

As before, Angela's harvest depends on her hours of work, through the production function. She works the land, and enjoys the remainder of the day as free time. In Unit 3 she consumed the grain that this activity produced. Recall that the slope of the feasible frontier is the **marginal rate of transformation (MRT)** of free time into grain.

Angela values both grain and free time. Again, we represent her preferences as indifference curves, showing the combinations of grain and free time that she values equally. Remember that the slope of the indifference curve is called the **marginal rate of substitution (MRS)** between grain and free time.

Angela works the land on her own

Figure 5.2 shows Angela's indifference curves and her feasible frontier. The steeper the indifference curve, the more Angela values free time relative to grain. You can see that the more free time she has (moving to the right), the flatter the curves—she values free time less.

In this unit, we make a particular assumption (called quasi-linearity) about Angela's preferences that you can see in the shape of her indifference curves. As she gets more grain, her MRS does not change. So the curves have the same slope as you move up the vertical line at 16 hours of free

> **marginal rate of transformation (MRT)** The quantity of some good that must be sacrificed to acquire one additional unit of another good. At any point, it is the slope of the feasible frontier. *See also: marginal rate of substitution.*

> **marginal rate of substitution (MRS)** The trade-off that a person is willing to make between two goods. At any point, this is the slope of the indifference curve. *See also: marginal rate of transformation.*

time. More grain does not change her valuation of free time relative to grain.

Why might this be? Perhaps she does not eat it all, but sells some and uses the proceeds to buy other things she needs. This is just a simplification (called quasi-linearity) that makes our model easier to understand. Remember: when drawing indifference curves for the model in this unit, simply shift them up and down, keeping the MRS constant at a given amount of free time.

Angela is free to choose her typical hours of work to achieve her preferred combination of free time and grain. Work through Figure 5.2 to determine the allocation.

Figure 5.2 shows that the best Angela can do, given the limits set by the feasible frontier, is to work for 8 hours. She has 16 hours of free time, and produces and consumes 9 bushels of grain. This is the number of hours of work where the marginal rate of substitution is equal to the marginal rate of transformation. She cannot do better than this! (If you're not sure why, go back to Unit 3 and check.)

A new character appears

But now, Angela has company. The other person is called Bruno; he is not a farmer but will claim some of Angela's harvest. We will study different rules of the game that explain how much is produced by Angela, and how it is divided between her and Bruno. For example, in one scenario, Bruno is the

Leibniz: Quasi-linear preferences (http://tinyco.re/L050401)

Leibniz: Angela's choice of working hours (http://tinyco.re/L050402)

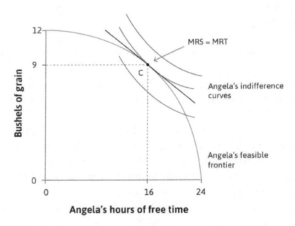

Figure 5.2 Independent farmer Angela's feasible frontier, best feasible indifference curve, and choice of hours of work.

1. The feasible frontier
The diagram shows Angela's feasible frontier, determined by her production function.

2. The best Angela can do
The best Angela can do, given the limits set by the feasible frontier, is to work for 8 hours, taking 16 hours of free time and producing 9 bushels of grain. At this point C, the marginal rate of substitution (MRS) is equal to the marginal rate of transformation (MRT).

3. MRS = MRT
The MRS is the slope of the indifference curve. The trade-off she is willing to make between grain and free time. The MRT is the slope of the feasible frontier: the trade-off she is constrained to make. At point C, the two trade-offs balance.

landowner and Angela pays some grain to him as rent for the use of the land.

Figure 5.3 shows Angela and Bruno's combined feasible frontier. The frontier indicates how many bushels of grain Angela can produce given how much free time she takes. For example, if she takes 12 hours free time and works for 12 hours, then she produces 10.5 bushels of grain. One possible outcome of the interaction between Angela and Bruno is that 5.25 bushels go to Bruno, and Angela retains the other 5.25 bushels for her own consumption.

Work through Figure 5.3 to find out how each possible allocation is represented in the diagram, showing how much work Angela did and how much grain she and Bruno each got.

Which allocations are likely to occur? Not all of them are even possible. For example, at point H Angela works 12 hours a day and receives nothing (Bruno takes the entire harvest), so Angela would not survive. Of the allocations that are at least possible, the one that will occur depends on the rules of the game.

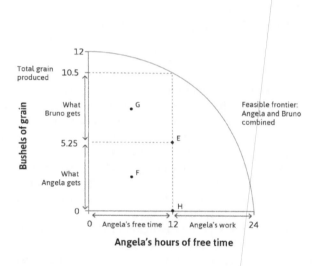

Figure 5.3 Feasible outcomes of the interaction between Angela and Bruno.

1. The combined feasible frontier
The feasible frontier shows the maximum amount of grain available to Angela and Bruno together, given Angela's amount of free time. If Angela takes 12 hours of free time and works for 12 hours then she produces 10.5 bushels of grain.

2. A feasible allocation
Point E is a possible outcome of the interaction between Angela and Bruno.

3. The distribution at point E
At point E, Angela works for 12 hours and produces 10.5 bushels of grain. The distribution of grain is such that 5.25 bushels go to Bruno and Angela retains the other 5.25 bushels for her own consumption.

4. Other feasible allocations
Point F shows an allocation in which Angela works more than at point E and gets less grain, and point G shows the case in which she works more and gets more grain.

5. An impossible allocation
An outcome at H—in which Angela works 12 hours a day, Bruno consumes the entire amount produced and Angela consumes nothing—would not be possible: she would starve.

EXERCISE 5.4 USING INDIFFERENCE CURVES

In Figure 5.3 (page 193), point F shows an allocation in which Angela works more and gets less than at point E, and point G shows the case in which she works more and gets more.

By sketching Angela's indifference curves, work out what you can say about her preferences between E, F and G, and how this depends on the slope of the curves.

QUESTION 5.2 CHOOSE THE CORRECT ANSWER(S)

Figure 5.3 (page 193) shows Angela and Bruno's combined feasible set, and four allocations that might result from an interaction between them.

From the figure, we can conclude that:

☐ If Angela has very flat indifference curves, she may prefer G to the other three allocations.
☐ If Angela has very steep indifference curves, she may prefer F to the other three allocations.
☐ Allocation G is the best of the four for Bruno.
☐ It is possible that Angela is indifferent between G and E.

5.5 TECHNICALLY FEASIBLE ALLOCATIONS

Initially Angela could consume (or sell) everything she produced. Now Bruno has arrived, and he has a gun. He has the power to implement any allocation that he chooses. He is even more powerful than the dictator in the dictator game (in which a Proposer dictates how a pie is to be divided). Why? Bruno can determine the size of the pie, as well as how it is shared.

Unlike the experimental subjects in Unit 4, in this model Bruno and Angela are entirely self-interested. Bruno wants only to maximize the amount of grain he can get. Angela cares only about her own free time and grain (as described by her indifference curves).

We now make another important assumption. If Angela does not work the land, Bruno gets nothing (there are no other prospective farmers that he can exploit). What this means is that Bruno's reservation option (what he gets if Angela does not work for him) is zero. As a result, Bruno thinks about the future: he will not take so much grain that Angela will die. The allocation must keep her alive.

technically feasible An allocation within the limits set by technology and biology.

First, we will work out the set of **technically feasible** combinations of Angela's hours of work and the amount of grain she receives: that is, all the combinations that are possible within the limitations of the technology (the production function) and biology (Angela must have enough nutrition to do the work and survive).

biologically feasible An allocation that is capable of sustaining the survival of those involved is biologically feasible.

Figure 5.4 shows how to find the technically feasible set. We already know that the production function determines the feasible frontier. This is the technological limit on the total amount consumed by Bruno and Angela, which in turn depends on the hours that Angela works. Angela's biological survival constraint shows the minimum amount of grain that she needs for each amount of work that she does; points below this line would leave her so undernourished or overworked that she would not survive. This constraint shows what is **biologically feasible**. Notice that if she expends more energy working, she needs more food; that's why the curve rises from right to left from point Z as her hours of work increase. The slope of the biological survival constraint is the marginal rate of substitution between free time and grain in securing Angela's survival.

Note that there is a maximum amount of work that would allow her barely to survive (because of the calories she burns up working). As we saw in Unit 2, throughout human history people crossed the survival threshold when the population outran the food supply. This is the logic of the Malthusian population trap. The productivity of labour placed a limit on how large the population could be.

The fact that Angela's survival might be in jeopardy is not a hypothetical example. During the Industrial Revolution, life expectancy at birth in Liverpool, UK, fell to 25 years: slightly more than half of what it is today in the poorest countries in the world. In many parts of the world today, farmers' and workers' capacity to do their jobs is limited by their caloric intake.

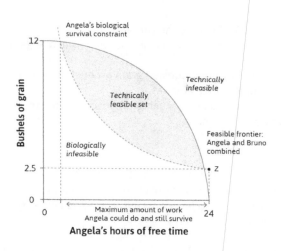

Figure 5.4 Technically feasible allocations.

1. The biological survival constraint
If Angela does not work at all, she needs 2.5 bushels to survive (point Z). If she gives up some free time and expends energy working, she needs more food, so the curve is higher when she has less free time. This is the biological survival constraint.

2. Biologically infeasible and technically infeasible points
Points below the biological survival constraint are biologically infeasible, while points above the feasible frontier are technically infeasible.

3. Angela's maximum working day
Given the feasible frontier, there is a maximum amount of work above which Angela could not survive, even if she could consume everything she produced.

4. The technically feasible set
The technically feasible allocations are the points in the lens-shaped area bounded by the feasible frontier and the biological survival constraint (including points on the frontier).

EXERCISE 5.5 CHANGING CONDITIONS FOR PRODUCTION
Using Figure 5.4 (page 195), explain how you would represent the effects of each of the following:

1. an improvement in growing conditions such as more adequate rainfall
2. Angela having access to half the land that she had previously
3. the availability to Angela of a better designed hoe making it physically easier to do the work of farming.

In Angela's case, it is not only the limited productivity of her labour that might jeopardize her survival, but also how much of what she produces is taken by Bruno. If Angela could consume everything she produced (the height of the feasible frontier) and choose her hours of work, her survival would not be in jeopardy since the biological survival constraint is below the feasible frontier for a wide range of working hours. The question of biological feasibility arises because of Bruno's claims on her output.

In Figure 5.4, the boundaries of the feasible solutions to the allocation problem are formed by the feasible frontier and the biological survival constraint. This lens-shaped shaded area gives the technically possible outcomes. We can now ask what will actually happen—which allocation will occur, and how does this depend on the institutions governing Bruno's and Angela's interaction?

QUESTION 5.3 CHOOSE THE CORRECT ANSWER(S)
Figure 5.4 (page 195) shows Angela and Bruno's feasible frontier, and Angela's biological survival constraint.

Based on this figure, which of the following is correct?

☐ If Angela works 24 hours she can survive.
☐ There is a technically feasible allocation in which Angela does not work.
☐ A new technology that boosted grain production would result in a bigger technically feasible set.
☐ If Angela did not need so much grain to survive the technically feasible set would be smaller.

5.6 ALLOCATIONS IMPOSED BY FORCE

With the help of his gun, Bruno can choose any point in the lens-shaped technically feasible set of allocations. But which will he choose?

He reasons like this:

BRUNO: For any number of hours that I order Angela to work, she will produce the amount of grain shown by the feasible frontier. But I'll have to give her at least the amount shown by the biological survival constraint for that much work, so that I can continue to exploit her. I get to keep the difference between what she produces and what I give her. Therefore I should find the hours of Angela's work for which the vertical distance between the feasible frontier and the biological survival constraint (Figure 5.5) is the greatest.

economic rent A payment or other benefit received above and beyond what the individual would have received in his or her next best alternative (or reservation option). *See also: reservation option.*

The amount that Bruno will get if he implements this strategy is his **economic rent**, meaning the amount he gets over what he would get if Angela were not his slave (which, in this model, we set at zero).

Bruno first considers letting Angela continue to work 8 hours a day, producing 9 bushels, as she did when she had free access to the land. For 8 hours of work she needs 3.5 bushels of grain to survive. So Bruno could take 5.5 bushels without jeopardizing his future opportunities to benefit from Angela's labour.

Bruno is studying Figure 5.5 and asks for your help. You have noticed that the MRS on the survival constraint is less than the MRT at 8 hours of work:

YOU: Bruno, your plan cannot be right. If you forced her to work a little more, she'd only need a little more grain to have the energy to work longer, because the biological survival constraint is relatively flat at 8 hours of work. But the feasible frontier is steep, so she would produce a lot more if you imposed longer hours.

You demonstrate the argument to him using the analysis in Figure 5.5, which indicates that the vertical distance between the feasible frontier and the biological survival constraint is the greatest when Angela works for 11 hours. If Bruno commands Angela to work for 11 hours, then she will produce 10 bushels and Bruno will get to keep 6 bushels for himself. We can use Figure 5.5 to find out how many bushels of grain Bruno will get for any technically feasible allocation.

The lower panel in the last step in Figure 5.5 shows how the amount Bruno can take varies with Angela's free time. The graph is hump-shaped, and peaks at 13 hours of free time and 11 hours of work. Bruno maximizes his amount of grain at allocation B, commanding Angela to work for 11 hours.

Notice how the slopes of the feasible frontier and the survival constraint (the MRT and MRS) help us to find the number of hours where Bruno can take the maximum amount of grain. To the right of 13 hours of free time (that is, if Angela works less than 11 hours) the biological survival constraint is flatter than the feasible frontier (MRS < MRT). This means that working more hours (moving to the left) would produce more grain than what Angela needs for the extra work. To the left of 13 hours of free time (Angela working more), the reverse is true: MRS > MRT. Bruno's economic rent is greatest at the hours of work where the slopes of the two frontiers are equal.

That is:

MRT of work hours into grain output
= MRS of work hours into subsistence requirements

QUESTION 5.4 CHOOSE THE CORRECT ANSWER(S)
Figure 5.5 (page 198) shows Angela and Bruno's feasible frontier, and Angela's biological survival constraint.

If Bruno can impose the allocation:

☐ He will choose the technically feasible allocation where Angela produces the most grain.
☐ His preferred choice will be where the marginal rate of transformation (MRT) on the feasible frontier equals the marginal rate of substitution (MRS) on the biological survival constraint.
☐ He will not choose 8 hours of work, because the MRS between Angela's work hours and subsistence requirements exceeds the MRT between work hours and grain output.
☐ He will choose 13 hours of free time for Angela, and consume 10 bushels of grain.

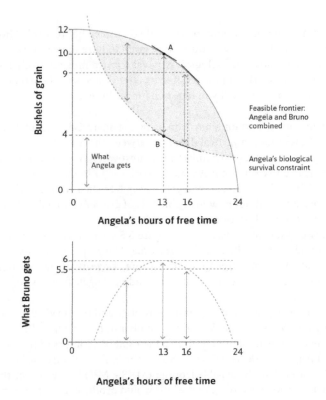

Figure 5.5 Coercion: The maximum technically feasible transfer from Angela to Bruno.

1. Bruno can command Angela to work
Bruno can choose any allocation in the technically feasible set. He considers letting Angela continue working 8 hours a day, producing 9 bushels.

2. When Angela works for 8 hours
Bruno could take 5.5 bushels without jeopardizing his future benefit from Angela's labour. This is shown by the vertical distance between the feasible frontier and the survival constraint.

3. The maximum distance between frontiers
The vertical distance between the feasible frontier and the biological survival constraint is greatest when Angela works for 11 hours (13 hours of free time).

4. Allocation and distribution at the maximum distance
If Bruno commands Angela to work for 11 hours, she will produce 10 bushels, and needs 4 to survive. Bruno will get to keep 6 bushels for himself (the distance AB).

5. At high working hours the survival frontier becomes steeper
If Bruno makes Angela work for more than 11 hours, the amount he can take falls as working hours increase.

6. The best Bruno can do for himself
Bruno gets the maximum amount of grain by choosing allocation B, where Angela's working time is such that the slope of the feasible frontier is equal to the slope of the biological survival constraint: MRT = MRS.

7. What Bruno gets
If we join up the points then we can see that the amount Bruno gets is hump-shaped, and peaks at 11 hours of work (13 hours of free time).

New institutions: Law and private property

The economic interaction described in this section takes place in an environment where Bruno has the power to enslave Angela. If we move from a scenario of coercion to one in which there is a legal system that prohibits slavery and protects **private property** and the rights of landowners and workers, we can expect the outcome of the interaction to change.

In Unit 1, we defined private property as the right to use and exclude others from the use of something, and the right to sell it (or to transfer these rights to others). From now on we will suppose that Bruno owns the land and can exclude Angela if he chooses. How much grain he will get as a result of his private ownership of the land will depend on the extent of his **power** over Angela in the new situation.

When people participate voluntarily in an interaction, they do so because they expect the outcome to be better than their reservation option—the next-best alternative. In other words, they do so in pursuit of **economic rents**. Economic rents are also sometimes called **gains from exchange**, because they are how much a person gains by engaging in the exchange compared to not engaging.

The sum of the economic rents is termed the surplus (or sometimes the **joint surplus**, to emphasize that it includes all of the rents). How much rent they will each get—how they will share the surplus—depends on their **bargaining power**. And that, as we know, depends on the institutions governing the interaction.

In the example above, Angela was forced to participate and Bruno chose her working hours to maximize his own economic rent. Next we look at the situation where she can simply say no. Angela is no longer a slave, but Bruno still has the power to make a take-it-or-leave-it offer, just like the Proposer in the ultimatum game.

5.7 ECONOMICALLY FEASIBLE ALLOCATIONS AND THE SURPLUS

We check back on Angela and Bruno, and immediately notice that Bruno is now wearing a suit, and is no longer armed. He explains that this is no longer needed because there is now a government with laws administered by courts, and professional enforcers called the police. Bruno now owns the land, and Angela must have permission to use his property. He can offer a contract allowing her to farm the land, and give him part of the harvest in return. But the law requires that exchange is voluntary: Angela can refuse the offer.

BRUNO: It used to be a matter of power, but now both Angela and I have property rights: I own the land, and she owns her own labour. The new rules of the game mean that I can no longer force Angela to work. She has to agree to the allocation that I propose.

YOU: And if she doesn't?

BRUNO: Then there is no deal. She doesn't work on my land, I get nothing, and she gets barely enough to survive from the government.

YOU: So you and Angela have the same amount of power?

BRUNO: Certainly not! I am the one who gets to make a take-it-or-leave-it offer. I am like the Proposer in the ultimatum game, except that this is no game. If she refuses she goes hungry.

---

private property The right and expectation that one can enjoy one's possessions in ways of one's own choosing, exclude others from their use, and dispose of them by gift or sale to others who then become their owners.

power The ability to do (and get) the things one wants in opposition to the intentions of others, ordinarily by imposing or threatening sanctions.

economic rent A payment or other benefit received above and beyond what the individual would have received in his or her next best alternative (or reservation option). *See also: reservation option.*
gains from exchange The benefits that each party gains from a transaction compared to how they would have fared without the exchange. *Also known as: gains from trade. See also: economic rent.*

surplus, joint The sum of the economic rents of all involved in an interaction. *Also known as: total gains from exchange or trade.*
bargaining power The extent of a person's advantage in securing a larger share of the economic rents made possible by an interaction.

YOU: But if she refuses you get zero?
BRUNO: That will never happen.

Why does he know this? Bruno knows that Angela, unlike the subjects in the ultimatum game experiments, is entirely self-interested (she does not punish an unfair offer). If he makes an offer that is just a tiny bit better for Angela than not working at all and getting subsistence rations, she will accept it.

Now he asks you a question similar to the one he asked earlier:

BRUNO: In this case, what should my take-it-or-leave-it offer be?

You answered before by showing him the biological survival constraint. Now the limitation is not Angela's survival, but rather her agreement. You know that she values her free time, so the more hours he offers her to work, the more he is going to have to pay.

YOU: Why don't you just look at Angela's indifference curve that passes through the point where she does not work at all and barely survives? That will tell you how much is the least you can pay her for each of the hours of free time she would give up to work for you.

reservation option A person's next best alternative among all options in a particular transaction. *Also known as: fallback option. See also: reservation price.*

reservation indifference curve A curve that indicates allocations (combinations) that are as highly valued as one's reservation option.

Point Z in Figure 5.6 is the allocation in which Angela does no work and gets only survival rations (from the government, or perhaps her family). This is her **reservation option**: if she refuses Bruno's offer, she has this option as a backup. Follow the steps in Figure 5.6 to see Angela's **reservation indifference curve**: all of the allocations that have the same value for her as the reservation option. Below or to the left of the curve she is worse off than in her reservation option. Above and to the right she is better off.

The set of points bounded by the reservation indifference curve and the feasible frontier is the set of all economically feasible allocations, now that Angela has to agree to the proposal that Bruno makes. Bruno thanks you for this handy new tool for figuring out the most he can get from Angela.

The biological survival constraint and the reservation indifference curve have a common point (Z): at that point, Angela does no work and gets subsistence rations from the government. Other than that, the two curves differ. The reservation indifference curve is uniformly above the biological survival constraint. The reason, you explain to Bruno, is that however hard she works along the survival constraint, she barely survives; and the more she works the less free time she has, so the unhappier she is. Along the reservation indifference curve, by contrast, she is just as well off as at her reservation option, meaning that being able to keep more of the grain that she produces compensates exactly for her lost free time.

EXERCISE 5.6 BIOLOGICAL AND ECONOMIC FEASIBILITY
Using Figure 5.6:

1. Explain why a point on the biological survival constraint is higher (more grain is required) when Angela has fewer hours of free time. Why does the curve also get steeper when she works more?
2. Explain why the biologically feasible set is not equal to the economically feasible set.
3. Explain (by shifting the curves) what happens if a more nutritious kind of grain is available for Angela to grow and consume.

We can see that both Angela and Bruno may benefit if a deal can be made. Their exchange—allowing her to use his land (that is, not using his property right to exclude her) in return for her sharing some of what she produces—makes it possible for both to be better off than if no deal had been struck.

- As long as Bruno gets some of the crop he will do better than if there is no deal.
- As long as Angela's share makes her better off than she would have been if she took her reservation option, taking account of her work hours, she will also benefit.

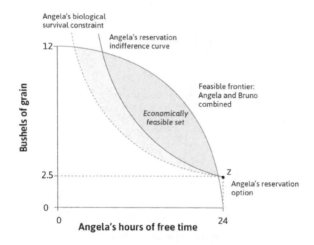

Figure 5.6 Economically feasible allocations when exchange is voluntary.

1. Angela's reservation option
Point Z, the allocation in which Angela does not work and gets only survival rations from the government, is called her **reservation option**.

2. Angela's reservation indifference curve
The curve showing all of the allocations that are just as highly valued by Angela as the reservation option is called her **reservation indifference curve**.

3. The economically feasible set
The points in the area bounded by the reservation indifference curve and the feasible frontier (including the points on the frontiers) define the set of all economically feasible allocations.

This potential for mutual gain is why their exchange need not take place at the point of a gun, but can be motivated by the desire of both to be better off.

All of the allocations that represent mutual gains are shown in the economically feasible set in Figure 5.6. Each of these allocations Pareto-dominates the allocation that would occur without a deal. In other words, Bruno and Angela could achieve a **Pareto improvement**.

> **Pareto improvement** A change that benefits at least one person without making anyone else worse off. *See also: Pareto dominant.*

This does not mean that both parties will benefit equally. If the institutions in effect give Bruno the power to make a take-it-or-leave-it offer, subject only to Angela's agreement, he can capture the entire surplus (minus the tiny bit necessary to get Angela to agree). Bruno knows this already.

Once you have explained the reservation indifference curve to him, Bruno knows which allocation he wants. He maximizes the amount of grain he can get at the maximum height of the lens-shaped region between Angela's reservation indifference curve and the feasible frontier. This will be where the MRT on the feasible frontier is equal to the MRS on the indifference curve. Figure 5.7a shows that this allocation requires Angela to work for fewer hours than she did under coercion.

So Bruno would like Angela to work for 8 hours and give him 4.5 bushels of grain (allocation D). How can he implement this allocation? All he has to do is to make a take-it-or-leave-it offer of a contract allowing Angela to work the land, in return for a land rent of 4.5 bushels per day. (This is a sharecropping contract, in which a landowner allows a farmer to use land in return for a share of the crop.) If Angela has to pay 4.5 bushels (CD in Figure 5.7a) then she will *choose* to produce at point C, where she works for 8 hours. You can see this in the figure; if she produced at any

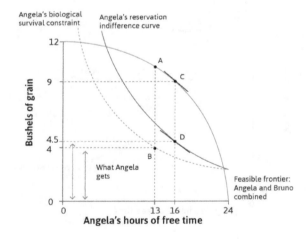

Figure 5.7a Bruno's take-it-or-leave-it proposal when Angela can refuse.

1. Bruno's best outcome using coercion
Using coercion, Bruno chose allocation B. He forced Angela to work 11 hours and received grain equal to AB. The MRT at A is equal to the MRS at B on Angela's biological survival constraint.

2. When Angela can say no
With voluntary exchange, allocation B is not available. The best that Bruno can do is allocation D, where Angela works for 8 hours, giving him grain equal to CD.

3. MRS = MRT again
When Angela works 8 hours, the MRT is equal to the MRS on Angela's reservation indifference curve, as shown by the slopes.

other point on the feasible frontier and then gave Bruno 4.5 bushels, she would have lower utility—she would be below her reservation indifference curve. But she can achieve her reservation utility by working for 8 hours, so she will accept the contract.

EXERCISE 5.7 WHY ANGELA WORKS FOR 8 HOURS

Angela's income is the amount she produces minus the land rent she pays to Bruno.

1. Using Figure 5.7a (page 202), suppose Angela works 11 hours. Would her income (after paying land rent) be greater or less than when she works 8 hours? Suppose instead, she works 6 hours, how would her income compare with when she works 8 hours?
2. Explain in your own words why she will choose to work 8 hours.

Since Angela is on her reservation indifference curve, only Bruno benefits from this exchange. All of the joint surplus goes to Bruno. His economic rent (equal to the land rent she pays him) is the surplus.

Remember that when Angela could work the land on her own she chose allocation C. Notice now that she chooses the same hours of work when she has to pay rent. Why does this happen? However much rent Angela has to pay, she will choose her hours of work to maximize her utility, so she will produce at a point on the feasible frontier where the MRT is equal to her MRS. And we know that her preferences are such that her MRS doesn't change with the amount of grain she consumes, so it will not be affected by the rent. This means that if she can choose her hours, she will work for 8 hours irrespective of the land rent (as long as this gives her at least her reservation utility).

Figure 5.7b shows how the surplus (which Bruno gets) varies with Angela's hours. You will see that the surplus falls as Angela works more or less than 8 hours. It is hump-shaped, like Bruno's rent in the case of coercion. But the peak is lower when Bruno needs Angela to agree to the proposal.

Leibniz: Angela's choice of working hours when she pays rent (http://tinyco.re/L050701)

EXERCISE 5.8 TAKE IT OR LEAVE IT?

1. Why is it Bruno, and not Angela, who has the power to make a take-it-or-leave-it offer?
2. Can you imagine a situation in which the farmer, not the landowner, might have this power?

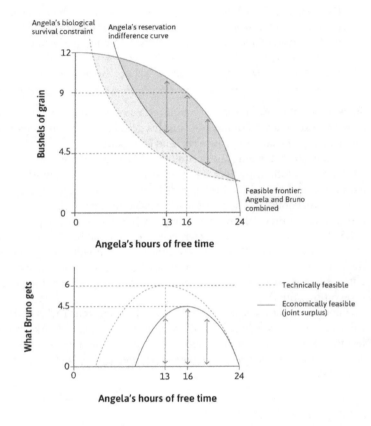

Figure 5.7b Bruno's take-it-or-leave-it proposal when Angela can refuse.

1. Angela's working hours when she was coerced
Using coercion, Angela was forced to work 11 hours. The MRT was equal to the MRS on Angela's biological survival constraint.

2. Bruno's best take-it-or-leave-it offer
When Bruno cannot force Angela to work, he should offer a contract in which Angela pays him 4.5 bushels to rent the land. She works for 8 hours, where the MRT is equal to the MRS on her reservation indifference curve.

3. The maximum surplus
If Angela works more or less than 8 hours, the joint surplus is less than 4.5 bushels.

4. Bruno's grain
Although Bruno cannot coerce Angela he can get the whole surplus.

5. Technically and economically feasible peaks compared
The peak of the hump is lower when Angela can refuse, compared to when Bruno could order her to work.

QUESTION 5.5 CHOOSE THE CORRECT ANSWER(S)
Figure 5.6 (page 201) shows Angela and Bruno's feasible frontier, Angela's biological survival constraint, and her reservation indifference curve.

Based on this figure, which of the following is correct?

☐ The economically feasible set is the same as the technically feasible set.
☐ For any given number of hours of free time, the marginal rate of substitution on the reservation indifference curve is smaller than that on the biological survival constraint.
☐ Some points are economically feasible but not technically feasible.
☐ If the ration Angela gets from the government increases from 2 to 3 bushels of grain, her reservation indifference curve will be above her biological survival constraint whatever her working hours.

QUESTION 5.6 CHOOSE THE CORRECT ANSWER(S)
Figure 5.7a (page 202) shows Angela and Bruno's feasible frontier, Angela's biological survival constraint and her reservation indifference curve. B is the outcome under coercion, while D is the outcome under voluntary exchange when Bruno makes a take-it-or-leave-it offer.

Looking at this graph, we can conclude that:

☐ With a take-it-or-leave-it offer, Bruno's economic rent is equal to the joint surplus.
☐ Both Bruno and Angela are better off under voluntary exchange than under coercion.
☐ When Bruno makes a take-it-or-leave-it offer, Angela accepts because she receives an economic rent.
☐ Angela works longer under voluntary exchange than under coercion.

5.8 THE PARETO EFFICIENCY CURVE AND THE DISTRIBUTION OF THE SURPLUS

Angela chose to work for 8 hours, producing 9 bushels of grain, both when she had to pay rent, and also when she did not. In both cases there is a surplus of 4.5 bushels: the difference between the amount of grain produced, and the amount that would give Angela her reservation utility.

The two cases differ in who gets the surplus. When Angela had to pay land rent, Bruno took the whole surplus, but when she could work the land for herself she obtained all of the surplus. Both allocations have two important properties:

- All the grain produced is shared between Angela and Bruno.
- The MRT on the feasible frontier is equal to the MRS on Angela's indifference curve.

This means that the allocations are Pareto efficient.

To see why, remember that Pareto efficiency means that no Pareto improvement is possible: it is impossible to change the allocation to make one party better off without making the other worse off.

The first property is straightforward: it means that no Pareto improvement can be achieved simply by changing the amounts of grain they each consume. If one consumed more, the other would have to have less. On the other hand, if some of the grain produced was not being consumed, then consuming it would make one or both of them better off.

The second property, MRS = MRT, means that no Pareto improvement can be achieved by changing Angela's hours of work and hence the amount of grain produced.

If the MRS and MRT were not equal, it would be possible to make both better off. For example, if MRT > MRS, Angela could transform an hour of her time into more grain than she would need to get the same utility as before, so the extra grain could make both of them better off. But if MRT = MRS, then any change in the amount of grain produced would only be exactly what is needed to keep Angela's utility the same as before, given the change in her hours.

Figure 5.8 shows that there are many other Pareto-efficient allocations in addition to these two. Point C is the outcome when Angela is an independent farmer. Compare the analysis in Figure 5.8 with Bruno's take-or-leave-it offer, and see the other Pareto-efficient allocations.

Figure 5.8 shows that in addition to the two Pareto-efficient allocations we have observed (C and D), every point between C and D represents a Pareto-efficient allocation. CD is called the **Pareto efficiency curve**: it joins together all the points in the feasible set for which MRS = MRT. (You will also hear it called the contract curve, even in situations where there is no contract, which is why we prefer the more descriptive term Pareto efficiency curve.)

At each allocation on the Pareto efficiency curve Angela works for 8 hours and there is a surplus of 4.5 bushels, but the distribution of the surplus is different—ranging from point D where Angela gets none of it, to point C where she gets it all. At the hypothetical allocation G, both receive an economic rent: Angela's rent is GD, Bruno's is GC, and the sum of their rents is equal to the surplus.

PARETO EFFICIENCY AND THE PARETO EFFICIENCY CURVE

- A **Pareto-efficient** allocation has the property that there is no alternative technically feasible allocation in which at least one person would be better off, and nobody worse off.
- The set of all such allocations is the **Pareto efficiency curve**. It is also referred to as the contract curve.

Leibniz: The Pareto efficiency curve (http://tinyco.re/L050801)

QUESTION 5.7 CHOOSE THE CORRECT ANSWER(S)

Figure 5.8 (page 207) shows the Pareto efficiency curve CD for the interaction between Angela and Bruno.

Which of the following statements is correct?

☐ The allocation at C Pareto-dominates the one at D.
☐ Angela's marginal rate of substitution is equal to the marginal rate of transformation at all points on the Pareto efficiency curve.
☐ The mid-point of CD is the most Pareto-efficient allocation.
☐ Angela and Bruno are indifferent between all the points on CD, because they are all Pareto efficient.

5.9 POLITICS: SHARING THE SURPLUS

Bruno thinks that the new rules, under which he makes an offer that Angela will not refuse, are not so bad after all. Angela is also better off than she had been when she had barely enough to survive. But she would like a share in the surplus.

She and her fellow farm workers lobby for a new law that limits working time to 4 hours a day, while requiring that total pay is at least 4.5 bushels. They threaten not to work at all unless the law is passed.

BRUNO: Angela, you and your colleagues are bluffing.

ANGELA: No, we are not: we would be no worse off at our reservation option than under your contract, working the hours and receiving the small fraction of the harvest that you impose!

Angela and her fellow workers win, and the new law limits the working day to 4 hours.

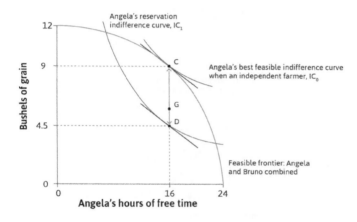

Figure 5.8 Pareto-efficient allocations and the distribution of the surplus.

1. The allocation at C
As an independent farmer, Angela chose point C, where MRT = MRS. She consumed 9 bushels of grain: 4.5 bushels would have been enough to put her on her reservation indifference curve at D. But she obtained the whole surplus CD—an additional 4.5 bushels.

2. The allocation at D
When Bruno owned the land and made a take-it-or-leave-it offer, he chose a contract in which the land rent was CD (4.5 bushels). Angela accepted and worked 8 hours. The allocation was at D, and once again, MRT = MRS. The surplus was still CD, but Bruno got it all.

3. Angela's preferences
Remember that Angela's MRS doesn't change as she consumes more grain. At any point along the line CD, such as G, there is an indifference curve with the same slope. So MRS = MRT at all of these points.

4. A hypothetical allocation
Point G is a hypothetical allocation, at which MRS = MRT. Angela works for 8 hours, and 9 bushels of grain are produced. Bruno gets grain CG, and Angela gets all the rest. Allocation G is Pareto efficient.

5. The Pareto efficiency curve
All the points making up the line between C and D are Pareto-efficient allocations, at which MRS = MRT. The surplus of 4.5 bushels (CD) is shared between Angela and Bruno.

How did things work out?

Before the short-hours law Angela worked for 8 hours and received 4.5 bushels of grain. This is point D in Figure 5.9. The new law implements the allocation in which Angela and her friends work 4 hours, getting 20 hours of free time and the same number of bushels. Since they have the same amount of grain and more free time, they are better off. Figure 5.9 shows they are now on a higher indifference curve.

The new law has increased Angela's bargaining power and Bruno is worse off than before. You can see she is better off at F than at D. She is also better off than she would be with her reservation option, which means she is now receiving an economic rent.

Angela's rent can be measured, in bushels of grain, as the vertical distance between her reservation indifference curve (IC_1 in Figure 5.9) and the indifference curve she is able to achieve under the new legislation (IC_2). We can think of the economic rent as:

- The maximum amount of grain per year that Angela would give up to live under the new law rather than in the situation before the law was passed.

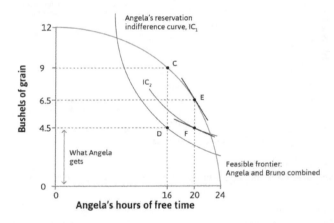

Figure 5.9 The effect of an increase in Angela's bargaining power through legislation.

1. Before the short hours law
Bruno makes a take-it-or-leave-it offer, gets grain equal to CD, and Angela works 8 hours. Angela is on her reservation indifference curve at D and MRS = MRT.

2. What Angela receives before legislation
Angela gets 4.5 bushels of grain: she is just indifferent between working for 8 hours and her reservation option.

3. The effect of legislation
With legislation that reduces work to 4 hours and keeps Angela's amount of grain unchanged, she is on a higher indifference curve at F. Bruno's grain is reduced from CD to EF (2 bushels).

4. MRT > MRS
When Angela works 4 hours, the MRT is larger than the MRS on the new indifference curve.

- Or (because Angela is obviously political) the amount she would be willing to pay so that the law passed, for example by lobbying the legislature or contributing to election campaigns.

QUESTION 5.8 CHOOSE THE CORRECT ANSWER(S)

In Figure 5.9 (page 208), D and F are the outcomes before and after the introduction of a new law that limits Angela's work time to four hours a day while requiring a minimum pay of 4.5 bushels. Based on this information, which of the following statements are correct?

☐ The change from D to F is a Pareto improvement.
☐ The new outcome F is Pareto efficient.
☐ Both Angela and Bruno receive economic rents at F.
☐ As a result of the new law, Bruno has less bargaining power.

5.10 BARGAINING TO A PARETO-EFFICIENT SHARING OF THE SURPLUS

Angela and her friends are pleased with their success. She asks what you think of the new policy.

YOU: Congratulations, but your policy is far from the best you could do.
ANGELA: Why?
YOU: Because you are not on the **Pareto efficiency curve**! Under your new law, Bruno is getting 2 bushels, and cannot make you work more than 4 hours. So why don't you offer to continue to pay him 2 bushels, in exchange for agreeing to let you keep anything you produce above that? Then you get to choose how many hours you work.

The small print in the law allows a longer work day if both parties agree, as long as the workers' reservation option is a 4-hour day if no agreement is reached.

YOU: Now redraw Figure 5.9 and use the concepts of the joint surplus and the Pareto efficiency curve from Figure 5.8 to show Angela how she can get a better deal.
YOU: Look at Figure 5.10. The surplus is largest at 8 hours of work. When you work for 4 hours the surplus is smaller, and you pay most of it to Bruno. If you increase the surplus, you can pay him the same amount, and your own surplus will be bigger—so you will be better off. Follow the steps in Figure 5.10 to see how this works.

The move away from point D (at which Bruno had all the bargaining power and obtained all the gains from exchange) to point H where Angela is better off consists of two distinct steps:

1. From D to F, the outcome is imposed by new legislation. This was definitely not win-win: Bruno lost because his economic rent at F is less than the maximum feasible rent that he got at D. Angela benefitted.
2. Once at the legislated outcome, there were many win-win possibilities open to them. They are shown by the segment GH on the Pareto efficiency curve. Win-win alternatives to the allocation at F are possible by definition, because F was not Pareto efficient.

> **Pareto efficiency curve** The set of all allocations that are Pareto efficient. Often referred to as the contract curve, even in social interactions in which there is no contract, which is why we avoid the term. *See also: Pareto efficient.*

Bruno wants to negotiate. He is not happy with Angela's proposal of H.

BRUNO: I am no better off under this new plan than I would be if I just accepted the legislation that the farmers passed.

YOU: But Bruno, Angela now has bargaining power, too. The legislation changed her reservation option, so it is no longer 24 hours of free time at survival rations. Her reservation option is now the legislated allocation at point F. I suggest you make her a counter offer.

BRUNO: Angela, I'll let you work the land for as many hours as you choose if you pay me half a bushel more than EF.

They shake hands on the deal.

Because Angela is free to choose her work hours, subject only to paying Bruno the extra half bushel, she will work 8 hours where MRT = MRS. Because this deal lies between G and H, it is a Pareto improvement over point F. Moreover, because it is on the Pareto-efficient curve CD, we know there are no further Pareto improvements to be made. This is true of every other allocation on GH—they differ only in the distribution of the mutual gains, as some favour Angela while others favour Bruno. Where they end up will depend on their bargaining power.

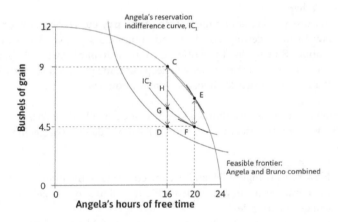

Figure 5.10 Bargaining to restore Pareto efficiency.

1. The maximum joint surplus
The surplus to be divided between Angela and Bruno is maximized where MRT = MRS, at 8 hours of work.

2. Angela prefers F to D
But Angela prefers point F implemented by the legislation, because it gives her the same amount of grain but more free time than D.

3. Angela could also do better than F
Compared to F, she would prefer any allocation on the Pareto efficiency curve between C and G.

4. Angela can propose H
At allocation H, Bruno gets the same amount of grain: CH = EF. Angela is better off than she was at F. She works longer hours, but has more than enough grain to compensate her for the loss of free time.

5. A win-win agreement by moving to an allocation between G and H
F is not Pareto efficient because MRT > MRS. If they move to a point on the Pareto efficiency curve between G and H, Angela and Bruno can both be better off.

QUESTION 5.9 CHOOSE THE CORRECT ANSWER(S)

In Figure 5.10 (page 210), Angela and Bruno are at allocation F, where she receives 3 bushels of grain for 4 hours of work.

From the figure, we can conclude that:

- ☐ All the points on EF are Pareto efficient.
- ☐ Any point in the area between G, H and F would be a Pareto improvement.
- ☐ Any point between G and D would be a Pareto improvement.
- ☐ They would both be indifferent between all points on GH.

5.11 ANGELA AND BRUNO: THE MORAL OF THE STORY

Angela's farming skills and Bruno's ownership of land provided an opportunity for mutual gains from exchange.

The same is true when people directly exchange, or buy and sell, goods for money. Suppose you have more apples than you can consume, and your neighbour has an abundance of pears. The apples are worth less to you than to your neighbour, and the pears are worth more to you. So it must be possible to achieve a Pareto improvement by exchanging some apples and pears.

When people with differing needs, property and capacities meet, there is an opportunity to generate gains for all of them. That is why people come together in markets, online exchanges or pirate ships. The mutual gains are the pie—which we call the surplus.

The allocations that we observe through history are largely the result of the institutions, including property rights and bargaining power, that were present in the economy. Figure 5.11 summarizes what we have learnt about the determination of economic outcomes from the succession of scenarios involving Angela and Bruno.

- Technology and biology determine whether or not they are able to mutually benefit, and the technically feasible set of allocations (Section 5.5). If Bruno's land had been so unproductive that Angela's labour could not produce enough to keep her alive, then there would have been no room for a deal.
- For allocations to be economically feasible, they must be Pareto improvements relative to the parties' reservation options, which may depend on institutions (such as Angela's survival rations from the government (Section 5.7) or legislation on working hours (Section 5.10)).
- The outcome of an interaction depends on people's preferences (what they want), as well as the institutions that provide their bargaining power (ability to get it), and hence how the surplus is distributed (Section 5.10).

The story of Angela and Bruno provides three lessons about efficiency and fairness, illustrated by Figure 5.10, to which we will return in subsequent units.

- When one person or group has power to dictate the allocation, subject only to not making the other party worse off than in their reservation option, the powerful party will capture the entire surplus. If they have done this, then there cannot be any way to make either of them better off without making the other worse off (point D in the figure). So this must be Pareto efficient!

- Those who consider their treatment unfair often have some power to influence the outcome through legislation and other political means, and the result may be a fairer distribution in their eyes or ours, but may not necessarily be Pareto efficient (point F). Societies may face trade-offs between Pareto-efficient but unfair outcomes, and fair but Pareto-inefficient outcomes.
- If we have institutions under which people can jointly deliberate, agree on, and enforce alternative allocations, then it may be possible to avoid the trade-off and achieve both efficiency and fairness—as Angela and Bruno did through a combination of legislation and bargaining between themselves (point H).

5.12 MEASURING ECONOMIC INEQUALITY

In our analysis of the interaction between Angela and Bruno, we have assessed the allocations in terms of Pareto efficiency. We have seen that they (or at least one of them) can be better off if they can negotiate a move from a Pareto-inefficient allocation to one on the Pareto efficiency curve.

But the other important criterion for assessing an allocation is fairness. We know that Pareto-efficient allocations can be highly unequal. In the case of Angela and Bruno, inequality resulted directly from differences in bargaining power, but also from differences in their *endowments*: that is, what they each owned before the interaction (their initial wealth). Bruno owned land, while Angela had nothing except time and the capacity to work. Difference in endowments, as well as institutions, may in turn affect bargaining power.

Max O. Lorenz. 1905. 'Methods of Measuring the Concentration of Wealth'. *Publications of the American Statistical Association* 9 (70).

It is easy to assess the distribution between two people. But how can we assess inequalities in larger groups, or across a whole society? A useful tool for representing and comparing distributions of income or wealth, and showing the extent of inequality, is the **Lorenz curve** (invented in 1905 by Max Lorenz (1876–1959), an American economist, while he was still a student). It indicates how much disparity there is in income, or any other measure, across the population.

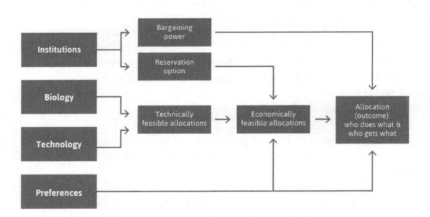

Figure 5.11 The fundamental determinants of economic outcomes.

The Lorenz curve shows the entire population lined up along the horizontal axis from the poorest to the richest. The height of the curve at any point on the horizontal axis indicates the fraction of total income received by the fraction of the population given by that point on the horizontal axis.

To see how this works, imagine a village in which there are 10 landowners, each owning 10 hectares, and 90 others who farm the land as sharecroppers, but who own no land (like Angela). The Lorenz curve is the blue line in Figure 5.12. Lining the population up in order of land ownership, the first 90% of the population own nothing, so the curve is flat. The remaining 10% own 10 hectares each, so the 'curve' rises in a straight line to reach the point where 100% of people own 100% of the land.

If instead each member of the population owned one hectare of land— perfect equality in land ownership—then the Lorenz curve would be a line at a 45-degree angle, indicating that the 'poorest' 10% of the population have 10% of the land, and so on (although in this case, everyone is equally poor, and equally rich).

The Lorenz curve allows us to see how far a distribution departs from this line of perfect equality. Figure 5.13 shows the distribution of income that would have resulted from the prize-sharing system described in the articles of the pirate ship, the *Royal Rover*, discussed in the introduction to this unit. The Lorenz curve is very close to the 45-degree line, showing how the institutions of piracy allowed ordinary members of the crew to claim a large share of income.

In contrast, when the Royal Navy's ships *Favourite* and *Active* captured the Spanish treasure ship *La Hermione*, the division of the spoils on the two British men-of-war ships was far less equal. The Lorenz curves show that ordinary crew members received about a quarter of the income, with the remainder going to a small number of officers and the captain. You can see that the *Favourite* was more unequal that the *Active*, with a lower share going to each crew member. By the standards of the day, pirates were unusually democratic and fair-minded in their dealings with each other.

Lorenz curve A graphical representation of inequality of some quantity such as wealth or income. Individuals are arranged in ascending order by how much of this quantity they have, and the cumulative share of the total is then plotted against the cumulative share of the population. For complete equality of income, for example, it would be a straight line with a slope of one. The extent to which the curve falls below this perfect equality line is a measure of inequality. *See also: Gini coefficient.*

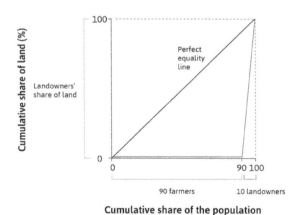

Figure 5.12 A Lorenz curve for wealth ownership.

The Gini coefficient

The Lorenz curve gives us a picture of the disparity of income across the whole population, but it can be useful to have a simple measure of the degree of inequality. You can see that more unequal distributions have a greater area between the Lorenz curve and the 45-degree line. The **Gini coefficient** (or Gini ratio) named after the Italian statistician Corrado Gini (1884–1965), is calculated as the ratio of this area to the area of the whole of the triangle under the 45-degree line.

If everyone has the same income, so that there is no income inequality, the Gini coefficient takes a value of 0. If a single individual receives all the income, the Gini coefficient takes its maximum value of 1. We can calculate the Gini for land ownership in Figure 5.14a as area A, between the Lorenz curve and the perfect equality line, as a proportion of area (A + B), the triangle under the 45-degree line:

$$\text{Gini} = \frac{A}{A+B}$$

Figure 5.14b shows the Gini coefficients for each of the Lorenz curves we have drawn so far.

Strictly speaking, this method of calculating the Gini gives only an approximation. The Gini is more precisely defined as a measure of the average difference in income between every pair of individuals in the population, as explained in the Einstein at the end of this section. The area method gives an accurate approximation only when the population is large.

> **Gini coefficient** A measure of inequality of any quantity such as income or wealth, varying from a value of zero (if there is no inequality) to one (if a single individual receives all of it).

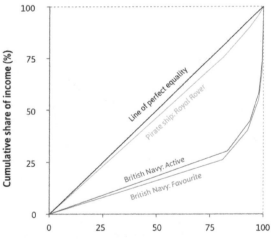

Figure 5.13 The distribution of spoils: Pirates and the Royal Navy.

Comparing income distributions and inequality across the world
To assess income inequality within a country, we can either look at total market income (all earnings from employment, self-employment, savings and investments), or **disposable income**, which better captures living standards. Disposable income is what a household can spend after paying tax and receiving transfers (such as unemployment benefit and pensions) from the government:

> **disposable income** Income available after paying taxes and receiving transfers from the government.

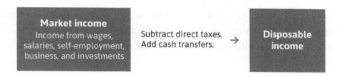

In Unit 1, we compared inequality in the income distributions of countries using the 90/10 ratio. Lorenz curves give us a fuller picture of how distributions differ. Figure 5.15 shows the distribution of market income in the Netherlands in 2010. The Gini coefficient is 0.47, so by this measure it has greater inequality than the *Royal Rover*, but less than the British Navy ships. The analysis in Figure 5.15 shows how redistributive government policies result in a more equal distribution of disposable income.

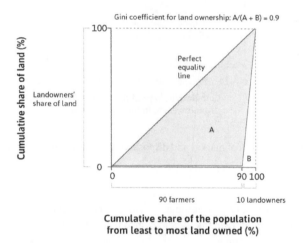

Figure 5.14a The Lorenz curve and Gini coefficient for wealth ownership.

Distribution	Gini
Pirate ship *Royal Rover*	0.06
British Navy ship *Active*	0.59
British Navy ship *Favourite*	0.6
The village with sharecroppers and landowners	0.9

Figure 5.14b Comparing Gini coefficients.

Notice that in the Netherlands, almost one-fifth of the households have a near-zero market income, but most nonetheless have enough disposable income to survive, or even live comfortably: the poorest one-fifth of the population receive about 10% of all disposable income.

There are many different ways to measure income inequality besides the Gini and the 90/10 ratio, but these two are widely used. Figure 5.16 compares the Gini coefficients for disposable and market income across a large sample of countries, ordered from left to right, from the least to the most unequal by the disposable income measure. The main reason for the substantial differences between nations in disposable income inequality is the extent to which governments can tax well off families and transfer the proceeds to the less well off.

LIS. *Cross National Data Center* (http://tinyco.re/0525655). Stefan Thewissen (University of Oxford) did the calculations in April 2015.

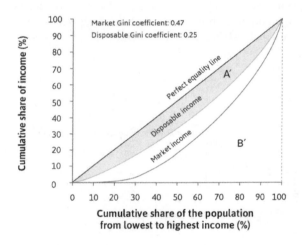

Figure 5.15 Distribution of market and disposable income in the Netherlands (2010).

1. The Lorenz curve for market income
The curve indicates that the poorest 10% of the population (10 on the horizontal axis) receive only 0.1% of total income (0.1 on the vertical axis), and the lower-earning half of the population has less than 20% of income.

2. The Gini for market income
The Gini coefficient is the ratio of area A (between the market income curve and the perfect equality line) to area A + B (below the perfect equality line), which is 0.47.

3. Disposable income
The amount of inequality in disposable income is much smaller than the inequality in market income. Redistributive policies have a bigger effect towards the bottom of the distribution. The poorest 10% have 4% of total disposable income.

4. The Gini for disposable income
The Gini coefficient for disposable income is lower: the ratio of areas A′ (between the disposable income curve and the perfect equality line) and A′ + B′ (below the perfect equality line) is 0.25.

Notice that:

- The differences between countries in disposable income inequality (the top of the lower bars) are much greater than the differences in inequality of market incomes (the top of the upper bars).
- The US and the UK are among the most unequal of the high-income economies.
- The few poor and middle-income countries for which data are available are even more unequal in disposable income than the US but …
- … (with the exception of South Africa) this is mainly the result of the limited degree of redistribution from rich to poor, rather than unusually high inequality in market income.

We study redistribution of income by governments in more detail in Unit 19 (Inequality).

QUESTION 5.10 CHOOSE THE CORRECT ANSWER(S)
Figure 5.15 (page 216) shows the Lorenz curve for market income in the Netherlands in 2010.

Which of the following is true?

☐ If area A increases, income inequality falls.
☐ The Gini coefficient can be calculated as the proportion of area A to area A + B.
☐ Countries with lower Gini coefficients have less equal income distributions.
☐ The Gini coefficient takes the value 1 when everyone has the same income.

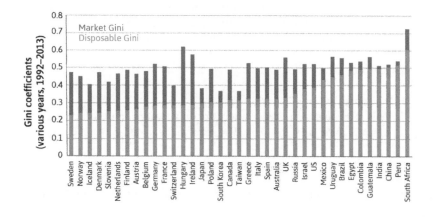

LIS. *Cross National Data Center*. Stefan Thewissen (University of Oxford) did the calculations in April 2015.

Figure 5.16 Income inequality in market and disposable income across the world.

EXERCISE 5.9 COMPARING DISTRIBUTIONS OF WEALTH
The table shows three alternative distributions of land ownership in a village with 100 people and 100 hectares of land. Draw the Lorenz curves for each case. For cases I and III calculate the Gini. For case II, show on the Lorenz curve diagram how the Gini coefficient can be calculated.

I	80 people own nothing	20 people own 5 hectares each	
II	40 people own nothing	40 people own 1 hectare each	20 people own 3 hectares each
III	100 people own 1 hectare each		

EINSTEIN

Inequality as differences among people
The Gini coefficient is a measure of inequality, precisely defined as:

g = half the relative mean difference in income
among all pairs of individuals in the population

To calculate g, you should know the incomes of every member of a population:

1. Find the difference in income between every possible pair in the population.
2. Take the mean of these differences.
3. Divide this number by the mean income of the population, to get the relative mean difference.
4. g = relative mean difference divided by two.

Examples:
There are just two individuals in the population and one has all the income. Assume their incomes are 0 and 1.

1. The difference between the incomes of the pair = 1.
2. This is the mean difference because there is just one pair.
3. Mean income = 0.5, so the relative mean difference = 1/0.5 = 2.
4. $g = 2/2 = 1$ (perfect inequality, as we would expect).

Two people are dividing a pie: one has 20%, and the other 80%.

1. The difference is 60% (0.60).
2. This is the mean difference (there are only two incomes, as before).
3. Mean income is 50% or 0.50. The relative mean difference is 0.6/0.5 = 1.20.
4. $g = 0.60$.

The Gini coefficient is a measure of how unequal their slices are. As an exercise, confirm that if the size of the smaller slice of the pie is σ, $g = 1 - 2\sigma$.

There are three people, and one has all of the income, which we assume is 1 unit.

1. The differences for the three possible pairs are 1, 1, and 0.
2. Mean difference = 2/3.
3. Relative mean difference = (2/3)(1/3) = 2.
4. g = 2/2 = 1.

Approximating the Gini using the Lorenz curve

If the population is large, we obtain a good approximation to the Gini coefficient using the areas in the Lorenz diagram: $g \approx A/(A + B)$.

But with a small number of people, this approximation is not accurate.

You can see this if you think about the case of 'perfect inequality' when one individual gets 100% of the income, for which the true Gini is 1, whatever the size of the population (we calculated it for populations of 2 and 3 above). The Lorenz curve is horizontal at zero up to the last individual, and then shoots up to 100%. Try drawing the Lorenz curves when the size of the population, N, is 2, 3, 10, and 20.

- When $N = 2$, $A/(A + B) = 0.5$, a very poor approximation to the true value, $g = 1$.
- When N is large, area A is not quite as big as area A + B, but the ratio is almost 1.

There is a formula that calculates the correct Gini coefficient from the Lorenz diagram:

$$g = \frac{N}{N-1} \frac{A}{A+B}$$

(Check for yourself that this works for the perfect inequality case when $N = 2$.)

5.13 A POLICY TO REDISTRIBUTE THE SURPLUS AND RAISE EFFICIENCY

Angela and Bruno live in the hypothetical world of an economic model. But real farmers and landowners face similar problems.

In the Indian state of West Bengal, home to more people than Germany, many farmers work as sharecroppers (bargadars in the Bengali language), renting land from landowners in exchange for a share of the crop.

The traditional contractual arrangements throughout this vast state varied little from village to village, with virtually all bargadars giving half their crop to the landowner at harvest time. This had been the norm since at least the eighteenth century.

But, like Angela, in the second half of the twentieth century many thought this was unfair, because of the extreme levels of deprivation among the bargadars. In 1973, 73% of the rural population lived in poverty, one of the highest poverty rates in India. In 1978, the newly elected Left Front government of West Bengal adopted new laws, called Operation Barga.

The new laws stated that:

- Bargadars could keep up to three-quarters of their crop.
- Bargadars were protected from eviction by landowners, provided they paid them the 25% quota.

Both provisions of Operation Barga were advocated as a way of increasing output. There are certainly reasons to predict that the size of the pie would increase, as well as the incomes of the farmers:

- *Bargadars had a greater incentive to work hard and well*: Keeping a larger share meant that there was a greater reward if they grew more crops.
- *Bargadars had an incentive to invest in improving the land*: They were confident that they would farm the same plot of land in the future, so would be rewarded for their investment.

Abhijit V. Banerjee, Paul J. Gertler, and Maitreesh Ghatak. 2002. 'Empowerment and Efficiency: Tenancy Reform in West Bengal'. *Journal of Political Economy* 110 (2): pp. 239–80.

West Bengal enjoyed a subsequent dramatic increase in farm output per unit of land, as well as farming incomes. By comparing the output of farms before and after the implementation of Operation Barga, economists concluded that both improved work motivation and investment occurred. One study suggested that Operation Barga was responsible for around 28% of the subsequent growth in agricultural productivity in the region. The empowerment of the bargadars also had positive spillover effects as local governments became more responsive to the needs of poor farmers.

Efficiency and fairness

Ajitava Raychaudhuri. 2004. *Lessons from the Land Reform Movement in West Bengal, India.* Washington, DC: World Bank.

Operation Barga was later cited by the World Bank as an example of good policy for economic development.

Figure 5.17 summarizes the concepts developed in this unit that we can use to judge the impact of an economic policy. Having gathered evidence to describe the resulting allocation, we ask: is it Pareto efficient, and fair? Is it better than the original allocation by these criteria?

The evidence that Operation Barga increased incomes indicates that the pie got larger, and the poorest people got a larger slice.

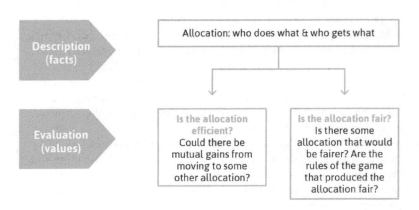

Figure 5.17 Efficiency and fairness.

In principle, the increase in the size of the pie means there could be mutual gains from the reforms, with both farmers and landowners made better off.

However, the actual change in the allocation was not a Pareto improvement. The incomes of some landowners fell following the reduction in their share of the crop. Nevertheless, in increasing the income of the poorest people in West Bengal, we might judge that Operation Barga was fair. We can assume that many people in West Bengal thought so, because they continued to vote for the Left Front alliance. It stayed in power from 1977 until 2011.

We do not have detailed information for Operation Barga, but we can illustrate the effect of the land reform on the distribution of income in the hypothetical village of the previous section, with 90 sharecroppers and 10 landowners. Figure 5.18 shows the Lorenz curves. Initially, the farmers pay a rent of 50% of their crop to the landowners. Operation Barga raises the farmer's crop share to 75%, moving the Lorenz curve towards the 45-degree line. As a result, the Gini coefficient of income is reduced from 0.4 (similar to the US) to 0.15 (well below that of the most equal of the rich economies, such as Denmark). The Einstein at the end of this section shows you how the Gini coefficient depends on the proportion of farmers and their crop share.

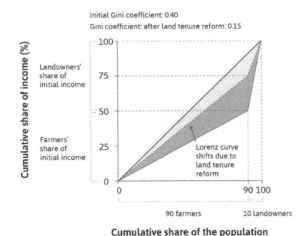

Initial Gini coefficient: 0.40
Gini coefficient: after land tenure reform: 0.15

Figure 5.18 Bargaining in practice: How a land tenure reform in West Bengal reduced the Gini coefficient.

EINSTEIN

The Lorenz curve and the Gini coefficient in a class-divided economy with a large population

Think about a population of 100 people in which a fraction n produce the output, and the others are employers (or landlords, or other claimants on income who are not producers).

Take, as an example, the farmers and landlords in the text (in West Bengal). Each of the $n \times 100$ farmers produces q and he or she receives a fraction, s, of this; so each of the farmers has income sq. The $(1 - n) \times 100$ employers each receive an income of $(1 - s)q$.

The figure below presents the Lorenz curve and the perfect equality line similar to Figure 5.18 in the text.

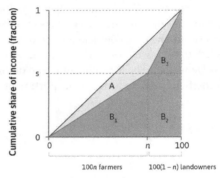

Figure 5.19 The Lorenz curve and the perfect equality line.

The slope of the line separating area A from B_1 is s/n (the fraction of total output that each farmer gets), and the slope of the line separating area A from B_3 is $(1 - s)/(1 - n)$, the fraction of total output that each landlord gets. We can approximate the Gini coefficient by the expression $A/(A + B)$, where in the figure $B = B_1 + B_2 + B_3$.

So we can express the Gini coefficient in terms of the triangles and rectangle in the figure. To see how, note that the area of the entire square is 1 while the area $(A+B)$ under the perfect equality line is $1/2$. The area A is $(1/2) - B$. Then we can write the Gini coefficient as

$$g = \frac{(0.5 - B_1 + B_2 + B_3)}{0.5} = 1 - 2(B_1 + B_2 + B_3)$$

We can see from the figure that

$$B_1 = \frac{ns}{2}$$
$$B_2 = (1 - n)s$$
$$B_3 = \frac{(1 - n)(1 - s)}{2}$$

so,

$$g = 1 - 2(\frac{ns}{2} + (1-n)s + \frac{(1-n)(1-s)}{2})$$
$$= 1 - (ns + 2s - 2ns + 1 - s + n + ns)$$
$$= n - s$$

This means that the Gini coefficient in this simple case is just the fraction of the total population producing the output (the farmers) minus the fraction of the output that they receive in income.

Inequality will increase in this model economy if:

- The fraction of producers in the economy increases but the total share of output they receive remains unchanged. This would be the case if some of the landlords became farmer tenants, each receiving a fraction s of the crop they produced.
- The fraction of the crop received by the producers falls.

5.14 CONCLUSION

Economic interactions are governed by institutions, which specify the rules of the game. To understand the possible outcomes, we first consider what allocations are technically feasible, given the limits imposed by biology and technology. Then, if participation is voluntary, we look for economically feasible allocations: those which could provide mutual gains (a surplus), and therefore are Pareto-improving relative to the reservation positions of the parties involved.

Which feasible allocation will arise depends on the bargaining power of each party, which determines how a surplus will be shared and in turn depends on the institutions governing the interaction. We can evaluate and compare allocations using two important criteria for judging economic interactions: fairness and Pareto efficiency.

Concepts introduced in Unit 5
Before you move on, review these definitions:

- Institutions
- Power
- Bargaining power
- Allocation
- Pareto criterion, Pareto domination and Pareto improvement
- Pareto efficiency
- Pareto efficiency curve
- Substantive and procedural concepts of fairness
- Economic rent (compared to land rent)
- Joint surplus
- Lorenz curve and Gini coefficient

5.15 REFERENCES

Banerjee, Abhijit V., Paul J. Gertler, and Maitreesh Ghatak. 2002. 'Empowerment and Efficiency: Tenancy Reform in West Bengal' (http://tinyco.re/9394444). *Journal of Political Economy* 110 (2): pp. 239–280.

Clark, Andrew E., and Andrew J. Oswald. 2002. 'A Simple Statistical Method for Measuring How Life Events Affect Happiness' (http://tinyco.re/7872100). *International Journal of Epidemiology* 31 (6): pp. 1139–1144.

Leeson, Peter T. 2007. 'An–arrgh–chy: The Law and Economics of Pirate Organization'. *Journal of Political Economy* 115 (6): pp. 1049–94.

Lorenz, Max O. 1905. 'Methods of Measuring the Concentration of Wealth' (http://tinyco.re/0786587). *Publications of the American Statistical Association* 9 (70).

Pareto, Vilfredo. 2014. *Manual of political economy: a variorum translation and critical edition*. Oxford, New York, NY: Oxford University Press.

Raychaudhuri, Ajitava. 2004. *Lessons from the Land Reform Movement in West Bengal, India* (http://tinyco.re/0335719). Washington, DC: World Bank.

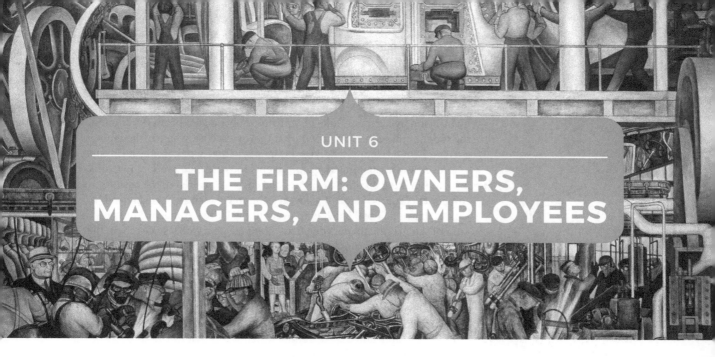

THE FIRM: OWNERS, MANAGERS, AND EMPLOYEES

HOW THE INTERACTIONS AMONG THE FIRM'S OWNERS, MANAGERS, AND EMPLOYEES INFLUENCE WAGES, WORK, AND PROFITS, AND HOW THIS AFFECTS THE ENTIRE ECONOMY

THEMES AND CAPSTONE UNITS
- 18: Global economy
- 19: Inequality
- 21: Innovation
- 22: Politics and policy

- The firm is an actor in the capitalist economy, and a stage on which interactions among the firm's employees, managers, and owners are played out.
- Hiring labour is different from buying other goods and services, and the contract between the employer and the employee is incomplete. It does not cover what the employer really cares about, which is how hard and well the employee works.
- Incomplete contracts arise when important information, such as the employee's effort, is asymmetric or non-verifiable.
- In economics, employment is modelled as a principal (the employer) interacting with an agent (the employee).
- The principal-agent model can be used to study other relationships with incomplete contracts, such as the interaction between a lender and a borrower.
- Firms do not pay the lowest wages possible. They set wages so that employees earn economic rents, to motivate them to work effectively, and stay with the firm.
- Working together in firms brings mutual gains: profit for owners, and economic rents for managers and employees. But rents also lead to involuntary unemployment in the economy.

Apple's iPhone and iPad are iconic American hi-tech products, yet neither is assembled in the US. Until 2011 a single company, Foxconn, produced every iPhone and iPad in factories in China, mainly so that Apple could take advantage of lower costs, including wages.

The components of the iPhone and iPad for the most part do not come from China, but are sourced from around the world. Components such as the flash memory, display module, and touch screen are made by a number of different companies including Toshiba and Sharp in Japan. The microprocessor is made by Samsung in South Korea and other components, by Infineon in Germany. Like other firms, Apple makes profits by finding the supplier that can provide inputs at the lowest cost, whether the input is a component or labour, wherever in the world that supplier may be located.

The cost of assembling the components into the final product in China is small—making up only 4% of the total cost—compared to the cost of components sourced from high-wage economies such as Germany and Japan. Almost half of Apple's employees in the US sell Apple products rather than making them, while firms compete on a global scale to win the lucrative business of supplying Apple with its components. The cost of producing the iPhone is far lower than the price Apple charges: in 2016, a 32Gb iPhone 7 cost $224.80 to manufacture. Its price in the US was $649.

Apple is not alone in outsourcing (or **offshoring**) production to countries that are not the main market for the goods produced. In most manufacturing industries, firms based in rich countries have transferred a significant proportion of production, which was previously done by local employees, to poorer countries where wages are lower. But Apple and other firms are looking for more than cheap labour. Wages in some of Apple's source countries such as Germany are higher than in the US.

Other industries, particularly garment manufacturing, have relocated primarily to low-wage economies. More than 97% of apparel and 98% of footwear sold in the US by American brands and retailers is made overseas. China, Bangladesh, Cambodia, Indonesia, and Vietnam are now among the world's main exporters of textiles and clothing. At the time of the Industrial Revolution, the world's largest exporter was Britain.

Also, in developing countries, additional business costs such as health and safety rules are far lower, and environmental regulations are often less strict.

Apple, Samsung, and Toshiba are business organizations called **firms**. Not everyone is employed in a firm. For example, many farmers, carpenters, software developers or personal trainers work independently, as neither employee nor employer. While some people work for governments and not-for-profit organizations, the majority of people in rich nations make their living by working in a firm.

Firms are major actors in the economy and we will use this and the next unit to explain how they work. A firm is often referred to as if it were a person: we talk about 'the price Apple charges'.

But while firms are actors—and in some legal systems are treated as if they were individuals—firms are also the stage on which the people who make up the firm (employees, managers, and owners) act out their sometimes common but sometimes competing interests. In our 'Economist in action' video Richard Freeman, an economist who specializes in labour markets, explains some of the consequences of outsourcing for these actors.

To understand the firm, we will model how employers set wages and employees respond. We have already seen, in earlier units, the importance of work, and firms, in the economy:

- Work is how people produce their livelihoods. In deciding how much time to spend working, people face a trade-off between free time and the goods that they can produce, or the wage income that they can earn.
- Production, wages, and living standards have grown through the innovation and adoption of new technologies by firms.

offshoring The relocation of part of a firm's activities outside of the national boundaries in which it operates. It can take place within a multinational company or may involve outsourcing production to other firms.

firm A business organization which pays wages and salaries to employ people, and purchases inputs, to produce and market goods and services with the intention of making a profit.

Richard Freeman: You can't outsource responsibility
http://tinyco.re/0004374

- If a production process requires labour to be combined with other inputs—like Angela's labour and Bruno's land—then a voluntary contract between the owners of those inputs can determine how the surplus from their interaction will be shared between the two parties, depending on their bargaining power.
- There are potential gains (to all concerned) from individuals specializing in tasks for which they have a comparative advantage.
- The division of labour may be coordinated through market exchange. In Unit 1, specialization in grain and apples was coordinated through buying and selling grain and apples. In Unit 5, the interaction between Angela and Bruno was coordinated by a contract trading the use of land for a share of the crop.
- Sometimes, however, people need to work together to produce something that will benefit all of them, and their success will depend on their preferences and strategies to discourage free riding.
- Another way that work may be coordinated and combined with other inputs is by organization within a firm. The firms in Unit 2 produced cloth, deciding how much coal to buy and how many workers to employ.

We illustrated each of these conclusions using models that illuminate some aspects of the economy, while setting aside others. In Unit 2, we did not consider how the length of the working day was determined while the economy was growing. In Unit 3, we did not model how the wage or the marginal rate of transformation of free time into goods was determined when we analysed a decision on working hours. In Unit 2 we told a story of conflicting interests over wages, but we did not model strategic interaction and bargaining until Units 4 and 5. And in Unit 5 we used the story of just two (imaginary) people called Bruno and Angela to model how bargaining may affect the Pareto efficiency and fairness of allocations.

In this unit, we study how, in the modern capitalist economy, the coordination of labour takes place within firms. We model how wages are determined when there are conflicts of interest between employers and employees, and look at what this means for the sharing of the mutual gains that arise from cooperation in a firm.

In Unit 7, we look at the firm as an actor in its relationship with other firms and with its customers.

6.1 FIRMS, MARKETS, AND THE DIVISION OF LABOUR

The economy is made up of people doing different things, for example producing Apple display modules or making clothing for export. Producing display modules also involves many distinct tasks, done by different employees within Toshiba or Sharp, the companies that make them for Apple.

Setting aside the work done in families, in a capitalist economy, the **division of labour** is coordinated in two major ways: firms and markets.

- Through firms, the components of goods are produced by different people in different departments of the firm, and assembled to produce the finished shirt or iPhone.
- Or components produced by groups of workers in different firms may be brought together through market interactions between firms.
- By buying and selling goods on markets, the finished iPhone gets from the producer into the pocket of the consumer, and the American Apparel shirt ends up on somebody's back.

So in this unit we study firms. In the units to follow, we study markets. Herbert Simon, an economist, used the view from Mars to explain why it is important to study both.

> **division of labour** The specialization of producers to carry out different tasks in the production process. *Also known as: specialization.*

Among the institutions of modern capitalist economies, the firm rivals the government in importance. John Micklethwait and Adrian Wooldridge explain how this happened. John Micklethwait and Adrian Wooldridge. 2003. *The Company: A Short History of a Revolutionary Idea*. New York, NY: Modern Library.

Why do firms work the way they do? For example, why do the owners of the firm hire the workers, rather than the other way around? Randall Kroszner and Louis Putterman summarize this field of economics. Randall S. Kroszner and Louis Putterman (editors). 2009. *The Economic Nature of the Firm: A Reader*. Cambridge: Cambridge University Press.

GREAT ECONOMISTS

Herbert Simon

Imagine a visitor approaching Earth from Mars, Herbert 'Herb' Simon (1916–2001) urged his readers. Looking at Earth through a telescope that revealed social structure, what would our visitor see? Companies might appear as green fields, he suggested, divisions and departments as faint contours within. Connecting these fields, red lines of buying and selling. Within these fields, blue lines of authority, connecting boss and employee, foreman and assembly-worker, mentor and mentee.

Traditionally, economists had focused on the market and the competitive setting of prices. But to a visitor from Mars, Simon suggested:

> Organizations would be the dominant feature of the landscape. A message sent back home, describing the scene, would speak of 'large green areas interconnected by red lines.' It would not likely speak of 'a network of red lines connecting green spots'. ('Organizations and Markets', 1991)

Herbert A. Simon. 1991. 'Organizations and Markets' (http://tinyco.re/2460377). *Journal of Economic Perspectives* 5 (2): pp. 25–44.

Trained as a political scientist, Simon's desire to understand society led him to study both institutions and the human mind—to open the 'black box' of motivations that economists had come to take for granted. He was celebrated in departments of computer science, psychology, and, of course, economics, for which he won the Nobel Prize in 1978.

A firm, he pointed out, is not simply an agent, shifting to match supply and demand. It is composed of individuals, whose needs and desires might conflict. In what ways could these differences be resolved? Simon asked, when would an individual shift from contract work (a 'sale' of a particular, predefined task) to an employment relation (where a boss dictates the task after the sale—the relationship at the heart of a firm)?

When the desired task is easy to specify in a contract, Simon explained that we could view this as simply work-for-hire. But high uncertainty (the employer not knowing in advance what needs to be done) would make it impossible to specify in a contract what the worker was to do and, in this case, the result would be an employer-employee relation that is characteristic of the firm.

Herbert A. Simon. 1951. 'A Formal Theory of the Employment Relationship' (http://tinyco.re/0460792). *Econometrica* 19 (3).

This early work showcased two of Simon's lasting interests: the complexity of economic relations, where one might sell an obligation that was incompletely described, and the role of uncertainty in changing the nature of decision making. His argument demonstrated the emergence of the 'boss'.

Understanding how contract work turns into employment only implies that we understand a particular relationship between two members of an organization. We have yet to explain the firm as a whole—the Martian's green fields.

What makes a good organization? This is a question for psychologists as much as economists, because we know that incentives that tie individual rewards to the success of the organization appear to have little effect.

Simon's intellectual career can be contrasted with another great economist, Friedrich Hayek, whose ideas we will examine in detail in Unit 11. Both were interested in how societies could thrive in the face of uncertainty and imperfect agents. For Hayek, the price mechanism was all: a device to collect and process vast quantities of information, and so synchronize systems of arbitrary size.

But for Simon, the price mechanism needed to be supplemented—even supplanted—by institutions and governments better equipped to handle uncertainty and rapid change. These alternative 'authority mechanisms' draw on partially understood aspects of the human psyche: loyalty, group identification, and creative satisfaction.

By the time of his death in 2001, Simon had seen many of his ideas reach the mainstream. Behavioural economics has roots in his attempts to build economic theories that reflect empirical data. Simon's view from Mars shows that economics could not be a self-contained science: an economist needs to be both a mathematician, working with decision-sets and utilities, and a social psychologist, reasoning about the motivations of human relationships.

The coordination of work

The way that labour is coordinated within firms is different to coordination through markets:

- *Firms represent a concentration of economic power*: This is placed in the hands of the owners and managers, who regularly issue directives with the expectation that their employees will carry them out. An 'order' in the firm is a command.
- *Markets are characterized by a decentralization of power*: Purchases and sales result from the buyers' and sellers' autonomous decision. An 'order' in a market is a request for a purchase that can be rejected if the seller pleases.

The prices that motivate and constrain people's actions in a market are the result of the actions of thousands or millions of individuals, not a decision by someone in authority. The idea of private property specifically limits the things a government or anyone else can do with your possessions.

In a firm, by contrast, owners or their managers direct the activities of their employees, who may number in the thousands or even millions. The managers of Walmart, the world's largest retailer, decide on the activities of 2.2 million employees, a larger number of people than any army in world history before the nineteenth century. Walmart is an exceptionally large firm, but it is not exceptional in that it brings together a large number of people who work together in a way coordinated (by the management) to make profits.

Unlike flash mobs, firms do not form spontaneously and then disappear. Like any organization, firms have a decision-making process and ways of imposing their decisions on the people in it. When we say that 'Apple outsourced its component production' or 'the firm sets a price of $10.75', we mean that the decision-making process in the firm resulted in these actions.

Figure 6.1 shows a simplified picture of the firm's actors and decision-making structure.

The dashed upward green arrows represent a problem of **asymmetric information** between levels in the firm's hierarchy (owners and managers, managers and workers). Since owners or managers do not always know what their subordinates know or do, not all of their directions or commands (grey downward arrows) are necessarily carried out.

This relationship between the firm and its employees contrasts with the firm's relationship to its customers, which we study in the next unit. The bakery firm cannot text its customers to tell them to 'Show up at 8 a.m. and purchase two loaves of bread at the price of €1 each'. It could tempt its customers with a special offer, but unlike the employer with its employees, it cannot require them to show up. When you buy or sell something, it is generally voluntary. In buying or selling you respond to prices, not orders.

The firm is different: it is defined by having a decision-making structure in which some people have power over others. Ronald Coase, the economist who founded the study of the firm as both a stage and an actor, wrote:

> If a workman moves from department Y to department X, he does not go because of a change in relative prices but because he is ordered to do so ... the distinguishing mark of the firm is the suppression of the price mechanism. ('The Nature of the Firm', 1937)

These two books describe the property rights, authority structures, and market interactions that characterize the modern capitalist firm.

Henry Hansmann. 2000. *The Ownership of Enterprise*. Cambridge, MA: Belknap Press.

Oliver E. Williamson. 1985. *The Economic Institutions of Capitalism*. New York, NY: Collier Macmillan.

asymmetric information Information that is relevant to the parties in an economic interaction, but is known by some but not by others. *See also: adverse selection, moral hazard.*

Ronald H. Coase. 1937. 'The Nature of the Firm' (http://tinyco.re/8128486). *Economica* 4 (16): pp. 386–405.

Coase pointed out that the firm in a capitalist economy is a miniature, privately owned, centrally planned economy. Its top-down decision-making structure resembles the centralized direction of production in entire economies that took place in many Communist countries (and in the US and the UK during the Second World War).

Ronald H. Coase. 1992. 'The Institutional Structure of Production' (http://tinyco.re/1636715). *American Economic Review* 82 (4): pp. 713–19.

Contracts and relationships

The difference between market interactions and relationships within firms is clear when we consider the differing kinds of **contracts** that form the basis of exchange.

A sale contract for a car transfers ownership, meaning that the new owner can now use the car and exclude others from its use. A rental contract on an apartment does not transfer ownership of the apartment (which would include the right to sell it); instead it gives the tenant a limited set of rights over the apartment, including the right to exclude others (including the landlord) from its use.

Under a **wage labour** contract, an employee gives the employer the right to direct him or her to be at work at specific times, and to accept the authority of the employer over the use of his or her time while at work.

The employer does not own the employee as a result of this contract. If the employer did, the employee would be called a slave. We might say that the employer has 'rented' the employee for part of the day. To summarize:

contract A legal document or understanding that specifies a set of actions that parties to the contract must undertake.

wage labour A system in which producers are paid for the time they work for their employers.

- Contracts for products sold in markets permanently transfer *ownership* of the good from the seller to the buyer.
- Contracts for labour temporarily transfer *authority* over a person's activities from the employee to the manager or owner.

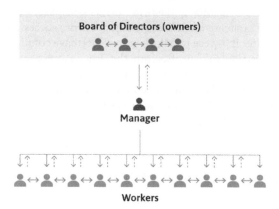

Figure 6.1 The firm's actors and its decision making and information structures.

1. Owners decide long-term strategies
The owners, through their board of directors, decide the long-term strategies of the firm concerning how, what, and where to produce. They then direct the manager(s) to implement these decisions.

2. Managers assign workers
Each manager assigns workers to the tasks required for these decisions to be implemented, and attempts to ensure that the assignments are carried out.

3. Flows of information
The green arrows represent flows of information. The upward green arrows are dashed lines because workers often know things that managers do not, and managers know things that owners do not.

Firms differ from markets in another way: social interactions within firms sometimes extend over decades, or even a lifetime. In markets, we shop around, so our interactions are typically short-lived and not repeated. One of the reasons for this difference is that working in a firm—as either a manager or an employee—means acquiring a network of associates who are essential for the job to be done well. Some of our workmates will become our friends. Managers and employees also acquire both technical and social skills that are specific to the firm they work for.

Oliver Williamson, an economist, termed these skills, networks, and friendships **relationship-specific** or **firm-specific assets** because they are valuable only while the worker remains employed in a particular firm. When the relationship ends, their value is lost to both sides. Think about how different this is to the social interactions in the market. Although you may know the face or even the name of a person from whom you buy, or to whom you sell something, the relationship is typically temporary, in which case this knowledge has little value.

This social aspect becomes important economically when economic changes disrupt social interactions.

Imagine how your life as a shopper changes if your local grocery store closes tomorrow. You would have to find a new place to shop, and it might take you a few minutes to learn where the various items you need are on display.

Now imagine what would change if the company in which you work goes out of business tomorrow. You would lose your network of work associates, your workplace friendships, and your firm-specific social and technical skills would suddenly have become useless to you. You might have to move to a new town. Your children would need to change school, so they would lose contact with their friends too.

Thus, the people making up the firm—owners, managers, and employees—are united in their common interest in the firm's success, because all of them would suffer if it were to fail. However, they have conflicting interests about how to distribute the profits from the firm's success amongst themselves (wages, managerial salaries, and owners' profits), and may disagree about other policies such as conditions of work, managerial perks, and who makes the key decisions—such as whether Apple should assemble iPhones in China or the US.

> **firm-specific asset** Something that a person owns or can do that has more value in the individual's current firm than in their next best alternative.

EXERCISE 6.1 THE STRUCTURE OF AN ORGANIZATION

In Figure 6.1 (page 231) we showed the actors and decision-making structure of a typical firm.

1. How might the actors and decision-making structure of three organizations, Google (http://tinyco.re/0428409), Wikipedia (http://tinyco.re/6233386), and a family farm compare with this?
2. Draw an organizational structure chart in the style of Figure 6.1 to represent each of these entities.

QUESTION 6.1 CHOOSE THE CORRECT ANSWER(S)
Which of the following statements is true?

☐ A labour contract transfers ownership of the employee from the employee to the employer.
☐ The office where the employee works is a relation-specific asset, because the employee cannot use it after leaving the firm.
☐ In a labour contract, one side of the contract has the power to issue orders to the other side, but this power is absent from a sale contract.
☐ A firm is a structure that involves decentralization of power to the employees.

6.2 OTHER PEOPLE'S MONEY: THE SEPARATION OF OWNERSHIP AND CONTROL

The firm's profits legally belong to the people who own the firm's assets, which include its capital goods. The owners direct the other members of the firm to take actions that contribute to the firm's profits. This in turn will increase the value of the firm's assets, and improve the wealth of the owners.

The owners take whatever remains after revenues (the proceeds from sale of the products) are used to pay employees, managers, suppliers, creditors, and taxes. Profit is the *residual*. It is what's left of the revenues after these payments. The owners claim it, which is why they are called **residual claimants**. Managers (unless they are also owners) are not residual claimants. Neither are employees.

This division of revenue has an important implication. If the firm's revenues increase because managers or employees do their job well, the owners will benefit, *but the managers and employees will not* (unless they receive a promotion, bonus, or salary increase). This is one reason we consider the firm as a stage, one on which not all the actors have the same interests.

In small enterprises, the owners are typically also the managers and so are in charge of operational and strategic decisions. As an example, consider a restaurant owned by a sole proprietor, who decides on the menu, hours of operation, marketing strategies, choice of suppliers, and the size and compensation of the workforce. In most cases the owner will try to maximize the profits of the enterprise by providing the kinds of food and ambience that people want, at competitive prices. Unlike Apple, the owner cannot outsource dishwashing or table service to a low-wage location.

In large corporations, there are typically many owners. Most of them play no part in the firm's management. The owners of the firm are the individuals and institutions, such as pension funds, that own the **shares** issued by the firm. By issuing shares to the general public, a company can raise capital to finance its growth, leaving strategic and operational decisions to a relatively small group of specialized managers.

These decisions include what, where, and how to manufacture the firm's products, or how much to pay employees and managers. The senior management of a firm is also responsible for deciding how much of the firm's profits are distributed to shareholders in the form of dividends, and how much is retained to finance growth. Of course, the owners benefit

residual claimant The person who receives the income left over from a firm or other project after the payment of all contractual costs (for example the cost of hiring workers and paying taxes).

share A part of the assets of a firm that may be traded. It gives the holder a right to receive a proportion of a firm's profit and to benefit when the firm's assets become more valuable. *Also known as: common stock.*

from the firm's growth because they own part of the value of the firm, which increases as the firm grows.

When managers decide on the use of other people's funds, this is referred to as the **separation of ownership and control**.

The separation of ownership and control results in a potential conflict of interest.

The decisions of managers affect profits, and profits decide the incomes of the owners. But it is not always in the interest of managers to maximize profits. They may choose to take actions that benefit themselves, at the expense of the owners. Perhaps they will spend as much as possible on their company credit card, or seek to increase their own power and prestige through empire-building, even if that is not in the interests of shareholders.

Even single owners of firms are not *required* to maximize their profits. Restaurant owners can choose menus they personally like, or waiters who are their friends. But unlike managers, when they lose profits as a result, the cost comes directly out of their pocket.

In the eighteenth century, Adam Smith observed the tendency of senior managers to serve their own interests, rather than those of shareholders. He said this about the managers of what were then called joint-stock companies:

> [B]eing the managers rather of other people's money than of their own, it cannot well be expected, that they should watch over it with the same anxious vigilance with which the partners in a [firm managed by its owners] frequently watch over their own … Negligence and profusion, therefore, must always prevail, more or less, in the management of the affairs of such a company. (*The Wealth of Nations*, 1776)

Smith had not seen the modern firm, but he understood the problems raised by the separation of ownership and control. There are two ways that owners can incentivize managers to serve their interests. They can structure contracts so that managerial compensation depends on the performance of the company's share price. Also, the firm's board of directors, which represents the firm's shareholders and typically has a substantial share in the firm (like a representative of a pension fund), can monitor the managers' performance. The board has the authority to dismiss managers, and shareholders in turn have the right to replace members of the board. The owners of large companies with many shareholders rarely exercise this authority, partly because shareholders are a large and diverse group that cannot easily get together to decide something. Occasionally, however, this **free-rider** problem is overcome and a shareholder with a large stake in a company may lead a shareholder revolt to change or influence senior management.

When we model the firm as an actor, we often assume that it maximizes profits. This is a simplification, but a reasonable one for most purposes:

- *Owners have a strong interest in profit maximization*: It is the basis of their wealth.
- *Market competition penalizes or eliminates firms that do not make substantial profits for their owners*: We saw this process in Unit 1 and Unit 2 as part of the explanation of the permanent technological revolution, and it applies to all aspects of the firms' decisions.

separation of ownership and control The attribute of some firms by which managers are a separate group from the owners.

free ride Benefiting from the contributions of others to some cooperative project without contributing oneself.

QUESTION 6.2 CHOOSE THE CORRECT ANSWER(S)

QUESTION 6.2 CHOOSE THE CORRECT ANSWER(S)

Which of the following statements about the separation of ownership and control is true?

☐ When the ownership and control of a firm is separated, the managers become the residual claimants.
☐ Managers always work to maximize the firm's profit.
☐ One way to address the problem associated with the separation of ownership and control is to pay the managers a salary that depends on the performance of the firm's share price.
☐ It is effective for shareholders to monitor the performance of the management, in a firm owned by a large number of shareholders.

6.3 OTHER PEOPLE'S LABOUR

The firm does not only manage, as Adam Smith put it, 'other people's money'. The decision-makers in a firm decide on the use of other people's labour too: the effort of their employees. People participate in firms because they can do better if they are part of the firm than if they are not. As in all voluntary economic interactions, there are mutual gains. But just as conflicts arise between owners and managers, there will generally be differences between owners and managers on the one hand, and employees on the other, about how the firm will use the strength, creativity, and other skills of its employees.

A firm's profits (before the payment of taxes) depend on three things:

- costs of acquiring the inputs necessary for the production process
- output (how much these inputs produce)
- sales revenues received from selling goods or services

Our focus here is how firms seek to minimize the cost of acquiring the necessary labour to produce the goods and services they sell. We have already seen in Unit 2 how firms might increase output without raising costs by adopting new technologies, and in Unit 7 we will study their sales decisions.

Hiring employees is different from buying other goods and services. When we buy a shirt or pay someone to mow a lawn, it is clear what we get for our cash. If we don't get it, we don't pay, but if we have already paid, we can go to court and get our money back.

But a firm cannot write an enforceable employment contract that specifies the exact tasks employees have to perform in order to get paid. This is for three reasons:

- When the firm writes a contract for the employment of a worker, it cannot know exactly what it will need the employee to do, because this will be determined by unforeseen future events.
- It would be impractical or too costly for the firm to observe exactly how much effort each employee makes in doing the job.
- Even if the firm somehow acquired this information, it could not be the basis of an enforceable contract.

To understand the last point, consider a restaurant owner, who would like her staff to serve customers in a pleasant manner. Imagine how difficult it would be for a court to decide whether the owner can withhold wages from a waiter because he had not smiled often enough.

An employment contract omits things that both the employees and the business owner care about: how hard and well the employee will work, and for how long the worker will stay. As a result of this **contractual incompleteness**, paying the lowest possible wage is almost never the firm's strategy to minimize the cost of acquiring the labour effort it needs.

> **incomplete contract** A contract that does not specify, in an enforceable way, every aspect of the exchange that affects the interests of parties to the exchange (or of others).

EXERCISE 6.2 INCOMPLETE CONTRACTS

Think of two or three jobs with which you are familiar, perhaps a teacher, a retail worker, a nurse, or a police officer.

In each case, indicate why the employment contract is necessarily incomplete. What important parts of the person's job—things that the employer would like to see the employee do or not do—cannot be covered in a contract, or if they are, cannot be enforced?

GREAT ECONOMISTS

Karl Marx

Adam Smith, writing at the birth of capitalism in the eighteenth century, was to become its most famous advocate. Karl Marx (1818–1883), who watched capitalism mature in the industrial towns of England, was to become its most famous critic.

Born in Prussia (now part of Germany), he distinguished himself as a student at a Jesuit high school only by his rebelliousness. In 1842 he became a writer and editor for the *Rheinische Zeitung*, a liberal newspaper, which was then closed by the government, after which he moved to Paris and met Friedrich Engels, with whom he collaborated in writing *The Communist Manifesto* (1848). Marx then moved to London in 1849. At first, Marx and his wife Jenny lived in poverty. He earned money by writing about political events in Europe for the *New York Tribune*.

Marx saw capitalism as just the latest in a succession of economic arrangements in which people have lived since prehistory. Inequality was not unique to capitalism, he observed—slavery, feudalism, and most other economic systems had shared this feature—but capitalism also generated perpetual change and growth in output.

He was the first economist to understand why the capitalist economy was the most dynamic in human history. Perpetual change arose, Marx observed, because capitalists could survive only by introducing new technologies and products, finding ways of lowering costs, and by reinvesting their profits into businesses that would perpetually grow.

This, he claimed, inevitably caused conflict between employers and workers. Buying and selling goods in an open market is a transaction between equals: nobody is in a position to order anyone else to buy or

Karl Marx. (1848) 2010. *The Communist Manifesto* (http://tinyco.re/0155765). Edited by Friedrich Engels. London: Arcturus Publishing.

sell. In the labour market, in which owners of capital are buyers and workers are the sellers, the appearance of freedom and equality was, to Marx, an illusion.

Employers did not buy the employee's work, because this cannot be purchased, as we have seen in this unit. Instead, the wage allowed the employer to rent the worker and to command workers inside the firm. Workers were not inclined to disobey because they might lose their jobs and join the 'reserve army' of the unemployed (the phrase that Marx used in his 1867 work, *Capital*). Marx thought that the power wielded by employers over workers was a core defect of capitalism.

Marx also had influential views on history, politics, and sociology. He thought that history was decisively shaped by the interactions between scarcity, technological progress, and economic institutions, and that political conflicts arose from conflicts about the distribution of income and the organization of these institutions. He thought that capitalism, by organizing production and allocation in anonymous markets, created atomized individuals instead of integrated communities.

In recent years, economists have returned to themes in Marx's work to help explain economic crises. These themes include the firm as an arena of conflict and of the exercise of power (this unit), the role of technological progress (Unit 1 and Unit 2), and the problems created by inequality (Unit 19).

Karl Marx. (1848) 2010. *The Communist Manifesto* (http://tinyco.re/0155765). Edited by Friedrich Engels. London: Arcturus Publishing. Karl Marx. 1906. *Capital: A Critique of Political Economy*. New York, NY: Random House.

Capital is long and covers many subjects, but you can use a searchable archive (http://tinyco.re/9166776) to find the passages you need.

Why is it not possible for firms just to pay employees according to how productive they are? For example, paying employees at a clothing factory $2 for each garment they finish. This method of payment, known as **piece rate**, provides the employee with an incentive to exert effort, because employees take home more pay if they make more garments.

In the late nineteenth century the pay of more than half of US manufacturing workers was based on their output, but piece rates are not widely used in modern economies. At the turn of the twenty-first century less than 5% of manufacturing workers in the US were paid piece rates and, beyond the manufacturing sector, piece rates are used even less often.

Why do most of today's firms not use this simple method to induce high effort from their employees?

piece-rate work A type of employment in which the worker is paid a fixed amount for each unit of the product made.

Susan Helper, Morris Kleiner, and Yingchun Wang. 2010. 'Analyzing Compensation Methods in Manufacturing: Piece Rates, Time Rates, or Gain-Sharing?' (http://tinyco.re/4437027). NBER Working Papers No. 16540, National Bureau of Economic Research, Inc.

- It is very difficult to measure the amount of output an employee is producing in modern knowledge- and service-based economies (think about an office worker, or someone providing home care for an elderly person).
- Employees rarely work alone, so measuring the contribution of individual workers is difficult (think about a team in a marketing company working on an advertising campaign, or the kitchen staff at a restaurant).

If piece rates are not practical, then what other method could a firm use to induce high effort from workers? How could the firm provide an incentive to do the job well, even though the worker is paid for time and not output? Just as the owners of the firm protect their interests by linking management pay to the firm's share price, the manager uses incentives so that employees will work effectively.

(p54)
Economic Rent = benefit from option taken - net benefit from next best option

"rent a worker's labor"

Economic Rent measures the value of a situation

QUESTION 6.3 CHOOSE THE CORRECT ANSWER(S)
Which of the following are reasons why employment contracts are incomplete?

☐ The firm cannot contract an employee not to leave.
☐ The firm cannot specify every eventuality in a contract.
☐ The firm is unable to observe exactly how an employee is fulfilling the contract.
☐ The contract is unfinished.

6.4 EMPLOYMENT RENTS

There are many reasons why people put in a good day's work. For many people, doing a good job is its own reward, and doing anything else would contradict their work ethic. Even for those not intrinsically motivated to work hard, feelings of responsibility for other employees or for one's employer may provide strong work motivation.

For some employees, hard work is a way to reciprocate a feeling of gratitude to the employer for providing a job with good working conditions. In other cases, firms identify teams of workers whose output is readily measured—for example, the percentage of on-time departures for airline staff—and pay a benefit to the whole group that is divided among team members.

But in the background, there is another reason to do a good job: the fear of being fired, or of missing the opportunity to be promoted into a position that has higher pay and greater job security.

Laws and practices concerning the termination of employment for cause (that is, because of inadequate or low quality work, not due to insufficient demand for the firm's product) differ among countries. In some countries, the owners of the firm have the right to fire a worker whenever they choose, while in others, dismissal is difficult and costly. But even in these cases, an employee has to fear the consequences of not working up to the employer's desired standards. Such a worker, for example, would be unlikely to achieve a position in the firm where she could count on remaining employed when lower demand for the firm's products results in other workers being dismissed.

Do workers care whether they lose their jobs?

If firms paid their employees the lowest wages they would be willing to accept, the answer would be no. Such a wage would make the worker indifferent between remaining in the job and losing it. But in practice most workers care very much. There is a difference between the value of the job (taking into account all the benefits and costs it entails) and the value of the next best option—which is being unemployed and having to search for a new job. In other words, there is an **employment rent**.

Employment rents can benefit owners and managers in two ways:

* *The employee is more likely to stay with the firm*: If she were to quit the job, the firm would need to pay to recruit and train someone else.
* *They can threaten to fire the worker*: Owners and managers exert power over employees because the employee has something to lose. The threat can be implicit or explicit, but it will make the worker perform in ways that she would not choose unless this was the case.

employment rent The economic rent a worker receives when the net value of her job exceeds the net value of her next best alternative (that is, being unemployed). *Also known as: cost of job loss.*

We can use the same reasoning in the employment of managers by the owners of the firm. The main reason owners wield power over managers is that they can fire them, and so eliminate their managerial employment rents.

HOW ECONOMISTS LEARN FROM FACTS

Managers exert power

These examples show the effect of the power that managers and owners exert.

- Labour economists Alan Krueger and Alexandre Mas unravel the mystery of why the tread on Bridgestone (Firestone) tyres was separating, endangering motorists and reducing profits.
- Barbara Ehrenreich worked undercover for minimum wage in motels and restaurants to see how America's poor live.
- Polly Toynbee, a British journalist, had previously done the same in the UK in 2003, taking jobs such as call centre employee and care home worker.
- Harry Braverman provides a history of what he calls the 'deskilling' process, and suggests how dumbing down jobs is a strategy for maximizing the employer's profits.

Alan B. Krueger and Alexandre Mas. 2004. 'Strikes, Scabs, and Tread Separations: Labor Strife and the Production of Defective Bridgestone/Firestone Tires'. *Journal of Political Economy* 112 (2): pp. 253–89.

Barbara Ehrenreich. 2011. *Nickel and Dimed: On (Not) Getting By in America*. New York, NY: St. Martin's Press.

Polly Toynbee. 2003. *Hard Work: Life in Low-pay Britain*. London: Bloomsbury Publishing.

Harry Braverman and Paul M. Sweezy. 1975. *Labor and Monopoly Capital: The Degradation of Work in the Twentieth Century*. 2nd ed. New York, NY: Monthly Review Press.

WHEN ECONOMISTS *AGREE*

Coase and Marx on the firm and its employees

The writer George Bernard Shaw (1856–1950) joked that 'if all economists were laid end to end, they would not reach a conclusion.'

This is funny, but not entirely true.

For example, the two leading economists of the early nineteenth century—Ricardo and Malthus—were political opponents. Ricardo often sided with businesspeople, for example in supporting freer imports of grain to Britain to reduce food prices and allow lower wages. Malthus opposed him and supported the Corn Laws (http://tinyco.re/6855467) that restricted grain imports, a position favoured by the landed gentry. But the two economists both proposed the same theory of land rents, which we still use today.

Even more striking is that two economists from different centuries and political orientations came up with similar ways of understanding the firm and its employees.

In the nineteenth century, Marx contrasted the way that buyers and sellers interact on a market, voluntarily engaging in trade, with how the firm is organized as a top-down structure, one in which employers issue orders and workers follow them. He called markets 'a very Eden of the innate rights of man', but described firms as 'exploit[ing] labour-power to the greatest possible extent.'

When Ronald Coase died in 2013, he was described by *Forbes* magazine as 'the greatest of the many great University of Chicago economists' (http://tinyco.re/6800200). The motto of *Forbes* is 'The capitalist tool', and the University of Chicago has a reputation as the centre of conservative economic thinking.

Yet, like Marx, Coase stressed the central role of authority in the firm's contractual relations:

> Note the character of the contract into which an [employee] enters that is employed within a firm ... for certain remuneration [the employee] agrees to obey the directions of the entrepreneur. (*The nature of the firm*, 1937)

Recall that Coase had also defined the firm by its political structure: 'If a workman moves from department Y to department X, he does not go because of a change in prices but because he is ordered to do so.' He sought to understand why firms exist at all, quoting his contemporary D. H. Robertson's description of them as 'islands of conscious power in this ocean of unconscious cooperation'.

Both based their thinking on careful empirical observation, and they arrived at a similar understanding of the hierarchy of the firm. They disagreed, however, on the consequences of what they observed: Coase thought that the hierarchy of the firm was a cost-reducing way to do business. Marx thought that the coercive authority of the boss over the worker limited the employee's freedom. Like Malthus and Ricardo, Coase and Marx disagreed. But like Malthus and Ricardo, they also advanced economics with a common idea.

Counting the cost of job loss

Recall that an economic rent measures the value of a situation—for example, having your current job—compared to what you would get if the current situation were no longer possible.

To calculate employment rent—or in other words, the net cost of job loss—we need to weigh up all the benefits and costs of working compared with being unemployed and searching for another job.

There are some costs of working, such as:

- *The disutility of work*: Employees must spend time doing things they would prefer not to do.
- *The cost of travelling to work every day*.

But there are many benefits, which would be lost if you lost your job:

- *Wage income*: This may be partially offset by an unemployment benefit or, in poorer countries, by the possibility of lower-paying self-employment or work on the family farm.
- *Firm-specific assets*: These include workplace friends, and perhaps the proximity of the workplace to your present home.
- *Medical insurance*: The employer may pay for the employee's healthcare in some countries.
- *The social status of being employed*: In Unit 13 we will see that the stigma of being unemployed is equivalent to a substantial financial cost for most people.

Even confining attention to the loss in wages, the cost is high. But how do we measure how high it is?

HOW ECONOMISTS LEARN FROM FACTS

How large are employment rents?

Setting aside the undoubtedly large but hard-to-measure psychological and social cost of losing one's job, estimating the cost of job loss (the size of the employment rent) is not simple.

Can we compare the economic situation of workers currently employed with the economic situation of unemployed people? No, because the unemployed are a different group of people, with different abilities and skills. Even if they were employed, they would be likely (on average) to earn less than people who currently have jobs.

An entire firm closing, or a mass layoff of workers, provides a **natural experiment** that can help. We could look at the earnings of workers before and after they lost their job during a major employment cutback. When a factory closes because the parent company has decided to relocate production to some other part of the world, for example, virtually all workers lose their jobs, and not just the ones who were most likely to lose their jobs through poor performance.

Louis Jacobson, Robert Lalonde, and Daniel Sullivan used such a natural experiment to estimate the cost of job loss. They studied experienced (not recently hired) full-time workers hit by mass layoffs in the US state of Pennsylvania in 1982. In 2014 dollars, those displaced had been averaging $50,000 in earnings in 1979. Those who were fortunate enough to find another job in less than three months took jobs that paid a lot less, averaging only $35,000: being laid off meant that their earnings declined by $15,000.

Four years later they were still making $13,300 less than similar workers who had been making the same initial wage, but whose firms did not lay off their workers. In the five years that followed their layoff they lost the equivalent of an entire year's earnings.

Many, of course, did not find work at all. They suffered even greater costs.

The year 1982 was not a good time to be looking for work in Pennsylvania, but similar estimates (from the US state of Connecticut between 1993 and 2004 for example) suggest that even in better times, employment rents are large enough that workers would worry about losing them.

natural experiment An empirical study exploiting naturally occurring statistical controls in which researchers do not have the ability to assign participants to treatment and control groups, as is the case in conventional experiments. Instead, differences in law, policy, weather, or other events can offer the opportunity to analyse populations as if they had been part of an experiment. The validity of such studies depends on the premise that the assignment of subjects to the naturally occurring treatment and control groups can be plausibly argued to be random.

Lori G. Kletzer. 1998. 'Job Displacement' (http://tinyco.re/ 8577746). *Journal of Economic Perspectives* 12 (1): pp. 115–36.

Kenneth A. Couch and Dana W. Placzek. 2010. 'Earnings Losses of Displaced Workers Revisited'. *American Economic Review* 100 (1): pp. 572–89.

Louis Jacobson, Robert J. Lalonde, and Daniel G. Sullivan. 1993. 'Earnings Losses of Displaced Workers'. *The American Economic Review* 83 (4): pp. 685–709.

QUESTION 6.4 CHOOSE THE CORRECT ANSWER(S)

In which of the following employment situations would the employment rent be high, *ceteris paribus*?

- ☐ In a job that provides many benefits, such as housing and medical insurance.
- ☐ In an economic boom, when the ratio of job-seekers to vacancies is low.
- ☐ When the worker is paid a high salary because she is a qualified accountant and there is a shortage of accountancy skills.
- ☐ When the worker is paid a high salary because the firm's customers know and trust her.

6.5 DETERMINANTS OF THE EMPLOYMENT RENT

To construct a model of how employment rents may be used to motivate employees to work hard, we consider Maria, an employee earning $12 an hour for a 35-hour working week. To determine her economic rent, we need to think how she would evaluate two aspects of her job:

- *The pay that she gets*: which is something she values.
- *How hard she works*: she would like to do no more work than is necessary.

utility A numerical indicator of the value that one places on an outcome, such that higher valued outcomes will be chosen over lower valued ones when both are feasible.

Using the concept of **utility** introduced in Unit 3, we can say that Maria's utility is increased by the goods and services she can buy with her wage, but reduced by the unpleasantness of going to work and working hard all day—the disutility of work.

Her disutility of work depends on how much effort she puts into her job. Suppose she spends half of her working time actually working, and half doing other things like checking Facebook. We represent this as an effort level of 0.5. Working this hard is equivalent to a cost of $2 per hour to Maria. To calculate her employment rent we first find her net utility of working and earning $12, compared with being unemployed and earning nothing:

$$\text{net utility per hour} = \text{wage} - \text{disutility of effort per hour}$$
$$= \$10$$

This is her employment rent *per hour*. The total employment rent (or cost of job loss), depends on how long she expects to remain unemployed. We will suppose that if she loses her job she can expect to remain unemployed for 44 weeks before finding another. The analysis in Figure 6.2 shows how to calculate the rent.

Her total employment rent is the employment rent per hour times the number of hours of work she will lose if her job is terminated. It is the shaded area in the figure.

$$\text{total employment rent} = \text{employment rent per hour} \times \text{expected lost hours of work}$$
$$= \$10 \text{ per hour} \times 1{,}540 \text{ hours}$$
$$= \$15{,}400$$

unemployment benefit A government transfer received by an unemployed person. *Also known as: unemployment insurance*

reservation wage What an employee would get in alternative employment, or from an unemployment benefit or other support, were he or she not employed in his or her current job.

People who lose their jobs can typically expect help from family and friends while they are out of work. Also, in many economies, people who lose their jobs receive **unemployment benefit** or financial assistance from the government. In poorer economies, they may be able to earn a small amount in informal self-employment.

If Maria receives an unemployment benefit or income from any of these sources, it will partially offset the lost wage income. Let us suppose that while Maria remains unemployed, she will receive a benefit equivalent to being paid $6 an hour for a 35-hour week. This is her **reservation wage**—it is always available to her, so she would be indifferent between having a job that paid $6 an hour, and not working. In Figure 6.2, without unemployment benefits, her reservation wage was zero. Figure 6.3 shows how this affects Maria's employment rent, assuming her effort and disutility of work are unchanged.

Our calculation of employment rent should take into account the reservation wage:

$$\text{employment rent per hour} = \text{wage} - \text{reservation wage} - \text{disutility of effort}$$
$$= \text{wage} - \text{unemployment benefit} - \text{disutility of effort}$$
$$= \$12 - \$6 - \$2$$
$$= \$4$$

And taking account of the duration of unemployment we see that:

$$\text{total employment rent} = \text{employment rent per hour} \times \text{expected hours of lost work time}$$
$$= \$4 \text{ per hour} \times 1{,}540 \text{ hours}$$
$$= \$6{,}160$$

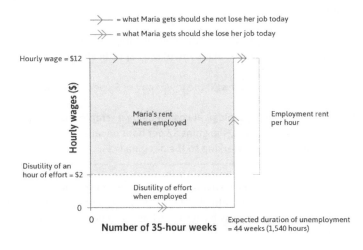

Figure 6.2 Maria's employment rent for a given effort and $12 wage in an economy without an unemployment benefit.

1. Maria's wage
Maria's hourly wage, after taxes and other deductions, is $12. Looking ahead from now (taken as time 0), she will continue to receive this wage for the foreseeable future if she keeps her job, indicated by the horizontal line at the top of the figure.

2. The disutility of working
Maria's current effort level is 0.5: she pursues non-work activities for half of the time on the job. Working this hard is equivalent to a cost of $2 per hour to Maria.

3. The net benefit of working
The difference between her wage and disutility of effort is the economic rent per hour that she receives while employed.

4. If Maria loses her job
If instead Maria were to lose her job at time 0, she would no longer receive her wages. This unfortunate state would persist as long as she remains unemployed, indicated by the horizontal line at the bottom of the figure.

5. The duration of unemployment
The expected duration of unemployment is 44 weeks, where she would have worked 35 hours per week. That is how long she will remain without pay (and without the disutility of working).

6. Maria finds a job
Maria expects to find another job at the same wage after 44 weeks.

7. Maria's employment rent
The shaded area is her total cost of job loss from the spell of unemployment, that is, her employment rent.

Unemployment benefits usually run out eventually: families and friends will not be able to help forever, and government unemployment benefits are often time-limited. If Maria's eligibility for unemployment benefits of $6 lasted only for 13 weeks, her reservation wage would not be $6—she would not be indifferent between a job that paid $6 an hour and unemployment. The employment rent would be higher and her reservation wage would be lower, because the average level of benefits she could expect over the 44-week period of unemployment would be much less than $6.

EXERCISE 6.3 ASSUMPTIONS OF THE MODEL

As in all economic models, our simplified representation of Maria's employment rent has deliberately omitted some aspects of the problem that might be important. For example, we have assumed that:

- Maria finds a job with the same pay after her spell of unemployment.
- She does not experience any psychological or social costs from being unemployed.

Redraw Figure 6.2 (page 243) to show how relaxing each of these assumptions would alter the employment rent. Specifically, assume:

- Maria can only find a job with the lower pay of $6 per hour after her spell of unemployment.
- She experiences a psychological cost of being unemployed of $1 per hour. When unemployed, she gains $2 per hour because there is no longer the disutility of working so the net gain is $1.

Our next step is to study the social interaction between the employer (who sets the wage knowing that it affects Maria's employment rent) and Maria herself, whose decision on how hard to work is influenced by the rent.

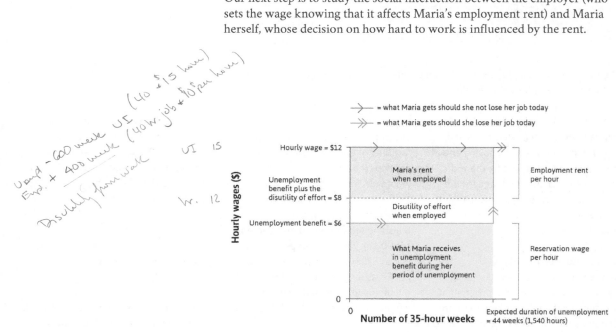

Figure 6.3 Maria's employment rent for a given effort and a $12 wage in an economy with an unemployment benefit of $6 of unlimited duration.

QUESTION 6.5 CHOOSE THE CORRECT ANSWER(S)
Maria earns $12 per hour in her current job and works 35 hours a week. Her disutility of effort is equivalent to a cost of $2 per hour of work. If she loses her job, she will receive unemployment benefit equivalent to $6 per hour. Additionally, being unemployed has psychological and social costs equivalent to $1 per hour. Then:

☐ The employment rent per hour is $3.
☐ Maria's reservation wage is $6 per hour.
☐ Maria's employment rent if she can get another job with the same wage rate after 44 weeks of being unemployed is $6,160.
☐ Maria's employment rent if she can only get a job at a lower wage rate after 44 weeks of being unemployed is more than $7,700.

6.6 WORK AND WAGES: THE LABOUR DISCIPLINE MODEL

When the cost of job loss (the employment rent) is large, workers will be willing to work harder in order to reduce the likelihood of losing the job. Holding constant other ways that it might influence the employment rent, a firm can increase the cost of job loss, and therefore the effort exerted by its employees, by raising wages.

We now represent this social interaction in the firm as a game played by the owners (through their managers) and the employees.

Remember that a game is a description of a social interaction, including:

- a list of the players
- the strategies they can adopt
- the order in which the players choose their actions
- what the players know when they choose their actions
- the outcomes for each of the players (their payoffs) for all of the strategies that may be chosen

As with other models, we ignore some aspects of their interaction to focus on what is important, following the priciple that sometimes we see more by looking at less.

On the stage of the firm, the cast of characters is just the owner (the employer) and a single worker, Maria. The game is sequential (one of them chooses first, like the ultimatum game that we saw in Section 10 of Unit 4) and is repeated in each period of employment. Here is the order of play:

1. *The employer chooses a wage*: This is based on his knowledge of how employees like Maria respond to higher or lower wages, and informs her that she will be employed in subsequent periods at the same wage—as long as she works hard enough.
2. *Maria chooses a level of work effort*: This is in response to the wage offered, taking into account the costs of losing her job if she does not provide enough effort.

The payoff for the employer is the profit. The greater Maria's effort, the more goods or services she will produce, and the more profit he will make.

Maria's payoff is her net valuation of the wage she receives, taking into account the effort she has expended.

If Maria's chooses her work effort as a best response to the employer's offer, and the employer chooses the wage that maximizes his profit given that Maria responds the way she does, their strategies are a **Nash equilibrium**.

> **Nash equilibrium** A set of strategies, one for each player in the game, such that each player's strategy is a best response to the strategies chosen by everyone else.

Employers typically hire work supervisors and may install surveillance equipment to keep watch on their employees, increasing the likelihood that the management will find out if a worker is not working hard and well. Here we will ignore these extra costs and just assume that the employer occasionally gets some information on how hard or well an employee is working. This is not enough to implement a piece-rate contract, but more than enough to fire a worker if the news is not good. Maria knows that the chance of the employer getting bad news decreases the harder she works.

To decide on the wage to set, the employer needs to know how the employee's work effort will respond to higher wages. So we will consider Maria's decision first.

The employee's best response

Maria's effort can vary between zero and one. We can think of this as the proportion of each hour that she spends working diligently (the rest of the time she is not working). An effort level of 0.5 indicates she is spending half the working day on non-work related activities such as checking Facebook, shopping online, or just staring out of the window.

We will assume that Maria's reservation wage is $6. Even if she put in no work whatsoever (and so endured no disutility of effort, spending all day on Facebook and day-dreaming) her job at a $6 wage would be no better than being without work. So she would not care one way or the other if her job ended. Her best response to a wage of $6 would be zero effort.

What if she were paid a higher wage?

For Maria, effort has a cost—the disutility of work—and a benefit: it increases the likelihood of her keeping the job, and the employment rent. In her choice of effort she needs to find a balance between these two.

A higher wage increases the employment rent and hence the benefit from effort, so it will lead her to choose a higher level of effort. Maria's best response (the effort she chooses) will increase with the level of the wage chosen by the employer.

> **worker's best response function (to wage)** The optimal amount of work that a worker chooses to perform for each wage that the employer may offer.

Figure 6.4 shows the effort Maria chooses for each level of the wage, referred to as her **best response curve**, or **best response function**. (Just like the production functions in Unit 3, it shows how one variable, in this case effort, depends on another, the wage.)

Point J in Figure 6.4 represents the situation in Figure 6.3 discussed at the end of the previous section. Maria's reservation wage is $6, she is paid $12, and chooses effort of 0.5.

The best response curve is concave. It becomes flatter as the wage and the effort level increase. This is because, as the level of effort approaches the maximum possible level, the disutility of effort becomes greater. In this case it takes a larger employment rent (and hence a higher wage) to get effort from the employee.

Seen from the standpoint of the owner or the employer, the best response curve shows how paying higher wages can elicit higher effort, but with diminishing marginal returns. In other words, the higher the initial wage, the smaller the increase in effort and output the employer gets from an extra $1 per hour in wages.

The best response curve is the frontier of the feasible set of combinations of wages and effort the firm can get from its employees, and the slope of the frontier is the marginal rate of transformation of wages into effort.

The lowest wage the firm could set for Maria would be the reservation wage, $6, where the best response curve hits the horizontal axis and effort is zero. So we can see that the firm would never offer the lowest wage possible, because she would not work.

We have drawn the best response function in Figure 6.4 under the assumption that unemployment is expected to last 44 weeks. If the expected duration were to change, the best response function would change too. If economic conditions worsened, increasing unemployment duration, Maria's employment rent would be higher. So for any wage, her best response would be to exert a higher level of effort.

Leibniz: The worker's best response function (http://tinyco.re/L060601)

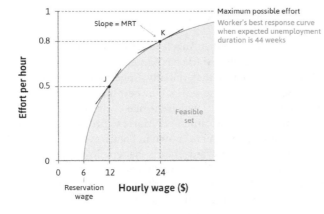

Expected Duration of Unempl.

Figure 6.4 Maria's best response to the wage. Point J refers to the information in Figure 6.3 (wage = $12, effort = 0.5 and expected duration of unemployment if she were to lose her job = 44 weeks).

1. Effort per hour
Effort per hour, measured on the vertical axis, varies between zero and one.

2. The relationship between effort and the wage
If Maria is paid $6 she does not care if she loses her job because $6 is her reservation wage. This is why she provides no effort at a $6 wage. If she is paid more, she provides more effort.

3. The worker's best response
The upward-sloping curve shows how much effort she puts in for each value of the hourly wage on the horizontal axis.

4. The effect of a wage increase when effort is low
When the wage is low, the best response curve is steep: a small wage increase raises effort by a substantial amount.

5. Diminishing marginal returns
At higher levels of wages, however, increases in wages have a smaller effect on effort.

6. The employer's feasible set
The best response curve is the frontier of the employer's feasible set of combinations of wages and effort that it gets from its employees.

7. The employer's MRT
The slope of the best response curve is the employer's marginal rate of transformation of higher wages into more worker effort.

QUESTION 6.6 CHOOSE THE CORRECT ANSWER(S)
Figure 6.4 (page 247) depicted Maria's best response curve when the expected duration of unemployment was 44 weeks. Which of the following statements is correct?

☐ If the expected unemployment duration increased to 50 weeks, Maria's best response to a wage of $12 would be an effort level above 0.5.
☐ If the unemployment benefit was reduced, then Maria's reservation wage would be higher than $6.
☐ Over the range of wages shown in the figure, Maria would never exert the maximum possible effort per hour.
☐ Increasing effort from 0.5 to 0.6 requires a bigger wage increase than increasing effort from 0.8 to 0.9.

6.7 WAGES, EFFORT, AND PROFITS IN THE LABOUR DISCIPLINE MODEL

Maria is not in the situation that Angela faced when Bruno could order her to work at the point of a gun. Maria has bargaining power because she can always walk away—an option that, initially, Angela did not have.

Maria chooses how hard she works. The best the owner can do is to determine the conditions under which she makes that choice. The owners and managers know that they cannot get Maria to provide more effort than is given by the best response curve shown in Figure 6.4. The fact that the best response curve slopes upwards means that employers face a trade-off. They can get more effort only by paying higher wages.

As we saw in Unit 2, to maximize profits, firms want to minimize the costs of production. In particular, they want to pay the lowest possible price for inputs. A company purchasing oil for use in the production process will look for the supplier that can provide it at the lowest price per litre, or equivalently, supply the most oil per dollar. Likewise, Maria provides an input to production, and her employer would like to purchase it at the lowest price. But this does not mean paying the lowest possible wage. We already know that if he paid the reservation wage, workers might show up (they wouldn't care one way or the other), but they would not work if they did.

The wage, w, is the cost to the employer of an hour of a worker's time. But what matters for production is not how many hours Maria provides, but how many units of effort: effort is the input to the production process. If Maria chooses to provide 0.5 units of effort per hour, and her hourly wage is w, the cost to the employer of a unit of effort is $2w$. In general, if she provides e units of effort per hour, the cost of a unit of effort is w/e.

So, to maximize profits, the employer should find a feasible combination of effort and wage that minimizes the cost per unit of effort, w/e.

Another way to say the same thing is that the employer should maximize the number of units of effort (sometimes called efficiency units) that he gets per dollar of wage cost, e/w.

The upward-sloping straight line in Figure 6.5 joins together a set of points that have the same ratio of effort to wages, w/e. If the wage is $10 per hour and a worker provides 0.45 units of effort per hour, the employer gets 0.045 efficiency units per dollar. Equivalently, a unit of effort costs

$10/0.45 = $22.2. The employer would be indifferent between this situation and one in which the wage is $20 with an effort of 0.9—the cost of effort is exactly the same at all points on the line. We will call this an <u>isocost line for effort</u>. Similarly to the isocost lines in Unit 2, these lines join points that have identical effects on the employer's costs. We can also think of it as an indifference curve for the employer.

To minimize costs, the employer will seek to reach the steepest isocost line for effort, where the cost of a unit of effort is lowest. But because he cannot dictate the level of effort, he has to pick some point on Maria's best response curve.

The best he can do is to set the wage at $12 on the isocost line that is tangent to Maria's best response curve (point A). Use the analysis in Figure 6.6 to see how the employer sets the wage.

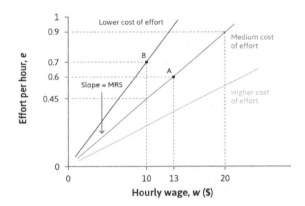

Figure 6.5 The employer's indifference curves: Isocost curves for effort.

1. An isocost line for effort
If $w = $10 and $e = 0.45$, $e/w = 0.045$. At every point on this line the ratio of effort to wages is the same. The cost of a unit of effort is $w/e = $22.22.

2. The slope of the isocost line
The line slopes upward because a higher effort level must be accompanied by a higher wage for the e/w ratio to remain unchanged. The slope is equal to $e/w = 0.045$, the number of units of effort per dollar.

3. Other isocost lines
On an isocost line, the slope is e/w, but the cost of effort is w/e. The steeper line has a lower cost of effort, and the flatter line has a higher cost of effort.

4. Some lines are better for the employer than others
A steeper line means lower cost of effort and hence higher profits for the employer. On the steepest isocost line he gets 0.7 units of effort for a wage of $10 (at B) so the cost of effort is $10/0.7 = $14.29 per unit. On the middle line he only gets 0.45 units of effort at this wage, so the cost of effort is $22.22, and profits are lower.

5. The slope is the MRS
The employer is indifferent between points on an isocost line. Like other indifference curves, the slope of the effort isocost line is the marginal rate of substitution: the rate at which the employer is willing to increase wages to get higher effort.

In Figure 6.6, the employer will choose point A, offering a wage of $12 per hour to hire Maria, who will exert effort of 0.5. The employer cannot do better than this point: any point with lower costs, for example, point B, is infeasible.

The employer minimizes costs and maximizes profit at the point where his MRS (the slope of his indifference curve or isocost line) equals the MRT (the slope of the best response curve, which is his feasible frontier). He balances the trade-off he is willing to make between wages and effort against the trade-off he is constrained to make by Maria's response.

This is a constrained choice problem, similar to the one in Unit 3. There, individuals maximizing utility chose working hours where MRS = MRT: the slope of their indifference curve equalled the slope of the feasible frontier determined by the production technology.

Leibniz: Finding the profit-maximizing wage (http://tinyco.re/L060701)

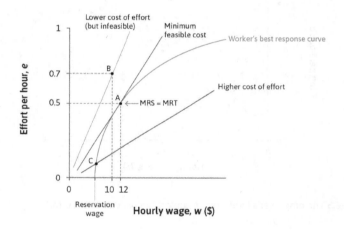

Figure 6.6 The employer sets the wage to minimize the cost of effort.

1. Minimizing the cost of effort
To maximize profits, the owner wants to obtain effort at the lowest cost. He will seek to get onto the steepest isocost line possible. But because he cannot dictate the level of effort, he has to pick some point on the worker's best response curve.

2. C is not the best the employer can do
Could this be a point such as C? No. It is clear that by paying more the owner will benefit from a lower wage-effort ratio.

3. Point A is the best the employer can do
The best he can do is the isocost line that is just touching (tangent to) the worker's best response curve.

4. MRS = MRT
At this point, the marginal rate of substitution (the slope of the isocost line for effort) is equal to the marginal rate of transformation of higher wages into greater effort (the slope of the best response function).

5. Point B
Points on steeper isocosts, such as Point B, would have lower costs for the employer but are infeasible.

6. Minimum feasible costs
Therefore $12 is the hourly wage that the employer should set to minimize costs and maximize profits.

When wages are set by the employer in this manner, they are sometimes called **efficiency wages** because the employer is recognizing that what matters for profits is e/w, the efficiency units per dollar of wage costs, rather than how much an hour of work costs.

What has the **labour discipline model** told us?

- *Equilibrium*: In the owner-employee game, the employer offers a wage and Maria provides a level of effort in response. Their strategies are a Nash equilibrium.
- *Rent*: In this allocation Maria provides effort because she receives an employment rent that she might lose if she were to slack off on the job.
- *Power*: Because Maria fears losing this economic rent, the employer is able to exercise power over her, getting her to act in ways that she would not do without this threat of job loss. This contributes to the profits of the employer.

Involuntary unemployment

When we think about the implications of the labour discipline model for the whole economy, it tells us something else, which may at first seem surprising:

There must always be **involuntary unemployment**.

Being unemployed involuntarily means not having a job, although you would be willing to work at the wage that other workers like you are receiving.

In developing our model we assumed that Maria could expect to be unemployed for 44 weeks before receiving another wage offer at the same level. But the model implies that there *must be* an extended period of unemployment.

To see why, try to imagine an equilibrium in the game between Maria and her employer in which he pays her a wage of $12 per hour, and if she lost her job she could immediately find another at the same wage. In that case, Maria's employment rent would be zero. She would be indifferent between keeping the job and losing it. So her best response would be an effort level of zero. But this could not be an equilibrium: the employer would not pay $12 an hour to someone who did no work.

If it were ever to happen that there were plenty of jobs available in the economy at $12 per hour, and no one was unemployed, such a situation could not last. Employers would offer higher wages to ensure that their workers had something to lose and would therefore work hard. But with higher wages, they would not be able to offer as many jobs. Workers who lost their jobs would no longer be able to find new ones easily. Jobs would be scarce and it might take weeks or months to find another. The economy would have moved to an equilibrium with higher wages and involuntary unemployment. Employees would be earning $16 an hour and those who lost their jobs would be willing to accept another at $16, but they would not immediately be able to find one.

In equilibrium, both wages and involuntary unemployment have to be high enough to ensure that there is enough employment rent for workers to put in effort.

Unemployment is an important concern for voters and the policymakers who represent them. We can use this model to see how policies that govern-

efficiency wages The payment an employer makes that is higher than an employee's reservation wage, so as to motivate the employee to provide more effort on the job than he or she would otherwise choose to make. *See also: labour discipline model, employment rent.*

labour discipline model A model that explains how employers set wages so that employees receive an economic rent (called employment rent), which provides workers an incentive to work hard in order to avoid job termination. *See also: employment rent, efficiency wages.*

unemployment, involuntary The state of being out of work, but preferring to have a job at the wages and working conditions that otherwise identical employed workers have. *See also: unemployment.*

ments pursue to alter the level of unemployment, or to provide income to unemployed workers, will affect the profits of firms and the effort level of their employees.

EXERCISE 6.4 THE EMPLOYER SETS THE WAGE
Would any of the following affect Maria's best response curve or the firm's isocost lines for effort in Figure 6.6 (page 250)? If so, explain how.

1. The government decides to increase childcare subsidies for working parents but not for those unemployed. Assume Maria has a child and is eligible for the subsidy.
2. Demand for the firm's output rises as celebrities endorse the good.
3. Improved technology makes Maria's job easier.

QUESTION 6.7 CHOOSE THE CORRECT ANSWER(S)
Figure 6.6 (page 250) depicts the efficiency wage equilibrium of a worker and a firm. According to this figure:

☐ Along the isocost line tangent to the best response curve, doubling of the per-hour effort from 0.45 to 0.90 would lead to an increased profit for the firm.
☐ The slope of each isocost line is the number of units of effort per dollar.
☐ At the equilibrium point, the marginal rate of transformation on the isocost line equals the marginal rate of substitution on the worker's best response curve.
☐ Points C and A both represent Nash equilibria because they are on the best response curve.

6.8 PUTTING THE MODEL TO WORK: OWNERS, EMPLOYEES, AND THE ECONOMY

Until now we have considered how the employer chooses a point on the best response function. But changes in <u>economic conditions or public policies</u> can shift the entire best response function, moving it to the right (or up) or to the left (or down).

The employee's incentive to choose a high level of effort depends on how much she has to lose (the employment rent), but also the likelihood of losing it. So the <u>position of the best response function depends</u> on:

- the utility of the things that can be bought with the wage
- the disutility of effort
- the reservation wage
- the probability of getting fired when working at each effort level

<u>If there are changes in any of these factors</u>, the best response curve will shift.

First, imagine how an increase in the unemployment rate affects the best response curve. When unemployment is high, workers who lose their jobs can expect a longer spell of unemployment. Recall that unemployment benefits (including support from family and friends) are limited, so the longer the expected spell of unemployment, the lower the level of the unemployment benefit per hour of lost work (or per week). So an increase in the duration of a spell of unemployment has two effects:

- *It reduces the reservation wage*: This increases the employment rent *per hour*.
- *It extends the period of lost work time*: This increases *total* employment rents (the cost of job loss).

Figure 6.7 shows the effects on the best response curve of a rise in unemployment, and also of a rise in unemployment benefits.

A rise in the level of unemployment shifts the best response curve to the left:

- For a given wage, say $18, the amount of effort that the worker will provide increases, improving the profit-making conditions for the employer.
- The wage that the employer would have to pay to get a given effort level, say 0.6, decreases.

A rise in unemployment benefits shifts the best response curve to the right, so it has the opposite effects.

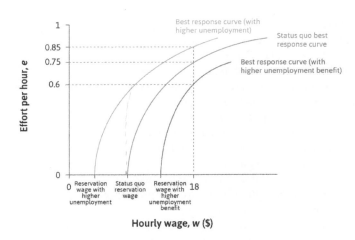

Figure 6.7 The best response curve depends on the level of unemployment and the unemployment benefit.

1. The status quo
The position of the best response curve depends on the reservation wage. It crosses the horizontal axis at this point.

2. The effect of unemployment benefits
A rise in the unemployment benefit increases the reservation wage and shifts the worker's best response curve to the right.

3. An increase in unemployment
If unemployment rises, the expected duration of unemployment increases. So the worker's reservation wage falls and the best response curve shifts to the left.

4. Effort changes for each wage
For a given hourly wage, say $18, workers put in different levels of effort when the levels of unemployment or unemployment benefit change.

Economic policies can alter both the size of the unemployment benefit and the extent of unemployment (and hence the duration of a spell of unemployment). These policies are often controversial. A rightward shift of the employee's best response function favours employees, who will put in less effort for any given wage, while a leftward shift favours owners, who will acquire the effort of their employees at a lower cost, raising profits.

EXERCISE 6.5 EFFORT AND WAGES

Suppose that, with the status quo best response curve in Figure 6.7 (page 253), the firm chooses the wage to minimize the cost of effort, and the worker's best response is an effort level of 0.6. If unemployment rose:

1. Would effort be higher or lower than 0.6 if the firm did not change the wage?
2. How would the firm change the wage if it wanted to keep the effort level at 0.6?
3. How would the wage change if the firm minimized the cost of effort at the new unemployment level?

HOW ECONOMISTS LEARN FROM FACTS

Workers speed up when the economy slows down

The idea that employment rents are an incentive for employees to work harder is illustrated in a study by Edward Lazear (an economic advisor to former US President George W. Bush) and his co-authors. They investigated a single firm during the global financial crisis, to see how the managers and workers reacted to the turbulent economic conditions. The firm specializes in technology-based services such as insurance-claims processing, computer-based test grading, and technical call centres, and operates in 12 US states. The nature of the work made it easy for the management of the firm to track the productivity of workers, which is a measure of worker effort.

It also allowed Lazear and his colleagues to use the firm's data from 2006–2010 to analyse the effect on worker productivity of the worst recession since the Great Depression.

When unemployment rose, workers could expect a longer spell of unemployment if they lost their job. Firms did not use their increased bargaining power to lower wages as they could have, fearing the reaction of their employees.

Lazear and his co-authors found that, in this firm, productivity increased dramatically as unemployment rose during the financial crisis. One possible explanation is that average productivity increased because management fired the least productive members of the workforce. But Lazear found that the effect was more due to workers putting in extra effort. The severity of the recession raised the workers' employment rent for any given wage, and they were therefore willing to work harder. We would predict from our model that the best response curve would have shifted to the left as a result of the recession. This meant that (unless employers lowered wages substantially) workers would work harder. Apparently, this is what happened.

Edward P. Lazear, Kathryn L. Shaw, and Christopher Stanton. 2016. 'Making Do with Less: Working Harder during Recessions'. *Journal of Labor Economics* 34 (S1 Part 2): pp. 333-360.

Our model shows that employers could have cut wages, while sustaining an employment rent sufficient to motivate hard work. An earlier recession provided another insight that helps to explain their reluctance to reduce wages in the crisis. Truman Bewley, an economist, was puzzled when he saw only a handful of firms in the northeast of the US cutting wages during the recession of the early 1990s. Most firms, like the one Lazear's team studied, did not cut their wages at all.

Bewley interviewed more than 300 employers, labour leaders, business consultants, and careers advisors in the northeast of the US. He found that employers chose not to cut wages because they thought it would hurt employee morale, reducing productivity and leading to problems of hiring and retention. They thought it would ultimately cost the employer more than the money they would save in wages.

Truman F. Bewley. 1999. *Why Wages Don't Fall during a Recession*. Cambridge, MA: Harvard University Press.

EXERCISE 6.6 LAZEAR'S RESULTS

Use the best response diagram to sketch the results found by Lazear and co-authors in their study of a firm during the global financial crisis.

1. Draw a best response curve for each of the following years and explain what it illustrates:
   (a) the pre-crisis period (2006)
   (b) the crisis years (2007–8)
   (c) the post-crisis year (2009)
   Assume that the employer did not adjust wages.
2. Is there a reason why a firm might not cut wages during a recession? Think about the research of Truman Bewley and the experimental evidence about reciprocity in Unit 4.

EXERCISE 6.7 OUTSOURCING COMES HOME

At the start of this unit, we discussed the decision by many clothing companies to outsource production to Bangladesh and other low-wage economies. Show your results in a single diagram.

1. Draw the best response curve of the workers in the high-wage home country in the absence of outsourcing (with the wage on the horizontal axis, and effort on the vertical axis).
2. In the same diagram show the best response curve of workers in the foreign low-wage country in the absence of outsourcing. (Assume that wages are measured in dollars in both cases.)
3. Show in your diagram what the home country employer will pay home country workers if outsourcing is not possible.
4. Show in your diagram what the home country employer will pay workers in the low-wage country if it switches production there (ignore the costs of moving production).
5. Now assume that outsourcing is possible and is widely practiced by many firms in the clothing industry. Show the best response function for home country workers under these conditions. Explain why this is different from your answer to 1. Show these outcomes in a diagram.

QUESTION 6.8 CHOOSE THE CORRECT ANSWER(S)
Which of the following statements are true?

☐ If unemployment benefits are increased, the minimum cost of a unit of effort for the employer will rise.
☐ If the wage doesn't change, employees will work harder in periods of high unemployment.
☐ If workers continue to receive benefits however long they remained unemployed, an increase in the level of unemployment will have no effect on the best response curve.
☐ If an employee's disutility of effort increases, the reservation wage will rise.

6.9 ANOTHER KIND OF BUSINESS ORGANIZATION

Even in capitalist economies, some business organizations have an entirely different structure to the one we have been analysing: their workers are the owners of the capital goods and other assets of the company, and they select managers who run the company on a day-to-day basis. This form of business organization is called a **worker-owned cooperative** or **cooperative firm**.

One well-known example of a cooperative is the large British retailer John Lewis Partnership (http://tinyco.re/2414644), founded in 1864 and held in trust for its employees since 1950. Every employee is a partner, and employee councils elect five out of seven members of the company board. The benefits for employees (pension, paid holidays, long-service sabbaticals, social activities) are generous, and the business' profits are shared out as a bonus, calculated as a percentage of each person's salary every year. The bonus normally ranges between 10% and 20% of pay, even after a significant chunk of the profits are retained for future investment. John Lewis is one of the country's most profitable and consistently successful retail businesses.

Worker-owned cooperatives are hierarchically organized, like conventional firms, but the directives issued from the top of the hierarchy come from people who owe their jobs to the worker-owners. Other than this, the main differences between conventional firms and worker-owned cooperatives are that the cooperatives need fewer supervisors and other management personnel to ensure that the worker-owners work hard and well. Fellow worker-owners will not tolerate a shirking worker because the shirker is reducing the profit share of the other workers. Reduced need for the supervision of workers is among the reasons that worker-owned cooperatives produce at least as much (if not more) per hour than their conventional counterparts.

Inequalities in wages and salaries within the company, for example between managers and production workers, are also typically less in worker-owned cooperatives than in conventional firms. And worker-owned cooperatives tend not to lay off workers when the economy goes into recession, offering their worker-owners a kind of insurance (often they cut back on the hours of all workers rather than terminating the employment of some).

Case studies show that in those unusual companies owned primarily by the workers themselves, work is done more intensely with less supervision.

---

cooperative firm A firm that is mostly or entirely owned by its workers, who hire and fire the managers.

During the twentieth century, worker-owned plywood producers successfully competed with traditional capitalist firms in the US. John Pencavel. 2002. *Worker Participation: Lessons from the Worker Co-ops of the Pacific Northwest*. New York, NY: Russell Sage Foundation Publications.

The knowledge-based economy is creating new forms of firms, neither capitalist nor worker-owned. Tim O'Reilly and Eric S. Raymond. 2001. *The Cathedral & the Bazaar: Musings on Linux and Open Source by an Accidental Revolutionary*. Sebastopol, CA: O'Reilly.

There have been many attempts to establish other types of business organization throughout recent history, but borrowing the funds to start and sustain worker-owned companies is often difficult because, as we will see in Unit 10, banks are often reluctant to lend funds (except at high interest rates) to people who are not wealthy.

EXERCISE 6.8 A WORKER-OWNED COOPERATIVE

In Figure 6.1 (page 231) we showed the actors and decision-making structure of a typical firm.

1. How do the actors and decision-making structure of John Lewis Partnership (http://tinyco.re/7059886) differ from that of a typical firm?
2. Redraw Figure 6.1 to show this.

GREAT ECONOMISTS

John Stuart Mill

John Stuart Mill (1806–1873) was one of the most important philosophers and economists of the nineteenth century. His book *On Liberty* (1859) parallels Adam Smith's *Wealth of Nations* in advocating limits on governmental powers, and is still an influential argument in favour of individual freedom and privacy.

Mill thought that the structure of the typical firm was an affront to freedom and individual autonomy. In *The Principles of Political Economy* (1848), Mill described the relationship between firm owners and workers as an unnatural one: 'To work at the bidding and for the profit of another, without any interest in the work … is not, even when wages are high, a satisfactory state to human beings of educated intelligence,' he wrote.

Attributing the conventional employer-employee relationship to the poor education of the working class, he predicted that the spread of education, and the political empowerment of working people, would change this situation:

> The relation of masters and work-people will be gradually superseded by partnership … perhaps finally in all, association of labourers among themselves. (*The Principles of Political Economy*, 1848)

EXERCISE 6.9 WAS MILL WRONG?

Why do you think Mill's vision of a post-capitalist economy of worker-owned cooperatives has not yet occurred?

Charles Fourier (1772–1837), a philosopher in France, envisioned a utopian world in which people would live in communities of between 1,600 and 1,800 people, called phalanxes. Fourier imagined that members would do all the industrial, craft, and agricultural activity, and would work hard because they did the jobs they liked. Who would clean the sewers and toilets, or put manure on gardens? Fourier suggested giving these jobs to children who love playing with dirt! Dozens of phalanxes existed in the mid-nineteenth century, with more than 40 in the US alone.

John Stuart Mill. 2002. *On Liberty* (http://tinyco.re/6454781). Mineola, NY: Dover Publications.

John Stuart Mill. 1994. *Principles of Political Economy* (http://tinyco.re/9348882). New York: Oxford University Press.

6.10 PRINCIPALS AND AGENTS: INTERACTIONS UNDER INCOMPLETE CONTRACTS

In the relationship between Maria and her employer, Maria's work effort matters to both parties but is not covered by the employment contract. This leads to the existence of employment rents. If they had been able to write a complete contract, the situation would have been quite different. The employer could have offered her an enforceable contract specifying both the wage and the exact level of effort she should provide, and if these terms were acceptable to her, she would have agreed and worked as required. To maximize his profit he would have chosen a contract that was only just acceptable, so she would not have earned any rents.

This example is not unusual. In practice, all employment relationships are governed by incomplete contracts. Employment contracts often do not even bother to mention that the worker should work hard and well. And there are many other ways in which we interact without a complete contract:

- People and banks lend money in return for a promise to repay the full amount plus the stipulated interest. But this may be unenforceable if the borrower is unable to repay.
- Owners of firms would like managers to maximize the value of the owners' assets, but managers have their own objectives (first class air travel, lavish offices) and managerial contracts often fall short of an enforceable requirement to maximize the owners' wealth.
- The contracts signed by tenants renting apartments may include clauses requiring that they maintain the value of the property. But aside from gross neglect, the liability for not maintaining the property is unenforceable.
- Insurance contracts require (but typically cannot enforce) that the people who purchase insurance should behave prudently and try not to take risks.
- Families devote a sizeable fraction of their budgets to purchasing educational and health services, the quality of which is rarely specified in a contract (and would be unenforceable if it were).
- Parents care for their children with the hope, but no contractual assurance, that their children will reciprocate when the parents are old and unable to work.

For these and a great many other exchanges, it appears that Emile Durkheim (1858–1917), the founder of modern sociology, was right when he observed that 'not everything in the contract is contractual.' As above, there is usually something that matters to at least one of the parties that cannot be written down in an enforceable contract.

Why are contracts incomplete?

Thinking about some examples of economic interactions, we can see that there are several reasons for the absence of a complete contract:

- *Information is not verifiable*: For a contract to be enforceable, relevant information must be observable by both parties, but also *verifiable* by third parties such as courts of law. The court must be able to establish whether or not the requirements of the contract were met. Verifiable information is often unavailable: for example, it may be impossible to prove whether the poor condition of a rented apartment is due to normal wear and tear or the tenant's negligence.

- *Time and uncertainty*: A contract is generally executed over a period of time, for example specifying that Party A does X now and Party B does Y later. But what B should do later may depend on things that are unknown when the contract is written. People are unlikely to be able to anticipate every possible thing that might happen in future—and trying to do so would probably not be cost-effective.
- *Measurement*: Many services and goods are inherently difficult to measure or describe precisely enough to be written into a contract. How would the restaurant owner measure how pleasantly his waiters interact with customers?
- *Absence of a judiciary*: For some transactions there are no judicial institutions (courts or other relevant third parties) capable of enforcing contracts. Many international transactions are of this type.
- *Preferences*: Even where the nature of the goods or services to be exchanged would permit a more complete contract, a less complete contract might be preferred. Intrusive surveillance of workers by employers may backfire if the employer's distrust angers the workers, leading to less satisfactory work performance. You do not necessarily want to know the exact quality of a concert before you buy the ticket—discovering it may be part of the experience.

Principal-agent models

Many contractual relationships can be modelled in the same way, as a game between two players, whom we call the principal and the agent, who face a conflict of interest. These are known as **principal-agent problems**. In the case of Maria and her employer, the employer is the principal. He would like to offer Maria, the agent, an employment contract, and she wants the job, but the amount of effort she will provide cannot be specified in the contract because it is not verifiable. This is a *problem* because there is a conflict of interest: he would prefer her to work hard, whereas Maria prefers an easy life.

Our model of Maria's employment is an example of a general class of principal-agent models, in which an action taken by the agent is 'hidden' from the principal, or 'unobservable'.

> **principal-agent relationship** This relationship exists when one party (the principal) would like another party (the agent) to act in some way, or have some attribute that is in the interest of the principal, and that cannot be enforced or guaranteed in a binding contract. *See also: incomplete contract. Also known as: principal-agent problem.*

- The agent can take some action (such as working hard),
- the principal benefits from this action,
- but taking the action is something the agent would not choose to do, perhaps because it is costly or unpleasant (this is the conflict of interest),
- and because information about the action is either not available to the principal or is not verifiable,
- there is no way that the principal can use an enforceable contract to *guarantee* that the action is performed.

In short: a **hidden action problem** occurs when there is a conflict of interest between the principal and the agent over some action that may be taken by the agent, and this action cannot be subjected to a complete contract. In these problems, information about the action is either *asymmetric* (the agent knows what action is taken, but the principal doesn't) or *unverifiable* (it cannot be used by a court to enforce a contract).

> **hidden actions (problem of)** This occurs when some action taken by one party to an exchange is not known or cannot be verified by the other. For example, the employer cannot know (or cannot verify) how hard the worker she has employed is actually working. *Also known as: moral hazard. See also: hidden attributes (problem of).*

The table in Figure 6.8 identifies the principals and agents in the examples from this section.

We study the banker-borrower principal-agent model in Unit 10. In Unit 12 we will introduce the second main class of principal-agent models, in which it is not the agent's action that cannot be contracted (hidden action) but rather something about the agent herself that is unknown to the principal (hidden attribute).

VERIFIABLE INFORMATION, ASYMMETRIC INFORMATION
Information is verifiable if it can be used in court to enforce a contract. Non-verifiable information, such as hearsay, cannot be used to enforce contracts.

Information that is known by one party but not another is asymmetric.

EXERCISE 6.10 PRINCIPAL-AGENT RELATIONSHIPS
For each of the following examples, explain who is the principal, who is the agent, and what aspects of their interaction are of interest to each and are not covered by a complete contract.

1. A company hires a security guard to protect its premises at night.
2. A charity wants to commission research to find out as much as possible about a new virus.

6.11 CONCLUSION

The products of people's labour may be transferred to others in markets, or within firms through employment contracts. To understand the role of the firm, we view it not only as an actor, but also a stage on which three sets of actors (owners, managers, and employees) interact. Principal-agent models help us understand how firms work by identifying the consequences of the conflicts of interest between the actors, when these cannot be resolved by complete contracts.

Employment contracts are incomplete: they can cover hours and some working conditions, but not the effort provided by the employee, which is not verifiable. So employers set wages that are higher than workers' reservation wages. Workers receive an employment rent, which motivates them to work hard and deters them from quitting. When all employers set wages in this way, there will be involuntary unemployment in the economy. Public policies such as the provision of unemployment benefits change workers' reservation wages and best response curves, and so affect the wage-setting process.

Principal	Agent	Action that is hidden, and not covered in the contract
Employer	Employee	Quality and quantity of work ✓
Banker	Borrower	Repayment of loan, prudent conduct ✓
Owner	Manager	Maximization of owners' profits
Landlord	Tenant	Care of the apartment
Insurance company	Insured	Prudent behavior
Parents	Teacher/doctor	Quality of teaching and care
Parents	Children	Care in old age

Figure 6.8 Hidden action problems.

> *Concepts introduced in Unit 6*
> Before you move on, review these definitions:
>
> - Division of labour
> - Separation of ownership and control
> - Firm-specific assets
> - Incomplete contract
> - Employment rent
> - Reservation wage
> - Worker's best response function
> - Involuntary unemployment
> - Asymmetric information
> - Verifiable information
> - Principal-agent relationship

6.12 REFERENCES

Bewley, Truman F. 1999. *Why Wages Don't Fall during a Recession*. Cambridge, MA: Harvard University Press.

Braverman, Harry, and Paul M. Sweezy. 1975. *Labor and Monopoly Capital: The Degradation of Work in the Twentieth Century*, 2nd ed. New York, NY: Monthly Review Press.

Coase, Ronald H. 1937. 'The Nature of the Firm' (http://tinyco.re/8128486). *Economica* 4 (16): pp. 386–405.

Coase, Ronald H. 1992. 'The Institutional Structure of Production' (http://tinyco.re/1636715). *American Economic Review* 82 (4): pp. 713–19.

Couch, Kenneth A., and Dana W. Placzek. 2010. 'Earnings Losses of Displaced Workers Revisited'. *American Economic Review* 100 (1): pp. 572–589.

Ehrenreich, Barbara. 2011. *Nickel and Dimed: On (Not) Getting By in America*. New York, NY: St. Martin's Press.

Hansmann, Henry. 2000. *The Ownership of Enterprise*. Cambridge, MA: Belknap Press.

Helper, Susan, Morris Kleiner, and Yingchun Wang. 2010. 'Analyzing Compensation Methods in Manufacturing: Piece Rates, Time Rates, or Gain-Sharing?' (http://tinyco.re/4437027). NBER Working Papers No. 16540, National Bureau of Economic Research, Inc.

Jacobson, Louis, Robert J. Lalonde, and Daniel G. Sullivan. 1993. 'Earnings Losses of Displaced Workers'. *The American Economic Review* 83 (4): pp. 685–709.

Kletzer, Lori G. 1998. 'Job Displacement' (http://tinyco.re/8577746). *Journal of Economic Perspectives* 12 (1): pp. 115–136.

Kroszner, Randall S., and Louis Putterman (editors). 2009. *The Economic Nature of the Firm: A Reader*, 3rd ed. Cambridge: Cambridge University Press.

Krueger, Alan B., and Alexandre Mas. 2004. 'Strikes, Scabs, and Tread Separations: Labor Strife and the Production of Defective Bridgestone/Firestone Tires'. *Journal of Political Economy* 112 (2): pp. 253–289.

Lazear, Edward P., Kathryn L. Shaw, and Christopher Stanton. 2016. 'Making Do with Less: Working Harder during Recessions'. *Journal of Labor Economics* 34 (S1 Part 2): pp. 333–360.

Marx, Karl. 1906. *Capital: A Critique of Political Economy* (http://tinyco.re/9166776). New York, NY: Random House.

Marx, Karl. 2010. *The Communist Manifesto* (http://tinyco.re/0155765). London: Arcturus Publishing.

Micklethwait, John, and Adrian Wooldridge. 2003. *The Company: A Short History of a Revolutionary Idea*. New York, NY: Modern Library.

Mill, John Stuart. 1994. *Principles of Political Economy* (http://tinyco.re/9348882). New York: Oxford University Press.

Mill, John Stuart. 2002. *On Liberty* (http://tinyco.re/6454781). Mineola, NY: Dover Publications.

O'Reilly, Tim, and Eric S. Raymond. 2001. *The Cathedral & the Bazaar: Musings on Linux and Open Source by an Accidental Revolutionary*. Sebastopol, CA: O'Reilly.

Pencavel, John. 2002. *Worker Participation: Lessons from the Worker Co-ops of the Pacific Northwest*. New York, NY: Russell Sage Foundation Publications.

Simon, Herbert A. 1951. 'A Formal Theory of the Employment Relationship' (http://tinyco.re/0460792). *Econometrica* 19 (3).

Simon, Herbert A. 1991. 'Organizations and Markets' (http://tinyco.re/2460377). *Journal of Economic Perspectives* 5 (2): pp. 25–44.

Toynbee, Polly. 2003. *Hard Work: Life in Low-pay Britain*. London: Bloomsbury Publishing.

Williamson, Oliver E. 1985. *The Economic Institutions of Capitalism*. New York, NY: Collier Macmillan.

UNIT 7

THE FIRM AND ITS CUSTOMERS

HOW A PROFIT-MAXIMIZING FIRM PRODUCING A DIFFERENTIATED PRODUCT INTERACTS WITH ITS CUSTOMERS

- Firms producing differentiated products choose price and quantity to maximize their profits, taking into account the product demand curve and the cost function.
- Technological and cost advantages of large-scale production favour large firms.
- The responsiveness of consumers to a price change is measured by the elasticity of demand, which affects the firm's price and profit margin.
- The gains from trade are shared between consumers and firm owners, but prices above marginal cost cause market failure and deadweight loss.
- Firms can increase profit through product selection and advertising. Those with fewer competitors can achieve higher profit margins, and monopoly rents.
- Economic policymakers use elasticities of demand to design tax policies, and reduce firms' market power through competition policy.

THEMES AND CAPSTONE UNITS
- 21: Innovation
- 22: Politics and policy

Ernst F. Schumacher's *Small is Beautiful*, published in 1973, advocated small-scale production by individuals and groups in an economic system designed to emphasize happiness rather than profits. In the year the book was published, the firms Intel and FedEx each employed only a few thousand people in the US. Forty years later, Intel employed around 108,000 people, and FedEx more than 300,000. Walmart had around 3,500 employees in 1973. In 2016 it employed 2.3 million.

Most firms are much smaller than this, but in all rich economies, most people work for large firms. In the US, 52% of private-sector employees work in firms with at least 500 employees. Firms grow because their owners can make more money if they expand, and people with money to invest get higher returns from owning stock in large firms. Employees in

Ernst F. Schumacher. 1973. *Small Is Beautiful: Economics as If People Mattered* (http://tinyco.re/3749799). New York, NY: HarperCollins. Note: link to first 80 pages only.

large firms are also paid more. Figure 7.1 shows the growth of some highly successful US firms.

What strategies can firms use to prosper and grow like the ones in Figure 7.1? The story of the British retailer Tesco, founded in 1919 by Jack Cohen, suggests one answer.

'Pile it high and sell it cheap,' was Jack Cohen's motto. He started as a street trader in the East End of London, and opened his first store 10 years later. Today, £1 in every £9 spent in a shop in the UK is spent in a Tesco store, and the company expanded worldwide in the 1990s. In 2014 Tesco had higher profits than any other retailer in the world except Walmart. Keeping the price low as Cohen recommended is one possible strategy for a firm seeking to maximize its profits: even though the profit on each item is small, the low price may attract so many customers that total profit is high.

Other firms adopt quite different strategies. Apple sets high prices for iPhones and iPads, increasing its profits by charging a price premium, rather than lowering prices to reach more customers. For example, between April 2010 and March 2012, profit per unit on Apple iPhones was between 49% and 58% of the price. During the same period, Tesco's operating profit per unit was between 6.0% and 6.5%.

A firm's success depends on more than getting the price right. Product choice and ability to attract customers, produce at lower cost and at a higher quality than their competitors all matter. They also need to be able to recruit and retain employees who can make all these things happen.

Figure 7.2 illustrates key decisions that a firm makes. In this unit, we will focus particularly on how a firm chooses the price of a product, and the quantity to produce. This will depend on the demand it faces—that is, the willingness of potential consumers to pay for its product—and its production costs.

The demand for a product will depend on its price, and the costs of production may depend on how many units are produced. But a firm can actively influence both consumer demand and costs in more ways than through price and quantity. As we saw in Unit 2, innovation may lead to new and attractive products, or to lower production costs. If the firm can innovate successfully it can earn economic rents—at least in the short term until others catch up. Further innovation may be needed if it is to stay

Jack Cohen, the founder of Tesco, began as a street market trader in the East End of London. The traders would gather at dawn each day and, at a signal, race to their favourite stall site, known as a pitch. Cohen perfected the technique of throwing his cap to claim the most desirable pitch. In the 1950s, Cohen began opening supermarkets on the US model, adapting quickly to this new style of operation. Tesco became the UK market leader in 1995, and now employs almost half a million people in Europe and Asia.

Today Tesco's pricing strategy aims to appeal to all segments of the market, labelling some of its own-brand products as Finest, and others as Value. The BBC Money Programme summarized the three Tesco commandments as 'be everywhere', 'sell everything', and 'sell to everyone'.

Erzo G. J. Luttmer. 2011. 'On the Mechanics of Firm Growth'. The Review of Economic Studies 78 (3): pp. 1042–68.

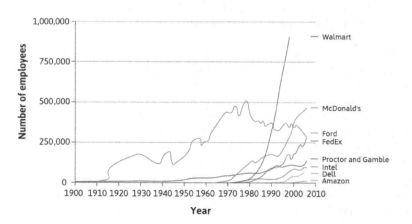

Figure 7.1 Firm size in the US: Number of employees (1900–2006).

ahead. Advertising can increase demand. And as we saw in Unit 6, the firm sets the wage, which is an important component of its cost. As we will see in later units, the firm also spends to influence taxes and environmental regulation in order to lower its production costs.

7.1 BREAKFAST CEREAL: CHOOSING A PRICE

To decide what price to charge, a firm needs information about demand: how much potential consumers are willing to pay for its product. Figure 7.3 shows the **demand curve** for Apple-Cinnamon Cheerios, a ready-to-eat breakfast cereal introduced by the company General Mills in 1989. In 1996, Jerry Hausman, an economist, used data on weekly sales of family breakfast cereals in US cities to estimate how the weekly quantity of cereal that customers in a typical city would wish to buy would vary with its price per pound (there are 2.2 pounds in 1 kg). For example, you can see from Figure 7.3 that if the price were $3, customers would demand 25,000 pounds of Apple-Cinnamon Cheerios. For most products, the lower the price, the more customers wish to buy.

If you were the manager at General Mills, how would you choose the price for Apple-Cinnamon Cheerios in this city, and how many pounds of cereal would you produce?

> **demand curve** The curve that gives the quantity consumers will buy at each possible price.

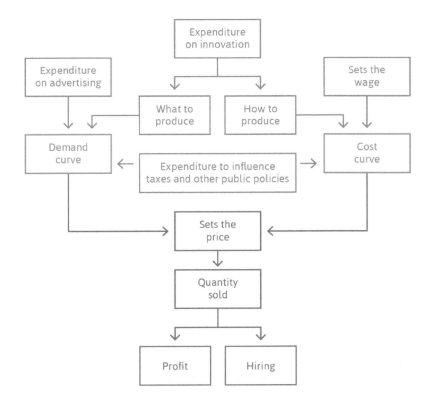

Figure 7.2 The firm's decisions.

HOW ECONOMISTS LEARN FROM FACTS

Estimating demand curves using surveys

Jerry Hausman used data on cereal purchases to estimate the demand curve for Apple-Cinnamon Cheerios. Another method, particularly useful for firms introducing completely new products, is a consumer survey. Suppose you were investigating the potential demand for space tourism. You could try asking potential consumers:

'How much would you be willing to pay for a 10-minute flight in space?'

But they may find it difficult to decide, or worse, they may lie if they think their answer will affect the price eventually charged. A better way to find out their true willingness to pay might be to ask:

'Would you be willing to pay $1,000 for a 10-minute flight in space?'

In 2011, someone did this, so now we know the consumer demand for space flight.

Whether the product is cereal or space flight, the method is the same. If you vary the prices in the question, and ask a large number of consumers, you would be able to estimate the proportion of people willing to pay each price. Hence you can estimate the whole demand curve.

'Willingness to Pay for a Flight in Space' (http://tinyco.re/7817145). Statista. Updated 20 October 2011.

Adapted from Figure 5.2 in Jerry A. Hausman. 1996. 'Valuation of New Goods under Perfect and Imperfect Competition' (http://tinyco.re/1626988). In *The Economics of New Goods*, pp. 207–248. Chicago, IL: University of Chicago Press.

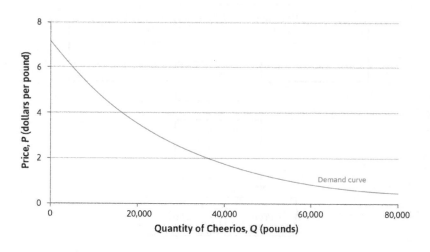

Figure 7.3 Estimated demand for Apple-Cinnamon Cheerios.

You need to consider how the decision will affect your profits (the difference between sales revenue and production costs). Suppose that the unit cost (the cost of producing each pound) of Apple-Cinnamon Cheerios is $2. To maximize your profit, you should produce exactly the quantity you expect to sell, and no more. Then revenue, costs, and profit are given by:

$$\text{total costs} = \text{unit cost} \times \text{quantity}$$
$$= 2 \times Q$$
$$\text{total revenue} = \text{price} \times \text{quantity}$$
$$= P \times Q$$
$$\text{profit} = \text{total revenue} - \text{total costs}$$
$$= P \times Q - 2 \times Q$$

So we have a formula for profit:

$$\text{profit} = (P - 2) \times Q$$

Using this formula, you could calculate the profit for any choice of price and quantity and draw the isoprofit curves, as in Figure 7.4. Just as indifference curves join points in a diagram that give the same level of utility, isoprofit curves join points that give the same level of total profit. We can think of the isoprofit curves as the firm's indifference curves: the firm is indifferent between combinations of price and quantity that give you the same profit.

QUESTION 7.1 CHOOSE THE CORRECT ANSWER(S)

A firm's cost of production is £12 per unit of output. If P is the price of the output good and Q is the number of units produced, which of the following statements is correct?

☐ Point $(Q, P) = (2{,}000, 20)$ is on the isoprofit curve representing the profit level £20,000.
☐ Point $(Q, P) = (2{,}000, 20)$ is on a lower isoprofit curve than point $(Q, P) = (1{,}200, 24)$.
☐ Points $(Q, P) = (2{,}000, 20)$ and $(4{,}000, 16)$ are on the same isoprofit curve.
☐ Point $(Q, P) = (5{,}000, 12)$ is not on any isoprofit curve.

QUESTION 7.2 CHOOSE THE CORRECT ANSWER(S)

Consider a firm whose unit cost (the cost of producing one unit of output) is the same at all output levels. Which of the following statements are correct?

☐ Each isoprofit curve depicts the firm's profit for different outputs for a given price of the output good.
☐ Isoprofit curves can be upward-sloping when at high profit levels.
☐ Every price-quantity combination lies on an isoprofit curve.
☐ Isoprofit curves slope downward when the price is above the unit cost.

To achieve a high profit, you would like both price and quantity to be as high as possible, but you are constrained by the demand curve. If you choose a high price, you will only be able to sell a small quantity; and if you want to sell a large quantity, you must choose a low price.

The demand curve determines what is feasible. Figure 7.5a shows the isoprofit curves and demand curve together. You face a similar problem to Alexei, the student in Unit 3, who wanted to choose the point in his feasible set where his utility was maximized. You want to choose a feasible price and quantity combination that will maximize your profit.

Your best strategy is to choose point E in Figure 7.5a: you should produce 14,000 pounds of cereal, and sell it at a price of $4.40 per pound, making $34,000 profit. Just as in the case of Alexei in Unit 3, your optimal combination of price and quantity involves balancing two trade-offs. As manager, we have assumed that you care about profit, rather than any particular combination of price and quantity.

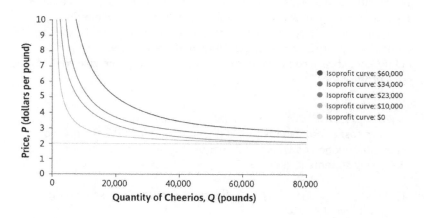

Figure 7.4 Isoprofit curves for the production of Apple-Cinnamon Cheerios. Note: Isoprofit data is illustrative only, and does not reflect the real-world profitability of the product.

1. Isoprofit curves
The graph shows a number of isoprofit curves for Cheerios.

2. Isoprofit curve: $60,000
You could make $60,000 profit by selling 60,000 pounds at a price of $3, or 20,000 pounds at $5, or 10,000 pounds at $8, or in many other ways. The curve shows all the possible ways of making $60,000 profit.

3. Isoprofit curve: $34,000
The $34,000 isoprofit curve shows all the combinations of P and Q for which profit is equal to $34,000.

4. Isoprofit curve: $23,000
The isoprofit curves nearer to the origin correspond to lower levels of profit.

5. Isoprofit curve: $10,000
The cost of each pound of Cheerios is $2, so profit = $(P - 2) \times Q$. This means that isoprofit curves slope downward. To make a profit of $10,000, P would have to be very high if Q was less than 8,000. But if $Q = 80,000$ you could make this profit with a low P.

6. Zero profits
The horizontal line shows the choices of price and quantity where profit is zero: if you set a price of $2, you would be selling each pound of cereal for exactly what it cost.

- The isoprofit curve is your indifference curve, and its slope at any point represents the trade-off you are *willing* to make between P and Q—your **MRS**. You would be willing to substitute a high price for a lower quantity if you obtained the same profit.
- The slope of the demand curve is the trade-off you are *constrained* to make—your **MRT**, or the rate at which the demand curve allows you to 'transform' quantity into price. You cannot raise the price without lowering the quantity, because fewer consumers will buy a more expensive product.

These two trade-offs balance at the profit-maximizing choice of P and Q.

The manager at General Mills probably didn't think about the decision in this way.

Perhaps the price was chosen more by trial and error, informed by past experience and market research. But we expect that a firm will find its way, somehow, to a profit-maximizing price and quantity. The purpose of our economic analysis is not to model the manager's thought process, but to understand the outcome, and its relationship to the firm's cost and consumer demand.

> **marginal rate of substitution (MRS)** The trade-off that a person is willing to make between two goods. At any point, this is the slope of the indifference curve. *See also: marginal rate of transformation.*
> **marginal rate of transformation (MRT)** The quantity of some good that must be sacrificed to acquire one additional unit of another good. At any point, it is the slope of the feasible frontier. *See also: marginal rate of substitution.*

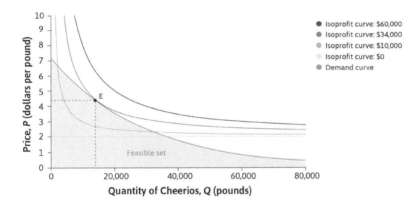

Legend:
- Isoprofit curve: $60,000
- Isoprofit curve: $34,000
- Isoprofit curve: $10,000
- Isoprofit curve: $0
- Demand curve

Demand curve data from Jerry A. Hausman. 1996. 'Valuation of New Goods under Perfect and Imperfect Competition'. In *The Economics of New Goods*, pp. 207–248. Chicago, IL: University of Chicago Press.

Figure 7.5a The profit-maximizing choice of price and quantity for Apple-Cinnamon Cheerios.

1. The profit-maximizing choice
The manager would like to choose a combination of P and Q on the highest possible isoprofit curve in the feasible set.

2. Zero profits
The horizontal line shows the choices of price and quantity where profit is zero: if you set a price of $2, you would be selling each pound of cereal for exactly what it cost.

3. Profit-maximizing choices
The manager would choose a price and quantity corresponding to a point on the demand curve. Any point below the demand curve would be feasible, such as selling 8,000 pounds of cereal at a price of $3, but you would make more profit if you raised the price.

4. Maximizing profit at E
You reach the highest possible isoprofit curve while remaining in the feasible set by choosing point E, where the demand curve is tangent to an isoprofit curve. The manager should choose $P = \$4.40$, and $Q = 14,000$ pounds.

Even from an economist's point of view, there are other ways to think about profit maximization. The lower panel of Figure 7.5b shows how much profit would be made at each point on the demand curve.

The graph in the lower panel is the profit function: it shows the profit you would achieve if you chose to produce a quantity, Q, and set the highest price that would enable you to sell that quantity, according to the demand function. And it tells us, again, that you would achieve the maximum profit of $34,000 with $Q = 14,000$ pounds of cereal.

Demand curve data from Jerry A. Hausman. 1996. 'Valuation of New Goods under Perfect and Imperfect Competition' (http://tinyco.re/1626988). In *The Economics of New Goods*, pp. 207–248. Chicago, IL: University of Chicago Press.

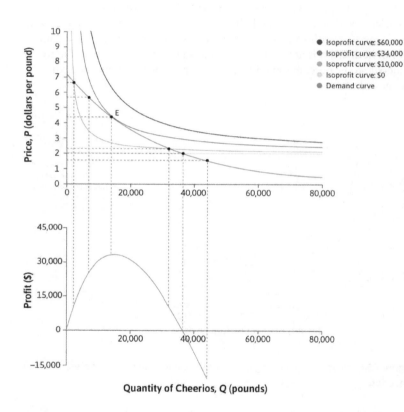

Figure 7.5b The profit-maximizing choice of price and quantity for Apple-Cinnamon Cheerios.

1. The profit function
The firm can calculate its profit at each point on the demand curve.

2. Profit at low quantities
When the quantity is low, so is the profit.

3. Increasing profits
As quantity increases, profit rises until...

4. Maximum profits
... profit reaches a maximum at E.

5. Falling profits
Beyond E the profit falls.

6. Zero profits
Profit falls to zero when the price is equal to the unit cost, $2.

7. Negative profits
To sell a very high quantity, the price has to be lower than the unit cost, so profit is negative.

QUESTION 7.3 CHOOSE THE CORRECT ANSWER(S)

The table represents market demand Q for a good at different prices P.

Q	100	200	300	400	500	600	700	800	900	1,000
P	£270	£240	£210	£180	£150	£120	£90	£60	£30	£0

The firm's unit cost of production is £60. Based on this information, which of the following is correct?

☐ At Q = 100, the firm's profit is £20,000.
☐ The profit-maximizing output is Q = 400.
☐ The maximum profit that can be attained is £50,000.
☐ The firm will make a loss at all outputs of 800 and above.

EXERCISE 7.1 CHANGES IN THE MARKET

Draw diagrams to show how the curves in Figure 7.5a (page 269) would change in each of the following cases:

1. A rival company producing a similar brand slashes its prices.
2. The cost of producing Apple-Cinnamon Cheerios rises to $3 per pound.
3. General Mills introduces a local advertising campaign costing $10,000 per week.

To make sketching the curves easier, assume the demand curve is linear. In each case, can you say what would happen to the price and the profit?

7.2 ECONOMIES OF SCALE AND THE COST ADVANTAGES OF LARGE-SCALE PRODUCTION

Why have firms like Walmart, Intel and FedEx grown so large? An important reason why a large firm may be more profitable than a small firm is that the large firm produces its output at lower cost per unit. This may be possible for two reasons:

- *Technological advantages*: Large-scale production often uses fewer inputs per unit of output.
- *Cost advantages*: In larger firms, fixed costs such as advertising have a smaller effect on the cost per unit. And they may be able to purchase their inputs at a lower cost because they have more bargaining power.

Economists use the term **economies of scale** or **increasing returns** to describe the technological advantages of large-scale production. For example, if doubling the amount of every input that the firm uses triples the firm's output, then the firm exhibits increasing returns.

> **economies of scale** These occur when doubling all of the inputs to a production process more than doubles the output. The shape of a firm's long-run average cost curve depends both on returns to scale in production and the effect of scale on the prices it pays for its inputs. *Also known as: increasing returns to scale. See also: diseconomies of scale.*

diseconomies of scale These occur when doubling all of the inputs to a production process less than doubles the output. *Also known as: decreasing returns to scale. See also: economies of scale.*

constant returns to scale These occur when doubling all of the inputs to a production process doubles the output. The shape of a firm's long-run average cost curve depends both on returns to scale in production and the effect of scale on the prices it pays for its inputs. *See also: increasing returns to scale, decreasing returns to scale.*

ECONOMIES AND DISECONOMIES OF SCALE

If we increase all inputs by a given proportion, and it:

- increases output more than proportionally, then the technology is said to exhibit **increasing returns to scale** in production or **economies of scale**,
- increases output less than proportionally, then the technology exhibits **decreasing returns to scale** in production or **diseconomies of scale**,
- increases output proportionally, then the technology exhibits **constant returns to scale** in production.

research and development
Expenditures by a private or public entity to create new methods of production, products, or other economically relevant new knowledge.

Economies of scale may result from specialization within the firm, which allows employees to do the task they do best, and minimizes training time by limiting the skill set that each worker needs. Economies of scale may also occur for purely engineering reasons. For example, transporting more of a liquid requires a larger pipe, but doubling the capacity of the pipe increases its diameter (and the material necessary to construct it) by much less than a factor of two. For proof, check *The size and cost of a pipe* in the Einstein at the end of this section.

But there are also built-in **diseconomies of scale**. Think of the firm's owners, managers, work supervisors and production workers. Suppose that each supervisor can direct 10 production workers, while each manager can direct 10 supervisors. If the firm employs 10 production workers, then the owner can do the management and supervision. If it employs 100 production workers, it needs to add a layer of 10 supervisors. If it grows to 1,000 production workers, it will need to recruit another layer of management to supervise the first layer of supervisors. So increasing production workers requires more than a proportional increase in supervision and management. The only way the firm could increase all inputs proportionally would be to reduce the intensity of supervision, with associated losses in productivity. We'll call this diseconomy of scale the *Dilbert law of firm hierarchy*, (after a Dilbert comic strip (http://tinyco.re/8720977)). See the Einstein at the end of this section for how to calculate the diseconomy of scale that our Dilbert law implies.

Cost advantages

Cost per unit may fall as the firm produces more output, even if there are constant or even decreasing returns to scale. This happens if there is a fixed cost that doesn't depend on the number of units—it will be the same whether the firm produces one unit, or many. An example would be the cost of **research and development** (R&D) and product design, acquiring a licence to engage in production, or obtaining a patent for a particular technique. Marketing expenses, such as advertising, are another fixed cost. The cost of a 30-second advertisement during the television coverage of the US Super Bowl football game in 2014 was $4 million, which would only be justifiable if a large number of units would be sold as a result.

A firm's attempt to gain favourable treatment by government bodies through lobbying, contributions to election campaigns, and public relations expenditures are also a kind of fixed cost. These expenses are more or less independent of the level of the firm's output.

Secondly, large firms are able to purchase their inputs on more favourable terms, because they have more bargaining power than small firms when negotiating with suppliers.

Demand advantages

Large size may benefit a firm in selling its product, not just in producing it. This occurs when people are more likely to buy a product or service if it already has a lot of users. For example, a software application is more useful when everybody is using a compatible version. These demand-side benefits of scale are called **network economies of scale**, and there are many examples in technology-related markets.

Because producing large amounts creates economies of scale, reduces costs, and increases demand, large-scale production is a powerful influence on firm size. Production by a small group of people is often too costly to compete with larger firms.

But while small firms typically either grow or die, there are limits to firm growth. We have already seen in Unit 6 that firms may outsource production of components. Firm growth is limited, in part, because sometimes it is cheaper to purchase part of the product than to manufacture it themselves. Apple would be gigantic if it decided that Apple employees would produce the touch screens, chipsets, and other components that make up the iPhone and iPad rather than purchasing these parts from Toshiba, Samsung, and other suppliers. Apple's outsourcing strategy limits the firm's size, and increases the size of Toshiba, Samsung, and other firms that produce Apple's components.

In the next section, we will model the way that a firm's costs depend on its scale of production.

> **network economies of scale** These exist when an increase in the number of users of an output of a firm implies an increase in the value of the output to each of them, because they are connected to each other.

QUESTION 7.4 CHOOSE THE CORRECT ANSWER(S)

Which of the following statements is correct?

- ☐ If a firm's technology exhibits constant returns to scale, doubling the inputs leads to doubling of the output level.
- ☐ If a firm's technology exhibits decreasing returns to scale, doubling the inputs more than doubles the output level.
- ☐ If a firm's technology exhibits economies of scale, costs per unit will fall as the firm expands its production.
- ☐ If a firm's technology exhibits diseconomies of scale, doubling the inputs leads to less than doubling of the output level.

EINSTEIN

The size and cost of a pipe

We can use simple mathematics to work out how much the cost of making a pipe increases when the area of the cross-section doubles. The formula for the area of a circle is:

$$\textbf{area of a circle} = \pi \times (\textbf{radius of circle})^2$$

Let us assume the area of the pipe was originally 10 cm², and then it was doubled in size to 20 cm². We can use the equation above to find the radius of the pipe in each case.

When the area of the pipe is 10:

$$\text{radius} = \sqrt{\frac{10}{\pi}} = 1.78 \text{ cm}$$

When the area of the pipe is 20:

$$\text{radius} = \sqrt{\frac{20}{\pi}} = 2.52 \text{ cm}$$

The cost of the material used to make a pipe of given length is proportional to its circumference. The formula for the circumference of a circle is:

$$\text{circumference} = 2 \times \pi \times \text{radius of a circle}$$

When the area of the pipe is 10:

$$\text{circumference} = 2 \times \pi \times 1.78 = 11.18 \text{ cm}$$

When the area of the pipe is 20:

$$\text{circumference} = 2 \times \pi \times 2.52 = 15.83 \text{ cm}$$

The pipe has doubled in capacity, but the circumference, and hence the cost, has only increased by a factor of:

$$\frac{15.83}{11.18} = 1.42$$

We can clearly see that the firm has benefitted from economies of scale.

Diseconomies of scale: CORE's Dilbert law of firm hierarchy
If every 10 employees at a lower level must have a supervisor at a higher level, then a firm that has 10^x production workers (the bottom of the ladder) will have x levels of management, 10^{x-1} supervisors at the lowest level, 10^{x-2} at the second lowest level, and so on.

A firm with 1 million (10^6) production workers will thus have 100,000 ($10^5 = 10^{6-1}$) lowest-level supervisors. Dilbert did not invent the law. He is too closely watched by his supervisor to have time for that. The CORE team did.

7.3 PRODUCTION: THE COST FUNCTION FOR BEAUTIFUL CARS

To set the price and the quantity produced for Apple-Cinnamon Cheerios, the manager needed to know the demand function and the production costs. Since we assumed that the cost of producing every pound of Cheerios was the same, the scale of production was determined by the demand for the good. In this section and the next, we will look at a different example, in which costs vary with the level of production.

Consider a firm that manufactures cars. Compared with Ford, which produces around 6.6 million vehicles a year, this firm produces specialty cars and will turn out to be rather small, so we will call it Beautiful Cars.

Think about the costs of producing and selling cars. The firm needs premises (a factory) equipped with machines for casting, machining, pressing, assembling, and welding car body parts. It may rent them from another firm, or raise financial capital to invest in its own premises and equipment. Then it must purchase the raw materials and components, and pay production workers to operate the equipment. Other workers will be needed to manage the production process, market, and sell the finished cars.

The firm's owners—the shareholders—would usually not be willing to invest in the firm if they could make better use of their money by investing and earning profits elsewhere. What they could receive if they invested elsewhere, per dollar of investment, is another example of **opportunity cost** (discussed in Unit 3), in this case called the **opportunity cost of capital**. Part of the cost of producing cars is the amount that has to be paid out to shareholders to cover the opportunity cost of capital—that is, to induce them to continue to invest in the assets that the firm needs to produce cars.

The more cars produced, the higher the total costs will be. The upper panel of Figure 7.6 shows how total costs might depend on the quantity of cars, Q, produced per day. This is the firm's cost function, $C(Q)$. From the cost function, we have worked out the average cost of a car, and how it changes with Q; the average cost curve (AC) is plotted in the lower panel.

We can see in Figure 7.6 that Beautiful Cars has decreasing average costs at low levels of production: the AC curve slopes downward. At higher levels of production, average cost increases so the AC curve slopes upward. This might happen because the firm has to increase the number of shifts per day on the assembly line. Perhaps it has to pay overtime rates, and equipment breaks down more frequently when the production line is working for longer.

Figure 7.7 shows how to find the **marginal cost** of a car, that is, the cost of producing one more car. In Unit 3, we saw that the marginal product for a given production function was the additional output produced when the input was increased by one unit, corresponding to the slope of the production function. Similarly, Figure 7.7 demonstrates that the marginal cost (MC) corresponds to the slope of the cost function.

By calculating the marginal cost at every value of Q, we have drawn the whole of the marginal cost curve in the lower panel of Figure 7.7. Since marginal cost is the slope of the cost function and the cost curve gets steeper as Q increases, the graph of marginal cost is an upward-sloping line. In other words, Beautiful Cars has increasing marginal costs of car production. It is the rising marginal cost that eventually causes average costs to increase.

Notice that in Figure 7.7 we calculated marginal cost by finding the change in costs, ΔC, from producing one more car. Sometimes it is more convenient to take a different increase in quantity. If we know that costs rise by $\Delta C = \$12,000$ when 5 extra cars are produced, then we could calculate $\Delta C / \Delta Q$, where $\Delta Q = 5$, to get an estimate for MC of $\$2,400$ per car. In general, when the cost function is curved, a smaller ΔQ gives a more accurate estimate.

opportunity cost When taking an action implies forgoing the next best alternative action, this is the net benefit of the foregone alternative.

opportunity cost of capital The amount of income an investor could have received by investing the unit of capital elsewhere.

fixed costs Costs of production that do not vary with the number of units produced.

marginal cost The effect on total cost of producing one additional unit of output. It corresponds to the slope of the total cost function at each point.

MARGINAL COST

At each point on the cost function, the marginal cost (MC) is the additional cost of producing one more unit of output, which corresponds to the slope of the cost function. If cost increases by ΔC when quantity is increased by ΔQ, the marginal cost can be estimated by:

$$MC = \frac{\Delta C}{\Delta Q}$$

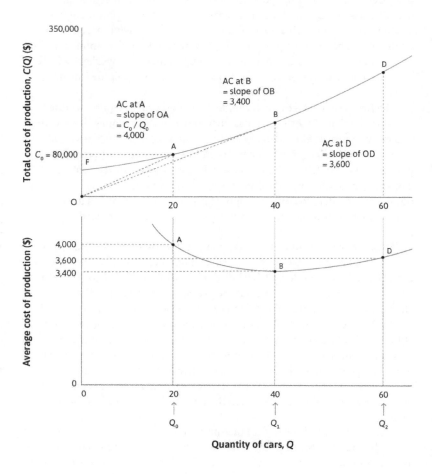

Figure 7.6 Beautiful Cars: Cost function and average cost.

1. The cost function
The top panel shows the cost function, $C(Q)$. It shows the total cost for each level of output, Q.

2. Fixed costs
Some costs do not vary with the number of cars. For example, once the firm has decided the size of its factory and invested in equipment, those costs will be the same irrespective of output. These are called **fixed costs**. So when $Q = 0$, the only costs are the fixed costs, F.

3. Total costs are increasing
As Q increases, total costs rise and the firm needs to employ more production workers. At point A, 20 cars are produced (we call this Q_0) costing $80,000 (we call this C_0).

4. Average cost
If the firm produces 20 cars per day, the average cost of a car is C_0 divided by Q_0, which is shown by the slope of the line from the origin to A. The average cost is now $80,000/20 = $4,000. We have plotted the average cost at point A on the lower panel.

5. Falling average cost
As output rises above A, fixed costs are shared between more cars. The average cost falls. At point B, the total cost is $136,000, average cost is $3,400.

6. Rising average cost
Average cost is lowest at point B. When production increases beyond B, the line to the origin gets gradually steeper again. At D average cost has risen to $3,600.

7. The average cost curve
We can calculate the average cost at every value of Q to draw the average cost (AC) curve in the lower panel.

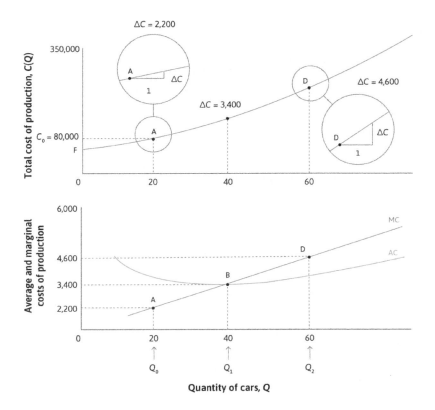

Figure 7.7 The marginal cost of a car.

1. Total cost, average cost and marginal cost
The upper panel shows the cost function (also called the total cost curve). The lower panel shows the average cost curve. We will plot the marginal costs in the lower panel too.

2. Total cost
Suppose the firm is producing 20 cars at point A. The total cost is $80,000.

3. Marginal cost
The marginal cost is the cost of increasing output from 20 to 21. This would increase total costs by an amount that we call ΔC, equal to $2,200. The triangle drawn at A shows that the marginal cost is equal to the slope of the cost function at that point.

4. Marginal cost at A
We have plotted the marginal cost at point A in the lower panel.

5. Marginal cost at D
At point D, where $Q = 60$, the cost function is much steeper. The marginal cost of producing an extra car is higher: $\Delta C = $4,600$.

6. Marginal cost at B
At point B, the curve is steeper than at A, but flatter than at D: MC = $3,400.

7. The cost function
Look at the shape of the whole cost function. When $Q = 0$ it is quite flat, so marginal cost is low. As Q increases, the cost function gets steeper, and marginal cost gradually rises.

8. The marginal cost curve
If we calculate marginal cost at every point on the cost function, we can draw the marginal cost curve.

Now look at the shapes of the AC and MC curves, shown again in Figure 7.8. You can see that the AC is downward-sloping at values of Q where the AC is greater than the MC, and it is upward-sloping where AC is less than MC. This is not just a coincidence: it happens whatever the shape of the total cost function. Follow the analysis in Figure 7.8 to see why this happens.

Leibniz: Average and marginal cost functions (http://tinyco.re/L070301)

QUESTION 7.5 CHOOSE THE CORRECT ANSWER(S)
Consider a firm with fixed costs of production. Which of the following statements about its average cost (AC) and marginal cost (MC) is correct?

☐ When AC = MC, the AC curve has a zero slope.
☐ When AC > MC, the MC curve is downward-sloping.
☐ When AC < MC, the AC curve is downward-sloping.
☐ The MC curve cannot be horizontal.

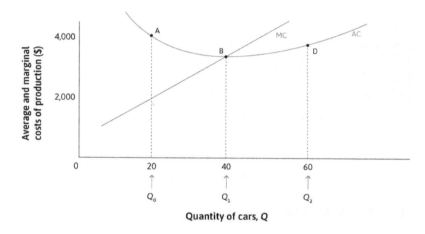

Figure 7.8 Average and marginal cost curves.

1. Average and marginal cost
The diagram shows both the average cost curve and the marginal cost curve.

2. MC < AC when Q = 20
Look at point A on the AC curve. When Q = 20, the average cost is $4,000, but the marginal cost is only $2,000. So if 21 cars rather than 20 are produced, that will reduce the average cost. Average cost is lower at Q = 21.

3. Average cost curve slopes downward when AC > MC
At any point, like point A, where AC > MC, the average cost will fall if one more car is produced, so the AC curve slopes downward.

4. Average cost curve slopes upward when AC < MC
At point D where Q = 60, the average cost is $3,600, but the cost of producing the 61st car is $4,600. So the average cost of a car will rise if 61 cars are produced. When AC < MC, the average cost curve slopes upward.

5. When AC = MC
At point B, where the average cost is lowest, the average and marginal costs are equal. The two curves cross. When AC = MC, the AC curve doesn't slope up or down: it is flat (the slope is zero).

QUESTION 7.6 CHOOSE THE CORRECT ANSWER(S)

Suppose that the unit cost of producing a pound of cereal is $2, irrespective of the level of output. Which of the following statements is correct?

☐ The total cost curve is a horizontal straight line.
☐ The average cost curve is downward-sloping.
☐ The marginal cost curve is upward-sloping.
☐ The average cost and the marginal cost curves coincide.

EXERCISE 7.2 THE COST FUNCTION FOR APPLE-CINNAMON CHEERIOS

Of course, cost functions can have different shapes from the one we drew for Beautiful Cars. For Apple-Cinnamon Cheerios, we assumed the average cost was constant, so that the unit cost of a pound of cereal was equal to $2, regardless of the quantity produced.

1. Draw the cost function (also called the total cost curve) for this case.
2. What do the marginal and average cost functions look like?
3. Now suppose that the marginal cost of producing a pound of Cheerios was $2, whatever the quantity, but there were also some fixed production costs. Draw the total, marginal, and average cost curves in this case.

Economists Rajindar and Manjulika Koshal studied the cost functions of universities in the US. They estimated the marginal and average costs of educating graduate and undergraduate students in 171 public universities in the academic year 1990–91. As you will see in Exercise 7.3, they found decreasing average costs. They also found that the universities benefitted from what are termed **economies of scope**: there were cost savings from producing several products—in this case graduate education, undergraduate education, and research—together.

If you want to know more about costs, George Stigler, an economist, has written an entertaining discussion of the subject in chapter 7 of his book.

economies of scope Cost savings that occur when two or more products are produced jointly by a single firm, rather being produced in separate firms.

Rajindar K. Koshal and Manjulika Koshal. 1999. 'Economies of Scale and Scope in Higher Education: A Case of Comprehensive Universities' (http://tinyco.re/8137580). *Economics of Education Review* 18 (2): pp. 269–77.

Economies of Scale and Scope. (http://tinyco.re/7593630) *The Economist*. Updated 20 October 2008.

George J. Stigler. 1987. *The Theory of Price*. New York, NY: Collier Macmillan.

EXERCISE 7.3 COST FUNCTIONS FOR UNIVERSITY EDUCATION

Below you can see the average and marginal costs per student for the year 1990–91 that Koshal and Koshal calculated from their research.

	Students	MC ($)	AC ($)	Total cost ($)
	2,750	7,259	7,659	21,062,250
	5,500	6,548	7,348	40,414,000
Undergraduates	8,250	5,838	7,038	
	11,000	5,125	6,727	73,997,000
	13,750	4,417	6,417	88,233,750
	16,500	3,706	6,106	100,749,000
	Students	MC ($)	AC ($)	Total cost ($)
	550	6,541	12,140	6,677,000
	1,100	6,821	9,454	10,339,400
Graduates	1,650	7,102	8,672	
	2,200	7,383	8,365	18,403,000
	2,750	7,664	8,249	22,684,750
	3,300	7,945	8,228	27,152,400

1. How do average costs change as the numbers of students rise?
2. Using the data for average costs, fill in the missing figures in the total cost column.
3. Plot the marginal and average cost curves for undergraduate education on a graph, with costs on the vertical axis and the number of students on the horizontal axis. On a separate diagram, plot the equivalent graphs for graduates.
4. What are the shapes of the total cost functions for undergraduates and graduates? (You could sketch them using what you know about marginal and average costs.) Plot them on a single chart using the numbers in the total cost column.
5. What are the main differences between the universities' cost structures for undergraduates and graduates?
6. Can you think of any explanations for the shapes of the graphs you have drawn?

7.4 DEMAND AND ISOPROFIT CURVES: BEAUTIFUL CARS

differentiated product A product produced by a single firm that has some unique characteristics compared to similar products of other firms.

Not all cars are the same. Cars are **differentiated products**. Each make and model is produced by just one firm, and has some unique characteristics of design and performance that differentiate it from the cars made by other firms.

We expect a firm selling a differentiated product to face a downward-sloping demand curve. We have already seen an empirical example in the case of Apple-Cinnamon Cheerios (another differentiated product). If the price of a Beautiful Car is high, demand will be low because the only consumers who will buy it are those who strongly prefer Beautiful Cars to all other makes. As the price falls, more consumers, who might otherwise have purchased a Ford or a Volvo, will be attracted to a Beautiful Car.

The demand curve

For any product that consumers might wish to buy, the product demand curve is a relationship that tells you the number of items (the quantity) they will buy at each possible price. For a simple model of the demand for Beautiful Cars, imagine that there are 100 potential consumers who would each buy one Beautiful Car today, if the price were low enough.

Each consumer has a **willingness to pay (WTP)** for a Beautiful Car, which depends on how much the customer personally values it (given the resources to buy it, of course). A consumer will buy a car if the price is less than or equal to his or her WTP. Suppose we line up the consumers in order of WTP, with the highest first, and plot a graph to show how the WTP varies along the line (Figure 7.9). Then if we choose any price, say $P = \$3{,}200$, the graph shows the number of consumers whose WTP is greater than or equal to P. In this case, 60 consumers are willing to pay $3,200 or more, so the demand for cars at a price of $3,200 is 60.

If P is lower, there are a larger number of consumers willing to buy, so the demand is higher. Demand curves are often drawn as straight lines, as in this example, although there is no reason to expect them to be straight in reality: we saw that the demand curve for Apple-Cinnamon Cheerios was not straight. But we do expect demand curves to slope downward: as the price rises, the quantity that consumers demand falls. In other words, when the available quantity is low, it can be sold at a high price. This relationship between price and quantity is sometimes known as the Law of Demand.

> **willingness to pay (WTP)** An indicator of how much a person values a good, measured by the maximum amount he or she would pay to acquire a unit of the good. *See also: willingness to accept.*

The Law of Demand dates back to the seventeenth century, and is attributed to Gregory King (1648–1712) and Charles Davenant (1656–1714). King was a herald at the College of Arms in London, who produced detailed estimates of the population and wealth of England. Davenant, a politician, published the Davenant-King Law of Demand in 1699, using King's data. It described how the price of corn would change depending on the size of the harvest. For example, he calculated that a 'defect', or shortfall, of one-tenth (10%) would raise the price by 30%.

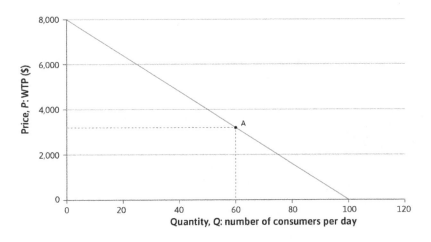

Figure 7.9 The demand for cars (per day).

The diagram depicts two alternative demand curves, D and D′, for a product. Based on this graph, which of the following are correct?

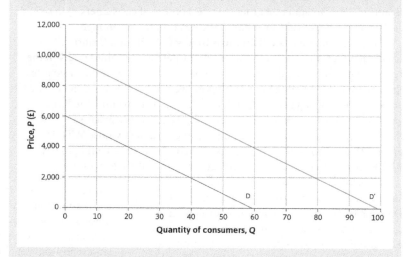

☐ On demand curve D, when the price is £5,000, the firm can sell 15 units of the product.
☐ On demand curve D′, the firm can sell 70 units at a price of £3,000.
☐ At price £1,000, the firm can sell 40 more units of the product on D′ than on D.
☐ With an output of 30 units, the firm can charge £2,000 more on D′ than on D.

Like the producer of Apple-Cinnamon Cheerios, Beautiful Cars will choose the price, P, and the quantity, Q, taking into account its demand curve and its production costs. The demand curve determines the feasible set of combinations of P and Q. To find the profit-maximizing point, we will draw the isoprofit curves, and look for the point of tangency as before.

The isoprofit curves

The firm's profit is the difference between its revenue (the price multiplied by quantity sold) and its total costs, $C(Q)$:

$$\text{profit} = \text{total revenue} - \text{total costs}$$
$$= PQ - C(Q)$$

economic profit A firm's revenue minus its total costs (including the opportunity cost of capital).
normal profits Corresponds to zero economic profit and means that the rate of profit is equal to the opportunity cost of capital.
See also: economic profit, opportunity cost of capital.

This calculation gives us what is known as the **economic profit**. Remember that the cost function includes the opportunity cost of capital (the payments that must be made to the owners to induce them to hold shares), which is referred to as **normal profits**. Economic profit is the additional profit above the minimum return required by shareholders.

Equivalently, profit is the number of units of output multiplied by the profit per unit, which is the difference between the price and the average cost:

$$\text{profit} = Q(P - \frac{C(Q)}{Q})$$
$$= Q(P - AC)$$

From this equation you can see that the shape of the isoprofit curves will depend on the shape of the average cost curve. Remember that for Beautiful Cars, the average cost curve slopes downward until $Q = 40$, and then upward. Figure 7.10 shows the corresponding isoprofit curves. They look similar to those for Cheerios in Figure 7.3, but there are some differences because the average cost function has a different shape. The lowest (lightest blue) curve shows the zero-economic-profit curve: the combinations of price and quantity for which economic profit is equal to zero, because the price is just equal to the average cost at each quantity.

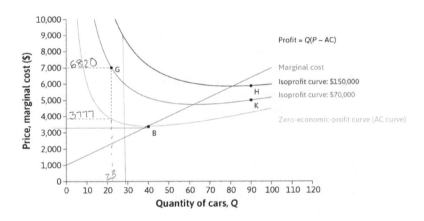

6820   Price
3777   AC
——————
3 043 Profit per unit
        * Q.

23 * 7000

Figure 7.10 Isoprofit curves for Beautiful Cars.

1. The zero-economic-profit curve
The lightest blue curve is the firm's average cost curve. If $P = AC$, the firm's economic profit is zero. So the AC curve is also the zero-profit curve: it shows all the combinations of P and Q that give zero economic profit.

2. The shape of the zero-economic-profit curve
Beautiful Cars has decreasing AC when $Q < 40$, and increasing AC when $Q > 40$. When Q is low, it needs a high price to break even. If $Q = 40$ it could break even with a price of $3,400. For $Q > 40$, it would need to raise the price again to avoid a loss.

3. AC and MC
Beautiful Cars has increasing marginal costs: the upward-sloping line. Remember that the AC curve slopes down if AC > MC, and up if AC < MC. The two curves cross at B, where AC is lowest.

4. Isoprofit curves
The darker blue curves show the combinations of P and Q giving higher levels of profit, so points G and K give the same profit.

5. Profit = $Q(P - AC)$
At G where the firm makes 23 cars, the price is $6,820 and the average cost is $3,777. The firm makes a profit of $3,043 on each car, and its total profit is $70,000.

6. Higher prices, higher profits
Profit is higher on the curves closer to the top-right corner in the diagram. Point H has the same quantity as K, so the average cost is the same, but the price is higher at H.

Notice that in Figure 7.10:

- Isoprofit curves slope downward at points where $P > $ MC.
- Isoprofit curves slope upward at points where $P < $ MC.

profit margin The difference between the price and the marginal cost.

The difference between the price and the marginal cost is called the **profit margin**. At any point on an isoprofit curve the slope is given by:

$$\text{slope of isoprofit curve} = -\frac{(P - \text{MC})}{Q}$$
$$= -\frac{\text{profit margin}}{\text{quantity}}$$

To understand why, think again about point G in Figure 7.10 at which $Q = 28$, and the price is much higher than the marginal cost. If you:

1. increase Q by 1
2. reduce P by $(P - \text{MC})/Q$

then your profit will stay the same because the extra profit of $(P - \text{MC})$ on car 29 will be offset by a fall in revenue of $(P - \text{MC})$ on the other 28 cars.

Leibniz: Isoprofit curves and their slopes (http://tinyco.re/L070401)

The same reasoning applies at every point where $P > $ MC. The profit margin is positive so the slope is negative. And it also applies when $P < $ MC. In this case, the profit margin is negative so an *increase* in price is required to keep profit constant when quantity rises by 1. The isoprofit curve slopes upward.

QUESTION 7.8 CHOOSE THE CORRECT ANSWER(S)

The diagram depicts the marginal cost curve (MC), the average cost curve (AC), and the isoprofit curves of a firm. What can we deduce from the information in the diagram?

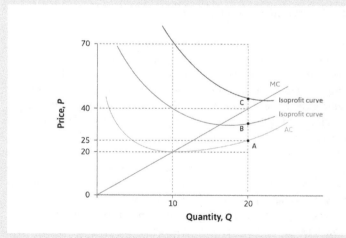

☐ The profit level at A is 500.
☐ The profit level at B is 150.
☐ The price at C is 50.
☐ The price at B is 36.

EXERCISE 7.4 LOOKING AT ISOPROFIT CURVES

The isoprofit curves for Cheerios are downward-sloping, but for Beautiful Cars they slope downward when Q is low and upward when Q is high.

1. In both cases the higher isoprofit curves get closer to the average cost curve as quantity increases. Why?
2. What is the reason for the difference in the shape of the isoprofit curves between the two firms?

7.5 SETTING PRICE AND QUANTITY TO MAXIMIZE PROFIT

In Figure 7.11 we have shown both the demand curve and the isoprofit curves for Beautiful Cars. What is the best choice of price and quantity for the manufacturer?

The only feasible choices are the points on or below the demand curve, shown by the shaded area on the diagram. To maximize profit the firm should choose the tangency point E, which is on the highest possible isoprofit curve.

The profit-maximizing price and quantity are $P^* = \$5,440$ and $Q^* = 32$, and the corresponding profit is $63,360. As in the case of Cheerios, the optimal combination of price and quantity balances the trade-off that the firm would be willing to make between price and quantity (for a given profit level), against the trade-off the firm is constrained to make by the demand curve.

The firm maximizes profit at the tangency point, where the slope of the demand curve is equal to the slope of the isoprofit curve, so that the two trade-offs are in balance:

- The demand curve is the feasible frontier, and its slope is the **marginal rate of transformation (MRT)** of lower prices into greater quantity sold.

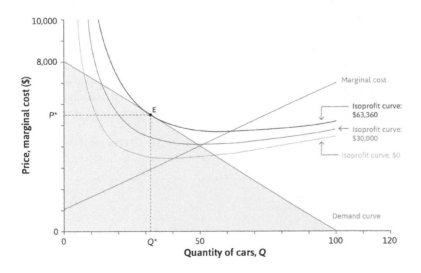

Figure 7.11 The profit-maximizing choice of price and quantity for Beautiful Cars.

- The isoprofit curve is the indifference curve, and its slope is the **marginal rate of substitution (MRS)** in profit creation, between selling more and charging more.

At E, the profit-maximizing point, MRT = MRS.

Leibniz: The profit-maximizing price (http://tinyco.re/L070501)

Compared with the multinational giants of the automobile industry, Beautiful Cars is a small firm: it chooses to make only 32 cars per day. In terms of its production levels (but not its prices) it is more similar to luxury brands like Aston-Martin, Rolls Royce and Lamborghini, each of which produces fewer than 5,000 cars a year. The size of Beautiful Cars is determined partly by its demand function—there are only 100 potential buyers per day, at any price. In the longer term, the firm may be able to increase demand by advertising: bringing its product to the attention of more consumers, and convincing them of its desirable qualities. But if it wants to expand production it will also need to look at its cost structure, as in Figure 7.7 (page 277). At present it has rapidly increasing marginal costs, so that average cost starts to rise when output per day exceeds 40. With its current premises and equipment it is difficult to produce more than 40 cars. Investment in new equipment may help to reduce its marginal cost, and might make expansion possible.

Constrained optimization

The profit-maximization problem is another **constrained choice problem**, like those in earlier units: Alexei's choice of study time, your own and Angela's choices of working hours, and the choice of the wage by Maria's employer.

Each of these problems has the same structure:

> **constrained choice problem** This problem is about how we can do the best for ourselves, given our preferences and constraints, and when the things we value are scarce. *See also: constrained optimization problem.*

- The decision-maker wants to choose the values of one or more variables to achieve a goal, or objective. For Beautiful Cars, the variables are price and quantity.
- The objective is to *optimize* something: to maximize utility, minimize costs, or maximize profit.
- The decision-maker faces a *constraint*, which limits what is feasible: Angela's production function, your budget constraint, Maria's best response curve, the demand curve for Beautiful Cars.

> **CONSTRAINED OPTIMIZATION**
> A decision-maker chooses the values of one or more variables
> - ... to achieve an objective
> - ... subject to a constraint that determines the feasible set

In each case, we have represented the decision-maker's choice graphically, by showing the indifference curves, which relate to the objective (iso-utility, isocost, or isoprofit), and the feasible set of outcomes, which is determined by the constraint. And we have found the solution of the problem at the tangency point where the MRS (slope of the indifference curve) is equal to the MRT (slope of the constraint).

Constrained optimization has many applications in economics; such problems can be solved mathematically, as well as graphically.

QUESTION 7.9 CHOOSE THE CORRECT ANSWER(S)
Figure 7.11 (page 285) depicts the demand curve for Beautiful Cars, together with the marginal cost and isoprofit curves. The quantity-price combination at point E is $(Q^*, P^*) = (32, 5,440)$. The average cost of producing 50 cars is the same as the average cost of producing 32. Suppose that the firm keeps the price at $P = \$5,440$ but now produces 50 cars instead of 32. Which of the following is correct?

☐ The firm will now sell all 50 cars at $5,440.
☐ The firm's profit will increase.
☐ The firm's profit remains the same.
☐ The firm's profit is now reduced.

QUESTION 7.10 CHOOSE THE CORRECT ANSWER(S)
Figure 7.11 (page 285) depicts the demand curve for Beautiful Cars, together with the marginal cost and isoprofit curves. At point E, the quantity-price combination is $(Q^*, P^*) = (32, 5,440)$ and the profit is $63,360.

Suppose that the firm chooses instead to produce $Q = 32$ cars and sets the price at $P = \$5,400$. Which of the following statements is correct?

☐ The profit remains the same at $63,360.
☐ The profit is reduced to $62,080.
☐ The average cost of production is $3,400.
☐ The firm is unable to sell all the cars.

QUESTION 7.11 CHOOSE THE CORRECT ANSWER(S)
Figure 7.11 (page 285) depicts the demand curve for Beautiful Cars, together with the marginal cost and isoprofit curves.

Suppose that the firm decides to switch from $P^* = \$5,440$ and $Q^* = 32$ to a higher price, and chooses the profit-maximizing level of output at the new price. Which of the following statements is correct?

☐ The quantity of cars produced is reduced.
☐ The marginal cost of producing an extra car is higher.
☐ The total cost of production is higher.
☐ The profit is increased due to the new higher price.

7.6 LOOKING AT PROFIT MAXIMIZATION AS MARGINAL REVENUE AND MARGINAL COST

In the previous section we showed that the profit-maximizing choice for Beautiful Cars was the point at which the demand curve was tangent to the highest isoprofit curve. To make maximum profit, it should produce $Q = 32$ cars and sell them at a price $P = \$5,440$.

We now look at a different method of finding the profit-maximizing point, without using isoprofit curves. Instead, we use the marginal revenue curve. Remember that if Q cars are sold at a price P, revenue R is given by $R = P \times Q$. The **marginal revenue**, MR, is the increase in revenue obtained by increasing the quantity from Q to $Q + 1$.

Figure 7.12a shows you how to calculate the marginal revenue when $Q = 20$: that is, the increase in revenue if quantity increases by one unit.

Figure 7.12a shows that the firm's revenue is the area of the rectangle drawn below the demand curve. When Q is increased from 20 to 21, revenue changes for two reasons. An extra car is sold at the new price, but since the new price is lower when $Q = 21$, there is also a loss of $80 on each of the other 20 cars. The marginal revenue is the net effect of these two changes.

In Figure 7.12b we find the marginal revenue curve, and use it to find the point of maximum profit. The upper panel shows the demand curve, and the middle panel shows the marginal cost curve. The analysis in Figure 7.12b shows how to calculate and plot the marginal revenue curve. When P is high and Q is low, MR is high: the gain from selling one more car is much greater than the total loss on the small number of other cars. As we move down the demand curve P falls (so the gain on the last car gets smaller), and Q rises (so the total loss on the other cars is bigger), so MR falls and eventually becomes negative.

The marginal revenue curve is usually (although not necessarily) a downward-sloping line. The lower two panels in Figure 7.12b demonstrate that the profit-maximizing point is where the MR curve crosses the MC curve. To understand why, remember that profit is the difference between revenue and costs, so for any value of Q, the change in profit if Q was increased by one unit (the marginal profit) would be the difference between the change in revenue, and the change in costs:

$$\text{profit} = \text{total revenue} - \text{total costs}$$
$$\text{marginal profit} = \text{MR} - \text{MC}$$

So:

- If MR > MC, the firm could increase profit by raising Q.
- If MR < MC, the marginal profit is negative. It would be better to decrease Q.

You can see how profit changes with Q in the lowest panel of 7.12b. Just as marginal cost is the slope of the cost function, marginal profit is the slope of the profit function. In this case:

- When $Q < 32$, MR > MC: Marginal profit is positive, so profit increases with Q.
- When $Q > 32$, MR < MC: Marginal profit is negative; profit decreases with Q.
- When $Q = 32$, MR = MC: Profit reaches a maximum.

> **marginal revenue** The increase in revenue obtained by increasing the quantity from Q to $Q + 1$.

Leibniz: Marginal revenue and marginal cost (http://tinyco.re/L070601)

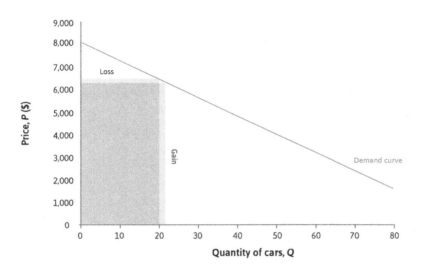

Revenue, $R = P \times Q$

$Q = 20$	$P = \$6,400$	$R = \$128,000$
$Q = 21$	$P = \$6,320$	$R = \$132,720$
$\Delta Q = 1$	$\Delta P = \$80$	$MR = \Delta R/\Delta Q = \$4,720$
Gain in revenue (21st car)		$\$6,320$
Loss of revenue ($80 on each of the other 20 cars)		$-\$1,600$
Marginal revenue		$\$4,720$

Figure 7.12a Calculating marginal revenue.

1. Revenue when $Q = 20$
When $Q = 20$, the price is $6,400, and revenue = $6,400 × 20, the area of the rectangle.

2. Revenue when $Q = 21$
If quantity is increased to 21, the price falls to $6,320. The change in price is $\Delta P = -\$80$. The revenue at $Q = 21$ is shown by the area of the new rectangle, which is $6,320 × 21.

3. Marginal revenue when $Q = 20$
The marginal revenue at $Q = 20$ is the difference between the two areas. The table shows that the area of the rectangle is larger when $Q = 21$. The marginal revenue is $4,720.

4. Why is MR > 0?
The increase in revenue happens because the firm gains $6,320 on the 21st car, and this gain is greater than the loss of 20 × $80 from selling the other 20 cars at a lower price.

5. Calculating the marginal revenue
The table shows that the marginal revenue can also be calculated as the difference between the gain of $6,320 and the loss of $1,600.

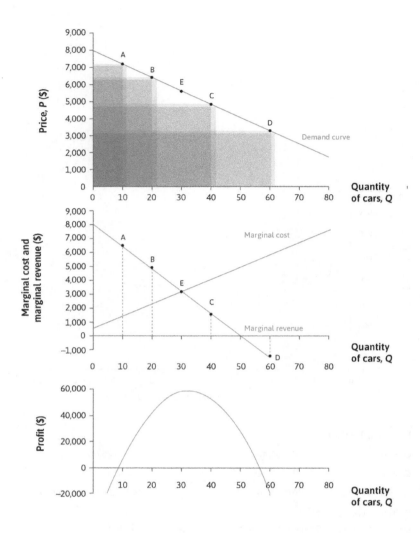

Figure 7.12b Marginal revenue, marginal cost, and profit.

1. Demand and marginal cost curves
The upper panel shows the demand curve, and the middle panel shows the marginal cost curve. At point A, $Q = 10$, $P = \$7,200$, revenue is $72,000.

2. Marginal revenue
The marginal revenue (middle panel) at A is the difference between the areas of the two rectangles: MR = $6,480.

3. Marginal revenue when $Q = 20$
Marginal revenue when $Q = 20$ and $P = \$6,400$ is $4,880.

4. Moving down the demand curve
As we move down the demand curve, P falls and MR falls by more. The gain on the extra car gets smaller, and the loss on the other cars is bigger.

5. MR < 0
At point D, the gain on the extra car is outweighed by the loss on the others, so the marginal revenue is negative.

6. The marginal revenue curve
Joining the points in the middle panel gives the marginal revenue curve.

7. MR > MC
MR and MC cross at point E, where $Q = 32$. MR > MC at any value of Q below 32: the revenue from selling an extra car is greater than the cost of making it, so it would be better to increase production.

8. MR < MC
When $Q > 32$, MR < MC: if the firm was producing more than 32 cars it would lose profit if it made an extra car, and it would increase profit if it made fewer cars.

QUESTION 7.12 CHOOSE THE CORRECT ANSWER(S)

This figure shows the marginal cost and marginal revenue curves for Beautiful Cars. Which of the following statements is correct, based on the information shown?

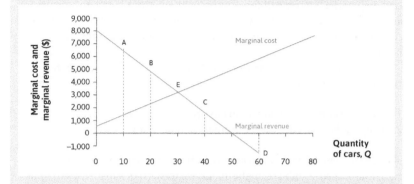

☐ When $Q = 40$, the marginal cost is greater than the marginal revenue so the firm's profit must be negative.

☐ Revenue is greater when $Q = 10$ than if $Q = 20$.

☐ The firm would not choose to produce at point E because marginal profit is zero.

☐ Profit is greater when $Q = 20$ than when $Q = 10$.

9. The firm's profit

In the lower panel we have plotted the firm's profit at each point on the demand curve. You can see that when $Q < 32$, MR > MC, and profit increases if Q increases. When $Q = 32$, profit is maximized. When $Q > 32$, MR < MC, and profit falls if Q rises.

7.7 GAINS FROM TRADE

Remember from Unit 5 that when people engage voluntarily in an economic interaction, they do so because it makes them better off: they can obtain a surplus called **economic rent**. The total surplus for the parties involved is a measure of the **gains from exchange** or gains from trade. We can analyse the outcome of the economic interactions between consumers and a firm just as we did for Angela and Bruno in Unit 5. We judge the total surplus, and the way it is shared, in terms of **Pareto efficiency** and fairness.

We have assumed that the rules of the game for allocating Cheerios and cars to consumers are:

1. A firm decides how many items to produce, and sets a price.
2. Then individual consumers decide whether to buy.

These rules reflect typical market institutions for the allocation of consumer goods, although we might imagine alternatives—maybe a group of people who wanted cars could get together to produce a specification, then invite manufacturers to tender for the contract.

In the interactions between a firm like Beautiful Cars and its consumers, there are potential gains for both, as long as the firm is able to manufacture a car at a cost less than the value of the car to a consumer. Recall that the demand curve shows the willingness to pay (WTP) of each of the potential consumers. A consumer whose WTP is greater than the price will buy the good and receive a surplus, since the value to her of the car is more than she has to pay for it.

Similarly, the marginal cost curve shows what it costs to make each additional car (if you start at $Q = 0$, the marginal cost curve shows how much it costs to make the first car, then the second, and so on). And if the marginal cost is lower than the price, the firm receives a surplus too. Figure 7.13 shows how to find the total surplus for the firm and its consumers, when Beautiful Cars sets the price to maximize its profits.

In Figure 7.13, the shaded area above $P*$ measures the **consumer surplus**, and the shaded area below $P*$ is the **producer surplus**. We see from the relative size of the two areas in Figure 7.13 that in this market, the firm obtains a greater surplus share.

As in the voluntary contracts between Angela and Bruno, both parties gain in the market for Beautiful Cars, and the division of the gains is determined by bargaining power. In this case the firm has more power than its consumers because it is the only seller of Beautiful Cars. It can set a high price and obtain a high share of the gains, knowing that consumers with high valuations of the car have no alternative but to accept. An individual consumer has no power to bargain for a better deal because the firm has many other potential customers.

---

economic rent A payment or other benefit received above and beyond what the individual would have received in his or her next best alternative (or reservation option). *See also: reservation option.*

gains from exchange The benefits that each party gains from a transaction compared to how they would have fared without the exchange. *Also known as: gains from trade. See also: economic rent.*

Pareto efficient An allocation with the property that there is no alternative technically feasible allocation in which at least one person would be better off, and nobody worse off.

CONSUMER SURPLUS, PRODUCER SURPLUS, PROFIT

- The consumer surplus is a measure of the benefits of participation in the market for consumers.
- The producer surplus is closely related to the firm's profit, but it is not quite the same thing. Producer surplus is the difference between the firm's revenue and the marginal costs of every unit, but it doesn't allow for the fixed costs, which are incurred even when $Q = 0$.
- The profit is the producer surplus minus fixed costs.
- The **total surplus** arising from trade in this market, for the firm and consumers together, is the sum of consumer and producer surplus.

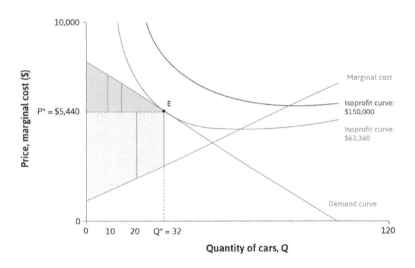

Figure 7.13 Gains from trade.

1. Gains from trade
When the firm sets its profit-maximizing price $P^* = \$5,440$ and sells $Q^* = 32$ cars per day, the 32nd consumer, whose WTP is $5,440, is just indifferent between buying and not buying a car, so that particular buyer's surplus is equal to zero.

2. A higher WTP
Other buyers were willing to pay more. The 10th consumer, whose WTP is $7,200, makes a surplus of $1,760, shown by the vertical line at the quantity 10.

3. What would the 15th customer have been willing to pay?
The 15th consumer has WTP of $6,800 and hence a surplus of $1,360.

4. The consumer surplus
To find the total surplus obtained by consumers, we add together the surplus of each buyer. This is shown by the shaded triangle between the demand curve and the line where price is P^*. This measure of the consumers' gains from trade is the **consumer surplus**.

5. The producer surplus for the 20th car
Similarly, the firm makes a producer surplus on each car sold. The marginal cost of the 20th car is $2,000. By selling it for $5,440, the firm gains $3,440, shown by the vertical line in the diagram between P^* and the marginal cost curve.

6. The total producer surplus
To find the total **producer surplus**, we add together the surplus on each car produced: this is the purple-shaded area.

7. The marginal car
The firm obtains a surplus on the marginal car: the 32nd and last car is sold at a price greater than marginal cost.

Pareto efficiency

Is the allocation of cars in this market **Pareto efficient**? The answer is no, because there are some consumers who do not purchase cars at the firm's chosen price, but who would nevertheless be willing to pay more than it would cost the firm to produce them. In Figure 7.13 we saw that Beautiful Cars makes a surplus on the *marginal car* (the 32nd one). The price is greater than the marginal cost. It could produce another car, and sell it to the 33rd consumer at a price lower than \$5,440 but higher than the production cost. This would be a **Pareto improvement**: both the firm and the 33rd consumer would be better off. In other words, the potential gains from trade in the market for this type of car have not been exhausted at E.

Suppose the firm had chosen instead point F, where the marginal cost curve crosses the demand curve. This point represents a Pareto-efficient allocation, with no further potential Pareto improvements—producing another car would cost more than any of the remaining consumers would pay. Figure 7.14 explains why the total surplus, which we can think of as the pie to be shared between the firm and its customers, would be higher at F.

The total surplus would be higher at the Pareto-efficient point (F) than at point E. Consumer surplus would be higher, because those who were

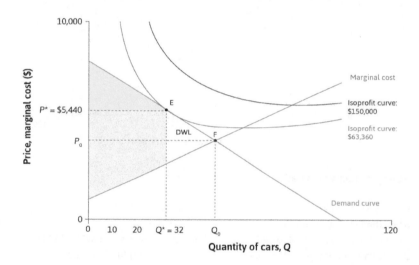

Figure 7.14 Deadweight loss.

1. Unexploited gains from trade
The firm's profit-maximizing price and quantity is at point E, but there are unexploited gains from trade. The firm could make one more car and sell it to the 33rd consumer for more than it would cost to produce.

2. A Pareto-efficient allocation
Suppose the firm chooses F instead, selling Q_0 cars at a price P_0 equal to the marginal cost. This allocation is Pareto efficient: making another car would cost more than P_0, and there are no more consumers willing to pay that much.

3. A higher consumer surplus
The consumer surplus is higher at F than at E.

4. A higher total surplus
The producer surplus is lower at F than at E, but the total surplus is higher.

5. Deadweight loss
At E, there is a deadweight loss equal to the area of the white triangle between $Q = 32$, the demand curve and the MC curve.

willing to buy at the higher price would benefit from the lower price, and additional consumers would also obtain a surplus. But Beautiful Cars will not choose F, because producer surplus is lower there (and you can see that it is on a lower isoprofit curve).

Since the firm chooses E, there is a loss of potential surplus, known as the **deadweight loss**. On the diagram it is the triangular area between $Q = 32$, the demand curve, and the marginal cost curve.

deadweight loss A loss of total surplus relative to a Pareto-efficient allocation.

It might seem confusing that the firm chooses E when we said that at this point it would be possible for both the consumers and the firm to be better off. That is true, but only if cars could be sold to other consumers at a lower price than to the first 32 consumers. The firm chooses E because that is the best it can do given the rules of the game (setting one price for all consumers). The allocation that results from price-setting by the producer of a differentiated product like Beautiful Cars is Pareto inefficient. The firm uses its bargaining power to set a price that is higher than the marginal cost of a car. It keeps the price high by producing a quantity that is too low, relative to the Pareto-efficient allocation.

As a thought experiment, imagine that the rules of the game were different, and the firm could charge separate prices to each buyer, just below the buyer's willingness to pay. Then the firm would definitely sell to any potential buyer whose willingness to pay exceeded the marginal cost, and as a result all mutually beneficial trades would take place. It would produce the Pareto-efficient quantity of cars.

To set individual prices in this way (called price discrimination), the firm would need to know the willingness to pay of every buyer. In this hypothetical case the deadweight loss would disappear. The firm would capture the entire surplus: there would be producer surplus, but no consumer surplus. We might think this unfair, but the market allocation would be Pareto efficient.

EXERCISE 7.5 CHANGING THE RULES OF THE GAME

1. Suppose that Beautiful Cars had sufficient information and so much bargaining power that it could charge each consumer, separately, the maximum they would be willing to pay. Draw the demand and marginal cost curves (as in Figure 7.14 (page 294)), and indicate on your diagram:
   (a) the number of cars sold
   (b) the highest price paid by any consumer
   (c) the lowest price paid
   (d) the consumer and producer surplus
2. Can you think of any examples of goods that are sold in this way?
3. Why is this not common practice?
4. Some firms charge different prices to different groups of consumers—for example, airlines may charge higher fares for last-minute travellers. Why would they do this and what effect would it have on the consumer and producer surpluses?
5. Suppose a competition policy has changed the rules of the game. How could this give consumers more bargaining power?
6. Under these rules, how many cars would be sold?
7. Under these rules, what would the producer and consumer surpluses be?

QUESTION 7.13 CHOOSE THE CORRECT ANSWER(S)
Which of the following statements is correct?

☐ Consumer surplus is the difference between the consumers' willingness to pay and what they actually pay.
☐ Producer surplus equals the firm's profit.
☐ Deadweight loss is the loss incurred by the producer for not selling more cars.
☐ All possible gains from trade are achieved when the firm chooses its profit-maximizing output and price.

7.8 THE ELASTICITY OF DEMAND

The firm maximizes profit by choosing the point where the slope of the iso-profit curve (MRS) is equal to the slope of the demand curve (MRT), which represents the trade-off that the firm is constrained to make between price and quantity.

So the firm's decision depends on how steep the demand curve is: in other words, how much consumers' demand for a good will change if the price changes. The **price elasticity of demand** is a measure of the responsiveness of consumers to a price change. It is defined as the percentage change in demand that would occur in response to a 1% increase in price. For example, suppose that when the price of a product increases by 10%, we observe a 5% fall in the quantity sold. Then we calculate the elasticity, ε, as follows:

price elasticity of demand The percentage change in demand that would occur in response to a 1% increase in price. We express this as a positive number. Demand is elastic if this is greater than 1, and inelastic if less than 1.

$$\varepsilon = -\frac{\% \text{ change in demand}}{\% \text{ change in price}}$$

ε is the Greek letter epsilon, which is often used to represent elasticity. For a demand curve, quantity falls when price increases. So the change in demand is negative if the price change is positive, and vice versa. The minus sign in the formula for the elasticity ensures that we get a positive number as our measure of responsiveness. So in this example we get:

$$\varepsilon = -\frac{-5}{10}$$
$$= 0.5$$

The price elasticity of demand is related to the slope of the demand curve. If the demand curve is quite flat, the quantity changes a lot in response to a change in price, so the elasticity is high. Conversely, a steeper demand curve corresponds to a lower elasticity. But they are not the same thing, and it is important to notice that the elasticity changes as we move along the demand curve, even if the slope doesn't.

Figure 7.15 shows (again) the demand curve for cars, which has a constant slope: it is a straight line. At every point, if the quantity increases by one ($\Delta Q = 1$), the price falls by $80 ($\Delta P = -\$80$):

$$\text{slope of the demand curve} = -\frac{\Delta P}{\Delta Q}$$
$$= -80$$

Since $\Delta P = -\$80$ when $\Delta Q = 1$ at every point on the demand curve, it is easy to calculate the elasticity at any point. At A, for example, $Q = 20$ and $P = \$6,400$. So:

$$\text{\% change in } Q = 100(\frac{\Delta Q}{Q}) = 100(\frac{1}{20}) = 5\%$$

$$\text{\% change in } P = 100(\frac{\Delta P}{P}) = 100(\frac{-80}{6400}) = -1.25\%$$

And so:

$$\varepsilon = -\frac{5}{-1.25}$$
$$= 4$$

The table in Figure 7.15 calculates the elasticity at several points on the demand curve. Use the steps in the analysis to see that, as we move down the demand curve, the same changes in P and Q lead to a higher percentage change in P and a lower percentage change in Q, so the elasticity falls.

We say that demand is elastic if the elasticity is higher than 1, and inelastic if it is less than 1. You can see from the table in Figure 7.15 that the marginal revenue is positive at points where demand is elastic, and negative where it is inelastic. Why does this happen? When demand is highly elastic, price will only fall a little if the firm increases its quantity. So by producing one extra car, the firm will gain revenue on the extra car without losing much on the other cars and total revenue will rise; in other words, MR > 0. Conversely, if demand is inelastic, the firm cannot increase Q without a big drop in P, so MR < 0. In the Einstein at the end of this section, we demonstrate that this relationship is true for all demand curves.

QUESTION 7.14 CHOOSE THE CORRECT ANSWER(S)
A shop sells 20 hats per week at $10 each. When it increases the price to $12, the number of hats sold falls to 15 per week. Which of the following statements are correct?

☐ When the price increases from $10 to $12, demand increases by 25%.
☐ A 20% increase in the price causes a 25% fall in demand.
☐ The demand for hats is inelastic.
☐ The elasticity of demand is approximately 1.25.

How does the elasticity of demand affect a firm's decisions? Remember that the car manufacturer's profit-maximizing quantity is $Q = 32$. You can see in Figure 7.15 that this is on the elastic part of the demand curve. The firm would never want to choose a point such as D where the demand curve is inelastic because the marginal revenue is negative there; it would always be better to decrease the quantity, since that would raise revenue and decrease costs. So the firm always chooses a point where the elasticity is greater than 1.

profit margin The difference between the price and the marginal cost.

Secondly, the firm's **profit margin** (the difference between the price and the marginal cost of production) is closely related to the elasticity of demand. Figure 7.16 represents a different situation of highly elastic demand. The demand curve is quite flat, so small changes in price make a big difference to sales. The profit-maximizing choice is point E. You can see that the profit margin is relatively small. This means that the quantity of cars it chooses to make is not far below the Pareto-efficient quantity, at point F, where the profit margin is zero.

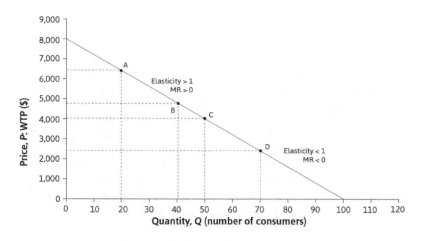

		Elasticity = − % Change in Q / % Change in P		
	A	B	C	D
Q	20	40	50	70
P	$6,400	$4,800	$4,000	$2,400
ΔQ	1	1	1	1
ΔP	−$80	−$80	−$80	−$80
% change in Q	5.00	2.50	2.00	1.43
% change in P	−1.25	−1.67	−2.00	−3.33
Elasticity	4.00	1.50	1.00	0.43
MR	$4,880	$1,680	$80	−$3,120

Figure 7.15 The elasticity of demand for cars.

1. This demand curve is a straight line
At each point on the demand curve if Q increases by 1, P changes by $\Delta P = -\$80$.

2. Elasticity at A
At point A, if $\Delta Q = 1$, the % change in Q is $100 \times 1/20 = 5\%$. Since $\Delta P = -\$80$, the % change in price is $100 \times (-80)/6,400 = -1.25\%$. The elasticity is 4.00.

3. Elasticity is lower at B than at A
At B, Q is higher, so the percentage change when $\Delta P = 1$ is lower. Similarly, P is lower and the percentage change in P is higher. So the elasticity at B is lower than at A. The table shows that it is 1.50.

4. As Q increases, elasticity decreases
The elasticity is equal to 1 at C, and below 1 at D.

5. The marginal revenue
The table also shows the marginal revenue at each point. When the elasticity is higher than 1, MR > 0. When the elasticity is below 1, MR < 0.

Figure 7.17 shows the decision of a firm with the same costs of car production, but less elastic demand for its product. In this case, the profit margin is high, and the quantity is low. When the price is raised, many consumers are still willing to pay. The firm maximizes profits by exploiting this situation, obtaining a higher share of the surplus, but the result is that fewer cars are sold and the unexploited gains from trade, shown by the deadweight loss, are high.

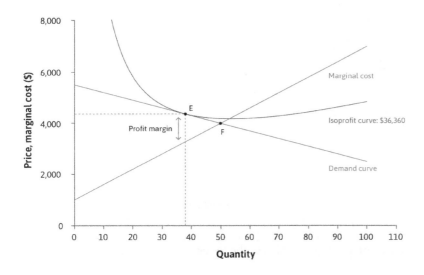

Figure 7.16 A firm facing highly elastic demand.

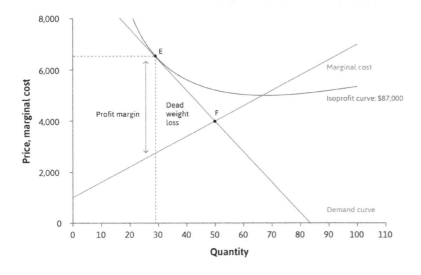

Figure 7.17 A firm facing less elastic demand.

price markup The price minus the marginal cost divided by the price. It is inversely proportional to the elasticity of demand for this good.

Leibniz: The elasticity of demand
(http://tinyco.re/L070801)

These examples illustrate that the lower the elasticity of demand, the more the firm will raise the price above the marginal cost to achieve a high profit margin. When demand elasticity is low, the firm has the power to raise the price without losing many customers, and the **markup**, which is the profit margin as a proportion of the price, will be high. The Einstein at the end of this section shows you that the markup is inversely proportional to the elasticity of demand.

QUESTION 7.15 CHOOSE THE CORRECT ANSWER(S)

The figure depicts two demand curves, D_1 and D_2.

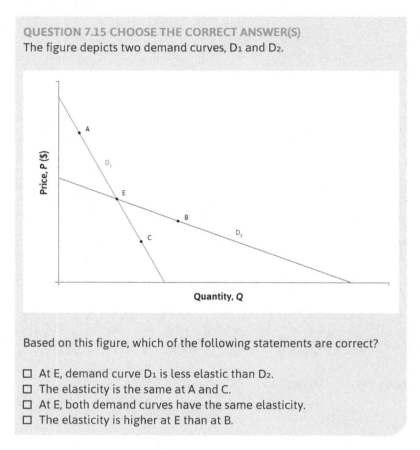

Based on this figure, which of the following statements are correct?

☐ At E, demand curve D_1 is less elastic than D_2.
☐ The elasticity is the same at A and C.
☐ At E, both demand curves have the same elasticity.
☐ The elasticity is higher at E than at B.

EINSTEIN

The elasticity of demand and the marginal revenue

The diagram shows how to obtain a general formula for the elasticity at a point (Q, P) on the demand curve.

It also shows how the elasticity is related to the slope of the demand curve. A flatter demand curve has a lower slope, indicating higher elasticity.

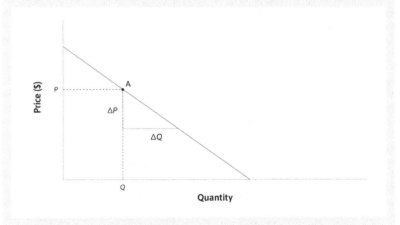

Figure 7.18 The elasticity of demand and the marginal revenue.

At point A, the price is P and the quantity is Q. If the quantity increases by ΔQ, the price falls: it changes by ΔP, which is negative.

$$\text{% change in } P = 100 \times \Delta P/P$$
$$\text{% change in } Q = 100 \times \Delta Q/Q$$
$$\text{Elasticity at A} = -\frac{\text{% change in } Q}{\text{% change in } P}$$
$$= -\frac{\Delta Q/Q}{\Delta P/P}$$
$$= -\frac{P}{Q} \times \frac{\Delta Q}{\Delta P}$$
$$\text{slope of demand curve} = \frac{\Delta P}{\Delta Q}$$
$$\text{Elasticity} = -\frac{P}{Q} \times \frac{1}{slope}$$

Suppose that the demand curve is elastic at A. Then the elasticity is greater than one:

$$-\frac{P\Delta Q}{Q\Delta P} > 1$$

Multiplying by $-Q\Delta P$ (which is positive):

$$P\Delta Q > -Q\Delta P$$

and rearranging, we get:

$$P\Delta Q + Q\Delta P > 0$$

Consider the special case when $\Delta Q = 1$. The inequality becomes:

$$P + Q\Delta P > 0$$

Now remember that the marginal revenue at point A is the change in revenue when Q increases by one unit. This change consists of the gain in revenue on the extra unit, which is P, and the loss on the other units, which is $Q\Delta P$. So this inequality tells us that the marginal revenue is positive.

We have shown that if the demand curve is elastic, MR > 0. Similarly, if the demand curve is inelastic, MR < 0.

The size of the markup chosen by the firm

We can find a formula that shows that the markup is high when the elasticity of demand is low.

We know that the firm chooses a point where the slope of the iso-profit curve is equal to the slope of the demand curve, and that the slope of the demand curve is related to the price elasticity of demand:

$$\varepsilon = -\frac{P}{Q} \times \frac{1}{\text{slope}}$$

Rearranging this formula:

$$\text{slope of demand curve} = -\frac{P}{Q} \times \frac{1}{\text{elasticity}}$$

We also know from Section 7.4:

$$\text{slope of isoprofit curve} = -\frac{(P - MC)}{Q}$$

When the two slopes are equal:

$$\frac{(P - MC)}{Q} = \frac{P}{Q} \times \frac{1}{\text{elasticity}}$$

Rearranging this gives us:

$$\frac{(P - MC)}{P} = \frac{1}{\text{elasticity}}$$

The left-hand side is the profit margin as a proportion of the price, which is called the markup. Therefore:

The firm's markup is inversely proportional to the elasticity of demand.

7.9 USING DEMAND ELASTICITIES IN GOVERNMENT POLICY

Measuring elasticities of demand is useful to policymakers. If the government puts a tax on a particular good, the tax will raise the price paid by consumers, so the effect of the tax will depend on the elasticity of demand:

- *If demand is highly elastic*: A tax will cause a large reduction in sales. That may be intentional, as when governments tax tobacco to discourage smoking because it is harmful to health.
- *If a tax causes a large fall in sales*: It also reduces potential tax revenue.

So a government wishing to raise tax revenue should choose to tax products with inelastic demand.

Several countries, including Mexico and France, have introduced taxes intended to reduce the consumption of unhealthy food and drink. A 2014 international study found worrying increases in adult and childhood obesity since 1980. In 2013, 37% of men and 38% of women worldwide were overweight or obese. In North America, the figures were 70% and 61%, but the obesity epidemic does not only affect the richest countries: the corresponding rates were 59% and 66% in the Middle East and North Africa.

Matthew Harding and Michael Lovenheim used detailed data on the food purchases of US consumers to estimate elasticities of demand for different types of food, to investigate the effects of food taxes. They divided food products into 33 categories and used a model of consumer decision making to examine how changes in their prices would change the share of each category in consumers' expenditure on food, and hence the nutritional composition of the diet, taking into account that the change in the price of any product would change the demand for that product and other products too. Figure 7.19 shows the prices and elasticities for some of the categories.

You can see that the demand for lower-calorie milk products (category 31) is the most price-responsive. If their price increased by 10%, the quantity purchased would fall by 19.72%. Demand for snacks and candy is quite inelastic, which suggests that it may be difficult to deter consumers from buying them.

EXERCISE 7.6 ELASTICITY AND EXPENDITURE

Figure 7.19 (page 304) shows the spending per week in each category of a US consumer whose total expenditure on food is $80, with typical spending patterns across food categories. Suppose that the price of category 30, high-calorie milk products, increased by 10%:

1. By what percentage would his demand for high-calorie milk products fall?
2. Calculate the quantity he consumes, in grams, before and after the price change.
3. Calculate his total expenditure on high-calorie milk products before and after the price change. You should find that expenditure falls.
4. Now choose a category for which the price elasticity is less than 1, and repeat the calculations. In this case you should find that expenditure rises.

Matthew Harding and Michael Lovenheim. 2013. 'The Effect of Prices on Nutrition: Comparing the Impact of Product- and Nutrient-Specific Taxes' (http://tinyco.re/9374751). SIEPR Discussion Paper No. 13-023.

For additional insight, this blog illustrates one reaction to Matthew Harding and Michael Lovenheim's research: *The Huffington Post*. 2014. 'There's An Easy Way To Fight Obesity, But Conservatives Will HATE It' (http://tinyco.re/0950519).

Harding and Lovenheim examined the effects of 20% taxes on sugar, fat and salt. A 20% sugar tax, for example, would increase the price of a product that contains 50% sugar by 10%. A sugar tax was found to have the most positive effect on nutrition. It would reduce sugar consumption by 16%, fat by 12%, salt by 10%, and calorie intake by 19%.

EXERCISE 7.7 FOOD TAXES AND HEALTH

Food taxes intended to shift consumption towards a healthier diet are controversial. Some people think that individuals should make their own choices, and if they prefer unhealthy products, the government should not interfere. In view of the fact that those who become ill will be cared for at some public expense, others argue that the government has a role in keeping people healthy.

In your own words, provide arguments for or against food taxes designed to encourage healthy eating.

Matthew Harding and Michael Lovenheim. 2013. 'The Effect of Prices on Nutrition: Comparing the Impact of Product- and Nutrient-Specific Taxes'. SIEPR Discussion Paper No. 13-023.

Category	Type	Calories per serving	Price per 100 g ($)	Typical spending per week ($)	Price elasticity of demand
1	Fruit and vegetables	660	0.38	2.00	1.128
2	Fruit and vegetables	140	0.36	3.44	0.830
15	Grain, pasta, bread	1,540	0.38	2.96	0.854
17	Grain, pasta, bread	960	0.53	2.64	0.292
28	Snacks, candy	433	1.13	4.88	0.270
29	Snacks, candy	1,727	0.68	7.60	0.295
30	Milk	2,052	0.09	2.32	0.1793
31	Milk	874	0.15	1.44	1.972

Figure 7.19 Price elasticities of demand for different types of food. See the Calories per serving to compare high and low calorie groups of each food type.

7.10 PRICE-SETTING, COMPETITION, AND MARKET POWER

Our analysis of the firm's pricing decisions applies to any firm producing and selling a product that is in some way different from that of any other firm. In the nineteenth century the French economist Augustin Cournot carried out a similar analysis using the example of bottled water from 'a mineral spring which has just been found to possess salutary properties possessed by no other'. Cournot referred to this as a case of **monopoly**—in a monopolized market there is only one seller. He showed, as we have done, that the firm would set a price greater than the marginal production cost.

> **monopoly** A firm that is the only seller of a product without close substitutes. Also refers to a market with only one seller. *See also: monopoly power, natural monopoly.*

Augustin Cournot and Irving Fischer. 1971. *Researches into the Mathematical Principles of the Theory of Wealth*. New York, NY: A. M. Kelley.

GREAT ECONOMISTS

Augustin Cournot

Augustin Cournot (1801–1877) was a French economist, now most famous for his model of oligopoly (a market with a small number of firms). Cournot's 1838 book *Recherches sur les Principes Mathématiques de la Théorie des Richesses* (Research on the Mathematical Principles of the Theory of Wealth) introduced a new mathematical approach to economics, although he feared it would 'draw on me … the condemnation of theorists of repute'. Cournot's work influenced other nineteenth century economists such as Marshall and Walras, and established the basic principles we still use to think about the behaviour of firms. Although he used algebra rather than diagrams, Cournot's analysis of demand and profit maximization is very similar to ours.

We saw in Section 7.6 that when the producer of a differentiated good sets a price above the marginal cost of production, the market outcome is not Pareto efficient. When trade in a market results in a Pareto-inefficient allocation, we describe this as a case of market failure.

The **deadweight loss** gives us a measure of the consequences of market failure: the size of the unexploited gains from trade. And we saw in Section 7.7 that the deadweight loss resulting from setting a price above marginal cost is high when the elasticity of demand is low.

So what determines the elasticity demand for a product, and why do some firms face more elastic demand than others? To answer this question, we need to think again about how consumers behave.

Markets with differentiated products reflect differences in the preferences of consumers. People who want to buy a car are looking for different combinations of characteristics. A consumer's willingness to pay for a particular model will depend not only on its characteristics, but also on the characteristics and prices of similar types of car sold by other firms.

> **MARKET FAILURE**
> Market failure occurs when markets allocate resources in a Pareto-inefficient way.

For example, Figure 7.20 shows the purchase prices of a three-door 1.0 litre hatchback in the UK in January 2014, which a consumer could find on a price comparison website.

Although the four cars are similar in their main characteristics, the website compares them on 75 other features, many of which differ between them.

When consumers can choose between several quite similar cars, the demand for each of these cars is likely to be quite elastic. If the price of the Ford Fiesta, for example, were to rise, demand would fall because people would choose to buy one of the other brands instead. Conversely, if the price of the Fiesta were to fall, demand would increase because consumers would be attracted away from the other cars. The more similar the other cars are to a Fiesta, the more responsive consumers will be to price differences. Only those with the highest brand loyalty to Ford, and those with a strong preference for a characteristic of the Ford that other cars do not possess, would fail to respond. Then the firm will have a relatively low price and profit margin.

In contrast, the manufacturer of a very specialized type of car, quite different from any other brand in the market, faces little competition and hence less elastic demand. It can set a price well above marginal cost without losing customers. Such a firm is earning **monopoly rents** (economic profits over and above its production costs) arising from its position as the only supplier of this type of car (likewise, an innovative firm earns rents while it is the only firm using a new technology: see Unit 2).

So a firm will be in a strong position if there are few firms producing close **substitutes** for its own brand, because it faces little competition. Then its elasticity of demand will be relatively low. We say that such a firm has **market power**. It will have sufficient bargaining power in its relationship with customers to set a high price without losing them to competitors.

Competition policy

This discussion helps to explain why policymakers may be concerned about firms that have few competitors. Market power allows them to set high prices, and make high profits, at the expense of consumers. Potential consumer surplus is lost both because few consumers buy, and because those who buy pay a high price. The owners of the firm benefit, but overall there is a deadweight loss.

A firm selling a niche product catering for the preferences of a small number of consumers (such as a Beautiful Car or a luxury brand like a Lamborghini) is unlikely to attract the attention of policymakers, despite the loss of consumer surplus. But if one firm is becoming dominant in a large market, governments may intervene to promote competition. In 2000

monopoly rents A form of economic profits, which arise due to restricted competition in selling a firm's product. *See also: economic profits.*

substitutes Two goods for which an increase in the price of one leads to an increase in the quantity demanded of the other. *See also: complements.*

market power An attribute of a firm that can sell its product at a range of feasible prices, so that it can benefit by acting as a price-setter (rather than a price-taker).

	Price
Ford Fiesta	£11,917
Vauxhall Corsa	£11,283
Peugeot 208	£10,384
Toyota IQ	£11,254

Figure 7.20 Car purchase prices in the UK (January 2014, Autotrader.com).

the European Commission prevented the proposed merger of Volvo and Scania, on the grounds that the merged firm would have a dominant position in the heavy trucks market in Ireland and the Nordic countries. In Sweden the combined market share of the two firms was 90%. The merged firm would have been almost a monopoly—the extreme case of a firm that has no competitors at all.

A particular concern is that when there are only a few firms in a market they may form a **cartel**: a group of firms that collude to keep the price high. By working together and behaving as a monopoly, rather than competing, they can increase profits. A well-known example is OPEC, an association of oil-producing countries. OPEC members jointly agree to set production levels to control the global price of oil. The OPEC cartel played a major role in sustaining high oil prices at a global level following the sharp increase in oil prices in 1973 and again in 1979. We return to study the causes of fluctuations in oil prices in Unit 11 and the effect of the oil price shocks on inflation and unemployment in Unit 15.

While cartels between private firms are illegal in many countries, firms often find ways to cooperate in the setting of prices so as to maximize profits. Policy to limit market power and prevent cartels is known as **competition policy**, or **antitrust policy** in the US.

Dominant firms may exploit their position by strategies other than high prices. In a famous antitrust case, the US Department of Justice accused Microsoft of behaving anti-competitively by 'bundling' its own Internet Explorer web-browser with its Windows operating system. In the 1920s, an international group of companies making electric light bulbs, including Philips, Osram, and General Electric, formed a cartel that agreed a policy of 'planned obsolescence' to reduce the lifetime of their bulbs to 1,000 hours, so that consumers would have to replace them more quickly. Despite its promise of 'always low prices', some people accuse Walmart of using its power unfairly, to reduce wages in the area around its stores, drive smaller retailers out of the market, or reduce the profits of its wholesale suppliers to unsustainable levels. A paper by John Vickers examines the economic basis for these claims.

> **cartel** A group of firms that collude in order to increase their joint profits.

> **competition policy** Government policy and laws to limit monopoly power and prevent cartels. *Also known as: antitrust policy.*

Richard J. Gilbert and Michael L. Katz. 2001. 'An Economist's Guide to US v. Microsoft' (http://tinyco.re/7683758). *Journal of Economic Perspectives* 15 (2): pp. 25–44.

Markus Krajewski. 2014. 'The Great Lightbulb Conspiracy' (http://tinyco.re/3479245). *IEEE Spectrum.* Updated 25 September.

Emek Basker. 2007. 'The Causes and Consequences of Wal-Mart's Growth' (http://tinyco.re/6525636). *Journal of Economic Perspectives* 21 (3): pp. 177–198.

John Vickers. 1996. 'Market Power and Inefficiency: A Contracts Perspective'. *Oxford Review of Economic Policy* 12 (4): pp. 11–26.

EXERCISE 7.8 MULTINATIONALS OR INDEPENDENT RETAILERS?
Imagine that you are a politician in a town where a multinational retailer is planning to build a new superstore. A local campaign is protesting that it will drive small independent retailers out of business, and thereby reduce consumer choice and change the character of the area. Supporters of the plan argue in turn that this will only happen if consumers prefer the supermarket.

Which side are you on?

QUESTION 7.16 CHOOSE THE CORRECT ANSWER(S)

Suppose that in a small town a multinational retailer is planning to build a new superstore. Which of the following arguments could be correct?

☐ The local protestors argue that the close substitutability of some of the goods sold between the new retailer and existing ones means that the new retailer faces inelastic demand for those goods, giving it excessive market power.

☐ The new retailer argues that the close substitutability of some of the goods implies a high elasticity of demand, leading to healthy competition and lower prices for consumers.

☐ The local protestors argue that once the local retailers are driven out, there will be no competition, giving the multinational retailer more market power and driving up prices.

☐ The new retailer argues that most of the goods sold by local retailers are sufficiently differentiated from its own goods that their elasticity of demand will be high enough to protect the local retailers' profits.

7.11 PRODUCT SELECTION, INNOVATION, AND ADVERTISING

The profits that a firm can achieve depend on the demand curve for its product, which in turn depends on the preferences of consumers and competition from other firms. But the firm may be able to move the demand curve to increase profits by changing its selection of products, or through advertising.

When deciding what goods to produce, the firm would ideally like to find a product that is both attractive to consumers and has different characteristics from the products sold by other firms. In this case demand would be high (many consumers would wish to buy it at each price) and the elasticity low. Of course, this is not likely to be easy. A firm wishing to make a new breakfast cereal, or type of car, knows that there are already many brands on the market. But technological innovation may provide opportunities to get ahead of competitors. After Toyota developed the first mass-produced hybrid car, the Prius, in 1997, there were for some years very few comparable cars available. Toyota effectively monopolized the hybrid market. By 2013 there were several competing brands, but the Prius remained the market leader, with more than 50% of hybrid sales.

If a firm has invented or created a new product, it may be able to prevent competition altogether by claiming exclusive rights to produce it, using patent or copyright laws. Ironically, in the 1970s a company called Parker Brothers spent years fighting in court to protect a monopoly that they had on a profitable board game called Monopoly. This kind of legal protection of monopoly may help to provide incentives for research and development of new products, but at the same time limits the gains from trade. In Unit 21, we analyse intellectual property rights in more detail.

Advertising is another strategy that firms can use to influence demand. It is widely used by both car manufacturers and breakfast cereal producers. When products are differentiated, the firm can use advertising to inform

John Kay. 'The Structure of Strategy' (reprinted from *Business Strategy Review* 1993) (http://tinyco.re/7663497).

Parker Brothers first marketed a property-trading board game under the name Monopoly in 1935. In a series of court cases in the 1970s, Parker Brothers attempted to prevent Ralph Anspach, an economics professor, from selling a game called Anti-Monopoly. Anspach claimed that Parker Brothers did not have exclusive rights to sell Monopoly, since the company had not originally invented it.

After the court ruled in favour of Anspach, many competing versions of Monopoly appeared on the market.

After a change in the law, Parker Brothers established the right to the Monopoly trademark in 1984, so Monopoly is now a monopoly again.

consumers about the existence and characteristics of its product, attract them away from its competitors, and create brand loyalty.

According to Schonfeld and Associates, a firm of market analysts, advertising on breakfast cereals in the US is about 5.5% of total sales revenue—about 3.5 times higher than the average for manufactured products. The data in Figure 7.21 is for the highest-selling 35 breakfast cereal brands sold in the Chicago area in 1991 and 1992. The graph shows the relationship between market share and quarterly expenditure on advertising. If you investigated the breakfast cereals market more closely, you would see that market share is not closely related to price. But it is clear from Figure 7.21 that the brands with the highest share are also the ones that spend the most on advertising. Matthew Shum, an economist, analysed cereal purchases in Chicago using this dataset, and showed that advertising was more effective than price discounts in stimulating demand for a brand. Since the most well-known brands were also the ones spending most on advertising, he concluded that its main function was not to inform consumers about the product, but rather to increase brand loyalty, and encourage consumers of other cereals to switch.

Matthew Shum. 2004. 'Does Advertising Overcome Brand Loyalty? Evidence from the Breakfast-Cereals Market' (http://tinyco.re/3909324). *Journal of Economics & Management Strategy* 13 (2): pp. 241–72.

7.12 PRICES, COSTS, AND MARKET FAILURE

Market failure occurs when the market allocation of a good is Pareto inefficient, and we have seen in this unit that one cause of market failure (we will see others in later units) is firms setting prices above the marginal cost of producing their goods.

Firms set prices above marginal costs when the goods they produce, like cars or breakfast cereals, are differentiated from those produced by other firms, so that they serve consumers with different preferences and face limited competition (or no competition, in the case of a monopolist producing a unique good). Firms can benefit from strategies that reduce competition, but without competition the deadweight loss may be high, so policymakers try to reduce the loss through competition policy.

Product differentiation is not the only reason for a price above marginal cost. A second important reason is decreasing average costs, perhaps due to economies of scale in production, fixed costs, or input prices declining as

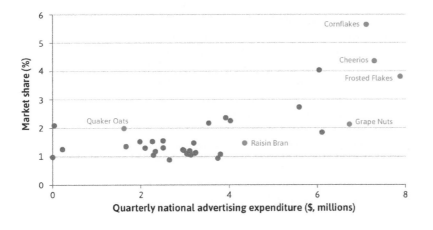

Figure 1 in Matthew Shum. 2004. 'Does Advertising Overcome Brand Loyalty? Evidence from the Breakfast-Cereals Market' (http://tinyco.re/3909324). *Journal of Economics & Management Strategy* 13 (2): pp. 241–72.

Figure 7.21 Advertising expenditure and market share of breakfast cereals in Chicago (1991–92).

the firm purchases larger quantities. In such cases, the average cost of production is greater than the marginal cost of each unit, and the average cost curve slopes downward. The firm's price must be at least equal to average cost—otherwise it makes a loss. And that means the price must be above the marginal cost.

Of course, decreasing average costs mean that firms can produce at lower cost per unit when operating at a large scale. In domestic utilities such as water, electricity and gas, there are high fixed costs of providing the supply network, irrespective of the quantity demanded by consumers. Utilities typically have increasing returns to scale. The average cost of producing a unit of water, electricity or gas will be very high unless the firm operates at a large scale. If a single firm can supply the whole market at lower average cost than two firms, the industry is said to be a **natural monopoly**.

natural monopoly A production process in which the long-run average cost curve is sufficiently downward-sloping to make it impossible to sustain competition among firms in this market.

In the case of a natural monopoly, policymakers may not be able to induce firms to lower their prices by promoting competition, since average costs would rise with more firms in the market. They may choose instead to regulate the firm's activities, limiting its discretion over prices in order to increase consumer surplus. An alternative is public ownership. The majority of water supply companies around the world are owned by the public sector, although in England and Wales in 1989, and in Chile in the 1990s, the entire water industry was privatized and is regulated by a public sector agency.

A different kind of example is a film production company. The company spends heavily on hiring actors, camera technicians, a director, purchasing rights to the script, and advertising the film. These are fixed costs (sometimes called first copy costs). The cost of making available additional copies of the film (the marginal cost) is typically low: the first copy is cheap to reproduce. This firm's marginal costs will be below its average costs (including the normal rate of profit). If it were to set a price equal to marginal cost it would go out of business.

The price of a differentiated product is above the marginal cost as a direct result of the firm's response to the absence of competing firms and price-insensitivity of consumers. The source of the problem in the cases of utilities and films is the cost structure, rather than lack of competition per se. Electricity is usually not a differentiated product, so buyers of electricity may be strongly price-sensitive, and the film industry is highly competitive. But price must be greater than marginal cost for firms to survive.

However, the two problems—limited competition and decreasing average costs—are often closely related because competition among firms with downward-sloping average cost curves tends to be winner-takes-all. The first firm to exploit the cost advantages of large size eliminates other firms and, as a result, eliminates competition too.

Whatever the underlying reason, a price above marginal cost results in market failure. Too little is purchased: there are some potential buyers whose willingness to pay exceeds the marginal cost but falls short of the market price—so they won't buy the good and there is a deadweight loss.

7.13 CONCLUSION

We have studied how firms producing differentiated goods choose the price and the quantity of output to maximize their profit. These decisions depend on the demand curve for the product—especially the elasticity of demand—and the cost structure for producing it. They will choose a price above the marginal cost of production—even more so when competition is limited and the elasticity of demand low.

Increasing returns in production and other cost advantages favour firms operating at large scale, where the unit cost is low. Innovation can also reduce costs and raise profits.

When the market price is above the marginal production cost, there is market failure: the allocation of the good is Pareto inefficient. Firms make economic profits, but consumer surplus is lower than it would be if the price was equal to the marginal cost, and there is a deadweight loss. So policymakers may be concerned when firms achieve a dominant position in a market. They can use competition policy and regulation to limit the exercise of market power.

Concepts introduced in Unit 7

Before you move on, review these definitions:

- Differentiated product
- Economies of scale
- Cost function
- Willingness to pay
- Demand curve
- Price-setting
- Consumer surplus
- Producer surplus
- Deadweight loss
- Market failure
- Elasticity of demand
- Profit margin

7.14 REFERENCES

Basker, Emek. 2007. 'The Causes and Consequences of Wal-Mart's Growth' (http://tinyco.re/6525636). *Journal of Economic Perspectives* 21 (3): pp. 177–198.

Cournot, Augustin, and Irving Fischer. 1971. *Researches into the Mathematical Principles of the Theory of Wealth*. New York, NY: A. M. Kelley.

Gilbert, Richard J., and Michael L. Katz. 2001. 'An Economist's Guide to US v. Microsoft' (http://tinyco.re/7683758). *Journal of Economic Perspectives* 15 (2): pp. 25–44.

Harding, Matthew, and Michael Lovenheim. 2013. 'The Effect of Prices on Nutrition: Comparing the Impact of Product- and Nutrient-Specific Taxes' (http://tinyco.re/9374751). SIEPR Discussion Paper No. 13-023.

Kay, John. 'The Structure of Strategy' (reprinted from *Business Strategy Review* 1993) (http://tinyco.re/7663497).

Koshal, Rajindar K., and Manjulika Koshal. 1999. 'Economies of Scale and Scope in Higher Education: A Case of Comprehensive Universities' (http://tinyco.re/8137580). *Economics of Education Review* 18 (2): pp. 269–277.

Krajewski, Markus. 2014. 'The Great Lightbulb Conspiracy' (http://tinyco.re/3479245). *IEEE Spectrum*. Updated 24 September 2014.

Schumacher, Ernst F. 1973. *Small Is Beautiful: Economics as If People Mattered* (http://tinyco.re/3749799). New York, NY: HarperCollins.

Shum, Matthew. 2004. 'Does Advertising Overcome Brand Loyalty? Evidence from the Breakfast-Cereals Market'. (http://tinyco.re/3909324). *Journal of Economics & Management Strategy* 13 (2): pp. 241–272.

Statista. 2011. 'Willingness to pay for a flight in space' (http://tinyco.re/7817145). Updated 20 October 2011.

Stigler, George J. 1987. *The Theory of Price*. New York, NY: Collier Macmillan.

The Economist. 2008. 'Economies of Scale and Scope' (http://tinyco.re/7593630). Updated 20 October 2008.

Vickers, John. 1996. 'Market Power and Inefficiency: A Contracts Perspective'. *Oxford Review of Economic Policy* 12 (4): pp. 11–26.

HOW MARKETS OPERATE WHEN ALL BUYERS AND SELLERS ARE PRICE-TAKERS

- Competition can constrain buyers and sellers to be price-takers.
- The interaction of supply and demand determines a market equilibrium in which both buyers and sellers are price-takers, called a competitive equilibrium.
- Prices and quantities in competitive equilibrium change in response to supply and demand shocks.
- Price-taking behaviour ensures that all gains from trade in the market are exhausted at a competitive equilibrium.
- The model of perfect competition describes idealized conditions under which all buyers and sellers are price-takers.
- Real-world markets are typically not perfectly competitive, but some policy problems can be analysed using this demand and supply model.
- There are important similarities and differences between price-taking and price-setting firms.

THEMES AND CAPSTONE UNITS

- 17: History, instability, and growth
- 18: Global economy
- 22: Politics and policy

Students of American history learn that the defeat of the southern Confederate states in the American Civil War ended slavery in the production of cotton and other crops in that region. There is also an economics lesson in this story.

At the war's outbreak on 12 April 1861, President Abraham Lincoln ordered the US Navy to blockade the ports of the Confederate states. These states had declared themselves independent of the US to preserve the institution of slavery.

As a result of the naval blockade, the export of US-grown raw cotton to the textile mills of Lancashire in England came to a virtual halt, eliminating three-quarters of the supply of this critical raw material. Sailing at night, a few blockade-running ships evaded Lincoln's patrols, but 1,500 were destroyed or captured.

313

excess demand A situation in which the quantity of a good demanded is greater than the quantity supplied at the current price. *See also: excess supply.*

We will see in this unit that the market price of a good, such as cotton, is determined by the interaction of supply and demand. In the case of raw cotton, the tiny quantities reaching England through the blockade were a dramatic reduction in supply. There was large **excess demand**—that is to say, at the prevailing price, the quantity of raw cotton demanded exceeded the available supply. As a result, some sellers realized they could profit by raising the price. Eventually, cotton was sold at prices six times higher than before the war, keeping the lucky blockade-runners in business. Consumption of cotton fell to half the prewar level, throwing hundreds of thousands of people who worked in cotton mills out of work.

Mill owners responded. For them, the price rise was an increase in their costs. Some firms failed and left the industry due to the reduction in their profits. Mill owners looked to India to find an alternative to US cotton, greatly increasing the demand for cotton there. The excess demand in the markets for Indian cotton gave some sellers an opportunity to profit by raising prices, resulting in increases in the prices of Indian cotton, which quickly rose almost to match the price of US cotton.

Responding to the higher income now obtainable from growing cotton, Indian farmers abandoned other crops and grew cotton instead. The same occurred wherever cotton could be grown, including Brazil. In Egypt, farmers who rushed to expand the production of cotton in response to the higher prices began employing slaves, captured (like the American slaves that Lincoln was fighting to free) in sub-Saharan Africa.

There was a problem. The only source of cotton that could come close to making up the shortfall from the US was in India. But Indian cotton differed from American cotton, and required an entirely different kind of processing. Within months of the shift to Indian cotton, new machinery was developed to process it.

As the demand for this new equipment soared, firms like Dobson and Barlow, who made textile machinery, saw profits take-off. We know about this firm, because detailed sales records have survived. It responded by increasing production of these new machines and other equipment. No mill could afford to be left behind in the rush to retool, because if it didn't, it could not use the new raw materials. The result was, in the words of Douglas Farnie, a historian who specialized in the history of cotton production, 'such an extensive investment of capital that it amounted almost to the creation of a new industry.'

The lesson for economists: Lincoln ordered the blockade, but in what followed, the farmers and sellers who increased the price of cotton were not responding to orders. Neither were the mill owners who cut back the output of textiles and laid off the mill workers, nor were the mill owners desperately searching for new sources of raw material. By ordering new machinery, the mill owners set off a boom in investment and new jobs.

All of these decisions took place over a matter of months, by millions of people, most of whom were total strangers to one another, each seeking to make the best of a totally new economic situation. American cotton was now scarcer, and people responded, from the cotton fields of Maharashtra in India to the Nile delta, to Brazil, and the Lancashire mills.

To understand how the change in the price of cotton transformed the world cotton and textile production system, think about the prices determined by markets as messages. The increase in the price of US cotton shouted: 'find other sources, and find new technologies appropriate for their use.' Similarly, when the price of petrol rises, the message to the car driver is: 'take the train', which is passed on to the railway operator: 'there are profits to be made by running more train services'. When the price of electricity goes up, the firm or the family is being told: 'think about installing photovoltaic cells on the roof.'

In many cases—like the chain of events that began at Lincoln's desk on 12 April 1861—the messages make sense not only for individual firms and families but also for society: if something has become more expensive then it is likely that more people are demanding it, or the cost of producing it has risen, or both. By finding an alternative, the individual is saving money and conserving society's resources. This is because, in some conditions, prices provide an accurate measure of the scarcity of a good or service.

In planned economies, which operated in the Soviet Union and other central and eastern European countries before the 1990s (discussed in Unit 1), messages about how things would be produced are sent deliberately by government experts. They decide what will be produced and at what price it will be sold. The same is true, as we saw in Unit 6, inside large firms like General Motors, where managers (and not prices) determine who does what.

The amazing thing about prices determined by markets is that individuals do not send the messages, but rather the anonymous interaction of sometimes millions of people. And when conditions change—a cheaper way of producing bread, for example—nobody has to change the message ('put bread instead of potatoes on the table tonight'). A price change results from a change in firms' costs. The reduced price of bread says it all.

This is explained in more detail in 'Who's in Charge?' (http://tinyco.re/9867111), Chapter 1 of Paul Seabright's book on how market economies manage to organize complex trades among strangers (follow the link to access Chapter 1 as a pdf). Paul Seabright. 2010. *The Company of Strangers: A Natural History of Economic Life* (Revised Edition). Princeton, NJ: Princeton University Press.

8.1 BUYING AND SELLING: DEMAND AND SUPPLY

In Unit 7 we considered the case of a good produced and sold by just one firm. There was one seller with many buyers in the market for that product. In this unit, we look at markets where many buyers and sellers interact, and show how the competitive market price is determined by both the preferences of consumers and the costs of suppliers. When there are many firms producing the same product, each firm's decisions are affected by the behaviour of competing firms, as well as consumers.

For a simple model of a market with many buyers and sellers, think about the potential for trade in second-hand copies of a recommended textbook for a university economics course. Demand for the book comes from students who are about to begin the course, and they will differ in their **willingness to pay (WTP)**. No one will pay more than the price of a new copy in the campus bookshop. Below that, students' WTP may depend on how hard they work, how important they think the book is, and on their available resources for buying books.

Figure 8.1 shows the demand curve. As in Unit 7, we line up all the consumers in order of willingness to pay, highest first. The first student is willing to pay $20, the 20th $10, and so on. For any price, *P*, the graph tells you how many students would be willing to buy: it is the number whose WTP is at or above *P*.

The demand curve represents the WTP of buyers; similarly, supply depends on the sellers' **willingness to accept (WTA)** money in return for books.

willingness to pay (WTP) An indicator of how much a person values a good, measured by the maximum amount he or she would pay to acquire a unit of the good. *See also: willingness to accept.*

Often when you buy something you don't need to think about your exact willingness to pay. You just decide whether to pay the asking price. But WTP is a useful concept for buyers in online auctions, such as eBay.

If you want to bid for an item, one way to do it is to set a maximum bid equal to your WTP, which will be kept secret from other bidders: this article explains how to do it on eBay (http://tinyco.re/0107311). eBay will place bids automatically on your behalf until you are the highest bidder, or until your maximum is reached. You will win the auction if, and only if, the highest bid is less than or equal to your WTP.

willingness to accept (WTA) The reservation price of a potential seller, who will be willing to sell a unit only for a price at least this high. *See also: willingness to pay.*

reservation price The lowest price at which someone is willing to sell a good (keeping the good is the potential seller's reservation option). *See also: reservation option.*

If you sell an item on eBay you can set a reserve price, which will not be disclosed to the bidders. This article explains eBay reserve prices (http://tinyco.re/9324100). You are telling eBay that the item should not be sold unless there is a bid at (or above) that price. So the reserve price should correspond to your WTA. If no one bids your WTA, the item will not be sold.

supply curve The curve that shows the number of units of output that would be produced at any given price. For a market, it shows the total quantity that all firms together would produce at any given price.

The supply of second-hand books comes from students who have previously completed the course, who will differ in the amount they are willing to accept—that is, their **reservation price**. Recall from Unit 5 that Angela was willing to enter into a contract with Bruno only if it gave her at least as much utility as her reservation option (no work and survival rations); here the reservation price of a potential seller represents the value to her of keeping the book, and she will only be willing to sell for a price at least that high. Poorer students (who are keen to sell so that they can afford other books) and those no longer studying economics may have lower reservation prices. Again, online auctions like eBay allow sellers to specify their WTA.

We can draw a **supply curve** by lining up the sellers in order of their reservation prices (their WTAs): see Figure 8.2. We put the sellers who are most willing to sell—those who have the lowest reservation prices—first, so the graph of reservation prices slopes upward.

For any price, the supply curve shows the number of students willing to sell at that price—that is, the number of books that will be supplied to the market. Notice that we have drawn the supply and demand curves as straight lines for simplicity. In practice they are more likely to be curves, with the exact shape depending on how valuations of the book vary among the students.

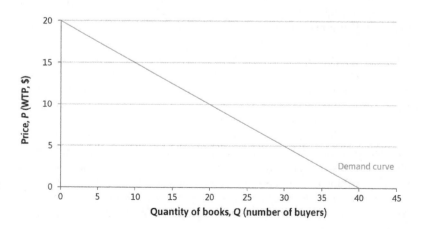

Figure 8.1 The market demand curve for books.

QUESTION 8.1 CHOOSE THE CORRECT ANSWER(S)

As a student representative, one of your roles is to organize a second-hand textbook market between the current and former first-year students. After a survey, you estimate the demand and supply curves. For example, you estimate that pricing the book at $7 would lead to a supply of 20 books and a demand of 26 books. Which of the following statements is correct?

☐ A rumour that the textbook may be required again in Year 2 would change the supply curve, shifting it upwards.
☐ Doubling the price to $14 would double the supply.
☐ A rumour that the textbook may no longer be on the reading list for the first-year students would change the demand curve, shifting it upwards.
☐ Demand would double if the price were reduced sufficiently.

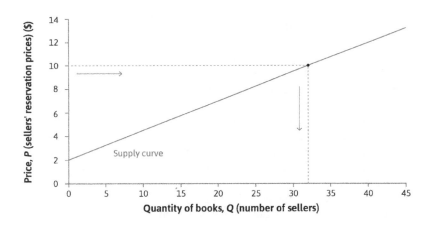

Figure 8.2 The supply curve for books.

1. Reservation price
The first seller has a reservation price of $2, and will sell at any price above that.

2. The 20th seller
The 20th seller will accept $7 …

3. The 40th seller
… and the 40th seller's reservation price is $12.

4. Supply curves slope upward
If you choose a particular price, say $10, the graph shows how many books would be supplied (Q) at that price: in this case, it is 32. The supply curve slopes upward: the higher the price, the more students will be willing to sell.

EXERCISE 8.1 SELLING STRATEGIES AND RESERVATION PRICES

Consider three possible methods to sell a car that you own:

- Advertise it in the local newspaper.
- Take it to a car auction.
- Offer it to a second-hand car dealer.

1. Would your reservation price be the same in each case? Why?
2. If you used the first method, would you advertise it at your reservation price?
3. Which method do you think would result in the highest sale price?
4. Which method would you choose?

8.2 THE MARKET AND THE EQUILIBRIUM PRICE

What would you expect to happen in the market for this textbook? That will depend on the market institutions that bring buyers and sellers together. If students have to rely on word-of-mouth, then when a buyer finds a seller they can try to negotiate a deal that suits both of them. But each buyer would like to be able to find a seller with a low reservation price, and each seller would like to find a buyer with a high willingness to pay. Before concluding a deal with one trading partner, both parties would like to know about other trading opportunities.

Traditional market institutions often brought many buyers and sellers together in one place. Many of the world's great cities grew up around marketplaces and bazaars along ancient trading routes such as the Silk Road between China and the Mediterranean. In the Grand Bazaar of Istanbul, one of the largest and oldest covered markets in the world, shops selling carpets, gold, leather, and textiles cluster together in different areas. In medieval towns and cities it was common for makers and sellers of a specific type of good to set up shops close to each other, so customers knew where to find them. The city of London is now a financial centre, but evidence of trades once carried out there can be found in surviving street names: Pudding Lane, Bread Street, Milk Street, Threadneedle Street, Ropemaker Street, Poultry Street, and Silk Street.

With modern communications, sellers can advertise their goods and buyers can more easily find out what is available, and where to buy it. But in some cases it is still convenient for many buyers and sellers to meet each other. Large cities have markets for meat, fish, vegetables or flowers, where buyers can inspect and compare the quality of the produce. In the past, markets for second-hand goods often involved specialist dealers, but nowadays sellers can contact buyers directly through online marketplaces such as eBay. Websites now help students sell textbooks to others in their university.

At the end of the nineteenth century, the economist Alfred Marshall introduced his model of supply and demand using a similar example to our case of second-hand books. Most English towns had a corn exchange (also known as a grain exchange)—a building where farmers met with merchants to sell their grain. Marshall described how the supply curve of grain would be determined by the prices that farmers would be willing to accept, and the demand curve by the willingness to pay of merchants. Then he argued that, although the price 'may be tossed hither and thither like a shuttlecock' in the 'higgling and bargaining' of the market, it would never be very far from the particular price at which the quantity demanded by merchants was equal to the quantity the farmers would supply.

Marshall called the price that equated supply and demand the *equilibrium price*. If the price was above the equilibrium, farmers would want to sell large quantities of grain. But few merchants would want to buy—there would be **excess supply**. Then, even the merchants who were willing to pay that much would realize that farmers would soon have to lower their prices and would wait until they did. Similarly, if the price was below the equilibrium, sellers would prefer to wait rather than sell at that price. If, at the going price, the amount supplied did not equal the amount demanded, Marshall reasoned that some sellers or buyers could benefit by charging some other price (in modern terminology, we would say that the going price was not a **Nash equilibrium**). So the price would tend to settle at an **equilibrium** level, where demand and supply were equated.

> **excess supply** A situation in which the quantity of a good supplied is greater than the quantity demanded at the current price. *See also: excess demand*.
>
> **Nash equilibrium** A set of strategies, one for each player in the game, such that each player's strategy is a best response to the strategies chosen by everyone else.
>
> **equilibrium (of a market)** A state of a market in which there is no tendency for the quantities bought and sold, or the market price, to change, unless there is some change in the underlying costs, preferences, or other determinants of the behaviour of market actors.

Marshall's argument was based on the assumption that all the grain was of the same quality. His supply and demand model can be applied to markets in which all sellers are selling identical goods, so buyers are equally willing to buy from any seller. If the farmers all had grain of different qualities, they would be more like the sellers of differentiated products in Unit 7.

GREAT ECONOMISTS

Alfred Marshall

Alfred Marshall (1842–1924) was a founder—with Léon Walras—of what is termed the neoclassical school of economics. His *Principles of Economics*, first published in 1890, was the standard introductory textbook for English speaking students for 50 years. An excellent mathematician, Marshall provided new foundations for the analysis of supply and demand by using calculus to formulate the workings of markets and firms,

> **marginal cost** The effect on total cost of producing one additional unit of output. It corresponds to the slope of the total cost function at each point.
>
> **marginal utility** The additional utility resulting from a one-unit increase of a given variable.

Alfred Marshall. 1920. *Principles of Economics* (http://tinyco.re/ 0560708), 8th ed. London: MacMillan & Co.

and express key concepts such as **marginal costs** and **marginal utility**. The concepts of consumer and producer surplus are also due to Marshall. His conception of economics as an attempt to 'understand the influences exerted on the quality and tone of a man's life by the manner in which he earns his livelihood …' is close to our own definition of the field.

Sadly, much of the wisdom in Marshall's text has rarely been taught by his followers. Marshall paid attention to facts. His observation that large firms could produce at lower unit costs than small firms was integral to his thinking, but it never found a place in the neoclassical school. This may be because if the average cost curve is downward-sloping even when firms are very large, there will be a kind of winner-takes-all competition in which a few large firms emerge as winners with the power to set prices, rather than taking the going price as a given. We return to this problem in Unit 12 and Unit 21.

Marshall would also have been distressed that *homo economicus* (whose existence we questioned in Unit 4) became the main actor in textbooks written by the followers of the neoclassical school. He insisted that:

> Ethical forces are among those of which the economist has to take account. Attempts have indeed been made to construct an abstract science with regard to the actions of an economic man who is under no ethical influences and who pursues pecuniary gain … selfishly. But they have not been successful. (*Principles of Economics*, 1890)

While advancing the use of mathematics in economics, he also cautioned against its misuse. In a letter to A. L. Bowley, a fellow mathematically inclined economist, he explained his own 'rules' as follows:

1. Use mathematics as a shorthand language, rather than as an engine of inquiry
2. Keep to them [that is, stick to the maths] till you have done
3. Translate into English
4. Then illustrate by examples that are important in real life
5. Burn the mathematics
6. If you can't succeed in 4, burn 3: 'This I do often.'

Marshall was Professor of Political Economy at the University of Cambridge between 1885 and 1908. In 1896 he circulated a pamphlet to the University Senate objecting to a proposal to allow women to be granted degrees. Marshall prevailed and women would wait until 1948 before being granted academic standing at Cambridge on a par with men.

But his work was motivated by a desire to improve the material conditions of working people:

> Now at last we are setting ourselves seriously to inquire whether it is necessary that there should be any so called lower classes at all: that is whether there need be large numbers of people doomed from their birth to hard work in order to provide for others the requisites of a refined and cultured life, while they themselves are prevented by their poverty and toil from having any share or part in that life. … The answer depends in a great measure upon facts and inferences, which are within the province of economics; and this is it which gives to economic studies their chief and their highest interest. (*Principles of Economics*, 1890)

Would Marshall now be satisfied with the contribution that modern economics has made to creating a more just economy?

To apply the supply and demand model to the textbook market, we assume that all the books are identical (although in practice some may be in better condition than others) and that a potential seller can advertise a book for sale by announcing its price on a local website. As at the Corn Exchange, we would expect that most trades would occur at similar prices. Buyers and sellers can easily observe all the advertised prices, so if some books were advertised at $10 and others at $5, buyers would be queuing to pay $5, and these sellers would quickly realize that they could charge more, while no one would want to pay $10 so these sellers would have to lower their price.

We can find the equilibrium price by drawing the supply and demand curves on one diagram, as in Figure 8.3. At a price $P^* = \$8$, the supply of books is equal to demand: 24 buyers are willing to pay $8, and 24 sellers are willing to sell. The equilibrium quantity is $Q^* = 24$.

The **market-clearing price** is $8—that is, supply is equal to demand at this price, so all buyers who want to buy and all sellers who want to sell can do so. The market is in equilibrium. In everyday language, something is in equilibrium if the forces acting on it are in balance, so that it remains still. Remember Fisher's hydraulic model of price determination from Unit 2: changes in the economy caused water to flow through the apparatus until it reached an equilibrium, with no further tendency for prices to change. We say that a market is in **equilibrium** if the actions of buyers and sellers have no tendency to change the price or the quantities bought and sold, unless

> **market-clearing price** At this price there is no excess supply or excess demand. *See also: equilibrium.*
> **equilibrium** A model outcome that is self-perpetuating. In this case, something of interest does not change unless an outside or external force is introduced that alters the model's description of the situation.

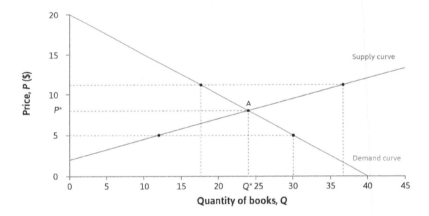

Figure 8.3 Equilibrium in the market for second-hand books.

1. Supply and demand
We find the equilibrium by drawing the supply and demand curves in the same diagram.

2. The market-clearing price
At a price $P^* = \$8$, the quantity supplied is equal to the quantity demanded: $Q^* = 24$. The market is in equilibrium. We say that the market clears at a price of $8.

3. A price above the equilibrium price
At a price greater than $8 more students would wish to sell, but not all of them would find buyers. There would be excess supply, so these sellers would want to lower their price.

4. A price below the equilibrium price
At a price less than $8, there would be more buyers than sellers—excess demand—so sellers could raise their prices. Only at $8 is there no tendency for change.

there is a change in market conditions such as the numbers of potential buyers and sellers, and how much they value the good. At the equilibrium price for textbooks, all those who wish to buy or sell are able to do so, so there is no tendency for change.

Price-taking

Will the market always be in equilibrium? As we have seen, Marshall argued that prices would not deviate far from the equilibrium level, because people would want to change their prices if there were excess supply or demand. In this unit, we study competitive market equilibria. In Unit 11 we will look at when and how prices change when the market is not in equilibrium.

In the market equilibrium that we have described for the textbook, individual students have to accept the prevailing price in the market, determined by the supply and demand curves. No one would trade with a student asking a higher price or offering a lower one, because anyone could find an alternative seller or buyer with a better price. The participants in this market are **price-takers**, because there is sufficient competition from other buyers and sellers so the best they can do is to trade at the same price. Any buyer or seller is of course free to choose a different price, but they cannot benefit by doing so.

We have seen examples where market participants do not behave as price-takers: the producer of a differentiated product can set its own price because it has no close competitors. Notice, however, that although the *sellers* of differentiated products are price-setters, the *buyers* in Unit 7 were price-takers. Since there are so many consumers wanting to buy breakfast cereals, an individual consumer has no power to negotiate a more advantageous deal, but simply has to accept the price that all other consumers are paying.

In this unit, we study market equilibria where both buyers and sellers are price-takers. We expect to see price-taking on both sides of the market where there are many sellers selling the identical goods, and many buyers wishing to purchase them. Sellers are forced to be price-takers by the presence of other sellers, as well as buyers who always choose the seller with the lowest price. If a seller tried to set a higher price, buyers would simply go elsewhere.

Similarly buyers are price-takers when there are plenty of other buyers, and sellers willing to sell to whoever will pay the highest price. On both sides of the market, competition eliminates bargaining power. We will describe the equilibrium in such a market as a **competitive equilibrium**.

A competitive market equilibrium is a Nash equilibrium, because given what all other actors are doing (trading at the equilibrium price), no actor can do better than to continue what he or she is doing (also trading at the equilibrium price).

Not all online markets for books are in competitive equilibrium. In one case when the conditions for equilibrium were not met, automatic price-setting algorithms raised the price of a book to $23 million! Michael Eisen, a biologist, noticed a classic but out-of-print text, *The Making of a Fly*, was listed for sale on Amazon by two reputable sellers, with prices starting at $1,730,045.91 (+$3.99 shipping). He watched over the next week as the prices rose rapidly, eventually peaking at $23,698,655.93, before dropping to $106.23. Eisen explains why in his blog.

Michael Eisen. 2011. 'Amazon's $23,698,655.93 book about flies' (http://tinyco.re/0044329). *It is NOT junk*. Updated 22 April 2011.

price-taker Characteristic of producers and consumers who cannot benefit by offering or asking any price other than the market price in the equilibrium of a competitive market. They have no power to influence the market price.

competitive equilibrium A market outcome in which all buyers and sellers are price-takers, and at the prevailing market price, the quantity supplied is equal to the quantity demanded.

EXERCISE 8.2 PRICE-TAKERS

Think about some of the goods you buy: perhaps different kinds of food, clothes, transport tickets, or electronic goods.

1. Are there many sellers of these goods?
2. Do you try to find the lowest price in each case?
3. If not, why not?
4. For which goods would price be your main criterion?
5. Use your answers to help you decide whether the sellers of these goods are price-takers. Are there goods for which you, as a buyer, are not a price-taker?

QUESTION 8.2 CHOOSE THE CORRECT ANSWER(S)

The diagram shows the demand and the supply curves for a textbook. The curves intersect at $(Q, P) = (24, 8)$. Which of the following is correct?

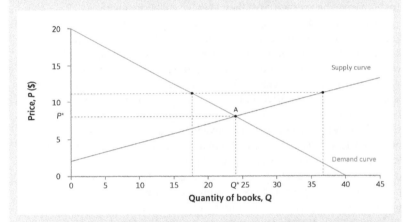

☐ At price $10, there is an excess demand for the textbook.
☐ At $8, some of the sellers have an incentive to increase their selling price to $9.
☐ At $8, the market clears.
☐ 40 books will be sold in total.

8.3 PRICE-TAKING FIRMS

In the second-hand textbook example, both buyers and sellers are individual consumers. Now we look at markets where the sellers are firms. We know from Unit 7 how firms choose their price and quantity when producing differentiated goods, and we saw that if other firms made similar products, their choice of price would be restricted (the demand curve for their own product would be almost flat) because raising the price would cause consumers to switch to other similar brands.

If there are many firms producing identical products, and consumers can easily switch from one firm to another, then firms will be price-takers in equilibrium. They will be unable to benefit from attempting to trade at a price different from the prevailing price.

To see how price-taking firms behave, consider a city where many small bakeries produce bread and sell it direct to consumers. Figure 8.4 shows what the market demand curve (the total daily demand for bread of all consumers in the city) might look like. It is downward-sloping as usual because at higher prices, fewer consumers will be willing to buy.

Suppose that you are the owner of one small bakery. You have to decide what price to charge and how many loaves to produce each morning. Suppose that neighbouring bakeries are selling loaves identical to yours at €2.35. This is the prevailing market price, and you will not be able to sell loaves at a higher price than other bakeries, because no one would buy—you are a price-taker.

Your marginal costs increase with your output of bread. When the quantity is small, the marginal cost is low, close to €1: having installed mixers, ovens and other equipment, and employed a baker, the additional cost to produce a loaf of bread is relatively small, but the average cost of a loaf is high. As the number of loaves per day increases, the average cost falls, but marginal costs begin to rise gradually because you have to employ extra staff and use equipment more intensively. At higher quantities the marginal cost is above the average cost; then average costs rise again.

The marginal and average cost curves are drawn in Figure 8.5. As in Unit 7, costs include the opportunity cost of capital. If price were equal to average cost ($P = AC$), your economic profit would be zero. You, the owner, would obtain a normal return on your capital. So the average cost curve (the leftmost curve in Figure 8.5) is the zero-economic-profit curve. The isoprofit curves show price and quantity combinations at which you would receive higher levels of profit. As we explained in Unit 7, isoprofit curves slope downwards where price is above marginal cost, and upwards where price is below marginal cost, so the marginal cost curve passes through the lowest point on each isoprofit curve. If price is above marginal cost, total profits can remain unchanged only if a larger quantity is sold for a lower price. Similarly, if price is below marginal cost, total profits can remain unchanged only if a larger quantity is sold for a higher price.

Figure 8.5 demonstrates how to make your decision. Like the firms in Unit 7, you face a constrained optimization problem. You want to find the point of maximum profit in your feasible set.

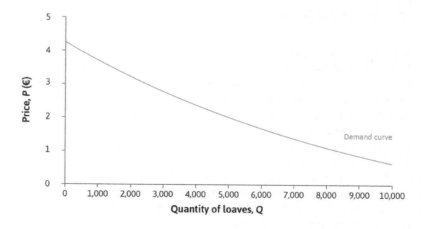

Figure 8.4 The market demand curve for bread.

Because you are a price-taker, the feasible set is all points where price is less than or equal to €2.35, the market price. Your optimal choice is $P^* = €2.35$ and $Q^* = 120$, where the isoprofit curve is tangent to the feasible set. The problem looks similar to the one for Beautiful Cars in Unit 7, except that for a price-taker, the demand curve is completely flat. For your bakery, it is not the *market* demand curve in Figure 8.4 that affects your own demand, it is the price charged by your competitors. This is why the horizontal line at P^* in Figure 8.5 is labelled as the firm's demand curve. If you charge more than P^*, your demand will be zero, but at P^* or less you can sell as many loaves as you like.

Figure 8.5 illustrates a very important characteristic of price-taking firms. They choose to produce a quantity at which the marginal cost is equal to the market price ($MC = P^*$). This is always true. For a price-taking firm, the demand curve for its own output is a horizontal line at the market price, so maximum profit is achieved at a point on the demand curve where

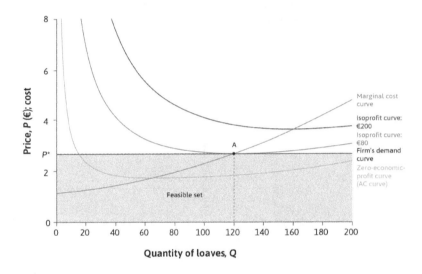

Figure 8.5 The profit-maximizing price and quantity for a bakery.

1. Marginal cost and isoprofit curves
The bakery has an increasing MC curve. On the AC curve, profit is zero. When MC > AC, the AC curve slopes upward. The other isoprofit curves represent higher levels of profit, and MC passes through the lowest points of all the isoprofit curves.

2. Price-taking
The bakery is a price-taker. The market price is $P^* = €2.35$. If you choose a higher price, customers will go to other bakeries. Your feasible set of prices and quantities is the area below the horizontal line at P^*.

3. The profit-maximizing price
The point of highest profit in the feasible set is point A, where the €80 isoprofit curve is tangent to the feasible set. You should make 120 loaves per day, and sell them at the market price, €2.35 each. You will make €80 of profit per day in addition to normal profits.

4. The profit-maximizing quantity
Your profit-maximizing quantity, $Q^* = 120$, is found at the point where $P^* = MC$: the marginal cost of the 120th loaf is equal to the market price.

the isoprofit curve is horizontal. And we know from Unit 7 that where isoprofit curves are horizontal, the price is equal to the marginal cost.

Another way to understand why a price-taking firm produces at the level of output where MC = P^* is to think about what would happen to its profits if it deviated from this point. If the firm were to increase output to a level where MC > P^*, the last unit would cost more than P^* to make, so the firm would make a loss on this unit and could make higher profits by reducing output. If it were to produce where MC < P^*, it could produce at least one more unit and sell it at a profit. Therefore it should raise output as far as the point where MC = P^*. This is where profits are maximized.

This is an important result that you should remember, but you need to be careful with it. When we make statements like 'for a price-taking firm, price equals marginal cost', we do not mean that the firm chooses a price equal to its marginal cost. Instead, we mean the opposite: the firm accepts the market price, and chooses its quantity so that the marginal cost is equal to that price.

Put yourself in the position of the bakery owner again. What would you do if the market price changed? Figure 8.6 demonstrates that as prices change you would choose different points on the marginal cost curve.

> **PRICE-TAKING FIRM**
> A price-taking firm maximizes profit by choosing a quantity where the marginal cost is equal to the market price (MC = P^*) and selling at the market price P^*.

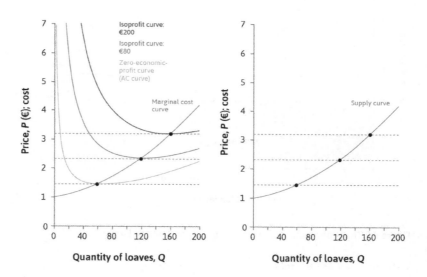

Figure 8.6 The firm's supply curve.

1. A change in price
When the market price is €2.35, you supply 120 loaves. What would you do if the price changed?

2. If the price rises
If P^* were to rise to €3.20, you could reach a higher isoprofit curve. To maximize profit you should produce 163 loaves per day.

3. If the price falls
If the price falls to €1.52 you could reach only the lightest blue curve. Your best choice would be 66 loaves, and your economic profit would be zero.

4. The marginal cost curve is the supply curve
In each case, you choose the point on your marginal cost curve where MC = market price. Your marginal cost curve is your supply curve.

For a price-taking firm, *the marginal cost curve is the supply curve*: for each price it shows the profit-maximizing quantity—that is, the quantity that the firm will choose to supply.

Notice, however, that if the price fell below €1.52 you would be making a loss. The supply curve shows how many loaves you should produce to maximize profit, but when the price is this low, the economic profit is nevertheless negative. On the supply curve, you would be minimizing your loss. If this happened, you would have to decide whether it was worth continuing to produce bread. Your decision depends on what you expect to happen in the future:

- If you expect market conditions to remain bad, it might be best to sell up and leave the market—you could obtain a better return on your capital elsewhere.
- If you expect the price to rise soon, you might be willing to incur some short-term losses, and it might be worth continuing to produce bread if the revenue helped you to cover the costs of maintaining your premises and retaining staff.

QUESTION 8.3 CHOOSE THE CORRECT ANSWER(S)

Figure 8.5 (page 325) shows a price-taking bakery's marginal and average cost curves, and its isoprofit curves. The market price for bread is $P^*=$ €2.35. Which of the following statements is correct?

☐ The firm's supply curve is horizontal.

☐ At the market price of €2.35, the firm will supply 62 loaves, at the point where the firm makes zero profit.

☐ At any market price, the firm's supply is given by the corresponding point on the average cost curve.

☐ The marginal cost curve is the firm's supply curve.

8.4 MARKET SUPPLY AND EQUILIBRIUM

The market for bread in the city has many consumers and many bakeries. Let's suppose there are 50 bakeries. Each one has a supply curve corresponding to its own marginal cost curve, so we know how much it will supply at any given market price. To find the market supply curve, we just add up the total amount that all the bakeries will supply at each price.

Figure 8.7 shows how this works if all the bakeries have the same cost functions. We work out how much one bakery would supply at a given price, then multiply by 50 to find total market supply at that price.

The market supply curve shows the total quantity that all the bakeries together would produce at any given price. It also represents the marginal cost of producing a loaf, just as the firm's supply curve does. For example, if the market price is €2.75, total market supply is 7,000. For every bakery, the marginal cost—the cost of producing one more loaf—is €2.75. And that means that the cost of producing the 7,001st loaf in the market is €2.75, whichever firm produces it. So the market supply curve is the market's marginal cost curve.

Now we know both the demand curve (Figure 8.4) and the supply curve (Figure 8.7) for the bread market as a whole. Figure 8.8 shows that the equilibrium price is exactly €2.00. At this price, the market clears: consumers demand 5,000 loaves per day, and firms supply 5,000 loaves per day.

Leibniz: Market supply curve
(http://tinyco.re/L080401)

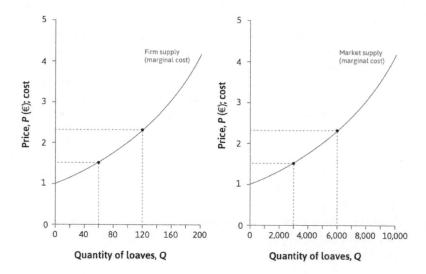

Figure 8.7 The firm and market supply curves.

1. The firm's supply curve
There are 50 bakeries, all with the same cost functions. If the market price is €2.35, each bakery will produce 120 loaves.

2. The market supply curve
When P = €2.35, each bakery supplies 50 loaves, and the market supply is 50 × 120 = 6,000 loaves.

3. Firm and market supply curves look similar
At a price of €1.52 they each supply 66 loaves, and market supply is 3,300. The market supply curve looks like the firm's supply curve, but the scale on the horizontal axis is different.

4. What if different firms had different costs?
If the bakeries had different cost functions, then at a price of €2.35 some bakeries would produce more loaves than others, but we could still add them together to find market supply.

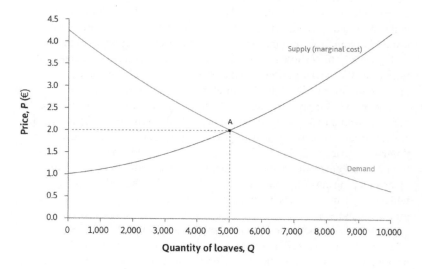

Figure 8.8 Equilibrium in the market for bread.

In the market equilibrium, each bakery is producing on its marginal cost curve, at the point where its marginal cost is €2.00. If you look back to the isoprofit curves in Figure 8.6, you will see that the firm is above its average cost curve, the isoprofit curve where economic profits are zero. So the owners of the bakeries are receiving economic rents (profit in excess of normal profit). Whenever there are economic rents, there is an opportunity for someone to benefit by taking an action. In this case, we might expect the economic rents to attract other bakeries into the market. We will see presently how this would affect the market equilibrium.

Leibniz: Market equilibrium
(http://tinyco.re/L080402)

QUESTION 8.4 CHOOSE THE CORRECT ANSWER(S)

There are two different types of producers of a good in an industry where firms are price-takers. The marginal cost curves of the two types are given below:

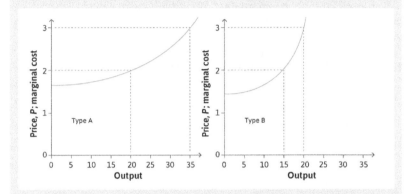

Type A is more efficient than Type B: for example, as shown, at the output of 20 units, the Type A firms have a marginal cost of $2, as opposed to a marginal cost of $3 for the Type B firms. There are 10 Type A firms and 8 Type B firms in the market. Which of the following statements is correct?

☐ At price $2, the market supply is 450 units.
☐ The market will supply 510 units at price $3.
☐ At price $2, the market's marginal cost of supplying one extra unit of the good will depend on the type of the firm that produces it.
☐ With different types of firms, we cannot determine the marginal cost curve for the market.

8.5 COMPETITIVE EQUILIBRIUM: GAINS FROM TRADE, ALLOCATION, AND DISTRIBUTION

Buyers and sellers of bread voluntarily engage in trade because both benefit. Their mutual benefits from the equilibrium allocation can be measured by the consumer and producer surpluses introduced in Unit 7. Any buyer whose willingness to pay for a good is higher than the market price receives a surplus: the difference between the WTP and the price paid. Similarly, if the marginal cost of producing a good is below the market price, the producer receives a surplus. Figure 8.9a shows how to calculate the total surplus (the gains from trade) at the competitive equilibrium in the market for bread, in the same way as we did for the markets in Unit 7.

When the market for bread is in equilibrium with the quantity of loaves supplied equal to the quantity demanded, the total surplus is the area below the demand curve and above the supply curve.

Notice how the equilibrium allocation in this market differs from the allocation of a differentiated product, Beautiful Cars, in Unit 7. The equilibrium quantity of bread is at the point where the market supply curve, which is also the marginal cost curve, crosses the demand curve, and the total surplus is the whole of the area between the two curves. Figure 7.13 showed that in the market for Beautiful Cars, the manufacturer chooses to produce

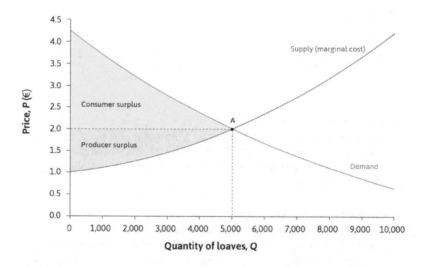

Figure 8.9a Equilibrium in the bread market: Gains from trade.

1. The consumer surplus

At the equilibrium price of €2 in the bread market, a consumer who is willing to pay €3.50 obtains a surplus of €1.50.

2. Total consumer surplus

The shaded area above €2 shows total consumer surplus—the sum of all the buyers' gains from trade.

3. The producer surplus

Remember from Unit 7 that the producer's surplus on a unit of output is the difference between the price at which it is sold, and the marginal cost of producing it. The marginal cost of the 2,000th loaf is €1.25; since it is sold for €2, the producer obtains a surplus of €0.75.

4. Total producer surplus

The shaded area below €2 is the sum of the bakeries' surpluses on every loaf that they produce. The whole shaded area shows the sum of all gains from trade in this market, known as the total surplus.

a quantity below the point where the marginal cost curve meets the demand curve, and the total surplus is lower than it would be at that point.

The competitive equilibrium allocation of bread has the property that *the total surplus is maximized*. Figure 8.9b shows that the surplus would be smaller if fewer than 5,000 loaves were produced. There would be consumers without bread who would be willing to pay more than the cost of producing another loaf, so there would be unexploited gains from trade. The total gains from trade in the market would be lower. We say there would be a **deadweight loss** equal to the triangle-shaped area. Producers would be missing out on potential profits, and some consumers would be unable to obtain the bread they were willing to pay for.

And if more than 5,000 loaves were produced, the surplus on the extra loaves would be negative: they would cost more to make than consumers were willing to pay. (Is the exchange of gifts at Christmas a similar case of deadweight loss?)

At the equilibrium, all the potential gains from trade are exploited. This property—that the combined consumer and producer surplus is maximized at the point where supply equals demand—holds in general: if both buyers and sellers are price-takers, the equilibrium allocation maximizes the sum of the gains achieved by trading in the market, relative to the original allocation. We demonstrate this result in our Einstein at the end of this section.

deadweight loss A loss of total surplus relative to a Pareto-efficient allocation.

Leibniz: Gains from trade
(http://tinyco.re/L080501)

Joel Waldfogel, an economist, gave his chosen discipline a bad name by suggesting that gift-giving at Christmas may result in a deadweight loss. If you receive a gift that is worth less to you than it cost the giver, you could argue that the surplus from the transaction is negative. Do you agree?

Joel Waldfogel. 1993. 'The Deadweight Loss of Christmas' (http://tinyco.re/0182759). *American Economic Review* 83 (5).

'Is Santa a Deadweight Loss?' (http://tinyco.re/7728778). *The Economist*. Updated 20 December 2001.

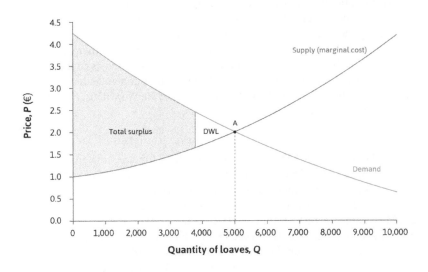

Figure 8.9b Deadweight loss.

Pareto efficient An allocation with the property that there is no alternative technically feasible allocation in which at least one person would be better off, and nobody worse off.

Pareto efficiency

At the competitive equilibrium allocation in the bread market, it is not possible to make any of the consumers or firms better off (that is, to increase the surplus of any individual) without making at least one of them worse off. Provided that what happens in this market does not affect anyone other than the participating buyers and sellers, we can say that the equilibrium allocation is **Pareto efficient**.

Pareto efficiency follows from three assumptions we have made about the bread market.

Price-taking

The participants are price-takers. They have no market power. When a particular buyer trades with a particular seller, each of them knows that the other can find an alternative trading partner willing to trade at the market price. Sellers can't raise the price because of competition from other sellers, and competition from other buyers prevents buyers from lowering it. Hence the suppliers will choose their output so that the marginal cost (the cost of the last unit produced) is equal to the market price.

In contrast, the producer of a differentiated good has bargaining power because it faces less competition: no one else produces an identical good. The firm uses its power to keep the price high, raising its own share of the surplus but lowering total surplus. The price is above marginal cost, so the allocation is Pareto inefficient.

A complete contract

The exchange of a loaf of bread for money is governed by a complete contract between buyer and seller. If you find there is no loaf of bread in the bag marked 'bread' when you get home, you can get your money back. Compare this with the incomplete employment contract in Unit 6, in which the firm can buy the worker's time, but cannot be sure how much effort the worker will put in. We will see in Unit 9 that this leads to a Pareto-inefficient allocation in the labour market.

No effects on others

We have implicitly assumed that what happens in this market affects no one except the buyers and sellers. To assess Pareto efficiency, we need to consider everyone affected by the allocation. If, for example, the early morning activities of bakeries disrupt the sleep of local residents, then there are additional costs of bread production and we ought to take the costs to the bakeries' neighbours into account too. Then, we may conclude that the equilibrium allocation is not Pareto efficient after all. We will investigate this type of problem in Unit 12.

Fairness

Remember from Unit 5 that there are two criteria for assessing an allocation: efficiency and fairness. Even if we think that the market allocation is Pareto efficient, we should not conclude that it is necessarily a desirable one. What can we say about fairness in the case of the bread market? We could examine the distribution of the gains from trade between producers and consumers: Figure 8.9a showed that both consumers and firms obtain a surplus, and in this example consumer surplus is slightly higher than producer surplus. You can see that this happens because the demand curve is relatively steep compared with the supply curve. Recall also from Unit 7 that a steep demand curve corresponds to a low elasticity of demand. Similarly, the slope of the supply curve corresponds to the elasticity of supply: in Figure 8.9a, demand is less elastic than supply.

In general, *the distribution of the total surplus between consumers and producers depends on the relative elasticities of demand and supply*.

We might also want to take into account the market participants' standard of living. For example, if a poor student buys a book from a rich student, we might think that an outcome in which the buyer paid less than the market price (closer to the seller's reservation price) would be better, because it would be fairer. Or, if the consumers in the bread market were exceptionally poor, we might decide that it would be better to pass a law setting a maximum bread price lower than €2.00 to achieve a fairer (although Pareto-inefficient) outcome. In Unit 11, we will look at the effect of regulating markets in this way.

The Pareto efficiency of a competitive equilibrium allocation is often interpreted as a powerful argument in favour of markets as a means of allocating resources. But we need to be careful not to exaggerate the value of this result:

- *The allocation may not be Pareto efficient*: We might not have taken everything into account.
- *There are other important considerations*: Fairness, for example.
- *Price-takers are hard to find in real life*: It is not as easy as you might think to find behaviour consistent with our simple model of the bread market (as we will see in Section 8.9).

Maurice Stucke. 2013. 'Is Competition Always Good?' (http://tinyco.re/8720076). *OUPblog*.

willingness to pay (WTP) An indicator of how much a person values a good, measured by the maximum amount he or she would pay to acquire a unit of the good. *See also: willingness to accept.*

willingness to accept (WTA) The reservation price of a potential seller, who will be willing to sell a unit only for a price at least this high. *See also: willingness to pay.*

EXERCISE 8.3 MAXIMIZING THE SURPLUS

Consider a market for the tickets to a football match. Six supporters of the Blue team would like to buy tickets; their valuations of a ticket (their **WTP**) are 8, 7, 6, 5, 4, and 3. The diagram below shows the demand 'curve'. Six supporters of the Red team already have tickets, for which their reservation prices (**WTA**) are 2, 3, 4, 5, 6, and 7.

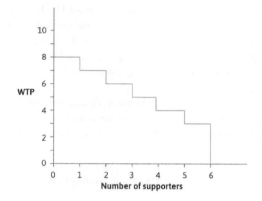

1. Draw the supply and demand 'curves' on a single diagram (Hint: the supply curve is also a step function, like the demand curve).
2. Show that four trades take place in equilibrium.
3. What is the equilibrium price?
4. Calculate the consumer (buyer) surplus by adding up the surpluses of the four buyers who trade.
5. Similarly calculate the producer (or seller) surplus.
6. Hence, find the total surplus in equilibrium.
7. Suppose that the market operates through bargaining between individual buyers and sellers. Find a way of matching the buyers and sellers so that more than four trades occur. (Hint: suppose the highest WTP buyer buys from the highest WTA seller.)
8. In this case, work out the surplus from each trade.
9. How does the total surplus in this case compare with the equilibrium surplus?
10. Starting from the allocation of tickets you obtained through bargaining, in which at least five tickets are owned by Blue supporters, is there a way through further trade to make one of the supporters better off without making anyone worse off?

EXERCISE 8.4 SURPLUS AND DEADWEIGHT LOSS

1. Sketch a diagram to illustrate the competitive market for bread, showing the equilibrium where 5,000 loaves are sold at a price of €2.00.
2. Suppose that the bakeries get together to form a cartel. They agree to raise the price to €2.70, and jointly cut production to supply the number of loaves that consumers demand at that price. Shade the areas on your diagram to show the consumer surplus, producer surplus, and deadweight loss caused by the cartel.
3. For what kinds of goods would you expect the supply curve to be highly elastic?
4. Draw diagrams to illustrate how the share of the gains from trade obtained by producers depends on the elasticity of the supply curve.

In Figure 8.9a (page 330), the market equilibrium output and price of the bread market is shown to be at $(Q^*, P^*) = (5,000, €2)$. Suppose that the mayor decrees that bakeries must sell as much bread as consumers want, at a price of €1.50. Which of the following statements are correct?

☐ The consumer and producer surpluses both increase.
☐ The producer surplus increases but the consumer surplus decreases.
☐ The consumer surplus increases but the producer surplus decreases.
☐ The total surplus is lower than at the market equilibrium.

QUESTION 8.6 CHOOSE THE CORRECT ANSWER(S)
Which of the following statements about a competitive equilibrium allocation are correct?

☐ It is the best possible allocation.
☐ No buyer's or seller's surplus can be increased without reducing someone else's surplus.
☐ The allocation must be Pareto efficient.
☐ The total surplus from trade is maximized.

EINSTEIN

Total surplus and WTP

However the market works, and whatever prices are paid, we can calculate the consumer surplus by adding together the differences between WTP and price paid for all the people who buy, and the producer surplus by adding together the difference between price received and marginal cost of every unit of output:

consumer surplus = sum of WTPs − sum of prices paid

producer surplus = sum of prices received − sum of MCs of each unit

Then when we calculate the total surplus, the prices paid and received cancel out:

total surplus = sum of WTPs of consumers − sum of MCs of producers

When buyers and sellers are price-takers, and the price equalizes supply and demand, the total surplus is as high as possible, because the consumers with the highest WTPs buy the product and the units of output with the lowest marginal costs are sold. Every trade involves a buyer with a higher WTP than the seller's reservation value, so the surplus would go down if we omitted any of them. And if we tried to include any more units of output in this calculation, the surplus would also go down because the WTPs would be lower than the MCs.

8.6 CHANGES IN SUPPLY AND DEMAND

Quinoa is a cereal crop grown on the Altiplano, a high barren plateau in the Andes of South America. It is a traditional staple food in Peru and Bolivia. In recent years, as its nutritional properties have become known, there has been a huge increase in demand from richer, health-conscious consumers in Europe and North America. Figures 8.10a–c show how the market changed. You can see in Figures 8.10a and 8.10b that between 2001 and 2011, the price of quinoa trebled and production almost doubled. Figure 8.10c indicates the strength of the increase in demand: spending on imports of quinoa rose from just $2.4 million to $43.7 million in 10 years.

For the producer countries these changes are a mixed blessing. While their staple food has become expensive for poor consumers, farmers—who are amongst the poorest—are benefiting from the boom in export sales. Other countries are now investigating whether quinoa can be grown in different climates, and France and the US have become substantial producers.

How can we explain the rapid increase in the price of quinoa? In this section, we look at the effects of changes in demand and supply in our simple examples of books and bread. At the end of this section you can apply the analysis to the real-world case of quinoa.

An increase in demand

In the market for second-hand textbooks, demand comes from new students enrolling on the course, and supply comes from students who took the course in the previous year. In Figure 8.11 we have plotted supply and demand for textbooks when the number of students enrolling remains stable at 40 per year. The equilibrium price is $8 and 24 books are sold, as shown by point A. Suppose that in one year the course became more popular. Figure 8.11 shows what would happen.

The increase in demand leads to a new equilibrium, in which 32 books are sold for $10 each. At the original price, there would be excess demand and sellers would want to raise their prices. At the new equilibrium, both price and quantity are higher. Some students who would not have sold their books at $8 will now sell at a higher price. Notice, however, that although

Jose Daniel Reyes and Julia Oliver. 'Quinoa: The Little Cereal That Could' (http://tinyco.re/9266629). *The Trade Post*. 22 November 2013. Underlying data from Food and Agriculture Organization of the United Nations. FAOSTAT *Database* (http://tinyco.re/4368803).

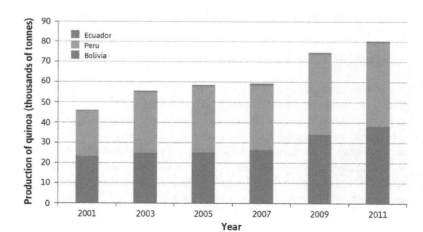

Figure 8.10a The production of quinoa.

demand has increased, not all the students who would have bought at $8 will purchase the book at the new equilibrium: those with WTP between $8 and $10 no longer want to buy.

When we say 'increase in demand', it's important to be careful about exactly what we mean:

- Demand is higher *at each possible price*, so the demand curve has shifted.
- In response to this shift there is a change in the price.
- This leads to an increase in the quantity supplied.
- This change is a movement *along* the supply curve.
- But the supply curve itself *has not shifted* (the number of sellers and their reserve prices have not changed), so we do not call this 'an increase in supply'.

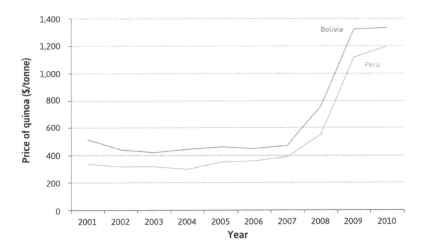

Figure 8.10b Quinoa producer prices.

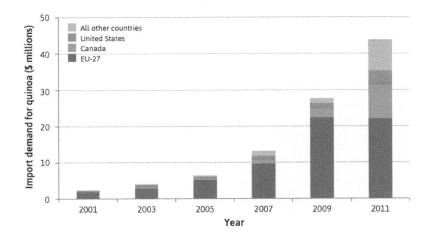

Figure 8.10c Global import demand for quinoa.

After an increase in demand, the equilibrium quantity rises, but so does the price. You can see in Figure 8.11 that the steeper (more inelastic) the supply curve, the higher the price will rise and the lower the quantity will increase. If the supply curve is quite flat (elastic), then the price rise will be smaller and the quantity sold will be more responsive to the demand shock.

An increase in supply due to improved productivity

In contrast, as an example of an increase in supply, think again about the market for bread in one city. Remember that the supply curve represents the marginal cost of producing bread. Suppose that bakeries discover a new technique that allows each worker to make bread more quickly. This will lead to a fall in the marginal cost of a loaf at each level of output. In other words, the marginal cost curve of each bakery shifts down.

Figure 8.12 shows the original supply and demand curves for the bakeries. When the MC curve of each bakery shifts down, so does the market supply curve for bread. Look at Figure 8.12 to see what happens next.

The improvement in the technology of breadmaking leads to:

- an increase in supply
- a fall in the price of bread
- a rise in the quantity sold

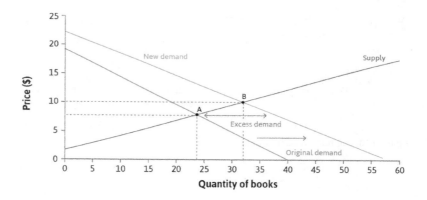

Figure 8.11 An increase in the demand for books.

1. The initial equilibrium point
At the original levels of demand and supply, the equilibrium is at point A. The price is $8, and 24 books are sold.

2. An increase in demand
If there were more students enrolling in one year, there would be more students wanting to buy the book at each possible price. The demand curve shifts to the right.

3. Excess demand when the price is $8
If the price remained at $8, there would be excess demand for books, that is, more buyers than sellers.

4. A new equilibrium point
There is a new equilibrium at point B with a price of $10, at which 32 books are sold. The increase in demand has led to a rise in the equilibrium quantity and price.

As in the example of an increase in demand, an adjustment of prices is needed to bring the market into equilibrium. Such shifts in supply and demand are often referred to as **shocks** in economic analysis. We start by specifying an economic model and find the equilibrium. Then we look at how the equilibrium changes when something changes—the model receives a shock. The shock is called **exogenous** because our model doesn't explain why it happened: the model shows the consequences, not the causes.

An increase in supply: More bakeries enter the market

Another reason for a change in market supply is the entry of more firms or the exit of existing firms. We analysed the equilibrium of the bread market in the case when there were 50 bakeries in the city. Remember from Section 8.4 that at the equilibrium price of €2, each bakery is on an isoprofit curve above the average cost curve. If economic profits are greater than zero, firms are receiving an economic rent, so other firms might want to invest in the baking business.

Leibniz: Shifts in demand and supply (http://tinyco.re/L080601)

> **shock** An exogenous change in some of the fundamental data used in a model.
> **exogenous** Coming from outside the model rather than being produced by the workings of the model itself. *See also: endogenous.*

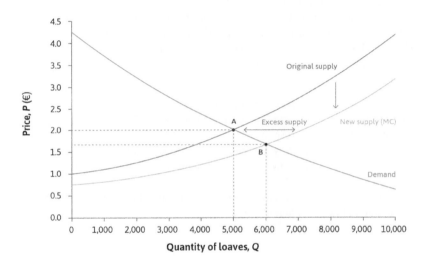

Figure 8.12 An increase in the supply of bread: A fall in MC.

1. The initial equilibrium point
The city's bakeries start out at point A, producing 5,000 loaves and selling them for €2 each.

2. A fall in marginal costs
The market supply curve then shifts because of the fall in the bakeries' marginal costs. The supply curve shifts down, because at each level of output, the marginal cost and therefore the price at which they are willing to supply bread is lower.

3. An increase in supply
The supply curve has shifted down. But another way to think of this change in supply is to say that the supply curve has shifted to the right. Since costs have fallen, the amount that bakeries will supply at each price is greater—an increase in supply.

4. Excess supply when the price is €2
The effect of the fall in marginal cost is an increase in market supply. At the original price, there is more bread than buyers want (excess supply). The bakeries would want to lower their prices.

5. The new equilibrium point
The new market equilibrium is at point B, where more bread is sold and the price is lower. The demand curve has not shifted, but the fall in price has led to an increase in the quantity of bread demanded, along the demand curve.

costs of entry Startup costs that would be incurred when a seller enters a market or an industry. These would usually include the cost of acquiring and equipping new premises, research and development, the necessary patents, and the cost of finding and hiring staff.

Since there is an opportunity for making greater than normal profit by selling bread in the city, new bakeries may decide to enter the market. There will be some **costs of entry**, for example, acquiring and equipping the premises, but provided these are not too high (or if premises and equipment can be easily sold if the venture doesn't work out) it will be worthwhile to do so.

Remember that we find the market supply curve by adding up the amounts of bread supplied by each firm, at each price. When more bakeries have entered, more bread will be supplied at each price level. Although the reason for the supply increase is different from the previous one, the effect on the market equilibrium is the same: a fall in price and a rise in bread sales. Figure 8.13 shows the effects on equilibrium. The bakeries once again start off at point A, selling 5,000 loaves of bread for €2. The entry of new firms shifts the supply curve outwards. There is more bread for sale at each price, so at the original price there would be excess supply. The new equilibrium is at point B with a lower price and higher bread sales.

The entry of new firms is unlikely to be welcomed by the existing bakeries. Their costs have not changed, but the market price has fallen to €1.75, so they must be making less profit than before. As we will see in Unit 11, the entry of new firms may eventually drive economic profits to zero, eliminating rents altogether.

EXERCISE 8.5 THE MARKET FOR QUINOA

Consider again the market for quinoa. The changes shown in Figures 8.10a–c (page 336) can be analysed as shifts in demand and supply.

1. Suppose there was an unexpected increase in demand for quinoa in the early 2000s (a shift in the demand curve). What would you expect to happen to the price and quantity initially?

2. Assuming that demand continued to rise over the next few years, how do you think farmers responded?
3. Why did the price stay constant until 2007?
4. How could you account for the rapid price rise in 2008 and 2009?
5. Would you expect the price to fall eventually to its original level?

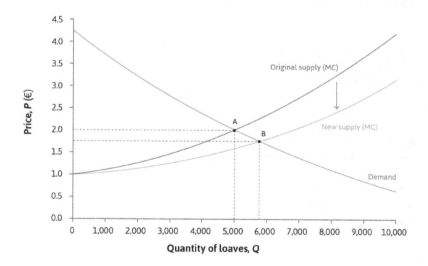

Figure 8.13 An increase in the supply of bread: More firms enter.

EXERCISE 8.6 PRICES, SHOCKS, AND REVOLUTIONS
Historians usually attribute the wave of revolutions in Europe in 1848 to long-term socioeconomic factors and a surge of radical ideas. But a poor wheat harvest in 1845 lead to food shortages and sharp price rises, which may have contributed to these sudden changes.

The table shows the average and peak prices of wheat from 1838 to 1845, relative to silver. There are three groups of countries: those where violent revolutions took place, those where constitutional change took place without widespread violence, and those where no revolution occurred.

1. Explain, using supply and demand curves, how a poor wheat harvest could lead to price rises and food shortages.
2. Find a way to present the data to show that the size of the price shock, rather than the price level, is associated with the likelihood of revolution.
3. Do you think this is a plausible explanation for the revolutions that occurred?
4. A journalist suggests that similar factors played a part in the Arab Spring in 2010 (http://tinyco.re/8936018). Read the post. What do you think of this hypothesis?

		Avg. price 1838–45	Max. price 1845–48
	Austria	52.9	104.0
	Baden	77.0	136.6
	Bavaria	70.0	127.3
	Bohemia	61.5	101.2
	France	93.8	149.2
	Hamburg	67.1	108.7
	Hessedarmstadt	76.7	119.7
Violent revolution 1848	Hungary	39.0	92.3
	Lombardy	88.3	119.9
	Mecklenburgschwerin	72.9	110.9
	Papal states	74.0	105.1
	Prussia	71.2	110.7
	Saxony	73.3	125.2
	Switzerland	87.9	146.7
	Württemberg	75.9	128.7
	Belguim	93.8	140.1
	Bremen	76.1	109.5
	Brunswick	62.3	100.3
Immediate constitutional change 1848	Denmark	66.3	81.5
	Netherlands	82.6	136.0
	Oldenburg	52.1	79.3
	England	115.3	134.7
	Finland	73.6	73.7
	Norway	89.3	119.7
No revolution 1848	Russia	50.7	44.1
	Spain	105.3	141.3
	Sweden	75.8	81.4

Berger, Helge, and Mark Spoerer. 2001. 'Economic Crises and the European Revolutions of 1848.' *The Journal of Economic History* 61 (2): pp. 293–326.

QUESTION 8.7 CHOOSE THE CORRECT ANSWER(S)
Figure 8.8 (page 328) shows the equilibrium of the bread market to be 5,000 loaves per day at price €2. A year later, we find that the market equilibrium price has fallen to €1.50. What can we conclude?

☐ The fall in the price must have been caused by a downward shift in the demand curve.
☐ The fall in the price must have been caused by a downward shift in the supply curve.
☐ The fall in price could have been caused by a shift in either curve.
☐ At a price of €1.50, there will be an excess demand for bread.

QUESTION 8.8 CHOOSE THE CORRECT ANSWER(S)
Which of the following statements are correct?

☐ A fall in the mortgage interest rate would shift up the demand curve for new houses.
☐ The launch of a new Sony smartphone would shift up the demand curve for existing iPhones.
☐ A fall in the oil price would shift up the demand curve for oil.
☐ A fall in the oil price would shift down the supply curve for plastics.

8.7 THE EFFECTS OF TAXES

Governments can use taxation to raise revenue (to finance government spending, or redistribute resources) or to affect the allocation of goods and services in other ways, perhaps because the government considers a particular good to be harmful. The supply and demand model is a useful tool for analysing the effects of taxation.

Using taxes to raise revenue

Raising revenue through taxation has a long history (see Unit 22). Take the taxation of salt, for example. For most of history, salt was used all over the world as a preservative, allowing food to be stored, transported, and traded. The ancient Chinese advocated taxing salt, since people needed it, however high the price. Salt taxes were an effective but often resented tool used by ruling elites in ancient India and medieval kings. Resentment of high salt taxes played an important part in the French Revolution, and Gandhi led protests against the salt tax imposed by the British in India.

Figure 8.14 illustrates how a salt tax might work. Initially the market equilibrium is at point A: the price is P^* and the quantity of salt traded is Q^*. Suppose that a sales tax of 30% is imposed on the price of salt, to be paid to the government by the suppliers. If suppliers have to pay a 30% tax, their marginal cost of supplying each unit of salt increases by 30%. So the supply curve shifts: the price is 30% higher at each quantity.

The new equilibrium is at point B, where a lower quantity of salt is traded. Although the consumer price has risen, note that it is not 30% higher than before. The price paid by consumers, P_1, is 30% higher than the price received by the suppliers (net of the tax), which is P_0. Suppliers receive a lower price than before, they produce less, and their profits will be lower. This illustrates an important feature of taxes: it is not necessarily the taxpayer who feels its main effect. In this case, although the suppliers pay the tax, the **tax incidence** falls partly on consumers and partly on producers.

Figure 8.15 shows the effect of the tax on consumer and producer surplus:

- *Consumer surplus falls*: Consumers pay a higher price, and buy less salt.
- *Producer surplus falls*: They produce less and receive a lower net price.
- *Total surplus is lower*: Even taking account of the tax revenue received by the government, the tax causes a deadweight loss.

When the salt tax is imposed, the total surplus from trade in the salt market is given by:

total surplus = consumer surplus + producer surplus + government revenue

Since the quantity of salt traded is no longer at the level that maximizes gains from trade, the tax has led to a deadweight loss.

> **tax incidence** The effect of a tax on the welfare of buyers, sellers, or both.

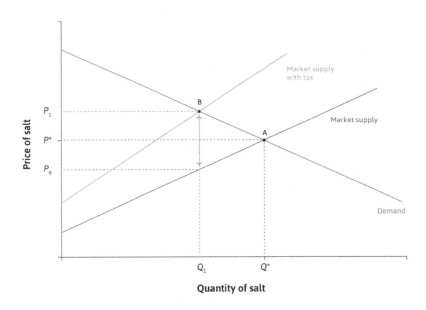

Figure 8.14 The effect of a 30% salt tax.

1. The initial equilibrium
Initially the market equilibrium is at point A. The price is P^* and the quantity of salt sold is Q^*.

2. A 30% tax
A 30% tax is imposed on suppliers. Their marginal costs are effectively 30% higher at each quantity. The supply curve shifts.

3. The new equilibrium
The new equilibrium is at B. The price paid by consumers has risen to P_1 and the quantity has fallen to Q_1.

4. The tax paid to the government
The price received by suppliers (after they have paid the tax) is P_0. The double-headed arrow shows the tax paid to the government on each unit of salt sold.

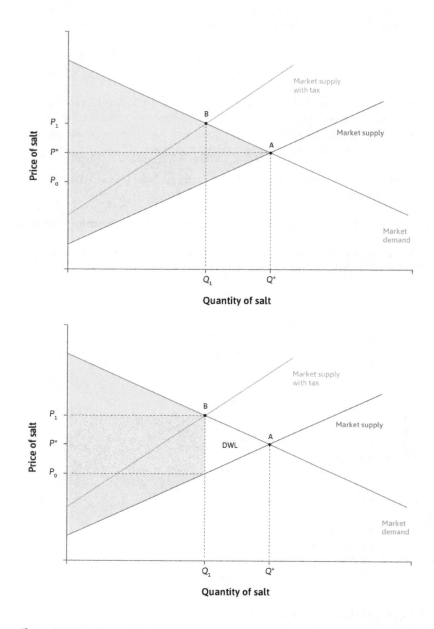

Figure 8.15 Taxation and deadweight loss.

1. Maximized gains from trade
Before the tax is imposed, the equilibrium allocation at A maximizes the gains from trade. In the upper panel the red triangle is the consumer surplus and the blue triangle is the producer surplus.

2. A tax reduces consumer surplus
The tax reduces the quantity traded to Q_1, and raises the consumer price from P^* to P_1. The consumer surplus falls.

3. A tax reduces producer surplus
The suppliers sell a lower quantity, and the price they receive falls from P^* to P_0. The producer surplus falls.

4. The tax revenue and deadweight loss
A tax equal to $(P_1 - P_0)$ is paid on each of the Q_1 units of salt that are sold. The green rectangular area is the total tax revenue. There is a deadweight loss equal to the area of the white triangle.

In general, taxes change prices, and prices change buyers' and sellers' decisions, which can cause deadweight loss. To raise as much revenue as possible, the government would prefer to tax a good for which demand is not very responsive to price, so that the fall in quantity traded is quite small—that is to say, a good with a low elasticity of demand. That is why the ancient Chinese recommended taxing salt.

We can think of the total surplus as a measure of the welfare of society as a whole (provided that the tax revenue is used for the benefit of society). So there is a second reason for a government that cares about welfare to prefer taxing goods with low elasticity of demand—the loss of total surplus will be lower. The overall effect of the tax depends on what the government does with the revenues that it collects:

- *The government spends the revenue on goods and services that enhance the wellbeing of the population*: Then the tax and resulting expenditure may enhance public welfare—even though it reduces the surplus in the particular market that is taxed.
- *The government spends the revenues on an activity that does not contribute to wellbeing*: Then the lost consumer surplus is just a reduction in the living standards of the population.

Therefore, taxes can improve or reduce overall welfare. The most that we can say is that taxing a good whose demand is inelastic is an efficient way to transfer the surplus from consumers to the government.

The government's power to levy taxes is a bit like the price-setting power of a firm that sells a differentiated good. It uses its power to raise the price and collect revenue, while reducing the quantity sold. Its ability to levy taxes depends on the institutions it can use to enforce and collect them.

One reason for the use of salt taxes in earlier times was that it was relatively easy for a powerful ruler to take full control of salt production, in some cases as a monopolist. In the notorious case of the French salt tax, the monarchy not only controlled all salt production; it also forced its subjects to buy up to 7 kg of salt each per year.

In March and April 1930, the artificially high price of salt in British colonial India provoked one of the defining moments of the Indian independence movement: Mahatma Gandhi's salt march to acquire salt from the Indian ocean. Similarly, in what came to be called the Boston tea party, in 1773 American colonists objecting to a British colonial tax on tea dumped a cargo of tea into the Boston harbour.

Resistance to taxes on inelastic goods arises for the very reason they are imposed: they are difficult to escape!

In many modern economies the institutions for tax collection are well-established, usually with democratic consent. Provided that citizens believe taxes have been implemented fairly, using them to raise revenue is accepted as a necessary part of social and economic policy. We will now look at another reason why governments may decide to levy taxes.

Jørgen Dejgård Jensen and Sinne Smed. 2013. 'The Danish Tax on Saturated Fat: Short Run Effects on Consumption, Substitution Patterns and Consumer Prices of Fats'. *Food Policy* 42: 18–31.

Using taxes to change behaviour

Policymakers in many countries are interested in the idea of using taxes to deter consumption of unhealthy foods with the objective of improving public health and tackling the obesity epidemic. In Unit 7, we looked at some data and estimates of demand elasticities for food products in the US, which help to predict how higher prices might affect people's diets there. Some countries have already introduced food taxes. Several, including France, Norway, Mexico, Samoa, and Fiji, tax sweetened drinks. Hungary's 'chips tax' is aimed at products carrying proven health risks, particularly those with high sugar or salt content. In 2011, the Danish government introduced a tax on products with high saturated fat content.

The level of the Danish tax was 16 Danish kroner (kr) per kilogram of saturated fat, corresponding to 10.4 kr per kg of butter. Note that this was a *specific tax*, levied as a fixed amount per unit of butter. A tax like the one we analysed for salt, levied as a percentage of the price, is known as an *ad valorem tax*. According to a study of the Danish fat tax, it corresponded to about 22% of the average butter price in the year before the tax. The study found that it reduced the consumption of butter and related products (butter blends, margarine, and oil) by between 15% and 20%. We can illustrate the effects in the same way as we did for the salt tax, using the supply and demand model (we are assuming here that butter retailers are price-takers).

Figure 8.16 shows a demand curve for butter, measured in kilograms per person per year. The numbers correspond approximately to Denmark's experience. We have drawn the supply curve for butter as almost flat, on the assumption that the marginal cost of butter for retailers does not change very much as quantity varies. The initial equilibrium is at point A, where the price of butter is 45 kr per kg, and each person consumes 2 kg of butter per year.

A tax of 10 kr per kg shifts the supply curve upwards and leads to a rise in price to 54 kr, and a fall in consumption to 1.6 kg. The consumer price rises by 9 kr—almost the full amount of the tax—and the suppliers' net revenue per kg of butter falls to 44 kr. In this case, although suppliers pay the tax, the tax incidence is felt mainly by consumers. Of the 10 kr tax per kg, the consumer effectively pays 9 kr, while the supplier or producer pays 1 kr. So the price received by the retailers, net of tax, is only 1 kr lower.

Figure 8.17 shows what happens to consumer and producer surplus as a result of the fat tax.

Again, both consumer and producer surpluses fall. The area of the green rectangle represents the tax revenue: with a tax of 10 kr per kg and equilibrium sales of 1.6 kg per person, tax revenue is $10 \times 1.6 = 16$ kr per person per year.

How effective was the fat tax policy? For a full evaluation of the effect on health we should look at all the foods taxed, and take into account the cross-price effects—the changes in consumption of other foods caused by the tax. The study of the Danish tax also allowed for the possibility that some retailers are not price-takers. Nevertheless, Figures 8.16 and 8.17 illustrate some important implications of the tax:

- *Consumption of butter products fell*: In this case by 20%. You can see this in Figure 8.16. In this respect, the policy was successful.
- *There was a large fall in surplus, especially consumer surplus*: You can see this in Figure 8.17. But recall that the government's aim when it

implemented the fat tax policy was not to raise revenue, but rather to reduce quantity. So the fall in consumer surplus was inevitable. The loss of surplus caused by a tax is a deadweight loss, which sounds negative. But in this case the policymaker might see it as a gain if the 'good', butter, is considered 'bad' for consumers.

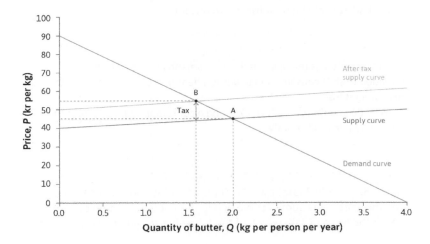

Figure 8.16 The effect of a fat tax on the retail market for butter.

1. Equilibrium in the market for butter
Initially the market for butter is in equilibrium. The price of butter is 45 kr per kg, and consumption of butter in Denmark is 2 kg per person per year.

2. The effect of a tax
A tax of 10 kr per kg levied on suppliers raises their marginal costs by 10 kr at every quantity. The supply curve shifts upwards by 10 kr.

3. A new equilibrium
The new equilibrium is at point B. The price has risen to 54 kr. Each person's annual consumption of butter has fallen to 1.6 kg.

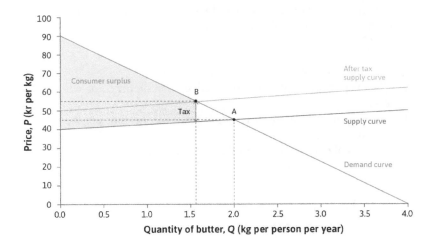

Figure 8.17 The effect of a fat tax on the consumer and producer surplus for butter.

One aspect of taxation not illustrated in our supply and demand analysis is the cost of collecting it. Although the Danish fat tax successfully reduced fat consumption, the government abolished it after only 15 months because of the administrative burden it placed on firms. Any taxation system requires effective mechanisms for tax collection, and designing taxes that are simple to administer (and difficult to avoid) is an important goal of tax policy. Policymakers who want to introduce food taxes will need to find ways of minimizing administrative costs. But since the costs cannot be eliminated, they will also need to consider whether the health gain (and reduction of costs of bad health) will be sufficient to offset them.

EXERCISE 8.7 THE DEADWEIGHT LOSS OF THE BUTTER TAX

Food taxes such as the ones discussed here and in Unit 7 are often intended to shift consumption towards a healthier diet, but give rise to deadweight loss.

Why do you think a policymaker and a consumer might interpret this deadweight loss differently?

QUESTION 8.9 CHOOSE THE CORRECT ANSWER(S)

Figure 8.14 (page 343) shows the demand and supply curves for salt, and the shift in the supply curve due to the implementation of a 30% tax on the price of salt. Which of the following statements are correct?

☐ In the post-tax equilibrium, the consumers pay P_1 and the producers receive P^*.
☐ The government's tax revenue is given by $(P^* - P_0)Q_1$.
☐ The deadweight loss is given by $(1/2)(P_1 - P_0)(Q^* - Q_1)$.
☐ As a result of the tax, the consumer surplus is reduced by $(1/2)(Q_1 + Q^*)(P_1 - P^*)$.

QUESTION 8.10 CHOOSE THE CORRECT ANSWER(S)

Figure 8.17 (page 347) shows the effect of a tax intended to reduce the consumption of butter. The before-tax equilibrium is at A = (2.0 kg, 45 kr) and the after-tax equilibrium is at B = (1.6 kg, 54 kr). The tax imposed is 10 kr per kg of butter. Which of the following statements is correct?

☐ The producers receive 45 kr per kg of butter.
☐ The tax policy would be more effective if the supply curve were less elastic.
☐ The very elastic supply curve implies that the incidence of the tax falls mainly on consumers.
☐ The loss of consumer surplus due to tax is $(1/2) \times 10 \times (2.0 - 1.6) = 2.0$.

8.8 THE MODEL OF PERFECT COMPETITION

To apply the model of supply and demand, we have assumed throughout this unit that buyers and sellers are price-takers. In what kinds of markets would we expect to see price-taking on both sides? To generate competition between sellers, and force sellers to act as price-takers, we need:

- *Many undifferentiated sellers*: As Marshall discussed, there must be many sellers, all selling identical goods. If their goods were differentiated, then each one would have some market power.
- *Sellers must act independently*: If they act as a cartel, for example, they are not price-takers—they can jointly choose the price.
- *Many buyers all wanting to buy the good*: Each of them will choose whichever seller has the lowest price.
- *Buyers know the sellers' prices*: If they do not, they cannot choose the lowest one.

Similarly, buyers must force each other to be price-takers:

- *There must be many buyers, competing with each other*: Then sellers have no reason to sell to someone who would pay less than everyone else.

A market with all of these properties is described as **perfectly competitive**. We can predict that the equilibrium in such a market will be a competitive equilibrium—so it will have the following characteristics:

- *All transactions take place at a single price*: This is known as the **law of one price**.
- *At that price, the amount supplied equals the amount demanded*: the market clears.
- No buyer or seller can benefit by altering the price they are demanding or offering. They are all **price-takers**.
- *All potential **gains from trade** are realized*.

Léon Walras, a ninteenth-century French economist, built a mathematical model of an economy in which all buyers and sellers are price-takers, which has been influential in how many economists think about markets.

> **PERFECT COMPETITION**
> A hypothetical market in which:
> - The good or service being exchanged is homogeneous (it does not differ from one seller to another).
> - There are large numbers of potential buyers and sellers of the good, each acting independently of the others.
> - Buyers and sellers can readily know the prices at which other buyers and sellers are exchanging the good.

> **perfectly competitive equilibrium** Such an equilibrium occurs in a model in which all buyers and sellers are price-takers. In this equilibrium, all transactions take place at a single price. This is known as the law of one price. At that price, the amount supplied equals the amount demanded: the market clears. No buyer or seller can benefit by altering the price they are demanding or offering. They are both price-takers. All potential gains from trade are realized. *See also: law of one price.*

> **law of one price** Holds when a good is traded at the same price across all buyers and sellers. If a good were sold at different prices in different places, a trader could buy it cheaply in one place and sell it at a higher price in another. *See also: arbitrage.*
> **gains from exchange** The benefits that each party gains from a transaction compared to how they would have fared without the exchange. *Also known as: gains from trade. See also: economic rent.*

GREAT ECONOMISTS

Léon Walras

Léon Walras (1834–1910) was a founder of the neoclassical school of economics. He was an indifferent student, and twice failed the entrance exam to the École Polytechnique in Paris, one of the most prestigious universities in his native France. He studied engineering at the School of Mines instead. Eventually his father, an economist, convinced him to take up the challenge of making economics into a science.

The pure economic science to which he aspired was the study of relationships among things, not people, and he had notable success in eliminating human relationships from his modelling. 'The pure theory of economics,' he wrote, 'resembles the physico-mathematical sciences in every respect.'

His device for simplifying the economy so that it could be expressed mathematically was to represent interactions among economic agents as if they were relationships among inputs and outputs, and to focus entirely on the economy in equilibrium. In the process the entrepreneur, a key actor in wealth creation from the Industrial Revolution to today, simply disappeared from Walrasian economics:

> Assuming equilibrium, we may even go so far as to abstract from entrepreneurs and simply consider the productive services as being, in a certain sense, exchanged directly for one another ...
> (*Elements of Theoretical Economics*, 1874)

Leon Walras. (1874) 2014. *Elements of Theoretical Economics: Or the Theory of Social Wealth*. Cambridge: Cambridge University Press.

Walras represented basic economic relationships as equations, which he used to study the workings of an entire economy composed of many interlinked markets. Prior to Walras, most economists had considered these markets in isolation: they would have studied, for example, how the price of textiles is determined on the cloth market, or land rents on the land market.

A century before Walras, a group of French economists called the physiocrats had studied the circulation of goods throughout the economy, as if the flow of goods from one sector to another in the economy was comparable to the circulation of blood in the human body (one of the leading physiocrats was a medical doctor). But the physiocrats' model was little more than a metaphor that drew attention to the interconnectedness of markets.

Walras used mathematics, rather than medical analogies, to create what is now called general equilibrium theory, a mathematical model of an entire economy in which all buyers and sellers act as price-takers and supply equals demand in all markets. Walras' work was the basis of the proof, much later, of the invisible hand theorem, giving the conditions under which such an equilibrium is Pareto efficient. The invisible hand game in Unit 4 is an example of the conditions in which the pursuit of self-interest can benefit everyone.

Walras had defended the right to private property, but to help the working poor he also advocated the nationalization of land and the elimination of taxes on wages.

Seven years after his death, the general equilibrium model was to play an important role in the debate about the feasibility and desirability of centralized economic planning compared to a market economy. In 1917, the Bolshevik Revolution in Russia put the economics of socialism and central planning on the agenda of many economists, but surprisingly, it was the defenders of central planning, not the advocates of the market, who used Walras' insights to make their points.

Friedrich Hayek, and other defenders of capitalism, criticized the Walrasian general equilibrium model. Their argument: by deliberately ignoring the fact that a capitalist economy is constantly changing, and therefore not taking into account the contribution of entrepreneurship and creativity in market competition, Walras had missed the true virtues of the market.

The model of perfect competition describes an idealized market structure in which we can be confident that the assumption of price-taking that underlies our model of supply and demand will hold. Markets for agricultural products such as wheat, rice, coffee, or tomatoes look rather like this, although goods are not truly identical, and it is unlikely that everyone is aware of all the prices at which trade takes place. But it is nevertheless clear that they have very little, if any, power to affect the price at which they trade.

In other cases—for example, markets where there are some differences in the quality of goods—there may still be enough competition that we can assume price-taking, in order to obtain a simple model of how the market works. A simplified model can provide useful predictions when the assumptions underlying it are only approximately true. Judging whether or not it is appropriate to draw conclusions about the real world from a simplified model is an important skill of economic analysis.

For example, we know that markets are not perfectly competitive when products are differentiated. Consumers' preferences differ, and we saw in Unit 7 that firms have an incentive to differentiate their product, if they can, rather than to supply a product similar or identical to others. Nevertheless, the model of supply and demand can be a useful approximation to help us to understand how some markets for non-identical products behave.

Figure 8.18 shows the market for an imaginary product called Choccos, for which there are close substitutes, as many similar products compete in the wider market for chocolate bars. Due to competition from other chocolate bars, the demand curve is almost flat. The range of feasible prices for Choccos is narrow, and the firm chooses a price and quantity where the marginal cost is close to the price. So this firm is in a similar situation to a firm in a perfectly competitive market. It is the equilibrium price in the larger market for chocolate bars that determines the feasible prices for Choccos—they have to be sold at a similar price to other chocolate bars.

The narrow range of feasible prices for this firm is determined by the behaviour of its competitors. So the main influence on the price of Choccos is not the firm, but the market for chocolate bars as a whole. Since all the firms will be producing at similar prices, which will be close to their marginal costs, we lose little by ignoring the differences between them and assuming that each firm's supply curve is its marginal cost curve, then finding the equilibrium in the wider market for chocolate bars.

We have already taken this approach when we analysed the Danish butter market. In practice, it is likely that some retailers who sell butter have some power to set prices. A local shop may be able to set a price that is higher than the price of butter elsewhere, knowing that some shoppers will find it convenient to buy rather than searching for a lower price. However, it is reasonable to assume that they don't have much wiggle room to set prices, and are strongly influenced by the prevailing market price. So price-taking is a good approximation for this market—good enough, at least, that the supply and demand model can help us to understand the impact of a fat tax.

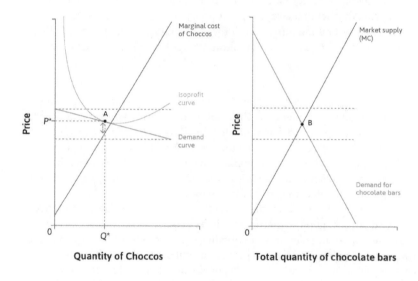

Figure 8.18 The market for Choccos and chocolate bars.

1. The market for Choccos
The left hand panel shows the market for Choccos, produced by one firm. There are many close substitutes in the wider market for chocolate bars.

2. The demand curve for Choccos
Due to competition from similar chocolate bars, the demand curve for Choccos is almost flat. The range of feasible prices is narrow.

3. The price of Choccos
The firm chooses a price P^* similar to its competitors, and a quantity where MC is close to P^*. Whatever the price of its competitors, it would produce close to its marginal cost curve. So the firm's MC curve is approximately its supply curve.

4. The market supply curve for chocolate bars
We can construct the market supply curve for chocolate bars in the right hand panel by adding the quantities from the marginal cost curves of all the chocolate bar producers.

5. The market demand curve for chocolate bars
If most consumers do not have strong preferences for one firm's product, we can draw a market demand curve for chocolate bars.

6. The demand curve for Choccos
The equilibrium price in the chocolate bar market (right-hand panel) determines the narrow range of prices from which the Chocco firm can choose (left-hand panel)—it will have to set a price quite close to that of other chocolate bars.

EXERCISE 8.8 PRICE-FIXING

We have used chocolate bars as a hypothetical example of an approximately competitive market. But in recent years, producers of best-selling chocolate bars worldwide have been accused of colluding with each other to keep prices high. Use the information in this article (http://tinyco.re/9016236) to explain:

1. In what ways does the market for chocolate bars fail to satisfy the conditions for perfect competition?
2. Each brand of chocolate bar faces competition from many other similar brands. Why, despite this, do some producers have considerable market power?
3. In what market conditions do you think price-fixing is most likely to occur, and why?

QUESTION 8.11 CHOOSE THE CORRECT ANSWER(S)

Look again at Figure 8.18 (page 352), which shows the market for Choccos and for all chocolate bars. Based on the two diagrams, which of the following statements is correct?

☐ The firm that makes Choccos chooses to produce at the bottom of the U-shaped isoprofit curve.
☐ All chocolate bars will be sold at the same price P^*.
☐ The existence of many competitors means that the firm is a price-taker.
☐ The market marginal cost (MC) curve is approximately the sum of the MC curves of all the producers of the chocolate bars.

8.9 LOOKING FOR COMPETITIVE EQUILIBRIA

If we look at a market in which conditions seem to favour perfect competition—many buyers and sellers of identical goods, acting independently—how can we tell whether it satisfies the conditions for a competitive equilibrium? Economists have used two tests:

1. Do all trades take place at the same price?
2. Are firms selling goods at a price equal to marginal cost?

The difficulty with the second test is that it is often difficult to measure marginal cost. But Lawrence Ausubel, an economist, was able to do this for the US bank credit card market in the 1980s. At this time 4,000 banks were selling an identical product: credit card loans. The cards were mostly Visa or Mastercard, but the individual banks decided the price of their loans—that is, the interest rate. The banks' cost of funds—the opportunity cost of the money loaned to credit card holders—could be deduced from other interest rates in financial markets. Although there were other components of marginal cost, the cost of funds was the only one that varied substantially over time. So if the credit card market were competitive, we would expect to see the interest rate on credit card loans rise and fall with the cost of funds.

Lawrence M. Ausubel. 1991. 'The Failure of Competition in the Credit Card Market'. *American Economic Review* 81 (1): pp. 50–81.

By comparing the credit card interest rate with the cost of funds over a period of eight years, Ausubel found that this didn't happen. When the cost of funds fell from 15% to below 7%, there seemed to be almost no effect on the price of credit card loans.

Why do the banks not cut their interest rates when their costs fall? He suggested two different possibilities:

- *It may be difficult for consumers to change credit card provider*: In that case, the banks are not forced to compete with each other, so they keep prices high when costs fall.
- *Banks might not be able to decide which of their customers are bad risks*: That would be a problem in this market, because the bad risks are most sensitive to prices. The banks do not want to lower their prices for fear of attracting the wrong kind of customer.

Perfect competition requires that consumers are sufficiently sensitive to prices to force firms to compete, and this may not be the case in any market where consumers have to search for products. If it takes time and effort to check prices and inspect products, they may decide to buy as soon as they find something suitable, rather than continue the search for the cheapest. When the Internet made online shopping feasible, many economists hypothesized that this would make retail markets more competitive: consumers would easily be able to check the prices of many suppliers before deciding to buy.

Glenn Ellison and Sara Fisher Ellison. 2005. 'Lessons About Markets from the Internet' (http://tinyco.re/4419622). *Journal of Economic Perspectives* 19 (2) (June): p. 139.

But often consumers are not very sensitive to prices, even in this environment. You can test the law of one price in online retail competition for yourself, by checking the prices of a particular product that should be the same wherever you buy it—a book or household appliance, for example—and comparing them. Figure 8.19 shows the prices of UK online retailers for a particular DVD in March 2014. The range of prices is high: the most expensive seller is charging 66% more than the cheapest.

From the early nineteenth century, the catches of Atlantic fisherman landed in the port of New York were sold at the Fulton Fish Market in Manhattan (in 2005, it relocated to the Bronx) to restaurants and retailers. It is still the largest market for fresh fish in the US, although fish are now brought in by road or air. Dealers do not display prices. Instead, customers can inspect the fish and ask for a price before making their decision, making it an institution that appears to encourage competition.

Kathryn Graddy. 2006. 'Markets: The Fulton Fish Market' (http://tinyco.re/4300778). *Journal of Economic Perspectives* 20 (2): pp. 207–220.

Kathryn Graddy, an economist who specializes in how prices are set, studied the Fulton Fish Market. There were about 35 dealers, with stalls close to each other, so customers could easily observe the quantity and quality of fish available and ask several dealers for a price. She used details of 3,357 sales of whiting by one dealer, including price, quantity, and quality of fish, and characteristics of the buyers.

Kathryn Graddy. 1995. 'Testing for Imperfect Competition at the Fulton Fish Market' (http://tinyco.re/8279962). *The RAND Journal of Economics* 26 (1): pp. 75–92.

Of course, prices were not the same for every transaction: quality varied, and fish supplies changed from day to day. But her surprising observation was that on average Asian buyers paid about 7% less per pound than white buyers (all of the dealers were white). There seemed to be no differences between the transactions with white and Asian buyers that could explain the different prices.

How could this happen? If one dealer was setting high prices for white buyers, why did other dealers not try to attract them to their own stalls by offering a better deal? Watch our interview with Graddy to find out how she collected her data, and what she discovered about the model of perfect competition.

Graddy observed that dealers knew that, in practice, white buyers were willing to take higher prices than Asian buyers. The dealers knew this without having to collude in setting their prices.

The examples in this section show that it is hard to find evidence of perfect competition. Nevertheless, we have seen that the model can be a useful approximation. Even if the conditions for perfect competition are not all satisfied, the model of supply and demand is a valuable tool for economic analysis, applicable when there is enough competition that individuals have little influence on prices.

In theory, the easy access to price information across the market should have allowed all buyers to quickly find very similar prices. But in practice, Graddy observed that bargaining occurred rarely, and then only with buyers of large quantities.

Kathryn Graddy: Fishing for perfect competition http://tinyco.re/ 7406838

EXERCISE 8.9 PRICE DISPERSION

Choose any published textbook that you have been using in your course. Go on to the web and find the price you can buy this book for from a number of different suppliers (Amazon, eBay, your local bookstore, and so on).

Is there dispersion in prices, and if so, how can you explain it?

EXERCISE 8.10 THE FULTON FISH MARKET

Watch Kathryn Graddy's video (http://tinyco.re/7406838).

1. How does she explain her evidence that the law of one price did not hold in the fish market?
2. Why did buyers and sellers not look for better deals?
3. Why did new dealers not enter the market in pursuit of economic rents?

The Hobbit: An Unexpected Journey

Supplier	Price including postage (£)
Game	14.99
Amazon UK	15.00
Tesco	15.00
Asda	15.00
Base.com	16.99
Play.com	17.79
Savvi	17.95
The HUT	18.25
I want one of those	18.25
Hive.com	21.11
MovieMail.com	21.49
Blackwell	24.99

Figure 8.19 Differing prices for the same DVD, from UK online retailers (March 2014).

8.10 PRICE-SETTING AND PRICE-TAKING FIRMS

We now have two different models of how firms behave. In the Unit 7 model, the firm produces a product that is different from the products of other firms, giving it market power—the power to set its own price. This model applies to the extreme case of a monopolist, who has no competitors at all, such as water supply companies, and national airlines with exclusive rights granted by the government to operate domestic flights. The Unit 7 model also applies to a firm producing differentiated products such as breakfast cereals, cars, or chocolate bars—similar, but not identical, to those of its competitors. In such cases, the firm still has the power to set its own price. But if it has close competitors, demand will be quite elastic and the range of feasible prices will be narrow.

In the supply-and-demand model developed in this unit, firms are price-takers. Competition from other firms producing identical products means that they have no power to set their own prices. This model can be useful as an approximate description of a market in which there are many firms selling very similar products, even if the idealized conditions for a perfectly competitive market do not hold.

In practice, economies are a mixture of more and less competitive markets. In some respects, firms act the same whether they are the single seller of a good or one of a great many competitors: all firms decide how much to produce, which technologies to use, how many people to hire, and how much to pay them so as to maximize their profits.

But there are important differences. Look back at the decisions made by price-setting firms to maximize profits (Figure 7.2). Firms in more competitive markets lack either the incentive or the opportunity to do some of these things.

A firm with a unique product will advertise (Buy Nike!) to shift the demand curve for its product to the right. But why would a single competitive firm advertise (Drink milk!)? This would shift the demand curve for all of the firms in the industry. Advertising in a competitive market is a **public good**: the benefits go to all of the firms in the industry. If you see a message like 'Drink milk!' it is probably paid for by an association of dairies, not by a particular one.

The same is true of expenditures to influence public policy. If a large firm with market power is successful, for example, in relaxing environmental regulations, then it will benefit directly. But activities like lobbying or contributing money to electoral campaigns will be unattractive to the competitive firm because the result (a more profit-friendly policy) is a public good.

Similarly, investment in developing new technologies is likely to be undertaken by firms facing little competition, because if they are successful in finding a profitable innovation, the benefits will not be lost to competitors also adopting it. However, one way that successful large firms can emerge is by breaking away from the competition and innovating with a new product. The UK's largest organic dairy, Yeo Valley, was once an ordinary farm selling milk, just like thousands of others. In 1994 it established an organic brand, creating new products for which it could charge premium prices. With the help of imaginative marketing campaigns it has grown into a company with 1,800 employees and 65% of the UK organic market.

The table in Figure 8.20 summarizes the differences between price-setting and price-taking firms.

public good A good for which use by one person does not reduce its availability to others. *Also known as: non-rival good. See also: non-excludable public good, artificially scarce good.*

Price-setting firm or monopoly	Firm in a perfectly competitive market
Sets price and quantity to maximize profits ('price-maker')	Takes market determined price as given and chooses quantity to maximize profits ('price-taker')
Chooses an output level at which marginal cost is less than price	Chooses an output level at which marginal cost equals price
Deadweight losses (Pareto inefficient)	No deadweight losses for consumers and firms (can be Pareto efficient if no one else in the economy is affected)
Owners receive economic rents (profits greater than normal profits)	If the owners receive economic rents, the rents are likely to disappear as more firms enter the market
Firms advertise their unique product	Little advertising: it costs the firm, but benefits all firms (it's a public good)
Firms may spend money to influence elections, legislation and regulation	Little expenditure by individual firms on this (same as advertising)
Firms invest in research and innovation; seek to prevent copying	Little incentive for innovation; others will copy (unless the firm can succeed in differentiating its product and escaping from the competitive market)

Figure 8.20 Price-setting and price-taking firms.

8.11 CONCLUSION

Buyers or sellers who have little influence on market prices, due to competition, are called price-takers. A market is in competitive equilibrium if all buyers and sellers are price-takers, and at the prevailing market price, the quantity supplied is equal to the quantity demanded (the market clears).

Price-taking firms choose their quantity so that the marginal cost is equal to the market price. The equilibrium allocation exploits all possible gains from trade.

The model of perfect competition describes a set of idealized market conditions in which we would expect a competitive equilibrium to occur. Markets for real goods don't conform exactly to the model. But price-taking can be a useful approximation, enabling us to use supply and demand curves as a tool for understanding market outcomes, for example, the effects of a tax, or a demand shock.

Concepts introduced in Unit 8
Before you move on, review these definitions:

- Price-taking firms
- Competitive equilibrium
- Exogenous shocks
- Taxation
- Model of perfect competition

8.12 REFERENCES

Ausubel, Lawrence M. 1991. 'The Failure of Competition in the Credit Card Market'. *American Economic Review* 81 (1): pp. 50–81.

Berger, Helge, and Mark Spoerer. 2001. 'Economic Crises and the European Revolutions of 1848'. *The Journal of Economic History* 61 (2): pp. 293–326.

Eisen, Michael. 2011. 'Amazon's $23,698,655.93 book about flies' (http://tinyco.re/0044329). *It is NOT junk.* Updated 22 April 2011.

Ellison, Glenn, and Sara Fisher Ellison. 2005. 'Lessons About Markets from the Internet' (http://tinyco.re/4419622). *Journal of Economic Perspectives* 19 (2) (June): p. 139.

Graddy, Kathryn. 1995. 'Testing for Imperfect Competition at the Fulton Fish Market' (http://tinyco.re/8279962). *The RAND Journal of Economics* 26 (1): pp. 75–92.

Graddy, Kathryn. 2006. 'Markets: The Fulton Fish Market' (http://tinyco.re/4300778). *Journal of Economic Perspectives* 20 (2): pp. 207–220.

Jensen, Jørgen Dejgård, and Sinne Smed. 2013. 'The Danish tax on saturated fat: Short run effects on consumption, substitution patterns and consumer prices of fats'. *Food Policy* 42: pp. 18–31.

Marshall, Alfred. 1920. *Principles of Economics* (http://tinyco.re/0560708), 8th ed. London: MacMillan & Co.

Reyes, Jose Daniel, and Julia Oliver. 2013. 'Quinoa: The Little Cereal That Could' (http://tinyco.re/9266629). *The Trade Post.* 22 November 2013.

Seabright, Paul. 2010. *The Company of Strangers: A Natural History of Economic Life* (Revised Edition). Princeton, NJ: Princeton University Press.

Stucke, Maurice. 2013. 'Is Competition Always Good?' (http://tinyco.re/8720076). *OUPblog.* Updated 25 March 2013.

The Economist. 2001. 'Is Santa a Deadweight Loss?' (http://tinyco.re/7728778). Updated 20 December 2001.

Waldfogel, Joel. 1993. 'The Deadweight Loss of Christmas' (http://tinyco.re/0182759). *American Economic Review* 83 (5).

Walras, Leon. (1874) 2014. *Elements of Theoretical Economics: Or the Theory of Social Wealth.* Cambridge: Cambridge University Press.

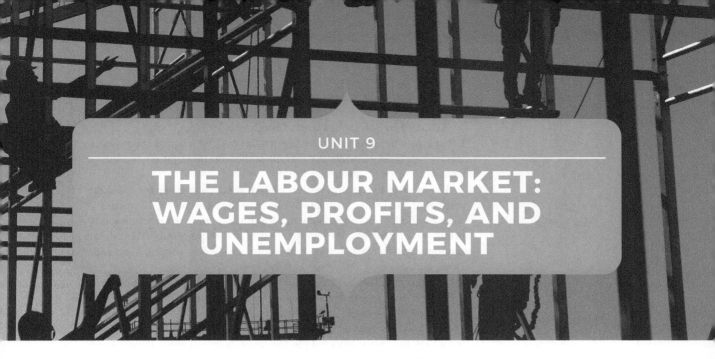

UNIT 9

THE LABOUR MARKET: WAGES, PROFITS, AND UNEMPLOYMENT

HOW THE ECONOMY-WIDE MARKET FOR LABOUR DETERMINES WAGES, EMPLOYMENT, AND THE DISTRIBUTION OF INCOME

THEMES AND CAPSTONE UNITS

- 17: History, instability, and growth
- 18: Global economy
- 19: Inequality
- 22: Politics and policy

- The labour market functions quite differently from the bread market described in the previous unit because firms cannot purchase the work of employees directly but only hire their time.
- As we saw in Unit 6, the principal-agent model is used to explain the conflict of interest between the employer and the employee over how hard the worker works, and why this issue cannot be resolved by a contract.
- The outcome of the wage-setting process across all firms in the economy is the wage-setting curve, which shows the wage associated with each unemployment rate.
- The prices that firms charge for their products are influenced by the demand for their goods and the cost of labour, the wage.
- The outcome of the price-setting process across all firms is the price-setting curve, which gives the value of the real wage that is consistent with a firm's profit-maximizing markup over production costs.
- Excess supply of labour (involuntary unemployment) is a feature of labour markets, even in equilibrium.
- If economy-wide demand for goods and services is too low, unemployment will be higher than its equilibrium level and may persist.
- Unions and public policies can affect labour market equilibrium.

As in many parts of the world, mining was a way of life for Doug Grey, a rigger who operated giant cranes at mines in the Northern Territory, Australia. In the 1990s, he helped construct the MacArthur River zinc mine, one of the world's largest, where his son Rob got his first job. 'I ended up driving ore trucks,' Rob reminisced, 'That was an awesome opportunity.'

Rob, it seemed then, had been born at the right time. He entered the labour market just as the worldwide natural resources boom was taking off, driven by the demand from the rapidly growing economy of China. Rob lived in Thailand for a time, spending little, and flying into his job in Borroloola.

About when Rob started work, Doug, the elder Grey, took a job at the Pilbara iron ore mine in Western Australia (WA), which paid about twice the average family income in Australia at the time. Both father and son were putting away substantial savings.

But by 2015 the natural resource boom was a distant memory, and the price of ore and zinc continued to plummet. Rob and his fellow miners were worried. 'Everybody knew the economic downturn and commodity prices were a problem. We had that in the back of our minds.' Their dream economy couldn't last. 'It was … obvious … that it was coming to an end,' Doug said.

And it did. In late 2015, Rob got the bad news: 'Two days into my break the general manager called and said, "thanks for your service, we appreciate it, we have to let you go."' His father, too, was laid off.

Driving ore trucks is Rob's passion and he still hopes to get back behind the wheel. But that is not going to happen, at least not at the Pilbara mine where his dad once worked. Faced with collapsing demand, the mining company cut production, and also sought to drastically reduce costs. As part of this process, they replaced human labour by machines wherever possible. In the Pilbara, *nobody* is behind the wheel of any of their giant robot ore trucks that are now being 'driven' by university graduates with joysticks 1,200 km away in Perth (we return to this process of automation and its effects on the labour market in Units 16 and 19).

The rise and fall of the Grey family's economic fortunes is all about the workings of the labour market in the mining and construction industries in Western Australia and the Northern Territory. Figure 9.1 shows that their experience was far from unusual. The boom in ore prices (in the top figure) made mining highly profitable, leading to strong demand for labour, which eventually dried up the pool of unemployed riggers and truck-drivers. Mining companies had no choice but to pay extraordinarily high salaries, and while the mining boom lasted, the companies remained highly profitable.

The downturn in commodity prices began in mid-2011 and unemployment began to rise. The Grey family's good fortunes lasted another four years.

In this unit, we describe how the labour market works and why even in equilibrium, the supply of labour (number of people seeking jobs) exceeds the demand for labour (number of jobs offered). Those without work in this situation are termed the **involuntary unemployed** (to distinguish them from those who are <u>unemployed by choice</u>, but are looking for a job).

9.1 THE WAGE-SETTING CURVE, THE PRICE-SETTING CURVE, AND THE LABOUR MARKET

In previous units we have looked at particular markets—buying and selling bread, for example—and sometimes at a single firm. Here we model the labour market of an entire economy, which determines the amount of unemployment in the population as a whole. We look at price-setting firms, selling differentiated products (as described in Unit 7), and a large number of identical workers who may be employed by the firms for the same wage set by the firm (as studied in Unit 6).

We consider the simple case in which the only input to production is labour, so that the only cost is the wage, and profits are determined by just three things: the **nominal wage** (the actual amount received in a particular currency), the price at which the firm sells its goods, and the average output produced by a worker in an hour.

nominal wage The actual amount received in payment for work, in a particular currency. *Also known as: money wage. See also: real wage.*

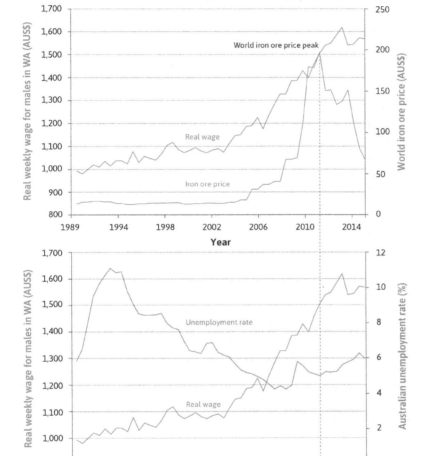

Australian Bureau of Statistics (http://tinyco.re/1648810) and International Monetary Fund (http://tinyco.re/8213274). Note: Unemployment rates are seasonally adjusted.

Figure 9.1 Real weekly earnings for males in Western Australia (left axis), world price of iron-ore and unemployment rate in Australia (right axis), (1989–2015).

1. Weekly earnings
The chart shows real weekly earnings for males in Western Australia, together with the world price of iron-ore in the top panel and the unemployment rate in Australia in the bottom panel.

2. Growth slows, unemployment rises
Following the peak in iron-ore prices, real wage growth slowed and unemployment began to rise.

The labour market

The labour market brings together two earlier themes: the firm and its employees (Unit 6) and the firm and its customers (Unit 7). Two things you have learned will be essential to seeing how the labour market functions.

Firms and employees

In order to motivate employees to work hard and well, firms must set the wage sufficiently high so that the worker receives an **employment rent**. This means there is a cost of job loss: she is better off being employed than being fired due to inadequate effort. If the worker is very likely to find alternative work if she is fired, which will be the case if the employment level in the economy is high, she will need a higher wage to work hard. Think of wage-setting as the business of the human resources (HR) department of the firm.

Firms and customers

In setting the price of the good they sell, firms face a trade-off between selling more goods and setting a higher price, due to the demand curve they face. To determine the price to set, the firm finds the markup over their production cost that balances the gains from a higher price against the losses from lower sales so as to maximize its profits. This profit-maximizing markup determines the division of the firm's revenues between profits and wages. Think of price setting as the business of the marketing department (MD) of the firm.

Wages and employment

We want to know how the real wage and the level of employment in the economy as a whole are determined. Keep in mind that the **real wage** is the nominal wage divided by the price level of a standard bundle of consumer goods, so it is determined both by the nominal wages paid by the firms and the prices they each set. Think about this in two stages:

- First, each firm decides what wage to pay, what price to charge for its products, and how many people to hire.
- Then, adding up all of these decisions across all firms gives the total employment in the economy and the real wage.

Here is how the first stage (choosing the wage, price, and employment) takes place in each firm:

- *The human resources department determines the lowest wage it can pay*: It must not undermine the workers' motivation to work, and its decision is based on the prices of other firms' products, the wages the other firms are paying, and the unemployment rate in the economy. This is the nominal wage set by the firm. It communicates this information to the MD.
- *The marketing department sets the price*: This is based on the firm's nominal wage and the shape and position of the demand curve facing the firm. For example, if the demand curve is elastic, indicating a high level of competition from other firms, it will set a lower price. Setting the price is the same thing as fixing the size of the markup over the cost of hiring labour. Given the position of the demand curve, which indicates the level of economy-wide demand, the MD then determines

---

employment rent The economic rent a worker receives when the net value of her job exceeds the net value of her next best alternative (that is, being unemployed). *Also known as: cost of job loss.* ✓

real wage The nominal wage, adjusted to take account of changes in prices between different time periods. It measures the amount of goods and services the worker can buy. *See also: nominal wage.*

the amount of output the firm will sell. It communicates this information to the production department (PD).

- The production department then calculates how many employees have to be hired to produce the output determined by the MD, based on the firm's production function.

The second stage—considering the outcome of all the firms' decisions added together—is more complicated. But the key idea is simple. Once all firms in the economy have made their wage and price (markup) decisions, the output per worker in the economy is divided into the real wage that a worker receives, and the real profits that the owner receives. If all firms are charging the same price and setting the same nominal wage, then a higher real wage (W/P) means a lower markup ($1 - (W/P)$). To understand how the real wage and employment are jointly determined in the labour market, we need two basic concepts:

- *The **wage-setting curve***: This gives the real wage necessary at each level of economy-wide employment to provide workers with incentives to work hard and well.
- *The **price-setting curve***: This gives the real wage paid when firms choose their profit-maximizing price.

In the next section we look at how employment and unemployment are measured. After that, we introduce the wage-setting curve using the model of wage-setting from Unit 6. Then we describe how a single firm determines its employment level using the model of price setting from Unit 7. This will provide a reason why the price-setting curve is essential to understanding the labour market in the economy as a whole. We then show how the two curves together determine the equilibrium level of employment, the real wage, and the distribution of income between wages and profits. Finally, we use this model to explore the effect of changes in public policy such as taxation of firms' profits and workers' wages, subsidies to firms for hiring more labour, changes in the unemployment insurance benefit received by those out of work, and changes in the degree of competition among firms.

<aside>
wage-setting curve The curve that gives the real wage necessary at each level of economy-wide employment to provide workers with incentives to work hard and well.

price-setting curve The curve that gives the real wage paid when firms choose their profit-maximizing price.
</aside>

QUESTION 9.1 CHOOSE THE CORRECT ANSWER(S)
Which of the following statements is correct?

- ☐ To maximize profits, firms set the wage at the level where the workers are indifferent between working and not working.
- ☐ Firms aim to set as high a price as possible.
- ☐ In equilibrium, the wage clears the labour market, so there is no unemployment.
- ☐ If all firms set the same price and pay the same nominal wage, then the higher the real wage that they pay, the lower is their markup.

9.2 MEASURING THE ECONOMY: EMPLOYMENT AND UNEMPLOYMENT

According to the standardized definition of the International Labour Organization (ILO) (http://tinyco.re/8208329), the **unemployed** are the people who:

- were without work during a reference period (usually four weeks), which means they were not in paid employment or self-employment
- were available for work
- were seeking work, which means they had taken specific steps in that period to seek paid employment or self-employment

> **unemployment** A situation in which a person who is able and willing to work is not employed.

Figure 9.2 provides an overview of the labour market and shows how these components fit together. We begin on the left-hand side with the population. The next box shows the **population of working age**. This is the total population, minus children and those over 64. It is divided into two parts: the **labour force** and those out of the labour force (known as **inactive**). People out of the labour force are not employed or actively looking for work, for example, people unable to work due to sickness or disability, or parents who stay at home to raise children. Only members of the labour force can be considered as employed or unemployed.

> **population of working age** A statistical convention, which in many countries is all people aged between 15 and 64 years.
> **inactive population** People in the population of working age who are neither employed nor actively looking for paid work. Those working in the home raising children, for example, are not considered as being in the labour force and therefore are classified this way.
> **labour force** The number of people in the population of working age who are, or wish to be, in work outside the household. They are either employed (including self-employed) or unemployed. *See also: unemployment rate, employment rate, participation rate.*

There are a number of statistics that are useful for evaluating labour market performance in a country and for comparing labour markets across countries. The statistics depend on the relative sizes of the boxes shown in Figure 9.2. The first is the **participation rate**, which shows the proportion of the working age population that is in the labour force. It is calculated as follows:

> **participation rate** The ratio of the number of people in the labour force to the population of working age. *See also: labour force, population of working age.*

$$\text{participation rate} = \frac{\text{labour force}}{\text{population of working age}}$$
$$= \frac{\text{employed} + \text{unemployed}}{\text{population of working age}}$$

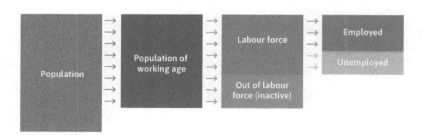

Figure 9.2 The labour market.

Next is the most commonly cited labour market statistic: the **unemployment rate**. This shows the proportion of the labour force that is unemployed. It is calculated as follows:

$$\text{unemployment rate} = \frac{\text{unemployed}}{\text{labour force}}$$

Lastly, we come to the **employment rate**, which shows the proportion of the population of working age that are in paid work or self-employed. It is calculated as follows:

$$\text{employment rate} = \frac{\text{employed}}{\text{population of working age}}$$

It is important to note that the denominator (the statistic on the bottom of the fraction) is different for the unemployment and the employment rate. Hence, two countries with the same unemployment rate can differ in their employment rates if one has a high participation rate and the other has a low one.

The table in Figure 9.3 provides a picture of the Norwegian and Spanish labour markets between 2000 and 2015, and shows how the labour market statistics relate to each other. It also shows that the structure of the labour market differs widely across countries. We can see that the Norwegian labour market worked better than the Spanish labour market in the last 15 years: Norway had a much higher employment rate and a much lower unemployment rate. Norway also had a higher participation rate, which is a reflection of the higher proportion of women in the labour force.

Norway and Spain are illustrations of two common cases. Norway is a low-unemployment, high-employment economy (the other Scandinavian countries—Sweden, Denmark, and Finland—are similar) and Spain is a high-unemployment, low-employment economy (the other southern European economies—Portugal, Italy and Greece—are other examples). Other combinations are possible, however: South Korea is an example of an economy that has both a low unemployment rate and a low employment rate.

unemployment rate The ratio of the number of the unemployed to the total labour force. (Note that the employment rate and unemployment rate do not sum to 100%, as they have different denominators.) *See also: labour force, employment rate.*

employment rate The ratio of the number of employed to the population of working age. *See also: population of working age.*

International Labour Association. 2015. *ILOSTAT Database* (http://tinyco.re/2173706).

	Norway	Spain
Number of persons, millions		
Population of working age	3.5	37.6
Labour force	2.5	21.6
Out of labour force (inactive)	1.0	16.0
Employed	2.4	18.1
Unemployed	0.1	3.5
Rates (%)		
Participation rate	2.5/3.5 = 71%	21.6/37.6 = 58%
Employment rate	2.4/3.5 = 69%	18.1/37.6 = 48%
Unemployment rate	0.1/2.5 = 4%	3.5/21.6 = 16%

Figure 9.3 Labour market statistics for Norway and Spain (averages over 2000–2015).

EXERCISE 9.1 EMPLOYMENT, UNEMPLOYMENT, AND PARTICIPATION

1. Visit the ILO's website and use the ILOSTAT Database (http://tinyco.re/ 2173706) to calculate the employment, unemployment, and participation rates for two economies of your choice.
2. Describe the differences in these two countries' data and compare them with Spain and Norway. Choose a visual representation of the data (for example, using the graph function of your spreadsheet software) and explain your choice.
3. After studying this unit, use the model of the labour market to suggest possible reasons for the differences in unemployment rates in these countries. You may need to find out more about the two countries' labour markets.

QUESTION 9.2 CHOOSE THE CORRECT ANSWER(S)
Which of the following statements is correct?

☐ participation rate = employed ÷ labour force
☐ unemployment rate = unemployed ÷ population of working age
☐ employment rate = employed ÷ population of working age
☐ employment rate + unemployment rate = 1

9.3 THE WAGE-SETTING CURVE: EMPLOYMENT AND REAL WAGES

We now build a model of the labour market that can help to explain differences in unemployment rates across countries, and changes over time within a country. To do this, we broaden the perspective from the single firm in Unit 6 to the whole economy, and we ask how changes in the unemployment rate affect the wage set by employers.

In Figure 9.4, the horizontal axis represents the proportion of the working-age population, and goes up to a value of 1. The vertical axis is the economy-wide wage.

- *The labour force is the vertical line furthest to the right*: it has a value less than 1, depending on the participation rate.
- *Inactive workers* are to the right of the labour force line.
- *The employment rate* is the vertical line to the left of the labour force, indicating the share of the population who are actually working.
- *The unemployment rate is the proportion of those in the labour force who are not employed*: that is, those workers in between the employment rate line and the labour force line.

Nash equilibrium A set of strategies, one for each player in the game, such that each player's strategy is a best response to the strategies chosen by everyone else.

The upward-sloping line is called the **wage-setting curve**. Like the best-effort response function of the employee on which it is based, the wage-setting curve is a mathematical version of an 'if-then' statement: if the employment rate is x, then the **Nash equilibrium** wage will be w. This means that at the employment rate x, the wage w is the result of both employers and employees doing the best they can in setting wages and responding to the wage with a given amount of effort, respectively.

This statement is true because the wage-setting curve for the whole economy is based directly on the employer's wage-setting decision and the employee's effort decision in an economy that is composed of many firms like the one we modelled in Unit 6.

We show how to do this in Figure 9.5 by bringing together Figure 9.4 (the economy-wide wage-setting curve) and Figure 6.6 (how the firm sets the wage). The top panel of Figure 9.5 shows the employee's best response curve at the two unemployment rates of 12% and 5%. As we saw in Unit 6, a higher unemployment rate reduces the reservation wage, because a worker faces a longer expected period of unemployment if he or she loses a job. This weakens the employees' bargaining power and shifts the best response curve to the left. With an unemployment rate of 12%, the reservation wage is shown by point F. The employer's profit-maximizing choice is point A with the low wage (w_L).

In the lower panel, we plot point A. The dashed line from unemployment of 12% indicates that the wage is set at w_L. We now assume a fixed size for the labour force and the horizontal axis gives the number of workers employed, N. As employment increases to the right, the unemployment rate falls.

Using exactly the same reasoning, we find the profit-maximizing wage set when unemployment is much lower at 5%. Both the reservation wage

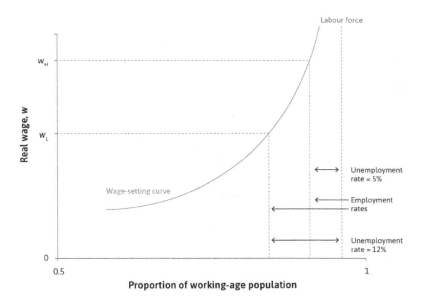

Figure 9.4 The wage-setting curve: Labour discipline and unemployment in the economy as a whole.

1. The wage-setting curve
The upward-sloping line is called the **wage-setting curve**.

2. The profit-maximizing wage when unemployment is high
At 12% unemployment in the economy, the employee's **reservation wage** is low and the worker will put in a high level of effort for a relatively low wage. The firm's profit-maximizing wage is therefore low.

3. The profit-maximizing wage when unemployment is low
At 5% unemployment in the economy, the employee's reservation wage is high and they will not put in much effort unless the wage is high. The firm's profit-maximizing wage is therefore higher.

and the wage set by the employer are higher, as shown by point B. This gives the second point on the wage-setting curve in the lower panel.

We derived the wage-setting curve as part of the labour discipline model, which was designed to illustrate how employees and firm owners (and their managers) interact when setting wages and determining the level of work effort. We will use the same model later when we describe policies to alter the level of unemployment in the entire economy. Later in this unit and in Units 16 and 17 we will look at the ways in which labour unions can affect the wage-setting process and so alter the workings of the labour market.

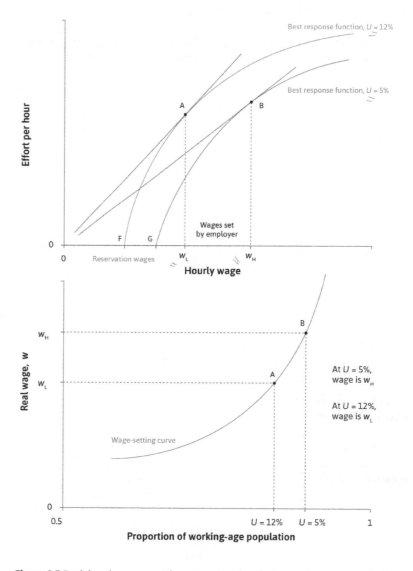

Figure 9.5 Deriving the wage-setting curve: Varying the unemployment rate in the economy.

Figure 9.6 is a wage-setting curve estimated from data for the US. Note that in Figure 9.6, the horizontal axis shows the unemployment rate explicitly, falling from left to right. By using data on unemployment rates and wages in local areas, economists can estimate and plot the wage-setting curve for an economy.

Wage-setting curves have been estimated for many economies. Read how it is done in an article by David Blanchflower and Andrew Oswald (http://tinyco.re/9574365).

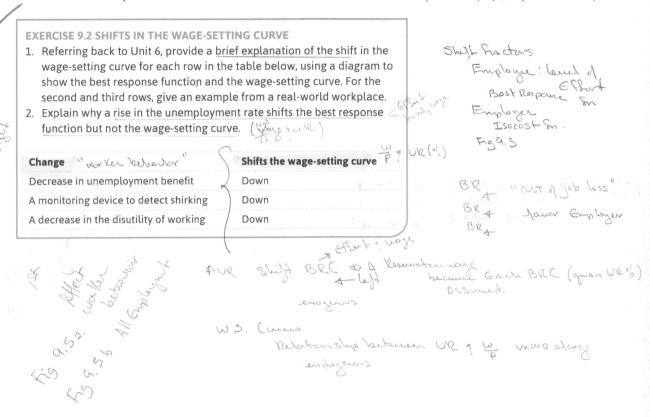

EXERCISE 9.2 SHIFTS IN THE WAGE-SETTING CURVE

1. Referring back to Unit 6, provide a brief explanation of the shift in the wage-setting curve for each row in the table below, using a diagram to show the best response function and the wage-setting curve. For the second and third rows, give an example from a real-world workplace.
2. Explain why a rise in the unemployment rate shifts the best response function but not the wage-setting curve.

Change	Shifts the wage-setting curve
Decrease in unemployment benefit	Down
A monitoring device to detect shirking	Down
A decrease in the disutility of working	Down

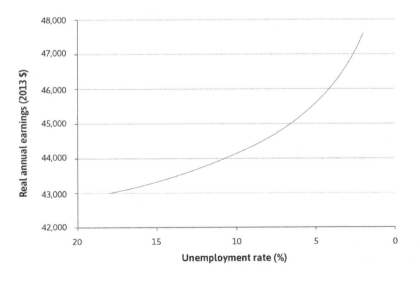

Estimated by Stephen Machin (UCL, 2015) from Current Population Survey microdata from the Outgoing Rotation Groups for 1979 to 2013.

Figure 9.6 A wage-setting curve estimated for the US economy (1979–2013).

QUESTION 9.3 CHOOSE THE CORRECT ANSWER(S)

Figure 9.5 (page 368) depicts the wage-setting curve and how it is derived using the best response function of the employees and the iso-cost lines for effort of the employers.

Based on this figure:

- ☐ A cut in the unemployment benefit would shift the best response function to the left, and raise the wage-setting curve.
- ☐ If the expected period of unemployment increased, it would shift the best response function to the right, raising the wage-setting curve.
- ☐ In a country where the stigma attached to unemployment is high, the wage-setting curve would be lower.
- ☐ A sudden drop in the working age population (due, for example, to the retirement of the baby-boomer generation) would shift the wage-setting curve lower.

9.4 THE FIRM'S HIRING DECISION

In order to understand the second component of the labour market model—the price-setting curve—we need to look more carefully at the firm's decision about how many people to hire, and how this depends on the amount that it produces. The amount produced depends on the amount that the firm is able to sell, which in turn depends on the price that it charges.

The firm's decision comes from the interaction between the firm's three departments. Recall in our model they are human resources (HR), the marketing department (MD), and the production department (PD). Remember this firm has only one input—labour—so the wage is the only cost. And to make things even simpler, we assume that one hour of labour produces one unit of output (average product of labour = $\lambda = 1$). So the wage the firm pays (W) is the cost of a unit of output (in the relevant currency unit). Note that W is the nominal wage and w is the real wage.

The process is summarized in the table in Figure 9.7.

labour productivity Total output divided by the number of hours or some other measure of labour input.

Once HR has set the wage at a level sufficient to motivate the workforce, the MD proceeds in two steps. Remember that the firm can set the price but not the quantity that it will be able to sell (quantity sold depends on the amount demanded at each price on the firm's demand curve). So first, as in Unit 7, the MD asks: which combinations of p and q are feasible? These combinations are shown by the demand curve, which will depend on the amounts that other firms are producing, the prices they are setting, the wages they are paying, and other influences on the total level of demand for goods in the economy.

Department	... knows	... and on this basis sets the firm's
Human resources	Prices, wages and employment in other firms	Nominal wage, W
Marketing	All of the above and firm's demand function	Price of output, p
Production	All of the above, plus **labour productivity** and amount the firm can sell	Employment, n

Figure 9.7 The three departments determine the firm's hiring.

Step two is to pick a point on the demand curve, so the MD looks at Figure 9.8 to determine how profitable each price-quantity combination would be. Using the value of W chosen by HR, the MD constructs the isoprofit curves shown. Recall that each curve is the collection of all combinations of price and quantity that will yield the firm the same level of profit, given the wage. Curves further out from the origin (higher price and quantity) indicate higher profits. Recall that:

$$\text{slope of the isoprofit curve} = \text{marginal rate of substitution}$$
$$= \frac{(p - W)}{q}$$

As in Unit 7, maximum profits occur at point B, where the demand curve is tangent to an isoprofit curve. The MD thus sets a price p^*, and calculates that it will be able to sell q^* units of the goods.

When the firm sells q^* goods at a price p^*, its total revenue is p^*q^*. Notice from the figure that once the firm has set a price, it has determined the division of the total revenue between profits and wages. This is based on the markup $(p - W)/p$ (or $1 - (W/p)$). As you have seen from Unit 7, this is greater when the demand curve is less elastic, indicating less intense competition.

The PD knows that each hour of a worker's time (working at the speed they are motivated to work by their employment rent and the threat of termination) produces a single unit of the good so it hires n^* workers' hours of labour, where $n^* = q^*$. This is the firm's (very simple) production function.

It will help in the next section to think about how the model explains what the firm would do if it found itself at a point like A. The MD would see that the firm was making lower profits because the isoprofit curve at A is lower than at point B. The MD would then raise the price and inform the

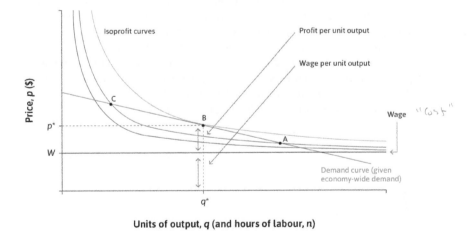

Figure 9.8 The firm's profit-maximizing choice of price, quantity, and employment.

1. Maximum profits
The maximum profits occur at point B where the firm's demand curve is tangent to an isoprofit curve.

2. The firm's price decision
This determines the division of the total revenue between profits and wages.

PD that it should produce less. Similarly, if the firm were at point C, the MD would lower its price and the PD would get the message to produce more, to meet the higher sales at the lower price.

QUESTION 9.4 CHOOSE THE CORRECT ANSWER(S)

Figure 9.8 (page 371) depicts the market's demand curve and the firm's isoprofit curves. Based on this information, which of the following statements is correct?

☐ The slope of the demand curve is the firm's marginal rate of substitution.

☐ Between points A and C, the firm would prefer point A as the output is higher.

☐ Having chosen its profit-maximizing price p*, the firm would then set its nominal wage level.

☐ If the firm finds itself producing at point C, it can increase its profit by selling more units at a lower price.

9.5 THE PRICE-SETTING CURVE: WAGES AND PROFITS IN THE WHOLE ECONOMY

We have seen in Figure 9.8 that when the firm sets the price as a markup on its wage cost, this means that the price per unit of output is split into the profit per unit and the wage cost per unit (Figure 9.8). For the economy as a whole, when all firms set prices this way, output per worker (labour productivity, or equivalently, the average product of labour, called lambda, λ) is split into real profit per worker Π/P and the real wage W/P (Figure 9.9).

Figure 9.9 shows the outcome of the price-setting decisions of firms in the whole economy and we use P to represent the economy-wide price level. The top horizontal line shows firms' revenues per worker in real terms: the average product of labour. What we call the price-setting 'curve' is not really much of a curve: it is just a single number that gives the value of the real wage that is consistent with the markup over costs, when all firms set their price to maximize their profits. The value of the real wage consistent with the markup does not depend on the level of employment in the economy, so it is shown as in Figure 9.9 as a horizontal line at the height of w^{PS}.

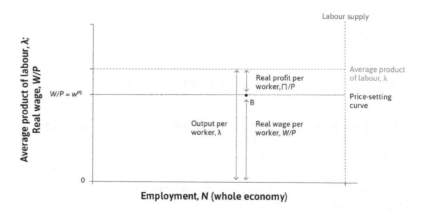

Figure 9.9 The price-setting curve.

Point B in Figures 9.9 and 9.10 on the price-setting curve shows the outcome of profit-maximizing price-setting behaviour of firms for the economy as a whole.

Now think about point A in Figure 9.10, which corresponds to point Ⓐ in Figure 9.8. Follow the steps in Figure 9.10 to see why the firm will raise its price so as to move towards higher profits at point Ⓑ The rise in price and the reduction in employment are indicated by the arrow at point A in Figure 9.10, which points down and to the left. It points down because the rise in prices implies a fall in the real wage, that is, the nominal wage divided by the price. It points left because a price increase implies a fall in output and employment.

EXERCISE 9.3 THE PRICE-SETTING CURVE

In your own words and using a diagram like Figure 9.8 (page 371), explain why prices would fall and employment would increase if the economy were at point C in Figure 9.10 (the opposite of what happens at point A).

In Figure 9.9, above the price-setting curve, like point Ⓐ firms raise prices and cut employment. Below the price-setting curve, at a point like Ⓒ firms lower prices and hire more people. Given the level of demand in the economy as a whole, firms' pricing and hiring behavior will push the economy

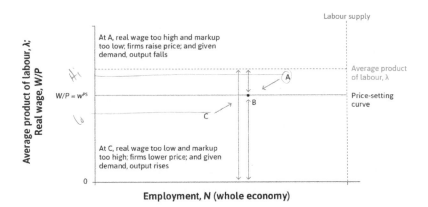

Figure 9.10 The price-setting curve.

1. Point A

Point A is above the price-setting curve, which means that the real wage is higher than is consistent with a firm's profit maximizing markup. If the real wage is too high, it means the markup is too low.

2. Point B

The firm will raise its price so as to move towards higher profits at point B. The increased price will mean that fewer goods are sold, and as this is true of all firms, total employment falls.

3. Point C

Below the price-setting curve, at a point like C, firms lower their prices and hire more people.

4. The profit-maximizing price

Point B is the firm's profit-maximizing price and profit margin. Given economy-wide demand, total profits are lower at A and C for firms facing the demand curve in Figure 9.8.

to a point on the price-setting curve so that the level of employment and real wage are at a point like B.

What will determine the height of the price-setting curve? There are many influences once we consider the impact of public policies (as we will see later in this unit), but two things have an important influence on the price-setting curve, even in the absence of government intervention:

- *Competition*: The intensity of competition in the economy determines the extent to which firms can charge a price that exceeds their costs, that is, the markup. The less the competition, the greater the markup. In Figure 9.8, a steeper demand curve, which results from less competition among firms, will lead to a higher markup and increase the profit per worker. Since this leads to higher prices across the whole economy, it implies lower real wages, pushing down the price-setting curve.
- *Labour productivity*: For any given markup, the level of labour productivity—how much a worker produces in an hour—determines the real wage. The greater the level of labour productivity (λ), the higher the real wage that is consistent with a given markup. In Figure 9.8, higher labour productivity shifts the dashed line upwards, and, keeping the markup unchanged, the price-setting curve will shift upwards, raising the real wage.

To understand more about the price-setting curve, read the Einstein at the end of this section.

QUESTION 9.5 CHOOSE THE CORRECT ANSWER(S)

The following diagram depicts the price-setting curve. Based on this information, which of the following statements is correct?

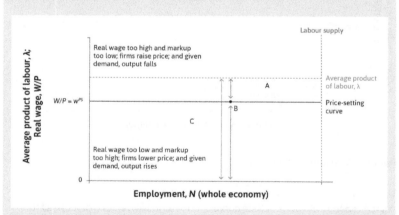

- ☐ At point A, the markup is too high, and therefore the firm will raise its price. This leads to lower demand for the good and hence lower employment towards B.
- ☐ At point C, the real wage is too low and the markup is too high. Therefore the firm is able to increase profit by lowering prices and hiring more workers.
- ☐ Higher competition implies a lower price-setting curve.
- ☐ For any given markup, higher labour productivity implies a lower price-setting curve, which means a lower real wage.

EINSTEIN

The price-setting curve

There are several steps to show how the price-setting curve for the economy as a whole results from the decisions of individual firms.

Step 1: The firm sets its price

To focus on what is essential, we assume the firm's only costs are the wages it pays. (We are setting aside the opportunity cost of the capital goods which the workers use in producing the firm's output.) We assume that on average a worker produces λ units of output, which does not vary with the number of workers employed. We use the Greek letter lambda (λ) for labour productivity. The firm pays the worker a wage W in dollars. Both labour productivity and wages can be measured per hour, per day or per year. In our numerical examples, we typically use hourly wages and productivity.

The unit labour cost is the wages paid to hire the amount of labour to produce one unit of the good. This is defined as:

$$\text{unit labour cost} = \frac{\text{nominal wage}}{\text{labour productivity}}$$
$$= \frac{W}{\lambda}$$

For example: if $W = \$30$ and $\lambda = 10$, then unit labour cost is $3, that is $30/10 units = $3 per unit.

Recall from Unit 7 that the firm chooses its price so that the markup is inversely proportional to the elasticity of the demand curve it faces:

$$\frac{(\text{price} - \text{marginal cost})}{\text{price}} = \frac{1}{\text{elasticity}}$$

Or because we have assumed that marginal and average costs are equal, that is, MC = AC, we can say that the markup is just the fraction of the price of a good that goes to the profits of the firm. The elasticity of the firm's demand curve is greater the more competition the firm faces from other firms, so the higher the elasticity, the lower the firm's price and markup. We call the markup μ (the Greek letter mu, rhyming with 'few'):

$$\mu = \frac{1}{\text{elasticity}} = \frac{P - C}{P} = \frac{\text{Profits per unit}}{\text{Price per unit}}$$

Using our assumptions, the firm's marginal (and average) cost is its unit labour cost (W/λ), and we can say that the firm sets its price, p, so that:

$$\mu = \frac{p - (\frac{W}{\lambda})}{p}$$
$$= 1 - \frac{\frac{W}{p}}{\lambda}$$

375

Rearranging, and multiplying each side by λ gives:

$$\frac{\frac{W}{P}}{\lambda} = 1 - \mu$$

$$\frac{W}{p} = \lambda(1 - \mu)$$

$$= \lambda - \lambda\mu$$

In words, this says:

real wage = output per worker(λ)
− real profit per worker($\lambda\mu$)

When the firm sets its profit-maximizing price, this splits output per worker into the part that goes to employees as wages and the part that goes to owners as profits.

Step 2: The price level in the economy as a whole and the real wage

From the employee's point of view, the real wage measures how much of her typical consumption she can purchase with an hour's earnings. Since she buys many different goods and services, this depends on prices set by the firms throughout the economy, not just her own firm. We call the average price of the goods and services the worker consumes, P, which is an average of the different levels of p set by individual firms across the economy.

The real wage is the nominal wage divided by the economy-wide price level, P.

$$\text{real wage} = \frac{\text{nominal wage}}{\text{price level}}$$

$$w = \frac{W}{P}$$

Step 3: Profits, wages, and the price-setting curve

We assume that the entire economy is made up of firms facing competition conditions similar to the single firm we have just studied. This means the price-setting problem from Step 1 applies to all firms in the economy, so we can use the price-setting equation to determine the economy-wide real wage:

$$\text{Price-setting curve} : \frac{W}{P} = \lambda(1 - \mu)$$

In words, this says that:

$$\text{real wage}(\frac{W}{P}) = \text{output per worker}(\lambda) -$$

$$\text{real profit per worker}(\lambda\mu)$$

This is the wage indicated by the price-setting curve.

9.6 WAGES, PROFITS, AND UNEMPLOYMENT IN THE WHOLE ECONOMY

By superimposing the wage-setting curve on the price-setting curve in Figure 9.11, we have a picture of the two sides of the labour market.

All of the points in the shaded area below the wage-setting curve are labeled 'no work done' because in this region the real wage is insufficient to motivate workers to work. In this situation, there is no work done and no profits, so nobody is hired: the only outcome possible in the long run if the real wage is below the wage-setting curve is zero employment. These shaded points are not feasible.

The equilibrium of the labour market is where the wage- and price-setting curves intersect. This is a **Nash equilibrium** because all parties are doing the best they can, given what everyone else is doing. Each firm is setting the nominal wage where the isocost curve is tangent to the best response function (Unit 6), and is setting the profit-maximizing price (Unit 7). Taking the economy as a whole, at the intersection of the wage and price setting curves (point X):

- The firms are offering the wage that ensures effective work from employees at least cost (that is, on the wage-setting curve). HR cannot recommend an alternative policy that would deliver higher profits.
- Employment is the highest it can be (on the price-setting curve), given the wage offered. The marketing department cannot recommend a change in price or output.
- Those who have jobs cannot improve their situation by changing their behaviour. If they worked less on the job, they would run the risk of becoming one of the unemployed, and if they demanded more pay, their employer would refuse or hire someone else.
- Those who fail to get jobs would rather have a job, but there is no way they can get one—not even by offering to work at a lower wage than others.

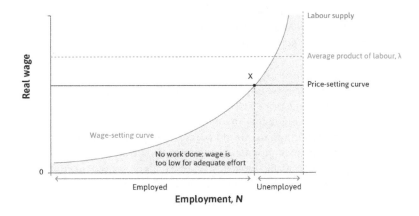

Figure 9.11 Equilibrium in the labour market.

Unemployment as a characteristic of labour market equilibrium
We have shown that unemployment can exist in Nash equilibrium in the labour market.

labour market equilibrium The combination of the real wage and the level of employment determined by the intersection of the wage-setting and price-setting curves. This is the Nash equilibrium of the labour market because neither employers nor workers could do better by changing their behaviour. *See also: equilibrium unemployment, inflation-stabilizing rate of unemployment.*

equilibrium unemployment The number of people seeking work but without jobs, which is determined by the intersection of the wage-setting and price-setting curves. This is the Nash equilibrium of the labour market where neither employers nor workers could do better by changing their behaviour. *See also: involuntary unemployment, cyclical unemployment, wage-setting curve, price-setting curve, inflation-stabilizing rate of unemployment.*

excess supply A situation in which the quantity of a good supplied is greater than the quantity demanded at the current price. *See also: excess demand.*

We now show why there will *always* be unemployment in **labour market equilibrium**, using the argument from Unit 6. This is called **equilibrium unemployment**.

Unemployment means that there are people seeking work but not finding it. This is also termed **excess supply** in the labour market, meaning that demand for labour at the given wage is lower than the number of workers willing to work at that wage. To understand why there will always be unemployment in labour market equilibrium, we refer to the labour supply curve.

In our model, we assume that the labour supply curve is vertical, meaning that higher wages do not lead more people to offer more hours at work. At higher wages some people seek (and find) more hours of work, and others seek (and find) shorter hours. You know from Unit 3 that the substitution effect of a wage increase (leading to the choice of more hours of work and less of free time) may be offset by the income effect. For simplicity we draw a supply curve such that the wage has no effect on the labour supply. But this is not important. The model would not be different if higher wages led to either more or fewer people seeking work. To see this, you can experiment with labour supply curves with different shapes in Figure 9.11.

Why will there always be some involuntary unemployment in labour market equilibrium?

- *If there was no unemployment*: The cost of job loss is zero (no employment rent) because a worker who loses her job can immediately get another one at the same pay.
- *Therefore some unemployment is necessary*: It means the employer can motivate workers to provide effort on the job.
- *Therefore the wage-setting curve is always to the left of the labour supply curve.*
- *It follows that in any equilibrium, where the wage and price-setting curves intersect, there must be unemployed people*: This is shown by the gap between the wage-setting curve and the labour supply curve.

Another way to see this is to look again at Figure 9.11. Notice that the wage-setting curve rises steeply when it comes close to the labour supply line, exceeding both the price-setting and labour productivity curves. This fact about our model highlights an important limit on policies to reduce unemployment. According to our model, any policy that comes close to entirely eliminating unemployment would put employers in a position that the best they could do would be to pay wages so high they would eliminate the employers' profits and drive the firms out of business.

EXERCISE 9.4 IS THIS REALLY A NASH EQUILIBRIUM?
In this model, the unemployed are no different from the employed (except for their bad luck). Imagine you are an employer, and one of the unemployed comes to you and promises to work at the same effort level as your current workers but at slightly lower wage.

1. How would you reply?
2. Does your reply help explain why unemployment must exist in a Nash equilibrium?

QUESTION 9.6 CHOOSE THE CORRECT ANSWER(S)
Figure 9.11 (page 377) depicts the labour market model. Consider now a reduction in the degree of competition faced by the firms. Which of the following statements is correct regarding the effects of reduced competition?

☐ The price-setting curve shifts up.
☐ The wage-setting curve shifts down.
☐ The equilibrium real wage falls.
☐ The unemployment level falls.

QUESTION 9.7 CHOOSE THE CORRECT ANSWER(S)
Which of the following statements is correct regarding the effects of a rise in the real wage on the labour supply of a worker?

☐ The income effect means that the worker will increase his labour supply.
☐ The substitution effect means that the worker will increase his consumption of free time.
☐ The income and substitution effects always enhance each other, leading to higher labour supply.
☐ At high wage levels, the income effect dominates the substitution effect, leading to lower labour supply.

9.7 HOW CHANGES IN DEMAND FOR GOODS AND SERVICES AFFECT UNEMPLOYMENT

derived demand

At the beginning of this unit, you read about the father and son working in the Australian minerals sector (Doug and Rob Grey). The boom and bust in their lives reflected changes in economic conditions in the Australian economy as a whole. The minerals boom had produced the large-scale construction of mining facilities in Western Australia, Queensland, and the Northern Territory. As construction was coming to an end on existing projects, global iron ore prices collapsed, with the result that new mines, ports and processing facilities were not started. In Figure 9.1, unemployment began to rise as the global price of iron ore plummeted.

Unemployment increased because the demand for labour in mining and in the related service activities shrank. Not only did the demand for minerals fall off, but demand also declined for the goods and services that the Grey family and others like them would have purchased if they had kept their jobs. As a result, demand for goods and services fell across the economy, and with it the derived demand for labour. The term 'derived demand for labour' is used to highlight the fact that the firms' demand for labour depends on the demand for their goods and services.

Economists use the term *aggregate*—meaning added up to measure the whole, not just the parts—to describe economy-wide facts or variables. Aggregate demand, for example, is the sum of the demand for all of the goods and services produced in the economy, whether from consumers, firms, the government, or buyers in other countries. The increase in unemployment caused by the fall in aggregate demand is called 'demand-deficient' unemployment—or, as we shall learn in Unit 13, **cyclical unemployment**.

How does this demand-deficient unemployment appear in our model of the labour market, and how does it relate to unemployment in the Nash equilibrium of the labour market?

Follow the steps in Figure 9.12 to compare unemployment in the labour market equilibrium (at X) with the unemployment caused by a low level of aggregate demand (at B). An unemployed person at X is **involuntarily unemployed** because that person would accept a job at the real wage shown by the intersection of the wage and price-setting curves.

An unemployed person at point B is also involuntarily unemployed. In fact, such a person would accept a job with a wage below the wage shown at B, and still be willing to work hard on the job.

> **cyclical unemployment** The increase in unemployment above equilibrium unemployment caused by a fall in aggregate demand associated with the business cycle. *Also known as: demand-deficient unemployment. See also: equilibrium unemployment.*

> **unemployment, involuntary** The state of being out of work, but preferring to have a job at the wages and working conditions that otherwise identical employed workers have. *See also: unemployment.*

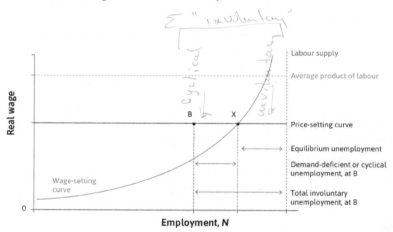

Figure 9.12 Equilibrium and demand-deficient (cyclical) unemployment.

1. Point X

At X, unemployment is at its labour market equilibrium level. Someone losing a job at X is not indifferent between being employed and unemployed because they experience a cost of losing the job.

2. Point B

At B, there are additional people looking for work who are also involuntarily unemployed. The additional unemployment at B is due to low aggregate demand and is called demand-deficient, or cyclical, unemployment.

3. The Nash equilibrium

At point B, total involuntary unemployment is given by the sum of cyclical and equilibrium unemployment. Point X is the Nash equilibrium of the labour market, which means that all actors are doing the best they can, given the actions of the other actors. No worker or firm can improve their position by changing their actions.

We term the level of joblessness at point X equilibrium unemployment, but what about point B? Could high demand-deficient unemployment be a long-term outcome? Will the behaviour of firms and workers result in the disappearance of the unemployment caused by insufficient aggregate demand?

We can see that B is not a Nash equilibrium. At this point the HR department—noting the high unemployment rate—would definitely say: 'With such high unemployment, we could pay our workers much less and they would still do their work!' Because the firm could make higher profits by lowering the wage, as long as it remained above the wage-setting curve, B is not a Nash equilibrium.

But even so, an outcome such as B could persist for a long time, without public policies to expand employment.

To see why, we first need to understand how a decision to lower the wage by HR departments across the economy could (under the right circumstances) lead to the disappearance of cyclical unemployment. Imagine the economy was at point B (with all firms at points like B in Figure 9.8). Then the following sequence would take place, initiated by HR:

- Lower wages would lower costs.
- The degree of competition facing the firm has not changed, so it would want to set a price to restore the profit-maximizing markup.
- Given the lower costs, firms would therefore cut prices.
- Because the demand curve facing the firm is downward-sloping they would sell more, expanding output and employment.

Figure 9.13 shows the firm's adjustment process. The wage is cut to the lower level by HR, and given the lower costs, the MD cuts the price to maximize profit. Firms would move to the right along their demand curve. Output and employment increase.

To see where the firm's price cutting will stop, think about the new iso-profit curves once the cost of hiring labour has declined. Remember from Unit 7 that as the cost (C) has fallen, at every point on the isoprofit curve is now at a higher profit level than was the case prior to the decline in wages.

Importantly, it is also steeper than before. Recall that the slope of the isoprofit curve is $(p − C)/q$ so that for example, at point B (q^*, p^*) the slope of the isoprofit curve with the higher wage is steeper.

Follow the steps in Figure 9.13 to see where the firm will set its price.

T. Bewley. 2007. 'Fairness, Reciprocity and Wage Rigidity'. *Behavioral Economics and its Applications*, edited by Peter Diamond and Hannu Vartiainen, pp. 157–188. Princeton, NJ: Princeton University Press.

C. M. Campbell and K. S. Kamlani. 1997. 'The reasons for wage rigidity: Evidence from a survey of firms'. *The Quarterly Journal of Economics* 112 (3) (August): pp. 759–789.

What could go wrong?

This process explains how wage and price cutting might lead the economy to move from B back to X. But real economies do not function so smoothly. What could possibly go wrong?

Worker resistance to a reduction in the nominal wage

The HR department would know that lowering the nominal wages of its employees would not be a simple matter, because it means that the actual monetary amount received by all existing workers would have to be smaller. As we saw in Unit 6, firms are often reluctant to cut nominal wages because it may reduce worker morale and result in conflict with employees. Strikes and worker resistance such as informal 'go slow' tactics would disrupt the production process. For these reasons the HR department might hesitate to impose nominal wage cuts on its workers.

Wage and price reductions might not lead to higher sales and employment

For the adjustment from B to X to occur, firms across the economy have to adjust wages and prices downward, and in response, firms and households have to increase their demand for goods and services by enough to restore economy-wide (or aggregate) demand to its level at point X. For the individual firm, a fall in price leads to higher sales. But falling prices across the economy can lead to cutbacks in spending, which shift the demand curves facing firms to the left. Falling prices can lead households to postpone

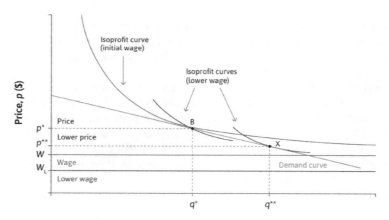

Figure 9.13 A firm raises output and employment following a cut in wages.

1. The new isoprofit curve
The new (lower wage) isoprofit curve passing through the original point B is now steeper than the demand curve, so the firm can do better by lowering its price and moving down the demand curve, selling more.

2. Maximum profits
It will continue doing this until it reaches a point on the demand curve where one of the new darker blue isoprofit curves is tangent to the demand curve. The firm maximizes profits at point X.

spending, as they hope to get better bargains later. The gap in spending would be exacerbated by such behaviour. Moreover, as wages fall people may spend less, reducing demand.

Thus, in the presence of deficient aggregate demand, the usual profit-seeking decisions of firms and the responses of consumers, when added up across the economy, cannot be guaranteed to move the economy from B to the Nash equilibrium at X.

The role of government policy

Fortunately, there is another way to get from B back to the Nash equilibrium. The government could adopt policies to increase its own spending and expand the demand facing the firms. In this case, at point B firms would find that they were producing less than the profit-maximizing amount and would employ more people, instead of wanting to reduce wages. Policies to affect the total demand in the economy are considered in Units 13–17.

Figure 9.14 illustrates this case. As before, the economy begins (following the fall in economy-wide demand) at point B. Rather than either waiting for a revival in aggregate demand (for example, through a recovery in global demand for minerals) or waiting for the process of wage and price reductions to spread across the economy, the government can increase the level of aggregate demand.

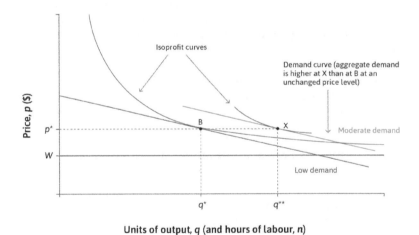

Figure 9.14 A firm raises output and employment following an increase in demand as a result of monetary or fiscal policy.

1. Before the increase in demand
As before, the firm begins at point B.

2. The demand curve shifts to the right
Remember, the isoprofit curves do not shift when the demand curve shifts. The firm moves on to a new higher isoprofit curve if demand rises as a result of higher economy-wide demand following monetary or fiscal policy actions.

monetary policy Central bank (or government) actions aimed at influencing economic activity through changing interest rates or the prices of financial assets. *See also: quantitative easing.*

fiscal policy Changes in taxes or government spending in order to stabilize the economy. *See also: fiscal stimulus, fiscal multiplier, aggregate demand.*

One method is for the central bank to make borrowing cheaper by reducing the interest rate. The aim is to provide incentives for people to bring forward some of their spending decisions, particularly on things that are often purchased with borrowed money such as housing and automobiles. We look closely at this **monetary policy** in Unit 10 (Banks, money and the credit market) and in Unit 15 (Inflation, unemployment and monetary policy). Other methods are for the government to increase its spending or reduce tax rates. These **fiscal policies** are the subject of Unit 14 (Unemployment and fiscal policy).

We can summarize what we have learned in Figures 9.15 a–c. When aggregate demand in the economy is too low, unemployment is higher than at the Nash equilibrium. The government or central bank can eliminate this demand-deficient unemployment through fiscal or monetary policy. These policies are likely to be a more rapid way of reducing unemployment compared to solely relying on the combination of downward adjustment of wages and prices by firms throughout the economy and increased demand by households and firms for goods and services.

The adjustment via fiscal or monetary policy is shown in Figure 9.15a, the adjustment via wage and price cuts is shown in Figure 9.15b, and the aggregate labour market is shown in Figure 9.15c.

EXERCISE 9.5 WAGES AND AGGREGATE DEMAND

We saw that if an economy has low aggregate demand with high cyclical unemployment, then automatic adjustment back to equilibrium could occur through a process of wage and price cuts. Imagine you are a worker and you see that many workers have lost their jobs while other workers are having their wages cut.

1. How might this affect your spending and saving decisions?
2. How might this affect adjustment back to equilibrium?

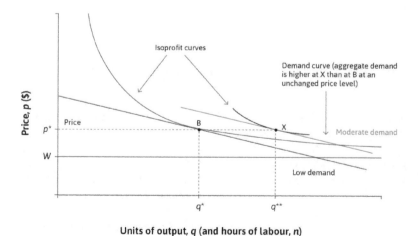

Figure 9.15a The firm: Adjustment to equilibrium unemployment at X via fiscal or monetary policy.

QUESTION 9.8 CHOOSE THE CORRECT ANSWER(S)

Figure 9.12 (page 380) depicts the labour market when there has been a negative aggregate demand shock. Based on this information, which of the following statements is correct?

☐ The new equilibrium B is a Nash equilibrium.
☐ At B, unemployment is purely cyclical.
☐ At B, the firms are able to make higher profits by lowering the wage.
☐ The adjustment back from B to X is immediate.

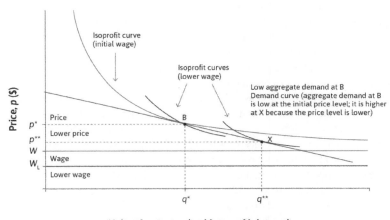

Figure 9.15b The firm: Adjustment to equilibrium unemployment at X via wage and price cuts.

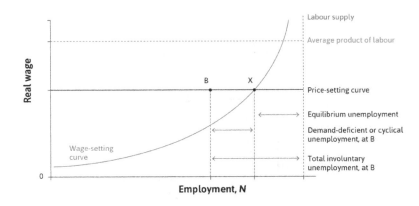

Figure 9.15c Aggregate labour market: cyclical and equilibrium unemployment.

9.8 LABOUR MARKET EQUILIBRIUM AND THE DISTRIBUTION OF INCOME

As we have seen, the labour market model determines not only the level of employment, unemployment, and the wage rate, but also the division of the economy's output between workers (both employed and unemployed) and employers. So the labour market model is also a model of the distribution of income in a simple economy in which there are just these two classes (employers, who are the owners of the firms, and workers), where some of the latter are without work.

As we did in Unit 5, we can construct the Lorenz curve and calculate the Gini coefficient for the economy in this model. Refer back to the Einstein in Unit 5 on the Lorenz curve and to the Einstein at the end of this section, which explain how to calculate the Gini coefficient with different kinds of information about a population.

In the left panel of Figure 9.16 we show the labour market of an economy with 80 identical employees of 10 identical firms. As you can see, there are 10 unemployed people. Each firm has a single owner. The economy is in equilibrium at point A, where the real wage is both sufficient to motivate workers to work and consistent with the firm's profit-maximizing price markup over costs ($w = 0.6$ in this case).

The right-hand panel shows the Lorenz curve for income in this economy. Because the unemployed people receive no income if there are no unemployment benefits, the Lorenz curve (the solid blue line) begins on the horizontal axis to the right of the left-hand corner. The price-setting curve in the left panel indicates that total output is divided up so that workers receive a 60% share and their employers receive the rest. In the right panel this is shown by the second 'kink' in the Lorenz curve, where we see that the poorest 90 people in the population (the 10 unemployed workers and the 80 employees, shown on the horizontal axis) receive 60% of the total output (on the vertical axis).

The size of the shaded area measures the extent of inequality, and the Gini coefficient is 0.36. To learn how to calculate the Gini coefficient from information like this see the Einstein at the end of this section.

The Lorenz curve is made up of three line segments with the beginning point having coordinates of (0, 0) and the endpoint (1, 1). The first kink in the curve occurs when we have counted all the unemployed people.

The second is the interior point, whose coordinates are (fraction of total number of economically active population, fraction of total output received

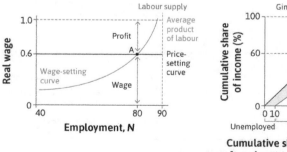

Figure 9.16 The distribution of income at labour market equilibrium.

in wages). The fraction of output received in wages, called the wage share in total income, s, is:

$$s = \text{wage share}$$
$$= \frac{\text{real wage per worker day}}{\text{output per worker day}}$$
$$= \frac{w}{\lambda}$$

Therefore the shaded area in the figure—and hence inequality measured by the Gini coefficient—will increase if:

- *A larger fraction of the employees are without work (higher unemployment rate)*: The first kink shifts right.
- *The real wage falls (or equivalently, the markup rises) and nothing else changes*: The second kink shifts down.
- *Productivity rises and nothing else changes (real wages do not rise)*: This implies that the markup rises, so again the second kink shifts down.

Factors that affect labour market equilibrium: Unemployment and inequality

What can change the level of employment and the distribution of income between profits and wages in equilibrium? Follow the steps in Figure 9.17 to see what would happen if there were an increase in the degree of competition faced by firms, perhaps as a result of a decrease in the barriers to firms from other countries competing in this economy's markets.

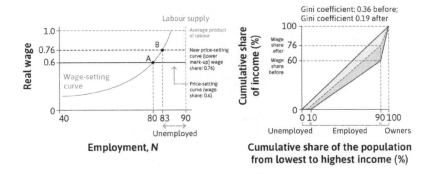

Figure 9.17 The effect of an increase in the extent of competition faced by firms: The price-setting curve shifts up and inequality falls.

1. The initial equilibrium
We start from the equilibrium at A with a Gini coefficient of 0.36. Suppose that the degree of competition faced by firms is increased.

2. A new equilibrium
The markup charged by firms in the market will decrease, and so the price-setting curve will be higher. The new equilibrium is at B.

3. A new Gini coefficient
At the new equilibrium there is a higher wage and a higher level of employment. Stronger competition means that firms have weaker market power: the share going to profits falls, and the share going to wages rises. Inequality falls: the new Gini coefficient is 0.19.

The markup would decrease, and as a result the real wage shown by the price-setting curve would increase, leading to a new equilibrium at point B with a higher wage and a higher level of employment. The share of output going to profits falls, and the share going to wages rises.

QUESTION 9.9 CHOOSE THE CORRECT ANSWER(S)

Figure 9.16 (page 386) is the Lorenz curve associated with a particular labour market equilibrium. In a population of 100, there are 10 firms, each with a single owner, 80 employed workers, and 10 unemployed workers. The employed workers receive 60% of the total income as wages. The Gini coefficient is 0.36. In which of the following cases would the Gini coefficient increase, keeping all other factors unchanged?

☐ A rise in the unemployment rate.
☐ A rise in the real wage.
☐ A rise in the workers' productivity while the real wage is unchanged.
☐ A rise in the degree of competition faced by the firms.

EINSTEIN

The Lorenz curve and the Gini coefficient in an economy with unemployed, employed, and employers (owners)

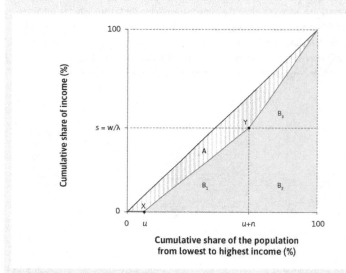

We now use the figure to derive an equation for the value of the Gini coefficient in terms of the following variables:

- u, the fraction of the population that is unemployed
- n, the fraction of the population that is employed
- w, the real wage
- q, output per employed worker
- $s = w/q$, the wage share received by workers

Recall that the Gini coefficient is equal to the area A divided by the area under the 45-degree line, and so it is equal to $A/0.5 = 2A$. We calculate A as $0.5 - B$ where $B = B_1 + B_2 + B_3$:

$$B_1 = \frac{1}{2}ns$$

$$B_2 = (1 - u - n)s$$

$$B_3 = \frac{1}{2}(1 - u - n)(1 - s)$$

Rearranging these variables gives us:

$$B = B_1 + B_2 + B_3$$
$$= \frac{1}{2}ns + (1 - u - n)s + \frac{1}{2}(1 - u - n)(1 - s)$$
$$= \frac{1}{2}(1 - u - n) + \frac{1}{2}(1 - u)s$$

This implies that the Gini coefficient is:

$$g = 2A$$
$$= 1 - (1 - u - n) - (1 - u)s$$
$$= u + n - (1 - u)s$$

Recall that $s = w/q$. What can we learn from the expression:

$$g = u + n - (1 - u)\frac{w}{q}?$$

- *If the class of employers gets relatively smaller:* Then $u + n$ rises. This implies that g rises, and point Y shifts right on the Lorenz curve: inequality goes up. This is because the same amount of profit is divided among fewer people, so they are even richer than before. This could depict the early evolution of capitalism from an economy of smallish family-owned firms and manufacturers, each employing a few workers, to a modern economy with concentrated wealth.
- *An increase in the wage share w/q, ceteris paribus, will reduce the Gini coefficient:* This shifts point Y upwards.
- *If all firms are cooperatives:* If there are no employers and the workers keep all that they produce ($w/q = 1$), then the Gini coefficient declines to $g = n - 1$ and point Y moves to the top right corner. If in addition there is no unemployment, then $u = 0$ and $n = 1$, so $g = 0$: there is perfect equality because everyone is a worker receiving an identical wage. This assumes productivity remains unchanged.
- *As we saw in the Einstein in Unit 5, this calculation does not work if the population is small:* In this case the formula we derived for the Gini coefficient does not equal 1 when a single person receives all of the income—as it should. To show this, suppose that $w = 0$, so the only income goes to the employers. Then in our formula above $g = u + n$. Now imagine that there are 10 people in the population, just one of whom is the employer. Then $g = 0.9$ when the Gini is really equal to 1. This is the small population bias. If you calculate the Gini coefficient by taking differences among pairs of people in the population, your result for g will not be subject to this small population bias. Alternatively, you can multiply the g calculated above by $N/(N - 1)$ to correct the bias, where N is the size of the population: multiplying 0.9 by 10/9 gives $g = 1$.

9.9 LABOUR SUPPLY, LABOUR DEMAND, AND BARGAINING POWER

Even though the supply of labour must always exceed demand for labour at the labour market equilibrium (there is always some involuntary unemployment), the supply of labour is still one of the important determinants of this Nash equilibrium. To see why this is so, imagine that there is immigration of people looking for employment (assume these immigrants are potential employees, as opposed to people who intend to start up a business), or that people who have stayed at home to raise children, or have retired, re-join the labour force.

What effect would this have? Let's look first at what happens to the wage-setting curve following an increase in labour supply:

- new jobseekers would enter the pool of unemployed
- which would increase the expected duration of a spell of unemployment
- by raising the cost of job loss, this increases the employment rent enjoyed by employed workers at the current wage and level of employment
- but firms would then be paying more than necessary to ensure worker motivation on the job …
- … therefore firms would lower their wages

This process is true for any point on the wage-setting curve, so it must be true of the entire curve. Therefore, the effect of an increase in labour supply is to shift the wage-setting curve downward.

Changes in labour supply: The effects of immigration

We use an increase in the labour supply due to immigration as an example. The labour supply curve would shift to the right, as shown in Figure 9.18.

In this story, the short-run impact of immigration is bad for existing workers in that country: wages fall and the expected duration of unemployment increases. In the long run, however, the increased profitability of firms leads to expanded employment that eventually (if no further changes take place) will restore the real wage and return the economy to its initial rate of unemployment. As a result, incumbent workers are no worse off. Immigrants are likely to be economically better off too—especially if they left their home country because it was difficult to make a living.

We summarize the effects of the increase in labour supply on the labour market:

- The shift downward in the wage-setting curve at the initial level of employment lowered the wage (to B).
- The reduction in the wage results in a reduction in the firms' marginal costs and with no change in the firm's demand conditions, the firms will hire additional workers.
- As a result, employment expands so that once again the economy is at the intersection of the price-setting curve and the new wage-setting curve, with higher employment.
- The increase in labour supply leads to a new equilibrium at higher employment because it shifts the wage-setting curve down. New hiring stops when the wage is once again at the level shown by the price-setting curve (at C). In the new equilibrium, employment is higher and the real wage is unchanged.

EXERCISE 9.6 IMMIGRATION OF ENTREPRENEURS
Suppose that some of the immigrants to the country decide to set up businesses, rather than become employees. Explain how you expect this to affect the wage-setting curve, the price-setting curve, and the labour market equilibrium.

QUESTION 9.10 CHOOSE THE CORRECT ANSWER(S)
Figure 9.16 (page 386) depicts the model of a labour market where there are 90 million workers. The current labour market equilibrium is at A. Now consider the case where the total labour supply is increased to 100 million. Based on this information, which of the following statements are correct regarding the adjustment process in the labour market?

☐ Initially, unemployment doubles.
☐ Higher unemployment results in a reduction in the employment rent enjoyed by workers employed at the current wage.
☐ The firms are required to raise wages to induce workers to work hard.
☐ The wage-setting curve shifts downward.

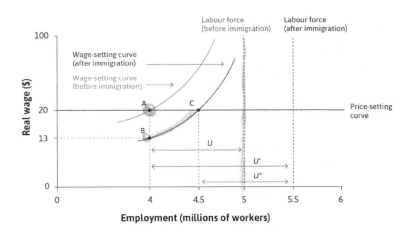

Figure 9.18 The effect of immigration on unemployment.

1. The initial situation
The economy starts at point A, employing 4 million workers at a wage of $20 per hour and a labour force of 5 million.

2. One million workers are unemployed
This is shown by the distance U.

3. Immigrant workers join the labour force
This increases the labour force from 5 million to 5.5 million workers.

4. The wage-setting curve shifts downward
At any level of employment there are now more unemployed workers. The rise in unemployment to 1.5 million is shown by distance U′. The threat of job loss is greater and firms can secure effort from the workforce at a lower wage.

5. Firms lower the wage
The wage is now set at point B on the wage-setting curve in the figure, with the wage at $13 an hour and employment still at 4 million.

6. Profits rise
This causes firms to hire more workers, which requires rising wages along the wage-setting curve. The labour market moves from point B to point C.

7. Employment and wages rise
They rise until they reach the price-setting curve, meaning profits are consistent with market competition again. At point C, employment is 4.5 million workers, the wage is $20, and unemployment has fallen back to 1 million workers, as shown by distance U″.

● ●●●

9.10 LABOUR UNIONS: BARGAINED WAGES AND THE UNION VOICE EFFECT

The labour market model presented so far is about firms and individual workers. But in many countries labour unions play a big part in how the labour market works. A **trade union** is an organization that can represent the interests of a group of workers in negotiations with employers over issues such as pay, working conditions, and working hours. The resulting contract is between the firm or organization representing employers and the labour union.

As you can see from Figure 9.19, the fraction of the workforce employed under collective bargaining agreements negotiated by labour unions varies greatly across countries, from virtually all workers in France and some northern European economies, to hardly any in the US and South Korea.

Labour unions and the bargained wage-setting curve

Where workers are organized into trade unions, the wage is not set by HR but instead is determined through a process of negotiation between union and firm. Although the wage must always be at least as high as the wage indicated by the wage-setting curve for the given level of unemployment, the bargained wage can be above the wage-setting curve. The reason is that now the employer's threat to dismiss the worker is not the only exercise of power that is possible. The union can threaten to 'dismiss' the employer (at least temporarily) by going on strike, that is, withdrawing the employees' labour from the firm.

We can think of a 'bargaining curve' lying above the wage-setting curve, which indicates the wage that the union-employer bargaining process will produce for every level of employment.

The relative bargaining power of the union and the employer determines how much this bargaining curve lies above the wage-setting curve. The union's power depends on the ability to withhold labour from the firm, so its bargaining strength will be greater if it can ensure that during a strike, no other workers will offer their services to the firm. This and the other

trade union An organization consisting predominantly of employees, the principal activities of which include the negotiation of rates of pay and conditions of employment for its members.

Sunny Freeman. 2015. 'What Canada can learn from Sweden's unionized retail workers' (http://tinyco.re/0808135). *Huffington Post Canada Business.* Updated 19 March 2015.

Barry T. Hirsch. 2008. 'Sluggish institutions in a dynamic world: Can unions and industrial competition coexist?' *Journal of Economic Perspectives* 22 (1) (February): pp. 153–176.

Jelle Visser. 2015. 'ICTWSS Data base. version 5.0.' (http://tinyco.re/8669300). *Amsterdam: Amsterdam Institute for Advanced Labour Studies AIAS.* Updated October 2015.

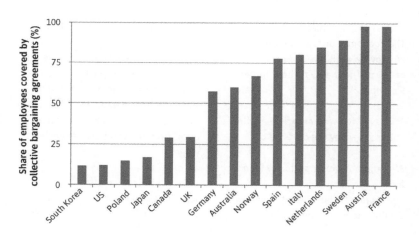

Figure 9.19 Share of employees whose wages are covered by collective bargaining agreements (early 2010s).

determinants of bargaining power depend on the laws and social norms that are in force in an economy. In many countries, for example, it is a serious violation of a social norm among workers to seek employment in a firm whose workers are on strike.

A powerful union, however, may not choose to raise the wage even if it has the power to do so. This is because even a very powerful union can only set the wage, and it cannot determine how many people the firm hires. Too high a wage may squeeze profits sufficiently to lead the firm to close down, or cut back on employment.

Unions may choose to restrain their use of bargaining power. If their wage-setting covers a substantial part of the economy, they will take into account the effect of their wage decision on the wages and employment of workers in the economy as a whole.

To see the difference that a labour union makes, let's see how the labour market would work if instead of the employer setting the wage and the employees individually responding, the process would now be:

1. The union sets the wage.
2. The employer informs workers that insufficient work will result in job termination.
3. Employees respond to the wage and the prospect of dismissal by choosing how hard to work.

In this case, the employer no longer sets the wage that maximizes profits (the point of tangency of the isocost line for effort and the best response curve at point A in Figure 9.20). Use the steps in Figure 9.20 to see what happens when the union rather than the firm sets the wage.

As shown in the figure, the wage will be higher than that preferred by the employer. Workers will now be working harder, but wages increase by more than productivity, so firms receive less effort for each dollar spent on wages. It follows that profits will be lower than without the union, that is, on the flatter isocost line passing through C.

By translating Figure 9.20 to the model of the labour market in Figure 9.21, we see that the bargained wage-setting curve lies above the wage-setting curve. Looking at the equilibrium where the bargained wage-setting curve intersects with the price-setting curve, the wage is unaffected, but the level of employment is lower.

Paradoxically, it seems that the union's success in bargaining would harm workers, since the real wage is unchanged and more people are out of work. But if we look at the data on union bargaining coverage and unemployment in Figure 9.22, it does not seem to be the case that unemployment is higher in countries where union bargains are important in wage-setting.

Austria, with almost all employees covered by union wage bargains, has a lower unemployment rate (averaged over 2000–2014) than the US, where fewer than one in five workers are covered by union contracts. Spain and Poland both had massive unemployment over this period, but union coverage was very high in Spain and very low in Poland.

So the fact that unions can push up the wage-setting curve to the new 'bargained wage-setting curve' must not be the entire story.

The union voice effect

Suppose that over time, the employer and the trade union had developed a constructive working relationship—for example, solving problems that arise in ways that benefit both employees and the owners. The employees may interpret the employer's recognition of the trade union, and its willingness to compromise with them over a higher wage, as a sign of goodwill.

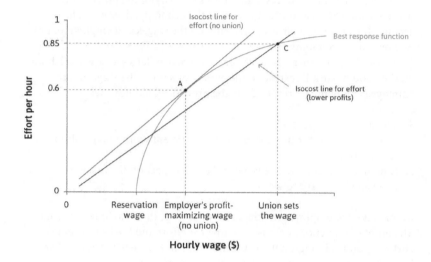

Figure 9.20 The union sets the firm's wage.

1. The employer sets the wage
At point A, the employer sets the wage that maximizes profits at the point of tangency of the isocost line and the best response function.

2. The union sets the wage instead
If the union sets the wage, it will be higher than that preferred by the employer, and effort levels correspondingly higher …

3. Higher effort but lower profits
… but profits would be lower (indicated by the flatter isocost line passing through C).

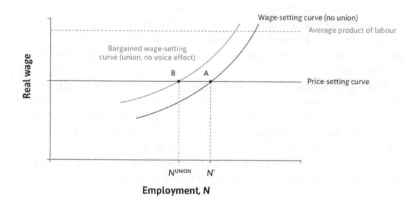

Figure 9.21 The bargained wage-setting curve when there is no union voice effect.

As a result, they might identify more strongly with their firm and experience effort as less of a burden than before, shifting their best response curve in Figure 9.23 up.

The result of the greater bargaining power of the workers, and their reciprocation of the company's worker-friendly policy, is shown as point D in the Figure 9.23. The wage is the same as in the previous case but because worker effort is higher, the firm's profits are higher. Note that in the example shown, the firm is still worse off than it was in the absence of the union.

With the new best response function, there is of course an outcome for a wage-setting firm that is even better than D—where the isocost curve is tangent to it (not shown). However, this is not feasible. The workers will not exert the higher effort in the absence of the negotiations about wages and conditions opened up by the union's role in wage-setting.

We have shown two effects of the presence of a labour union, which we can now represent in the labour market diagram:

- It may be able to get the firm to pay a wage greater than the minimum necessary to induce the employees to work (the bargaining curve is above the wage-setting curve).
- Providing employees with both recognition and a voice in how decisions are made may lower the disutility of effort and thus reduce the lowest wage necessary to motivate employees to work effectively.

The two effects are illustrated in Figure 9.24. In this figure, we show the case in which the equilibrium level of employment is higher and unemployment lower with the union (point Y) than without (point X). This is because the second effect (called the 'union voice effect') that shifts the wage-setting curve down was greater than the bargaining effect that shifts the wage-setting curve up.

But it could have worked out the other way around. The bargained wage effect could have been greater than the union voice effect, in which case the

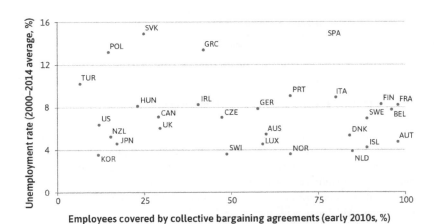

Jelle Visser. 2015. 'ICTWSS Data base. version 5.0.' (http://tinyco.re/8669300). *Amsterdam: Amsterdam Institute for Advanced Labour Studies AIAS.* Updated October 2015.

Figure 9.22 Collective wage bargaining coverage and unemployment across the OECD.

effect of unions would have been to reduce employment in the labour market equilibrium.

This provides a reason why the data in Figure 9.22 do not show any clear correlation (either positive or negative) of the extent of union contracts and the amount of unemployment.

Unions may also affect the average productivity of labour, which will shift the price-setting curve. If unions foster cooperation with management in solving production problems, average product and the price-setting curve will rise (leading to higher wages and less unemployment). If unions resist productivity improvements such as the introduction of new machinery or changes in work rules, then the effect will go in the opposite direction.

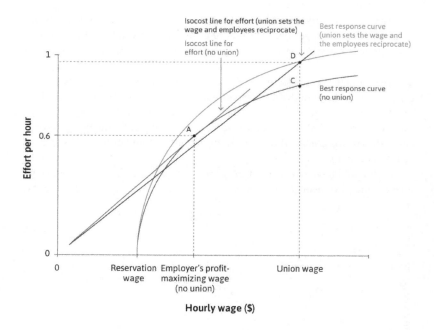

Figure 9.23 Union sets the firm's wage and employees reciprocate.

1. The employer sets the wage
At point A, the employer sets the wage that maximizes profits at the point of tangency of the isocost line and the best response curve.

2. The employer recognizes a trade union
If the employees interpret the employer's recognition of the trade union, and its willingness to compromise with them over a higher wage, as a sign of goodwill, the best response curve shifts up.

3. The effect of a worker-friendly policy
The result of the greater bargaining power of the workers, and their reciprocation of the company's worker-friendly policy, is shown as point D.

QUESTION 9.11 CHOOSE THE CORRECT ANSWER(S)
Figure 9.20 (page 394) depicts the effect of union wage-setting. What can we conclude from this figure?

☐ Compared to A, at C the effort per hour is higher and therefore the firm's profit is higher.
☐ The resulting bargained wage-setting curve will be above the wage-setting curve with no union.
☐ The effect of a strong union will always be to increase unemployment.
☐ Under union wage-setting, the firm is still setting the wage that maximizes its profits.

9.11 LABOUR MARKET POLICIES TO ADDRESS UNEMPLOYMENT AND INEQUALITY

Like when we studied the effect of taxes on prices and quantities of goods in Unit 8, we now use the labour market model we have constructed (the two curves) to see how a policy change will shift one or both of these curves. The effect of a policy is determined by how it changes the point of intersection of the two curves.

The objectives of labour market policies typically include reducing unemployment and raising wages (particularly of the least well off). Later (in Units 13–16) we will see that other objectives include reducing the economic insecurity to which families are exposed because of periods of unemployment.

The effect of policies that shift the price-setting curve

Education and training
Consider an improvement in the quality of education and training that future employees receive, which increases the productivity of labour. What is the effect of this productivity increase on real wages and equilibrium employment?

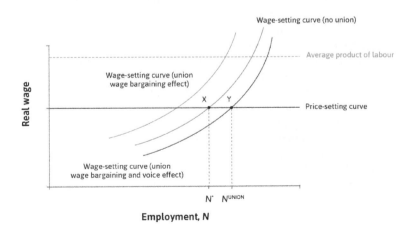

Figure 9.24 The bargained wage-setting curve and labour market equilibrium when there is a union voice effect.

The markup chosen by the firm when it sets its price to maximize its profits is determined by the amount of competition that the firm faces, so it is unaffected by the increase in productivity.

This markup determines the distribution of the firm's revenue between the employees and the owners, and so this has not changed either—wages remain the same fraction of revenue. So since the firm's output per worker has risen, real wages and the price-setting curve must also rise. The outcome is a rise in both equilibrium employment and the real wage.

A wage subsidy

A policy that has been advocated to increase employment is a subsidy paid to firms in proportion to the wages it pays its workers. For example, suppose that hiring a worker for an hour would cost the firm $40 in wages, but it would receive a 10% subsidy of that amount from the government, or $4. So the net wage cost to the firm would now be $36.

How would this affect the price-setting curve? The costs of the firm have now fallen, but as above, the optimal markup that the firm will use to determine its price has not changed, so the firm will lower its price to restore the old markup. When all firms do this, the prices of goods that the worker consumes fall, and real wages rise.

The effect, as above, is to shift upwards the price-setting curve. In both cases—education and training or a wage subsidy—the effect is to move the new labour market equilibrium up and right along with wage-setting curve to both higher wages and greater employment in the economy as a whole.

The full effect of each of these policies would have to take account of how the education and training or the wage subsidy were financed, but to allow a simple illustration of how the model works here, we assume that the funds necessary for these programs could be raised without affecting the labour market.

The effect of policies that shift the wage-setting curve

An example of how economic policy affects the wage-setting curve is shown in Figure 9.25. Throughout this example, the unemployment rate is held constant at 12% and we vary the unemployment benefit to which the worker is entitled. A higher unemployment benefit increases the reservation wage and shifts the best response curve to the right: the higher reservation wage at a higher unemployment benefit level is shown by point G. The employer sets a higher wage (point C). Work through the steps to see what happens to the wage-setting curve and unemployment.

There are policies that would affect the third curve in the figure (the labour supply curve). We have already seen how immigration policies could affect the supply of labour and hence the workings of the labour market. Other policies affecting the supply of labour include policies to enhance women's employment opportunities such as subsidized childcare, and a reduction in discrimination against disadvantaged minorities. These policies work initially by increasing the pool of people without jobs and therefore shifting downwards the wage-setting curve, as in the case of immigration.

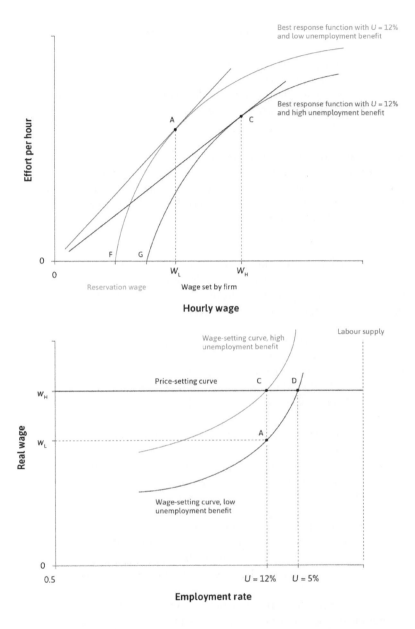

Figure 9.25 Deriving the wage-setting curve: Varying the unemployment benefit level in the economy.

1. The firm sets the wage
When unemployment is 12%, and the unemployment benefit is low, the firm sets the wage at point A in the upper panel, which corresponds to point A in the lower panel.

2. Higher unemployment benefit
There is a new wage-setting curve, which goes through point C.

3. The price-setting curve
We introduce the price-setting curve to find the labour market equilibrium. With the low unemployment benefit the equilibrium unemployment rate is 5% at D, but with the higher unemployment benefit the rate rises to 12% at C.

9.12 LOOKING BACKWARD: BARISTAS AND BREAD MARKETS

We have devoted an entire unit to the labour market for two reasons:

- Its functioning is very important for how well the economy serves the interests of the population.
- It is different enough from the way that many familiar markets work that it is essential to know these differences to understand how the economy works.

A good way to review these differences is to contrast the market for bread that we used to illustrate the model of a competitive equilibrium of price takers in the previous unit with the market for, say, baristas (which, for readers unfamiliar with Italian-inspired coffee shops, are those who make espresso-based coffee drinks).

Taking a price, setting a price

Recall that in the equilibrium of the bread market, neither bread consumers nor bakeries selling bread could benefit by offering to pay a different price or setting a different price from the one that prevailed in other transactions throughout the market. Buyers and sellers were price-takers in equilibrium:

- *No buyer could benefit from offering to pay less than the prevailing price*: No bakery would agree to the sale.
- *No buyer could benefit by offering to pay more than the going price*: This would just be throwing away money. Buyers in the bread market are price-takers because they wish to purchase bread at the lowest possible price.
- *No seller (a bakery) could benefit from setting a higher price*: There would be no customers.
- *No seller could benefit by offering a lower price*: This would be throwing away money. They can have as many customers as they like at the existing price.

> **reservation wage** What an employee would get in alternative employment, or from an unemployment benefit or other support, were he or she not employed in his or her current job.

Now think about a buyer in the labour market. This is an employer who buys the employee's time. The price is the wage. An employer who acts like a bread-buyer would offer the employee the lowest wage that the individual would accept to take the job. This lowest possible wage is the **reservation wage**.

We know from Unit 6 that an employer who did this would be disappointed. The worker who is paid just a reservation wage does not worry about losing the job, and so would have little incentive to work hard for the employer. Instead, we saw that employers choose a wage to balance their wage costs against the positive effects that a higher wage has on the employee's motivation to work.

Complete and incomplete contracts

In the bread market, the sales contract between buyer and seller is for bread, and if you buy bread you get what you want. It's a complete contract (remember, a contract need not be in writing and it need not be signed to be enforceable: your receipt is enough to get a refund if the bag labelled 'fresh bread' turned out to contain a week-old loaf when you got home).

In contrast, in the labour market, the employment contract is usually for the employee's work time and not for the work itself. Because it is the employee's work that produces the firm's goods and is essential to the firm's profits, this means the contract is an **incomplete contract**: something that matters to one of the parties to the exchange is not covered in the contract.

The implication is that, in contrast to the bread market, for a buyer in the labour market, paying more than is necessary to buy the employee's time is not throwing away money; it is the way that employers get what they want (work) and how they make profits. And because they are deciding on the price (that is, the wage) that they will offer the worker, they are price-setters and not price-takers. This is why Unit 8's model of the competitive equilibrium of price-takers does not work in the labour market.

Pareto efficiency and unexploited opportunities for mutual gains
In Unit 4, you encountered many situations in which the Nash equilibrium of some social interaction is not Pareto efficient. Examples include the prisoners' dilemma and the public goods game.

- *We use the Nash equilibrium*: This concept helps us predict what outcomes we will observe when people interact.
- *We use Pareto efficiency*: This concept evaluates whether there is some other outcome in which all parties might have done better (or at least as well).

Recall from Unit 8 that in the model we illustrated with the bread market, there were no unexploited opportunities for mutual gain at the competitive equilibrium (where the demand and supply curves intersect). In this situation, it is not possible to make one of the buyers or sellers better off—by having one of them trade more or less with their exchange partner, for example—without making at least one of them worse off. The outcome therefore was Pareto efficient.

This is not the case in the labour market. Competition among many buyers (firms hiring employees) and sellers (people seeking work) results in an equilibrium outcome—the wage w^* and the level of employment N^*—that is not Pareto efficient. What this means is that there is some *other* outcome—a different wage and level of employment that is feasible from the standpoint of the available resources and technology—that both employers and employees would prefer.

To see this, imagine that we are at the equilibrium of the labour market and one of the unemployed workers (identical to those employed) goes to an employer and says: 'Give me a break. I'll work as hard as the rest of your work force, but you can pay me a little less.'

The employer thinks: 'If I pay him a slightly lower wage, and if he works as hard as the rest, then my profits will go up.'

For the unemployed worker, getting a job makes a big difference. She now receives an employment rent, which measures how much better it is for her to have a job than not. The deal is a good one for her despite the fact that the employment rent she receives is slightly lower than that received by other workers (because her wage is slightly lower).

This little example shows that there is some other technically feasible outcome—employ $N^* + 1$ workers at the wage w^* for N^* of them and w^* minus a little bit for the last worker hired—that would be an improvement

incomplete contract A contract that does not specify, in an enforceable way, every aspect of the exchange that affects the interests of parties to the exchange (or of others).

for both the unemployed worker and the employer. So the outcome (N^*, w^*) is Pareto inefficient.

But if that is the case, why doesn't the employer hire the unemployed person? The answer is that the deal, while technically feasible, is not economically possible. This is because there is no way to enforce the unemployed person's promise to work as hard as the rest in return for a slightly lower wage. Remember the w^* on the wage-setting curve is the minimum the firm can pay to identical workers to ensure work effort is adequate. The problem thus goes back to a fundamental fact about the relationship between the firm and its employees: the contract is incomplete in that it cannot ensure a given level of effort from the worker. The Nash equilibrium in the labour market is Pareto inefficient.

The politics and sociology of markets

Here is another difference between the bread market and the barista market. The baker probably does not know the name of the person buying the bread, or anything about the buyer other than that he is offering the right price for the loaf. The buyer most likely cares equally little about the baker other than the taste of the bread.

Now think about the barista. What are the chances that she does not know the name of her immediate supervisor? And vice versa?

Why the difference? The bread market tends to be a one-off interaction among virtual strangers, while the labour market is an ongoing interaction among people who not only know each other's names but also care about what the other person is like.

The barista's supervisor cares about what the barista is like because her personality, loyalty to the brand, and her respect for social norms such as honesty and hard work will influence the quality and quantity of effort that she puts into the job. The buyer of the bread does not care about these aspects of the baker because what matters is the quality of the loaf, which can be easily determined, and a new bakery readily found if the taste is not right.

Another major difference is that the supervisor directs what the barista does—to dress a certain way, to show up at work at a certain time, and to not waste time on the job—with the expectation that she will comply with his orders. Because she receives an employment rent which she would lose if he were to dismiss her, he can exercise power over her, getting her to do things that she might not do without the threat of dismissal.

This is not the case in the bread market. If the buyer complains about the baker's attire, he would be invited to shop elsewhere. The difference is that neither the buyer nor the seller in the bread market is receiving a rent. For each of them, the transaction they are undertaking yields them benefits virtually identical to their next best alternative. When both can walk away at virtually no cost, then neither can exercise power over the other.

These are some of the differences—both economic and also political and sociological—between the bread market and the barista market. These are also the reasons why the model of the bread market with price-taking buyers and sellers, and market clearing in equilibrium, does not work for the labour market. The table in Figure 9.26 summarizes the differences.

Market	Bread: a market clearing equilibrium of price-takers	Baristas: price-setting by employers and equilibrium unemployment
Buyers	Individual consumers	Firms (employers)
Sellers	Firms (shops)	Individual workers
What is sold?	A loaf of bread	The worker's time
What does the buyer want?	A loaf of bread	The employee's effort on the job; not the worker's time
Competition among sellers?	*Yes*: There are many bakeries competing to sell bread.	*Yes*: There are many actual or would-be baristas competing to sell their time.
Is the contract complete?	*Yes*: If the bag labeled bread did not contain bread, you get your money back.	*No*: The firm's profits depend on the worker's effort per hour/week/month worked, which is not in the contract.
Price-taking buyers?	*Yes*: Individual buyers cannot bargain for a lower price than others are willing to pay (and would not want to pay more).	*No*: The buyer (the firm) sets the wage to minimize the cost of getting the worker to work; it cannot benefit by offering the lowest wage at which the worker (the seller) would accept the job.
Is there excess supply or demand in equilibrium?	*No*: The market clears. Sales take place at the lowest price the seller would accept.	*Yes*: Firms offer a wage higher than the worker's reservation wage (minimum price the seller would accept) to maximize their profits.

Figure 9.26 Differences between the labour market and competitive goods markets.

QUESTION 9.12 CHOOSE THE CORRECT ANSWER(S)
Which of the following statements are correct?

☐ Contracts are complete in both competitive goods markets and labour markets.
☐ In a competitive goods market the buyers are price-takers, while in a labour market the buyers of employment (the firms) are price-setters.
☐ There is no economic rent for either the buyers or the sellers in competitive goods markets. In contrast, in labour markets the sellers receive economic rents.
☐ Social norms do not affect the outcomes in either goods markets or in labour markets.

9.13 CONCLUSION

The model of the labour market is quite different from the model of equilibrium of price-taking buyers and sellers in Unit 8. The most obvious difference is that the labour market does not clear, even in equilibrium.

Involuntary unemployment at labour market equilibrium is unavoidable, because:

- *Employers and workers have a conflict of interest*: This is over how hard employees work.
- *Employers cannot write a complete contract with their employees*: They cannot specify the quality and quantity of work effort they will receive.

The extent of equilibrium unemployment is affected by how governments regulate labour and other markets. In Units 16 and 17 we shall see how these policies and the behaviour of labour unions and employers have affected the unemployment experience of different countries over the past few decades.

Unemployment can be higher than equilibrium unemployment as a result of a fall in the economy-wide demand for goods and services. In the example of the Greys in Australia, this was due to global movements in demand for commodities. But there are many other causes of fluctuations in aggregate demand that will be explored in the coming units.

Where unemployment is raised above the equilibrium level because of a lack of aggregate demand, governments and central banks can use fiscal and monetary policies to reduce it. This is likely to work better than relying on firms to cut wages and prices, and on households and firms to respond to those falling wages and prices by increasing their purchases.

The **principal-agent model** of the employer and the employee that we have used in this unit will appear in a new setting in the next unit: the credit market. Whereas in the labour market the principal is the employer and the agent the worker, in the credit market the principal is the lender and the agent the borrower. We saw here that in the labour market equilibrium there will be some people involuntarily unemployed, seeking a job and willing to work at the going wage rate. So, also, we will see that in the credit market there will be people seeking loans and willing to pay the going rate of interest, but unable to get a loan.

principal-agent relationship This relationship exists when one party (the principal) would like another party (the agent) to act in some way, or have some attribute that is in the interest of the principal, and that cannot be enforced or guaranteed in a binding contract. *See also: incomplete contract. Also known as: principal-agent problem.*

Concepts introduced in Unit 9
Before you move on, review these definitions:

- Wage-setting curve, price-setting curve
- Labour force, inactive population, participation rate
- Employment rate, unemployment rate
- Involuntary unemployment
- Equilibrium unemployment
- Cyclical unemployment
- Nominal wage, real wage
- Labour productivity
- Monetary policy, fiscal policy
- Trade union

9.14 REFERENCES

Bewley, T. 2007. 'Fairness, Reciprocity and Wage Rigidity'. *Behavioral Economics and its Applications*, eds. Peter Diamond and Hannu Vartiainen, pp. 157–188. Princeton, NJ: Princeton University Press.

Campbell, C. M., and K. S. Kamlani. 1997. 'The Reasons For Wage Rigidity: Evidence From a Survey of Firms'. *The Quarterly Journal of Economics* 112 (3) (August): pp. 759–789.

Carlin, Wendy and David Soskice. 2015. *Macroeconomics: Institutions, Instability, and the Financial System*. Oxford: Oxford University Press. Chapters 2 and 15.

Council of Economic Advisers Issue Brief. 2016. *Labor Market Monopsony: Trends, Consequences, and Policy Responses* (http://tinyco.re/7588734).

Freeman, Sunny. 2015. 'What Canada can learn from Sweden's unionized retail workers' (http://tinyco.re/0808135). *Huffington Post Canada Business*. Updated 19 March 2015.

Hirsch, Barry T. 2008. 'Sluggish institutions in a dynamic world: Can unions and industrial competition coexist?'. *Journal of Economic Perspectives* 22 (1) (February): pp. 153–176.

UNIT 10

BANKS, MONEY, AND THE CREDIT MARKET

HOW CREDIT, MONEY, AND BANKS EXPAND OPPORTUNITIES FOR MUTUAL GAIN, AND THE FACTORS THAT LIMIT THEIR CAPACITY TO ACCOMPLISH THIS

- People can rearrange the timing of their spending by borrowing, lending, investing, and saving.
- While mutual gains motivate credit market transactions, there is a conflict of interest between borrowers and lenders over the rate of interest, the prudent use of loaned funds, and their repayment.
- Borrowing and lending is a principal-agent relationship, in which the lender (the principal) cannot guarantee repayment of the loan by the borrower (the agent) by means of an enforceable contract.
- To solve this problem, lenders often require borrowers to contribute some of their own funds to a project.
- As a result, people with limited wealth are sometimes unable to secure loans, or can only do so at higher interest rates.
- Money is a medium of exchange consisting of bank notes and bank deposits, or anything else that can be used to purchase goods and services, and is accepted as payment because others can use it for the same purpose.
- Banks are profit-maximizing firms that create money in the form of bank deposits in the process of supplying credit.
- A nation's central bank creates a special kind of money called legal tender and lends to banks at its chosen policy interest rate.
- The interest rate charged by banks to borrowers (firms and households) is largely determined by the policy interest rate chosen by the central bank.

THEMES AND CAPSTONE UNITS
- 17: History, instability, and growth
- 18: Global economy
- 19: Inequality
- 22: Politics and policy

The market town of Chambar in southeastern Pakistan serves as the financial centre for 2,400 farmers in surrounding villages. At the beginning of the kharif-planting season in April, when they sow cotton and other cash crops, they will buy fertilizer and other inputs. Months have passed since they sold the last harvest and so the only way they can buy inputs is to borrow, promising to repay at the next harvest. Others borrow to pay for medicines or doctors. But few of them have ever walked through the shiny glass and steel doors of the JS Bank on Hyderabad Road. Instead, they visit one of approximately 60 moneylenders.

If they are seeking a first-time loan, they will be questioned intensively by the moneylender, asked for references from other farmers known to the lender, and in most cases given a small trial loan as a test of creditworthiness. The lender will probably visit to investigate the condition of the farmer's land, animals, and equipment.

The lenders are right to be wary. If the farmer's crop fails due to the farmer's lack of attention, the lender loses money. Unlike many financial institutions, lenders do not usually require that the farmer set aside some property or belongings (called **collateral**) that would become the lender's property if the farmer were unable to repay the loan—for example, some gold jewellery.

If the would-be first-time borrower looks reliable or trustworthy enough, he will be offered a loan. In Chambar, this is at an average interest rate of 78% per annum. If the borrower is paying the loan back in four months (the growing period of the crop prior to harvest), 100 rupees borrowed before planting will be paid back as 126 rupees. Knowing that more than half the loan applications are refused, the borrower would consider himself fortunate.

And indeed he would be, at least compared to some people 12,000 km away in New York, who take out short-term loans to be repaid when their next paycheck comes in. These payday loans bear interest rates ranging from 350% to 650% per annum, much higher than the legal maximum interest rate in New York (25%). In 2014, the 'payday syndicate' offering these loans was charged with criminal usury in the first degree.

Given the interest rate, is lending in Chambar likely to be exceptionally profitable? The evidence suggests it is not. Some of the funds lent to farmers are borrowed from commercial banks like the JS Bank at interest rates averaging 32% per annum, representing a cost to the moneylenders. And the costs of the extensive screening and collection of the debts further reduces the profits made by the lenders.

Partly as a result of the careful choices made by the moneylenders, default is rare: fewer than one in 30 borrowers fail to repay. By contrast, default rates on loans made by commercial banks are much higher: one in three. The moneylenders' success in avoiding default is based on their accurate assessment of the likely trustworthiness of their clients.

Money and trust are more closely related than you might think.

On 4 May 1970, a notice appeared in the *Irish Independent* newspaper in the Republic of Ireland, titled 'Closure of Banks'. It read:

> As a result of industrial action by the Irish Bank Officials' Association … it is with regret that these banks must announce the closure of all their offices in the Republic of Ireland … from 1 May, until further notice.

Banks in Ireland did not open again until 18 November, six-and-a-half months later.

Irfan Aleem. 1990. 'Imperfect information, screening, and the costs of informal lending: A study of a rural credit market in Pakistan' (http://tinyco.re/4382174). *The World Bank Economic Review* 4 (3): pp. 329–349.

collateral An asset that a borrower pledges to a lender as a security for a loan. If the borrower is not able to make the loan payments as promised, the lender becomes the owner of the asset.

Jessica Silver-Greenberg. 2014. 'New York Prosecutors Charge Payday Loan Firms with Usury' (http://tinyco.re/8917188). DealBook.

Did Ireland fall off a financial cliff? To everyone's surprise, instead of collapsing, the Irish economy continued to grow much as before. A two-word answer has been given to explain how this was possible: Irish pubs. Andrew Graham, an economist, visited Ireland during the bank strike and was fascinated by what he saw:

> Because everyone in the village used the pub, and the pub owner knew them, they agreed to accept deferred payments in the form of cheques that would not be cleared by a bank in the near future. Soon they swapped one person's deferred payment with another thus becoming the financial intermediary. But there were some bad calls and some pubs took a hit as a result. My second experience is that I made a payment with a cheque drawn on an English bank (£1 equalled 1 Irish punt at the time) and, out of curiosity, on my return to England, I rang the bank (in those days you could speak to someone you knew in a bank) and they told me my cheque had duly been paid in but that on the back were several signatures. In other words, it had been passed on from one person to another exactly as if it were money.

The Irish bank closures are a vivid illustration of the definition of money: it is anything accepted in payment. At that time, notes and coins made up about one-third of the money in the Irish economy, with the remaining two-thirds in bank deposits. The majority of transactions used cheques, but paying by cheque requires banks to ensure that people have the funds to back up their paper payments.

In a functioning banking system the cheque is cashed at the end of the day, and the bank credits the current account of the shop. If the writer of the cheque does not have enough money to cover the amount, the bank bounces the cheque, and the shop owner knows immediately that he has to collect in some other way. People generally avoid writing bad cheques as a result.

Credit or debit cards were not yet widely used. Today, a debit card works by instantly verifying the balance of your bank account and debiting from it. If you get a loan to buy a car, the bank credits your current account and you then write a cheque, use a credit or debit card, or initiate a bank transfer to the car dealer to buy the car. This is money in a modern economy.

So what happens when the banks close their doors and everyone knows that cheques will not bounce, even if the cheque writer has no money? Will anyone accept your cheques? Why not just write a cheque to buy the car when there is not enough money in your current account or in your approved overdraft? If you start thinking like this, you would not trust someone offering you a cheque in exchange for goods or services. You would insist on being paid in cash. But there is not enough cash in circulation to finance all of the transactions that people need to make. Everyone would have to cut back, and the economy would suffer.

How did Ireland avoid this fate? As we have seen, it happened at the pub. Cheques were accepted in payment as money, because of the trust generated by the pub owners. Publicans (owners of the pubs) spend hours talking and listening to their patrons. They were prepared to accept cheques, which could not be cleared in the banking system, as payment from those judged to be trustworthy. During the six-month period that the banks were closed, about £5 billion of cheques were written by individuals and businesses, but not processed by banks. It helped that Ireland had one pub for every 190 adults at the time. With the assistance of pub and shop owners who knew

Felix Martin. 2013. *Money: The Unauthorised Biography*. London: The Bodley Head.

Antoin E. Murphy. 1978. 'Money in an Economy without Banks: The Case of Ireland'. *The Manchester School* 46 (1) (March): pp. 41–50.

Jonathan Morduch. 1999. 'The Microfinance Promise' (http://tinyco.re/7650659). *Journal of Economic Literature* 37 (4) (December): pp. 1569–1614.

their customers, cheques could circulate as money. With money in bank accounts inaccessible, the citizens of Ireland created the amount of new money needed to keep the economy growing during the bank closure.

Irish publicans and the moneylenders in the market town of Chambar would perhaps not recognize, among the many things they had in common, that they were creating money, and they would not know that in doing so they were providing a service essential to the functioning of their respective economies.

Not everyone passes the trustworthiness tests set by pub owners and moneylenders, of course. And, in Chambar and New York, some of those who do pay much higher interest rates than others.

10.1 MONEY AND WEALTH

Borrowing and lending money, and the trust that makes this possible, are about shifting consumption and production over time. The moneylender offers funds to the farmer to purchase fertilizer now, and he will pay back after the crop matures, as long as it was not destroyed by a drought. The payday borrower will be paid at the end of the month but needs to buy food now. She wants to bring some of her future buying power to the present.

The passage of time is an essential part of concepts such as money, income, wealth, consumption, savings, and investment.

Money

money A medium of exchange consisting of bank notes and bank deposits, or anything else that can be used to purchase goods and services, and is accepted as payment because others can use it for the same purpose.

Money is a medium of exchange consisting of bank notes and bank deposits, or anything else that can be used to purchase goods and services, and is accepted as payment because others can use it for the same purpose. The 'because' is important and it distinguishes exchange facilitated by money from barter exchange. In a barter economy I might exchange my apples for your oranges because I want some oranges, not because I intend to use the oranges to pay my rent. Money makes more exchanges possible because it's not hard to find someone who will be happy to have your money (in exchange for something), whereas unloading a large quantity of apples could be a problem. This is why barter plays a limited role in virtually all modern economies.

David Graeber. 2012. 'The Myth of Barter' (http://tinyco.re/6552964). *Debt: The First 5,000 years.* Brooklyn, NY: Melville House Publishing.

For money to do its work, almost everyone must believe that if they accept money from you in return for handing over their good or service, then they will be able to use the money to buy something else in turn. In other words, they must trust that others will accept your money as payment. Governments and banks usually provide this trust. But the Irish bank closure shows that, when there is sufficient trust among households and businesses, money can function in the absence of banks. The publicans and shops accepted a cheque as payment, even though they knew it could not be cleared by a bank in the foreseeable future. As the bank dispute went on, the cheque presented to the pub or shop relied on a lengthening chain of uncleared cheques received by the person or business presenting the cheque. Some cheques circulated many times, endorsed on the back by the pub or shop owner, just like a bank note.

This is the fundamental characteristic of money. It is a medium of exchange.

Money allows purchasing power to be transferred among people so that they can exchange goods and services, even when payment takes place at a later date (for example, through the clearing of a cheque or settlement of credit card or trade credit balances). Therefore, money requires trust to function.

Wealth

One way to think about **wealth** is that it is the largest amount that you could consume without borrowing, after having paid off your debts and collected any money owed to you—for example if you sold your house, car, and everything you owned.

The term wealth is also sometimes used in a broader sense to include immaterial aspects such as your health, skills, and ability to earn an income (your **human capital**). But we will use the narrower definition of material wealth in this unit.

Income

Income is the amount of money you receive over some period of time, whether from market **earnings**, investments, or from the government.

Since it is measured over a period of time (such weekly or yearly), it is a **flow** variable. Wealth is a **stock** variable, meaning that it has no time dimension. At any moment of time it is just there. In this unit we only consider after-tax income, also known as disposable income.

To remember the difference between wealth and income, think of filling a bathtub, as in Figure 10.1. Wealth is the amount (stock) of water in the tub, while income is the flow of water into the tub. The inflow is measured by litres (or gallons) per minute; the stock of water is measured by litres (or gallons) at a particular moment in time.

As we have seen, wealth often takes physical forms such as a house, or car, or office, or factory. The value of this wealth tends to decline, either due to use or simply the passage of time.

This reduction in the value of a stock of wealth over time is called **depreciation**. Using the bathtub analogy, depreciation would be the amount of evaporation of the water. Like income, it is a flow (you could measure it in litres per year), but a negative one. So when we take account of depreciation we have to distinguish between net income and gross income. Gross income is the flow into the bathtub (remember that income means disposable or after-tax income), while net income is this flow less depreciation. **Net income** is the maximum amount that you could consume and leave your wealth unchanged.

wealth Stock of things owned or value of that stock. It includes the market value of a home, car, any land, buildings, machinery or other capital goods that a person may own, and any financial assets such as shares or bonds. Debts are subtracted—for example, the mortgage owed to the bank. Debts owed to the person are added.

human capital The stock of knowledge, skills, behavioural attributes, and personal characteristics that determine the labour productivity or labour earnings of an individual. Investment in this through education, training, and socialization can increase the stock, and such investment is one of the sources of economic growth. Part of an individual's endowments. *See also: endowment.*

income The amount of profit, interest, rent, labour earnings, and other payments (including transfers from the government) received, net of taxes paid, measured over a period of time such as a year. The maximum amount that you could consume and leave your wealth unchanged. *Also known as: disposable income. See also: pre-tax income.*
earnings Wages, salaries, and other income from labour.

flow A quantity measured per unit of time, such as annual income or hourly wage.
stock A quantity measured at a point in time. It's units do not depend on time. *See also: flow.*

depreciation The loss in value of a form of wealth that occurs either through use (wear and tear) or the passage of time (obsolescence).
net income Gross income minus depreciation. *See also: income, gross income, depreciation.*

consumption (C) Expenditure on consumer goods including both short-lived goods and services and long-lived goods, which are called consumer durables.

saving When consumption expenditure is less than net income, saving takes place and wealth rises. *See also: wealth.*
investment (I) Expenditure on newly produced capital goods (machinery and equipment) and buildings, including new housing.

Expenditure

The tub also has an outflow pipe or drain. The flow through the drain is called **consumption** expenditure, and it reduces wealth just as net income increases it.

An individual (or household) saves when consumption is less than net income, so wealth increases. Wealth is the accumulation of past and current saving. One form that **saving** can take is the purchase of a financial asset such as shares (or stocks) in a company or a government bond. Although in everyday language these purchases are sometimes referred to as 'investment', in economics, **investment** means expenditure on capital goods, which are goods such as machinery or buildings.

The distinction between investment and purchasing shares or bonds is illustrated by a sole-proprietor business. At the end of the year, the owner decides what to do with her net income. Out of the net income, she decides on her consumption expenditure for the year ahead and saves the remainder. By default, the saving would take the form of bank deposits since her income would be paid into the bank. With her savings, she could buy financial assets such as shares or bonds, which provide funds to businesses or the government. Or, instead, she could spend on new assets to expand her business, which would be considered an investment.

QUESTION 10.1 CHOOSE THE CORRECT ANSWER(S)
Which of the following statements are correct?

☐ Your material wealth is the largest amount that you can consume without borrowing, which includes the value of your house, car, financial savings, and human capital.
☐ Net income is the maximum amount that you can consume and leave your wealth unchanged.
☐ In economics, investment means saving in financial assets such as stocks and bonds.
☐ Depreciation is the loss in your financial savings due to unfavourable movements in the market.

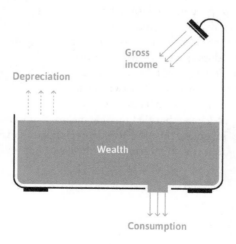

Figure 10.1 Wealth, income, depreciation, and consumption: The bathtub analogy.

Mr Bond has wealth of £500,000. He has a market income of £40,000 per year, on which he is taxed 30%. Mr Bond's wealth includes some equipment, which depreciates by £5,000 every year. Based on this information, which of the following statements is correct?

☐ Mr Bond's disposable income is £40,000.
☐ Mr Bond's net income is £28,000.
☐ The maximum amount of consumption expenditure possible for Mr Bond is £23,000.
☐ If Mr Bond decides to spend 60% of his net income on consumption and the rest on investment, then his investment is £9,200.

10.2 BORROWING: BRINGING CONSUMPTION FORWARD IN TIME

To understand borrowing and lending we will use feasible sets and indifference curves. In Units 3 and 5 you studied how Alexei and Angela make choices between conflicting objectives such as free time and grades or bushels of grain. They made choices from the feasible set, based on preferences described by indifference curves that represented how much they valued one objective relative to the other.

Here you will see that the same feasible set and indifference curve analysis applies to choosing between having something now, and having something later. In earlier units we saw that giving up free time is a way of getting more goods, or grades, or grain. Now we see that giving up some goods to be enjoyed now will sometimes allow us to have more goods later. The **opportunity cost** of having more goods now is having fewer goods later.

Borrowing and lending allow us to rearrange our capacity to buy goods and services across time. Borrowing allows us to buy more now, but constrains us to buy less later. To see how this works, think about Julia, who needs to consume now but has no money today. She knows that in the next period (later) she will have $100 from her paycheck or harvest. Julia's situation is shown in Figure 10.2. Each point in the figure shows a combination of Julia's capacity to consume things, now and later. We assume that she spends everything that she has, so each point in the figure gives her consumption now (measured on the horizontal axis) and later (measured on the vertical axis).

Initially Julia is at the point labelled 'Julia's endowment' in Figure 10.2. To consume now, Julia is considering taking out a payday loan (or she could be a farmer borrowing to finance her consumption before she can harvest and sell her crop).

Julia could, for example, borrow $91 now and promise to pay the lender the whole $100 that she will have later. Her total repayment of $100 would include the principal (how much she borrowed) plus the interest charge at the rate r, or:

$$\text{repayment} = \text{principal} + \text{interest}$$
$$= 91 + 91r$$
$$= 91(1 + r)$$
$$= \$100$$

opportunity cost When taking an action implies forgoing the next best alternative action, this is the net benefit of the foregone alternative.

interest rate The price of bringing some buying power forward in time. *See also: nominal interest rate, real interest rate.*

And if 'later' means in one year from now, then the annual **interest rate**, *r*, is:

$$\text{interest rate} = \frac{\text{repayment}}{\text{principal}} - 1$$
$$= \frac{100}{91} - 1$$
$$= 0.1 = 10\%$$

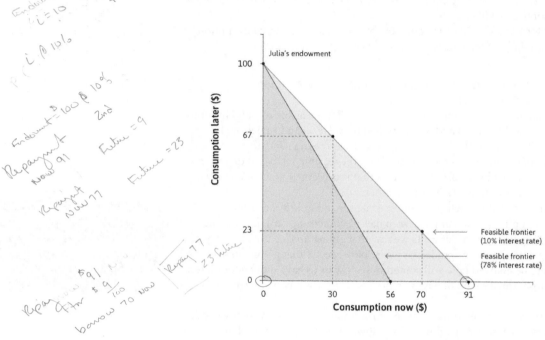

Figure 10.2 Borrowing, the interest rate, and the feasible set.

1. Julia has nothing
Julia has no money now, but she knows that in the next period she will have $100.

2. Bringing future income to the present
Julia could, for example, borrow $91 now and promise to pay the lender the $100 that she will have later. The interest rate would be 10%.

3. Borrowing less
At the same interest rate (10%), she could also borrow $70 to spend now, and repay $77 at the end of the year. In that case she would have $23 to spend next year.

4. Borrowing even less
At the same interest rate (10%), she could also borrow $30 to spend now, and repay $33 at the end of the year. In that case she would have $67 to spend next year.

5. Julia's feasible set
The boundary of Julia's feasible set is her feasible frontier, shown for the interest rate of 10%.

6. Julia's feasible frontier
Juila can borrow now and choose any combination on her feasible frontier.

7. A higher interest rate
If, instead of 10%, the interest rate is 78%, Julia can only borrow a maximum of $56 now.

8. The feasible set
The feasible set with the interest rate of 78% is the dark shaded area, while the feasible set with an interest rate of 10% is the dark shaded area plus the light shaded area.

You can think of the interest rate as the price of bringing some buying power forward in time.

At the same interest rate (10%), she could also borrow $70 to spend now, and repay $77 at the end of the year, that is:

$$\text{repayment} = 70 + 70r$$
$$= 70(1 + r)$$
$$= \$77$$

In that case she would have $23 to spend next year. Another possible combination is to borrow and spend just $30 now, which would leave Julia with $67 to spend next year, after repaying her loan.

All of her possible combinations of consumption now and consumption later (($91, $0), ($70, $23) ($30, $67), and so on) generate the feasible frontier shown in Figure 10.2, which is the boundary of the feasible set when the interest rate is 10%.

The fact that Julia can borrow means that she does not have to consume only in the later period. She can borrow now and choose any combination on her feasible frontier. But the more she consumes now, the less she can consume later. With an interest rate of $r = 10\%$, the opportunity cost of spending one dollar now is that Julia will have to spend $1.10 = 1 + r$ dollars less later.

One plus the interest rate $(1 + r)$ is the marginal rate of transformation of goods from the future to the present, because to have one unit of the good now you have to give up $1 + r$ goods in the future. This is the same concept as the marginal rate of transformation of goods, grain, or grades into free time that you encountered in Units 3 and 5.

But suppose that, instead of 10%, the interest rate is now 78%, the average rate paid by the farmers in Chambar. At this interest rate Julia can now only borrow a maximum of $56, because at 78% the interest on a loan of $56 is $44, using up all $100 of her future income. Her feasible frontier therefore pivots inward and the feasible set becomes smaller. Because the price of bringing buying power forward in time has increased, the capacity to consume in the present has fallen, just as your capacity to consume grain would fall if the price of grain went up (assuming you are not a producer of grain).

Of course the lender will benefit from a higher interest rate, as long as the loan is repaid, so there is a conflict of interest between the borrower and the lender.

10.3 IMPATIENCE AND THE DIMINISHING MARGINAL RETURNS TO CONSUMPTION

Given the opportunities for bringing forward consumption shown by the feasible set, what will Julia choose to do? How much consumption she will bring forward depends on how impatient she is. She could be impatient for two reasons:

- She prefers to smooth out her consumption instead of consuming everything later and nothing now.
- She may be an impatient type of person.

Smoothing

She would like to smooth her consumption because she enjoys an additional unit of something more when she has not already consumed a lot of it. Think about food—the first few bites of a dish are likely to be much more pleasurable than bites from your third serving. This is a fundamental psychological reality, sometimes termed the law of satiation of wants.

More generally, the value to the individual of an additional unit of consumption in a given period declines the more that is consumed. This is called **diminishing marginal returns to consumption**. You have already encountered something similar in Unit 3, in which Alexei experienced diminishing marginal returns to free time. Holding his grade constant, the more free time he had, the less each additional unit was worth to him, relative to how important the grade would be.

Use the analysis in Figure 10.3a to see how Julia can choose her consumption now and later, and how her preferences can be represented by indifference curves. Diminishing marginal returns to consumption in each period mean that Julia would like to smooth her consumption, that is, to avoid consuming a lot in one period and little in the other.

Pure impatience, or how impatient you are as a person

If Julia knows she can have two meals tomorrow but she has none today, then we have seen that diminishing marginal returns to consumption could explain why she might prefer to have one meal today and one tomorrow instead. Note that Julia would opt for the meal now not because she is an impatient person, but because she does not expect to be hungry in the future. She prefers to smooth her consumption of food.

But there is a different reason for preferring the good now, called **pure impatience**. To see whether someone is impatient as a person, we ask whether she values a good now more highly than later, when her initial endowment is having the same amount in both periods. There are two reasons for pure impatience:

- *Myopia (short-sightedness)*: People experience the present satisfaction of hunger or some other desire more strongly than they imagine the same satisfaction at a future date.
- *Prudence*: People know that they may not be around in the future, and so choosing present consumption may be a good idea.

To see what pure impatience means, we compare two points on the same indifference curve in Figure 10.3b. At point A she has $50 now and $50 later. We ask how much extra consumption she would need to have later in order to compensate her for losing $1 now. Point B on the same indifference curve gives us the answer. If she had only $49 now, she would need $51.50 later in order to stay on the same indifference curve and be equally happy. So she needed $1.50 later to compensate for losing $1 now. Julia has pure impatience because rather than preferring to perfectly smooth her consumption, she places more value on an additional unit of consumption today than in the future.

The slope of the indifference curve of 1.5 (in absolute value) at point A in Figure 10.3b means that she values an extra unit of consumption now 1.5 times as much as an extra unit of consumption later.

---

diminishing marginal returns to consumption The value to the individual of an additional unit of consumption declines, the more consumption the individual has. *Also known as: diminishing marginal utility.*

---

pure impatience This is a characteristic of a person who values an additional unit of consumption now over an additional unit later, when the amount of consumption is the same now and later. It arises when a person is impatient to consume more now because she places less value on consumption in the future for reasons of myopia, weakness of will, or for other reasons.

IMPATIENCE

Any preference to move consumption from the future to the present. This preference may be derived from:
- pure impatience
- diminishing marginal returns to consumption

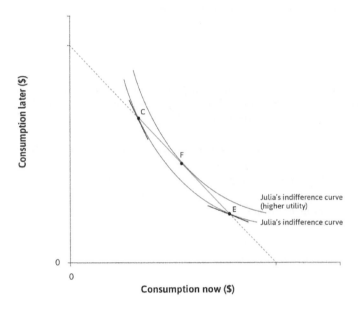

Figure 10.3a Consumption smoothing: Diminishing marginal returns to consumption.

1. Julia's choices
The dashed line shows the combinations of consumption now and consumption later from which Julia can choose.

2. Diminishing marginal returns to consumption
Julia's indifference curve is bowed toward the origin as a consequence of diminishing marginal returns to consumption in each period: the more goods she has in the present, the less she values an additional one now relative to more in the future. The slope of the indifference curve is the marginal rate of substitution (MRS) between consumption now and consumption later.

3. What choices would Julia make?
The MRS at C is high (the slope of her indifference curve is steep): Julia has little consumption now and a lot later, so diminishing marginal returns mean that she would like to move some consumption to the present. The MRS at E is low: She has a lot of consumption now and less later, so diminishing marginal returns mean that she would like to move some consumption to the future. So she will choose a point between C and E.

4. MRS falls
We can see that the MRS is falling as we move along the indifference curve from C to E: the slope is steeper at C than at E.

5. Julia's optimal choice
Given the choice shown by the line CE, Julia will choose point F. It is on the highest attainable indifference curve. She prefers to smooth consumption between now and later.

EXERCISE 10.1 THE CONSEQUENCES OF PURE IMPATIENCE

1. Draw the indifference curves of a person who is more impatient than Julia in Figure 10.3b, for any level of consumption now and consumption later.
2. Draw a set of indifference curves for Julia if she does not experience diminishing marginal returns to consumption but has pure impatience. Would she then want to smooth her consumption?
3. Draw a set of indifference curves for Julia if she does not experience diminishing marginal returns to consumption and has no pure impatience.

QUESTION 10.3 CHOOSE THE CORRECT ANSWER(S)

Figure 10.3a (page 417) depicts Julia's indifference curves for consumption in periods 1 (now) and 2 (later). Based on this information, which of the following statements is correct?

☐ The slope of the indifference curve is the marginal rate of substitution between the consumption in the two periods.
☐ The marginal return to consumption in period 1 is higher at E than at C.
☐ Julia's consumption is more equal (more 'smoothed') at C than at E. Therefore she prefers consumption choice C to E.
☐ Consuming exactly the same amount in the two periods is Julia's most preferred choice.

You value extra spending now @ 1.5 times greater than the extra spending in the future!

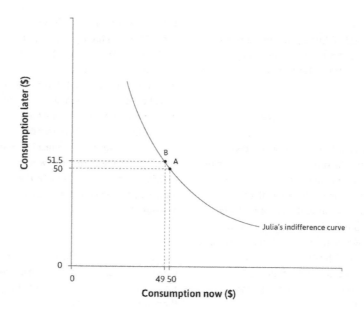

Figure 10.3b Pure impatience.

10.4 BORROWING ALLOWS SMOOTHING BY BRINGING CONSUMPTION TO THE PRESENT

How much will Julia borrow? If we combine Figures 10.2 and 10.3a we will have the answer. As in the other examples of a feasible set and indifference curves, Julia wishes to get to the highest possible indifference curve, but is limited by her feasible frontier. The highest feasible indifference curve when the interest rate is 10% will be the one that is tangent to the feasible frontier, shown as point E in Figure 10.4.

Here, she chooses to borrow and consume $58 and repay $64 later, leaving her $36 to consume later. We know that at this tangency point, the slope of the indifference curve is equal to the slope of the feasible frontier (otherwise the curves would cross). We define a person's **discount rate**, ρ (economists use the Greek letter rho, which rhymes with 'toe'), as the slope of the indifference curve minus one, which is a measure of how much Julia values an extra unit of consumption now, relative to an extra unit of consumption later.

For example, in Figure 10.3b, $\rho = 50\%$ at point A because an extra unit of consumption today was worth 1.5 extra units later. This means that Julia borrows just enough so that:

slope of the indifference curve (MRS) = slope of the feasible frontier (MRT)

We know that:

$$MRS = 1 + \rho$$
$$MRT = 1 + r$$

So:

$$MRS = MRT$$
$$1 + \rho = 1 + r$$

If we subtract 1 from both sides of this equation we have:

$$\rho = r$$
$$\text{discount rate} = \text{rate of interest}$$

Her discount rate ρ depends on both her desire to smooth consumption and on her degree of pure impatience.

Use the analysis in Figure 10.4 to see how Julia will choose consumption when the interest rate is 10% and when it is 78%.

> **A PERSON'S DISCOUNT RATE**
> A person's **discount rate**, ρ, is a measure of a person's impatience: how much she values an extra unit of consumption now over an extra unit of consumption later. This is the slope of her indifference curve between consumption now and consumption later, minus one.
>
> Her discount rate depends on two factors:
> * *Her desire to smooth consumption*: This is affected by the situation she is in (the current distribution of consumption now and later).
> * *Her pure impatience as a person*: This is also sometimes referred to as her subjective discount rate because it is based in part on her psychology.

> **EXERCISE 10.2 INCOME AND SUBSTITUTION EFFECTS**
> 1. Use Figure 10.4 (page 420) to show that the difference in current consumption at the lower and higher interest rate (at E and G), namely $23, is composed of an income effect and a substitution effect. It will be helpful to review income and substitution effects from Unit 3 before doing this.
> 2. Why do the income and substitution effects work in the same direction in this example?

QUESTION 10.4 CHOOSE THE CORRECT ANSWER(S)

Figure 10.4 depicts Julia's choice of consumptions in periods 1 and 2. She has no income in period 1 (now) and an income of $100 in period 2 (later). The current interest rate is 10%. Based on this information, which of the following statements is correct?

☐ At F, the interest rate exceeds Julia's discount rate (degree of impatience).

☐ At E, Julia is on the highest possible indifference curve given her feasible set.

☐ E is Julia's optimal choice, as she is able to completely smooth out her consumption over the two periods and consume the same amount.

☐ G is not a feasible choice for Julia.

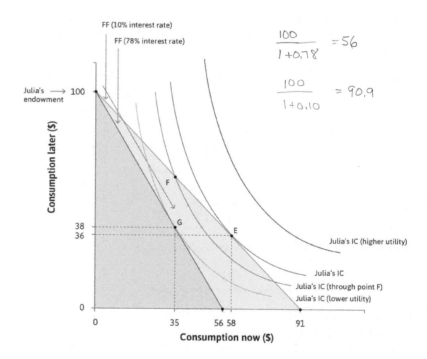

Figure 10.4 Moving consumption over time by borrowing.

1. Julia's feasible frontier
Julia wishes to get to the highest indifference curve but is limited by her feasible frontier.

2. Julia's best option
When the interest rate is 10%, the highest attainable indifference curve will be the one that is tangent to the feasible frontier shown as point E.

3. MRS and MRT
At this point, MRS = MRT.

4. The decision to borrow
At point F, her discount rate, ρ, exceeds r, the interest rate, so she would like to bring consumption forward in time. Similar reasoning eliminates all points on the feasible frontier except E.

5. An increase in the interest rate
If the interest rate at which she can borrow increases, the feasible set gets smaller.

6. The effect of a higher interest rate
The best Julia can do now is to borrow less ($35 instead of $58), as shown by point G.

10.5 LENDING AND STORING: SMOOTHING AND MOVING CONSUMPTION TO THE FUTURE

Now think about Marco, an individual facing a different situation from Julia who was considering a payday loan, or a farmer in Chambar seeking a loan until the harvest. While Julia is deciding how much to borrow, Marco has some goods or funds worth $100, but does not (yet) anticipate receiving any income later. Julia and Marco will both get $100 eventually, but time creates a difference. Marco's wealth, narrowly defined, is $100. Julia's wealth is zero.

We saw that Julia, who will earn $100 in the future, wants to borrow. The situation that she is in gives her a strong desire to smooth by borrowing. Think about what Julia's indifference curve, passing through her endowment point, might look like. As shown in Figure 10.5, it is very steep. Because she currently has nothing, she has a strong preference for increasing consumption now.

This is called Julia's **reservation indifference curve**, because it is made of all of the points at which Julia would be just as well off as at her reservation position, which is her endowment with no borrowing or lending (Julia's endowment and reservation indifference curves are similar to those of Angela, the farmer, in Unit 5).

Look at Marco's indifference curve passing through his endowment point, which is $100 now and nothing later. As shown in Figure 10.5, it is quite flat now, indicating that he is looking for a way to transfer some of his consumption to the future.

Marco and Julia's indifference curves and hence their pure impatience are similar. They differ according to their situation, not their preferences. Julia borrows because she is poor in the present, unlike Marco, and that is why she is impatient—she needs to smooth her consumption.

reservation indifference curve A curve that indicates allocations (combinations) that are as highly valued as one's reservation option.

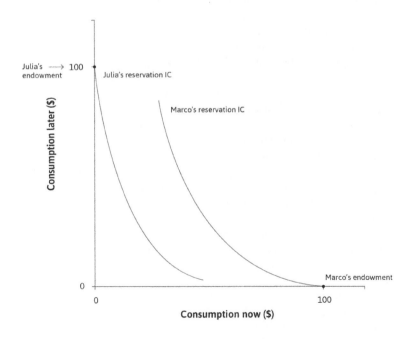

Figure 10.5 Reservation indifference curves and endowments.

Marco has $100 worth of grain just harvested, and no debts to pay off. He could consume it all now, but as we have seen, this would probably not be the best he could do given the circumstances:

- We have assumed his income in the future is zero.
- Like Julia, he has diminishing marginal returns to consumption of grain.

In order to smooth, he wishes to move some goods to the future. He could store the grain, but if he did, mice would eat some of it. Mice are a form of depreciation. The grain they eat represents a reduction in Marco's wealth due to the passage of time. So, taking account of the mice, if he consumed nothing at all during this period he would have just $80 worth of grain a year later. This means that the cost of moving grain from the present to the future is 20% per year.

In Figure 10.6, we see that Marco's endowment is on the horizontal axis, as he has $100 of grain available now. The dark line shows Marco's feasible frontier using storage, and the dark shaded area shows his feasible set. If this were the only option, and if his indifference curves were as indicated, he would definitely store some of the grain. In Figure 10.6, some part of his feasible frontier lies outside his endowment indifference curve, so he can do better by storing some grain.

But how much? Like Julia, Marco will find the amount of storage that gets him to the highest feasible indifference curve by finding the point of tangency between the indifference curve and the feasible frontier. This is point H, so he will eat $68 of the grain now, and consume $26 of it later (mice ate $6 of the grain). At point H, Marco has equated his MRS between consumption now and in the future to the MRT, which is the cost of moving goods from the present to the future.

He could avoid the mice by selling the grain and putting $100 under his mattress. His feasible frontier would then be a straight line (not shown) from consumption now of $100, to consumption later of $100. We are assuming that his $100 note will not be stolen and that $100 will purchase the same amount of grain now and later because there is no inflation (we explain inflation, and its effects, in Unit 13). Under these assumptions, storing money under the mattress is definitely better than storing grain when there are mice.

A better plan, if Marco could find a trustworthy borrower, would be to lend the money. If he did this and could be assured of repayment of $(1 + r)$ for every $1 lent, then he could have feasible consumption of $100 \times (1 + r)$ later, or any of the combinations along his new feasible consumption line. The light line in Figure 10.6 shows the feasible frontier when Marco lends at 10%. As you can see from the figure, compared to storage or putting the money under his mattress, his feasible set is now expanded by the opportunity to lend money at interest. Marco is able to reach a higher indifference curve.

As we have seen, in a contemporary economy, there are a variety of financial instruments that Marco can use to shift consumption to the future by lending such as term deposits, or bonds issued by companies or by the government.

If Marco faced an investment opportunity that meant he could invest his asset today and have it be worth more in a year—for instance, if he owns land where he could use the grain as seed and cultivate more grain—then that would similarly expand his feasible set.

10.6 INVESTING: ANOTHER WAY TO MOVE CONSUMPTION TO THE FUTURE

If Marco owns some land, he could do even better. He could invest the grain (planting it as seed and feeding it to his draft animals to help him work the fields until harvest). This opportunity to invest will further expand his feasible set. Suppose that if he were to invest all of his grain, he could harvest $150 worth of grain later, as shown in Figure 10.7. He has invested $100, harvested $150, and so earned a profit of $150 − $100 = $50, or a profit rate (profits divided by the investment required) of $50/$100 = 50%. The slope of the red line is −1.5, where the absolute value (1.5) is the marginal rate of transformation of investment into returns, or 1 plus the rate of return on the investment.

If Marco could get a loan at 10%, he would quickly see that he would be better off with an entirely new plan: invest everything he has, with a harvest next year of $150, but also borrow now in order to be able to consume more both now and in the future. This 'invest-it-all' plan is shown in

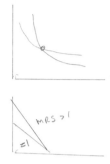

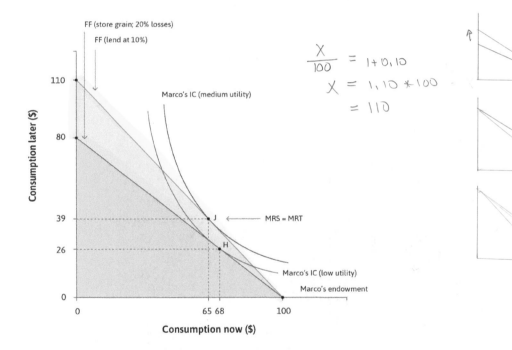

Figure 10.6 Smoothing consumption by storing and lending.

1. Marco has wealth today
Marco has $100 of grain available now.

2. Marco's feasible frontier
The dark line shows Marco's feasible frontier using storage, and the shaded area shows his feasible set.

3. Marco's preferences
Marco's reservation indifference curve goes through his endowment.

4. Marco's decision to store
Point H on Marco's indifference curve denotes the amount of storage that he will choose.

5. Marco's decision to lend
The light line shows the feasible frontier when Marco lends at 10%.

6. The effect of the decision to lend
Marco is now able to reach a higher indifference curve.

Figure 10.8. The plan shifts Marco's feasible frontier out even further, as shown by the dotted red line. Marco ends up consuming at a new point, L, with more both now and in the future.

Figure 10.9 summarizes how the 'invest-it-all and borrow' plan works compared to the other options.

The feasible sets for all of Marco's options are shown in Figure 10.10.

Let's return to how Marco differs from Julia. Compare the feasible sets of Julia shown in Figure 10.4 and of Marco, whose options are shown in Figure 10.10.

Three differences between Marco and Julia explain the disparity in their outcomes.

- *Marco starts with an asset while Julia starts with nothing*: Julia has the prospect of a similar asset later, but this puts the two on opposite sides of the credit market.
- *Marco has a productive investment opportunity while Julia does not.*
- *Marco and Julia may face different interest rates*: The less-obvious difference is that if Marco (after investing his entire asset at a 50% return)

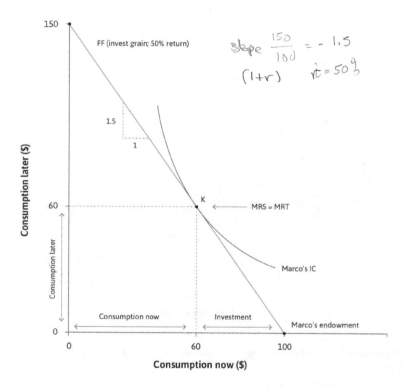

Figure 10.7 Investing in a high-return project.

1. The return on investment
If Marco were to invest all of his grain, he could harvest $150 worth of grain later.

2. The return on investment
The slope of the red line is –1.5, where the absolute value (1.5) is 1 plus the rate of return on the investment.

3. Marco's optimal choice
Marco chooses to consume $60 now and $60 later, as shown by point K. At this point, the feasible frontier is tangent to an indifference curve.

wants to move his buying power forward in time, he borrows against his future income at a rate of 10%. Julia, lacking assets like the poor farmers in Chambar, may have no alternative but to borrow at the higher rate of 78%. The paradox is that Marco can borrow at a low interest rate *because he does not need to borrow.*

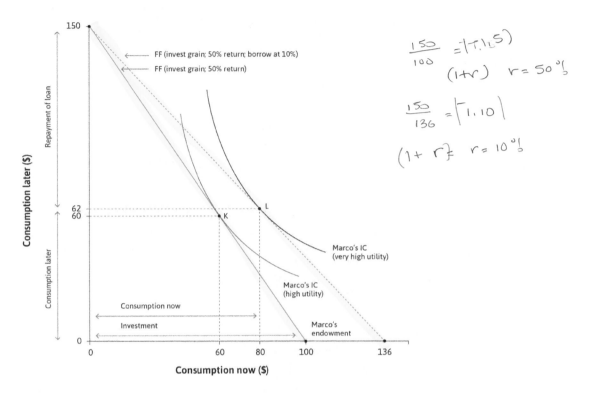

Figure 10.8 Borrowing to invest in a high-return project.

1. Marco's optimal choice when he can invest
His optimal choice when he can invest is at point K.

2. Marco gets a loan
If he could get a loan at 10%, he would be better off by investing everything he has. This expands his feasible set, as shown by the dotted red line.

3. Optimal choice after getting a loan
Marco ends up consuming at point L, with $80 now and $62 in the future.

Plan (points in Figures 10.6 and 10.8)	Rate of return or interest	Consumption now, consumption later	Investment	Ranking by utility (or combined consumption)
Storage (H)	−20% (loss)	$68, $26	n/a	Worst ($94)
Lending only (J)	10%	$65, $39	n/a	Third best ($104)
Investment only (K)	50%	$60, $60	$40	Second best ($120)
Investment and borrowing (L)	50% (investment), −10% (lending)	$80, $62	$100	Best ($142)

Figure 10.9 Storage, lending, investment, and borrowing provide Marco with many feasible sets.

To summarize, borrowing, lending, storing, and investing are ways of moving goods consumption forward (to the present) or backwards (to the future) in time.

People engage in these activities because:

- *They can increase their utility by smoothing consumption*: Or, if they have pure impatience, by moving consumption to the present.
- *They can increase their consumption in both periods*: By lending, or investing.

People differ in which of these activities they engage (some borrowing, some lending) because:

- *They have differences in their situation*: For example, having an income now or later will affect their discount rates and their opportunities. Also, some have investment opportunities (like Marco), while others do not.
- *They differ in their level of pure impatience.*

EXERCISE 10.3 AN INCREASE IN THE INTEREST RATE

1. Use a diagram like Figure 10.4 (page 420) to show the income and the substitution effects of an increase in the interest rate for Marco who receives his endowment today.
2. Compare these effects with those for Julia in Exercise 10.2 and explain your results.

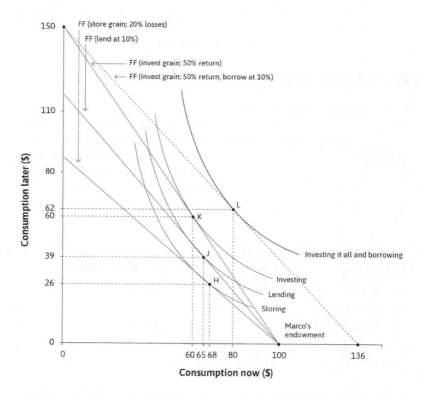

Figure 10.10 Options for the individual (Marco) who starts with assets.

EXERCISE 10.4 LIFETIME INCOME
Consider an individual's income over his or her lifetime from leaving school to retirement. Explain how an individual may move from a situation like Julia's to one like Marco's over the course of their lifetime (assume that their pure impatience remains unchanged over their lifetime).

QUESTION 10.5 CHOOSE THE CORRECT ANSWER(S)
Figure 10.6 (page 423) depicts Marco's choice of consumption in periods 1 (now) and 2 (later). He has $100 worth of grain in period 1 and no income in period 2. Marco has two choices. In scheme 1, he can store the grain that he does not consume in period 1. This results in a loss of 20% of the grain due to pests and rotting. In scheme 2, he can sell the grain that he does not consume and lend the money at 10%. Based on this information, which of the following statements is correct?

☐ With scheme 1, if Marco consumes $68 worth of grain in period 1, he can consume $32 worth of grain in period 2.
☐ With scheme 2, if Marco consumes $68 worth of grain in period 1, he can consume $35 worth of grain in period 2.
☐ The marginal rate of transformation is higher under scheme 1 than under scheme 2.
☐ Marco will always be on a higher indifference curve under scheme 2 than under scheme 1.

QUESTION 10.6 CHOOSE THE CORRECT ANSWER(S)
Figure 10.10 (page 426) depicts four possible feasible frontiers for Marco, who has $100 worth of grain in period 1 (now) and no income in period 2 (later). In scheme 1, he can store the grain that he does not consume in period 1. This results in 20% loss of the grain due to pests and rotting. In scheme 2, he can sell the grain that he does not consume and lend the money at 10%. In scheme 3, he can invest the remaining grain (for example by planting it as seed) for a return of 50%. Finally in scheme 4, he can invest the entire amount of grain and borrow against his future income at 10%. Based on this information, which of the following statements is correct?

☐ 20% depreciation from storage means that Marco is worse off at H than at his initial endowment of consuming all $100 worth of grain in period 1.
☐ The consumption choice J can only be attained under scheme 2.
☐ If the rate of lending increases, the feasible frontier for scheme 2 tilts inwards from the point 100 on the horizontal axis (becomes flatter).
☐ If the rate of borrowing increases, the feasible frontier for scheme 4 tilts inwards from the point 150 on the vertical axis (becomes steeper).

10.7 ASSETS, LIABILITIES, AND NET WORTH

We will see that a person's wealth is an important aspect of their situation in the process of borrowing, lending, and investing, and that those with more wealth like Marco have opportunities not available to those with less wealth, like Julia. **Balance sheets** are an essential tool for understanding how wealth changes when an individual or a firm borrows and lends.

A balance sheet summarizes what the household or firm owns, and what it owes to others. What you own (including what you are owed by others) is called your **assets**, and what you owe others is called your **liabilities** (to be liable means to be responsible for something, in this case to repay your debts to others). The difference between your assets and your liabilities is called your **net worth**. The relationship between assets, liabilities, and net worth is shown in Figure 10.11.

When the components of an equation are such that by definition, the left-hand side is equal to the right-hand side, it is called an accounting identity, or identity for short. The balance sheet identity states:

$$\text{assets} \equiv \text{liabilities} + \text{net worth}$$

Net worth is accumulated savings over time. We can also turn the identity around by subtracting liabilities from both sides, so that:

$$\text{net worth} \equiv \text{assets} - \text{liabilities}$$
$$\equiv \text{what the household owns or is owed}$$
$$- \text{what the household owes to others}$$

In the bathtub analogy, the water in the bathtub represents wealth as accumulated savings, and is the same as net worth. As we saw, net worth or wealth increases with income, and declines with consumption and depreciation. For a household, income increases bank deposits, while consumption is paid with bank deposits. Because bank deposits are an asset for their owner, these operations affect the asset side of the household's balance sheet.

But your wealth or net worth does not change when you lend or borrow. This is because a loan creates both an asset and a liability on your balance sheet: if you borrow money you receive cash as an asset, while the debt is an equal liability.

balance sheet A record of the assets, liabilities, and net worth of an economic actor such as a household, bank, firm, or government.

asset Anything of value that is owned. *See also: balance sheet, liability.*
liability Anything of value that is owed. *See also: balance sheet, asset.*
net worth Assets less liabilities. *See also: balance sheet, equity.*

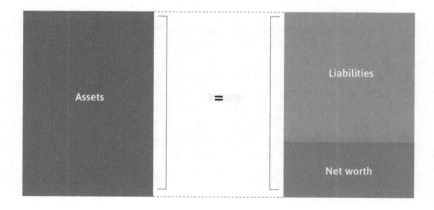

Figure 10.11 A balance sheet.

Julia started off with neither assets nor liabilities and a net worth of zero, but on the basis of her expected future income she borrowed $58 when the interest rate was 10% (point E in Figure 10.4). At this time her asset is the $58 in cash that she is holding, while her liability is the loan that she has to pay back later. We record the value of the loan as $58 now, since that is what she received for getting into debt (her liability rises to $64 later only once interest has been added). This is why taking out the loan has no effect on her current net worth—the liability and the asset are equal to one another, so her net worth remains unchanged at zero. In Figure 10.12 this is recorded in her balance sheet under the heading 'Now (before consuming)'.

She then consumes the $58—it flows out through the bathtub drain, to use our earlier analogy. Since she still has the $58 liability, her net worth falls to –$58. This is recorded in Figure 10.12 in her balance sheet under the heading 'Now (after consuming)'.

Later, she receives income of $100 (an inflow to the bathtub). Also, because of accumulated interest, the value of her loan has risen to $64. So her net worth becomes $100 – $64 = $36. Again, we suppose that she then consumes the $36, leaving her with $64 in cash to pay off her debt of $64. At this point her net worth falls back to zero. The corresponding balance sheets are also shown in Figure 10.12.

Now – before consuming

Julia's assets		Julia's liabilities	
Cash	$58	Loan	$58

Net worth = $58 – $58 = $0

Now – after consuming

Julia's assets		Julia's liabilities	
Cash	0	Loan	$58

Net worth = –$58

Later – before consuming

Julia's assets		Julia's liabilities	
Cash	$100	Loan	$64

Net worth = $100 – $64 = $36

Later – after consuming

Julia's assets		Julia's liabilities	
Cash	$64	Loan	$64

Net worth = 0

Figure 10.12 Julia's balance sheets.

QUESTION 10.7 CHOOSE THE CORRECT ANSWER(S)

The following diagram depicts Julia's choice of consumption in periods 1 (now) and 2 (later) when the interest rate is 78%. She has no income in period 1 and an income of $100 in period 2. She chooses the consumption choice G. Based on this information, which of the following statements regarding Julia's balance sheet is correct?

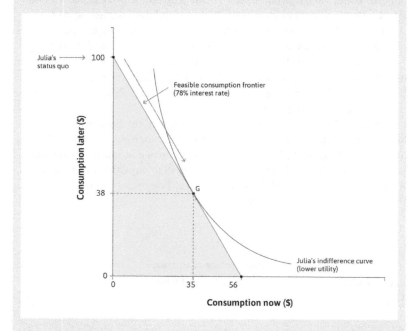

☐ The asset after borrowing but before consumption in period 1 is 56.
☐ The net worth after consumption in period 1 is 0.
☐ The liability before consumption in period 2 is 35.
☐ The asset after consumption but before repaying the loan in period 2 is 62.

●●
10.8 BANKS, MONEY, AND THE CENTRAL BANK

Among the moneylenders in Chambar, the profitability of their lending business depends on:

- the cost of their borrowing
- the default rate on the loans they extended to farmers
- the interest rate they set

The closure of Irish banks for six months revealed how money can be created in an economy and how it depends on trust.

These case studies and the two-period model provide much of what we need in order to understand the role of the financial system in the economy. But we must introduce two more actors on the economic stage: banks and the central bank.

A **bank** is a firm that makes profits through its lending and borrowing activities. The terms on which banks lend to households and firms differ from their borrowing terms. The interest they pay on deposits is lower than the interest they charge when they make loans, and this allows banks to make profits.

To explain this process, we first have to explore in more detail the concept of money.

We saw that anything that is accepted as payment can be counted as money. But money in this sense is different from legal tender, which is also called **base money** or high-powered money. Unlike bank deposits or cheques, legal tender has to be accepted as payment by law. It comprises cash (notes and coins) and accounts held by commercial banks at the **central bank**, called commercial bank reserves. Reserves are equivalent to cash because a commercial bank can always take out reserves as cash from the central bank, and the central bank can always print any cash it needs to provide. As we will see, this is not the case with accounts held by households or businesses at commercial banks—commercial banks do not necessarily have the cash available to satisfy all their customers' needs.

Most of what we count as money is not legal tender issued by the central bank, but instead is created by commercial banks when they make loans. We explain using bank balance sheets.

Unlike our earlier example in which a bank deposit arises from a loan, let us suppose in this case that Marco has $100 in cash and he puts it in a bank account in Abacus Bank. Abacus Bank will put the cash in a vault, or it will deposit the cash in its account at the central bank. Abacus Bank's balance sheet gains $100 of base money as an asset, and a liability of $100 that is payable on demand to Marco, as shown in Figure 10.13a.

Abacus Bank's assets		Abacus Bank's liabilities	
Base money	$100	Payable on demand to Marco	$100

Figure 10.13a Marco deposits $100 in Abacus Bank.

Marco wants to pay $20 to his local grocer, Gino, in return for groceries, so he instructs Abacus Bank to transfer the money to Gino's account in Bonus Bank (he could do this by paying Gino using a debit card). This is shown on the balance sheets of the two banks in Figure 10.13b: Abacus Bank's assets and liabilities both go down by $20, while Bonus Bank's assets are increased by this addition of $20 of base money, and its liabilities increase by $20 payable on demand to Gino.

Abacus Bank's assets		Abacus Bank's liabilities	
Base money	$80	Payable on demand to Marco	$80

Bonus Bank's assets		Bonus Bank's liabilities	
Base money	$20	Payable on demand to Gino	$20

Figure 10.13b Marco pays $20 to Gino.

bank A firm that creates money in the form of bank deposits in the process of supplying credit.

TYPES OF MONEY

Money is a medium of exchange used to purchase goods or services. It can take the form of bank notes, bank deposits, or whatever else one purchases things with.

- **Base money** (also known as legal tender): Cash and the balances held by commercial banks in their accounts at the central bank, known as reserves.
- **Bank money**: Money in the form of bank deposits created by commercial banks when they extend credit to firms and households.
- **Broad money**: The stock of money in circulation, which is the sum of base money (excluding legal tender held by banks) and bank money.

central bank The only bank that can create a country's legal tender. Usually part of the government. Commercial banks have accounts at this bank, holding legal tender.

This illustrates the payment services provided by banks. So far we have just considered transactions using base money, or legal tender. We now show how banks create money in the process of making loans.

Suppose that Gino borrows $100 from Bonus Bank. Bonus Bank lends him the money by crediting his bank account with $100, so he is now owed $120. But he owes a debt of $100 to the bank. So Bonus Bank's balance sheet has expanded. Its assets have grown by the $100 it is owed by Gino, and its liabilities have grown by the $100 it has credited to his bank account, shown in Figure 10.13c.

Bonus Bank's assets		Bonus Bank's liabilities	
Base money	$20		
Bank loan	$100	Payable on demand to Gino	$120
Total	**$120**		

Figure 10.13c Bonus Bank gives Gino a loan of $100.

Bonus Bank has now expanded the money supply: Gino can make payments up to $120, so in this sense the money supply has grown by $100—even though base money has not grown. The money created by his bank is called **bank money**.

Base money remains essential, however, partly because customers sometimes take out cash, but also because when Gino wants to spend his loan, his bank has to transfer base money. Suppose Gino employs Marco to work in his shop, and pays him $10. Then Bonus Bank has to transfer $10 of base money from Gino's bank account to Marco's bank account in Abacus Bank. This transaction is shown in Figure 10.13d.

Abacus Bank's assets		Abacus Bank's liabilities	
Base money	$90	Payable on demand to Marco	$90

Bonus Bank's assets		Bonus Bank's liabilities	
Base money	$10		
Bank loan	$100	Payable on demand to Gino	$110
Total	**$110**		

Figure 10.13d Gino pays Marco $10.

In practice, banks make many transactions to one another in a given day, most cancelling each other out, and they settle up at the end of each day. So at the end of each day, each bank will transfer or receive the net amount of transactions they have made. This means they do not need to have available the legal tender to cover all transactions or demand for cash.

Note that if Marco and Gino were customers of the same bank, there will be no loss of base money. This is one reason why banks fight to get a larger share of deposits.

Because of the loan, the total 'money' in the banking system has grown, as Figure 10.13e shows.

Creating money may sound like an easy way to make profits, but the money banks create is a liability, not an asset, because it has to be paid on

Abacus Bank and Bonus Bank's assets		Abacus Bank and Bonus Bank's liabilities	
Base money	$100		
Bank loan	$100	Payable on demand	$200
Total	**$200**		

Figure 10.13e The total money in the banking system has grown.

demand to the borrower. It is the corresponding loan that is an asset for the bank. Banks make profits out of this process by charging interest on the loans. So if Bonus Bank lends Gino the $100 at an interest rate of 10%, then next year the bank's liabilities have fallen by $10 (the interest paid on the loan, which is a fall in Gino's deposits). This income for the bank increases its accumulated profits and therefore its net worth by $10. Since net worth is equal to the value of assets minus the value of liabilities, this allows banks to create positive net worth.

Base money (excluding legal tender held by banks) plus bank money is called **broad money**. Broad money is money in the hands of the non-bank public.

The ratio of base money to broad money varies across countries and over time. For example, before the financial crisis, base money comprised about 3–4% of broad money in the UK, 6–8% in South Africa, and 8–10% in China.

By taking deposits and making loans, banks provide the economy with the service of **maturity transformation**. Bank depositors (individuals or firms) can withdraw their money from the bank without notice. But when banks lend, they give a fixed date on which the loan will be repaid, which in the case of a **mortgage** loan for a house purchase, may be 30 years in the future. They cannot require the borrower to repay sooner, which allows those receiving bank loans to engage in long-term planning. This is called maturity transformation because the length of a loan is termed its maturity, so the bank is engaging in short-term borrowing and long-term lending. It is also called liquidity transformation: The lenders' deposits are liquid (free to flow out of the bank on demand) whereas bank loans to borrowers are illiquid.

While maturity transformation is an essential service in any economy, it also exposes the bank to a new form of risk (called **liquidity risk**), aside from the possibility that its loans will not be repaid (called **default risk**).

Banks make money by lending much more than they hold in legal tender, because they count on depositors not to need their funds all at the same time. The risk they face is that depositors can all decide they want to withdraw money instantaneously, but the money won't be there. In Figure 10.13e, the banking system owed $200 but only held $100 of base money. If all customers demanded their money at once, the banks would not be able to repay. This is called a **bank run**. If there's a run, the bank is in trouble. Liquidity risk is a cause of bank failures.

maturity transformation The practice of borrowing money short-term and lending it long-term. For example, a bank accepts deposits, which it promises to repay at short notice or no notice, and makes long-term loans (which can be repaid over many years). *Also known as: liquidity transformation*

mortgage (or mortgage loan) A loan contracted by households and businesses to purchase a property without paying the total value at one time. Over a period of many years, the borrower repays the loan, plus interest. The debt is secured by the property itself, referred to as collateral. *See also: collateral.*

liquidity risk The risk that an asset cannot be exchanged for cash rapidly enough to prevent a financial loss.
default risk The risk that credit given as loans will not be repaid.

bank run A situation in which depositors withdraw funds from a bank because they fear that it may go bankrupt and not honour its liabilities (that is, not repay the funds owed to depositors).

Once people become frightened that a bank is experiencing a shortage of liquidity, there will be a rush to be the first to withdraw deposits. If everyone tries to withdraw their deposits at once, the bank will be unable to meet their demands because it has made long-term loans that cannot be called in at short notice.

'The Fear Factor' (http://tinyco.re/6787148). *The Economist*. Updated 2 June 2012.

Like any other firm in a capitalist system, banks can also fail by making bad investments, such as by giving loans that do not get paid back. But in some cases, banks are so large or so deeply involved throughout the financial system that governments decide to rescue them if they are at risk of going bankrupt. This is because, unlike the failure of a firm, a banking crisis can bring down the financial system as a whole and threaten the livelihoods of people throughout the economy. In Unit 17 we will see how bank failures were involved in the global financial crisis of 2008.

QUESTION 10.8 CHOOSE THE CORRECT ANSWER(S)
Which of the following statements is correct?

☐ Money is the cash (coins and notes) used as the medium of exchange to purchase goods and services.
☐ Bank money is the total money in the savers' deposit accounts at the bank.
☐ Base money is broad money minus bank money.
☐ Liquidity transformation occurs when the banks transform illiquid deposits into liquid loans.

10.9 THE CENTRAL BANK, THE MONEY MARKET, AND INTEREST RATES

interest rate (short-term) The price of borrowing base money.

Commercial banks make money out of banking services and loans. But for that they need to be able to make transactions, for which they need base money. There is no automatic relationship between the amount of base money they require and the amount of lending they do. Rather, they need whatever amount of base money will cover the net transactions they have to make on a daily basis. The price of borrowing base money is the **short-term interest rate**.

Suppose in the above example that Gino wants to pay $50 to Marco (and there are no other transactions that day). Gino's bank, Bonus Bank, doesn't have enough base money to make the transfer to Abacus Bank, as we can see from its balance sheet in Figure 10.13f.

So Bonus Bank has to borrow $30 of base money to make the payment. Banks borrow from each other in the money markets since, at any moment, some banks will have excess money in their bank account, and others not enough. They could try to induce someone to deposit additional money in another bank account, but deposits also have costs due to interest payments, marketing, and maintaining bank branches. Thus, cash deposits are only one part of bank financing.

But what determines the price of borrowing in the money market (the interest rate)? We can think in terms of supply and demand:

Bonus Bank's assets		Bonus Bank's liabilities	
Base money	$20		
Bank loan	$100	Payable on demand to Gino	$120
Total	**$120**		

Figure 10.13f Bonus Bank does not have enough base money to pay $50 to Abacus Bank.

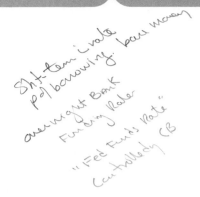

- The demand for base money depends on how many transactions commercial banks have to make.
- The supply of base money is simply a decision by the central bank.

Since the central bank controls the supply of base money, it can also decide the interest rate. The central bank intervenes in the money market by saying it will lend whatever quantity of base money is demanded at the interest rate (i) that it chooses.

The technicalities of how the central bank implements its chosen policy interest rate vary among central banks around the world. The details can be found on each central bank's website.

Banks in the money market will respect that price: no bank will borrow at a higher rate or lend at a lower rate, since they can borrow at rate i from the central bank. This i is also called the base rate, official rate or **policy rate**.

The base rate applies to banks that borrow base money from each other, and from the central bank. But it matters in the rest of the economy because of its knock-on effect on other interest rates. The average interest rate charged by commercial banks to firms and households is called the **bank lending rate**. This rate will typically be above the policy interest rate, to ensure that banks make profits (it will also be higher for borrowers perceived as risky by the bank, as we saw earlier). The difference between the bank lending rate and the base rate is the markup or spread on commercial lending.

In the UK, for example, the policy interest rate set by the Bank of England was 0.5% in 2014, but few banks would lend at less than 3%. In emerging economies this gap can be quite large, owing to the uncertain economic environment. In Brazil, for instance, the central bank policy rate in 2014 was 11% but the bank lending rate was 32%.

The central bank does not control this markup, but generally the bank lending rate goes up and down with the base rate, just as other firms typically vary their prices according to their costs.

Figure 10.14 greatly simplifies the financial system. In this model, we show savers facing just two choices: to deposit money in a bank current account, which we assume pays no interest, or buy **government bonds** in the money market. The interest rate on government bonds is called the **yield**. Read the Einstein at the end of this section for an explanation of these bonds, and why the yield on government bonds is close to the policy interest rate. We also give an explanation of what are called **present value** calculations, which are essential for you to understand how assets like bonds are priced.

We have now seen a model of how the central bank sets the policy interest rate and how this affects the lending interest rate. But why should a central bank do this at all? To understand the role of the central bank, we must look at two questions:

- *How does the lending rate affect spending in the economy?* We will answer this question in Section 10.11.
- *Why does the central bank wish to affect spending by changing the interest rate (as mentioned in Figure 10.14)?* We will answer this much larger question in Units 13–15, when we explain fluctuations in employment and inflation in the economy as a whole, and reasons why central banks are frequently given responsibility for moderating those fluctuations by changing the interest rate.

policy (interest) rate The interest rate set by the central bank, which applies to banks that borrow base money from each other, and from the central bank. *Also known as: base rate, official rate. See also: real interest rate, nominal interest rate.*

lending rate (bank) The average interest rate charged by commercial banks to firms and households. This rate will typically be above the policy interest rate: the difference is the markup or spread on commercial lending. *Also known as: market interest rate. See also: interest rate, policy rate.*

government bond A financial instrument issued by governments that promises to pay flows of money at specific intervals.
yield The implied rate of return that the buyer gets on their money when they buy a bond at its market price.
present value The value today of a stream of future income or other benefits, when these are discounted using an interest rate or the person's own discount rate. *See also: net present value.*

Adapted from Figure 5.12 in Chapter 5 of Wendy Carlin and David Soskice. 2015. *Macroeconomics: Institutions, Instability, and the Financial System.* Oxford: Oxford University Press.

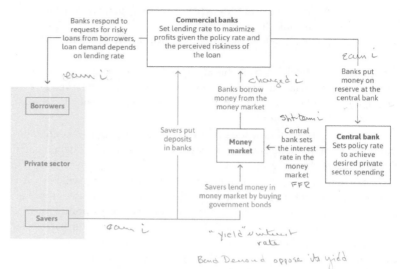

Figure 10.14 Banks, the central bank, borrowers, and savers.

EXERCISE 10.5 INTEREST RATE MARKUPS

Use the websites of two central banks of your choice to collect data on the monthly policy interest rate and the mortgage interest rate between 2000 and the most recent year available.

1. Plot the data, with the date on the horizontal axis and the interest rate on the vertical axis.
2. How does the banking markup (interest rate margin) compare between the two countries?
3. Do banking markups change over time? Suggest possible reasons for what you observe.

EINSTEIN

Present value (PV)

Assets like shares in companies, bank loans, or bonds typically provide a stream of income in the future. Since these assets are bought and sold, we have to ask the question: how do we value a stream of future payments? The answer is the present value (PV) of the expected future income.

To make this calculation, we have to assume that people participating in the market to buy and sell assets have the capability to save and borrow at a certain interest rate. So, imagine you face an interest rate of 6% and are offered a financial contract that says you will be paid €100 in one year's time. That contract is an asset. How much would you be willing to pay for it today?

You would not pay €100 today for the contract, because if you had €100 today, you could put it in the bank and get €106 in a year's time, which would be better than buying the asset.

Imagine you are offered the asset for €90 today. Now you will want to buy it, because you could borrow €90 today from the bank at 6%, and in a year's time you would pay back €95.40 while you receive €100 from the asset, making a profit of €4.60.

The break-even price (PV) for this contract would make you indifferent between buying the contract and not buying it. It has to be equal to whatever amount of money would give you €100 in a year's time if you put it in the bank today. With an interest rate of 6%, that amount is:

$$PV = \frac{100}{1 + 6\%} = \frac{100}{1.06} = 94.34$$

€94.34 today is worth the same to you as €100 in a year's time, because if you put €94.34 in the bank, then it would be worth €100 in a year. Equivalently, if you borrowed €94.34 today from the bank to buy the asset, you would have to pay back €100 in a year's time, exactly offsetting the €100 the asset gives you.

We say that the income next year is discounted by the interest rate: a positive interest rate makes it worth less than income today.

The same logic applies further in the future, where we allow for interest compounding over time. If you receive €100 in t years time, then today its value to you is:

$$PV = \frac{100}{1.06^t}$$

Now suppose an asset gives a payment each year for T years, paying X_t in year t, starting next year in year 1. Then each payment X_t has to be discounted according to how far in the future it is. So with an interest rate of i the PV of this asset is:

$$PV = \frac{X_1}{(1 + i)^1} + \frac{X_2}{(1 + i)^2} + ... + \frac{X_T}{(1 + i)^T}$$

The present value of these payments obviously depends on the amounts of the payments themselves. But it also depends on the interest rate: if the interest rate increases, then the PV will decline, because future payments are discounted (their PV reduced) by more. Note that it is easy to adjust the present value formula to take into account different interest rates for years 1, 2, and so on.

Net present value (NPV)

This logic applies to any asset that provides income in the future. So if a firm is considering whether or not to make an investment, they have to compare the cost of making the investment with the present value of the profits they expect it to provide in the future. In this context we consider the net present value (NPV), which takes into account the cost of making the investment as well as the expected profits. If the cost is c and the present value of the expected profits is PV, then the NPV of making the investment is:

$$NPV = PV - c$$

If this is positive then the investment is worth making, because the expected profits are worth more than the cost (and vice versa).

Bond prices and yields

A bond is a particular kind of financial asset, where the bond issuer promises to pay a given amount over time to the bondholder. Issuing or selling a bond is equivalent to borrowing, because the bond issuer receives cash today and promises to repay in the future. Conversely, a bond buyer is a lender or saver, because the buyer gives up cash today, expecting to be repaid in the future. Both governments and firms borrow by issuing bonds. Households buy bonds as a form of saving both directly and indirectly through pension funds.

Bonds typically last a predetermined amount of time, called the maturity of the bond, and provide two forms of payment: the face value F, which is an amount paid when the bond matures, and a fixed payment every period (for example, every year or every 3 months) until maturity. In the past, bonds were physical pieces of paper and when one of the fixed payments was redeemed, a coupon was clipped from the bond. For this reason, the fixed payments are called coupons and we label them C.

As we saw in the calculation of PV, the amount that a lender will be willing to pay for a bond will be its present value, which depends on the bond's face value, the series of coupon payments, and also on the interest rate. No one will buy a bond for more than its present value because they would be better off putting their money in the bank. No one will sell a bond for less than its present value, because they would be better off borrowing from the bank. So:

price of bond = discounted present value of coupons
+ discounted present value of the face value when it matures

Or, for a bond with a maturity of T years:

$$P = \underbrace{\frac{C}{(1+i)^1} + \frac{C}{(1+i)^2} + \dots + \frac{C}{(1+i)^T}}_{\text{coupons}} + \underbrace{\frac{F}{(1+i)^T}}_{\text{face value}}$$

An important characteristic of a bond is its yield. This is the implied rate of return that the buyer gets on their money when they buy the bond at its market price. We calculate the yield using an equation just like the PV equation. The yield y will solve the following:

$$P = \underbrace{\frac{C}{(1+y)^1} + \frac{C}{(1+y)^2} + \dots + \frac{C}{(1+y)^T}}_{\text{coupons}} + \underbrace{\frac{F}{(1+y)^T}}_{\text{face value}}$$

arbitrage The practice of buying a good at a low price in a market to sell it at a higher price in another. Traders engaging in arbitrage take advantage of the price difference for the same good between two countries or regions. As long as the trade costs are lower than the price gap, they make a profit. *See also: price gap.*

If the interest rate stays constant, as we have assumed, then the yield will be the same as that interest rate. But in reality, we cannot be sure how interest rates are going to change over time. In contrast, we know the price of a bond, its coupon payments, and its face value, so we can always calculate a bond's yield. Buying a bond with yield y is equivalent to saving your money at the guaranteed constant interest rate of $i = y$.

Since a saver (a lender) can choose between buying a government bond, lending the money in the money market, or putting it into a bank account, the yield on the government bond will be very close to the rate of interest in the money market. If it weren't, money would be switched very quickly from one asset to the other by traders until the rates of return were equalized, a strategy called **arbitrage**.

Let's take a numerical example: a government bond with a face value of €100, yearly coupon of €5, and a maturity of 4 years. The nominal interest rate in the money market is 3%, and we use this to discount the cash flows we receive.

So the price of this bond is given by:

$$P = \frac{5}{(1.03)^1} + \frac{5}{(1.03)^2} + \frac{5}{(1.03)^3} + \frac{5}{(1.03)^4} + \frac{100}{(1.03)^4}$$
$$= 4.85 + 4.71 + 4.58 + 4.44 + 88.85$$
$$= 107.43$$

We would be willing to pay at most €107.43 for this bond today, even though it generates €120 of revenue over four years. The yield is equal to the interest rate of 3%. If the central bank raises the policy interest rate, then this will reduce the market price of the bond, increasing the yield in line with the interest rate.

10.10 THE BUSINESS OF BANKING AND BANK BALANCE SHEETS

To understand the business of banking in more detail, we can look at a bank's costs and revenues:

- *The bank's operational costs*: These include the administration costs of making loans. For example, the salaries of loan officers who evaluate loan applications, the costs of renting and maintaining a network of branches and call centres used to supply banking services.
- *The bank's interest costs*: Banks must pay interest on their liabilities, including deposits and other borrowing.
- *The bank's revenue*: This is the interest on and repayment of the loans it has extended to its customers.
- *The bank's expected return*: This is the return on the loans it provides, taking into account the fact that not all customers will repay their loans.

Like moneylenders, if the risk of making loans (the default rate) is higher, then there will be a larger gap (or spread or markup) between the interest rate banks charge on the loans they make and the cost of their borrowing.

The profitability of the business depends on the difference between the cost of borrowing and the return to lending, taking account of the default rate and the operational costs of screening the loans and running the bank.

A good way to understand a bank is to look at its entire balance sheet, which summarizes its core business of lending and borrowing. Banks borrow and lend to make profits:

- *Bank borrowing is on the liabilities side*: Deposits, and borrowing (secured and unsecured) are recorded as liabilities.
- *Bank lending is on the assets side.*

As we saw above:

$$\text{net worth} \equiv \text{assets} - \text{liabilities}$$

Another way of saying this is that the net worth of a firm, like a bank, is equal to what is owed to the shareholders or owners. This explains why net worth is on the liabilities side of the balance sheet. If the value of the bank's assets is less than the value of what the bank owes others, then its net worth is negative, and the bank is **insolvent**.

Let's examine the asset side of the bank balance sheet:

> **insolvent** An entity is this if the value of its assets is less than the value of its liabilities. *See also: solvent.*

- (1) *Cash and central bank reserves*: Item 1 on the balance sheet is the cash it holds, plus the bank's balance in its account at the central bank, called its reserve balances. Cash and reserves at the central bank are the bank's readily accessible, or **liquid**, funds. This is base money and amounts to a tiny fraction of the bank's balance sheet—just 2% in this example of a typical contemporary bank. As we saw above, money created by the central bank is a very small proportion of the broad money that circulates in the economy.
- (2) *Bank's own financial assets*: These assets can be used as collateral for the bank's borrowing in the money market. As we discussed above, they borrow to replenish their cash balances (item 1, Figure 10.15) when depositors withdraw (or transfer) more funds than the bank has available.
- (3) *Loans to other banks*: A bank will also have loans to other banks on its balance sheet.
- (4) *Loans to households and firms*: The bank's lending activities are the largest item on the asset side. The loans made by the bank to households and firms make up 55% of the balance sheet in Figure 10.15. This is the bank's core business. Some of this will be secured lending. A loan is secured if the borrower has provided collateral. In the case of housing loans, called mortgages, the value of the house is the collateral. Other bank loans are unsecured, like overdrafts, credit card balances, and consumer loans.
- (5) *Bank assets* such as buildings and equipment will be recorded on the asset side of the balance sheet.

Assets (owned by the bank or owed to it)		% of balance sheet	Liabilities (what the bank owes households, firms and other banks)		% of balance sheet
Cash reserve balances at the central bank (1)	Owned by the bank: immediately accessible funds	2	Deposits (1)	Owned by households and firms	50
Financial assets, some of which (government bonds) may be used as collateral for borrowing) (2)	Owned by the bank	30	Secured borrowing (collateral provided) (2)	Includes borrowing from other banks via the money market	30
Loans to other banks (3)	Via the money market	11	Unsecured borrowing (no collateral provided) (3)		16
Loans to households (4)		55			
Fixed assets such as buildings and equipment (5)	Owned by the bank	2			
Total assets		100	Total liabilities		96
Net worth = total assets − total liabilities = equity (4)					4

Figure 10.15 A simplified bank balance sheet.
Adapted from Figure 5.9 in Chapter 5 of Wendy Carlin and David Soskice. 2015. *Macroeconomics: Institutions, Instability, and the Financial System.* Oxford: Oxford University Press.

On the liability side of the bank balance sheet, there are three forms of bank borrowing, shown in Figure 10.15:

- (1) The most important one is *bank deposits*, making up 50% of the bank's balance sheet in this example. The bank owes these to households and firms. As part of its profit-maximization decision, the bank makes a judgement about the likely demand by depositors to withdraw their deposits. Across the banking system withdrawals and deposits occur continuously, and when the cross-bank transactions are cleared, most cancel each other out. Any bank must ensure that it has cash and reserves at the central bank to meet the demand by depositors for funds, and the net transfers they have made that day. Holding cash and reserves for this purpose has an opportunity cost, because those funds could instead be lent out in the money market in order to earn interest, so banks aim to hold the minimum prudent balances of cash and reserves.

(2) and (3) on the liabilities side of the balance sheet are what the bank has borrowed from households, firms, and other banks in the money market.

- Some of this is *secured borrowing*: The bank provides collateral using its financial assets (which appear on the left-hand side of the balance sheet in item (2)).
- Some borrowing is *unsecured*.

Item (4) on the balance sheet is the bank's **net worth**. This is the bank's **equity**. It comprises the shares issued by the bank and the accumulated profits, which have not been paid out as dividends to shareholders over the years. For a typical bank, its equity is only a few per cent of its balance sheet. The bank is a very debt-heavy company.

We can see this from real-world examples illustrated in Figures 10.16 and 10.17.

Figure 10.16 shows the simplified balance sheet of Barclays Bank (just before the financial crisis) and Figure 10.17 shows the simplified balance sheet of a company from the non-financial sector, Honda.

Current assets refers to cash, inventories, and other short-term assets. Current liabilities refer to short-term debts and other pending payments.

A way of describing the reliance of a company on debt is to refer to its **leverage ratio** or gearing.

Unfortunately the term *leverage ratio* is defined differently for financial and non-financial companies (both definitions are shown in Figures 10.16 and 10.17). Here, we calculate the leverage for Barclays and Honda using the definition used for banks: total assets divided by net worth. Barclays' total assets are 36 times their net worth. This means that given the size of its liabilities (its debt), a very small change in the value of its assets $(1/36 \approx 3\%)$ would be enough to wipe out its net worth and make the bank insolvent. By contrast, using the same definition we see that Honda's leverage is less than three. Compared to Barclays, Honda's equity is far higher in relation to its assets.

> **leverage ratio (for banks or households)** The value of assets divided by the equity stake in those assets.

> **LEVERAGE FOR NON-BANKS**
> This is defined differently from leverage for banks. For companies, the leverage ratio is defined as the value of total liabilities divided by total assets. For an example of the use of the leverage definition for non-banks, see: Marina-Eliza Spaliara. 2009. 'Do Financial Factors Affect the Capital–labour Ratio? Evidence from UK Firm-Level Data'. *Journal of Banking & Finance* 33 (10) (October): pp. 1932–1947.

Another way to say this is that Honda finances its assets by a mixture of debt (62%) and equity (38%), whereas Barclays finances its assets with 97% debt and 3% equity.

Assets		Liabilities	
Cash reserve balances at the central bank	7,345	Deposits	336,316
Wholesale reserve repo lending	174,090	Wholesale repo borrowing secured with collateral	136,956
Loans (for example mortgages)	313,226	Unsecured borrowing	111,137
Fixed assets (for example buildings, equipment)	2,492	*Trading portfolio liabilities*	71,874
Trading portfolio assets	177,867	*Derivative financial instruments*	140,697
Derivative financial instruments	138,353	*Other liabilities*	172,417
Other assets	183,414		
Total assets	996,787	Total liabilities	969,397
		Net worth	
		Equity	27,390
Memorandum item: Leverage ratio (total assets/net worth)		996,787/27,390 = 36.4	

Figure 10.16 Barclays Bank's balance sheet in 2006 (£m).

Barclays Bank. 2006. *Barclays Bank PLC Annual Report* (http://tinyco.re/7943148). Also presented as Figure 5.10 in Chapter 5 of Wendy Carlin and David Soskice. 2015. *Macroeconomics: Institutions, Instability, and the Financial System*. Oxford: Oxford University Press.

Assets		Liabilities	
Current assets	5,323,053	Current liabilities	4,096,685
Finance subsidiaries-receivables, net	2,788,135	Long-term debt	2,710,845
Investments	668,790	Other liabilities	1,630,085
Property on operating leases	1,843,132		
Property, plant and equipment	2,399,530		
Other assets	612,717		
Total assets	13,635,357	Total liabilities	8,437,615
		Net worth	
		Equity	5,197,742
Memorandum item: Leverage ratio as defined for banks (total assets/net worth)		13,635,357/5,197,742 = 2.62	
Memorandum item: Leverage ratio as defined for non-banks (total liabilities/total assets)		8,437,615/13,635,357 = 61.9%	

Figure 10.17 Honda Motor Company's balance sheet in 2013 (¥m).

Honda Motor Co. 2013. *Annual Report.*

QUESTION 10.9 CHOOSE THE CORRECT ANSWER(S)

The following example is a simplified balance sheet of a commercial bank. Based on this information, which of the following statements is correct?

Assets		Liabilities	
Cash and reserves	£2m	Deposits	£45m
Financial assets	£27m	Secured borrowing	£32m
Loans to other banks	£10m	Unsecured borrowing	£20m
Loans to households and firms	£55m		
Fixed assets	£6m		
Total assets	£100m	Total liabilities	£97m

☐ The bank's base money consists of cash and reserves and financial assets.
☐ Secured borrowing is borrowing with zero default risk.
☐ The bank's net worth is its cash and reserves of £2 million.
☐ The bank's leverage is 33.3.

10.11 THE CENTRAL BANK'S POLICY RATE CAN AFFECT SPENDING

Households and firms borrow to spend: the more it costs to borrow (equivalently, the higher the interest rate), the less they spend now. This allows the central bank to influence the amount of spending in the economy, which then affects firms' decisions about how many people to employ and what prices to set. In this way, the central bank can affect the level of unemployment and inflation (rising prices), as we shall see in detail in Units 13 to 15.

To see the effect of a lower interest rate on consumption spending, we return to Julia, who has no wealth, but expects to receive $100 one year from now. Use the analysis in Figure 10.18 to see how the interest rate affects her decision over how much to spend now.

In many rich countries, when people borrow it is most often to purchase a car or a home (mortgages for housing are less common in countries where financial markets are less developed). Loans for this purpose are readily available even to people of limited wealth because, unlike loans to purchase food or daily consumption items, mortgage loans purchase a car or house that can be signed over to the bank as collateral. This insures the bank against default risk. For this reason, an important channel for the effects of

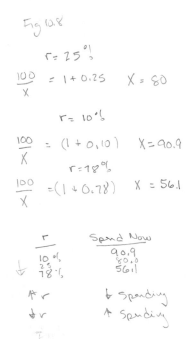

Fig 10.8

$r = 25\%$

$\dfrac{100}{X} = 1 + 0.25 \qquad X = 80$

$r = 10\%$

$\dfrac{100}{X} = (1 + 0.10) \qquad X = 90.9$

$r = 78\%$

$\dfrac{100}{X} = (1 + 0.78) \qquad X = 56.1$

r	Spend Now
10%	90.9
25%	80.0
78%	56.1

↑ r → ↓ Spending

↓ r → ↑ Spending

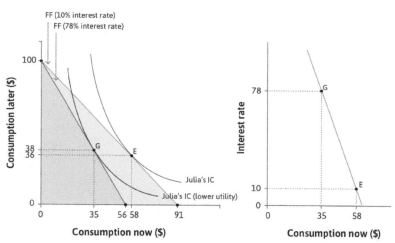

Figure 10.18 Interest rates and consumption spending.

1. Julia has no wealth now
She expects to receive $100 in one year.

2. The moneylender's interest rate
At the moneylender's interest rate of 78%, she borrowed in order to spend $35 now (point G).

3. A lower interest rate
At the interest rate of 10% she would borrow and spend $58 now (point E).

4. As the interest rate falls …
The right-hand panel of the figure traces out Julia's consumption spending now as the interest rate falls, with G and E corresponding to the same points in the left-hand panel.

5. Julia's demand curve
The downward-sloping line is Julia's demand for loans, which also shows her expenditure now.

the interest rate on domestic spending in many rich economies is through its effect on home purchases and consumer durables such as automobiles. The interest rates set by central banks can help to moderate ups and downs in spending on housing and consumer durables, and so smooth out the fluctuations in the whole economy.

QUESTION 10.10 CHOOSE THE CORRECT ANSWER(S)

The following diagram depicts Julia's choice of consumptions in periods 1 (now) and 2 (later) under different interest rates. She has no income in period 1 but an income in period 2 against which she can borrow. Based on this information, which of the following statements are correct?

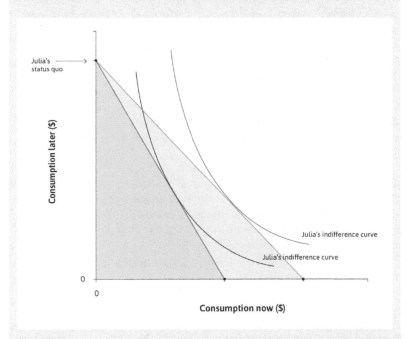

- ☐ A cut in the interest rate increases the marginal rate of transformation of consumption from period 2 to period 1.
- ☐ Julia will unambiguously increase her consumption in period 1 after an interest rate cut.
- ☐ Julia will unambiguously decrease her consumption in period 2 after an interest rate cut.
- ☐ The graph of interest rate (vertical axis) versus period-1 consumption (horizontal axis) is downward sloping.

EXERCISE 10.6 INTEREST RATES AND CONSUMPTION SPENDING

Think about the income and substitution effects of a rise in the interest rate, as analysed in Exercise 10.2 and 10.3. Comment on whether a rise in the interest rate would be expected to reduce consumption expenditure in an economy in which a proportion of households are like Julia, and a proportion are like Marco.

10.12 CREDIT MARKET CONSTRAINTS: A PRINCIPAL-AGENT PROBLEM

Lending is risky. A loan is made now and has to be repaid in the future. Between now and then, unanticipated events beyond the control of the borrower can occur. If the crops in Chambar, Pakistan were destroyed by bad weather or disease, the moneylenders would not be repaid even though the farmers were hard-working. The obsolescence of the skill you have invested in using your student loan is an unavoidable risk, and will mean the loan may not be repaid. The interest rate set by a bank or a moneylender would be greater if the default risk due to unavoidable events was greater.

But lenders face two further problems. When loans are taken out for investment projects, the lender cannot be sure that a borrower will exert enough effort to make the project succeed. Moreover, often the borrower has more information than the lender about the quality of the project and its likelihood of success. Both of these problems arise from the difference between the information the borrower and the lender have about the borrower's project and actions.

This creates a conflict of interest. If the project doesn't succeed because the borrower made too little effort, or because it just wasn't a good project, the lender loses money. If the borrower were using only her own money, it is likely that she would have been more conscientious or maybe not engaged in the project at all.

The relationship between the lender and the borrower is a **principal-agent problem**. The lender is the 'principal' and the borrower is the 'agent'. The principal-agent problem between borrower and lender is similar to the 'somebody else's money' problem discussed in Unit 6. In that case, the manager of a firm (the agent) is making decisions about the use of the funds supplied by the firm's investors (the principals), but they are not in a position to require him to act in a way that maximizes their wealth, rather than pursuing his own objectives.

In the case of borrowing and lending, it is often not possible for the lender (the principal) to write a contract that ensures a loan will be repaid by the borrower (the agent). The reason is that it is impossible for the lender to ensure by contract that the borrower will use the funds in a prudent way that will allow repayment according to the terms of the loan.

The table in Figure 10.19 compares two principal-agent problems.

One response of the lender to this conflict of interest is to require the borrower to put some of her wealth into the project (this is called **equity**). The more of the borrower's own wealth is invested in the project, the more closely

> **principal-agent relationship** This relationship exists when one party (the principal) would like another party (the agent) to act in some way, or have some attribute that is in the interest of the principal, and that cannot be enforced or guaranteed in a binding contract. *See also: incomplete contract. Also known as: principal-agent problem.*
> **collateral** An asset that a borrower pledges to a lender as a security for a loan. If the borrower is not able to make the loan payments as promised, the lender becomes the owner of the asset.

	Actors	Conflict of interest over	Enforceable contract covers	Left out of contract (or unenforceable)	Result
Labour market (Units 6 and 9)	Employer Employee	Wages, work (quality and amount)	Wages, time, conditions	Work (quality and amount), duration of employment	Effort under-provided; unemployment
Credit market (Unit 12)	Lender Borrower	Interest rate, conduct of project (effort, prudence)	Interest rate	Effort, prudence, repayment	Too much risk, credit constraints

Figure 10.19 Principal-agent problems: The credit market and the labour market.

aligned her interests are with those of the lender. Another common response, whether the borrowers are home buyers in New Zealand or car buyers in New Orleans, is to require the borrower to set aside property that will be transferred to the lender if the loan is not repaid (this is called **collateral**).

Equity or collateral reduces the conflict of interest between the borrower and the lender. The reason is that when the borrower has some of her money (either equity or collateral) at stake:

- *She has a greater interest in working hard*: She will try harder to make prudent business decisions to ensure the project's success.
- *It is a signal to the lender*: It signals that the borrower thinks that the project is of sufficient quality to succeed.

But there is a hitch. If the borrower had been wealthy, she could either use her wealth as collateral and as equity in the project, or she could have been on the other side of the market, lending money. Typically the reason why the borrower needs a loan is that she is not wealthy. As a result, she may be unable to provide enough equity or collateral to sufficiently reduce the conflict of interest and hence the risk faced by the lender, and the lender refuses to offer a loan.

This is called **credit rationing**: those with less wealth borrow on unfavourable terms compared with those with more wealth, or are refused loans entirely.

Borrowers whose limited wealth makes it impossible to get a loan at any interest rate are termed **credit-excluded**. Those who borrow, but only on unfavourable terms, are termed **credit-constrained**. Both are sometimes said to be wealth-constrained, meaning that their wealth limits their credit market opportunities. Adam Smith had credit rationing in mind when he wrote:

> Money, says the proverb, makes money. When you have got a little it is often easy to get more. The great difficulty is to get that little. (*An Inquiry into the Nature and Causes of the Wealth of Nations*, 1776)

The relationship between wealth and credit is summarized in Figure 10.20.

The exclusion of those without wealth from credit markets or their borrowing on unfavourable terms is evident in these facts:

- *In a survey, one in eight US families had their request for credit rejected by a financial institution*: The assets of these credit-constrained families were 63% lower than the unconstrained families. 'Discouraged borrowers' (those who did not apply for a loan because they expected to be rejected) had even lower wealth than the rejected applicants.
- *Credit card borrowing limits are often increased automatically*: If borrowing increases in response to an automatic change in the borrowing limit, we can conclude that the individual was credit-constrained. The authors of this study suggested that approximately two-thirds of US families may be credit-constrained or excluded.
- *Inheritance leads the self-employed to considerably increase the scale of their operations*: An inheritance of £5,000 in 1981 (around $24,000 today) doubled a typical British youth's likelihood of setting up a business.

Those seeking loans to purchase a car are often required to allow a device to be installed in the vehicle that is controlled by the bank, which will disable the ignition of the car if the loan payments are not made as required, as this *New York Times* video shows. The practice has not made lenders very popular. http://tinyco.re/2009482

credit rationing The process by which those with less wealth borrow on unfavourable terms, compared to those with more wealth.

credit-excluded A description of individuals who are unable to borrow on any terms. *See also: credit-constrained.*
credit-constrained A description of individuals who are able to borrow only on unfavourable terms. *See also: credit-excluded.*

Adam Smith, 'Of the Profits of Stock' (http://tinyco.re/9527891). In *An Inquiry into the Nature and Causes of the Wealth of Nations*, 1776.

David Gross and Nicholas Souleles. 2002. 'Do Liquidity Constraints and Interest Rates Matter for Consumer Behavior? Evidence from Credit Card Data'. *The Quarterly Journal of Economics* 117 (1) (February): pp. 149–185.

- *Owning a house can be used as collateral*: A 10% rise in value of housing assets that could be used as collateral to secure loans in the UK increases the number of startup businesses by 5%.
- *Asset-poor people in the US frequently take out short-term 'payday loans'*: In the state of Illinois, the typical short-term borrower is a low-income woman in her mid-thirties ($24,104 annual income), living in rental housing, borrowing between $100 and $200, and paying an average annual rate of interest of 486%.
- *Poor and middle-income Indian farmers could substantially raise their incomes if they did not face credit constraints*: Not only do they generally underinvest in productive assets, but the assets they hold are biased towards those they can sell in times of need (bullocks) and against highly profitable equipment (irrigation pumps), which have little resale value.

Samuel Bowles. 2006. *Micro-economics: Behavior, Institutions, and Evolution (the Roundtable Series in Behavioral Economics)*. Princeton, NJ: Princeton University Press.

QUESTION 10.11 CHOOSE THE CORRECT ANSWER(S)

Which of the following statements are correct regarding the principal-agent problem?

☐ A principal-agent problem exists in loans due to a positive possibility of the principal not being repaid.

☐ The principal-agent problem can be resolved by writing a binding contract for the borrower to exert full effort.

☐ One solution for the principal-agent problem in loans is for the borrower to provide equity.

☐ The principal-agent problem leads to credit rationing in the loans market.

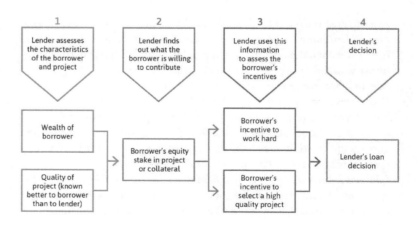

Figure 10.20 Wealth, project quality, and credit.

Jonathan Morduch. 1999. 'The Microfinance Promise'. *Journal of Economic Literature* 37 (4) (December): pp. 1569–1614.

EXERCISE 10.7 MICROFINANCE AND LENDING TO THE POOR
Read the paper 'The Microfinance Promise' (http://tinyco.re/2004502). The Grameen Bank in Bangladesh makes loans available to groups of individuals who together apply for individual loans, under the condition that the loans to the group members will be renewed in the future if (but only if) each member has repaid the loan on schedule.

Explain how you think such an arrangement would affect the borrower's decision about what to spend the money on, and how hard she will work to make sure that repayment is possible.

10.13 INEQUALITY: LENDERS, BORROWERS, AND THOSE EXCLUDED FROM CREDIT MARKETS

Long before there were the employers, employees, and the unemployed that we studied in the previous unit, there were lenders and borrowers. Some of the first written records of any kind were records of debts. Differences in income between those who lend (people like Marco) and those who borrow (people like Julia) remain an important source of economic inequality today.

We can analyse inequalities between borrowers and lenders (and among the borrowing class) using the same Lorenz curve and Gini coefficient model that we used to study inequality among employers and employees.

Here is an illustration. An economy is composed of 90 farmers who borrow from 10 lenders, and use the funds to finance the planting and tending of their crops. The harvest (on average) is sold for an amount greater than the farmer's loan, so that for every euro borrowed and invested the farmer gains income of $1 + \Pi$, where Π is called the rate of profit.

Following the harvest, the farmers repay the loans with interest, at rate i. We simplify by assuming that all of the loans are repaid and that all lenders lend the same amount to the farmers at the same interest rate.

Since each euro invested produces total revenue of $1 + \Pi$, each farmer produces income (revenue less costs) of Π. But this income is divided between the lender, who receives an income of i for every euro lent, and the borrower who receives the remainder, namely $\Pi - i$. So the lender receives a share of i/Π of total output, and the borrower receives a share of $1 - (i/\Pi)$.

Thus if $i = 0.10$ and $\Pi = 0.15$ then the lenders' share of total income is 2/3 and the borrowers' is 1/3.

Inequality in this economy is depicted in Figure 10.21. The Gini coefficient is 0.57.

In the previous sections we showed why some would-be borrowers (those unable to post collateral or lacking their own funds to finance a project) might be excluded entirely from borrowing even if they would be willing to pay the interest rate. How does this affect the Lorenz curve and the Gini coefficient?

To explore this, imagine that 40 of the prospective borrowers are excluded (and since they cannot borrow, they receive no income at all) and that nothing else in the situation changes (i and Π remain unchanged).

The dashed line in Figure 10.21 shows the new situation. The new Gini coefficient is 0.70, showing an increase in inequality as the result of the credit market exclusion of the poor.

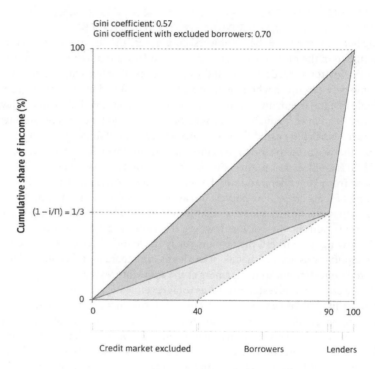

Gini coefficient: 0.57
Gini coefficient with excluded borrowers: 0.70

Figure 10.21 Inequality in a borrowing and lending economy. Note: The Gini coefficient when there are no borrowers excluded is 0.57; when 40 are excluded, it is 0.70.

1. A model economy of lenders and borrowers

An economy is composed of 90 farmers who borrow from 10 lenders. Since $i = 0.10$ and $\Pi = 0.15$, the lenders' share of total income is 2/3 and the borrowers' is 1/3. The Gini coefficient is 0.57.

2. Some borrowers are credit market excluded

Suppose that 40 of the prospective borrowers are excluded. Since they cannot borrow, they receive no income at all.

3. Inequality increases

When some prospective borrowers are excluded, the Gini coefficient increases to 0.70.

QUESTION 10.12 CHOOSE THE CORRECT ANSWER(S)

In an economy with a population of 100, there are 80 farmers and 20 lenders. The farmers use the funds to finance the planting and tending of their crops. The rate of profit for the harvest is 12.5%, while the interest rate charged is 10%. Compare the following two cases:

1. Case A: All farmers are able to borrow.
2. Case B: Only 50 farmers are able to borrow.

Based on this information, which of the following statements is correct?

☐ The share of total output received by the farmers who can borrow is 25%.
☐ The Gini coefficient for Case A is 0.5.
☐ The Gini coefficient for Case B is 0.6.
☐ There is a 10% increase in the Gini coefficient in Case B compared to Case A.

This example illustrates the fact that one cause of inequality in an economy is that some people (like Marco) are in a position to profit by lending money to others, just as others (like Bruno in Unit 5) are in a position to profit by employing others.

Bruno and Marco are probably not the best-loved characters in the economy. For similar reasons, banks are not the most popular or trusted institutions. In the US, for example, 73% of people expressed 'a great deal' or 'quite a lot' of confidence in the military in 2016, exactly the same as the level a decade earlier. By contrast, in 2016, only 27% expressed a degree of confidence in banks, down from 49% a decade earlier. Surveys show that the public in Germany, Spain and many other countries hold their banks in low esteem. This has particularly been the case since the financial crisis of 2008.

It is sometimes said that rich people lend on terms that make them rich, while poor people borrow on terms that make them poor. Our example of Julia and Marco made it clear that one's view of the interest rate—as a cost for Julia and as a source of income for Marco—depends on one's wealth. People with limited wealth are credit-constrained, which limits their ability to profit from the investment opportunities that are open to those with more assets.

It is also true that, in determining the rate of interest at which an individual will borrow, the lender often has superior bargaining power, and so can set a rate that enables him to capture most of the mutual gains from the transaction.

But do banks and the financial system make some people poor and other people rich? To answer this question, compare banks to other profit-making firms. Both are owned by wealthy people, who profit from the business they do with poorer people. Moreover, they often transact on terms (rates of interest, wages) that perpetuate the lack of wealth of borrowers and employees.

✓

EXERCISE 10.8 UNPOPULAR BANKS

Why do you think that banks tend to be more unpopular than other profit-making firms (Honda or Microsoft, for example)?

But even those who dislike banks do not think that the less wealthy would be better off in their absence, any more than that the less wealthy would benefit if firms ceased to employ labour. Banks, credit, and money are essential to a modern economy—including to the economic opportunities of the less well off—because they provide opportunities for mutual gains that occur when people can benefit by moving their buying power from one time period to another, either borrowing (moving it to the present) or lending (the opposite).

✓

EXERCISE 10.9 LIMITS ON LENDING

Many countries have policies that limit how much interest a moneylender can charge on a loan.

1. Do you think these limits are a good idea?
2. Who benefits from the laws and who loses?
3. What are likely to be the long-term effects of such laws?
4. Contrast this approach to helping the poor gain access to loans with the Grameen Bank in Exercise 10.7.

10.14 CONCLUSION

As the Irish bank closure showed, money and credit are so fundamental to economic interactions that people find ways to recreate money even when formal institutions fail. Indeed, archaeologists have discovered evidence of lending and the use of money to denominate debts and to facilitate exchange, from long before banks or governments existed. This is because substantial mutual gains are made possible when a group of people develop sufficient trust in each other and in a particular medium of exchange.

In modern economies, the creation of money is inextricably tied up with the creation of credit, or the process of lending by commercial banks whose actions are regulated by government and managed by the central bank. Borrowing and lending allows people to smooth consumption when they have irregular incomes, to satisfy their impatience, or to finance investment that can increase their future consumption possibilities. The credit market produces mutual gains for borrowers and lenders but, like many economic transactions, the distribution of those gains via the interest rate represents a conflict of interest.

> *Concepts introduced in Unit 10*
> Before you move on, review these definitions:
>
> - Money, broad money, base money, bank money
> - Wealth
> - Income
> - Diminishing marginal returns to consumption
> - A person's discount rate
> - Pure impatience
> - Collateral
> - Balance sheet, assets, liabilities, net worth, equity, solvency
> - Leverage ratio
> - Credit-constrained, credit-excluded
> - The central bank's policy interest rate

10.15 REFERENCES

Aleem, Irfan. 1990. 'Imperfect information, screening, and the costs of informal lending: A study of a rural credit market in Pakistan' (http://tinyco.re/4382174). *The World Bank Economic Review* 4 (3): pp. 329–349.

Bowles, Samuel. 2006. *Microeconomics: Behavior, institutions, and evolution (the roundtable series in behavioral economics)*. Princeton, NJ: Princeton University Press.

Carlin, Wendy and David Soskice. 2015. *Macroeconomics: Institutions, Instability, and the Financial System*. Oxford: Oxford University Press. Chapters 5 and 6.

Graeber, David. 2012. 'The Myth of Barter' (http://tinyco.re/6552964). In *Debt: The First 5,000 years*. Brooklyn, NY: Melville House Publishing.

Gross, David, and Nicholas Souleles. 2002. 'Do Liquidity Constraints and Interest Rates Matter for Consumer Behavior? Evidence from Credit Card Data'. *The Quarterly Journal of Economics* 117 (1) (February): pp. 149–185.

Martin, Felix. 2013. *Money: The Unauthorised Biography*. London: The Bodley Head.

Morduch, Jonathan. 1999. 'The Microfinance Promise' (http://tinyco.re/7650659). *Journal of Economic Literature* 37 (4) (December): pp. 1569–1614.

Murphy, Antoin E. 1978. 'Money in an Economy Without Banks: The Case of Ireland'. *The Manchester School* 46 (1) (March): pp. 41–50.

Silver-Greenberg, Jessica. 2014. 'New York Prosecutors Charge Payday Loan Firms with Usury' (http://tinyco.re/8917188). DealBook.

Spaliara, Marina-Eliza. 2009. 'Do Financial Factors Affect the Capital–labour Ratio? Evidence from UK Firm-level Data'. *Journal of Banking & Finance* 33 (10) (October): pp. 1932–1947.

The Economist. 2012. 'The Fear Factor' (http://tinyco.re/6787148). Updated 2 June 2012.

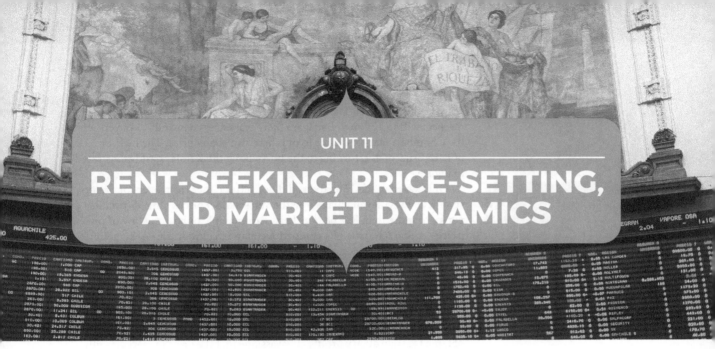

RENT-SEEKING, PRICE-SETTING, AND MARKET DYNAMICS

RENT-SEEKING EXPLAINS WHY PRICES CHANGE (AND WHY SOMETIMES THEY DON'T), AND HOW MARKETS WORK (SOMETIMES FOR BETTER, SOMETIMES FOR WORSE)

THEMES AND CAPSTONE UNITS

- 17: History, instability, and growth
- 18: Global economy
- 19: Inequality
- 21: Innovation
- 22: Politics and policy

- Prices are messages about conditions in the economy, and provide motivation for acting on this information.
- People take advantage of rent-seeking opportunities when competitive markets are not in equilibrium, often profiting by setting a price different from what others are setting.
- This rent-seeking process may eventually equate supply to demand.
- Prices in financial markets are determined through trading mechanisms and can change from minute to minute in response to new information and changing beliefs.
- Price bubbles can occur, for example in markets for financial assets.
- Governments and firms sometimes set prices and adopt other policies such that markets do not clear.
- Economic rents help explain how markets work.

Fish and fishing are a major part of the life of the people of Kerala in India. Most of them eat fish at least once a day, and more than a million people are involved in the fishing industry. But before 1997, prices were high and fishing profits were limited due to a combination of waste and the bargaining power of fish merchants, who purchased the fishermen's catch and sold it to consumers.

When returning to port to sell their daily catch of sardines to the fish merchants, many fishermen found that the merchants already had as many fish as they needed that day. They would be forced to dump their worthless catch back into the sea. A lucky few returned to the right port at the right time when demand exceeded supply, and they were rewarded by extraordinarily high prices.

On 14 January 1997, for example, 11 boatloads of fish brought to the market at the town of Badagara found the market oversupplied, and jettisoned their catch. There was excess supply of 11 boatloads. But at fish markets within 15 km of Badagara there was excess demand: 15 buyers left the Chombala market unable to purchase fish at any price. The luck, or lack of it, of fishermen returning to the ports along the Kerala coast is illustrated in Figure 11.1.

Only seven of the 15 markets did not suffer either from over- or under-supply. In these seven villages (on the vertical line) prices ranged from Rs4 per kg to more than Rs7 per kg. This is an example of how the **law of one price**—a characteristic of a competitive market equilibrium—is sometimes a poor guide to how actual markets function.

When the fishermen have bargaining power because there is excess demand, they get much higher prices. In markets with neither excess demand nor excess supply, the average price was Rs5.9 per kg, shown by the horizontal dashed line. In markets with excess demand, the average was Rs9.3 per kg. The fishermen fortunate enough to put in at these markets obtained extraordinary profits, if we assume that the price in markets with neither excess demand nor supply was high enough to yield economic profits. Of course, on the following day they may have been the unlucky ones who found no buyers at all, and so would dump their catch into the sea.

This all changed when the fishermen got mobile phones. While still at sea, the returning fishermen would phone the beach fish markets and pick the one at which the prices that day were highest. If they returned to a high-priced market they would earn an economic rent (that is, income in excess of their next best alternative, which would be returning to a market with no excess demand or even one with excess supply).

By gaining access to real-time market information on relative prices for fish, the fishermen could adjust their pattern of production (fishing) and distribution (the market they visit) to secure the highest returns.

A study of 15 beach markets along 225 km of the northern Kerala coast found that, once the fishermen used mobile phones, differences in daily

law of one price Holds when a good is traded at the same price across all buyers and sellers. If a good were sold at different prices in different places, a trader could buy it cheaply in one place and sell it at a higher price in another. *See also: arbitrage.*

Robert Jensen. 2007. 'The Digital Provide: Information (Technology), Market Performance, and Welfare in the South Indian Fisheries Sector.' *The Quarterly Journal of Economics* 122 (3) (August): pp. 879–924.

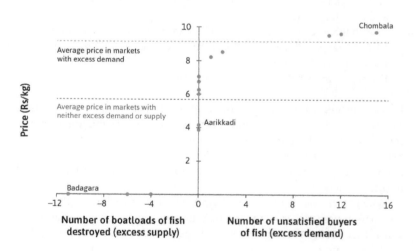

Figure 11.1 Bargaining power and prices in the Kerala wholesale fish market (14 January 1997). (Note: Two markets had the same outcome, with a price of Rs4 per kg.)

prices among the beach markets were cut to a quarter of their previous levels. No boats jettisoned their catches. Reduced waste and the elimination of the dealers' bargaining power raised the profits of fishermen by 8% at the same time as consumer prices fell by 4%.

Mobile phones allowed the fishermen to become very effective rent-seekers, and their rent-seeking activities changed how Kerala's fish markets worked: they came close to implementing the law of one price, virtually eliminating the periodic excess demand and supply, to the benefit of fishermen and consumers (but not of the fish dealers who had acted as middlemen).

This happened because the Kerala sardine fishermen could respond to the information given by the prices at different beaches. It is another example of the idea we introduced in Unit 8 to explain the effect of the American Civil War on markets for cotton: that prices can be messages. For the economist Friedrich Hayek, this was the key to understanding markets.

GREAT ECONOMISTS

Friedrich Hayek

The Great Depression of the 1930s ravaged the capitalist economies of Europe and North America, throwing a quarter of the workforce out of work in the US. During the same period, the centrally planned economy of the Soviet Union continued to grow rapidly under a succession of five-year plans. Even the arch-opponent of socialism, Joseph Schumpeter, had conceded:

'Can socialism work? Of course it can ... There is nothing wrong with the pure theory of socialism.'

Friedrich Hayek (1899–1992) disagreed. Born in Vienna, he was an Austrian (later British) economist and philosopher who believed that the government should play a minimal role in the running of society. He was against any efforts to redistribute income in the name of social justice. He was also an opponent of the policies advocated by John Maynard Keynes designed to moderate the instability of the economy and the insecurity of employment.

Hayek's book *The Road to Serfdom* was written against the backdrop of the Second World War, when economic planning was being used both by German and Japanese fascist governments, by the Soviet communist authorities, and by the British and American governments. He argued that well-intentioned planning would inevitably lead to a totalitarian outcome.

His key idea about economics revolutionized how economists think about markets. It was that prices are messages. They convey valuable information about how scarce a good is, but information that is available only if prices are free to be determined by supply and demand, rather than by the decisions of planners. Hayek even wrote a comic book (http://tinyco.re/9802258), which was distributed by General Motors, to explain how this mechanism was superior to planning.

Friedrich A. Hayek. 1994. *The Road to Serfdom* (http://tinyco.re/0683881). Chicago, Il: University of Chicago Press.

But Hayek did not think much of the theory of competitive equilibrium that we explained in Unit 8, in which all buyers and sellers are price-takers. 'The modern theory of competitive equilibrium,' he wrote, '*assumes* the situation to exist which a true explanation ought to account for as the effect of the competitive process.'

In Hayek's view, assuming a state of equilibrium (as Walras had done in developing general equilibrium theory) prevents us from analysing competition seriously. He defined competition as 'the action of endeavouring to gain what another endeavours to gain at the same time.' Hayek explained:

> Now, how many of the devices adopted in ordinary life to that end would still be open to a seller in a market in which so-called 'perfect competition' prevails? I believe that the answer is exactly none. Advertising, undercutting, and improving ('differentiating') the goods or services produced are all excluded by definition—'perfect' competition means indeed the absence of all competitive activities. (*The Meaning of Competition*, 1946)

The advantage of capitalism, to Hayek, is that it provides the right information to the right people. In 1945, he wrote:

> Which of these systems [central planning or competition] is likely to be more efficient depends mainly on the question under which of them we can expect [to make fuller use] of the existing knowledge. This, in turn, depends on whether we are more likely to succeed in putting at the disposal of a single central authority all the knowledge which ought to be used but which is initially dispersed among many different individuals, or in conveying to the individuals such additional knowledge as they need in order to enable them to dovetail their plans with those of others. (*The Use of Knowledge in Society*, 1945)

Hayek's challenging ideas, and their application, are still fiercely debated today.

'Keynes and Hayek: Prophets for Today' (http://tinyco.re/0417474). *The Economist*. Updated 14 March 2014.

> **exogenous** Coming from outside the model rather than being produced by the workings of the model itself. See also: endogenous.
> **endogenous** Produced by the workings of a model rather than coming from outside the model. See also: exogenous

Unit 8 introduced the concept of competitive market equilibrium, a situation in which the actions of the buyers and sellers of a good have *no tendency to change its price, or the quantity traded,* and the market clears. We saw that changes from the outside called **exogenous** shocks, like an increase in the demand for bread or a new tax, will alter the equilibrium price and quantity.

The opposite of exogenous is **endogenous**, meaning 'coming from the inside' and resulting from the workings of the model itself. In this unit, we will study how prices and quantities change through endogenous responses to exogenous shocks and the real-world competition that Hayek complained was absent from the model of competitive equilibrium. We will see that rent-seeking behaviour by market participants can bring about market clearing, move markets to different equilibria in the long run, cause bubbles and crashes, or lead to the development of secondary markets in response to price controls.

11.1 HOW PEOPLE CHANGING PRICES TO GAIN RENTS CAN LEAD TO A MARKET EQUILIBRIUM

When Lincoln's decision to blockade the southern ports led to a drastic shortage of cotton on the world market (Unit 8), people saw the opportunity to benefit by changing the price. In turn, these price changes sent a message to producers and consumers around the world to change their behaviour.

The blockade was an exogenous shock that changed the market equilibrium. In a competitive equilibrium, all trades take place at the same price (the market-clearing price), and buyers and sellers are price-takers. An exogenous shift in supply or demand means that the price has to change if the market is to reach the new equilibrium. The following example shows how this can happen.

Figure 11.2 shows the competitive equilibrium in a market for hats. At point A, the equilibrium price equalizes the number of hats demanded by consumers to the number produced and sold by hat-sellers. At this point, no one can benefit by offering or charging a different price, given the price everyone else is offering or charging—it is a Nash equilibrium. Follow the steps in Figure 11.2 to see how an increase in the demand for hats gives hat-sellers an opportunity to benefit.

At the original point of competitive equilibrium (A) the price was $8, and all buyers and sellers were acting as price-takers. When demand increases, the buyers or sellers do not immediately know that the equilibrium price has risen to $10. If everyone were to remain a price-taker, the price would not change. But when demand shifts, some of the buyers or sellers will realize that they can benefit by being a price-*maker*, and decide to charge a different price from the others.

For example, when a hat-seller notices that every day there are customers wishing to buy hats, but none left on the shelf, she realizes that some customers would have been happy to pay more than the going price, and that some who paid the going price for their hat would have been willing to pay more. So the hat-seller will raise her price the next day—price-taking is no longer her best strategy, and she becomes a price-maker. She does not know exactly where the new demand curve is, but she cannot fail to see the people who want to buy hats go home disappointed.

By raising the price she raises her profit rate, and earns an economic rent (at least temporarily)—that is, she makes higher profits than are necessary to keep her hat business going. Moreover, because her price now exceeds her marginal cost, she will produce and sell more hats. The same is true of other hat-sellers who will experiment with higher prices and increased outputs.

As a result of the rent-seeking behaviour of hat-sellers, the industry adjusts to the new equilibrium at point C in Figure 11.2. At this point the market again clears, supply is equal to demand, and none of the sellers or buyers can benefit from charging a price different from $10. They all return to being price-takers, until the next change in supply or demand comes along.

When a market is not in equilibrium, both buyers and sellers can act as price-makers, transacting at a price different from the previous equilibrium price. If we start from the original equilibrium and take the opposite case of a fall in demand for hats, there will be excess supply at the going price of $8. A customer at the hat shop might say to the hat-seller: 'I see you have quite a few unsold hats piling up on your shelf. I'd be happy to buy one of those for $7.' To the buyer this would be a bargain. But it's also a good deal for the seller, because at the reduced level of sales, $7 is still greater than the hat-seller's marginal cost of producing the hat.

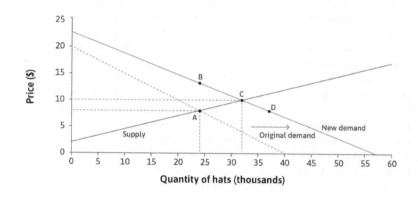

Figure 11.2 An increase in demand in a competitive market: Opportunities for rent-seeking.

1. Equilibrium
At point A, the market is in equilibrium at a price of $8. The supply curve is the marginal cost curve, so the marginal cost of producing a hat is $8.

2. An exogenous demand shock
The shock shifts the demand curve to the right.

3. Excess demand
At the going price, the number of hats demanded exceeds the number supplied (point D).

4. Raising the price
When demand has increased, a hat-seller who observes more customers will realize that she can make higher profits by raising the price. She could sell as many hats at any price between A and B.

5. Increasing quantity
If she sells the same quantity as before at a higher price, the price exceeds the marginal cost of a hat. She earns an economic rent. But she could do even better by increasing the quantity as well.

6. A new equilibrium
As a result of the rent-seeking behaviour of hat-sellers, the hat industry adjusts. Prices and quantities increase until a new equilibrium emerges at point C.

Market equilibration through rent-seeking

The hats example illustrates how markets adjust to equilibrium through the pursuit of **disequilibrium economic rents**:

- *When a market is in competitive equilibrium*: If there is an exogenous change in demand or supply, there will be either excess demand or excess supply at the original price.
- Then, there are *potential rents*: Some buyers are willing to pay prices that are different from the original price, but above the marginal cost for the seller.
- *While the market is in disequilibrium*: Buyers and sellers can gain these rents by transacting at different prices. They become *price-makers*.
- This process continues *until there is a new competitive equilibrium*: At this point there is no excess demand or supply, and buyers and sellers are price-takers again.

Notice how market equilibration through rent-seeking resembles the process of technological improvement through rent-seeking modelled in Unit 2. There the exogenous change was the possibility of adopting a new technology. The first firm to do so gained **innovation rents**: profits in excess of the normal profit rate. This process went on until the innovation was widely diffused in the industry and prices had adjusted so that there were no further innovation rents to be had.

disequilibrium rent The economic rent that arises when a market is not in equilibrium, for example when there is excess demand or excess supply in a market for some good or service. In contrast, rents that arise in equilibrium are called equilibrium rents.

innovation rents Profits in excess of the opportunity cost of capital that an innovator gets by introducing a new technology, organizational form, or marketing strategy. *Also known as: Schumpeterian rents.*

EINSTEIN

Equilibration through rent-seeking in an experimental market

Economists have studied the behaviour of buyers and sellers in laboratory experiments to assess whether prices do adjust to equalize supply and demand. In the first such experiment, done in 1948, Edward Chamberlin gave each member of a group of Harvard students a card designating them as 'buyers' or 'sellers' and stating their willingness to pay or reservation price in dollars. They could then bargain amongst themselves, and he recorded the trades that took place. He found that prices tended to be lower, and the number of trades higher, than the equilibrium levels. Chamberlin would repeat the experiment every year. One of the students who took part in 1952, Vernon Smith, later conducted his own experiments and won a Nobel Prize in economics as a result.

He modified the rules of the game so that participants had more information about what was happening: buyers and sellers called out prices that they were willing to offer or accept. When anyone agreed to a proposed deal, a trade took place and the two participants dropped out of the market. His second modification was to repeat the game several times, with the participants keeping the same card in each round.

Figure 11.3 shows his results. There were 11 sellers, with reservation prices between $0.75 and $3.25, and 11 buyers with WTP in the same range. The diagram shows the corresponding supply and demand functions. You can see that, in equilibrium, six trades will take place at a price of $2. But the participants did not know this, since they did not know the price on anyone else's card. The right-hand-side of the diagram shows the price for each trade that occurred. In the first period there were five trades, all at prices below $2. But by the fifth period most prices were very close to $2, and the number of trades was equal to the equilibrium quantity.

Vernon L. Smith. 1962. 'An Experimental Study of Competitive Market Behavior' (http://tinyco.re/3095861). *Journal of Political Economy* 70 (3) (January): p. 322.

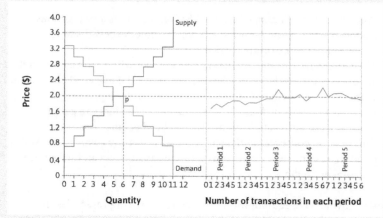

Figure 11.3 Vernon Smith's experimental results.

Smith's experiment provides some support for applying the model of competitive equilibrium to describe markets in which goods are identical—there are enough buyers and sellers, and they are well informed about the trading of others. The outcome was close to equilibrium even in the first period, and converged quickly towards it in subsequent periods as the participants learned more about supply and demand. The competitive model does not capture the rent-seeking behaviour during periods of adjustment in the experiment, but it correctly predicts the eventual outcome to be the price-taking equilibrium.

EXERCISE 11.1 A SUPPLY SHOCK AND ADJUSTMENT TO A NEW MARKET
Consider a market in which bakeries supply bread to the restaurant trade.
A new technology becomes available to the bakeries, shifting the supply
curve as shown in the figure.

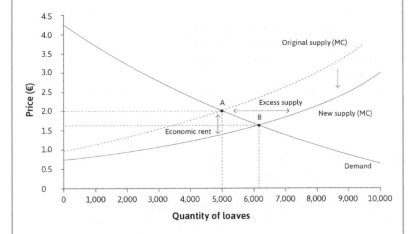

1. Explain why the bakeries would want to increase sales. Why can they
   not do so at the original price?
2. Describe how the actions of bakeries could adjust the industry to a new
   equilibrium.
3. Is it always the seller who benefits from the economic rents that arise
   when the market is in disequilibrium?
4. What action might restaurants take while the market is not in equilibrium?

EXERCISE 11.2 COTTON PRICES AND THE AMERICAN CIVIL WAR
Read the introduction to Unit 8 and the 'Great Economist' box about
Friedrich Hayek in this unit. Use the supply-and-demand model to
represent:

1. The increase in the price of US raw cotton (show the market for US raw
   cotton, a market with many producers and buyers).
2. The increase in the price of Indian cotton (show the market for Indian
   raw cotton, a market with many producers and buyers).
3. The reduction in textile output in an English textile mill (show a single
   firm in a competitive product market).

In each case, indicate which curve(s) shift and explain the result.

QUESTION 11.2 CHOOSE THE CORRECT ANSWER(S)

Figure 11.2 (page 460) shows the hat market before and after a demand shift. Based on this information, which of the following statements are correct?

☐ After the demand increase, sellers will initially sell more hats at $8.
☐ The adjustment to the new equilibrium is driven by the rent-seeking behaviour of the buyers and the sellers.
☐ While the market adjusts, some buyers may pay more for a hat than others.
☐ The new equilibrium price may be anywhere between A and B.

11.2 HOW MARKET ORGANIZATION CAN INFLUENCE PRICES

Social interactions and market organization can both have a powerful impact on prices. Data from fish markets (which are good for comparison because fish are relatively homogeneous) show how influential both can be.

On the eastern coast of Italy, the Ancona fish market (http://tinyco.re/5538756) uses a Dutch auction system. When a crate of fish goes down a conveyor belt, a screen displays the initial price of the crate. That price declines incrementally until a seller pushes a button to buy the case. Transactions occur every four seconds on three active belts and €25 million of fish are sold annually. An auctioneer decides the initial prices, and buyers representing supermarkets and restaurants compete to determine final prices.

The Marseille fish market uses a different system. Sellers agree a price with each buyer who approaches their stand. This is called pairwise trading. If Paul is a seller, and buyer George approaches his stand to purchase a box of sardines, Paul offers him a price. That price may differ from the price Paul offers his next buyer. There is minimal haggling but George is free to reject a price and find another seller.

Some individual vendors in the Marseille market vary the prices of the same fish to different consumers by up to 30%. An individual buyer can end up paying very different amounts for different transactions of the same fish. Despite this, there is a typical downward-sloping relationship between price and quantity in the aggregate market.

Alan Kirman used data on buyer loyalty to explain this kind of **price discrimination**. The Marseille market is composed of approximately 45 sellers and 500 buyers, many of whom are retailers like those in Ancona. Some buyers are extremely loyal to certain fishmongers, and others circulate. More loyal customers pay slightly *higher* prices than their less loyal counterparts. Kirman's data reveal that this arrangement has led to higher profits for sellers and higher payoffs for 90% of loyal customers.

How does this make sense? Buyer payoffs come from both price and the satisfaction of demand. Imagine you are a buyer. On your first day at the Marseille market you are equally likely to buy from any of the fishmongers. You buy cod from Sarah and your supermarket makes a profit, making you more likely to return to Sarah next day. In this way, your past experiences inform your present decisions.

After continuing to buy from Sarah for some time, she begins serving you cod before her other customers as a reward for your loyalty. So you keep buying from Sarah because you are more likely to get all of the fish

price discrimination A selling strategy in which different prices are set for different buyers or groups of buyers, or prices vary depending on the number of units purchased.

that you demand. The benefits of being a loyal customer are especially apparent when the weather limits the quantity of fish available.

Now imagine you are the fishmonger. Seller payoffs come from profits and the satisfaction of your supply. By increasing the number of loyal customers you have, your revenue becomes more reliable and your demand predictions become more accurate.

If you give loyal customers priority over others—perhaps by serving them first—you improve their experience buying from you, making them more likely to return. Over time these customers become so loyal that they will remain despite a small increase in the prices that you charge them.

In this manner, individual relationships and past experiences influence prices. The pairwise trading structure allows for customer loyalty to have a heavy influence on prices in the Marseille market.

Remarkably something very similar happens in Ancona, which has been studied by Mauro Gallegati and his co-authors. Figure 11.4 shows that some individual buyers in the market have very atypical price-quantity relationships. But as shown in Figure 11.5, the aggregate price quantity relationship is standard. Even without face-to-face interaction, buyer loyalty is present and some consumers are more likely to buy from certain ships. Unlike the Marseille market, however, many of these loyal customers pay *lower* prices than their less loyal counterparts. This is puzzling, since there is no face-to-face contact between buyers and sellers. The authors believe that this is due to a complex learning process.

Another noteworthy fact about the Ancona market is that prices fall during the day. In this case, why don't buyers simply wait for better prices? Once again we must consider a trade-off—if buyers wait until later in the day, it becomes more likely that they will not be able to buy the fish that they want. Many buyers may not be willing to accept that risk and will pay higher prices to guarantee that they get their fish. Consistent with this explanation, prices rise sharply at the end of the day when total supply is low.

Prices ultimately come from the interests of and relationships between buyers and sellers. Market organization determines precisely how these relationships influence prices.

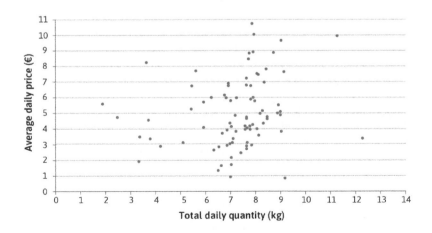

Mauro Gallegati, Gianfranco Giulioni, Alan Kirman, and Antonio Palestrini. 2011. 'What's that got to do with the price of fish? Buyers behavior on the Ancona fish market' (http://tinyco.re/6460122). *Journal of Economic Behavior & Organization* 80 (1) (September): pp. 20–33.

Figure 11.4 The price-quantity relationship for a single buyer in the Ancona fish market.

11.3 SHORT-RUN AND LONG-RUN EQUILIBRIA

When we modelled equilibrium in the market for bread in Unit 8, we assumed that there were a fixed number of bakeries (50) in the city. We worked out the industry supply curve by adding together the amounts of bread each bakery would supply at each price, and then found the equilibrium price and quantity.

But we also saw that at the equilibrium price, the bakeries were earning rents (their economic profits were greater than zero), providing an opportunity for other firms to benefit by entering the market. Entry of new firms would shift market supply, leading to a new equilibrium. This is an example of how rent-seeking can move a market to a different equilibrium in the long run.

Figure 11.6 shows the bread market equilibrium with 50 bakeries at point A in the right-hand panel: 5,000 loaves are sold at €2 each. The left-hand panel shows the isoprofit and marginal cost curves for each bakery (assuming they are identical) and the point where it produces when the price is €2: it produces 100 loaves (where price equals marginal cost). And we can see that at point A it is above the average cost curve, earning a positive economic profit.

The market equilibrium at point A is described as a **short-run equilibrium**. The phrase 'short-run' is used to indicate that we are holding something constant for now, although it might change in future. In this case, we mean that point A is the equilibrium *while the number of firms in the market remains constant*. But because firms are earning rents, we do not expect this situation to last. Follow the steps to see what happens in the longer run.

When the **long-run equilibrium** is reached at point C, the price of bread is equal to both the marginal and the average cost ($P = MC = AC$), and every bakery's economic profit is zero.

In the long run, profits to be made in the bread market are no higher than the profits that potential bakery owners could make by using their assets elsewhere. And, if any owners could do better by putting their premises to a different use (or by selling them and investing in a different business) we would expect them to do so. Although no one would be

short-run equilibrium An equilibrium that will prevail while certain variables (for example, the number of firms in a market) remain constant, but where we expect these variables to change when people have time to respond to the situation.

long-run equilibrium An equilibrium that is achieved when variables that were held constant in the short run (for example, the number of firms in a market) are allowed to adjust, as people have time to respond the situation.

Mauro Gallegati, Gianfranco Giulioni, Alan Kirman, and Antonio Palestrini. 2011. 'What's that got to do with the price of fish? Buyers behavior on the Ancona fish market'. *Journal of Economic Behavior & Organization* 80 (1) (September): pp. 20–33.

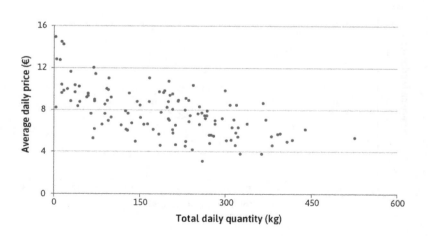

Figure 11.5 The aggregate price-quantity relationship in the Ancona market.

earning more than normal profits, no one should be earning less than normal profits either.

We can use Figure 11.6 to work out how many bakeries there will be in the long-run equilibrium. The left-hand panel shows that the price must be €1.52, because that is the point on the firm's supply curve where the firm makes normal profits ($P = MC = AC$), and each bakery produces 66 loaves. From the demand curve in the right-hand panel, we can deduce that at this price the quantity of bread sold will be 6,500 loaves. So the number of bakeries in the market must be 6,500/66 = 98.

Notice how the short-run and long-run equilibrium differ. In the short run, the number of firms is *exogenous*—it is assumed to remain constant at 50. In the long run, the number of bakeries can change through the endogenous rent-seeking responses of firms. The number of firms in the long-run equilibrium is *endogenous*—it is determined by the model.

The concepts of short- and long-run equilibria don't have much to do with specific periods of time, except that some variables (such as the market price and the quantity produced by individual firms) can adjust more

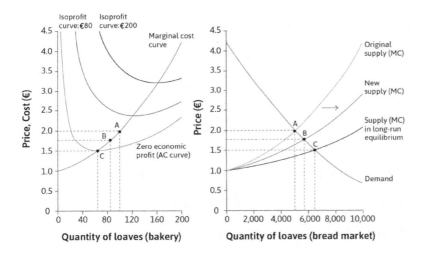

Figure 11.6 The market for bread in the short run and the long run.

1. The short-run equilibrium
Initially there are 50 bakeries. The market is at a short-run equilibrium at point A. The price of a loaf of bread is €2, and the bakeries' profits are above the normal level. They are earning rents, so more bakeries will wish to enter.

2. More firms enter
When new firms enter, the supply curve shifts to the right. The new equilibrium is at point B. The price has fallen to €1.75. There are more bakeries selling more bread in total, but each one is producing less than before and making less profit.

3. Price is still greater than average cost
At B, the price is still above the average cost—bakeries are making greater-than-normal profits. This is still only a short-run equilibrium, because more firms will want to enter.

4. The long-run equilibrium
More bakeries will enter, lowering the market price, until the price is equal to the average cost of a loaf, and bakeries are making normal profits. The long-run equilibrium is at point C.

quickly than others (such as the number of firms participating in a market). So what we mean by the short run and the long run depends on the model. The short-run equilibrium is achieved when everyone has done the best they can from adjusting the easily adjustable variables while the others remain constant. The long-run equilibrium happens when these other variables have adjusted too.

Short-run and long-run elasticities

Remember from Unit 8 that when demand for a good increases, the increase in the quantity sold depends on the elasticity of the supply curve (that is, the marginal cost curve). So if the demand for bread increases, a steep (inelastic) supply curve means that the price of bread rises a lot in the short run while the number of bakeries is fixed, with a relatively small rise in quantity. But in the longer run, this will lead to more bakeries entering, so the price falls, and quantity increases more. We say that, because of the possibility of entry and exit of firms, the supply of bread *is more elastic in the long run.*

The distinction between the short run and the long run applies in many economic models. Besides the number of firms in an industry, there are lots of other economic variables that adjust slowly, and it is useful to distinguish between what happens before and after they adjust.

In the next section, we will see another example: both the supply and the demand for oil are more elastic in the long run, because producers can eventually build new oil wells, and consumers can switch to different fuels for cars or heating. What we mean by the short run in this case is the period during which firms are limited by their existing production capacity, and consumers by the cars and heating appliances they currently own.

QUESTION 11.3 CHOOSE THE CORRECT ANSWER(S)

Figure 11.6 (page 467) shows the market for bread in the short run, with 50 bakeries, and in the long run when more bakeries can enter. All bakeries are identical. Which of the following statements is correct?

☐ The supply curve of each bakery shifts as more bakeries enter the market.
☐ A and B cannot be long-run equilibria, as the bakeries are making a positive economic rent.
☐ More bakeries will want to enter the market when C is reached.
☐ Bakeries will want to leave the market when C is reached, because they don't make any profit.

11.4 PRICES, RENT-SEEKING, AND MARKET DYNAMICS AT WORK: OIL PRICES

Figure 11.7 plots the real price of oil in world markets (in constant 2014 US dollars) and the total quantity consumed globally from 1865 to 2014. To understand what drives the large fluctuations in the oil price, we can use our supply and demand model, distinguishing between the short run and the long run.

We know that prices reflect scarcity. If a good becomes scarcer, or more costly to produce, the supply will fall and price will tend to rise. For more than 60 years, oil industry analysts have been predicting that demand would soon outstrip supply: production would reach a peak and prices would then rise as world reserves declined. 'Peak oil' is not evident in Figure 11.7. One reason is that rising prices provide incentives for further exploration. Between 1981 and 2014, more than 1,000 billion barrels were extracted and consumed, yet world reserves of oil more than doubled from roughly 680 billion barrels to 1,700 billion barrels.

Prices have risen strongly in the twenty-first century and an increasing number of analysts are predicting that conventional oil, at least, has reached a peak. But unconventional resources such as shale oil are now being exploited. Perhaps it will be climate change policies, rather than resource depletion, that eventually curb oil consumption.

What makes the price messages in Figure 11.7 hard to read is the sharp swings from high to low and back again over short periods of time. These fluctuations cannot be explained by looking at oil reserves, because they reflect short-run scarcity. Both supply and demand are inelastic in the short run.

Short-run supply and demand

On the demand side, the main use of oil products is in transport services (air, road, and sea). Demand is inelastic in the short run because of the limited substitution possibilities. For example, even if petrol prices rise substantially, in the short run most commuters will continue to use their existing cars to travel to work because of the limited alternatives immediately available to them. So the short-run demand curve is steep.

Traditional oil extraction technology is characterized by a large up-front investment in expensive oil wells that can take many months or longer to construct, and once in place, can keep pumping until the well is depleted or oil can no longer be profitably extracted. Once the well is drilled, the cost of extracting the oil is relatively low, but the rate at which the oil is pumped faces capacity constraints—producers can get only so many barrels per day from a well. This means that, taking existing capacity as fixed in the short run, we should draw a short-run supply curve that is initially low and flat,

R. G. Miller and S. R. Sorrell. 2013. 'The Future of Oil Supply' (http://tinyco.re/6167443). *Philosophical Transactions of the Royal Society A: Mathematical, Physical and Engineering Sciences* 372 (2006) (December).

Nick A. Owen, Oliver R. Inderwildi, and David A. King. 2010. 'The status of conventional world oil Reserves—Hype or cause for concern?' *Energy Policy* 38 (8) (August): pp. 4743–4749.

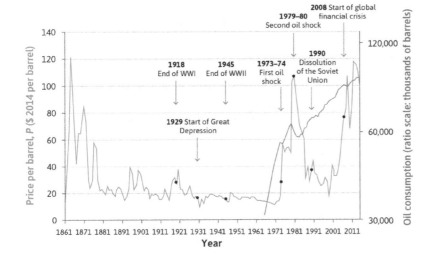

BP. (2015) *BP Statistical Review of World Energy June 2015*.

Figure 11.7 World oil prices in constant prices (1865–2014) and global oil consumption (1965–2014).

and then turns upwards very steeply as capacity constraints are hit. We also need to allow for the **oligopolistic** structure of the world market for crude oil. The Organization of Petroleum Exporting Countries (OPEC) is a cartel with a dozen member countries that currently accounts for about 40% of world oil production. OPEC sets output quotas for its members. We can represent this in our supply and demand diagram by a flat marginal cost line that stops at the total OPEC production quota. At that point, the line becomes vertical. This is not because of capacity constraints, but because OPEC producers will not sell any more oil.

Figure 11.8 assembles the market supply curve by adding the OPEC production quota to the non-OPEC supply curves (remember we obtain market supply curves by adding the amounts supplied by each producer at each price) and combines it with the demand curve to determine the world oil price.

> **oligopoly** A market with a small number of sellers, giving each seller some market power.

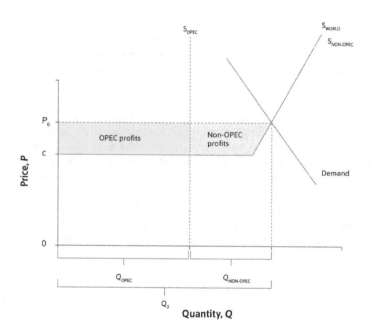

Figure 11.8 The world market for oil.

1. OPEC supply
OPEC's members can increase production easily within their current capacity, without increasing their marginal cost c. OPEC quotas limit their total production to Q_{OPEC}.

2. The non-OPEC supply
Non-OPEC countries can produce oil at the same marginal cost c until they get close to capacity, when their marginal costs rise steeply.

3. World supply curve
Total world supply is the sum of production by OPEC and other countries at each price.

4. The equilibrium oil price
The demand curve is steep: world demand is inelastic in the short run. In equilibrium, the price is P_0 and total oil consumption Q_0 is equal to Q_{OPEC} + $Q_{non-OPEC}$.

5. Profit
OPEC's profit is $(P_0 - c) \times Q_{OPEC}$, the area of the rectangle below P_0. Non-OPEC profit is the rest of the shaded area below P_0.

The 1970s oil price shocks

In 1973 and 1974, OPEC countries imposed a partial oil embargo in response to the 1973–4 Middle East war, and in 1979 and 1980, oil production by Iran and Iraq fell because of the supply disruptions following the Iranian Revolution and the outbreak of the Iran–Iraq war. These are represented in Figure 11.9 by a leftward shift of the world supply curve S_{world}, driven by a reduction in the volume of OPEC production to Q'_{OPEC}. Total production and consumption falls, but because demand is very price-inelastic, the percentage increase in price is much larger than the percentage decrease in quantity. This is what we see in the data in Figure 11.7. The oil price (in 2014 US dollars) goes from $18 per barrel in 1973 to $56 in 1974, and then to $106 in 1980, but the declines in world oil consumption after these price shocks are small by comparison (–2% between 1973 and 1975, and –10% between 1979 and 1983).

The 2000–2008 oil price shock

The years 2000 to 2008 were a period of rapid economic growth in industrializing countries, especially China and India. The **income elasticity of demand** for oil and oil products is higher in these countries than in developed market economies, and demand for car ownership and tourist air travel is growing relatively rapidly as they become wealthier. This increase in income moves the demand curve to the right, as shown in Figure 11.10. In this case, it is the inelastic short-run supply curve for oil that accounts for the big increase in price and only a modest increase in world oil consumption. The sharp price decrease in 2009 has the same explanation but in reverse: the financial crisis of 2008–9 was a negative demand shock that moved the demand curve to the left, so world consumption fell by about 3%, and the price of crude fell from over $100 per barrel in the summer of 2008 to $40–50 in early 2009.

> **income elasticity of demand** The percentage change in demand that would occur in response to a 1% increase in the individual's income.

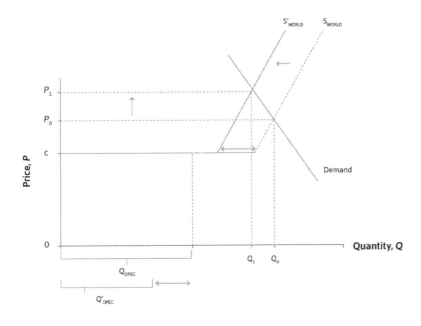

Figure 11.9 The OPEC oil price shocks of the 1970s: OPEC decreases output.

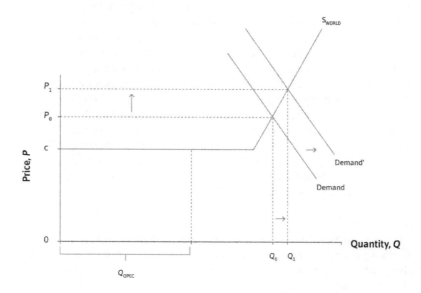

Figure 11.10 The oil price shocks of 2000–8: Economic growth increases world demand.

EXERCISE 11.3 THE WORLD MARKET FOR OIL
Using the supply and demand diagram:

1. Illustrate what happens when economic growth boosts world demand
   (a) in the short run
   (b) in the long run as producers invest in new oil wells
   (c) in the long run as consumers find substitutes for oil
2. Similarly, describe the short and long-run consequences of a negative supply shock similar to the 1970s shock.
3. If you observed an oil price rise, how in principle could you tell whether it was driven by supply-side or demand-side developments?
4. How would the diagram, and the response to shocks, be different if there were:
   (a) a competitive market composed of many producers?
   (b) a single monopoly oil producer?
   (c) an OPEC cartel controlling 100% of world oil production and seeking to maximize the combined profits of its members?
5. Why would individual OPEC member countries have an incentive to produce more than the quota assigned to them?
6. Does this logic carry over to the situation in the real world where there are also non-OPEC producers?

EXERCISE 11.4 THE SHALE OIL REVOLUTION

An important development in the past 10 years has been the re-emergence of the US as a major oil producer via the 'shale oil revolution'. Shale oil is extracted using the technology of hydraulic fracturing or 'fracking': injecting fluid into ground at high pressure to fracture the rock and allow extraction. In a speech called 'The New Economics of Oil' (http://tinyco.re/4892492) in October 2015, Spencer Dale, group chief economist at oil producer BP plc, explained how shale oil production differs from traditional extraction.

1. According to Dale, how has the shale oil revolution affected the world market for oil?
2. How will the world oil market be different in future?
3. Explain how our supply and demand diagram should be changed if his analysis is correct.

11.5 THE VALUE OF AN ASSET: BASICS

People buy fish, hats, and fuel for their consumption value: to eat, wear, or burn them (respectively). Markets for **assets** can work differently because buyers have a second motive: not only to benefit in some way while owning the asset, but also to be able to sell it later. So what determines the value of an asset, whether it is real estate, an artwork, or a financial asset, such as shares in a firm?

Remember from Unit 6 that the profits of a firm belong to its shareholders in direct proportion to the shares that each holds. These profits are typically divided between dividends paid directly to shareholders, and retained earnings used to maintain and expand the firm's ability to generate revenues. But since the future is so uncertain, how should these shares be valued?

Two important determinants of the value of a financial asset (also called a *security*) are the size of the cash flows that it is expected to generate, and uncertainty in one's forecasts of these cash flows.

Bonds

It is easiest to start with an asset that promises a fixed stream of payments at specified dates over a finite period. Suppose investors are completely confident that the promised payments will be made. The best example of this is a **government bond** issued by a country with a negligible likelihood of default, such as the US or Switzerland (this case was analysed in the Einstein in Unit 10).

Investors will be willing to buy and hold the asset only if its rate of return—the future payments relative to the price at which it can be bought or sold—compares well with interest rates on similar assets elsewhere in the economy. The promised stream of payments is fixed, so the lower the price of the asset, the greater will be the interest rate that it yields to a buyer. In other words, the price of the asset will be inversely related to the interest rate that the asset yields. If other interest rates in the economy rise, the interest rate on bonds will have to rise too—so the price of bonds will fall.

Now consider **corporate bonds**, which are not risk-free. The greater the risk of default, the higher will be the interest rate that investors demand in order to hold the asset. If two bonds promise exactly the same stream of

asset Anything of value that is owned. *See also: balance sheet, liability.*

government bond A financial instrument issued by governments that promises to pay flows of money at specific intervals.

bond A type of financial asset for which the issuer promises to pay a given amount over time to the holder. *Also known as: corporate bonds.*

473

payments, the riskier one will have a lower price. Investors will earn a higher interest rate if they buy the riskier bond and it happens not to default, but face a greater risk that the promised payments will not all materialize.

Stocks

Stocks (also called **shares**) differ from bonds in two important respects: there is no specific promised stream of payments, and the time period over which payments will be made is not fixed. Firms expected to generate greater net earnings will have higher valuations, and if expectations change, so will the value of the shares. But like bonds, their value will also depend on interest rates elsewhere in the economy, and on how risky the earnings are thought to be.

Risk

But how should the risk of an asset be assessed? Answering this question requires us to understand the distinction between **systematic risk** and **idiosyncratic risk**. The earnings of a firm may rise above or fall short of expectations for various reasons. Some events—such as changes in trade policy, interest rates, or economy-wide demand for goods and services — simultaneously affect broad classes of financial assets. Other events—such as a successful drug trial, or lawsuit alleging safety problems for a vehicle— affect only the specific firms that stand to lose or gain. The first source of risk is called systematic or **undiversifiable**, the second idiosyncratic or **diversifiable**.

A third type of risk, **systemic risk**, usually refers to risks that threaten the financial system itself. We will examine examples of systemic risk, such as the 2008 financial crisis, in Unit 17.

An important insight in the economics of finance is that diversifiable risk is essentially irrelevant in the valuation of securities, because investors can almost eliminate it by constructing portfolios that contain a large number of assets, each of which has a very small weight. In any given period some of the firms in the portfolio will experience positive shocks, and some negative, but as long as shocks are truly idiosyncratic, they will tend to cancel each other out and the portfolio itself will be largely unaffected.

Systematic risk is different. It arises from shocks that affect large classes of securities simultaneously and cannot be diversified away. Different firms are exposed to different levels of systematic risk, depending on the degree to which their earnings are correlated with those of the market as a whole. For example, the earnings of Ford or Chrysler are heavily dependent on economic conditions in the economy as a whole, since people postpone purchases of cars during economic downturns. In contrast, utility companies providing gas and electricity to residential customers are sheltered from such risks since energy consumption is not very sensitive to economic conditions.

Investors will demand higher average returns from shares in companies with high levels of systematic risk, since their earnings will tend to be volatile in ways that cannot be easily diversified away. The rate of return that will induce investors to buy shares in a company is sometimes called the required rate of return, or the **market capitalization rate**. *Ceteris paribus*, this rate will be higher for companies subject to greater systematic risk. So for any given beliefs about expected future earnings, share values will be higher for companies with lower market capitalization rates.

share A part of the assets of a firm that may be traded. It gives the holder a right to receive a proportion of a firm's profit and to benefit when the firm's assets become more valuable. *Also known as: common stock.*

systematic risk A risk that affects all assets in the market, so that it is not possible for investors to reduce their exposure to the risk by holding a combination of different assets. *Also known as: undiversifiable risk.*

idiosyncratic risk A risk that only affects a small number of assets at one time. Traders can almost eliminate their exposure to such risks by holding a diverse portfolio of assets affected by different risks. *Also known as: diversifiable risk.*

systemic risk A risk that threatens the financial system itself.

This insight was developed by William Sharpe, John Lintner, and others in the 1960s, building on prior work by Harry Markowitz.

market capitalization rate The rate of return that is just high enough to induce investors to hold shares in a particular company. This will be high if the company is subject to a high level of systematic risk.

Trading strategies

The share price computed from such considerations—anticipated future earnings and the level of systematic risk—is sometimes called the **fundamental value of a share** or security. Many institutional investors, including actively managed mutual funds and some hedge funds, adopt trading strategies based on buying assets that they perceive to be priced below their fundamental values, and selling those that are overpriced relative to fundamentals.

However, there are other trading strategies that are not based on an assessment of fundamental value at all. For instance, some traders look for evidence of *momentum* in asset prices, buying because they expect prices to rise further, or selling because they expect prices to fall. An investor might be willing to pay more than the fundamental value of a security if she believes that the price will rise even further above this value. In this case, the buyer could make a gain by buying at a low price and selling at a higher price, even if the fundamental value of the security had not changed.

Buying and selling assets based on an assessment of their fundamental values is a form of **speculation**, motivated by a belief that prices will soon return to their fundamental values. Buying and selling based on perceived *momentum* is also an example of speculation, motivated by a belief that short-run trends have a degree of persistence. These strategies, and many others, are present in modern financial markets. They determine the behaviour of prices, and the possibility of bubbles and crashes (as we shall see in later sections).

> **fundamental value of a share** The share price based on anticipated future earnings and the level of systematic risk, which can be interpreted as a measure of the benefit today of holding the asset now and in the future.

> **speculation** Buying and selling assets in order to profit from an anticipated change in their price.

HOW ECONOMISTS LEARN FROM FACTS

The wisdom of crowds: The weight of stock (oxen) and the value of stocks

What is the right price for, say, a share in Facebook? Would it be better for the price to be set by economic experts, rather than determined in the market by the actions of millions of people, few of whom have expert knowledge about the economy or the company's prospects?

Economists are far from understanding the details of how this mechanism actually works. But an important insight comes from an unusual source: a guessing game played in 1907 at an agricultural fair in Plymouth, England. Attendees at the fair were presented with a live ox. For sixpence (2.5p), they could guess the ox's 'dressed' weight, meaning how much saleable beef could be obtained. The entrant whose answer written on a ticket came closest to the answer would win the prize.

The polymath Francis Galton later obtained the tickets associated with that contest. He found that a player chosen at random missed the correct weight by an *average* of 40 lbs. But what he called the '*vox populi*' or 'voice of the people'—the *median* value of all the guesses—was remarkably close to the true value, deviating by only 9 lbs (less than 1%).

The insight that is relevant to economics is that the average of a large number of not-very-well-informed people is often extremely accurate. It is possibly more accurate than the estimate of an experienced veterinarian or ox breeder.

Galton's use of the median to aggregate the guesses meant that *vox populi* was the voice of the (assumed) most informed player but it was the guesses of all the others that picked out this most informed player.

Vox populi was obtained by taking all of the information available, including the hunches and fancies that drove outliers high or low.

Galton's result is an example of the 'Wisdom of the Crowd'. This concept is particularly interesting for economists because it contains, in a stylized format, many of the ingredients that go into a good price mechanism.

As Galton himself noted, the guessing game had a number of features contributing to the success of *vox populi*. The entry fee was small, but not zero, allowing many to participate, but deterring practical jokers. Guesses were written and entered privately, and judgements were uninfluenced 'by oratory and passion'. The promise of a reward focused the attention.

Although many participants were well informed, many were less so and, as Galton noted, were guided by others at the fair and their imagination. Galton's choice of the median value would reduce (but not eliminate) the influence of these less-informed guessers, preventing individual wild guesses (say, those 10 times the true value) from pulling the *vox populi* away from the views of the group as a whole.

The stock market represents another expression of *vox populi*, where people guess at the value of a company, often but not always quite accurately tracking changes in the quality of management, technology, or market opportunities.

The wisdom of crowds also explains the success of prediction markets. The Iowa Electronic Markets (http://tinyco.re/0124936), run by the University of Iowa, allows individuals to buy and sell contracts that pay off depending on who wins an upcoming election. The prices of these assets pool the information, hunches, and guesses of large numbers of participants. Such prediction markets–often called political stock markets—can provide uncannily accurate forecasts of election results months in advance, sometimes better than polls and even poll-aggregation sites. Other prediction markets allow thousands of people to bet on such events as who will win the Oscar for best female lead. It was even proposed to create a prediction market for the next occurrence of a major terrorist attack in the US.

QUESTION 11.4 CHOOSE THE CORRECT ANSWER(S)
Which of the following statements is correct?

☐ The fundamental value of the shares in a firm is determined by expected future profits and systematic risk.
☐ If there is no new information regarding the future profitability or systematic risk of a firm, but its share price keeps rising, the fundamental value must be increasing.
☐ Buying a share at a price above its fundamental value in the hope that someone else would buy it from you at an even higher price is guaranteed to lose money.
☐ All investors always agree on the fundamental value of the shares in a firm.

11.6 CHANGING SUPPLY AND DEMAND FOR FINANCIAL ASSETS

Prices in financial markets are constantly changing. The graph in Figure 11.11 shows how News Corp's (NWS) share price on the Nasdaq **stock exchange** fluctuated over one day in May 2014 and, in the lower panel, the number of shares traded at each point. Soon after the market opened at 9.30 a.m., the price was $16.66 per share. As investors bought and sold shares through the day, the price reached a low point of $16.45 at both 10 a.m. and 2 p.m. By the time the market closed, with the share price at $16.54, nearly 556,000 shares had been traded.

At any time when the market for shares in News Corp is open, each of the existing shareholders has a reservation price, namely the least price at which the shareholder would be willing to sell. Others are in the market to buy, as long as they can find an acceptable price. As traders' beliefs about the profitability of News Corp change, their willingness to buy and sell changes. To see how the prices of financial assets are affected by such shifts in demand and supply, follow the steps in Figure 11.12. The curves show the hourly volume of shares that would be demanded and supplied at each price.

In practice, stock markets don't operate in fixed time periods, such as an hour. Trade takes place continuously and prices are always changing, through a trading mechanism known as a *continuous double auction*.

> **stock exchange** A financial marketplace where shares (or stocks) and other financial assets are traded. It has a list of companies whose shares are traded there.

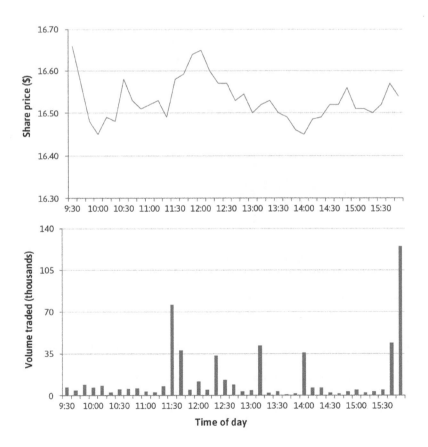

Bloomberg L.P. (http://tinyco.re/ 9335006), accessed 28 May 2014.

Figure 11.11 News Corp's share price and volume traded (7 May 2014).

limit order An announced price and quantity combination for an asset, either to be sold or bought.
order book A record of limit orders placed by buyers and sellers, but not yet fulfilled.

Anyone wishing to buy can submit a price and quantity combination known as a **limit order**. For instance, a limit order to buy 100 shares in News Corp at a price of $16.50 per share indicates that the buyer commits to buying 100 shares, as long as they can be obtained at a price no greater than $16.50 per share. This is the buyer's reservation price. Similarly, a limit sell order indicates a commitment to sell a given quantity of shares, as long as the price is no less than the amount specified (the seller's reservation price).

When a limit buy order is placed, one of two things can happen. If a previously placed limit sell order exists that has not yet been filled, and it offers the required number of shares at a price that is at or below the amount indicated by the buyer, a trade occurs. If there is no such order available, then the limit order is placed in what is called an **order book** (which is really just an electronic record), and becomes available to trade against new sell orders that arrive.

Orders to buy are referred to as *bids*, and orders to sell as *asks*. The order book lists bids in decreasing order of price, and asks in increasing order. The top of the book for shares in NWS at around midday on 8 May 2014 looked like the table in Figure 11.13.

Figure 11.12 Good news about profitability.

1. The initial equilibrium
Initially the market is in equilibrium at A: 6,000 shares are sold per hour at a price of $16.50.

2. Good news about profitability
Some good news about the future profitability of News Corp simultaneously shifts the demand curve ...

3. Good news about profitability
... and the supply curve.

4. A new equilibrium
The new temporary market equilibrium is at B. The price has risen from $16.50 to $16.65. In this illustration, demand changes more than supply, so volume rises too.

Given this situation, a buy order for 100 shares at $16.57 would remain unfilled and would enter the book at the top of the bid column. However, a bid for 600 shares at $16.60 would be filled immediately, since it can be matched against existing limit sell orders. 500 shares would trade at $16.59 apiece, and 100 shares would trade at $16.60. Whenever a buy order is immediately filled, trade occurs at the best possible price for the buyer (the ask price). Similarly, if a sell order is placed and immediately filled from existing orders, trade occurs at the best possible price for the seller (the bid price).

We can now see how prices in such a market change over time. Someone who receives negative news about News Corp, such as a rumour that a board member is about to resign, and believes this information has not yet been incorporated into the price, may place a large sell order at a price below $16.56, which will immediately trade against existing bids. As these trades occur, bids are removed from the order book and the price of the stock declines. Similarly, in response to good news, orders to buy at prices above the lowest ask will trade against existing sell orders, and transactions will occur at successively increasing prices.

Since the price fluctuates, it is not easy to think of this market as being in equilibrium. But it is nevertheless the case that the price is always adjusting to reconcile supply and demand and hence clear the market.

Financial assets provide another example of markets equilibrating through economic rent-seeking:

- Those who believe they will benefit from buying News Corp shares at a particular price lodge a bid at that price.
- Those who believe they will benefit by selling lodge an ask at a particular price.
- The price at any moment reflects the aggregate outcome of the rent-seeking behaviour of all the actors in the market—including those who are simply holding on to their shares.

Watch our video in which Rajiv Sethi, one of the authors of this unit, demonstrates how orders are processed in a continuous double auction. http://tinyco.re/3679850

EXERCISE 11.5 SUPPLY AND DEMAND CURVES

1. Use the data from the NWS order book in Figure 11.13 to plot supply and demand curves for shares.
2. Explain why the two curves do not intersect.

Bid		Ask	
Price ($)	Quantity	Price ($)	Quantity
16.56	400	16.59	500
16.55	400	16.60	700
16.54	400	16.61	800
16.53	600	16.62	500
16.52	200	16.63	500

Figure 11.13 A continuous double auction order book: Bid and ask prices for News Corp (NWS) shares.

Yahoo Finance (http://tinyco.re/6764389), accessed 8 May 2014.

QUESTION 11.5 CHOOSE THE CORRECT ANSWER(S)

The figure shows an order book for News Corp shares. Which of the following statements about this order book is correct?

Bid		Ask	
Price ($)	Quantity	Price ($)	Quantity
16.56	400	16.59	500
16.55	400	16.60	700
16.54	400	16.61	800
16.53	600	16.62	500
16.52	200	16.63	500

☐ A buyer wants 500 shares at $16.59.
☐ A limit buy order at $16.56 means that the buyer would pay at least $16.56 per share.
☐ A limit sell order for 100 shares at $16.58 will be unfilled.
☐ A limit buy order for 600 shares at $16.59 will be filled with 500 shares bought at $16.59 and the remaining 100 shares at $16.60.

11.7 ASSET MARKET BUBBLES

The flexibility demonstrated by News Corp stock prices is common in markets for other financial assets such as government bonds, currencies under floating exchange rates, **commodities** such as gold, crude oil and corn, and tangible assets such as houses and works of art.

But share prices are not only volatile hour-by-hour and day-by-day. They can also display large swings, often referred to as **bubbles**. Figure 11.14 shows the value of the Nasdaq Composite Index between 1995 and 2004. This index is an average of prices for a set of stocks, with companies weighted in proportion to their market capitalization. The Nasdaq Composite Index at this time included many fast-growing and hard-to-value companies in technology sectors.

The index began the period at less than 750, and rose in five years to more than 5,000 with a remarkable annualized rate of return of around 45%. It then lost two-thirds of its value in less than a year, and eventually bottomed out at around 1,100, almost 80% below its peak. The episode has come to be called the *tech bubble*.

Information, uncertainty, and beliefs

The term **bubble** refers to a sustained and significant departure of the price of any asset (financial or otherwise) from its fundamental value.

Sometimes, new information about the fundamental value of an asset is quickly and reliably expressed in markets. Changes in beliefs about a firm's future earnings growth result in virtually instantaneous adjustments in its share price. Both good and bad news about patents or lawsuits, the illness or departure of important personnel, earnings surprises, or mergers and acquisitions can all result in active trading—and swift price movements.

Because stock price movements often reflect important information about the financial health of a firm, traders who lack this information can try to deduce it from price movements. Using Hayek's language, changes in

commodities Physical goods traded in a manner similar to stocks. They include metals such as gold and silver, and agricultural products such as coffee and sugar, oil and gas. Sometimes more generally used to mean anything produced for sale.

asset price bubble Sustained and significant rise in the price of an asset fuelled by expectations of future price increases.

prices are messages containing information. If markets are to work well, traders must respond to these messages. But when they interpret a price increase as a sign of further price increases (**momentum trading** strategies) the result can be self-reinforcing cycles of price increases, resulting in asset price bubbles followed by sudden price declines, called crashes.

Three distinctive and related features of markets may give rise to bubbles:

- *Resale value:* The demand for the asset arises both from the benefit to its owner (for example, the flow of dividends from a stock, or the enjoyment of having a painting by a well-known artist in your living room) and because it offers the opportunity for speculation on a change in its price. Similarly, a landlord may buy a house both for the rental income and also to create a capital gain by holding the asset for a period of time and then selling it. People's beliefs about what will happen to asset prices differ, and change as they receive new information or believe others are responding to new information.
- *Ease of trading:* In financial markets, the ease of trading means that you can switch between being a buyer and being a seller if you change your mind about whether you think the price will rise or fall. Switching between buying and selling is not possible in markets for ordinary goods and services, where sellers are firms with specialized capital goods and skilled workers, and buyers are other types of firms, or households.
- *Ease of borrowing to finance purchases:* If market participants can borrow to increase their demand for an asset that they believe will increase in price, this allows an upward movement of prices to continue, creating the possibility of a bubble and subsequent crash.

momentum trading Share trading strategy based on the idea that new information is not incorporated into prices instantly, so that prices exhibit positive correlation over short periods.

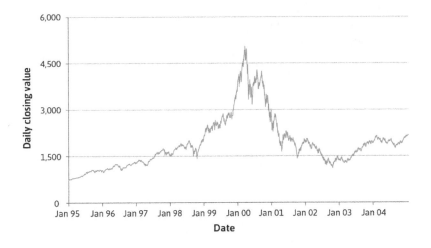

Yahoo Finance (http://tinyco.re/6764389), accessed 14 January 2014.

Figure 11.14 The tech bubble: Nasdaq Composite Index (1995–2004).

WHEN ECONOMISTS DISAGREE

Do bubbles exist?

The price movements in Figure 11.14 (and Figure 11.20 in the next section), give the impression that asset prices can swing wildly, bearing little relation to the stream of income that might reasonably be expected from holding them.

But do bubbles really exist, or are they an illusion based only on hindsight? In other words, is it possible to know that a market is experiencing a bubble before it crashes? Perhaps surprisingly, some prominent economists working with financial market data disagree on this question. They include Eugene Fama and Robert Shiller, two of the three recipients of the 2013 Nobel Prize.

Fama denies that the term 'bubble' has any useful meaning at all:

> These words have become popular. I don't think they have any meaning … It's easy to say prices went down, it must have been a bubble, after the fact. I think most bubbles are twenty-twenty hindsight. Now after the fact you always find people who said before the fact that prices are too high. People are always saying that prices are too high. When they turn out to be right, we anoint them. When they turn out to be wrong, we ignore them. They are typically right and wrong about half the time.

Eugene Fama, quoted in 'Interview with Eugene Fama' (http://tinyco.re/0438887), *The New Yorker*. (2010).

This is an expression of what economists call the *efficient market hypothesis*, which claims that all generally available information about fundamental values is incorporated into prices virtually instantaneously. Robert Lucas—another Nobel laureate, firmly in Fama's camp—explained the logic of this argument in 2009, in the middle of the financial crisis:

> One thing we are not going to have, now or ever, is a set of models that forecasts sudden falls in the value of financial assets, like the declines that followed the failure of Lehman Brothers in September. This is nothing new. It has been known for more than 40 years and is one of the main implications of Eugene Fama's efficient-market hypothesis … If an economist had a formula that could reliably forecast crises a week in advance, say, then that formula would become part of generally available information and prices would fall a week earlier.

Tim Harford. 2012. 'Still Think You Can Beat the Market?' (http://tinyco.re/7063932). *The Undercover Economist*. Updated 24 November 2012.

If the efficient market hypothesis is accurate, how could the 2008 financial crisis happen? Robert Lucas on Fama's efficient market hypothesis: Robert Lucas. 2009. 'In Defence of the Dismal Science' (http://tinyco.re/6052194). *The Economist*. Updated 6 August 2009.

Responding to Lucas, Markus Brunnermeier explains why this argument is not watertight:

> Of course, as Bob Lucas points out, when it is commonly known among all investors that a bubble will burst next week, then they will prick it already today. However, in practice each individual investor does not know when other investors will start trading against the bubble. This uncertainty makes each individual investor nervous about whether he can be out of (or short) the market sufficiently long until the bubble finally bursts. Consequently, each investor is reluctant to lean against the wind. Indeed, investors may in fact prefer to ride a bubble for a long time such that price corrections only occur after a long delay, and often abruptly. Empirical research on stock price predictability supports this view. Furthermore, since funding frictions limit arbitrage activity, the fact that you can't make money does not imply that the 'price is right'.
>
> This way of thinking suggests a radically different approach for the future financial architecture. Central banks and financial regulators have to be vigilant and look out for bubbles, and should help investors to synchronize their effort to lean against asset price bubbles. As the current episode has shown, it is not sufficient to clean up after the bubble bursts, but essential to lean against the formation of the bubble in the first place.

Shiller has argued that relatively simple and publicly observable statistics, such as the ratio of stock prices to earnings per share, can be used to identify bubbles as they form. Leaning against the wind by buying assets that are cheap based on this criterion, and selling those that are dear, can result in losses in the short run, but long-term gains that, in Shiller's view, exceed the returns to be made by simply investing in a diversified basket of securities with similar risk attributes.

In collaboration with Barclays Bank, Shiller has launched a product called an exchange-traded note (ETN) that can be used to invest in accordance with his theory. This asset is linked to the value of the cyclically adjusted price-to-earnings (CAPE) ratio, which Shiller believes is predictive of future prices over long periods. So this is one economist who has put his money where his mouth is: you can follow the fluctuation of Shiller's index on Barclays Bank's website (http://tinyco.re/7309155).

Brunnermeier argues Lucas was right to emphasize that financial market frictions are a counter-argument to the efficient market hypothesis: Markus Brunnermeier. 2009. 'Lucas Roundtable: Mind the Frictions' (http://tinyco.re/0136751). *The Economist*. Updated 6 August 2009.

Robert J. Shiller. 2003. 'From Efficient Markets Theory to Behavioral Finance' (http://tinyco.re/3989503). *Journal of Economic Perspectives* 17 (1) (March): pp. 83–104.

Burton G. Malkiel. 2003. 'The Efficient Market Hypothesis and Its Critics' (http://tinyco.re/4628706). *Journal of Economic Perspectives* 17 (1) (March): pp. 59–82.

The classic examination of bubbles was made by John Maynard Keynes in Chapter 12 of his General Theory. John Maynard Keynes. 1936. *The General Theory of Employment, Interest and Money* (http://tinyco.re/6855346). London: Palgrave Macmillan.

So there are two quite different interpretations of the 'tech bubble' episode in Figure 11.14:

John Cassidy. 2010. 'Interview with Eugene Fama' (http://tinyco.re/4647447). *The New Yorker*. Updated 13 January 2010.

Robert J. Shiller. 2015. *Irrational Exuberance*, Chapter 1 (http://tinyco.re/4263463). Princeton, NJ: Princeton University Press.

- *Fama's view*: Asset prices throughout the episode were based on the best information available at the time and fluctuated because information about the prospects of the companies was changing sharply. In John Cassidy's 2010 interview with Fama in *The New Yorker*, he describes many of the arguments for the existence of bubbles as 'entirely sloppy'.
- *Shiller's view*: Prices in the late 1990s had been driven up simply by expectations that the price would still rise further. He called this '**irrational exuberance**' among investors. The first chapter of his book *Irrational Exuberance* explains the idea.

irrational exuberance A process by which assets become overvalued. The expression was first used by Alan Greenspan, then chairman of the US Federal Reserve Board, in 1996. It was popularized as an economic concept by the economist Robert Shiller.

EXERCISE 11.6 MARKETS FOR GEMS
A *New York Times* article (http://tinyco.re/6343875), describes how the worldwide markets for opals, sapphires, and emeralds are affected by discoveries of new sources of gems.

1. Explain, using supply and demand analysis, why Australian dealers were unhappy about the discovery of opals in Ethiopia.
2. What determines the willingness to pay for gems? Why do Madagascan sapphires command lower prices than Asian ones?
3. Explain why the reputation of gems from particular sources might matter to a consumer. Shouldn't you judge how much you are willing to pay for a stone by how much you like it yourself?
4. Do you think that the high reputation of gems from particular origins necessarily reflects true differences in quality?
5. Could we see bubbles in the markets for gems?

QUESTION 11.6 CHOOSE THE CORRECT ANSWER(S)
Which of the following statements about bubbles is correct?

☐ A bubble occurs when the fundamental value of a share rises too quickly.
☐ A bubble is less likely to occur in a market where people can easily switch from buying to selling.
☐ Momentum trading strategies make bubbles more likely to occur.
☐ Bubbles can only occur in financial markets.

11.8 MODELLING BUBBLES AND CRASHES

We have seen that bubbles could occur in markets for financial assets because demand depends, in part, on expectations about the prices at which they may be resold in future. This argument might also apply to durable goods—such as houses, paintings, and 'collectibles' like vintage cars or stamps. Can we apply our model of price-taking buyers and sellers to such markets?

Figure 11.15 illustrates the supply and demand for shares in a (so far) hypothetical firm called the Flying Car Corporation (FCC). Initially the share price is $50 on the lowest demand curve. When potential traders and investors receive good news about expected future profitability, the demand curve shifts to the right, and the price increases to $60 (for simplicity, we assume that the supply curve doesn't move).

Initially the exogenous rise in demand has the same effect as in the markets for bread and hats. Follow the steps in Figure 11.15 to see what happens next.

The sequence of events in Figure 11.15 can happen if individuals interpret a price rise to mean that other people have received news that they hadn't heard themselves, and adjust their own expectations upwards. Or they may think there is an opportunity for speculation: to buy the stock now and sell to other buyers at a profit later. Either way, the initial increase in demand creates a **positive feedback**, leading to further increases in demand.

This does not happen in the bread market. People do not respond to a rise in bread price by buying more bread and filling their freezer. To model markets for assets like shares, paintings, or houses, we need to allow for the additional effects of beliefs about future prices. Figure 11.16 contrasts two alternative scenarios following an exogenous shock of good news about future profits of FCC that raises the price from $50 to $60 as in Figure 11.15.

In the left-hand panel, beliefs dampen price rises: some market participants respond to the initial price rise with scepticism about whether the fundamental value of FCC is really $60, so they sell shares, taking a

positive feedback (process) A process whereby some initial change sets in motion a process that magnifies the initial change. *See also: negative feedback (process).*

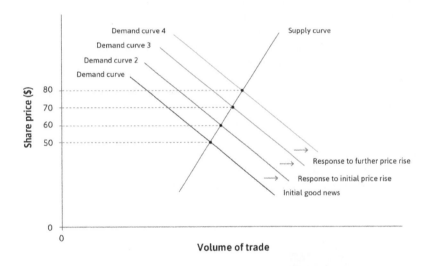

Figure 11.15 The beginning of a bubble in FCC shares.

1. The initial price
Initially the price of a share in a firm called the Flying Car Corporation (FCC) is $50 on the lowest demand curve.

2. The response to good news
When potential traders and investors receive good news about expected future profitability, the demand curve shifts to the right, and the price increases to $60.

3. The effect of a price rise
Observing the price rise, potential buyers treat it as further good news. The demand curve shifts up simply because the price has increased, and the price rises again to $70.

4. The beginning of a bubble
This further rise may lead to another shift in demand, continuing the process.

485

profit from the higher price. This behaviour reduces the price and it falls to a value somewhat above its initial level, where it stabilizes. The news has been incorporated into a price between \$50 and \$60, reflecting the aggregate of beliefs in the market about the new fundamental value of FCC.

By contrast, in the right panel beliefs amplify price rises. When demand rises, others believe that the initial rise in price signals a further rise in future. These beliefs produce an increase in the demand for FCC shares. Other traders see that those who bought more shares in FCC benefited as its price rose and so they follow suit. A self-reinforcing cycle of higher prices and rising demand takes hold.

If beliefs dampen price changes and restore the market to equilibrium after a price shock, we say that the equilibrium is **stable**. Figure 11.17 shows how we can model the process of price adjustment in the case of a stable equilibrium. The left-hand panel shows supply and demand curves for FCC shares, with an equilibrium price P_0 corresponding to their fundamental value. The right-hand panel shows the relationship between prices in successive periods of time, called the *price dynamics curve* (PDC). If P_t, the price in period t, is equal to P_0, then the price in the next period, P_{t+1}, will be the same, because at the equilibrium there is no tendency for change. But if the current price P_t is not at the equilibrium, the PDC shows what the price will be in the next period. Follow the steps in Figure 11.7 to see how, with a PDC like the one shown here, the market will return to equilibrium after a shock.

In Figure 11.17, the PDC is flatter than the 45° line, so when the price is above the equilibrium, it will adjust downwards again until equilibrium is restored. This PDC represents the case in which beliefs about the fundamental value of the asset dominate any tendency to interpret the price rise as a signal of further price rises.

Let's now suppose that following the initial increase in the share price P_1, demand *increases*: shares in FCC are now seen as a better investment. Even if everyone knows that the fundamental value of the shares is still P_0, some people believe that the price will continue to rise for some time. If the conviction takes hold that the price will increase further, then owning more shares is a good strategy. There will be a capital gain from holding them because they can be sold later for more than the price paid to acquire them.

Beliefs dampen price rises

Beliefs amplify price rises: a bubble

Figure 11.16 Positive vs negative feedback.

In this case, as shown in the left-hand panel of Figure 11.18, the higher price shifts the demand curve to the right. In the right-hand panel, the PDC is steeper than the 45° line. This tells us that the price next period is further from the equilibrium at P_0 than the price this period. This PDC represents the case of an **unstable equilibrium**.

In the next period the price rises again. In a self-reinforcing bubble, this process can continue indefinitely—at least until something happens to change the expectation of continuously rising prices (and of a growing deviation of the price from its fundamental value).

Instability caused by self-reinforcing price expectations can only happen in markets for goods that can be resold, like financial assets or durable goods. There is no point buying more vegetables, fish, or fashion items in the hope of making a capital gain on them, because the fish and vegetables will rot, and fashions will change. However, in the markets for tulip bulbs in the seventeenth century, office space in Tokyo in the late 1980s, and houses in Las Vegas in the 2000s (see Exercise 11.10), people continued buying as prices rose, accelerating prices further, because they expected to benefit by reselling the asset.

In Unit 17 we will use a model with a price dynamics curve to look at the role of the housing market in the financial crisis of 2008. In Unit 20, a similar model helps explain how humans interact with the natural environment and why in some situations we observe both stabilizing processes and vicious circles of runaway environmental collapse.

> **unstable equilibrium** An equilibrium such that, if a shock disturbs the equilibrium, there is a subsequent tendency to move even further away from the equilibrium.

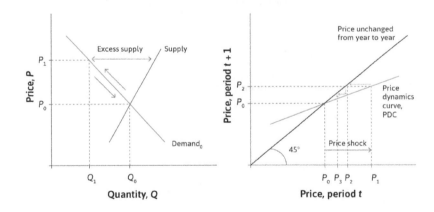

Figure 11.17 A stable equilibrium in the market for FCC shares.

1. The equilibrium price
The left-hand panel shows the supply and demand curves in a market where the equilibrium price is P_0. The 45° line on the right shows that when the price in period t is P_0, the price in period $t + 1$ will be the same. There is no tendency to change.

2. A price shock
Suppose that, following a temporary blip in demand for shares, the price in this market is P_1. There is excess supply.

3. The price adjusts
The PDC shows that if the price this period is P_1, then it will be P_2 next period.

4. Beliefs dampen prices
Since the PDC is flatter than the 45° line, P_2 is closer to the equilibrium than P_1. Investors are influenced by their beliefs about the fundamental value of FCC, which is P_0.

5. Moving back to equilibrium
Prices get closer to P_0. The process continues until equilibrium is regained.

Leibniz: Price bubbles
(http://tinyco.re/L110801)

How do bubbles come to an end?

A bubble bursts when some participants in the market perceive a danger that the price will fall. Then would-be buyers hold back, and those who hold the assets will try to get rid of them. The process in Figure 11.15 is reversed. Figure 11.19 uses the supply and demand model to illustrate what happens. At the top of the bubble the shares trade at $80. Both the supply and demand curves shift when the bubble bursts, and the price collapses from $80 to $54—leaving those who owned shares when the price was $80 with large losses.

If the price of an asset has been driven up solely by beliefs about future price rises, there should be opportunities for those who are well informed about the value to profit from their superior information. So if the rise in the Nasdaq index in Figure 11.14 was indeed a bubble, why did those who identified it as a bubble fail to profit by placing gigantic bets on a major price decline?

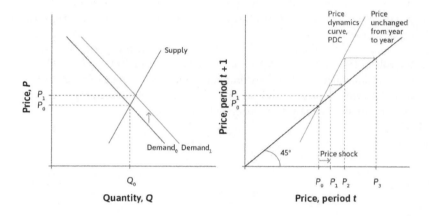

Figure 11.18 An unstable equilibrium.

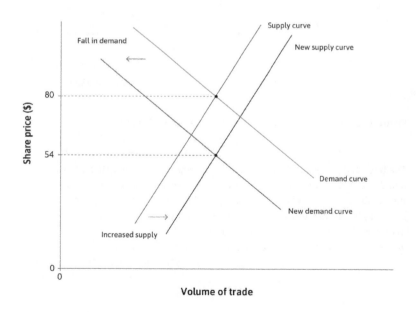

Figure 11.19 The collapse of FCC's share price.

As it happens, many large investors did 'lean against the wind' by placing bets on the bubble bursting, including some well-known fund managers on Wall Street. They did so by **selling short** (shorting): borrowing shares at the current high price and immediately selling them, with the intention of buying them back cheaply (to return to the owner) after the price crashed. But this is an extremely risky strategy, since it requires accuracy in timing the crash—if prices continue to rise, the losses can become unsustainable. You may be right about the bubble but if you get the timing wrong, then when you are due to buy the shares and return them to the owner, the price is higher than it was when you sold them. You will make a loss and may not be able to repay your loan.

Indeed, many of those buying an asset may also be convinced of an eventual crash, but hoping to exit the market before it happens. This was the case during the tech bubble when Stanley Druckenmiller, manager of the Quantum Fund with assets of $8 billion, held shares in technology companies that he knew were overvalued. After prices collapsed and inflicted significant losses on the fund, he used a baseball metaphor to describe his error. 'We thought it was the eighth inning, and it was the ninth,' he explained, 'I overplayed my hand.'

short selling The sale of an asset borrowed by the seller, with the intention of buying it back at a lower price. This strategy is adopted by investors expecting the value of an asset to decrease. *Also known as: shorting.*

EXERCISE 11.7 WHAT IS THE FUNDAMENTAL VALUE OF A BITCOIN?

A bubble may have occurred in the market for the virtual currency called Bitcoin. Bitcoin was introduced by a group of software developers in 2009. Where it is accepted, it can be transferred from one person to another as payment for goods and services.

Unlike other currencies it is not controlled by a single entity such as a central bank. Instead it is 'mined' by individuals who lend their computing power to verify and record Bitcoin transactions in the public ledger. At the start of 2013, a Bitcoin could be purchased for about $13. On 4 December 2013 it was trading at $1,147. It then lost more than half its value in two weeks. These and subsequent price swings are shown in Figure 11.20.

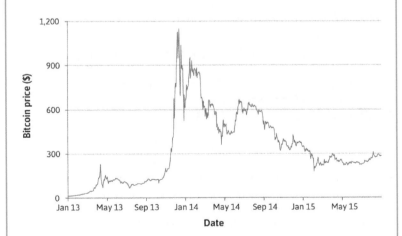

Figure 11.20 The value of Bitcoin (2013–2015).

Use the models in this section, and the arguments for and against the existence of bubbles, to provide an account of the data in Figure 11.20.

Coindesk.com. 2015. *Bitcoin News, Prices, Charts, Guides & Analysis* (http://tinyco.re/8792662) and Bitcoincharts (http://tinyco.re/4434190). Both accessed August 2016.

Charles P. Kindleberger.
2005. *Manias, Panics, and Crashes: A History of Financial Crises (Wiley Investment Classics)*
(http://tinyco.re/6810098).
Hoboken, NJ: Wiley, John & Sons.

EXERCISE 11.8 THE BIG TEN ASSET PRICE BUBBLES OF THE LAST 400 YEARS

According to Charles Kindleberger, an economic historian, asset price bubbles have occurred across a wide variety of countries and time periods. The bubbles of the last 100 years have predominantly been focused on real estate, stocks, and foreign investment.

- 1636: The Dutch tulip bubble
- 1720: The South Sea Company
- 1720: The Mississippi Scheme
- 1927–29: The 1920s stock price bubble
- 1970s: The surge in loans to Mexico and other developing economies
- 1985–89: The Japanese bubble in real estate and stocks
- 1985–89: The bubble in real estate and stocks in Finland, Norway and Sweden
- 1990s: The bubble in real estate and stocks in Thailand, Malaysia, Indonesia and several other Asian countries between 1992 and 1997, and the surge in foreign investment in Mexico 1990–99
- 1995–2000: The bubble in over-the-counter stocks in the US
- 2002–07: The bubble in real estate in the US, Britain, Spain, Ireland, and Iceland

Pick one of these asset price bubbles, find out more about it, and then:

1. Tell the story of this bubble using the models in this section.
2. Explain the relevance to your story, if any, of the arguments in the 'Do bubbles exist?' box in Section 11.7 about the existence of bubbles.

QUESTION 11.7 CHOOSE THE CORRECT ANSWER(S)
Which of the following statements about asset prices are correct?

☐ A bubble occurs when beliefs about future prices amplify a price rise.
☐ When positive feedback occurs, the market is quickly restored to equilibrium.
☐ Negative feedback is when prices give traders the wrong information about the fundamental value.
☐ When beliefs dampen price rises, the market equilibrium is stable.

QUESTION 11.8 CHOOSE THE CORRECT ANSWER(S)
Which of the following statements about short selling (shorting) is correct?

☐ Shorting is used to benefit from a price fall.
☐ Shorting involves selling shares that you currently own.
☐ The maximum loss a trader can incur by shorting is the price he receives from the sale of the shares.
☐ Shorting is a sure way of profiting from a suspected bubble.

11.9 NON-CLEARING MARKETS: RATIONING, QUEUING, AND SECONDARY MARKETS

Tickets for Beyoncé's 2013 world tour sold out in 15 minutes for the Auckland show in New Zealand, in 12 minutes for three UK venues, and in less than a minute for Washington DC in the US. When American singer Billy Joel announced a surprise concert in his native Long Island, New York in October 2013, all available tickets were snapped up in minutes. In both cases it's safe to say that there were many disappointed buyers who would have paid well above the ticket price. At the price chosen by the concert organizers, demand exceeded supply.

We see excess demand for tickets for sporting events, too. The London organizing committee for the 2012 Olympic games received 22 million applications for 7 million tickets. Figure 11.21 is a stylized representation of the situation for one Olympic event.

The number of available tickets, 40,000, is fixed by the capacity of the stadium. The ticket price at which supply and demand are equal is £225. The organizing committee do not choose this price, but a lower price of £100; at this price 70,000 tickets are demanded. There is excess demand of 30,000 tickets.

Some of those who obtain tickets for a popular event may be tempted to sell them rather than use them. In Figure 11.21, anyone who buys a ticket for £100 with the intention of reselling could sell it for at least £225, receiving a rent of £125 (compared with the next best alternative of not buying a ticket).

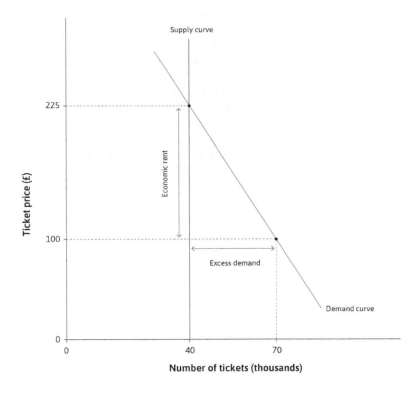

Figure 11.21 Excess demand for tickets.

The potential for rents may create a parallel or secondary market. In the case of tickets for concerts and sporting events, part of the initial demand comes from scalpers: people who plan to resell at a profit. Tickets appear almost instantly on peer-to-peer trading platforms such as StubHub (http://tinyco.re/6667216) or Ticketmaster (http://tinyco.re/0560780), listed at prices that may be multiples of what was originally paid. In the last few days of the 2014 Winter Olympics in Sochi, tickets for the Olympic Park with a face value of 200 roubles were sold outside the Park for up to 4,000 roubles.

Prices in the secondary market equate demand and supply, and allocations are accordingly made to those with the greatest willingness to pay. The assumption that this market-clearing price will be much higher than the listed price is responsible, in part, for the initial frenzied demand for tickets. Nevertheless, some individuals who buy at the lower prices hold on to their tickets, and attend an event that they would otherwise be unable to afford.

Event organizers may try to prevent scalping. In Sochi, the security officers were supposed to intervene. But prevention is increasingly difficult, as online sales provide new opportunities for scalping on a large scale using 'ticket-bots': software that automatically buys tickets within moments of their release. The *New York Times* estimated that scalpers made $15.5 million (http://tinyco.re/8299453) from just 100 performances of the Broadway musical *Hamilton* in the summer of 2016.

rationed goods Goods that are allocated to buyers by a process other than price (such as queueing, or a lottery).

In the case of the London Olympics, the organizing committee set the price, and the tickets were allocated by lottery. This is an example of goods being **rationed** rather than allocated by price. The organizers could have chosen a much higher price (£225 for the event in Figure 11.21), which would have cleared the market. But that would have meant that people willing to pay less than £225 would not have seen the event. By allocating the tickets through a lottery, some people with a lesser willingness to pay (perhaps because they had limited incomes) would also get to see the Games.

There was much public debate about the process, and some anger, but IOC President Jacques Rogge defended it as 'open, transparent and fair'.

There are other cases where the producer of a good chooses to operate with persistent excess demand. The New York restaurant Momofuku Ko offers a 16-course tasting menu at lunch for $175, and has just 12 seats. Online reservations may be made one week in advance, open at 10 a.m. daily, and typically sell out in three seconds. In 2008, the proprietor David Chang sold a reservation at a charity auction for $2,870. Even taking into account the willingness of individuals to pay more for an item when the proceeds go to charity, this suggests substantial excess demand for reservations—but he has not raised the price.

EXERCISE 11.9 IOC POLICY

1. Do you think the IOC policy of using a lottery is fair?
2. Is it Pareto efficient? Explain why or why not.
3. Using the criteria of fairness and Pareto efficiency, how would you judge the widely criticized practice of 'scalping' tickets.
4. Can you think of any other arguments for or against scalping?

EXERCISE 11.10 THE PRICE OF A TICKET

Explain why the seller of a good in fixed supply (such as concert tickets or restaurant reservations) might set a price that the seller knows to be too low to clear the market.

QUESTION 11.9 CHOOSE THE CORRECT ANSWER(S)

Figure 11.21 (page 491) is a stylized representation of the market for an event at the 2012 London Olympic Games. 40,000 tickets were allocated by lottery, at £100 each.

Assume that buyers could resell their tickets in the secondary market. Which of the following statements is correct?

- ☐ The market cleared at £100.
- ☐ The probability of obtaining a ticket was 4/7.
- ☐ The economic rent earned by those selling in the secondary market was £100.
- ☐ The lottery organizers should have chosen a price of £225.

11.10 MARKETS WITH CONTROLLED PRICES

In December 2013, on an unusually cold and snowy Saturday in New York City, demand for taxi services rose appreciably. The familiar metered yellow and green cabs, which operate at a fixed rate (subject to minor adjustments for peak and night-time hours), were hard to find. Those looking for taxis were accordingly rationed, or faced long waiting times.

But there was an alternative available—another example of a secondary market: the on-demand, app-based taxi service called Uber, which by March 2017 would be operating in 81 countries. This recent entrant in the local transportation market uses a secret algorithm that responds rapidly to changing demand and supply conditions.

Standard cab fares do not change with the weather, but Uber's prices can change substantially. On this December night, Uber's surge-pricing algorithm resulted in fares that were more than seven times Uber's standard rate. This spike in pricing choked off some demand and also led to some increased supply, as drivers who would have clocked off remained on the road and were joined by others.

City authorities often regulate taxi fares as part of their transport policy, for example to maintain safety standards, and minimize congestion. In some countries, local or national government also controls housing rents. Sometimes this is to protect tenants, who may have little bargaining power in their relationships with landlords, or sometimes because urban rents would be too high for key groups of workers.

Figure 11.22 shows a situation in which local government might decide to control the housing rent in a city (note that here we mean *rent* in the everyday sense of a payment from tenant to landlord for use of the accommodation). Initially the market is in equilibrium, with 8,000 tenancies at a rent of €500—the market clears. Now suppose that there is an increase in demand for tenancies. Rents will rise, because the supply of rental housing is inelastic, at least in the short run: it would take time to build new houses, so more tenancies can only be supplied immediately if some owner-occupiers decide to become landlords and live elsewhere themselves.

Suppose that the city authorities are concerned that this rise would be unaffordable for many families, so they impose a **rent ceiling** at €500. Follow the steps in Figure 11.22 to see what happens.

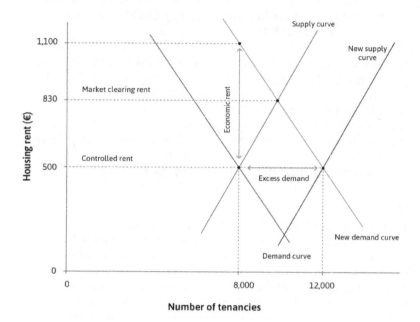

Figure 11.22 Housing rents and economic rents.

1. The market clears
Initially the market clears with 8,000 tenancies at rent of €500.

2. An increase in demand
Now suppose that there is an increase in demand for tenancies.

3. Rent increases
The supply of housing for rent is inelastic, at least in the short run. The new market-clearing rent, €830, is much higher.

4. A rent ceiling?
Suppose the city authorities impose a rent ceiling at €500. Landlords will continue to supply 8,000 tenancies, so there is excess demand.

5. The short side of the market
When the price is below the market-clearing level, the suppliers are on the **short side of the market**. They, not the demanders, determine the number of tenancies.

6. Some people would pay much more
There are 12,000 people on the long side of the market. Only 8,000 obtain tenancies. There are 8,000 people willing to pay €1,100 or more, but tenancies are not necessarily allocated to the people with highest willingness to pay.

7. A secondary market
If it were legal, some tenants could sublet their accommodation at €1,100, obtaining an economic rent of €600 (the difference between €1,100 and the controlled rent of €500).

8. The long-run equilibrium
The long-run solution for making more tenancies available at a reasonable rent is for the city authorities to encourage house-building so as to shift out the supply curve.

With a controlled price of €500 there is excess demand. In general a controlled price will not clear the market, and trade will then take place on the **short side** of the market: that is, the quantity traded will be whichever is lower of the quantities supplied and demanded. In Figure 11.22, the price is low and suppliers are on the short side. If the price were high (above the market-clearing price), demanders would be on the short side.

When the rent is €500, the number of tenancies will be 8,000. Of the 12,000 people on the long side of the market, 8000 would pay €1,100 or more, but tenancies are not allocated to those with highest willingness to pay. Those lucky enough to obtain tenancies may be anywhere on the new demand curve above €500.

The rent control policy puts more weight on maintaining a rent that is seen to be fair, and affordable by existing tenants who might otherwise be forced to move out, than it does on Pareto efficiency. The scarcity of rental accommodation gives rise to a potential economic rent: if it were legal (it usually isn't), some tenants could sublet their accommodation, obtaining an economic rent of €600 (the difference between €1,100 and €500).

If the increase in demand proves to be permanent, the long-run solution for the city authorities may be policies that encourage house-building, shifting out the supply curve so that more tenancies are available at a reasonable rent.

> **short side (of a market)** The side (either supply or demand) on which the number of desired transactions is least (for example, employers are on the short side of the labour market, because typically there are more workers seeking work than there are jobs being offered). The opposite of short side is the long side. *See also: supply side, demand side.*

This brief economic analysis of rent controls in Paris points out the counter-productive effects: Jean Bosvieux and Oliver Waine. 2012. 'Rent Control: A Miracle Solution to the Housing Crisis?' (http://tinyco.re/0599316). *Metropolitics.* Updated 21 November 2012.

Richard Arnott, on the other hand, argues that economists should rethink their traditional opposition to rent control: Richard Arnott. 1995. 'Time for Revisionism on Rent Control?' (http://tinyco.re/7410213). *Journal of Economic Perspectives* 9 (1) (February): pp. 99–120.

> **EXERCISE 11.11 WHY NOT RAISE THE PRICE?**
> Discuss the following statement: 'The sharp increase in cab fares on a snowy day in New York led to severe criticism of Uber on social media, but a sharp increase in the price of gold has no such effect.'

QUESTION 11.10 CHOOSE THE CORRECT ANSWER(S)
Figure 11.22 (page 494) illustrates the rental housing market. Initially, the market clears at €500 with 8,000 tenancies. Then, there is an outward shift in the demand curve, as shown in the diagram. In response, the city authority imposes a rent ceiling of €500 and prohibits subletting. Based on this information, which of the following statements are correct?

☐ There are 4,000 potential tenants who are left unhoused.
☐ The market would clear at €1,100.
☐ If subletting was possible, then those renting could earn an economic rent of €330.
☐ Excess demand could be eliminated in the long run by building more houses.

11.11 THE ROLE OF ECONOMIC RENTS

An economic rent is a payment or other benefit that someone receives that is superior to his or her next best alternative. Throughout this unit, we have seen how economic rents play a role in the changes that take place in the economy.

- In the real case of the Kerala fisherman, and the hypothetical market for hats, rent-seeking by buyers or sellers in response to a situation of excess supply or demand brought about a market-clearing equilibrium.
- In the model of the bread market, rents (economic profits) can arise in a short-run equilibrium in which the number of firms is fixed. In the long run, other bakeries enter the market in pursuit of these rents.
- In the world oil market, rents for oil producers arise from the constraints on producers and consumers that make supply and demand curves inelastic in the short-run, but in turn provide incentives for building new wells for exploration.
- In asset markets, rents arise when the price deviates from the fundamental value of the asset, providing opportunities for speculation and creating the potential for bubbles.
- In markets that do not clear because prices are controlled, excess demand gives rise to a potential economic rent, which leads (unless prevented by regulation) to the development of a clearing secondary market.
- Another example, from Unit 2, is the innovation rent obtained by early innovators, which provides the incentive to adopt a new technology.

disequilibrium rent The economic rent that arises when a market is not in equilibrium, for example when there is excess demand or excess supply in a market for some good or service. In contrast, rents that arise in equilibrium are called equilibrium rents.

equilibrium rent Rent in a market that is in equilibrium. *Also known as: stationary or persistent rents.*

In each of these examples, rents arise because of some kind of disequilibrium, or short-run constraint—we call them *dynamic* or **disequilibrium rents**. They set in motion a process—rent-seeking—that ultimately creates an equilibrium in which these kinds of rents no longer exist. In contrast, we have also seen examples of *persistent* or *stationary rents*. The main examples are shown in the table in Figure 11.23.

Type	Description	Unit
Bargaining	In a bargaining situation, how much the outcome exceeds the reservation option (next best alternative)	4.5
Employment	Wages and conditions above an employee's reservation option providing an incentive to work hard	6.9
Monopoly	Profits above economic profits made possible by limited competition	7
Government-induced	Payments above the actor's next best alternative not competed away because of government regulation (for example rent control, intellectual property rights)	9

Figure 11.23 Examples of stationary rents.

In the models studied in this unit, we have seen that if markets do not clear, there are disequilibrium rents that give incentives for people to change the prices or quantities at which they transact, and so bring about market clearing. The labour market (see Unit 9) is different: it does not clear in equilibrium. Employees therefore receive a rent—the difference between the wage and their reservation option. But in this case it is a persistent or **equilibrium rent**: because a contract to work hard is unenforceable there is no way any buyer (the employer) or seller (the worker) can benefit by changing his or her price or quantity.

Economic rents and rent-seekers often have a bad name in economics. People disapprove because they think about rents as those arising from government-created monopolies (taxi licenses, intellectual property rights) or privately created monopolies. These rents indicate that the good or service will be sold at a price exceeding its marginal cost, and so the markets for these goods are not Pareto efficient.

But we have now seen the usefulness of some economic rents. They encourage innovation, provide incentives for employees to work hard, encourage new entrants to a market and thereby lower prices for consumers, and can bring an out-of-equilibrium market to a Pareto-efficient equilibrium.

QUESTION 11.11 CHOOSE THE CORRECT ANSWER(S)
Which of the following are stationary rents?

- ☐ Innovation rent where firms make positive economic profits from a new invention.
- ☐ Employment rent where the wage is set high to induce workers to work hard.
- ☐ Monopoly rent where firms make excess profits due to limited competition.
- ☐ Speculative rent where profits are made by correctly betting on the price changes in a bubble.

11.12 CONCLUSION

Prices are messages about the conditions in a market economy. In situations of market disequilibrium, or short-run equilibrium arising from temporary constraints, people act on price messages if they are able to do so, in pursuit of economic rents. In markets for goods this often leads in the long run to market clearing and the eventual disappearance of the rents.

Assets are purchased partly for their resale value. In markets for financial assets, supply and demand shift rapidly as traders receive new information. The price adjusts in a continuous double auction to reconcile supply and demand. Prices in asset markets send messages to traders about future prices, which can cause the price to deviate from the fundamental asset value; in this case rent-seeking may create a bubble or a crash.

Sometimes suppliers or regulators choose to override price messages, leading to excess supply or demand, for example for concert tickets, taxi cabs, or housing tenancies. Economic rents can then persist—unless a secondary market is allowed to develop.

> *Concepts introduced in Unit 11*
> Before you move on, review these definitions:
>
> - Market equilibration through rent-seeking
> - Long-run and short-run equilibria
> - Fundamental value of an asset
> - Continuous double auction
> - Order book
> - Price bubble
> - Stable and unstable equilibria
> - Secondary market
> - Dynamic and stationary economic rents

11.13 REFERENCES

Arnott, Richard. 1995. 'Time for Revisionism on Rent Control?' (http://tinyco.re/7410213). *Journal of Economic Perspectives* 9 (1) (February): pp. 99–120.

Bosvieux, Jean, and Oliver Waine. 2012. 'Rent Control: A Miracle Solution to the Housing Crisis?' (http://tinyco.re/0599316). *Metropolitics*. Updated 21 November 2012.

Brunnermeier, Markus. 2009. 'Lucas Roundtable: Mind the frictions' (http://tinyco.re/0136751). *The Economist*. Updated 6 August 2009.

Cassidy, John. 2010. 'Interview with Eugene Fama' (http://tinyco.re/4647447). *The New Yorker*. Updated 13 January 2010.

Harford, Tim. 2012. 'Still Think You Can Beat the Market?' (http://tinyco.re/7063932). *The Undercover Economist*. Updated 24 November 2012.

Hayek, Friedrich A. 1994. *The Road to Serfdom* (http://tinyco.re/0683881). Chicago, Il: University of Chicago Press.

Keynes, John Maynard. 1936. *The General Theory of Employment, Interest and Money* (http://tinyco.re/6855346). London: Palgrave Macmillan.

Kindleberger, Charles P. 2005. *Manias, Panics, and Crashes: A History of Financial Crises (Wiley Investment Classics)* (http://tinyco.re/6810098). Hoboken, NJ: Wiley, John & Sons.

Lucas, Robert. 2009. 'In defence of the dismal science' (http://tinyco.re/6052194). *The Economist*. Updated 6 August 2009.

Malkiel, Burton G. 2003. 'The Efficient Market Hypothesis and Its Critics' (http://tinyco.re/4628706). *Journal of Economic Perspectives* 17 (1) (March): pp. 59–82.

Miller, R. G., and S. R. Sorrell. 2013. 'The Future of Oil Supply' (http://tinyco.re/6167443). *Philosophical Transactions of the Royal Society A: Mathematical, Physical and Engineering Sciences* 372 (2006) (December).

Owen, Nick A., Oliver R. Inderwildi, and David A. King. 2010. 'The Status of Conventional World Oil Reserves—Hype or Cause for Concern?' (http://tinyco.re/9394545). *Energy Policy* 38 (8) (August): pp. 4743–4749.

Shiller, Robert J. 2003. 'From Efficient Markets Theory to Behavioral Finance' (http://tinyco.re/3989503). *Journal of Economic Perspectives* 17 (1) (March): pp. 83–104.

Shiller, Robert J. 2015. 'The Stock Market in Historical Perspective' (http://tinyco.re/4263463). In *Irrational Exuberance*. Princeton, NJ: Princeton University Press.

The Economist. 2014. 'Keynes and Hayek: Prophets for Today' (http://tinyco.re/0417474). Updated 14 March 2014.

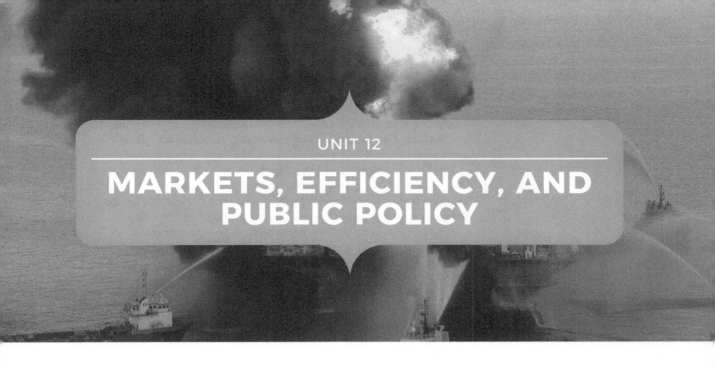

UNIT 12

MARKETS, EFFICIENCY, AND PUBLIC POLICY

WHEN MARKET-DETERMINED PRICES INDUCE PEOPLE TO ACCOUNT FOR THE FULL EFFECTS OF THEIR ACTIONS ON OTHERS, OUTCOMES ARE EFFICIENT. WHEN PRICES DO NOT CAPTURE SIGNIFICANT EFFECTS, MARKETS FAIL, AND OTHER REMEDIES ARE NEEDED

THEMES AND CAPSTONE UNITS

- 17: History, instability, and growth
- 19: Inequality
- 20: Environment
- 21: Innovation
- 22: Politics and policy

- These external effects arise when property rights and legal contracts do not cover some of the effects of the decision-maker's actions. For example, one cannot sue the smoker for the damages experienced from second-hand smoke.
- Property rights and contracts that would reward actors for the positive external effects imposed on others, and make them liable to pay damages for the negative effects, are infeasible when the necessary information is not available to one or more of the parties or cannot be used in a court of law.
- Policies can address market failures by inducing actors to internalize these effects, for example by subsidizing a firm's R&D when it may benefit other firms, or by imposing taxes that raise the price of goods whose production or use is environmentally destructive.
- Other policies can directly regulate the actions of firms and households, for example by banning the use of chemicals such as pesticides that impose costs on others.
- Private bargaining among parties can sometimes constrain actors to take account of the effect of their actions on others, for example a merger between a firm emitting pollutants and a firm suffering damage as a result.
- For moral and political reasons, some goods and services, such as our vital organs, emergency medical care, or our votes are not traded on markets, but are allocated by other means.

501

The logic of Adam Smith's famous claim, that the businessman in pursuit of his own interest is 'led by an invisible hand' to promote the interests of society, is the basis of the economic model of a perfectly competitive market (see Unit 8). Price-taking firms and consumers, each pursuing their own private objectives, implement market outcomes that are Pareto efficient.

Friedrich Hayek explained how Smith's invisible hand could work (see Unit 11). Prices send messages about the real scarcity of goods and services, messages that motivate people to produce, consume, invest, and innovate in ways that make the best use of an economy's productive potential.

It is this process that allows the market system—many markets interlinked—to coordinate the division of labour through the exchange of goods among entire strangers from the four corners of the world, without centralized direction.

Hayek suggested we think of the market as a giant information-processing machine that produces prices, which provide information that guides the economy, usually in desirable directions. The remarkable thing about this massive computational device is that it's not really a machine at all. Nobody designed it, and nobody is at the controls. When it works well, we use phrases like 'the magic of the market'.

But sometimes the magic fails. The happy coincidence of private motives and socially valued outcomes summarized by Smith's phrase is an attribute of a model—a very useful one for many purposes—but not a description of how real markets work in general, and therefore not a good guide to public policy.

In this unit, we will consider cases in which prices send the wrong messages. Smith explained that, in areas such as education and the legal system, government policies are needed to promote social wellbeing and ensure that markets work well. Smith was also clear that there were some things that should not be bought and sold in markets. The modern equivalents might include human kidneys, votes, a good school, or life-saving medical care.

Here are two cases in which Hayek's and Smith's logic fails:

1. *Pesticides:* The pesticide chlordecone was used on banana plantations in the Caribbean islands of Guadeloupe and Martinique (both part of France) to kill the banana weevil. It was perfectly legal, and to the plantation owners it was an effective way of reducing costs and boosting the plantations' profits.

   As the chemical was washed off the land into rivers that flowed to the coast, it contaminated freshwater prawn farms, the mangrove swamps where crabs were caught, and what had been rich coastal spiny lobster fisheries. The livelihoods of fishing communities were destroyed and those who ate contaminated fish fell ill.

   The fact that this pesticide was a grave danger to humans had been known since the time it was introduced, when workers in the US producing the chemical reported symptoms of neurological damage, leading to its prohibition in 1976. The French government received reports on contamination in Guadeloupe a few years later, but waited until 1990 to ban the substance, and were pressured by banana plantation owners to give them a special exemption until 1993.

   Twenty years later, fishermen protesting the slow pace of French government assistance in addressing the fallout from the contamination

Paul Seabright. 2010. 'Chapter 1'. In *The Company of Strangers: A Natural History of Economic Life* (http://tinyco.re/2891054). Princeton, NJ: Princeton University Press. pp. 9–10.

demonstrated in the streets of Fort de France (the largest town in Martinique) and barricaded the port. Looking back, Franck Nétri, a Gaudeloupean fisherman, worried: 'I've been eating pesticide for 30 years. But what will happen to my grandchildren?'

He was right to worry. In 2012, the fraction of Martiniquean men suffering from prostate cancer was the highest in the world and almost twice that of the second-highest country, and the mortality rate was well over four times the world average. Neurological damage in children, including cognitive performance, has also been documented.

2. *Antibiotics:* Since the discovery of penicillin in 1928, the development of antibiotics has brought huge benefits to mankind. Diseases that were once fatal are now treated easily with medicines that are cheap to produce. But the World Health Organization has recently warned that we are heading for a 'post-antibiotic era' as many bacteria are becoming resistant: 'Unless we take significant actions to … change how we produce, prescribe and use antibiotics, the world will lose more and more of these global public health goods and the implications will be devastating.'

> **social dilemma** A situation in which actions taken independently by individuals in pursuit of their own private objectives result in an outcome which is inferior to some other feasible outcome that could have occurred if people had acted together, rather than as individuals.

Overuse of antibiotics is an example of a **social dilemma** (see Unit 4), in which the unregulated pursuit of self-interest leads to outcomes that are Pareto inefficient. Bacteria become resistant to antibiotics when we use them too often, in the wrong dosage, or for conditions that are not caused by bacteria. In India, for example, antibiotics are easily available over the counter in pharmacies without a doctor's prescription.

Doctors recognize that leaving the allocation of antibiotics to the market has damaging consequences. Following the advice of unlicensed private medical practitioners, people use antibiotics when other treatments would be better. To save money, the patients often stop taking the antibiotics when they feel a little better. This is exactly the pattern of use that will produce antibiotic-resistant pathogens. But for the patient, the treatment worked, and the unlicensed doctor's business will prosper.

Contamination by pesticides and the creation of superbugs are quite similar problems. Let's think of these issues as a doctor would.

First, we diagnose the problem. In the case of chlordecone, the problem is that the actions of the banana plantation owners endanger the fishermen's livelihood and health, but these costs of using the pesticide do not show up anywhere in the profit-and-loss calculations of the owners or the price of pesticides. The overuse of antibiotics occurs because the user does not take account of the costs that will be imposed on others when antibiotic superbugs proliferate.

Our diagnosis: Actors do not take account of the costs their decisions impose on others.

Next, we aim to devise a treatment. In some cases, the treatment is obvious. Chlordecone was simply banned in France and the US, and its use could have been vastly reduced if the plantation owners had been required (by law or by private agreement with those affected) to pay the damages that their pesticide use inflicted on the fishing communities and others.

In other cases, like the misuse of antibiotics by both patients and medical practitioners, effective treatments are more difficult to devise, and may necessarily involve an ethical appeal to the actors' sense of responsibility towards others.

Our suggested treatment: Either directly regulate the actions that impose costs on others, or force the decision-maker to bear these costs.

To understand why **markets fail** in cases like these, it is helpful to remember the conditions that are needed for markets to work well. As we saw in Unit 1, **private property** is a key requirement for a market system. If something is to be bought and sold, then it must be possible to claim the right to own it. A purchase is simply a transfer of ownership rights from the seller to the buyer. You would hesitate to pay for something unless you believed that others would acknowledge (and if necessary protect) your right to keep it.

So for a market to work effectively (or even to exist), other social institutions and social norms are required. Governments provide a system of laws and law enforcement that guarantee **property rights** and enforce **contracts**. **Social norms** dictate that you respect the property rights of others, even when enforcement is unlikely or impossible.

private property The right and expectation that one can enjoy one's possessions in ways of one's own choosing, exclude others from their use, and dispose of them by gift or sale to others who then become their owners.

property rights Legal protection of ownership, including the right to exclude others and to benefit from or sell the thing owned.

contract A legal document or understanding that specifies a set of actions that parties to the contract must undertake.

social norm An understanding that is common to most members of a society about what people should do in a given situation when their actions affect others.

Douglass North argued that institutions were not only necessary for the good functioning of the economy, but also the fundamental cause of long-run growth: Douglass C. North. 1990. *Institutions, Institutional Change and Economic Performance.* Cambridge: Cambridge University Press.

Daron Acemoglu, Simon Johnson, and James Robinson argue that institutions are fundamental for growth. They also provide evidence based on the European colonial history and the division of Korea: Acemoglu, Daron, Simon Johnson, and James A. Robinson. 2005. 'Institutions as a Fundamental Cause of Long-Run Growth' (http://tinyco.re/2662186). In *Handbook of Economic Growth, Volume 1A.*, edited by Philippe Aghion and Steven N. Durlauf, North Holland. Daron Acemoglu and James A. Robinson. 2012. *Why Nations Fail: The Origins of Power, Prosperity and Poverty*, 1st ed. New York, NY: Crown Publishers.

Whenever you agree with a seller to pay a certain amount of money in exchange for a good—say, a pair of shoes—you implicitly enter into a contract with the seller. If you have the protection of a legal system, you can expect the contract to be honoured. When you get home and open the box the shoes will be there, and if they fall apart within days you will receive a refund. It is the government that determines the rules of the game in which market trade takes place. Of course, enforcement by a court is rarely necessary because of social norms that motivate both buyers and sellers to play by the rules of the game, even in cases where there is not an actual contract or a transfer of a title of ownership.

More complex transactions require explicit written contracts that can be used in court as evidence that the parties agreed to a transfer of ownership. For example, an author may sign a contract that gives a publisher the sole right to publish a book. Contracts govern relationships that are to be maintained over a period of time, particularly employment. In the labour market, a court upholds the right of the worker to work no more than the contracted hours and to receive the agreed-upon pay.

Laws and legal traditions can also help markets function when they provide compensation for individuals who are harmed by the actions of others. Liability law, for example, ensures that if a firm sells a car with a design fault and someone is injured as a result, the firm must pay for the damage. Employers usually have a duty of care towards their employees, requiring them to provide a safe working environment, and incurring fines or other penalties when they do not.

Many of the problems we investigate in this unit arise because of difficulties of guaranteeing property rights or writing appropriate contracts. There are goods—like clean rivers—that matter to people but cannot easily be bought and sold. We begin with a closer look at the diagnosis and treatment of a case like the pesticides in Martinique and Guadeloupe.

Marcel Fafchamps and Bart Minten. 1999. 'Relationships and Traders in Madagascar'. *Journal of Development Studies* 35 (6) (August): pp. 1–35.

EXERCISE 12.1 PROPERTY RIGHTS AND CONTRACTS IN MADAGASCAR

Marcel Fafchamps and Bart Minten studied grain markets in Madagascar in 1997, where the legal institutions for enforcing property rights and contracts were weak. Despite this, they found that theft and breach of contract were rare. The grain traders avoided theft by keeping their stocks very low, and if necessary, sleeping in the grain stores. They refrained from employing additional workers for fear of employee-related theft. When transporting their goods, they paid protection money and travelled in convoy. Most transactions took a simple 'cash and carry' form. Trust was established through repeated interaction with the same traders.

1. Do these findings suggest that strong legal institutions are not necessary for markets to work?
2. Consider some market transactions in which you have been involved. Could these markets work in the absence of a legal framework, and how would they be different if they did?
3. Can you think of any examples in which repeated interaction helps to facilitate market transactions?
4. Why might repeated interaction be important even when a legal framework is present?

12.1 MARKET FAILURE: EXTERNAL EFFECTS OF POLLUTION

When markets allocate resources in a Pareto-inefficient way, we describe this as a **market failure**. We encountered one cause of market failure in Unit 7: a firm producing a differentiated good (such as a car) that chooses its price and output level such that the price is greater than the marginal cost. In contrast, we know from Unit 8 that a competitive market allocation maximizes the total surplus of the producers and consumers, and is Pareto efficient, as long as no one else is affected by the production and consumption of the good.

market failure When markets allocate resources in a Pareto-inefficient way.

But the market allocation of the good is unlikely to be Pareto efficient if the decisions of producers and consumers affect others in ways that they do not adequately take into account. This is another cause of market failure. When we analyse gains from trade in such cases, we have to consider not only the consumer and producer surplus, but also the costs or benefits that other parties who are neither buyers nor sellers may experience. For example, the superbug that emerges as a result of the sale and overuse of an antibiotic may kill someone who had no part in the sale and purchase of the antibiotic.

We will analyse the gains from trade in a case where the production of a good creates an **external cost**: pollution. Our example is based on the real-world case of the plantations' use of the pesticide chlordecone to control the banana weevil, which we discussed earlier.

external effect A positive or negative effect of a production, consumption, or other economic decision on another person or people that is not specified as a benefit or liability in a contract. It is called an external effect because the effect in question is outside the contract. *Also known as: externality. See also: incomplete contract, market failure, external benefit, external cost.*

marginal private cost (MPC) The cost for the producer of producing an additional unit of a good, not taking into account any costs its production imposes on others. *See also: marginal external cost, marginal social cost.*

marginal social cost (MSC) The cost of producing an additional unit of a good, taking into account both the cost for the producer and the costs incurred by others affected by the good's production. Marginal social cost is the sum of the marginal private cost and the marginal external cost.

marginal private benefit (MPB) The benefit (in terms of profit, or utility) of producing or consuming an additional unit of a good for the individual who decides to produce or consume it, not taking into account any benefit received by others.

marginal social benefit (MSB) The benefit (in terms of utility) of producing or consuming an additional unit of a good, taking into account both the benefit to the individual who decides to produce or consume it, and the benefit to anyone else affected by the decision.

To see why this is called an **external effect** (or sometimes an **externality**), imagine for a minute that the same company owned the banana plantations and fisheries, and hired fishermen and sold what they caught for profit. The owners of the company would decide on the level of pesticide to use, taking account of its downstream effects. They would trade-off the profits from the banana part of their business against the losses from the fisheries.

But this was not the case in Martinique and Guadeloupe. The plantations owned the profits from banana production, which were increased by using pesticide. The fisherman 'owned' the losses from fishing. The pollution effect of the pesticide was external to the people making the decision on its use. Joint ownership of the plantations and fisheries would have internalized this effect, but the plantations and fisheries were under separate ownership.

To model the implications of this kind of external effect, Figure 12.1 shows the marginal costs of growing bananas on an imaginary Caribbean island where a fictional pesticide called Weevokil is used. The marginal cost of producing bananas for the growers is labelled as the **marginal private cost (MPC)**. It slopes upward because the cost of an additional tonne of bananas increases as the land is more intensively used, requiring more Weevokil. Use the analysis in Figure 12.1 to compare the MPC with the **marginal social cost (MSC)**, which includes the costs borne by fishermen whose waters are contaminated by Weevokil.

You can see in Figure 12.1 that the marginal social cost of banana production is higher than the marginal private cost. To focus on the essentials, we will consider a case in which the wholesale market for bananas is competitive, and the market price is $400 per tonne. If the banana plantation owners wish to maximize their profit, we know that they will choose their output so that price is equal to their marginal cost—that is, the marginal private cost. Figure 12.2 shows that their total output will be 80,000 tonnes of bananas (point A). Although 80,000 tonnes maximizes profits for banana producers, this does not include the cost imposed on the fishing industry, so it is not a Pareto-efficient outcome.

To see this, think about what would happen if the plantations were to produce less. The fishermen would benefit but the owners of the plantations would lose. So on the face of it, it appears that producing 80,000 tonnes must be Pareto efficient. But let's imagine that the fishermen could persuade the plantation owners to produce one tonne less. The fishermen would gain $270—they would no longer suffer the loss of revenue from fishing that is caused by the production of the 80,000th tonne of bananas. The plantations would lose hardly anything. Their revenues would fall by $400, but their costs would fall by almost exactly this amount because, when producing 80,000 tonnes, the marginal private cost is equal to the price ($400).

So if the fishermen paid the plantation owners any amount between just greater than zero and just less than $270, *both groups would be better off* with 79,999 tonnes of bananas.

What about another payment to get the plantations to produce 79,998 tonnes instead? You can see that because the marginal external cost imposed on the fishermen is still much higher than the surplus received by the plantations on the next tonne (the difference between the price and the MPC), such a payment would also make both parties better off.

By how much could the fishermen persuade the plantations to reduce production? Look at the point in Figure 12.2 at which the price of bananas is equal to the marginal social cost. At this point, 38,000 tonnes of bananas are produced. If the payments by the fishermen to the plantations resulted in them producing just 38,000 tonnes, then the fishermen could no longer benefit by making further payments in return for reduced output. If production were lowered further, the loss to the plantations (the difference between price and marginal cost) would be greater than the gain to the fishermen (the difference between private and social cost, shaded). At this point, the maximum payment the fishermen would be willing to make would not be enough to induce the plantations to cut production further. So 38,000 tonnes is the Pareto-efficient level of banana output.

marginal external cost (MEC) The cost of producing an additional unit of a good that is incurred by anyone other than the producer of the good. *See also: marginal private cost, marginal social cost.*

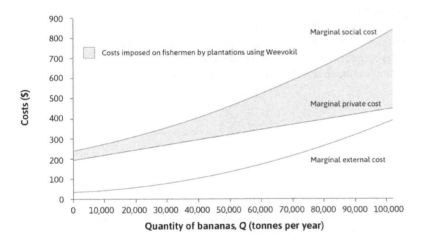

Figure 12.1 Marginal costs of banana production using Weevokil.

1. The marginal private cost
The purple line is the marginal cost for the growers: the **marginal private cost (MPC)** of banana production. It slopes upward because the cost of producing an additional tonne increases as the land is more intensively used, requiring more Weevokil.

2. The marginal external cost
The orange line shows the marginal cost imposed by the banana growers on fishermen—the **marginal external cost (MEC)**. This is the cost of the reduction in quantity and quality of fish caused by each additional tonne of bananas.

3. The marginal social cost
Adding together the MPC and the MEC, we get the full marginal cost of banana production: the **marginal social cost (MSC)**. This is the green line in the diagram.

4. The total external cost
The shaded area in the figure shows the total costs imposed on fishermen by plantations using Weevokil. It is the sum of the differences between the marginal social cost and the marginal private cost at each level of production.

To summarize:

- *The plantations produce 80,000 tonnes of bananas*: At this point price equals MPC.
- *The Pareto-efficient level of output is 38,000 tonnes of bananas*: Price equals MSC.
- *When production is 38,000 tonnes it is not possible for the plantations and fishermen to both be made better off*.
- *If a single company owned both the banana plantations and fisheries*: This company would choose to produce 38,000 tonnes because, for the single owner, price would be equal to MPC at 38,000 tonnes.

In general, pollutants like Weevokil have negative external effects, sometimes called *environmental spillovers*. They bring *private benefits* to those who decide to use them, but by damaging the environment—water resources, in this case—they impose *external costs* on other firms or on households that rely on environmental resources. For society as a whole, this is a market failure: compared with the Pareto-efficient allocation, the pollutant is overused, and too much of the associated good (bananas, in our example) is produced.

Leibniz: External effects of pollution (http://tinyco.re/L120101)

The features of this case of market failure are summarized in the table below. In the following sections, we will summarize other examples of market failure in a similar table. At the end of this unit, we will bring all the examples together in Figure 12.13 so that you can compare them.

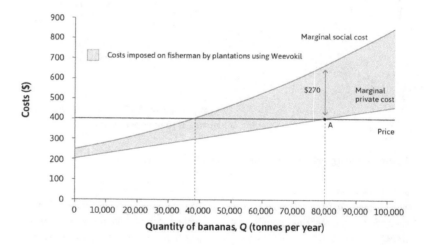

Figure 12.2 The plantations' choice of banana output.

Decision	How it affects others	Cost or benefit	Market failure (misallocation of resources)	Terms applied to this type of market failure
A firm uses a pesticide that runs off into waterways	Downstream damage	Private benefit, external cost	Overuse of pesticide and overproduction of the crop for which it is used	Negative external effect, environmental spillover

Figure 12.3 Market failure: Water pollution.

QUESTION 12.1 CHOOSE THE CORRECT ANSWER(S)

A factory is situated next to a dormitory for nurses who work night shifts. The factory produces 120 humanoid robots a day. The production process is rather noisy, and the nurses often complain that their sleep is disturbed. Based on this information, which of the following statements is correct?

☐ The marginal private cost is the factory's total cost of producing 120 robots a day.

☐ The marginal social cost is the noise cost incurred by the nurses from production of an additional robot.

☐ The marginal external cost is the cost to the factory, plus the noise cost incurred by the nurses, when an additional robot is produced.

☐ The total external cost is the total costs per day imposed on the nurses by the factory's production.

12.2 EXTERNAL EFFECTS AND BARGAINING

To demonstrate that the market allocation of bananas (producing 80,000 tonnes, using Weevokil) is not Pareto efficient, we showed that the fishermen could pay the plantation owners to produce fewer bananas, and both would be better off.

Does this suggest a remedy for this market failure that might be implemented in the real world?

It does. The fishermen and the plantation owners could negotiate a private bargain. Solutions of this type are often called *Coasean* bargaining, after Ronald Coase who pioneered the idea that private bargaining might be preferable to dealing with external effects by governmental intervention. He argued that the two parties to the exchange often have more of the information necessary to implement an efficient outcome than the government does.

GREAT ECONOMISTS

Ronald Coase

You have already met Ronald Coase (1910–2013). He was featured in Unit 6 for his representation of the firm as a political organization. He is also known for his idea that private bargaining could address market failures.

He explained that when one party is engaged in an activity that has the incidental effect of causing damage to another, a negotiated settlement between the two may result in a Pareto-efficient allocation of resources. He used the legal case of Sturges v Bridgman (http://tinyco.re/2709868) to illustrate his argument. The case concerned Bridgman, a confectioner (candy-maker) who for many years had been using machinery that generated noise and vibration. This caused no external effects until his neighbour Sturges built a consulting room on the boundary of his property, close to the confectioner's kitchen. The courts granted the doctor an injunction that prevented Bridgman from using his machinery.

Coase pointed out that once the doctor's right to prevent the use of the machinery had been established, the two sides could modify the outcome. The doctor would be willing to waive his right to stop the noise in return for a compensation payment. And the confectioner would be willing to pay if the value of his annoying activities exceeded the costs that they imposed on the doctor.

Also, the court's decision in favour of Sturges rather than Bridgman would make no difference to whether Bridgman continued to use his machinery. If the confectioner had been granted the right to use it, the doctor would have paid him to stop if, and only if, the doctor's costs were greater than the confectioner's profits.

In other words, private bargaining would ensure that the machinery was used if, and only if, its use, alongside a compensation payment, made both better off. Private bargaining would ensure Pareto efficiency. Bargaining gives the confectioner an incentive to take into account not only the marginal private costs of using the machine to produce candy, but also the external costs imposed on the doctor. That is, the confectioner takes account of the entire social cost. To the confectioner, the price of using the annoying machinery during the doctor's visiting hours would now send the right message. Private bargaining could be a substitute for legal liability. It ensures that those harmed would be compensated, and that those who could inflict harm would make efforts to avoid harmful behaviour.

To summarize:

- The court's role was to establish the initial property rights of the two parties: Bridgman's right to make noise or Sturges' right to quiet.
- Then, as long as private bargaining exhausted all the potential mutual gains, the result would (by definition) be Pareto efficient, independently of which party owned the initial rights.
- We might object that the court's decision resulted in an unfair distribution of profits, but however one evaluates this concern (or if, like Coase himself, one puts 'questions of equity aside'), the outcome would be Pareto efficient.

transaction costs Costs that impede the bargaining process or the agreement of a contract. They include costs of acquiring information about the good to be traded, and costs of enforcing a contract.

But Coase emphasized that his model could not be directly applied to most situations because of the costs of bargaining and other impediments that prevent the parties from exploiting all possible mutual gains. Costs of bargaining, sometimes called **transaction costs**, may prevent Pareto efficiency. If the confectioner cannot find out how badly the noise affects the doctor, the doctor has an incentive to overstate the costs to get a better deal. Establishing each party's actual costs and benefits is part of the cost of the transaction, and this cost might be too high to make a bargain possible.

Coase's analysis suggests that a lack of established property rights, and other impediments leading to high transaction costs, may stand in the way of using bargaining to resolve externalities. We know from the experiments in Unit 4 that bargaining may also fail if one party regards the outcome as unfair. But with a clear legal framework in which one side initially owned the rights to produce (or to prevent production of) the externality, as long as these rights were tradable between the two parties there might be no need for further intervention.

Until now you have probably thought about property rights as referring to goods that are typically bought and sold in markets, like food, clothes, or houses. Coase's approach suggests that we could think of other rights—in his example, the right to make a noise or to have a quiet work environment—as goods that can be bargained over and traded in return for money.

Let's see how a private bargain might solve the pesticide problem. Initially it is not illegal to use Weevokil: the allocation of property rights is such that the plantations have the right to use it, and choose to produce 80,000 tonnes of bananas. This allocation and the associated incomes and environmental effects represent the **reservation option** of the plantation owners and fishermen. This is what they will get if they do not come to some agreement.

For the fishermen and the plantation owners to negotiate effectively, they would each have to be organized so that a single person (or body) could make agreements on behalf of the entire group. So let's imagine that a representative of an association of fishermen sits down to bargain with a representative of an association of banana growers. To keep things simple we will assume that, at present, there are no feasible alternatives to Weevokil, so they bargain only over the output of bananas.

Both sides should recognize that they could gain from an agreement to reduce output to the Pareto-efficient level. In Figure 12.4, the situation before bargaining begins is point A, and the Pareto-efficient quantity is 38,000 tonnes. The total shaded area shows the gain for the fishermen (from cleaner water) if output is reduced from 80,000 to 38,000. But reducing banana production will lead to lower profits for the plantations. Use the analysis in Figure 12.4 to see that the fall in profit is smaller than the gain for the fishermen, so there is a net social gain that they could agree to share.

Since the gain to the fishermen would be greater than the loss to the plantations, the fishermen would be willing to pay the banana growers to reduce output to 38,000 tonnes if they had the funds to do so.

The **minimum acceptable offer** from the fishermen depends on what the plantations get in the existing situation, which is their reservation profit (shown by the blue area labelled 'loss of profit'). If plantation owners agreed to this minimum payment to compensate them for their loss of profit, the fishing industry would achieve a net gain from the agreement equal to the net social gain, while plantations would be no better (and no worse) off.

The maximum the fishing industry would pay is determined by their **fallback (reservation) option**, as in the case of the plantations. It is the sum of the blue and green areas. In this case, the plantations would get all of the net social gain while the fishermen would be no better off. As in the cases of bargaining in Unit 5, the compensation they agree on, between these maximum and minimum levels, will be determined by the bargaining power of the two groups.

You may think it unfair that the fishermen need to pay for a reduction in pollution. At the Pareto-efficient level of banana production, the fishing industry is still suffering from pollution, and it has to pay to stop the pollution getting worse. This happens because we have assumed that the plantations have a legal right to use Weevokil.

An alternative legal framework could give the fishermen a right to clean water. If that were the case, the plantation owners wishing to use Weevokil could propose a bargain in which they paid the fishermen to give up some of their right to clean water to allow the Pareto-efficient level of banana

reservation option A person's next best alternative among all options in a particular transaction. *Also known as: fallback option. See also: reservation price.*

minimum acceptable offer In the ultimatum game, the smallest offer by the Proposer that will not be rejected by the Responder. Generally applied in bargaining situations to mean the least favourable offer that would be accepted.

production, which will be a much more favourable outcome for the fishermen. In principle, the bargaining process would result in a Pareto-efficient allocation independently of whether the initial rights were granted to the plantations (right to pollute) or to the fishermen (right to unpolluted water). But the two cases differ dramatically in the distribution of the benefits of solving the market failure.

As Coase acknowledged, practical obstacles to bargaining may prevent the achievement of Pareto efficiency:

- *Impediments to collective action:* Private bargaining may be impossible if there are many parties on both sides of the external effect, for example many fishermen and many plantation owners. Each side needs to find someone they trust to bargain for them, and agree how payments will be shared within each industry. The individuals representing the two groups would be performing a public service that might be difficult to secure.
- *Missing information:* Devising the payment scheme makes it necessary to measure the costs of Weevokil, not just in aggregate, but to each fisherman. We also need to establish the exact origin of the pollutant, plantation by plantation. Only when we have this information can we calculate the size of the payment that each fisherman has to pay, and how much each plantation should receive. It's easy to see that it is far harder to make a polluting industry accountable for the damage it does

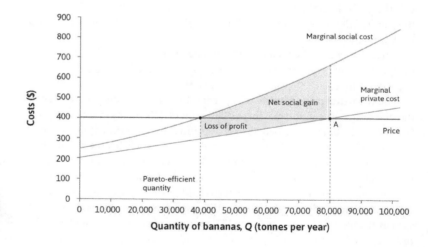

Figure 12.4 The gains from bargaining.

1. The status quo
The situation before bargaining is represented by point A, and the Pareto-efficient quantity of bananas is 38,000 tonnes. The total shaded area shows the gain for fishermen if output is reduced from 80,000 to 38,000 (that is, the reduction in the fishermen's costs).

2. Lost profit
Reducing output from 80,000 to 38,000 tonnes reduces the profits of plantations. The lost profit is equal to the loss of producer surplus, shown by the blue area.

3. The net social gain
The net social gain is the gain for the fishermen minus the loss for the plantations, shown by the remaining green area.

than to calculate the liability for damage done, for example, by a single reckless driver.

- *Tradability and enforcement:* The bargain involves the trading of property rights, and the contract governing the trade must be enforceable. Having agreed to pay thousands of dollars, the fishermen must be able to rely on the legal system if a plantation owner does not reduce output as agreed. This may require the fishermen and the courts to discover information about the plantation's operations that are not publicly known or available.
- *Limited funds:* The fishermen may not have enough money (we have seen in Unit 10 why they would probably not be able to borrow large sums) to pay the plantations to reduce output to 38,000 tonnes.

The pesticide example illustrates that although correcting market failures through bargaining may not require direct government intervention, it does require a legal framework for enforcing contracts so that property rights are tradable and so that all parties stick to the bargains they make. Even with this framework, the problems of collective action, missing information, and enforcement of what will inevitably be complex contracts make it unlikely that Coasean bargaining alone can address market failures.

> According to the 1992 Rio Declaration of the United Nations: 'National authorities should endeavour to promote the internalization of environmental costs and the use of economic instruments, taking into account the approach that the polluter should, in principle, bear the cost of pollution, with due regard to the public interest and without distorting international trade and investment.' Several of the approaches we describe in this unit are consistent with this principle. Either giving the fisherman a right to clean water or enforcing compensation means that the plantations will have to pay at least as much as the costs incurred by the fishing industry. A tax also means that the polluter pays, although it pays the government rather than the fishing industry.

EXERCISE 12.2 BARGAINING POWER

In the example of plantation owners and fishermen, can you think of any factors that might affect the bargaining power of these parties?

EXERCISE 12.3 A POSITIVE EXTERNALITY

Imagine a beekeeper, who produces honey and sells it at a constant price per kilogram.

1. Draw a diagram with the quantity of honey on the horizontal axis, showing the marginal cost of honey production as an upward-sloping line, and the price of honey as a horizontal line. Show the amount of honey that the profit-maximizing beekeeper will produce.
2. For the beekeeper, the **marginal private benefit** of producing a kilo of honey is equal to the price. But since the bees benefit a neighbouring farmer, by helping to pollinate her crops, honey production has a positive external effect. Draw a line on your diagram to represent the **marginal social benefit** of honey production. Show the quantity of honey that would be Pareto efficient. How does it compare with the quantity chosen by the beekeeper?
3. Explain how the farmer and beekeeper could both be made better off through bargaining.

> **marginal private benefit (MPB)** The benefit (in terms of profit, or utility) of producing or consuming an additional unit of a good for the individual who decides to produce or consume it, not taking into account any benefit received by others.

QUESTION 12.2 CHOOSE THE CORRECT ANSWER(S)

The graph depicts the MPC and MSC of the robot factory production in Question 12.1.

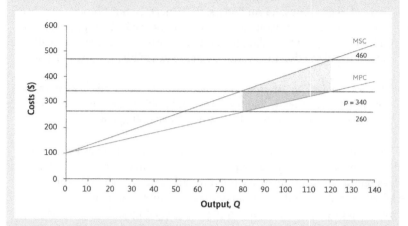

The robot market is competitive and the market price is £340. Currently the factory is producing an output of 120, but 80 would be Pareto efficient. Which of the following statements is correct?

☐ To reduce output to 80, the factory's minimum acceptable payment would be £1,600.
☐ The maximum that the nurses are willing to pay to induce the factory to reduce the output to 80 is £2,400.
☐ The factory would not reduce its output to 80 unless it received at least £4,000.
☐ The net social gain from the output reduction to 80 depends on the amount paid by the nurses to the factory.

QUESTION 12.3 CHOOSE THE CORRECT ANSWER(S)

Consider the situation where the noise of a factory's production affects nurses in the dormitory next door. If there are no transaction costs to impede Coasean bargaining, which of the following statements is correct?

☐ Whether the final output level will be Pareto efficient depends on who has the initial property rights.
☐ The nurses would be better off in the bargained allocation if they initially had a right to undisturbed sleep than they would if the factory has the right to make noise.
☐ If the factory has the right to make noise, it will prefer not to bargain with the nurses.
☐ If the nurses have the initial rights, they will obtain all of the net social gain from robot production.

12.3 EXTERNAL EFFECTS: POLICIES AND INCOME DISTRIBUTION

Suppose in the case of our Weevokil example that Coasean bargaining proves to be impractical, and that the fisherman and plantation owners cannot resolve the Weevokil problem privately. We will continue to assume that it is not possible to grow bananas without using Weevokil. What can the government do to achieve a reduction in the output of bananas to the level that takes into account the costs for the fishermen? There are three ways this might be done:

- regulation of the quantity of bananas produced
- taxation of the production or sale of bananas
- enforcing compensation of the fishermen for the costs imposed on them

Each of these policies has different distributional implications for the fisherman and plantation owners.

Regulation

The government could cap total banana output at 38,000 tonnes, the Pareto-efficient amount. This looks like a straightforward solution. On the other hand, if the plantations differ in size and output, it may be difficult to determine and enforce the right quota for each one.

This policy would reduce the costs of pollution for the fishermen, but it would lower the plantations' profits. They would lose their surplus on each tonne of bananas between 38,000 and 80,000.

Taxation

Figure 12.5 shows the MPC and MSC curves again. At the Pareto-efficient quantity (38,000 tonnes), the MSC is $400 and the MPC is $295. The price is $400. If the government puts a tax on each tonne of bananas produced, equal to $400 − $295 = $105 (the marginal external cost), then the after-tax price received by plantations will be $295. Now, if plantations maximize their profit, they will choose the point where the after-tax price equals the marginal private cost and produce 38,000 tonnes, the Pareto-efficient quantity. Use the analysis in Figure 12.5 to see how this policy works.

The tax corrects the price message, so that the plantations face the full marginal social cost of their decisions. When the plantations are producing 38,000 bananas, the tax is exactly equal to the cost imposed on the fishermen. This approach is known as a **Pigouvian tax**, after the economist Arthur Pigou who advocated it. It also works in the case of a positive external effect: if the marginal social benefit of a decision is greater than the marginal private benefit, this becomes a Pigouvian subsidy, which can ensure that the decision-maker takes this **external benefit** into account.

Pigouvian tax A tax levied on activities that generate negative external effects so as to correct an inefficient market outcome. *See also: external effect, Pigouvian subsidy.*

external benefit A positive external effect: that is, a positive effect of a production, consumption, or other economic decision on another person or people that is not specified as a benefit in a contract. *Also known as: external economy. See also: external effect.*

The distributional effects of taxation are different from those of regulation. The costs of pollution for fishermen are reduced by the same amount, but the reduction in banana profits is greater, since the plantations pay taxes as well as reducing output, and the government receives tax revenue.

Leibniz: Pigouvian taxes
(http://tinyco.re/L120301)

Enforcing compensation

The government could require the plantation owners to pay compensation for costs imposed on the fishermen. The compensation required for each tonne of bananas will be equal to the difference between the MSC and the MPC, which is the distance between the green and purple lines in Figure 12.6. Once compensation is included, the marginal cost of each tonne of bananas for the plantations will be the MPC plus the compensation, which is equal to the MSC. So now the plantations will maximize profit by choosing point P_2 in Figure 12.6 and producing 38,000 tonnes. The shaded area shows the total compensation paid. The fishermen are fully compensated for pollution, and the plantations' profits are equal to the true social surplus of banana production.

The effect of this policy on the plantations' profits is similar to the effect of the tax, but the fishermen do better because they, rather than the government, receive payment from the plantations.

Diagnosis and treatment in the case of chlordecone

When we identified 38,000 tonnes as the Pareto-efficient level of output in our model, we assumed that growing bananas inevitably involves Weevokil pollution. So our diagnosis was that too many bananas were being produced, and we looked at policies for reducing production. But that was not the case in Guadaloupe and Martinique, where there were alternatives to chlordecone. If alternatives to Weevokil were available, it would be inefficient to restrict output to 38,000 tonnes, because if the plantations could choose a different production method and the corresponding profit-

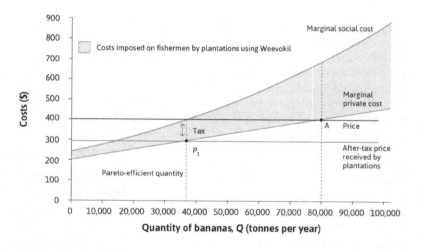

Figure 12.5 Using a tax to achieve Pareto efficiency.

1. The marginal external cost
At the Pareto-efficient quantity, 38,000 tonnes, the MPC is $295. The MSC is $400. So the marginal external cost is MSC − MPC = $105.

2. Tax = MSC − MPC
If the government puts a tax on each tonne of bananas produced equal to $105, the marginal external cost, then the after-tax price received by plantations will be $295.

3. The after-tax price is $295
To maximize profit, the plantations will choose their output so that the MPC is equal to the after-tax price. They will choose point P_1 and produce 38,000 tonnes.

maximizing output, they could be better off, and the fishermen no worse off.

So the problem was caused by the use of chlordecone, not the production of bananas.

The market failure occurred because the price of chlordecone did not incorporate the costs that its use inflicted on the fishermen, and so it sent the wrong message to the firm. Its low price said: 'use this chemical, it will save you money and raise profits', but if its price had included the full external costs of its use, it might have been high enough to have said: 'think about the downstream damage, and look for an alternative way to grow bananas'.

In this situation, a policy of requiring the plantations to compensate the fishermen would have given them the incentive to find production methods that caused less pollution and could, in principle, have achieved an efficient outcome.

But the other two policies would not do so. Rather than taxing or regulating banana production, it would be better to regulate or tax the sale or the use of chlordecone, to motivate plantations to find the best alternative to intensive chlordecone use.

In theory, if the tax on a unit of chlordecone was equal to its marginal external cost, the price of chlordecone for the plantations would be equal to its marginal social cost, so it would be sending the right message. They could then choose the best production method taking into account the high cost of chlordecone, which would involve reducing its use or switching to a different pesticide, and determine their profit-maximizing output. As with the banana tax, the profits of the plantations and the pollution costs for the fishermen would fall, but the outcome would be better for the plantations, and possibly the fishermen also, if chlordecone rather than bananas were taxed.

Unfortunately, none of these remedies was used for 20 years in the case of chlordecone, and the people of Guadaloupe and Martinique are still living with the consequences. In 1993, the government finally recognized that the marginal social cost of chlordecone use was so high that it should be banned altogether.

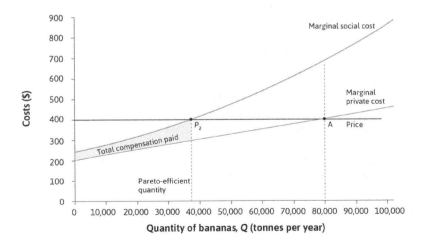

Figure 12.6 The plantations compensate the fishermen.

In Guadaloupe and Martinique, nothing was done to reduce chlordecone pollution until 1993, although chlordecone was first listed as carcinogenic in 1979. It was obvious that the external costs were much higher than in our case of Weevokil, damaging the health of islanders as well as the livelihood of fishermen. In fact, the marginal social cost of any bananas produced with the aid of chlordecone was higher than their market price, justifying an outright ban on its use. The pollution turned out to be much worse than anyone realized at the time, and is likely to persist in the soil for 700 years. In 2013, fishermen in Martinique barricaded the port of Fort de France until the French government agreed to allocate $2.6 million in aid.

There are limits to how well governments can implement Pigouvian taxes, regulation and compensation—often for the same reasons as for Coasean bargaining:

- *The government may not know the degree of harm suffered by each fisherman*: As a result, it can't create the best compensation policy.
- *Marginal social costs are difficult to measure*: While the plantations' marginal private costs are probably well known, it is harder to determine marginal social costs, such as the pollution costs, to either individuals or to society as a whole.
- *The government may favour the more powerful group*: In this case it could impose a Pareto-efficient outcome that is also unfair.

GREAT ECONOMISTS

Arthur Pigou

Arthur Pigou (1877–1959) was one of the first neoclassical economists to focus on welfare economics, which is the analysis of the allocation of resources in terms of the wellbeing of society as a whole. Pigou won awards during his studies at the University of Cambridge in history, languages, and moral sciences (there was no dedicated economics degree at the time). He became a protégé of Alfred Marshall. Pigou was an outgoing and lively person when young, but his experiences as a conscientious objector and ambulance driver during the First World War, as well as anxieties over his own health, turned him into a recluse who hid in his office except for lectures and walks.

Pigou's economic theory was mainly focused on using economics for the good of society, which is why he is sometimes seen as the founder of welfare economics.

His book *Wealth and Welfare* was described by Schumpeter as 'the greatest venture in labour economics ever undertaken by a man who was primarily a theorist', and provided the foundation for his later work, *The Economics of Welfare*. Together, these works built up a relationship between a nation's economy and the welfare of its people. Pigou focused on happiness and wellbeing. He recognized that concepts such as political freedom and relative status were important.

Pigou believed that the reallocation of resources was necessary when the interests of a private firm or individual diverged from the interests of society, causing what we would today call externalities. He suggested taxation could solve the problem: Pigouvian taxes are intended to ensure that producers face the true social costs of their decisions.

Arthur Pigou. 1912. *Wealth and Welfare* (http://tinyco.re/2519065). London: Macmillan & Co.

Arthur Pigou. (1920) 1932. *The Economics of Welfare* (http://tinyco.re/2042156). London: Macmillan & Co.

Despite both being heirs to Marshall's new school of economics, Pigou and Keynes did not see eye-to-eye. Keynes's work, *The General Theory of Employment, Interest and Money*, contained a critique of Pigou's *The Theory of Unemployment*, and Pigou felt that Keynes's material was becoming too dogmatic and turning students into 'identical sausages'.

Although overlooked for much of the twentieth century, Pigou's work paved the way for much of labour economics and environmental policy. Pigouvian taxes were largely unrecognized until the 1960s, but they have become a major policy tool for reducing pollution and environmental damage.

The online version of Keynes's *The General Theory* (http://tinyco.re/ 2987470) allows you to search for his critique of Pigou: John Maynard Keynes. 1936. *The General Theory of Employment, Interest and Money*. London: Palgrave Macmillan.

Now we can extend the table we started to create in Section 12.1 (Figure 12.3). Look at the fifth column in Figure 12.7, which is new: it adds the possible remedies for the problem of negative external effects.

EXERCISE 12.4 PIGOUVIAN SUBSIDY

Consider the beekeeper and neighbouring farmer in Exercise 12.3. Why might they be unable to bargain successfully to achieve a Pareto-efficient outcome in practice? Use the diagram you drew to show how the government might improve the situation by subsidizing honey production. Describe the distributional effects of this subsidy, and compare it to the Pareto-efficient bargaining outcome.

EXERCISE 12.5 COMPARING POLICIES

Consider the three policies of regulation, taxation, and compensation arrangements discussed above. Evaluate the strengths and weaknesses of each policy from the standpoint of Pareto efficiency and fairness.

Decision	How it affects others	Cost or benefit	Market failure (misallocation of resources)	Possible remedies	Terms applied to this type of market failure
A firm uses a pesticide that runs off into waterways	Downstream damage	Private benefit, external cost	Overuse of pesticide and overproduction of the crop for which it is used	Taxes, quotas, bans, bargaining, common ownership of all affected assets	Negative external effect, environmental spillover

Figure 12.7 Water pollution market failure, with remedies.

QUESTION 12.4 CHOOSE THE CORRECT ANSWER(S)

The graph shows the MPC and MSC of robot production for the factory situated next to a dormitory for nurses who work nightshifts.

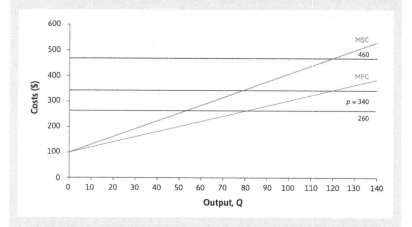

The market for robots is competitive and the market price is £340. The initial output is 120 but the government uses a Pigouvian tax to reduce this to the efficient level of 80. Which of the following statements is correct?

☐ Under the Pigouvian tax, the factory's surplus will be £6,400.
☐ The required Pigouvian tax is £120 per robot.
☐ The nurses are at least as well off as they would be under Coasean bargaining.
☐ The nurses obtain no benefit from the imposition of the Pigouvian tax.

●●●

12.4 PROPERTY RIGHTS, CONTRACTS, AND MARKET FAILURES

In taking an action so as to maximize profits (choosing the level of banana production or the choice of pesticide) the plantation owners did not take account of the external costs they imposed on the fishermen. And they had no reason to take account of them: they had the right to pollute the fisheries.

The same is true for the overuse of antibiotics. A self-interested person has no reason to use antibiotics sparingly, because the superbug that may be created will probably infect someone else.

If the prices of chlordecone and the antibiotic were high enough, there would be no overuse. But the prices of these goods were based on the costs of production, and excluded costs that their use would inflict on others. As you have seen, the private cost to the user (how much he paid to acquire the good) fell short of the social cost for this reason.

Another example: when fuel costs are low, more people decide to drive to work rather than taking the train. The information conveyed by the low price does not include the environmental costs of deciding to drive. The effects on the decision-maker are termed private costs and benefits, while the total effects, including those inflicted or enjoyed by others, are social costs and benefits.

Costs inflicted on others (such as pollution and congestion that are worse because you drive to work) are termed **external diseconomies** or **negative externalities**, while uncompensated benefits conferred on others are **external economies** or **positive externalities**.

We can understand why these and other market failures are common by thinking about how they could be avoided.

How could the cost of driving to work accurately reflect all of the costs incurred by anyone, not just the private costs made by the decision-maker? The most obvious (if impractical) way would be to require the driver to pay everyone affected by the resultant environmental damage (or traffic congestion) an amount exactly equal to the damage inflicted. This is of course impossible to do, but it sets a standard of what has to be done or approximated if the 'price of driving to work' is to send the correct message.

Something like this approach applies if you drive recklessly on the way to work, skid off the road, and crash into somebody's house. Tort law (the law of damages) in most countries would require you to pay for the damage to the house. You are held liable for the damages so that you would pay the cost you had inflicted on another.

Knowing this, you might think twice about driving to work (or at least slow down a bit when you are late). It will change your behaviour and the allocation of resources.

But while tort law in most countries covers some kinds of harm inflicted on others (reckless driving), other important external effects of driving your car (such as adding to air pollution or congestion) would not be covered . Here are two further examples:

- *A firm operates an incinerator that produces fumes:* The fumes lower the surrounding air quality. Those being polluted do not have a right to clean air, which is the right that would be the basis for a claim for compensation from the firm. So the firm does not have to pay these costs.
- *You play music loudly at night and disturb the sleep of the people next door:* Sleeping neighbours do not have an enforceable right not to be woken by your music. There is no way that your neighbours can make you pay them compensation for the inconvenience you cause.

Legal systems also fail to provide compensation for the benefits that one's actions confer on others:

- *A firm trains a worker who quits for a better job:* The skills of the trained worker go with them to the new job. Therefore, even though a different firm receives the benefit, the firm that paid for the training cannot collect compensation from the new firm.
- *Kim, the farmer in Unit 4, contributes to the cost of an irrigation project while other farmers free-ride on Kim's contribution:* Kim has no way of claiming payment for this public-spirited act. The free-riders will not compensate Kim.
- *A country invests in reducing carbon emissions that lowers the risks of climate change for other countries:* As we saw in Unit 4, unless a treaty guarantees compensation for the costs of reduced emissions, other countries do not need to pay for this. The environmental improvement for the other countries is an uncompensated benefit.

external diseconomy A negative effect of a production, consumption, or other economic decision, that is not specified as a liability in a contract. Also known as: external cost, negative externality. See also: external effect.
external economy A positive effect of a production, consumption, or other economic decision, that is not specified as a benefit in a contract. Also known as: external benefit, positive externality. See also: external effect.

incomplete contract A contract that does not specify, in an enforceable way, every aspect of the exchange that affects the interests of parties to the exchange (or of others).

missing market A market in which there is some kind of exchange that, if implemented, would be mutually beneficial. This does not occur due to asymmetric or non-verifiable information.

verifiable information Information that can be used to enforce a contract.

asymmetric information Information that is relevant to the parties in an economic interaction, but is known by some but not by others. *See also: adverse selection, moral hazard.*

Market failures occur in these examples because the external benefits and costs of a person's actions are not owned by anyone. Think about waste. If you redecorate your house and you tear up the floor or knock down a wall, you own the debris and you have to dispose of it, even if you need to pay someone to take it away. But this is not the case with fumes from the incinerator or loud music at night. You do not have a contract with the incinerator company specifying at what price you are willing to accept fumes, or with your neighbour about the price of the right to play music after 10pm. In these cases economists say that we have 'incomplete, missing, or unenforceable property rights'—or, simply, **incomplete contracts**.

We saw an important example of an incomplete contract in Unit 6. In the employment relationship, the employer can pay for the worker's time, but the contract cannot specify how much effort is to be put in. Likewise, the external effects of a person's actions are effects that are not governed by contracts. Another way to express the problem is to say that there is no market within which these external effects can be compensated. So economists also use the term **missing markets** to describe problems like this.

In the case of Weevokil pollution:

- *The fishermen's property rights were incomplete*: They did not own a right to clean water in their fisheries, which would enable them to receive compensation for pollution, and they could not purchase such a right.
- *There was no market for clean water.*

Why don't countries just rewrite their laws to reward people for the benefits they confer on others, and make decision-makers pay for the costs they inflict on others?

In Unit 6, we reviewed the reasons why the kinds of complete contracts that would enforce these objectives are incomplete or unenforceable. These are that necessary information is either not available or not **verifiable**, the external effects are too complex or difficult to measure to be written into an enforceable contract, or there may be no legal system to enforce the contract (as in pollution, which crosses national borders). You can see in our example that it would not be possible to write a complete set of contracts in which each individual fisherman could receive compensation from each plantation for the effects on that fisherman of its individual decisions.

For these and other reasons, in most cases it is impractical to use tort law to make people liable for the costs they inflict on others, because we don't have that information. And it is equally infeasible to use the legal system to compensate people for the beneficial effects they have on others, for example, to pay those who keep beautiful gardens an amount equal to the pleasure this confers on those who pass their house. A court would have to know how much that pleasure was worth to each passerby.

In the five bulleted examples earlier in this section, the reason why uncompensated external costs and benefits occur is the same:

- Some information that is of concern to someone other than the decision-maker is non-verifiable or **asymmetric information**.
- Therefore, there can be no contract or property rights ensuring that external effects will be compensated.
- As a result, some of the social costs or benefits of the decision-maker's actions will not be included (or will not be sufficiently important) in the decision-making process.

12.5 PUBLIC GOODS

The irrigation projects that we studied in Unit 4 are another example of a good that may not be provided efficiently in the market system. We described irrigation systems as a **public good**. When one farmer incurs a cost to provide irrigation, all farmers benefit. This creates a social dilemma. If farmers act independently, they all have an incentive to free-ride, in which case no one will provide irrigation. Only by finding ways of working together can they achieve the outcome that benefits them all.

The defining characteristic of a public good is that if it is available to one person it can be available to everyone at no additional cost. An irrigation system is a public good for the community where it is located. There are other examples that are public goods for a whole country, like national defence (if one person is protected from foreign invasion, this will be true of others, too) and weather forecasting (if I can tune in and find out if it's likely to rain today, so can you). These are services that are typically provided by governments rather than the market.

Knowledge is also a public good. You can use your knowledge of a recipe for baking a cake or the rules of multiplication without affecting the ability of others to use the same knowledge. (This creates a problem for firms investing in research—if competing firms can freely appropriate the knowledge that they produce, their incentive to innovate is reduced.) And the environment provides public goods. Enjoying a view of the setting sun does not deprive anyone else of their enjoyment.

In all of these cases, once the good is available at all, the marginal cost of making it available to additional people is zero. Goods with this characteristic are also called **non-rival goods**.

A good is termed public if once available to one person, it can be available to everyone at no additional cost and its use by one person does not reduce its availability to others. This character of a public good is called non-rival because potential users are not in competition (rivals) with each other for the good.

Note that some economists add that others cannot be excluded from the goods' use. These goods are called **non-excludable public goods**. We consider the non-rival character of a public good to be its defining characteristic, whether others can be excluded or not.

For some public goods, it is possible to exclude additional users, even though the cost of their use is zero. Examples are satellite TV, the information in a **copyrighted** book, or a film shown in an uncrowded cinema: it costs no more if an additional viewer is there, but the owner can nonetheless require that anyone who wants to see the film must pay. The same goes for a quiet road on which tollgates have been erected. Drivers can be

public good A good for which use by one person does not reduce its availability to others. Also known as: non-rival good. See also: non-excludable public good, artificially scarce good.

non-excludable public good A public good for which it is impossible to exclude anyone from having access. See also: artificially scarce good.

copyright Ownership rights over the use and distribution of an original work.

artificially scarce good A public good that it is possible to exclude some people from enjoying. *Also known as: club good.*

private good A good that is both rival, and from which others can be excluded.

common-pool resource A rival good that one cannot prevent others from enjoying. *Also known as: common property resource.*

excluded (unless they pay the toll) even though the marginal cost of an additional traveller is zero.

Public goods for which it is feasible to exclude others are sometimes called **artificially scarce goods** or **club goods** (because they function like joining a private club: when the golf course is not crowded, adding one more member costs the golf club nothing, but the club will still charge a membership fee).

The opposite of a non-excludable public good is a **private good**. We have seen many examples: loaves of bread, dinners in restaurants, rupees divided between Anil and Bala (Unit 4), and boxes of breakfast cereal. All of these goods are both rival (more for Anil means less for Bala) and excludable (Anil can prevent Bala from taking his money).

There is a fourth kind of good that is rival, but not excludable, called a **common-pool resource**. An example is fisheries that are open to all. What one fisherman catches cannot be caught by anyone else, but anyone who wants to fish can do so. We can also think of busy public roads as a common-pool resource. Anyone who chooses to use them may do so, but each user makes the road more congested and slows down the journeys of others. The table in Figure 12.8 summarizes the four kinds of goods.

Figure 12.8 shows four distinct categories of goods. But the extent of rivalry or excludability in goods is a matter of degree. For some kinds of goods, the cost of additional users is not literally zero (which is what pure non-rivalry would require) but instead very small. An example is a medical drug that cost millions in research funds to create the first pill, but only pennies per application to make treatments available to additional users once created.

'Goods' in economics are things that people want to use or consume. But there are also 'bads': things that people don't want, and might be willing to pay to *not* have, such as household refuse, or unpleasant-smelling drains. These are *private bads*. Analogously, we can define *public bads*: air pollution, for example, is a bad that affects many people simultaneously. It is non-rival in the sense that one person suffering its effects does not reduce the suffering of the others.

As can be seen from the examples, whether a good is private or public depends not only on the nature of the good itself, but on legal and other institutions:

- Knowledge that is not subject to copyright or other intellectual property rights would be classified as a **non-excludable public good** …
- … But when the author uses copyright law to create a monopoly on the right to reproduce that knowledge, it is a **public good** that is **artificially scarce**.

	Rival	Non-rival
Excludable	Private goods (food, clothes, houses)	Public goods that are artificially scarce (subscription TV, uncongested tollroads, knowledge subject to intellectual property rights, Unit 21)
Non-excludable	Common-pool resources (fish stocks in a lake, common grazing land, Units 4 and 20)	Non-excludable public goods and bads (view of a lunar eclipse, public broadcasts, rules of arithmetic or calculus, national defence, noise and air pollution, Units 20 and 21)

Figure 12.8 Private goods and public goods.

- Common grazing land is a **common-pool resource** …
- … But if the same land is fenced to exclude other users, it becomes a **private good**.

Markets typically allocate private goods. But for the other three kinds of good, markets are either not possible or likely to fail. There are two reasons:

- *When goods are non-rival, the marginal cost is zero:* Setting a price equal to marginal cost (as is necessary for a Pareto-efficient market transaction) will not be possible unless the provider is subsidized.
- *When goods are not excludable there is no way to charge a price for them:* The provider cannot exclude people who haven't paid.

So when goods are not private, public policy may be required to allocate them. National defence is a responsibility of the government in all countries. Environmental policy addresses problems of common-pool resources and public bads such as pollution, and carbon emissions (see Unit 20). Governments also adopt a range of policies to address the problem of knowledge as a public good, such as issuing **patents** to give firms an incentive to undertake research and development (R&D) (see Unit 21).

Market failure in the case of public goods is closely related to the problems of **external effects**, absent **property rights**, and **incomplete contracts** that we have been discussing in this unit. A community irrigation system is a public good, so if one farmer decides to invest in an irrigation project, this confers an **external benefit** on the other farmers. Since her private benefit is less than the overall social benefit, she will invest too little from the point of view of the community, or she may not invest at all. There is no market in which the beneficiaries of the irrigation system pay the providers for the benefits they obtain, and it would be difficult to write complete contracts between all the farmers to achieve a Pareto-efficient irrigation level.

Similarly, we analysed Weevokil pollution as a problem in which the decisions of banana plantations imposed a negative external effect on fisherman. The private cost of using Weevokil was below the social cost, so the pesticide was overused. But we can also interpret the plantations as contributing to a **public bad**, from which all of the fishermen suffer.

The user of a common-pool resource imposes an external cost on other users. By driving your car on a busy road, for example, you contribute to the congestion experienced by other drivers.

Thus, any of the examples of non-private goods introduced in this section can be described using the framework we set up in Section 12.3 to summarize cases of market failure. They are summarized in the table in Figure 12.9.

patent A right of exclusive ownership of an idea or invention, which lasts for a specified length of time. During this time it effectively allows the owner to be a monopolist or exclusive user.

public bad The negative equivalent of a public good. It is non-rival in the sense that a given individual's consumption of the public bad does not diminish others' consumption of it.

EXERCISE 12.7 RIVALRY AND EXCLUDABILITY

For each of the following goods or bads, decide whether they are rival and whether they are excludable, and explain your answer. If you think the answer depends on factors not specified here, explain how.

1. A free public lecture held at a university lecture theatre
2. Noise produced by aircraft around an international airport
3. A public park
4. A forest used by local people to collect firewood
5. Seats in a theatre to watch a musical
6. Bicycles available to the public to hire to travel around a city

QUESTION 12.5 CHOOSE THE CORRECT ANSWER(S)

Which of the following statements is correct?

☐ Some public goods are rival.
☐ A public good must be non-excludable.
☐ A good cannot be rival and non-excludable.
☐ If a good is non-rival, then the cost of an additional person consuming it is zero.

Decision	How it affects others	Cost or benefit	Market failure (misallocation of resources)	Possible remedies	Terms applied to this type of market failure
You take an international flight	Increase in global carbon emissions	Private benefit, external cost	Overuse of air travel	Taxes, quotas	Public bad, negative external effect
You travel to work by car	Congestion for other road users	Private cost, external cost	Overuse of cars	Tolls, quotas, subsidized public transport	Common-pool resource, negative external effect
A firm invests in R&D	Other firms can exploit the innovation	Private cost, external benefit	Too little R&D	Publicly funded research, subsidies for R&D, patents	Public good, positive external effect

Figure 12.9 Examples of market failure, with remedies.

12.6 MISSING MARKETS: INSURANCE AND LEMONS

We know that a common reason for contracts to be incomplete is that information about an important aspect of the interaction is unavailable, or unverifiable. In particular, information is often **asymmetric**—that is, one party knows something relevant to the transaction that the other doesn't know.

One form of asymmetric information is a **hidden action**. In Unit 6 we studied the case of the employee whose choice of how hard to work is hidden from the employer. This causes a problem known as **moral hazard**. There is a conflict of interest because the employee would prefer not to work as hard as the employer would like, and work effort cannot be specified in the contract. We saw in Unit 9 how the employer's response (paying a wage above the reservation level) led to a Pareto-inefficient outcome in the labour market.

In this section, we introduce a second form of asymmetric information, that of **hidden attributes**. When you want to purchase a used car, for example, the seller knows the quality of the vehicle. You do not. This attribute of the car is hidden from the prospective buyer. Hidden attributes can cause a problem known as **adverse selection**.

Hidden actions and moral hazard

The problem of hidden action occurs when some action taken by one party to an exchange is not known or cannot be verified by the other. For example, the employer cannot know (or cannot verify) how hard the worker she has employed is actually working.

The term moral hazard originated in the insurance industry to express the problem that insurers face, namely, the person with home insurance may take less care to avoid fires or other damages to his home, thereby increasing the risk above what it would be in absence of insurance. This term now refers to any situation in which one party to an interaction is deciding on an action that affects the profits or wellbeing of the other but which the affected party cannot control by means of a contract, often because the affected party does not have adequate information on the action. It is also referred to as the 'hidden actions' problem.

Hidden attributes and adverse selection

The problem of hidden attributes occurs when some attribute of the person engaging in an exchange (or the product or service being provided) is not known to the other parties. An example is that the individual purchasing health insurance knows her own health status, but the insurance company does not.

The term adverse selcetion refers to the problem faced by parties to an exchange in which the terms offered by one party will cause some exchange partners to drop out. An example is the problem of asymmetric information in insurance: if the price is sufficiently high, the only people who will seek to purchase medical insurance are people who know they are ill (but the insurer does not). This will lead to further price increases to cover costs. Also referred to as the 'hidden attributes' problem (the state of already being ill is the hidden attribute), to distinguish it from the 'hidden actions' problem of moral hazard.

George Akerlof, an economist, was the first to analyse this problem in 1970. Initially his paper on the subject was rejected by two economics journals for being trivial. Another returned it, saying that it was incorrect. Thirty-one years later, he was awarded the Nobel Prize for his work on asymmetric information. Akerlof and co-author Robert Shiller give a simple explanation of the so-called market for lemons in this book: George A. Akerlof and Robert J. Shiller. 2015. *Phishing for Phools: The Economics of Manipulation and Deception*. Princeton, NJ: Princeton University Press.

Hidden attributes and adverse selection

A famous example of how hidden attributes may result in a market failure is known as the market for lemons. A 'lemon' is slang for a used car that you discover to be defective after you buy it. The model describes a used car market:

- Every day, 10 owners of 10 used cars consider selling.
- The cars differ in quality, which we measure by the true value of the car to its owner. Quality ranges from zero to $9,000 in equal steps: there is one worthless car, one worth $1,000, another worth $2,000, and so on. The average value of the cars is thus $4,500.
- There are many prospective buyers and each would happily buy a car for a price equal to its true value, but not more.
- Sellers do not expect to receive the full value of their vehicle, but they are willing to sell if they can get more than half the true value. So the total surplus on each car—the gain from trading it—will be half the price of the car.

If prospective buyers were able to observe the quality of every car, then buyers would approach each seller and bargain over the price, and by the end of the day all of the cars (except for the entirely worthless one) would be sold at a price somewhere between their true value and half the true value. The market would have assured that all mutually beneficial trades would take place.

But, on any day, there is a problem: potential buyers have no information about the quality of any car that is for sale. All they know is the true value of the cars sold the previous day. The most that prospective buyers are willing to pay for a car will be the average value of the cars sold the day before.

Now suppose that 10 cars had been offered on the market the day before. We use a proof by contradiction to show that one by one, the sellers of the highest quality cars will drop out of the market, until there is no market for used cars. Consider the market today:

- Yesterday all the cars (as we assumed at the start) were put on the market and sold.
- The average value of these cars was $4,500, so the most a buyer is willing to pay today will be $4,500.
- At the beginning of the day, each prospective seller considers selling his or her car, expecting a price of $4,500 at the most. Most of the owners are happy, because it is more than half the true value of their car.
- But one owner isn't pleased. The owner of the best car would not sell unless the price exceeds half the value of his car: more than $4,500.
- Prospective buyers will not pay this price. So today the owner of the best car will not offer it for sale. No one with a car worth $9,000 will be willing to participate in this market.
- The rest of the cars will sell today: their value averages $4,000.
- Tomorrow buyers will know the average value of the cars sold today. And so tomorrow, buyers will decide they will be willing to pay at most $4,000 for a car.
- The owner of tomorrow's highest-quality car (the one worth $8,000) will know this, and know that she will not get her minimum price, which is greater than $4,000. Tomorrow, she will not offer her car for sale.

- As a result, the average quality of cars sold on the market tomorrow will be $3,500, which means the owner of the third-best car will not put his car up for sale the day after tomorrow.
- And so it goes on, until, at some point next week, only the owner of a lemon worth $1,000 and a totally worthless car will remain in that day's market.
- If cars of these two values had sold the previous day, then, the next day, buyers will be willing to pay at most $500 for a car.
- Knowing this, the owner of the car worth $1,000 will decide she would rather keep her car.
- The only car on the market will be worth nothing. Cars that remain in this market are lemons, because only the owner of a worthless car would be prepared to offer that car for sale.

Economists call processes like this **adverse selection** because the prevailing price selects which cars will be left in the market. If any cars are traded, they will be the lower quality ones. The selection of cars is adverse for buyers. In the example above, there are no cars left at all—the market disappears altogether.

Adverse selection in the insurance market
The *market for lemons* is a well-known term in economics, but the lemons problem—that is, the **problem of hidden attributes**—is not restricted to the used car market.

Another important example is health insurance. Imagine hypothetically that you will be born into a population in which you do not know whether you will be a person with a serious health problem, or might contract such a problem later in life, or perhaps be entirely healthy until old age. There is a health insurance policy available covering any medical services you may need, and the premium is the same for everyone—it is set according to the average expected medical costs of people in the population, so that for the insurance company the premiums will cover the total expected payout, assuming everyone signs up. Would you buy this health insurance policy?

In this situation, most people would be happy to purchase the policy, because serious illness imposes high costs that are often impossible for an average family to pay. The costs of protecting you and your family from a financial catastrophe (or the possibility that you can't afford healthcare when you need it) are worth the insurance premium.

The assumption that you do not know anything about your health status in this thought experiment is unrealistic. It is another use of John Rawls' veil of ignorance that we discussed in Unit 5. Thinking about this problem as an impartial observer highlights the importance of the veil of ignorance assumption.

Though everyone would have bought insurance if they did not know about their future health status, the situation changes dramatically if we can choose whether to buy health insurance without the veil of ignorance,

adverse selection The problem faced by parties to an exchange in which the terms offered by one party will cause some exchange partners to drop out. An example is the problem of asymmetric information in insurance: if the price is sufficiently high, the only people who will seek to purchase medical insurance are people who know they are ill (but the insurer does not). This will lead to further price increases to cover costs. Also referred to as the 'hidden attributes' problem (the state of already being ill is the hidden attribute), to distinguish it from the 'hidden actions' problem of moral hazard. *See also: incomplete contract, moral hazard, asymmetric information.*

hidden attributes (problem of) This occurs when some attribute of the person engaging in an exchange (or the product or service being provided) is not known to the other parties. An example is that the individual purchasing health insurance knows her own health status, but the insurance company does not. *Also known as: adverse selection. See also: hidden actions (problem of).*

that is, knowing our health status. In this situation, information is asymmetric. Look at the situation from the standpoint of the insurance company:

- *People are more likely to purchase insurance if they know that they are ill*: So the average health of people buying insurance will be lower than the average health of the population.
- *This information is asymmetric*: The person buying the insurance knows how healthy he or she is, but the insurance company does not.
- *Insurance companies will be profitable only if they charge higher prices*: These prices will be higher than they would charge if all members of the population were forced to purchase the same insurance.
- *This leads to adverse selection*: In which case, the price will be high enough that only people who knew they were ill would wish to purchase insurance.
- *This leads to even higher prices for insurance*: To remain in business, the insurance companies will now have to raise prices again. Eventually the vast majority of the people purchasing insurance will be those who know they already have a serious health problem.
- *Healthy people are priced out of the market*: Those who want to buy insurance in case they fall ill in the future will not buy insurance.

This is another example of a **missing market**: many people will be uninsured. It is a market that could exist, but only if health information were symmetrical and verifiable (ignoring for the moment the problem of whether everyone would want to share their health data). It could provide benefits to both insurance company owners and people who wanted to insure themselves. Not having such a market is Pareto inefficient.

To address the problem of adverse selection due to asymmetric information, and the resulting missing markets for health insurance, many countries have adopted policies of compulsory enrolment in private insurance programs or universal tax-financed coverage.

Moral hazard in the insurance market

Hidden attributes are not the only problem facing insurers, whether private or governmental. There is also a **problem of hidden actions**. Buying an insurance policy may make the buyer more likely to take exactly the risks that are now insured. For example, a person who has purchased full coverage for his car against damage or theft may take less care in driving or locking the car than someone who had not purchased insurance.

Insurers typically place limits on the insurance they sell. For example, coverage may not apply (or may be more expensive) if someone other than the insured is driving, or if the car is usually parked in a place where a lot of cars are stolen. These provisions can be written into an insurance contract.

But the insurer cannot enforce a contract about how fast you drive or whether you drive after having had a drink. These are the actions that are hidden from the insurer because of the asymmetric information: you know these facts, but the insurance company does not.

This is a problem of **moral hazard**, similar to the one of labour effort. They are both **principal-agent problems**: the agent (an insured person, or employee) chooses an action (how careful to be, or how hard to work) that matters to the principal (the insurance company, or the employer), but cannot be included in the contract because it is not verifiable.

hidden actions (problem of) This occurs when some action taken by one party to an exchange is not known or cannot be verified by the other. For example, the employer cannot know (or cannot verify) how hard the worker she has employed is actually working. *Also known as: moral hazard. See also: hidden attributes (problem of).*

Though seemingly very different, these moral hazard problems are similar in an important respect to chlordecone pollution, and to public goods and common-pool resources in the previous section. In every case, someone makes a decision that has external costs or benefits for someone else: in other words, costs or benefits that are uncompensated. For example in the moral hazard case, the insured person (the agent) decides how much care to take. Taking care has an external benefit for the insurer (principal) but is costly for the agent, so consequently we have a market failure: the level of care chosen is too low.

So these problems of moral hazard (and also the adverse selection problems described earlier in this section) can be placed within the framework of external effects and market failure we are using throughout this unit. The problems arising from asymmetric information are summarized in the table in Figure 12.10.

> **moral hazard** This term originated in the insurance industry to express the problem that insurers face, namely, the person with home insurance may take less care to avoid fires or other damages to his home, thereby increasing the risk above what it would be in absence of insurance. This term now refers to any situation in which one party to an interaction is deciding on an action that affects the profits or wellbeing of the other but which the affected party cannot control by means of a contract, often because the affected party does not have adequate information on the action. It is also referred to as the 'hidden actions' problem. *See also: hidden actions (problems of), incomplete contract, too big to fail.*
>
> **principal-agent relationship** This relationship exists when one party (the principal) would like another party (the agent) to act in some way, or have some attribute that is in the interest of the principal, and that cannot be enforced or guaranteed in a binding contract. *See also: incomplete contract. Also known as: principal-agent problem.*

EXERCISE 12.8 HIDDEN ATTRIBUTES

Identify the hidden attributes in the following markets and how they may impede market participants from exploiting all of the possible mutual gains from exchange:

1. A second-hand good being sold on eBay (http://tinyco.re/2913411), Craigslist (http://tinyco.re/2392254) or a similar online platform
2. Renting apartments through Airbnb (http://tinyco.re/2409089)
3. Restaurants of varying quality

Explain how the following may facilitate mutually beneficial exchanges, even in the presence of hidden attributes:

4. Electronic ratings shared among past and prospective buyers and sellers
5. Exchanges among friends, and friends of friends
6. Trust and social preferences
7. Intermediate buyers and sellers, such as used car dealers

QUESTION 12.6 CHOOSE THE CORRECT ANSWER(S)

There are 10 cars on the market, of which six are good quality cars worth $9,000 to buyers, and the others are lemons, worth zero. There are many potential buyers who do not know the quality of each car, but they know the proportion of good quality cars, and are willing to pay the average value. All sellers are happy to accept a price at least half the value of their car. Based on this information, which of the following statements is correct?

☐ The buyers are willing to pay at most $4,500.
☐ Only the lemons will be sold in this market.
☐ All cars will be sold at a price of $5,400.
☐ All cars will be sold at a price of $4,500.

QUESTION 12.7 CHOOSE THE CORRECT ANSWER(S)

In which of the following cases is there an adverse selection problem?

☐ A motor insurance market, in which the insurers do not know how carefully the insured people drive.

☐ A health insurance market, in which the insurers do not know whether or not the applicants for insurance are habitual smokers.

☐ Online sales of nutritional supplements, when consumers cannot tell whether their contents are as claimed by sellers.

☐ A firm that employs home-workers, but cannot observe how hard they are working.

12.7 INCOMPLETE CONTRACTS AND EXTERNAL EFFECTS IN CREDIT MARKETS

We discussed borrowing and lending in Unit 10. Borrowing and lending is a **principal-agent problem** in which the prudent use of the borrowed funds; hard work to ensure the success of the project for which the funds were borrowed; and the repayment of the loan, cannot be secured by means of an enforceable contract.

As a result, the decisions of the borrower—hard work, prudence—have **external effects** on the lender. What the borrower does affects the profits of the lender but is 'external' to the contract. They are not covered in the contract because critical information that would be necessary to write them into a contact—how prudently the borrower ran the project, or how hard she worked for its success—is not available to the lender, and even if it were, in most cases it would not be sufficient to enforce the necessary contracts.

Notice how similar this is to the problems of an employee making effort or an insured person taking care. They are all **moral hazard** problems.

Decision	How it affects others	Cost or benefit	Market failure (misallocation of resources)	Possible remedies	Terms applied to this type of market failure
An employee on a fixed wage decides how hard to work	Hard work raises employer's profits	Private cost, external benefit	Too little effort, wage above reservation wage, unemployment	More effective monitoring, performance-related pay, reduced conflict of interest between employer and employee	Incomplete labour contract, hidden action, moral hazard
Someone who knows he has a serious health problem buys insurance	Loss for insurance company	Private benefit, external cost	Too little insurance offered, insurance premiums too high	Mandatory purchase of health insurance, public provision, mandatory health information sharing	Missing markets, adverse selection
Someone who has purchased car insurance decides how carefully to drive	Prudent driving contributes to insurance company's profits	Private cost, external benefit	Too little insurance offered, insurance premiums too high	Installing driver monitoring devices	Missing markets, moral hazard

Figure 12.10 Asymmetric-information market failures, with remedies.

The fundamental problem in the case of credit is that because the borrower may not repay the loan in the event of a failed project, she will take risks that she would have avoided if she had to bear the full cost of a bad outcome. This means that the project is more likely to fail, imposing costs on the lender.

As we saw in Unit 10, this will make the lender reluctant to make loans unless the borrower can be given an incentive not to take undue risk, either by investing some of her own funds in the project for which she is seeking funding (**equity**) or by providing **collateral** to the lender. This means that a person with little wealth may not be able to get a loan, even for a project that would have used the resources in a highly productive way, for example a new business, the cost of a license to practice a trade, or training.

To put it another way, lenders are willing to trade-off project quality to get a borrower who has more equity or more collateral. Sometimes a high-quality project from a poor would-be borrower is not funded by the lender, while a rich individual with a middling project gets a loan, as illustrated in Figure 12.11.

Thus poor borrowers may be **credit-constrained** or **credit-excluded**. This is another form of market failure, which arises particularly when wealth is very unequally distributed. Remember from Unit 10 how the Grameen Bank addressed this problem by making groups of borrowers jointly responsible for loan repayment, giving them an incentive to work hard and take prudent decisions without the need for equity or collateral.

Credit market failures also occur for another reason. When a bank makes a loan, it takes account of the possibility that it may not be repaid: if the interest rate it can charge is sufficiently high, even quite risky loans (like payday loans) may be a good bet. But the bank also worries about what might happen to its profits should most of its borrowers be unable to pay, as would happen if it had extended mortgages for home purchases during a boom in housing prices, and then the housing bubble burst. The bank could fail.

If the owners of the bank would bear all of the costs of a bankruptcy, then they would make strenuous efforts to avoid it. But the owners are unlikely to bear the full costs, for two reasons:

- *The bank will typically have borrowed from other banks:* Just like the farmer borrowing to plant his crop, the bank owners will know that some of the costs of bankruptcy will be borne by other banks that will not be repaid.
- *'Too big to fail':* If the bank is sufficiently important in the economy, then the prospect of its failure is likely to provoke a bailout of the bank by the government, subsidizing it with tax revenue.

So again, the bank owners know that others (taxpayers or other banks) will bear some of the costs of their risk-taking. They then take more risks than

equity An individual's own investment in a project. This is recorded in an individual's or firm's balance sheet as net worth. *See also: net worth. An entirely different use of the term is synonymous with fairness.*

collateral An asset that a borrower pledges to a lender as a security for a loan. If the borrower is not able to make the loan payments as promised, the lender becomes the owner of the asset.

credit-constrained A description of individuals who are able to borrow only on unfavourable terms. *See also: credit-excluded.*
credit-excluded A description of individuals who are unable to borrow on any terms. *See also: credit-constrained.*

too big to fail Said to be a characteristic of large banks, whose central importance in the economy ensures they will be saved by the government if they are in financial difficulty. The bank thus does not bear all the costs of its activities and is therefore likely to take bigger risks. *See also: moral hazard.*

	Rich	Poor
High quality project	Loan granted	No loan
Intermediate quality project	Loan granted	No loan
Low quality project	No loan	No loan

Figure 12.11 Project quality and wealth of borrower.

they would if they were to bear all of the costs of their actions. Like environmental spillovers, excess risk-taking by banks and borrowers is a **negative external effect** leading to a **market failure**.

Those who may get stuck with the risk-taker's losses try to protect themselves. Governments seek to regulate the banking system, limiting bank leverage so that banks would theoretically have sufficient resources to repay their debts.

We can add the credit market examples to our table of market failures in Figure 12.12.

QUESTION 12.8 CHOOSE THE CORRECT ANSWER(S)
Which of the following statements is correct?

☐ The problem with the credit market is that rich people will always get a loan irrespective of the quality of their project.
☐ It is easier for rich people to get loans because they are able to provide equity or collateral.
☐ Banks are described as 'too big to fail' when their large size makes them safe institutions.
☐ Banks that are 'too big to fail' are careful not to make risky loans.

12.8 THE LIMITS OF MARKETS

Markets might seem to be everywhere in the economy, but this is not the case. Recall Herbert Simon's image from Unit 6 of a Martian viewing the economy. The Martian mainly sees green fields, which are firms. They are connected by red lines representing buying and selling in markets, but many resource allocation decisions are made within the firms. Families, similarly, do not allocate resources among parents and children by buying and selling. Governments use the political process rather than market competition to determine where, and by whom, schools will be built and roads maintained.

Why are some goods and services allocated in markets, while firms, families, and governments allocate others? This is an old question, and there are two basic answers.

First, some kinds of activities are better carried out by families, some by governments, some by firms, and some by markets. It is hard to see, for

Decision	How it affects others	Cost or benefit	Market failure (misallocation of resources)	Possible remedies	Terms applied to this type of market failure
Borrower devotes insufficient prudence or effort to the project in which the loan is invested	Project more likely to fail, resulting in non-repayment of loan	Private benefit, external cost	Excessive risk, too few loans issued	Redistribute wealth, common responsibility for repayment of loans (Grameen Bank)	Moral hazard, credit market exclusion
Bank that is 'too big to fail' makes risky loans	Taxpayers bear costs if bank fails	Private benefit, external cost	Excessively risky lending	Regulation of banking practices	Moral hazard

Figure 12.12 Credit market failures, with remedies.

example, how conceiving and raising children could be effectively carried out by firms or markets. A combination of families and governments (schooling) does the job in most societies.

What determines the balance between firms and markets?

Ronald Coase provided an explanation of the relative importance of firms and markets. Firms exist because for some things, 'in-house' production is more profitable than acquiring the same thing by purchase. The extent of the market is determined by the firm's decision about which components of a product to produce and which ones to buy. Coase explained that the boundaries of this divide between the firm and the market are set by the relative costs of the 'make it' and 'buy it' options.

Coase's explanation underlines an important fact that is often lost in sometimes heated debates about the merits of decentralized systems of organization-like markets, as opposed to more centralized ones like governments. What he showed is that there are some things that centralized systems (like the firm) are better at, and others that are better handled by the market. And the beauty of this demonstration is that it is not a judgement by some possibly biased observer: it is the verdict of the market itself. Competition among firms ultimately punishes firms that overdo the 'make it' option by overextending the boundaries of the centralized system through internal expansion. And market competition equally punishes the firms that fail to take advantage of centralized decision making by overly opting for the 'buy it' option.

The second answer to the question why some goods are allocated in markets and some in other institutions is quite different from Coase's explanation of the boundaries of the firm. People disagree about the appropriate extent of the market, some thinking that some things that are now for sale should be allocated by other means, while others think that markets should take a larger role in the economy.

Those who wish to limit the extent of the market often make two arguments:

- *Repugnant markets*: Marketing some goods and services—vital organs, or human beings—violates an ethical norm, or undermines the dignity of those involved.
- **Merit goods**: It is widely held that some goods and services (called merit goods) should be available to people independently of their ability or willingness to pay.

Repugnant markets

In most countries, there are well-established institutions that allow parents to voluntarily give up a baby for adoption. But laws typically prevent parents from selling their infants. Commercial surrogacy—a couple providing a newborn infant to another couple for pay—is not legal in most countries (though it is in some states in the US, India, and Russia).

Why do most countries ban the buying and selling of babies? Is it not true that a market for infants would provide parents wishing to sell and would be parents wishing to buy with opportunities for mutual gains from exchange?

Virtually all countries ban the sale of human organs for transplant. But economic reasoning might hold that it is wrong to prevent these transactions if both parties enter into them voluntarily.

merit goods Goods and services that should be available to everyone, independently of their ability to pay.

One reason we might object is that the sale may not be truly voluntary, because poverty might force people to enter into a transaction they might later regret. A second reason would be a belief that putting a price on a baby, or a body part, violates a principle of human dignity. It corrupts our attitudes towards others.

Alvin Roth, an economist who won a Nobel Prize for his work, calls these *repugnant markets*.

The philosophers Michael Walzer and Michael Sandel have discussed the moral limits of markets. Some market transactions conflict with the way we value humanity, such as buying and selling people as slaves; others with principles of democracy, such as allowing people to sell their votes. We have seen some of the advantages of allocating resources using markets and the price system. In that analysis we implicitly assumed that exchanging the good for money did not affect its intrinsic value to the buyer and seller.

But parents' attitudes to babies and voters' appreciation of their democratic rights might both be altered if they were bought and sold. When we consider whether it would be beneficial to introduce a new market, or monetary incentives, we should think about whether this might crowd out other social norms or ethical preferences.

Merit goods

There are some goods and services that are considered special in that they should be made available to all people, even those who lack the ability or willingness to pay for them. These are called **merit goods**, and they are provided by governments rather than allocated by a market governed by the willingness to pay.

In most countries, primary education is provided free to all children and financed by taxation. Basic health care—at least emergency care—is also often available to all, irrespective of the ability to pay. The same holds in many countries for legal representation at trial: a person unable to pay for a lawyer should be assigned legal representation without charge. Personal security—protection from criminal assault or home fires, for example—is typically ensured in part by publically provided police protection and fire-fighting services.

Why should merit goods be provided to people free of charge? People of limited income do not have access to a great many things. They typically live in sub-standard and often unhealthy housing, and have very limited opportunities for recreational travel. Why are basic health care and schooling, legal representation, and police and fire protection different? The answer is that in many countries, these goods and services are considered the right of every citizen.

Alvin E. Roth. 2007. 'Repugnance as a Constraint on Markets' (http://tinyco.re/2118641). *Journal of Economic Perspectives* 21 (3): pp. 37–58.

Michael Sandel. 2009. *Justice.* London: Penguin.

Michael Walzer. 1983. *Spheres of Justice: A Defense of Pluralism and Equality.* New York, NY: Basic Books.

Michael Sandel investigating the moral limits of his audience in his TED Talk 'Why we shouldn't trust markets with our civic life'.
http://tinyco.re/2385666

EXERCISE 12.9 CAPITALISM AMONG CONSENTING ADULTS

Should all voluntary contractual exchanges be allowed among consenting adults?

What do you think about the following (hypothetical) exchanges? You may assume in each case that the people involved are sane, rational adults who have thought about the alternatives and consequences of what they are doing. In each case, decide whether you approve, and whether you think the transaction should be prohibited.

1. A complicated medical procedure has been discovered that cures a rare form of cancer in patients who would otherwise certainly die. Staff shortages make it impossible to treat all those who would benefit, and the hospital has established a policy of first come, first served. Ben, a wealthy patient who is at the bottom of the list, offers to pay Aisha, a poor person on the top of the list, $1 million to exchange places. If Aisha dies (which is very likely), then her children will inherit the money. Aisha agrees.
2. Melissa is 18. She has been admitted to a good university but does not have any financial aid, and cannot get any. She signs a four-year contract to be a stripper on the Internet and will begin work when she is 19. The company will pay her tuition fees.
3. Space Marketing Inc. announces plans to launch giant billboards made from Mylar sheets into low orbit. Companies would pay more than $1 million dollars to display advertisements. Logos, about the size of the moon, will be visible to millions of people on Earth.
4. You are waiting in line to buy tickets for a movie that is almost sold out. Someone from the back of the line approaches the person in front of you and offers her $25 to let him in front of her.
5. A politically apathetic person, who never votes, agrees to vote in an election for the candidate who pays him the highest amount.
6. William and Elizabeth are a wealthy couple who give birth to a baby with a minor birth defect. They sell this baby to their (equally wealthy) neighbours and buy a child without any birth defects from a family who need the money.
7. A care home for elderly people advertises for nurses, saying, 'Jamaicans preferred'. The director justifies it by saying: 'In our experience, Jamaican nurses are the most efficient'.
8. A well-informed and sane adult, with an adequate income, decides that he would like to sell himself to become the slave of another person. He finds a buyer willing to pay his asking price. The aspiring slave will give the price paid by the buyer to his children to further their education.

12.9 MARKET FAILURE AND GOVERNMENT POLICY

Figure 12.13 brings together the examples we have seen in which markets fail to allocate resources efficiently. At first sight they seem different from each other, but in each one, we can identify an external benefit or cost that a decision-maker does not take into account. The table in Figure 12.14 shows that the fundamental source of market failure is an information problem: some important aspect of an interaction that cannot be observed by one of the parties, or cannot be verified by a court.

The table in Figure 12.13 also shows some possible remedies. Governments play an important role in the economy in their attempts to diminish the inefficiencies associated with many kinds of market failure. However, the same information problems can hamper a government seeking to use taxes, subsidies, or prohibitions to improve on the market outcome. For example, the French government eventually decided to ban the use of chlordecone rather than collect the information necessary to devise a tax on banana production or provide compensation to the fisheries.

Sometimes a combination of remedies is the best way to cope with these information problems and resulting market failures. An example is car insurance. In many countries, third-party insurance (covering damage to others) is compulsory to avoid the adverse selection problem that would occur if only the accident-prone drivers purchased insurance. To address the moral hazard problem of hidden actions, insurers sometimes require the installation of on-board monitoring devices so that prudent driving habits can be an enforceable part of the insurance contract.

Looking ahead: A broader role for governments

Most of the models so far in this course are *microeconomic* models: that is, models of the interactions between individual employers and employees, borrowers and lenders, firms and their customers, and firms competing with other firms. We have seen in this unit that problems of Pareto inefficiency may arise in these interactions, and governments have a role in addressing them. Governments also address problems of inequality and poverty by redistributing income from richer to poorer households. But public policies are aimed at many other objectives, including:

- *Moderating fluctuations in employment and inflation:* In Unit 10 you learned that except for the very wealthy, people cannot borrow enough to sufficiently smooth their consumption over time in response to changes in their employment status and other shocks. Governments can help by adopting policies that moderate the fluctuations in people's real incomes and employment (Units 13–15).
- *Wages, profits, and productivity in the long run:* In Units 2, 6, and 9 you studied how wages, profits, and the productivity of labour are determined. Governments have a role here, too, in adopting policies that will affect the bargaining power of employers and their workers, and in boosting the productivity of labour.

Decision	How it affects others	Cost or benefit	Market failure (misallocation of resources)	Possible remedies	Terms applied to this type of market failure
A firm uses a pesticide that runs off into waterways	Downstream damage	Private benefit, external cost	Overuse of pesticide and overproduction of the crop for which it is used	Taxes, quotas, bans, bargaining, common ownership of all affected assets	Negative external effect, environmental spillover
You take an international flight	Increase in global carbon emissions	Private benefit, external cost	Overuse of air travel	Taxes, quotas	Public bad, negative external effect
You travel to work by car	Congestion for other road users	Private cost, external cost	Overuse of cars	Tolls, quotas, subsidized public transport	Common-pool resource, negative external effect
A firm invests in R&D	Other firms can exploit the innovation	Private cost, external benefit	Too little R&D	Publicly funded research, subsidies for R&D, patents	Public good, positive external effect
An employee on a fixed wage decides how hard to work	Hard work raises employer's profits	Private cost, external benefit	Too little effort; wage above reservation wage; unemployment	More effective monitoring, performance-related pay, reduced conflict of interest between employer and employee	Incomplete labour contract, hidden action, moral hazard
Someone who knows he has a serious health problem buys insurance	Loss for insurance company	Private benefit, external cost	Too little insurance offered; insurance premiums too high	Mandatory purchase of health insurance, public provision, mandatory health information sharing	Missing markets, adverse selection
Someone who has purchased car insurance decides how carefully to drive	Prudent driving contributes to insurance company's profits	Private cost, external benefit	Too little insurance offered; insurance premiums too high	Installing driver monitoring devices	Missing markets, moral hazard
Borrower devotes insufficient prudence or effort to the project in which the loan is invested	Project more likely to fail, resulting in non-repayment of loan	Private benefit, external cost	Excessive risk; too few loans issued to poor borrowers	Redistribute wealth; common responsibility for repayment of loans (Grameen Bank)	Moral hazard, credit market exclusion
Bank that is 'too big to fail' makes risky loans	Taxpayers bear costs if bank fails	Private benefit, external cost	Excessively risky lending	Regulation of banking practices	Moral hazard
A monopoly, a firm producing a differentiated good, or a firm with declining AC sets P > MC (Unit 7)	Price is too high for some potential buyers	Private benefit, external cost	Too low a quantity sold	Competition policy, public ownership of natural monopolies	Imperfect competition, decreasing average costs, natural monopoly

Figure 12.13 Market failures with remedies.

Question	Answer
Why do market failures happen?	People, guided only by market prices, do not take account of the full effect of their actions on others
Why is the full effect of their actions on others not taken into account?	There are external benefits and costs that are not compensated by payments
Why are some benefits or costs not compensated?	No markets exist in which they can be traded
Why not? And why can't private bargaining and payments solve the problem?	The required property rights and contracts cannot be enforced by courts of law
What prevents property rights and contracts from being enforceable?	Asymmetric or non-verifiable information

Figure 12.14 Market failures and information problems.

Understanding these aspects of public policy as well as policies concerning the global economy, the environment, inequality, and innovation, requires that we now develop a model of the economy as a whole, sometimes called *macroeconomics*. Our understanding of the labour market from Units 6 and 9, the credit market from Unit 10 and this unit and the process of innovation from Unit 2 provide the basis for our understanding of how the economy considered as a whole works. This will be the subject of the next unit.

EXERCISE 12.10 MARKET FAILURE
Construct a table like the one in Figure 12.13 (page 539) to analyse the possible market failures associated with the decisions below. In each case, can you identify which markets or contracts are missing or incomplete?

1. You inoculate your child with a costly vaccination against an infectious disease.
2. You use money that you borrow from the bank to invest in a highly risky project.
3. A fishing fleet moves from the overfished coastal waters of its own country to international waters.
4. A city airport increases its number of passenger flights by allowing nighttime departures.
5. You contribute to a Wikipedia page.
6. A government invests in research in nuclear fusion.

12.10 CONCLUSION

Pareto-inefficient market outcomes (market failure) can result from limited competition, average costs declining with output, or external effects. Externalities occur when some aspect of an exchange is not covered by an enforceable property right or contract, as a result of asymmetric or non-verifiable information. Examples include employment, credit, and insurance contracts (which may be affected by problems of moral hazard and adverse selection), and public goods and bads (such as knowledge and pollution).

Both Coasean bargaining and Pigouvian taxes and subsidies can improve on market outcomes in these cases, but both are limited by the same problems of asymmetric and non-verifiable information that is the reason for the market failure.

Repugnance and other moral objections to exchanging some goods for money, and the crowding-out effects of monetary incentives, provide reasons why some goods and services are not allocated using markets.

> *Concepts introduced in Unit 12*
> Before you move on, review these definitions:
>
> - Market failure
> - External effect (externality)
> - Marginal social cost
> - Pigouvian tax (or subsidy)
> - Coasean bargaining
> - Asymmetric information
> - Moral hazard
> - Adverse selection
> - Public good
> - Repugnant markets
> - Merit good

12.11 REFERENCES

Acemoglu, Daron, and James A. Robinson. 2012. *Why Nations Fail: The Origins of Power, Prosperity and Poverty*, 1st ed. New York, NY: Crown Publishers.

Acemoglu, Daron, Simon Johnson, and James A. Robinson. 2005. 'Institutions as a Fundamental Cause of Long-Run Growth' (http://tinyco.re/2662186). In *Handbook of Economic Growth, Volume 1A.*, eds. Philippe Aghion and Steven N. Durlauf. North Holland.

Akerlof, George A., and Robert J. Shiller. 2015. *Phishing for Phools: The Economics of Manipulation and Deception*. Princeton, NJ: Princeton University Press.

Fafchamps, Marcel, and Bart Minten. 1999. 'Relationships and Traders in Madagascar'. *Journal of Development Studies* 35 (6) (August): pp. 1–35.

Keynes, John Maynard. 1936. *The General Theory of Employment, Interest and Money* (http://tinyco.re/6855346). London: Palgrave Macmillan.

North, Douglass C. 1990. *Institutions, Institutional Change and Economic Performance*. Cambridge: Cambridge University Press.

Pigou, Arthur. 1912. *Wealth and Welfare* (http://tinyco.re/2519065). London: Macmillan & Co.

Pigou, Arthur. (1920) 1932. *The Economics of Welfare* (http://tinyco.re/2042156). London: Macmillan & Co.

Roth, Alvin E. 2007. 'Chapter 1: Repugnance as a Constraint on Markets' (http://tinyco.re/2118641). *Journal of Economic Perspectives* 21 (3): pp. 37–58.

Sandel, Michael. 2009. *Justice*. London: Penguin.

Seabright, Paul. 2010. 'Chapter 1: Who's in Charge?'. In *The Company of Strangers: A Natural History of Economic Life* (http://tinyco.re/2891054). Princeton, NJ, United States: Princeton University Press.

Walzer, Michael. 1983. *Spheres of Justice: A Defense of Pluralism and Equality*. New York, NY: Basic Books.

ECONOMIC FLUCTUATIONS AND UNEMPLOYMENT

HOW ECONOMIES FLUCTUATE BETWEEN BOOMS AND RECESSIONS AS THEY ARE CONTINUOUSLY HIT BY GOOD AND BAD SHOCKS

- Fluctuations in the total output of a nation (GDP) affect unemployment, and unemployment is a serious hardship for people.
- Economists measure the size of the economy using the national accounts: these measure economic fluctuations and growth.
- Households respond to shocks by saving, borrowing, and sharing to smooth their consumption of goods and services.
- Due to limits on people's ability to borrow (credit constraints) and their weakness of will, these strategies are not sufficient to eliminate shocks to their consumption.
- Investment spending by firms (on capital goods) and households (on new housing) fluctuates more than consumption.

Losing your job hurts. It causes stress. Following the global financial crisis in 2008, unemployment went up, as did the number of searches for antistress medication on Google. By plotting the increase in search intensity against the increase in the unemployment rate in the different states of the US (Figure 13.1), we see that states that had a larger increase in the unemployment rate between 2007 and 2010, also had a larger increase in searches for antistress medication. This suggests that higher unemployment is related to higher stress. We say the two are correlated.

The upward-sloping line summarizes the data by finding the line that best fits the scatter of points. This is called a line of best fit or a **linear regression line**. When a line of best fit is upward sloping, it means that higher values of the variable on the horizontal axis (in this case the rise in unemployment) are associated with higher values of the variable on the vertical axis (in this case, the increase in Google searches for antistress medication).

THEMES AND CAPSTONE UNITS
- 17: History, instability, and growth
- 18: Global economy
- 21: Innovation
- 22: Politics and policy

Andrew E. Clark and Andrew J. Oswald. 2002. 'A Simple Statistical Method for Measuring How Life Events Affect Happiness' (http://tinyco.re/7872100). *International Journal of Epidemiology* 31 (6): pp. 1139–1144.

reverse causality A two-way causal relationship in which A affects B and B also affects A.
linear regression line The best-fitting line through a set of data.

The Spurious Correlations website shows how dangerous it is to draw a conclusion from correlation. James Fletcher. 2014. 'Spurious Correlations: Margarine Linked to Divorce?' (http://tinyco.re/6825314). *BBC News*.

Yann Algan, Elizabeth Beasley, Florian Guyot, and Fabrice Murtin. 2014. 'Big Data Measures of Human Well-Being: Evidence from a Google Stress Index on US States'. *Sciences Po Working Paper*.

Many kinds of evidence show that being unemployed or fearing unemployment is a major source of unhappiness for people. It ranks alongside major disease and divorce as a stressful life event.

Economists have estimated that becoming unemployed produces more unhappiness than is measured solely by the loss of earnings from being out of work. Economists Andrew Clark and Andrew Oswald have measured the effect of important life events on how happy people claim to be when they are asked. In 2002, they calculated that the average British person would need to be compensated by £15,000 ($22,500) per month after losing their job in order to be as happy as they were when they were employed. This is considerably larger than the loss of earnings (which at the time were £2,000 per month on average).

The compensation needed to restore wellbeing is an enormous amount, much greater than the monetary loss associated with a spell of unemployment. The reason is that unemployment dramatically reduces self-esteem and leads to a much greater reduction in happiness. As we saw in Unit 1, wellbeing depends on more than just income.

Correlation may not be causation

Can we draw the conclusion from the data in Figure 13.1 that higher unemployment *causes* higher stress? Maybe we have it the wrong way round, and actually Google searches cause unemployment. Economists call this **reverse causality**. We can rule this out because it is unlikely that individual Google searches on the side effects of antidepressants could cause an increase in unemployment at the state level. Yet there are other possible explanations for this pattern.

A natural disaster like Hurricane Katrina (http://tinyco.re/7393966) in the US state of Louisiana in 2005 could have triggered an increase in both stress and unemployment. This is an example where a third factor—in this case, the weather—might account for the positive **correlation** between searches for antidepressants and unemployment. It warns us to be careful in concluding that an observed correlation implies a causal relationship between variables.

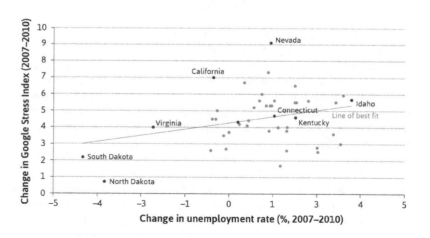

Figure 13.1 Changes in unemployment and wellbeing during the financial crisis: Evidence from the US states (2007–2010).

To establish a causal relationship between variables, economists devise experiments (http://tinyco.re/8046664) (like those in Unit 4) or exploit natural experiments (like the comparison of East and West Germany in Unit 1 or the estimate of the size of employment rents in Unit 6).

In Exercise 13.1, we show you a tool that you can use to examine your ideas about how the overall wellbeing in a country can be compared with wellbeing in other countries. What is your recipe for a better life in your country? How important do you think unemployment is? Do other things matter more or just as much—for example, good education, clean air, a high level of trust among citizens, high income, or not too much inequality?

In this unit, we learn about why economies go through upswings, during which unemployment falls, and downswings, during which it rises. We focus on the total spending (by households, firms, the government and people outside the home economy) on the goods and services produced by people employed in the home economy.

correlation A statistical association in which knowing the value of one variable provides information on the likely value of the other, for example high values of one variable being commonly observed along with high values of the other variable. It can be positive or negative (it is negative when high values of one variable are observed with low values of the other). It does not mean that there is a causal relationship between the variables. *See also: causality, correlation coefficient.*

EXERCISE 13.1 THE OECD BETTER LIFE INDEX

The Better Life Index (http://tinyco.re/2887644), was created by the Organization for Economic Cooperation and Development (OECD). It lets you design a measure of the quality of life in a country by deciding how much weight to put on each component of the index.

1. Should a better life index include the following elements: income, housing, jobs, community, education, environment, civic engagement, health, life satisfaction, safety, and work-life balance? For each of these elements, explain why or why not.
2. Use the Better Life Index tool to create your own better life index for the country where you are living. How does this country score on the topics that are important to you?
3. Rank the countries in the database using your own newly created better life index, and compare it with a ranking based exclusively on income.
4. For both of these indices, choose two countries with contrasting rankings and briefly suggest why this may be the case.

The OECD is an international organization based in Paris, with 35 member countries, most with high levels of GDP per capita. It was formed in 1948 to facilitate postwar reconstruction in Western Europe. The OECD is an important source of internationally comparable statistics on economic and social performance.

13.1 GROWTH AND FLUCTUATIONS

Economies in which the capitalist revolution has taken place have grown over the long run, as illustrated in the hockey stick charts for GDP per capita in Unit 1.

But growth has not been smooth. Figure 13.2 shows the case of the British economy, for which data over a long period is available. The first chart shows GDP per person (per capita) of the population from 1875. This is part of the hockey stick graph from Unit 1. The chart next to it shows the same data but plots the **natural logarithm** ('log') of GDP per capita. This is a way of presenting the ratio scale that we used in Unit 1.

logarithmic scale A way of measuring a quantity based on the logarithm function, $f(x) = \log(x)$. The logarithm function converts a ratio to a difference: $\log(a/b) = \log a - \log b$. This is very useful for working with growth rates. For instance, if national income doubles from 50 to 100 in a poor country and from 1,000 to 2,000 in a rich country, the absolute difference in the first case is 50 and in the second 1,000, but $\log(100) - \log(50) = 0.693$, and $\log(2,000) - \log(1,000) = 0.693$. The ratio in each case is 2 and $\log(2) = 0.693$.

See the Einstein at the end of this section to explore the relationship between plotting the log of a variable and the use of a ratio scale on the vertical axis.

By looking at the graph in levels of GDP per capita in the left-hand panel of Figure 13.2, it is hard to tell whether the economy was growing at a steady pace, accelerating, or decelerating over time. Transforming the data into natural logs in the right-hand panel allows us to answer the question about the pace of growth more easily. For example, for the period after the First World War, a straight line from 1921 to 2014 fits the data well. For a graph in which the vertical axis represents the log of GDP per capita, the slope of the line (the dashed black line) represents the average annual growth rate of the series. Immediately we notice that growth was steady from 1921 to 2014 (with a little uptick during the Second World War). You can see that a line drawn through the log series from 1875 to 1914 is flatter than the line from 1921, indicating that the growth rate was lower.

We will explore long-run growth further in Units 16 and 17. In this unit we focus on fluctuations. These are the deviations from the dotted black line showing the long-run growth rate in Figure 13.2.

The top panel of Figure 13.3 plots the annual growth rate of UK **GDP** between 1875 and 2014. Since we want to focus on the size of the economy and how it changes from year to year, we will examine total GDP rather than GDP per capita.

gross domestic product (GDP) A measure of the market value of the output of the economy in a given period.

Ryland Thomas and Nicholas Dimsdale. (2017). 'A Millennium of UK Data' (http://tinyco.re/5827360). Bank of England OBRA dataset.

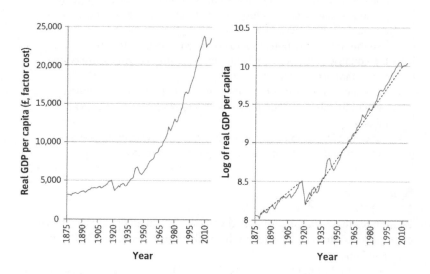

Figure 13.2 UK GDP per capita (1875–2014).

1. Annual growth rate after 1921
In the right-hand panel, the slope of the line (the dashed black line) represents the average annual growth rate from 1921 to 2014. It was 2.0% per annum. We can see that growth was steady.

2. Annual growth rate 1875 to 1914
A line drawn through the log series from 1875 to 1914 is flatter than the line from 1921. The average growth rate in that period was only 0.9% per annum.

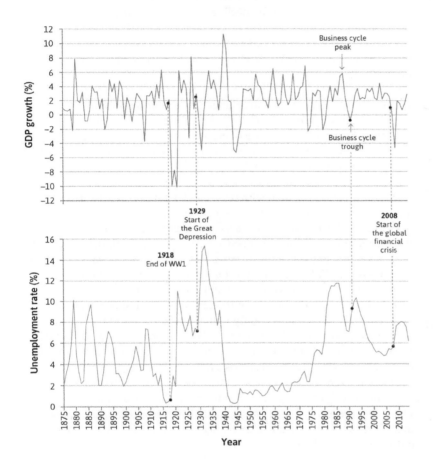

Ryland Thomas and Nicholas Dimsdale. (2017). 'A Millennium of UK Data' (http://tinyco.re/5827360). Bank of England OBRA dataset.

Figure 13.3 UK GDP growth and unemployment rate (1875–2014).

1. UK GDP growth and unemployment
The panels show UK GDP growth and the unemployment rate for the period 1875–2014.

2. Peaks and troughs
The arrows highlight the peak and trough of a business cycle during the late 1980s and early 1990s.

3. The global financial crisis
In the twenty-first century, the 2008 financial crisis followed a period in which fluctuations were limited.

4. Downturns and unemployment
We can see that downturns in the business cycle are associated with rising unemployment. In the business cycle of the early 1990s, unemployment continued to rise for a time after the growth rate began to rise.

recession The US National Bureau of Economic Research defines it as a period when output is declining. It is over once the economy begins to grow again. An alternative definition is a period when the level of output is below its normal level, even if the economy is growing. It is not over until output has grown enough to get back to normal. The latter definition has the problem that the 'normal' level is subjective.

It is clear from the ups and downs of the series in Figure 13.3 that economic growth is not a smooth process. We often hear about economies going through a boom or a **recession** as growth swings from positive to negative, but there is no standard definition of these words. The National Bureau of Economic Research (NBER) (http://tinyco.re/3195217), a US organization, defines it like this: 'During a recession, a significant decline in economic activity spreads across the economy and can last from a few months to more than a year.' An alternative definition says that an economy is in recession during a period when the level of output is below its normal level. So we have two definitions of recession:

- *NBER definition*: output is declining. A recession is over once the economy begins to grow again.
- *Alternative definition*: the level of output is below its normal level, even if the economy is growing. A recession is not over until output has grown enough to get back to normal.

There is a practical problem with the second definition: it is a matter of judgement, and sometimes controversy, over what an economy's *normal* output would be (we return to this issue in later units, where we will see that 'normal output' is often defined as that consistent with stable inflation).

business cycle Alternating periods of faster and slower (or even negative) growth rates. The economy goes from boom to recession and back to boom. *See also: short-run equilibrium*.

The movement from boom, to recession, and back to boom is known as the **business cycle**. In Figure 13.3 you will notice that in addition to the yearly change in GDP, in which recessions measured by negative growth seem to happen about twice every 10 years, there are less frequent episodes of much larger fluctuations in output. In the twentieth century, the big downward spikes coincided with the end of the First and Second World Wars, and with the economic crisis of the Great Depression. In the twenty-first century, the global financial crisis followed a period in which fluctuations were limited.

In the lower part of Figure 13.3 you can see that the unemployment rate varies over the business cycle. During the Great Depression, unemployment in the UK was higher than it had ever been, and it was particularly low during the World Wars.

> **EXERCISE 13.2 DEFINING RECESSIONS**
> A recession can be defined as a period when output is declining, or as a period when the level of output is below normal (sometimes referred to as its 'potential level'). Look at this article (http://tinyco.re/2305833), especially Figures 5, 6, and 7, to find out more.
>
> 1. Consider a country that has been producing a lot of oil and suppose that from one year to the next its oil wells run out. The country will be poorer than previously. According to the two definitions above, is it in a recession?
> 2. Does knowing whether a country is in recession make a difference to policymakers whose job it is to manage the economy?

QUESTION 13.1 CHOOSE THE CORRECT ANSWER(S)

The following is the graph of the natural log of UK real GDP per capita between 1875 and 2014:

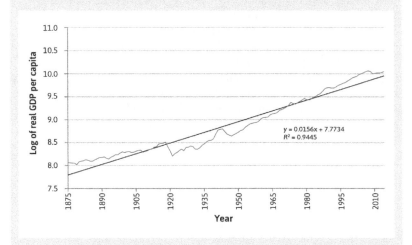

Based on this information, which of the following statements is correct?

☐ The graph shows that real GDP per capita in the UK in 1955 was about £8,000.

☐ The slope of the best-fit straight line is the average annual growth rate.

☐ The graph shows that the average growth rate was lower in the decades after 1921 than in the decades before 1918.

☐ The graph of real GDP per capita plotted using a ratio scale would look very different to the graph above.

EINSTEIN

Ratio scales and logarithms

In Unit 1, we made frequent use of a ratio or log scale on the vertical axis to display long-run data. For example, we used ratio scales with the units doubling in Figure 1.1b and rising tenfold in Figure 1.2. The ratio scale is also called a logarithmic (or log) scale. We can write a scale where the tick marks on the vertical axis double like this:

$$2^0, 2^1, 2^2, \ldots$$

Or a scale where they rise tenfold, like this:

$$10^0, 10^1, 10^2, \ldots$$

The first is called a logarithmic scale in base 2; the second is in base 10.

As we saw in the charts in Unit 1, if the data forms a straight line on a ratio (logarithmic) scale, then the growth rate is constant. A different method of using this property of logarithms is to first convert the data into natural logs and then plot it on a scale that is linear in logs.

Natural logs use base e, where e is a number (approximately 2.718) that has mathematically useful properties.

We can use a calculator or a spreadsheet program to convert levels into natural logs. As you can see, when applied to this data, it converts the curved line in Figure 13.2 in the left-hand panel into one that is almost a straight line in the right-hand one.

Using the chart functions in Microsoft Excel helps illustrate the relationship between plotting the data with a ratio scale on the vertical axis (Figure 13.4a, which uses the doubling or base 2 scale) and transforming the data into natural logs and plotting on a linear scale (in logs) on the axis (Figure 13.4b). Note that the tick marks double from 4,096 to 8,192 to 16,384 in Figure 13.4a and rise from 8.5 to 9 to 9.5 in Figure 13.4b.

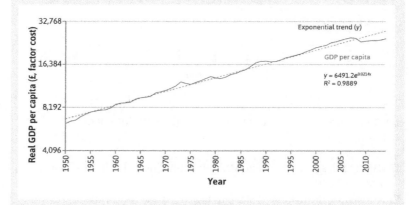

Figure 13.4a The ratio scale and an exponential function.

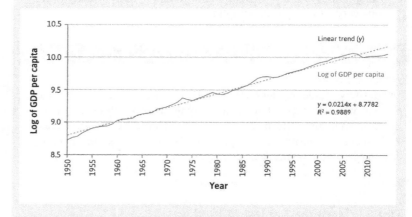

Figure 13.4b The linear scale in natural logs and a linear function.

In each chart, a line appears alongside the data series. Using Excel, we created Figure 13.4a by selecting Analysis/Trendline, and then selecting 'Exponential'. Excel finds the line or curve that best fits the data points: since the scale is a ratio scale, a straight line is displayed. The equation of the line is given. Other spreadsheet or graphing software offers similar features.

We can see that the exponential function uses what is called base e in contrast to base 2 (doubling) or base 10 (increasing tenfold). The exponent on e tells us the compound annual growth rate of the series: it is 0.0214 × 100 = 2.14% per annum.

In Figure 13.4b, if we use Excel to select the 'Fit a linear function' option, a straight line appears. This time, we see an equation for a straight line with intercept 8.7782 and slope 0.0214. Now the slope of the line tells us the exponential, or equivalently, the compound annual growth rate of the series: 0.0214 × 00 = 2.14% per annum.

In summary:

- When a data series is plotted, either using a ratio scale or by transforming the data into natural logs, and the outcome is approximately linear, it means that the growth rate of the series is approximately constant. This constant growth rate is called an exponential growth rate.
- The exponential growth rate (known also as the compound annual growth rate or CAGR) is the slope of the line when the natural logarithm of the data series is plotted.
- Notice the persistent deviation of the British economy from the trend line following the 2008 financial crisis.

13.2 OUTPUT GROWTH AND CHANGES IN UNEMPLOYMENT

We saw in Figure 13.3 that unemployment goes down in booms and up in recessions.

Figure 13.5 shows the relationship between output and unemployment fluctuations, known as **Okun's law**. Arthur Okun, an advisor to US President Kennedy, noticed that when a country's output growth was high, unemployment tended to decrease. Okun's law has been a strong and stable empirical relationship in most economies since the Second World War.

Figure 13.5 plots the change in the unemployment rate (vertical axis) and the growth rate of output (horizontal axis) for six countries: higher output growth is clearly associated with a decrease in unemployment. In each country chart, there is a downward-sloping line that best fits the points. In the US, for example, the slope of the line implies that, on average, a 1% increase in the output growth rate decreases the unemployment rate by roughly 0.38 percentage points. We say that **Okun's coefficient** is −0.38 in the US. Our Einstein at the end of this section shows how to derive the coefficient.

The dot labeled 2009 in each graph in Figure 13.5 shows the changes in real GDP and unemployment that occurred from 2008 to 2009, during the recession that followed the global financial crisis. We can see that in 2009, all four of the advanced economies experienced their worst output contraction in 50 years. As predicted by Okun's law, unemployment rose in Spain, Japan, and the US.

In each of these three countries, however, the increase in unemployment was higher than Okun's law predicted: the red dot is well above the black line of best fit. Germany looks very different: Okun's law predicted a rise in

Okun's law The empirical regularity that changes in the rate of growth of GDP are negatively correlated with the rate of unemployment. *See also: Okun's coefficient.*

Okun's coefficient The change in the unemployment rate in percentage points predicted to be associated with a 1% change in the growth rate of GDP. *See also: Okun's law.*

unemployment of 1.65 percentage points in Germany but, as the red dot shows, German unemployment hardly changed in 2009. An economic policymaker would surely want to know how Germany managed to protect jobs in the face of the largest decline in the economy's output in 50 years. We will see why this occurred later in this unit.

Brazil and Malaysia also experienced contractions in output and increases in unemployment in 2009. However, like most developing economies, they were hit less hard by the crisis than the advanced economies. Also, Malaysia had recently experienced a much worse contraction during the East Asian crisis in 1998, when growth was –7.4%—bad enough that it would not fit on our chart.

We can summarize the relationship between output, unemployment, and wellbeing like this:

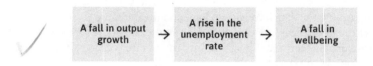

OECD. 2015. *OECD Statistics* (http://tinyco.re/9377362); The World Bank. 2015. *World Development Indicators* (http://tinyco.re/9263826).

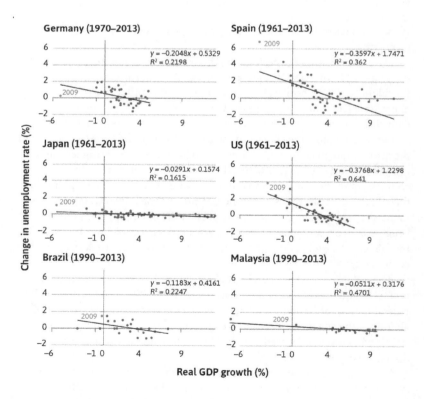

Figure 13.5 Okun's law for selected economies.

EXERCISE 13.3 OKUN'S LAW

1. Look at the regression lines (the lines of best fit) in Figure 13.5 (page 552). What prediction does the regression line show for unemployment when the economy is not growing? Are the results the same for all the countries?
2. Assume that the population in the economy is growing. Can you use this assumption to provide an explanation for your results in question 1? What else might explain the differences between countries?

QUESTION 13.2 CHOOSE THE CORRECT ANSWER(S)

The following graph shows the relationship between real GDP growth and change in unemployment for the US between 1961 and 2013.

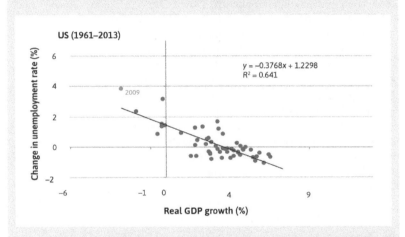

The equation shown is the regression result for the best-fitting line. Based on this information, which of the following statements is correct?

☐ The unemployment rate remains stable when there is zero real GDP growth.

☐ Okun's coefficient for the US is 1.2298.

☐ From the regression result, policy makers can be sure that a 1% increase in real GDP next year will definitely lead to a fall in the unemployment rate of 0.38%.

☐ With real GDP falling by 2.8% in 2009, the predicted rise in the unemployment rate would have been 2.3%.

EINSTEIN

Okun's law

This is defined as:

$$\Delta u_t = \alpha + \beta(\text{GDP growth}_t)$$

Δu_t is the change in unemployment rate at time t, (GDP growth$_t$) is the real GDP growth at time t, α is the intercept value, and β is a coefficient determining how real GDP growth is predicted to be translated into a change in unemployment rate. Okun's Law is an empirical linear relationship that associates real GDP growth with changes in unemployment. The coefficient β, called Okun's coefficient, is generally found to be negative, suggesting that a positive real GDP growth will be associated with a fall in the unemployment rate.

The estimated Okun's law relationship for Germany, for the period 1970–2013, has coefficients $\beta = -0.20$ and $\alpha = 0.53$.

When we estimate a line of best fit, we also measure the R-squared (R^2), which is a statistic that lies between 0 and 1. It measures how closely the observed data fits the line that we draw through them, with 1 being a perfect fit, and 0 representing no observable relationship between the observations and the prediction. In our case, the R^2 statistic measures how well Okun's law approximates the data for real GDP growth and unemployment changes. The R^2 statistic is 0.22 for Germany for the period 1970–2013, which is much lower than for the estimated Okun's law equation for the US, which is 0.64.

To work out the predicted percentage change in unemployment for Germany in 2009 using the Okun's law equation, we simply plug in the value of real GDP growth for Germany in 2009 and solve the equation as follows:

$$\Delta u_{2009} = 0.53 + (-0.20) \times (-5.1) = 1.58$$

Okun's law predicts that the fall in GDP of 5.1% in 2009 in Germany should have been associated with an increase in unemployment by 1.58 percentage points.

13.3 MEASURING THE AGGREGATE ECONOMY

Economists use what are called aggregate statistics to describe the economy as a whole (known as the aggregate economy, meaning simply the sum of its parts brought together).

In Figure 13.5, **aggregate output** (GDP) is the output of all producers in a country, not just those of some region, firm, or sector. Recall from Unit 1 that Diane Coyle, an economist who specializes in how we measure GDP, describes it as:

aggregate output The total output in an economy, across all sectors and regions.

> Everything from nails to toothbrushes, tractors, shoes, haircuts, management consultancy, street cleaning, yoga teaching, plates, bandages, books, and the millions of other services and products in the economy.

The **national accounts** are statistics published by national statistical offices that use information about individual behaviour to construct a quantitative picture of the economy as a whole. There are three different ways to estimate GDP:

- *Spending:* The total spent by households, firms, the government, and residents of other countries on the home economy's products.
- *Production:* The total produced by the industries that operate in the home economy. Production is measured by the **value added** by each industry: this means that the cost of goods and services used as inputs to production is subtracted from the value of output. These inputs will be measured in the value added of other industries, which prevents double-counting when measuring production in the economy as a whole.
- *Income:* The sum of all the incomes received, comprising wages, profits, the incomes of the self-employed, and taxes received by the government.

The relationship between spending, production, and incomes in the economy as a whole can be represented as a circular flow: the national accounts measurement of GDP can be taken at the spending stage, the production stage, or the income stage. If accurate measurement were possible, the total of expenditure, output, and incomes in a year would be the same so the point at which the measurement is taken would not matter.

This is because any spending on a good or a service, which must have been produced, is income for whomever sold that output. If you buy a taco from a street vendor for 20 pesos, then your expenditure is 20 pesos, the value added of the taco whose production was necessary for this sale is 20 pesos, and the income received by the street vendor is also 20 pesos. The same point applies if you purchase a car for $20,000, a massage for $50, or insurance for $20 per month.

Households and firms both receive income and spend it. Figure 13.6 shows the circular flow between households and firms (ignoring the role of government and purchases from and sales abroad for now).

In the model of the economy in Figure 1.12, we looked at the physical flows among households, firms, and the biosphere instead of the circular flow of income. In Unit 20, we look at how the interaction of households and firms with the biosphere can be measured.

> **national accounts** The system used for measuring overall output and expenditure in a country.
> **value added** For a production process this is the value of output minus the value of all inputs (called intermediate goods). The capital goods and labour used in production are not intermediate goods. The value added is equal to profits before taxes plus wages.

In eighteenth century France, a group of economists, called the Physiocrats, studied the economy and compared the way it functioned to the circular flow of blood in the human body. This was a forerunner to how we think today about the circular flow in the economy that allows us to calculate GDP. Money flows from the spender to the producer, from the producer to its employees or shareholders, and then is spent again on further output, continuing the cycle.

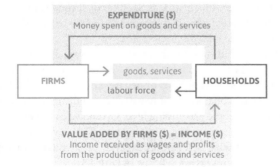

Figure 13.6 The circular flow model: Three ways to measure GDP.

imports (M) Goods and services produced in other countries and purchased by domestic households, firms, and the government.
exports (X) Goods and services produced in a particular country and sold to households, firms and governments in other countries.

GDP can be defined according to any of these three perspectives. But we have to be careful in the definition because, while it is always the case that one person's expenditure is another person's income, globalization means that often the two people are in different countries. This is the case with **imports** and **exports**: someone in China may buy rice from someone in Japan, implying that the expenditure is Chinese while the income is Japanese.

How do we account for these transactions? Since GDP is defined as *domestic* product, it counts as Japanese GDP because the rice was produced (and sold) by Japan. So exports are included in GDP because they are part of domestic production, but imports are not because they are produced elsewhere. For this reason, GDP is defined to include exports and exclude imports:

- as the value added of domestic production, or as expenditure on domestic production
- as income due to domestic production

The circular flow model in Figure 13.6 considered only households and firms, but the government, and the public services the government provides, can be incorporated in a similar way. Households receive some goods and services that are supplied by the government, for which they do not pay at the point of consumption. A good example is primary school education.

The consumption and production of these services can be visualized using the circular flow model:

- *Households to government:* Households pay taxes.
- *Government to households:* These taxes pay for the production of public services used by households.

In this way the government can be seen as another producer, like a firm—with the difference that the taxes paid by a particular household pay for public services in general, and do not necessarily correspond to the services received by that household. In Unit 19, we will look at how the payment of taxes and the receipt of public services or benefits varies across households. Since public services are not sold in the market, we also have to make a further assumption: that the value added of government production is equal to the amount it costs the government to produce.

So we can say that if, for example, citizens on average pay $15,000 per year in taxes (the expenditure), that is $15,000 of revenues to the government (the income), which uses it to produce $15,000 worth of public goods and services (the value added).

The fact that expenditure, output, and incomes are all equal means that we can use any one of these perspectives to help us understand the others. We described recessions as periods of negative output growth. But this means they must also be periods of negative expenditure growth (output will only decline if people are buying less). Often, we can even say that output declines because people are buying less. This is very useful because we know a lot about what determines expenditure, which in turn helps us to understand recessions, as we will see in Unit 14.

13.4 MEASURING THE AGGREGATE ECONOMY: THE COMPONENTS OF GDP

Figure 13.7 shows the different components of GDP from the expenditure side, as measured in the national accounts for economies on three different continents: the US, the Eurozone, and China.

Consumption (C)

Consumption includes the goods and services purchased by households. Goods are normally tangible things. Goods like cars, household appliances, and furniture that last for three years or more are called durable goods; those that last for shorter periods are non-durable goods. Services are things that households buy that are normally intangible, such as transportation, housing (payment of rent), gym membership, and medical treatment. Household spending on durable goods like cars and household equipment is counted in consumption in the national accounts, although as we will see, in economic terms the decision to buy these long-lasting items is more like an investment decision.

From the table in Figure 13.7 we see that in the advanced countries, consumption is by far the largest component of GDP, close to 56% in the Eurozone and 68% in the US. This contrasts with China, where final consumption of households accounts for 37% of GDP.

Investment (I)

This is the spending by firms on new equipment and new commercial buildings; and spending on residential structures (the construction of new housing).

Investment in the unsold output that firms produce is the other part of investment that is recorded as a separate item in the national accounts. It is called the change in **inventories** or stocks. Including changes in stocks is essential to ensuring that when we measure GDP by the output method (what is produced), it is equal to GDP measured by the expenditure method (what is spent, including investment by firms in unsold inventories).

Investment represents a much lower share of GDP in OECD countries, roughly one-fifth of GDP in the US and the Eurozone. In contrast, investment accounts for almost half of GDP in China.

consumption (C) Expenditure on consumer goods including both short-lived goods and services and long-lived goods, which are called consumer durables.

investment (I) Expenditure on newly produced capital goods (machinery and equipment) and buildings, including new housing.

inventory Goods held by a firm prior to sale or use, including raw materials, and partially-finished or finished goods intended for sale.

$$GDP(Y) = C + I + G + NX$$
$$I^v + I^p$$
$$AE = C + I^p + G + NV$$
$$I^v \rightarrow inventory$$

	US	Eurozone (19 countries)	China
Consumption (C)	68.4%	55.9%	37.3%
Government spending (G)	15.1%	21.1%	14.1%
Investment (I)	19.1%	19.5%	47.3%
Change in inventories	0.4%	0.0%	2.0%
Exports (X)	13.6%	43.9%	26.2%
Imports (M)	16.6%	40.5%	23.8%

OECD. 2015. *OECD Statistics* (http://tinyco.re/9377362); The World Bank. 2015. *World Development Indicators* (http://tinyco.re/9263826). OECD reports a statistical discrepancy for China equal to -3.1% of GDP.

Figure 13.7 Decomposition of GDP in 2013 for the US, the Eurozone, and China.

Government spending on goods and services (G)

This represents the consumption and investment purchases by the government (consisting of central and local government, often called 'general government'). Government consumption purchases are of goods (such as office equipment, software, and cars) and services (such as wages of civil servants, armed services, police, teachers, and scientists). Government investment spending is on the building of roads, schools, and defence equipment. Much of **government spending** on goods and services is for health and education.

Government transfers in the form of benefits and pensions, such as Medicare in the US, or social security benefits in Europe, are not included in *G* because households receive them as income: when they are spent, they are recorded in *C* or *I*. It would be double-counting to record this spending in *G* too.

The share of government spending on goods and services is slightly higher in Europe (21.1%) than in the US (15.1%). Remember, this excludes transfers (such as benefits and pensions). The greater difference in the role of the government between Europe and the US comes from those transfers. In 2012, total government spending including transfers was 57% of GDP in France, compared to 40% of GDP in the US.

Exports (X)

Domestically produced goods and services that are purchased by households, firms, and governments in other countries.

Imports (M)

Goods and services purchased by households, firms, and governments in the home economy that are produced in other countries.

Net exports (X − M)

Also called the **trade balance**, this is the difference between the values of exports and imports (*X* − *M*).

In 2010, the US had a trade deficit of 3.4% of GDP and China had a trade surplus of 3.6% of GDP. The trade balance is a **deficit** if the value of exports minus the value of imports is negative; it is called a **trade surplus** if it is positive.

$GDP(Y) = AD$

GDP (Y)

To calculate GDP, which is the **aggregate demand** for what is produced in the country, we add the purchases by those in other countries (exports) and subtract the purchases by home residents of goods and services produced abroad (imports). Taking China as an example, its GDP is the aggregate demand for China's output, which includes its exports less its imports.

Working with national accounts data is a way of learning about the economy, and an easy way to do this is to use the Federal Reserve Economic Data (FRED) (http://tinyco.re/3965569). To learn more about the country where you live and how it compares to other countries, try Exercise 13.4 for yourself.

In most countries, private consumption spending makes up the largest share of GDP (see Figure 13.7 to check). Investment spending accounts for a much smaller share (China's very high level of investment, shown in Figure 13.7, is exceptional). We use the data in the national accounts to

---

government spending (G) Expenditure by the government to purchase goods and services. When used as a component of aggregate demand, this does not include spending on transfers such as pensions and unemployment benefits. *See also: government transfers*

government transfers Spending by the government in the form of payments to households or individuals. Unemployment benefits and pensions are examples. Transfers are not included in government spending (G) in the national accounts. *See also: government spending (G)*

trade balance Value of exports minus the value of imports. *Also known as: net exports. See also: trade deficit, trade surplus.*

trade deficit A country's negative trade balance (it imports more than it exports). *See also: trade surplus, trade balance.*

trade surplus A country's positive trade balance (it exports more than it imports). *See also: trade deficit, trade balance.*

aggregate demand The total of the components of spending in the economy, added to get GDP: $Y = C + I + G + X - M$. It is the total amount of demand for (or expenditure on) goods and services produced in the economy. *See also: consumption, investment, government spending, exports, imports.*

calculate how much each component of expenditure contributes towards GDP fluctuations.

The equation below shows how GDP growth can be broken down into the contributions made by each component of expenditure. We can see that the contribution of each component to GDP growth depends on both the share of GDP that the component makes up and its growth over the previous period.

$$
\text{percentage change in GDP} = \begin{array}{l} (\text{percentage change in consumption} \times \\ \text{share of consumption in GDP}) \\ + \\ (\text{percentage change in investment} \times \\ \text{share of investment in GDP}) \\ + \\ (\text{percentage change in government spending} \times \\ \text{share of government spending in GDP}) \\ + \\ (\text{percentage change in net exports} \times \\ \text{share of net exports in GDP}) \end{array}
$$

The table in Figure 13.8 shows the contributions of the components of expenditure to US GDP growth. The data is for 2009, in the middle of the recession caused by the global financial crisis. We can see that:

- Although investment makes up less than one-fifth of US GDP, it was much more important in accounting for the contraction in the economy than the fall in consumption spending.
- Although consumption makes up about 70% of US GDP, the effect of investment on GDP was more than three times larger.
- In contrast to consumption and investment, government expenditure contributed positively to GDP growth. The US government used fiscal stimulus to prop up the economy whilst private sector demand was depressed.
- Net exports also contributed positively to GDP, which reflects both the stronger performance of emerging economies in the aftermath of the crisis and the collapse in import demand that accompanied the recession.

Shortcomings of GDP as a measure
Three things need to be kept in mind when using the concept of GDP:

1. *It is a conventional measure of the size of an economy*: We examined what GDP includes in Unit 1. In Unit 20, the concept of green growth accounting is introduced, which shows how to calculate the size of the economy and its growth taking into account environmental degradation.
2. *Distinguish aggregate GDP from GDP per capita*: This is especially import- ant when discussing growth. In this section, the focus has been on GDP

	GDP	Consumption	Investment	Government spending	Net exports
2009	−2.8	−1.06	−3.52	0.64	1.14

Figure 13.8 Contributions to percentage change in real GDP in the US in 2009.

Federal Reserve Bank of St. Louis. 2015. *FRED* (http://tinyco.re/3965569). Note that in the national accounts, govern- ment investment is counted as government spending and not invest- ment.

and the contributions of the different components of demand to its growth. In other contexts, the relevant concept is a per capita measure. To see the difference, note that GDP in the UK grew by 7% between 2007 and 2015 but GDP per capita grew by only 0.8%. The explanation is that there was a large increase in immigration.

3. *GDP per capita is a flawed measure of living standards*: Recall from Unit 1 that Robert Kennedy's 1968 speech at the University of Kansas (http://tinyco.re/9533853) highlighted these flaws (search for 'Gross National Product' in the text).

EXERCISE 13.4 HOW TO USE FRED

If you want real-time macroeconomic data on the German unemployment rate or China's output growth, you do not need to learn German and Chinese, or struggle to get to grips with national archives, because FRED does it for you! FRED is a comprehensive up-to-date data source maintained by the Federal Reserve Bank of St Louis in the US, which is part of the US central banking system. It contains the main macroeconomic statistics for almost all developed countries going back to the 1960s. FRED also allows you to create your own graphs and export data into a spreadsheet.

To learn how to use FRED to find macroeconomic data, follow these steps:

- Visit the FRED website (http://tinyco.re/8136544).
- Use the search bar and type 'Gross Domestic Product' (GDP) and the name of a major global economy. Select the annual series for both nominal (current prices) and real (constant prices) GDP for this country. Click the 'Add to Graph' button at the bottom of the page.

Use the graph you created to answer these questions:

1. What is the level of nominal GDP in your chosen country this year?
2. FRED tells you that the real GDP is chained in a specific year (this means that it is evaluated in terms of constant prices for that year). Note that the real GDP and the nominal GDP series cross at one point. Why does this happen? " base year "

From the FRED graph, keep only the real GDP series. FRED shows recessions in shaded areas for the US eco-

nomy using the NBER definition, but not for other economies. For other economies, assume that a recession is defined by two consecutive quarters of negative growth. At the bottom of the graph page, select 'Create your own data transformation' and click on 'Percent change from one year' (FRED gives you a hint about how to calculate a growth rate at the bottom of the page: notes on growth rate calculation and recessions). The series now shows the percentage change in real GDP.

3. How many recessions has your chosen economy undergone over the years plotted in the chart?
4. What are the two biggest recessions in terms of length and magnitude?

Now add to the graph the quarterly unemployment rate for your chosen economy (click on 'Add data series' under the graph and search for 'Unemployment' and your chosen country name).

5. How does the unemployment rate react during the two main recessions you have identified?
6. What was the level of the unemployment rate during the first and the last quarter of negative growth for those two recessions?
7. What do you conclude about the link between recession and the variation in unemployment?

Note: To make sure you understand how these FRED graphs are created, you may want to extract the data into a spreadsheet, and create a graph showing the growth rate of real GDP and the evolution of the unemployment rate since 1948 for the US economy.

(Graph 2)

(Graph 1)

QUESTION 13.3 CHOOSE THE CORRECT ANSWER(S)
Which of the following statements is correct regarding measuring GDP?

☐ GDP can be measured either as the total spending on domestically produced goods and services, or the total value added in domestic production, or the sum of all incomes received from domestic production.
☐ Both exports and imports are included in the measurement of GDP.
☐ Government production is not included in the GDP.
☐ The value added of government production is computed using the price that public goods and services are sold at in the market.

QUESTION 13.3 CHOOSE THE CORRECT ANSWER(S)
Which of the following statements is correct regarding measuring GDP?

☐ GDP can be measured either as the total spending on domestically produced goods and services, or the total value added in domestic production, or the sum of all incomes received from domestic production.
☐ Both exports and imports are included in the measurement of GDP.
☐ Government production is not included in the GDP.
☐ The value added of government production is computed using the price that public goods and services are sold at in the market.

QUESTION 13.4 CHOOSE THE CORRECT ANSWER(S)
Which of the following would increase GDP?

☐ A decline in imports, holding all other components of GDP constant.
☐ An increase in remittances paid to domestic residents by relatives living abroad.
☐ An increase in government spending.
☐ A decline in exports.

13.5 HOW HOUSEHOLDS COPE WITH FLUCTUATIONS

Economies fluctuate between good and bad times. So far we have studied industrialized economies, but this is equally true in economies based on agriculture. Figure 13.9a illustrates fluctuations in production in the largely agrarian British economy between 1550 and 1700. Just as we divided GDP into different components from the expenditure side, we can also divide it into different sectors on the production side. Figure 13.9a shows the growth rate of real GDP and of the three main sectors: agriculture, industry, and services. Follow the analysis in Figure 13.9a to see how the agricultural sector drove fluctuations in GDP.

Figure 13.9b shows the growth rates of real GDP and agriculture in India since 1960. In 1960 agriculture comprised 43% of the economy, which had declined to 17% in 2014. Partly due to modern farming methods, agriculture in modern India is not as volatile as it was in Britain before 1700. But it remains nearly twice as volatile as GDP as a whole.

To help us to think about the costs and causes of economic fluctuations, we begin with an agrarian economy. In an economy based on agricultural production, the weather—along with war and disease—is a major cause of good and bad years. The term **shock** is used in economics to refer to an unexpected event, for example, extreme weather or a war. As we know, people think about the future and usually they anticipate that unpredictable events may occur. They also act on these beliefs. In a modern economy, this is the basis of the insurance industry. In an agrarian economy, households also anticipate that both bad luck and good harvests can occur.

How do households cope with fluctuations that can cut their income in half from one season to the next?

shock An exogenous change in some of the fundamental data used in a model.

Stephen Broadberry, Bruce M. S. Campbell, and Alexander Klein. 2015. *British Economic Growth, 1270–1870*. Cambridge: Cambridge University Press.

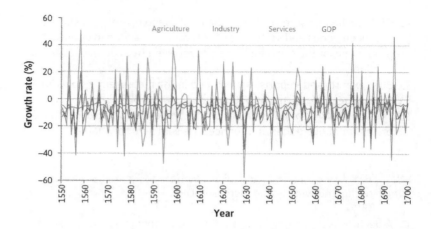

Figure 13.9a The role of agriculture in the fluctuations of the aggregate economy in Britain (1550–1700).

1. GDP growth between 1550 and 1700
The figure shows the growth rate of real GDP and its three main sectors at this time.

2. Agriculture
Clearly the agricultural sector is much more volatile than other sectors.

3. Industry
In this period the average difference in the output of the agricultural sector from one year to the next is three times larger than that of the industrial sector …

4. Services
… and more than 10 times larger than that of the services sector.

5. Agriculture drove fluctuations in GDP
Between 1552 and 1553, the agricultural sector expanded by 41% and GDP rose by 17%. In the next year the agricultural sector contracted by 16% and the economy shrank by 8%.

The World Bank. 2015. *World Development Indicators* (http://tinyco.re/9263826).

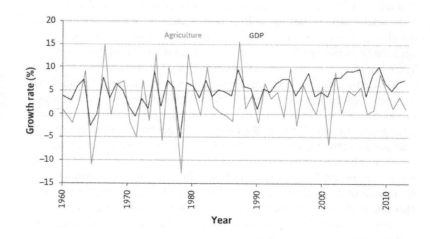

Figure 13.9b The role of agriculture in the fluctuations of the aggregate economy in India (1961–2014).

We can distinguish between two situations:

- *Good or bad fortune strikes the household:* For example, when disease affects a family's animals, or when a family member who plays an important role in farming is injured.
- *Good or bad fortune strikes the economy as a whole:* For example, when drought, disease, floods, a war, or an earthquake affects a whole area.

Household shocks

People use two strategies to deal with shocks that are specific to their household:

- **Self-insurance**: Households that encounter an unusually high income in some period will save, so that when their luck reverses, they can spend their savings. As we saw in Unit 10, they may also borrow in bad times if they can, depending on how credit-constrained they are. It is called self-insurance because other households are not involved.
- **Co-insurance**: Households that have been fortunate during a particular period can help a household hit by bad luck. Sometimes this is done among members of extended families or among friends and neighbours. Since the mid-twentieth century, particularly in richer countries, co-insurance has taken the form of citizens paying taxes, which are then used to support individuals who are temporarily out of work, called unemployment benefits.

Informal co-insurance among family and friends is based on both reciprocity and trust: you are willing to help those who have helped you in the past, and you trust the people who you helped to do the same in return. **Altruism** towards those in need is also usually involved, although co-insurance can work without it.

These strategies reflect two important aspects of household preferences:

- *People prefer a smooth pattern of consumption:* As we saw in Unit 10, they dislike consumption that fluctuates as a result of bad or good shocks such as injury or good harvests. So they will self-insure.
- *Households are not solely selfish:* They are willing to provide support to each other to help smooth the effect of good and bad luck. They often trust others to do the same, even when they do not have a way of enforcing this. Altruistic and reciprocal preferences remain important even when co-insurance takes the form of a tax-supported unemployment benefit, because these are among the motives for supporting the public policies in question.

Economy-wide shocks

Co-insurance is less effective if the bad shock hits everyone at the same time. When there is a drought, flood, or earthquake, it is more difficult for an agrarian economy to protect the wellbeing of the people who are affected. For example, it is not usually possible to store produce from a bumper harvest long enough to get through the next bad harvest, which may take several years to arrive.

But when these shocks hit, co-insurance may be even more necessary, as community survival requires that less badly hit households help the worst-hit households. In farming economies of the past that were based in volatile

self-insurance Saving by a household in order to be able to maintain its consumption when there is a temporary fall in income or need for greater expenditure.
co-insurance A means of pooling savings across households in order for a household to be able to maintain consumption when it experiences a temporary fall in income or the need for greater expenditure.

'New Cradles to Graves' (http://tinyco.re/8856321). *The Economist*. Updated 8 September 2012.

altruism The willingness to bear a cost in order to benefit somebody else.

Michael Naef and Jürgen Schupp report comparisons between surveys and experiments using trust. Michael Naef and Jürgen Schupp. 2009. 'Measuring Trust: Experiments and Surveys in Contrast and Combination' (http://tinyco.re/3956674). IZA Discussion Paper No. 4087.

climates, people practised co-insurance based on trust, reciprocity, and altruism. These are norms, like the fairness norm we discussed in Unit 4, and they probably emerged and persisted because they helped people to survive in these regions that were often hit by bad weather shocks. Recent research suggests that they seem to have persisted even after climate had become largely unimportant for economic activity.

The evidence for this is that people in the regions with high year-to-year variability in rainfall and temperature during the past 500 years now display high levels of trust, and have more modern day co-insurance institutions such as unemployment benefit payments and government assistance for the disabled and poor.

Ruben Durante. 2010. 'Risk, Cooperation and the Economic Origins of Social Trust: An Empirical Investigation' (http://tinyco.re/7674543). Sciences Po Working Paper.

EXERCISE 13.5 HEALTH INSURANCE

1. Think about the health insurance system in your country. Is this an example of co-insurance or self-insurance?
2. Can you think of other examples of both co-insurance and self-insurance? In each case, consider what kinds of shocks are being insured against and how the scheme is financed.

QUESTION 13.5 CHOOSE THE CORRECT ANSWER(S)

Figure 13.9a (page 562) plots the growth rate of real GDP, as well as the growth rates of the agricultural, industrial, and service sectors between 1550 and 1700 in Britain.

Which of the following statements can be deduced from the graph?

☐ The average growth rate of the agricultural sector was higher than that of the service sector for the period shown.
☐ The growth rate of the industrial sector was more volatile than that of the service sector.
☐ The agricultural sector largely drove fluctuations in GDP.
☐ The recession around 1560 was caused by contractions in all three sectors.

13.6 WHY IS CONSUMPTION SMOOTH?

A basic source of stabilization in any economy comes from the desire of households to keep the level of their consumption of goods and services constant. Keeping a steady level of consumption means households have to plan. They think about what might happen to their income in the future, and they save and borrow to smooth the bumps in income. This is the self-insurance we discussed above.

We have seen that this behaviour occurs in agrarian societies faced by weather and war shocks, but modern households also try to smooth their consumption. One way to visualize this behaviour is to focus on predictable events. A young person thinking about life can imagine getting a job, then enjoying a period of working life with income higher than the starting salary, followed by years in retirement when income is lower than during working life.

As we saw in Unit 10, people prefer to smooth their consumption because there are diminishing marginal returns to consumption at any given time. So having a lot of consumption later and little now, for example, is worse than having some intermediate amount of consumption in the two periods (Figure 10.3a).

The person contemplating a future promotion and planning their spending would be in a position similar to Julia in Unit 10 (Figure 10.2), who had limited funds in the present but knew she would have more later, and consequently was interested in moving some of her future buying power to the present by borrowing. The model of decision making for the individual that we introduced in Unit 3 and Unit 10 is the basis for thinking about consumption throughout a person's life. It predicts that, although income fluctuates throughout our lives, our desired consumption is smoother.

We can use Figure 13.10 to visualize an individual's tendency to smooth consumption expenditure. In this simple example, before starting work, the individual's income and consumption expenditure are the same—we assume, for example, that parents support their children until the children start work. Follow the analysis in Figure 13.10 to see their income and con-sumption over time.

A notable feature of Figure 13.10 is that consumption changes before income does.

Like a family in an agrarian economy that begins saving for a daughter's dowry before she is old enough to marry, the individual shown in Figure 13.10 anticipates receiving higher income after a promotion, and adjusts consumption upward ahead of time. As we have seen in Unit 10, this assumes that the individual can borrow. Maybe it is possible to convince

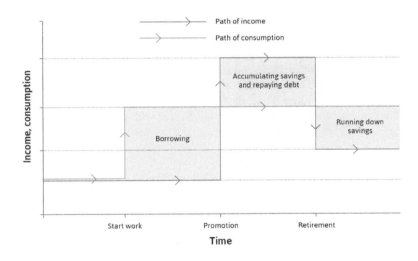

Figure 13.10 Consumption smoothing through our lifetime.

1. Income over time
The blue line shows the path of income over time: it starts low, rises when the individual is promoted and falls at retirement.

2. Consumption expenditure
This is the red line. It is smooth (flat) from the point at which the individual first gets a job.

3. The individual borrows while young
At this time income is low. The individual saves and repays the debt when older and earning more, and finally runs down savings after retirement, when income falls again.

the bank that the job is secure and prospects are good. If so, the individual can probably get a mortgage now, and live in a more comfortable house with a higher standard of living than would be the case if long-term earnings were to remain at the starting salary. The labels on Figure 13.10 show that the individual borrows while young and income is low, saves and repays the debt when older and earning more, and finally runs down savings after retirement, when income falls again.

The model of decision making highlights the desire of households for a smooth path of consumption. We next ask what happens when something unexpected occurs to disturb the lifetime consumption plan. What if the individual shown in the figure encounters an unexpected income shock? The consumption-smoothing model suggests that:

- *The individual will make a judgement*: This will be about whether the shock is temporary or permanent.
- *If the shock is permanent*: We should adjust the red line in Figure 13.10 up or down to reflect the new long-run level of consumption that the individual adopts, consistent with the new pattern of forecast income.
- *If the shock is temporary*: Little will change. A temporary fluctuation in income has almost no effect on the lifetime consumption plan, because it makes only a small change to lifetime income.

To summarize, when individuals and households behave in the way shown in Figure 13.10, shocks to the economy will be dampened because spending decisions are based on long-term considerations. They aim to avoid fluctuations in consumption even when income fluctuates.

What limits a household's consumption smoothing? Many individuals and households are not able to make or implement long-term consumption plans. Making plans can be difficult because of a lack of information. Even if we have information, we may not be able to use it to predict the future with confidence. For example, it is often very hard to judge whether a change in circumstances is temporary or permanent.

There are three other things that constrain the ways in which households can smooth their consumption when faced with income shocks. The first two concern limits on self-insurance, the third is a limit on co-insurance:

- *Credit constraints or credit market exclusion:* Introduced in Unit 10, this restricts a family's ability to borrow in order to sustain consumption when income has fallen.
- *Weakness of will:* A characteristic of human behaviour that leads people to be unable to carry out the plans—for example, saving in anticipation of a negative income shock—that they know would make them better off.
- *Limited co-insurance:* So that those with a fall in income cannot expect much support in sustaining their incomes from others more fortunate than them.

Credit constraints

As we saw in Unit 10, the amount a family can borrow is limited, particularly if it is not wealthy. Households with little money cannot borrow at all, or only at extraordinarily high interest rates. Thus the people who most need credit to smooth their consumption are often unable to do

In *Portfolios of the Poor: How the World's Poor Live on $2 a Day*, Daryl Collins, Jonathan Morduch, Stuart Rutherford, and Orlanda Ruthven show how poor households manage finances to avoid literally living hand-to-mouth. 'Smooth Operators' (http://tinyco.re/7009658). *The Economist.* Updated 14 May 2009. Some of the stories can be read online (http://tinyco.re/8070650).

so. The credit constraints and credit market exclusion discussed in Units 10 and 12 help explain why borrowing is often not possible.

Figure 13.11 shows the reaction of two different types of households to an anticipated rise in income. Households that are able to borrow as much as they like are in the top panel. Credit-constrained households that are unable to get a loan or take out a credit card are in the bottom panel. Follow the analysis in Figure 13.11 to see how the two households react to two key events:

1. News is received that income will rise at a predictable time in the future (for example, a promotion or a bequest).
2. The household's income actually rises (the promotion happens, the inheritance comes through).

We can think about these decisions using the two-period model of borrowing and lending from Unit 10, shown in Figure 13.12. First consider a household that receives the same income, y, this period and next period, indicated by the endowment point A in Figure 13.12. The interest rate is r

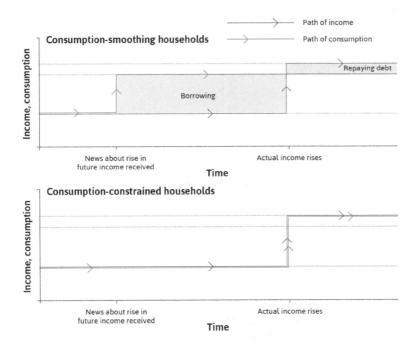

Figure 13.11 Consumption when credit constraints bind: An anticipated rise in income.

1. Income over time
The blue lines on the figure show that the path of income over time is the same in both households.

2. Consumption smoothing
The red line in the top panel shows that, in a consumption-smoothing household, consumption changes immediately once the household receives the news.

3. The effect of credit constraints
On the other hand, a credit-constrained household that cannot borrow has to wait until the income arrives before adjusting its standard of living.

so if the household can borrow and save, then it can choose any point on the budget constraint, which has the slope $-(1 + r)$. The budget constraint is another term for the frontier of the feasible set with the slope of $-(1 + r)$ which we used in Unit 10.

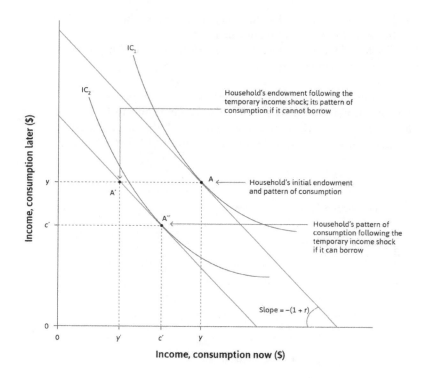

Figure 13.12 Credit-constrained and unconstrained households: An unanticipated temporary fall in income.

1. Same income in both periods
Consider a household that receives the same income, y, this period and next period, indicated by the endowment point A.

2. An unconstrained household
The interest rate is r so if the household can borrow and save, then it can choose any point on the budget constraint, which has the slope $-(1 + r)$.

3. Preference for smoothing
Assume that the household prefers to consume the same amount each period, shown by the point A where the indifference curve is tangent to the budget constraint.

4. A negative shock
Now suppose that the household experiences an unexpected negative temporary shock to its income this year, such as a bad harvest, which lowers this year's income to y', leaving expected income next year unaffected at y.

5. The budget constraint
If it can borrow and save, then its budget constraint has a slope of $-(1 + r)$ and passes through point A'.

6. The highest indifference curve
The highest curve that touches this budget constraint does so at point A'', showing that the household prefers to smooth consumption, consuming c' in both periods. The household borrows c' − y' now and repays $(1 + r)(c' − y')$ next period following the shock.

We learn from this example that:

- Without borrowing or lending, the endowment point and pattern of consumption coincide.
- Compared with the smoothing household, the credit-constrained household consumes less this period and more next period.

We can also see that the indifference curve that passes through A′ (not shown) is lower than the one that passes through A″. So the household that can smooth consumption by borrowing is better off than the credit-constrained household.

A temporary change in income affects the current consumption of credit-constrained households more than it does that of the unconstrained.

Weakness of will

In Figure 13.13, an individual learns that income is going to fall in the future. This could be because of retirement or job loss. It could also be because the individual is becoming pessimistic. Perhaps the newspapers predict an economic crisis. In the top panel of Figure 13.13 we again show a household behaving in a forward-looking manner to smooth consumption. The bottom panel shows a household with **weakness of will** that consumes all its income today even though it implies a large reduction in consumption in the future.

This feature of human behaviour is familiar to many of us. We often lack willpower.

The problem of not being able to save obviously differs from the problem of not being able to borrow: saving is a form of self-insurance and doesn't involve anyone else.

weakness of will The inability to commit to a course of action (dieting or foregoing some other present pleasure, for example) that one will regret later. It differs from impatience, which may also lead a person to favour pleasures in the present, but not necessarily act in a way that one regrets.

HOW ECONOMISTS LEARN FROM FACTS

My diet starts tomorrow

Economists have conducted experiments to test for behaviour that would help to explain why we don't save even when we can. For example, Daniel Read and Barbara van Leeuwen conducted an experiment with 200 employees at firms in Amsterdam. They asked them to choose today what they thought they would eat next week. The choice was between fruit and chocolate.

When asked, 50% of subjects replied that they would eat fruit next week. But, when next week came, only 17% actually chose to eat fruit. The experiment shows that, although people may plan to do something that they know will be beneficial (eat fruit, save money), when the time comes they often don't do it.

Read: Daniel, and Barbara van Leeuwen. 1998. 'Predicting Hunger: The Effects of Appetite and Delay on Choice'. *Organizational Behavior and Human Decision Processes* 76 (2): pp. 189–205.

Limited co-insurance

Most households lack a network of family and friends who can help out in substantial ways over a long period when a negative income shock occurs. As we have seen, unemployment benefits provide this kind of co-insurance—the

OECD. 2010. *Employment Outlook 2010: Moving Beyond the Jobs Crisis* (http://tinyco.re/5607435).

citizens who turn out to be lucky in one year insure those who are unlucky. But in many societies the coverage of these policies is very limited.

A vivid demonstration of the value of smoothing through co-insurance is the experience of Germany during the drastic reduction in income experienced by that economy in 2009 (see Figure 13.5). When the demand for firms' products fell, workers' hours of work were cut, but as a result of both government policy and agreements between firms and their employees, very few Germans lost their jobs, and many of those at work were still paid as if they were working many more hours than they did. The result was that although aggregate income fell, consumption did not—and unemployment did not increase.

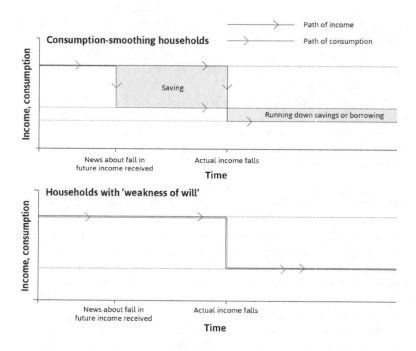

Figure 13.13 Consumption when households are weak-willed: An anticipated fall in income.

1. The path of income
The blue lines in the figure show that income follows the same path in both sets of households.

2. Consumption smoothing
The red line in the top panel shows the consumption path for a consumption-smoothing household. When it receives news of the imminent fall in income, it immediately starts saving to supplement consumption when income falls.

3. A weak-willed household
In contrast, the weak-willed household does not react to the news, and keeps consumption high until income falls.

But most empirical evidence shows that credit constraints, weakness of will, and limited co-insurance mean that, for many households, a change in income results in an equal change in consumption. In the case of a negative income shock such as the loss of a job, this means that the income shock will now be passed on to other families who would have produced and sold the consumption goods that are now not demanded.

We will see in the next unit how the initial shock in income may be multiplied (or amplified) by the fact that families are limited in their ability to smooth their consumption. This in turn helps us understand the business cycle and how policymakers may or may not help to manage it.

Empirical evidence shows that, even when income changes in predictable ways, consumption responds. Tullio Jappelli and Luigi Pistaferri. 2010. 'The Consumption Response to Income Changes' (http://tinyco.re/3409802). *VoxEU.org*.

EXERCISE 13.6 CHANGES IN INCOME, CHANGES IN CONSUMPTION
Take the situation in Figure 13.12 (page 568). Begin at point A′ for the credit-constrained households and at point A for the consumption smoothing (unconstrained) households.

1. For each household type, explain the relationship between the change in income and the change in consumption when income returns to normal after the temporary decline.
2. Based on this analysis, explain the predicted relationship between temporary changes in income and consumption for an economy with a mixture of the two household types.

QUESTION 13.6 CHOOSE THE CORRECT ANSWER(S)
Figure 13.12 (page 568) shows the consumption choice of a consumer over two periods. His initial endowment is (y, y), that is, an income y in both periods, which is depicted by point A. If possible, the consumer prefers to consume the same amount in both periods. The interest rate is r.

Now assume that there has been a temporary shock such that the income in period 1 is reduced to $y′$, while the period 2 income is expected to return to y. Assume that a credit-constrained consumer is not able to borrow at all. Based on this information, which of the following statements is correct?

☐ If the consumer is credit-constrained, then he will consume less in period 2 than he would have done without the temporary shock.
☐ If the consumer is not credit-constrained, then he will be able to borrow to consume the same amount as he would have done in both periods without the temporary shock.
☐ If the consumer is not credit-constrained, then he will borrow $y - c′$ in period 1 in order to smooth out his consumption in the two periods.
☐ If the consumer is not credit-constrained, then he will consume $c′$ in both periods such that $c′ = y - (c′ - y′)(1 + r)$ (income minus repayment in period 2).

QUESTION 13.7 CHOOSE THE CORRECT ANSWER(S)

The following diagram shows the path of income for a household that receives news about an expected rise and fall in future income at the depicted times.

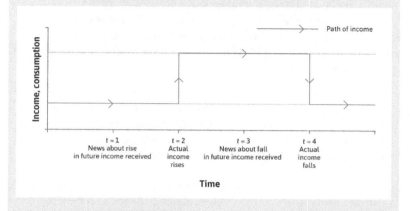

Assume that the household prefers to smooth out its consumption if it can. Based on this information, which of the following statements is correct?

☐ If the household is not credit-constrained, then it will consume the same level after $t = 1$.

☐ If the household is credit-constrained and has 'weakness of will', then its consumption will match precisely its income path.

☐ If the household is not credit-constrained but has 'weakness of will', then it will borrow at $t = 1$ and save at $t = 3$.

☐ If the household is credit-constrained but does not have 'weakness of will', then it will borrow at $t = 1$ and save at $t = 3$.

13.7 WHY IS INVESTMENT VOLATILE?

Households tend to smooth their consumption spending when they can, but there is no similar motivation for a firm to smooth investment spending. Firms increase their stock of machinery and equipment and build new premises whenever they see an <u>opportunity to make profits</u>. But, unlike eating and most other consumption expenditures, investment expenditures can be postponed. There are several reasons why this is likely to produce clusters of investment projects at some times, while few projects at other times.

In Unit 2, we saw how firms responded to profit opportunities in the Industrial Revolution by innovating. This helps explain why investment occurs in waves. When an innovation like the spinning jenny is introduced, firms using the new technology can produce output at lower cost or produce higher-quality output. They expand their share of the market. Firms that fail to follow may be forced out of business because they are unable to make a profit using the old technology. But new technology means that firms must install new machines. As firms do this, there is an investment boom. This will be amplified if the firms producing the machinery and equipment need to expand their own production facilities to meet the extra demand expected.

In this case, investment by one firm pushes other firms to invest: if they don't, they may lose market share or even be unable to cover their costs and eventually have to leave the industry. But investment by one firm can also pull other firms to invest by helping to increase their market and potential profits.

An example of push investment is the hi-tech investment boom in the US. From the mid-1990s, new information and communications technology (ICT) was introduced into the US economy on a large scale. Figure 13.14 shows the sustained growth of investment in new technologies through the second half of the 1990s.

As we saw in Unit 11, investment in new technology can lead to a stock market bubble and over-investment in machinery and equipment. The chart shows in dotted orange the behaviour of the US stock market index on which hi-tech companies are listed. This is the Nasdaq index, introduced in Unit 11.

The index rose strongly from the mid-1990s to an all-time peak in 1999 as stock market investors' confidence in the profitability of new tech firms grew. Investment in IT equipment (the red line) grew rapidly as a result of this confidence, but dropped sharply following the collapse in confidence that caused the fall of the stock market index. This suggests that over-investment in machinery and equipment had occurred: investment did not begin growing again until 2003. Robert Shiller, the economist, argued that the Nasdaq index was driven high by what he called 'irrational exuberance', as you might recall from Unit 11. Beliefs in the future of hi-tech led not only to share prices rising to levels that were unsustainable, but also to excessive investment in machinery and equipment in the hi-tech sector.

Credit constraints are another reason for the clustering of investment projects and the volatility of aggregate investment. In a buoyant economy, profits are high and firms can use these profits to finance investment projects. Access to external finance from sources outside the firm is also easier: in the US hi-tech boom, for example, the expansion of the Nasdaq exchange reflected the appetite of investors to provide finance by buying shares (stocks) in firms in the emerging ICT industries.

To understand how one firm's investment can induce another firm to invest, think of a local economy comprising of just two firms. Firm A's machinery and equipment are not fully used, so the firm can produce more

Robert Shiller has explained in a *VoxEU podcast* (http://tinyco.re/9820978) how animal spirits contribute to the volatility of investment.

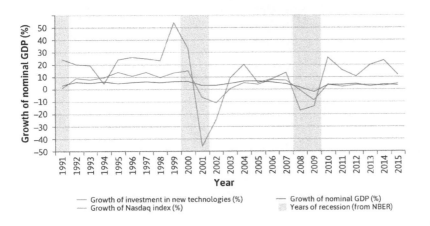

US Bureau of Economic Analysis. 2015. *Fixed Assets Accounts Tables* (http://tinyco.re/7765843). Note: the series are in current US dollars. Nasdaq value is the yearly average of the close price value of the Nasdaq. Investment in new technologies is the investment in information processing equipment, computers and peripheral equipment, communication equipment, communication structure, and IPPR investments for software, semiconductors, and other electronic components and computers.

Figure 13.14 Investment in new technologies and the dotcom bubble (1991–2015).

if it hires more employees. But there is not enough demand to sell the products it would produce. This situation is called low **capacity utilization**. The owners of Firm A have no incentive to hire more workers or to install additional machinery (that is, to invest).

Firm B has the same problem. Because of low capacity utilization, profits are low for both. Thus when we think about both firms together we have a vicious circle:

If the owners of both A and B decide to invest and hire at the same time, they would employ more workers, who would spend more, increasing the demand for the products of both firms. The profits of both would rise, and we have a virtuous circle:

These two circles highlight the role of expectations of future demand, which depend on the behaviour of other actors. A game similar to those studied in Unit 4 can illustrate how to get out of the vicious circle and into the virtuous one. As in every game, we specify:

- *The actors*: The two firms.
- *The actions that they can take*: Invest, or do not invest.
- *The information they have*: They decide simultaneously, so they do not know what the other has done.
- *The payoff*: The profits resulting from each of the four pairs of actions that they could possibly take.

capacity utilization rate A measure of the extent to which a firm, industry, or entire economy is producing as much as the stock of its capital goods and current knowledge would allow.

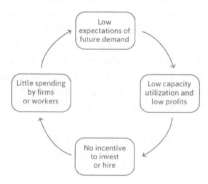

Figure 13.15 Negative expectations of future demand create a vicious circle.

Figure 13.16 Positive expectations of future demand create a virtuous circle.

The four possible outcomes of the interaction and the payoffs are given in Figure 13.17.

From this figure you can see what happens when the virtuous (both invest) and vicious (neither invest) circles occur. Note what happens if one of the firms invests but the other does not. If Firm A invests and B does not (the upper-right cell in the figure) then A pays to install new equipment and premises, but because the other firm did not invest there is no demand for the products that the new capacity could produce; so A makes a loss. But had B known that A would invest, then B would have made higher profits by investing as well (getting 100 rather than only 80). On the other hand, had B known that A was not going to invest, then it would have done better to also not invest.

In this game, the two firms will do better if they do the same thing, and the best outcome is when both firms invest. This is another reason that investment tends to fluctuate a lot. If owners of firms think that other firms will not invest, then they will not invest, confirming the pessimism of the other owners. This is why the vicious circle is self-reinforcing. The virtuous circle is self-reinforcing for the same reason. Optimism about what other firms will do leads to investment, which sustains the optimism.

There are two **Nash equilibria** in this game (upper-left and lower-right). To find the Nash equilibria use the 'dot' and 'circle' method of Unit 4, beginning with A's best responses to B's choices. If B invests, A's best response is also to invest so a dot goes into the upper-left cell. If B does not invest, A chooses also not to invest so we place a dot in the bottom right-hand cell. Notice that A does not have a dominant strategy. Now, we consider B's best responses. If A invests, B's best response is to invest and if A does not invest, B chooses not to invest. The circles showing B's best responses coincide with the dots: B also does not have a dominant strategy. Where the dots and circles coincide, there are Nash equilibria.

The Nash equilibrium (lower-right) in which both firms have low capacity utilization and low hiring and investment is not Pareto efficient, because there is a change in which both make higher profits, namely if both firms decide to invest. This situation is like the driving on the right or left side of the road game, discussed in Unit 4, or the interaction described in Figure 4.15 concerning specialization in different crops, or global climate change described in Figure 4.17b. These are all called **coordination games**.

Nash equilibrium A set of strategies, one for each player in the game, such that each player's strategy is a best response to the strategies chosen by everyone else.

	B's profit	
	B invests	B does not invest
A invests	100 / 100	80 / −40
A does not invest	−40 / 80	10 / 10

Figure 13.17 Investment decisions as a coordination game.

Eurostat. 2015. *Confidence Indicators by Sector*. Federal Reserve Bank of St. Louis. 2015. FRED (http://tinyco.re/3965569).

COORDINATION GAME

A game in which there are two Nash equilibria and in which one may be Pareto superior to the other is called a coordination game.

- Driving on the right or the left is a coordination game in which neither equilibrium is preferable to either player.
- In the crop specialization coordination game in Unit 4 (Figure 4.15), specialization in the 'right' crops (a different crop for the two farmers, which their land is more suited for) is better for both than the 'wrong specialization'.
- In the investment coordination game (Figure 13.17), an outcome in which both invest is better for both than neither investing.

The name is very apt here because to make the move from the vicious to the virtuous circle, the firms have to coordinate in some way (both agree to invest) or develop optimistic beliefs about what the other will do. This kind of optimism is often called business confidence, and it has a major role in the fluctuations in the economy as a whole. As we will see in the next unit, under some circumstances, government policy can also help shift an economy from the Pareto-inefficient outcome to the Pareto-efficient outcome.

We can generalize the argument about the role of coordination in investment to say that investment spending by firms will respond positively to the growth of demand in the economy. Once an increase in aggregate spending on home's production of goods and services (that is, on $C + I + G + X - M$) occurs, this helps to coordinate the forward-looking plans of firms about their future capacity needs, and stimulates investment spending.

Figure 13.18 illustrates the relationship between the growth of aggregate demand (excluding investment), business confidence, and investment for the Eurozone. The business confidence indicator moves closely with aggregate demand (excluding investment) and investment.

Therefore we would expect the data from the national accounts to confirm that consumption spending is smoother and investment spending more volatile than GDP in the economy as a whole.

As expected, Figures 13.19a and 13.19b show that investment is much more volatile than consumption in two rich countries (the UK and the US) and two middle-income countries (Mexico and South Africa). The upward and downward spikes in the red series for investment are larger than those for the green series for consumption.

A close look at the charts for the rich countries also shows that, as predicted, consumption is less volatile than GDP. The purple peaks and troughs for GDP are larger than the green ones for consumption. This is less evident in the middle-income countries, perhaps because households are more credit-constrained and therefore are less able to borrow in order to smooth their consumption.

How volatile is government spending? Unlike investment, government spending (the G in the national accounts) does not respond to innovation or fluctuate with business confidence. We would predict it to be less volatile than investment. And net exports? The demand for exports will fluctuate

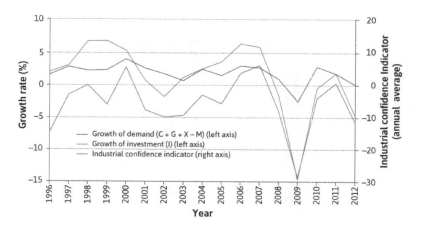

Figure 13.18 Investment and business confidence in the Eurozone (1996–2012).

with the business cycle in other countries, and will be affected more by the booms and recessions of the countries that are large export markets. Find out about the volatility of government spending and net exports by consulting FRED.

EXERCISE 13.7 CONSULTING FRED

For your own country, use data from FRED to construct charts for the growth rate of real GDP, consumption, investment, net exports, and government expenditure.

1. How has government expenditure evolved in your own country throughout the period for which data is available?
2. Comment on the relationship between the growth rate of output and government spending during this period.
3. Describe the volatility of government spending and net exports relative to that of GDP and suggest an explanation for the patterns you observe.

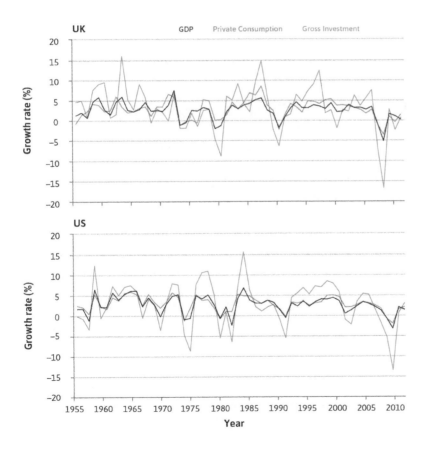

Federal Reserve Bank of St. Louis. 2015. FRED (http://tinyco.re/3965569).

Figure 13.19a Growth rates of consumption, investment, and GDP in the UK and US, per cent per annum (1956–2012).

OECD. 2015. *OECD Statistics* (http://tinyco.re/9377362); The World Bank. 2015. *World Development Indicators* (http://tinyco.re/9263826).

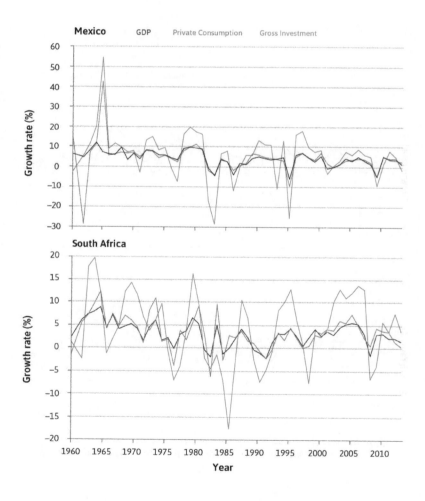

Figure 13.19b Growth rates of consumption, investment, and GDP in Mexico and South Africa (1961–2012).

QUESTION 13.8 CHOOSE THE CORRECT ANSWER(S)

Consider a local economy comprising of just two firms, Firm A and Firm B. Currently both firms have low capacity utilization. The following table shows the profits (or losses if negative) when the firms invest or do not invest:

		Firm B's profit	
		Firm B invests	Firm B does not invest
Firm A's profit	Firm A invests	150 / 100	80 / −20
	Firm A does not invest	−40 / 60	40 / 20

Based on this information, which of the following statements is correct?

- ☐ Investing is a dominant strategy for both firms.
- ☐ The only Nash equilibrium is for both firms to invest.
- ☐ Firm A investing and Firm B not investing is a Pareto-inefficient Nash equilibrium.
- ☐ To achieve the Pareto-efficient Nash equilibrium, the firms have to coordinate in some way or develop business confidence.

13.8 MEASURING THE ECONOMY: INFLATION

In Figures 13.20a and 13.20b we repeat the graphs from Figure 13.3, showing the growth rate of GDP and the unemployment rate in the UK from 1875 to 2014.

In Figure 13.20c, we show the rate of inflation over this period. **Inflation** is an increase in the general price level in the economy, usually measured over a year. For the British economy, inflation ranges from a low level, with prices actually falling (called **deflation**) for much of the inter-war period before and after the Great Depression, to a peak of nearly 25% per annum in 1975.

Previously we saw that the downward spikes of economic crises were associated with upward spikes of unemployment; we now see that inflation was especially low in the 1930s and especially high in the 1970s. The peak in inflation followed the first of two oil price shocks (1973 and 1979) that were major disturbances to the global economy.

Figure 13.21 shows average rates of inflation in different regions of the world, and how they have changed over time. Upward spikes in inflation have tended to occur in periods of economic crisis, but the general trend worldwide since the 1970s has been a decline in inflation rates. The figure also shows that inflation tends to be higher in poor than in rich countries. For instance, since 2000, inflation has averaged 6.0% in sub-Saharan Africa

> **inflation** An increase in the general price level in the economy. Usually measured over a year. *See also: deflation, disinflation.*
> **deflation** A decrease in the general price level. *See also: inflation.*

Aggregate prices
⇒ Average (general) price
level   Δ in rate (%)
Inflation
Disinflation
Deflation

and 6.6% in south Asia, in contrast to only 2.2% in the high-income OECD countries.

What is inflation?

Take your favourite chocolate bar. If its price goes up during the year from 50p to 55p, how do you know that is a symptom of inflation in the economy? It could just be that the chocolate bar has become more expensive relative to everything else, as a result of a rightward shift in the demand curve or a leftward shift in the supply curve of the kind we studied in Unit 8. To see what has happened to prices across the economy, take a giant shopping basket and fill it with every product and service that you buy in January. Has the

Ryland Thomas and Nicholas Dimsdale. (2017). 'A Millennium of UK Data' (http://tinyco.re/5827360). Bank of England OBRA dataset.

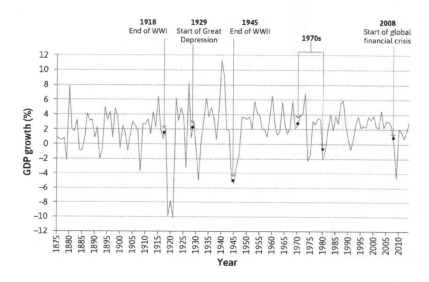

Figure 13.20a UK GDP growth (1875–2014).

Ryland Thomas and Nicholas Dimsdale. (2017). 'A Millennium of UK Data' (http://tinyco.re/5827360). Bank of England OBRA dataset.

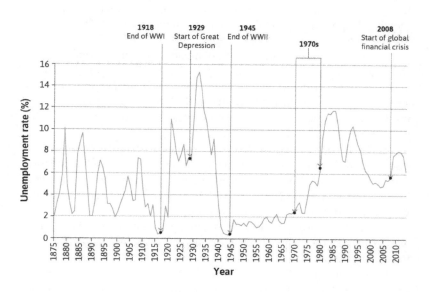

Figure 13.20b UK unemployment rate (1875–2014).

price of this same giant basket increased when you check the prices in January the following year? And what about the baskets of other people?

To answer this question, and to understand how inflation is measured, it's best to listen to the people who work it out. In the UK, the Office for National Statistics (ONS) does this. Until 2016 Richard Campbell was the head of the team in charge of measuring inflation, and while he was at the ONS he made an animation (http://tinyco.re/4099871) to explain how the task is done.

The **Consumer Price Index (CPI)** measures the general level of prices that consumers have to pay for goods and services, including consumption taxes. The basket of goods and services is chosen to reflect the spending of a typical household in the economy. For this reason, the change in the CPI, or CPI inflation, is often considered to measure changes in the 'cost of living'.

The CPI is based on what consumers actually buy. It includes the prices of food and drink, housing, clothing, transportation, recreation, education,

consumer price index (CPI) A measure of the general level of prices that consumers have to pay for goods and services, including consumption taxes.

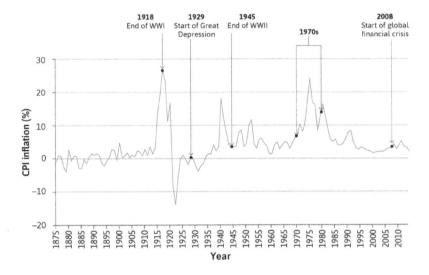

Figure 13.20c UK inflation rate (1875–2014).

Ryland Thomas and Nicholas Dimsdale. (2017). 'A Millennium of UK Data' (http://tinyco.re/5827360). Bank of England OBRA dataset.

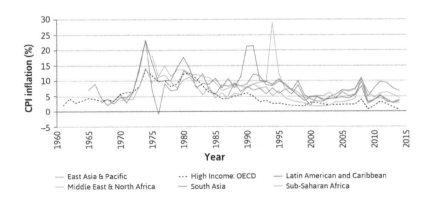

Figure 13.21 Inflation levels and volatility in high- and low-income economies.

The World Bank. 2015. *World Development Indicators* (http://tinyco.re/9263826).

CPI + consumed domestically
+ imports
– exclude exports

communications, medical care, and other goods and services. The goods and services in the basket <u>are weighted</u> according to the fraction of household spending they account for. The <u>CPI excludes exports</u>, which are consumed by foreign residents, but <u>includes imports</u>, which are consumed by households in the home economy. The change in the CPI over the past year is commonly used as a measure of inflation.

The **GDP deflator** is a price index like the CPI, but it tracks the change in prices of <u>all domestically produced</u> final goods and services. Instead of a basket of goods and services, the GDP deflator tracks the price changes of the <u>components of domestic GDP</u>, that is, of $C + I + G + X - M$ (the GDP <u>deflator includes exports</u>, which are produced by the home economy, but <u>excludes imports</u>, which are produced abroad).

> **GDP deflator** A measure of the level of prices for domestically produced output. This is the ratio of nominal (or current price) GDP to real (or constant price) GDP.

The GDP deflator can also be expressed as the ratio of nominal (or current price) GDP to real (or constant price) GDP. The GDP deflator series is most commonly used to transform a nominal GDP series into a real GDP series. As we saw in Section 1.2 and Unit 1's Einstein section, the real GDP series shows how the size of the home economy changes over time, taking into account changes in the price of domestically produced goods and services.

GDP deflator "domestically produced".
+ exports
– exclude imports

EXERCISE 13.8 MEASURING INFLATION

After watching Richard Campbell's animation (http://tinyco.re/4099871), answer these questions:

1. How do we construct a giant representative shopping basket for the whole population?
2. If inflation this year is 2.5%, then what is the current price of the representative shopping basket that cost £100 last year?

The official national inflation rate does not necessarily reflect your own personal inflation rate. If you want to calculate your own personal inflation rate and how it deviates from the national one, some national statistics agencies offer a personal inflation calculator, such as Statistics Netherlands (http://tinyco.re/0093731) or Statistics South Africa (http://tinyco.re/7543547). Your own office of national statistics may also have a personal inflation calculator.

3. Using a personal inflation calculator, calculate your personal inflation rate and comment on how and why it differs from the official inflation rate for your country.

EXERCISE 13.9 THE CPI AND THE GDP DEFLATOR

1. Use the data from FRED to construct charts for real GDP growth, the unemployment rate, and the inflation rate for the US. Select the period from 1960 until the most recent year available. In addition, download the data for the US GDP deflator (search for GDPDEF).

    Use the data you downloaded to answer the following questions (remember that the CPI is calculated from the price of goods consumed in the home country, while the GDP deflator is calculated from the price of the goods produced in the home country):

2. The main difference in the evolution of the series for the CPI and the GDP deflator takes place in 1974–75 and 1979–2000. What could explain this pattern? (Hint: think about the likely impact of an oil crisis on the price of imported goods and, in particular, on your own transport and fuel bills.)
3. What do you notice about the evolution of unemployment and inflation in the early 1980s?
4. Now construct the same charts for your own country. Write a brief report on the evolution of inflation, unemployment, and the real GDP growth rate over the same period.

13.9 CONCLUSION

In this unit, we have introduced two essential tools for understanding the economy: the national accounts used to measure aggregate economic activity, and a set of models that allow us to organize the data in ways that illuminate economic fluctuations. Economists are often asked to provide forecasts about the future development of the economy, and they use both data and models to do this. We have learnt in this unit that households and firms make forecasts when deciding on their spending.

In the following two units, we focus on government policy. We shall see that in order to make good forecasts and good policies, the government and central bank need to take into account how households and firms think about the future and what may disrupt their plans.

Concepts introduced in Unit 13

Before you move on, review these definitions:

*   Recession
*   Okun's law
*   Circular flow of production, income, and spending
*   Aggregate demand and its components: Y, C, I, G, X, M
*   Government transfer payments
*   Self-insurance and co-insurance
*   Capacity utilization rate
*   Investment as a coordination game
*   Inflation, CPI, and GDP deflator

13.10 REFERENCES

Carlin, Wendy and David Soskice. 2015. *Macroeconomics: Institutions, Instability, and the Financial System*. Oxford: Oxford University Press. Chapters 1 and 10.

Clark, Andrew E., and Andrew J. Oswald. 2002. 'A Simple Statistical Method for Measuring How Life Events Affect Happiness' (http://tinyco.re/7872100). *International Journal of Epidemiology* 31 (6): pp. 1139–1144.

Collins, Daryl, Jonathan Morduch, Stuart Rutherford, and Orlanda Ruthven. 2009. *Portfolios of the Poor* (http://tinyco.re/8070650). Princeton: Princeton University Press.

Durante, Ruben. 2010. 'Risk, Cooperation and the Economic Origins of Social Trust: An Empirical Investigation' (http://tinyco.re/7674543). Sciences Po Working Paper.

Fletcher, James. 2014. 'Spurious Correlations: Margarine Linked to Divorce?' (http://tinyco.re/6825314). *BBC News*.

Jappelli, Tullio, and Luigi Pistaferri. 2010. 'The Consumption Response to Income Changes' (http://tinyco.re/3409802). *VoxEU.org*.

Naef, Michael, and Jürgen Schupp. 2009. 'Measuring Trust: Experiments and Surveys in Contrast and Combination' (http://tinyco.re/3956674). IZA discussion Paper No. 4087.

OECD. 2010. *Employment Outlook 2010: Moving Beyond the Jobs Crisis* (http://tinyco.re/5607435).

Shiller, Robert. 2009. 'Animal Spirits' (http://tinyco.re/9820978). *VoxEU.org podcast*. Updated 14 August 2009.

The Economist. 2009. 'Smooth Operators' (http://tinyco.re/7009658). Updated 14 May 2009.

The Economist. 2012. 'New Cradles to Graves' (http://tinyco.re/8856321). Updated 8 September 2012.

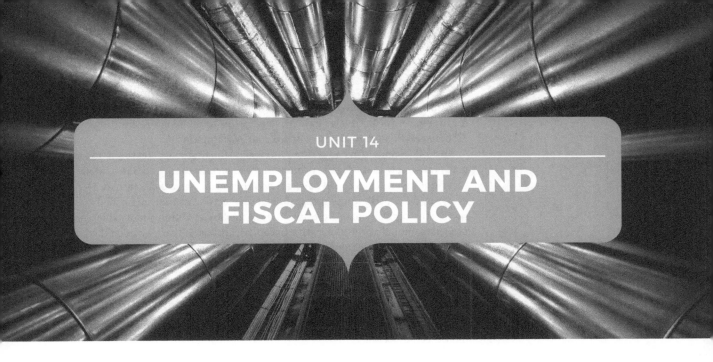

UNEMPLOYMENT AND FISCAL POLICY

HOW GOVERNMENTS CAN MODERATE COSTLY FLUCTUATIONS IN EMPLOYMENT AND INCOME

- Fluctuations in aggregate demand affect GDP growth through a multiplier process, because households face limits to their ability to save, borrow, and share risks.
- An increase in the size of government following the Second World War coincided with smaller economic fluctuations.
- Governments can use changes in taxes or government spending to stabilize the economy, but bad policy can destabilize it.
- If a single household saves, its wealth necessarily increases, but if all households save this may not be true, because without additional spending by the government or firms to counteract the fall in demand, aggregate income will fall.
- Every national economy is embedded in the world economy. This is a source of shocks, both good and bad, and places constraints on the kinds of policies that can be effective.

THEMES AND CAPSTONE UNITS

- 17: History, instability, and growth
- 18: Global economy
- 21: Innovation
- 22: Politics and policy

In August 1960, three months before he was elected US president, the 43-year-old Senator John F. Kennedy found time to spend the day cruising Nantucket Sound on his boat, the Marlin. His crew for the day included John Kenneth Galbraith and Seymour Harris, both Harvard economists, and Paul Samuelson, an economist at MIT and later also a Nobel laureate. They had not been recruited for their nautical skills. In fact, apart from Harris, the senator did not even know them.

The future president wanted to learn 'the new economics', which John Maynard Keynes, an economist who we will learn more about in Section 14.6, had formulated in response to the Great Depression. When Kennedy was a teenager in the decade before the Second World War, the US and many other countries experienced a drastic fall in output (we can see this for the US in Figure 14.1) and massive unemployment that persisted for more than 10 years.

Kennedy had a lot to learn. He admitted that he had barely passed the only economics course he took at Harvard. He would later spend a day at the America's Cup sailing races being tutored by Harris, who assigned texts for him to read. Harris later gave private lessons to the senator, shuttling by air between Boston, where he worked, and Washington DC.

In 1948, Samuelson had written *Economics*, the first major textbook to teach these new ideas. Harris promoted the same economic ideas in a book that he edited in 1948 called *Saving American Capitalism*, a collection of 31 essays by 24 contributors. At that time, it seemed that capitalism needed saving: the centrally planned economies of the Soviet Union and its allies, a model promoted as the alternative to capitalism, had entirely avoided the Great Depression. Kennedy needed economics to understand policies that could promote economic growth, reduce unemployment, but also avoid economic instability.

We have seen in Unit 13 that instability in the economy as a whole is characteristic not only of economies dominated by agriculture, but also of capitalist economies. Figure 14.1 shows the annual growth of real GDP in the US economy since 1870.

A dramatic reduction in the severity of business cycles occurred after the end of the Second World War. Figure 14.1 shows another important development at that time: the increasing role of the government in the economy. The red line shows the share of federal (national), local, and state government tax revenue as a share of GDP. This is a good measure of the size of the government relative to that of the economy.

The share of employment in agriculture, which we have seen was one cause of volatility in the economy, fell from 50% in the 1870s to 20% by the

The Maddison Project. 2013. *2013 Version* (http://tinyco.re/7749051); US Bureau of Economic Analysis. 2016. *GDP & Personal Income* (http://tinyco.re/9376977); World Bank; Wallis, John Joseph. 2000. 'American Government Finance in the Long Run: 1790 to 1990' (http://tinyco.re/5867884). *Journal of Economic Perspectives* 14 (1) (February): pp. 61–82.

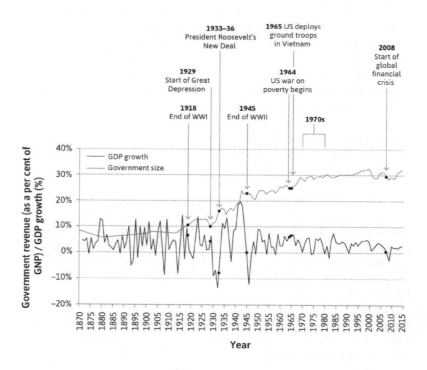

Figure 14.1 Fluctuations in output and the size of government in the US (1870–2015).

beginning of the Second World War, yet there was no sign of the economy becoming more stable over this period. As we have seen, households try to smooth fluctuations in their consumption but they can't always do this successfully, partially because there are limits to how much they can borrow.

The fact that the fluctuations in output growth dramatically reduced while the size of government expanded does not mean that increased government spending stabilized the economy (remember: statistical correlations do not mean causation). But there are good reasons to think that the increase in the red line was part of the reason for the smoothing of the black line. In this unit, we ask why the increased role of the government in the economy is part of the explanation for the more stable economy in the second half of the twentieth century.

What Harris taught Kennedy was influenced by the contrast between the volatility of the economy before the Second World War, and the steadier growth and absence of deep recessions afterwards. Why do economies experience unemployment, inflation, and instability in output, and what kinds of policies might address these problems?

In Unit 13, we took the household's viewpoint of the business cycle, which allowed us to establish why fluctuations in employment and income are costly, and how households try to limit the consequences for their wellbeing. In this unit, we take the policymaker's viewpoint. As we saw in Figure 14.1, the big increase in the size of government after the Second World War was accompanied by a reduction in the size of business cycle fluctuations. After 1990, the business cycle in advanced economies became even smoother, until the global financial crisis in 2008. This led to the period from the early 1990s to the late 2000s being called the **great moderation**.

> **great moderation** Period of low volatility in aggregate output in advanced economies between the 1980s and the 2008 financial crisis. The name was suggested by James Stock and Mark Watson, the economists, and popularized by Ben Bernanke, then chairman of the Federal Reserve.

14.1 THE TRANSMISSION OF SHOCKS: THE MULTIPLIER PROCESS

In a capitalist economy, private investment spending is driven by expectations about future post-tax profits. As we saw in Unit 13, spending on investment projects tends to occur in clusters. Two reasons for this observation are:

- Firms may adopt a new technology at the same time.
- Firms may have similar beliefs about expected future demand.

We need a tool to help us understand how decisions of firms (and households) to raise or reduce investment spending will affect the economy as a whole. You will recall that some households are able to completely smooth temporary bumps in their income, but that in credit-constrained households, higher income from getting a job or moving from part-time to full-time work will also lead to higher consumption spending.

As a result, changes in current income influence spending, affecting the income of others, so indirect effects through the economy amplify the direct effect of a shock to **aggregate demand** (often shortened to AD) created by an investment boom.

We will show how economists answer such questions as 'how large would the total direct and indirect impact of a rise in investment spending be?' or, 'what would be the effect of lower government spending?'

> **aggregate demand** The total of the components of spending in the economy, added to get GDP: $Y = C + I + G + X - M$. It is the total amount of demand for (or expenditure on) goods and services produced in the economy. *See also: consumption, investment, government spending, exports, imports.*

2 Questions

A statistic called the **multiplier** provides one way of answering this question. Imagine there is a new technology. New spending takes place in the economy as a result; output of the new capital goods rises, as do the incomes of the people producing them. The circular flow of expenditure, income, and output previously shown in Figure 13.6 illustrates this process.

- *If the total increase in GDP is equal to the initial increase in spending*: We say that the multiplier is equal to 1.
- *If the total increase in GDP is greater or less than the initial increase in spending*: We say that the multiplier is greater than 1 or less than 1.

multiplier process A mechanism through which the direct and indirect effect of a change in autonomous spending affects aggregate output. *See also: fiscal multiplier, multiplier model.*
consumption function (aggregate) An equation that shows how consumption spending in the economy as a whole depends on other variables. For example, in the multiplier model, the other variables are current disposable income and autonomous consumption. *See also: disposable income, autonomous consumption.*

To see why GDP may rise by more than the initial increase in investment spending, we explain what economists call the **multiplier process**. We do this by combining the very different behaviour of consumption-smoothing and non-smoothing households to represent consumption spending for the economy as a whole. In this **aggregate consumption function**, consumption depends on current income, among other things. Recall that in the model of Unit 13, consumption-smoothing households will not increase their consumption one-for-one, or even at all, in response to a temporary €1 increase in their income. Credit-constrained and other households who do not smooth, on the other hand, will increase their current consumption by €1 in response to a temporary €1 increase in their income.

In 2008, when governments considered temporary increases in government spending and tax cuts in response to the recession that followed the global financial crisis, the size of the multiplier became the subject of a debate among policymakers and economists. We return to this debate later in the unit.

As we shall see, the multiplier is greater than 1 if the additional consumption spending resulting from a temporary €1 increase in income is greater than zero but less than €1 (say, for example, 60 cents).

After explaining how this is a consequence of the multiplier process, we will show that the validity of the assumptions we make in the multiplier model depend on the state of the economy.

14.2 THE MULTIPLIER MODEL

We begin with a simple model that excludes the government and foreign trade. In this model, there are two types of expenditure:

- **consumption**
- **investment**

We assume that aggregate consumption spending has two parts:

consumption (C) Expenditure on consumer goods including both short-lived goods and services and long-lived goods, which are called consumer durables.
investment (I) Expenditure on newly produced capital goods (machinery and equipment) and buildings, including new housing.

- *A fixed amount*: How much people will spend, independent of their income. This fixed amount, also known as **autonomous consumption**, is shown as c_0 on the vertical axis of Figure 14.2.
- *A variable amount*: This depends on current income, and is an upward-sloping red line in Figure 14.2.

So we can write consumption spending in the form of an equation, which we call the **aggregate consumption function**:

aggregate consumption = autonomous consumption
+ consumption that depends on income

$$C = c_0 + c_1 Y$$

The term c_1 gives the effect of one additional unit of income on consumption, called the **marginal propensity to consume (MPC)**. In Figure 14.2, the slope of the consumption line is equal to the marginal propensity to consume. A steeper consumption line means a larger consumption response to a change in income. A flatter line means that households are smoothing their consumption so that it does not vary much when their incomes change. We assume that the marginal propensity to consume is positive, but less than one. This means that only part of an increase in income is consumed; the rest is saved.

We will work with an aggregate consumption function in which the marginal propensity to consume, c_1, equals 0.6. This means that an additional unit of income (Euros in this case) increases consumption by €1 × 0.6 = 60 cents.

Naturally, this average number hides large variation across households, who differ in their wealth and in the credit constraints they face. Most households have little wealth, and even in rich countries about one in four households are credit-constrained. As we saw in Unit 13, weakness of will also plays a role. So, both for households that are credit-constrained and for those that do not save ahead of anticipated declines in income, consumption closely tracks income.

autonomous consumption Consumption that is independent of current income.

marginal propensity to consume (MPC) The change in consumption when disposable income changes by one unit.

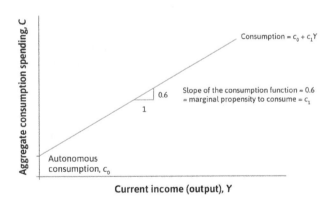

Figure 14.2 The aggregate consumption function.

1. Autonomous consumption
This is the fixed amount that households will spend that does not depend on their current level of income.

2. Consumption that depends on income
The upward-sloping line denotes the part of consumption that depends on current income (and hence on current output).

3. The marginal propensity to consume
The slope of the consumption line is equal to the marginal propensity to consume.

Households with low wealth smooth consumption very little if their income falls sharply. The marginal propensity to consume for this group is closer to 0.8. For the small fraction of households who hold the majority of wealth, however, current income plays a very small role in determining consumption, and their marginal propensity to consume is closer to zero. This means that for rich households, an increase in current income of €1 would raise their consumption by just a few cents.

The term c_0 in the aggregate consumption function captures all the other influences on consumption that are not related to current income. Taken literally, it is how much a person with no income would consume, but this is not the best way to think about it. It is just the consumption that is independent of income, and for this reason we call it **autonomous consumption**.

Since the consumption function only explicitly includes current income, expectations about *future* income will be included in autonomous consumption. To see what this means in practice, recall from Unit 13 that consumption will change as a result of people becoming more or less optimistic about their future employment and earnings prospects.

Figure 14.3 illustrates how expectations affected consumption in the financial crisis of 2008 and highlights the exceptional nature of this episode. The figure shows how consumer confidence changed in the US over the course of the crisis. The consumer sentiment index that we have used is the University of Michigan Surveys of Consumers (http://tinyco.re/7469765). It is based on monthly interviews with 500 households, and asks how they view prospects for their own financial situation and for the general economy over the short and long term. The figure also plots the evolution of a number of key macroeconomic indicators: disposable income, consumption of durable goods like cars and home furnishings, and consumption of non-durable goods, such as food. All of the series in Figure 14.3 are shown as index numbers, with the first quarter of 2008 as the base year.

We notice:

- *Consumption of non-durable goods went down slightly more than disposable income*: It fell by 3% during the period. Contrary to the predictions of

Federal Reserve Bank of St. Louis. 2015. FRED (http://tinyco.re/5104028).

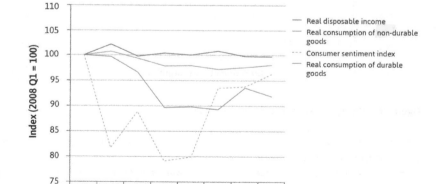

Figure 14.3 Fear and household consumption in the US during the global financial crisis (2008 Q1–2009 Q4).

consumption smoothing, households were sufficiently worried about their future prospects that they made adjustments to their spending on non-durables.

• *Consumption of durables decreased much more dramatically than disposable income*: It decreased by 10% in the first year.

Why the sudden drop in consumption of consumer durables? An important reason is that households were suddenly fearful about the future of their jobs, as shown by the sharp decline in the consumer sentiment index in Figure 14.3. The collapse of the investment bank Lehman Brothers in September 2008 (http://tinyco.re/3073658), worries about the stability of the banking system, and a higher burden of household debt due to falling house prices led households with mortgages to postpone purchases of expensive items like cars and fridges. It's important to remember that spending on consumer durables can easily be postponed. In this sense it is more like an investment than a consumption decision (even though consumer durables are counted as part of consumption in the national accounts). As a result, we would expect the series for consumer durables to be more volatile than for non-durable consumption.

We now show how a shock is transmitted through the economy. In Figure 14.4 we show the amount of output produced by the economy (on the horizontal axis) and the demand for output (on the vertical axis). Everything is measured in real terms because we are interested in how changes in aggregate demand create changes in output and employment.

The 45-degree line from the origin of the diagram shows all the combinations in which output is equal to aggregate demand. This corresponds to the circular flow discussed in Unit 13, where we saw that spending on goods and services in the economy (aggregate demand) is equal to production of goods and services in the economy (aggregate output). You can see this because with a 45-degree line the horizontal distance (output) is equal to the vertical distance (aggregate demand). We can therefore say that:

output = aggregate demand for goods produced in the home economy
$$Y = AD$$

But how do we know where the economy is on the 45-degree line? Is it at a position of low output, which would mean high unemployment, or is it at a position of high output, which would mean low unemployment?

We determine this position by analysing the individual components of aggregate demand. We assume that firms are willing to supply any amount of the goods demanded by those making purchases in the economy; they are not operating at full **capacity utilization**. Because we have assumed that there is no government spending or trade with other economies, in this model there are just two components of aggregate spending:

• *Consumption*: We take the consumption line introduced in Figure 14.2. Because the marginal propensity to consume is less than one, the consumption line is flatter than the 45-degree line, which has a slope of one.
• *Investment*: We assume investment does not depend on the level of output.

goods market equilibrium The point at which output equals the aggregate demand for goods produced in the home economy. The economy will continue producing at this output level unless something changes spending behaviour. *See also: aggregate demand.*

capacity utilization rate A measure of the extent to which a firm, industry, or entire economy is producing as much as the stock of its capital goods and current knowledge would allow.

The equation for aggregate demand is therefore:

$$\text{aggregate demand} = \text{consumption} + \text{investment}$$
$$AD = C + I$$
$$= c_0 + c_1 Y + I$$

So adding investment to the consumption line simply leads to a parallel upward shift. In this respect, investment is similar to autonomous consumption. We can see from Figure 14.4 that the aggregate demand line has an intercept of $c_0 + I$, a slope of c_1, and is flatter than the 45-degree line.

In Figure 14.4 we now have a picture showing how the level of output in the economy is determined. Output is equal to aggregate demand (the 45-degree line), and aggregate demand is equal to $c_0 + c_1 Y + I$ (the flatter line), so the economy must be at point A where the two lines cross.

The same figure tells us the effect of a change in autonomous consumption (c_0) or investment. We study this change exactly as we did the changes in supply and demand in Unit 11: we see how the change makes the old outcome no longer an equilibrium, and then we locate the new equilibrium. The expected change is the movement from the old to the new equilibrium.

Changes in autonomous consumption or investment displace the old equilibrium because they change aggregate demand, which in turn alters

(p 557)

$$GDP(Y) = C + I + G + NX$$
$$AE = C + I^P + G + NX$$
$$\underline{}I^U$$

$$AD = C + I + G + NX$$

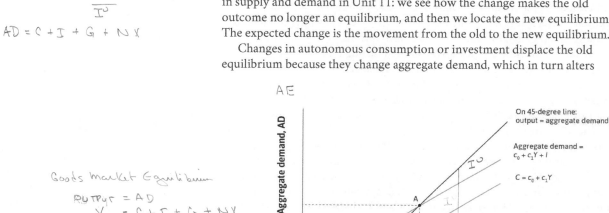

AE

Goods market Equilibrium

OUTPUT = AD

$$Y = C + I + G + NX$$

$$AE = C + \underline{I^P} + G + NX$$
$$ I^U$$

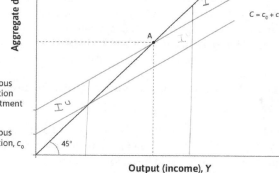

Figure 14.4 Goods market equilibrium: The multiplier diagram.

1. Goods market equilibrium

Point A is called a **goods market equilibrium**: the economy will continue producing at that output level unless something changes spending behaviour.

2. The 45-degree line

The 45-degree line from the origin of the diagram shows all the combinations in which output is equal to aggregate demand, meaning the economy is in goods market equilibrium.

3. Consumption

The first component of aggregate demand is consumption, which is represented by the consumption line introduced in Figure 14.2.

4. Investment

Adding investment to the consumption line simply leads to a parallel upward shift of the aggregate demand line.

the level of output and employment. In Figure 14.5, we take the multiplier diagram and reduce investment. We choose a reduction in investment of €1.5 billion. Follow the steps in Figure 14.5 to see what happens.

We trace the effect of the fall in investment through the economy in Figure 14.5. The first-round effect is that the fall in investment cuts aggregate demand by €1.5 billion. But lower spending also means lower production and lower incomes, and firms will fire workers as a result, leading to a further decline in spending. Think of credit-constrained households where some members lose their job: they would like to keep consumption stable, but when their income falls they are unable to borrow enough to sustain that level of consumption, so they reduce their spending, which leads to further cuts in production and incomes. The consumption equation tells us that this kind of behaviour leads to a fall in aggregate con-

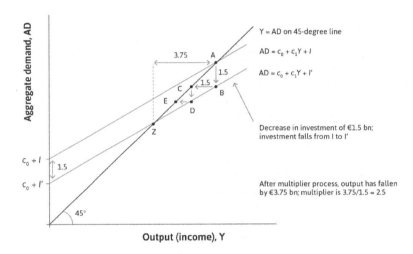

$$\frac{3.75}{1.5} = 2.5 \text{ multiplied effect}$$

Figure 14.5 The multiplier in action: An investment-led recession.

1. Goods market equilibrium
The economy starts at point A, in goods market equilibrium.

2. A fall in investment
The fall in investment cuts aggregate demand by €1.5 billion, and the economy moves vertically downward from point A to point B.

3. Firms cut back
With demand lower, firms cut back production and reduce employment. With output and employment lower, incomes fall by €1.5 billion. This is the move from B to C.

4. A fall in consumption
Once households' incomes fall, they reduce their consumption, because they may be credit-constrained. The consumption equation tells us that this kind of behaviour initially leads to a fall in aggregate consumption of 0.6 times the fall in income. This is the distance from point C to point D.

5. Firms cut back again
Firms respond by cutting production, output falls, and the economy moves from point D to point E.

6. ... and so on
The process will go on until the economy reaches point Z.

7. The new aggregate demand line
This goes through point Z and shows the new goods market equilibrium of the economy following the investment shock.

8. The fall in output as a result of the shock
The total fall in output exceeds the initial size of the decline in investment; output has fallen by €3.75 billion.

9. The multiplier is equal to 2.5
The total change in output is 2.5 times larger than the initial change in investment.

sumption of 0.6 times the fall in income. The process will go on until the economy reaches point Z.

Following the investment shock, the intercept of the line has moved down by €1.5 billion, causing a parallel shift in the aggregate demand line. Output has fallen by €3.75 billion, more than the fall in investment of €1.5 billion: this is the multiplier process.

In this case, the multiplier is equal to 2.5, because the total change in output is 2.5 times larger than the initial change in investment. A multiplier of 2.5 is unrealistically large. As we shall see in the next section, once taxes and imports are introduced in the model, the multiplier shrinks.

We call the model of aggregate demand that includes the multiplier process the **multiplier model**. This is a summary:

multiplier model A model of aggregate demand that includes the multiplier process. *See also: fiscal multiplier, multiplier process.*

- *A fall in demand leads to a fall in production and an equivalent fall in income*: This leads to a further (smaller) fall in demand, which leads to a further fall in production, and so on.
- *The multiplier is the sum of all these successive decreases in production*: Eventually, output has fallen by a larger amount than the initial shift in demand. Output is a multiple of the initial shift.
- *Production adjusts to demand*: Firms supply the amount of goods demanded at the prevailing price. When demand falls, firms adjust production down. The model assumes that they do not adjust their prices.

Note that the economy we are studying is one in which we assume there are underutilized resources in the form of spare capacity in production facilities and underemployed labour. We also assume that wages are not affected by changes in the level of output. For the multiplier process to work in the same way in response to a rise in investment, the assumption of spare capacity and fixed wages means that costs will not rise when output goes up, so firms will be happy to supply the extra output demanded without adjusting their prices. Otherwise some of the increased spending will translate into higher prices or wages rather than higher real output—as we discuss in the next unit.

If the economy is not characterized by spare capacity and constant wages, the multiplier will be smaller than what we find here.

We can also show the effect on output by combining the two equations that determine the lines in the multiplier diagram. The 45-degree line is simply the equation $Y = AD$. Combining this with the equation for AD gives us:

$$Y = AD = C + I$$
$$= c_0 + c_1 Y + I$$

Collecting terms on the left hand side,

$$Y(1 - c_1) = c_0 + I$$

We then divide through by $(1 - c_1)$:

$$Y = \frac{1}{1 - c_1} \times (c_0 + I)$$

We can now calculate how much output will increase or decrease using the value of the multiplier times the change in **autonomous demand**.

Discover another way to summarize our findings from the diagram algebraically in the Einstein at the end of this section.

The change in output in Figure 14.5 is 2.5 times greater than the initial shock to investment, which means that the shock has been amplified. In algebra, we write this as $\Delta Y = k\Delta I$, and say it as 'delta Y (the change in output) is equal to k, the multiplier, times delta I (the change in investment)'.

> **autonomous demand** Components of aggregate demand that are independent of current income.

QUESTION 14.1 CHOOSE THE CORRECT ANSWER(S)

Figure 14.2 (page 589) depicts a consumption function of an economy, where C is the aggregate consumption spending and Y is the current income of the economy.

Based on this information, which of the following statements is correct?

☐ The marginal propensity to consume (MPC) is the proportion of current income spent on consumption, C/Y.

☐ The MPC is given by the line's intercept on the vertical axis.

☐ The MPC is normally less than 1 as some households are able to smooth their consumption.

☐ If the current income of a country is $Y = \$100$ trillion and the MPC = 0.6, then the aggregate consumption spending is $C = \$60$ trillion.

QUESTION 14.2 CHOOSE THE CORRECT ANSWER(S)

The following diagram depicts the change in the aggregate goods market equilibrium when there is a €2 billion increase in investment.

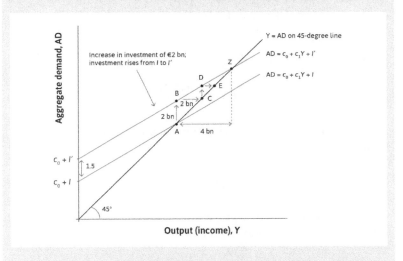

The economy's marginal propensity to consume is 0.5. Based on this information, which of the following statements is correct?

☐ The new goods market equilibrium after the investment increase is E.

☐ Aggregate demand increases by a total of €2 billion × 0.5 = €1 billion due to the increase in investment.

☐ The multiplier is 2.

☐ The distance between C and D is three-quarters the distance between A and B (€1.5 billion).

Calculating the multiplier

We consider the effect of an increase in investment of €1.5 billion. We can summarize our findings from the multiplier diagram by doing some algebra. To get the multiplier, we can calculate the total increase in production after $n + 1$ rounds of the process. Each round of the process matches the circular flow diagram. The first-round increase in demand and production is €1.5 billion. The second-round increase in demand and production is ($c_1 \times$ €1.5 billion), the third-round increase in demand and production is $c_1 \times (c_1 \times$ €1.5 billion) = ($c_1^2 \times$ €1.5 billion), and so on.

Following this logic, the total increase in demand and production after $n + 1$ rounds is the total sum of these changes:

$$1.5 + c_1(1.5) + c_1^2(1.5) + ... + c_1^n(1.5) = 1.5(1 + c_1 + c_1^2 + ... + c_1^n)$$

Because the marginal propensity to consume is lower than one, we can show that the total sum in the brackets reaches a limit of $1/(1 - c_1)$ as n gets large. This is because the term in the brackets is, mathematically, a geometric series. We show this as follows.

If k is the multiplier, we have:

$$k = 1.5(1 + c_1 + c_1^2 + ... + c_1^n)$$

Now multiply both sides by $(1 - c_1)$ to get:

$$
\begin{aligned}
k(1 - c_1) &= (1 + c_1 + c_1^2 + ... + c_1^n)(1 - c_1) \\
&= (1 + c_1 + c_1^2 + ... + c_1^n) - (c_1 + c_1^2 + c_1^3 + ... + c_1^{n+1}) \\
&= 1 - c_1^{n+1}
\end{aligned}
$$

Now divide again by $(1 - c_1)$:

$$k = \frac{(1 - c_1^{n+1})}{(1 - c_1)}$$

As n gets large, assuming $c_1 < 1$, the numerator tends to 1. So, in the limit:

$$k = \frac{1}{1 - c_1}$$

In the example, the marginal propensity to consume is, on average, 0.6. This implies that the multiplier is equal to:

$$\frac{1}{1 - c_1} = \frac{1}{1 - 0.6} = 2.5$$

We can then apply the multiplier to the initial change in investment of €1.5 billion to find the sum of all the successive increases in production triggered by the initial hike in investment and aggregate demand: 2.5 × €1.5 billion = €3.75 billion.

14.3 HOUSEHOLD TARGET WEALTH, COLLATERAL, AND CONSUMPTION SPENDING

From Unit 13, we know that consumption is the largest component of GDP in most economies. Therefore an important part of understanding changes in output and employment is understanding why consumption changes.

We saw that a shock to investment shifts the aggregate demand curve, and is transmitted through the economy as households adjust their spending in response to changes in income. We focused on incomplete consumption smoothing, such as credit constraints. This behaviour is reflected in the size of the multiplier and the *slope* of the aggregate demand curve. But consumption and saving behaviour can also *shift* the aggregate demand curve.

A shift in aggregate demand can be caused by a shift in autonomous consumption, represented by the term c_0 in the aggregate consumption function, $C = c_0 + c_1 Y$. A change in c_0 will in turn produce a multiplier response of output and employment through the circular flow of expenditure, output, and income in the same way as the fall in investment in the previous section was multiplied.

Think about a family with a **mortgage** on its house. If the price of houses falls, the family will be concerned that its wealth, too, has fallen. A likely reaction to this is for the household to save more. This is called **precautionary saving**. One way to analyse this behaviour is to assume that households have in mind a **target wealth** that they aim to hold.

When something happens to affect the stock of the household's wealth relative to this target, it reacts by either increasing or decreasing its savings to restore wealth back to its target level. If this adjustment involves precautionary saving, it is modelled as a fall in autonomous consumption.

In 1929, a downturn in the US business cycle that initially appeared similar to others in the preceding decade turned into a large-scale economic disaster—the **Great Depression**.

The fall in output and employment during the Great Depression highlights two ways in which aggregate consumption might fall—credit constraints in the multiplier process, and changes in wealth relative to target wealth.

To understand the economic mechanisms at work in the Great Depression, we use the multiplier diagram shown in Figure 14.6. Point A shows the initial situation of the economy in the third quarter of 1929. There was then a fall in investment. This shifts the aggregate demand curve from the pre-crisis to the crisis level. The dotted line from point B shows the level of output that would have been observed in the business cycle trough if the usual multiplier process had been at work. There would have been a recession, but no Great Depression. But the downturn was made much worse because there was a fall in the demand for consumer goods, even by those who kept their jobs.

Consumption was cut back through two mechanisms:

- *The shift from A to B*: As output and employment fell, some households cut spending on housing and consumer durables because they were credit-constrained, and therefore unable to borrow in the deteriorating conditions. Some economists have estimated that the size of the multiplier at the time was about 1.8.
- *The shift from B to C*: Even households that remained in work cut back spending because it became increasingly clear that the downturn was the

mortgage (or mortgage loan) A loan contracted by households and businesses to purchase a property without paying the total value at one time. Over a period of many years, the borrower repays the loan, plus interest. The debt is secured by the property itself, referred to as collateral. *See also: collateral.*

precautionary saving An increase in saving to restore wealth to its target level. *See also: target wealth.*

target wealth The level of wealth that a household aims to hold, based on its economic goals (or preferences) and expectations. We assume that households try to maintain this level of wealth in the face of changes in their economic situation, as long as it is possible to do so.

Great Depression The period of a sharp fall in output and employment in many countries in the 1930s.

Christina D. Romer. 1993. 'The Nation in Depression' (http://tinyco.re/4965855). *Journal of Economic Perspectives* 7 (2) (May): pp. 19–39.

new reality, not a temporary shock. This shifted the consumption function down and pulled the economy further into depression from B to C in Figure 14.6.

Research done since the Great Depression (which we examine in more depth in Unit 17) provides a number of explanations for the fall in autonomous consumption in the US:

- *Uncertainty:* Uncertainty about the state of the economy provoked by the dramatic stock market crash of October 1929 made both firms and households more cautious, prompting them to postpone purchases of machinery and equipment and consumer durables.
- *Pessimism and the desire to save more:* Households also became more pessimistic about their ability to maintain current levels of spending, as they feared unemployment and lower earnings in the future. Their assessment of their material wealth was also affected as the prices of houses and financial assets fell. The 1920s had seen a build-up of debt by households, as they were able to use instalment agreements for the first time to buy consumer durables.
- *The banking crisis and the collapse of credit:* A third factor that shifted the aggregate demand line down to the level labelled 'trough' was the banking crisis of 1930 and 1931, which affected both consumption and

Robert J. Gordon. 1986. *The American Business Cycle: Continuity and Change* (http://tinyco.re/5375612). Chicago, Il: University of Chicago Press.

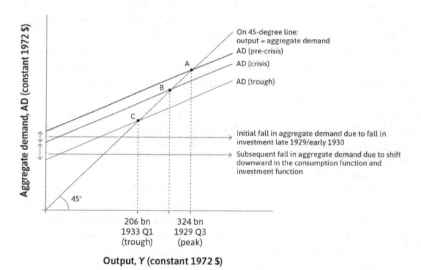

Figure 14.6 Aggregate demand in the Great Depression

1. The 1929 peak
Point A shows the initial situation of the economy.

2. A fall in investment
This shifts the aggregate demand curve from the pre-crisis to the crisis level.

3. A normal recession
The economy would normally be at point B.

4. The 1933 trough
However, instead of a typical downswing (from A to B), output fell by much more than can be explained by the multiplier process alone, which is shown by the move from B to C.

investment. There was a wave of failures of small, weak, and largely unregulated banks across the US. The system of small banks was vulnerable to panic. Savers began to fear that they would not be able to get access to their deposits. As explained in Unit 10, as panic spread from bank to bank, bank runs affected the entire banking system. With the collapse of the banking system, households lost deposits and small firms lost their access to credit.

To illustrate why households who were not affected by credit constraints nevertheless cut consumption, we look at the composition of a household's wealth or assets. In Unit 10 we introduced the concept of wealth by comparing it with the volume of water in a bathtub. At that time we focused on material wealth. In Figure 14.7 we extend the concept of wealth to broad wealth so as to include the household's expected future earnings from employment, known as the value of its **human capital**.

Follow the analysis in Figure 14.7 to see the composition of the household's broad wealth, which is equal to the value of all its assets, minus its debt (which we assume is a mortgage on the house).

As we shall see:

- *If target wealth is above expected wealth*: The household will increase savings and decrease consumption.
- *If target wealth is below expected wealth*: The household will decrease savings and increase consumption.

In early 1929, how would a household with the wealth position shown in column A of Figure 14.8 have interpreted news about factory closures, the collapse of the stock market, and bank failures? How would it have adjusted spending on consumer durables, housing, and non-durables? Answers to these questions help tell us why the Great Depression happened.

- *Before the Depression:* Viewed from early in 1929 (column A in Figure 14.8), households are shown as making consumption decisions in line with their expectations: total wealth is equal to target wealth.
- *The Depression:* By late 1929 (column B), the downturn was underway and beliefs had changed. With job losses throughout the economy, households revised expected earnings downward. Falling asset prices (of shares and houses) reduced the value of the household's material wealth. The result was a gap between the household's target wealth and expected wealth. This helps to explain the cutback in consumption by households who could (and in an ordinary downturn, would) have helped to smooth a temporary fall in aggregate demand. Instead, these households increased their saving. This fall in autonomous consumption is part of the explanation for the downward shift of the aggregate demand curve from crisis to trough in Figure 14.6.
- *The **financial accelerator**, collateral, and credit constraints:* Changes in household wealth affect consumption through another channel. In Unit 10, we saw that having collateral may enable a household to borrow. An important example is the case of home loans, where the bank extends a loan using the value of the house as collateral. If the value of your house falls, the bank will be willing to lend less, making you more credit-constrained, which may reduce your consumption.

human capital The stock of knowledge, skills, behavioural attributes, and personal characteristics that determine the labour productivity or labour earnings of an individual. Investment in this through education, training, and socialization can increase the stock, and such investment is one of the sources of economic growth. Part of an individual's endowments. *See also: endowment.*

equity An individual's own investment in a project. This is recorded in an individual's or firm's balance sheet as net worth. *See also: net worth. An entirely different use of the term is synonymous with fairness.*

financial accelerator The mechanism through which firms' and households' ability to borrow increases when the value of the collateral they have pledged to the lender (often a bank) goes up.

The same mechanisms are at work if house prices increase, which will tend to increase consumption:

- *For those who are not credit-constrained:* If the value of your house increases, this improves your net worth and raises your wealth relative to target. We would predict that this would reduce your precautionary savings, increasing consumption.
- *For those who are credit-constrained:* A rise in the price of your house can lead you to increase your consumption spending because the higher collateral enables you to borrow more.

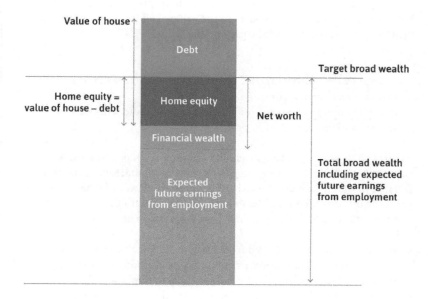

Figure 14.7 Household wealth: Key concepts.

1. Expected future earnings from employment
These are represented by the orange rectangle.

2. Financial wealth
This is the green rectangle.

3. The household's ownership stake in the house
This is the blue rectangle.

4. The household's total broad wealth
This is the sum of the green, blue, and orange rectangles.

5. Households also hold debt
This is shown by the red rectangle.

6. The household's net worth
Also called material wealth. We find it by taking the total assets (excluding expected future earnings), which is the value of the house plus financial wealth, and then subtracting the debt it owes.

7. The value of the house
This is equal to the household's **equity** in the house, plus what it owes to the bank (the mortgage).

8. Target wealth
For the household shown in the figure, expected broad wealth (orange + green + blue) is equal to target wealth.

EXERCISE 14.1 A HOUSEHOLD'S BALANCE SHEET

Consider a family of two parents and two children who have a mortgage on their home. They have paid off half the mortgage. The family also owns a car and a portfolio of shares in companies. They spend their income on food, clothing, and private school fees, and have retirement savings held in a pension fund.

1. Which of these items would be on a balance sheet for the household?
2. Using the example of the bank's balance sheet in Figure 10.16 as a guide, construct an annual balance sheet for your hypothetical household. You may want to research the typical values for these items for a family of this type.

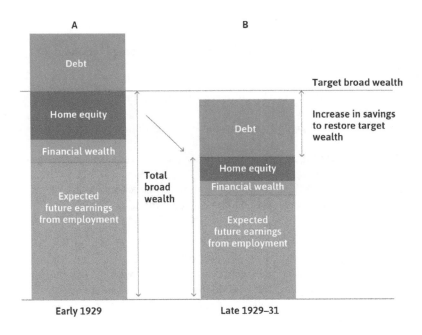

Figure 14.8 The Great Depression: Households cut consumption to restore their target broad wealth.

1. Before the Depression
Households are making consumption decisions in line with their expectations about their net worth and future earnings from employment. This is shown by the fact that total wealth is equal to target wealth.

2. The Depression
In late 1929, column B, the downturn was underway and beliefs had changed.

3. Precautionary saving
The result was a gap between the household's target wealth and expected wealth. Households increased their savings.

EXERCISE 14.2 HOUSING IN FRANCE AND GERMANY

In France and Germany, it is difficult for a household to increase its borrowing based on an increase in the market value of the house. In addition, large down-payments (as a percentage of the house price) are required for house purchases.

1. On the basis of this information, how would you expect a rise in house prices in France or Germany to affect spending by households?
2. In the US or UK, loans are more easily available based on a rise in home equity and only a small down-payment is required. How would you expect your answer to question 1 to change when considering the US or UK?
3. What do you conclude about the role of the financial accelerator in France and Germany compared with the UK and the US?

Note: A December 2014 VoxEU article, 'Combatting Eurozone deflation: QE for the people' (http://tinyco.re/4854300), tells you more about the influence of a change in house prices on spending in Europe and the US.

QUESTION 14.3 CHOOSE THE CORRECT ANSWER(S)

Which of the following statements is correct regarding household wealth?

☐ A household's material wealth is its financial wealth plus the value of its house.
☐ The total broad wealth equals material wealth plus expected future earnings.
☐ A household adjusts its precautionary saving in response to changes in its target wealth.
☐ If the household's target wealth is above its expected wealth, then it will decrease savings and increase consumption.

14.4 INVESTMENT SPENDING

In Unit 13, we contrasted the volatility of investment with the smoothness of consumption spending. But how do firms make investment decisions? Think of the manager or owner of a firm deciding what to do with their accumulated profits. There are four choices:

1. *Dividends:* Allocate the funds to managerial or employee salaries, or to dividends for owners.
2. *Saving:* Buy an interest-bearing financial asset such as a bond, or retire (pay off) existing debt.
3. *Investment abroad:* Build new productive capacity in another country.
4. *Investment at home:* Build new capacity in the home country.

The fourth choice is called investment in our model (the third choice is also investment, but since it is spent in the foreign country it is measured in the foreign country's national accounts as part of its I, not in the home country's).

If we assume that there is no reason to change salaries then we can also break down the owner's decision as we did Marco's decision in Unit 10:

- *The owner has the choice to consume now or consume later*: Taking the revenue as dividends means the owner can, if desired, simply consume the extra income now.
- *If the decision is to consume later*: The owner can either save (lend by buying a financial asset such as a bond or retire debt) or invest in a new project.
- *If the decision is to invest*: Whether the owner does it in the home country or abroad will depend on the expected rate of profit for the potential investment projects in the two locations.

The desirability of consuming more now rather than later depends on the owner's discount rate (ρ), as discussed in Unit 10. The owner will compare this to the return they can get by not consuming now. If the firm saves by buying a financial asset then the return is the interest rate r. If the firm invests in productive capacity then the return will be the profit rate on investment, which we will call Π as in Unit 10:

- *If ρ is greater than both r and Π*: The owner will keep the funds and increase consumption spending.
- *If r is greater than ρ and Π*: The decision will be to repay debt or purchase a financial asset.
- *If Π is greater than ρ and r*: The owner will invest (either at home or abroad).

Because of these options, the interest rate is one of the factors determining whether investment takes place. We saw in Unit 10 that this can be altered by central bank policy (**monetary policy**). The interest rate is the opportunity cost of purchases of machinery, equipment, and structures that increase the capital stock—if you have money available, you could save it with a return of r instead of investing it. Alternatively, if you do not have money available, then the cost of borrowing for investment is also r. If we rank investment projects by their expected post-tax rate of profit, then a lower interest rate raises the number of projects for which the expected rate of profit is greater than the interest rate. We saw this when Marco faced the decision of whether or not to invest (Figure 10.10). Thus a higher interest rate reduces investment, and a lower interest rate increases it.

Figure 14.9 illustrates this fact for an economy consisting of two firms, A and B. For each firm in this example, there are three investment projects of different scale and rate of return. They are shown in decreasing order of the expected rate of profit. Follow the analysis in Figure 14.9 to see how the interest rate determines which investment projects go ahead. The lower panel aggregates the two firms to show how investment in the economy as a whole responds to a change in the interest rate.

In Figures 14.10a–c, we look at how a change in profit expectations affects investment.

In the two-firm economy in Figure 14.10a, the expected rate of profit for each project rises because of an improvement in the supply-side conditions in the economy. The height of each column rises, and as a result, there is more investment at a given interest rate.

monetary policy Central bank (or government) actions aimed at influencing economic activity through changing interest rates or the prices of financial assets. *See also: quantitative easing.*

An upward shift can be caused by a fall in expected input prices, such as a forecast fall in the price of energy or wages, or a fall in taxation over the life of the project.

Another example of a positive supply effect is an improvement in the security of property rights so that there is a smaller chance that the government or another powerful actor (such as a landowner, like Bruno in Unit 5, who might threaten a smallholder) will take over ownership of the investment project. This is called a fall in the **risk of expropriation** and is an example of an improvement in the business environment.

> **expropriation risk** The probability that an asset will be taken from its owner by the government or some other actor.

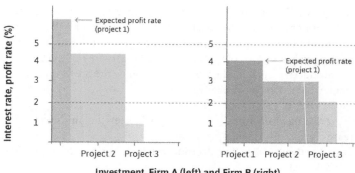

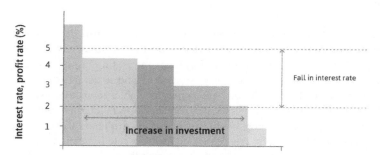

Figure 14.9 Investment, expected rate of profit, and the interest rate in an economy with two firms.

1. Firm A
Firm A has three investment projects of different scale and rate of profit. They are shown in decreasing order of the expected rate of profit.

2. Firm B
Firm B also has three different investment projects.

3. The decision to invest
If the interest rate remains at 5%, Firm A goes ahead with project 1 and Firm B does not invest at all. But if the interest rate was 2%, A would undertake projects 1 and 2 and B would undertake all three of its projects.

4. The decision to invest
The lower panel aggregates the potential investments of the two firms, arranged by the expected profit rate as before.

5. Aggregate investment increases
Investment in the economy increases after a fall in the interest rate. Five projects go ahead, instead of just one.

In Figure 14.10b, the height of the columns remains unchanged, but their width (representing the amount of investment that is profitable in many projects) has increased. This is the result of a permanent increase in demand and the lack of sufficient capacity to meet forecast sales.

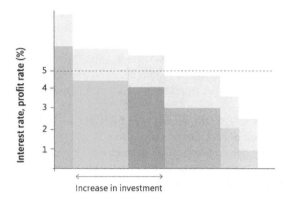

Figure 14.10a The aggregate economy, where the expected rate of profit rises for a given set of projects (supply effect).

1. Interest rate at 5%
With the interest rate equal to 5%, only one project will go ahead.

2. Improvement in supply conditions
The improvement in supply conditions increases the expected rate of profit for each project.

3. Effect on investment
For the same interest rate, investment rises: two more projects go ahead.

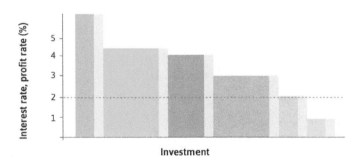

Figure 14.10b The aggregate economy, where the desired capacity rises for each project (demand effect).

1. Interest rate at 2%
With the interest rate equal to 2%, and the initial desired capacity, investment is shown by the darker coloured blocks.

2. Higher forecast demand
Pressure on existing capacity from higher forecast demand raises the desired size of each project, so investment rises to include the lighter coloured blocks.

investment function (aggregate) An equation that shows how investment spending in the economy as a whole depends on other variables, namely, the interest rate and profit expectations. See also: interest rate, profit.

In an economy with many thousands of firms, a downward-sloping line (as in Figure 14.10c) represents the potential investment projects. This is called the **aggregate investment function**. The response of investment to a change in the interest rate is shown as a shift from C to E. Figure 14.10c also shows the effect of a change in the profitability of investment, which arises from supply and demand effects and raises investment from C to D for the same interest rate.

The empirical evidence suggests that business spending on machinery and equipment is not very sensitive to the interest rate. The limited effect of changes in the interest rate on business investment (illustrated by the steepness of the lines in the figure) highlights the importance of the supply- and demand-side factors that shift the investment function (Figures 14.10a and 14.10b).

The interest rate affects investment spending outside the business sector through its effects on households' decisions to purchase new or larger homes, which influence new housing construction. The interest rate also has substantial effects on the demand for durable consumer goods, such as cars and home appliances, which are often purchased using credit.

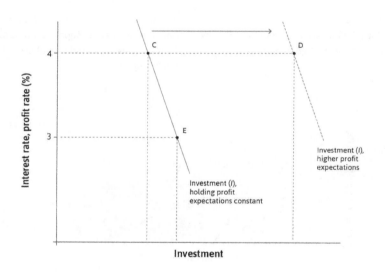

Figure 14.10c Aggregate investment function: Effects of the interest rate and profit expectations.

1. Potential investment projects
In an economy with many thousands of firms, all their potential investment projects are represented by a downward-sloping aggregate investment function.

2. Investment increases
In response to a fall in the interest rate, investment increases from C to E.

3. An increase in profit expectations
This shifts the investment function to the right: if the interest rate is held constant at 4%, investment increases from C to D.

QUESTION 14.4 CHOOSE THE CORRECT ANSWER(S)

Figure 14.9 (page 604) depicts possible investment projects for Firms A and B.

Based on this information, which of the following statements is correct?

☐ Both firms only undertake their project 1 when the interest rate is 5%.

☐ The central bank can ensure that all projects will be undertaken by cutting the interest rate to 1.5%.

☐ When the demand is expected to permanently increase beyond the capacity of existing plants and equipment, the level of investment increases due to an upward shift in the expected profit rate.

☐ An expected rise in energy prices leads to a fall in the expected profit rates, resulting in fewer projects being profitable at a given interest rate. This results in reduced investment.

QUESTION 14.5 CHOOSE THE CORRECT ANSWER(S)

Figure 14.10c (page 606) depicts the aggregate investment function of an economy.

Based on this information, which of the following statements is correct?

☐ *Ceteris paribus*, an increase in the interest rate would lead to a fall in investment due to an inward shift of the investment line.

☐ A rise in corporate tax would shift the investment line outwards.

☐ A forecast of a permanent demand increase shifts the investment line outwards.

☐ A steeper line indicates the higher sensitivity of the level of aggregate investment to changes in interest rate.

14.5 THE MULTIPLIER MODEL: INCLUDING THE GOVERNMENT AND NET EXPORTS

Here we add governments and central banks to the model so that we can show how they can stabilize (or destabilize) the economy after a shock. As before, we assume that firms are willing to supply any amount of goods demanded, so:

$$\text{output} = \text{aggregate demand}$$
$$Y = AD$$

We saw in Unit 13 that when we include the government and interactions with the rest of the world through exports and imports, aggregate demand can be split into these components:

$$\text{aggregate demand} = \text{consumption}$$
$$+ \text{ investment}$$
$$+ \text{ government spending}$$
$$+ \text{ net exports}$$

To understand the aggregate demand function as shown above, it is useful to go through each component in turn:

Consumption

Household consumption spending depends on post-tax income. The government charges a tax t, which we assume is proportional to income. The income left after the payment of tax, $(1 - t)Y$, is called disposable income. The marginal propensity to consume, c_1, is the fraction of disposable income (not pre-tax income) consumed. This means that in the aggregate consumption function:

- Spending on consumption is written as: $C = c_0 + c_1(1 - t)Y$.
- All of the influences on consumption apart from current disposable income are included in autonomous consumption, c_0, and will therefore shift the consumption function in the multiplier diagram. These include wealth and target wealth, collateral effects, and changes in the interest rate.

Investment

We have just seen that investment spending will be influenced by the interest rate and the expected post-tax rate of profit. In the aggregate investment function:

- Spending on investment is a function of the interest rate and the expected post-tax rate of profit.
- *Ceteris paribus,* a higher interest rate reduces investment spending, shifting down the aggregate demand curve.
- A higher expected post-tax rate of profit raises investment spending, shifting up the aggregate demand curve.

Government spending

Much of government spending (excluding transfers) is on general public services, health, and education. Government spending does not change in a systematic way with changes in income. It is referred to as **exogenous**.

An increase in government spending shifts the aggregate demand curve up in the multiplier diagram.

> **exogenous** Coming from outside the model rather than being produced by the workings of the model itself. *See also: endogenous.*

Net exports

The home economy sells goods and services abroad, which are its exports. The amount of foreign goods the home economy demands (its imports) will depend on domestic incomes. The fraction of each additional unit of income that is spent on imports is termed the **marginal propensity to import** (m), which must be between 0 and 1. So we have:

> **marginal propensity to import** The change in total imports associated with a change in total income.

$$\text{net exports} = X - M$$
$$= X - mY$$

If a country's costs of production fall so that it can sell its goods at a lower price on world markets compared to the prices of other countries, the demand for its exports will increase, and domestic demand for imports will fall. We will see in the next unit that the **exchange rate** affects the prices of a country's goods on world markets. Growth in world markets also increases exports. For now, however, we will ignore these effects and assume that exports are also exogenous.

Putting together each of the components of aggregate demand we have:

> **exchange rate** The number of units of home currency that can be exchanged for one unit of foreign currency. For example, the number of Australian dollars (AUD) needed to buy one US dollar (USD) is defined as number of AUD per USD. An increase in this rate is a depreciation of the AUD and a decrease is an appreciation of the AUD.

$$AD = c_0 + c_1(1 - t)Y + I + G + X - mY$$

Both taxes and imports reduce the size of the multiplier. Recall that the multiplier tells us the amount by which an increase in spending (such as a rise in autonomous consumption, investment, government spending, or exports) raises GDP in the economy. When we include taxation and imports in the model, the indirect multiplier effect of a given rise in spending on GDP is smaller. This is because some household income goes straight to the government as taxation, and some is used to buy goods and services produced abroad. Because we assume that the government does not increase its spending when taxes go up, and foreign buyers do not import more of our goods when we import more of theirs, this means that some of an autonomous increase in income does not lead to further indirect increases in income in the domestic economy. Like saving, taxation and imports are referred to as leakages from the circular flow of income. The result is to reduce the indirect effects of an autonomous change in spending on aggregate demand, output, and employment.

To summarize:

- *A higher marginal propensity to import reduces the size of the multiplier*: This makes the aggregate demand curve flatter.
- *An increase in exports shifts the aggregate demand curve up in the multiplier diagram.*
- *An increase in the tax rate reduces the size of the multiplier*: This makes the aggregate demand curve flatter.

The Einstein at the end of this section shows you how to calculate the size of the multiplier in the model once the tax rate and imports are included. To illustrate, we assume a tax rate of 20% (0.2) and a marginal propensity to import of 0.1. Before we introduced the government, we set the marginal propensity to consume, c_1, at 0.6. If we use these numbers in the formula for the multiplier that we calculate in the Einstein, we get the result that the value of the multiplier is $k = 1.6$, compared to 2.5 without including taxation and imports. In the next section we look at how economists have estimated the size of the multiplier from data, why their estimates differ, and why it matters.

EXERCISE 14.3 THE MULTIPLIER MODEL

Consider the multiplier model discussed above.

1. Compare two economies, which differ only in their share of credit-constrained households but are identical otherwise. In which economy is the multiplier larger? Illustrate your answer using a diagram.
2. On the basis of your comparison of the two economies, would you expect the multiplier in an economy to vary over its business cycle?
3. Some economists estimated the size of the multiplier in the Great Depression to be equal to 1.8. Explain how the following characteristics of the US economy at the time could have affected its value:
   (a) the size of government (see Figure 14.1)
   (b) the fact that there were no unemployment benefits
   (c) the fact that the share of imports was small

QUESTION 14.6 CHOOSE THE CORRECT ANSWER(S)

The aggregate demand of an open economy is given by the after-tax domestic consumption C, the investment I (which depends on the interest rate r), the government spending G and net exports $X - M$:

$$AD = C + I + G + X - M$$
$$= c_0 + c_1(1 - t)Y + I + G + X - mY$$

c_0 is autonomous consumption, c_1 is the marginal propensity to consume, and m is the marginal propensity to import. In the economy's equilibrium this equals its output: $AD = Y$. Solving for Y yields:

$$Y = \left(\frac{1}{1 - c_1(1 - t) + m}\right)(c_0 + I(r) + G + X)$$

Given this equation, which of the following increases the multiplier?

☐ A fall in government spending.
☐ A fall in the interest rate.
☐ A fall in the marginal propensity to import.
☐ A rise in the tax rate.

EINSTEIN

The multiplier in an economy with a government and foreign trade

We can again use the fact that there is equilibrium in the goods market when output is equal to aggregate demand to find the multiplier (equilibrium is where the aggregate demand line crosses the 45-degree line in the multiplier diagram). The aggregate demand equation can be rearranged to solve for output and consequently the multiplier:

$$\text{output} = \text{aggregate demand}$$
$$\text{output} = \text{consumption}$$
$$+ \text{ investment}$$
$$+ \text{ government spending}$$
$$+ \text{ net exports}$$

Therefore:

$$Y = c_0 + c_1(1-t)Y + I(r) + G + X - mY$$
$$Y(1 - c_1(1-t) + m) = c_0 + I(r) + G + X$$
$$Y = \underbrace{\frac{1}{(1 - c_1(1-t) + m)}}_{\text{multiplier}} \times \underbrace{(c_0 + I(r) + G + X)}_{\text{demand that doesn't depend on income}}$$

We can see that the multiplier is smaller when we introduce the government and foreign trade:

$$\frac{1}{(1 - c_1(1-t) + m)} < \frac{1}{(1 - c_1)}$$

The reason is that the denominator on the left-hand side is larger than on the right:

$$1 - c_1(1-t) + m > 1 - c_1$$

14.6 FISCAL POLICY: HOW GOVERNMENTS CAN DAMPEN AND AMPLIFY FLUCTUATIONS

There are three main ways that government spending and taxation can dampen fluctuations in the economy:

- *The size of government:* Unlike private investment, government spending on consumption and investment is usually stable. Spending on health and education, which are the two largest government budget items in most countries, does not fluctuate with capacity utilization or with business confidence. These kinds of government spending stabilize the economy. As we have also seen, a higher tax rate dampens fluctuations because it reduces the size of the multiplier.
- *The government provides unemployment benefits:* Although households save to smooth fluctuations in income, few households save enough (that is, self-insure) to cope with an extended period of unemployment. So unemployment benefits help households to smooth consumption. Other programs to redistribute income to the poor have the same smoothing effect.
- *The government can intervene:* It can intervene deliberately to stabilize aggregate demand using **fiscal policy**.

Could workers insure privately against job loss? There are also three reasons why the private market fails, and therefore governments provide unemployment insurance in the form of unemployment benefits:

- *Correlated risk*: In a recession, job loss will be widespread. This means that there will be a surge in insurance claims across the economy and a private provider may be unable to pay out on the scale required. It also means **co-insurance** among a group of neighbours or family members may be of limited use, as the need for help may arise in many households at the same time.
- *Hidden actions*: As we saw in Unit 12, the insurance company cannot observe the reason for the job loss so it would have to insure the employee against a firm cutting back employment due to lack of demand, as well as the worker being fired for inadequate work. This creates a **moral hazard**, because a well-insured person is expected to make less of an effort on the job.
- *Hidden attributes*: Suppose you learn that your firm is in difficulty, but the insurance company does not. This is another example of **asymmetric information**. You will therefore buy insurance when you learn of the likely closure of the firm, and it will be provided at good rates because the insurance company does not know that you are likely to make a claim on them. Workers who know their firm is performing well will not buy insurance. The hidden attributes problem will be true about individuals (hardworking or lazy), as well as firms (successful or failing). The good prospects (those who enjoy working hard, for example) will shun the insurance and the insurer will be left with those likely to face the extra risks of losing their job.

The system of unemployment benefits is part of the **automatic stabilization** that characterizes modern economies. We have already seen another automatic stabilizer: a proportional tax system reduces the size of the multiplier and dampens the business cycle.

fiscal policy Changes in taxes or government spending in order to stabilize the economy. *See also: fiscal stimulus, fiscal multiplier, aggregate demand.*

co-insurance A means of pooling savings across households in order for a household to be able to maintain consumption when it experiences a temporary fall in income or the need for greater expenditure.

hidden actions (problem of) This occurs when some action taken by one party to an exchange is not known or cannot be verified by the other. For example, the employer cannot know (or cannot verify) how hard the worker she has employed is actually working. *Also known as: moral hazard. See also: hidden attributes (problem of).*

In our list, the third role of government in dampening fluctuations is the use of fiscal policy in deliberate stabilization policies: an increase in government spending or cuts in taxation to support aggregate demand in a downturn; or trimming spending and raising taxes to rein in a boom. It can be cumbersome to have these fiscal policy measures approved by a parliament, which has power over budgetary decisions, which is one reason why stabilization policy is often handled through monetary, rather than fiscal, policy. But fiscal policy can also play an important role in stabilization, as we now consider, especially in particularly large downturns.

The paradox of thrift and the fallacy of composition

By comparing a household with the economy as a whole, we better understand the nature of an increase in the government's deficit in a recession. Faced with a household budget deficit, a family worried about their falling wealth cuts spending and saves more. We saw exactly this behaviour in Figure 14.8 when households increased their savings in 1929. Keynes showed that the wisdom of family precautionary saving does not apply to the government when the economy is in a recession.

Compare the attempt to save more by a single household and by all households in the economy simultaneously. Think of a single household cutting expenditures and putting its additional savings in a sock. The money is in the sock for when the household decides it is wise to spend it.

Now, assume that all households cut expenditures and put additional savings in their socks. Assuming nothing else in the economy changes, the additional saving causes lower aggregate consumption spending in the economy. What happens? From the previous section, we can model this as a fall in autonomous consumption, c_0: the aggregate demand curve shifts down. The economy moves through the multiplier process to a lower level of output, income, and employment. The aggregate attempt to increase savings led to a fall in aggregate income, which is known as the **paradox of thrift**. The fact that what is true for one part of the economy is not true of the whole economy is known as the **fallacy of composition**.

A single household can increase its savings if it anticipates bad luck, and the saving will be there if it is unlucky—for example, if someone becomes ill or loses a job. However, if every household does this when the economy is in a recession, this behaviour causes the bad luck: more people lose their jobs. The reason is that in the economy as a whole, spending and earning go together. My spending is your income. Your spending is my income.

moral hazard This term originated in the insurance industry to express the problem that insurers face, namely, the person with home insurance may take less care to avoid fires or other damages to his home, thereby increasing the risk above what it would be in absence of insurance. This term now refers to any situation in which one party to an interaction is deciding on an action that affects the profits or wellbeing of the other but which the affected party cannot control by means of a contract, often because the affected party does not have adequate information on the action. It is also referred to as the 'hidden actions' problem. *See also: hidden actions (problems of), incomplete contract, too big to fail.*

hidden attributes (problem of) This occurs when some attribute of the person engaging in an exchange (or the product or service being provided) is not known to the other parties. An example is that the individual purchasing health insurance knows her own health status, but the insurance company does not. *Also known as: adverse selection. See also: hidden actions (problem of).*

asymmetric information Information that is relevant to the parties in an economic interaction, but is known by some but not by others. *See also: adverse selection, moral hazard.*

automatic stabilizers Characteristics of the tax and transfer system in an economy that have the effect of offsetting an expansion or contraction of the economy. An example is the unemployment benefits system.

paradox of thrift If a single individual consumes less, her savings will increase; but if everyone consumes less, the result may be lower rather than higher savings overall. The attempt to increase saving is thwarted if an increase in the saving rate is unmatched by an increase in investment (or other source of aggregate demand such as government spending on goods and services). The outcome is a reduction in aggregate demand and lower output so that actual levels of saving do not increase.

fallacy of composition Mistaken inference that what is true of the parts (for example a household) must be true of the whole (in this case the economy as a whole). *See also: paradox of thrift.*

What can be done? The government can allow the automatic stabilizers to operate and help absorb the shock. In addition, it can provide an economic stimulus (such as a temporary increase in government spending or a temporary cut in taxation) until business and consumer confidence return and the private sector regains its willingness to spend. Budget deficits rise, but this avoids a deep recession, as Keynes realized.

When a government cuts taxes or increases government spending G in a recession, it is called a **fiscal stimulus**. The aim is to counteract the fall in aggregate demand from the private sector. A tax cut is intended to encourage the private sector to spend more, while an increase in G is a direct addition to aggregate demand. Figure 14.11a shows how an increase in G can offset a decline in private consumption, such as that described by the paradox of thrift. Like an exogenous increase in investment, the rise in G operates via the multiplier, so the increase in output will typically be greater than the increase in G.

> **fiscal stimulus** The use by the government of fiscal policy (via a combination of tax cuts and spending increases) with the intention of increasing aggregate demand. *See also: fiscal multiplier, fiscal, policy, aggregate demand.*

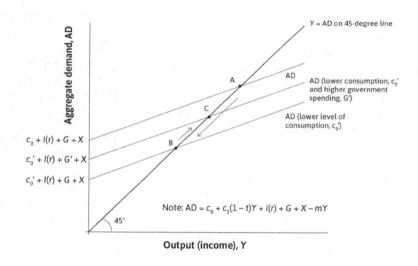

Figure 14.11a Fiscal expansion can offset a decline in private consumption.

1. Goods market equilibrium
The economy starts at point A, in goods market equilibrium, at which aggregate demand is equal to output.

2. The economy moves into recession
This occurs after a fall in consumer confidence, reducing c_0. The aggregate demand line shifts downward and the economy moves from point A to point B.

3. Fiscal stimulus: a rise in G
Suppose that the government then increases spending, from G to G', in order to counteract the decline in aggregate demand. AD shifts back up and the economy moves to point C.

GREAT ECONOMISTS

John Maynard Keynes

John Maynard Keynes (1883–1946) and the Great Depression of the 1930s changed the course of economic thought. Until then, most economists had seen unemployment as the result of some kind of imperfection in the labour market. If this market worked optimally it would equate the supply of, and demand for, workers. The massive and persistent unemployment in the decade prior to the Second World War led Keynes to look again at the problem of joblessness.

Keynes was born into an academic family in Cambridge, UK. He studied mathematics at King's College, Cambridge and then became an economist and prominent follower of the renowned Cambridge professor, Alfred Marshall. Before the First World War, Keynes was a world authority on the quantity theory of money and the gold standard, and held conservative views on economic policy, arguing for a limited role of government. But his views would soon change.

In 1919, following the end of the First World War, Keynes published *The Economic Consequences of the Peace*, which opposed the Versailles settlement that ended the war. This book instantly made him a global celebrity. Keynes rightly argued that Germany could not pay large reparations for the war, and that an attempt to make Germany do this would help provoke a worldwide economic crisis. In 1925, Keynes opposed Britain's return to the gold standard, arguing that this policy would lead to a contraction of the economy. In 1929 there was a financial crash and global crisis. The Great Depression followed. In 1931 Britain was driven off the gold standard.

In response to these dramatic events, Keynes explained that the orthodox monetary policies required by the gold standard would worsen the depression, and that the world needed policies to increase aggregate demand. In 1936, he published *The General Theory of Employment, Interest and Money* in which he set out an economic model to explain these views. *The General Theory* immediately became world famous, particularly for the idea of the multiplier, which is explained in this unit. In *The General Theory*, Keynes reasoned that if interest rates were already very low, then fiscal expansion would be necessary to alleviate depression. Such was the lasting influence of his work that the initial response in many countries to the global economic crisis of 2008 was to apply such Keynesian policies.

During the Second World War, Keynes turned to postwar reconstruction, determined to ensure that the mistakes that followed the First World War would not be repeated. In 1944, with Harry Dexter White of the US, he led an international conference at Bretton Woods in New Hampshire that resulted in the creation of a new international monetary system, managed by the International Monetary Fund, or IMF.

John Maynard Keynes. 2005. *The Economic Consequences of the Peace*. New York, NY: Cosimo Classics.

John Maynard Keynes. 1936. *The General Theory of Employment, Interest and Money* (http://tinyco.re/6855346). London: Palgrave Macmillan.

The Bretton Woods system was designed to avoid the mistakes Keynes had unsuccessfully warned against in the aftermath of the First World War, and to ensure that a country that was in recession (and had balance of payments difficulties) would not need to follow the contractionary policies required by the gold standard. A country like this could use fiscal policy to pursue full employment, while at the same time it could devalue its exchange rate to encourage exports, reduce imports, and achieve a satisfactory balance of payments position.

Keynes led a remarkably varied life. He was an academic, a senior civil servant, owner of the *New Statesman* magazine, financial speculator, chairman of an insurance company, and member of the British House of Lords. He was also the founder of the Arts Council of Great Britain and chairman of the Covent Garden Opera Company. He was married to the Russian ballerina Lydia Lopokova and was a key member of the Bloomsbury Group, a remarkable circle of artistic and literary friends in London, which included the novelist Virginia Woolf.

In 1926, in a pamphlet entitled *The End of Laissez-Faire*, he wrote:

> For my part I think that capitalism, wisely managed, can probably be made more efficient for attaining economic ends than any alternative system yet in sight, but that in itself it is in many ways extremely objectionable. Our problem is to work out a social organization which shall be as efficient as possible without offending our notions of a satisfactory way of life.

John Maynard Keynes. 2004. *The End of Laissez-Faire*. Amherst, NY: Prometheus Books.

How governments can amplify fluctuations

Keynes' argument refers to the cell in the bottom right of Figure 14.12 at the end of this section: poor policymaking that amplifies the business cycle.

Sometimes a government chooses to raise taxes or cut spending during a recession because it is concerned about the effect of a recession on its **budget balance**. The government budget balance is the difference between government revenue less transfers, T, and government spending, G, that is, $(T - G)$. As we have seen, if the economy is in recession, government transfers, like unemployment benefits, rise while tax revenues fall, so the government's budget balance deteriorates and may become negative.

When the government's budget balance is negative, this is called a **government budget deficit**—government spending on goods and services, including investment spending, plus spending on transfers (such as pensions and unemployment benefits) is greater than government tax revenue. A **government budget surplus** is when tax revenue is greater than government spending. To summarize:

government budget balance The difference between government tax revenue and government spending (including government purchases of goods and services, investment spending, and spending on transfers such as pensions and unemployment benefits). *See also: government budget deficit, government budget surplus.*

government budget deficit When the government budget balance is negative. *See also: government budget balance, government budget surplus.*

government budget surplus When the government budget balance is positive. *See also: government budget balance, government budget deficit.*

- *Budget in balance*: $G = T$
- *Budget deficit*: $G > T$
- *Budget surplus*: $G < T$

The worsening of the government's budgetary position in a recession is part of its stabilizing role. Conversely, when the government chooses to override the stabilizers to reduce its deficit, this may amplify fluctuations in the economy.

Suppose a government tries to improve its budgetary position in a recession by cutting its spending. This, like a tax increase, is referred to as austerity policy. Follow the analysis in Figure 14.11b to see how austerity policy can reinforce a recession by further reducing aggregate demand.

Does this argument mean that governments should never impose austerity in order to reduce a fiscal deficit? No—just that a recession is not a wise time to do it. Running government deficits under the wrong economic conditions can be harmful. In a well-designed policy framework, there will be constraints on government action, as we will see in Section 14.8.

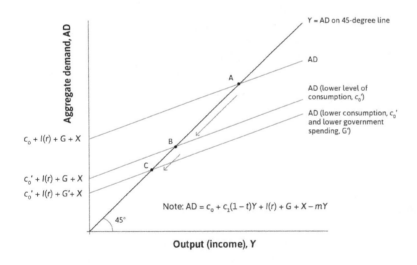

Figure 14.11b Government austerity can worsen a recession.

1. Goods market equilibrium
The economy starts at point A in goods market equilibrium, at which aggregate demand is equal to output.

2. The economy moves into recession
This occurs after a fall in consumer confidence, reducing c_0. The aggregate demand line shifts downward and the economy moves from point A to point B.

3. Austerity policy
Suppose that the government then reduces spending from G to G′, in a bid to offset the deterioration of its budget balance. The recession then feeds back to raise government transfers and reduce tax revenue.

negative feedback (process) A process whereby some initial change sets in motion a process that dampens the initial change. *See also: positive feedback (process).*

positive feedback (process) A process whereby some initial change sets in motion a process that magnifies the initial change. *See also: negative feedback (process).*

The table in Figure 14.12 summarizes the lessons so far. The first row gives examples of how household behaviour may either smooth or disrupt the economy. The terms **negative** and **positive feedback** are used to refer to dampening and amplifying mechanisms in the business cycle.

EXERCISE 14.4 SPENDING CUTS IN A RECESSION
Assume the government is initially in budget balance.

1. Does the government's budget balance improve, deteriorate, or remain unchanged if the government cuts its spending in a recession, *ceteris paribus*? To answer this question, use the example in Figure 14.11b (page 617). Assume the budget was in balance at point A. Once at B, the government cuts G in an attempt to improve its budget balance. Assume there are no unemployment benefits and a linear tax.
2. Evaluate the government's policy.

QUESTION 14.7 CHOOSE THE CORRECT ANSWER(S)
Which of the following statements is correct?

☐ Maintaining fiscal balance in a recession helps to stabilize the economy.
☐ Automatic stabilizers refer to the fact that economic shocks are partly offset by households smoothing their consumption in the face of variable income.
☐ The multiplier on a fiscal stimulus is higher when the economy is functioning at full capacity.
☐ A fiscal stimulus can be implemented by raising spending to directly increase demand, or by cutting taxes to increase private sector demand.

	Dampening mechanisms offset shocks (stabilizing)	Amplifying mechanisms reinforce shocks (may be destabilizing)
Private sector decisions	• Consumption smoothing	• Credit constraints limit consumption smoothing • Rising value of collateral (house prices) can increase wealth above the target level and raise consumption • Rising capacity utilization in a boom encourages investment spending, adding to the boom
Government and central bank decisions	• Automatic stabilizers (for example unemployment benefits) • Stabilization policy (fiscal or monetary)	• Policy mistakes such as limiting the scope of automatic stabilizers in a recession or running deficits during low demand periods while not running surpluses during booms

Figure 14.12 The role of the private sector and the government in the business cycle.

14.7 THE MULTIPLIER AND ECONOMIC POLICYMAKING

In the multiplier model, we have used simple ways of modelling aggregate consumption, investment, trade, and government fiscal policy. This means there are a small number of variables from which the size of the multiplier is calculated (the marginal propensity to consume, the marginal propensity to import, and the tax rate). When we apply the model to the real world, it is important to realize that there is no single multiplier that applies at all times.

The multiplier will be a different size if the economy is operating at full capacity utilization and low unemployment than in a recession. With fully employed resources, a 1% increase in government spending would displace or **crowd out** some private spending in the economy. To consider an extreme case, if all workers are employed, then an increase in government employment can only come about by taking workers out of the private sector. If increased government production were offset exactly by reduced private sector production, then the multiplier would be zero.

We would not normally expect a government to undertake a fiscal expansion when unemployment is very low—although it may in exceptional circumstances like war, as the US did in the later years of the Second World War and in the Vietnam War.

The size of the multiplier will also depend on the expectations of firms and businesses. The economy is not like a bicycle tyre, from which air can be pumped in or let out to keep the pressure at the right level. Households and firms react to policy changes, but they also anticipate them. For example, if firms anticipate that the government will stabilize the economy following a negative shock, this will support business confidence, and the policymaker will be able to use a smaller stimulus. Alternatively, if households think that higher government spending will be followed by higher taxes, those who have the ability to save may put aside more of their money to pay the extra taxes. If this happened, it would reduce the impact of the stimulus.

When the financial crisis in 2008 led to the biggest fall in GDP in many economies since the Great Depression, the world's policymakers expected an answer from economists: would fiscal policy help to stabilize the economy? The multiplier model, inspired by Keynes' analysis of the Great Depression, suggested that it would. But by 2008, many economists doubted that the Keynesian model was still relevant. The crisis has revived interest in it and has led to a greater, though not complete, consensus among economists about the size of the multiplier (see below).

In 2012 a study published by Alan Auerbach and Yuriy Gorodnichenko, two economists, showed how the multiplier varies in size according to whether the economy is in a recession or in an expansion. This is exactly the insight that policymakers needed in 2008.

For the US, their study suggested a $1 increase in government spending in the US raises output by about $1.50 to $2.00 in a recession, but only about $0.50 in an expansion. Auerbach and Gorodnichenko extended their research to other countries and found similar results. They also found that the effect of autonomous increases in spending in one country had spillover effects on the countries with which they trade. These effects were about the same magnitude as the indirect effects of second, third, and further rounds of spending in the home country.

> **CROWDING OUT**
> The effect of an increase in government spending in reducing private spending, as would be expected for example in an economy working at full capacity utilization, or when a fiscal expansion is associated with a rise in the interest rate.

This is a summary of the paper published in 2012: Alan Auerbach and Yuriy Gorodnichenko. 2015. 'How Powerful Are Fiscal Multipliers in Recessions?' (http://tinyco.re/3018428). *NBER Reporter 2015 Research Summary.*

HOW ECONOMISTS LEARN FROM FACTS

The Mafia and the multiplier

It may surprise you that economists have used the Italian government's struggle against the Mafia to uncover the size of the multiplier, but that's what Antonio Acconcia, Giancarlo Corsetti, and Saverio Simonelli were able to do. Adopting the **natural experiment** method to address the problem of **reverse causality**, they used data on Mafia-related dismissals of local politicians to isolate the variation in public spending that is not caused by variations in output.

After legal changes in 1991, the central government dismissed provincial councils in Italy who were revealed to have close links with the Mafia, and appointed new officials in their place. These technocrats cut local spending by 20% on average. The change in public spending occurred because of the Mafia links, through their effect on the replacement of government officials. And because there is no direct causal link from proximity to the Mafia to the variation in output, proximity to the Mafia can be used to uncover the causal effect of a change in public spending on output. This situation is illustrated in Figure 14.13.

natural experiment An empirical study exploiting naturally occurring statistical controls in which researchers do not have the ability to assign participants to treatment and control groups, as is the case in conventional experiments. Instead, differences in law, policy, weather, or other events can offer the opportunity to analyse populations as if they had been part of an experiment. The validity of such studies depends on the premise that the assignment of subjects to the naturally occurring treatment and control groups can be plausibly argued to be random.
reverse causality A two-way causal relationship in which A affects B and B also affects A.

Antonio Acconcia, Giancarlo Corsetti, and Saverio Simonelli. 2014. 'Mafia and Public Spending: Evidence on the Fiscal Multiplier from a Quasi-Experiment'. *American Economic Review* 104 (7) (July): pp. 2185–2209.

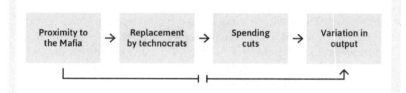

Figure 14.13 Using Mafia proximity to estimate the multiplier.

Using this method, the researchers were able to estimate multipliers of 1.5 at the local level.

Economists have used their ingenuity to come up with methods of estimating the size of the multiplier and the implication of its operation for jobs. Using the US stimulus program that was implemented in the wake of the financial crisis (the American Recovery and Reinvestment Act of 2009 (http://tinyco.re/7003843), a $787 billion fiscal stimulus), we would expect that US states that were more severely hit by the financial crisis would have had higher unemployment and attracted more stimulus spending by the government. So unemployment causes more spending in those states. This makes it difficult to estimate the effect of higher spending on output and unemployment, which is what we want to do if we want to know the size of the multiplier.

One approach to get around this problem of reverse causality is to make use of the fact that some of the spending in the US stimulus program was distributed to US states using a formula that was unrelated to the severity of the recession experienced in each state. For example, some road-repair expenditures funded by the stimulus package were based on the length of highway in each state.

Given the formula for allocating road-building funds and the fact that more miles of highway has no direct effect on the change in unemployment, this allows us to answer the question: were more jobs created in states that received more stimulus spending?

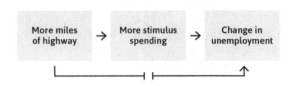

Figure 14.14 Using US stimulus highway spending to estimate the multiplier.

The results of studies using this approach estimated a multiplier of 2, and suggest that the American Recovery and Reinvestment Act created between 1 million and 3 million new jobs.

In spite of scepticism among some economists before the 2008 crisis that the multiplier was greater than one, policymakers around the world embarked on fiscal stimulus programs in 2008–09. Fiscal stimulus was credited with helping to avert another Great Depression, as we will see in Unit 17.

WHEN ECONOMISTS DISAGREE

How responsive is the economy to government spending?
There are few questions in economic policy discussed as heatedly in the years since the financial crisis in 2008 as the size of the fiscal multiplier: what is the effect on GDP of a 1% increase in government spending?

Much of the heat is generated by political differences among those involved. People who favour greater government expenditure tend to think the multiplier is large, while those who would like a smaller government tend to think that it is small. (We don't know whether this correlation is because their beliefs about government influence their estimates of the size of the multiplier, or the other way round.)

This debate has been going on since the first theoretical formalization of the multiplier by John Maynard Keynes in the 1930s. The recent economic crisis has revitalized it for two reasons:

1. *Monetary policy could not be used*: Following the financial crisis, several major economies remained in recession despite central banks cutting interest rates to very close to zero. As we will see in the next unit, interest rates cannot be cut below zero, so governments wanted to

Sylvain Leduc and Daniel Wilson. 2015. 'Are State Governments Roadblocks to Federal Stimulus? Evidence on the Flypaper Effect of Highway Grants in the 2009 Recovery Act' (http://tinyco.re/3885744). Federal Reserve Bank of San Francisco Working Paper 2013–16 (September).

The debate continues. Here are some easily available resources:

Miguel Almunia, Agustín Bénétrix, Barry Eichengreen, Kevin H. O'Rourke, and Gisela Rua. 2010. 'From Great Depression to Great Credit Crisis: Similarities, Differences and Lessons.' *Economic Policy* 25 (62) (April): pp. 219–65.
Tim Harford. 2010. 'Stimulus Spending Might Not Be as Stimulating as We Think' (http://tinyco.re/8583440). *Financial Times*.
Paul Krugman. 2012. 'A Tragic Vindication' (http://tinyco.re/6611089). Paul Krugman – *New York Times* Blog. Updated 9 October 2012.
Jonathan Portes. 2012. 'What Explains Poor Growth in the UK? The IMF Thinks It's Fiscal Policy' (http://tinyco.re/8763401). *National Institute of Economic and Social Research Blog*. Updated 9 October 2012.
Noah Smith. 2013. 'Why the Multiplier Doesn't Matter' (http://tinyco.re/7260376). *Noahpinion*. Updated 7 January 2013.
Simon Wren-Lewis. 2012. 'Multiplier Theory: One Is the Magic Number' (http://tinyco.re/7820994). *Mainly Macro*. Updated 24 August 2012.

know if the fiscal stimulus of an increase in government spending would help stabilize the economy.

2. *Arguments about whether austerity works*: After the Eurozone crisis in 2010, many European countries that were in recession adopted austerity measures of cutting government spending, with the objective of bringing their public finances back to balance.

In both stimulus and austerity, the success of the policy depends on the size of the multiplier. If the multiplier is negative—which could happen if a rising fiscal deficit causes a large reduction in confidence—a stimulus package would lead to a reduction in GDP, and an austerity policy would cause GDP to rise. If the multiplier is positive but less than 1, a fiscal stimulus would raise GDP but by less than the increase in government spending. If, as in our multiplier model, the multiplier is greater than 1, a fiscal stimulus would raise GDP by more than the increase in government spending and a policy of austerity would reinforce the recession conditions.

International Monetary Fund. 2012. *World Economic Outlook October: Coping with High Debt and Sluggish Growth* (http://tinyco.re/ 5970823).

Depending on methodologies and assumptions, economists have put forward different estimates of multipliers, from negative numbers to values greater than 2. For instance, members of President Obama's Council of Economic Advisors estimated the multiplier as 1.6 when they prepared the American Recovery and Reinvestment Act of 2009. The International Monetary Fund presented estimates in 2012 that multipliers in advanced economies were, after the crisis, between 0.9 and 1.7.

To be effective, government spending needs to put resources that would otherwise be idle into productive use. These resources can be unemployed (or underemployed) workers, as well as offices, shops, or factories functioning with spare capacity. When an economy functions at full capacity (with no idle resources), extra government spending will crowd out private spending.

Robert J. Barro. 2009. 'Government Spending Is No Free Lunch.' *The Wall Street Journal*.

Paul Krugman. 2009. 'War and Non-Remembrance' (http://tinyco.re/ 8410113). Paul Krugman – *New York Times* Blog.

Robert Barro and Paul Krugman, the economists, disagreed about the size of the multiplier in the weeks that followed the enactment of the American Recovery and Reinvestment Act in early 2009. Using data on government defence spending during the Second World War, Barro concluded that the multiplier was not larger than 0.8. That is, spending $1 on military equipment yielded only 80 cents of output. However, Krugman responded that in wartime there are no idle productive resources to take advantage of. People of working age were in work supporting the war effort in factories, and the government used rationing to depress private consumption.

In the recessions that followed the Eurozone crisis in 2010, just as new economic research was finding evidence that multipliers in recessions were well above one, many European governments implemented fiscal austerity to balance their budgets. These countries had poor growth outcomes—another sign that, in deep recessions, the multiplier is greater than one. But some Eurozone countries had no choice but to adopt austerity policies. As we will see in the next section, they had lost the ability to borrow.

EXERCISE 14.5 METHODS TO ESTIMATE THE MULTIPLIER
Consider the three methods discussed in this unit that have been used to estimate the size of the multiplier: the Mafia-related dismissals in Italy, the stimulus highway spending in the US, and wartime defence spending in the US.

Why do you think estimates of the size of the multiplier vary? Use the material in this unit to support your explanation.

EXERCISE 14.6 CONTRIBUTIONS TO CHANGE IN REAL GROSS DOMESTIC PRODUCT OVER THE BUSINESS CYCLE
In the table in Figure 13.8 (page 559) we showed the contributions of the main components of expenditure (C, I, G, and $X - M$) made to US GDP growth during the recession of 2009. We can use FRED to see whether these contributions changed during the recovery phase of the recession.

Go to the FRED website (http://tinyco.re/8136544). Search for 'Contribution to GDP' using the search bar, and select these four annual series:

- Contribution to percentage change in real gross domestic product: Personal consumption expenditures
- Contribution to percentage change in real gross domestic product: Gross private domestic investment
- Contribution to percentage change in real gross domestic product: Government consumption expenditure and gross investment
- Contributions to percentage change in real gross domestic product: Net exports of goods and services

Click the 'Add to Graph' button to create a graph of the four series. Use the 'Add Data Series' option to add a series for the growth of real GDP.

1. Do the contributions to GDP add up approximately to the growth of GDP?

Now use the data you have downloaded to carry out the following tasks for the period from 2007 to 2014:

2. Describe the contributions to US GDP growth in the recession (2008 Q1 to 2009 Q2) and in the recovery phase from 2009 Q3 of the business cycle. If you analyse the data using the FRED graph, you will see the recession shaded in the chart. Prepare a table like the one in Figure 13.8 (page 559).
3. What might explain the differences seen in the role of consumption and investment during the recession and recovery phases of the business cycle?
4. From the contribution to GDP growth of government consumption and investment expenditure, what can you infer about the US government's fiscal policy during the crisis?

Note: To make sure you understand how these FRED graphs are created, you may want to extract the data into your spreadsheet and reproduce the series.

EXERCISE 14.7 THE FALL OF FRANCE
In an article from August 2014, 'The Fall of France' (http://tinyco.re/ 7111032), Paul Krugman criticizes the austerity policy implemented in France.

Use what you have learned about the fiscal multiplier to explain why, in Krugman's opinion, fiscal austerity in France (and more generally in Europe) would fail (explain carefully what you think Krugman means by 'fail').

EXERCISE 14.8 STIMULUS WITHOUT MORE DEBT

Read 'Stimulus, Without More Debt' (http://tinyco.re/9857908) by Robert Shiller.

Assume the economy is in a recession. The government has a high level of debt and wants to set a balanced budget, that is, $G = T$. How can the government achieve a fiscal stimulus effect on GDP whilst keeping the budget balanced?

To answer the question, take the following steps:

- Show how this is possible in a multiplier diagram, ensuring that you label the relevant intercepts and angles. Make the diagram sufficiently accurate so that the exact size of the multiplier is visible.
- Explain in words how the government can achieve such a fiscal stimulus effect whilst keeping the budget balanced.
- Derive the balanced budget multiplier using algebra. (Hint: You will need to write down expressions for the change in GDP associated with a change in both G and T and set these equal to each other.)
- Comment briefly on any disadvantages you see with the use of this balanced budget fiscal stimulus.

You can make the following assumptions:

- Assume a lump sum tax. This means that the tax does not depend on the level of income, $T = T$, rather than our usual assumption that $T = tY$.
- Also assume that the country does not have any imports or exports.

QUESTION 14.8 CHOOSE THE CORRECT ANSWER(S)

Which of the following statements is correct regarding the multiplier?

☐ Economists tend to agree on their estimates of the multiplier.
☐ Reverse causation can be a problem when estimating the multiplier empirically.
☐ If households anticipate that increased government spending will be funded by future tax increases, then the multiplier will be higher.
☐ If firms anticipate that the government's fiscal policy will be effective, then the multiplier will be higher.

14.8 THE GOVERNMENT'S FINANCES

From the paradox of thrift, we learned that in a recession, it is counterproductive for the government to offset the automatic stabilization of the economy. We have also learned that using a fiscal stimulus to boost aggregate demand in a deep recession can be justified, under conditions in which the multiplier is greater than one. So why are stimulus policies often followed by policies of austerity? The answer is the **government's debt**. To understand why, we turn to the government's revenue and its expenditure.

government debt The sum of all the bonds the government has sold over the years to finance its deficits, minus the ones that have matured.

Revenue

Governments raise revenue in the form of income taxes and taxes on spending, often called Value Added Tax (VAT) or sales tax. They also raise money from a variety of other sources including taxes on products like alcohol, tobacco, and petrol—and on wealth, including through inheritance taxes.

Expenditure

Government expenditure includes health, education, and defence, as well as public investment such as roads and schools.

Government revenue is also used to fund social security transfers, which include unemployment benefits, pensions, and disability benefits. The government also has to pay interest on its debt. Transfers and interest payments are paid out of government revenues, but they do not count in G because the government is not spending money on goods or services.

Government primary deficit

The government deficit, excluding interest payments on its debt, is called the **primary budget deficit** and is measured by $G − T$, where T is tax revenue minus transfers (assumed to be tY in the multiplier model with a proportional tax rate, t). If the initial situation is one of a zero primary deficit, then it automatically worsens in a business cycle downturn. When the downturn reverses, the government's primary budget deficit will decline, and in the upswing, the government will have higher revenues than spending.

When there is a budget deficit, this means the government must borrow to cover the gap between its revenue and its expenditure. The government borrows by selling bonds. Firms and households buy the bonds. Households usually buy them indirectly, because they are bought by pension funds, from which households buy pensions. The sale of bonds adds to the government's debt.

Because of the existence of global financial markets, foreigners can also buy home country bonds. Government bonds are attractive to investors because they pay a fixed interest rate and because they are generally considered a safe investment: the default risk on government bonds is usually low. Investors are likely to want to hold a mixture of safe and risky assets, and government bonds are normally at the safe end of the spectrum.

A **sovereign debt crisis** is a situation in which government bonds come to be considered risky. Such crises are not uncommon in developing and emerging economies, but they are rare in advanced economies. However, in 2010, there was an increase in interest rates on bonds issued by the Irish, Greek, Spanish, and Portuguese governments, which was a signal of a sharp increase in default risk—the likelihood that the government would be unable to make the required payments on its debt. It marked the start of the Eurozone crisis. Governments of countries experiencing a sovereign debt crisis may have no alternative to austerity policies if they can no longer borrow, because in this case they cannot spend more than the tax revenue they receive.

A large stock of debt relative to GDP can be a problem because, like a household, the government has to pay interest on its debt and it has to raise revenue to pay the interest, which may require raising tax rates. However, governments are not like households in that there is no point at which they need to have paid off all their stock of debt—as one set of bonds matures, governments will typically issue more bonds, maintaining a stock of debt (this is called rolling over debt, which firms also typically do to finance their operations). Indeed, because government bonds are generally seen as a safe

primary deficit The government deficit (its revenue minus its expenditure) excluding interest payments on its debt. *See also: government debt.*

sovereign debt crisis A situation in which government bonds come to be considered so risky that the government may not be able to continue to borrow. If so, the government cannot spend more than the tax revenue they receive.

asset outside periods of crisis, there is usually demand for **government debt** from private investors. As the long-run data for the UK in Figure 14.15 makes clear, there are no general rules about how much debt is safe for governments to have.

Figure 14.15 shows the path of UK government debt from 1700 to 2014. The level of indebtedness of a government is measured in relation to the size of the economy, that is, as a percentage of GDP. The two big upward spikes in the British debt to GDP ratio in the twentieth century were caused by the need for the government to borrow to finance the war effort.

Financial crises also raise government debt. Governments borrow both to bail out failing banks and to support the economy in the lengthy recessions that follow financial crises. The UK's debt-to-GDP ratio rapidly doubled to more than 80% after the 2008 global financial crisis.

Note also that, although the UK government emerged from the Second World War with a very high level of debt, it fell rapidly in the following decades: from 260% of GDP to 50% by the 1980s. Why? The British government ran a primary budget surplus in every year except one from 1948 until 1973, which helped to reduce the debt-to-GDP ratio. But the ratio may also fall even when there is a primary budget deficit, as long as the growth rate of the economy is higher than the interest rate. During the period of rapid reduction of the British debt ratio, in addition to the primary surpluses, there was moderate growth, low nominal interest rates set by the government, and moderate inflation.

Why does inflation help a country reduce its debt ratio? Because the face value of government bonds (the level of debt) is denominated in nominal terms. For instance, the issue of 10-year bonds in 1950 would promise to repay £1 million in 1960. So if inflation was moderately high during the 1950s, then nominal GDP would be growing fast while that £1 million owed in 1960 would remain constant, meaning the debt would have shrunk relative to GDP. As we discuss further in Unit 15, inflation reduces the real value of debt.

Ryland Thomas and Nicholas Dimsdale. (2017). 'A Millennium of UK Data' (http://tinyco.re/5827360). Bank of England OBRA dataset.

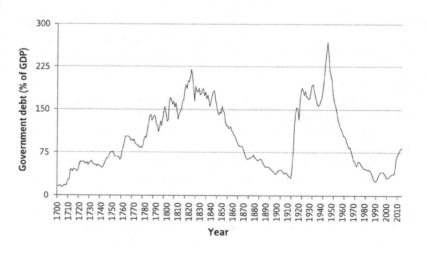

Figure 14.15 UK government debt as a percentage of GDP (1700–2014).

For many advanced economies, there have been extended periods in which the growth rate has been higher than the interest rate. Brad DeLong, an economist, has pointed out that this has been true for the US for almost all of the last 125 years.

Bradford DeLong. 2015. 'Draft for Rethinking Macroeconomics Conference Fiscal Policy Panel' (http://tinyco.re/4631043). *Washington Center for Equitable Growth.* Updated 5 April 2015.

EXERCISE 14.9 EFFICIENCY AND FAIRNESS

How would you use the criteria of **Pareto improvement** and **fairness** to evaluate the use of stimulus policies and bank bailouts following the global financial crisis of 2007–2008?

Hint: you might want to look back at Sections 5.2 and 5.3 in Unit 5, where the concepts are explained.

Pareto improvement A change that benefits at least one person without making anyone else worse off. *See also: Pareto dominant.*

fairness A way to evaluate an allocation based on one's conception of justice.

'A Load to Bear' (http://tinyco.re/9740912). *The Economist.* Updated 26 November 2009.

Countries with aging populations have demographic trends that imply upward pressure on the debt-to-GDP ratio, because the proportion of government revenue spent on state pensions, healthcare, and social care for the elderly will increase. Many governments and voters are facing a difficult choice: do they limit benefits, or put up taxes?

The lessons from our discussion of fiscal policy and government debt are:

- *Automatic stabilizers play a useful role*: Over the course of the business cycle, they contribute to economic wellbeing.
- *If additional fiscal stimulus is used, this ought to be reversed later*: This reversal can take place when the economy is growing again. If a stimulus is not reversed, the government debt-to-GDP ratio will rise.
- *Financial crises and wars increase government debt.*
- *Inflation reduces the debt burden of the government*: Likewise, deflation increases it.
- *An ever-increasing debt ratio is unsustainable*: But there is no rule that says exactly how much debt is problematic.
- *If the growth rate is below the interest rate, it is necessary to run primary government surpluses as they stabilize and reduce the debt ratio*: Attempting to reduce the debt ratio rapidly, however, is counterproductive if it depresses growth.

To get a feel for the effects of policy interventions, *The Economist* provides a modelling tool (http://tinyco.re/3107039) to experiment as a hypothetical policymaker. Try different combinations of primary budget balance, growth rate, nominal interest rate, and inflation rate as methods of preventing the debt ratio from continuously rising in a country of your choice.

14.9 FISCAL POLICY AND THE REST OF THE WORLD

In Unit 13 we saw that agrarian economies suffered shocks from wars, disease, and the weather. In Unit 11, we saw that the American Civil War affected economies including Brazil, India and the UK. In modern economies, what happens in the rest of the world is a source of shocks, and also affects how domestic economic policy works. To avoid making mistakes, policymakers need to know about these interactions.

Foreign markets matter

Fluctuations in growth in important markets abroad can explain why the economy moves into an upswing or downswing: this is a change in the net export component of aggregate demand, that is, $(X - M)$. China, for example, is a very important market for Australian exports (32% of Australian exports went to China in 2013, accounting for 6.5% of Australian aggregate demand). When the Chinese economy slowed down from a growth rate of 10.6% in 2010 to 7.8% in 2013, this was transmitted directly to a slowdown in growth in Australia via a fall in net exports.

Similarly, the slowdown in the Eurozone because of the 2010 crisis that followed the 2008 global financial crisis, was an important reason for the sluggishness of the British economy's exit from recession. This is because a high proportion of UK exports go to the EU. For example, 44% of the UK's exports went to the EU in 2013, accounting for 13% of UK aggregate demand.

Imports dampen domestic fluctuations

As we have seen, the size of the multiplier is reduced by the marginal propensity to import. When autonomous demand goes up, it stimulates spending, and some of the products bought are produced abroad. This dampens the domestic upswing.

Trade constrains the use of fiscal stimulus

Trade with other countries constrains the ability of domestic fiscal policymakers to use stimulus policies in a recession. A striking example comes from France in the 1980s. At the start of the 1980s, the French economy remained weak following the oil shocks of the 1970s, which disrupted the world economy. In 1981, the socialist candidate François Mitterrand won the presidential election. His appointed prime minister, Pierre Mauroy, implemented a program to stimulate aggregate demand through increased government spending and tax cuts (in the multiplier model, this is a rise in G and a fall in t, the tax rate).

In Figure 14.16, we show what happened in France and in its biggest trading partner, Germany. The blue bars show the outcomes for France and the red bars show the outcomes for Germany. The figure presents the outcomes for three years. In the first year, there was no stimulus, in the second, there was a fiscal stimulus in France, and the third year was the year following the stimulus.

If you look at Figure 14.16, you will see that the budget balance in France (measured as $(T - G)/Y$) becomes negative. We can read this as saying that from a balanced budget in 1980, there was a budget deficit of nearly 3% of GDP in 1982, which increased further by 1983.

Meanwhile, in Germany, the budget remained close to balance through the three years. The budget surpluses were 0%, 0%, and 0.2% respectively.

The expansionary demand policy in France was an exception in Europe. There was an initial boost to French growth in 1982 (from 1.6% to 2.4%) but it quickly vanished, with growth falling back to 1.2% in 1983. Why?

The upturn in the French economy led French households to increase their spending, but much of this was on foreign goods. The French stimulus spilled over to countries that produced more competitive products, like Japan (electronic goods) and Germany (cars). There was a surge of imports into France: measured relative to the level in 1979, imports were higher by 17.9%, as shown in Figure 14.16. Germany's exports were higher by 17.1% in 1982 and by nearly 14% in 1983. As a result, GDP growth was higher in Germany than in France in 1983. The French stimulus policy mostly bene-fitted its trading partners who had more competitive goods. France slipped behind the pack of European countries, with lower growth and a high gov-ernment budget deficit (above 3% in 1983).

The failure of Mitterrand's policy was reflected in economic terms by pressure on the French franc (the unit of currency during the period). Between 1981 and 1983, the French government had to devalue the franc three times in an effort to make French goods more competitive with those produced abroad. Mauroy stepped down in 1984 and the new prime minister introduced an austerity policy.

The Mitterrand experiment highlights the limits of using a fiscal stimulus to successfully stabilize a deep recession. In the case of France, the policy was badly designed and it delayed the adjustment of the French eco-nomy to the shocks that had affected it in the 1970s. Note that the problem in France was not only high unemployment. Injecting more aggregate demand stimulated spending, but not spending on French output.

The multiplier was very low and the spillover effects to other economies meant that most of the stimulus leaked out of France. Had the major Euro-pean economies adopted fiscal expansionary policies simultaneously the results would have been different, as the spillover effects of Germany, say, would have stimulated the French economy. This is an example of poor policymaking due to a failure to understand the country's links with the rest of the world. It would fit in the final row of the third column in Figure 14.12 (page 618).

A fiscal stimulus may not be the only (or best) policy option in a recession: Olivier Blanchard, the former chief economist of the IMF, explains how fiscal consolidation worked in the case of Latvia in 2008, even though he had initially advised against it.

Olivier Blanchard. 2012. 'Lessons from Latvia' (http://tinyco.re/8173211). *IMFdirect – The IMF Blog*. Updated 11 June 2012.

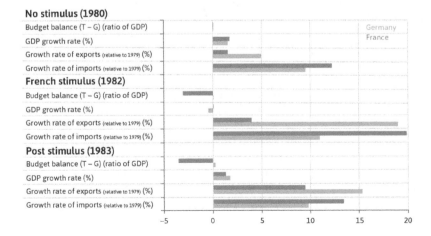

OECD. 2015. OECD Statistics (http://tinyco.re/9377362).

Figure 14.16 Successes and failures of the French fiscal stimulus (1980–1983).

coordination game A game in which there are two Nash equilibria, of which one may be Pareto superior to the other. *Also known as: assurance game.*

EXERCISE 14.10 COORDINATING A STIMULUS
Assume the world is made up of just two countries, or blocs, called North and South. The world is in a deep recession. The situation can be described using the **coordination game** used for investment in Unit 13. Here the two strategies are Stimulus and No stimulus.

Explain in words how the coordination game reflects the problems faced by policymakers in the two countries that arise because of their interdependence.

QUESTION 14.9 CHOOSE THE CORRECT ANSWER(S)
Figure 14.16 (page 629) shows the effects of France's increased government spending and tax cuts in 1982 on the economies of France and Germany.

Based on this information, which of the following statements are correct?

☐ The French budget balance worsened by more than 3% as a result of the fiscal expansion.
☐ The fiscal expansion successfully resulted in a long-run shift in the French GDP growth rate to above 2%.
☐ The German economy benefitted from the spillover effect of higher French imports of German goods.
☐ Fiscal expansionary policy should never be adopted by European economies, as they have high levels of trade with each other.

14.10 AGGREGATE DEMAND AND UNEMPLOYMENT

We now have two models for thinking about total output, employment, and the unemployment rate in the economy:

supply side (aggregate economy) How labour and capital are used to produce goods and services. It uses the labour market model (also referred to as the wage-setting curve and price-setting curve model). *See also: demand side (aggregate economy).*

demand side (aggregate economy) How spending decisions generate demand for goods and services, and as a result, employment and output. It uses the multiplier model. *See also: supply side (aggregate economy).*

multiplier model A model of aggregate demand that includes the multiplier process. *See also: fiscal multiplier, multiplier process.*

- *The **supply side** (labour market) model*: One model, set out in Unit 9, is of the supply side of the economy and focuses on how labour is employed to produce goods and services. This is called the labour market model (or the wage-setting curve and price-setting curve model).
- *The **demand side** (**multiplier**) **model**: The other is of the demand side of the economy and explains how spending decisions generate demand for goods and services and, as a result, employment and output. This is the multiplier model.

When we put the models together, we will be able to explain how the economy fluctuates around the long-run labour market equilibrium over the business cycle.

The labour market model from Unit 9 is shown in Figure 14.17, and the equilibrium in the labour market is where the wage- and price-setting curves intersect. We will see that the economy tends to fluctuate over the business cycle around the unemployment rate shown at point A. In the example in Figure 14.17, the unemployment rate at equilibrium is 5%.

Figure 14.18 places the multiplier diagram beneath the labour market diagram. Note that in the labour market diagram, the horizontal axis measures the number of workers, so we can measure employment and unemployment along it. In the multiplier diagram, output is on the horizontal axis. The **production function** connects employment and output, and in this model, the production function is very simple.

We assume that labour productivity is constant and equal to λ ('lambda'), so the production function is:

$$Y = \lambda N$$

To allow us to draw the demand-side model underneath the supply-side model, we assume λ = 1, and so $Y = N$.

Short-term fluctuations in employment are caused by changes in aggregate demand. As we saw in Unit 9, when employment is below the labour market equilibrium because of deficient aggregate demand, the additional unemployment is called **cyclical unemployment**. If there is excess demand, above labour market equilibrium, then unemployment is below its equilibrium level.

In Figure 14.19, the economy is initially at labour market equilibrium at point A with unemployment of 5%. The level of output here is called the normal level of output. This means that the level of aggregate demand must be as shown by the aggregate demand curve labelled 'normal'. Any other level of aggregate demand would produce a different level of employment.

In our study of business cycle fluctuations using the multiplier model, we have made a number of *ceteris paribus* assumptions. We have assumed that prices, wages, the capital stock, technology, and institutions are constant. We use the term **short run** to refer to these assumptions. The purpose of the model is to predict what happens to output, aggregate demand, and employment when there is a demand shock (a shock to

production function A graphical or mathematical expression describing the amount of output that can be produced by any given amount or combination of input(s). The function describes differing technologies capable of producing the same thing.

cyclical unemployment The increase in unemployment above equilibrium unemployment caused by a fall in aggregate demand associated with the business cycle. *Also known as: demand-deficient unemployment. See also: equilibrium unemployment.*

short run (model) The term does not refer to a period of time, but instead to what is exogenous: prices, wages, the capital stock, technology, institutions. *See also: price, wages, capital, technology, institutions, medium run (model), long run (model).*

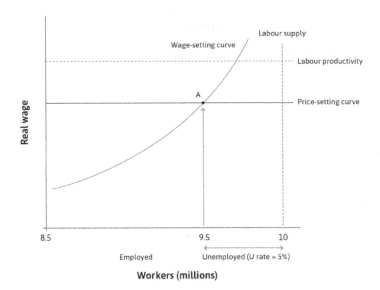

Figure 14.17 The supply side of the aggregate economy: The labour market.

investment, consumption or exports), or when policymakers use fiscal policy or monetary policy to shift the aggregate demand curve.

medium run (model) The term does not refer to a period of time, but instead to what is exogenous. In this case capital stock, technology, and institutions are exogenous. Output, employment, prices, and wages are endogenous. *See also: capital, technology, institutions, short run (model), long run (model)*.

Notice that in Figure 14.19, the labour market is not in equilibrium when output is higher or lower than normal. The labour market model is a **medium-run** model where wages and prices can change, unlike in the multiplier model, which is a **short-run** model. So a short-run equilibrium in the multiplier model may not be a medium-run equilibrium in the labour market model.

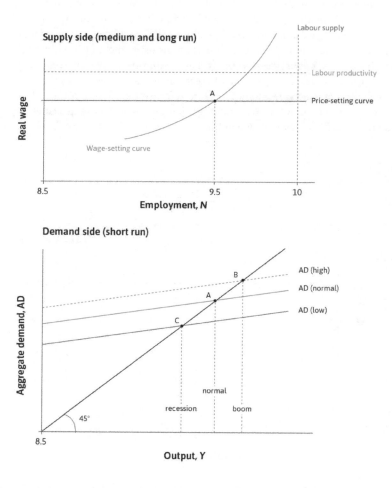

Figure 14.18 The supply side and the demand side of the aggregate economy.

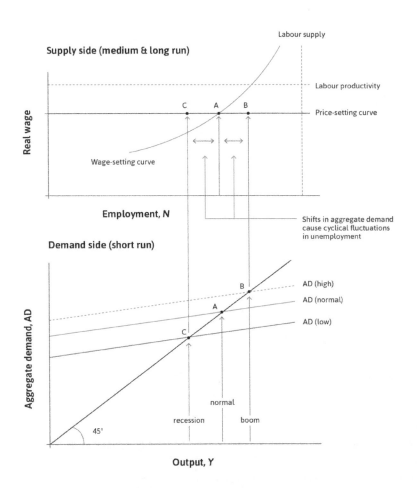

Figure 14.19 Business cycle fluctuations around equilibrium unemployment.

1. Labour market equilibrium
The economy is initially at labour market equilibrium at point A with unemployment of 5%. The level of aggregate demand must be as shown by the aggregate demand curve labelled 'normal'.

2. A boom
Consider a rise in investment that shifts the aggregate demand curve up to AD (high), so that output and employment rise. The economy is at B: with the boom, unemployment falls below 5%. The additional employment is called cyclical employment.

3. A slump
If the aggregate demand curve shifts down, then through the multiplier process, output and employment fall to C. Unemployment rises above 5%. The additional unemployment is called cyclical unemployment.

long run (model) The term does not refer to a period of time, but instead to what is exogenous. A long-run cost curve, for example, refers to costs when the firm can fully adjust all of the inputs including its capital goods; but technology and the economy's institutions are exogenous. *See also: technology, institutions, short run (model), medium run (model).*

- *In Unit 15, the business cycle*: We develop the model in Figure 14.19 by asking what happens to wages and prices in a boom and in a recession.
- *In Unit 16, the long run*: We use the wage-setting curve and the price-setting curves to study the **long run**, where output, employment, prices and wages can change, as well as institutions and technologies. We ask how changes in basic institutions and policies such as the weakening of trade unions, the increase in competition in markets for goods and services, or new labour-saving technologies will affect the aggregate economy.

The table in Figure 14.20 summarizes the different models we will use to study the aggregate economy.

Unit	Run	What is exogenous?	What is endogenous	Problem to be addressed	Appropriate policies	Model to use
13, 14	Short	Prices, wages, capital stock, technology, institutions	Employment, demand, output	Demand shifts affect unemployment	Demand side	Multiplier
14, 15	Medium	Capital stock, technology, institutions	Employment, demand, output, prices, wages	Demand and supply shifts affect unemployment, inflation and equilibrium unemployment	Demand side, supply side	Labour market; Phillips curve
16	Long	Technology, institutions	Employment, demand, output, prices, wages and capital stock	Shifts in profit conditions and changes in institutions affect equilibrium unemployment and real wages	Supply side	Labour market model with firm entry and exit

Figure 14.20 Models to study the aggregate economy.

QUESTION 14.10 CHOOSE THE CORRECT ANSWER(S)

The following are the labour market and the multiplier diagrams, representing the medium-run supply side and the short-run demand side of the aggregate economy, respectively:

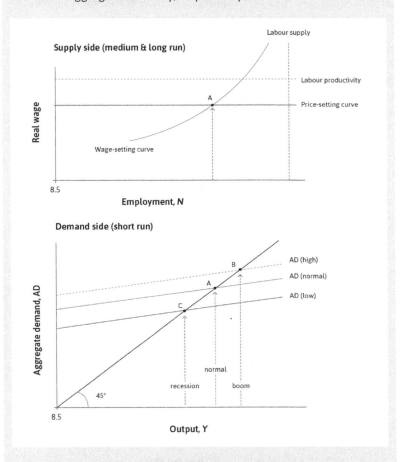

Assume that the economy's production function is given by $Y = N$, where Y is the output and N is the employment. Based on this information, which of the following statements is correct?

☐ A rise in investment shifts the AD curve up, resulting in a higher aggregate output. This causes the price-setting curve to shift up in the short run, leading to higher employment.

☐ A fall in autonomous consumption shifts the AD curve down, resulting in a lower aggregate output. This causes the wage-setting curve to shift to the left in the short run, leading to higher unemployment.

☐ Labour productivity shifts with the changes in aggregate demand in the short run.

☐ The shifts in the aggregate demand cause short-run cyclical fluctuations in unemployment around the medium-run level shown in the labour market diagram.

14.11 CONCLUSION

Economies often experience shocks to aggregate demand, such as a decline in business investment or an increase in desired savings by households. These shocks tend to be amplified by the process described by the multiplier. In addition to their first-round effects, there are second-round or other indirect effects due to further declines in spending.

In the second half of the twentieth century, the advanced economies enjoyed a great decline in economic instability, which was due in part to larger governments and the existence of automatic stabilizers that moderated swings in aggregate demand.

While active fiscal policy played its part, it had a mixed record. France discovered in the early 1980s that a poorly planned fiscal expansion can lead to a fiscal deficit with little benefit to the domestic economy.

In 2008, the world was reminded that even the rich countries can suffer from economic crises, and the importance of fiscal policy in deep recessions was reaffirmed. Unfortunately for the Eurozone, the hardest-hit countries were unable to implement the necessary fiscal stimulus because of fears of sovereign debt crises.

Concepts introduced in Unit 14

Before you move on, review these definitions:

- Multiplier process, multiplier model
- Marginal propensity to consume, marginal propensity to import
- Consumption function
- Investment function
- Goods market equilibrium
- Autonomous consumption, autonomous demand
- Target wealth
- Financial accelerator
- Automatic stabilizer
- Fiscal stimulus
- Paradox of thrift
- Government budget balance, deficit, surplus
- Primary deficit
- Government debt
- Sovereign debt crisis
- Positive and negative feedback
- Supply and demand sides of aggregate economy
- Business cycle fluctuations
- Long run, medium run, short run

14.12 REFERENCES

Acconcia, Antonio, Giancarlo Corsetti, and Saverio Simonelli. 2014. 'Mafia and Public Spending: Evidence on the Fiscal Multiplier from a Quasi-Experiment'. *American Economic Review* 104 (7) (July): pp. 2185–2209.

Almunia, Miguel, Agustín Bénétrix, Barry Eichengreen, Kevin H. O'Rourke, and Gisela Rua. 2010. 'From Great Depression to Great Credit Crisis: Similarities, Differences and Lessons' (http://tinyco.re/9513563). *Economic Policy* 25 (62) (April): pp. 219–265.

Auerbach, Alan, and Yuriy Gorodnichenko. 2015. 'How Powerful Are Fiscal
    Multipliers in Recessions?' (http://tinyco.re/3018428). *NBER Reporter
    2015 Research Summary*.

Barro, Robert J. 2009. 'Government Spending Is No Free Lunch'
    (http://tinyco.re/3208655). *Wall Street Journal*.

Blanchard, Olivier. 2012. 'Lessons from Latvia' (http://tinyco.re/8173211).
    IMFdirect – The IMF Blog. Updated 11 June 2012.

Carlin, Wendy and David Soskice. 2015. *Macroeconomics: Institutions,
    Instability, and the Financial System*. Oxford: Oxford University Press.
    Chapter 14.

DeLong, Bradford. 2015. 'Draft for Rethinking Macroeconomics
    Conference Fiscal Policy Panel' (http://tinyco.re/4631043).
    Washington Center for Equitable Growth. Updated 5 April 2015.

Harford, Tim. 2010. 'Stimulus Spending Might Not Be As Stimulating As
    We Think' (http://tinyco.re/8583440). Undercover Economist Blog,
    The Financial Times.

International Monetary Fund. 2012. *World Economic Outlook October:
    Coping with High Debt and Sluggish Growth* (http://tinyco.re/5970823).

Keynes, John Maynard. 1936. *The General Theory of Employment, Interest and
    Money* (http://tinyco.re/6855346). London: Palgrave Macmillan.

Keynes, John Maynard. 2004. *The End of Laissez-Faire*. Amherst, NY:
    Prometheus Books.

Keynes, John Maynard. 2005. *The Economic Consequences of Peace*. New
    York, NY: Cosimo Classics.

Krugman, Paul. 2009. 'War and Non-Remembrance'. (http://tinyco.re/
    8410113). Paul Krugman – *New York Times* Blog.

Krugman, Paul. 2012. 'A Tragic Vindication' (http://tinyco.re/6611089).
    Paul Krugman – *New York Times* Blog.

Leduc, Sylvain, and Daniel Wilson. 2015. 'Are State Governments
    Roadblocks to Federal Stimulus? Evidence on the Flypaper Effect of
    Highway Grants in the 2009 Recovery Act' (http://tinyco.re/
    3885744). Federal Reserve Bank of San Francisco Working Paper
    2013–16 (September).

Portes, Jonathan. 2012. 'What Explains Poor Growth in the UK? The IMF
    Thinks It's Fiscal Policy' (http://tinyco.re/8763401). *National Institute
    of Economic and Social Research Blog*. Updated 9 October 2012.

Romer, Christina D. 1993. 'The Nation in Depression'. (http://tinyco.re/
    4965855). *Journal of Economic Perspectives* 7 (2) (May): pp. 19–39.

Shiller, Robert. 2010. 'Stimulus, Without More Debt' (http://tinyco.re/
    9857908). *The New York Times*. Updated 25 December 2010.

Smith, Noah. 2013. 'Why the Multiplier Doesn't Matter' (http://tinyco.re/
    7260376). *Noahpinion*. Updated 7 January 2013.

The Economist. 2009. 'A Load to Bear' (http://tinyco.re/9740912). Updated
    26 November 2009.

Wren-Lewis, Simon. 2012. 'Multiplier theory: One is the Magic Number'
    (http://tinyco.re/7820994). *Mainly Macro*. Updated 24 August 2014.

INFLATION, UNEMPLOYMENT, AND MONETARY POLICY

HOW THE RATE OF UNEMPLOYMENT AND THE LEVEL OF OUTPUT IN THE ECONOMY AFFECT INFLATION, THE CHALLENGES THIS POSES TO POLICYMAKERS, AND HOW THIS KNOWLEDGE CAN SUPPORT EFFECTIVE POLICIES TO STABILIZE EMPLOYMENT AND INCOMES

THEMES AND CAPSTONE UNITS
- 17: History, instability, and growth
- 18: Global economy
- 19: Inequality
- 21: Innovation
- 22: Politics and policy

- When unemployment is low, inflation tends to rise. When unemployment is high, inflation falls.
- Policymakers and voters prefer low unemployment and low inflation (but not a falling price level).
- They typically cannot have both and face a trade-off instead.
- There is an inflation-stabilizing rate of unemployment, and a wage-price inflation spiral develops if unemployment is kept lower than this.
- Monetary policy affects aggregate demand and inflation through a variety of channels.
- Adverse shocks, such as an oil price increase, can lead to higher unemployment and higher inflation.
- Many governments have given responsibility for monetary policy—often described as inflation targeting—to central banks.

Before his successful 1992 US presidential campaign, Bill Clinton's electoral strategists had decided that two of their campaign issues should be health policy and 'change'. But it was the third focus of his campaign—the recession of 1991—that resonated with the public. The reason was the phrase the campaign workers used: 'The economy, stupid!'

The 1991 recession meant that many Americans lost their jobs, and the Clinton campaign slogan brought this issue to the attention of the voters. When the ballots were counted in November 1992, Clinton received almost 6 million more votes than George H. W. Bush, the incumbent president.

In a democracy, election outcomes are always affected by the state of the economy, and how the public judges the economic competence of the government and the opposition. Two important measures of this economic performance are unemployment and inflation. In Unit 13 we saw that unemployment undermines our wellbeing, but inflation worries us too. Figure 15.1 shows that in US presidential elections, the margin of victory of the ruling party is higher when inflation is lower.

So if you are a politician worrying about your citizens' concerns as well as your own career, you should minimize both unemployment and inflation. Is this possible?

We get an insight by looking at how a German minister of finance, trained as an economist, handled his dual role as a politician (at an election rally in the evening) and as an economist (in his office the next day).

Helmut Schmidt was called the 'super minister' in the West German government of Chancellor Willy Brandt because he was both minister of economics and minister of finance.

At an election rally in 1972, he claimed that: 'Five per cent inflation is easier to bear than five per cent unemployment.' He promised that his party would prioritize lower unemployment whilst keeping inflation low and stable.

The following day Professor Otto Schlecht, head of the economics policy department at the Federal Ministry of Economics, said to Schmidt: 'Herr Minister, what you said yesterday, which is in the newspapers this morning, is false.'

Schmidt replied: 'I agree that what I said was technically wrong. But you cannot advise me about what I decide is politically expedient to say to an election rally in front of 10,000 Ruhr miners in the Westfalenhalle in Dortmund.'

Helmut Schmidt's commitment at the rally and his explanation afterward, show two things about the relationship between economics and politics. The first is that politicians are elected to office, and so respond to the views of voters. The second is that politicians as policymakers face constraints on their choice of policies. They can't just promise the economic outcomes that voters care about—in Schmidt's case: low unemployment, and low and stable inflation. The economist in Schmidt was well aware of the constraints but, at the rally, he was speaking as a politician.

Helmut Schmidt (1918–2015) was West German Chancellor from 1974 until 1982. In 1972, inflation in West Germany was 5.5% (up from 5.2% the previous year) and unemployment was 0.7% (up from 0.5% the previous year). By 1975, inflation was 5.9% and unemployment was 3.1%.

Inflation before 1950: Michael Bordo, Barry Eichengreen, Daniela Klingebiel, and Maria Soledad Martinez-Peria. 2001. 'Is the Crisis Problem Growing More Severe?'. *Economic Policy* 16 (32) (April): pp. 52–82; CPI after 1950: Federal Reserve Bank of St. Louis. 2015. FRED (http://tinyco.re/3965569); Electoral results: US National Archives. 2012. '1789–2012 Presidential Elections' (http://tinyco.re/6521380). US Electoral College.

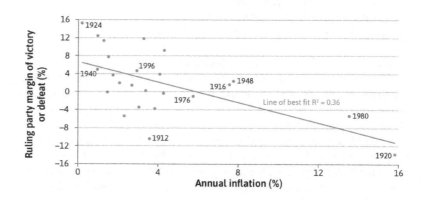

Figure 15.1 Inflation and presidential election victory in the US (1912–2012).

While the policymaker wants to deliver both low unemployment and low inflation, the economy operates in such a way that when unemployment goes down, inflation tends to go up. And when inflation falls, unemployment tends to go up. This is a problem we have seen before: policymakers must deliver what is feasible, and this involves trading one objective off against the other. Another way to say this: more inflation is the **opportunity cost** of lower unemployment, and more unemployment is the opportunity cost of less inflation. Moreover, the economy is subject to shocks that can make both inflation and unemployment worse, limiting the set of feasible outcomes. And experience from the late 1960s showed that inflation would carry on rising if unemployment were too low. This was the setting for Helmut Schmidt's reflections on his election promise.

Following the experience of rising inflation across the world, during the late 1980s there was a rethinking of how macroeconomic policy should be designed. In the 1990s, the policy known as **inflation targeting** by central banks was widely adopted. Many governments delegated the management of fluctuations in the economy to the central bank, with fiscal policy playing a lesser role, and recognized that policies to improve the supply side of their economies—such as increasing competition and better functioning labour markets—were necessary if they wanted to achieve a lower rate of unemployment compatible with low and stable inflation.

As we saw in Unit 11, prices are messages. They send signals about scarce resources. We looked at how shifts in demand or supply for a good resulted in a change in its price relative to other goods and services, and how this signalled a change in the relative scarcity of the good or service. In this unit, we look not at relative prices but at inflation or deflation: a rise or fall in prices in general. We begin by asking how inflation got a bad name.

15.1 WHAT'S WRONG WITH INFLATION?

Before we turn to the question, we need to clarify a few terms.

What is the difference between **inflation**, **deflation**, and **disinflation**?

A car analogy is a useful way to think about these differences. We can compare what happens to the price level in the economy with a car's initial location and the distance covered when it travels at different speeds:

- *Zero inflation:* A constant price level from year to year means that inflation is zero. This is like a stationary car: the car's location is constant and the distance travelled per hour is zero.
- *Inflation:* Now, consider a rate of inflation, such as 2% per year. This means that the price level goes up by 2% each year. This is the case of a car travelling at a constant speed: a car travelling at 20 km per hour means that the distance from the initial location increases by 20 km each hour. After two hours, the car is 40 km away from its initial location; after another hour, it is 60 km away, and so on.
- *Deflation:* Deflation is when the price level falls. This is equivalent to the car travelling backward at 20 km per hour. After an hour, the car is 20 km behind its initial location, and so on.
- *Rising inflation:* If the rate of inflation is increasing, the price level is increasing at an increasing rate. Suppose now that the rate of inflation increases from 2% to 4% to 6% in successive years, so the economy experiences rising inflation. This is the case of a car accelerating: the distance travelled from the starting point is increasing at an increasing

opportunity cost When taking an action implies forgoing the next best alternative action, this is the net benefit of the foregone alternative.

inflation targeting Monetary policy regime where the central bank changes interest rates to influence aggregate demand in order to keep the economy close to an inflation target, which is normally specified by the government.

inflation An increase in the general price level in the economy. Usually measured over a year. *See also: deflation, disinflation.*
deflation A decrease in the general price level. *See also: inflation.*
disinflation A decrease in the rate of inflation. *See also: inflation, deflation.*

rate, for example from 20 km per hour in the first hour to 40 km per hour in the second hour, and so on. After two hours, the car is 60 km away from its initial location.

- *Falling inflation:* This is called **disinflation** and is equivalent to a car reducing its speed, for example from 60 km per hour to 40 km per hour to 20 km per hour. Once the speed reaches zero, the car's location does not change. The equivalent in the economy is that when inflation falls to zero, the price level does not change.

We have seen why voters dislike unemployment. But why do voters dislike inflation? For some people in the economy, such as some pensioners, incomes are fixed in nominal terms, meaning that they receive a fixed number of yuan or dollars or euros. If prices rise during the year, these households can buy fewer goods and services at the end of the year than they could at the beginning. They are worse off and will tend to vote against a party they believe will permit higher inflation.

Whether one loses or benefits from inflation also depends on which side of the credit market one is on. Julia the borrower and Marco the lender (in Unit 10) have a conflict about the interest rate at which Julia borrows. They also have differing interests about inflation, because if prices rise before Julia repays her loan, Marco will find that he can buy less with the repayment than would have been the case if there were zero inflation.

More generally, using the same logic as we used when discussing the government's debt in the previous unit, inflation means that:

- *Borrowers with nominal debt will benefit:* Those with mortgages on fixed **nominal interest rate** loans, for example, will benefit from inflation, because the debt stays the same in nominal terms, and so becomes smaller in real terms.
- *Lenders with nominal assets will lose:* Banks or others who have loaned money at fixed nominal interest rates will lose, because when the sum is repaid it will be worth less in terms of the goods or services it can buy. Very high inflation will wipe out the value of nominal assets, which happened in Zimbabwe in 2008–2009.

To take account of inflation when analysing borrowing and lending, we use what is termed the **real interest rate**, which is defined as follows and is also known as the **Fisher equation**:

$$\text{real interest rate (\% per annum)} = \text{nominal interest rate (\% per annum)} - \text{the inflation rate (\% per annum)}$$

The real interest rate measures the buying power of the repayment of a loan at the prices that exist when the loan is repaid. To see what this means, let's suppose Julia were to borrow $50 from Marco with a repayment of $55 next year. The nominal interest rate is 10%. But if next year's prices were 6% higher than this year's (6% inflation rate), then what Marco could buy with the repayment is not 10% more than he could have bought with the sum he loaned to Julia, but instead only 4%. The real interest rate is 4%.

In addition to redistributing income from creditors (those with assets) and those on nominally fixed incomes (like pensioners) to debtors, in some cases inflation can also make the economy work less well. While there is no evidence that moderate inflation is bad for the economy, when inflation is

---

DESCRIBING A CHANGE IN PRICE LEVEL
- **Inflation**: The price level is rising
- **Deflation**: The price level is falling
- **Disinflation**: The *inflation rate* is falling

nominal interest rate The interest rate uncorrected for inflation. It is the interest rate quoted by high-street banks. See also: *real interest rate, interest rate.*

real interest rate The interest rate corrected for inflation (that is, the nominal interest rate minus the rate of inflation). It represents how many goods in the future one gets for the goods not consumed now. See also: *nominal interest rate, interest rate.*

'In Dollars They Trust' (http://tinyco.re/3392021). *The Economist.* Updated 27 April 2013.

Fisher equation The relation that gives the real interest rate as the difference between the nominal interest rate and expected inflation: real interest rate = nominal interest rate – expected inflation.

high it is often also volatile and therefore hard to predict. Large price changes create uncertainty, and make it more difficult for individuals and firms to make decisions based on prices.

In an environment of high and volatile inflation, it is hard to separate the signal about the scarcity of resources (sent by **relative prices**) from the noise of erratically rising prices. Firms might find it harder to know which sector to invest in, or which crop would be better to plant (quinoa or barley, for example); individuals would find it harder to decide whether quinoa has become more expensive relative to other sources of protein. Moreover, in an inflationary environment, firms have to update their prices more frequently than they would prefer. This requires time and resources, referred to as **menu costs**.

Would households and firms be better off with falling prices? No. A sustained fall in the price level is undesirable for many of the same reasons that inflation is undesirable, and could have even more dramatic economic consequences. When prices are falling, households will postpone consumption (particularly of expensive items such as fridges, televisions, and cars) because they expect goods will be cheaper in the future. Similarly, deflation increases the debt burden of borrowers, for the same reason that inflation reduces it.

As we have seen in Unit 14, a rise in the debt burden depresses consumption because some affected households save to restore their target wealth and others find themselves credit-constrained. The fall in consumption will induce a drop in aggregate demand and economic activity. Weaker aggregate spending will tend to depress prices further and can trigger a vicious circle of falling prices and economic stagnation.

This happened in Japan. The Japanese economy was one of the great success stories of the period after the Second World War. The upward slope of its hockey stick was remarkably steep, as you saw in Unit 1. Living standards, as measured by GDP per capita, went from less than one-fifth of the level in the US in 1950 to more than 70% by 1980. But in the past 25 years, Japan has faced low growth and rising unemployment. For the first time for an advanced economy in the postwar period, there has been persistent deflation: deflation was observed in 12 years out of 21 between 1995 and 2015.

Many economists think that a little bit of inflation is a good thing, as long as it remains stable. In the next unit we will see one reason why this is the case. The process of innovation and change that characterizes a dynamic economy means that, in any given year, workers in some firms and sectors will be more in demand than in others. With rising prices, a fall in real income among the losers may be masked by the fact that nominal incomes are rising, or at least not falling. For example, many people will not even notice a slight fall in their real wage due to modest inflation, but nobody would fail to notice a reduction in his or her nominal wage. With some low inflation, the adjustment of workers and resources between different firms and industries in response to changes in relative wages can take place without losers experiencing falling nominal wages. Inflation greases the wheels of the labour market.

Another important reason to prefer a bit of inflation to none is that it gives monetary policy more room to manoeuvre. As we will see later, positive inflation allows the *real* interest rate to go lower in order to offset a major recession than if inflation is zero.

relative price The price of one good or service compared to another (usually expressed as a ratio).

menu costs The resources used in setting and changing prices.

QUESTION 15.1 CHOOSE THE CORRECT ANSWER(S)

The following table shows the annual inflation rate (the GDP deflator) of Japan, the UK, China, and South Sudan in the period 1996–2015 (Source: World Bank).

	1996–2000	2001–2005	2006–2010	2011–2015
Japan	−1.9%	−0.9%	-0.5%	1.6%
UK	2.1%	1.7%	1.8%	1.8%
China	8.1%	2.4%	2.1%	0.8%
South Sudan	54.1%	6.5%	0.6%	−18.7%

Based on this information, which of the following statements is correct?

☐ Japan experienced a persistent period of disinflation before 2011.
☐ In the UK, the price of goods and services remained stable between 2001 and 2015.
☐ China has been experiencing deflationary pressure throughout the period 1996–2015.
☐ South Sudan's price level is higher in 2015 than it was in 1996.

QUESTION 15.2 CHOOSE THE CORRECT ANSWER(S)

The following table shows the nominal interest rate and the annual inflation rate (the GDP deflator) of Japan in the period 1996–2015 (Source: World Bank).

	1996–2000	2001–2005	2006–2010	2011–2015
Interest rate	1.5%	1.4%	1.3%	1.2%
Inflation rate	−1.9%	−0.9%	−0.5%	1.6%

Based on this information, which of the following statements are correct?

☐ The real interest rate in 1996–2000 was −0.4%.
☐ Japan's real interest rate has been rising consistently over this period.
☐ Japan's real interest rate turned from being positive to negative during the period.
☐ The real interest rate has been falling faster than the nominal interest rate.

15.2 INFLATION RESULTS FROM CONFLICTING AND INCONSISTENT CLAIMS ON OUTPUT

Inflation arises from conflicts among economic actors, when they are powerful enough that their claims on goods and services are inconsistent.

To see how this works, think of an economy composed of many firms (each of which is owned by a single individual) and their employees, who are also the consumers of the various goods produced by the firms. To keep track of what is happening in the firms, we assume that prices are set by the marketing department and wages by the human resources (HR) department.

Initially the marketing department in each firm is setting prices based on the markup that maximizes its profits, given the degree of competition in the markets in which it sells (as we saw in Units 7 and 9). And the HR department is also setting the real wage for its workers (which is the nominal wage in the firm, divided by the price level in the economy) as the lowest wage consistent with workers actually working, given the level of unemployment in the economy (as we saw in Units 6 and 9).

If, once all firms have set their wages and prices, the wage rate and the price level are consistent with the firms maximizing their profits, then there will be no reason for either prices or wages to be changed. At this unemployment rate, the price level is constant (inflation is zero). This is the level of unemployment where the wage-setting and price-setting curves intersect, that is, the labour market Nash equilibrium that we saw in Unit 9.

Suppose now that the government adopts **protectionist policies**, which make it difficult for foreign firms to enter its markets. Then the markets facing the firm become less competitive, so that the firm can charge a higher markup on its costs. If this is the case across the economy, the resulting increase in the price level will lower the real wage of the workers. But while the owner of an individual firm is happy with the higher price that the marketing department can now charge, the workers are unhappy with the fall in the real wage. The result is that workers now lack the motivation to work. So the HR department of the firm will raise its nominal wage, and all other firms will do the same. Both prices and wages have risen and the economy experiences inflation.

Will it end there? No. The nominal wage increase has raised the cost of production to firms and they will use this as the basis of their markup pricing, leading to a further increase in prices and a fall in the real wage, which the HR department will correct by again raising the nominal wage. The process of rising wages and prices will continue as long as:

- firms are powerful enough to charge the higher markup
- workers at the given unemployment rate have enough bargaining power to require the initial real wage in order to motivate them to work

In the example given, inflation rose while unemployment did not change, following a change in the competitive conditions facing firms that allowed them to raise their markup, increasing the owners' profits. But there are other ways that the process could have begun from the same starting point. Suppose the degree of competition in product markets remains the same, but the level of employment rises. At the new lower level of unemployment the firms would want to pay workers a higher (real) wage to keep them working. This induces the marketing departments of firms to raise their prices, so as to maintain the markup that competitive conditions allowed. And the inflationary process would begin.

To summarize, inflation may result from:

- *An increase in the bargaining power of firms over their consumers:* This is caused by a reduction in competition, which allows firms to charge a higher markup. It is a downward shift of the price-setting curve.
- *An increase in the bargaining power of workers over firms:* This allows them to get a higher wage in return for working hard.

> **protectionist policy** Measures taken by a government to limit trade; in particular, to reduce the amount of imports in the economy. These are designed to protect local industries from external competition. They can take different forms, such as taxes on imported goods or import quotas.

645

There are two ways that the <u>increase in the bargaining power of workers</u> could take place:

- *A shift upward of the wage-setting curve:* The wage they would receive is higher at every level of employment.
- *An increase in the level of employment, moving along the wage-setting curve:* In this case, the wage-setting curve is unchanged.

We studied reasons for the shift in the wage-setting curve, such as improved generosity of unemployment benefits or stronger trade unions, in Unit 9. The movement along the wage-setting curve, rather than a shift in the curve, is what we will analyse next.

Figure 15.2 summarizes three causes of inflation. In Section 15.3, we explain how the changes in bargaining power illustrated in Figure 15.2 translate into inflation. The third cause—higher employment may result in inflation—came to light when William (Bill) Phillips, the economist, published a scatter plot of annual **wage inflation** and unemployment in the British economy. This is shown in Figure 15.3.

> **wage inflation** An increase in the nominal wage. Usually measured over a year. *See also: nominal wage.*

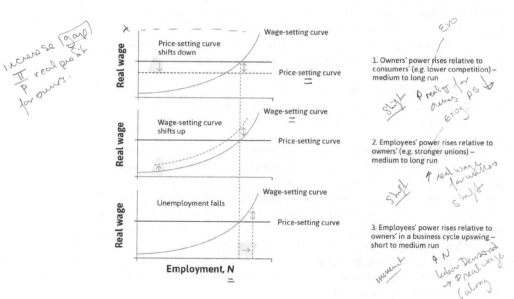

Figure 15.2 Three causes of inflation: changes in bargaining power.

1. Owners' power rises relative to consumers'
For example, due to lower competition (medium- to long-run effect).

2. Employees' power rises relative to owners'
For example, due to stronger unions (medium- to long-run effect).

3. Employees' power rises relative to owners'
For example, due to a business cycle upswing (short- to medium-run effect).

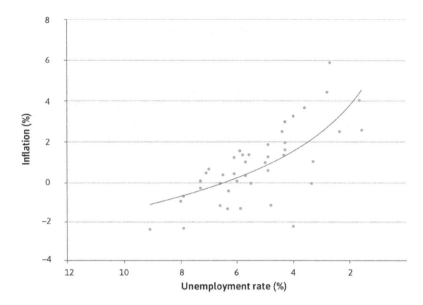

Ryland Thomas and Nicholas Dimsdale. (2017). 'A Millennium of UK Data' (http://tinyco.re/5827360). Bank of England OBRA dataset.

Figure 15.3 Phillips's original curve: Wage inflation and unemployment (1861–1913).

GREAT ECONOMISTS

Bill Phillips

A. W. ('Bill') Phillips (1914–1975) was an unusually colourful character for a world-renowned economist. Raised in New Zealand, Phillips spent time as a crocodile hunter, a movie director, and a prisoner of war in Indonesia during the Second World War, before finally becoming a professor at the London School of Economics.

Phillips had engineering know-how, and while studying sociology in London in 1949, he built a hydraulic machine to model the British economy. The Monetary National Income Analogue Computer (http://tinyco.re/0194162) (MONIAC) used transparent pipes and coloured water to bring economists' equations to life. It was like the hydraulic economy model produced by Irving Fisher half a century earlier (mentioned in Unit 2), but much more elaborate. MONIAC had tanks for each of the components of domestic GDP, such as investment, consumption, and government expenditures. Imports and exports were shown by water being added or drained from the model. The machine could be used to model the effect on the economy of shocks to different variables, such as tax rates and government spending, which would set in motion flows between the tanks. Working versions of the machine

A. W. Phillips. 1958. 'The Relation Between Unemployment and the Rate of Change of Money Wage Rates in the United Kingdom, 1861–1957' (http://tinyco.re/5934214). *Economica* 25 (100): p. 283.

Phillips curve An inverse relationship between the rate of inflation and the rate of unemployment.

can still be found in the London Science Museum and universities around the world.

In a 1958 paper, Phillips made another major contribution to the study of economics. By drawing a scatterplot of the data for the rates of unemployment and inflation in the British economy between 1861 and 1913, he found that low rates of unemployment were associated with high rates of inflation, and high unemployment with low inflation. The relationship has since been referred to as the **Phillips curve**.

QUESTION 15.3 CHOOSE THE CORRECT ANSWER(S)
The following diagram depicts the model of the labour market:

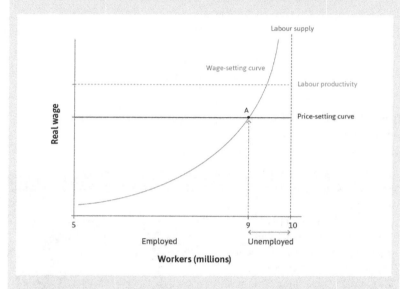

Suppose now that the government adopts policies that make it difficult for foreign firms to enter its markets. Assume that the level of employment and the labour supply remain constant. Which of the following statements regarding mechanisms by which inflation is created are correct?

☐ With reduced competition, firms can now charge a higher markup on their costs, raising the price-setting curve.
☐ With the labour market not in equilibrium at the lower real wage, the workers now lack the motivation to work at the given unemployment rate. Therefore the wage is increased, described by an upward shift in the wage-setting curve.
☐ If the firms are able to continue charging the new higher markup, now applied to the new higher wage, the price rises again, lowering the real wage to the price-setting curve.
☐ After the price rise, if the workers are able to continue demanding the initial real wage as the minimum level required to motivate them to work, the wage rises again, increasing the real wage to the level on the wage-setting curve.

QUESTION 15.4 CHOOSE THE CORRECT ANSWER(S)
The following diagram depicts the model of the labour market:

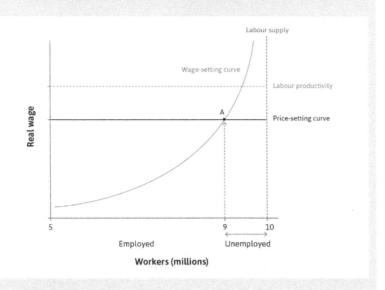

Suppose there is an increase in workers' bargaining power that causes inflation. Which of the following statements are correct?

☐ Workers' bargaining power can increase due to an increase in unemployment benefits, resulting in a rise in the wage-setting curve.
☐ Workers' bargaining power can increase due to an increase in the unemployment level along a given wage-setting curve.
☐ After the initial increase in the workers' bargaining power, the firms adjust the wages and prices by shifting the wage-setting curve, creating inflation.
☐ After the initial increase in the workers' bargaining power, the firms adjust the wages and prices, creating inflation. Neither the wage nor the price-setting curve shifts.

15.3 INFLATION, THE BUSINESS CYCLE, AND THE PHILLIPS CURVE

When central banks report their interest rate decision to the public, they normally justify a rise in the interest rate by saying that forecast inflation is up. They are raising the interest rate to dampen aggregate demand, raise cyclical unemployment, and as a result, bring inflation back toward target.

Conversely, if they are announcing a lower interest rate, they explain that this is because there is a danger of inflation falling too low (possibly into deflation). Just as a reduction in aggregate demand and employment will bring inflation down, a rise in aggregate demand and employment will increase inflation.

To model inflation, we assume that the HR departments of firms set nominal wages (for example, in dollars, pounds, or euros) once a year, and that the marketing departments set prices immediately after wages. The real wage that employees care about is their nominal wage relative to the economy-wide level of prices, and is defined as:

$$w = \frac{W}{P}$$

It is the **real wage** on the vertical axis in the labour market diagram in Question 15.4.

To see how inflation comes about in a business cycle upswing, we begin with the economy at the labour market equilibrium and with constant prices, and consider a rise in aggregate demand, which reduces unemployment below the equilibrium.

- *When unemployment is low, the HR department needs to set higher wages:* The cost of job loss is low and workers expect higher real wages if they are to work effectively.
- *Higher wages mean higher costs for firms:* The marketing department will raise prices to cover the higher costs. As long as competitive conditions have not changed, the firm's markup will be unchanged.
- *The price level will have gone up:* Once all firms in the economy have set higher prices, the economy has experienced wage and price inflation. And real wages have not increased: the percentage increase in W equals the percentage increase in P, so W/P is unchanged.

What happens next? We assume that aggregate demand remains high enough to keep unemployment below the labour market equilibrium. At the next annual round of wage-setting, the HR department is in the same position as the previous year: with continuing low unemployment, workers are disappointed with their real wage. It must raise nominal wages. When costs go up, the marketing department raises prices once more. This is called the **wage-price spiral**. It explains why, at low unemployment, the price level rises, not just in the year that unemployment fell, but year after year.

If there is a recession instead of a boom, the wage-price spiral operates in reverse, and the price level falls year after year.

We now ask why prices would have been constant year after year before the boom in aggregate demand reduced unemployment. We will see that when the labour market is in equilibrium (the normal phase of the business cycle), there is no pressure for wages and prices to change. From Unit 9 we know that labour market equilibrium is where the wage-setting curve and the price-setting curve intersect. But why is this unemployment rate so special for the rate of inflation?

In Figure 15.4a, it is only at point (A), where the real wage on the wage-setting curve coincides with the real wage on the price-setting curve, that the labour market is at a Nash equilibrium. As we saw in Unit 9, at this point both workers and firms are doing the best that they can, given the actions of the other. At A, the claims of owners for profits and of workers for wages add up exactly to the size of the pie (the sum of the double-headed arrows showing the profits per worker and real wages is equal to output per worker, which is shown by the red dashed line). This means that the HR department will have no reason to raise wages, and with no increase in costs, the marketing department will keep prices unchanged. The real wage will remain constant and no one will be disappointed.

real wage The nominal wage, adjusted to take account of changes in prices between different time periods. It measures the amount of goods and services the worker can buy. *See also: nominal wage.*

wage-price spiral This occurs if an initial increase in wages in the economy is followed by an increase in the price level, which is followed by an increase in wages and so on. It can also begin with an initial increase in the price level.

In an economy at the unemployment rate at labour market equilibrium (point A), wages and prices will be stable and inflation will be zero.

We now use the labour market diagram to show what happens in a boom, when unemployment is lower than at A. Figure 15.4b shows how workers' claims to real wages and firms' claims to real profits sum to more than total productivity when unemployment is below equilibrium, and sum to less than total productivity when unemployment is above equilibrium. When unemployment is below equilibrium this leads to upwards pressure on wages and prices, or a rising wage-price spiral. When unemployment is above equilibrium it leads to downwards pressure on wages and prices, or a declining wage-price spiral.

If we sketch the relationship between inflation and unemployment from the three phases of the business cycle, we get something similar to the one Phillips discovered in the data: when unemployment is lower, inflation is higher and vice versa.

The big message from the model of inflation and conflict over the pie is that if employment is above or below the labour market equilibrium then the price level is either rising or falling. When the real wage given by the wage-setting curve and that given by the price-setting curve are not equal, we say there is a **bargaining gap** equal to the vertical distance between the two curves.

> **bargaining gap** The difference between the real wage that firms wish to offer in order to provide workers with incentives to work, and the real wage that allows firms the markup that maximizes profits given the degree of competition.

- *If unemployment is lower than at the equilibrium:* There is a positive bargaining gap and there is inflation.
- *If unemployment is higher than at the equilibrium:* There is a negative bargaining gap and there is deflation.
- *If there is labour market equilibrium:* The bargaining gap is zero and the price level is constant.

For example, if the wage on the price-setting curve is 100 and on the wage-setting curve it is 101, the bargaining gap is 1%.

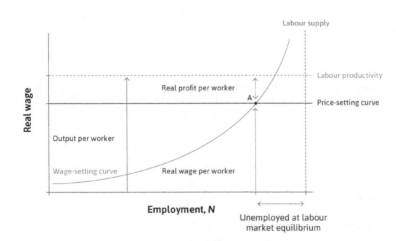

Figure 15.4a Inflation and conflict over the pie: Stable price level at labour market equilibrium.

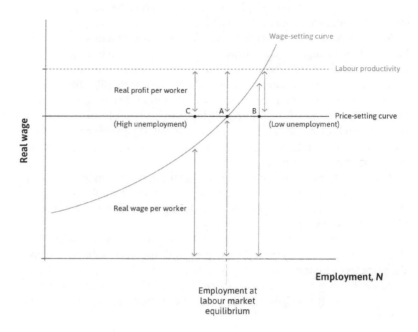

Figure 15.4b Inflation and conflict over the pie at low and high unemployment.

1. Labour market equilibrium at A
At A, the economy is at labour market equilibrium. The real wage on the wage-setting curve is equal to that on the price-setting curve, so firms' claims to real profit per worker plus the workers' claims to real wages sum to labour productivity.

2. Low unemployment at B
At low unemployment, the real wage required so that workers will work hard increases so the claims of workers for wages and owners for profits are inconsistent: they sum to more than labour productivity.

3. High unemployment at C
At high unemployment, workers are in a weaker bargaining position. The claims of workers and owners sum to less than labour productivity.

The bargaining gap and the Phillips curve

We can summarize the causal chain from the bargaining gap to inflation like this:

Bargaining gap (%)	→	Increase in wages (%)	→	Increase in unit costs (%)	→	Increase in prices (%) = inflation (%)

Remember, the triple bar indicates that inflation is defined as the percentage increase in prices. So, to work out the inflation rate, we use the following:

$$\begin{aligned} \text{inflation (\%)} &\equiv \text{increase in prices (\%)} \\ &= \text{increase in costs per unit of output (\%)} \\ &= \text{increase in wages (\%) (if wages are the only costs)} \\ &= \text{bargaining gap (\%)} \end{aligned}$$

In Figure 15.4c, we draw a new diagram beneath the wage-setting curve and price-setting curve. This is the Phillips curve diagram, with inflation on the vertical axis and employment on the horizontal axis. If we begin with employment at the labour market equilibrium, and inflation of zero, we note that the economy can remain here: there is no pressure for the price level to rise or fall. This gives a point on the Phillips curve. Now consider a higher level of employment due to stronger aggregate demand. A positive bargaining gap opens up and wages and prices will rise. Firms increase wages in response to the fall in unemployment. The price level rises as firms put up their prices in response to the rise in their labour costs. If the bargaining gap is 1%, prices and wages will rise by 1%. This gives a second point on the Phillips curve.

As long as employment remains above the labour market equilibrium, employees will be disappointed at the end of the year. Their real wage will not have risen by 1% as they had anticipated, so they will bargain for

> **BARGAINING GAP**
>
> The difference between the real wage that firms wish to offer in order to provide workers with incentives to work (the wage-setting curve), and the real wage that allows firms the markup on costs required to motivate them to continue in business (the price-setting curve).
>
> - When the bargaining gap is positive, the real wage on the wage-setting curve is above the price-setting curve, and the claims of employers and owners to output per worker are inconsistent.
> - The percentage bargaining gap is equal to the wage on the wage-setting curve, minus the wage on the price-setting curve, divided by the wage on the price-setting curve.

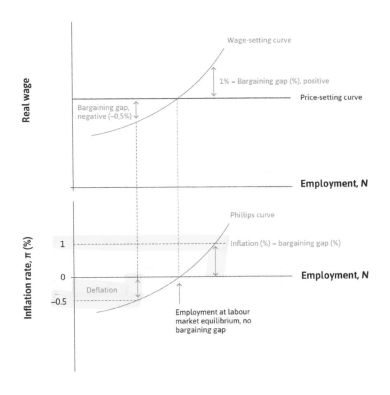

Figure 15.4c Bargaining gaps, inflation, and the Phillips curve.

1. Labour market equilibrium
The bargaining gap is zero and inflation is zero.

2. Low unemployment
The bargaining gap is positive and inflation is positive.

3. High unemployment
The bargaining gap is negative and inflation is negative.

another 1% rise. The result: wages and prices will rise by 1% the following year as well: firms will put up wages by 1% to take the real wage up to the wage-setting curve, and they will put up prices by 1% in response to that cost increase. We will observe lower unemployment and higher inflation as in Phillips' original empirical scatter plot.

To complete the picture, we include the multiplier model beneath the labour market and Phillips diagrams to bring the short- and medium-run models together. This highlights that:

- *At a higher level of aggregate demand (a boom) inflation is positive*: Unemployment is lower, which means there is a positive bargaining gap, so wages and prices are rising continuously.
- *At a lower level of aggregate demand (a recession), there is deflation*: Unemployment is higher, which means there is a negative bargaining gap.

EXERCISE 15.1 THE BARGAINING GAP IN A RECESSION

Suppose the economy is initially at labour market equilibrium with stable prices (inflation is zero). At the beginning of year 1, investment declines and the economy moves into recession with high unemployment.

1. Explain why a negative bargaining gap arises.
2. Assume the negative bargaining gap is 1%. Draw a diagram with years on the horizontal axis and the price level on the vertical axis. Starting from a price index of 100, sketch the path of the price level for the 5 years that follow, assuming the bargaining gap remains at –1%.
3. Who are the winners and losers in this economy?

EXERCISE 15.2 POSITIVE AND NEGATIVE SHOCKS

Draw a labour market diagram where the economy is at labour market equilibrium with stable prices. Now consider:

- A positive shock to aggregate demand that reduces the unemployment rate by 2 percentage points.
- A negative shock that increases it by 2 percentage points.

1. What happens to the bargaining gap in each case?
2. What would you expect to happen to the price level in each case? Explain your answers.

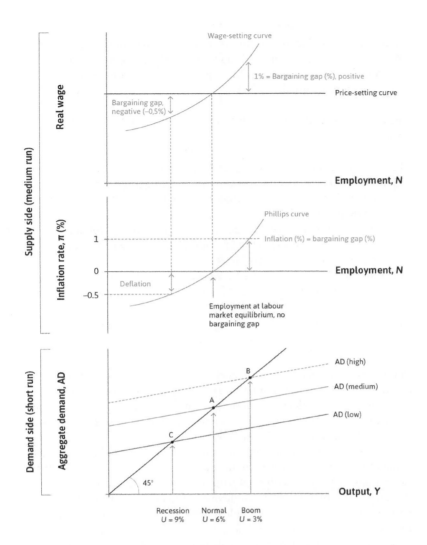

Figure 15.4d The short- and medium-run models: Aggregate demand, employment, and inflation.

1. Labour market equilibrium
When the level of aggregate demand produces employment at labour market equilibrium (a normal level of activity), the price level is stable (inflation is zero).

2. A boom
At a higher level of aggregate demand (a boom), there is a positive bargaining gap and inflation is positive.

3. A recession
At a lower level of aggregate demand (a recession), there is a negative bargaining gap and deflation.

See Figure 15.4d (page 655) for diagrams of the labour market model, the Phillips curve, and the multiplier model of aggregate demand. The unemployment rates and the bargaining gaps at different states of the economy are shown.

Based on this information, which of the following statements is correct?

☐ There is no inflation when the unemployment rate is zero.
☐ In the boom shown, the upward shift in the aggregate demand curve reduces the unemployment rate, which in turn creates a bargaining gap of 1%.
☐ In the recession shown, the downward shift in the aggregate demand curve increases the unemployment rate, which in turn creates a bargaining gap of 0.5%.
☐ The resulting Phillips curve shows a positive correlation between the unemployment rate and inflation rate.

15.4 INFLATION AND UNEMPLOYMENT: CONSTRAINTS AND PREFERENCES

Phillips' original curve, and the model in Figure 15.4d, suggest that there is a lasting trade-off between inflation and unemployment. For example, with the Phillips curve in the figure, if the government is happy to have inflation of 1% each year, then it can support a boom level of aggregate demand with an unemployment rate of 3% year after year.

If it prefers stable prices (zero inflation), then it needs to keep aggregate demand at the normal level, with unemployment of 6%. This suggests that the Phillips curve is a **feasible set** from which the policymaker can select the desired combination of unemployment and inflation. The policymaker prefers low inflation and high employment, and those preferences can be represented in the usual way in the form of indifference curves.

Work through the steps of the analysis in Figure 15.5 to see how the policymaker's preferences are described by indifference curves.

Note first some important features of the diagram. Typically when drawing indifference curves, a choice further from the origin is preferred since more of what is on each axis is preferred. In this case, the policymaker's best outcome is shown by point F, with inflation at the target and full employment. As we saw at the end of Section 15.1, the policymaker is likely to prefer low (stable) inflation to zero. This means the indifference curves become vertical at, say, 2% inflation. Above target inflation, the indifference curves are positively sloped, as getting employment closer to full employment is worth accepting higher (above target) inflation. Below the target, the indifference curves are negatively sloped, as getting employment closer to full employment is worth accepting lower (below target) inflation.

We assume that there are diminishing marginal returns to the two targets of high employment and low inflation. This implies that when the outcome is further from the inflation target but closer to full employment, the indifference curve is flatter because the policymaker places more value on getting closer to the inflation target. Conversely, when the outcome is

feasible set All of the combinations of the things under consideration that a decision-maker could choose given the economic, physical or other constraints that he faces. *See also: feasible frontier.*

further from full employment but closer to the inflation target, the indifference curve is steeper because the policymaker places more value on getting closer to full employment.

In the right-hand panel of the figure, the indifference curves and the Phillips curve are shown. The policymaker sees the Phillips curve as the feasible set and will try to use monetary or fiscal policy to choose the level of aggregate demand so that employment is at C. This is the indifference curve closest to the best outcome of F, which is consistent with the Phillips curve trade-off.

In this example, the policymaker prefers a combination of unemployment of 3% and inflation of 5% to another feasible combination of unemployment of 6% and a stable price level (zero inflation).

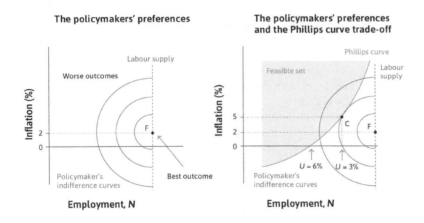

Figure 15.5 The Phillips curve and the policymaker's preferences.

1. The policymaker's preferences
The figure shows the policymaker's indifference curves.

2. High employment and inflation
When employment and inflation are very high, the indifference curve is flat.

3. Lower employment and inflation
When inflation and employment are lower, the indifference curve is steeper.

4. Inflation at 2%
The indifference curve is vertical when inflation is at 2%.

5. Full employment
The indifference curve is horizontal when employment = labour supply.

6. The policymaker's preferred outcome
F marks the policymaker's preferred combination of inflation and unemployment.

7. The feasible set
The policymaker chooses from the feasible set on the Phillips curve.

8. The preferred feasible outcome
This is on the Phillips curve at point C.

EXERCISE 15.3 THE PHILLIPS CURVE AND THE POLICYMAKER'S PREFERENCES

The following questions refer to Figure 15.5 (page 657).

1. What would the policymaker's indifference curves look like if the policymaker cared only about low unemployment?
2. Which point on the Phillips curve would that policymaker choose?
3. What would the policymaker's indifference curves look like if the policymaker cared only about low inflation?
4. Which point on the Phillips curve would this policymaker choose?
5. What would the indifference curves look like if, to be re-elected, the policymaker needed the support of pensioners more than that of working-age people?

15.5 WHAT HAPPENED TO THE PHILLIPS CURVE?

The model in Figure 15.5 suggests that a policymaker who is able to adjust the level of aggregate demand can pick any combination of inflation and unemployment along the Phillips curve. But the data in Figure 15.6 suggests that the trade-off between inflation and unemployment is not a stable one. There is a mass of data points and no discernible, positively sloped Phillips curve.

Figure 15.6 shows the inflation and unemployment combinations for the US for each year between 1960 and 2014. Note that on the horizontal axis, the scale for the unemployment rate declines as we move to the right in the figure. A Phillips curve sketched through the observations in the 1960s gives a reasonably good picture of the inflation-unemployment trade-off in that decade. But that curve clearly does not fit in other periods. The figure shows how the Phillips curve changed over time.

Milton Friedman. 1968. 'The Role of Monetary Policy'. *American Economic Review* 58 (1): pp. 1–17.

In his presidential address to the American Economic Association in December 1967, Milton Friedman provided an explanation for why the Phillips curve is not stable. He referred to the recent experience in the US. Since 1966 unemployment had been steady, averaging 3.7%, but inflation had increased from 3.0% to 4.2%. He said that the only way unemployment could be kept as low as 3% was by allowing inflation to keep increasing: 'There is always a temporary trade-off between inflation and unemployment; there is no permanent trade-off,' he claimed. This is what Helmut Schmidt knew, but did not want to admit to the voters, in 1972.

If there is no permanent trade-off, then the Phillips curve is not a feasible set in the same way as the feasible consumption frontier was: the feasible consumption frontier stays in place when a different point on it is chosen. By contrast, Friedman, supported by evidence from many countries from the late 1960s, showed that if a government tries to keep unemployment 'too low' the result will be not just higher inflation, but rising inflation as well.

Inflation means rising prices. Rising inflation means prices increasing at an ever-faster rate. This means that the Phillips curve would keep shifting upward.

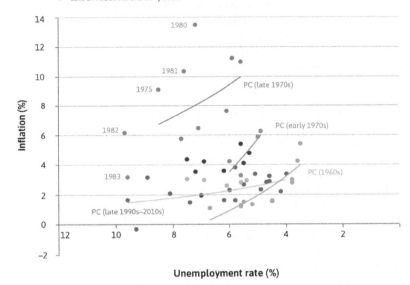

Federal Reserve Bank of St. Louis. 2015. FRED (http://tinyco.re/3965569).

Figure 15.6 Phillips curves in the US (1960–2014).

1. Where is the Phillips curve?
The figure shows the inflation and unemployment combinations for the US for each year between 1960 and 2014.

2. A shifting curve
We can use the figure to show how the Phillips curve shifted over time.

3. The 1960s
The Phillips curve (PC) for the 1960s shows the economy was in a good state. The US could achieve combinations of relatively low inflation and unemployment.

4. The 1970s
In the early 1970s, the Phillips curve appears to have shifted up.

5. The 1970s
The curve shifts up again in the late 1970s.

6. The 1980s
And up again in the early 1980s, further worsening the trade-off between unemployment and inflation.

7. The 1990s
In the late 1990s to the present, the Phillips curve is low and flat.

15.6 EXPECTED INFLATION AND THE PHILLIPS CURVE

We now explain why the Phillips curve shifts: why does inflation keep rising when governments try to keep unemployment too low? We will show that there is only one unemployment rate at which inflation is stable, and that this is the labour market Nash equilibrium.

We need to go back to two familiar points:

- *People are forward-looking:* We explained this in Units 6, 9, 10 and 13. They take actions now in anticipation of things they expect to happen. To stress this, economists say that 'expectations matter'.
- *People treat prices as messages:* Friedrich Hayek taught us this (see Unit 11). Therefore people also treat changes in prices as messages about what will happen in the future, just as people treat a build-up of clouds as a prediction of rain.

expected inflation The opinion that wage- and price-setters form about the level of inflation in the next period. *See also: inflation.*

With these two building blocks, we can see why Friedman was right. As well as the battle for the pie between workers and the owners of firms that is the fundamental cause of rising prices, Friedman showed that, at low unemployment, inflation keeps increasing. This is because of the way that wage- and price-setters form their views about what will happen to inflation, which is called **expected inflation**. The behaviour of inflation will reflect both elements.

Introducing expected inflation

We introduce the role of expected inflation by returning to the Phillips curve.

Look at Figure 15.7. You will notice that at the labour market equilibrium with an unemployment rate of 6%, the inflation rate is 3% and not zero as in Figure 15.4d.

If wage- and price-setters expect prices to rise by 3% per annum, and the level of aggregate demand is 'normal' and keeps unemployment at 6%, then the economy can remain at the labour market equilibrium with inflation remaining constant at 3% per annum. Every year, wages and prices will rise by 3% and the real wage will remain at the intersection of the wage- and price-setting curves. This is point A.

Now consider a boom, which takes the economy to lower unemployment at point B. What will happen to inflation? Workers expect prices to rise by 3% and will require a nominal wage increase of 3% just to keep their real wage unchanged. But they require an additional 2% rise to give them an expected real wage rise on the wage-setting curve, so wages increase by 5%. With their costs rising by 5%, firms will increase prices by 5%. In the boom, inflation will be 5%. This gives a Phillips curve like the one we have seen before. The only difference is that inflation at labour market equilibrium is 3% rather than zero.

When inflation is not zero, we can summarize the causal chain from expected inflation and the bargaining gap to inflation like this:

To work out the inflation rate:

inflation (%) ≡ increase in prices (%)
= increase in costs per unit of output (%)
= increase in wages (%) (if wages are the only costs)
= expected inflation (%) + bargaining gap (%)

But Friedman pointed out that with low unemployment, inflation would not remain at 5% at point B. To see why, we ask what happens next.

The shifting Phillips curve

With low unemployment continuing, workers will be disappointed with the outcome, since they did not achieve their expected real wage. Why not? Workers expected a 2% real wage increase at B from their nominal pay rise of 5% (to give the real wage on the wage-setting curve), but they did not get this because firms raised their prices by 5%.

But the story does not end there. We know that both parties cannot be satisfied with the outcome at low unemployment, because their claims add up to more than the size of the pie. Now, we assume that workers expect

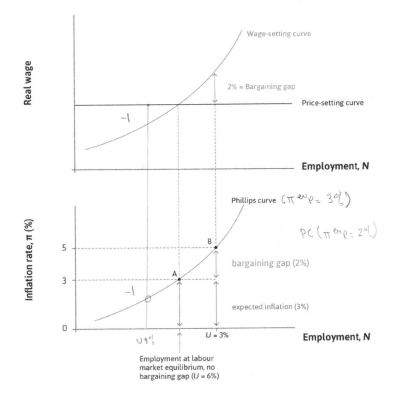

Figure 15.7 Bargaining gaps, expected inflation, and the Phillips curve.

1. Labour market equilibrium
At labour market equilibrium, inflation is 3% as expected.

2. A boom
At lower unemployment, the bargaining gap is 2%.

3. The new rate of inflation, 5%
At B, inflation is equal to expected inflation plus the bargaining gap.

inflation next year to be equal to inflation last year. So at the next wage-setting round, the human resources department has to take into account the fact that their employees expect prices to rise by 5%. Another interpretation is that HR includes inflation over the past year in the wage settlement, to make up for the shortfall in the real wage that workers experienced because inflation turned out to be higher than expected. So in order to achieve another real wage increase of 2%, the HR department sets a wage increase of 7%. The process continues with the rate of inflation increasing over time.

The table in Figure 15.8 summarizes the situation. We compare the situation over a three-year period with unemployment at two levels: 6% and 3%.

The first column of Figure 15.8 reflects forward-looking behaviour. Expected inflation over the year ahead is based on the previous year's inflation. The second column shows the unemployment rate. The third column shows the bargaining gap. The fourth column is the inflation outcome, which reflects expectations and the bargaining gap.

We can summarize the causal chain from the last period's inflation rate to this period's inflation rate like this:

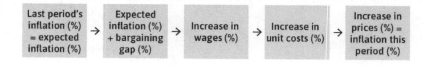

To work out the inflation rate:

inflation (%) ≡ increase in prices (%)
= increase in costs per unit of output (%)
= increase in wages (%) (if wages are the only costs)
= expected inflation (%) + bargaining gap (%)
= last period's inflation + bargaining gap (%)

We can show the data in the table in Figure 15.8 and in the Phillips curve and labour market diagrams in Figure 15.9. The stable inflation case is at point A with unemployment of 6% and inflation of 3%, year after year. At low unemployment (3%), the Phillips curve shifts up from the one through

	Year	Expected inflation (previous year's inflation)	Unemployment	Bargaining gap	Inflation outcome: expectations plus bargaining gap
Stable inflation	1	3%	6%	0%	3%
	2	3%	6%	0%	3%
	3	3%	6%	0%	3%
Rising inflation	1	3%	3%	2%	5%
	2	5%	3%	2%	7%
	3	7%	3%	2%	9%

Figure 15.8 Unstable Phillips curves: Expected inflation and the bargaining gap.

point B to the one through point C when expected inflation rises from 3% to 5%.

By plotting the path of inflation over time in Figure 15.10 we can see the distinctive contributions of the bargaining gap and expected inflation to inflation. In this example, the bargaining gap opens up in year 1 because of the move to low unemployment. The assumption that unemployment remains below the **inflation-stabilizing rate** is reflected in the persistence of the bargaining gap. Inflation rises in every period because the previous period's inflation feeds into expected inflation and therefore into wage and price inflation. Note that the real wage does not change, but remains on the price-setting curve.

> **inflation-stabilizing rate of unemployment** The unemployment rate (at labour market equilibrium) at which inflation is constant. Originally known as the 'natural rate' of unemployment. *Also known as: non-accelerating rate of unemployment, stable inflation rate of unemployment. See also: equilibrium unemployment.*

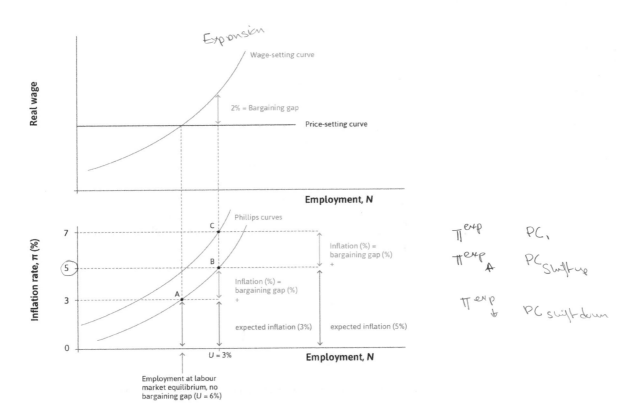

Figure 15.9 Inflation expectations and Phillips curves.

1. Labour market equilibrium at A
Inflation is 3% as expected.

2. A boom: First period at B
At lower unemployment, the bargaining gap is 2%. Inflation is equal to expected inflation plus the bargaining gap.

3. A boom: Next period at C
Next period, with unemployment still low at 3%, inflation is equal to expected inflation plus the bargaining gap. The Phillips curve has shifted up because expected inflation increased.

EXERCISE 15.4 A NEGATIVE AGGREGATE DEMAND SHOCK WITH HIGH UNEMPLOYMENT

Copy Figure 15.9 (page 663), making sure you leave plenty of space to the left of the 6% unemployment marker. Assume that from an initial position at A, there is a negative shock to private sector demand such as depressed private investment, which raises unemployment to 9%.

1. Show the inflation, expected inflation, and the bargaining gap at the new level of unemployment on your diagram.
2. What do you predict will happen to inflation over the following two years, assuming there is no further change in unemployment?
3. Draw the Phillips curves and write a brief explanation of your findings.

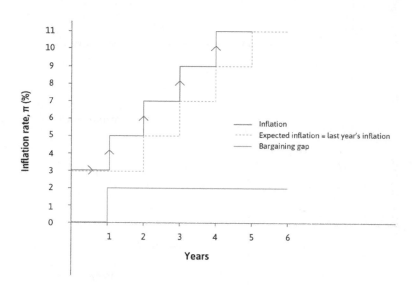

Figure 15.10 Inflation, expected inflation, and the bargaining gap.

1. A zero bargaining gap
Inflation is as expected: 3%.

2. Year 1
At the start of year 1 following the opening up of the bargaining gap and after wages and prices have been adjusted, inflation is equal to the bargaining gap (2%) plus expected inflation (3%).

3. Year 2
At the start of year 2, with no change in the bargaining gap, inflation goes up to 7%, equal to the bargaining gap plus expected inflation.

4. ... and each year afterwards
As long as the bargaining gap remains unchanged, inflation rises each year.

EXERCISE 15.5 INFLATION, EXPECTED INFLATION, AND THE BARGAINING GAP

Use the same axes as in Figure 15.10 (page 664) to plot inflation, expected inflation, and the bargaining gap in a single diagram. Assume that the price level is constant in period zero. The economy is hit by a recession at the beginning of period 1 and unemployment remains at a constant high level until the beginning of period 6.

1. Plot the path of the bargaining gap.
2. Plot the path of inflation and expected inflation.
3. Give a brief explanation of why the bargaining gap might have disappeared and state any other assumptions you are making. Summarize your findings.

QUESTION 15.6 CHOOSE THE CORRECT ANSWER(S)

Figure 15.6 (page 659) is a scatter plot of the inflation rate and the unemployment rate for the US for each year between 1960 and 2014.

Based on this information, which of the following statements is correct?

☐ The Phillips curve is stable over the years.
☐ The Phillips curve shifted higher over the period.
☐ In the 1960s, the Phillips curve suggests a trade-off of a 2% fall in the unemployment rate and a 2–3% rise in the inflation rate.
☐ In the most recent period, the US economy has been able to lower its inflation rate with little effect on the unemployment rate.

QUESTION 15.7 CHOOSE THE CORRECT ANSWER(S)

Figure 15.9 (page 663) depicts the diagrams of the labour market model and the Phillips curve that incorporates inflation expectations.

Based on this information, which of the following statements is correct?

☐ The labour market equilibrium occurs at zero inflation and 6% unemployment rate.
☐ With the fall in the unemployment rate to 3%, the Phillips curve shifts up immediately.
☐ The bargaining gap returns to zero after the first round of wage- and price-setting.
☐ Upward shifts of the Phillips curve represent a rising inflation rate for a given unemployment rate.

15.7 SUPPLY SHOCKS AND INFLATION
Friedman was correct in two ways:

- Expected inflation shifts the Phillips curve.
- Policymakers were wrong to think of the Phillips curve as a feasible set from which they could simply select the most electorally popular combination of inflation and unemployment.

But there are other causes of high and rising inflation. The Phillips curve will shift up if the price-setting curve shifts down or the wage-setting curve shifts up. Recall Figure 15.2: if the power of owners of firms relative to consumers increases, the marketing department raises prices and kicks off a wage-price spiral. In that example, owners of firms in the home economy became more powerful because the government adopted policies that made it more difficult for foreign firms to enter the economy. Similarly, a wage-price spiral can begin if the power of employees increases relative to owners—as would be the case if trade unions become more powerful and exercise that power to achieve higher wage increases from the HR department.

Shocks that move the Phillips curve by changing the labour market equilibrium are described as **supply shocks**, because the labour market represents production or supply in the economy. They are different from **demand shocks**, like a change in investment or in consumption, which work via their effect on aggregate demand. While a negative demand shock will increase unemployment and reduce inflation, a negative supply shock can lead to increased unemployment and inflation at the same time.

Changes in the global economy can also cause supply shocks that trigger inflation. A particularly important change for understanding the shifts in Phillips curves, such as those for the US economy shown in Figure 15.6, is a change in the world oil price (we look at other possible causes in Units 16 and 17). The labour market model and the Phillips curve can explain why a one-off increase in the world oil price can lead to a combination of:

- a one-off increase in the price level (inflation) at the time of the shock, *and*
- rising inflation over time

To do this, we show that a rise in the oil price:

- *Shifts the price-setting curve down:* This leads to a positive bargaining gap and inflation.
- *Shifts the Phillips curve up:* It will continue to shift up as expected inflation rises.

An increase in the oil price pushes down the price-setting curve. A typical firm uses imported oil in the production process. With increased costs for oil, the firm's profits can only remain unchanged if real wages fall. At the level of the economy as a whole, the national pie to be divided between owners and employees shrinks when more has to be paid for imports.

We show in the Einstein at the end of this section how to modify the price-setting curve once firms in the economy use imported materials in production.

supply shock An unexpected change on the supply side of the economy, such as a rise or fall in oil prices or an improvement in technology. *See also: wage-setting curve, price-setting curve, Phillips curve.*

demand shock An unexpected change in aggregate demand, such as a rise or fall in autonomous consumption, investment, or exports. *See also: supply shock.*

A rise in the oil price creates a bargaining gap and triggers a wage-price spiral through its effect on the price level. Firms raise their prices to protect their profit margins when the cost of imported oil rises. Firms across the economy will behave this way so the price level will rise. This reduces the real wage of employees, so the price-setting curve shifts down (to see how firms set their prices following an oil price rise, see the Einstein at the end of this section). At the initial employment level this opens up a bargaining gap between the real wage on the price-setting curve and the real wage on the wage-setting curve. That is, the rise in prices satisfies firms, but the corresponding fall in real wages does not satisfy workers.

In Figure 15.11, the price-setting curve shifts down following the oil shock. In this example, a bargaining gap of 2% opens up between the wage-setting curve and the post-shock price-setting curve. This fits the scenario in Figure 15.10, where a bargaining gap of 2% appears at the beginning of year 1. This increases inflation from its pre-existing level of 3% to 5% and as expected inflation adjusts, inflation rises thereafter every year. The Phillips curve shifts up year by year.

As long as employment remains at its pre-oil-shock level, inflation will increase every period, as illustrated in Figure 15.10. The new labour market equilibrium and post-shock inflation-stabilizing employment level is shown in Figure 15.11. Unemployment is higher at the new labour market

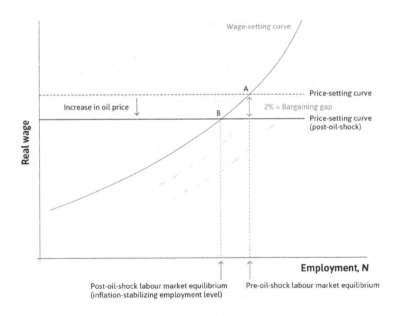

Figure 15.11 An oil shock and the price-setting curve.

1. Labour market equilibrium
The economy is initially at point A.

2. An oil shock
The oil price increases and shifts the price-setting curve down.

3. The bargaining gap
If aggregate demand is maintained to keep the economy at A, there is a positive bargaining gap. Inflation will increase year by year.

4. A new equilibrium
There is a new labour market equilibrium at B with higher unemployment.

equilibrium where the post-shock price-setting curve intersects the wage-setting curve.

Shocks to the world oil price are a major source of macroeconomic disturbance.

Following the early 1970s oil shock, for example, US inflation jumped from 6.2% in 1973 to 9.1% in 1975 and unemployment went from 4.9% to 8.5% at the same time.

This pattern was common across the developed world. For example, in the same period, inflation in Spain rose from 11.4% to 17% and unemployment increased from 2.7% to 4.7%.

We can see from Figure 15.12 that there were two big recessions in the UK in the 1970s. They were due to the oil shocks of 1973–74 and 1979–80, which were associated with a rise in both unemployment and inflation to their highest levels since the Second World War (you can see the effect on inflation in Figure 13.19a and Figure 13.19b).

High inflation in the 1970s and early 1980s was associated with high unemployment in many countries. Unemployment in the UK peaked at nearly 12% in the mid-1980s.

The model helps us to understand why the rise in the oil price led to rising inflation and high unemployment. But it also helps to explain the role that high unemployment played in bringing inflation down.

In the model, the only ways that high inflation can be brought down are:

- a reduction in the bargaining gap
- a fall in expected inflation

If unemployment is sufficiently high, then there will be a negative bargaining gap and inflation will fall. Remember that for the bargaining gap to be negative, unemployment has to rise above the new higher inflation-stabilizing unemployment rate. Once inflation begins to fall, it will continue to fall as the Phillips curve shifts downwards and the economy follows the path shown in Figure 15.10 in reverse.

Figure 15.13 shows a scatterplot of unemployment and inflation for the British economy from 1950 to 2014. Instead of fitting Phillips curves to the

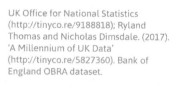

UK Office for National Statistics (http://tinyco.re/9188818); Ryland Thomas and Nicholas Dimsdale. (2017). 'A Millennium of UK Data' (http://tinyco.re/5827360). Bank of England OBRA dataset.

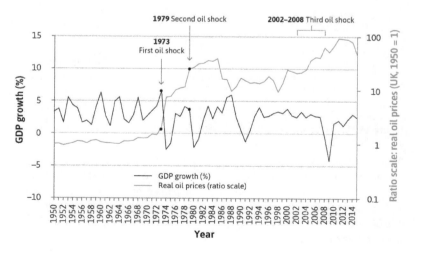

Figure 15.12 UK GDP growth and real oil prices (1950–2015).

observations, as in Figure 15.6, the points are joined and dated. This helps us to follow the path taken by the economy. Notice the large increase in unemployment in the 1980s associated with bringing inflation down. This is sometimes referred to as the cost of disinflation.

But there's a puzzle here: why did the third oil shock from 2002–08 not lead to increased inflation, just like the earlier ones? This section should have provided you with some starting points to investigate this, and a speech given in 2006 by David Walton, an economist, will help you. If you read both carefully, you might ask the following questions:

David Walton. 2006. 'Has Oil Lost the Capacity to Shock?' (http://tinyco.re/ 8182920). *Oxonomics* 1 (1): pp. 9–12.

- *Was the unit cost increase smaller due to less energy-intensive production?* This would have made the increase in the materials cost per unit of output smaller and reduced the size of the initial downward shift in the price-setting curve.
- *Did the wage-setting curve shift downwards at the same time as the third oil price shock?* This also would have reduced or perhaps even eliminated the bargaining gap opened up by the oil price shock.
- *Did a wage-price spiral fail to develop because expected inflation did not adjust upward, as in the past oil shocks?*

What could stop expected inflation rising? In the next section, we examine the role of monetary policy.

EXERCISE 15.6 AN OIL SHOCK

Think about the three questions related to oil shocks that we listed above. In each case:

1. Explain the mechanism linking the oil shock to inflation using a diagram.
2. Identify some evidence (for example, data or commentary in the economics press) that is consistent with the hypothesis proposed.

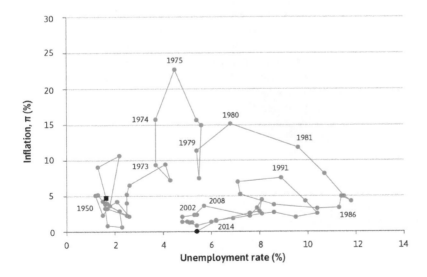

UK Office for National Statistics (http://tinyco.re/9188818); Ryland Thomas and Nicholas Dimsdale. (2017). 'A Millennium of UK Data' (http://tinyco.re/5827360). Bank of England OBRA dataset.

Figure 15.13 UK Inflation and unemployment rate (1950–2015).

EINSTEIN

The price-setting curve with imported materials

In the Einstein in Unit 9, we explained how the price-setting curve for the economy as a whole results from the decisions of individual firms. Here we take a shortcut and go straight to the economy as a whole. Firms in the economy use both the products of other firms in the economy and imported products as inputs. The cost of these inputs will be affected by wage costs and costs of imported materials. Once we put together all the firms in an economy, we have only two types of cost: labour and imported materials. (Here we are setting aside the opportunity cost of the capital goods used in production that are the property of the firm owners and the basis of their profits.)

In Unit 9, we assumed that other than the firm's own capital goods, there were no inputs other than labour and hence no costs other than wages. In this case, the value of a firm's output was the same as the firm's value added. Expressed on a per worker basis this was divided into wage and profits:

output per worker = value added per worker
= wage + profit per worker

Here, there are imported materials such as oil that are necessary to produce the output. As a result, the firm's costs include not only wages but also the costs of purchasing these imported materials.

output per worker = wage
+ profit per worker
+ imported materials costs per worker
= value added per worker
+ imported materials costs per worker

This makes it clear that unlike in Unit 9 where there were just two claimants on the value of the output (wages and profits), we now have three: labour costs, imported materials costs, and profits. This affects the price-setting curve, as we shall see.

In the Unit 9 Einstein, λ represented value added per worker, or labour productivity. Now, where we have inputs other than labour, we define q as the units of output per worker, which is not the same thing as labour productivity because output now exceeds value added by the value of imported inputs.

Since output per worker is q and the nominal wage is W, the firm's unit labour cost (ulc) is:

$$\text{ulc} \equiv \frac{W}{q}$$

Now the firm's cost per unit is its unit labour cost (ulc) plus its unit imported materials cost (umc).

So unit costs (uc) are:

$$\text{uc} = \text{umc} + \text{ulc}$$

We define the markup, μ, as the share of the price that represents profits to the firm (what is left over after subtracting unit costs):

$$\mu \equiv \frac{(P - \text{umc} - \text{ulc})}{P}$$

$$\equiv 1 - \frac{\text{umc}}{P} - \frac{\text{ulc}}{P}$$

Note that umc/P is the imported materials cost as a share of the price of a unit of output, while ulc/P is the wage cost as a share of the price of a unit of output. For example, suppose the price per unit is $5, imported materials cost $1 per unit and labour costs $2.50 per unit. Then imported materials comprise 20% of the cost, wages another 50%, and the share of profit, or the markup, is:

$$\mu = 1 - \frac{1}{5} - \frac{2.5}{5} = 0.3$$

which is 30%.

Substituting ulc = W/q gives us:

$$\mu = 1 - \frac{\text{umc}}{P} - \frac{W/q}{P}$$

Multiplying each side by q and rearranging, and remembering that P is both the price of the individual firm's output and the general price level in the economy, we get the price-setting curve:

$$\frac{W}{P} \equiv q(1 - \mu - \frac{\text{umc}}{P})$$

This shows that the real wage per worker is equal to output per worker, q, minus a share μ that goes as profits to the owner, minus a share umc/P that goes to foreign producers who supply the imported materials. Any increase in unit materials costs such as a rise in the price of oil will shift the price-setting curve down.

In the absence of imported materials, $q = \lambda$ and umc = 0, and we get the familiar expression for the price-setting curve from Unit 9:

$$\frac{W}{P} \equiv \lambda(1 - \mu)$$

An equivalent but alternative version of the markup equation is provided in the next section.

The markup price-setting equation for the firm

As we saw in the Einstein in Unit 9, the price set by a profit maximizing firm is a markup on its costs, where the markup μ is the share of the price that was the firm's profits, and is lower the more competition there is in the product market.

When explaining the process of inflation, economists often simplify by setting aside changes in the degree of competition so as to focus on the ways that increasing costs contribute to price increases. For this it is useful to have an equation describing how firms will set different prices as their costs change, assuming that the degree of competition in product markets (and therefore μ) is unchanged.

For this purpose economists use the following equation:

$$P = (1 + m)(\text{unit costs})$$
$$= (1 + m)(\text{umc} + \text{ulc})$$

where the percentage markup on costs is m, umc is the unit cost of materials, and ulc is the unit cost of labour.

The markup price-setting equation says that if unit costs are $3.00 and the markup m is 10%, the price will be $3.30. So the extra $0.30 charged above unit costs is equal to 10% of those costs. If we want to know μ in this case, we ask what the extra $0.30 is as a share of the total price, rather than as a share of the cost. Then μ = $0.30/$3.30 = 0.09 or 9%.

One advantage of using m is that it makes it easy to see that if the markup is fixed, then a rise in unit costs must imply a proportionate price rise (for example, an increase in unit costs of 5% must imply a price rise of 5%). This follows directly from the markup price-setting equation above.

We can also ask what happens to P when just one part of the costs rise, such as the imported materials cost. Assuming m remains constant, the percentage change in the price is equal to the percentage change in total unit costs:

$$\frac{\Delta P}{P} = \frac{(1 + m)\Delta(\text{umc} + \text{ulc})}{(1 + m)(\text{umc} + \text{ulc})}$$
$$= \frac{\Delta\text{umc}}{(\text{umc} + \text{ulc})} + \frac{\Delta\text{ulc}}{(\text{umc} + \text{ulc})}$$

We now divide both the numerator and the denominator of the first term on the right hand side by umc, and the second term by ulc:

$$\frac{\Delta P}{P} = \frac{\Delta\text{umc}/\text{umc}}{(\text{umc} + \text{ulc})/\text{umc}} + \frac{\Delta\text{ulc}/\text{ulc}}{(\text{umc} + \text{ulc})/\text{ulc}}$$

This is equivalent to:

$$\frac{\Delta P}{P} \equiv \frac{\Delta\text{umc}}{\text{umc}} \times \frac{\text{umc}}{(\text{umc} + \text{ulc})} + \frac{\Delta\text{ulc}}{\text{ulc}} \times \frac{\text{ulc}}{(\text{umc} + \text{ulc})}$$

In words, the percentage change in P is equal to the percentage change in umc times umc's share of unit costs, plus the percentage change in ulc times ulc's share of unit costs. For example, suppose the markup is 60% and unit cost is $5, of which $4 is labour cost and $1 is imported materials, so the price is $P = 1.6 \times \$5 = \$8$. Wages are 80% of the cost, so if wages go up 10% then the price will rise by 80% × 10% = 8%. In this example, unit costs rise to $4.4 + $1 = $5.4 and the price rises to $P = 1.6 \times \$5.4 = \$8.64$ (a rise of 8%). Equally, if the price of imports, such as oil, were to rise by 10% then the price would rise by 20% × 10% = 2%.

15.8 MONETARY POLICY

We use the Phillips curve and the policymaker's indifference curves to look at shocks and policy responses. Before doing so, we need to recall how monetary policy affects the economy.

As we saw, we can explain why people might dislike rising or volatile inflation, but most people have no reason to object to a (slowly) rising price level. In fact, many central banks around the world have policies to target an inflation rate of 2%. They either set this objective for themselves, or the government sets the objective for them. It means they are doing best if prices rise each year by a rate close to 2%.

When central banks target an inflation rate of 2%, the best answer to the question 'why does the price level rise at 2%?' becomes 'because the central bank makes it happen'.

As we first saw in Unit 10, when inflation is forecast to be higher or lower than this, the central bank can take action to adjust the level of aggregate demand and employment so as to steer the economy toward a 2% target.

When they can, central banks use changes in the policy interest rate as their monetary policy instrument to stabilize the economy. Monetary policy relies on the <u>central bank being able to control interest rates</u>, and on changes in interest rates influencing <u>aggregate demand</u>. For example, higher interest rates make it more expensive to borrow money to spend. It is important to remember that it is the real interest rate that affects spending. But when the central bank sets the policy rate, it sets it in nominal terms. So by setting a particular nominal rate it is aiming for a specific real interest rate, and it therefore takes account of the effect of expected inflation (see our Einstein at the end of this section for more about the Fisher equation).

The transmission of monetary policy

Figure 15.14 shows how the Bank of England views the transmission of monetary policy from its interest rate decision to aggregate demand and inflation in 'normal' situations—that is, when the interest rate is its policy instrument.

Look at the boxes in the first column of Figure 15.14.

Market interest rates

In Unit 10 we explained that, although the central bank sets the **policy interest rate**, commercial banks set the **market interest rate** (also referred to as the **bank lending rate**) that households and firms pay when they take out loans. When the central bank cuts the policy rate to stimulate spending, the market interest rate typically falls by approximately the same amount. To set the policy rate, the central bank will therefore work backwards, starting with its desired level of aggregate demand:

policy (interest) rate The interest rate set by the central bank, which applies to banks that borrow base money from each other, and from the central bank. *Also known as: base rate, official rate. See also: real interest rate, nominal interest rate.*
lending rate (bank) The average interest rate charged by commercial banks to firms and households. This rate will typically be above the policy interest rate: the difference is the markup or spread on commercial lending. *Also known as: market interest rate. See also: interest rate, policy rate.*

1. It will estimate a target for the total aggregate demand, Y, to stabilize the economy, based on the labour market equilibrium and the Phillips curve.
2. It will then estimate the **real interest rate**, r, which will produce this level of aggregate demand, based on shifting the aggregate demand line into the desired position in the multiplier diagram.
3. Finally it calculates the nominal policy rate, i, that will produce the appropriate market interest rate.

Think about how a fall in the market interest rate affects the decision to build a new house. The cost of taking out a loan to finance the construction of the house will fall, so as the interest rate falls, investors will consider more new housing projects to be financially viable. Through this channel, a lower policy rate will raise investment by businesses and households, and a higher policy rate will lower it (see Figure 14.9).

Asset prices

This refers to financial assets in the economy such as government bonds and shares issued by companies. When the central bank changes the interest rate, this has a ripple effect through all the interest rates in the economy, from mortgage rates to the interest rates on 20-year government bonds. As we saw in the Einstein in Unit 10, when the interest rate goes down, the price of the asset goes up. So a fall in interest rates will be expected to feed through to spending, because households who own the assets will feel wealthier.

Profit expectations and confidence

In Units 13 and 14 we stressed the importance of profit expectations and confidence for the investment decisions of firms. When setting the interest rate, the central bank tries to build confidence through consistent policymaking and good communication with the public. If it lowers the policy rate and explains its reasoning, this can lead firms to expect higher

The Bank of England.

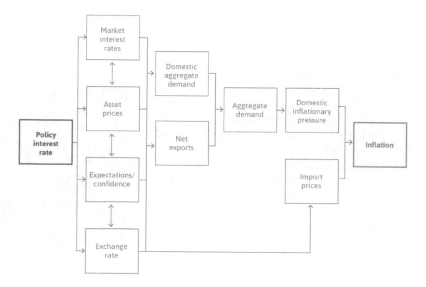

Figure 15.14 Monetary policy transmission mechanisms.

demand, who will therefore increase investment. Similarly, if it increases the confidence of households that they will not lose their jobs, then they may also increase their spending.

Exchange rate

We return in the next section to the way monetary policy affects aggregate demand through the exchange rate channel: this will shift the aggregate demand line by changing net exports, $(X - M)$.

In the multiplier model of aggregate demand, the transmission channels from the policy rate to domestic aggregate demand are reflected in the investment function (including new housing), which shifts when the real interest rate changes. We write this function $I(r)$. The expectations and asset price effects will shift the investment function as we saw in Figure 14.5, and the consumption function, by changing c_0 (Figure 14.11a).

In the multiplier diagram, the intercept of the aggregate demand line with the vertical axis includes investment, which means that the line shifts whenever the interest rate is changed by the central bank, or when business confidence changes. If the central bank is trying to boost the economy in a business cycle downturn, it cuts the interest rate. By signalling its willingness to support growth, the central bank also aims to influence the confidence of decision-makers in firms and households and help shift the economy from the low-investment equilibrium illustrated in the coordination game in Figure 13.17 to a high-investment equilibrium.

Figure 15.15 shows how monetary policy can be employed to stabilize the economy following a downturn caused by a drop in consumption (for example, as a result of a fall in consumer confidence). Follow the steps in the analysis in Figure 15.15 to see how a cut in the real interest rate brings the economy out of recession. In this example, we assume that the decline in the interest rate to r' only increases investment and not autonomous consumption, which remains at c_0'.

A warning

Using simple diagrams like Figure 15.15 may give the impression that the central bank is able to stabilize the economy by accurate diagnosis of a shock and precise intervention with a change in the interest rate. This is far from the case! The economy emits all kinds of noisy signals and it is difficult to decide, for example, whether a downturn is a temporary blip or signifies a long-term weakness. The models we use help us to organize our thinking about the causal links in the economy and what policies might be warranted. They do not give a complete recipe for effective stabilization.

Figure 15.15 shows how the central bank could attempt to counteract a recession. But how should the central bank react to a consumption boom? It needs the opposite policy. A boom will shift the aggregate demand line upwards, so the central bank must pursue policies that dampen demand and return the aggregate demand line back to its starting point. The central bank can do this by raising the interest rate.

But why would it want to curtail a boom? From the Phillips curve, we know that a boom leads to higher inflation, and, if expectations adjust to past inflation, to rising inflation. High and rising inflation imposes costs on the economy.

We have shown how monetary policy can be used by the central bank to stabilize the economy in a recession. The government could also have played this role by cutting taxes, or by boosting spending.

policy i rate ⇒ DD
Inv. demand → r
  $I(r)$

Expectations &
Asset prices Effects
  ⇒ $I(r)$
  c_0

675

Why monetary policy, and what are its limits? Fiscal policy is complicated to adjust and inflexible. Instead, to keep aggregate demand close to the level it desires, the central bank can adjust the interest rate up and down by small amounts month-by-month.

There are two important limitations, however, to the usefulness of monetary policy in stabilization:

- *The short-term nominal interest rate cannot go below zero*: But this is the central bank's policy instrument.
- *A country without its own currency does not have its own monetary policy.*

The zero lower bound

'Controlling Interest' (http://tinyco.re/7889919). *The Economist.* Updated 21 September 2013.

If the policy interest rate were negative, people would simply hold cash rather than put it in the bank, because they would have to pay the bank for holding their money (that's what a negative interest rate means). This is the **zero lower bound** on the nominal interest rate. It matters because when the economy is in a slump, a nominal interest rate of zero may not be low enough to achieve a sufficiently low real interest rate to drive up interest-sensitive spending and get the economy going again. Remember that the real interest rate is equal to the nominal interest rate minus inflation. So the zero lower bound on the nominal interest rate means that the lower bound on the real interest rate is equal to *minus* the inflation rate. Policy interest

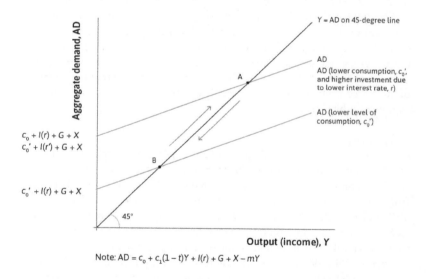

Note: $AD = c_0 + c_1(1 - t)Y + I(r) + G + X - mY$

Figure 15.15 The use of monetary policy to stabilize the economy in a recession.

1. Goods market equilibrium
The economy starts in goods market equilibrium at point A.

2. A recession
Consumption then falls, which shifts the aggregate demand line down and the economy enters a recession, moving from point A to point B.

3. Monetary policy
To stabilize the economy, the central bank stimulates investment by lowering the real interest rate from r to r'. This policy shifts the aggregate demand curve upward, pulling the economy out of recession and back to its starting point.

rates were reduced close to zero in many economies after the global financial crisis, but this was not enough to restore aggregate demand to the labour market equilibrium. For this reason, some economists argue that countries with inflation targets of 2% should raise them to 4% in order to allow real interest rates to become more negative in a slump.

This is also why economies that were badly hit by the global financial crisis introduced a new kind of monetary policy called **quantitative easing (QE)**. The aim of QE is to increase aggregate demand by buying assets, even when the policy interest rate is zero.

How is QE supposed to work?

- *The central bank buys bonds and other financial assets:* It creates additional base money for this purpose.
- *This raises demand for bonds and other financial assets:* So the central bank shifts the demand curve for those assets to the right, which pushes up the price. This also decreases the yield and interest rate on bonds, as explained in the Einstein in Unit 10.
- *This boosts spending:* Particularly on housing and consumer durables, because both the cost of borrowing and return to holding financial assets has gone down.

So, even when the interest rate the central bank directly controls is stuck at zero, it can use QE to try to reduce the interest rate on a variety of other financial assets. The empirical evidence suggests that the effects of QE in boosting aggregate demand are positive but small.

No national monetary policy

Monetary policy may not be available to a country. Members of the Eurozone gave up their own monetary policy when they joined the currency union. The Eurozone is called a **common currency area** (or currency union) because all the members use the euro. This means there is just one monetary policy for the whole of the Eurozone. The European Central Bank (ECB) in Frankfurt sets the policy interest rate, because it controls the base money used by all banks in the Eurozone. This interest rate may be more appropriate for some members than for others. In particular, after the financial crisis, unemployment was low and falling in Germany but in the southern Eurozone countries such as Spain and Greece, it was high and rising fast. There were many complaints that the ECB's monetary policy remained too restrictive for too long for the needs of the latter countries.

zero lower bound This refers to the fact that the nominal interest rate cannot be negative, thus setting a floor on the nominal interest rate that can be set by the central bank at zero. *See also: quantitative easing.*

quantitative easing (QE) Central bank purchases of financial assets aimed at reducing interest rates on those assets when conventional monetary policy is ineffective because the policy interest rate is at the zero lower bound. *See also: zero lower bound.*

common currency area A group of countries that use the same currency. This means there is just one monetary policy for the group. *Also known as: currency union.*

EXERCISE 15.7 FISCAL OR MONETARY POLICY?
Think back to the discussion of the government finances in Unit 14.

1. In the event of a financial crisis, would it be preferable for the government to stabilize the economy using fiscal or monetary policy?
2. What are the dangers of using fiscal policy?
3. When might the government have no choice but to use fiscal policy?

QUESTION 15.8 CHOOSE THE CORRECT ANSWER(S)
Which of the following statements is correct regarding monetary policy?

☐ When interest rates go down, asset prices go up.
☐ The zero lower bound refers to the central bank's inability to set the real interest rate to below zero.
☐ Quantitative easing involves the central bank lowering its official interest rate.
☐ Interest rates cannot be set in a currency union.

EINSTEIN

The real interest rate and the Fisher equation

From Unit 10, the interest rate tells you how many dollars (or euros, pounds, or the currency you use) you will have to pay in the future in exchange for borrowing $1 today. If you are a lender, it tells you how many dollars you will receive in the future by giving up the use of $1 today.

The interest rates that you see quoted in bank windows or bank websites are nominal interest rates. That is to say, they do not take inflation into account. If you are a lender, what you really want to know is how many goods you will get in the future in exchange for the goods you don't consume now. If you are a borrower, what matters is how many goods you will have to give up in the future to pay the interest, rather than the total interest measured in dollars. The opportunity cost of the loan is the goods you have to give up, not the money you have to give up. To make this distinction, you need to take account of inflation.

Households and firms make decisions based on real interest rates. Firms will judge which investment projects are worth undertaking using real interest rates, and lenders will charge a higher level of interest on their loans if inflation is expected to erode their lending margins in the future.

The equation for the real interest rate is known as the **Fisher equation**, named after Irving Fisher, whose physical model of the economy we saw in Unit 2. The Fisher equation states that the real interest rate (per cent per annum) equals the nominal interest rate (per cent per annum) minus the inflation expected over the year ahead:

$$r = i - \pi^e$$

When evaluating an investment project, the expected inflation rate needs to be taken into account. For a given nominal interest rate, higher inflation reduces the real interest rate, reducing the real cost of borrowing. We can also see that when prices are expected to fall over the year ahead—that is, expected inflation is negative, or deflation is expected—it raises the real interest rate above the nominal interest rate. At the higher real interest rate, some investment projects that would have been undertaken in the absence of forecast deflation are ruled out.

15.9 THE EXCHANGE RATE CHANNEL OF MONETARY POLICY

Monetary policy in the US works mainly through the effect of changes in the interest rate on investment, particularly on new housing and consumer durables. But in many other economies, especially smaller ones, an important channel for monetary policy is through the effect of interest rate changes on the **exchange rate** and the economy's competitiveness in international markets, and hence on net exports.

Why does the interest rate affect the exchange rate? Much of the demand for different countries' currencies comes from international investors who want to hold and trade financial assets from around the world. These investors prefer to earn a higher return, so they prefer assets with a high yield, or interest rate. For this reason, if a country's central bank lowers the interest rate, demand for that country's bonds declines: international investors are less attracted to their financial assets. With the demand for bonds lower, the demand for the currency to buy those bonds declines. The decline in demand for the currency will lead to depreciation, that is, a decline in its price in terms of other currencies.

Take the case of a slowdown in the Australian economy caused by a decline in investment demand. The Reserve Bank of Australia responds to this by cutting the interest rate. This lowers the yield on Australian financial assets, making them less attractive to international investors. For example, when the Reserve Bank of Australia reduces the interest rate, there is less demand for three-month or ten-year Australian government bonds. If the demand for Australian financial assets like government bonds goes down, then the demand for the Australian dollars needed to buy them also goes down.

Because of this, the cut in the interest rate leads to a depreciation of the Australian dollar, which means that it will buy a smaller number of US dollars, Chinese yuan, euros, or any other currency. Depreciation makes Australian exports and home-produced goods more competitive, boosting aggregate demand and stabilizing the economy. Both higher export demand for home-built products (X) and lower demand from Australians for goods and services produced abroad (M) raise aggregate demand in the home economy.

The foreign exchange market is a market in which currencies are traded against each other, such as the Australian dollar (AUD) and the US dollar (USD). The exchange rate is defined as the number of units of home currency for one unit of foreign currency, in other words:

$$\text{exchange rate of the Australian dollar} = \frac{\text{number of AUD}}{\text{one USD}}$$

When one USD buys more AUD, the AUD is said to have depreciated. When one AUD buys more USD, the AUD is said to have appreciated.

A depreciation of the home country's exchange rate makes their exports cheaper, and imports from abroad more expensive. For example, if a T-shirt in Australia costs 20 AUD, and the exchange rate with the USD is 1.07 (remember this is the number of AUD for one USD), then the T-shirt costs 20/1.07 = 18.69 USD in the US. Equivalently, a T-shirt sold for 18.69 USD in the US would cost 20 AUD in Australia. If the exchange rate of the Australian dollar then depreciates to 1.25, what happens to the price of

> **exchange rate** The number of units of home currency that can be exchanged for one unit of foreign currency. For example, the number of Australian dollars (AUD) needed to buy one US dollar (USD) is defined as number of AUD per USD. An increase in this rate is a depreciation of the AUD and a decrease is an appreciation of the AUD.

exports and imports of T-shirts in Australia? Exports of Australian T-shirts become cheaper; a 20 AUD T-shirt now costs only 16 USD in the US rather than 18.69 USD. In contrast, imports of US T-shirts into Australia become more expensive—a 18.69 USD T-shirt now costs 23.36 AUD rather than 20 AUD.

Figure 15.16 is a rough summary of the chain of events in Australia.

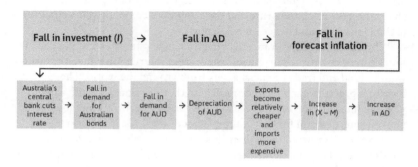

Figure 15.16 A cut in Australia's interest rate.

EXERCISE 15.8 WHY BONDS?

Explain why a change in the central bank's policy interest rate affects the exchange rate through the market for financial assets (such as government bonds).

QUESTION 15.9 CHOOSE THE CORRECT ANSWER(S)

The following is a table of the British pound (GBP) exchange rate against the dollar (USD) and euro (Source: Bank of England):

	24 Nov 2014	**23 Nov 2015**
USD/GBP	1.5698	1.5131
euro/GBP	1.2622	1.4256

In this table, the exchange rates are defined as the number of USD or euro per GBP. Based on this information, which of the following statements are correct?

☐ USD appreciated against GBP over the year.
☐ GBP depreciated against euro over the year.
☐ Exports of British goods were cheaper in the US in November 2015 than a year before.
☐ Imports from Europe were more expensive in Britain in November 2015 than a year before.

15.10 DEMAND SHOCKS AND DEMAND-SIDE POLICIES

To see how policymakers respond to **demand shocks** in practice, think about the recession in the US after the bursting of the tech bubble. The table in Figure 15.17 illustrates the fiscal and monetary policy mix used during the US recession in 2001 when after a decade of expansion, the growth rate of the US economy slowed.

The top row shows that the annual growth rate of real GDP decreased from 4.1% to 0.9%. The bottom two rows in Figure 15.17 show that the slowdown led to rising unemployment and falling inflation, exactly as we would expect from a negative demand shock. The end of the boom of the late 1990s, during which firms had been over-optimistic about the profits to be made on investment in new technology and had overestimated the need for new capacity in ICT-producing industries, triggered the slowdown (see Unit 11 for more about the tech bubble and Figure 14.5 for the model of investment with supply and demand effects shifting the investment function).

The recession and the policy response

The figure shows that the contribution of non-residential investment to the percentage change in GDP was much larger than either residential investment or government expenditure in 2000. It fell in 2001, pulling the economy into recession.

The recession could have been much worse in the absence of the strong response from monetary and fiscal policy.

In 2001, the Federal Reserve started rapidly decreasing the nominal interest rate, from a high of 6.2% on average in 2000, to 3.9% in 2001, and a low of 1.1% in 2003.

- *Monetary policy:* We can see from Figure 15.17 that this large drop in nominal interest rates helped boost residential investment in 2001 and 2002. Its contribution to growth became much larger than before. It also helped non-residential investment to recover, but the adjustment was slower: the contribution of non-residential investment to growth became positive only in 2003.

		2000	2001	2002	2003
Real gross gomestic product (annual % change)		4.1	0.9	1.8	2.8
Contribution to % change in GDP	**Change in non-residential investment**	1.15	−1.2	−0.66	0.69
	Change in residential investment	−0.07	0.09	0.39	0.66
	Change in government expenditure	0.10	0.88	0.74	0.36
	Change in other contributions	2.92	1.13	1.33	1.09
Federal Reserve nominal interest rate (annual average, %)		6.24	3.89	1.67	1.13
Unemployment rate (%)		4	4.47	5.8	6
Inflation rate (%)		3.4	2.8	1.6	2.3

Figure 15.17 The policy mix: Fiscal and monetary policy in the US following the collapse of the tech bubble.

Federal Reserve Bank of St. Louis. 2015. FRED (http://tinyco.re/3965569).

'Bush's Push' (http://tinyco.re/
1194788). *The Economist*. Updated
6 January 2003.

- *Fiscal policy:* To compensate for the stagnation in firms' private investment, the government used expansionary fiscal policy. It introduced large tax cuts and increased spending in 2001 and 2002. The multiplier model helps explain the logic of the government's policy, and the large increase in the contribution of public expenditure to growth in 2001 and 2002.

We can see from Figure 15.17 that the swift action of the government and central bank helped to stabilize the economy. Inflation and GDP growth bounced back rapidly from the recession. Unemployment was slower to react, however, continuing to creep up in 2003. In fact, the US unemployment rate did not drop all the way down to its 2000 level, perhaps suggesting that the US economy was operating above capacity in the run-up to the tech bubble.

The recession and the model

We can apply the model we have developed to the case of a slump in investment spending in the US economy in Figure 15.18. From the multiplier diagram in the lower panel, we know that a fall in investment spending shifts the aggregate demand line down, and leads to a new goods market equilibrium in the economy with lower output and higher unemployment. Figure 15.17 showed that this is what happened in the US after the tech bubble ended. Unemployment increased from 4% in 2000 to 6% in 2003, and inflation fell from 3.4% in 2000 to 1.6% in 2002.

Following the logic of the Phillips curve, inflation will fall in response to a rise in unemployment. Work through the steps of the analysis in Figure 15.18 to see the consequences of the shock, and the government's response of a fiscal stimulus and the Federal Reserve's response of looser monetary policy.

Note that now, the best outcome for the policymaker is not full employment. Rather, it is the level of employment (and unemployment) that maintains labour market equilibrium, to avoid consistently rising or falling inflation. In Figure 15.18, point X is the policymaker's best outcome. Inflation is at target and employment is consistent with constant inflation. It is clear from the indifference curves that the recession reduces wellbeing in the economy.

EXERCISE 15.9 A CONSTRUCTION BOOM

1. What happens when there is a positive shock to aggregate demand from a boom in the construction of new housing? Explain using the multiplier diagram and the Phillips curve diagram.
2. What would you expect the central bank to do?

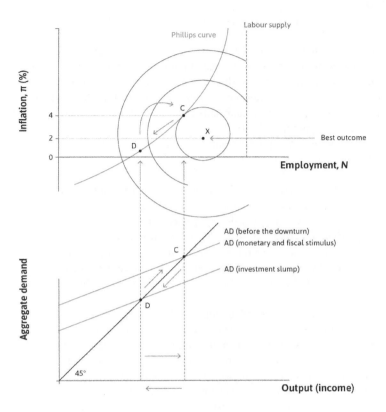

Figure 15.18 A policy intervention to restore employment and output after a fall in investment.

1. Before the downturn
The economy is at point C.

2. The investment slump
This shifts aggregate demand down. The economy moves to a situation with higher unemployment and lower inflation (from point C to point D).

3. Both the central bank and the government respond
A cut in the interest rate and fiscal stimulus via tax cuts and increased government spending shifts the aggregate demand line back to its starting position.

4. The effect of intervention
The increase in output from higher aggregate spending reduces unemployment and raises inflation. The economy moves back along the Phillips curve to point C.

15.11 MACROECONOMIC POLICY BEFORE THE GLOBAL FINANCIAL CRISIS: INFLATION-TARGETING POLICY

The 25 years before the global financial crisis in 2008 came to be known as the **great moderation**. A look back at Figure 15.12 tells us why. Despite a major oil shock in the 2000s, the British economy and many other economies continued to experience steady growth, low inflation and low unemployment. This is a remarkable contrast with the high inflation and high unemployment of the 1970s.

There were two important features of the 1990s and 2000s prior to the crisis:

- *Central banks were made independent of government control:* Monetary policy was placed in the hands of these independent central banks in most advanced and many developing countries.
- *Inflation targeting:* These banks used their policy instruments to keep the economy close to a target rate of inflation. As shown in Figure 15.19, by 2012, 28 countries had adopted inflation targeting, usually with a band (range) of what was judged an acceptable level of inflation.

Why make central banks independent and give them inflation targets? The lessons of Figure 15.6 about the instability of Phillips curves, and the high costs of unemployment incurred by countries in the 1980s as they brought inflation down, created the impetus. Policymakers globally believed there would be an inflation-stabilizing unemployment rate.

Beginning in the 1990s, governments increasingly took the view that central banks should be given responsibility for keeping the economy close to a target rate of inflation. This is typically around 2% in developed economies, but higher in some developing economies, as the table in Figure 15.19 shows. Since many voters will prefer lower unemployment even if it comes with higher inflation, as we saw in Section 15.1, how can central banks credibly commit not to deviate from their announced inflation target?

To tackle this concern, many countries increased the independence of the central bank. Politicians, like the West German superminister Helmut Schmidt, may want to promise lower unemployment now—even if this leads to rising inflation later—to be re-elected. Making the central bank independent, with an explicit inflation target, makes it easier for the central bank to resist political pressure. This prevents a wage-price spiral. The central bank is committed to act to keep inflation close to the target and this, in turn, is expected to help keep the inflation rate expected by workers and firms close to target.

Figure 15.20 illustrates the relationship between the degree of central bank independence in the mid-1980s, and average inflation between 1962 and 1990, across OECD countries. There is a strong negative correlation between the two variables. Countries with little central bank independence in the mid-1980s were those where inflation was, on average, higher over the 30-year period.

We can't conclude from this correlation how, or even if, central bank independence limited inflation, but many suspected that central bank independence would make it easier to control inflation. As a result, the high-inflation countries granted much more independence to their central bank, with a low inflation target embedded in official statutes.

---

great moderation Period of low volatility in aggregate output in advanced economies between the 1980s and the 2008 financial crisis. The name was suggested by James Stock and Mark Watson, the economists, and popularized by Ben Bernanke, then chairman of the Federal Reserve.

inflation targeting Monetary policy regime where the central bank changes interest rates to influence aggregate demand in order to keep the economy close to an inflation target, which is normally specified by the government.

New Zealand, which had high inflation in 1989, pioneered inflation targeting. Inflation fell and remained low. Other high-inflation countries soon followed, in particular Mediterranean countries like Portugal, Greece, Spain, Italy, and France.

This evidence suggests that central bank independence does help to reduce inflation.

Under the policy of inflation targeting, whenever the economy was experiencing lower unemployment than the inflation-stabilizing rate (moving to the northeast on a Phillips curve and on to a less favourable

Country	Inflation targeting adoption rate	Inflation rate at adoption date (%)	2010 end-of-year inflation (%)	Target inflation rate (%)
New Zealand	1990	3.30	4.03	1–3
Canada	1991	6.90	2.23	2 ± 1
UK	1992	4.00	3.39	2
Australia	1993	2.00	2.65	2–3
Sweden	1993	1.80	2.10	2
Czech Republic	1997	6.80	2.00	3 ± 1
Israel	1997	8.10	2.62	2 ± 1
Poland	1998	10.60	3.10	2.5 ± 1
Brazil	1999	3.30	5.91	4.5 ± 1
Chile	1999	3.20	2.97	3 ± 1
Colombia	1999	9.30	3.17	2–4
South Africa	2000	2.60	3.50	3–6
Thailand	2000	0.80	3.05	0.5–3
Hungary	2001	10.80	4.20	3 ± 1
Mexico	2001	9.00	4.40	3 ± 1
Iceland	2001	4.10	2.37	2.5 ± 1.5
Korea, Republic of (South Korea)	2001	2.90	3.51	3 ± 1
Norway	2001	3.60	2.76	2.5 ± 1
Peru	2002	−0.10	2.08	2 ± 1
Phillipines	2002	4.50	3.00	4 ± 1
Guatemala	2005	9.20	5.39	5 ± 1
Indonesia	2005	7.40	6.96	5 ± 1
Romania	2005	9.30	8.00	3 ± 1
Serbia	2006	10.80	10.29	4–8
Turkey	2006	7.70	6.40	5.5 ± 2
Armenia	2006	5.20	9.35	4.5 ± 1.5
Ghana	2007	10.50	8.58	8.5 ± 2
Albania	2009	3.70	3.40	3 ± 1

Figure 15.19 Countries who had inflation-targeting central banks by 2012.

Sarwat Jahan. 2012. 'Inflation Targeting: Holding the Line' (http://tinyco.re/5875915). *International Monetary Fund Finance & Development*.

indifference curve), the central bank would raise the interest rate and dampen aggregate demand. Similarly, following a fall in aggregate demand (as a result of a fall in business confidence, for example) and facing the threat of recession, the central bank would cut the interest rate and bring the economy back toward its inflation target. We described the actions of the Federal Reserve in these terms in Figure 15.17.

Figure 15.21 shows the Phillips curve and indifference curves for an economy with an inflation-targeting central bank. The economy has stable inflation at point X, where inflation is at the policymaker's 2% target and unemployment at labour market equilibrium is 6%. Labour market equilibrium, and hence the inflation-stabilizing rate of unemployment, will be different in different countries. For example, during the 2000s, it was estimated at 5.9% in the UK, and 7.7% in Germany.

If an aggregate demand shock reduces unemployment below 6%, inflation rises along the Phillips curve. In response, the central bank would

CPI inflation: OECD. 2015. *OECD Statistics* (http://tinyco.re/9377362). Independence of central bank: Vittorio Grilli, Donato Masciandaro, Guido Tabellini, Edmond Malinvaud, and Marco Pagano. 1991. 'Political and Monetary Institutions and Public Financial Policies in the Industrial Countries' (http://tinyco.re/7432619). *Economic Policy* 6 (13): pp. 341–392.

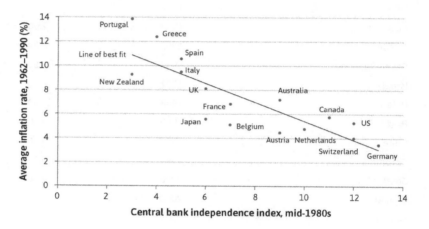

Figure 15.20 Inflation and central bank independence: OECD countries.

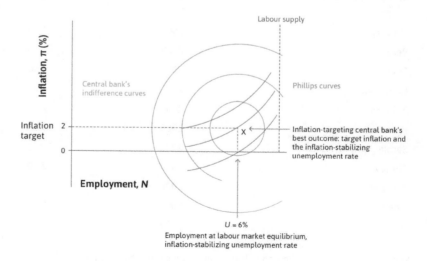

Figure 15.21 The economy's inflation-stabilizing unemployment rate.

raise the interest rate to reduce aggregate demand and raise unemployment. Unless the central bank acts promptly, a wage-price spiral can begin, with the Phillips curve shifting upward. Likewise, if inflation should fall below target, the central bank will lower the interest rate to put upward pressure on inflation.

The commitment of central banks to an inflation target helps explain why the third oil shock in the 2000s did not provoke a return to the high inflation of the 1970s. The commitment meant that even if the inflation rate rose temporarily, no one expected it to last because the central bank was committed to preventing it. With stable inflation expectations, there was no reason for a wage-price spiral to begin.

QUESTION 15.10 CHOOSE THE CORRECT ANSWER(S)

Figure 15.21 (page 686) depicts the Phillips curve and the indifference curves of an economy. This economy has an independent central bank with an inflation target of 2%.

Based on this information, which of the following statements is correct?

☐ The central bank will try to achieve zero unemployment while keeping the inflation at 2%.

☐ The shape of the indifference curves indicates that the central bank is willing to trade higher inflation for lower unemployment at all times.

☐ Consider an aggregate demand shock that increases unemployment. Without monetary or fiscal policy to counter the negative bargaining gap, the Phillips curve would shift down.

☐ Consider an aggregate demand shock that increases unemployment. The central bank would raise the interest rate to put downward pressure on inflation, in order to bring it back to the target rate.

15.12 ANOTHER REASON FOR RISING INFLATION AT LOW UNEMPLOYMENT

Why is there a trade-off in the economy between unemployment and inflation? So far, the answer is that when unemployment is high in the economy, employees face a high cost of job loss, and employers will be able to get workers to work conscientiously at a lower wage than would be the case when unemployment is lower.

But there is a second reason for the relationship between low unemployment and high inflation. In Figure 15.22, the horizontal axis shows the degree of capacity utilization in the economy. When capacity utilization rises as we move to the right along the horizontal axis, fewer machines are idle, there are fewer empty tables in restaurants, and other indicators (for example, more people working overtime shifts) show a reduction of spare capacity in factories and shops. In Unit 14 we explained the usual response of firms to rising capacity utilization: that they increase investment to expand their ability to meet orders.

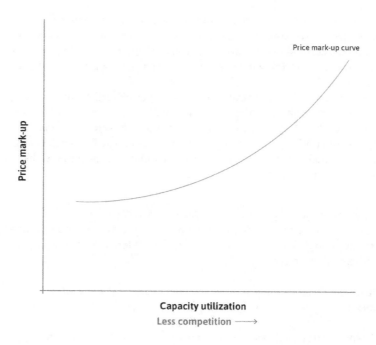

Figure 15.22 Price responses to rising employment and capacity utilization.

capacity-constrained A situation in which a firm has more orders for its output than it can fill. *See also: low capacity utilization.*

However, building new plants and installing new equipment takes time. Meanwhile, at current prices, firms have more orders than they can fill. Economists say they are **capacity-constrained**. They lose nothing by raising prices in these conditions. Moreover, their competitors—firms producing similar products—are capacity-constrained too, so these firms face less competition, meaning that their demand curves are now steeper (less price-elastic). So all firms will tend to respond to higher capacity utilization by raising the markup of prices above costs, and this will kick off a wage-price spiral.

15.13 CONCLUSION

Voters want the economy to operate with low unemployment and low but positive inflation. But achieving this outcome is not easy. In the short run there is a trade-off between inflation and unemployment, which means that policy makers could choose to reduce unemployment at a cost of higher inflation. But this can lead to higher inflation expectations and a wage-price spiral, which means that inflation is not just temporarily higher, but continues to rise over time.

Central banks are believed to be more likely to consider the future impact of their actions than politicians, who respond to short-term demo-cratic pressures. For this reason, many countries have adopted inflation targeting with independent central banks, who rely on the nominal interest rate as their policy tool in response to both supply and demand shocks.

The new macroeconomic policy framework of inflation targeting seemed to be working well when tested by the oil shock in the 2000s. Then came the global financial crisis, which rocked the consensus. Many central banks hit the zero lower bound for nominal interest rates, leading to a renewed interest in fiscal policy as a stabilization tool.

Concepts introduced in Unit 15

Before you move on, review these definitions:

- Disinflation, expected inflation
- Real interest rate
- Conflicting claims on output
- Phillips curve, shifting Phillips curve
- Bargaining gap
- Policymaker's preferences
- Monetary policy transmission, exchange rate channel
- Exchange rate
- Quantitative easing
- Supply shocks, demand shocks
- Central bank independence
- Inflation target
- Capacity-constrained firms

15.14 REFERENCES

Carlin, Wendy and David Soskice. 2015. *Macroeconomics: Institutions, Instability, and the Financial System*. Oxford: Oxford University Press. Chapters 3, 4, 9–13.

Friedman, Milton. 1968. 'The Role of Monetary Policy' (http://tinyco.re/4959694). *The American Economic Review* 58 (1): pp. 1–17.

Phillips, A W. 1958. 'The Relation Between Unemployment and the Rate of Change of Money Wage Rates in the United Kingdom, 1861–1957' (http://tinyco.re/5934214). *Economica* 25 (100): p. 283.

The Economist. 2003. 'Bush's Push' (http://tinyco.re/1194788). Updated 6 January 2003.

The Economist. 2013. 'Controlling Interest' (http://tinyco.re/7889919). Updated 21 September 2013.

The Economist. 2013. 'In Dollars They Trust' (http://tinyco.re/3392021). Updated 27 April 2013.

Walton, David. 2006. 'Has Oil Lost the Capacity to Shock?' (http://tinyco.re/8182920). *Oxonomics* 1 (1): pp. 9–12.

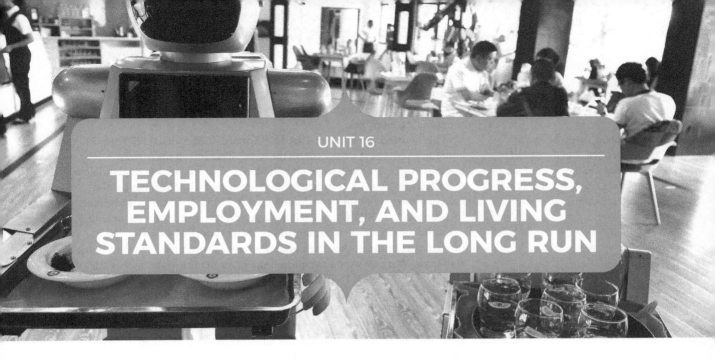

TECHNOLOGICAL PROGRESS, EMPLOYMENT, AND LIVING STANDARDS IN THE LONG RUN

HOW LONG-TERM TRENDS AND DIFFERENCES IN LIVING STANDARDS AND UNEMPLOYMENT BETWEEN COUNTRIES ARE THE RESULT OF TECHNOLOGICAL PROGRESS, INSTITUTIONS, AND POLICIES

- The increasing use of machinery and other capital goods in production, along with technological progress made possible by increasing knowledge, have been the foundation for rising living standards in the long run.
- The 'creative destruction' of older ways of producing goods and organizing production has led to continuous job loss as well as job creation, but not higher unemployment in the long run.
- A country's economic institutions and policies can be evaluated by their capacity to keep involuntary unemployment low and to sustain increases in real wages.
- Many successful economies have provided extensive forms of co-insurance against the job losses arising from both creative destruction and competition from other economies, so that most citizens of these nations welcome both technological change and the global exchange of goods and services.
- The main difference between high-performing economies and laggards is that the institutions and policies of high performers incentivize their main actors to increase the size of the pie, rather than fighting over the size of their slice.

In 1412, the city council of Cologne prohibited the production of a spinning wheel by a local craftsman because it feared unemployment among textile manufacturers that used the hand spindle. In the sixteenth century, new ribbon-weaving machines were banned in large parts of Europe. In 1811, in the early stage of the Industrial Revolution in England, the Luddite movement protested forcefully against new labour-saving

THEMES AND CAPSTONE UNITS
- 17: History, instability, and growth
- 18: Global economy
- 19: Inequality
- 21: Innovation
- 22: Politics and policy

Eric Hobsbawm and George Rudé. 1969. *Captain Swing*. London: Lawrence and Wishart.

691

Jeremy Rifkin. 1996. *The End of Work: The Decline of the Global Labor Force and the Dawn of the Post-Market Era.* New York, NY: G. P. Putnam's Sons.

machinery, such as spinning machines that allowed one worker to produce the amount of yarn previously produced by 200 workers. The movement was led by a young unskilled artisan, Ned Ludd, who allegedly destroyed the spinning machines.

The Swiss economist Jean-Charles-Léonard de Sismondi (1773–1842) contemplated a new world 'where the King sits alone on his island, endlessly turning cranks to produce, with automatons, all that England now manufactures'. The increasing use of information technology has caused contemporary economists, including Jeremy Rifkin, to voice the same fears.

Sismondi and Rifkin made plausible arguments. But as we saw in Unit 1, as a result of labour-saving innovations, many countries moved to the upward part of the hockey stick and experienced sustained growth in living standards. Workers were paid more–remember the real wage hockey stick from Unit 2 (Figure 2.1). The 'end of work' also hasn't happened yet, though in 1935 Bertrand Russell, a philosopher, expressed anticipation rather than fear of the end of work (http://tinyco.re/2000918), arguing that: '[T]here is far too much work done in the world, that immense harm is caused by the belief that work is virtuous, and that what needs to be preached in modern industrial countries is quite different from what always has been preached.'

Technological progress has not created rising unemployment rates. Instead it has raised the lowest wage that firms can pay while still covering their costs. As a result, technological progress expands the resources the firm has to invest in increasing production, and it also incentivizes continued investment. By focusing only on the destruction of jobs, those who worry about the end of work have ignored the fact that labour-saving technological progress also induces the investment that helps to create jobs.

In most economies for which data is available, at least 10% of jobs are destroyed every year, and about the same number of new ones are created. In France or the UK, every 14 seconds a job is destroyed and another one created. This is part of the creative destruction process at the heart of capitalist economies that we described in Units 1 and 2.

Those who lose their jobs bear substantial costs in the short run. The short run may not seem very short to them: it can last years or even decades. Those who benefit may be the children of the handloom weaver displaced by the power loom, or the children of the unemployed typist who was displaced by the computer. They benefit by finding a job in an occupation that is more productive than the job their parents did, and they may share in the benefit from the new goods and services that are available because the power loom or the computer exist.

The destructive part of creative destruction affects occupations that may often be concentrated in particular regions, with large losses in wages and jobs. Families and communities who are the losers often take generations to recover. Like 'short run', the term 'average' often hides the costs to the workers displaced and communities destroyed by the introduction of new technologies.

Today, for example, information and communication technology (ICT) is reshaping our societies. ICT is replacing much of routine labour, in many cases further impoverishing the already poor. People who would have previously anticipated rising living standards have fewer job opportunities.

Nevertheless, most people benefit from the fall in prices due to the new technology. For better or worse, creative destruction as a result of techno-logical progress is part of the dynamism of the capitalist economic system. And while lives have been disrupted and the environment increasingly threatened by this dynamism, the introduction of improved technologies is also the key to <u>rising living standards in the long run</u>. We shall see that:

- technological change is constantly putting people out of work
- but the countries that have avoided high levels of unemployment are among those in which the productivity of labour has increased the most

Figure 16.1 shows unemployment rates for 16 OECD countries from 1960 to 2014.

Unemployment rates were low and quite similar in the 1960s, and then diverged in the 1970s, reflecting in part the different responses to the oil shocks described in Unit 14. Of these countries, only Japan (JPN), Austria (AUT), and Norway (NOR) had unemployment rates that stayed below 6% over the entire period. In Spain (SPA), unemployment was around 20% from the mid 1980s to the end of the 1990s. It then halved in the 2000s before jumping back above 20% following the financial crisis and Eurozone crisis from 2009. In this respect Germany (GER) is unusual: unemployment fell in the years following the global financial crisis.

While there has been no upward trend in unemployment rates over the long run, there have been two important developments in the labour market that have accompanied the growth in living standards. As we saw in Unit 3 (Figure 3.1), average annual hours worked by people with jobs have fallen. In addition, a larger fraction of adults are working for pay, which is mainly due to the rise in the proportion of women who do paid work.

The <u>patterns of unemployment</u> in Figure 16.1 are not explained by national differences in the rate of innovation, or waves of innovation over time. They <u>reflect differences in the institutions and policies</u> in force in the countries.

As production has become more capital-intensive, how have living standards improved over the long run without producing mass unemployment?

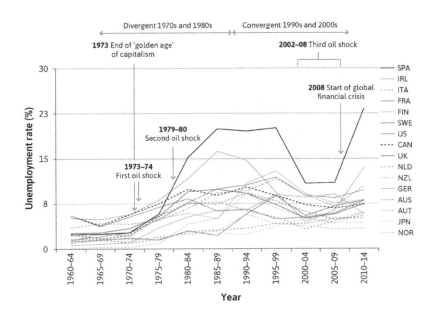

Data from 1960–2004: David R Howell, Dean Baker, Andrew Glyn, and John Schmitt. 2007. 'Are Protective Labor Market Institutions at the Root of Unemployment? A Critical Review of the Evidence' (http://tinyco.re/ 2000761). *Capitalism and Society* 2 (1) (January). Data from 2005 to 2012: OECD. 2015. *OECD Statistics* (http://tinyco.re/9377362).

Figure 16.1 Unemployment rates in selected OECD countries (1960–2014).

We begin by studying the accumulation of capital (the increasing stock of machinery and equipment) and infrastructure (such as roads and ports), which have always been fundamental to the dynamism of capitalism.

EXERCISE 16.1 WEALTH AND LIFE SATISFACTION

As we saw in Unit 3, technological progress increases your hourly productivity. This means that by working the same number of hours you could thus produce and consume more, or you can produce and consume the same amount of goods while working fewer hours and enjoying more free time.

The economist Oliver Blanchard argues that the difference in output per capita between the US and France is partially due to the fact that relative to those in the US, the French have used some of the increase in productivity to enjoy more free time rather than raise consumption (http://tinyco.re/2128090).

1. Think about two countries, one that has lower GDP per capita due to fewer hours worked, and another that has higher GDP per capita due to more hours worked (such as France and the US). Assuming that overall life satisfaction consists only of free time and consumption, in which country would you expect overall life satisfaction to be higher, and why? Clearly state any assumptions you make about the preferences of residents in each country.
2. Considering only working hours and GDP per capita, which country (France or the US) would you prefer to live in, and why? How would your answer change if you considered other factors as well?

QUESTION 16.1 CHOOSE THE CORRECT ANSWER(S)

Figure 16.1 (page 693) is a graph of unemployment rates for 16 OECD countries from 1960 to 2014.

Based on this information, which of the following statements is correct?

☐ There is no correlation between unemployment rates across countries.
☐ There has been a clear upward trend in unemployment in all countries in the last 30 years.
☐ The unemployment rates of different countries were affected very differently by the oil shocks of the 1970s.
☐ The unemployment rate rose in all countries following the 2008 global financial crisis.

16.1 TECHNOLOGICAL PROGRESS AND LIVING STANDARDS

In Unit 2 we saw how firms could earn Schumpeterian **innovation rents** by introducing new technology. Firms that fail to innovate (or copy other innovators) are unable to sell their product for a price above the cost of production, and eventually fail. This process of **creative destruction** led to sustained increases in living standards on average because technological progress and the accumulation of **capital goods** are complementary: each provides the conditions necessary for the other to proceed.

- *New technologies require new machines*: The accumulation of capital goods is a necessary condition for the advance of technology, as we saw in the case of the spinning jenny.
- *Technological advance is required to sustain the process of capital goods accumulation*: It means that the introduction of increasingly capital-intensive methods of production continues to be profitable.

The second point here needs explanation. Start with the production function that we used in Units 2 and 3. We discovered that output depends on labour input, and that the function describing this relationship shifts upward with technological progress, so that the same amount of labour now produces more output. In Unit 3 the farmer had a fixed amount of land: we assumed the amount of capital goods was fixed. But as we have seen, the amount of capital goods which the modern worker uses is vastly greater than that used by farmers in the past.   " Endogenous "

Now we include capital goods (machinery, equipment, and structures) explicitly in the production function. If you look at the horizontal axis in Figure 16.2, you will see that it records the amount of capital goods per worker. This is a measure of what is called the **capital intensity** of production. On the vertical axis, we have the amount of output per worker, also known as **labour productivity**.

As was the case in Unit 3, the production function describes diminishing marginal returns: as the worker works with more capital goods, output increases, but at a diminishing rate (Charlie Chaplin showed in the 1936 film *Modern Times* (http://tinyco.re/2139871) that there is a limit to the number of machines a worker can make use of). This means that with increasing quantities of capital goods, we have a diminishing marginal product of capital goods. The slope of the production function at each level of capital per worker shows the marginal product of capital. It shows how much output increases if capital equipment per worker increases by one unit.

The magnified section at point A in Figure 16.2 shows how the marginal product of capital is calculated: note that Y/worker is used as shorthand for output per worker, and the marginal product of capital (MPK) is $\Delta Y/\Delta K$. The marginal product of capital at each level of capital per worker is the slope of the tangent to the production function at that point.

Previous Leibnizes have showed how to use calculus to calculate the MPK at any point on a given production function. Take a moment to have another look at them.

innovation rents Profits in excess of the opportunity cost of capital that an innovator gets by introducing a new technology, organizational form, or marketing strategy. *Also known as: Schumpeterian rents.*

creative destruction Joseph Schumpeter's name for the process by which old technologies and the firms that do not adapt are swept away by the new, because they cannot compete in the market. In his view, the failure of unprofitable firms is creative because it releases labour and capital goods for use in new combinations.

capital goods The equipment, buildings, raw materials, and other inputs used in producing goods and services, including where applicable any patents or other intellectual property that is used.

capital-intensive Making greater use of capital goods (for example machinery and equipment) as compared with labour and other inputs. *See also: labour-intensive.*

labour productivity Total output divided by the number of hours or some other measure of labour input.

Leibniz: Malthusian economics
Leibniz: Labour and production

concave function A function of two variables for which the line segment between any two points on the function lies entirely below the curve representing the function (the function is convex when the line segment lies above the function).

We can see from Figure 16.2 that the marginal product of capital is falling as we move along the production function. A production function that exhibits diminishing returns to capital is **concave**. Concavity captures the fact that output per worker increases with capital per worker, but less than proportionally.

Concavity means that an economy will not be able to sustain growth in output per worker simply by adding more of the same type of capital. At a certain point, the marginal productivity of capital becomes so low that it is not worth investing any further. As we saw in Unit 14, business owners will invest domestically only if the return is higher than the return to buying

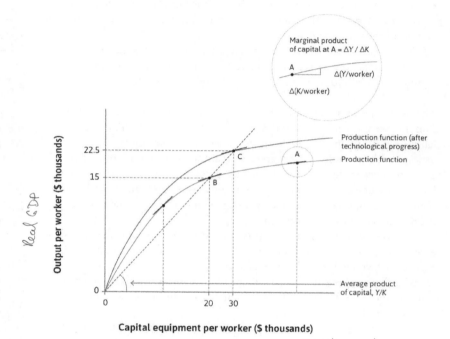

Figure 16.2 The economy's production function and technological progress.

1. Diminishing returns to capital
The production function is characterized by diminishing returns to capital.

2. The marginal product of capital
The magnified section at point A shows how the marginal product of capital is calculated: it is the slope of the tangent to the production function at A.

3. Higher capital intensity
The marginal product of capital is falling as we move along the production function to higher capital intensity.

4. Technological progress
This rotates the production function upward.

5. The original production function
At point B on the original production function, capital per worker is $20,000 and output per worker is $15,000.

6. After technological progress
Consider point C on the new production function (after technological progress), at which capital per worker has risen to $30,000 and output per worker has risen to $22,500.

7. The slope of the production function
We have chosen point C so that the slope of the production function, and therefore the marginal product of capital, is the same as at point B.

8. The average product of capital
The dotted blue line goes from the origin through the production functions for the old and new technologies. Its slope is the average product of capital.

bonds (the yield) or investing abroad, and at the same time, high enough that they do not simply want to spend their profits on consumption goods.

Sustained economic growth requires technological change that increases the marginal productivity of capital. This rotates the production function upwards and makes it profitable to invest domestically, leading to increased capital intensity. Follow the steps in the analysis in Figure 16.2 to see how the combination of technological change and capital investment raises output per worker.

New technology can also refer to new ways of organizing work. Remember that a technology is a set of instructions for combining inputs to make output. The managerial revolution in the early twentieth century called **Taylorism** is a good example: labour and capital equipment were reorganized in a streamlined way, and new systems of supervision were introduced to make workers work harder. More recently, the information technology revolution allows one engineer to be connected with thousands of other engineers and machines all over the world. The ICT revolution therefore rotates the production function upward, increasing its slope at every level of capital per worker.

In Figure 16.2, you can see a dotted blue line from the origin through the production functions for the old and new technologies. The slope of this line tells us the amount of output per unit of capital goods at the point where it intersects the production function: it is the amount of output per worker divided by the capital goods per worker. From the diagram, we note that points B and C on the two production functions have the same output per unit of capital goods.

To see how technological progress and capital accumulation shaped the world, we focus on the countries that have been the technology leaders. Britain was the technological leader from the Industrial Revolution until the eve of the First World War, when the US took over leadership. Figure 16.3 has capital per worker on the horizontal axis and output per worker on the vertical axis.

We can now look at the path traced out over time by the UK and the US. Looking first at Britain, the data begins in 1760 (the bottom corner of the chart) and ends in 1990 with much higher capital intensity and productivity. The bottom right-hand side of the diagram shows the same points in the familiar hockey-stick chart for GDP per worker. As Britain moved up the hockey stick over time, both capital intensity and productivity rose. In the US, productivity overtook the UK by 1910 and has remained higher since. In 1990, the US had higher productivity and capital intensity than the UK.

Figure 16.3 shows that the countries that are rich today have seen labour productivity rise over time as they became more capital-intensive. For example, if we look at the US, capital per worker (measured in 1985 US dollars) rose from $4,325 in 1880 to $14,407 in 1953, and $34,705 in 1990. Alongside this increase in capital intensity, US labour productivity rose from $7,400 in 1880 to $21,610 in 1953, to $36,771 in 1990. John Habakkuk, an economic historian, has argued that wages were high for factory workers in the US in the late nineteenth century because they had the option to move to the west of the country: therefore the factory owners had the incentive to develop labour-saving technology.

Productivity growth has reduced labour input per unit of output: the fear of the Luddites and the forecasts of the 'end of work' authors was that this would cause permanent job loss.

Taylorism Innovation in management that seeks to reduce labour costs, for example by dividing skilled jobs into separate less-skilled tasks so as to lower wages.

John Habakkuk. 1967. *American and British Technology in the Nineteenth Century: The Search for Labour Saving Inventions.* United Kingdom: Cambridge University Press.

From Figure 16.3 it is clear that the historical paths traced out by these economies are not curved like the single production function in Figure 16.2. This is because they experienced a combination of capital accumulation and technological progress. Successfully growing economies move along paths similar to the blue dotted line between B and C in Figure 16.2.

We know from Unit 1 that other countries moved up the hockey stick at very different times. Consider Japan, Taiwan and India in Figure 16.3. Notice that by 1990, capital per worker in Japan was not only higher than in the US, but also almost twice as high as in Britain. Japan had reached this level in less than half the time it took Britain. Taiwan in 1990 was also more capital-intensive than Britain. The lead in <u>mass production</u> and <u>science-based industries</u> that the US had established was eroded as other countries invested in education and research, and adopted American management techniques.

Interpreting Figure 16.3 using the model of the production function in Figure 16.2 shows that countries adopted <u>more capital-intensive methods of production as they became richer.</u> However, while Japan and Taiwan both experienced substantial technological progress, the fact that output per worker remained below that of both the US and Britain means that they remained on a lower production function.

Richard R Nelson and Gavin Wright. 1992. 'The Rise and Fall of American Technological Leadership: The Postwar Era in Historical Perspective' (http://tinyco.re/2811203). *Journal of Economic Literature* 30 (4) (December): pp. 1931–1964.

Robert C. Allen. 2012. 'Technology and the Great Divergence: Global Economic Development Since 1820'. *Explorations in Economic History* 49 (1) (January): pp. 1–16.

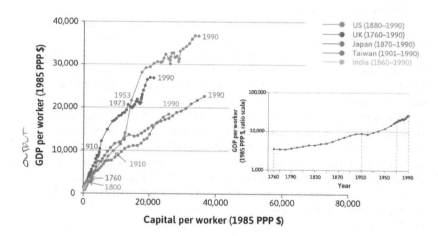

Figure 16.3 Long-run growth trajectories of selected economies.

1. The UK

The data begins in 1760 at the bottom corner of the chart, and ends in 1990 with much higher capital intensity and productivity.

2. GDP per worker

The bottom right-hand side of the diagram shows the same points in the familiar hockey-stick chart for GDP per worker, using the ratio scale.

3. The US

In the US, productivity overtook the UK by 1910 and has remained higher since.

4. Japan, Taiwan, and India

The paths of Japan, Taiwan, and India show that moving along the hockey-stick curve of living standards requires capital accumulation and the adoption of new technology.

To summarize:

- *Technological progress shifted the production function up*: It was stimulated by the prospect of innovation rents.
- *This offset the diminishing marginal returns to capital*: Capital productivity, measured by the slope of a ray from the origin, remained roughly constant over time in the technology leaders.

Technological progress played a crucial role in preventing diminishing returns from ending the long-run improvement in living standards resulting from the accumulation of capital goods.

QUESTION 16.2 CHOOSE THE CORRECT ANSWER(S)

The following diagram shows an economy's production function before and after technological progress:

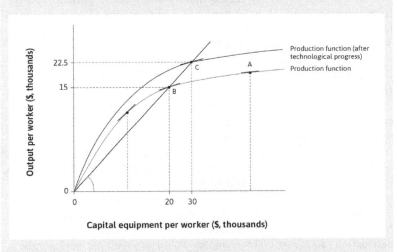

Based on this information, which of the following statements is correct?

☐ The average product of capital at A is 20,000 / 15,000 = 1.33.
☐ The marginal product of capital at A is (22,500 – 15,000) / (30,000 – 20,000) = 0.75.
☐ The concavity of the production function indicates a diminishing marginal product of capital.
☐ As a result of a technological progress, the marginal product of capital rises but the average product of capital remains constant, for a given level of capital per worker.

●●●
16.2 THE JOB CREATION AND DESTRUCTION PROCESS

Labour-saving technological progress of the type illustrated in Figures 16.2 and 16.3 allows more outputs to be produced with a given amount of labour, and it also contributes to the expansion of production. By incentivizing investment, it compensates for some of the jobs it has destroyed, and may even create more jobs than previously existed. When more jobs are created than destroyed in a given year, employment increases. When more jobs are destroyed than created, employment decreases.

We know that at any moment there are some people who are involuntarily unemployed. They would prefer to be working, but don't have a job. The number of unemployed people is a **stock** variable, measured without a time dimension. It changes from day to day, or year to year, as some of the jobless are hired (or give up seeking work), other people lose a job, and yet others decide to seek work for the first time (young people leaving school or university, for example). Those without work are sometimes called the 'pool' of the unemployed: people getting a job or ceasing to look for one exit the pool, while those who lose their jobs enter the pool. The number of people getting and losing jobs is a **flow** variable.

The total job reallocation process is the sum of job creation and destruction. Compared to that, the net growth of employment is typically small and positive.

Figure 16.4 shows the job destruction, job creation, and net employment growth in some countries. Note that in the UK from 1980 to 1998, more jobs were destroyed than created: net employment growth was negative. Across a set of countries at different stages of development, and with different openness to international trade, we see a fairly similar rate of job reallocation. In most countries, about one-fifth of jobs are created or destroyed each year, in spite of widely varying rates of net employment growth.

Now imagine an economic system in which new jobs are created at a rate of 2% each year, and job destruction is banned (that is, the job destruction rate is zero). This economy would also see a net employment growth of 2%. This is what a planner might seek to do. Figure 16.4 shows

> **stock** A quantity measured at a point in time. It's units do not depend on time. *See also: flow.*
> **flow** A quantity measured per unit of time, such as annual income or hourly wage.

John Haltiwanger, Stefano Scarpetta, and Helena Schweiger. 2014. 'Cross Country Differences in Job Reallocation: The Role of Industry, Firm Size and Regulations' (http://tinyco.re/2719834). *Labour Economics* (26): pp. 11–25.

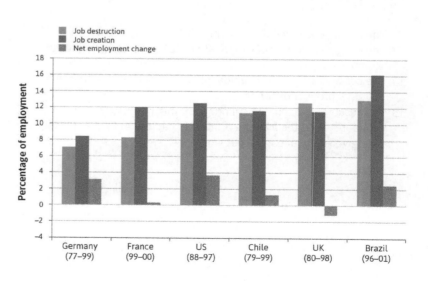

Figure 16.4 Job destruction, job creation, and net employment across countries.

this is not the way a capitalist economy works in practice: there is no planner. Competition and the prospect of gaining economic rents both mean that creating some jobs often implies destroying others.

To understand how job creation and destruction take place in an industry, we look at the impact of the information technology revolution in the US retail sector since the 1990s. The adoption of systems that electronically link cash registers to scanners, credit card processing machines, and to management systems for both inventories and customer relationships allowed tremendous increases in output per worker. Think of the volume of retail transactions handled per cashier in a new retail outlet.

Research shows that labour productivity growth in the retail sector was entirely accounted for by more productive new establishments (such as retail units or plants) displacing much less productive existing establishments (including older establishments of the same firm, as well as shops and plants owned by others, where jobs were lost).

We showed the massive expansion of employment in the US firm Walmart in Figure 7.1 of Unit 7. Walmart's growth was partly based on opening more efficient out-of-town stores, made possible by new retail and wholesale technologies.

For the manufacturing sector, detailed evidence collected from all the firms in the economy shows how productivity growth takes place through the creation and destruction of jobs inside firms, and by their entry and exit. Data for Finland in the years from 1989 to 1994, for example, shows that 58% of productivity growth took place within firms (similar to the Walmart example). The exit of low-productivity firms contributed to a quarter of the increase, and 17% was contributed by the reallocation of jobs and output from low- to high-productivity firms.

The French construction industry provides another example of the reallocation of work from weaker to stronger firms. According to the French National Institute of Statistics, more of the jobs in the economy were destroyed than created in firms with very low productivity (in the bottom 25%). Between 1994 and 1997, these firms created 7.1% of new jobs and destroyed 16.1%, implying that employment in those firms shrank by 9.0%. In contrast, job creation exceeded destruction (17.1% against 11.8%) in the top 25% of construction firms.

EXERCISE 16.2 SCHUMPETER REVISITED

1. In Unit 2 we discussed how Joseph Schumpeter characterized capitalist economies by the process of 'creative destruction'. In your own words, explain what this term means.
2. Based on this definition, give examples of destruction and creation, and identify the winners and the losers in the short and long run.

bargaining power The extent of a person's advantage in securing a larger share of the economic rents made possible by an interaction.

procyclical Tending to move in the same direction as aggregate output and employment over the business cycle. See also: countercyclical.

countercyclical Tending to move in the opposite direction to aggregate output and employment over the business cycle.

acyclical No tendency to move either in the same or opposite direction to aggregate output and employment over the business cycle.

co-insurance A means of pooling savings across households in order for a household to be able to maintain consumption when it experiences a temporary fall in income or the need for greater expenditure.

Beveridge curve The inverse relationship between the unemployment rate and the job vacancy rate (each expressed as a fraction of the labour force). Named after the British economist of the same name.

We met the concept of co-insurance in Unit 13, when we explained how households that have been fortunate during a particular period use their savings to help a household hit by bad luck, and in Unit 14, when we explained how correlated risk limits the usefulness of co-insurance, helping to explain the government's role in providing co-insurance through a system of unemployment benefits.

16.3 JOB FLOWS, WORKER FLOWS, AND THE BEVERIDGE CURVE

Jobs are created and destroyed by business owners and managers seeking to gain Schumpeterian innovation rents, and in response to the pressure of competition in markets for goods and services. For most workers this means that nothing is permanent: in the course of a lifetime, people move in and out of many jobs (often not by choice). Sometimes people move from job to job, but they move in and out of unemployment too.

In Unit 5, we looked at the decisions of an employer (Bruno) and an employee (Angela) about her work hours and rent. Once Bruno's gun was replaced by a legal system and contracts, we saw that taking a job was a voluntary arrangement entered into for mutual gain. The balance of **bargaining power** may have been unequally distributed but the exchange was, nevertheless, voluntary.

When a worker leaves a job, it may be voluntary, but it can also be an involuntary temporary lay-off (dictated by product demand conditions facing the firm), or a redundancy (the job has been eliminated).

Jobs are also created, as can be seen by the movement of job destruction and creation in the US in Figure 16.5. Job creation is strongly **procyclical**: this means that it rises in booms, and falls during recessions. Conversely, job destruction is **countercyclical**: it rises during recessions (if the change in a variable was not correlated with the business cycle, it would be called **acyclical**). The next section will show how aggregate policies interact with those movements in job flows and worker flows.

This intense job reallocation process and the ability of the government to provide **co-insurance** led the English economist and politician Lord William Beveridge (1879–1963) to become the founding father of the UK social security system. He is also remembered among economists because, like Bill Phillips, they bestowed on Beveridge one of their highest honours: they named the **Beveridge curve** after him.

The Beveridge curve

Beveridge suggested a simple relationship between job vacancy rates (the number of jobs available for workers) and the level of unemployment (the number of workers looking for jobs), expressed as a fraction of the labour force.

Beveridge noticed that when unemployment was high, the vacancy rate was low; and when unemployment was low, the vacancy rate was high:

- *During recessions, there will be high unemployment*: When the demand for a firm's product is declining or growing slowly, firms can manage with their current staff even if a few of them quit or retire. As a result, they advertise fewer positions. In the same conditions of weak demand for firms' products, people will be laid off or their jobs entirely eliminated.
- *During booms, unemployment will decline*: The number of vacant jobs posted by firms increases, and more workers will be employed to cope with rising demand for products.

The downward-sloping relationship between the vacancy rate and the unemployment rate over the business cycle is illustrated in Figure 16.6, which shows two examples of what came to be called the Beveridge curve, using data from Germany and the US. Each dot represents a quarter, from 2001 Q1 until 2015 Q2.

Why are there vacant jobs that are not filled, and unemployed people looking for a job at the same time? We can think of matching being tricky in many parts of life. For example, think of our love lives: how often are we looking for the perfect partner but are unable to find someone suitable?

Some factors prevent newly unemployed people from being matched with newly posted jobs (we call this process **labour market matching**):

labour market matching The way in which employers looking for additional employees (that is, with vacancies) meet people seeking a new job.

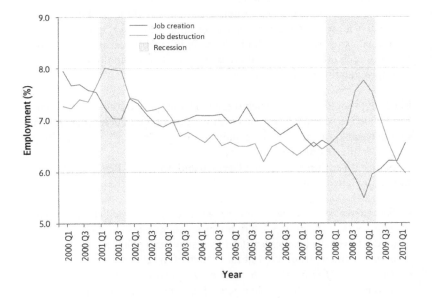

Steven J. Davis, R. Jason Faberman, and John C Haltiwanger. 2012. 'Recruiting Intensity During and After the Great Recession: National and Industry Evidence' (http://tinyco.re/2991501). *American Economic Review* 102 (3): pp. 584–588.

Figure 16.5 Job creation and destruction during business cycles in the US (2000 Q1–2010 Q2).

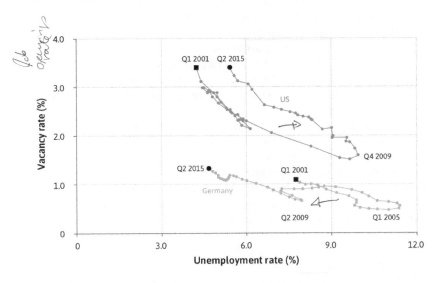

OECD Employment Outlook and OECD Labour Force Statistics: OECD. 2015. *OECD Statistics* (http://tinyco.re/9377362).

Figure 16.6 Beveridge curves for the US and Germany (2001 Q1–2015 Q2).

- *A mismatch between the location and nature of the workers looking for jobs and the jobs available for workers*: This is sometimes a matter of skills required by firms and the skills of jobseekers. For example, research explains that one of the reasons for inefficiency in the US labour market in recent years (http://tinyco.re/2991501) has been that vacancies are concentrated in a few industries. The telephone engineer whose job was recently eliminated may not have the computer skills required to fill the vacancies in the company's billing department. Or the redundant workers and the vacancies may be located in different parts of the country. Travelling to another area to find a job would mean severing ties with neighbours, schools, and relatives.

Natasha Singer. 2014. 'In the Sharing Economy, Workers Find Both Freedom and Uncertainty' (http://tinyco.re/2844216). *The New York Times*. Updated 16 August 2014.

- *Either jobseekers or those seeking to hire may not have relevant information*: As we have seen in Unit 6, economic actors with different skills and needs— jobseekers and firms in this example—look for opportunities for mutual gains from trade. But the firm and the jobseeker may not know about each other (although there is evidence that technology is improving this matching process).

Matching should be easier when there is a larger pool of the unemployed from which to select. Observing a combination of high unemployment and a large number of vacancies is an indicator of inefficiency in the matching process in the labour market.

Notice three things about the German and American Beveridge curves shown in Figure 16.6:

- *Both curves slope downward, as expected*: The US data oscillates between vacancy rates of about 3% with unemployment rates between 3% and 4% (at the top of the business cycle), to vacancy rates of a little over 2% and unemployment around 6% (at the trough of the cycle).
- *The position of each nation's Beveridge curve is different*: The German labour market appears to do a better job of matching workers seeking jobs to firms seeking workers. To see this, notice that the vacancy rate in Germany for every year is lower than in the US for any year, although the two countries experienced a common range of unemployment rates. So, fewer job openings were wasted in Germany.
- *Both the curves shifted over the course of the decade*: The German curve, having established itself over the period 2001 Q1 to 2005 Q1, turned towards the origin and established a new Beveridge curve in the period 2009 Q2 to 2012 Q1. The latter Beveridge curve was closer to the origin, with a smaller sum of the vacancy rate and the unemployment rate than before.

Michael Burda and Jennifer Hunt. 2011. 'The German Labour-Market Miracle' (http://tinyco.re/2090811). *VoxEU.org*. Updated 2 November 2011.

How did this improvement in the German labour market occur? New policies called the Hartz reforms seemed to have worked. Enacted between 2003 and 2005, the Hartz reforms provided more adequate guidance to unemployed workers in finding work and reduced the level of unemployment benefits sooner, so as to provide the unemployed with a stronger motive to search.

The US curve shifted too, but unlike Germany, conditions deteriorated. For the period 2001 Q1 to 2009 Q2, the US seems as if it is moving along a curve. After that the curve moves out from the origin and then seems to establish a new curve, above and to the right of the older one, suggesting the American labour market became less efficient in matching workers to jobs. Between 2001 and 2008, business-cycle movements displaced workers in all industries all over the country in the usual way, so there wasn't much of a geographical and skills mismatch between workers looking for work and vacant jobs, so why did the Beveridge curve move?

- *Many redundancies in one industry*: The global financial crisis between 2008 and 2009, and the recession that followed, particularly affected the housing construction industry. There was a skill-based mismatch between the unemployed and vacancies available.
- *The collapse of US housing prices*: When house prices fell, many homeowners were trapped in a house that was worth less than they had paid for it. They could not sell their house and move to an area with more job vacancies, and this restricted their choice of jobs.

Vincent Sterk. 2015. 'Home Equity, Mobility, and Macroeconomic Fluctuations' (http://tinyco.re/2186300). *Journal of Monetary Economics* (74): pp. 16–32.

The result was that the economy moved to a situation where, for a given level of vacancies, there was a higher rate of unemployment.

EXERCISE 16.3 BEVERIDGE CURVES AND THE GERMAN LABOUR MARKET

According to the Beveridge curves, the German labour market does a better job at matching workers with job openings, but over some intervals (for example, 2001 Q1 to 2005 Q1), average unemployment in Germany in Figure 16.6 (page 703) was higher than in the US.

Consider the possible role of aggregate demand (Section 13.2 on Okun' law, and Section 14.10 on aggregate demand and unemployment). What kind of data could be used to find support for your hypothesis?

QUESTION 16.3 CHOOSE THE CORRECT ANSWER(S)

The graph shows the plot of Beveridge curves for the US and Germany for the period 2001 Q1 to 2015 Q2.

Based on this information, which of the statements below is correct?

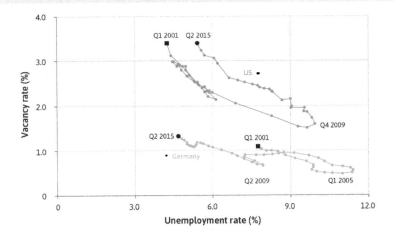

- ☐ The Beveridge curves depict the negative relationship between the vacancy rate and the employment rate.
- ☐ The US labour market was better at matching workers with vacancies during the financial crisis of 2008–9.
- ☐ The US Beveridge curve shifted after the financial crisis, improving the matching rate.
- ☐ The matching rate in Germany improved after its Beveridge curve shifted around 2007.

16.4 INVESTMENT, FIRM ENTRY, AND THE PRICE-SETTING CURVE IN THE LONG RUN

In Figure 16.1 we saw the remarkable divergence in unemployment rates across advanced economies that began in the 1970s. In the most recent period shown on the chart, European countries like Spain, Greece, or France experienced very high unemployment rates, ranging from around 10% in France to more than 20% in Spain, while in other countries, especially those in East Asia (South Korea, Japan) and in northern Europe (Austria, Norway, Netherlands, Switzerland, and Germany), unemployment was between 5% and 6%.

To explain the main trends over time and differences in the unemployment rate among countries, we extend concepts from earlier units to model the long run. In this long-run model, things that may change slowly and which are assumed to be constant in medium- or short-run models—such as the size of the capital stock, and the firms operating in the economy—can fully adjust to a change in economic conditions.

Determinants of economic performance in the long run

In the long run, the unemployment rate will depend on how well a country's policies and institutions address the two big incentive problems of a capitalist economy:

- *Work incentives*: Wage and salary workers must work hard and well, even though it is difficult to design and enforce contracts that accomplish this (as we saw in Unit 6).
- *Investment incentives*: The owners of firms must invest in job creation when they could invest abroad, or simply use their profits to buy consumption goods and not invest at all. As we saw in Unit 14, firms considering investment decisions will take account not only of the rate of profit after taxes, but also the risk of adverse changes such as hostile legislation or even confiscation of their property, which is referred to as **expropriation risk**. Just as workers cannot be forced to work hard but have to be motivated to do so, firms cannot be forced to create new jobs or to maintain existing ones.

David G Blanchflower and Andrew J Oswald. 1995. 'An Introduction to the Wage Curve' (http://tinyco.re/ 2712192). *Journal of Economic Perspectives* 9 (3): pp. 153–167.

Solving both problems simultaneously would mean a low level of unemployment at the same time as rapidly rising wages. But ways of addressing one of these problems may make it difficult to address the other. For example, policies that lead to very high wages may induce employees to work hard, but leave owners of firms with little incentive to invest in creating new productive capacity and jobs.

In the next section we will see that countries differ in how successfully they address these two incentive problems simultaneously.

The **wage-setting curve** that we have used in Units 6, 9, 14, and 15 shows that wages must be higher when unemployed workers expect to find a new job easily or when they receive a generous unemployment benefit, both of which reduce the expected cost of job loss. This is why the wage-setting curve is positively related to the employment level, and why an increase in the unemployment benefit will shift the curve upward, as this research demonstrates.

wage-setting curve The curve that gives the real wage necessary at each level of economy-wide employment to provide workers with incentives to work hard and well.

The necessary incentives for investment by owners of firms are represented by the **price-setting curve** in the labour market model (see Unit 9).

We will extend the labour market model to the long run by allowing firms to enter and exit, and owners to expand the capital stock or allow it to shrink. To simplify, let's assume that firms are all of a given size, and that the capital stock grows or shrinks simply by the addition or subtraction of firms. We assume that there are constant returns to scale so that in the long run, percentage increases in employment are matched by the same percentage increase in capital.

We define the long-run equilibrium in the labour market as a situation in which not only real wages and the employment level, but also the number of firms, is constant (remember that equilibrium is always defined by what is unchanging, unless there is some force for change from things not considered in the model).

There are two conditions that determine how the number of firms may change:

- *Firm exit due to a low markup*: Owners may withdraw their funds or even close firms if the existing markup is too low, meaning that the expected rate of profit after taxes is not attractive relative to the alternative uses to which the owners could put their assets. These alternative uses could be investing in foreign subsidiaries, outsourcing part of the production process, buying government bonds, or distributing its profits as dividends to the owners. In this case, the number of firms falls.
- *Firm entry due to a high markup*: If the markup is sufficiently high, the resulting high profit rate will attract new firms to enter the economy.

When is firm exit due to too low a markup likely to happen? This will occur when the economy is highly competitive as a result of a great number of competing firms, resulting in a high elasticity of demand for the firm's products and hence a small markup. When there are 'too many' firms to sustain a high enough markup, then firms will exit, which will tend to raise the markup.

Similarly, when there are few firms in the economy, the degree of competition will be limited, the markup will be high, and the resulting profit rate will be sufficient to attract new firms to enter. As a result, the economy will become more competitive and the markup will fall.

This means that the markup has a tendency to self-correct. If it is too low then firms will exit and it will rise, and if it is too high then firms will enter and it will decline.

Figure 16.7a illustrates this process by showing how the number of firms and the profit-maximizing markup are related. For each number of firms, the downward-sloping line gives the markup that maximizes the firm's profits. It slopes downward because:

- The more firms there are, the more competitive the economy is.
- This means a higher elasticity of demand facing the firms when they sell their products (less 'steep' demand curves).
- The markup that maximizes the firm's profits will fall, because, as we saw in Unit 7, the markup, μ, is 1/(elasticity of demand).

> **price-setting curve** The curve that gives the real wage paid when firms choose their profit-maximizing price.

The other line in the figure is horizontal and shows the markup that is just sufficient to retain the existing number of firms, which we call μ^*. Follow the steps in the analysis in Figure 16.7a to see why the number of firms will be stable at 210.

Now, using Figure 16.7a, think what would occur if as a result of a change of government, the risk of expropriation of private property by the government decreased. This is an improvement in the conditions for operating a business, and could include changes in legislation that reduce the probability that the government will take over firms or implement unpredictable changes in taxation. With <u>better business conditions</u>, a lower markup is required for firms to operate in this economy. Follow the steps in Figure 16.7b to see how this leads to an increase in the number of firms in equilibrium.

From the equilibrium markup to the price-setting curve in the long run

As before, once we know the markup μ^* and the average product of labour λ, we know the real wage w that must result: it is the share of the average product of labour (or, equivalently, of output per worker) that is not claimed by the employer through the markup. With constant returns to scale, if capital per worker remains constant, higher employment is consistent with constant output per worker: the long-run price-setting curve is flat. We note as well that in the model, the unemployed and employed workers are identical because of the presence of involuntary unemployment in the labour market equilibrium.

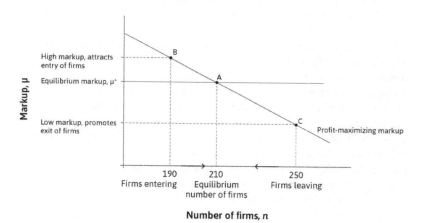

Figure 16.7a Firm entry, exit, and the equilibrium markup.

1. The profit-maximizing markup
The downward sloping line gives the markup that maximizes the firm's profits, for a given number of firms. The number of firms is constant and equal to 210 at the equilibrium markup, μ^*.

2. Competition and number of firms
The more firms there are, the more competitive the economy, which will result in a higher elasticity of demand and a lower markup.

3. Firm exit
With 250 firms, the markup is below μ^* and firms will leave the economy.

4. Firm entry
With 190 firms, the economy is at B and the markup exceeds μ^*, so new firms will enter.

The long-run price-setting curve is given by:

$$w = \lambda(1 - \mu^*)$$

As Figure 16.8 shows, this fact allows us to translate the equilibrium markup into the real wage paid, which fixes the height of the price-setting curve. In the left-hand panel, the equation of the long-run price-setting curve is drawn as a horizontal line, with the equilibrium markup on the horizontal axis and the wage on the vertical axis: with a zero markup, the wage is equal to output per worker; and when the markup is equal to 1 (or equivalently 100%), the wage is equal to zero.

The right-hand panel of Figure 16.8 shows the long-run price-setting curve at different levels of the long-run equilibrium markup. By employment on the horizontal axis in the long-run model, we mean employment with constant capital per worker. We can summarize the factors that will shift the long-run price-setting curve through their effects on either output per worker or the markup.

The long-run price-setting curve is higher: (lower bg. markup)

- the higher the output per worker
- the lower the long-run markup at which firm entry and exit are zero

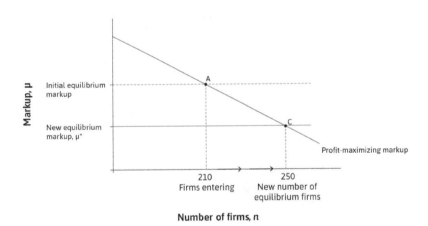

Figure 16.7b An improvement in conditions for doing business: Firm entry, exit, and the equilibrium markup.

1. An improvement in conditions for doing business
This lowers the equilibrium markup. The existing markup at A is now 'too high'.

2. New firms enter the market
The economy grows until there are 250 firms.

What lowers the markup at which entry and exit are zero?

- higher competition
- lower risk of expropriation of owners in the home economy
- higher quality environment for doing business: for example, better human capital or infrastructure
- lower expected long-run tax rate
- lower opportunity cost of capital: for example, a lower interest rate on bonds
- lower expected profits on foreign investments
- lower expected long-term cost of imported materials

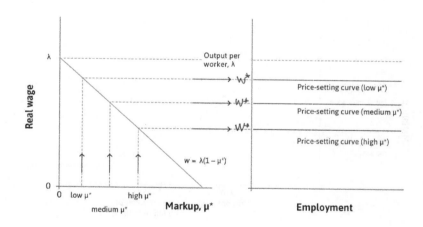

Figure 16.8 Changes in the long-run markup shift the price-setting curve.

1. The-long run price-setting curve
In the left-hand panel, the equation of the long-run price-setting curve is shown as a downward-sloping line in the diagram, with the equilibrium markup on the horizontal axis and the wage on the vertical axis.

2. A low markup
A low long-run equilibrium markup is associated with a higher long-run price-setting curve.

3. A high markup
Long-run price-setting curves are lower for higher markups.

EXERCISE 16.4 MEASURING THE CONDITIONS FOR INVESTMENT

Go to the World Bank's *Doing Business* database (http://tinyco.re/2588313).

1. In the 'Topics' section, collect (download) data on three characteristics of the business environment that will affect the long-run markup, for 20 countries of your choice. Justify your choice of characteristics.

Now go to the World Bank's *DataBank* database (http://tinyco.re/2009817).

2. Download GDP per capita data for the 20 countries of your choice. For each characteristic, create a scatterplot with the characteristic of the business environment (rank) on the horizontal axis, and GDP per capita on the vertical axis. Summarize the relationship between the two variables (if any).
3. Explain why a good business environment may raise GDP per capita.
4. Why might high GDP per capita improve the business environment?
5. From your answers to questions 3 and 4, explain the potential challenges when interpreting the relationship between two variables using a scatterplot.

QUESTION 16.4 CHOOSE THE CORRECT ANSWER(S)

Figure 16.8 (page 710) depicts the graphs of the long-run price-setting curve and the markup at which firm entry and exit are both zero.

Based on this information, which of the following statements is correct?

☐ An increase in the degree of competition in the economy will lower the price-setting curve.
☐ A lower interest rate leads to a lower price-setting curve.
☐ Lower worker productivity leads to a higher price-setting curve for a given markup μ^*.
☐ Higher risk of expropriation of businesses overseas results in a higher price-setting curve.

QUESTION 16.5 CHOOSE THE CORRECT ANSWER(S)

Which of the following statements is correct regarding the model of the labour market?

☐ In the short- and medium-run models the amount of capital is fixed, while in the long-run model the amount of capital can vary.
☐ Labour-saving technological progress raises unemployment in both the short and long run.
☐ In the long-run model, firms enter the market when the markup is low.
☐ In the long-run model, the markup is independent of the number of firms.

711

16.5 NEW TECHNOLOGY, WAGES, AND UNEMPLOYMENT IN THE LONG RUN

We have seen that, contrary to the fears of the Luddites, the constant increase in the amount produced in an hour of work has not resulted in ever-increasing unemployment. It is wages that on average have risen, not unemployment.

In many countries, the combination of technological progress and investment that raises the capital stock roughly doubled the productivity of labour each generation. Our model showed the result: a rise in the real wage that was consistent with profits high enough to motivate firm owners to continue investing, rather than using their wealth in other ways.

The Luddites were right to be concerned about the hardships experienced by those thrown out of work. What they missed is that the additional profits made possible by the introduction of the new technologies provided a kind of self-corrective: additional investments that would sooner or later result in the creation of new jobs.

The upward shift in the price-setting curve is illustrated in Figure 16.9a, which shows the status quo ('old technology') with the long-run equilibrium at A, and a technological advance that shifts the long-run equilibrium to B. At point B, the real wage is higher and so is the employment rate, in other words, unemployment is lower. The model shows that technological progress need not raise unemployment in the economy as a whole.

Before examining the experiences of unemployment in different countries, we need to understand:

- *What determines the rate of increase in the productivity of labour?* This accounts for the upward shift in the price-setting curve.
- *How does the economy shift from A to B?* Both are long-run equilibria in the labour market.   more

New knowledge and new technology: The innovation diffusion gap

It often takes years, if not decades, before an improved technology is widely introduced in an economy. This **diffusion gap** causes differences between the productivity of labour in the most advanced firms and the firms that lag technologically.

In the UK, one study found that the top firms are more than five times as productive as the bottom firms. Similar differences in productivity have been found in firms in India and China. In Indonesia's electronics industry—a part of the highly competitive global market—data from the late 1990s show that the firms at the 75th percentile were eight times as productive as those in the 25th percentile.

The low-productivity firms manage to stay in business because they pay lower wages to their employees, and in many cases earn a lower rate of profit on the owner's capital as well. Closing diffusion gaps can greatly increase the speed at which new knowledge and management practices are in widespread use.

This may occur when a union bargains for wages such that equivalent workers are paid the same throughout the economy. One consequence of this is that the least productive firms (which are also those paying low wages) will experience wage increases, making some of these firms unprofitable and putting them out of business. The union might also

diffusion gap The lag between the first introduction of an innovation and its general use. *See also: diffusion.*

support government policies that complement its role in hastening the exit of unproductive firms, raising average productivity in the economy and shifting up the price-setting curve. In this case, associations of workers can help bring about creative destruction instead of resisting it.

Associations of owners may also be part of the process of creative destruction by not seeking to prolong the life of unproductive firms, knowing that their demise is part of the process of making the pie larger. But in many cases, employees and owners of the lagging firms do not act in this way. They gain protection through subsidies, tariff protection, and bailouts that guarantee, at least for a time, the survival of the unproductive firm and its jobs.

The rate at which the economy's price-setting curve shifts upward depends on which of these attitudes towards the process of creative destruction is predominant. Economies differ greatly in this respect.

Adjustment to technological change: The employment and wage adjustment gap

Economies differ too in how they make the journey from the status-quo equilibrium like A to a new equilibrium such as B in Figure 16.9b.

Recall that the price-setting curve in the long-run model is the level of the real wage such that firms will neither enter nor leave the economy. So the move from point A (at 6% unemployment) to point B (at 4% unemployment) occurred because firms entered the economy, a process that takes some time. What happened along the way? Follow the steps in the analysis in Figure 16.9b to see one possible path.

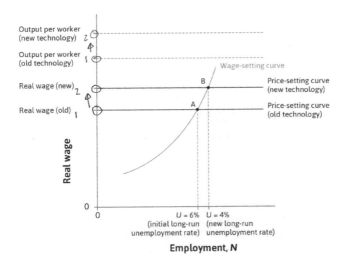

Figure 16.9a The long-run unemployment rate and new technology.

1. The long-run equilibrium before the new technology is introduced
This is at point A.

2. A technological advance
This shifts output per worker and the price-setting curve upwards.

3. The long run equilibrium effect on employment
At point B, the real wage is higher and unemployment is lower.

Was this a win-win journey? Only if you compare the start and end points or have a sufficiently long time horizon. The time between the introduction of new technology and the new long-run equilibrium is usually measured in years or even decades, not weeks or months. Younger workers might have more to gain from the eventual higher wages and employment, but older workers might never experience the outcome at B.

Also, note that in Figure 16.9b, we assumed that the real wage did not decline in the short run. But if the economy were to move to point D, firms could lower the real wage so that it lies on the wage-setting curve at the new level of unemployment. This is more likely to happen if the new investment that would take the economy to point E is slow in arriving. In that case, wages may fall under the pressure of greater unemployment before employment adjusts upwards.

We have already seen that in Britain, the adjustment to the technological progress in the eighteenth and nineteenth centuries (the Industrial Revolution) was not rapid. There was a prolonged delay before real wages began to rise continually, starting around 1830.

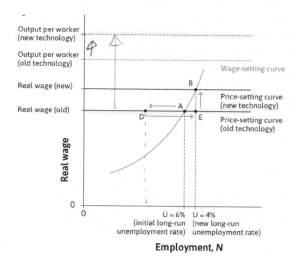

Figure 16.9b The long-run unemployment rate and new technology.

1. The response to new technology
A new technology means that fewer workers can produce the same output. How does the economy adjust?

2. The implementation of the new technology
The new technology initially displaces a substantial number of workers from their jobs. At point D, the wage is the same but there are fewer jobs.

3. Economic profits are high at D
New firms will be attracted to the economy and investment will rise. Unemployment eventually falls as the economy moves from D to E.

4. Wages rise
With lower unemployment, firms have to set higher wages to secure adequate worker effort, so wages go up.

5. A new equilibrium
Adjustment stops when the economy is at point B, with higher real wages and lower long-run unemployment.

Just as was the case with the diffusion gap, public policies, trade union, and employer association practices can alter the size of this employment and wage **adjustment gap**. Government policy can help reallocate workers to new firms and sectors by providing job-matching and retraining services, and by providing generous but time-limited unemployment benefits. This helps workers released from failing firms to move quickly to better ones.

The size of these adjustment gaps also depends on institutions and policies that could ease or hamper the creation of jobs in new sectors. If the wage is below the price-setting curve, profits are sufficient to create new investment and form new firms. This is part of the process of adjusting to creative destruction. Some countries have well-designed product-market regulation and competition policy that make it easier to start a new business. In others, incumbent businesses have succeeded in making it difficult for new firms to enter, which slows or even prevents the economy moving to point B.

Looking back at Figure 16.1, you may wonder why the unemployment rate does not shrink continuously in a world with continuous technological progress. The reason is that other forces in the economy lead to the wage-setting curve shifting upwards. Trade unions could be responsible for this shift (as in Unit 9), but there are other explanations:

- *Unemployment benefits*: Elected members of government may adopt more generous unemployment benefits as the economy adjusts to the new technology. They wish to assist those out of work. This improves the reservation position of workers and shifts the wage-setting curve up.
- *Rural wages*: Technological improvements in the countryside and migration from rural areas to cities associated with the implementation of new technology in manufacturing may raise rural incomes and therefore increase the workers' reservation option, which lowers the cost of losing a manufacturing job. As a result, urban employers must pay more to induce employees to work. This situation could occur in developing countries with large rural sectors.

We further explore these forces in Unit 17, when we investigate the golden age of capitalism following the Second World War.

Lessons from creative destruction and consumption smoothing

By this time, you may have noticed two recurring themes in this course:

- *Creative destruction*: Improvements in living standards often occur by a process of technological progress in which jobs, skills, entire sectors, and communities become obsolete and are abandoned. We study this process in Units 1, 2, 16, and 21.
- *Consumption smoothing*: Households faced with shocks to their income seek to even out the ups and downs of their standard of living through borrowing, unemployment benefits, mutual assistance among family and friends, and other forms of co-insurance. We studied this process in Units 10, 13, and 14.

The two themes above are related. People suffering from job destruction will suffer less if they can smooth their consumption. Economies differ greatly in the extent to which their policies, culture, and institutions allow

adjustment gap The lag between some outside change in labour market conditions and the movement of the economy to the neighbourhood of the new equilibrium.

consumption smoothing. In those that do this well, resistance to the creative-destructive forces of technological progress is likely to be low. In those that do not, owners and employees alike will try to find ways to resist (or halt) the process of creative destruction, preferring to defend their firm's assets and existing jobs.

The attitude of unions to the process of job destruction and creation is an example. In countries with adequate consumption-smoothing opportunities, trade unions tend not to insist on a worker's right to keep a particular job. Instead they demand adequate new job opportunities, and support in searching and training for new work.

In other countries, unions and government policy seek to protect the status quo matching of workers to jobs, for example by making it more difficult to terminate a labour contract, even when the worker has performed inadequately. This **employment protection legislation** may be harmful to labour market performance by enlarging the diffusion and adjustment gaps, and slowing the rate of technical progress, while at the same time pushing the wage-setting curve up.

These differing responses to the opportunities and challenges presented by creative destruction will help us understand why some economies performed better than others in recent history.

employment protection legislation
Laws making job dismissal more costly (or impossible) for employers.

Samuel Bentolila, Tito Boeri, and Pierre Cahuc. 2010. 'Ending the Scourge of Dual Markets in Europe' (http://tinyco.re/ 2724010). VoxEU.org. Updated 12 July 2010.

In our 'Economist in action' video, John Van Reenen uses the game of cricket to explain how the economy's average productivity is affected by the survival of low productivity firms. http://tinyco.re/ 4455896

QUESTION 16.6 CHOOSE THE CORRECT ANSWER(S)
Watch our 'Economist in action' video featuring John van Reenen about the determinants of the productivity of firms. Based on the video, which of the following statements is correct?

☐ The huge variation in productivity across countries and firms is due to differences in management practices.
☐ A country's openness to foreign direct investment (FDI) is more important for improving productivity than creative destruction.
☐ The 'creative' part of creative destruction is effective in improving productivity in the short and long run.
☐ A country's openness to imports can affect its productivity.

QUESTION 16.7 CHOOSE THE CORRECT ANSWER(S)
Figure 16.9b (page 714) depicts the long-run adjustment process in the labour market after technological progress.

Based on this information, which of the following statements is correct?

☐ The new technology does not cause any increase in unemployment, either in the short run or in the long run.
☐ At D firms increase investment, and hence employment, due to the large gap between the real wage paid and the workers' wage-setting curve.
☐ Lower unemployment at E implies a higher wage required to induce workers to exert high effort, resulting in the higher real wage at B.
☐ The adjustment from equilibrium A to the new equilibrium at B is immediate.

16.6 TECHNOLOGICAL CHANGE AND INCOME INEQUALITY

What happens to the distribution of income in an economy when a new technology is introduced that raises the productivity of labour? Think about the case we just studied in Figures 16.9a and 16.9b, where we highlight the contrast between the **short-run** immediate impact, and the **long-run** outcome that results once the higher profits, made possible by the innovation, have motivated additional investments by firm owners.

In the short run, the economy moves from point A to point D in Figure 16.9b. The new technology raises output per worker and reduces the number of people employed. For those employed at D, we assume that in the short run the real wage is unaffected.

What is the effect on inequality in the short run, at point D? Inequality increases for two reasons: first, because of the rise in the number of unemployed workers with low or no income, and second because in the short run only the employers reap the benefit of the new technology. The employers' share of output goes up. This is summarized in the first row of Figure 16.10. Of course, had wages at D fallen to meet the wage-setting curve at the new unemployment rate, this would have exacerbated the rise in inequality.

But this is not where the process ends. Point D in Figure 16.9b is not a Nash equilibrium because at the new level of productivity and the old real wage, firms are making sufficient profits to either attract new firms to enter or to incentivize existing firms to expand their output. Looking back to Figure 16.9b, the economy expands and more people are employed. This also pushes wages up along the wage-setting curve. This process will continue until the wage is sufficiently high that firms stop expanding or entering the economy, that is until the economy reaches point B, the new Nash equilibrium.

Comparing the new Nash equilibrium at point B with the initial one at point A, both workers and employers benefit from the new technology. The wage share is back at its initial level and inequality is lower at B because the unemployment rate is lower. Note that although the wage share at B is no higher than at A, real wages are higher.

The long-run effect of the change in technology was to slightly reduce inequality because:

- the share of output going to employees was restored to its pre-existing level in the long run due to an increase in real wages
- the higher real wage allowed employers to maintain motivation for workers to work hard at a lower level of unemployment

short run (model) The term does not refer to a period of time, but instead to what is exogenous: prices, wages, the capital stock, technology, institutions. *See also: price, wages, capital, technology, institutions, medium run (model), long run (model).*

long run (model) The term does not refer to a period of time, but instead to what is exogenous. A long-run cost curve, for example, refers to costs when the firm can fully adjust all of the inputs including its capital goods; but technology and the economy's institutions are exogenous. *See also: technology, institutions, short run (model), medium run (model).*

	In Figure 16.9b	Employment	Unemployment	Wage share	Inequality
Short run (number of firms and their capital stock do not change)	A to D	Down	Up	Down	Up
Long run (outcome adjusts fully to the new Nash equilibrium of the model, no change in wage-setting curve)	A to B	Up	Down	No change	Slightly down

Figure 16.10 Effects of technological improvements on the labour market model: Short and long run.

To see the effect on inequality, we will represent the initial situation by a Lorenz curve (introduced in Unit 5 and used also in Units 9 and 10), and then see how its shape changes. In Figure 16.11, the unemployed, workers, and employers are shown on the horizontal axis.

The solid line in Figure 16.11 is the Lorenz curve corresponding to the situation at point A in Figure 16.9b. When unemployment increases to D (on the horizontal axis), the Lorenz curve shifts out to the dashed one. The kink is lower, reflecting the lower wage share at point D. In the long run, unemployment falls to B and the wage share returns to its initial level. The Lorenz curve shifts inwards.

Follow the steps in the analysis in Figure 16.11 to see how the Lorenz curve changes on the way to the new equilibrium.

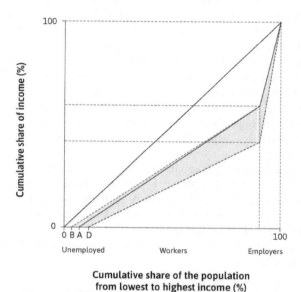

Figure 16.11 Effects of a new technology on inequality: Short and long run.

1. Unemployment before a new technology is introduced

The economy starts in long-run equilibrium before the new technology, with a share A of the population being unemployed (corresponding to point A in Figure 16.9b).

2. The implementation of the new technology

This displaces some workers from their jobs so that unemployment now increases to D (corresponding to point D in Figure 16.9b). We assume that wages remain the same for the remaining workers, so since output per worker has risen, wages as a share of output declines.

3. Economic profits are high

New firms will be attracted to the economy and investment will rise, so existing firms will expand. Unemployment eventually falls to the level shown by point B, the new long-run equilibrium.

EXERCISE 16.5 TECHNOLOGICAL PROGRESS AND INEQUALITY

The Einstein in Unit 9 showed that the Gini coefficient g can be calculated from the three groups of people in the economy-wide labour market as follows:

$$g = u + n - (1 - u)\frac{w}{\lambda}$$

Here, u represents the fraction unemployed, n the fraction of the labour force in employment, the quantity $1 - n - u$ the fraction of the labour force that are employers, w the real wage, and λ the output per worker. The expression w/λ is the fraction of total output that workers' wages can purchase, called the wage share. This is clear because wn is total wages paid, and λn is total output produced.

In the initial Lorenz curve (prior to the technical change), suppose there were 6 unemployed, 84 employed workers and 10 employers, with wages sufficient to purchase 60% of output.

1. Confirm that the Gini coefficient in this case would be 0.336.
2. Now suppose that technological progress leads to 4 workers losing their jobs while output stays constant, and the wage level of the remaining workers also stays constant, so profits increase by the amount that the total wage bill has dropped. What is the new wage share? What is the new Gini coefficient?
3. In the long run, assume there are 4 unemployed, 86 employed, and 10 employers, and the wage share returns to 60%. What is the Gini coefficient now? In your own words, explain why inequality increased in the short run and fell in the long run.

QUESTION 16.8 CHOOSE THE CORRECT ANSWER(S)

Does the introduction of a new labour-saving technology results in ...?

☐ Higher wage share of output and higher Gini coefficient in the short run.
☐ Lower wage share of output and higher Gini coefficient in the short run.
☐ Lower wage share of output and lower Gini coefficient in the short run.
☐ Higher unemployment, lower wage share of output, and higher Gini coefficient in the long run.

16.7 HOW LONG DOES IT TAKE FOR LABOUR MARKETS TO ADJUST TO SHOCKS?

How long is the long run? In 1923, John Maynard Keynes wrote:

John Maynard Keynes. 1923. *A Tract on Monetary Reform*. London, Macmillan and Co.

> The long run is a misleading guide to current affairs. *In the long run we are all dead.* Economists set themselves too easy, too useless a task if in tempestuous seasons they can only tell us that when the storm is past the ocean is flat again. (*A Tract on Monetary Reform*)

What you think about Keynes' quote, especially the italicized part, may depend on your age (he was 40 at time and would live another 23 years). The sea is flat in equilibrium, in Keynes' metaphor, but if you are interested in safe navigation what may be more important is what happens in the passage from one equilibrium to another, in other words, getting through the storm. Keynes advocated what we have earlier termed a dynamic view of the economy, that is, one that focuses on changes.

In Section 16.5 we studied how, if the labour market is knocked out of equilibrium by a labour-saving innovation that puts employees out of work, there may be a new long-run equilibrium in which the displaced workers are re-employed at higher wages. Keynes' point is that good economic policies have to be based on an understanding of how the economy gets from one equilibrium to the other and how long it takes.

But many economists since have taken what Keynes called the 'easy' approach and just focused on one or more equilibria. When something changes (like a new technology), economists compare the equilibrium before and after the change. This is termed the comparative static approach (static means unchanging, so the idea is to compare two things that are different–the before and after–but are themselves static.)

Hal Varian (1947–), an important American economic theorist, points out the difficulties in knowing what happens out of equilibrium and so tells the readers of his popular microeconomics text (http://tinyco.re/2912410): 'we will generally ignore the question of how the equilibrium is reached, and focus only on the issue of how firms behave in the equilibrium.'

Varian is right: it is important to know what happens in equilibrium and how the level of employment, wages, and profits that occur in equilibrium will differ depending on conditions and policies adopted. It is also not true that in the long run 'we' are all dead, unless the only people you count as 'we' are those alive now, not future generations who will live after you and experience the long run effects of the policies adopted now. And we know from Unit 4 that people do care about the wellbeing of others, so the long run matters even if it is very long.

If when things change, the economy moves quickly from one equilibrium to another, the comparative static approach advocated by Varian makes sense. If the process of equilibration takes a long time or if we cannot even be sure that the economy will move to another equilibrium (see 'Do bubbles exist?' in Unit 11 (page 482)), then Keynes' emphasis on the dynamics of the adjustment process seems appropriate.

In Unit 11 we explained that when a market is not in equilibrium, there are opportunities for economic actors to benefit by changing the price or quantity they are selling or buying. These so-called rent-seeking activities are part of the process by which a new equilibrium is established. In a fish market, for example, rent seeking just means offering or charging a different price, and the process of getting to a new equilibrium is relatively quick.

But in the labour market, if competition from other firms has reduced the demand for the good you are producing and put you out of work, the process is going to be slower. The reason is that the rent seeking that may bring about a new equilibrium may involve you retraining to develop a new set of skills, or you may have to uproot your family and seek work in a new location.

The debate on how quickly the US labour markets would adjust to the 'shock' of competition from imports of manufactured goods from China is a case in point. Around the turn of the current century after more than a decade of rapidly rising imports from China, there was a consensus among US economists that imports were not having any major negative effect on wages or employment, in part because workers producing goods competing with imports could easily relocate to other regions. In another of our earlier 'Economist in action' videos (http://tinyco.re/0004374) on global production and outsourcing, Richard Freeman asked if wages in the US were 'being set in Beijing' and answered with a resounding 'no'.

Yet evidence was accumulating even then that the adjustment of the US economy to the China shock was not going to be a simple textbook comparative static jump from one equilibrium to another. Most economists did not then anticipate the extent to which China would quickly come to dominate global production of manufactured goods: having produced one-twentieth of the world's manufactured goods in 1990, a quarter of a century later it produced a quarter of the global total.

But it was not just the unexpected size of the China shock that overturned the optimism of many economists; the labour market's adjustment did not work as quickly as they had assumed.

The impact on US labour markets was geographically concentrated: parts of the state of Tennessee specializing in furniture production and facing competition from China were hard hit, while nearby Alabama specializing in heavy industry was barely affected since China did not export heavy industrial goods. The geographical concentration of the effects of the China shock has allowed economists to study how labour markets adjusted.

They found that in US labour markets, the long run is a very long time. 'China exposed' regions suffered major losses in manufacturing employment; many of the jobless found it impossible to find work locally and gave up, they left the labour force. Very few left the region. Localities hit by import competition in the 1990s continued to be depressed into the second decade of this century. Between 1999 and 2011, the China shock led to a loss of 2.4 million jobs.

The conclusion of a major study of the China shock sounded more like Keynes than Varian. If one had to project the impact for the US labour market with nothing to go on other than a standard undergraduate economics textbook, one would predict large movements of workers between US tradable industries (meaning, exporting or competing with imports), for example, from apparel and furniture to pharmaceuticals and jet aircraft. You would also expect limited reallocation of jobs from tradables to non-tradables, and no net impacts on US aggregate employment. The reality of adjustment to the China trade shock has been very different.

Adjustment to the introduction of labour-saving machinery, which we have studied in this unit, is likely to be similarly slow. In Unit 18 we return to China in the world economy, and show that the response to the China shock in Germany was quite different.

Kathryn Graddy: Fishing for perfect competition http://tinyco.re/7406838

Richard Freeman: You can't outsource responsibility http://tinyco.re/0004374

EconTalk. 2016. 'David Autor on Trade, China, and U.S. Labor Markets' (http://tinyco.re/2829759). Library of Economics and Liberty. Updated 26 December 2016.

David Autor and Gordon Hanson. *NBER Reporter 2014 Number 2: Research Summary. Labor Market Adjustment to International Trade* (http://tinyco.re/2846538).

16.8 INSTITUTIONS AND POLICIES: WHY DO SOME COUNTRIES DO BETTER THAN OTHERS?

What do we mean by 'good' performance or a 'good' outcome? The answer matters because citizens who vote for parties with alternative economic programs, and policymakers who attempt to improve those programs, will need some concept of what is desirable—either for the individual, the policymaker, or the nation.

As we saw in Unit 3, people value their free time as well as their access to goods. We should include their reward per hour of work in our evaluation of outcomes. In any given year, a 'good' performance is one in which unemployment is low and real wages per hour are high. Putting this into a dynamic setting, and evaluating an economy over many years, we judge performance as 'good' if a country combines rapid growth of real wages per worker hour with low unemployment.

There are of course other dimensions of long-run economic performance that most people care about. We may care whether or not the distribution of economic rewards is fair, whether or not the economy's relationship with the natural environment is sustainable, or about the extent to which households are subjected to economic insecurity through business cycle fluctuations. But here we focus solely on the growth in real wages per hour and the unemployment rate.

We use the labour market model and the Beveridge curve to see that achieving good performance requires an economy to have two capacities:

- *To raise the price-setting curve and restrain the upward shift of the wage-setting curve*: So that both hourly wage growth and the long-run employment rate are high.
- *To adjust rapidly and fully*: So that the entire economy can take advantage of opportunities from technological change.

Technological change means jobs disappearing in firms in which new technology substitutes for workers. Jobs also disappear as new firms enter and those unable to adapt to the new conditions shut down. The Beveridge curve highlights the importance of matching workers and vacancies in the labour market. In Figure 16.9b, we saw that the impact of new technology is initially to displace workers: the Beveridge curve summarizes the economy's ability to rapidly redeploy displaced workers, shortening the period the economy spends in the short-run situation (point D, Figure 16.9b).

Figure 16.12 shows long-run performance (over a 40-year period) for a group of advanced economies. It uses the criteria of real wage growth and unemployment rates. We study a long period because we do not want our evaluation of long-term performance to be affected by the particular phase of the business cycle in which a country finds itself (it will look much better at the peak than at the trough). We use wages in manufacturing because they are measured in ways that are more accurately comparable across nations—although this is not ideal, because the share of employment in manufacturing shrinks over time and varies across countries.

Good performance places a country in the top-left corner of Figure 16.12, with high wage growth and low unemployment; bad performance places a country in the bottom-right corner. Since we value both high wage growth and low unemployment, we may be prepared to tolerate low wage growth if it is associated with a lower level of unemployment. This means that we can represent a citizen's indifference curve as a ray from the origin. Steeper rays are better, and a country's performance is measured by the steepness of a ray from the origin to that country's observation. If you look at Figure 16.12, and take Belgium (BEL) as an example: a Belgian citizen would prefer to be on a steeper ray, like that of Germany (GER), with lower unemployment and higher wage growth.

The two rays in Figure 16.12 divide the countries into three groups. The high performers over the 40-year period from 1970 to 2011 are Norway and Japan. The low performers are Belgium, Italy, US, Canada, and Spain. The poor performance of the US is in part due to the fact that it started with higher wages in 1970, because it was the world's technology leader during this period (as we saw in Figure 16.3). This meant that other nations could learn from it, rapidly raising their productivity. Similar arguments apply to Canada. For this reason we do not take these two countries as representative of the low performers, although real wages have grown much more slowly than productivity in the US, so most US citizens did not benefit very much from economic growth in this period.

Notice that successful countries used different combinations of policies and institutions. Some of the best performers (on steeper rays from the origin) like Norway, Finland, Sweden, and Germany have powerful unions, while the Nordic countries (including Denmark) have some of the most generous unemployment benefits in the world.

Figure 16.13 reproduces the unemployment data from Figure 16.1, but with two of the high performers and two of the low performers from Figure 16.12 highlighted. The differences between Japan and Norway on one hand, and Italy and Spain on the other, centre on unemployment rather than real wage growth. In Figure 16.13 you can see how unemployment behaved differently following the oil shocks of the 1980s, and after the financial crisis.

We shall see that the model in this unit provides a useful framework for understanding the high and low performers of the labour market. We will now show how to use the model to explain the way that institutions and policies affect real wage growth and unemployment in the long run.

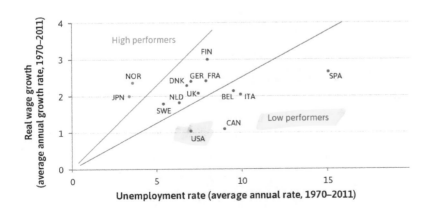

OECD. 2015. *OECD Statistics* (http://tinyco.re/9377362); BLS data for Spanish real wages available only from 1979. Spanish real wage growth for 1970–1979 has therefore been estimated using Tables 16.25 and 16.5 from Barciela López, Carlos, Albert Carreras, and Xavier Tafunell. 2005. *Estadísticas históricas de España: Siglos XIX-XX*. Bilbao: Fundación BBVA.

Figure 16.12 Long-run unemployment and real wage growth across the OECD (1970–2011).

EXERCISE 16.6 YOU ARE THE POLICYMAKER

Refer to Figure 16.12 (page 723) to answer the following questions:

1. Using the same axes, draw the indifference curves of a citizen or policymaker who cares only about wage growth.
2. According to the data in the figure, which countries would be the high performers and which would be the low performers?
3. Using the same axes, draw your indifference curves if you only cared about the unemployment rate. Which countries would be the high and low performers in this case?
4. Using the same axes, draw an indifference curve based on your own personal preferences over wage growth and unemployment, and justify your choice.
5. Now considering your preferences over other economic factors, which country in the figure would you choose to live in, and why? Explain which economic factors you included in your decision.

Data from 1960–2004: David R. Howell, Dean Baker, Andrew Glyn, and John Schmitt. 2007. 'Are Protective Labor Market Institutions at the Root of Unemployment? A Critical Review of the Evidence' (http://tinyco.re/2000761). *Capitalism and Society* 2 (1) (January). Data from 2005 to 2012: OECD harmonized unemployment rates, OECD. 2015. *OECD Statistics* (http://tinyco.re/9377362).

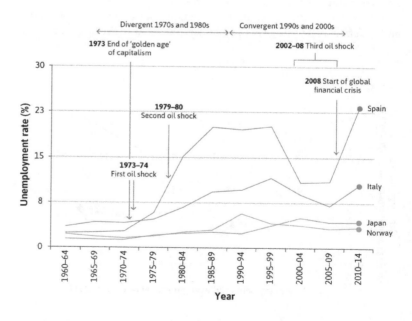

Figure 16.13 Unemployment rates of two high and two low labour market performers (1960–2014).

QUESTION 16.9 CHOOSE THE CORRECT ANSWER(S)

The following graph plots the real wage growth of different countries against their unemployment rate, averaged over the period 1970–2011.

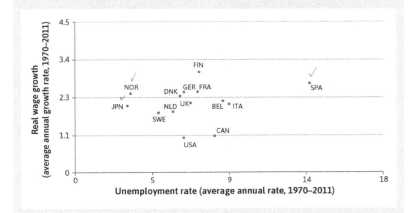

Based on this information, which of the following statements is correct?

☐ If you only cared about unemployment, then Finland is the country with the best performance.

☐ If you only cared about wage growth, then European countries have outperformed North American countries.

☐ If you cared about both unemployment and wage growth, then Spain is one of the best-performing countries.

☐ If you cared about both unemployment and wage growth, then Finland has unambiguously outperformed Norway.

●●●●●

16.9 TECHNOLOGICAL CHANGE, LABOUR MARKETS, AND TRADE UNIONS

Policies and institutions make a difference. The models shed light on the experience of some of the best and worst performers. We take three countries as examples: Norway and Japan as good performers, and Spain as a poor performer.

In Norway and Spain, unions are important, but not in Japan. In Norway, more than half of all wage and salary workers are trade union members, and union wage deals affect most workers in the economy. In Spain, although union wage deals are important for the entire economy, less than one-fifth of Spanish workers are in unions.

Figure 16.14 provides information on the importance of union wage deals and unemployment. On the horizontal axis, we plot the percentage of employees whose wages are determined by union wage deals. As you can see, in some European countries, union wage deals cover almost all employees. And in the set of countries with coverage of more than 80%, unemployment rates range from less than 4% (Netherlands) to almost 14% (Spain). Figure 16.14 suggests that there is no tendency for unemployment to be higher in countries in which unions are more influential in wage-setting. Low unemployment is found in countries extending across the

725

whole range of union strength. Compare South Korea and the Netherlands, Japan and Austria, or the US and Sweden.

Just as the employer does not offer the lowest wage possible, most unions do not seek the highest wage they could win in bargaining. Employers offer wages above the minimum because they cannot control how hard the worker works. Unions do not bargain for the maximum wage possible (the wage that would leave none of the pie for the owners) because unions cannot control the firm's decisions about hiring, firing, and investment, and higher wages may reduce employment by reducing the firm's profits.

A union organized across many firms and sectors will not exploit all the bargaining power it possesses. It knows that large wage gains will lead to:

- *In the **medium run***: Restrictive aggregate demand policies, as the government and central bank seek to keep inflation close to target (as we saw in Unit 15).
- *In the **long run***: The exit of firms and a smaller stock of capital goods, which will slow the rate of productivity growth.

Unions that act this way are called **inclusive trade unions**. Non-inclusive unions may bargain for high wages in their own corner of the economy without regard for the effects on other firms or workers, both employed and unemployed. Employers' associations that take account of the interests of all businesses, including those that might enter an industry and compete with its incumbent firms, are called inclusive business or employers' associations. When unions and businesses act in an inclusive manner there is also more likely to be a positive union voice effect. As discussed in Unit 9, this lowers the disutility of work, helping to push down the wage-setting curve.

The Nordic case: Inclusive unions and employers' associations

This inclusive behaviour is exactly what the trade unions and employers' associations of Norway (as well as in the other Nordic countries) did over this period: their centralized wage bargaining insisted on a common wage for a given kind of labour, depriving low-productivity firms of access to

medium run (model) The term does not refer to a period of time, but instead to what is exogenous. In this case capital stock, technology, and institutions are exogenous. Output, employment, prices, and wages are endogenous. *See also: capital, technology, institutions, short run (model), long run (model).*

inclusive trade union A union, representing many firms and sectors, which takes into account the consequences of wage increases for job creation in the entire economy in the long run.

OECD. 2015. *OECD Statistics* (http://tinyco.re/9377362). Labour force statistics. Visser, Jelle. 2016. 'ICTWSS: Database on Institutional Characteristics of Trade Unions, Wage Setting, State Intervention and Social Pacts in 51 countries between 1960 and 2014' (http://tinyco.re/2809024) *Amsterdam Institute for Advanced Labour Studies (AIAS).*

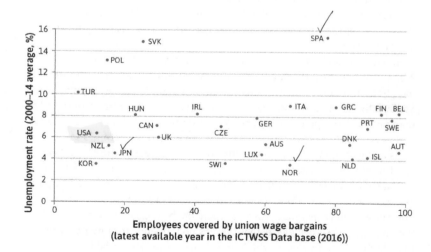

Figure 16.14 Union wage bargaining coverage and unemployment across the OECD (2000–2014).

inexpensive labour and driving many of them out of business. As workers were quickly redeployed to employment in more productive firms, the main impact was to raise average labour productivity, pushing up the price-setting curve and allowing higher wages.

Inclusive trade unions also support generous income floors and high-quality publicly provided healthcare, occupational retraining, and educational services—all of which reduce the risk to which most individuals are exposed. This has the effect of making the creative destruction of technological change less destructive for people's personal lives and allows them to be generally more open to change and to risk-taking. Both of these attributes are essential for a technologically dynamic society.

These so-called 'active labour market policies' improve the matching process between workers looking for work and job vacancies available for workers. A result is that workers whose jobs are eliminated (for example, by the failure of low-productivity firms under the pressure of centrally bargained uniform wages) can find an alternative job more quickly. The result is a Beveridge curve closer to the origin, superior to both the German and US Beveridge curves (shown in Figure 16.6). It is far inside that of Spain, as we see in Figure 16.15.

An inclusive union knows that the economy has to respect the two major incentive problems of a capitalist economy: providing incentives for workers to work and for employers to invest. In some cases—for example, in Sweden with its highly centralized trade union federation—trade union leaders knew and persuaded their members that in the long run, pushing down the wage-setting curve will increase employment and will not reduce wages.

As a result, the inclusive unions of the Nordic countries (Norway, Sweden, Finland, and Denmark) set their wage demands in accordance with the productivity of labour. When it rose they demanded a fair share. They had bargaining power from low unemployment, high membership, and their ability to implement wage agreements across the economy, but they did not use this power to push the wage-setting curve up unless it was warranted by productivity growth. These unions also supported legislation and policies that make working less onerous, shifting downward the wage-setting curve, and further expanding long-run employment.

Adrian Wooldridge. 2013. 'Northern Lights' (http://tinyco.re/2892712). *The Economist*. Updated 2 February 2013.

Torben M Andersen, Bengt Holmström, Seppo Honkapohja, Sixten Korkman, Hans Tson Söderström, and Juhana Vartiainen. 2007. *The Nordic Model: Embracing Globalization and Sharing Risks* (http://tinyco.re/2490148). Helsinki: Taloustierto Oy.

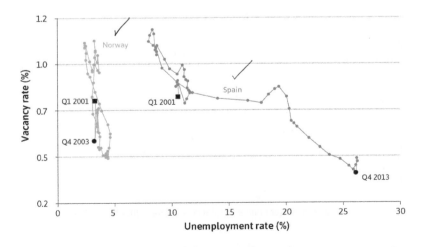

OECD Employment Outlook: OECD. 2015. *OECD Statistics* (http://tinyco.re/9377362).

Figure 16.15 Beveridge curves for Spain and Norway (2001 Q1 – 2013 Q4).

The Japanese case: Inclusive employers' associations

In contrast to the Nordic countries, Japanese unions are weak, but workers are well organized in the large companies. Employers' associations are strong and work to coordinate wage-setting among the large firms. These associations therefore operate in a similar way to the unions in Norway: the impact of wage decisions on the economy as a whole is taken into account when wages are set. Specifically, the corporations deliberately do not compete in hiring workers, so as to avoid raising wages.

The Spanish case: Non-inclusive unions

Unions protect jobs in Spain, supported by government policy. Wage-setters in Spain are strong enough to wield power, but are not inclusive. A combination of non-inclusive unions and supportive government legislation that protects jobs may help to account for the poor performance of the Spanish labour market.

Based on the model, we would predict high unemployment in Spain, and low unemployment in Norway and Japan. And that is what we see in the data.

Unemployment benefits and unemployment

The employment-enhancing effects of inclusive trade union and government co-insurance policies may help to explain an apparent anomaly: countries with generous unemployment benefits do not have higher rates of unemployment (see Figure 16.16).

This is anomalous, because in our model an increase in the unemployment benefit would, *ceteris paribus*, reduce the workers' cost of job loss, and shift the wage-setting curve up.

The contrast between unemployment rates and benefits in Norway and Italy illustrates the point. An unemployed person gets a benefit of almost 50% of previous gross earnings in Norway, and unemployment is low; in contrast, benefits in Italy offer a 10% **gross replacement rate**, and unemployment is much higher than in Norway. The implication is that countries that are able to implement generous but well-designed unemployment insurance schemes, coordinated with job placement services and other active labour market policies, can achieve low rates of unemployment. Providing people with oppor-

gross unemployment benefit replacement rate The proportion of a worker's previous gross (pre-tax) wage that is received (gross of taxation) when unemployed.

OECD. 2015. *OECD Statistics* (http://tinyco.re/9377362).

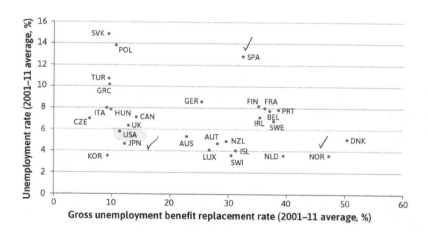

Figure 16.16 Unemployment benefit generosity and unemployment rates across the OECD (2001–2011).

tunities to smooth consumption may make them readier to embrace new technology, which will shift the price-setting curve upward.

EXERCISE 16.7 UNEMPLOYMENT RATES AND LABOUR MARKET INSTITUTIONS

Some people have argued that high unemployment in some European countries relative to the US during the 1990s and 2000s was due to the existence of rigid labour market institutions (for example, powerful unions, generous unemployment benefits, and strong employment protection legislation).

1. Using Figure 16.1 (page 693), check if the unemployment rate has always been higher in most European countries compared to the US.
2. From what you have learned from this section, and by looking at Figures 16.1, 16.14 (page 726), and 16.16 (page 728), evaluate the claim that high unemployment in Europe was due to the existence of rigid labour market institutions.

You can read more about the role of institutions in European unemployment in these papers. Olivier Blanchard and Justin Wolfers. 2000. 'The Role of Shocks and Institutions in the Rise of European Unemployment: The Aggregate Evidence'. *The Economic Journal* 110 (462) (March): pp. 1–33. David R Howell, Dean Baker, Andrew Glyn, and John Schmitt. 2007. 'Are Protective Labor Market Institutions at the Root of Unemployment? A Critical Review of the Evidence' (http://tinyco.re/2000761). *Capitalism and Society* 2 (1) (January).

QUESTION 16.10 CHOOSE THE CORRECT ANSWER(S)

The following is a plot of unemployment rate and trade union density for the period 2000–2012. Trade union density is defined as the fraction of employees who are union members.

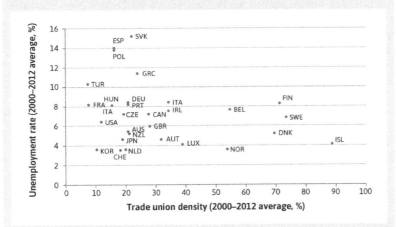

Based on this information, which of the following statements is correct?

☐ High trade union density is a necessary condition for a low unemployment rate.

☐ Low trade union density results in high unemployment.

☐ Considering only the Nordic countries (Norway, Denmark, Sweden, and Finland), it can be concluded that high trade union density leads to a low unemployment rate.

☐ Given the trade union density, the relative unemployment outcomes indicate that inclusiveness of trade unions is higher in Norway than in Belgium.

16.10 CHANGES IN INSTITUTIONS AND POLICIES

We have seen that differences in institutions and policies make a big difference for employment and wage growth, and that citizens of Spain might wish to have institutions like those of Japan or a Nordic country. But changing institutions is difficult because it inevitably creates winners and losers.

Countries that changed their policies changed their fortunes. Both the UK and the Netherlands suffered sharply increased unemployment rates in the 1970s and early 1980s due to the first and second oil shocks (which shifted the price-setting curve down) and the increased bargaining power of labour (which shifted the wage-setting curve up). These effects are illustrated in Figure 16.17. But a change in policy eventually turned the bad news around. In the UK, the unemployment rate fell from 11.6% in 1985 to 5.1% in 2002, and in the Netherlands it fell from 9.2% to 2.8% over the same period.

Both countries turned around their economies and shifted the wage-setting curves down, but they used different institutions and policies:

- *In the Dutch case*: Institutions became more inclusive, moving in a Nordic direction by common agreement.
- *In the British case*: Policy reduced the power of the non-inclusive unions and increased competition in labour markets.

In the Netherlands, a key component was an agreement in 1982 between employers and unions called the Wassenaar Accord. Unions offered wage restraint (a downward shift in the wage-setting curve) and in exchange, the employers agreed to a reduction in working hours. The union agreed that the reduction in working hours would not increase labour costs (and hence would not shift the price-setting curve down).

Stephen Nickell and Jan van Ours. 2000. 'The Netherlands and the United Kingdom: A European Unemployment Miracle?' *Economic Policy* 15 (30): pp. 136–180.

David R. Howell, Dean Baker, Andrew Glyn, and John Schmitt. 2007. 'Are Protective Labor Market Institutions at the Root of Unemployment? A Critical Review of the Evidence' (http://tinyco.re/2000761). *Capitalism and Society* 2 (1) (January). Data from 2005 to 2012: OECD harmonized unemployment rates, OECD. 2015. *OECD Statistics* (http://tinyco.re/9377362).

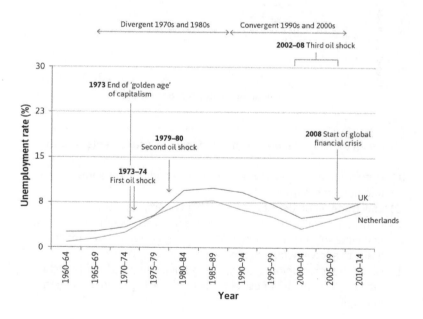

Figure 16.17 Different ways of pushing down the wage-setting curve: The Netherlands and the UK.

In the Dutch case, unions and employers' associations were capable of coordinating wage-setting to achieve a better macroeconomic outcome. They were powerful enough that they could ensure their members stuck to the agreement. The unions were exercising bargaining restraint in the interests of improved performance of the labour market, and hence in the economy as a whole.

In the UK, the wage-setting curve also shifted down but in this case, it was because of a fall in union power brought about by changing industrial relations legislation, which weakened the ability of the non-inclusive unions to organize strike action.

EXERCISE 16.8 THE LABOUR MARKET MODEL

Explain how to use the labour market model (wage-setting curve and price-setting curve) to show the changes in labour market performance of the UK and the Netherlands from the early 1970s to the early 2000s, as discussed in this section. The article by Nickell and van Ours (2000) referenced above is a good research resource for this question.

16.11 SLOWER PRODUCTIVITY GROWTH IN SERVICES, AND THE CHANGING NATURE OF WORK

The rise and fall of manufacturing employment

As discussed in Unit 1, before the Industrial Revolution most of the output of the economy was made by family members. They were not employees but instead were independent producers of the goods and services both for their own use (called home production) and for sale to others. The Industrial Revolution and the emergence of the capitalist economic system shifted labour from the family and the farm to firms: independent producers became employees.

Due to technological progress in machine-based production, manufactured goods became cheaper. As a result, textiles and clothing once produced in the home were now purchased and paid for with the wages gained through industrial and other employment. The result was a sustained increase in employment in the industrial sector of the economy. Manufacturing makes up most of the employment in **industry**, and the terms manufacturing and industry are often used interchangeably.

> **industry** Goods-producing business activity: agriculture, mining, manufacturing, and construction. Manufacturing is the most important component.

Labour-saving innovation also made farming more productive. And as people became richer they spent less of their budget on food. Therefore the fraction of the labour force engaged in farming fell.

For many, the shift out of farming and the rise of manufacturing employment meant an improvement in economic opportunities, especially when the trade unions and worker-based political parties forced employers to improve industrial working conditions.

This did not last forever though. Figure 16.18 shows that for most of the world's large economies, the era of expanding manufacturing employment ended sometime in the third quarter of the twentieth century. Just as manufacturing had initially displaced agriculture as the main kind of employment, the production of services rather than goods has replaced manufacturing. Follow the steps in the analysis in Figure 16.18 to see how major industrial economies passed through stages of rising and falling manufacturing employment at different times.

The economics of slower productivity growth in services

The amount of labour devoted to agriculture has declined in all of the countries shown in Figure 16.18. Fewer than one in 20 workers in rich countries work in agriculture. The recent big shift in work has been from the production of goods (manufacturing and agriculture) to the production of services. We know that output per hour of labour (productivity) is growing more slowly in the production of services than in manufacturing. This has two effects:

- *An employment shift*: To produce the same mix of goods and services it now takes relatively less labour devoted to goods and more to services.
- *A consumption shift*: The costs of producing goods have fallen relative to the costs of producing services, and so the prices of goods have fallen relative to the prices of services. This leads people to buy more goods and fewer services than they otherwise would have done.

The first of these effects has been stronger than the second.

To see how this process works, let's simplify by using a model in which only the first effect occurs. So we assume that people consume a given ratio

US Bureau of Labor Statistics. 2004. *International Labor Comparisons (ILC)* (http://tinyco.re/2780183). Updated 14 October; International Labour Association. 2015. *ILOSTAT Database* (http://tinyco.re/2040567); The Conference Board. *International Comparisons of Annual Labor Force Statistics, 2013* (http://tinyco.re/2640734).

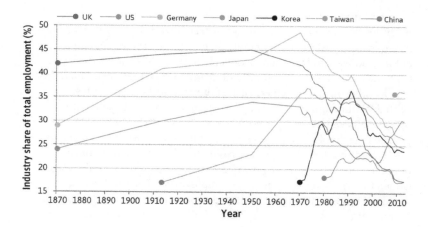

Figure 16.18 The rise and fall of the share of employment in industry (1870–2013).

1. The shift of employment out of industry
This was led by the UK and the US around 1950, followed by Japan and Germany about 20 years later.

2. South Korea's rise to industrial prominence
This began only in the last quarter of the twentieth century, yet the share of manufacturing employment in South Korea was already falling by the end of the century.

3. Manufacturing in Taiwan and Germany
Taiwan now has a larger share of the labour force in manufacturing than Germany.

4. Manufacturing in China
Unlike the other countries in the figure, in China labour continued to be pulled into the manufacturing sector in the first decade of the 21st century.

of goods (shirts, for example) and services (haircuts). The examples illustrate the reason for slower productivity growth in services: it takes about as long today to cut someone's hair as it did 100 or even 200 years ago, but to produce a shirt it takes much less time than it did 200 years ago (probably less than a fifth).

Figure 16.19 shows the model. The total amount of labour employed in the economy is assumed to be 1 (it could be 1 million hours, for example). If all of this labour is devoted to the production of goods, 1 unit of goods is produced. And the same is true of services: if all the labour produces services, then 1 unit of services is produced.

The solid red line is the feasible frontier, showing the amounts of goods and services that are possible given the existing technologies and the amount of labour employed. We assume that the same number of units of goods and services are consumed, so in the figure the quantity of services and the quantity of goods consumed both equal half a unit in the first period. In the second period, productivity rises in manufacturing while staying constant in services, meaning that the cost and hence the price of goods declines relative to services. Follow the steps in the analysis to see the effect on employment.

Labour has shifted from goods production to services production. This model is designed to illustrate why the shift took place. Two things left out of the model have, in reality, reduced the shift, and a third one has increased it:

- *Productivity increases in some services reduces the shift*: We assumed that there was no productivity increase in services. But think of the kinds of services we have discussed in this unit, such as the sharing of music or other forms of digital information, where the productivity advances have been large. If productivity in services increased, then in our model it would at least partially offset the shift in labour. We will see just below, however, that much of the service sector of the economy is made up of such things as personal care, which is more like haircuts than the reproduction of music.
- *Substitution of goods for services reduces the shift*: We increase the proportion of goods we consume if their relative price falls. By assuming that the ratio of goods (shirts) to services (haircuts) did not change, we ignored this process. It would partially offset the decline in goods employment.
- *An increase in relative demand for services increases the shift*: We also ignored the possibility that as incomes rise, people choose to spend more of their budget on services. Remember that services include tourism and other forms of recreation, and also include health, education, and care, which may not be paid directly out of the household's disposable income. This would reinforce the shift of labour into services. We have seen this before: it is equivalent to the earlier shift of labour out of agriculture that occurred when the share of food in household budgets shrank.

However, in the countries showing a decline in goods employment relative to services, the net effect of the things we have excluded from the model did not completely offset the deindustrialization of the workforce.

Another complicating factor is that some countries are net importers of goods while others are net exporters, meaning that many goods are purchased in a different country from where they were produced. This is part of the explanation for why different countries have different patterns for the hump-shaped relationship shown in Figure 16.18. International trade and the opportunities for specialization that came with it accelerated the decline in the goods-producing share of employment in some countries (the US and the UK, for example), but slowed it down in others (Germany, South Korea).

China's growing share of employment in goods reflects the forces seen elsewhere in the now-rich countries and its specialization in exporting manufactured goods. The Einstein at the end of this section illustrates the logic behind Figure 16.19 and analyses the result of a productivity increase in goods production.

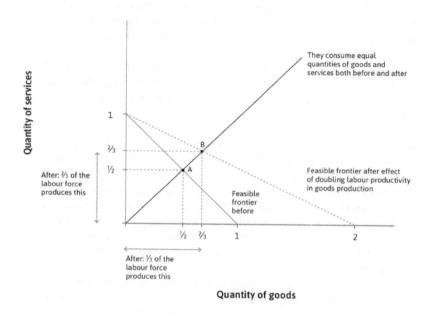

Figure 16.19 Increased productivity in goods production raises the fraction of workers in services.

1. The feasible frontier
The solid red line is the feasible frontier and shows the amounts of goods and services that can be produced given the existing technologies and labour available.

2. Equal split of goods and services
We assume equal amounts of goods and services are consumed: at A, the amount consumed of each equals 1/2.

3. Manufacturing productivity increases
The productivity of labour in the production of goods doubles, but productivity remains unchanged in services. The new feasible frontier is shown as the dashed line.

4. More goods, more services
If people continue to consume equal amounts of goods and services, the economy will be at point B with production and consumption of 2/3 units of each.

5. A shift in employment
At B, labour has shifted from the production of goods to the production of services: 1/3 of the labour produces goods, and 2/3 produces services.

EINSTEIN

How faster productivity growth in goods production may shift employment from goods to services

This Einstein explains the logic behind Figure 16.19 and explains why a productivity increase in goods production shifts employment to firms that produce services. We define λ_s as the productivity of labour in services. Then $\lambda_s = Q_s/L_s$, the quantity of services divided by the amount of labour employed to produce it. In our model, the following equation holds:

$$\lambda_s L_s = Q_s = Q_g = \lambda_g L_g$$

- $\lambda_s L_s = Q_s$: The productivity of labour in services multiplied by the amount of labour in services is equal to the amount of services produced.
- $Q_s = Q_g$: The output of goods must be the same as the output of services. This isn't always true, but we defined it that way in our model.
- $Q_g = \lambda_g L_g$: The output of goods is equal to the productivity of labour in the production of goods multiplied by the amount of labour employed in producing goods.

We can now equate the first and last terms of the above equation to give us an expression for the amount of labour that must be employed in the two sectors, given the productivity levels in each sector, if they produce an equal number of units of output:

$$\lambda_s L_s = \lambda_g L_g$$

We then rewrite this expression, using the fact that the total amount of labour in the two sectors sums to one:

$$\lambda_s L_s = \lambda_g L_g = \lambda_g (1 - L_s)$$

Then we rearrange the equation using the first and last terms to get an expression for the amount of labour engaged in service production:

$$L_s = \frac{\lambda_g}{\lambda_g + \lambda_s}$$

In the figure, productivity in both of the two sectors was 1, so the amount of labour engaged in goods production was 1/2. When the productivity of labour in goods production doubles:

$$L_s = \frac{2}{2+1} = \frac{2}{3}$$

This is the share of labour devoted to the production of services after the increase in productivity of the labour used in the production of goods.

16.12 WAGES AND UNEMPLOYMENT IN THE LONG RUN

We have learned that national economies differ not only in how rapidly they adjust to the opportunities offered by technological change and other changes of circumstance, but also in the wages and employment that they can sustain in the long run.

These depend on many of the characteristics of economies that we have analysed in earlier units. Figure 16.20 summarizes the determinants of the unemployment rate and the growth rate of real wages, and notes the units where these concepts are discussed.

Figure 16.21 builds on Figure 16.20 by showing the institutions and policies that can affect the growth of real wages and the unemployment rate.

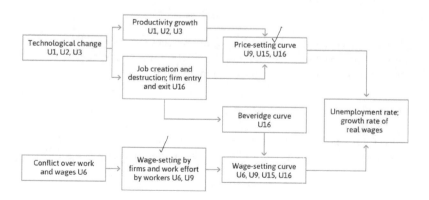

Figure 16.20 Determinants of the unemployment rate and the growth rate of real wages in the long run.

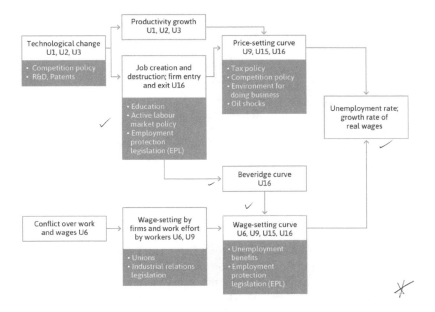

Figure 16.21 The institutions, policies, and shocks that can influence unemployment and real wages.

16.13 CONCLUSION

Unemployment is a market failure: it means that there are people willing to work at the current market wage but cannot find a willing employer. Job destruction is a constant feature of capitalist economies, in which technological changes tend to raise productivity and put some workers out of their jobs. But a well-functioning economy will also feature high levels of investment that ensure that jobs are created at least as fast as they are destroyed.

Ensuring that firms will invest both in technological progress and in job creation is one of the fundamental incentive problems of a capitalist economy. The other is ensuring that workers have the incentive to put in sufficient effort to do their jobs. We have analysed these incentives using the price-setting curve and the wage-setting curve, which show respectively the maximum wage that firms can pay and still remain in the industry, and the minimum wage that can be paid to get sufficient effort from workers.

The main difference between the high-performing economies and the laggards is that in high-performing economies, institutions and policies work so that the incentives of the main actors are to increase the size of the pie, rather than wasting resources fighting over the size of the slice.

> *Concepts introduced in Unit 16*
> Before you move on, review these definitions:
>
> • Creative destruction
> • Marginal product of capital
> • Job creation, job destruction
> • Diminishing marginal product of capital
> • Beveridge curve
> • Labour market matching
> • Long-run price-setting curve
> • Equilibrium markup
> • Diffusion gap, adjustment gap

16.14 REFERENCES

Andersen, Torben M., Bengt Holmström, Seppo Honkapohja, Sixten Korkman, Hans Tson Söderström, and Juhana Vartiainen. 2007. *The Nordic Model: Embracing Globalization and Sharing Risks* (http://tinyco.re/2490148). Helsinki: Taloustierto Oy.

Autor, David, and Gordon Hanson. *NBER Reporter 2014 Number 2: Research Summary. Labor Market Adjustment to International Trade* (http://tinyco.re/2846538).

Bentolila, Samuel, Tito Boeri, and Pierre Cahuc. 2010. 'Ending the Scourge of Dual Markets in Europe' (http://tinyco.re/2724010). *VoxEU.org*. Updated 12 July 2010.

Blanchard, Olivier, and Justin Wolfers. 2000. 'The Role of Shocks and Institutions in the Rise of European Unemployment: The Aggregate Evidence'. *The Economic Journal* 110 (462): pp. 1–33.

Blanchflower, David G., and Andrew J. Oswald. 1995. 'An Introduction to the Wage Curve' (http://tinyco.re/2712192). *Journal of Economic Perspectives* 9 (3): pp. 153–167.

Burda, Michael, and Jennifer Hunt. 2011. 'The German Labour-Market Miracle' (http://tinyco.re/2090811). *VoxEU.org*. Updated 2 November 2011.

Carlin, Wendy and David Soskice. 2015. *Macroeconomics: Institutions, Instability, and the Financial System*. Oxford: Oxford University Press. Chapters 8, 15.

EconTalk. 2016. 'David Autor on Trade, China, and U.S. Labor Markets' (http://tinyco.re/2829759). Library of Economics and Liberty. Updated 26 December 2016.

Habakkuk, John. 1967. *American and British Technology in the Nineteenth Century: The Search for Labour Saving Inventions*. United Kingdom: Cambridge University Press.

Hobsbawm, Eric, and George Rudé. 1969. *Captain Swing*. London: Lawrence and Wishart.

Howell, David R., Dean Baker, Andrew Glyn, and John Schmitt. 2007. 'Are Protective Labor Market Institutions at the Root of Unemployment? A Critical Review of the Evidence' (http://tinyco.re/2000761). *Capitalism and Society* 2 (1).

Keynes, John Maynard. 1923. *A Tract on Monetary Reform*. London, Macmillan and Co.

Nelson, Richard R., and Gavin Wright. 1992. 'The Rise and Fall of American Technological Leadership: The Postwar Era in Historical Perspective' (http://tinyco.re/2811203). *Journal of Economic Literature* 30 (4) (December): pp. 1931–1964.

Nickell, Stephen, and Jan van Ours. 2000. 'The Netherlands and the United Kingdom: A European Unemployment Miracle?'. *Economic Policy* 15 (30) (April): pp. 136–180.

Rifkin, Jeremy. 1996. *The End of Work: The Decline of the Global Labor Force and the Dawn of the Post-Market Era*. New York, NY: G. P. Putnam's Sons.

Singer, Natasha. 2014. 'In the Sharing Economy, Workers Find Both Freedom and Uncertainty' (http://tinyco.re/2844216). *The New York Times*. Updated 16 August 2014.

Sterk, Vincent. 2015. 'Home Equity, Mobility, and Macroeconomic Fluctuations' (http://tinyco.re/2186300). *Journal of Monetary Economics* 74 (September): pp. 16–32.

Wooldridge, Adrian. 2013. *Northern Lights* (http://tinyco.re/2892712). Updated 2 February 2013.

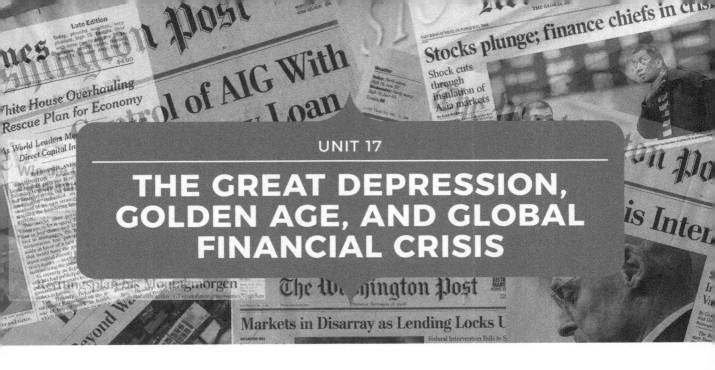

ECONOMISTS HAVE LEARNED DIFFERENT LESSONS FROM THREE PERIODS OF DOWNTURN AND INSTABILITY THAT HAVE INTERRUPTED OVERALL IMPROVEMENTS IN LIVING STANDARDS IN HIGH INCOME ECONOMIES SINCE THE END OF THE FIRST WORLD WAR

- There have been three distinctive economic epochs in the hundred years following the First World War—the roaring twenties and the Great Depression, the golden age of capitalism and stagflation, and the great moderation and subsequent financial crisis of 2008.

- The end of each of these epochs—the stock market crash of 1929, the decline in profits and investment in the late 1960s and early 1970s culminating in the oil shock of 1973, and the financial crisis of 2008, respectively—was a sign that institutions that had governed the economy to that point had failed.

- The new institutions marking the golden age of capitalism—increased trade union strength and government spending on social insurance—addressed the aggregate demand problems highlighted by the Great Depression and were associated with rapid productivity growth, investment, and falling inequality.

- Nevertheless, the golden age ended with a crisis of profitability, investment, and productivity, followed by stagflation.

- The policies adopted in response to the end of the golden age restored high profits and low inflation at the cost of rising inequality, but did not restore the investment and productivity growth of the previous epoch, and made economies vulnerable to debt-fuelled financial booms. One of these booms precipitated a global financial crisis in 2008.

Before dawn on Saturday, 7 February 2009, 3,582 firefighters began deploying across the Australian state of Victoria. It would be the day remembered by Australians as Black Saturday: the day that bushfires devastated 400,000 hectares, destroyed 2,056 homes, and took 173 lives.

But when the fire brigades suited up that morning, there had not been any reports of fire. What had mobilized every firefighter in Victoria was the McArthur Forest Fire Danger Index (FFDI), which the previous day exceeded what (until then) had been its calibrated maximum of 100—a level that had been reached only during the bushfires of January 1939. When the FFDI exceeds 50, it indicates 'extreme' danger. A value above 100 is 'catastrophic' danger. On 6 February 2009 it had hit 160.

Later there would be accusations, trials and even a Royal Commission to determine who or what had caused Australia's worst natural disaster. There were many possible causes: lightning strikes, sparks from farm machinery, faulty power lines, or even arson.

A single spark or a lightning strike did not cause Black Saturday. Every day sparks ignite small bush fires, and on that day alone the Royal Commission reported 316 separate grass, scrub or forest fires. This was not a calamity because of any one of these local fires, but because of conditions that transformed easily contained bushfires into an unprecedented disaster.

Small causes are sometimes magnified into large effects. Avalanches are another natural example. In electricity grids, a failure of one link in the net-work overloads other links, leading to a cascade of failures and a blackout.

Small causes with big consequences are found in economics too, for example in the **Great Depression** of the 1930s and the **global financial crisis** of 2008.

Although recessions are characteristic of capitalist economies, as we have seen, they rarely turn into episodes of persistent contraction. This is because of a combination of the economy's self-correcting properties and successful intervention by policymakers. Specifically:

- *Households take preventative measures that dampen rather than amplify shocks* (Unit 13).
- *Governments create automatic stabilizers* (Unit 14).
- *Governments and central banks take actions to produce negative rather than positive feedbacks when shocks occur* (Units 14 and 15).

But, like Black Saturday, occasionally a major economic calamity occurs. In this unit, we look at three crises that have punctuated the last century of unprecedented growth in living standards in the rich countries of the world—the Great Depression of the 1930s, the end of the **golden age of capitalism** in the 1970s, and the global financial crisis of 2008.

The global financial crisis in 2008 took households, firms, and govern-ments around the world by surprise. An apparently small problem in an obscure part of the housing market in the US caused house prices to plummet, leading to a cascade of unpaid debts around the world, and a collapse in global industrial production and world trade.

To economists and historians, the events of 2008 looked scarily like what had happened at the beginning of the Great Depression in 1929. For the first time they found themselves fretting about the level of the little-known Baltic Dry Index (http://tinyco.re/4186755), a measure of shipping prices for commodities like iron, coal, and grain. When world trade is booming, demand for these commodities is high. But the supply of freight capacity is inelastic, so shipping prices rise and the Index goes up. In May 2008, the Baltic Dry Index reached its highest level since it was first published in

Philip Ball. 2002. 'Blackouts Inherent in Power Grid.'. *Nature News*. Updated 8 November 2002.

Philip Ball. 2004. 'Power Blackouts Likely.' *Nature News*. Updated 20 January 2004.

Great Depression The period of a sharp fall in output and employ-ment in many countries in the 1930s.
global financial crisis This began in 2007 with the collapse of house prices in the US, leading to the fall in prices of assets based on subprime mortgages and to widespread uncertainty about the solvency of banks in the US and Europe, which had borrowed to purchase such assets. The ramifications were felt around the world, as global trade was cut back sharply. Goverments and central banks responded aggressively with stabilization policies.
golden age (of capitalism) The period of high productivity growth, high employment, and low and stable inflation extending from the end of the Second World War to the early 1970s.

1985. But the reverse is also true—by December, many more people were checking the Index because it had fallen by 94%. The fall told them that, thousands of miles from the boarded-up houses of bankrupt former homeowners in Arizona and California where the crisis had begun, giant $100-million freighters were not moving because there was no trade for them to carry.

In 2008 economists remembered the lessons of the Great Depression. They encouraged policymakers globally to adopt a coordinated set of actions to halt the collapse in aggregate demand, and to keep the banking system functioning.

But economists also share some of the responsibility for the policies that made this crisis more likely. For 30 years, unregulated financial and other markets had been stable. Some economists incorrectly assumed that they were immune to instability. So the events of 2008 also show how a failure to learn from history helps create the next crisis.

How did a small problem in the US housing market send the global economy to the brink of a catastrophe?

- *The dry undergrowth:* In Unit 18, you will see that there was rapid growth in the globalization of international capital markets, measured by the amount of foreign assets owned by domestic residents. At the same time, the globalization of banking was occurring. Some of the unregulated expansion of lending by global banks ended up financing mortgage loans to so-called **subprime borrowers** in the US.
- *The spark:* Falling real estate prices meant that banks with very high leverage, and therefore with thin cushions of net worth (equity), in the US, France, Germany, the UK and elsewhere quickly became insolvent.
- *The **positive feedback** mechanism:* Fear was transmitted around the world and customers cancelled orders. Aggregate demand fell sharply. The high degree of interconnection among global banks and the possibility of massive transactions in a matter of seconds made excessive leverage an increasingly dangerous source of instability.
- *The complacent policymakers:* With few exceptions, most policymakers and the economists whose advice they sought still believed that the financial sector was able to regulate itself. The international central bank for central banks—the Bank for International Settlements in Basel— allowed banks great scope to choose their level of leverage. Banks could use their own models to calculate the riskiness of their assets. They could meet the international regulatory standards for leverage by understating the riskiness of their assets, and by parking these risky assets in what are called shadow banks, which they owned but which were outside the scope of banking regulations. All of this was entirely legal. Many economists continued to believe that economic instability was a thing of the past, right up to the onset of the crisis itself. It is as if Australian firefighters had watched the Forest Fire Danger Index hit 160, but did nothing because they didn't believe a fire was possible.

In 1666 the Lord Mayor of London was called to inspect a fire that had recently started in the city. It might have been halted, had he permitted the demolition of the surrounding houses. But he judged that the risk the fire posed was small, and feared the cost of compensating the owners of the houses. The fire spread, and the Great Fire of London ultimately destroyed most of the city. Like the Lord Mayor, policymakers in the twenty-first

For a list of booms, banking busts and crises see Table 8, Chapter 10 of: Carmen M Reinhart and Kenneth S Rogoff. 2009. *This Time Is Different: Eight Centuries of Financial Folly*. Princeton, NJ: Princeton University Press.

subprime borrower An individual with a low credit rating and a high risk of default. *See also: subprime mortgage.*

positive feedback (process) A process whereby some initial change sets in motion a process that magnifies the initial change. *See also: negative feedback (process).*

Baumslag Webb and Rupert Read. 2017. 'How Should Regulators deal with Uncertainty? Insights from the Precautionary Principle'. *Bank Underground.*

743

century were reluctant to impose stronger regulations on the financial sector because they would have reduced the sector's profitability. They did not appreciate the much larger cost that their failure to regulate would cause the economy.

Some of those involved admitted afterwards that their belief in the stability of the economy had been wrong. For example, Alan Greenspan, who had been in charge of the US central bank (the Federal Reserve) between 1987 and 2006, admitted this error to a US government committee hearing.

HOW ECONOMISTS LEARN FROM FACTS

'I made a mistake'
On 23 October 2008, a few weeks after the collapse of the US investment bank Lehman Brothers, former US Federal Reserve chairman Alan Greenspan admitted that the accelerating financial crisis had shown him 'a flaw' in his belief that free, competitive markets would ensure financial stability. In a hearing of the US House of Representatives Committee on Oversight and Government Reform, Greenspan was questioned by the chair of the House Committee, Congressman Henry Waxman:

WAXMAN: Well, where did you make a mistake then?
GREENSPAN: I made a mistake in presuming that the self-interest of organizations, specifically banks and others, was best capable of protecting [the banks'] own shareholders and their equity in the firms … So the problem here is that something which looked to be a very solid edifice, and, indeed, a critical pillar to market competition and free markets, did break down. And I think that, as I said, shocked me. I still do not fully understand why it happened and, obviously, to the extent that I figure out where it happened and why, I will change my views. If the facts change, I will change.
WAXMAN: You had a belief that [quoting Greenspan] 'free, competitive markets are by far the unrivalled way to organize economies. We have tried regulation, none meaningfully worked.' You have the authority to prevent irresponsible lending practices that led to the subprime mortgage crisis. You were advised to do so by many others. [Did you] make decisions that you wish you had not made?
GREENSPAN: Yes, I found a flaw …
WAXMAN: You found a flaw?
GREENSPAN: I found a flaw in the model … that defines how the world works, so to speak.
WAXMAN: In other words, you found that your view of the world was not right, it was not working.
GREENSPAN: Precisely. That's precisely the reason I was shocked, because I had been going for 40 years or more with very considerable evidence that it was working exceptionally well.

As the financial crisis unfolded in the summer and autumn of 2008, economists in government, central banks, and universities diagnosed a crisis of aggregate demand and bank failure. Many of the key policymakers in this crisis were economists who had studied the Great Depression.

They applied the lessons they had learned from the Great Depression in the US: cut interest rates, provide liquidity to banks, and run fiscal deficits.

In November 2008, ahead of the G20 summit in Washington, British Prime Minister Gordon Brown told reporters: 'We need to agree on the importance of coordination of monetary and fiscal policy. There is a need for urgency. By acting now we can stimulate growth in all our economies. The cost of inaction will be far greater than the cost of any action.'

A direct comparison between the first 10 months of the Great Depression and the 2008 financial crisis shows that the collapse of industrial production in the world economy was similar (compare January 1930 and January 2009 in Figure 17.1a). But lessons had been learned: in 2008, monetary and fiscal policy responses were much larger and more decisive than in 1930, as shown in Figures 17.1b and 17.1c.

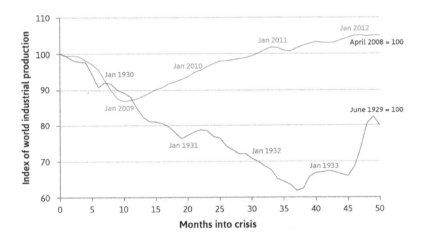

Miguel Almunia, Agustín Bénétrix, Barry Eichengreen, Kevin H. O'Rourke, and Gisela Rua. 2010. 'From Great Depression to Great Credit Crisis: Similarities, Differences and Lessons.' *Economic Policy* 25 (62): pp. 219–65. Updated using CPB Netherlands Bureau for Economic Policy Analysis. 2015. 'World Trade Monitor.'

Figure 17.1a The Great Depression and the global financial crisis: Industrial production.

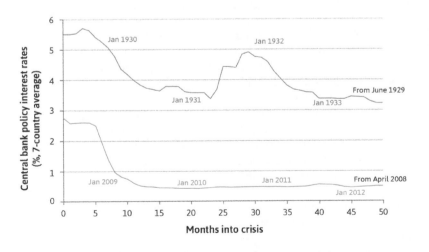

As in Figure 17.1a, updated using national central bank data.

Figure 17.1b The Great Depression and the global financial crisis: Monetary policy.

As in Figure 17.1a, updated using International Monetary Fund. 2009. *World Economic Outlook: January 2009*; International Monetary Fund. 2013. 'IMF Fiscal Monitor April 2013: Fiscal Adjustment in an Uncertain World, April 2013.' April 16.

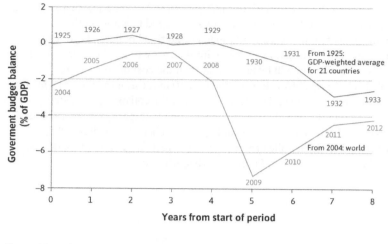

Figure 17.1c The Great Depression and the global financial crisis: Fiscal policy.

17.1 THREE ECONOMIC EPOCHS

In the past 100 years, the economies we often refer to as 'advanced' (basically meaning 'rich'), including the US, western Europe, Australia, Canada, and New Zealand, have seen average living standards measured by output per capita grow six-fold. Over the same period, hours of work have fallen. This is a remarkable economic success, but it has not been a smooth ride.

Units 1 and 2 told the story of how rapid growth began. In Figures 13.2 and 13.3, we contrasted the steady long-run growth rate from 1921 to 2011 with the fluctuations of the business cycle, which go from peak to peak every three to five years.

In this unit we will study three distinctive epochs. Each begins with a period of good years (the light shading in Figure 17.2), followed by a period of bad years (the dark shading):

- *1921 to 1941:* The crisis of the Great Depression is the defining feature of the first epoch. It inspired Keynes' concept of **aggregate demand**, now standard in economics teaching and policymaking.
- *1948 to 1979:* The golden age epoch stretched from the end of the Second World War to 1979, and is named for the economic success of the 1950s and 1960s. The golden age ended in the 1970s with a crisis of profitability and productivity, and the emphasis in economics teaching and policymaking shifted away from the role of aggregate demand toward **supply-side problems**, such as productivity and decisions by firms to enter and exit markets.
- *1979 to 2015:* In the most recent epoch, the global financial crisis caught the world by surprise. The potential of a debt-fuelled boom to cause havoc was neglected during the preceding years of stable growth and seemingly successful macroeconomic management, which had been called the **great moderation**.

The term 'crisis' is routinely applied to the first and the last of these episodes because they represented an unusual but recurrent cataclysmic divergence from the normal ups-and-downs of the economy. In the second epoch, the end of the golden age also marked a sharp deviation from what

aggregate demand The total of the components of spending in the economy, added to get GDP: $Y = C + I + G + X - M$. It is the total amount of demand for (or expenditure on) goods and services produced in the economy. *See also: consumption, investment, government spending, exports, imports.*

supply side (aggregate economy) How labour and capital are used to produce goods and services. It uses the labour market model (also referred to as the wage-setting curve and price-setting curve model). *See also: demand side (aggregate economy).*

great moderation Period of low volatility in aggregate output in advanced economies between the 1980s and the 2008 financial crisis. The name was suggested by James Stock and Mark Watson, the economists, and popularized by Ben Bernanke, then chairman of the Federal Reserve.

had become normal. The three unhappy surprises that ended the epochs are different in many respects, but they share a common feature: positive feedbacks magnified the effects of routine shocks that would have been dampened under other circumstances.

What does Figure 17.2 show?

- *Productivity growth:* A broad measure of economic performance is the growth of hourly productivity in the business sector. Productivity growth hit low points in the Great Depression, at the end of the golden age epoch in 1979, and in the wake of the financial crisis. The golden age of capitalism got its name due to the extraordinary productivity growth until late in that epoch. The dashed blue lines show the average growth of productivity for each sub-period.
- *Unemployment:* High unemployment, shown in red, dominated the first epoch. The success of the golden age was marked by low unemployment as well as high productivity growth. The end of the golden age produced spikes in unemployment in the mid 1970s and early 1980s. In the third epoch, unemployment was lower at each successive business cycle trough until the financial crisis, when high unemployment re-emerged.

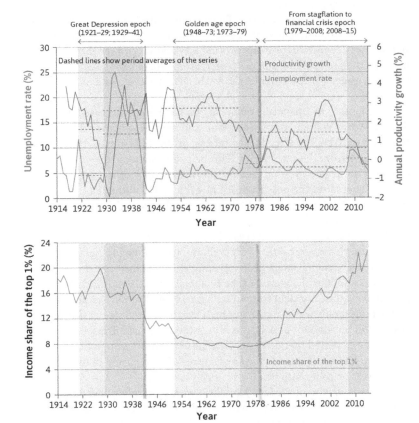

United States Bureau of the Census. 2003. Historical Statistics of the United States: Colonial Times to 1970, Part 1. United States: United States Govt Printing Office; Facundo Alvaredo, Anthony B Atkinson, Thomas Piketty, Emmanuel Saez, and Gabriel Zucman. 2016. 'The World Wealth and Income Database (WID).'; US Bureau of Labor Statistics; US Bureau of Economic Analysis.

Figure 17.2 Unemployment, productivity growth, and inequality in the US (1914–2015).

- *Inequality:* Figure 17.2 also presents data on inequality for the US: the income share of the top 1%. The richest 1% had nearly one-fifth of income in the late 1920s just before the Great Depression. Their share then steadily declined until a U-turn at the end of the golden age eventually restored the income share of the very rich to 1920s levels.

We saw in earlier units that continuous technological progress has characterized capitalist economies, driven by the incentives to introduce new technology. Based on their expected after-tax profits, entrepreneurs make investment decisions to get a step ahead of their competitors. Productivity growth reflects their collective decisions to invest in new machinery and equipment that embody improvements in technology. Figure 17.3 shows the growth rate of the capital stock and the profit rate of firms in the non-financial corporate sector of the US economy (before and after the payment of taxes on profits).

The data in Figure 17.3 illustrates that capital stock growth and firm profitability tend to rise and fall together. As we saw in Unit 14, investment is a function of expected post-tax profits, and expectations will be influenced by what has happened to profitability in the recent past. Once firms make a decision to invest, there is a lag before the new capital stock is ordered and installed.

As profitability was restored following the collapse of the stock market in 1929 and the banking crises of 1929–31, investment recovered and the capital stock began to grow again. During the golden age, profitability and investment were both buoyant. A closer look at Figure 17.3 is revealing. Investment depends on post-tax profitability and we can see that the gap between the pre-tax (red) and post-tax (green) rate of profit declined during the golden age. The lower panel shows the **effective tax rate** on corporate profits.

Wars have to be financed, and the tax on businesses increased during the Second World War and the Korean War, and more slowly over the course of the Vietnam War. The effective tax rate on profits fell from 8% to 2% during the 30 years from the early 1950s. This helped to stabilize the post-tax rate of profit. In the late 1970s and early 1980s, taxes on profits were cut sharply. Thereafter the pre-tax profit rate fluctuated without a trend. But in spite of the stabilization of profitability in the third epoch, the growth rate of the capital stock fell.

On the eve of the financial crisis, Figures 17.2 and 17.3 show that the richest Americans were doing very well. But this did not stimulate investment, with the capital stock growing more slowly than at any time since the Second World War. The onset of the financial crisis also coincided with a peak in private sector debt (shown in Figure 17.4). Debt in financial firms and in households was at a postwar high (relative to the size of GDP). The swelling in the amount of debt was clearest for financial firms, but households also increased their debt-to-GDP ratio steadily through the 2000s.

Figure 17.5a summarizes the key features of each period in the US economy over the past century.

The three epochs of modern capitalism were worldwide phenomena, but some countries experienced them differently compared to the US. By 1921, the US had been the world productivity leader for a decade, and the world's largest economy for 50 years. Its global leadership in technology and its global firms help explain rapid catch-up growth in Europe and Japan during the golden age. On either side of the golden age, the crises that began in the

> **effective tax rate on profits** This is calculated by taking the before-tax profit rate, subtracting the after-tax profit rate, and dividing the result by the before-tax profit rate. This fraction is usually multiplied by 100 and reported as a percentage.

$$\frac{C-P}{P} \not= 100$$

US in 1929 and 2008 became global crises. Figure 17.5b summarizes important differences between the US and other rich countries.

The three epochs of modern capitalism are very different, as Figures 17.5a and 17.5b show. We need to use the full range of tools of analysis we have developed in previous units to understand their dynamics, and how one epoch is related to another.

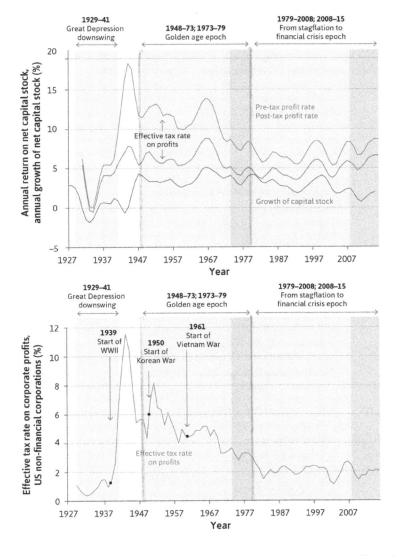

US Bureau of Economic Analysis.

Figure 17.3 Upper panel: Capital stock growth and profit rates for US non-financial corporations (1927–2015). Lower panel: Effective tax rate on profits for US non-financial corporations (1929–2015).

US Federal Reserve. 2016. 'Financial Accounts of the United States, Historical.' December 10; US Bureau of Economic Analysis.

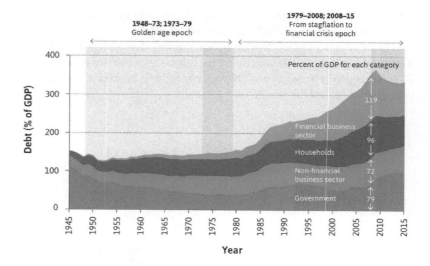

Figure 17.4 Debt as a percentage of GDP in the US: Households, non-financial business sector, financial business sector, and the government (1945–2015).

Name of Period	Dates	Important features of the US economy
1920s	1921–1929	Low unemployment High productivity growth Rising inequality
Great Depression	1929–1941	High unemployment Falling prices Unusually low growth rate of business capital stock Falling inequality
Golden age	1948–1973	Low unemployment Unusually high productivity growth Unusually high growth rate of capital stock Falling effective tax rate on corporate profits Falling inequality
Stagflation	1973–1979	High unemployment and inflation Low productivity growth Lower profits
1980s and the great moderation	1979–2008	Low unemployment and inflation Falling growth rate of business capital stock Sharply rising inequality Rising indebtedness of households and banks
Financial crisis	2008–2015	High unemployment Low inflation Rising inequality

Figure 17.5a The performance of the US economy over a century.

QUESTION 17.1 CHOOSE THE CORRECT ANSWER(S)

The following figure shows the unemployment rate (left-hand axis) and productivity growth (right-hand axis) in the US between 1914 and 2015.

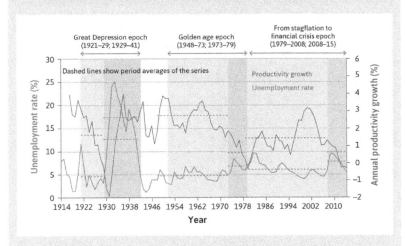

Based on this information, which of the following statements is correct?

☐ The US has been able to achieve increasingly lower unemployment rates in its boom years through this period.

☐ There was a consistent and significant fall in productivity growth during the Great Depression era.

☐ The US economy's performance in 1979–2008 was less strong than during the other two boom periods, with a higher average unemployment rate and lower average productivity growth.

☐ The unemployment rate reached in the recent financial crisis was the highest since the stagflation years of 1973–79.

Name of Period	Differences between US and other rich countries
Great Depression	US: Large, sustained downturn in GDP starting from 1929 UK: Avoided a banking crisis, experienced a modest fall in GDP
Golden age	US: Technology leader Outside US: Diffusion of technology creates catch-up growth, improving productivity
Financial crisis	US: Housing bubble creates banking crisis Germany, Nordic countries, Japan, Canada, Australia: Did not experience bubble, largely avoided financial crisis
International openness (all three periods)	More important in most countries than in the US

Figure 17.5b A cross-national comparison of the Great Depression, the golden age, and the financial crisis: Distinctive features of the US.

QUESTION 17.2 CHOOSE THE CORRECT ANSWER(S)

The following figure shows the income share of the top 1% richest households in the US between 1914 and 2013.

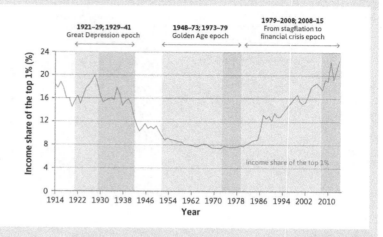

Based on this information, which of the following statements are correct?

- ☐ Inequality always rises in boom years.
- ☐ Inequality can either rise or fall during recessions.
- ☐ The great moderation era was distinct from the other two boom periods in that inequality rose during the period.
- ☐ The top 1% richest US households received nearly one-fifth of the total income in 2010.

17.2 THE GREAT DEPRESSION, POSITIVE FEEDBACKS, AND AGGREGATE DEMAND

Capitalism is a dynamic economic system, and as we saw in Unit 13, booms and recessions are a recurrent feature even when weather-driven fluctuations in agricultural output are of limited importance in the economy. But not all recessions are equal. In Unit 14, we saw that in 1929 a downturn in the US business cycle similar to others in the preceding decade transformed into a large-scale economic disaster—the Great Depression.

The story of how the Great Depression happened is dramatic to us, and must have been terrifying to those who experienced it. Small causes led to ever-larger effects in a downward spiral, like the cascading failures of an electricity grid during a blackout. Three simultaneous positive feedback mechanisms brought the American economy down in the 1930s:

- *Pessimism about the future:* The impact of a decline in investment on unemployment and of the stock market crash of 1929 on future prospects spread fear among households. They prepared for the worst by saving more, bringing about a further decline in consumption demand.
- *Failure of the banking system:* The resulting decline in income meant that loans could not be repaid. By 1933, almost half of the banks in the US had failed, and access to credit shrank. The banks that did not fail raised interest rates as a hedge against risk, further discouraging firms from

investing and curbing household spending on automobiles, refrigerators, and other durable goods.

- *Deflation:* Prices fell as unsold goods piled up on store shelves.

Deflation affects aggregate demand through several routes. The most important channel operated through the effect of deflation on those with high debts. Since debts were denominated in nominal terms, deflation pushed up their real value. This positive feedback channel was new because in earlier episodes of deflation levels of debt had been much lower. Households stopped buying cars and houses, and many debtors become insolvent, creating problems for both borrowers and the banks. One-fifth of those in owner-occupied and rented accommodation were in default. Farmers were among those with high levels of debt. Prices of their produce were falling, pulling down their incomes directly and pushing up the burden of their debt. They responded to this by increasing production, which made the situation worse by reducing prices further. When prices are falling, people also postpone the purchase of durables, which further reduces aggregate demand.

Few people understood these positive feedback mechanisms at the time, and the government's initial attempts to reverse the downward spiral failed. This was partly because the government's actions were based on mistaken economic ideas. It was also because even if they had pursued ideal policies, the government's share of the economy was too small to counter the powerful destabilizing trends in the private sector.

Figure 17.6 shows the fall in industrial production that started in 1929. In 1932 it was less than 60% of the 1929 level. This was followed by a recovery, until it fell again by 20% in 1937. Unemployment remained above 10% until 1941, the year the US entered the Second World War. Consumer prices fell with GDP from 1929 to 1933 and remained stable until the early 1940s.

> **deflation** A decrease in the general price level. *See also: inflation.*

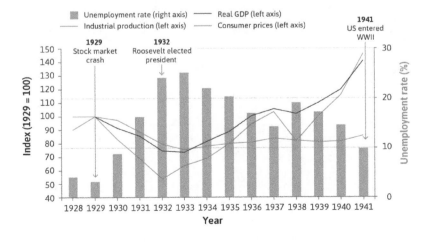

United States Bureau of the Census. 2003. [Historical Statistics of the United States: Colonial Times to 1970, Part 1] (tinyco.re/9147417). United States: United States Govt Printing Office; Federal Reserve Bank of St Louis (FRED).

Figure 17.6 The effect of the Great Depression on the US economy (1928–1941).

EXERCISE 17.1 FARMERS IN THE GREAT DEPRESSION

During the Great Depression, demand for agricultural output fell. Faced with falling prices for agricultural output and with high levels of debt, farmers increased production. The response of farmers may have made sense from an individual point of view, but collectively it made the situation worse. Using wheat farmers as an example, and assuming that wheat farms are all identical, draw diagrams of an individual price-taking farm's cost curves and industry-wide supply and demand to illustrate this situation. Explain your reasoning.

17.3 POLICYMAKERS IN THE GREAT DEPRESSION

Just as the day of Australia's major bushfire is now called Black Saturday, the day that the Great Depression started is now known as Black Thursday. On Thursday 24 October 1929, the US Dow Jones Industrial Average fell 11% on opening, starting three years of decline for the US stock market. Figure 17.7 shows the business cycle upswings and downswings from 1924 to 1941.

The <u>long downswing</u> from the third quarter of 1929 until the first quarter of 1933 was <u>driven by big falls in household</u> and <u>business investment</u> (the red bar), and <u>in consumption of non-durables</u> (the green bar). Recall that in Figure 14.6 we used the multiplier model to describe how this shock created a fall in aggregate demand, and in Figure 14.8 we described a model of how households had cut consumption to restore their target wealth, to understand the observed behaviour of households and firms in the Great Depression.

In Unit 14, we showed how <u>government policy could amplify or dampen fluctuations</u>. In the opening years of the Great Depression, government

[margin handwriting: Multiplier Model]

Appendix B in Robert J. Gordon. 1986. *The American Business Cycle: Continuity and Change*. Chicago, Il: University of Chicago Press.

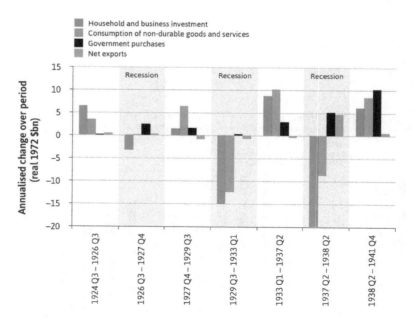

Figure 17.7 Changes in the components of aggregate demand during upswings and downswings (1924 Q3–1941 Q4).

policy both amplified and prolonged the shock. Initially, government purchases and net exports hardly changed. As late as April 1932 President Herbert Hoover told Congress that 'far-reaching reduction of governmental expenditures' was necessary, and advocated a balanced budget. Hoover was replaced by Franklin Delano Roosevelt in 1932, at which point government policy changed.

Austerity policy!

Fiscal policy in the Great Depression

Fiscal policy made little contribution to recovery until the early 1940s. Estimates suggest that output was 20% below the full employment level in 1931, for example, which means that the small budget surplus in that year would have implied a large cyclically adjusted surplus, given the decline in tax revenues in the depressed economy.

CFP

Under Roosevelt, from 1932 to 1936 the government ran deficits. When the economy went into recession in 1938–39, the deficit shrank from its peak of 5.3% in 1936 to 3% in 1938. This was another mistake that reinforced the downturn. The big increase in military spending from early 1940 (well before the US entered the Second World War in late 1941) contributed to the recovery.

Monetary policy in the Great Depression

Monetary policy prolonged the Great Depression. The real interest rate data in Figure 17.8 suggest that monetary policy was contractionary in the US economy from 1925 onwards: the real interest rate increased, reaching a peak of 13% in 1932. Once the downturn began in 1929, this policy stance reinforced, rather than offset, the decline of aggregate demand. But note that the nominal interest rate was falling after its peak in 1929; the real interest rate went up because prices were falling too. Interest-sensitive spending on buildings and consumer durables decreased sharply.

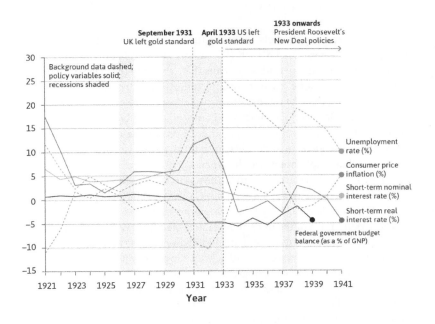

Milton Friedman and Anna Jacobson J. Schwartz. 1982. *Monetary Trends in the United States and the United Kingdom, Their Relation to Income, Prices, and Interest Rates, 1867–1975*. Chicago, Il: University of Chicago Press; United States Bureau of the Census. 2003. Historical Statistics of the United States: Colonial Times to 1970, Part 1. United States: United States Govt Printing Office; Federal Reserve Bank of St Louis (FRED).

Figure 17.8 Policy choices in the Great Depression: The US (1921–1941).

gold standard The system of fixed exchange rates, abandoned in the Great Depression, by which the value of a currency was defined in terms of gold, for which the currency could be exchanged. *See also: Great Depression.*

zero lower bound This refers to the fact that the nominal interest rate cannot be negative, thus setting a floor on the nominal interest rate that can be set by the central bank at zero. *See also: quantitative easing.*

New Deal US President Franklin Roosevelt's program, begun in 1933, of emergency public works and relief programs to employ millions of people. It established the basic structures for modern state social welfare programs, labour policies, and regulation.

THE GREAT DEPRESSION
The period during the 1930s in which there was a sharp fall in output and employment, experienced in many countries.

- Countries that left the gold standard earlier in the 1930s recovered earlier.
- In the US, Roosevelt's New Deal policies accelerated recovery from the Great Depression, partly by causing a change in expectations.

The gold standard

The US was still on what was known as the **gold standard**. This meant that the US authorities promised to exchange dollars for a specific quantity of gold (the promise was to pay an ounce of gold for $20.67). Under the gold standard, the authorities had to continue to pay out gold at the fixed rate and, if there was a fall in demand for US dollars, gold would flow out of the country. To prevent this, either the country's tradable goods had to become more competitive (boosting gold inflows through higher net exports) or gold had to be attracted through capital inflows. This could done by either putting up the nominal interest rate or keeping it high relative to the interest rate in other countries. To avoid contributing to the gold outflow, policymakers were reluctant to push the interest rate down to the **zero lower bound**. This closed off the possibility of using monetary policy to counteract the recession.

Unless wages decline rapidly to raise international competitiveness and boost the inflow of gold through higher exports and lower imports, sticking to the gold standard in a recession is destabilizing, as it will amplify the downturn. There was a very large outflow of gold from the US after the UK left the gold standard in September 1931. One reason for speculation against the US dollar (that is, investors selling dollars for gold) was that there were expectations that the US would also abandon the gold standard and devalue the dollar. If it did, those holding dollars would lose.

A change in expectations

In 1933 Roosevelt began a program of changes to economic policy:

- *The **New Deal***: This committed federal government spending to a range of programs to increase aggregate demand.
- *The US left the gold standard*: In April 1933 the US dollar was devalued to $35 per ounce of gold, and the nominal interest rate was reduced to close to the zero lower bound (see Figure 17.8).
- *Roosevelt also introduced reforms to the banking system*: This followed bank runs in 1932 and early 1933.

The change in people's beliefs about the future was just as important as these policy changes. On 4 March 1933, in his inaugural address as president, Roosevelt had told Americans that: 'the only thing we have to fear is fear itself—nameless, unreasoning, unjustified terror'.

We have seen that the terrors of consumers and investors in 1929 had been justified. But due to a combination of Roosevelt's New Deal policies and early signs of recovery that were already present before he became president, households and firms began to think that prices would stop falling and that employment would expand.

Figure 17.9 adds a third column to the model of household wealth that we first encountered in Figure 14.8. Column C shows the household's perspective from late 1933. By that time, output and employment were growing. With much of the uncertainty about the future resolved, households re-evaluated their expected wealth (including their expected earnings from employment). They reversed the cutbacks in consumption because they saw no need to make additional savings. To the extent that they now expected their income prospects and asset prices to return to pre-crisis levels, consumption would be restored. Any increase in wealth above target due to the increased savings during the Great Depression years (shown by wealth above target in column C) would create an additional boost to consumption.

The slow path to recovery had begun. But the US economy would not return to pre-Great Depression levels of employment until Roosevelt was in his third term as president and the Second World War had begun.

EXERCISE 17.2 ADVANTAGES AND DISADVANTAGES OF FIXED EXCHANGE RATES

In an 'Economist in action' video, Barry Eichengreen, an economist and economic historian, discusses fixed exchange rate systems such as the gold standard in the Great Depression and the euro system in the aftermath of the financial crisis.

1. According to the video, what are some advantages and disadvantages of fixed exchange rate systems?
2. How can countries that are in these exchange rate systems effectively respond to economic shocks? What are some features of the euro system that make it difficult to respond effectively?

Barry Eichengreen: Pegged exchange rates http://tinyco.re/6433456

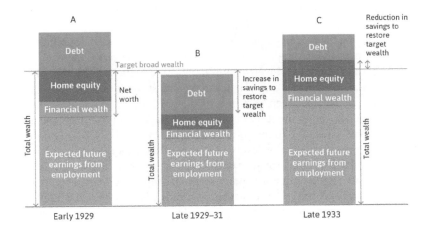

Figure 17.9 The Great Depression and recovery: Households cut consumption to restore target wealth in the depression; and increased consumption from 1933.

See p. 715

QUESTION 17.3 CHOOSE THE CORRECT ANSWER(S)

Franklin Roosevelt became the US President in 1933. In the period after he became the president:

- The federal government deficit increased to 5.6% of GNP in 1934.
- The short-term nominal interest rate fell from 1.7% in 1933 to 0.75% in 1935.
- The CPI fell by 5.2% in 1933 and rose by 3.5% in 1934.
- The US left the gold standard in April 1933.
- The New Deal was launched in 1933 and included proposals to increase federal government spending in a wide range of programs and reforms to the banking system.

Which of the following statements is correct regarding the years immediately after Roosevelt became the US president?

- ☐ A change in the expectations of consumers of their future earnings, as a result of the New Deal, would have contributed to an expansion in the economy's aggregate demand.
- ☐ The value of the US dollar increased as the result of the abandonment of the gold standard and allowed the nominal interest rate to be cut to close to zero.
- ☐ The real interest rate rose after 1933.
- ☐ Fiscal contraction from the increased government deficit would have contributed to the economy escaping from the Depression.

17.4 THE GOLDEN AGE OF HIGH GROWTH AND LOW UNEMPLOYMENT

The years from 1948 until 1973 were remarkable in the history of capitalism. In the US, we saw in Figure 17.2 that productivity growth was more rapid and unemployment was lower than in the other periods. But this 25-year golden age of capitalism was not confined to the US. Japan, Australia, Canada, New Zealand, and countries across western Europe experienced a golden age as well. Unemployment rates were historically low (see Figure 16.1). Figure 17.10 shows data from 1820 to 1913 for 13 advanced countries, and for 16 countries from 1950 to 1973.

The growth rate of GDP per capita was more than two-and-a-half times as high during the golden age as in any other period. Instead of doubling every 50 years, living standards were doubling every 20 years. The importance of saving and investment is highlighted in the right panel, where we can see that the capital stock grew almost twice as fast during the golden age as it did between 1870 and 1913.

Figure 17.11 shows the story of how western European countries and Japan (almost) caught up to the US. In this figure, the level of GDP per hour worked in the US is set at the level of 100 throughout, and so the figure tells us nothing about the performance of the US itself (we have to use Figure 17.2 for that). However, it is a striking way to represent the starting point of economies relative to the US immediately after the Second World War and their trajectories in the years that followed. This was known as **catch-up growth**.

THE GOLDEN AGE OF CAPITALISM

The period of high productivity growth, high employment, and stable inflation extending from the end of the Second World War to the early 1970s.

- The gold standard was replaced by the more flexible **Bretton Woods system**.
- Employers and employees shared the benefits of technological progress, thanks to the **postwar accord**.
- The golden age ended with a period of **stagflation** in the 1970s.

The three large defeated countries (Germany, Italy, and Japan) were furthest behind in 1950. Japan's GDP per hour worked was less than one-fifth the level of the US. Clearly, growth of all of these economies was faster than the US during the golden age: all moved much closer to the level of US productivity.

What was the secret of golden age performance in the productivity leader (the US) and in the follower countries?

- *Changes in economic policymaking and regulation:* These resolved the problems of instability that characterized the Great Depression.
- *New institutional arrangements between employers and workers:* These created conditions in which it was profitable for firms to innovate. In the US, the technology leader, this meant new technologies, while the follower countries often adopted improved technology and management already in use in the US. Because trade unions and workers' political parties were now in a stronger position to bargain for a share of the productivity gains, they supported innovation—even when it meant temporary job destruction.

After the Second World War, governments had learned the lessons of the Great Depression. This affected national and international policymaking. Just as Roosevelt's New Deal signalled a new policy regime and raised expectations in the private sector, postwar governments provided reassurance that policy would be used to support aggregate demand if necessary.

Postwar governments were larger in all of these countries and grew throughout the 1950s and 1960s. Figure 14.1 showed the decline in output fluctuations after 1950, and the much larger size of government in the US. In Unit 14, we saw how a larger government provides more automatic stabilization for the economy. The modern welfare state was built in the 1950s, and unemployment benefits were introduced. This also formed part of the automatic stabilization.

catch-up growth The process by which many (but far from all) economies in the world close the gap between the world leader and their own economy.

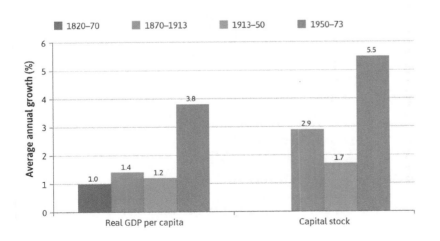

Table 2.1 in Andrew Glyn, Alan Hughes, Alain Lipietz, and Ajit Singh. 1989. 'The Rise and Fall of the Golden Age'. In *The Golden Age of Capitalism: Reinterpreting the Postwar Experience*, edited by Stephen A. Marglin and Juliet Schor. New York, NY: Oxford University Press. Data from 1820 to 1913 for 13 advanced countries, and for 16 countries from 1950.

Figure 17.10 The golden age of capitalism in historical perspective.

Bretton Woods system An international monetary system of fixed but adjustable exchange rates, established at the end of the Second World War. It replaced the gold standard that was abandoned during the Great Depression.

Given the cost of adherence to the gold standard during the Great Depression, it was clear that a new policy regime for international economic relations had to be put in place. The new regime was called the **Bretton Woods system**. It was named after the ski resort in New Hampshire where representatives of the major economies, including Keynes, created a system of rules that was more flexible than the gold standard. Exchange rates were tied to the US dollar rather than gold, and if countries became very uncompetitive—if they faced a 'fundamental disequilibrium' in external accounts, in the words of the agreement— devaluations of the exchange rate were permitted. When a currency like the British pound was devalued (as occurred in November 1967) it became cheaper to buy pounds. This boosted the demand for British exports and reduced the demand of British residents for goods produced abroad. The Bretton Woods system worked fairly well for most of the golden age.

17.5 WORKERS AND EMPLOYERS IN THE GOLDEN AGE
High investment, rapid productivity growth, rising wages, and low unemployment defined the golden age. How did this virtuous circle work?

- *After-tax profits in the US economy remained high:* This persisted from the end of the Second World War through the 1960s (look again at Figure 17.3), and the situation was similar in other advanced economies.
- *Profits led to investment:* The widespread expectation that high profits would continue in the future provided the conditions for sustained high levels of investment (refer back to the model of investment spending in Section 14.4).
- *High investment and continued technological progress created more jobs:* Unemployment stayed low.
- *The power of workers:* Trade unions and political movements allied with employees were sufficiently strong to secure sustained increases in wages. But accords between unions and employers meant that unions tended to act in an inclusive manner (Unit 16), and sustained the union

The Conference Board. 2016. 'Total Economy Database.'

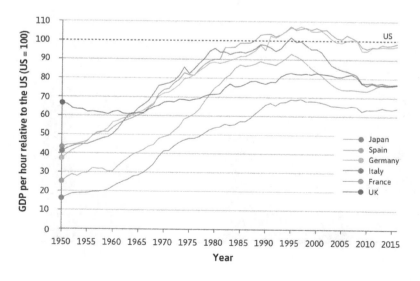

Figure 17.11 Catching up to the US during the golden age and beyond (1950–2016).

voice effect (Unit 9), encouraging cooperation between workers and firms in the face of new technology adoption.

Follow the steps in the analysis in Figure 17.12 to see how these four bullet points explaining the golden age can be translated into shifts in the price-setting curve and the wage-setting curve. Recall from Unit 16 that the price-setting curve shows the real wage consistent with employers maintaining investment at a level that keeps employment constant. This means that a real wage below the price-setting curve will encourage firms to enter or raise their investment, and employment rises.

In the US, technological progress was rapid in the golden age as the innovations developed during the Great Depression and the Second World War were embodied in new capital equipment. The new technologies and new management techniques already in use in the US could also be used in the catch-up economies. In many of these countries golden age growth was even faster than at the technology frontier as defined by the US in Figure 17.11.

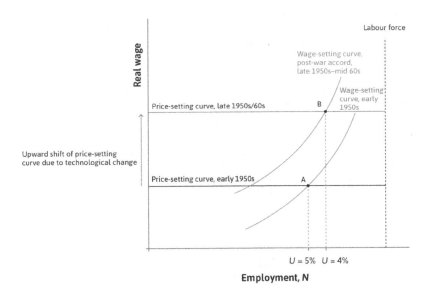

Figure 17.12 The golden age: Using the wage- and price-setting curves.

1. The beginning of the golden age
Suppose that the US economy was at point A at the beginning of the golden age, with unemployment of 5%.

2. Technological progress
This shifts the price-setting curve up (to the one labelled 'late 1950s/60s'). This stimulates high investment, consistent with the data for the growth of the capital stock in the US shown in Figure 17.3.

3. The wage-setting curve shifts up, but less than the price-setting curve
Strong unions and favourable government policies increased labour's bargaining power. But through accords with employers, the resulting upward shift in the wage-setting curve was modest.

4. The actors agree
At point B, unions and employers agree about the scope for wage increases.

The strength of unions in wage-setting and the improvement in unemployment insurance during the 1950s and 60s are illustrated as an upward shift of the wage-setting curve in Figure 17.12. The outcome observed, with wages growing in line with productivity at low unemployment, is illustrated by point B.

Both trade unions and governments were important in this process. Between 1920 and 1933, trade unions in the US lost two-fifths of their members. During the 1930s, changes in the laws affecting trade unions, as well as the hardship of the Great Depression, reversed this decline. High demand for labour during the Second World War strengthened labour's bargaining power, but trade union membership as a fraction of total employment peaked in the early 1950s. There was a subsequent steady decline during the next 50 years.

Figure 17.13 shows both the growth of the government and the historically high level of trade union membership in the US. As we have seen, larger government partly reflected the new entitlements to unemployment benefits. In the wage- and price-setting curve model, higher unemployment benefits and stronger trade unions shift the wage-setting curve upwards, but when unions are inclusive and when there is a strong union voice effect, then this upwards shift is restrained.

Unions would tend to act in an inclusive manner, meaning that they refrained from using the full extent of their bargaining power (for example, in firms or plants where they had a very strong position). Instead, they cooperated in an economy-wide bargain designed to keep wage growth consistent with the constraint imposed by the price-setting curve. In return, employers would maintain investment at a level sufficient to keep unemployment low. This unwritten but widely observed pattern of sharing the gains to technological progress between employees and employers is termed the **postwar accord**.

postwar accord An informal agreement (taking different forms in different countries) among employers, governments, and trade unions that created the conditions for rapid economic growth in advanced economies from the late 1940s to the early 1970s. Trade unions accepted the basic institutions of the capitalist economy and did not resist technological change in return for low unemployment, tolerance of unions and other rights, and a rise in real incomes that matched rises in productivity.

John Joseph Wallis. 2000. 'American Government Finance in the Long Run: 1790 to 1990'. *Journal of Economic Perspectives* 14 (1): pp. 61–82; Gerald Mayer. 2004. Union Membership Trends in the United States. Washington, DC: Congressional Research Service; US Bureau of Economic Analysis.

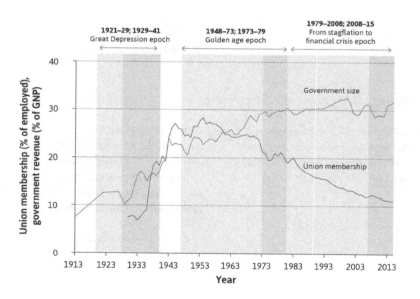

Figure 17.13 Trade union membership and the size of government in the US (1913–2015).

These postwar accord relationships between employers, unions, and governments, which sustained high productivity growth, high real wage growth, and low unemployment, differed across countries. In Scandinavia, Austria, Belgium, Netherlands, Switzerland, and West Germany, wage-setting was either centralized in a single union, or coordinated among unions or employers' associations, resulting in wage restraint. In technologically advanced sectors in France and Italy, governments intervened to set wages in dominant state-owned firms, creating wage guidance across the economy. The outcome was similar to the result in the countries with centralized wage-setting.

Where there was little cooperation between employers and unions, a country's performance in the golden age was worse. In Figure 17.11, the UK's relatively poor golden age performance shows up clearly. It started with higher productivity than the other large countries shown (that is, its productivity level in 1950 was the closest to that of the US) but was overtaken by France, Italy, and West Germany in the 1960s.

The British industrial relations system made an accord difficult. It combined very strong union power at the factory level with fragmented unions, which were unable to cooperate in the economy as a whole. The strength of local union shop stewards (representatives) in a system of multiple unions per plant led unions to attempt to outdo each other when negotiating wage deals, and created opposition to the introduction of new technology and new ways of organizing work.

The problems of the British economy were compounded because markets of British firms in former colonies were protected from competition, which weakened pressure to innovate. In the creative destruction process, competition creates incentives for firms to get a step ahead of their rivals and reduces the number of low-productivity firms. When competition is weak, existing firms and jobs are protected. The employers and workers in these firms share the monopoly rents, but the overall size of the pie is reduced because technological progress is slower.

In the US and the successful catch-up countries, postwar accords succeeded in creating the conditions for a high profit and high investment equilibrium. It delivered rapid productivity and real wage growth at low unemployment, but the British experience during the 1950s and 1960s (Figure 17.11) emphasizes that there is nothing automatic about achieving this outcome.

QUESTION 17.4 CHOOSE THE CORRECT ANSWER(S)

Figure 17.12 (page 761) describes the movements in employment, profits and wages in the 1950s to 1960s using the labour market model.

Which of the following statements is correct regarding this period?

☐ The rise in the wage-setting curve due to stronger trade unions and higher unemployment benefits led to postwar innovation. This shifted the price-setting curve up.

☐ A rise in the wage-setting curve depresses profits and reduces investment. This conflict of interest between workers and employers means that low unemployment, high profits, and high investment would not have been sustainable.

☐ The substantial increase in the bargaining power of trade unions and political movements allied with workers meant that they could demand the highest possible wages, pushing the wage-setting curve to its highest possible level.

☐ Continuing technological progress owing to widespread expectations of sustained high profits, together with high wages resulting from the strong bargaining power of trade unions, created a virtuous circle of high investment, rapid productivity growth, rising wages, and low unemployment.

17.6 THE END OF THE GOLDEN AGE

stagflation Persistent high inflation combined with high unemployment in a country's economy.

The virtuous circle of the golden age began to break down in the late 1960s, in part as a result of its own successes. Years of low unemployment convinced workers that they had little chance of losing their jobs. Their demands for improvements in working conditions and higher wages drove down the profit rate. The postwar accord and its rationale of enlarging the pie gave way to a contest over the size of the slice that each group could get. This set the stage for the period of combined inflation and stagnation called **stagflation** that would follow.

Greater industrial strife in the late 1960s in leading economies signalled the breakdown of the golden age postwar accords. Figure 17.14 plots the days on strike per 1,000 industrial workers in advanced economies from 1950 to 2002. As strike activity peaked, wages measured relative to share prices increased rapidly. The postwar accords that helped create the golden age collapsed.

Workers also demanded policies to redistribute income to the less well off and to provide more adequate social services, making it difficult for

Andrew Glyn. 2006. *Capitalism Unleashed: Finance, Globalization, and Welfare.* Oxford: Oxford University Press.

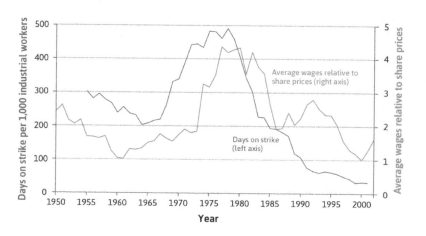

Figure 17.14 The end of the golden age: Strikes and wages relative to share prices in advanced economies (1950–2002).

governments to run a budget surplus. In the US, additional military spending to fund the Vietnam War added to aggregate demand, keeping the economy at unsustainably high levels of employment.

The process is represented in Figure 17.15 by an upward shift in the wage-setting curve (to the one labelled 'late 1960s/early 70s'). At the same time, economy-wide productivity growth slowed (see Figure 17.2 for the US data). As the gap between the technology frontier in the US and in the catch-up countries in western Europe narrowed, it was more difficult to get easy gains from technology transfer (see Figure 17.11).

In 1973, the first oil price shock occurred. In Figure 17.15, this contributes to the downward shift of the price-setting curve (see the price-setting curve labelled '1973–79' and refer back to Figure 15.11). Higher imported oil costs reduce the maximum real wage that workers can get if firms are to keep their profit margin unchanged.

What happened?

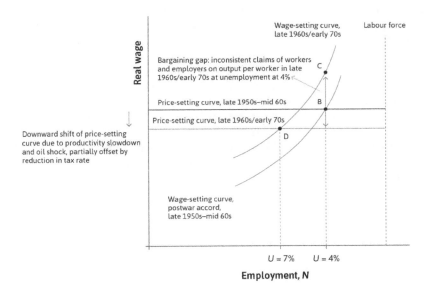

Figure 17.15 The end of the golden age: Using the wage and price-setting curves. (Note that the real wage on the vertical axis is measured post-tax and in terms of consumer prices.

1. The postwar accord collapses
The upward shift in the wage-setting curve represents the collapse of postwar accords during the late 1960s and early 1970s.

2. The first oil shock (1973)
In 1973, the first oil price shock occurred. This pushed the price-setting curve down.

3. Inflation-stabilizing unemployment increases
The combination of a downward shift in the price-setting curve and an upward shift in the wage-setting curve meant that the sustainable long-term unemployment rate increased to 7%, shown at point D.

4. A bargaining gap develops
The double-headed arrow at low unemployment shows the situation in the early 1970s.

Wages did not rise to the level of point C. Under the impact of the upward pressure on wages and the oil price shock, the economy contracted and unemployment began to rise. But even a significant reduction in employment (short of increasing the unemployment rate to 7%) did not eliminate the bargaining gap shown in the figure. A result was an increase in the rate of inflation, as is shown in Figure 17.16.

Because of the strong bargaining position of workers in the early 1970s in most of the high-income economies, the oil price shock primarily hit employers, redistributing income from profits to wages (Figure 17.15). The era of fair-shares bargaining under the postwar accords was coming to a close.

In the US and most of the high-income countries, unions were strong enough to defend their share of the pie even after the oil price increase and they chose to do so. In terms of the model, this meant wages were above the new price-setting curve. This cut into profits, so investment fell and the rate of productivity growth slowed. As predicted by the model in Figure 17.15, the outcome was rising inflation (Figure 17.16), falling profits (Figure 17.3), weak investment (Figure 17.3), and high unemployment (Figure 17.16).

In a handful of countries with inclusive and powerful trade unions (as described in Unit 16), the accord survived. In Sweden, for example, the powerful centralized labour movement restrained its wage claims to preserve profitability, investment, and high levels of employment (Figure 16.1).

The end of the golden age set off a new economic crisis, one that was very different from the Great Depression. The economic downturn of the 1930s had been propelled by problems of aggregate demand and for this reason it has been called a **demand-side** crisis. The end of the golden age has been called a **supply-side** crisis, because problems on the supply side of the economy depressed the profit rate, the rate of investment, and the rate of productivity growth.

demand side (aggregate economy)
How spending decisions generate demand for goods and services, and as a result, employment and output. It uses the multiplier model. *See also: supply side (aggregate economy).*

supply side (aggregate economy)
How labour and capital are used to produce goods and services. It uses the labour market model (also referred to as the wage-setting curve and price-setting curve model). *See also: demand side (aggregate economy).*

OECD. 2016. 'OECD Statistics'.

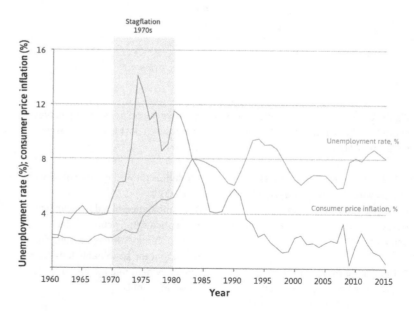

Figure 17.16 After the golden age: Unemployment and inflation in advanced economies (1960–2015).

The period that ensued came to be called **stagflation** because it combined high unemployment and high inflation. If the golden age was an unusual time during which everything went right at once, stagflation was an unusual time in which everything went wrong.

According to the Phillips curve model of Unit 15, inflation goes up when unemployment goes down; this is a movement along the Phillips curve. Figure 17.16 summarizes the unemployment and inflation data for the advanced economies from 1960–2013.

Just as the Phillips curve predicts, for most of the period, inflation and unemployment were negatively correlated: as unemployment rose, inflation fell and vice versa. But as we saw in Figure 15.6, the entire Phillips curve shifted upward during this period, as a bargaining gap opened and expected inflation increased. Look at the shaded part of Figure 17.16: inflation and unemployment rose together, giving this period its name.

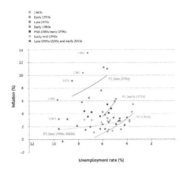

Figure 15.6 (page 659) shows the inflation and unemployment combinations for the US for each year between 1960 and 2014.

QUESTION 17.5 CHOOSE THE CORRECT ANSWER(S)

Figure 17.14 (page 764) is a graph of days on strike per 1,000 industrial workers (left-hand axis) and the average wages relative to share prices (right-hand axis) in advanced economies between 1950 and 2002.

Based on this information, which of the following statements is correct?

- ☐ Strikes are beneficial to all workers.
- ☐ Nearly half of the workers went on strike at the peak of the strike activity between 1975 and 1980.
- ☐ The postwar accord of cooperation between employers and employees broke down in the late 1960s.
- ☐ The first oil shock of 1973 triggered a sharp rise in average wages.

QUESTION 17.6 CHOOSE THE CORRECT ANSWER(S)

Figure 17.15 (page 765) describes the movements in employment, profits, and wages in the 1950s to 1970s using the labour market model.

Which of the following statements is correct regarding this period?

- ☐ The collapse of postwar accords in the late 1960s/early 70s led to workers demanding higher wages, leading to an upward shift in the wage-setting curve.
- ☐ The reduction in the tax rate introduced to counter the effect of the oil shock led to the fall in the price-setting curve.
- ☐ The rise in the wage-setting curve led to the wage rate rising to point C.
- ☐ The economy swiftly settled at the new labour market equilibrium at D, with stable inflation, unemployment, profits, and wages.

QUESTION 17.7 CHOOSE THE CORRECT ANSWER(S)

Figure 17.16 (page 766) is a graph of the unemployment rate and consumer price inflation in advanced economies between 1960 and 2013.

Based on this information, which of the following statements is correct?

☐ As predicted by the Phillips curve, the unemployment rate rises whenever inflation falls and vice versa throughout the period depicted.

☐ The unemployment rate and the inflation rate were consistently positively correlated during the stagflation period of the 1970s.

☐ Stagflation was caused by the shifting up of the Phillips curve, propelled by higher inflation expectations.

☐ The end of stagflation was characterized by falls in both the unemployment rate and the inflation rate.

17.7 AFTER STAGFLATION: THE FRUITS OF A NEW POLICY REGIME

The third major epoch during the last 100 years of capitalism began in 1979. Across the advanced economies, policymakers focused on restoring the conditions for investment and job creation. Expanding aggregate demand would not help: what would have been part of the solution during the Great Depression had now become part of the problem.

Arrangements based on accords between workers and employers continued in some northern European and Scandinavian countries. Elsewhere, employers abandoned the accord, and policymakers turned to different institutional arrangements as the basis for restoring the incentives for firms to invest.

The new policies were called **supply-side reforms**, aimed to address the causes of the supply-side crisis of the 1970s. The policies were centred on the need to shift the balance of power between employer and worker in the labour market, and in the firm. Government policy at this time achieved this goal in two main ways:

- *Restrictive monetary and fiscal policy*: Governments showed that they were prepared to allow unemployment to rise to unprecedented levels, weakening the position of workers and restoring the consistency of claims on output per worker as the basis of modest and stable inflation.
- *Shifting the wage-setting curve down*: As we saw in Unit 15, these policies included cuts in unemployment benefits and the introduction of legislation to reduce trade union power.

Figure 17.16 illustrates the new policy environment. Unemployment increased rapidly from 5% to 8% in the early 1980s. This was the price of restoring conditions for profit and investment, and for reducing inflation from greater than 10% to 4%. Policymakers were prepared to depress aggregate demand and tolerate high unemployment until inflation fell.

The increased unemployment beginning with the first oil price shock in 1973 had two effects:

supply-side policies A set of economic policies designed to improve the functioning of the economy by increasing productivity and international competitiveness, and by reducing profits after taxes and costs of production. Policies include cutting taxes on profits, tightening conditions for the receipt of unemployment benefits, changing legislation to make it easier to fire workers, and the reform of competition policy to reduce monopoly power. *Also known as: supply-side reforms.*

- *It reduced the bargaining gap in Figure 17.15*: This brought down inflation (shown in Figure 17.16).
- *It put labour unions and workers on the defensive*: The cost of job loss rose and employees had less bargaining power.

Figure 17.17 shows the development of productivity (output per hour) and real wages in manufacturing in the US from the beginning of the golden age. Index numbers are used for each series to highlight the growth of real wages relative to that of output per hour worked. Real wage growth in line with output per hour is not inevitable. In Unit 2, Figure 2.1, when looking at the growth of real wages in England since the thirteenth century, we saw that institutions (social movements, changes in the voting franchise and in laws) played a vital role in translating productivity growth into real wage growth.

The figure shows two dramatically different periods:

- *Before 1973*: Fair-shares bargaining meant that wages and productivity grew together.
- *After 1973*: Productivity growth was not shared with workers. For production workers in manufacturing, real wages barely changed in the 40 years after 1973.

By the mid-1990s, the effects of the new supply-side policy regime were becoming clear. The period from this time until the global financial crisis of 2008 was called the **great moderation** because inflation was low and stable, and unemployment was falling. Although wage growth fell well below productivity growth, policymakers no longer thought of this as a bug; it was a feature of the new regime. The third oil shock that occurred in the 2000s was a good test of the regime. As we saw in Unit 15, it was less disruptive than the two oil shocks in the 1970s.

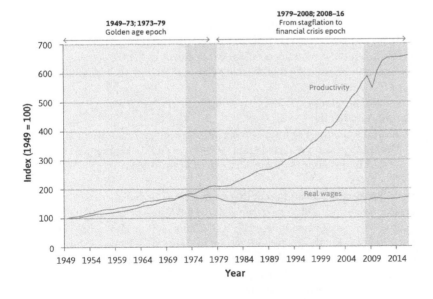

US Bureau of Labor Statistics. Note: 'production workers' exclude supervisory employees such as foremen and managers.

Figure 17.17 The golden age and its aftermath: Real wages and output per production worker in manufacturing in the US (1949–2016).

While the new regime appeared to have the virtue of macroeconomic stability, in countries where the bargaining power of workers had been most curtailed, like the US and the UK, the cost was the dramatic rise in inequality that we saw in Figure 17.2.

In virtually all of the advanced economies, the new supply-side policies redistributed income from wages to profits. In the US (Figure 17.3), the after-tax profit rate gradually increased between the 1970s and 2008. But investment responded only weakly to the profit incentives, so that the rate of growth of the capital stock declined.

Supply-side policy advisors could not recreate the improbable package of high employment, high investment, and growing wages of the golden age. The growth of profits unmatched by investment in new equipment would also help to cause the next crisis.

EXERCISE 17.3 WORKERS' BARGAINING POWER

In the light of the Great Depression, most advanced economies adopted policies after the Second World War that strengthened the bargaining power of employees and labour unions. By contrast, after the golden age, the policies chosen weakened workers' bargaining power.

1. Explain the reasons for these contrasting approaches.
2. Discuss the possible role of weaker worker bargaining power in the run-up to the global financial crisis.

17.8 BEFORE THE FINANCIAL CRISIS: HOUSEHOLDS, BANKS, AND THE CREDIT BOOM

The great moderation masked three changes that would create the environment for the global financial crisis. While to some extent these changes were shared across most advanced economies, actors in the US economy played a pivotal role in the global financial crisis, just as they had during the Great Depression:

- *Rising debt*: The sum of the debt of the government and of non-financial firms changed relatively little as a proportion of GDP between 1995 and 2008, but the mountainous shape of total debt in the US economy shown in Figure 17.4 was created by growth in household and financial sector debt.
- *Increasing house prices*: The rise in house prices became more pronounced after 1995.
- *Rising inequality*: The long-run decline in inequality that began after the Great Depression reversed after 1979 (Figure 17.2). Workers no longer shared in the gains from productivity (Figure 17.17).

How can we make an argument that connects the financial crisis to the great moderation, and to long-run rising debt, house prices, and inequality? We use what we learned in Units 9, 10, 13, and Section 17.4 to help us. We know that during the great moderation, from the mid-1990s to the eve of the financial crisis, the real wages of those with earnings in the bottom 50% hardly grew. Relative to the earnings of the top 50%, they lost out. One way they could improve their consumption possibilities was to take out a home loan. Before the 1980s, financial institutions had been restricted in the kinds of loans they could make and in the interest rates they could charge. **Financial deregulation** generated aggressive competition for customers, and gave those customers much easier access to credit.

THE GREAT MODERATION AND THE GLOBAL FINANCIAL CRISIS

The great moderation was a period of low volatility in output between the mid-1980s and 2008. It was ended by the global financial crisis, triggered by falling US house prices from 2007 onwards.

- At the onset of the crisis, government and central bank stabilization policies, notably including **bank bailouts**, avoided a repeat of the Great Depression.
- Nevertheless, there followed a sustained global fall in aggregate output, popularly known as the **great recession**.

---

financial deregulation Policies allowing banks and other financial institutions greater freedom in the types of financial assets they can sell, as well as other practices.
bank bailout The government buys an equity stake in a bank or some other intervention to prevent it from failing.
great recession The prolonged recession that followed the global financial crisis of 2008.

Housing booms and the financial accelerator

When households borrow to buy a house, this is a secured or collateralized loan. As part of the mortgage agreement, the bank can take possession of the house if the borrower does not keep up repayments. Collateral plays an important role in sustaining a house price boom. When the house price goes up—driven, for example, by beliefs that a further price rise will occur—this increases the value of the household's collateral (see the left-hand diagram in Figure 17.18). Using this higher collateral, households can increase their borrowing, and move up the housing ladder to a better property. This, in turn, pushes up house prices further and sustains the bubble, because the banks extend more credit based on the higher collateral. Increased borrowing, made possible by the rise in the value of the collateral, is spent on goods and services as well as on housing.

When house prices are expected to rise, it is attractive to households to increase their borrowing. Suppose a house costs $200,000, and the household makes a down payment of 10% ($20,000). This means it borrows $180,000. Its initial **leverage ratio**, in this case the value of its assets divided by its equity stake in the house, is 200/20 = 10. Suppose the house price rises by 10% to $220,000. The return to the equity the household has invested in the house is 100% (since the value of the equity stake has risen from $20,000 to $40,000: it has doubled). Households who are convinced

leverage ratio (for banks or households) The value of assets divided by the equity stake in those assets.

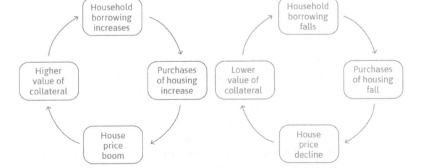

On the way up   **On the way down**

Figure 17.18 The housing market on the way up and on the way down.

Adapted from figure in Hyun Song Shin. 2009. 'Discussion of 'The Leverage Cycle' by John Geanakoplos'.

that house prices will rise further will want to increase their leverage: that is how they get a high return. The increase in collateral, due to the rise in the price of their house, means they can satisfy their desire to borrow more.

The mechanism through which a rise in the value of collateral leads to an increase in borrowing and spending by households and firms is called the **financial accelerator** (see Section 14.3 for these details). The left-hand side of Figure 17.18 shows the outcome of the interaction between the bubble in house prices and its transmission through the economy via the financial accelerator during a boom. On the right-hand side, we see what happens when house prices decline. The value of collateral falls and the household's spending declines, pushing house prices down.

The assets and liabilities of a household can be represented in its balance sheet, and this can be used to explain the interaction of a house price bubble and the financial accelerator. The house is on the asset side of the household's balance sheet. The mortgage owed to the bank is on the liabilities side. When the market value of the house falls below what is owed on the mortgage, the household has negative net worth. This condition is sometimes referred to as the household being 'underwater'. Using the example above, if the leverage ratio is 10, a fall in the house price by 10% wipes out the household's equity. A fall of more than 10% would place the household underwater.

As we saw with households in the Great Depression, if a decline in net worth means that a household is below its target wealth, it responds by cutting what it spends. When a housing bubble is forming, the rise in the value of collateral reinforces the boom by boosting both borrowing and spending; on the way down, the fall in the value of house increases household debt and the household reduces spending. Rising house prices immediately before 2008 were prices that sent the 'wrong' message. We know that resources were misallocated, because the US and some countries in Europe were left with thousands of abandoned houses.

Financial deregulation and subprime borrowers

In the boom period when house prices were expected to rise, the riskiness of home loans to the banks making them fell and, as a result, banks extended more loans. The opportunities for poor people to borrow for a home loan expanded as lenders asked for lower deposits, or even no deposit at all. This is shown in Figure 17.19. The financial accelerator mechanism is an example of positive feedback: from higher collateral, to more borrowing, to further increases in house prices.

Figure 17.20 shows the contrast between the material wealth of a household in the bottom and top fifth of households, according to their net worth in 2007. Using the definitions introduced in Section 13.3 and used in Section 17.4, the household's material wealth is equal to the value of its house (which will by definition be equal to the sum of the debt outstanding and the household's home equity) minus the mortgage debt, plus financial wealth (net of non-housing debt).

The left-hand bar is the poorest 20% of households. The right-hand bar is the richest 20%. The data is shown in a way that allows us to compare the assets and liabilities (debt) of the two groups. In each case, the total of debt plus assets is made equal to 100%. This means we cannot compare the absolute amount of wealth or debt held by each group, but the data allows us to see clearly the type of asset (housing or financial) each household type holds, and how much debt each type has relative to the assets it holds. This

---

financial accelerator The mechanism through which firms' and households' ability to borrow increases when the value of the collateral they have pledged to the lender (often a bank) goes up.

tells us a lot about how a fall in house prices would affect the spending behaviour of each type.

The left-hand bar represents borrower households. These are poor households, normally only able to borrow when they have housing collateral to use as security. They have little financial wealth, as shown by the size of the green rectangle. These households have much more debt than equity in their houses, and are vulnerable to a fall in house prices.

Rich households have a lot of assets, mainly in the form of financial wealth: bank account and money market deposits, government and corporate bonds, and shares. They also have little debt. These are the saver households of Unit 10.

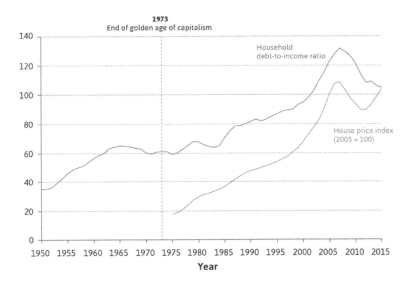

US Federal Reserve. 2016. 'Financial Accounts of the United States, Historical'. December 10; US Bureau of Economic Analysis; Federal Reserve Bank of St Louis (FRED).

Figure 17.19 The household debt-to-income ratio and house prices in the US (1950–2015).

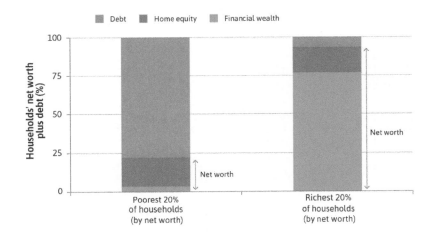

Adapted from Figure 2.1 in Atif Mian and Amir Sufi. 2014. *House of Debt: How They (and You) Caused the Great Recession, and How We Can Prevent It from Happening Again.* Chicago, Il: The University of Chicago Press.

Figure 17.20 Household wealth and debt in the US: Poorest and richest quintiles by net worth (2007).

derivative A financial instrument in the form of a contract that can be traded, whose value is based on the performance of underlying assets such as shares, bonds or real estate. *See also: collateralized debt obligation.*

collateralized debt obligation (CDO) A structured financial instrument (a derivative) consisting of a bond or note backed by a pool of fixed-income assets. The collapse in the value of the instruments of this type that were backed by subprime mortgage loans was a major factor in the financial crisis of 2007–2008.

mortgage-backed security (MBS) A financial asset that uses mortgages as collateral. Investors receive payments derived from the interest and principal of the underlying mortgages. *See also: collateral.*

credit ratings agency A firm which collects information to calculate the credit-worthiness of individuals or companies, and sells the resulting rating for a fee to interested parties.

Financial deregulation and bank leverage
In the context of the deregulated financial system, banks increased their borrowing:

- to extend more loans for housing
- to extend more loans for consumer durables like cars and furnishings
- to buy more financial assets based on bundles of home loans

The combination of the great moderation, rising house prices, and the development of new, apparently less risky financial assets such as the **derivatives** called **collateralized debt obligations** (**CDOs**), based on bundles of home loans called **mortgage-backed securities** (**MBSs**), made it profitable for banks to become more highly leveraged.

Figure 17.21 shows the leverage of US investment banks and all UK banks. In the US, the leverage ratio of investment banks was between 12 and 14 in the late 1970s, rising to more than 30 in the early 1990s. It hit 40 in 1996 and peaked at 43 just before the financial crisis. By contrast, the leverage of the median UK bank remained at the level of around 20 until 2000. Leverage then increased very rapidly to a peak of 48 in 2007. In the 2000s, British and European global banks, including firms called shadow banks, increased borrowing to buy CDOs and other financial assets that originated in the US housing market.

Leverage increased because of financial deregulation and the business model of banks. But why were savers prepared to continue lending to the increasingly leveraged financial system and, indirectly, to the highly leveraged household sector?

Firms called **credit ratings agencies** (the big three are Fitch Ratings, Moody's and Standard & Poor's) assess the risk of financial products, and part of their role is to provide evidence to reassure lenders that their investments are safe. After almost 20 years of the great moderation, economic crises seemed like a historical idea, and so these companies gave the highest ratings (meaning the lowest risk) to many of the assets created from **subprime mortgages**.

US Federal Reserve. 2016. 'Financial Accounts of the United States, Historical.' December 10; Bank of England. 2012. Financial Stability Report, Issue 31.

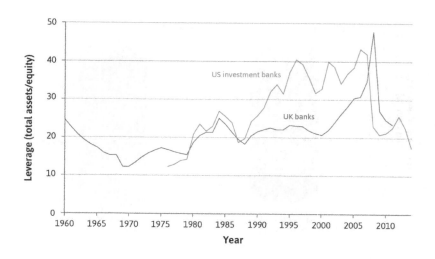

Figure 17.21 Leverage ratio of banks in the UK and US (1960–2014).

The subprime housing crisis of 2007

The interrelated growth of the indebtedness of poor households in the US and global banks meant that when homeowners began to default on their repayments in 2006, the effects could not be contained within the local or even the national economy. The crisis caused by the problems of subprime mortgage borrowers in the US spread to other countries. Financial markets were frightened on 9 August 2007 when French bank BNP Paribas halted withdrawals from three investment funds because it could not 'fairly' value financial products based on US mortgage-based securities—it simply did not know how much they were worth.

The recession that swept across the world in 2008–09 was the worst contraction of the global economy since the Great Depression. Unlike the bushfires in southeastern Australia in 2009, the financial crisis took the world by surprise. The world's economic policymakers were unprepared. They discovered belatedly that a long period of calm in financial markets could make a crisis more likely.

This was an argument that Hyman Minsky, the economist, had made long before the great moderation. Minsky developed these ideas while a professor of economics at the University of California, Berkeley, and so he may even have been thinking of fires. In northern Mexico, the fire management authorities allow small fires to burn, and as a result dry undergrowth does not accumulate. Major fires are more frequent across the US border in California, where small fires are quickly extinguished.

In 1982, Minsky wrote *Can 'It' Happen Again?* about the way in which tranquil conditions lead firms to choose riskier methods of financing their investment. His warning went unheeded. Instead of producing increased vigilance, the calm conditions of the great moderation bred complacency among regulators and economists. It was the increasingly risky behaviour of banks, as Minsky had predicted, that created the conditions for the crisis.

> **subprime mortgage** A residential mortgage issued to a high-risk borrower, for example, a borrower with a history of bankruptcy and delayed repayments. *See also: subprime borrower.*

> Hyman P. Minsky. 1982. *Can 'It' Happen Again? Essays on Instability and Finance.* Armonk, NY: M. E. Sharpe.

GREAT ECONOMISTS

Hyman Minsky

Hyman Minsky (1919–1996) was an American economist who developed a financial theory of the business cycle. His ideas have attracted renewed attention among both academics and banking and finance professionals since the global economic crisis of 2008.

Minsky argued that macroeconomic fluctuations could not be properly understood without taking account of the manner in which business investment is financed. At a time when most economists viewed firms as the location of a production function, Minsky focused instead on the assets and liabilities on the firm's balance sheet. The assets, including plant and equipment, but also less tangible assets such as patents, copyrights, and trademarks, are expected to generate a stream of revenues stretching far into the future. The liabilities include the firm's obligations to its

hedge finance Financing used by firms to fulfil contractual payment obligations using cashflow. Term coined by Hyman Minsky in his Financial Instability Hypothesis. *See also: speculative finance.*

speculative finance A strategy used by firms to meet payment commitments on liabilities using cash flow, although the firm cannot repay the principal in this way. Firms in this position need to 'roll over' their liabilities, usually by issuing new debt to meet commitments on maturing debt. Term coined by Hyman Minsky in his Financial Instability Hypothesis. *See also: hedge finance.*

creditors, and imply a stream of payments due at various points in time.

New investment by the firm expands its capacity to produce goods and services, and thus alters its expected stream of revenues. If it is financed by debt, it also changes the firm's financial obligations at future dates. In deciding how to finance its investment, the firm faces a choice:

- *Issue long-term debt*: It anticipates that revenues would be sufficient to cover obligations at all points in time.
- *Issue short-term debt*: This debt needs to be repaid before the anticipated revenues are available. It creates the need for further borrowing to repay debt at the end of this term.

In general, long-term borrowing is more expensive, since lenders demand a higher interest rate. But short-term borrowing is risky, because the firm may be unable to refinance debt as it comes due. Even if it can refinance, it may be forced to borrow at high rates if credit availability is constrained.

Firms that chose the safer but more expensive option, matching revenues and debt obligations, were said by Minsky to be engaged in **hedge finance**. Those that took the cheaper but more risky option, borrowing short-term to finance long-term investments, were engaging in **speculative finance**.

A key component of Minsky's theory concerned the manner in which the distribution of financial practices in the economy changed over time. As long as financial market conditions remained relatively tranquil, so that rolling over short-term debt was easy, firms with the most aggressive financial practices would prosper at the expense of those that were the most prudent. Not only would the most aggressive firms grow faster, they would also attract imitators, and the distribution of financial practices in the economy would become increasingly speculative. There would be a rise in the demand for refinancing short-term debt, and hence an increase in financial fragility: a severe financial market disruption, with a contraction in credit or a spike in short-term interest rates, would become increasingly likely.

In Minsky's view, this process leads inevitably to a crisis because, as long as a crisis is averted, the most aggressive financial practices proliferate and financial fragility continues to rise. When a crisis finally occurs, the most aggressive firms will suffer disproportionately and the prudent firms will prosper. The sharp shift in the aggregate distribution of financial practices lowers fragility and sets the stage for the process to begin again. In Minsky's words:

> Stability—even of an expansion—is destabilizing in that more adventurous financing of investment pays off to the leaders, and others follow. (*John Maynard Keynes*, 1975)

In other words, a period like the great moderation sows the seeds of the next financial crisis.

In 2007, Charles Prince, chief executive of Citigroup, explained to the *Financial Times* the difficulty of resisting 'adventurous financing' during booms. 'As long as the music is playing, you've got to get up and dance,' he said in July, as the global economy hurtled towards a crisis deeper than anything seen since the Great Depression, 'We're still dancing'.

EXERCISE 17.4 HOUSEHOLD WEALTH AS A BALANCE SHEET

1. Show the information in Figure 17.20 (page 773) in the form of a balance sheet, for one household from the lowest and one from the highest net worth quintile (use the balance sheets in Figures 10.16 and 10.17 as a guide). Assume that the sum of assets and liabilities is $200,000 for the poorer household and $600,000 for the richer household, both households have some savings, and that assets do not depreciate.

Think about the proportions of debt held by these households that might consist of mortgage debt. Now consider the relative effects on the households of a fall in house prices.

2. Define negative equity as a situation where the market value of a house is less than the debt secured on it. In your example balance sheet for the poorer family, calculate the fall in house prices that would push this household into negative equity.
3. If house prices fell by just enough to push the household into negative equity, would this household be insolvent? Explain.

QUESTION 17.8 CHOOSE THE CORRECT ANSWER(S)

Figure 17.19 (page 773) shows the household debt-to-income ratio and the house prices in the US between 1950 and 2014. Based on this information, which of the following statements is correct?

☐ The real value of household debt more than doubled from the end of the golden age to the peak on the eve of the financial crisis.
☐ The causality is from the house price to household debt, that is, higher house prices encourage higher debt, but not the other way round.
☐ A household debt-to-income ratio of over 100 means that the household is bankrupt.
☐ Subprime mortgages partly explain the rise in debt in the US prior to the financial crisis.

QUESTION 17.9 CHOOSE THE CORRECT ANSWER(S)

Figure 17.21 (page 774) is the graph of leverage of banks in the UK and the US between 1960 and 2014.

The leverage ratio is defined as the ratio of the banks' total assets to their equity. Which of the following statements are correct?

☐ A leverage ratio of 40 means that only 2.5% of the asset is funded by equity.
☐ The total asset value of US banks doubled between 1980 and later 1990s.
☐ A leverage ratio of 25 means that a fall of 4% in the asset value would make a bank insolvent.
☐ UK banks increased their leverage rapidly in the 2000s in order to make more loans to UK house buyers.

17.9 MODELLING HOUSING BUBBLES

In Unit 11 (Section 11.8), we introduced the concepts of stable and unstable equilibria. Here we develop those concepts further. We will show that a market like the housing market can have a stable equilibrium at a low price and another stable equilibrium at a high price level. In between is an unstable equilibrium. This is represented by an S-shaped price dynamics curve (PDC).

Figure 17.22 reproduces diagrams from Figures 11.18 and 11.19. The left hand panel shows what happens at an unstable equilibrium. Beginning at the price P_0, an increase in the price leads away from equilibrium because it is interpreted as a sign that the price will rise further, which drives up demand for houses as people demand more of the asset they believe will increase in value. If at the price P_0 something were to occur that lowered the price, a similar process would take the price even lower, as people would take that to be a signal that houses are falling in value, and so would be less likely to buy.

The right-hand panel shows how a stable equilibrium is one in which initial price changes are dampened rather than exaggerated as a result of what is called negative feedback. Here a rise in price leads to a fall in demand for houses, which depresses the price. Eventually the price returns to the initial level. This is a stable equilibrium.

The process that leads a market to adjust to a small shock by returning to its pre-existing equilibrium is called a **negative feedback process** because the initial price change causes further price changes (feedbacks) that are in the opposite direction (negative) of the initial change. A **positive feedback process** is one in which some initial change leads to further changes in the same direction (positive).

In order to see how a market could have two equilibria and how movement from one to the other could represent a price bubble or a price crash, we can combine the stable and unstable equilibria in the two panels of Figure 17.22 into the S-shaped figure shown in Figure 17.23. Notice that at A the PDC has a slope that is steeper than 45 degrees (like the left panel in Figure 17.22). So point A is an unstable equilibrium and the price will not remain here if it is disturbed by either a price rise or fall no matter how small: positive feedbacks will lead the price away from the equilibrium.

negative feedback (process) A process whereby some initial change sets in motion a process that dampens the initial change. *See also: positive feedback (process).*

positive feedback (process) A process whereby some initial change sets in motion a process that magnifies the initial change. *See also: negative feedback (process).*

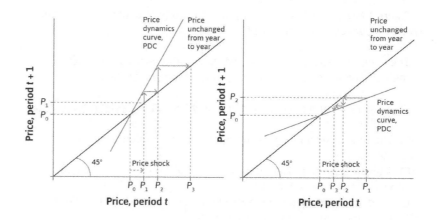

Figure 17.22 Unstable and stable equilibria in the housing market.

There will be a house price bubble if the price increases at A, and a crash if the price decreases.

Notice that at points C and B the PDC is flatter that the 45-degree line, so for these points the right panel of Figure 17.22 explains what will happen if the market is at either one of these points and something shifts the price up or down. Because of negative feedback, the initial shock will be dampened and the price will return to the equilibrium value.

Point A is called a **tipping point.** For a price above A, prices increase continuously until point B; for a price below A, prices decrease continuously until point C. The direction of the change in price switches from rising to falling at the tipping point A.

Remember that at B, house prices are high, but stable. They will remain unchanged at the high level from year to year. Even if there are blips up or down, we know that the price will return to its level at B.

But now suppose that at the high price (point B) some people 'get cold feet'. They think prices are far too high given the fundamentals of house affordability (the demand side) and the supply of houses. 'These high prices can never last,' they say to themselves. They begin to think that house prices will fall: 'It's time to sell so that when prices fall, I can get a better house for the same money.' Owners with a mortgage start to worry that lower house prices could leave them with negative equity in their house, that is, a situation in which the market value of the house is less than the mortgage they owe to the bank.

These people will believe that house prices are going to be lower next period than shown by B. This is represented in Figure 17.24 by a downward shift of the S-shaped price dynamics curve to the darker blue one. As more people come round to the view that prices will fall and sell their houses, the S-shaped curve shifts down and prices fall along the broken arrow from B to Z.

Once sentiment in the housing market has shifted sufficiently that the S-shaped curve (now dark blue) is below the 45-degree line, there is no tipping point left. The market collapses to K. This model helps to explain the fear that a bubble in the housing market can be followed by a devastating crash. Note that the financial accelerator is part of the reason why these collapses can be so large and why the new equilibrium can be so far below the old equilibrium.

> **TIPPING POINT**
> An unstable equilibrium at the boundary between two regions characterized by distinct movements in some variable. If the variable takes a value on one side of the tipping point, the variable moves in one direction; on the other, it moves in the other direction. A ridge dividing two valleys is a tipping point; for example, water falling on one side runs away from the ridge in one direction towards an inland lake while water falling on the other side (even very close to the ridge) flows in the other direction towards the sea. In the case of the housing bubble, beyond a certain price (the tipping point price), prices will increase creating a bubble and below that price they fall (a bust).

> **EXERCISE 17.5 DIFFERENCES BETWEEN EQUILIBRIUM AND STABILITY**
> Explain in your own words, giving examples, the difference between the terms equilibrium and stability.

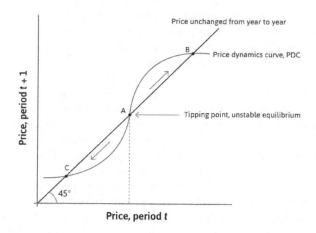

Figure 17.23 Unstable and stable equilibria in the housing market: The S-shaped PDC.

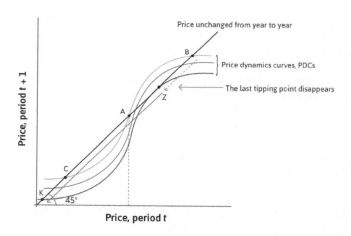

Figure 17.24 A tipping point in the housing market.

1. An equilibrium at B
At Point B, house prices are high, but stable.

2. Some owners get 'cold feet'
Suppose some people start to believe that prices are too high and sell their houses. This is shown by a downward shift of the S-shaped price dynamics curve to the darker blue one.

3. A change in sentiment
As more people come round to the view that prices will fall and also sell, the S-shaped curve shifts down and prices fall along the broken arrow from B to Z.

4. Prices collapse
The sentiment in the housing market has shifted so much that there is no tipping point left. The market collapses to K.

QUESTION 17.10 CHOOSE THE CORRECT ANSWER(S)
Figure 17.24 (page 780) shows some S-shaped price dynamics curves for the housing market.

Based on the figure, which of the following statements is true?

☐ The parts of the PDC where the slope is less than 45 degrees represent a negative feedback process.
☐ Points Z and K represent unstable equilibria.
☐ A positive feedback process means that housing prices are always increasing.
☐ Optimism about housing prices would shift the PDC upwards.

17.10 THE FINANCIAL CRISIS AND THE GREAT RECESSION

Rising house prices in the US in the 2000s were driven by the behaviour of lenders, encouraged by government policy, to extend loans to poorer households. They were able to fund these subprime loans by packaging them into financial derivatives, which banks and financial institutions across the world were eager to buy. Rising house prices created the belief that prices would continue to rise, which shifted the demand curve for housing further to the right by providing households with access to loans based on housing collateral.

Follow the steps in the analysis in Figure 17.25 to see the housing price cycle on the way down from its peak in mid-2006. It illustrates how a small initial fall in prices led to a further collapse in demand as people started to believe that house prices would fall further. This change in beliefs resulted in the downward shift in the PDC in Figure 17.24, creating a new lower equilibrium value for house prices.

In Figure 17.26 you can see the contribution of the components of GDP to growth in the 18 months before the crisis in the US economy, then in the five quarters of recession from the start of 2008, followed by the recovery phase to the end of 2010. The fall in residential investment (the red bar) was the most important feature of the onset phase. At that stage, it was the only drag on growth. This was the consequence of the fall in house prices that began in late 2006. During the recession, a further fall in housing investment was compounded by a fall in non-residential investment and consumption.

Just as in the Great Depression, the fall in consumption was not simply due to the multiplier process. Households stopped buying new houses, but also cut spending on consumer durables. The financial accelerator mechanism helps to explain the transmission of falling house prices through the fall in the value of collateral to aggregate demand. Cutbacks in spending on new housing and on consumer durables were concentrated among the poorer households who had taken out subprime mortgages. The timing of the collapse of demand is consistent with the central role played by housing and debt in the financial crisis. There was also a fall in investment. Orders for new equipment were cancelled and factories closed. Workers were laid off and job creation slumped.

We can link the pattern of aggregate demand in Figure 17.26 to the decisions of households by using a diagram similar to the one we developed for the Great Depression. This is Figure 17.27. These two figures are dif-

Bank for International Settlements. 2015. 'Residential Property Price Statistics'. Updated November 20, and other national sources.

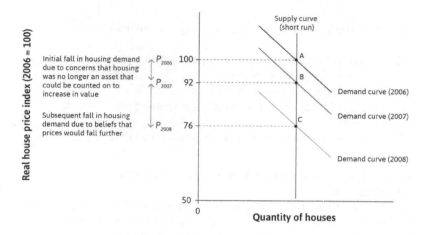

Figure 17.25 The financial crisis: The US housing price collapse.

1. The US economy (2006)

The housing market in the US economy in 2006 is shown at point A.

2. House prices fall (2007)

House prices began to decline in 2007 as demand shifted downwards from A to B, pushing the house price index down to 92 from its peak of 100.

3. A positive feedback process

Once prices were falling, the belief that prices would fall further became widespread. This led to further declines in demand, all the way down to C. The house price index fell to a level of 76 in 2008.

US Bureau of Economic Analysis.

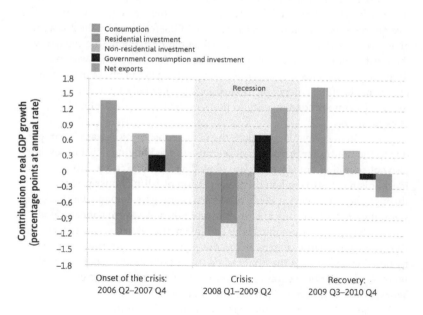

Figure 17.26 Aggregate demand and the financial crisis in the US (2006 Q2–2010 Q4).

ferent ways of looking at the same developments: Figure 17.27 is an individual household's view of the unfolding crisis, while Figure 17.26 is the same process from the perspective of the whole economy.

Column A in Figure 17.27 shows the situation in the 1980s. The 1990s to mid-2000s, as we saw, was a period of rapidly rising house prices. Column B shows the outcome by 2006. In the figure, the house price is the sum of the blue box for home equity, and the red box for debt (the mortgage). The increase in house prices increased home equity and pushed up households' assessment of their wealth, which was inflated by the expectation that house prices would continue to rise. One effect was that they uprated their target wealth. But target wealth did not grow as much as perceived wealth, so they also borrowed more in order to consume more. This meant that home equity grew, but so did debt. The higher level of household debt is shown by the larger debt rectangle in column B.

From 2006, house prices in the US began to fall. The household's viewpoint in 2008 and 2009 is shown in column C. Rising unemployment led to a downward re-evaluation of expected future earnings from employment. Household net worth shrank, as we can see in column C. Note that the size of the debt rectangle has not changed between columns B and C.

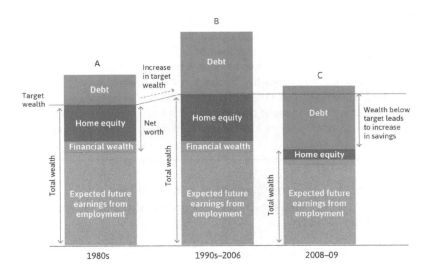

Figure 17.27 The financial crisis: Housing boom, household debt, and house price crash.

1. The great moderation (1980s)
Column A shows the situation in the 1980s.

2. Rising house prices (1990s–2006)
Through the 1990s and especially in the early 2000s, rising house prices increased total wealth, so households increased consumption by increasing debt.

3. Falling house prices (2006–2009)
Rising unemployment led to a downward re-evaluation of expected future earnings from employment. Household net worth shrank.

4. Wealth is below target
The fall in house and asset prices, combined with lower expected earnings, reduced wealth below target. Households cut consumption and increased savings.

The combined effect of the fall in house and asset prices, the increased debt acquired in the boom years, and lower expected earnings, had the effect of reducing wealth below target. As a result, households cut consumption and increased savings. This is shown in column C by the double-headed arrow labelled 'Wealth below target leads to increase in savings'.

The household shown in Figure 17.27 still has positive net worth following the fall in house and asset prices in the crisis. This is shown by the sum of the red, blue, and green rectangles in column C. But the behaviour of households whose net worth became negative following the fall in house prices was an important feature of the great recession that followed the financial crisis in the US. To show this in a diagram like Figure 17.27, the debt rectangle would slide down into the box labelled 'expected earnings from employment', wiping out the blue, green, and orange rectangles, reducing total wealth, and increasing the gap between expected and target wealth. It is easy to see how households in the bottom quintile shown in Figure 17.20 went underwater in 2008 and 2009. In the US in 2011, 23% of properties with a mortgage were worth less than that mortgage. Households in this position would have cut consumption as they paid down their debt to restore their financial position.

EXERCISE 17.6 THE CRISIS AND THE MULTIPLIER

1. Show the features of the 2008 crisis in the multiplier diagram, using Figure 14.6 (page 598) for the Great Depression as a model. Use the concepts of the consumption function, a house price bubble, the financial accelerator, and positive feedback in your answer.
2. How can you represent the role played by the higher marginal propensity to consume of households in the bottom quintile in your analysis? Refer to Figure 17.20 (page 773) and assume the economy is closed.

QUESTION 17.11 CHOOSE THE CORRECT ANSWER(S)

Figure 17.26 (page 782) depicts the US aggregate demand between 2006 Q2 and 2010 Q4.

Based on this information, which of the following statements is correct?

☐ The fall in residential investment was the sole cause of the financial crisis.

☐ In the recession, not only did households stop purchasing new houses and other consumption goods, but also firms stopped investing.

☐ Government consumption and investment have been supporting economic growth throughout the period considered.

☐ Household consumption in housing and other goods recovered promptly since the end of the crisis.

17.11 THE ROLE OF BANKS IN THE CRISIS

House prices and bank solvency

The financial crisis was a banking crisis—and it was global, as BNP Paribas demonstrated in August 2007 when it would not pay out to bondholders in one of its investment funds. The banks were in trouble because they had become highly leveraged and were vulnerable to a fall in the value of the financial assets that they had accumulated on their balance sheets (refer back to Figure 17.21 for the leverage of US and UK banks). The values of the financial assets were in turn based on house prices.

With a ratio of net worth to assets of 4%, as in the example of the bank in Figure 11.14, a fall in the value of its assets of an amount greater than this will render a bank insolvent. House prices fell much more than 4% in many countries in the recent financial crisis. In fact, the peak-to-trough fall in house price indices for Ireland, Spain, and the US were 50.3%, 31.6%, and 34.6% respectively. This created a problem of solvency for the banks. Just as with the underwater households, banks were in danger of their net worth being wiped out. It is relatively easy for a household to calculate whether this has happened, but not for a bank.

Unlike a house, obscure financial assets on (or often designed to be kept off) a bank's balance sheet, with acronyms like CDO, CDS, CLO, and even CDO^2, were hard to value. This made it difficult to judge which banks were in trouble.

Bank liquidity and the credit crunch

Doubts about the solvency of banks created another problem in the financial system—the problem of **liquidity risk**, which we introduced in Unit 10. A characteristic feature of banking is the mismatch between short-term liabilities, which it owes to depositors, and long-term assets, which are loans owed to the bank. Consequently, banks rely on the money market, where banks borrow from and lend to each other on a short-term basis, to fund themselves when they need short-term liquidity. But the operation of the money market relies on borrowers and lenders having trust in the solvency of those with whom they trade. The expected profit on a loan is the interest rate multiplied by the probability that the borrower will not default:

liquidity risk The risk that an asset cannot be exchanged for cash rapidly enough to prevent a financial loss.

$$\text{Expected profitability of loan} = (1 + r)(1 - \text{probability of default})$$

Therefore, as people feared that those to whom they were lending were more likely to default, they would only lend at a high interest rate. In many cases, banks or others operating in the money markets simply refused to lend at all. Newspapers called it the 'credit crunch'.

In Unit 10, we learnt that the interest rate in the money market is tied tightly to the policy interest rate set by the central bank. This relationship broke down in the credit crunch. Borrowing on the interbank market became much more expensive and hampered the ability of central banks to stabilize the economy. Even when the central banks reduced the interest rate close to the zero lower bound, the fear that banks would default kept money market rates high. This led to high mortgage lending rates: high money-market interest rates raised a bank's funding costs, as discussed in Unit 10.

Fire sales: A positive feedback process

The forced sale of assets, known informally as a **fire sale**, is a positive feedback process. In the financial crisis, the fire sale is an external effect for both the housing market and the markets for financial assets, and both affected the solvency of banks.

fire sale The sale of something at a very low price because of the seller's urgent need for money.

In the housing case, it is easy to visualize. Think of a household that is underwater and cannot repay a housing loan. Its debt exceeds the market value of the house. The household is under pressure to sell quickly in order to pay off as much of the mortgage as they can, to avoid continuing interest payments. If the housing market is undergoing a crash, then they may have to accept a drastically reduced price for the house (which may still be better for them than continuing to pay interest on the whole mortgage). This is a market failure because the fire sale has an external effect, conferring a cost (a fall in price) on other owners of the same type of asset.

In the financial crisis, banks as well as households faced massive losses in the value of their financial assets and were under pressure to sell them at reduced prices in order to repay debts (for example, to depositors who wanted their deposits back). Since many banks were desperately trying to sell at the same time, these asset prices plunged. This in turn further threatened the solvency of banks and other financial institutions as part of the positive feedback loop.

Governments rescue banks

Across the advanced economies, banks failed and were rescued by governments. To find out more about how they did this, and for more background on how the financial system failed during the crisis, we suggest reading *The Baseline Scenario* (http://tinyco.re/4748992).

In Unit 10 we highlighted the fact that banks do not bear all the costs of bankruptcy. The bank owners know that others (taxpayers or other banks) will bear some of the costs of the banks' risk-taking activity. So the banks take more risks than they would take if they bore all the costs of their actions. Excess risk-taking by banks is a negative external effect leading to a market failure. And it arises because of the principal-agent problem between the government (the principal) and the agent (the bank). The government is the principal because it has a direct interest in (and is held responsible for) maintaining a healthy economy, and will bear the cost of bank bailout as a consequence of excessive risk-taking by banks. Governments cannot write a complete set of rules that would align the interests of the banks with those of the government or the taxpayer.

Banks are rescued because the failure of a bank is different from the failure of a typical firm or household in a capitalist economy. Banks play a central role in the payments system of the economy and in providing loans to households and to firms. Chains of assets and liabilities link banks, and those chains had extended across the world in the years before the crisis.

The interconnectedness of banks was vividly illustrated in the credit crunch, where liquidity dried up in the money markets because each bank doubted the solvency of other banks. The event associated most closely with the financial crisis, the bankruptcy of US investment bank Lehman Brothers on 15 September 2008, showed how interconnected banks were (and are). This was not the beginning of the crisis—we have seen that the contraction of aggregate demand in the US began with the troubles in the housing market—but it signalled its escalation at the national and global level.

Thus the banking system, like an electricity grid, is a network. The failure of one of the elements in this connected network—whether a household or another bank—creates pressure on every other element. Just as happens in an electricity grid, the process in a banking system may create a cascade of subsequent failures, as occurred between 2006 and 2008.

In our 'Economist in action' video, Joseph Stiglitz, one of the few economists who warned repeatedly about the risks inherent in the financial system in the lead-up to the financial crisis, explains the combination of incentives, external effects, and positive feedback processes that led to this cascade of financial failure.

Joseph Stiglitz on why the financial crisis was a market failure.
http://tinyco.re/7394572

EXERCISE 17.7 HOW CONVENTIONAL WISDOM ON FINANCIAL MARKETS CONTRIBUTED TO THE GLOBAL FINANCIAL CRISIS

In the 'Economist in action' video of Joseph Stiglitz he explains that the financial crisis was a market failure. Watch it, and consider these questions:

1. What assumptions were made about financial markets before the crisis, and which assumption was particularly problematic?
2. How did incentives given to banks play a role in the recent financial crisis?

EXERCISE 17.8 BEHAVIOUR IN THE FINANCIAL CRISIS

'The Crisis of Credit Visualized' is an animated explanation of the behaviour of households and banks in the financial crisis available on YouTube.

1. Use the models discussed in this unit to explain the story told in the video.
2. Are there parts of the video that you cannot explain using the models and concepts from this unit?

The Crisis of Credit Visualized.
http://tinyco.re/3866047

QUESTION 17.12 CHOOSE THE CORRECT ANSWER(S)

Which of the following statements are correct regarding fire sales in the housing market?

☐ A household is underwater when the value of the house it owns is less than the value of the mortgage on the house.
☐ A fire sale occurs when a household cannot repay its mortgage and sells its house.
☐ Fire sales have a positive externality for prospective buyers who are able to purchase the foreclosed houses cheaply.
☐ Fire sales have a negative externality on other owners of similar assets by lowering the value of their assets.

17.12 THE ECONOMY AS TEACHER

Economists learned about the importance of aggregate demand from the Great Depression, but it gave them an undue confidence that a combination of fiscal and monetary policy would virtually eliminate unemployment in the long run. In Section 17.6, we saw the limits to this policy when the golden age broke down, with intensified conflict between workers and employers reflected in rising inflation.

The dominance of the prevailing Keynesian aggregate demand-oriented view helps explain most economists' failure to diagnose the supply-side nature of the first oil shock in 1973. Figure 17.28 illustrates this policy mistake for the US. The doubling of the oil price (in real terms) is indicated by the increase in the index from 5 to 10 in the chart in 1973. From Unit 15 and this unit, we know that when the national economic pie is reduced by a commodity price shock, this will intensify the conflict of interest over its division, and so inflation increased to more than 10% in 1974. Yet policy-makers were focused on the effect of the oil price shock in reducing aggregate demand and raising unemployment. They responded by loosening monetary policy (look at the falling nominal and real interest rates). Fiscal policy was not tightened.

A different response followed the second oil shock in 1979. The focus was on the need to reduce inflation and to restore expected profits. Instead of attempting to support aggregate demand, policymakers paid attention to the upward pressure on inflation created by the oil shock. Monetary and fiscal policy were directed toward the control of inflation as advocated by Milton Friedman a decade earlier; policy was tightened and governments were prepared to allow unemployment to rise in order to reduce inflation.

Expressed in terms of the labour market model, policymakers now recognized that the oil shock raised the inflation-stabilizing unemployment rate, which led them to implement supply-side policies to weaken trade unions (to shift the wage-setting curve down) and to increase competition in monopolized industries such as telecommunications (to shift the price-setting

Federal Reserve Bank of St Louis (FRED); Congressional Budget Office; US Bureau of Labor Statistics.

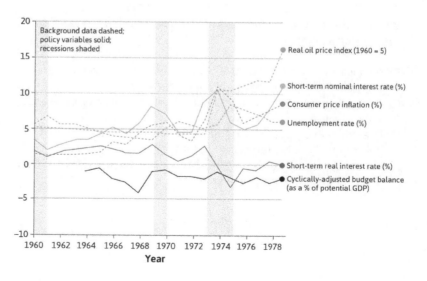

Figure 17.28 Policy choices during the end of the golden age: The US (1960–79).

curve up). These policies were closely associated with Prime Minister Margaret Thatcher in the UK and President Ronald Reagan in the US.

By extending deregulation from labour and product markets to the financial system, policymakers of the post-1979 epoch created the conditions in which financial practices that led to the global financial crisis could proliferate. Hyman Minsky had warned as early as 1982 how this could occur in tranquil macroeconomic circumstances.

Some had echoed Minsky's thinking well before the crisis. For example, in September 2000, Sir Andrew Crockett, general manager at the Bank for International Settlements, told banking supervisors:

> The received wisdom is that risk increases in recessions and falls in booms. In contrast, it may be more helpful to think of risk as increasing during upswings, as financial imbalances build up, and materializing in recessions.

Andrew Crockett. 2000. 'Marrying the Micro- and Macro-Prudential Dimensions of Financial Stability' (http://tinyco.re/5128318). Speech to International Conference of Banking Supervisors, Basel, 20–21 September.

In the table in Figure 17.29 we summarize the lessons for economists from each epoch.

We can draw three conclusions:

1. *Economists have learned from the successes and the failures of the three epochs:* Though the process has been slow, economics today is the result of this process.
2. *Successful policies in each epoch did not prevent positive feedback processes that contributed to subsequent crises:* Each epoch succeeded initially

Epoch	Dates	Prior conventional wisdom	Economic outcomes	What economists learned	Primary author
1920s and the Great Depression	1921–1941	Markets are self-correcting, efficient, and ensure the full use of resources.	Collapse of aggregate demand, high and persistent unemployment.	Instability is an intrinsic feature of the aggregate economy and aggregate demand can be stabilized by government policy.	Keynes
Golden age of capitalism and its demise	1945–1979	Government policy can implement an employment target by picking a point on the Phillips curve.	Late-60s decline in profits, investment, and productivity growth. Stable Phillips curve trade-off disappears.	With given institutions, the need to maintain profits, investment, and productivity growth can limit the ability of a government to implement sustainable low unemployment using aggregate demand policies.	Friedman
From stagnation to the financial crisis	1979–2016	Instability has been purged from capitalist dynamics; minimally regulated financial markets work well.	Financial and housing market crash of 2008.	Debt-fuelled financial and housing bubbles can co-exist with low and stable inflation, and will destabilize an economy in the absence of appropriate regulations.	Minsky

Figure 17.29 The economy as teacher: What economists learned in the three epochs.

because the policies and institutions that had been adopted addressed the shortcomings of the previous epoch. But then policymakers and economists have been taken by surprise when virtuous circles have turned into vicious circles.

3. *No school of thought has policy advice that would have been good in every epoch:* The value of competing approaches and insights depends on the situation. Ideas from both Friedman and Keynes have been essential to what economists have learned.

When Germany invaded France in 1914 at the beginning of the First World War, the French soldier André Maginot was wounded in the attack. When he later became minister of war he was determined to construct an impregnable line of defence, which we remember as the Maginot Line, in case German soldiers tried to march into France again.

But come the beginning of the Second World War, Germany's *blitzkrieg* (lightning war) attack used tanks and motorized troop carriers. The Germans didn't breach the Maginot line, they just drove around it.

Economists today are trying to avoid Maginot's error. A careful study of the economic history of the past century will help us to not simply fight the 'last war', but to prepare for whatever new difficulties will arise.

EXERCISE 17.9 BANKING REGULATIONS CAN HELP BRING ON FINANCIAL CRISES

An 'Economist in action' video shows Anat Admati, an economist, explaining the problems with the regulation of the banking system.

1. Using housing prices as an example, explain the upsides and downsides of leverage.
2. According to the video, what is the key difference between banks and other corporations, and why is this dangerous for the banking system?
3. What are some factors that contribute to the fragility and riskiness of the banking system, and how can we prevent future financial crises from occurring?

Anat Admati: What's wrong with banking (and what to do about it).
http://tinyco.re/8573554

EXERCISE 17.10 HOOVER'S BALANCED BUDGET

On 4 April 1932, as the US economy spiraled downward, President Hoover wrote to the US Congress to advocate a balanced budget and cuts in government spending.

Read Hoover's letter (http://tinyco.re/5833681) and write a critique of it, using the economics concepts from Units 13 to 17.

EXERCISE 17.11 AUSTERITY POLICY

In Unit 14, we introduced the **paradox of thrift** and examined the use of **austerity policies** in many countries before their economies had recovered from the recession that followed the 2008 crisis.

Were the lessons of the Great Depression forgotten when austerity policies were introduced? An analysis written by Barry Eichengreen and Kevin O'Rourke (http://tinyco.re/9442518) will help you answer this question.

17.13 CONCLUSION

One hundred years ago, economists believed that the private economy is always reliably self-correcting. Now they understand that governments can greatly increase their capacity to self-correct through automatic stabilizers such as unemployment insurance. They also understand that government policies, such as financial regulations, are essential to reduce the likelihood of financial crises—and when crises do hit, it falls to the government to rescue the financial sector and the economy.

Economists learned the importance of aggregate demand and positive feedback processes from the Great Depression. In response, after the Second World War, new policy regimes and institutions were developed at the national and international level. Based on accords between workers and firms in an environment of rapid productivity growth, they led to a golden age of shared prosperity in many countries.

This regime broke down in the face of slowing productivity growth and the first oil price shock. Macroeconomic stability in the great moderation was regained at the cost of rising inequality in many countries. Both the stability itself and the rising inequality sowed the seeds of the next crisis by leading to a build-up of private sector debt that resulted in the global financial crisis. Government support for the financial sector and aggregate demand averted another Great Depression, though not a lengthy recession.

The quick adoption of these policies in many countries was in important measure the result of what economists had learned since the Great Depression about the importance of aggregate demand. Economists continue learning about how the aggregate economy works, addressing critical issues such as the causes of instability in financial and housing markets and the determinants of aggregate investment. Greater understanding in these and other areas of economics will contribute to a more informed public debate on policies to ensure sustainable and secure improvements in living standards for all.

paradox of thrift If a single individual consumes less, her savings will increase; but if everyone consumes less, the result may be lower rather than higher savings overall. The attempt to increase saving is thwarted if an increase in the saving rate is unmatched by an increase in investment (or other source of aggregate demand such as government spending on goods and services). The outcome is a reduction in aggregate demand and lower output so that actual levels of saving do not increase.

austerity A policy where a government tries to improve its budgetary position in a recession by increasing its saving. See also: *paradox of thrift*.

Concepts introduced in Unit 17
Before you move on, review these definitions:

- Positive feedback (process)
- Global financial crisis
- Golden age of capitalism
- Great Depression
- Gold standard
- Catch-up growth
- Subprime mortgage
- Stagflation
- Effective tax rate on profits
- Postwar accord
- Financial deregulation
- Great moderation
- Great recession
- Bank bailouts

17.14 REFERENCES

Ball, Philip. 2002. 'Blackouts Inherent in Power Grid' (http://tinyco.re/9262695). *Nature News*. Updated 8 November 2002.

Ball, Philip. 2004. 'Power Blackouts Likely' (http://tinyco.re/7102799). *Nature News*. 20 January 2004.

Carlin, Wendy and David Soskice. 2015. *Macroeconomics: Institutions, Instability, and the Financial System*. Oxford: Oxford University Press. Chapters 6 and 7.

Crockett, Andrew. 2000. 'Marrying the Micro- and Macro-Prudential Dimensions of Financial Stability' (http://tinyco.re/5128318). Speech to International Conference of Banking Supervisors, Basel, 20–21 September.

Eichengreen, Barry, and Kevin O'Rourke. 2010. 'What Do the New Data Tell Us?' (http://tinyco.re/9442518). *VoxEU.org*. Updated 8 March 2010.

Mian, Atif, Amir Sufi, and Francesco Trebbi. 2013. 'The Political Economy of the Subprime Mortgage Credit Expansion' (http://tinyco.re/4522161). *Quarterly Journal of Political Science* 8: pp. 373–408.

Minsky, Hyman P. 1975. *John Maynard Keynes* (http://tinyco.re/9354915). New York, NY: McGraw-Hill.

Minsky, Hyman P. 1982. *Can 'It' Happen Again? Essays on Instability and Finance*. Armonk, NY: M. E. Sharpe.

Reinhart, Carmen M., and Kenneth S. Rogoff. 2009. *This Time Is Different: Eight Centuries of Financial Folly*. Princeton, NJ: Princeton University Press.

Shin, Hyun Song. 2009. 'Discussion of "The Leverage Cycle" by John Geanakoplos' (http://tinyco.re/7184580). Discussion prepared for the 2009 NBER Macro Annual.

Webb, Baumslag, and Robert Read. 2017. *How Should Regulators deal with Uncertainty? Insights from the Precautionary Principle* (http://tinyco.re/7250222). Bank Underground.

Wiggins, Rosalind, Thomas Piontek, and Andrew Metrick. 2014. 'The Lehman Brothers Bankruptcy A: Overview' (http://tinyco.re/8750749). Yale Program on Financial Stability Case Study 2014-3A-V1.

UNIT 18
THE NATION AND THE WORLD ECONOMY

HOW THE INTEGRATION OF NATIONAL ECONOMIES INTO A GLOBAL SYSTEM OF TRADE AND INVESTMENT PROVIDES OPPORTUNITIES FOR MUTUAL GAINS AND CONFLICTS OVER THE DISTRIBUTION OF THE GAINS

- Globalization is a term referring to the integration of the world's markets in goods and services, as well as flows of investment and people across national boundaries.
- Globalization has led to the prices of goods converging across countries, but much less so of wages.
- Nations tend to specialize in the production of the goods and services in which they are relatively low-cost producers, for example because of economies of scale, an abundance of the relevant resources or skills, or public policies.
- This specialization allows for mutual gains for the people of trading countries.
- Increased trade and specialization may benefit some groups within a country while harming others, for example, those producing goods that compete with imports.
- When evaluating government policy and international agreements, we may look at whether they fully exploit the mutual gains made possible, distribute those gains fairly, and reduce the economic insecurities involved in the globalization process.

In December 1899, the steamship *Manila* docked in Genoa, Italy, and offloaded her cargo of grain grown in India. The Suez Canal had opened 30 years earlier, slashing the cost of moving agricultural commodities from south Asia to European markets. Italian bakers and shoppers were delighted at the low prices. Italian farmers were not. After a couple of months in Genoa, the *Manila* headed west. She carried 69 people in steerage (the cheapest possible passage), who were abandoning their homeland in search of a livelihood in the US.

793

The low prices were made possible by a revolution in transportation and farming technology. As with the opening of the Suez Canal, the expansion of the railway system to the fields of North America, the Russian plain and northern India, and the development of steam-powered ships like the *Manila,* had cut the cost of transporting grain to distant markets. Across the vast plains of the American midwest, new strains of wheat, newly developed reapers and sowers, and improved drainage technologies had created a hi-tech, capital-intensive form of farming that was as productive as anywhere in the world.

Across Europe, parliaments and state bodies struggled to adjust to the grain price shock. In France and Germany, farmers and their advocates prevailed. Despite the benefits of lower grain prices to families, and despite the protests of workers who consumed the grain, governments imposed **tariffs** to protect the incomes of farmers.

Denmark, among other countries, responded differently. Instead of protecting grain farmers from cheap imports, the government helped them to start dairy farming instead. Using cheap imported grain as an input, farmers responded to the incentives to produce milk, cheese, and other commodities that could not be transported cheaply over long distances. In turn, cheaper grain meant families could increase spending on these dairy products.

In Italy, the children of some farmers took up jobs in the booming textile industry, which was exporting to the rest of the world. Many bankrupted farmers made the trip to the US. They slept on the decks of empty freighters that were returning to the US to pick up grain for Europe. About 750,000 Europeans made this voyage each year during the decade after the *Manila*'s visit to Genoa. Some of their grandchildren would end up as American farmers, growing grain in Kansas.

There were big winners and big losers from the grain price shock. Many of the changes made economic sense. For example, the world's grain was now grown increasingly in places where it could be produced most efficiently. But tariffs designed to protect the farmers of Germany and France held back this reallocation, preventing owners and workers in other sectors of the economy from enjoying lower grain prices. This continues to this day—rich countries still commonly protect their agricultural sectors through subsidies.

The battle line was not between rich and poor, or landlords and tenants, or employers and employees. The conflict was between the producers of different commodities. Those involved in manufacturing welcomed the expansion of trade with the US, while those farming grain did not.

Globalization is the word commonly used to describe our increasingly interconnected world. This term refers not only to the trade in grain and migration across national borders illustrated by the *Manila,* but also to non-economic aspects of international integration, such as the International Criminal Court (http://tinyco.re/2116436), the flow of ideas across borders, or our increasingly similar taste in music.

In Unit 6, we looked at firms like Apple that choose to produce their goods in other parts of the world where costs are lower. This **offshoring** is an important dimension of globalization, and it can involve outsourcing

tariff A tax on a good imported into a country.

[handwritten note:] tariffs are imposed to protection of select group(s) @ Expense of all other groups

In the European Union, the Common Agricultural Policy seeks to protect the agricultural sector for member countries. In the US, the most recent legislation supporting the sector is The Agricultural Act of 2014, known as 'The Farm Bill'.

globalization A process by which the economies of the world become increasingly integrated by the freer flow across national boundaries of goods, investment, finance, and to a lesser extent, labour. The term is sometimes applied more broadly to include ideas, culture, and even the spread of epidemic diseases.

offshoring The relocation of part of a firm's activities outside of the national boundaries in which it operates. It can take place within a multinational company or may involve outsourcing production to other firms.

[handwritten margin note:] Competition

production to other companies, or it can take place within the boundaries of a multinational company. For example, Figure 18.1 shows that the Ford Motor Company operates offices or plants in 22 countries outside the US. The company started offshoring a year after it was founded, first in Canada in 1904, and began manufacturing in many other countries soon afterwards, for example in Australia (1925) and even the Soviet Union (1930). In 2016 this 'American' company had 201,000 employees, 144,000 of them located outside the US.

In the case of a <u>multinational compan</u>y, owners, managers and employees in many countries have become part of the <u>same unified, transnational structure</u>. This is because the costs of doing business within the company are lower than the costs of doing business with other companies. But, as we saw with the cotton market in Units 8 and 11, globalization not only involves the <u>integration of firms</u> in different countries; it involves the <u>integration of markets</u> themselves, bringing sellers and buyers in different countries closer together.

You have already learned the <u>basic concepts</u> that you need to understand the global economy:

- Exchange involves the possibility of <u>mutual gains</u> and also conflicts over how these gains will be distributed.
- The resulting outcomes may not be Pareto efficient (there may be technically feasible mutual gains that remain unrealized).
- The resulting distribution may seem unfair in the eyes of many.
- <u>Well-designed government policies</u> can improve the efficiency or fairness of the outcomes.

While this is true of any set of market exchanges, when goods, services, people, and financial assets cross national boundaries, governments have additional powers and policies that include:

- *Imposition of tariffs:* These are taxes on imports that effectively discriminate against goods produced in other countries.
- *Immigration policies:* Governments regulate the movement of people between nations in a way that would not be possible (or acceptable) within most nations.

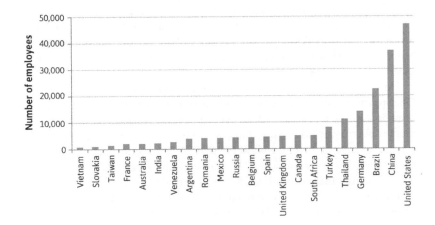

Figure 18.1 Ford employees across the world in 2014.

- *Capital controls:* Limits on the ability of individuals or firms to transfer financial assets among countries.
- *Monetary policies:* They affect the exchange rate, and so alter the relative prices of imported and exported goods.

While national boundaries give governments additional policy tools, they also limit the reach of governments. Within a nation, governments generally succeed in protecting private property rights where these exist, and in enforcing contracts. Because there is no world government (and international agencies are often weak), enforcing contracts and protecting property rights globally is sometimes impossible.

This raises controversial questions about the fairness of the distribution of mutual gains from exchange. The conflicting interests sometimes coincide with national differences between poorer and richer economies. It is tempting, though often inaccurate as we will see, to consider these conflicts as 'us' at home versus 'them' abroad.

In this unit, we will consider three markets that became more integrated with globalization: international markets for goods and services (trade), international labour markets (migration), and international capital markets (international capital flows, which are flows of savings and investment).

18.1 GLOBALIZATION AND DEGLOBALIZATION IN THE LONG RUN

merchandise trade Trade in tangible products that are physically shipped across borders.

The trade in goods, sometimes called **merchandise trade**, concerns tangible products that are physically shipped across borders by road, rail, water, or air. Trade of this sort has been happening for millennia, although the nature of the goods traded, and the distances over which they have been shipped, have changed dramatically. Trade in services is a more recent phenomenon, although it has also been occurring for centuries. Services that are commonly traded across borders are tourism, financial services, and legal advice. Many traded services make merchandise trade easier or cheaper—for example, shipping services, or insurance and financial services.

The UK became the leading provider of these services during the nineteenth century, when it was the most advanced industrial economy, the major naval and imperial power, and the most important trading nation. Nowadays, countries also export educational services (for example, people travel from all over the world to study in US or European universities), consulting services, and medical services. India has become a major exporter of software-related services. For example, the ebook for the CORE project was initially developed in Bangalore. We will study these service exports together with merchandise trade, since the same principles can help us to understand them.

How can we measure the extent of globalization in goods and services? One approach would simply be to measure the amount of trade in a country or region, or the world as a whole, over time. If it increased, we conclude that the country, region or the whole world was becoming more globalized. It is common to measure trends in the share of imports, exports, or total trade (imports plus exports) in GDP as an indicator of globalization, so as to take account of the growth of GDP as well as trade.

Figure 18.2 shows world merchandise exports (which excludes services), expressed as a share of world GDP, between 1820 and 2011. The share rose by a factor of 8 between 1820 and 1913, from 1% to 8%. In 1950, the share was lower (5.5%) but recovered rapidly during the prosperous postwar period. It reached 10.5% in 1973, 17% in 1998, and 26% in 2011. In the long run, the trend has clearly been upwards, with a sharp acceleration from the 1990s onwards. However, this trend was interrupted between 1914 and 1945, which included two world wars and the Great Depression.

A second method is to measure the additional costs associated with exporting goods relative to selling them domestically. When the costs of trading between countries fall, then in economic terms, the world has shrunk. It is as if countries were closer. In Unit 8, you learned about Alfred Marshall and his model of supply and demand. We saw that the **law of one price** holds in markets with many potential buyers and sellers, where all goods are identical and where buyers and sellers are aware of all trading opportunities. But this assumes that it is costless to take advantage of those trading opportunities. If, on the other hand, trading between markets in two countries is costly because of transport costs, trade barriers, or other factors, then there is no reason to suppose that prices will be the same in both.

Consider the market for a good that is produced in (and exported from) one country and consumed in (and imported into) another. Let's use the example of Japan exporting cars to the US. To keep the analysis straightforward, imagine that these are the two only countries in the world, that the Japanese do not consume cars, and that the US does not produce any cars itself. This means that everything that is produced is traded. The blue line in Figure 18.3 represents the supply curve in Japan: it is an upward-sloping function of the price in Japan. The red line represents the demand curve in the US. It is a downward-sloping function of the price in that country.

Let t be the cost of shipping a car from Japan to the US, including all transportation costs, trade taxes and so on. If the market is competitive, then the total cost of obtaining a car in the US will be the cost of buying it in Japan, plus the trade cost t. t is a measure of the **price gap** between cars in Japan and cars in the US. Follow the analysis in Figure 18.3 to see how changes in trade costs are reflected in price gaps.

- In the right circumstances, globalization can benefit both exporting producers and importing consumers.
- It does so by bringing them closer together, and it leads to an increase in both the supply of exports and the demand for imports.

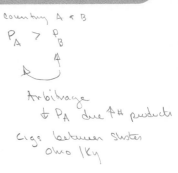

> **law of one price** Holds when a good is traded at the same price across all buyers and sellers. If a good were sold at different prices in different places, a trader could buy it cheaply in one place and sell it at a higher price in another. *See also: arbitrage.*
>
> **price gap** A difference in the price of a good in the exporting country and the importing country. It includes transportation costs and trade taxes. When global markets are in competitive equilibrium, these differences will be entirely due to trade costs. *See also: arbitrage.*

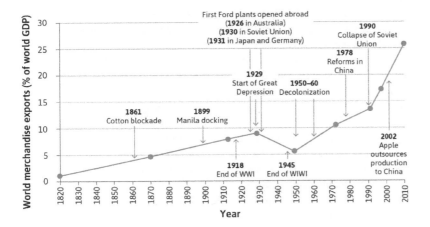

Figure 18.2 World merchandise exports as a share of world GDP (1820–2011).

(1) Appendix I in Angus Maddison. 1995. *Monitoring the World Economy, 1820–1992*. Washington, DC: Development Centre of the Organization for Economic Co-operation and Development; (2) Table F-5 in Angus Maddison. 2001. *The World Economy: A Millennial Perspective (Development Centre Studies)*. Paris: Organization for Economic Co-operation and Development; (3) World Trade Organization. 2013. *World Trade Report* (http://tinyco.re/2912108). Geneva: WTO; (4) International Monetary Fund. 2014. *World Economic Outlook Database: October 2014* (http://tinyco.re/2218637).

arbitrage The practice of buying a good at a low price in a market to sell it at a higher price in another. Traders engaging in arbitrage take advantage of the price difference for the same good between two countries or regions. As long as the trade costs are lower than the price gap, they make a profit. *See also: price gap.*

The concept of **arbitrage** explains why the price gap should tend to equal the sum of all trade costs. By buying at a low price in export markets and selling at a higher price in import markets, traders can make a profit as long as the price gap is higher than the total costs of trade. When traders engage in arbitrage in this fashion, they lower the supply of the good in the export market, driving up its price, and they increase the supply of the good in the import market, lowering its price. Both of these effects cause the price gap to decline. This should continue until price gaps have been driven down to the trade cost, and further arbitrage is unprofitable. A high price gap reflects a world in which trade is expensive and globalization is limited. A low price gap, on the other hand, reflects a much more globalized world in which trade is cheap.

This means we can learn about globalization from data on prices:

- *Globalization should lead to falling import prices*: But if we observe falling import prices, this does not necessarily mean that globalization is

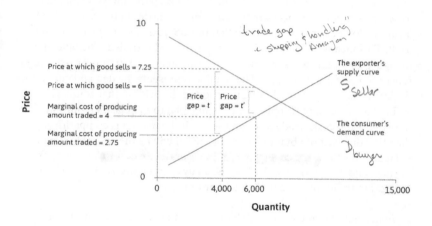

Figure 18.3 The market for cars: Price gaps reflect trade costs.

1. The exporter's supply curve
The blue line represents the supply curve in the producing (exporting) country, which is Japan. It is an upward-sloping function of the price in that country.

2. The consumer's demand curve
The red line represents the demand curve in the consuming (importing) country, which is the US. It is a downward-sloping function of the price in that country.

3. A competitive market
If the market is competitive, then the price of the car in the US will be the cost of buying it in Japan, plus the trade cost t. Let us assume that the cost of shipping a unit of the good is 4.5. We will show that 4,000 cars will be produced.

4. Why 4,000?
Because at that quantity, the difference between the supply curve and the demand curve is equal to the trade cost, 4.5. The marginal cost in Japan will be 2.75, while the customers in the US are willing to pay 7.25 per unit.

5. The effect of globalization
If we think of globalization as a process, then a world that is becoming more globalized is one in which trade costs are falling. In the figure, this is represented by a decline in trade costs from t to t'.

6. The price gap declines
As can be seen, falling trade costs imply a decline in the price gap between the import price and the export price, and an increase in the number of cars traded from 4,000 to 6,000.

occurring. The demand for the good in question may simply have declined (or the supply may have increased).

- *Globalization should also lead to rising export prices*: But rising export prices do not necessarily imply globalization. Demand for the good in question may simply be rising (or the supply may have declined).
- *Declining price gaps between importing and exporting countries are a much surer sign of globalization*: This is particularly true if we can also observe rising trade volumes.

For example, Figure 18.4 shows unmistakable evidence of declining transatlantic trade costs during the nineteenth century. The wheat price gap between the UK and the US (expressed as a percentage) fluctuated wildly before 1840 or so, around a roughly constant trend. It then started to decline at about the same time that shipping costs started to fall, a result of the introduction of steamships on long-distance routes. The price gap had almost vanished by 1914. At the same time, the volume of wheat shipped across the Atlantic rose dramatically.

The transatlantic trade in wheat is not an isolated example. International price gaps fell sharply on many routes and for many commodities between 1815 and 1914, the first epoch of modern globalization.

Figure 18.5 gives 'American-Anglo' price gaps (the reverse of Figure 18.4) for a variety of commodities between 1870 and 1913. For agricultural commodities such as wheat and animal products, British prices were higher than American ones, so the price gaps are the percentage by which the British price exceeded the American price. In the case of industrial commodities such as cotton textiles or iron bars, American prices were higher than British ones, so the price gaps quoted are the percentage by which prices in Boston or Philadelphia exceeded prices in Manchester or London. In nearly all cases price gaps fell (sugar is the outstanding exception), indicating that transatlantic commodity markets were becoming better integrated. Much like the dramatic reduction in grain prices in Genoa after the opening of the Suez Canal, which we discussed in the introduction to this unit, price gaps between the US and the UK reduced over time because of a revolution in transportation and improvements in farming and production technology. This is hardly an isolated example.

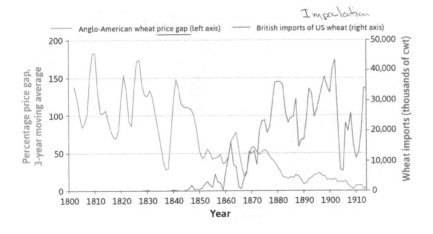

Figure 3 in Kevin H. O'Rourke and Jeffrey G. Williamson. 2005. 'From Malthus to Ohlin: Trade, Industrialization and distribution since 1500'. *Journal of Economic Growth* 10 (1) (March): pp. 5–34.

Figure 18.4 The Anglo-American wheat trade (1800–1914).

There exists evidence of similar convergence for Liverpool-Bombay cotton, London-Calcutta jute, and London-Rangoon rice prices.

Railways were probably even more important than steamships in integrating global commodity markets. Without them, it would have been prohibitively expensive to ship grain and other goods to and from the interior of continents and coastal seaports. Where price gaps fell less sharply during the late nineteenth century, this was often because of tariffs—taxes on imports—which were rising in several countries for reasons that we will discuss later, and which counteracted the effects of declining transport costs.

Transatlantic shipments of wheat fell after 1914, and price gaps rose, suggesting a rise in trade costs and therefore deglobalization. International price gaps rose during the interwar period for many agricultural commodities, because governments raised tariffs in response to unemployment and economic insecurity. When a country undertakes **protectionist policies**, its government is taking steps to limit trade, in particular by reducing the amount of imports coming into the economy. This is often done to protect domestic industries against foreign competition (hence protectionism), but it also means consumers have to pay more for imports. Protectionist measures include taxes to raise the domestic price of imports (a **tariff**) and quantitative restrictions on imports (a **quota**).

The post-1945 period was one of 'reglobalization', which began slowly but then accelerated, especially after 1990. Agricultural markets were largely protected for much of the period, and there is no reason to suppose that international price gaps for agricultural commodities fell sharply. The markets for industrial goods and components, on the other hand, were liberalized, and several studies have found evidence of declining international price gaps in the late twentieth century.

Economists have measured trade costs indirectly, by looking at trade between pairs of countries. This shows the long-term changes in impediments to trade, and can separate the effects of distance between the countries from national policies of those countries. If trade between Germany and France, for example, increased from one year to the next, but it did not increase between these two countries and their other trading

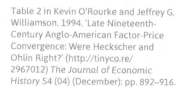

protectionist policy Measures taken by a government to limit trade; in particular, to reduce the amount of imports in the economy. These are designed to protect local industries from external competition. They can take different forms, such as taxes on imported goods or import quotas.

quota A limit imposed by the government on the volume of imports allowed to enter the economy during a specific period of time.

Table 2 in Kevin O'Rourke and Jeffrey G. Williamson. 1994. 'Late Nineteenth-Century Anglo-American Factor-Price Convergence: Were Heckscher and Ohlin Right?' (http://tinyco.re/2967012) *The Journal of Economic History* 54 (04) (December): pp. 892–916.

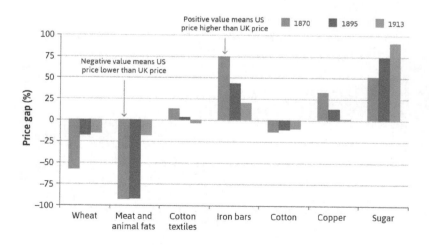

Figure 18.5 Commodity price gaps between the US and UK (1870–1913).

partners at the same time, we can interpret this as an indirect measure of declining trade costs for this pair of countries.

If we sum total trade costs each year for all major economies, we have an indicator of the process of globalization. Figures 18.6 and 18.7 do this for the period 1870 to 2000.

Trade costs declined substantially from 1870 to 1913, reflecting declining transport costs and reductions in tariffs. Trade costs then rose in the interwar period because of rising tariffs. This was particularly the case following the onset of the Great Depression in 1929: countries attempted to solve unemployment problems by discouraging imports.

From 1970, trade costs started to fall worldwide again as countries began to reliberalize trade, and transport technologies improved. Tariffs tend to be higher in low-income countries than in rich countries, in part because alternative methods of raising government revenue such as the income tax are difficult to administer in developing countries. As Figure 18.7 shows, however, most countries have reduced their tariffs in recent decades.

The price evidence therefore suggests interrupted commodity market integration over the past 150 years. Nineteenth century integration was briefly reversed, followed by reintegration after the Second World War. We call these two periods of integration **Globalization I and Globalization II**.

> **Globalization I and II** Two separate periods of increasing global economic integration: the first extended from before 1870 until the outbreak of the First World War in 1914, and the second extended from the end of the Second World War into the twenty-first century. *See also: globalization.*

EXERCISE 18.1 PRICE GAPS THAT DID AND DIDN'T FALL

Figure 18.5 (page 800) shows the price gap of different commodities between the US and UK over time. Can you think of a reason why price gaps for meat and animal fats such as butter did not start to fall until 1895? Propose an explanation for the smaller price gaps and the more rapid fall for copper as compared with iron ore. What might account for the increase in the price gap for sugar?

1870 – WWI
WWII – 2000's

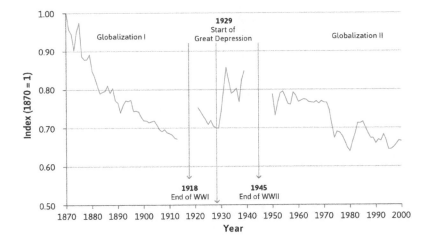

David S. Jacks, Christopher M. Meissner, and Dennis Novy. 2011. 'Trade Booms, Trade Busts, and Trade Costs'. *Journal of International Economics* 83 (2) (March): pp. 185–201. Note: Presented as an index, with 1870 = 1.

Figure 18.6 Impediments to trade (1870–2000).

EXERCISE 18.2 LEARNING MORE ABOUT TARIFFS
Download the World Bank data set, 'Trends in average MFN applied tariff rates in developing and industrial countries, 1981–2010' (http://tinyco.re/2008507). This data was used to produce Figure 18.7.

1. Choose one country from each income category (code 1 to 4) and plot the evolution of tariffs in these four countries. Use your plots to describe how tariffs in your chosen countries have changed over time.
2. Evidence from other studies suggests that on average, tariffs tend to be higher in lower-income countries than in high-income countries, but that most countries have reduced tariffs substantially in recent decades. Do your plots support this claim? Suggest an explanation for some of the observed differences between your chosen countries (if any). (As a starting point you may want to consider your chosen countries' membership of global trade agreements such as GATT/WTO (http://tinyco.re/2336439) or the EU (http://tinyco.re/2809410), and also whether the country has followed the structural adjustment programs of the IMF (http://tinyco.re/2776457)).

QUESTION 18.1 CHOOSE THE CORRECT ANSWER(S)
Figure 18.3 (page 798) depicts the supply curve in the exporting country and the demand curve in the importing country in a market for a traded good. Assume that the good is produced exclusively in the exporting country and consumed exclusively in the importing country.

Based on this information, which of the following statements is correct?

☐ At quantity 4,000, the price received by the producers is 7.25.
☐ At quantity 6,000, the price paid by the consumer is 4.
☐ The price gap represents the trade costs, such as transportation costs and trade taxes.
☐ Increasing the quantity sold to 6,000 causes the price gap to fall to 2.

The World Bank. 2011. 'Data on Trade and Import Barriers' (http://tinyco.re/2008507). Note: 3-year centred moving average.

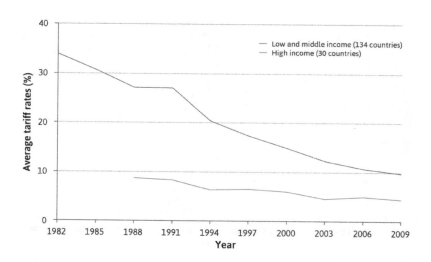

Figure 18.7 Average tariff rates, per cent (1981–2010).

QUESTION 18.2 CHOOSE THE CORRECT ANSWER(S)
Figure 18.6 (page 801) is a graph of an index that represents trade costs. A higher index represents higher trade costs and less globalization. Based on this information, which of the following statements are correct?

☐ The graph suggests a consistent decline in trade costs since 1870.
☐ Attempts by countries to address their unemployment problems after the 1929 Great Depression seem to have led to a decline in globalization.
☐ There does not seem to be any evidence of increased globalization after the Second World War.
☐ The graph suggests that commodity market integration over the past 150 years was one of interrupted integration.

18.2 GLOBALIZATION AND INVESTMENT

As in commodity markets, in international capital markets there is a similar pattern of nineteenth century globalization, followed by a brief episode of interwar deglobalization, and late twentieth century reglobalization.

If countries existed in isolation, they would have to finance their investment needs using their own savings. If this were the case, they could not spend more than they earned in a year, and all their income would have to be spent domestically. Domestic expenditure would have to equal domestic income. In reality, we see lending and borrowing across borders, between individuals, financial institutions, companies, and governments. To keep the language simple, let's talk about countries lending to or borrowing from other countries, bearing in mind the fact that these countries are not actors themselves but are made up of many individuals, companies, and institutions. A country can spend more than it earns by borrowing from abroad. Similarly a country can decide not to use its savings to finance domestic investment, and instead lend it abroad and earn a return on these foreign loans. In this case, its savings will exceed domestic investment, or (equivalently) its income will be higher than its expenditure.

We use the balance of payments accounts to track lending and borrowing abroad. We first need to explain how lending and borrowing abroad is related to international trade in goods and services. This is because imports represent payments from the domestic economy to the rest of the world, while exports represent payments from the rest of the world to the domestic economy. The **balance of payments** records the sources and uses of foreign exchange. If the records of transactions were complete, the balance would sum to zero because the source and use of each dollar crossing an international border could be accounted for (in reality, an entry called 'errors and omissions' is added to the balance of payments accounts to make it sum to zero).

To see how the balance of payments accounts work, think first about an economy where the only international payments are due to trade. If the home country imports more than it exports, then its

BALANCE OF PAYMENTS ACCOUNT (BP)
Records all payment transactions between the home country and the rest of the world and is divided into two parts: the current account and the capital and financial account.

$$BP \equiv CA + \text{(capital and financial account)}$$

If there is a current account surplus, this is a source of foreign exchange and it is either used to purchase foreign assets such as factories (FDI) or financial assets (recorded as a private net capital outflow) or it adds to the home country's official foreign exchange reserves. As a consequence, the home country's wealth rises. The opposite is the case for a current account deficit.

Financial capital markets

Balance of Payments

residents are making more international payments than they are receiving. For example, a country buying a higher value of imports from the US than it receives from selling its exports to the US needs to get hold of the US dollars—by borrowing from the US or the rest of the world—to cover the difference.

Conversely, if the home country is exporting more than it is importing, then its nationals must be lending to their trading partners so they can pay for the exports. These loans are a use of foreign exchange for the home country, and a source of foreign exchange for its trade partners.

Thus a trade deficit will imply that the country is borrowing, while a trade surplus implies it is lending (which is equivalent to saving, as we saw in Unit 10).

foreign portfolio investment The acquisition of bonds or shares in a foreign country where the holdings of the foreign assets are not sufficiently great to give the owner substantial control over the owned entity. Foreign direct investment (FDI), by contrast, entails ownership and substantial control over the owned assets. *See also: foreign direct investment.*
foreign direct investment (FDI) Ownership and substantial control over assets in a foreign country. *See also: foreign portfolio investment.*

remittances Money sent home by international migrant workers to their families or others in the migrants' home country. In countries which either supply or receive large numbers of migrant workers, this is an important international capital flow.

There are other reasons that people in one country make payments to people in another. The most important is the purchase of assets in another country. If a US company purchases shares in a company in China, it is making a payment for a Chinese asset. This implies a payment from the US to China. This is a use of foreign exchange called **foreign portfolio investment**. Similarly, if a US company purchases a factory in China, this is a use of foreign exchange called **foreign direct investment (FDI)**.

In subsequent years, however, the US company will receive dividends from its portfolio investment or profits from its direct investment, which will be sent back ('repatriated') to the US company. These repatriated profits are payments from China to the US. They are recorded in the US balance of payments as a source of foreign exchange.

Other important international payments include money sent home by migrant workers to their families (called **remittances**) and official aid flows, mostly from the governments of rich to poor countries.

CURRENT ACCOUNT (CA)
The sum of all payments made to a country minus all payments made by the country.

$$\text{current account} \equiv \text{exports - imports}$$
$$+ \text{ net earnings from assets abroad}$$
$$CA \equiv X - M + NINV$$

Since the current account includes all international payments, it also tells us directly whether a country is borrowing or lending:

- **CA deficit**: This means the country is borrowing—it has to do so to cover the excess payments it is making to the rest of the world.
- **CA surplus**: This means the country is lending (saving) to allow other countries to send it the excess payments.

All of these international payments are tracked in the balance of payments accounts, and the net value of these payments is called the **current account (CA)**—so the CA is the sum of all payments made to a country minus all payments made by the country. A country might have a trade deficit—that is, import more than it is exporting—but still have a current account surplus if it is receiving more than enough income from its foreign investments, remittances or foreign aid to pay the difference. In this case it will not need to borrow. For simplicity we ignore remittances and international aid and assume that the current account is equal to exports (X) minus imports (M) plus net earnings from assets owned abroad.

The borrowing and lending tracked by the current account are known as **net capital flows**. In this context, capital refers to money that is being lent and borrowed, rather than capital goods. A country that is borrowing (has a CA deficit) is receiving net capital flows—it is borrowing cash in order to cover its CA deficit. This cash will have to be paid back in the future, so capital inflows also represent rising foreign debt for the country. If the borrowed money is used for productive investments though, the investment can help generate the income needed to repay the debt. Thus, when a country wants to invest more than it can afford using its own savings, borrowing from abroad can be used to finance the extra investment.

Historically, increased trade tends to lead to larger CA imbalances. That is, when countries trade more, they also tend to borrow and lend more. The measure shown in Figure 18.8 is the sum of the absolute values of the current account balances of 15 countries from 1870 to 2014. We add up the absolute value of the current accounts to capture both borrowing and lending across countries.

As with commodity trade (Figure 18.6), the volume of capital flows in Figure 18.8 reflects a pattern of interrupted globalization. During the late nineteenth century there were huge capital flows from northwest Europe where there were **current account surpluses**—the UK especially, but also France and Germany—which financed investment in railways and infrastructure in countries such as Argentina, Australia, Canada, and the US. These were all countries with abundant and underexploited natural resources, especially land, but railways had to be extended into the interior in order to exploit these resources, and the land had to be settled with immigrants. In Europe, the countries that succeeded in attracting foreign investment during this period, such as Russia and Sweden, were also relatively resource-abundant. The investments made a healthy return, since

current account deficit The excess of the value of a country's imports over the combined value of its exports plus its net earnings from assets abroad. *See also: current account, current account surplus.*

current account surplus The excess of the combined value of its exports and net earnings from assets abroad over the value of its imports. *See also: current account, current account deficit.*

net capital flows The borrowing and lending tracked by the current account. *See also: current account, current account deficit, current account surplus.*

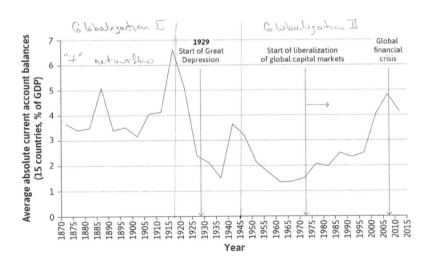

(1) Figure 2.2 from Maurice Obstfeld and Alan M. Taylor. 2005. *Global Capital Markets: Integration, Crisis, and Growth (Japan–US Center UFJ Bank Monographs on International Financial Markets).* Cambridge: Cambridge University Press; (2) International Monetary Fund. 2014. *World Economic Outlook Database: October 2014* (http://tinyco.re/2218637). Note: The data shown in the figure is the average absolute current account balance (as a percentage of GDP) for 15 countries in five-year blocks (from 1870–74 through to 2010–14). The countries in the sample are Argentina, Australia, Canada, Denmark, Finland, France, Germany, Italy, Japan, Netherlands, Norway, Spain, Sweden, UK, US. Data for 2014 is an IMF estimate.

Figure 18.8 International capital flows (1870–2014).

they increased the productive capacity of the borrowing countries, who were able to pay back the loans with interest based on the increased incomes that they enjoyed as a result.

In the interwar period these capital flows fell sharply—especially after the beginning of the Great Depression in 1929, which had led many countries to impose strict limits on the movement of capital across frontiers. These limits on capital flows meant that countries had to keep their **current account deficits** and surpluses relatively low— they prevented the capital inflows that would be required to finance large current account deficits. Unlike international trade, which resumed growth soon after the end of the Second World War, capital controls persisted for longer and only started to be relaxed in the 1970s and 1980s. Since then capital flows have increased sharply, although not yet to their dizzying heights of the early twentieth century.

Figure 18.9 shows how international asset holdings evolved during the twentieth century. The pattern is U-shaped. For the rich countries that dominated international lending, the share of foreign assets divided by GDP was high in the early part of the century, but collapsed in the 1930s. After 1945, New York took over from London as the global financial centre and the US eclipsed Britain as the dominant international asset holder.

To measure price gaps in international capital markets, we need prices of identical financial assets in different countries. Where researchers have been able to locate such prices, they have found that the late nineteenth century saw significant globalization in capital flows.

For most of the nineteenth century, if a would-be arbitrageur in New York (or London) wished to act on a price gap between New York and London, the speed at which information travelled limited his opportunities (we tracked the speed at which information travelled over the past 1,000 years in Unit 1). Information about price gaps travelled on ships that crossed the Atlantic. By the time the arbitrageur learned of the price gap, the information was already several days out of date. To act on it, he had to send written instructions to his agent in the other city to buy or sell. These

(1) Figure 2.2 from Maurice Obstfeld and Alan M. Taylor. 2005. *Global Capital Markets: Integration, Crisis, and Growth (Japan-US Center UFJ Bank Monographs on International Financial Markets)*. Cambridge: Cambridge University Press; (2) Lane, Philip R., and Gian-Maria Milesi-Ferretti. 2007.'Europe and Global Imbalances' (http://tinyco.re/2740164). IMF Working Papers 07 (144). The series shows the ratio of international assets to the GDP of the sample of countries in each year.

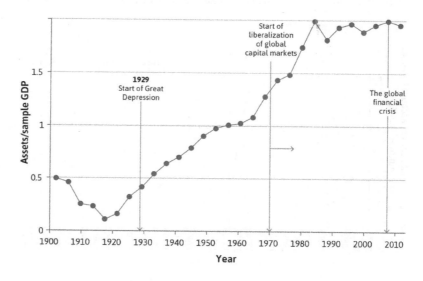

Figure 18.9 International asset holdings (1900–2014).

instructions travelled by ship too. It took a large price gap, therefore, to create speculation, since prices may have changed by the time the orders made it across the Atlantic.

In 1866, investors in London and New York (and their agents) could, for the first time, communicate with each other on the same day. They were using the first transatlantic telegraph cable, running from Ireland to Newfoundland in Canada. Once the cable was installed, investors could act immediately when they heard of a potential arbitrage opportunity, and price gaps immediately collapsed.

In most countries, residents and companies do the majority of invest-ment. One dimension of globalization is the foreign direct investment (FDI) mentioned earlier by companies abroad, including subsidiaries. Unlike the use of savings to buy foreign bonds or shares in a foreign company (portfolio investment), the intention of FDI is to exercise control over the use of resources in the foreign company.

Figure 18.10 shows the destination of investments by US companies when they invested directly in other companies abroad between 2001 and 2012. Perhaps surprisingly, when US firms chose to produce outside the US, they mostly went to countries in Europe; and in Europe, largely to countries in which wages were higher than in the US. The Netherlands, Germany, and the UK alone received more US investment than Asia and Africa combined. In this respect the location of Ford plants around the world shown in Figure 18.1 is not typical, because Ford has far more employees in China, Brazil, Thailand, and South Africa combined than in Germany, UK, Canada, Belgium, and France combined.

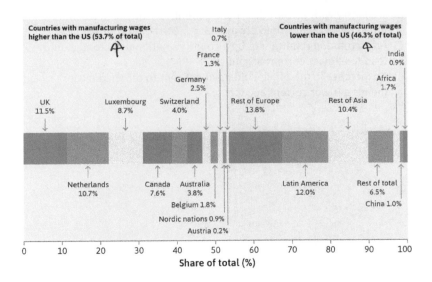

Figure 18.10 Foreign direct investment: Investment by US firms in other countries according to whether wages are lower or higher than in the US (2001–2012).

United Nations Conference on Trade and Development. 2014. *Bilateral FDI Statistics* (http://tinyco.re/2945855). Note: Data is for US FDI flows abroad. The countries shown to have manufacturing wages higher than the US are those that are classified by the US BLS International Labor Comparisons as having higher hourly compensation in manufacturing than the US on average over the 2005–09 period.

EXERCISE 18.3 INTERNATIONAL CAPITAL FLOWS: DOES CAPITAL FLOW FROM RICHER TO POORER COUNTRIES?

1. China has enjoyed a period of rapid development over recent decades. Using data from FRED (http://tinyco.re/3965569), plot China's current account balance over the period 1998–2012, and describe how it has evolved since the late 1990s (Hint: search for 'total current account balance for China'). Make sure to highlight whether it is a CA surplus or deficit.
2. On the same graph, plot the current account balance of the US over the same time period, and compare it with China's current account balance (you can also find the data for the US at FRED by searching for 'total current account balance for United States').
3. What does your graph suggest about capital flows between richer and poorer countries? Read the 2007 article 'The paradox of capital' (http://tinyco.re/9576333) by Eswar Prasad, Raghuram Rajan and Arvind Subramanian, who are IMF economists. Explain what is meant by 'capital flowing uphill' and whether or not it is a paradox.
4. Look at Figure 18.8 (page 805) and note that international capital flows (as measured by average absolute current account balances as a proportion of GDP) in the first decades of the twenty-first century are similar to those of the late nineteenth century. Using the discussion of capital flows in this section and in the article from question 3, was capital 'flowing uphill' during Globalization I or Globalization II? Why, or why not?

QUESTION 18.3 CHOOSE THE CORRECT ANSWER(S)

Which of the following statements regarding current accounts is correct, *ceteris paribus*?

☐ An increase in the trade surplus would lead to a decrease in a country's current account.
☐ A country with zero trade balance but historically high foreign direct investment would always have a current account deficit.
☐ An increase in remittances by a country's nationals abroad would lead to a lower current account.
☐ An increase in the official aid payment sent to other countries means a lower current account.

18.3 GLOBALIZATION AND MIGRATION

In the late nineteenth century, declining transport costs and rising wages made passage to America affordable for millions. Since then, labour migration is probably the dimension of globalization along which international economic integration has advanced the least. Indeed, labour into and out of some countries is less mobile internationally today than it was in 1913. Figure 18.11 plots immigration into the US as a percentage of the increase in the US population. During the late nineteenth and early twentieth century immigrants accounted for more than half of the increase in the US population, their numbers more than equalling the number of births minus the number of deaths. Restrictive legislation curbed immigration between the world wars. Although the contribution of immigrants to the growth in population has been rising again since the Second World War, it has not matched the growth before 1914. The low figures from the mid-1940s to the 1970s can in part also be explained by the relatively high birth rate in the US over this period.

There were relatively few institutional barriers to immigration in the late nineteenth century. Today, migrants without appropriate documentation may be deported or imprisoned. This meant that when Europe was experiencing its population boom, as death rates fell sharply and birth rates fell only with a lag, it was able to ship its surplus population to what the fifteenth-century explorer Amerigo Vespucci had named the 'New World' in America. Today's lower-income countries are not so fortunate. Immigration barriers were already in place during the late nineteenth century, but they became much stricter during and after the First World War, and rich countries retain strict immigration barriers to this day.

Thus the movement of goods and finance between countries is easier, and greater in magnitude, than the movement of people. Sending your money or your goods to some distant economy is much easier than sending yourself. You might have to learn an entirely new language or culture, not to mention leaving behind family and your home community. This is one reason why, for labour, there is nothing equivalent to the reduction in price gaps for goods that we discussed above. There is no tendency of wages in different countries around the world to become more similar.

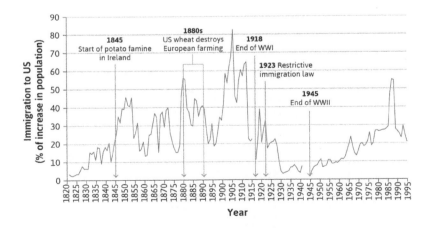

Susan B. Carter, Michael R. Haines, Richard Sutch, and Scott Sigmund Gartner (editors). 2006. *Historical Statistics of the United States: Earliest Times to the Present*. New York: Cambridge University Press.

Figure 18.11 Immigration into the US as a percentage of the change in US population (1820–1998).

Figure 18.12 shows the trends in wages paid to manufacturing workers expressed as a ratio of the wages of US manufacturing workers. It indicates, for example, that in the late 1970s, workers in Finland were paid 80% of the wage of US workers but, by 2012, they were paid more than 20% more.

There are three developments that we can see in Figure 18.12:

- Like France, many other European countries caught up with the US in manufacturing wages, in some cases surpassing them by more than 40% (Norway and Sweden).
- Wages in South Korea and Japan rapidly converged towards the US wage level.
- A number of low-wage countries (for example, Sri Lanka) remained far behind, some falling even further behind (Mexico).

In conclusion, there was a dramatic increase in the integration of the world economy during the nineteenth century, which was marked by increasing volumes of trade and corresponding reduction in price gaps, as well as the movement of capital. This was followed by a brief period of deglobalization during the Great Depression and the Second World War, and renewed globalization afterwards, especially since the 1990s. These three waves of globalization, deglobalization, and reglobalization are equivalent to those in Figure 18.4.

Trade costs and barriers to the mobility of capital and labour fell in the nineteenth century, largely as a result of steam-driven transportation technologies. They rose again in the interwar period, largely due to government intervention—taxes and other barriers to trade, capital controls and immigration restrictions—and fell again in the late twentieth century, as a result of more liberal policies and technological change. National boundaries, however, have continued to be important barriers to the global integration of labour markets.

US Bureau of Labor Statistics. 2015. *International Labor Comparisons* (http://tinyco.re/2780183). Note: (1) Data is for hourly compensation costs in manufacturing, which includes total hourly direct pay (pre-tax), employer social insurance expenditures, and labour-related taxes. National currency data converted into US dollars at the average daily exchange rate for the reference year; (2) Graph of Sri Lanka shows most recent available data, for the year 2008.

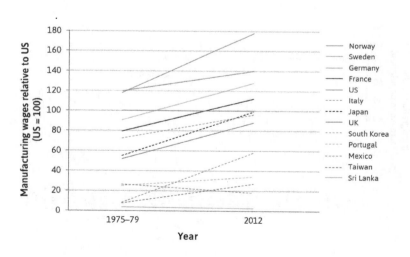

Figure 18.12 Manufacturing wages relative to the US (1975–79 and 2012).

QUESTION 18.4 CHOOSE THE CORRECT ANSWER(S)

Figure 18.11 (page 809) depicts the level of immigration into the US as a percentage of the change in the US population.

Based on this information, which of the following statements is correct?

☐ In the decade prior to the First World War, the number of immigrants was higher than the number of births minus the number of deaths.
☐ Wars cause permanent declines in the level of migration.
☐ As with trade in goods and capital flows, there is evidence of a continued trend of 'reglobalization' in migration since the end of the Second World War.
☐ The trend in the graph suggests that with high migration over the past 150 years the wages in different countries around the world should now be similar.

18.4 SPECIALIZATION AND THE GAINS FROM TRADE AMONG NATIONS

The result of this process of global economic integration means that today virtually all nations are part of a global economy characterized by:

- *Specialization*: Particular locations specialize in the production of distinct goods.
- *International trade*: These goods are then exchanged with other locations specializing in other goods.

Specialization entails trade because by producing a narrower range of goods and services than you use, you must engage in trade to acquire the ones you do not produce. International trade is the outcome of specialization among countries.

Machine tools (such as precision-cutting tools) produced in southern Germany are used in the production of computers in coastal south China running software produced in Bangalore and California. These are then flown on aircraft produced near Seattle in the US to be sold to users throughout the world. Producers of these commodities put food on their table grown in the Canada or Ukraine and wear shirts made in Mauritius.

As these examples show, trade and specialization are two sides of the same process. Each provides the conditions necessary for the other. In the absence of trade, machine tool workers in Stuttgart could not eat bread made from grain grown in Ukraine or Canada and wear clothes made in Mauritius. If they had to provide for themselves, many of them would be farmers or clothing workers. In the absence of specialization, there would be little to trade.

In Section 1.8, you met Greta and Carlos, who each wanted to consume both apples and wheat. With their own land and labour they each could have produced both crops, and been entirely self-sufficient. But they found that they could be better off by specializing; Carlos producing only apples and Greta producing only wheat.

> **specialization** This takes place when a country or some other entity produces a more narrow range of goods and services than it consumes, acquiring the goods and services that it does not produce by trade.

[handwritten margin note: Exchange involves possibility of mutual gain & conflict over how gains are distributed]

comparative advantage A person or country has comparative advantage in the production of a particular good, if the cost of producing an additional unit of that good relative to the cost of producing another good is lower than another person or country's cost to produce the same two goods. *See also: absolute advantage.*

economies of scale These occur when doubling all of the inputs to a production process more than doubles the output. The shape of a firm's long-run average cost curve depends both on returns to scale in production and the effect of scale on the prices it pays for its inputs. *Also known as: increasing returns to scale. See also: diseconomies of scale.*

The two were better off by specializing because their land differed in what it was best at producing. While Carlos could produce 50 times as many apples as tonnes of wheat on his land if he produced just one crop, Greta could only produce 25 times as many apples as tonnes of wheat (again, if she produced just one or the other). Although Greta could produce more of either crop than could Carlos, Carlos had a **comparative advantage** in producing apples (in terms of productivity, he was less inferior to her in producing that crop compared to the other). Make sure you understand the term comparative advantage and Figures 1.9a and b before going on.

We are going to use the same reasoning to explain why entire countries specialize in some goods and services, and some in others.

For Greta and Carlos, the reason for specialization was that they had different land. In the same way, the natural resources and climate of countries differ. It would be very costly to produce bananas in Germany given the climate, and this is one of the reasons why Germans make their living doing other things. But there are many other reasons for specialization.

Suppose instead that Greta and Carlos had identical plots of land and the same set of skills. They are equally adept at growing either wheat or apples, but the production of both apples and wheat is subject to **economies of scale**. This would mean, for example, that doubling the amount of land and their own time devoted to the production of, say, apples would more than double the quantity of apples produced. Whether or not this is a reasonable assumption depends on the production technology of each good.

So we will replace Figure 1.9a, which showed the case of specialization based on factor endowments, with Figure 18.13. In the table in this figure, you see that if 25 hectares (and a proportional amount of either Greta's or Carlos' labour is devoted to the production of apples), 625 apples will be produced. If the land devoted to apple production is doubled to 50 (with half of labour time still applied to its production) apple production increases by a factor of four, to 2,500.

Imagine the two working as self-sufficient farmers, each with 100 hectares, dividing their land and labour equally between the two crops. They would each have 250 tonnes of wheat and 2,500 apples to consume.

But if either one of them were to specialize in wheat and the other in apples and then share the resulting crops equally, they could have four times as much wheat and apples as they would have in the absence of specialization. The important point here is that it doesn't matter who specializes in what. The advantage of specialization does not come from any difference between the endowments (skills, land) of Greta and Carlos but instead from the fact that people each producing a lot of one thing may be more efficient than them producing lesser amounts of many things.

Area of land used in production (hectares)	1	25	50	75	100
Wheat (tonnes)	0.1	62.5	250	562.5	1,000
Apples	1	625	2,500	5,625	10,000

Figure 18.13 Economies of scale in the production of wheat and apples. Note that the entries in the 'Apples' row are just the square of the amount of land devoted to the production of apples, and the 'Wheat' row is just one-tenth of the number of apples produced in each column.

We'll get back to Carlos and Greta in the next section, but what do the examples featuring them tell us about global integration and trade between nations? For example, why do southern Germans specialize in producing machine tools, high-end automobiles and other manufactured goods, while the southern coast of China is the world centre of manufacturing computers that run on US-produced software, while Mauritians produce shirts, and the residents of Alberta, Canada grow grain? There are two kinds of answers:

- *Economies of scale, agglomeration, and other positive feedbacks:* The production of aircraft is subject to extraordinary economies of scale. The Boeing Plant in Everett, Washington is the largest building in the world (over 13 million cubic metres in volume). Writing computer code is not subject to economies of scale, but good software is produced in areas in which a very large number of people are working on similar tasks, sharing information and innovating.
- *Differences between regions:* Alberta has an appropriate climate and soil for growing grain. The production of clothing requires a lot of labour but not an extensive amount of capital goods, fitting the availability of these factors of production in Mauritius. German apprenticeship training schemes support the high level of skills needed for the machine tool industry.

The distinctive aspect of the first source of specialization is its accidental quality. Why Everett, Washington rather than Osaka, Japan? Why is Bangalore a software hub, and not Singapore or Sydney?

To explain specialization we often need to draw on both types of explanation. German machine tool production, for example, benefits not only from the high level of skill of the German workforce but also from economies of co-location, called **economies of agglomeration**. Firms also share information and develop common industry standards for components, and they stimulate research in the region, from which they benefit.

Figure 18.14 (page 814) summarizes our explanation of specialization and trade.

ECONOMIES OF AGGLOMERATION
The cost reductions that firms may enjoy when they are located close to other firms in the same or related industries.

Don't confuse this with *economies of scale* or *economies of scope*, which apply to a single firm as it grows.

EXERCISE 18.4 ASSESS SOME COUNTRY PRODUCTION SPECIALIZATION PATTERNS
Choose a few goods and services not discussed in this unit (for example, wine, automobiles, professional services such as accounting and auditing, consumer electronics, bicycles, or fashion goods). Use Figure 18.14 (page 814), along with what you know or can research about your chosen products, to provide an explanation of country specialization patterns.

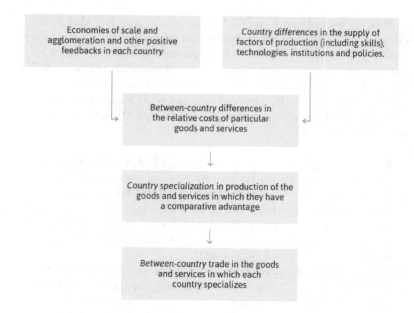

Figure 18.14 Between-country cost differences, specialization, and trade.

18.5 SPECIALIZATION, FACTOR ENDOWMENTS, AND TRADE BETWEEN COUNTRIES

In this section, we look in more detail at trade specialization based on factor endowments, extending the analysis in Section 1.8. We show how trade between the people of different nations—specialized in the production of different things—can result in mutual gains, and also in conflicts over how these gains are distributed.

Imagine Greta lives on Wheat Island and Carlos lives on Apple Island. The land on each island can be used for growing both wheat and apples, and they consume both wheat and apples in order to survive. For the example in this section, we will use the numbers shown in Figure 18.15, and assume that Greta and Carlos each have 100 hectares of land. We have already seen that Greta is lucky. Wheat Island has better soil for both crops. She has an **absolute advantage** in both crops. Although Carlos' land is worse overall for producing both crops, his disadvantage is less, relative to Greta, in apples than in wheat.

Remember, even those who have an absolute advantage in nothing at all will specialize in the thing at which they are least bad, and get the other goods they consume by exchange. Similarly, people who are better at producing everything will specialize in the goods at which they are

absolute advantage A person or country has this in the production of a good if the inputs it uses to produce this good are less than in some other person or country. *See also: comparative advantage.*

	Production if 100% of time is spent on one good, per hectare of land
Greta	1,250 apples or 100 tonnes of wheat
Carlos	1,000 apples or 40 tonnes of wheat

Figure 18.15 Absolute and comparative advantage in the production of apples and wheat.

comparatively best, while importing other goods. Both Greta and Carlos can benefit from specialization and trade.

To see how this works, follow the analysis in Figure 18.16a.

Diversification in the absence of trade

In the absence of trade, Carlos and Greta do best by selecting a point on the highest indifference curve possible, given the constraint of their feasible production frontier. In our simple example, the feasible production frontier is also the feasible consumption frontier, because each person spends time producing only wheat and apples, and can consume only the amount they produce. Follow the analysis in Figure 18.16b to how Carlos and Greta make their production and consumption decisions.

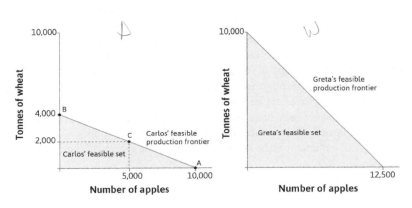

Figure 18.16a Carlos' (Apple Island's) and Greta's (Wheat Island's) feasible production frontiers.

1. Carlos' production
The left-hand panel of the figure shows the combinations of wheat and apples that Carlos can produce in a year. If he produces only apples and has 100 hectares of land, he can produce 10,000 of them. This is shown by point A on the horizontal axis.

2. Specialization in wheat
Similarly, if Carlos produces only wheat then he can produce 4,000 tonnes, as shown by point B on the vertical axis.

3. The feasible production frontier
The red line that joins points A and B is the feasible production frontier for Carlos. It shows all the combinations of wheat and apples that can be produced by Carlos in a year.

4. Carlos's choice
He can choose to produce any combination on (or inside) the frontier. For example, he could produce 2,000 tonnes of wheat and 5,000 apples, as shown by point C.

5. Carlos' feasible set
He can produce anywhere between the origin and the feasible production frontier. The red shaded area shows his feasible set.

6. The feasible production frontier for Greta
This is shown in the right hand panel. Greta can produce more of both goods than Carlos can. If she only produces a single good, she can produce either 12,500 apples or 10,000 tonnes of wheat with 100 hectares of land.

7. Wheat Island has an absolute advantage
It has this advantage in producing both goods because Greta can produce more of both of them. Graphically, Greta's feasible set includes Carlos' within it.

Trade and specialization

What will happen when Greta and Carlos are able to trade? The decision to trade could be made for a number of reasons, such as the development of a new technology (maybe a boat) or the removal of barriers to trade (perhaps the end of a feud between the two islands). As we learnt in Unit 1, it is the relative, not the absolute, cost of producing the two goods that matters for mutually beneficial trade.

We will show that both Carlos and Greta gain when one island specializes in the production of wheat and the other specializes in the production of apples. Carlos can produce 4,000 tonnes of wheat a year, or 10,000 apples. In order to produce one more tonne of wheat, Carlos has to produce 2.5 fewer apples, so the marginal rate of transformation between tonnes of wheat and apples is 2.5. Since it takes the same amount of inputs (land and labour) to produce one tonne of wheat as it does to produce 2.5 apples, a tonne of wheat will cost the same as 2.5 apples. Thus the relative price of wheat to apples will be 2.5. The relative price is another way of referring to the marginal rate of transformation or the opportunity cost.

Greta is more productive in producing both goods. Greta can produce 10,000 tonnes of wheat in a year, or 12,500 apples. The relative price of wheat to apples on Wheat Island is therefore 1.25. Wheat Island therefore has a comparative advantage in producing wheat.

The relative price of apples is simply the inverse of the relative price of wheat, so if Wheat Island has a comparative advantage in producing wheat, then Apple Island will have a comparative advantage in producing apples. Figure 18.17 summarizes the key numbers from the example. The relative

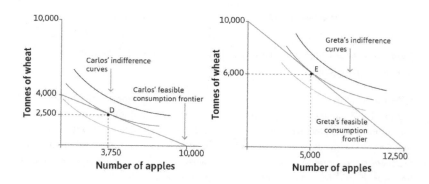

Figure 18.16b Carlos' (Apple Island's) and Greta's (Wheat Island's) utility-maximizing choices of consumption.

1. Carlos' feasible consumption frontier
This is in the left-hand panel, coinciding with his feasible production frontier.

2. Carlos' indifference curves
The shape of the indifference curves represents Carlos' preferences over wheat and apples.

3. The highest indifference curve Carlos can attain
It will be the one that is tangent to his feasible consumption frontier. He will choose to consume 2,500 tonnes of wheat a year and 3,750 apples, as shown by point D.

4. Greta's superior productivity
This means she can consume more of both goods than Carlos. We assume her preferences are the same as Carlos' (the indifference curves are the same shape). She consumes 6,000 tonnes of wheat a year and 5,000 apples, as shown by point E.

prices of the good for which each island has a comparative advantage are shown in bold.

Gains from trade

When there is no trade (autarky, closed economies), the feasible production frontier is also the feasible consumption frontier. From Figure 18.16b, we can see that when the economies are closed, total production between the two countries is 2,500 + 6,000 = 8,500 tonnes of wheat and 3,750 + 5,000 = 8,750 apples. When countries fully specialize however, Greta is able to produce 10,000 tonnes of wheat and Carlos can produce 10,000 apples, so there is more of both goods overall. As long as they can trade, they can both consume more of each good and can, ideally, both be better off.

If we assume that there are no trade costs, it is obvious that the relative price of wheat and apples is the same in each country when they trade. What will the new price be? From Carlos' point of view, the supply of wheat has increased more than the supply of apples, so the price of wheat relative to apples will go down to something less than 2.5. Equally, from Greta's point of view the supply of wheat has increased by less than the supply of apples, so the relative price of wheat will go up for her to something higher than 1.25. When trading, the prices will lie between the prices experienced by the two economies when they are closed.

To see what happens when they trade, work through the analysis in Figure 18.18.

Because both countries are now specializing in the good in which they have a comparative advantage, the new consumption frontiers are above their production frontiers. For each country, the two frontiers meet at the point at which they do not trade, which given full specialization, correspond to each axis. We can see that specialization and international trade have led to an increase in the size of the feasible consumption set for both countries. Note that through trade, Greta cannot consume more than the maximum amount of apples Carlos can produce (10,000), which is why her feasible consumption frontier does not extend beyond 10,000 apples.

If we look back to Figure 18.16b we can see that any expansion of their feasible sets makes it possible for both Carlos and Greta to reach a higher level of utility (a higher indifference curve), so trade has been mutually beneficial.

Specialization has enlarged the feasible consumption set of both in the same way that borrowing and investing increased the feasible consumption set of Marco in Unit 10. By investing, Marco specialized in having income in the future, which increased the total income he earned over all periods.

	Apple Island (Carlos)	Wheat Island (Greta)
Tonnes of wheat produced per year	400	1,000
Number of apples produced per year	1,000	1,250
Relative price of wheat	1,000/400 = 2.5	**1,250/1,000 = 1.25**
Relative price of apples	**400/1,000 = 0.4**	1,000/1,250 = 0.8

Figure 18.17 An island has a comparative advantage in producing a good when it is relatively cheaper in their economy (in the absence of trade).

Then, by borrowing, he imported some of his future income to the present so that he could consume in both periods.

The relative price determines the extent to which trade increases the feasible set of each island. This, in turn, depends on how the price is determined. Suppose that Greta can unilaterally determine the price. To increase her gains from trade, Greta will choose a price that increases the amount of apples she receives for each tonne of wheat she sells to Carlos. Intuitively, Greta wants the good she produces to command a higher price. If we assume that she has chosen a price of wheat of 2.25, then how does this affect the expansion of the feasible sets? Follow the analysis in Figure 18.19 to find out.

Of course, if Greta could set any price she wished, she could have set an even higher price. If she set the price at 2.5 apples per tonne, she would eliminate Carlos' gains from trade entirely. At this price Carlos would be equally well off if he produced his own wheat and would have no reason to engage in trade with Greta. When the people of a country are better able to influence the price in their favour, we say they have **bargaining power**.

> **bargaining power** The extent of a person's advantage in securing a larger share of the economic rents made possible by an interaction.

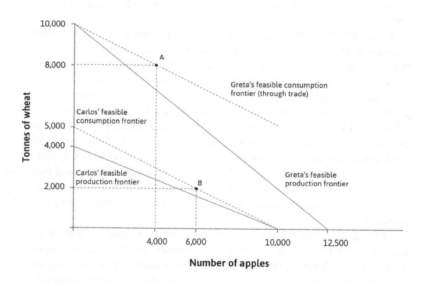

Figure 18.18 The effect of trade and specialization on Carlos' and Greta's feasible consumption frontiers.

1. Before specialization and trade
The figure shows the feasible production frontiers for Carlos and Greta.

2. The effect of specialization and trade
The dotted red lines show the outward shift of the feasible consumption frontiers due to specialization and trade. We assume that the relative price of wheat after specialization and trade is 2 (an arbitrary price in between 1.25 and 2.5).

3. Consumption after specialization and trade
Carlos specializes in apples, producing 10,000, and exports (10,000 – 6,000 = 4,000) apples to Greta, who specializes in wheat, producing 10,000 tonnes and exports (10,000 – 8,000 = 2,000) tonnes of wheat to Carlos.

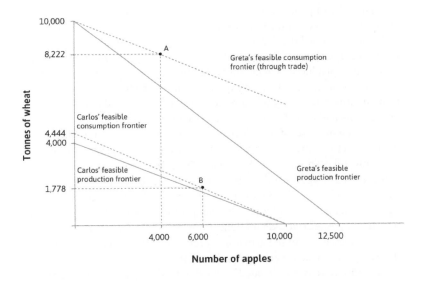

Figure 18.19 The effect of trade and specialization on the feasible consumption frontiers for Carlos and Greta, when Greta is able to dictate the price.

1. Feasible production frontiers
The figure starts with the same feasible production frontiers as Figure 18.18.

2. After trade
Greta now dictates the relative price of wheat to be 2.25. Trade still shifts out both feasible sets, but it shifts Greta's by more. This means trade and specialization will increase the utility of both Carlos and Greta, but will increase Greta's utility by more.

3. At the new price
Greta has to give up fewer tonnes of wheat to get 4,000 apples. She is better off than she was at a price of 2 in Figure 18.18. In contrast, Carlos is worse off relative to the price of 2. He gets fewer tonnes of wheat in return for the same number of apples.

GREAT ECONOMISTS

David Ricardo

David Ricardo (1772–1823) developed the theory of comparative advantage. He was also the first economist to warn that a rapidly growing capitalist economy would confront the limits of its natural environment.

The son of a successful stockbroker and the third of 17 children, Ricardo grew up in London and eloped at the age of 21, which led to a long period of estrangement from his parents. He went on to build a huge fortune through trading in stocks before interesting himself in political economy. He entered parliament (by purchasing a seat, which then was possible) where, besides his contributions on economic questions, he favoured liberal social causes such as religious tolerance, freedom of speech, and opposition to slavery.

Ricardo's central contribution to economic theory was an analysis of the principles of production and distribution in a growing capitalist economy with a large agrarian sector. In *An Essay on Profits*, published in 1815, he developed the Ricardian model, which came to dominate British economic thought for much of the next 50 years. In this model, agricultural production relied on three inputs: labour, capital, and land. As production and population expanded, either existing land had to be farmed more intensively with greater doses of capital and labour, or less fertile plots had to be brought into production.

Drawing on ideas of diminishing returns, he explained how this would lead to a squeeze on profits and the eventual stagnation of the economy. Like Thomas Malthus, whose ideas we studied in Unit 2, he reasoned that wages could not be below subsistence. As farming expanded to less good land, the price of food and hence wages would have to increase. A result would be that profits (which Ricardo presumed would be invested) would fall. Rents (presumed to be spent on luxuries) would increase due to the growing scarcity of land. The result would be the eventual slowdown and stagnation of the economy.

Ricardo therefore advocated a repeal of tariffs on the import of grains (known as the Corn Laws), which his friend Malthus defended. Ricardo reasoned that if Britain could acquire more of its food from the US and elsewhere, then paying workers a subsistence wage would cost less to the employers, raising the rate of profit and investment. Importing grain rather than growing it in Britain would make land less scarce and therefore limit the landlord's share of total output. The result, according to Ricardo, would be continued growth rather than stagnation.

His greatest work, *On the Principles of Political Economy and Taxation* (published in 1817), introduced the labour theory of value, later used by Karl Marx. This theory holds that the value of goods is proportional to the amount of labour required, directly or indirectly, in their production. Wassily Leontief (1906–1999) devised a way that these values could

David Ricardo. 1815. *An Essay on Profits*. London: John Murray.

David Ricardo. 1817. *On The Principles of Political Economy and Taxation* (http://tinyco.re/2109109). London: John Murray.

be calculated (see 'When economists disagree: Heckscher–Ohlin, and the Leontief Paradox' later in this unit).

In *Principles,* Ricardo laid out the principle of comparative advantage, recognizing that two countries could trade to the mutual advantage of each, even if one of them was absolutely better at producing all goods.

Ricardo is not as famous an economist as Smith, Malthus, Mill, or Marx, but he is greatly respected for the theory of comparative advantage. In addition, his method of structuring thought using an abstract model as a guide to economic understanding makes him a very modern great economist.

EXERCISE 18.5 COMPARATIVE ADVANTAGE

Suppose that there are only two countries in the world, Germany and Turkey, each with four workers. Within a given time period, each worker in Germany can produce three cars or two televisions, and each worker in Turkey can produce two cars or three televisions.

1. Draw the feasible production frontier for each country, with televisions on the horizontal axis and cars on the vertical axis. In the absence of trade, what is the relative price of cars in each country?
2. Suppose that, in the absence of trade, Germany consumes nine cars and two televisions while Turkey consumes two cars and nine televisions. Mark these consumption points as G and T, respectively. Draw the feasible consumption frontier for each country in the absence of trade. Comment on the relationship between the production and consumption frontiers you have drawn for each country.
3. Now suppose Germany and Turkey start trading. What is the range of possible values for the world relative price of cars? If the world relative price of cars is $P_C/P_{TV} = 1$, in which good will each country specialize?
4. Now use the world relative price given above to draw the feasible consumption frontier of each country in the figures you have drawn. Use these figures to explain whether or not each country gains from trade.
5. What is the marginal rate of transformation between cars and televisions in each country? Explain the relationship between comparative advantage and the marginal rate of transformation between goods.

EXERCISE 18.6 POWER AND BARGAINING

Going back to our example of Carlos and Greta, assume that Greta has the power to set the relative price. Based on what you have learned in Unit 4 about how people play the ultimatum game, how do you think Carlos would react to a price offer of 2.4 apples per tonne of wheat?

QUESTION 18.5 CHOOSE THE CORRECT ANSWER(S)

The following diagram shows Carlos' and Greta's feasible production frontiers and their utility-maximizing choices of consumption between wheat and apples under autarky (no trade).

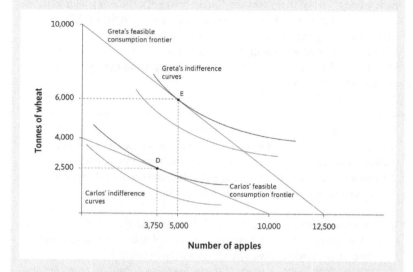

Based on this information, which of the following statements is correct?

☐ Carlos will choose to consume 10,000 apples.
☐ Greta can consume 3,750 apples and 2,500 tonnes of wheat but will choose not to do so.
☐ Greta has an absolute advantage in the production of wheat, while Carlos has an absolute advantage in the production of apples.
☐ Regardless of the shape of the indifference curves (which could be different from those depicted in the diagram), Greta will always choose to consume more of both goods than Carlos.

QUESTION 18.6 CHOOSE THE CORRECT ANSWER(S)

Figure 18.18 (page 818) depicts the feasible frontier and the consumption frontier of Carlos and Greta if they specialize and trade. The resulting relative price of wheat is assumed to be 2.

Let the resulting consumption be at A and B, respectively, for Greta and Carlos. Then which of the following statements is correct?

☐ As Greta has the absolute advantage in production of both goods, she will produce both apples and wheat.
☐ Carlos produces 6,000 apples and 2,000 tonnes of wheat, while Greta produces 4,000 apples and 8,000 tonnes of wheat.
☐ Carlos trades 4,000 of his apples for 2,000 tonnes of Greta's wheat.
☐ Greta is better off while Carlos is worse off as a result of the trade.

QUESTION 18.7 CHOOSE THE CORRECT ANSWER(S)
The following diagram shows Alex's and Jose's feasible production
frontiers for oranges and melons.

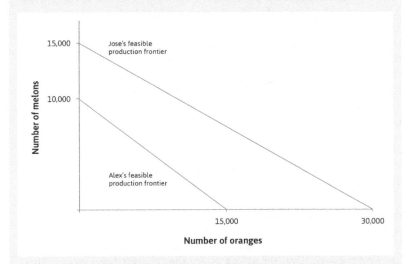

Based on this information, which of the following statements are
correct?

☐ Jose has an absolute advantage in the production of both melons
and oranges.
☐ Jose has a comparative advantage in the production of melons.
☐ With trade and specialization, Jose will specialize in the production
of oranges while Alex will specialize in the production of melons.
☐ The relative price of melons after trade will be 1.75.

18.6 WINNERS AND LOSERS FROM TRADE AND SPECIALIZATION

Carlos and Greta both benefit from trade, so why are imports and exports
often controversial? Unlike our story, in the real world there are almost
always winners and losers. The processes of specialization and exchange
affect regions, industries, and household types differently. Had the bakers
and shoppers of Genoa known that cheap grain was aboard the *Manila* they
would have cheered her into port, while local farmers may have secretly
prayed for a shipwreck.

Nations are composed of people with differing economic interests. They
are not like our islands with only Greta and Carlos. Therefore, to understand these issues we need to go further than assuming a single individual
or a set of identical individuals inhabits each nation.

To think about winners and losers from trade, we begin with a model of
two stylized countries, which we call the US and China, where
specialization is based on factor endowments. The US is an advanced economy with a long tradition of manufacturing. China is less developed, but
has become the world's second-largest economy by exporting
manufactured goods. Let us imagine, unrealistically, that the US and China
produce only two goods, which are produced under constant returns to
scale: passenger aircraft and consumer electronics (like games consoles,

823

personal computers, and TVs). Furthermore, we assume (more realistically this time) that the US has an absolute advantage in producing both goods, and a comparative advantage in producing aircraft.

We assume that aircraft production is capital-intensive and that capital is relatively abundant in the US. In contrast, China has a comparative advantage in consumer electronics production, which is more labour-intensive and China has an abundance of labour relative to capital. Given these assumptions, when the economies begin to trade with one another, the US will specialize in the production of aircraft, whereas China will specialize in the production of consumer electronics.

Opening trade between the US and China in aircraft and consumer electronics has the following effects:

- It increases the consumption possibility set for both countries.
- Conflicts of interest emerge between the countries.
- Conflicts of interest emerge within each country.

As we have seen, the relative price of the two goods affects how the gains from trade are divided between the countries. The usual forces of demand and supply affect the relative price, but the balance of bargaining power between the two affects the price too. For the US and China, and all other countries in the real world, relative prices are subject to the same forces. In Unit 15, for example, we investigated the macroeconomic consequences of oil price shocks. But what caused the increase in the relative price of oil?

cartel A group of firms that collude in order to increase their joint profits.

- *The first and second oil shocks (1970s):* Relative price increases were due to political developments in the Middle East and to the ability of oil producers to exert monopoly power through a **cartel**. The exercise of monopoly power by producers shifted the supply curve upward.
- *The third oil shock (2000s):* The growth of China and other emerging economies caused a large increase in global demand. The global demand curve for oil shifted to the right.

The beneficiaries of a rise in relative price are the inhabitants of the country that specializes in producing that product. But do all citizens benefit? Not everyone in a country is the same. For example, some people have only their labour to sell. Others have accumulated wealth, which they can use to invest in firms.

In the example of the US and China, after trade the US specializes in producing aircraft and China specializes in consumer electronics. Trade and specialization mean that resources shift from one industry to another. Workers previously employed in electronics in the US must try to find work in the expanding aircraft manufacturing businesses. Similarly, in China, employment will expand in consumer electronics production. In the short run at least, those workers employed in the industry that their nation does not specialize in will lose out. For now, let us ignore any effect that trade has on the total size of the economy. We will return to this shortly.

The increase in production of aircraft in the US increases the demand for the factor of production used intensively in that industry: capital. In China, it increases demand for labour instead.

- *The winners in the US:* The owners of capital benefit more from trade than workers, because capital becomes relatively scarce as production of aircraft rises. Since the wealthy tend to hold proportionally more of their wealth in capital than the poor, we would predict a rise in inequality.

- *The winners in China:* Workers are in higher demand as consumer electronics production expands. Wages rise as firms compete for workers. As we have seen in Unit 6, lower unemployment lowers the cost of job loss, and firms raise wages. Workers benefit more from trade than the owners of capital, hence we would expect inequality to fall.

Trade and specialization in the US involves transferring labour and capital from electronics production to aircraft production. Think of what happens when one unit of capital, such as a factory, shifts from electronics to aircraft production. An electronics factory closes, laying off X workers, and an aircraft factory opens, hiring Y workers. Which is bigger, X or Y?

The answer: X is bigger than Y, since one unit of capital provides the tools and equipment necessary to employ more workers in electronics than in aircraft production (since electronics is relatively labour-intensive). Thus, when capital shifts from electronics production to aircraft production, there is a net loss of jobs. This is of course also assuming that workers do not need to re-skill and, more generally, that there are no other frictions in the labour market. These factors would result in a greater loss of jobs in the short run.

In this case, US workers are losing out, and US employers are winning. Workers are working for lower wages, and profits rise. The effect of imports of labour-intensive electronics and the shift in US production to less labour-demanding goods (aircraft) is that employers capture most of the gains from trade. As consumers of electronics, both employers and workers benefit. This is an example of a general principle about who benefits from international trade: The owners of relatively scarce factors of production in their own country prior to trade (US labour in our example) lose from specialization and trade, and the owners of relatively abundant factors (owners of capital in the US) gain.

The reasoning behind this principle is as follows:

- Factors that are relatively scarce in their own countries, compared with in the rest of the world, are relatively expensive compared to prices elsewhere when there is no trade. When their economies start trading with the rest of the world their price is dragged down towards the world average, because they are effectively competing with their abundant counterparts in the rest of the world.
- The same reasoning applies in reverse to factors that are relatively abundant in their own countries relative to the rest of the world.

So, in the US in this example, workers are initially relatively scarce and lose from trade, while employers gain; in China workers are initially relatively abundant and gain from trade, while employers lose. The key to understanding this is to focus on the change in relative scarcity once labour and capital embodied in traded goods and services can flow across borders.

This, however, ignores the overall increase in the size of the economy resulting from trade. This could benefit everyone in the economy and could therefore offset the losses experienced by the disadvantaged group (in this case, the US workers).

Figure 18.20 illustrates the two dimensions of conflict arising from international trade.

On the left we have the US and Chinese economies with limited specialization and trade. To make comparison easy, the economies are normalized to a size of one, and the numbers in the pies show both the proportion and size (in brackets) of the slice of the economic pie that accrue to workers (red) and the owners of capital (blue). On the right we show the US and Chinese economies with greater specialization and trade.

The gains from specialization and trade are clear from the fact that the total size of each economy on the right is larger. The size of the US economy has increased by 30% and the size of the Chinese economy has increased by 40%. The prices at which they have traded (as determined by bargaining) have resulted, in this case, in China securing more of the gains from trade.

But notice too that China's shift into labour-intensive electronics has raised labour's share of China's larger pie, and reduced the share of profits. Both capital and labour in China are, however, better off with higher specialization and trade, as the absolute size of the slices going to workers and the owners of capital have both increased (0.5 < 0.84 and 0.5 < 0.56).

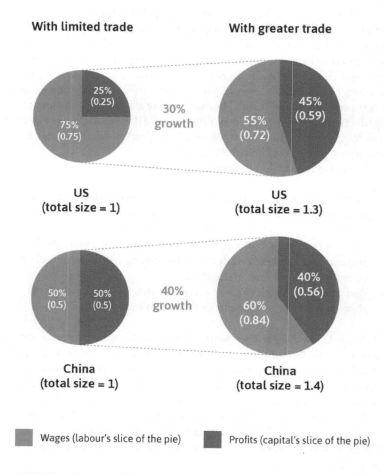

Figure 18.20 The winners and losers from trade between the US and China.

The story is different in the US. The owners of capital goods (employers) now have a larger slice of the US's larger pie, but the US workers' slice is not only proportionally smaller (75% > 55%), but also smaller in absolute size (0.75 > 0.715). So even after we take the growth of the economy into account, US workers are the losers. US employers, Chinese employers, and Chinese workers are all winners.

The same logic would continue to apply if we considered other factors of production. For example, consider two industries that require employees with different levels of skills and education: a skill-intensive industry (information technology) and a non skill-intensive industry (consumer electronics assembly). If a rich economy, relatively abundant in skilled labour, starts trading with a poor, unskilled, labour-abundant country, then unskilled workers in rich countries (and skilled workers in poor countries) will lose out relative to skilled workers in rich countries (and unskilled workers in poor countries), who will gain.

You might think that this would affect the way that different groups viewed trade. Indeed, there is considerable survey evidence that unskilled workers in rich countries are more protectionist than skilled workers, but unskilled workers in poor countries are more in favour of trade than skilled workers. Of course, as illustrated in Figure 18.20, if the gains from trade are large enough it could still be the case that the members of the group that is relatively less well off within a country are made better off in absolute terms by the specialization and trade.

The example of the US and China shown in this section does not only have relevance for the wave of globalization after 1945. One hundred years ago, when Eli Heckscher and Bertil Ohlin, two Swedish economists, were working on better understanding patterns of specialization and trade, they were motivated by the globalization of the late nineteenth century. One difference between then and now is the factors of production involved. While our example of the US and China focused on capital- and labour-intensive manufactured goods, the globalization of the late nineteenth century involved the exchange of land-intensive agricultural goods (food and raw materials such as cotton) for labour-intensive manufactures.

The agricultural goods were exported by land-abundant (and labour-scarce) countries such as the US, Canada, Australia, Argentina, and Russia; the manufactured goods were exported by labour-abundant (and land-scarce) countries in northwest Europe, such as Britain, France, and Germany. In this context, the big losers were European landowners and workers in land-abundant regions; the big winners were European workers and the owners of land in the New World and other land-abundant economies. In Unit 2 we saw that workers in England gained economically, relative to landowners, from the middle of the nineteenth century onwards.

The same happened in other land-scarce, labour-abundant societies in Europe and elsewhere (for example, Japan). Meanwhile, the ratio of land rents to wages rose strongly in land-abundant, labour-scarce regions: not just the New World economies mentioned earlier, but also in areas such as the Punjab, which was a major exporter of agricultural products.

Not surprisingly, European landowners objected to this, and in countries such as France and Germany they succeeded in getting governments to impose tariffs on agricultural imports. There was thus a political backlash against globalization. Governments raised trade costs in the form of tariffs to counteract the impact of the fall in other trade costs, notably transportation.

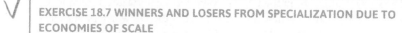

EXERCISE 18.7 WINNERS AND LOSERS FROM SPECIALIZATION DUE TO ECONOMIES OF SCALE

Suppose there are two countries that are identical in their factor endowments. Both would like to consume both passenger cars and commercial vehicles, industries in which there are economies of scale. In the absence of trade, each country would have both industries. If they could trade, both could benefit by specializing and taking advantage of economies of scale to lower their costs of production.

Assume that once trade becomes possible, country A specializes in producing passenger cars and country B specializes in producing commercial vehicles. Because of economies of scale, the cost of passenger cars relative to commercial vehicles is lower in country A than in country B.

1. Explain why we would expect to observe trade in similar products, known as intra-industry trade, when production technology is characterized by economies of scale.
2. Who are the winners and losers in this example? How does your result compare with that of the winners and losers in the example of the US and China, where specialization is based on relative factor endowments?

QUESTION 18.8 CHOOSE THE CORRECT ANSWER(S)

Figure 18.20 (page 826) is a diagram that describes the effects of trade on the employers and the workers in the US and China. The initial size of each economy is normalized to one. The US has the comparative advantage in the capital-intensive goods, while China has the comparative advantage in the labour-intensive goods. As a result of trade the US's economy is assumed to grow by 30% and that of China by 40%.

Based on this information, which of the following statements is correct?

☐ Specialization means that China will produce all the capital-intensive goods.
☐ The US has the stronger bargaining power in the determination of the relative price after trade.
☐ In the US, the employers are better off while the workers are worse off as a result of trade.
☐ In China, the workers are better off while the employers are worse off as a result of trade.

EXERCISE 18.8 THE COLLAPSE OF THE SOVIET UNION

In the late 1980s and early 1990s, the Soviet Union collapsed. The Soviet Union comprised Russia and some of the countries that now make up eastern Europe and central Asia. It was a planned economy, run from Moscow by the Communist Party. Following this collapse, countries in the former Soviet Union and elsewhere in the former Soviet bloc—with a total of close to 300 million workers—opened their borders to international trade.

1. Assume that Germany was a capital-intensive country, while the former Soviet bloc states were labour-intensive. Use the analysis in this section to identify likely winners and losers from this shock to global trade in:
   (a) Germany
   (b) the countries of the former Soviet bloc
2. What other information would you need to know about these countries to identify the actual winners and losers?

18.7 WINNERS AND LOSERS IN THE VERY LONG RUN AND ALONG THE WAY

In our example of the US and China, the short-run effect of trade was to raise the profits of US employers while depressing the wages of US workers. This would provide US employers with incentives to invest more in building additional capacity to produce aircraft. Our analysis of wages and employment in the long run (in Unit 16) provides a lens for us to study what will happen next.

Specializing in the production of the good in which it has a comparative advantage increases the productivity of US labour (workers have moved from producing electronics to producing aircraft, where they are more productive). This shifts up the price-setting curve and output per worker. So, in this respect, specialization according to comparative advantage is similar to technological progress as analysed in Unit 16. It may be worth reviewing the key concepts in that unit before continuing on here.

Use the analysis in Figure 18.21 to follow through the impact effect and adjustment process. We start with the US wage-setting curve and the price-setting curve before specialization and trade with China. The economy starts at point A with unemployment at the long-run rate of 6%.

When the economy has come to the new intersection of the price- and wage-setting curves, will the US economy now employ more or fewer workers than before?

As shown in the analysis in Figure 18.21, the answer depends on the change to the wage-setting curve. Historically, in many countries, integration into the world economy was accompanied by unemployment in some sectors of the economy. In addition, economic fluctuations due to international price changes produced variations in cyclical unemployment. The result was an increase in voters' demands for more adequate unemployment insurance policies, and a strengthening of employment protection and other policies to protect households from shocks to income and employment. Voters supported these policies for the same reason that households seek to smooth consumption. These effects would shift the wage-setting curve up.

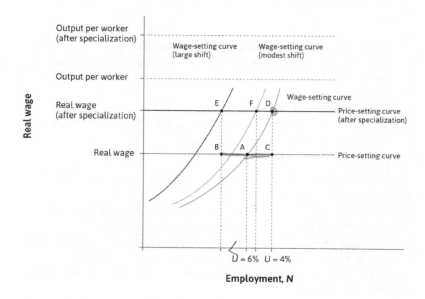

Figure 18.21 The long-run effect of specialization on unemployment in the US.

1. Unemployment at the long-run rate
The economy starts at point A (U = 6%).

2. The US specializes in the production of aircraft
It has a comparative advantage. By specializing in the good it is relatively best at, this increases the average productivity of US labour, shifting up output per worker and therefore, the price-setting curve.

3. Workers producing consumer electronics are laid off
US consumers are now buying their DVD players from China. Some are hired in producing aircraft, but not all, because productive capacity in that sector is limited. The economy moves from point A to point B and unemployment rises.

4. US aircraft manufacturing firms are making large profits
They expect this will continue in the future. They build new production capacity, expanding the demand for labour and re-employing the former electronics workers. The economy moves from point B to point C, and unemployment falls to 4% below its original level.

5. Increased demand for labour
The demand increases workers' bargaining power. Wages increase. This process stops when the economy has come to the new intersection of the price- and wage-setting curves at point D.

6. The wage-setting curve
It may also shift if workers demand more generous unemployment benefits because of the increased job turnover due to the effects of trade. If it shifts a lot, specialization might imply a reduction in total employment. For example, at point E in the figure, unemployment is higher than the original long-run rate of 6%.

7. Specialization and unemployment
However, if there were only a modest shift in the wage-setting curve, employment would have risen as a result of specialization, as shown by point F.

As we saw in Unit 17, in the era after the Second World War, many countries integrated their economies into the world economy and at the same time developed income-smoothing policies, commonly termed the **welfare state**. In Nordic countries, for example, trade unions agreed to unimpeded imports. In return they won support for unemployed workers, and policies to retrain workers displaced by imports increased.

The rapid growth in world trade among the high-income countries following the Second World War took place alongside the development of the welfare state and falling inequality. Unemployment remained low during this period, as we saw in Units 16 and 17. Specialization in this period was based on trade among quite similar countries—US and western European economies, for example—and it rested to a considerable extent on economies of scale and agglomeration economies. Much of it was so-called intra-industry trade where countries were trading similar goods (exporting and importing different kinds of cars and commercial vehicles, for example, as in Exercise 18.7).

The process of specialization created winners and losers—including winner companies like BMW and Ford, and entire winner industries like machine tools in Germany and aircraft production in the US, benefiting owners and employees alike. And, unlike specialization based on factor endowments, trade based on economies of scale does not separate out the winners and losers according to the factor of production that is the main endowment on which a person's income depends (for example labour or capital).

The renewed growth of global integration following the collapse of the Soviet Union and the opening up of China to trade from the early 1990s has been accompanied by rising inequality in many high-income countries, along with geographically concentrated job losses in labour markets affected by imports from China. For these particular displaced workers it was not much reassurance to know that a new equilibrium would eventually be reached in which workers would on average be better off.

With the help of the labour market model in Figure 18.21, we can see the common features of a trade shock and a technology shock. In Section 16.7, we contrasted the benefits of these shocks in the very long run with the costly adjustment as jobs are lost before new ones are created in different industries (and locations). The evidence reported there from the 'China shock' that began in the early 1990s highlighted that job losses were concentrated geographically and persisted for decades. Tennessee, which specialized in furniture, suffered massive, long-lasting job losses, while nearby Alabama, which produced goods that were not exported by China, did not.

Not all countries were affected in the same way by the China trade shock. Recent research shows that in Germany, the new opportunities to trade with low wage countries in eastern Europe arising after the fall of the Berlin Wall, and to trade with China, slowed down the loss of manufacturing jobs. Although jobs in industries competing with imports shrank, jobs in exporting industries were about the same in 2014 as in 1997. One explanation for the difference between the effects in China and the US is that among the capital-intensive countries, Germany was more successful than the US in expanding its markets in China. Comparing Germany and the US, Germany's specialization in exports of machine tools, other capital goods (for use in Chinese factories), and transport equipment matched the demand from rapidly industrializing China.

welfare state A set of government policies designed to provide improvements in the welfare of citizens by assisting with income smoothing (for example, unemployment benefits and pensions).

Wolfgang Dauth, Sebastian Findeisen, and Jens Südekum. 2017. 'Sectoral Employment Trends in Germany: The Effect of Globalization on their Micro Anatomy' (http://tinyco.re/2554801). VoxEU.org. Updated 26 January 2017.

QUESTION 18.9 CHOOSE THE CORRECT ANSWER(S)

Figure 18.21 (page 830) is the long-run labour market model for the US as a result of specialization according to its comparative advantage.

The US has a comparative advantage in the production of capital-intensive aircraft, while China, its trade partner, has a comparative advantage in the production of labour-intensive consumer electronics. Before trade, the German labour market equilibrium is at A. Which of the following statements are correct?

☐ As a result of specialization, at first both worker productivity and the total employment level rise.
☐ With the rise in productivity, the firms expand employment resulting in a lower unemployment rate.
☐ With lower unemployment, workers demand higher wages for high effort, resulting in a higher price-setting curve.
☐ The wage-setting curve rises if workers demand unemployment insurance as a result of globalization. Then the long-run employment level is unambiguously lower than at A.

18.8 MIGRATION: GLOBALIZATION OF LABOUR

Just as the Italian farmers had not been happy to see the cheap Indian grain being offloaded from the steamer *Manila* in Genoa, workers in North America did not always welcome Europeans in search of a more affluent life, like the 69 passengers sailing west on the *Manila* after leaving Genoa on their way to New York. Immigration hurt unskilled workers in the New World. Where unskilled wages lagged furthest behind average incomes, immigration barriers were raised the most.

This resulted in another type of globalization backlash during the first period of globalization in the nineteenth and early twentieth centuries: gradually rising barriers to immigration.

In Unit 9, we analysed the effect of immigration on unemployment (see Figure 9.18 (page 391)). The model helps us to see why opposition to immigration was common among workers in land-abundant economies like the US or Canada at that time and in many countries since. When new people arrive in a nation they are unemployed, so we might expect the first impact of immigration to be that it increases unemployment. This means that immigration also increases the cost of job loss for residents, because the worker who loses a job is now in a larger pool of unemployed workers. Workers have more to fear from losing their jobs, and firms will be able to make employees work effectively at a lower wage.

This is not the end of the story. Firms are now getting work at lower wages, and so are more profitable. As a result they will seek to expand production. To do this, they will invest in new machinery. This will increase labour demand in the rest of the economy, and when the new capacity is ready, firms will hire more workers. Return to the analysis in Figure 9.18 (page 391) to follow the steps from the impact effect to the long-run outcome.

In this story, the short-run impact of immigration is bad for existing workers in that country: wages fall and the expected duration of unemployment increases. The short run may last for years or even decades.

In the longer run, the increased profitability of firms leads to expanded employment that eventually will restore the real wage and return the economy to its initial rate of unemployment (if no further changes in the situation take place, like another wave of immigration). As a result, incumbent workers are no worse off. Immigrants are likely to be economically better off too—especially if they left their home country because it was difficult to make a living.

EXERCISE 18.9 THE ECONOMIC EFFECTS OF IMMIGRATION
1. Summarize the evidence on migrants' skills suggested in the video.
2. Use the labour market model to show what may happen to wages and employment after an influx of migrant workers.
3. What is the evidence on the effect of immigration on wages in Britain reported in the video? Compare this with your prediction from question 2. Try to modify the price- and wage-setting model to come up with an explanation of this evidence.

18.9 GLOBALIZATION AND ANTI-GLOBALIZATION

As the nineteenth-century examples of European agricultural protection and New World immigration restrictions show, globalization can undermine itself. It produces winners and losers. We have seen that by allowing countries to specialize, globalization of trade in goods and services can expand the consumption possibilities of all nations. But the freer movement of capital around the world in search of profit-making opportunities also allows businesses to seek countries with lax environmental regulation and low taxation or where workers do not have rights to organize in trade unions.

So governments that wish to attract overseas investments are often under pressure to oppose policies that would address problems of environmental sustainability and economic justice. The freer movement of goods and capital, as we saw in Units 13 to 15, also limits the effectiveness of policies to stabilize aggregate demand and employment. The movement of labour from one country to another creates gains for some, but threatens losses for others.

If the losers, whether from the mobility of goods, investment or people, are ignored, globalization may turn out to be politically unsustainable in a democracy.

These concerns have been analysed by Dani Rodrik, an economist, who developed what he calls the fundamental political **trilemma of the world economy**. His trilemma refers to three things, all of which are valued, but which (according to Rodrik) cannot all occur at the same time. Rodrik's trilemma is really just another trade-off, like that between low inflation and low unemployment (it's hard to have both), except that Rodrik's trade-off is in three dimensions.

He defines the three dimensions as:

1. *Hyperglobalization:* A world in which there are virtually no political or cultural barriers to the location of goods and investment.
2. *Democracy within nation states:* This means (as we said in Unit 1) that the government respects both individual liberty and political equality.
3. *National sovereignty:* Each national government can pursue policies that it chooses without any significant limits imposed on it by other nations or by global institutions.

The economic effects of immigration are widely debated among the public. This interview from 2006 with Christian Dustmann, an economist who specializes in the effects of migration, captures this debate—in particular the impact of migrant workers on the British town of Swindon. http://tinyco.re/2964221

trilemma of the world economy The likely impossibility that any country, in a globalized world, can simultaneously maintain deep market integration (across borders), national sovereignty, and democratic governance. First suggested by Dani Rodrik, an economist.

Dani Rodrik. 2012. *The Globalization Paradox: Democracy and the Future of the World Economy*. United States: W. W. Norton & Company.

hyperglobalization An extreme (and so far hypothetical) type of globalization in which there is virtually no barrier to the free flows of goods, services, and capital. *See also: globalization.*

As an example of one of the tensions among these objectives, according to Rodrik, **hyperglobalization** means that countries have to compete with each other for investment, with the result that wealth owners will seek locations for their investments in which labour has fewer rights and the environment is less protected. This makes it difficult for national governments to adopt regulatory standards or other policies, or raise taxes on mobile capital or highly paid workers, even when citizens think that fairness requires this. Implementing hyperglobalization may be impossible in a democratic society. The outcome may therefore either be the demise of hyperglobalization (top row of Figure 18.22) or the demise of democracy (middle row).

Figure 18.22 illustrates the three possible outcomes of Rodrik's political trilemma.

Let us take each row of the table in turn to clarify the trade-offs.

- *Hyperglobalization is ruled out (top row)*: This happens if national sovereignty and democracy at the national level endure. The reason is that there have to be limits on labour and capital mobility in order to

Adapted from Dani Rodrik. 2012. *The Globalization Paradox: Democracy and the Future of the World Economy.* United States: W. W. Norton & Company.

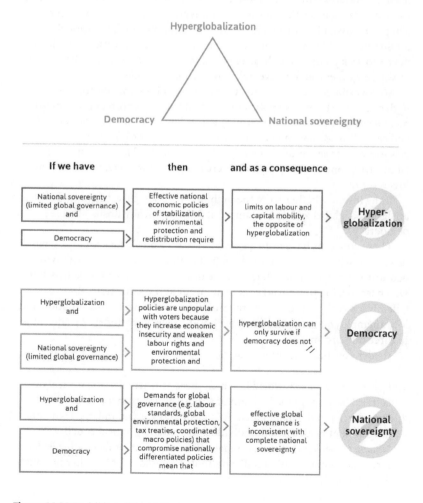

Figure 18.22 Rodrik's political trilemma.

deliver effective national policies of stabilization, environmental sustainability, and redistribution that will be demanded by a democratic electorate.

• *Democracy is ruled out (middle row)*: Hyperglobalization policies can only be implemented by the national government if the citizens' opposition to them is weakened by a dilution of democratic processes.

• *National sovereignty is ruled out (bottom row)*: If hyperglobalization policies are accompanied by supranational institutions that can prevent a **race to the bottom** in environmental and labour standards, for example, and therefore gain democratic support, this restricts the ability of countries to choose national policies independently.

A way of understanding the bottom row is to think of existing arrangements in a federation like the US or Germany. There is free flow of goods, investment, and people across states of the federation. The race to the bottom is prevented by federal legislation and by democratic elections at federal level. This restricts the ability of the states to implement policies that would interfere with the benefits of 'hyperglobalization' across the whole country, with the protection of standards and the operation of stabilization policy.

A second example is the political integration of Europe over the last few decades. It happened, in part, so that governments could obtain the benefits of free trade, plus the free movement of capital and labour, while retaining some ability at the supranational EU-wide level to regulate profit-making in the interests of fairness and economic stability.

The obvious problem is how to make sure that this EU-wide or global governance is democratic as well as technocratic, and to allow voters to change the system if they don't like it.

Other supranational governance initiatives include world agreements on climate change, and efforts by the International Labour Organization to require that all nations meet at least minimal standards for the treatment of labour (eliminating child labour or the physical coercion of employees, for example).

race to the bottom Self-destructive competition between national or regional governments, resulting in lower wages and less regulation to attract foreign investment in a globalized economy.

EXERCISE 18.10 RODRIK'S TRILEMMA
Watch Dani Rodrik's 'Economist in action' video.

1. According to the video, what are some of the benefits and trade-offs due to globalization?
2. State some historical examples of the policy trilemma that were given in the video.

Use Rodrik's trilemma and other information you can find to describe:

3. The popular support that led to the election of Donald Trump as president of the US in 2016.
4. The popular support that led to the vote in 2016 for 'Brexit', that is, for the UK to leave the European Union.

Dani Rodrik explains in our 'Economist in action' video that economics is a science of trade-offs, and that we can have too much globalization. His 'Globalization Trilemma' shows that when economies are increasingly globalized, they must 'give up some sovereignty or some democracy'.
http://tinyco.re/8475334

EXERCISE 18.11 EXAMINE THE RESPECTIVE STRENGTHS AND COSTS OF ECONOMIC INDEPENDENCE, AND INTERDEPENDENCY

In an essay titled 'National Self-Sufficiency', published in 1933, John Maynard Keynes warned of the consequences of globalization before the word even existed:

> We each have our own fancy. Not believing that we are saved already, we each should like to have a try at working out our own salvation. We do not wish, therefore, to be at the mercy of world forces working out, or trying to work out some uniform equilibrium according to the ideal principles, if they can be called such, of laissez-faire capitalism ... We wish for the time at least ... to be our own masters and to be as free as we can ... to make our own favourite experiments towards the ideal social republic of the future.

It became conventional wisdom that global integration would eventually make the idea of national economic sovereignty impractical. A third of a century after Keynes wished for time 'to be our own masters', Charles Kindleberger, an international trade economist, wrote that:

> The nation-state is just about through as an economic unit ... It is too easy to get about.
>
> Two-hundred-thousand-ton tankers ... airbuses and the like will not permit the sovereign independence of the nation-state in economic affairs. (*American Business Abroad*, 1969)

1. Explain in your own words Keynes' case in favour of 'national self-sufficiency' and Kindleberger's claim that 'the national state is ... through'.
2. Frame the views of Keynes and Kindleberger in terms of Rodrik's Trilemma, and use the data in this unit and other units to assess their statements. (You may want to recall the role of economic policies in helping nations adjust to technological change and trade in Sections 16.8–16.10, and look ahead to the data on the size of the government and how this has changed over time in Unit 22.)

18.10 TRADE AND GROWTH

What are the best policies for governments to adopt if they seek to promote long-run growth in living standards? Some argue that it is a choice between two policy extremes:

- Seal the national borders and withdraw from the world economy!
- Let trade, immigration, and investment across national boundaries take place in the absence of government regulation of any kind!

Few (if any) economists advocate either policy. The question is how to exploit the contributions of the global economy to a nation's wellbeing, while minimizing the ways in which integration into the global economy may retard it. Among the growth-enhancing aspects of greater global economic integration are:

- *Competition:* Limiting the impediments to trade in goods and services among nations increases the degree of competition faced by firms in the local economy. This means that firms that fail to adopt new technologies and other cost-cutting methods are more likely to fail and to be replaced by more dynamic firms. The result will be an increase in the rate of technological progress.
- *The size of the market:* A firm that can export to the world market has the opportunity (if it can meet the competition) of selling far more than it could were it restricted to the domestic market. This allows lower-cost production, which benefits home-economy buyers, employees, and owners of these successful firms, as well as external buyers.

Ways that greater integration into the global economy might retard growth include:

- *Learning by doing in infant industries:* In addition to economies of scale, another factor contributing to cost reductions is termed **learning by doing**. Even if the firm never achieves large-scale production, costs of production typically fall over time. Tariffs protecting infant industries can give firms the time and possibly the scale of operation necessary to become competitive.
- *Disadvantageous specialization:* For reasons of history, some countries may specialize in sectors where there is a lot of potential for innovation, whereas others specialize in sectors with little such potential. Many Latin American countries, for example, slowed growth by specializing in low-innovation sectors such as natural resource extraction. Developing new specializations may require direct government intervention, including **infant industry** protection.

It is clear from Figure 18.23 that during the second period of globalization, workers in some countries—China and South Korea for example—have seen rapid increases in their income levels. But the same figure also makes it clear that in other countries, such as Mexico and Sri Lanka, workers have seen few benefits from the increasingly integrated world economy.

There has not been a unique route to economic success during the past 150 years. For example:

- *Early protectionism in Germany and the US:* These countries developed modern manufacturing sectors behind high tariff barriers that sheltered them from British competition. In the late nineteenth century, the correlation between tariffs and economic growth across relatively rich countries was positive. In particular, higher manufacturing tariffs were associated with higher growth. During the interwar period, tariffs were also positively correlated with growth.
- *Scandinavian prosperity through openness:* These countries have been very open to trade for more than 100 years and have prospered. So as to mitigate the fluctuations in household income associated with changes in international prices, they also have high tax rates to support generous social insurance and subsidies for retraining.

infant industry A relatively new industrial sector in a country that has relatively high costs, because its recent establishment means that it has few benefits from learning by doing, its small size deprives it of economies of scale, or a lack of similar firms means that it does not benefit from economies of agglomeration. Temporary tariff protection of this sector or other support may increase productivity in an economy in the long run.
learning by doing This occurs when the output per unit of inputs increases with greater experience in producing a good or service.

- *Picking national winners:* Many East Asian governments have promoted trade while influencing its pattern by favouring certain industries, or even certain firms, and by directing firms to compete in export markets whilst providing some protection from import competition.
- *Two directions after 1945:* On the one hand, countries in East Asia that encouraged their firms to compete in international markets grew faster than Latin American countries that were more closed to international trade. On the other hand, after those Latin American countries reduced their tariffs in the early 1990s, their subsequent economic growth rates were lower than during the more closed period 1945 to 1980.

If there is a lesson from this, it is that success does not depend on whether a country is more or less integrated into the world economic system—more or fewer exports and imports, for example, or a greater amount of international investment by its firms—but rather on how well economic integration is managed by policies that promote growth.

EXERCISE 18.12 THE EFFECT OF TRADE ON GROWTH

The empirical evidence on how trade affects growth is mixed.

1. Suppose you are a consultant with the World Trade Organization (http://tinyco.re/2008074) and are asked to design an empirical study to find the effect of a country's openness to trade on growth. How would you approach this exercise? (Hint: see Section 1.9, the introduction to Unit 13, and Section 14.7 for some ways that economists learn from data.)

2. How would you measure openness to trade (tariffs, export ratios, or other indices of openness)? Discuss the advantages and limitations of your chosen method.

3. Explain the problems you would face in designing a convincing study. Hint: think back to the examples given in Section 1.9, the introduction to Unit 13, and Section 14.7 about the ways that it is sometimes possible to establish that something (like trade, in this example) causes something else (like growth or lack of growth).

---

(1) Andrew Glyn. 2006. *Capitalism Unleashed: Finance, Globalization, and Welfare.* Oxford: Oxford University Press; (2) National Bureau of Statistics of China. *Annual Data* (http://tinyco.re/2297128); (3) Bank of England; (4) US Bureau of Labor Statistics. 2015. *International Labor Comparisons* (http://tinyco.re/2780183). Note: Annual US BLS data for Mexico, the Philippines and Sri Lanka has been smoothed using a backward-looking five-year moving average.

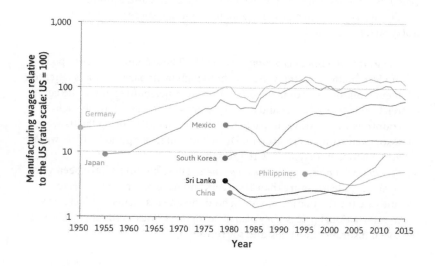

Figure 18.23 Catching up and stagnating: Manufacturing wages relative to the US (1950–2015).

WHEN ECONOMISTS DISAGREE

Heckscher–Ohlin, the Leontief paradox, and the new trade theory
It was once thought that if countries were identical none would have a comparative advantage in the production of any good, and there would be no reason for them to specialize and to exchange goods. For example, Eli Heckscher (1879–1952) and Bertil Ohlin (1899–1979) reasoned that, when accounting for comparative advantage and trade, the key differences between countries were the relative scarcity of land, labour, or capital. Canada and the US had abundant land relative to the amount of labour, and hence would specialize in and export agricultural goods. With more capital and less labour than China, Germany would export capital-intensive goods to China.

Wassily Leontief (1906–1999) challenged the widely accepted Heckscher-Ohlin theory in 1953. Using a method of input-output analysis that he had invented, he measured the amount of labour and capital goods used in the production of the goods exported from, and imported to, the US. He determined, for example, the amount of labour required:

- to produce a car
- to produce the steel, that went into the car
- to produce the coal, that fired the steel plant, that produced the steel, that went into the car

… and so on.

Based on the Heckscher–Ohlin theory he expected that, because the US was the most capital-abundant country in the world when measured by the stock of machinery, buildings and other capital goods per worker, its exports would be capital-intensive and its imports labour-intensive. He found the opposite.

For more than 50 years, economists have struggled to resolve this so-called **Leontief paradox**. Leontief speculated that the US might be labour-abundant if instead of simply measuring the quantity of employees, we include cultural and organizational factors that support a high level of effective work per employee. While his hypothesis has not yet been adequately tested empirically, it reminds us that culture and institutions may be an essential part of explaining how an economy works and may be a source of comparative advantage.

During the 1980s, economists Avinash Dixit, Elhanan Helpman, Paul Krugman, and others, developed models of trade in which trade was not due to differences between countries, but instead to increasing returns to scale. As we have seen in this unit if, through specialization, trade allows countries to reap greater economies of scale, this makes trade a good idea even if the countries do not differ in endowments, including culture and institutions. This 'new trade theory' supports arguments for tariff protection. For example, increasing returns means monopoly profits—so perhaps it would be a good thing if your country gets these profits, rather than someone else. Read Paul Krugman's Nobel lecture, and an earlier paper that he wrote on free trade, to find out more.

Leontief paradox The unexpected finding by Wassily Leontief that exports from the US were labour-intensive and its imports capital-intensive, a result that contradicts what the economic theories predicted: namely that a country abundant in capital (like the US) would export goods that used a large quantity of capital in their production.

Paul Krugman. 2009. 'The Increasing Returns Revolution in Trade and Geography.' In *The Nobel Prizes 2008* , edited by Karl Grandin. Stockholm: The Nobel Foundation.
Krugman, Paul. 1987. 'Is Free Trade Passé?' *Journal of Economic Perspectives* 1 (2): pp. 131–44.

18.11 CONCLUSION

The world's economies are now part of an integrated global system. Major companies consider the entire world when deciding where to produce and where to sell their goods and services. Investors, likewise, choose where to hold their assets, whether financial or real, on the basis of calculations of expected returns after taxes in all the regions of the world. But we have also seen that labour has for the most part not been globalized, and for political, cultural, and language reasons remains largely national. National borders remain an essential fact of the global economy. National governments remain major actors in affecting the course of their own and other economies.

Globalization has brought about important changes. In the eighteenth century, at the birth of economics as a discipline, goods were traded across national boundaries, and investments were made in far-flung parts of the world; but for the most part the nation and its economy had the same boundaries.

The world today looks quite different. Trading of goods and services and investment are now integrated into the world financial system in which transactions are made electronically in milliseconds.

Economists can help to design and evaluate policies that secure the greatest possible mutual gains among the world's people participating in this new dynamic and cosmopolitan economy. They can also identify groups whose livelihoods are under threat from the globalization process and propose policies to ensure that the gains made possible from worldwide investment and exchange are fairly shared.

Concepts introduced in Unit 18
Before you move on, review these definitions:

- Globalization and hyperglobalization
- Specialization
- Comparative advantage
- Price gap, trade costs, arbitrage
- Globalization I and II
- Tariff
- Current account (CA), CA deficit, CA surplus, net capital flows
- Balance of payments accounts
- International capital flows
- Gains from trade
- Foreign direct investment (FDI)
- Foreign portfolio investment
- Economies of agglomeration
- Learning by doing
- Infant industries

18.12 REFERENCES

Dauth, Wolfgang, Sebastian Findeisen, and Jens Südekum. 2017. *Sectoral employment trends in Germany: The effect of globalisation on their micro anatomy* (http://tinyco.re/2554801). *VoxEU.org.* Updated 26 January 2017.

Krugman, Paul. 1987. 'Is Free Trade Passé?' *Journal of Economic Perspectives* 1 (2): pp. 131–44.

Krugman, Paul. 2009. 'The Increasing Returns Revolution in Trade and Geography'. In *The Nobel Prizes 2008*, ed. Karl Grandin. Stockholm: The Nobel Foundation.

Ricardo, David. 1815. *An Essay on Profits*. London: John Murray.

Ricardo, David. 1817. *On The Principles of Political Economy and Taxation* (http://tinyco.re/2109109). London: John Murray.

Rodrik, Dani. 2012. *The Globalization Paradox: Democracy and the Future of the World Economy*. United States: W. W. Norton & Company.

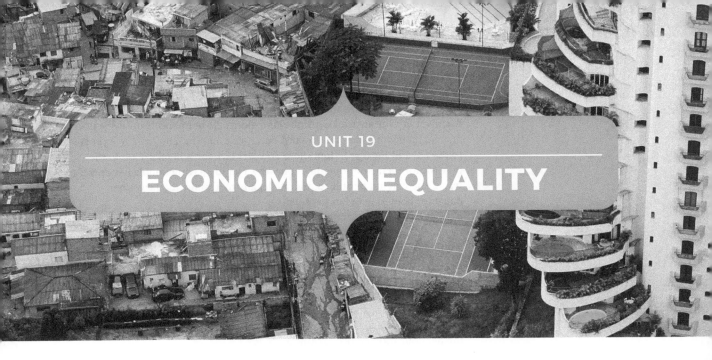

ECONOMIC DISPARITIES ARE MOSTLY A MATTER OF WHERE YOU WERE BORN, WHO YOUR PARENTS ARE, AND (IN SOME COUNTRIES) YOUR GENDER. WELL-DESIGNED POLICIES AND INSTITUTIONS CAN REDUCE INEQUALITIES WITHOUT LOWERING AVERAGE LIVING STANDARDS

- Having declined for most of the twentieth century, inequality of income then increased in the US, the UK, India, and many other countries.
- Nonetheless, because of the rapid economic growth of China and India, countries with very large populations, income inequality among all people in the world has declined since the end of the twentieth century.
- Discrimination based on race, gender, or religion, and other forms of unequal opportunity mean that otherwise identical people will have different incomes and economic opportunities, contributing to inequality.
- Income disparities among people are due to what they own (for example, a piece of land), are (male or female), or have (particular skills) that enable them to receive income.
- The institutions and policies in force in a society and the technologies used in production influence these determinants of income.
- Some inequalities provide incentives to study and work hard, and to take the risks associated with innovation and investment.
- But inequalities also restrict economic opportunities of the less well off and may also result in a more conflict-ridden society and impose costs, impairing economic performance.
- Well-designed and implemented government policies can limit unfair economic inequality while raising average living standards, as has been done in many countries.

It is 1975. Renfu is the child of a local Communist Party leader. In 10 years, he will attend Tsinghua University, an elite engineering university in Beijing, and will join the Communist Party himself. In 20 years, he will run a state-owned enterprise. In 30 years, he will be CEO of the company after it is privatized, and be highly ranked within the Party.

However, Yichen, whose parents have no party connections, will not go to university, but instead work the land alongside her parents until she is 16, and then work at a state-owned enterprise making car parts for export to the US and Europe. When she is 30 years old, she will take a job in the new Motorola factory opening in nearby Tianjin, paying double her current wage. She will not be able to migrate legally to Tianjin and leaves her daughter behind with her parents.

Yichen and Renfu are hypothetical people. We could have inserted a disclaimer: 'All characters appearing in this work are fictitious…' But that would not be entirely true—they illustrate the divergent histories of real people alive today.

Let's also consider two other hypothetical people living in the US, also in 1975. Mark and Stephanie, both 17, live in Gary, Indiana. Mark is about to finish high school and start working in the local unionized steel mill with his father, where the pay is good and he doesn't have to spend four years in further education before earning a wage.

In the 1981 recession, Mark will lose his job. He will try to use his mechanical ability to open a car parts business. With little wealth of his own to post as collateral, he will not be able to obtain a bank loan, so he will move south to another factory. This one is non-unionized, and he will make less money than he did in Gary. In 2008, during the recession, his factory will replace him with a KUKA Robotics Corporation Titan industrial robot.

Stephanie, both of whose parents are doctors, decides she will attend Indiana University Bloomington, majoring in psychology. Afterwards she will work for a large financial corporation in Chicago and, after a series of promotions, becomes a vice-president for human resources. She will invest her savings in the stock market, which yields an average return of more than 10% for many years, and will benefit from government tax cuts that favour high earners.

These four people had very different life outcomes. Is there anything wrong with that? Each of the four made good choices knowing what they could have known at the time, everybody worked hard, and yet they had very different lives. We might say that they simply drew different hands in the card game of life.

Their parents are an important difference in the hands that they drew. This starts with the fact that Yichen and Renfu were born in China, and Mark and Stephanie in the US. The parents of the two in China were likely to be equally poor, although Communist Party members enjoyed a higher level of social prestige and education. The gap in wealth between the two sets of American parents would probably have been larger. If Mark was black the gap would be greater than if he was white, but his family would still have been far better off in material terms than both the Chinese families.

In 2017, the children of Stephanie and Renfu, who have been relatively successful in each country, will have access to a variety of opportunities not available to the children of Yichen and Mark. In China, Renfu's children will attend better schools and have better job prospects because of their father's connections. With luck, they may attend a US university, gain valuable work experience in the university-trained, English-speaking global labour market, and return to China with salaries many times those of the average Chinese citizen.

Yichen's daughter will not obtain a high-quality primary or secondary education. This is because the hukou restrictions mean she must go to school in Yichen's rural home district and not in Tianjin, where her mother works. Nevertheless, most likely she will be better off over her lifetime than her parents, and will certainly be better off than her grandparents.

In the US, Stephanie's children will attend either a public school in her expensive neighbourhood, well funded by local property taxes, or an expensive private school. They will get early access to a much larger vocabulary, form lifelong friendships with other kids from their privileged background, and engage in a variety of interesting extracurricular experiences that help their educational performance and will help them get admission to elite universities. This will translate into average lifetime earnings of close to $800,000 greater than the earnings of those whose education finishes at high school level.

Mark's children will have to deal with poorly funded public schools, the absence of union jobs, a minimum wage that will be worth less in real terms than it was in their parents' generation, and changes in technology and trade that will amplify the effects of these problems. The life trajectories of these four people illustrate just a few of the global changes in the distribution of income that have occurred in the past 40 years.

Inequality exists across many dimensions, including income, wealth, education, health, and other opportunities. In this unit, we will focus primarily on inequalities in wealth and income, both because they have been studied extensively by economists and because they are strongly related to other forms of inequality. We begin with three sets of facts:

- *Inequality of income*: In the next section, we survey evidence from around the globe about inequalities in income and how they have changed in the past century.
- *Accidents of birth*: We then look at inequality through an alternative lens. Accidents of birth influence one's income, whether it be one's nation, race, gender, wealth, or even the quality and extent of one's schooling.
- *The future of inequality*: The last set of facts offers a glimpse into the future of the rich economies, looking at the kinds of jobs available as automation and the global relocation of industrial production accelerate the transition from a manufacturing to a service-producing economy.

We then ask why inequality is widely seen as a problem, and provide a way to approach the question of whether there is too much (or too little) inequality. We present a model of the causes of economic inequality in order to understand how public policies and other changes can alter the degree of economic inequality. And we then use this model to explain both recent changes in the levels of economic inequality in a number of countries, and the effects of government policies on the degree of inequality.

Mary C. Daly and Leila Bengali. 2014. 'Is It Still Worth Going to College?'. *Federal Reserve Bank of San Francisco*. May 5.

Branko Milanovic. 2007. *Worlds Apart: Measuring International and Global Inequality*. Princeton, NJ: Princeton University Press.

Branko Milanovic. 2012. *The Haves and the Have-Nots: A Brief and Idiosyncratic History of Global Inequality*. New York, NY: Basic Books.

You can find an interactive version of this figure at http://tinyco.re/7434364.

You can find an interactive version of this figure at http://tinyco.re/7434364.

EXERCISE 19.1 INCOME VARIATION ACROSS AND WITHIN COUNTRIES
In Unit 1, Figure 1.2 (page 4) showed the distribution of income across and within countries in 2014. The height of each bar in the chart varies along two axes. The first axis of variation, from left to right of the figure, is a ranking of countries according to gross domestic income per capita from the poorest on the left (Liberia), to the richest on the right (Singapore). The second axis, from the front to the back of the figure, shows the distribution of income from poor to rich within each country.

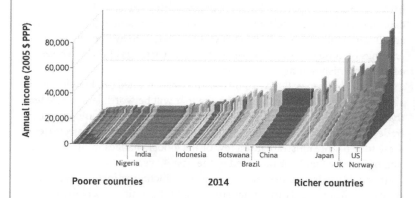

Go back over the stories of Mark, Renfu, Stefanie, and Yichen and make your guess about which decile fits each of the fictional characters. Briefly justify your choice.

19.1 INEQUALITY ACROSS THE WORLD AND OVER TIME

As you know from Unit 5, we can use Lorenz curves to estimate Gini coefficients, which measure the degree of inequality in wealth, income, earnings (income from work in the form of salaries and wages), years of schooling, and other indicators of economic or social success.

Wealth, earnings, market income and disposable income
Figure 19.1 shows data on three dimensions of inequality (wealth, earnings, and disposable income) in three economies. Recall that wealth is the value of the assets owned by a household (net of their debts). Earnings are income from labour, including from wages, salaries, and self-employment. Market income is the sum of:

- all income received as earnings
- all income received from business owned by the household or from investments

Finally, disposable income is the income that a family can spend

- after paying taxes
- after receiving any monetary transfers from the government such as unemployment benefit and pensions

Two things stand out in Figure 19.1:

- *Wealth is much more unequally distributed than earnings, and earnings are much more unequally distributed than disposable income*: Though the differences among the three measures of inequality are much smaller in Japan than in Sweden and the US.
- *Sweden has much lower disposable income inequality than the other two countries*: This is due to its relatively modest inequality in earnings and more importantly, to its system of taxes and transfers which benefits the less well off. It is not due to greater equality in Sweden's distribution of wealth. As you can see from the graph, wealth is distributed almost as unequally in Sweden as in the US.

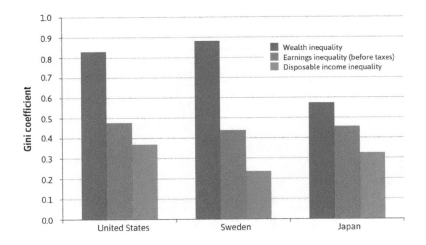

Mattia Fochesato and Samuel Bowles. 2013. 'Wealth Inequality from Prehistory to the Present: Data, Sources and Methods.' Dynamics of Wealth Inequality Project, Behavioral Sciences Program, Santa Fe Institute; Mattia Fochesato and Samuel Bowles. 2017. 'Technology, Institutions and Wealth Inequality in the Very Long Run'. Santa Fe Institute; Chen Wang and Koen Caminada. 2011. 'Leiden Budget Incidence Fiscal Redistribution Dataset'. Version 1. Leiden Department of Economics Research.

Figure 19.1 Inequality in wealth, earnings, and disposable income: US, Sweden, and Japan (2000s).

Facundo Alvaredo, Anthony B. Atkinson, Thomas Piketty, Emmanuel Saez, and Gabriel Zucman. 2016. 'The World Wealth and Income Database (WID)' (http://tinyco.re/5262390). Anthony B. Atkinson and Thomas Piketty, eds. 2007. *Top Incomes Over the Twentieth Century: A Contrast between Continental European and English-Speaking Countries*. Oxford: Oxford University Press.

Explore the top incomes in countries that you are interested in the World Wealth and Income Database (http://tinyco.re/5262390).

Income inequalities over time and among countries

Another way to measure inequality focuses on the very rich, providing an answer to the question: what fraction of total income or wealth belongs to the richest 1% or 10% of the population? This indicator has the advantage that it can be measured over hundreds of years, because the very rich have long been required to pay taxes, and hence we have reasonably good information on their incomes and wealth. Figure 19.2 shows the fraction of all wealth held by the richest 1%, for all countries on which long-run data is available.

There appear to be three distinct periods: the eighteenth and nineteenth centuries up to about 1910 show increasing wealth inequality (excepting Norway and Denmark), the twentieth century until 1980 shows decreasing wealth inequality, and the period since shows a modest increase in wealth inequality.

Figure 19.3 presents similar data for the share of income before taxes and transfers (rather than wealth) received by the top 1% of income earners. As in Figure 19.2 there are cross-country differences. For example, in recent years the US is much more unequal than China, India, or the UK. But there are also common trends, similar to the second and third periods in the distribution of wealth: a trend towards less inequality in much of the first three quarters of the twentieth century, followed by an increase in inequality since about 1980.

But this sharp U-turn towards greater inequality did not occur in all countries, including most of the major economies of the continent of Europe. These are shown in Figure 19.4.

Adapted from Figure 19 of Daniel Waldenström and Jesper Roine. 2014. 'Long Run Trends in the Distribution of Income and Wealth' (http://tinyco.re/8651400). In *Handbook of Income Distribution: Volume 2a*, edited by Anthony Atkinson and Francois Bourguignon. Amsterdam: North-Holland. Data.

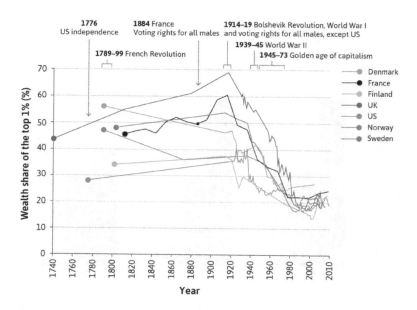

Figure 19.2 Share of total wealth held by the richest 1% (1740–2011).

Looking at Figures 19.2 to 19.4, one can see that:

- *There are common trends across most of the countries for which we have data*: For example, a fall in inequality between 1920 and 1980.
- *Countries differ greatly in what happened since 1980*: In some of the world's largest economies—China, India, and the US—inequality rose steeply, while in others—Denmark, France, and the Netherlands—inequality remained close to historically modest levels.

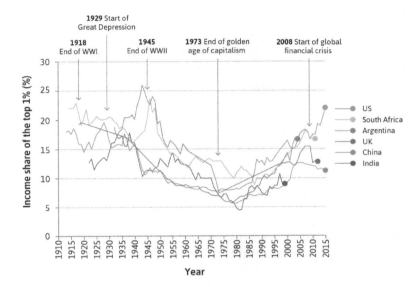

Facundo Alvaredo, Anthony B. Atkinson, Thomas Piketty, Emmanuel Saez, and Gabriel Zucman. 2016. 'The World Wealth and Income Database (WID)'.

Figure 19.3 The share of total income received by the top 1% (1913–2015).

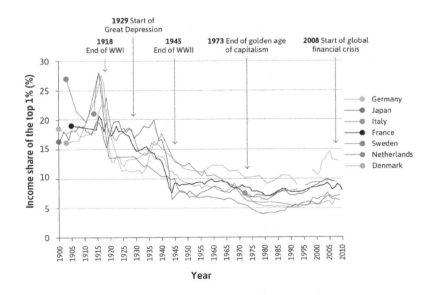

Facundo Alvaredo, Anthony B. Atkinson, Thomas Piketty, Emmanuel Saez, and Gabriel Zucman. 2016. 'The World Wealth and Income Database (WID)'.

Figure 19.4 Declining share of the top 1% in some European economies and Japan (1900–2013).

Thomas Piketty. 2014. *Capital in the Twenty-First Century.* Cambridge, MA: Harvard University Press.

Thomas Piketty, Professor of Economics at the Paris School of Economics, explains how he 'tries to be useful' by collecting long-run data on the distribution of wealth.
http://tinyco.re/8537633

We used data created by Thomas Piketty and his collaborators to create Figures 19.3 and 19.4. He is an economist and author of the bestselling economics book *Capital in the Twenty-First Century.* In our 'Economist in action' video, he examines economic inequality from the French Revolution to today, and explains why careful study of the facts is essential.

Inequalities between and within nations

At the beginning of Unit 1 you read that prior to the emergence of capitalism, the income a daughter or a son received depended on where their parents were on the economic ladder. It mattered much less in which part of the world the son or daughter was born.

The economic take-off of the first capitalist economies changed this.

The 'great divergence' in Unit 1 resulted because the kink in the hockey stick for per capita income came earlier for some countries (Britain, Italy, and Japan in Figure 1.1a), later for others (China and India), and is yet to occur for still others (Nigeria and Argentina) (see also Figure 1.11). The result of the uneven timing of the capitalist revolution around the world was a widening of inequalities among the people of the world, which occurred over the nineteenth and twentieth centuries until very recently. Even the poor in North America and Europe became richer than the rich elsewhere.

How do we measure global inequality? Think about the Lorenz curve constructed by lining up all the individuals in the world from lowest to highest income, irrespective of the country people live in. You know from Figure 1.2 that the poorest 20%—the part of the Lorenz curve extending from zero to 0.20 on the horizontal axis—would be very flat: this would represent most of the populations of Liberia and Nigeria, and middle and lower income people in Indonesia and India for example. If we construct the entire Lorenz curve, we can calculate the Gini coefficient for the whole world. This is shown for market income in Figure 19.5. For example, in 2003 the worldwide Gini coefficient was 0.69. We can see that inequality among the world's individuals is high but has fallen very recently.

The other series in Figure 19.5 (the red line) presents global inequality in a different way. It focuses on the income differences *between* countries. Imagine that everyone in each country earned the average income for that country. In this thought experiment, everyone in the UK would earn exactly the UK's average income, whereas everyone in China would earn exactly the Chinese average income. What would income inequality look like in this hypothetical example?

The red line shows the result of performing this calculation. In our thought experiment, the only source of inequality in the world would be inequality across countries. Inequality is reduced, but substantial inequalities still exist due to the vast differences in income between countries.

You can see that the Gini coefficient for all individuals in the world in 1988 (the beginning of the blue line) was 0.69, and this number would have been 0.60 had there been perfect equality within each country (the red line). As a result, we see that 87% of global inequality in income is accounted for by our measure of inequality between countries (that is because 0.60/0.69 = 0.87, or 87%).

The figure also shows that between-country inequality has been falling rapidly: by 2013, 76% of global inequality was between-country inequality (0.47/0.62 = 0.76).

The most recent Gini coefficient for the whole world is 0.62. You know that this is closer to 1 (one person has all the income in the world) than to 0 (no income differences in the world). But how much inequality does this really indicate? To see how to interpret the Gini coefficient, read the Einstein: 'The Gini Coefficient and worldwide income differences', which is at the end of this section.

Figure 19.5 has three main messages for us:

- *Most of the inequality in the world is between individuals in different countries (the red series)*: It is not between individuals in the same country (the difference between the blue and red series).
- *But this is changing*: The world's two largest and once very poor economies—India and China—raised their average incomes more rapidly than the richer countries, reducing between-country inequality, and because inequalities across individuals in these countries and many other large nations became greater, increasing within-country inequality.
- *Inequality between individuals is declining*: The net result of these opposite trends is that inequality among the individuals of the world has started to decline.

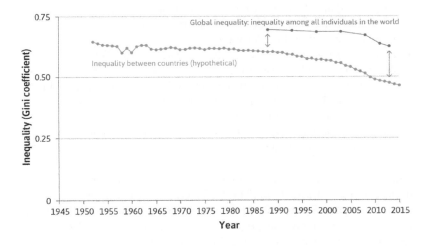

Branko Milanovic. 2012. 'Global Income Inequality by the Numbers: In History and Now—an Overview'. Policy Research Working Paper 6259. The World Bank. Inequality between countries (hypothetical) refers to the thought experiment in which everyone in the same country has the same income.

Figure 19.5 Global and between-country income inequality (1952–2015).

1. Inequality among the world's individuals falls (1986–2013)
The blue line shows income inequality among all individuals in the world. It is, effectively, the world's Gini coefficient.

2. The hypothetical inequality between countries falls…
The red curve shows the between-country income inequality between 1952 and 2015. To calculate it, we assume everyone in a given country had the same income. Since the 1980s, inequality started to decline rapidly.

3. … and within-country inequality rises
The decline in between-country inequality accelerated as the growth of the world's largest poor countries, China and India, took off. But inequality within countries, including China and India, increased.

A glimpse into the future of the rich economies: The missing middle?

The increased inequality that has occurred within many developed countries has been associated with a changing distribution of jobs. Low-paying jobs and high-paying jobs have increased in number while middle-income jobs have become scarcer. The result—more jobs at the top and the bottom of the economic ladder, and fewer on the middle rungs—has been termed 'the missing middle'.

The data in Figure 19.6 illustrate both trends for the US economy. We have used the US economy as an illustration because of the quality of the available data, but similar trends are evident in other high-income countries.

Figure 19.6 arranges jobs from the highest paid (in hourly wages) at the top to the lowest paid jobs at the bottom, and estimates growth or contraction of employment on the horizontal axis.

Notice these things about the data:

- *The missing middle*: Both high-wage and (especially) low-wage occupations are adding many jobs, but employment gains among the occupations with wages in between are more limited.
- *Jobs replace work once done by family members*: The biggest increases are in human services, most of them in health-related professions. These growing occupations substitute for work once done primarily by family members, such as personal care aides and home health care aides.
- *Machines do routine work*: Digitalization reduces the demand for jobs that involve routine tasks, such as postal mail sorters and machine operators. The tasks that machines are not replacing tend to be either well paid (personal financial advisors, nurse practitioners) or poorly paid, such as those taking care of the elderly at home.
- *High-wage job gainers work with information technologies*: Growing occupations with high wages (outside human services) such as operations researchers, statisticians, and web developers are those in which digital information processing has greatly increased the productivity of workers with the right kinds of skills.
- *Workers with average wages are the losers*: Occupations with job losses tend to have near-average wages or less.

Figure 19.6 only showed occupations for which gains or losses are projected to be at least 20% of their 2014 level and change by at least 10,000 employees. But as Figure 19.7 shows, this pattern holds when we look at all jobs in the US economy. The projected trends shown in Figures 19.6 and 19.7 have been underway in the US since at least the 1970s.

Note: Figure 19.6 shows only the occupations that are projected to undergo changes of 10,000 employees or more. The term 'various' indicates similar occupations. The blue dots are the occupations related to machine operators (sewing machine operators, textile machine operators, switchboard operators, machine operators, and molding). The horizontal dashed line is the average hourly wage across all occupations in the US in June 2015. The C-shaped line is a second-order polynomial that fits the data shown in the chart.

The dot labelled '1997' shows the mean hourly wage machine operators would have earned in 2015 had their wage remained in the same proportion to the mean wage as in 1997.

EXERCISE 19.2 INEQUALITIES AMONG YOUR CLASSMATES
1. Using this Gini coefficient calculator (http://tinyco.re/2316743), calculate the degree of inequality of height among your classmates.
2. Why is this Gini coefficient so much smaller than it was for wealth in Figure 19.1?
3. Now use the calculator to compute the Gini coefficient for another measure (for example, age, weight, commuting time to university, number of siblings, or grade in the last exam).
4. Explain any differences between this Gini coefficient and that for wealth.

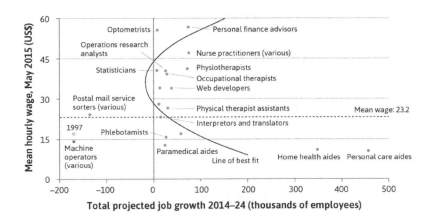

US Bureau of Labor Statistics. 2014. 'Employment Projections'. US Bureau of Labor Statistics. 2015. 'Occupational Employment Statistics'.

Figure 19.6 The missing middle in the US (2014–24): Occupations forecast to undergo job changes of 10,000 employees or more.

1. Estimated projected US jobs growth
Figure 19.6 arranges jobs from the highest paid (in hourly wages) at the top to the lowest paid jobs at the bottom, and estimates growth or contraction of employment on the horizontal axis.

2. Skilled US workers' wages have fallen
Due to the combined effect of automation and the 'China effect', the wages of machine operator occupations fell from 73% of the mean wage in 1997 to 61% in 2014.

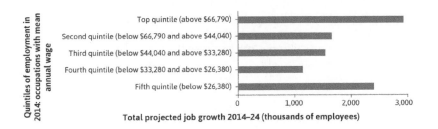

US Bureau of Labor Statistics. 2014. 'Employment Projections'. US Bureau of Labor Statistics. 2015. 'Occupational Employment Statistics'.

Figure 19.7 The missing middle in the US (2014–24): Job growth is highest in the top fifth and bottom fifth of occupations in the US, by mean annual earnings.

QUESTION 19.1 CHOOSE THE CORRECT ANSWER(S)

Figure 19.1 (page 847) shows the inequality in wealth, earnings, and disposable income in the US, Sweden, and Japan using the Gini coefficient.

Based on this information, which of the following statements are correct?

☐ Wealth is much more unequally distributed than earnings in all three countries.
☐ Sweden is an unambiguously more unequal society than Japan.
☐ Of the three countries, the US is the most unequal society.
☐ Sweden attains its relatively equal disposable income distribution through its system of taxes and transfers.

QUESTION 19.2 CHOOSE THE CORRECT ANSWER(S)

In Thomas Piketty's 'Economist in action' video (page 850), which of the following were NOT among the reasons that Piketty gave for the fall in the incomes of the very rich during the twentieth century?

☐ the First World War
☐ the Great Depression
☐ the Russian Revolution
☐ the Second World War

QUESTION 19.3 CHOOSE THE CORRECT ANSWER(S)

Figure 19.6 (page 853) is a scatterplot of occupations for the US economy, with the 2015 mean hourly wages on the vertical axis and the 2014–24 projected job growth on the horizontal axis:

Based on this information, which of the following statements is correct?

☐ Occupations with the biggest projected growth are those that benefit from innovations that increase automation.
☐ Occupations with substantial projected job losses are those with the highest wages, which would encourage employers to invest in automation.
☐ The high wage occupations with projected job growth are either in human services or occupations in which digital information processing has greatly increased the productivity of high skill workers.
☐ There is no particular pattern between the mean average wage and the projected job growth.

EINSTEIN

The Gini coefficient and worldwide income differences

In Unit 5 you learned that the Gini coefficient is a measure of inequality that is defined as half of the relative mean differences in incomes between all pairs of people in a population.

Recall that the mean difference in incomes among all pairs in the population which we denote as Δ can be expressed as the income of the richer of the pair (y^r) minus the income of the poorer of the pair (y^p) summed over all of the pairs in the population, and then divided by the number of pairs in the population (n). The relative mean difference is this quantity divided by mean income, y.

So half of the relative mean difference is:

$$g = (\frac{1}{2})(\frac{\Delta}{y})$$

By rearranging this equation, you can see that the average difference between the two paired people will be the mean income times twice the Gini coefficient:

$$\Delta = 2yg$$

But there is a more interesting interpretation of the Gini coefficient. If we have drawn all possible pairs from the world's population, the mean income in the world ($\bar{y}$) will be:

$$\bar{y} = \frac{1}{2}(\frac{1}{n}\sum_{i=1}^{n}y_i^r + \frac{1}{n}\sum_{i=1}^{n}y_i^p)$$

$$= \frac{1}{2}(\bar{y}^r + \bar{y}^p)$$

where we defined $\bar{y}^r$ and $\bar{y}^p$ are the average incomes of the richer and the poorer of each of the pairs, respectively. So we can now rewrite the expression for the Gini coefficient in terms of $\bar{y}^r$ and $\bar{y}^p$:

$$g = (\frac{1}{2})2(\frac{\bar{y}^r - \bar{y}^p}{\bar{y}^r + \bar{y}^p})$$

By rearranging and dividing through by $\bar{y}^p$, we have:

$$g(\bar{y}^r + \bar{y}^p) = \bar{y}^r - \bar{y}^p$$

$$g(\frac{\bar{y}^r}{\bar{y}^p} + 1) = \frac{\bar{y}^r}{\bar{y}^p} - 1$$

$$g\frac{\bar{y}^r}{\bar{y}^p} + g = \frac{\bar{y}^r}{\bar{y}^p} - 1$$

$$g + 1 = \frac{\bar{y}^r}{\bar{y}^p}(1 - g)$$

$$\frac{g + 1}{1 - g} = \frac{\bar{y}^r}{\bar{y}^p}$$

Using this final expression, if the Gini coefficient for the world is 0.62, then:

$$\frac{\bar{y}^r}{\bar{y}^p} = \frac{g+1}{1-g} = \frac{0.62+1}{1-0.62} = 4.26$$

This says that if the Gini coefficient is 0.62, then across all of the pairs in the population or across a large random sample of the population, the better off of the two is on average 4.26 times richer than the less well off.

EXERCISE 19.3 ANOTHER WAY TO INTERPRET GINI COEFFICIENTS

Use Figure 5.16 (page 217) to estimate the Gini coefficient for disposable income in Denmark and South Africa. In explaining the difference in income inequality between these two countries, you could use the information in the Gini as follows: if two people are chosen at random from the population of the country, what is the average ratio of the richer person's income to that of the poorer person's? To allow you to translate data on the Gini coefficient into this ratio, use the formula in the Einstein to construct a table of the richer/poorer ratio for Gini coefficients ranging from 0.0 to 0.9 (in increments of 0.1). Graph your results. Explain the difference in inequality between Denmark and South Africa using your results. What does the formula imply if the Gini coefficient is equal to 1?

19.2. ACCIDENTS OF BIRTH: ANOTHER LENS TO STUDY INEQUALITY

Scholars have recently asked 'big questions' about inequality.

Daron Acemoglu and James A. Robinson. 2012. *Why Nations Fail: The Origins of Power, Prosperity, and Poverty*. New York, NY: Crown Publishing Group.

Angus Deaton. 2013. *The Great Escape: Health, Wealth, and the Origins of Inequality*. Princeton, NJ: Princeton University Press.

Jared Diamond. 1999. *Guns, Germs, and Steel: The Fates of Human Societies*. New York, NY: Norton, W. W. & Company.

Kent Flannery and Joyce Marcus. 2014. *The Creation of Inequality: How Our Prehistoric Ancestors Set the Stage for Monarchy, Slavery, and Empire*. Cambridge, MA: Harvard University Press.

Much of the inequality in the world today can be traced to differences among people in things over which they have virtually no control, such as their race, sex, nation, or parents. We call these differences 'accidents of birth'.

To see how important accidents of birth can be, try the following thought experiment. Go back to Figure 1.2 (page 4). Suppose that all you care about is income, and you can choose either:

- the income decile you are in, but the country you are born in will be decided by chance
- the country you are born in, but the decile you are in within the country will be decided by chance

Did you choose option 1 (the decile) or option 2 (the country)?

If you chose option 1, you would of course choose to be in the top decile, so you would be somewhere at the back of Figure 1.2. But where? You would have an equal chance of being born in Nigeria on the left-hand side or in the UK on the right-hand side.

If you chose option 2, you could select one of countries at the right-hand end with the highest average income. You are as likely to be in the lowest decile, at the front of the figure, as in the highest decile, at the back.

One's citizenship is one of the great accidents of birth affecting income. Passports and borders limit the economic opportunities people from different countries face. People with the same education, capacities, and ambition but born on different sides of a national border face very different life chances, whether that is the border between Mexico and the US, The

People's Democratic Republic of Korea (North Korea) and South Korea, or the Mediterranean Sea that divides North Africa from Europe. Even where migration is allowed, migrants are often denied access to political and labour rights, as in the Gulf States and some East Asian countries.

Gender and other forms of categorical inequality

Inequalities based on accidents of birth also exist within countries:

- *Caste*: Vast disparities in life chances in India, for example, follow from long-established hereditary and hierarchical 'caste' boundaries. Caste is a social status that ranges from high-status Brahmins to Dalits (once called 'untouchables').
- *Formalized discrimination*: Until 1994, apartheid in South Africa formalized inequality with a complex system of racial barriers.
- *Colonists and indigenous people*: In Australia, the US, and much of Latin America, extraordinary economic and social inequality exists between descendants of European colonists and those who arrived tens of thousands of years earlier, called indigenous people.

Inequalities based on one's ethnic identity or caste are examples of **categorical inequality** (also known as **group inequality**), meaning economic differences among people who are treated as being in different social categories as defined by more powerful social classes. The Indian castes are categories, as are those of 'African', 'White', 'Coloured' and 'Asian' in South Africa. Categorical inequalities are for the most part based on accidents of birth, because one is born into membership in one of the categories, and switching category is typically difficult if not impossible.

To understand how easily segregation by race or some other categorical characteristic arises, take two minutes to play the online game *The Parable of the Polygons* (http://tinyco.re/4763470).

The most common form of categorical inequality is that between men and women. There are many economic differences between men and women on average. This is a bit puzzling because other than differing biological roles in reproduction, men and women are so similar: similar parents, similar schools (in most countries), similar genetic inheritance on matters affecting intellectual skills and so on. But it is clear that the economy treats men and women differently. This is much more true in some countries than in others, but it is true for all countries.

Income disparities between men and women among otherwise similar individuals are one measure of this inequality. Figure 19.8 shows the expected lifetime earnings (labour income) of men and women in the US, who work full time from the time they leave school until retirement. As a result, any differences in the figure are not due to women having more time out of the labour force (on average) because of child rearing.

Because the quality of schooling does not differ between males and females on average (and girls tend to do as well on most tests), the gender differences in pay are not due to differences in cognitive ability or quality of schooling. Yet for every level of schooling, women can expect to earn much less than men.

The figure also shows, however, that additional schooling contributes to higher lifetime incomes, and that those women who complete university (a bachelor's degree) can expect to earn much more than men who ended their schooling after secondary school.

categorical inequality Inequality between particular social groups (identified, for instance, by a category such as race, nation, caste, gender or religion). *Also known as: group inequality.*

In many parts of the world girls receive considerably less schooling than boys, but as Figure 19.9 shows, girls go to school for the same number of years on average as boys in both the US and France, and longer in Brazil. Countries in which women have historically suffered extraordinary social and economic disadvantages, such as China and Indonesia, have virtually eliminated the gender gap in years of schooling, and India, though far behind, is rapidly closing it.

Intergenerational inequality

In addition to categorical differences such as nation, gender, race, or ethnic group, a second source of economic inequality within a nation is inherited. You may be rich or poor simply because your parents were rich or poor.

Two hundred years ago, in most countries it was taken for granted that somebody would expect a life of poverty simply because her parents had been poor, or that someone else would inherit the ownership of his father's

Adapted from Figure 5 in Anthony P. Carnevale, Stephen J. Rose, and Ban Cheah. 2011. *The College Payoff*. Georgetown University Center on Education and the Workforce. (Note: The average for males is $2,520,286, while for females it is $1,909,714.)

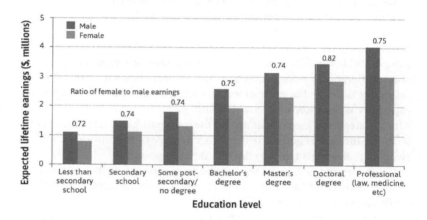

Figure 19.8 Categorical inequality: Schooling and lifetime earnings for men and women in the US.

The World Bank. 2016. IIASA/VID Educational Attainment Model. Dataset produced by the International Institute for Applied Systems Analysis (IIASA) in Luxemburg, Austria and the Vienna Institute of Demography, Austrian Academy of Sciences. Educational Attainment Statistics.

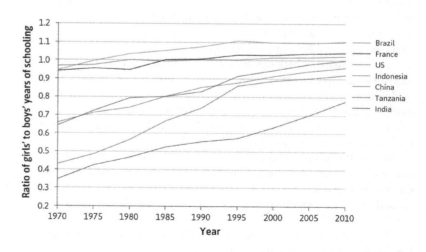

Figure 19.9 Categorical inequality: Average years of schooling, girls relative to boys (1970–2010).

company and social status, without having to prove that he was the best person for the job. The inheritance of inequality from one generation to the next seemed to be part of the natural order of things.

But this has changed with the spread of public education and, in many countries, with the decline in discrimination against poor people due to their race, religion, or simply their humble origins. In some countries, the economic status of one's parents matters a great deal for the economic success of their children; in other countries, differences among parents are only weakly transmitted to their offspring.

The expression **intergenerational transmission of economic differences** refers to the processes by which the economic status of the adult sons and daughters comes to resemble the economic status of the parents. The transmission process takes many forms:

- Children inherit the wealth of their parents.
- The genetic makeup of the children is similar to the parents.
- Through parental influence in child rearing, parents and children tend to share similar preferences, social norms, and knowledge, skills and social connections acquired outside formal schooling.

Intergenerational inequality occurs where these processes result in similarity between the economic status of parents and their children: the children of the well off become rich themselves, while the children of the less well off stay poor.

Economists and sociologists measure intergenerational inequality by ranking parents by their incomes or wealth, and then looking at what income or wealth their kids end up with when they become adults. They confirm that there is substantial intergenerational inequality. Kids whose parents had a high income are likely to grow up to have high incomes themselves, and kids from low-income families are likely to have low incomes as adults.

This is what we see in Figure 19.10, which gives measures of the intergenerational inequality of men in the US (left panel) and Denmark (the right panel), based on their labour earnings (wages or salaries). The tall bar on the left in the US panel means that among those whose fathers were in the bottom fifth of the earnings distribution, 40% were themselves in the poorest fifth, while 7% ended up in the top fifth of the earnings distribution. By contrast, 36% of those born to the richest fifth were themselves in the richest fifth—the tall purple bar on the right.

One of the reasons that children of the rich tend to be richer than the children of the poor is the financial support that rich parents give to their children, both during the parents' lifetimes and at death in the form of inheritances. The data in Figure 19.10, however, is based on labour earnings, not inherited wealth. The earnings of parents and their children appear to be similar in the US, partly because children of well off parents receive more, higher-quality, schooling. They also benefit from the networks and connections of their parents, which improve access to the labour market.

The data from Denmark in the right panel suggests a more level playing field. Only 25% of those born to parents in the poorest fifth of the population end up in the poorest fifth themselves, compared to 40% in the US. This suggests that those born to relatively poor parents are less disadvantaged in Denmark. Similarly, 33% of those born to parents in the

intergenerational transmission of economic differences The processes by which the economic status of the adult sons and daughters comes to resemble the economic status of the parents. *See also: intergenerational elasticity, intergenerational mobility.*

intergenerational inequality The extent to which differences in parental generations are passed on to the next generation, as measured by the intergenerational elasticity or the intergenerational correlation. *See also: intergenerational elasticity, intergenerational mobility, intergenerational transmission of economic differences.*

Samuel Bowles and Herbert Gintis. 2002. 'The Inheritance of Inequality' (http://tinyco.re/8562867). *Journal of Economic Perspectives* 16 (3): pp. 3–30.

Gregory Clark. 2015. *The Son Also Rises: Surnames and the History of Social Mobility*. Princeton, NJ: Princeton University Press.

richest fifth end up in the richest fifth themselves, compared to 36% in the US. Based on this data, we would conclude that intergenerational inequality is lower in Denmark than in the US, though it still does not appear to be a completely level playing field.

A measure that can summarize the overall rate of intergenerational inequality in a society is the **intergenerational elasticity** of income or wealth. To see what this measures, consider two pairs of fathers and children. The father in the first pair is richer than the father in the second. The intergenerational elasticity measures how much richer the child of the well off father will be than the child of the poorer father. An elasticity of 0.5, for example, means that if one father is 10% richer, then his child, when grown up, will be on average 5% richer than the other child. The higher the intergenerational elasticity, the greater the degree of intergenerational transmission of economic status and the greater the level of intergenerational inequality. In a society with a high intergenerational elasticity, **intergenerational mobility** is low.

intergenerational elasticity When comparing parents and grown offspring, the percentage difference in the second generation's status that is associated with a 1% difference in the adult generation's status. *See also: intergenerational inequality, intergenerational mobility, intergenerational transmission of economic differences.*

The term intergenerational elasticity has nothing to do with the usual meaning of the word elastic. But, like the price elasticity of demand for a good, it concerns the percentage change in something that is associated with a percentage change in something else.

intergenerational mobility Changes in the relative economic or social status between parents and children. Upward mobility occurs when the status of a child surpasses that of the parents. Downward mobility is the converse. A widely used measure of intergenerational mobility is the correlation between the positions of parents and children (for example, in their years of schooling or income). Another is the intergenerational elasticity. *See also: intergenerational elasticity, intergenerational transmission of economic differences.*

What is the relationship between a measure of intergenerational inequality such as the intergenerational elasticity and the extent of inequality among the members of a population at a given point in time? You can think of many reasons why the two would go together.

Figure 19.11 presents evidence on the relationship between intergenerational elasticity for earnings and earnings inequality at a particular time. We refer to earnings inequality at a particular time, which we measure using the Gini coefficient for income, as cross-sectional inequality. Note that we do not include the effects of taxes and government transfers in Figure 19.11 when we measure both income inequality and intergenerational transmission of earnings, because we are interested in the movements of these two dimensions of inequality that are independent of government policy.

Table 14 in Markus Jäntti, Bernt Bratsberg, Knut Røed, Oddbjørn Raaum, Robin Naylor, Eva Österbacka, Anders Björklund, and Tor Eriksson. 2006. 'American Exceptionalism in a New Light: A Comparison of Intergenerational Earnings Mobility in the Nordic Countries, the United Kingdom and the United States.' Discussion Paper Series 1938. Institute for the Study of Labor.

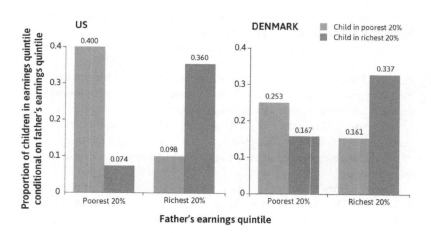

Figure 19.10 Intergenerational inequality in earnings: The US and Denmark.

The figure shows that for the countries considered, inequality in earnings at any particular point in time tends to be higher when intergenerational inequality is high. The US, UK, and Italy are examples of countries that have both high cross-sectional inequality and high intergenerational inequality. In other countries (Norway, Denmark, Finland) both intergenerational inequality and cross-sectional inequality are quite limited. But some countries differ according to which type of inequality is most pronounced. Compare, for example, Canada and Switzerland.

Does cross-sectional inequality cause intergenerational inequality, or the other way around, or both, or neither? We know that societies with a strong culture of fairness and equal treatment, such as Denmark, adopt policies to reduce inequality between people at a given moment, including offering generous benefits to unemployed and retired individuals through the welfare state. At the same time, they also attempt to limit intergenerational inequality by providing equal opportunities for high-quality education, and through other policies that would reduce intergenerational transmission of economic status. This is part of the explanation of the contrast between Denmark and the US in Figure 19.10.

Another likely source of the correlation in Figure 19.11 is that in any period (a generation for example), some individuals experience good luck—for example, living in a region that experienced an economic boom, while others experience bad luck—serious illness (their own or a family member), unplanned pregnancy, business failure, or because technological change or shifts in demand make their skills less valuable. These 'shocks' create more inequality in any given generation.

But if having high-income parents gives their sons and daughters economic advantages when they grow up, then these shocks live on even after the parents pass away. A person's father may have been rich just by good fortune, but his son and daughter will also be rich (or at least richer than they would have been) by inheritance.

Thus, in countries where intergenerational inequality is substantial, for example in the US, Italy, and the UK, high or low incomes resulting from good luck or bad luck are passed on to the next generation, and added to whatever shocks of good or bad fortune that the next generation

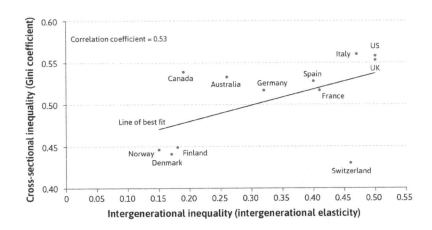

Miles Corak. 2013. 'Inequality from Generation to Generation: The United States in Comparison.' In *The Economics of Inequality, Poverty, and Discrimination in the 21st Century*, edited by Robert S. Rycroft. Santa Barbara, CA: Greenwood Pub Group; Wen-Hao Chen, Michael Förster, and Ana Llena-Nozal. 2013. 'Globalisation, Technological Progress and Changes in Regulations and Institutions: Which Impact on the Rise of Earnings Inequality in OECD Countries?'. Working Paper Series 597. LIS.

Figure 19.11 Intergenerational and cross-sectional inequality.

861

experiences. As a result, intergenerational inequality contributes to cross-sectional inequality.

You now know some basic facts about inequalities around the world. Knowing these facts, we ask what, if anything, is wrong with economic inequality?

EXERCISE 19.4 HOW INEQUALITIES OF BIRTH PERSIST BETWEEN GENERATIONS

1. Go back to the stories of Yichen, Renfu, Stephanie, and Mark and indicate all of the accidents of birth that affected their economic successes or failures.
2. Give some reasons why the intergenerational inequality and inequality between members of a population at a given moment in time are positively correlated.

QUESTION 19.4 CHOOSE THE CORRECT ANSWER(S)

Figure 19.10 (page 860) shows the proportion of children in earnings quantile conditional on their father's earnings quantile in the US and Denmark, respectively.

Based on this information, which of the following statements is correct?

☐ The data provides support for the 'American Dream', a term coined in 1931 by James Truslow Adams that refers to 'a dream of social order in which each man and woman shall be able to attain to the fullest stature of which they are innately capable ... regardless of the fortuitous circumstances of birth or position' (in *The Epic of America*, 1931).

☐ In the US, 7.4% of those from the poorest 20% of families managed to move up to become part of the richest 20%.

☐ In Denmark, it is far more difficult for the richest families to preserve their status for the next generation than in the US.

☐ The figure suggests that there is very little governments can do to reduce intergenerational transmission of economic status.

19.3 WHAT (IF ANYTHING) IS WRONG WITH INEQUALITY?

In November 2016, we asked students beginning economics at Humboldt University in Berlin, 'What is the most pressing issue that economists today should address?' Their replies are shown in the word cloud in Figure 19.12, in which the size of the word or phrase indicates the frequency with which that term was mentioned. Students in other universities around the world gave similar answers.

Perceived, ideal and actual inequalities

One of the reasons why inequality is seen as a problem is that many people think there is too much of it.

Michael Norton, a professor of business administration, and Daniel Ariely, a psychologist and behavioural economist, asked a large sample of Americans how they thought the wealth of the US should be distributed: what fraction of it, for example, should go to the wealthiest 20%? They also asked them to estimate what they thought the distribution of wealth actually was.

Figure 19.13 gives the results, with the top three bars showing the distribution that different groups of respondents considered would be ideal, and the fourth bar the wealth distribution that they thought actually existed in the US. The top bar shows that Americans thought that, ideally, the richest 20% should own a little more than 30% of total wealth—some inequality was desirable, but not a lot. Now contrast this with the fourth bar ('Estimated'), which shows that they thought that the richest 20% owned about 60% of the wealth. The bottom bar shows the actual distribution. In reality, the richest fifth owns 85% of the wealth. The actual distribution is much more unequal than the public's estimate—and contrasts sharply with the lower inequality that people would like to see.

Different groups largely agree on the ideal distribution of wealth. Americans with an annual income greater than $100,000 thought that the share going to the top 20% should be slightly larger than those who earned less than $50,000 thought it should be. Not shown in the figure: Democratic Party voters wished for a more equal distribution than Republican Party voters, and women preferred more equality than did men. The differences between these groups, however, were small.

Michael I. Norton and Daniel Ariely. 2011. 'Building a Better America—One Wealth Quintile at a Time' (http://tinyco.re/3629531). *Perspectives on Psychological Science* 6 (1): pp. 9–12.

Figure 19.12 Inequality is one of the main problems that students think economics should address.

When is inequality unfair?

Although there seems to be a consensus on the ideal outcome in the US, policies that would redistribute income and wealth are controversial and debated passionately—as they are in most countries. Differences in self-interest contribute to the arguments. Richer Americans, for example, tend to oppose redistribution that favours the poor, while poorer Americans support it.

But, as the experiments in Unit 4 would lead us to expect, self-interest is just part of the explanation. People differ also because they hold different beliefs about why the poor are poor and how the rich became rich. In laboratory settings, people often express strong feelings of fairness, and give up considerable sums of money to ensure that outcomes are consistent with ideas of economic justice.

For example, Responders in the ultimatum game reject what they consider an unfair offer, preferring to receive nothing and to impose the same fate on the Proposer than to agree to being treated unfairly. Both rich and poor may think that high levels of inequality are unfair and that the government should reduce economic disparities, even if it means voting for policies that would reduce the disposable income of the voter.

In Unit 5, you read about contrasting ideas about fairness, not based on how people play in experimental games, but instead on moral principles. Procedural theories, which are ideas of fairness based on how the inequality came to be, focus not on *how* poor or rich someone is, but instead on *why* the person is poor or rich.

Christina Fong, an economist, wanted to know if people in the US think this way when it comes to their political support or opposition to policies to raise the incomes of the poor, financed by general taxation. She found that a person who thinks that hard work and risk-taking are essential to economic success is much less likely to support redistribution to the poor than one who thinks that the key to success is inheritance, being white, your connections, or who your parents are.

The results of her study are in Figure 19.14. Notice that white people who think that being white is important to getting ahead strongly support redistribution to the poor—evidently because they think that the process that determines economic success is unfair.

Adapted from Figures 2 and 3 in Michael I. Norton and Daniel Ariely. 2011. 'Building a Better America—One Wealth Quintile at a Time'. *Perspectives on Psychological Science* 6 (1): pp. 9–12.

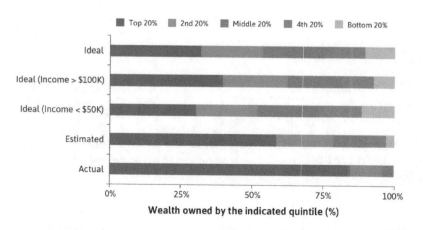

Figure 19.13 Ideal, estimated, and actual distribution of wealth for people in the US.

This suggests that for many people, the question 'how much inequality is too much?' cannot be answered unless we know why a family or person is rich or poor. Many people think it is unfair if income depends substantially on what we call an 'accident of birth' (categorical inequality)—your race, your sex, or your country. Inequalities based on hard work or taking risks are less likely to be seen as a problem.

EXERCISE 19.5 ESTIMATED, IDEAL, AND ACTUAL DISTRIBUTIONS OF WEALTH

Use this Gini coefficient calculator (http://tinyco.re/2316743) to determine the Gini coefficients for wealth ownership given by the estimated, ideal, and actual distributions in Figure 19.13 (page 864). Note: You will have to estimate the data visually from the chart.

EXERCISE 19.6 A LEVEL PLAYING FIELD

When people think about 'too much inequality', some think about the Gini coefficient measuring inequality at a point in time, while others are more interested in intergenerational inequality.

1. Use an example of two fictional families in each country to explain the combination of cross-sectional and intergenerational income inequality in Canada and Switzerland shown in Figure 19.11 (page 861).

Now think about the indifference curves that you could draw in this figure that would indicate the combinations

of inequality and intergenerational inequality that would be equally fair in your judgement.

2. If you cared only about the Gini coefficient and you disliked inequality, what would they look like?
3. If you cared only about the intergenerational elasticity and you disliked inequality, what would your indifference curves look like?
4. On Figure 19.11, draw indifference curves according to your personal preferences for cross-sectional and intergenerational inequality. Use your indifference curves to rank the countries from the fairest to the least fair.

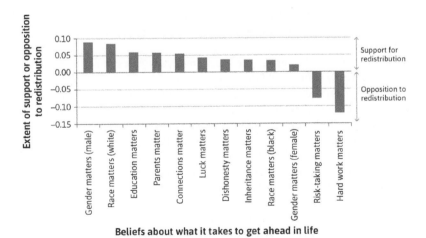

Figure 5.3 in Samuel Bowles. 2012. *The New Economics of Inequality and Redistribution.* Cambridge: Cambridge University Press; Christina Fong, Samuel Bowles, and Herbert Gintis. 2005. 'Strong Reciprocity and the Welfare State'. In *Handbook of Giving, Reciprocity and Altruism.* Edited by Serge-Christophe Kolm and Jean Mercier Ythier. Amsterdam: Elsevier.

Figure 19.14 How beliefs about what it takes to get ahead predict whether people in the US support or oppose government programs to redistribute income to the poor.

19.4 HOW MUCH INEQUALITY IS TOO MUCH (OR TOO LITTLE)?

We know that accidents of birth matter. But even if the playing field were level (that is, accidents of birth did not matter), we would still face a question: how rich should the winners be compared to the losers?

A lens for looking at unfairness: The veil of ignorance.

To think about this question, transport yourself to a hypothetical world in which you (perhaps along with other fellow citizens) are asked to design your model society. There will be two groups or classes of equal size, one called 'richer' and the other 'poorer'. You will get to live in the society you design after you have answered the question 'how rich should the richer class be and how poor should the poorer class be?'

But there is a hitch: which class you get to be in will be determined by the flip of a coin *after you have decided how unequal the society will be.*

This thought experiment is what the American philosopher John Rawls, whom we encountered in Unit 5, termed choosing a social contract from behind a veil of ignorance. The 'veil of ignorance' ensures that we do not know which position we would occupy in the society we were designing.

Behind the curious device of the veil is an important concept. Rawls' fundamental idea is that justice should be impartial. It should not favour one group over another, and the veil of ignorance invites you to think this way (because you do not yet know which group you are going to be in). Rawls asked us to think about justice as if:

> [N]o one knows his place in society, his class position or social status; nor does he know his fortune in the distribution of natural assets and abilities, his intelligence and strength, and the like. (*A Theory of Justice*, 1971)

This does not tell us the answer to how much inequality there should be, but it does suggest a way to look at it.

Feasible inequality

Economics gives us tools for studying what combinations of the income of the rich and the poor are feasible, and how we might reason about which ones are preferable to others.

Let's try one way to answer the question of 'how rich should the richer class be and how poor should the poorer class be'. Let's say there should be no difference between the incomes of the rich and the poor. Suppose that, in this case, both classes would receive $100,000 annually (per adult). This is shown by point E (for Equality) in Figure 19.15, where the 45-degree line gives all of the points of equal income between the two classes (so there is really no meaning to 'rich' and 'poor'). The figure shows the annual income per adult of the poor and the rich on separate axes.

Would this be your choice? In this version of an ideal society, you would not run the risk of ending up poorer than others after the coin flip. But as an economist you might think that complete equality in the society would mean that there were insufficient incentives for people to work, study, and take risks innovating and investing, so that at least some inequality could actually be better for everyone.

In the figure, points between E and R show possible combinations in which the rich are richer than the poor, but where the poor also are richer than they would be under complete equality. To put it another way, from any one of these points, including point E, there is a win-win possibility: giving more income to the rich allows the poor to have more income as well.

Comparing the two points, you can see that E is Pareto inefficient because both the rich and poor are better off at R than at E. The income distribution at R is also the one at which the poor are as rich as they can possibly be in this economy, as indicated by the feasible frontier. This is the point that Rawls favoured (and why we called it point R).

Would you choose R? Notice that, above R, the frontier is very steep. This means that it's possible to make the rich much richer by making a small reduction in the income of the poor.

The red curved line passing through R and E (and the other points above R) is the frontier of the feasible set of income distributions for the economy in question. We assume that a government can adopt policies to bring about any one of these economically feasible points, but in Unit 22 we will

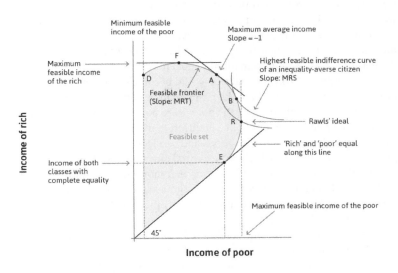

Figure 19.15 Choosing between feasible income distributions.

1. Equality between rich and poor
Point E shows the case in which rich and poor receive the same income.

2. Rawls' ideal
Rawls' preferred point is R, where the poor are as rich as possible.

3. The feasible set
The red curved line made passing through R and E (and the other points above R) is the frontier of the feasible set of income distributions of this economy. Its slope is the MRT.

4. Maximum expected income
If you were interested in maximizing your expected income then you would choose point A, where the income gains of the rich are exactly offset by income losses by the poor, so the marginal rate of transformation is equal to one.

5. If you knew you would be rich
If you could rig the coin flip so that you knew you would end up rich (and you had no concern about fairness) you would select point F.

6. The worst solution for the poor
Point D denotes the minimal income of the poor and, like E, is not Pareto efficient.

7. Inequality aversion
An inequality-averse citizen with indifference curves as depicted by the blue curves would choose point B.

introduce limits on the government's ability to do so, which would have the effect of shrinking the feasible set. As with all feasible frontiers, the slope is a marginal rate of transformation. In this case, the transformation is of income losses of the poor into income gains for the rich.

$$\text{slope of the feasible frontier} = \text{MRT}$$
$$= \frac{\text{income gains for the rich}}{\text{income losses for the poor}}$$

If the point R had been proposed, would you want to consider other points higher up on the feasible frontier? Remember, after the coin flip, you will get either the income of the rich or that of the poor with equal probability (one half), so you know that:

$$\text{expected income} = 0.5 \times (\text{income of the rich}) + 0.5 \times (\text{income of the poor})$$

As long as income gains for the rich come at little expense of income losses for the poor, you would definitely do better to move above point R. If you were interested in maximizing your expected income and did not care about the degree of inequality, then you would choose point A, where the income gains of the rich are exactly offset by income losses by the poor, so the marginal rate of transformation is equal to one.

But after point A, the inequalities would become so severe that the average income would fall, and the rich would be getting a larger slice of a smaller pie. This might occur if the poor were not fed enough to work hard, or were angry enough about their condition to motivate the rich to divert some economic resources from goods and services production into protecting their wealth, which reduces total output. By looking ahead to Figure 19.30c, you will see data showing that more unequal societies (such as the US, UK, and Italy) devote more resources to workers employed in private and public security activities than do other more equal countries with similar GDP per capita.

Like the feasible set when Angela and Bruno were bargaining in Unit 5, there is a minimum level of income that the poor can get. This minimum could be set by their biological survival needs, or perhaps by the fact that if income fell below this level they would revolt. Notice that if the poor were to be even poorer than at point F, the rich would also suffer. So like point E (maximal equality), point D (minimal income of the poor) is not Pareto efficient.

In the figure we have considered the following income distributions:

- E: complete equality
- R: the distribution with the highest income for the poor
- A: the highest average income of rich and poor
- F: the maximum income of the rich
- D: the distribution in which the poor are at their minimum feasible living standard

A preference for fairness

Which would you choose? Points between D and F are easy to eliminate from the running, as they are all inferior to point F for both classes. And the same goes for points between E and R. Eliminating all Pareto-inefficient distributions from consideration means that no points in the interior (inside) of the feasible set would be considered.

That leaves points between F and R. How will you choose among them? To answer this, you need to consult your indifference curves. In this case, an indifference curve gives combinations of the incomes of the two classes that you value equally.

Curves further away from the origin are preferred (more income for both groups is always better). The slope of these indifference curves is the marginal rate of substitution between income for the rich and income for the poor.

$$\text{slope of indifference curves} = \text{MRS}$$
$$= \frac{\text{marginal value of poor income}}{\text{marginal value of rich income}}$$

You would then maximize your utility by finding the point on the feasible frontier at which the marginal rate of transformation is equal to the marginal rate of substitution. If you wished to maximize your own expected income, then you would place an equal value on the income of the rich and the poor because you are equally likely to be one or the other.

But you might care about the condition of the poorer class even if you were lucky enough to be assigned to the richer class in the coin flip (remember, you have to make your choice before you know your assignment). That is, you might be **inequality averse**, caring about your own payoffs but also disliking inequality across groups. In this case, you would have an indifference curve like the blue one shown in the figure. You would choose point B, somewhere between Rawls' ideal (the highest feasible income of the poor) and point A, the highest average income.

The familiar graph of the feasible set and a family of indifference curves helps to clarify the choices about inequality and fairness that a citizen or group of citizens may wish to make. But it does not tell us how any of the points on the feasible frontier might actually be implemented. Changing the level of inequality in a society requires altering one or more of the causes of the current state of inequality. To understand income inequality, we first have to understand the factors that determine an individual's income.

inequality aversion A dislike of outcomes in which some individuals receive more than others.

QUESTION 19.5 CHOOSE THE CORRECT ANSWER(S)
Figure 19.15 (page 867) shows the feasible frontier of the incomes of the rich and the poor.

Which of the following statements is correct?

☐ E, the point of maximum equality, is Pareto efficient.
☐ For the inequality-averse citizen shown, any point between R and F on the frontier is preferable to any point inside the frontier.
☐ If you had a 50-50 chance of being rich or poor, then your expected income is maximized at point B.
☐ Between D and F, lower income for the poor leads also to lower income for the rich.

19.5 ENDOWMENTS, TECHNOLOGY, AND INSTITUTIONS

Income and endowments

In this section, we provide a framework that helps explain why different individuals receive different incomes.

An individual's income depends on things that they own, or are, or have that allow them to receive income. These things affecting a person's income are called **endowments** and include:

- *Their financial wealth*: Their savings or stocks or bonds that they own, on which they receive interest or dividends.
- *The physical assets they own*: For example, land or the buildings and machinery of a company on which they may receive profits or rents, and which they can use as collateral.
- *Their schooling and work experience*, which affects their value to an employer and therefore their earnings on the labour market (sometimes termed their **human capital**).
- *Their race, gender, age, and other aspects* that may affect wages, access to credit, or other exchanges.
- *Their citizenship* and whether the individual has a visa, which determine whether they can legally work in a particular country and therefore their earnings on the labour market.
- *Any other attribute*, or possession, or capacity that affects the income an individual will receive.

As a result, we can think of an individual's income as depending on:

- their endowments
- the income resulting from each item in the set of their endowments

So, for example, consider a person, Ella, whose endowment is the ability to work full time (1,750 hours) at a wage based on her skill as a medical technician (€30 per hour). She also receives a child benefit of €2,000 as an entitlement from the government for her child. Her endowment would be the following list:

- ability to work 1,750 hours of labour per annum as a medical technician
- the right to a child benefit to assist in caring for her child

She has been able to secure only half-time work (875 hours) so the annual income she derived from all sources is: (875 hours × €30) + (1 child grant × €2,000) = €26,250.

Now consider Kamal, who recently inherited a sum from his late father sufficient to start a small business. He was previously working as the manager of a similar small firm for €120,000 per year. Kamal's endowment is:

- ability to work full time using skills and experience as a manager
- ownership of the buildings, equipment, and other assets of his firm, worth €8 million

If he did not manage the firm himself, he would have to hire a full time manager with similar skills and experience, costing him €120,000. Last year, his firm's (accounting) profit was €600,000 without counting Kamal's

endowment The facts about an individual that may affect his or her income, such as the physical wealth a person has, either land, housing, or a portfolio of shares (stocks). Also includes level and quality of schooling, special training, the computer languages in which the individual can work, work experience in internships, citizenship, whether the individual has a visa (or green card) allowing employment in a particular labour market, the nationality and gender of the individual, and even the person's race or social class background. *See also: human capital.*

human capital The stock of knowledge, skills, behavioural attributes, and personal characteristics that determine the labour productivity or labour earnings of an individual. Investment in this through education, training, and socialization can increase the stock, and such investment is one of the sources of economic growth. Part of an individual's endowments. *See also: endowment.*

own efforts as a manager, worth €120,000 a year. So his income is the €600,000 in profit, which we divide into the returns to his managerial efforts (€120,000) and the returns to the ownership of assets (€480,000).

By studying why people have differing endowments, and what determines the income associated with each of the endowments, we can understand income inequality.

The factors influencing individual income can be understood using the model of cause-and-effect relationships in Figure 19.16. The arrows point from a cause to an effect.

Both institutions and technologies are part of the explanation of differing endowments among individuals. Inherited wealth gave Kamal a valuable asset, while subsidized higher education helped Ella qualify as a medical technician. Both are examples of the effect of institutions on endowments.

We have seen that intergenerational inequality will be greater where inheritances are not heavily taxed and where educational policies allow the wealthy to acquire more and better education for their children. If marriage customs result in spouses having similar levels of wealth—called 'positive assortment'—this will contribute to inequalities in endowments. Elite private universities, for example, contribute to positive assortment because like exclusive social clubs, they provide meeting and matching opportunities for the sons and daughters of the wealthy. These are also examples of institutions influencing differences in endowments.

Technology matters, too. Where there are strong economies of scale such as in the technology of digital platforms, these will support the winner-take-all forms of competition that we explain in Unit 21. In this setting, a few people—the winners—will end up with substantial endowments in the form of valuable financial or real assets, while the rest end up with little.

The value of a particular endowment, say a programming skill or ownership of a 3D printer, depends on both technology and institutions, as well as on other factors, including supply and demand. The demand for Ella's skill was limited, perhaps due to cuts in health care spending, so she was unable to work full time. Next year Kamal's firm may face competition from a new

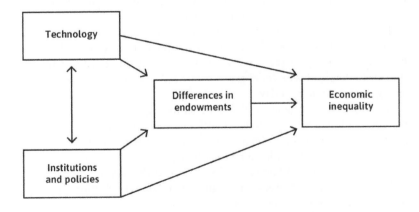

Figure 19.16 The causal relationships between technology, institutions and policies, endowments, and inequality.

competitor, making the 7.5% rate of return ($600,000/$8,000,000) that he made this year impossible. Both are examples of how institutions affect the income provided by an asset.

Technology matters, too. Being physically strong was a valuable endowment in agriculture—at least until mechanization made it less important in determining earnings. In that case a change in technology (mechanization) reduced the demand for a particular kind of skill, and so its value (relative to other skills) fell. The value of land, for example, will depend on how productive it is in growing marketable crops (technology) and whether it is zoned for commercial or residential uses (institutions).

Using the model to review inequality from previous units

In previous units, we studied how differences in endowments determined economic outcomes, including inequality. Figure 19.17 summarizes these situations, starting with the interaction in Unit 5 between Bruno, the landlord, and Angela, the farmer he employed.

Recall that how much Bruno got and the inequality between them depended on:

- *Their endowments*: The fact that Bruno owned the land meant he could exclude Angela from working on it
- *Angela's productivity as a worker*: This is determined by Angela's endowment of skills and capacities, as well as the available technology.
- *Angela's reservation option*: What Angela would get if she were to refuse to work for Bruno or he refused to hire her. This is an important influence on her bargaining power in her dealings with Bruno. It is determined by her endowments and the institutions or policies in place.

The endowments of the pairs of individuals in Figure 19.17 appear in the second column of the figure. In the first example, Bruno owns the land and Angela only owns her time and capacity to work. This inequality in land ownership matters because it determines who has to work for whom, and who can earn income from allowing others to work with their capital goods or their land.

Endowments matter in another way, because they change Angela's reservation option. If Angela owned land that she could work herself, then Bruno would need to pay her at least enough to ensure that she would rather work for him than work on her own land.

Recall that a change in institutions and policies can change Angela's reservation option. Before the rule of law, the institutions were such that Bruno could simply coerce her to work, and the only thing that constrained the size of the surplus he could get was the need to keep Angela healthy enough to work the next day.

The institutional change, which gave her the right to say no, improved this reservation option. Bruno had to offer Angela a deal that would make her better off working for him than not working. Angela's new 'right to say no' raised the value of her labour endowment.

In the last column of Figure 19.17 we consider the way that changes in technology affect the degree of inequality. In the row concerning the firm's owners and employees, a labour-saving technology, as we saw in Unit 16, can—at least initially—reduce the number of workers a firm needs, making employees more vulnerable to job loss and reducing the likelihood of getting another job at the same wage for those who have been fired.

Situation, actors and unit	Endowment	Reservation option	Conflict over?	Institutions and policies (examples)	Technology (examples)
Landlord and farmer: Bruno and Angela (Unit 5)	Bruno owns the land; Angela has 24 hours of potential labour	Bruno: rent land to another farmer; Angela: government support	Rent paid by Angela to Bruno and the hours that Angela works	Angela's reservation option (which depends on whether slavery is legal) and legislation limiting work hours.	Angela's increased productivity due to an improvement in seeds allows Bruno a larger surplus when he has all the bargaining power.
Borrowing, lending and investment: Julia and Marco (Unit 10)	Julia: $100 next year; Marco: $100 now	Julia: consume nothing now, $100 later; Marco: consume some now, store and consume some later	Julia benefits from a low interest rate and Marco benefits from a high interest rate.	Competition among lenders and interest rate regulation	An improvement in storage technology (for example less loss of grain to the mice) makes it easier for Marco to move his goods forward in time, and also raises the rate of return on his investments.
Specialization and trade: Greta and Carlos (Unit 18)	The skills and resources of each that determine their feasible consumption set in the absence of specialization and trade	Both: the utility they would enjoy if they did the best possible without trading	Price at which they exchange the good in which they specialize when they trade	Price-setting power by either Greta or Carlos	An improvement in the technology of the good in which one specializes will benefit both, the larger gains going to the person with price-setting power.
Firm: owners and employees (Unit 6)	Owner: ownership of the firm; Employee: capacity to work given her skills	Owner: hire some other employee; Employee: unemployment insurance and job search	Wage, working conditions, effort on the job	Level of unemployment insurance, employment level, and legislation regulating work conditions	A new technology may increase the productivity of the employee's effort, increasing the employer's profits (short run) and increasing employment and the real wage (long run). It may also affect how easily the employer can monitor the employee's effort.
Banana plantation: owners and downstream fishing communities (Unit 12)	Owners: the land and other capital goods of the plantation; Fishing communities: their boats and capacity to catch fish, access to fisheries	Owners: raise bananas without using Weevokil pesticide; Fishing communities: convert to farming	Use of polluting chemical, possible compensation for destruction of fisheries or commitment not to use Weevokil	Regulations governing the use of pollutants and enforcement of private agreements made between the parties	A new pesticide technology could reduce or increase the conflict between the two groups depending on its external effects.

Figure 19.17 Inequality: Endowments, reservation options, conflicts, institutions, and technologies.

Like technology, institutions and policies affect the value of endowments. In the example of Ella, the medical technician, her specialized skills are part of her endowment but their paid value (€30 per hour in the example) will depend on institutions. If gender discrimination is a common practice of employers, then her skills might be worth less. If a license is required to do this work, then the value of her skills will be greater if she is licensed. These are examples of institutions and policies affecting the value of endowments.

The credit market in Unit 10 is another example. Recall that Julia's endowment is $100 next year. What she can consume now depends on her wealth (what is in the bathtub), and that depends on the institutions and policies determining whether she can borrow, and the interest rate at which she can borrow.

If her only option is the village moneylender in Chambar or a payday lender in New York, she faces a high interest rate and her wealth (now) is much lower than $100. If she can borrow at a low interest rate, her wealth is quite close to $100. If she can't borrow at all, then there is nothing in the bathtub and her wealth now is zero.

How endowments, technology, institutions, and inequality interact over time

Endowments and the income that they provide are constantly changing as people acquire more skills or as the value of some endowment—such as a piece of land or a rental apartment—falls. Figure 19.16 illustrated the causes of economic inequality. In Figure 19.18, we illustrate inequality as a cause of changes in institutions, technology, and differences in endowments.

The arrow from economic inequality to differences in endowments in the next period captures the fact that the children of richer parents may end up with more and higher quality education, or with greater inherited wealth.

Economic inequality may also influence institutions and policies. An example we shall see in Unit 22 is that in most countries—even democracies—a wealthy person typically has more influence on what the government does than does a poor person. A greater gap between the rich and the poor could increase the political advantage of the wealthy, resulting in policies favouring those with higher incomes.

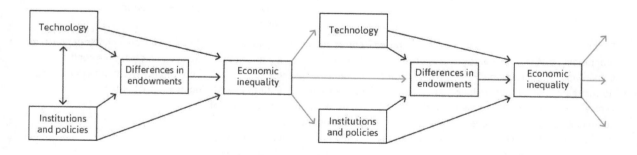

Figure 19.18 Economic inequality over time. The red arrows show that economic inequality in one period has effects on technologies, institutions and policies, and differences in endowments in the future.

> **EXERCISE 19.7 YICHEN, RENFU, MARK, AND STEPHANIE**
> Consider the economic situation of Yichen, Renfu, Mark, and Stephanie, discussed at the start of this unit. Give examples of how technology, institutions, and differences in endowments explain economic inequality between these actors, and how inequality between them could change over time.

19.6 INEQUALITY, ENDOWMENTS, AND PRINCIPAL-AGENT RELATIONSHIPS

Recall that the labour and credit market models in Units 9 and 10 provided the background for our macroeconomic models of the functioning of the whole economy and for the study of how shocks and policies affect economy-wide employment, incomes, and inflation. We used the Lorenz curve to summarize the effects on inequality. And in explaining the model of inequality in Figure 19.16, we used examples from the labour and credit markets.

The **principal-agent models** also give us a new way to study an important dimension of inequality: differences in power affect the type of choices that a person may feasibly make. Principals are in a position to exercise power over agents, but agents rarely can exercise power over principals. Here is why.

The employer (the owner or the manager who is the principal in the labour market) has the power to determine what the firm will produce, using what technology, and in which country to locate production. They also have the power to set the wage and the tasks that a worker is directed to perform, and can also fire the worker. The worker chooses how to go about her work within limits that the employer sets.

Recall that in order to motivate the worker to work hard and well, the employer sets a wage so that the employee is better off with the job than she would be without it, receiving an economic rent. The employer can fire the worker and deprive her of the employment rent she would otherwise receive. The fear of losing this rent is an important reason for the worker to carry out the employer's wishes. It is also the reason why the employer has power over the employee.

The worker could, of course, quit. But this does not make the relationship equal when it comes to power. If she is receiving an economic rent she would penalize herself by quitting, and her employer would just replace her with someone currently unemployed.

We can contrast this with the relationships among price-taking buyers and sellers at the equilibrium of a competitive market. None of these traders is in a position to demand that any other trader act in one way or another. Think about the buyer, for example, who orders the seller to make the good available at a lower price, threatening not to buy otherwise. What would the seller do? Nothing. The seller can sell as much as she wishes at the going price (remember, the demand curve facing an individual firm is flat).

A second contrast is with the interactions we studied in Unit 4 where the actions open to all parties were identical—for example, either use integrated pest management or chemical fertilizers, either learn C++ or Java.

Like the relationship between the employer and employee, the other principal-agent models we have seen reflect the unequal relationships between groups of people with differing endowments, such as landlords and tenant farmers, and borrowers and lenders.

principal-agent relationship This relationship exists when one party (the principal) would like another party (the agent) to act in some way, or have some attribute that is in the interest of the principal, and that cannot be enforced or guaranteed in a binding contract. See also: incomplete contract. Also known as: principal-agent problem.

Figure 19.19 illustrates how the credit and labour markets influence the relationships among the groups of lenders and borrowers, and employers and employees.

Starting at the upper left of the figure, wealthy individuals can use their wealth to purchase the capital goods to become employers and they can also lend to others. Among the less wealthy, there will be some successful borrowers who can as a result also become employers. Those with even less wealth cannot borrow (they are the credit market excluded that you studied in Unit 10, or can only borrow where the house provides the collateral for the mortgage), and must seek work as employees. Employers then hire employees from among the less wealthy, with some remaining unemployed (due to the workings of the labour market that you studied in Units 6, 9, and 15).

Horizontal arrows indicate a principal-agent relationship. Lenders and employers are the principals in the figure; their common red colour indicates this similarity. Agents—successful borrowers, and employees—are coloured green to distinguish them from would-be agents (credit market excluded and unemployed) who are coloured purple. You definitely do not want to be in the purple boxes. But even if you are an agent lucky enough to be in one of the green boxes, the principal can put you back in the purple box just by refusing to deal with you. This is why lenders and employers have power over borrowers and employees.

Figure 19.19 helps us understand why some people end up as principals (employers, for example) while others end up as agents (employees). If one is wealthy, one can be both a lender and an employer. There is some truth to the saying that 'people are born into their position in the economic order'. This was literally true in some economies of the past. For example, the

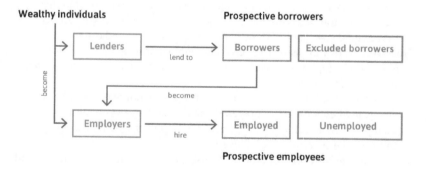

Figure 19.19 The credit and labour markets shape the relationships between groups with different endowments.

1. A model economy
Consider an economy with wealthy individuals and employees.

2. Credit market excluded
Those without wealth (collateral) or insufficient wealth are excluded from the credit market.

3. Wealthy individuals and successful borrowers
These people can purchase capital goods so as to become employers.

4. Those who are not wealthy
These are employees or unemployed.

5. Employers hire employees on the labour market
This excludes the unemployed.

position of the slave was perpetuated by the enslavement of their children as a matter of law.

Something similar can occur in places where wealth is inherited from parent to child. The children of employees (who inherit little wealth) are also more likely to become the next generation's workers than are the children of employers. You already saw that the children of well off parents in the US also tend to have high incomes when they become adults (Figure 19.10).

But look again at that figure: there is some mobility among the income groups even in the US and there is very little intergenerational inequality in Denmark. Becoming an employer requires that one has sufficient wealth. But inheriting wealth from a parent is not the only way, and in some countries not even the most important way to acquire wealth. The wealth necessary to become an employer may be acquired by saving. It may also be acquired by developing a great project and persuading investors called 'venture capitalists' to fund it.

We have also seen in Units 13 and 16 that there are transitions by individuals between boxes over their life-time. A younger person may initially be a borrower and then be a lender later in life; a spell of unemployment can be followed by one of employment.

QUESTION 19.6 CHOOSE THE CORRECT ANSWER(S)
Which of the following statements are correct?

☐ Endowments are facts about an individual that may affect his or her income.
☐ Having or not having a degree does not constitute a difference in endowments if it is a matter of individual choice.
☐ All individuals have the same reservation option irrespective of their endowments.
☐ A visa (permission to work for a non-citizen) is not an element of an individual's endowment because it cannot be sold.

19.7 PUTTING THE MODEL TO WORK: EXPLAINING CHANGES IN INEQUALITY

The model presented in the previous section helps us to understand why individuals have different incomes. To understand inequality, however, we need to consider the changes across the entire income distribution. In this section, we will apply the labour market model from Unit 9, in combination with our understanding of the determinants of individuals' income, to look at the effect on inequality of:

- an increase in the educational level of the workforce
- a reduction in discrimination against a segment of the workforce
- automation of production reducing the demand for some skills and increasing others

You may wish to review the workings of the labour market model described in Unit 9 before proceeding.

A more educated and more productive workforce

What will be the consequences if workers have acquired more schooling? We expect additional schooling to increase productivity, meaning that a unit of effort by a more educated worker produces more goods per hour using the same technology. The direct effect of additional schooling on an individual is therefore to improve their endowment of labour. Holding everything else equal, the increased productivity means that any individual can get paid a higher wage for their labour.

However, what if the entire workforce becomes more educated? This could be the result, for instance, of an increase in the compulsory schooling age. At the pre-existing real wage, the result of higher productivity will be a higher profit for the firms. This shifts the price-setting curve upwards, as shown in the left panel of Figure 19.20. With higher profits, new firms enter and existing firms hire additional workers, which reduces the unemployment rate. Lower unemployment in turn makes it easier for a dismissed worker to find a new job. It therefore increases the workers' reservation position, raising the wage. Workers both possess a better, higher-productivity endowment of labour time and enjoy better prices for their endowment.

The effects on inequality are shown in the right panel of Figure 19.20. There are now fewer unemployed workers. The segment of the Lorenz curve representing employed workers is now flatter because even though the real wage has risen, a larger fraction of the work force (85% instead of 80%) receives the same 60% of the (now increased) total output.

The line segment for the owners is unaffected because the same 10% of the population continue to receive 40% of the output; like the wages of workers, their profits are up because more is being produced. In this example, the effect of the increased education and productivity of the workforce on inequality is to reduce the Gini coefficient from 0.36 to 0.33.

A reduction in labour market segmentation

Until now we have assumed that all workers receive the same wage in a single labour market, but in reality there are many distinct labour markets. In what is termed the **primary labour market**, workers may be represented by trade unions, and enjoy high wages and job security. 'Job ladders' allow promotion to better paying and more secure jobs. Primary labour market jobs are frequently referred to as 'good jobs'.

Workers in the secondary labour market are on short-term contracts with limited wages and job security, and tend to be young or from popula-tions discriminated against by race or ethnic group. In many European countries, these are called 'zero-hours contracts' because the employer does not commit to providing work for any particular number of hours. The **secondary labour market** is also referred to as the 'gig economy' in which freelance work or very short-term contracts are the norm, rather than permanent jobs. For any given endowment of skills, these workers will usually receive a lower income than the workers in the primary labour market. Institutions therefore benefit the workers in the primary labour market and disadvantage workers in the secondary market, increasing income inequality.

Figure 19.21 shows a Lorenz curve for an economy with **labour market segmentation**, with a low-wage segment and an equal number of high-wage primary segment workers. The owners are not segmented because they can easily invest their wealth in firms in either or both sectors and, as a consequence, the rate of return will be the same in both sectors. The elimination of labour market segmentation means that all workers receive the same wage, but unless this affects the relative bargaining power of workers and owners, it does not alter the share of the output going to workers as a whole. This demonstrates how institutional change can reduce inequality by aligning the wages individuals receive for their endowments.

The figure illustrates the fact that much of the inequality in modern economies is among employees (from secondary labour market workers to very highly paid professionals), and that reducing these inequalities can significantly reduce the Gini coefficient. Where trade unions have reduced labour market segmentation and narrowed the wage differentials among workers, inequality is lower. An example is the so-called solidarity wage policy introduced in Sweden, which we will discuss in Unit 22.

> **segmented labour market** A labour market whose distinct segments function as separate labour markets with limited mobility of workers from one segment to the other (including for reasons of racial, language, or other forms of discrimination). *See also: primary labour market, secondary labour market.*

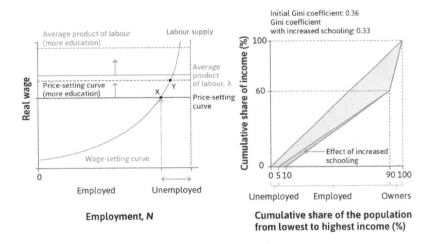

Figure 19.20 The effect of a more educated workforce on inequality among employers, employees, and the unemployed: The economy-wide labour market and the Lorenz curve.

1. Our model economy
Consider how the economy described in the left panel, with its initial equilibrium at point X, changes when workers (both employed and unemployed) get more education.

2. Worker productivity rises, shifting up the price-setting curve
The wage consistent with the price-setting firm's profit maximizing markup is now higher.

3. Firms enter
In response to higher profits, production expands, which reduces the unemployment rate. Since this increases the reservation position of employees, it induces firms to set a higher wage. The new labour market equilibrium is at Y.

4. Inequality falls
The Lorenz curve shifts up, as fewer workers are unemployed. The percentage division of output between workers and owners remains unchanged.

Automation

> **automation** The use of machines that are substitutes for labour.

Automation is a term used to describe new technologies that allow machines to do the work that people used to do. Technological innovations that replace labour have been an essential part of the capitalist economy since the introduction of the spinning jenny in the eighteenth century, which we described in Unit 2. As we saw in Unit 16, new technologies typically put some people out of work, while increasing the demand for the

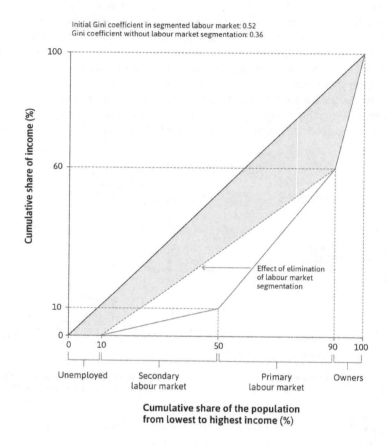

Figure 19.21 The effect of labour market segmentation.

1. A model economy with labour market segmentation
Forty workers in the secondary labour segment of the market receive just 10% of the economy's output; the 40 workers in the primary labour market receive half of the output (they are paid five times as much as the secondary workers). The 10 owners receive 40% of the output (they are paid 16 times as much as the secondary workers).

2. Elimination of labour market segmentation
All 80 workers now receive the same pay, and as a whole receive 60% of the output of the economy. The secondary workers' wages have risen, while the primary sector workers' wages have fallen.

3. Effect on inequality
The Gini coefficient, which had been 0.52 under labour market segmentation, has fallen to 0.36.

skills of other workers. We can study these effects using the Lorenz curve and the Gini coefficient derived from it.

To see how, consider a hypothetical economy in Figure 19.22, before and after it introduces machines that perform routine operations that had always been done by humans. We'll call these machines 'robots'. The solid blue Lorenz curve depicts the distribution of income between five employers and 95 workers before the introduction of the robots. Five of the workers are unemployed, and among the 90 who are employed, all receive the same wage, whether they do routine or non-routine work.

The slope of the flatter of the two upward-sloping lines is an indication of how much workers are paid relative to their productivity. We see that the 90 employed workers receive 60% of the income of the economy. So each receives 0.60/90 or two-thirds of a per cent of what the economy produces. The slope of the steeper solid line shows that five owners receive 40% of the income, so that each receives 8% (= 0.40/5) of the output of the entire economy.

To understand the short-run impact of the plan to introduce robots, think about the skill endowments of the workers. Sixty of them are doing routine jobs that were once relatively well paid, such as machine tending or mail sorting, that can now be done by robots. Others have the training to not just operate machinery, but to design, repair, and calibrate machinery, and manage its deployment.

The short-run effects depend on the kinds of work a worker does:

- *The robots are labour-replacing*: For routine jobs in which the machines and skills are substitutes, the value of a worker's endowment is reduced by the new technology because the robot can replace the worker.
- *The robots are labour-enhancing*: For those jobs in which the machines and skills are complements, the value of a worker's endowment is increased by the new technology.

These two effects are shown in the new (dashed) Lorenz curve depicting the short-run effects of the new technology on workers who previously earned two-thirds of a per cent of output each. At least some of the 60 workers for whom the robots are labour-replacing lose their job. Five of them have now joined the unemployed; the machines have replaced their labour. Those who remain employed have suffered a fall in their bargaining power (because they too can be replaced). These 55 workers now receive 25% of the output of the economy, and their earnings fall to 0.5% of the total output each.

On the other hand, the 30 workers with skills that are complementary to the robots have gained. They now receive 35% of the output of the economy, or a little more than 1% each.

The effect of automation thus can be similar to the effect of labour market segmentation, but in the case of robots, the segregation of workers depends on whether their skills are easily substituted by machines (the losers) or instead are complementary to the machines (the gainers).

The result is that the Gini coefficient increases from 0.38 to 0.53, shown by the new Lorenz curve falling further below the perfect equality line.

An example of the effect of automation is the introduction of automatic teller machines (ATMs) by banks. Surely this would have increased unemployment among human bank tellers?

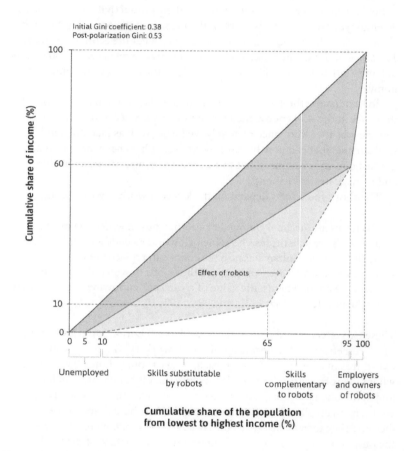

Initial Gini coefficient: 0.38
Post-polarization Gini: 0.53

Figure 19.22 The effect of robots on inequality: polarization of the labour market.

1. The Lorenz curve before the introduction of the robots
The solid blue Lorenz curve shows the distribution of income among the unemployed, employees, and owners. All workers, whether doing routine or non-routine work, earn the same wage.

2. The introduction of robots replaces and cheapens routine labour
After the introduction of robots, 5 more workers—those who were doing routine work that robots now can do—become unemployed. The remaining 55 routine workers now receive just 10% of the economy's output.

3. The robots make some workers' labour more valuable
Thirty of the employees have skills complementary to the machines. They earn higher wages.

4. The effect of the robots on inequality
The introduction of robots polarizes the labour market and increases the Gini coefficient.

James Bessen, an economist, looked at the employment levels in the US and found that the number of bank tellers continued to rise even after the machines were installed. Rather than doing mechanical tasks, they were now providing other services such as advice to customers.

Bessen also found employment increased among bookkeepers and retail sales staff despite automation of some of their tasks, but on the other hand, technology did displace the jobs of travel agents. Automation was complementary to the skills of some bookkeepers and bank tellers, but it was a substitute for the skills of travel agents.

What determines whether automation increases or decreases wages and employment? We can use an analysis similar to the one we did in Unit 16. There are two contradictory effects.

On one hand:

- *Labour-replacing automation reduces the demand for some types of labour*: this sends workers into unemployment.
- *This reduces the reservation option of all workers*: It lowers the wage that firms have to set to maintain their desired level of work effort.

On the other hand:

- *The increase in labour productivity increases profits.*
- *This motivates and finances an expansion of the capital stock of the economy.*
- *The increase in capital stock creates additional employment opportunities*: It reduces unemployment and increases the wage required to motivate workers along the wage-setting curve.

As we saw in Unit 16, adjustment of local labour markets to labour-saving technology and competition from imports may take a very long time.

The model cannot determine whether the new Nash equilibrium in the labour market will result in a more equal distribution of income or a less equal one. Inequality among workers will be greater due to the fact that the robots created winners and losers among employees, by raising the value of some labour endowments (the engineers) and lowering the value of the labour endowments of others (the routine workers). If the level of unemployment goes back down to its pre-automation level, and if the firm's markup on costs is unaffected, then the only durable effect will be greater inequality among workers, resulting in an increase in the Gini coefficient.

A government observing the process of automation might respond with levying taxes on the enhanced profits of the owners and on the incomes of the workers with increased wages. In designing the taxes, it would need to take into account their effect on the behaviour of workers and employers. The revenue from these taxes can be used to finance:

- *Additional employment and opportunities for career progression and rising wages*: These opportunities could be in human services such as health and care, where jobs are non-routine but often poorly paid.
- *Opportunities for workers with routine skills to upgrade their endowments*: Their labour becomes machine-enhanced rather than machine-replaceable; for example, a former drill press operator learning how to code.

James Bessen. 2015. *Learning by Doing: The Real Connection between Innovation, Wages, and Wealth*. New Haven, CT: Yale University Press.

Diane Coyle. 2015. 'Thinking, Learning and Doing' (http://tinyco.re/6552078). *Enlightenment Economics Blog*. Updated 23 October 2015.

Listen to James Bessen talk about his book in a May 2016 episode of the EconTalk podcast (http://tinyco.re/6669867).

> **EXERCISE 19.8 HOW AUTOMATION AFFECTS EMPLOYMENT**
> Return to Figures 19.6 (page 853) and 19.7 (page 853). Use what you have learned in this section about robots as substitutes or complements to employees' endowments to explain some of the patterns in job growth shown in these figures.

> **QUESTION 19.7 CHOOSE THE CORRECT ANSWER(S)**
> Which of the following statements regarding segmented labour markets are correct?
>
> ☐ The 'gig economy' is not part of the primary labour market.
> ☐ Workers in the secondary labour market are better paid than those in the primary labour market.
> ☐ Trade unions have attempted to reduce hours of work by introducing zero hours contracts.
> ☐ Primary labour market jobs are concentrated in agriculture.

19.8 PREDISTRIBUTION

Governments influence the degree of inequality in the economy. They do this in two ways:

- **Redistribution**: By taxes and transfers that result in a distribution of disposable income that differs from the distribution of market income (as we saw in Figure 19.1) and by expenditure that provides public services to households.
- **Predistribution**: By affecting the endowments that people have and the value of those endowments, leading to a change in the inequality in market income (going back to Figure 19.1 again, here governments affect the distribution of earnings before taxes and transfers or the distribution of privately held wealth).

Examples of predistribution that you have already seen include:

- *Increased education of the workforce*: This changes the endowments of employees, adding skills and other work relevant capacities that will affect market incomes.
- *Eliminating or reducing labour market segmentation*: This—and other anti-discrimination policies—will alter the prices (wages) that a person's endowment will be paid in the labour market. In particular, it raises the value of the endowments of people who otherwise would suffer discrimination.

Other aspects of predistribution affect the basic institutional structure of the economy. By defining and enforcing the legal framework in which the employers, banks, employees, unions, borrowers, and other key economic actors interact, governments affect the distribution of market income. Using the legal system, governments can also alter which property rights are protected, for example banning slavery, legalizing unions (Units 9 and 16), establishing trading rights in emissions (Unit 18), or setting the duration of intellectual property rights and patents (Unit 21). All of these

redistribution policy Taxes, monetary, and in-kind transfers of the government that result in a distribution of final income that differs from the distribution of market income. *See also: predistribution policy.*

predistribution policy Government actions that affect the endowments people have and their value, including the distribution of market income and the distribution of privately held wealth. Examples include education, minimum wage, and anti-discrimination policies. *See also: redistribution policy.*

statutory minimum wage A minimum level of pay laid down by law, for workers in general or of some specified type. The intention of a minimum wage is to guarantee living standards for the low-paid. Many countries, including the UK and the US, enforce this with legislation. *Also known as: minimum wage.*

measures can change the relative bargaining power between groups as well as their reservation options, which in turn will change the distribution of income.

Finally, governments can change the set of contracts that are allowed, which alters the distribution of income. We discussed one example in Unit 5, when we saw the effect of legislation that limited the maximum hours that employees could work.

Another important example of predistribution by limiting the kinds of contracts that are allowed is a **statutory minimum wage**, which prohibits contracts with wages below a certain level. This affects the value of a worker's endowment of labour, but it may also affect the likelihood that the worker will be able to find a job. The costs of the minimum wage could be fewer jobs.

Arin Dube, an economist, studied differential changes in minimum wages in bordering local areas in the US. In our 'Economist in action' video he explains that he found that raising the minimum wage had a little negative impact on employment but increased the income of poor workers on average.

Ensuring high-quality early childhood education is another predistribution policy. In our 'Economist in action' video, James Heckman, a Nobel-prize-winning economist from the University of Chicago, shows how economists can learn from experiments and other data about how to level the playing field for children growing up poor.

Figure 19.23 lists a set of policies that can reduce inequality in market incomes, drawn from this and other units.

Arin Dube describes his study that found that, on average, raising the minimum wage increased the income of poor workers.
http://tinyco.re/3737648

Arindrajit Dube, T. William Lester, and Michael Reich. 2010. 'Minimum Wage Effects across State Borders: Estimates Using Contiguous Counties' (http://tinyco.re/5393066). *Review of Economics and Statistics* 92 (4): pp. 945–64.

James Heckman describes why investing in the early years of disadvantaged children's lives is both fair and efficient.
http://tinyco.re/3964341

James J. Heckman. 2013. *Giving Kids a Fair Chance*. Cambridge, MA: MIT Press.

EXERCISE 19.9 NON-COMPETE CONTRACTS IN THE LABOUR MARKET MODEL

Legislation can rule out particular kinds of contracts, such as those that prohibit employees from leaving their firm to work for a competitor. The justification offered for these **non-compete contracts** is that workers leaving a firm may take with them industrial or trade secrets that would benefit the competition. But in the US, non-compete clauses are even included in contracts of fast-food workers. Use the labour market model to explain why employers would introduce non-compete contracts in sectors where industrial secrets are not an issue.

non-compete contract A contract of employment containing a provision or agreement by which the worker cannot leave to work for a competitor. This may reduce the reservation option of the worker, lowering the wage that the employer needs to pay.

QUESTION 19.8 CHOOSE THE CORRECT ANSWER(S)

According to our 'Economist in action' video of Arin Dube, which of the following was a finding of his study of the minimum wage increase?

☐ Increasing the minimum wage increased worker turnover.
☐ A 10% increase in minimum wage resulted in a 4% increase in earnings.
☐ A 10% increase in minimum wage resulted in a 4% decrease in employment.
☐ There was a minimal negative effect on employment.

Endowment	Policy	Direct effect	Indirect effect	Unit
Labour	Free high-quality primary education for all children	Increases opportunities for poorer children to attain more advanced levels of schooling, which increases the market value of their endowment of labour	Raises average productivity of labour, shifting up price-setting curve, which increases wages and employment (*ceteris paribus*)	U19
Labour	Raise the share of the harvest going to the farmer	Increases the value of the farmer's endowment of labour	Raises farmers' incomes	U5
Labour	Eliminate ethnic, racial, or gender discrimination	Increases the value of the labour endowment of those targeted by discrimination	Raises incomes of targeted groups	U19
Labour	Minimum wage	Increases value of labour endowments among those who were previously unable to work for more than the minimum wage	Raises incomes of the poor and reduces incomes of employers (unless employment effects dominate)	U19
Labour	Laws and policies to increase workers' bargaining power (for example trade unions)	Increases value of labour endowments of trade union members and improves working conditions	Raises incomes of trade union members (unless negative employment or productivity effects dominate) and reduces incomes of employers	U9, U16, U19
Ownership of firms	Policies to ensure competition	Reduces price markup	Raises real wages, reduces profits	U7, U9, U16
Intellectual property	Restrict IPRs (for example shorter patents or copyrights)	Reduces value of endowment of intellectual property among IPR holders.	May discourage innovation but enables quicker diffusion of innovations	U21
Professional license	Allow easier access to licenses (for example for taxis)	Increases supply and reduces incomes of license holders.	Greater equality (if license holders are richer than average)	U19

Figure 19.23 Predistribution policies that can reduce inequality in market incomes.

19.9 EXPLAINING RECENT TRENDS IN INEQUALITY IN MARKET INCOME

Can these policies or other changes help explain the trends in market income inequality? Figure 19.24 indicates three of these trends and suggests possible explanations based on the models you have learned.

To explain the reduction in between-country inequality (and the associated reduction in between-household inequality) in the world, think of the world as a single capitalist economy with a labour market that is segmented along national lines. To do this, we propose a very simple economy of the 'world' with just two 'countries': China and Europe-and-North-America. So instead of two labour market segments in the same country, there are two countries, a low-wage country and a high-wage country, a little like China and the US in Unit 18.

Just as it is not easy for workers to move up from the secondary to the primary labour market within a country, the global economy has nationally segmented labour markets because of the barriers facing workers who would like to relocate from one country to the other. And, just as in the national economy, owners are not segmented. They invest their wealth wherever it will get the highest return. As we saw in Unit 18, globalization is only partial: the world labour market is far from integrated while capital mobility is high, because money does not need a green card or a work visa to be allowed to 'work' in a country.

The process of globalization has been associated with a reduction in global labour market inequality, as the once-low wages in successful exporter countries like China begin to catch up with wages in the higher-wage economies like France. A second effect has been a vast increase in the amount of labour that is now available for employment in the global capitalist economy, and this has been associated with an increase in the share of income going to owners of firms rather than employees.

Trends	Data	Contributing causes	Models
Declining within-country inequality (1920–1980)	Figures 19.2, 19.3, 19.4	Increasing education and productivity reduced unemployment. Reduced labour market segmentation and other sources of inequality among workers. Technological improvements that were complementary to low and middle-skill workers.	Figure 19.20, Figure 19.21
Stable or rising within-country inequality (1980–2017)	Figures 19.2, 19.3, 19.4, 19.6, 17.3 (upper panel)	Increased inequality among workers due to new technologies that were complementary to the skills of higher paid workers, and substitutes for workers doing routine tasks. Weaker trade unions and conservative political parties in power saw bargaining power shift in favour of employers, whilst the resulting higher profits after taxes were not translated into expanding employment (in some countries).	Figure 19.22
Stable or decreasing between-country inequality (1995–2017)	Figure 19.5	Reduced global labour market segmentation due to rapid growth of labour productivity and demand in China and other poorer countries.	Figure 19.24

Figure 19.24 Using economic models to explain trends in inequality in market income.

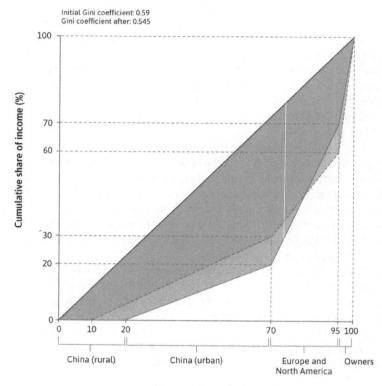

Initial Gini coefficient: 0.59
Gini coefficient after: 0.545

Cumulative share of the world's income recipients (%)

China (rural)   China (urban)   Europe and   Owners
North America

Figure 19.25 The 'world' as a unified capitalist economy with a segmented labour market.

The red segment shows the impact of globalization increasing inequality by reducing wages in the rich countries relative to their employers while the green part shows the effects of greater incomes among poor employees in 'China'.

1. The world before China took off
Much of the hypothetical Chinese economy is initially rural and not directly engaged in the capitalist economy. The Chinese urban labour force—half of the hypothetical world's total labour force—receives just 20% of the world's income. The European and North American labour force—half the size of China's—receives twice as much. The world Gini coefficient is 0.59.

2. China takes off
The rural sector in China has shrunk to 10%, increasing China's share of the labour force engaged in the global capitalist economy, which now receives the same share of world income as the European and North American workers (30% each).

3. A new labour-abundant and more equal world with winners and losers
Red shading shows owners' share of world output increasing from 30% to 40% while Western workers lose income. But the dashed Lorenz curve and disappearing green-shaded portions show an increased income share for poorer workers. The world Gini falls from 0.59 to 0.545.

19.10 REDISTRIBUTION: TAXES AND TRANSFERS

Differences among economies in the extent and nature of redistribution

Our models of wages and profits try to explain market income. But that is not the amount of income that people have to spend, nor does it include things essential to our livelihoods that we do not purchase, but instead acquire as a matter of citizenship.

Disposable income, as you know, is the income a person has after paying any income taxes and social security contributions, and after receiving any government transfers. But this is not an adequate measure of a household's living standard because it does not include the effects of indirect taxes, such as value added tax, and the extent to which free or subsidized public services such as public education and health are available to households.

These public expenditures are called **in-kind transfers** because they are a transfer to households in the form of free or subsidized services, rather than in the form of cash. When we take into account both indirect taxes and in-kind transfers, we arrive at a third income concept, called final income. Final income is the most complete measure of the living standard of a household. It tells us the value of all the goods and services that the household is able to consume. Figure 19.26 summarizes the relationship between these three income concepts.

Figure 19.27 shows the Gini coefficients for market income, disposable income, and final income for three large middle-income countries. In South Africa, direct taxes and transfers reduce the Gini by 0.08, from 0.77 to 0.69. Indirect taxes and public services reduce the Gini by a further 0.09 to 0.60 for final income, but it remains exceptionally unequal. Brazil had much higher inequality than Mexico in both market income and disposable income, but the Gini coefficient for final income falls to almost the same level as Mexico's, at 0.44 compared to 0.43.

> **in-kind transfers** Public expenditure in the form of free or subsidized services for households rather than in the form of cash transfers.

The welfare state

The policies that turn market income into final income are often referred to as the **welfare state**. These policies can be broken down into the taxation side and the expenditure side. The taxation side is any policy that collects revenue for the government, while the expenditure side is any policy that either gives money to households, or spends money on their behalf. We will see more about the composition of government expenditures in Unit 22.

In countries where redistribution reduces inequality by a lot, most of this work is done by expenditures, rather than taxation.

In the 28 countries in the European Union, the average Gini in 2015 for market income is 0.46, which taxes and transfers reduce to 0.27 for disposable income. But taxes only achieve 0.04 of that redistribution, with the remaining 0.15 driven by transfers to households. This doesn't mean

> **welfare state** A set of government policies designed to provide improvements in the welfare of citizens by assisting with income smoothing (for example, unemployment benefits and pensions).

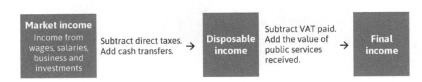

Figure 19.26 Different income concepts.

that they have low tax rates, but instead it means that rich and poor pay similar shares of their incomes in taxes. On the other hand, poorer households benefit proportionally much more from expenditures.

Transfers, both in cash and in kind, have a large impact on inequality. But in most cases this is not their purpose. Most transfers are justified for other reasons, and reducing inequality is just a desirable side effect. Public education, for instance, has many justifications, including as an investment in human capital that makes the country more productive. Public health subsidies are often justified on the basis of a basic human right to life and to good health.

The welfare state is often represented and debated as a system of redistribution from the rich to the poor. But it is equally seen, and often defended, as redistribution from the lucky to the unlucky. Parts of the welfare state also redistribute from the young to the old.

In countries with large welfare states, much of the expenditure is on forms of **social insurance**, which includes assistance to poor households, but also includes public pensions, unemployment benefits, social housing, child benefits, and other expenditures that are targeted at groups that are not defined by low income. Public pensions transfer income to the old. Child benefits, like expenditures on public education, transfer income to the young (or those who care for them). Since they are paid for by taxes contributed by working adults, they are a way for society to enable people to smooth incomes throughout their lifetimes. We receive income from the government when we are very young and very old, when our incomes are low or zero, and we pay some of it back to the government when we are of working age and receiving a salary.

Similarly, public unemployment insurance is a way for people of working age to smooth their incomes in the face of the risk of unemployment. We pay while we are working, and we receive payments if we are out of work.

These forms of social insurance are not targeted specifically at poor people. But they have a large impact on inequality because *most* retired people and unemployed people would be very poor if they did not receive social insurance payments. In fact, in the European Union, public pensions

Data on the Gini coefficient for the EU was taken from 'Effects of tax-benefit components on inequality (Gini index), 2011–2015 policies', which you can access on the Euromod statistics website (http://tinyco.re/7634364).

social insurance Expenditure by the government, financed by taxation, which provides protection against various economic risks (for example, loss of income due to sickness, or unemployment) and enables people to smooth incomes throughout their lifetime. *See also: co-insurance.*

Nora Lustig, Carola Pessino and John Scott (2014), 'The Impact of Taxes and Social Spending on Inequality and Poverty in Argentina, Bolivia, Brazil, Mexico, Peru, and Uruguay: Introduction to the Special Issue' (http://tinyco.re/7128629). *Public Finance Review* Vol. 42 (3): pp. 287–303; Gabriela Inchauste, Nora Lustig, Mashekwa Maboshe, Catriona Purfield and Ingrid Woolard. (2015). 'The Distributional Impact of Fiscal Policy in South Africa' (http://tinyco.re/2381815). Commitment to Equity Working Paper No. 29, February 2015.

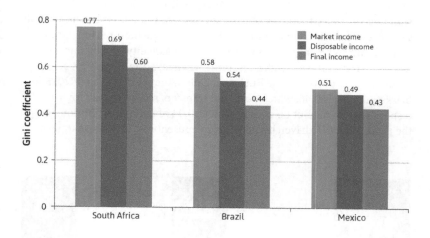

Figure 19.27 Gini coefficients for market income, disposable income, and final income.

are the policy with the greatest impact on inequality. They reduce the average Gini coefficient by 0.11, more than all other transfers combined.

Figure 19.28 shows the average household market income and disposable income in the UK in a single year, by age of the household's primary earner. Households whose primary earner is less than 25 years old have an average household market income of £24,108 and an average household disposable income of £24,735. The richest group of households is those whose primary earner is aged 40–44 years old, and incomes decline rapidly after 60–64 years, as primary earners tend to retire. Disposable income is higher than market income for the under-25s and the over-65s, when market income is at its lowest, and conversely for those aged 25–64, when household income is at its highest.

If we hypothetically imagine that there is one household at each age group, the Gini coefficient for market income would be 0.249 while for disposable income it would be 0.139—the tax and benefit system as a whole reduces inequality because it effectively redistributes from richer households to poorer households. But the figure demonstrates that much of this result could be due to redistribution from those of working age to the retired.

Progressive and regressive redistribution

When the direct effect of a tax or transfer policy (compared to what would happen in the absence of the policy) is a reduction in inequality, it is called **progressive**. We have just seen that expenditures are more progressive than taxes. If a policy's direct effect is a rise in inequality it is called **regressive**. Policies that are neither progressive nor regressive are called **distributionally neutral**.

For an expenditure or transfer to be progressive, it has to increase the incomes of poorer households by more than richer households, in percentage terms. This guarantees that it will reduce the Gini coefficient, and lead to a shift upwards in the Lorenz curve. Note that this

progressive (policy) An expenditure or transfer that increases the incomes of poorer households by more than richer households, in percentage terms. *See also: regressive (policy).*
regressive (policy) An expenditure or transfer that increases the incomes of richer households by more than poorer households, in percentage terms. *See also: progressive (policy).*
distributionally neutral A policy that is neither progressive or regressive so that it does not alter the distribution of income. *See also: progressive (policy), regressive (policy).*

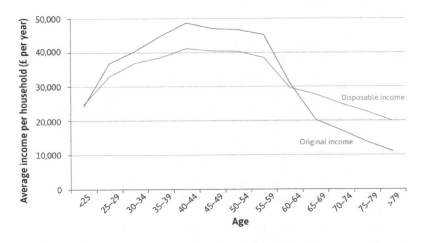

Effects of taxes and benefits on household income (http://tinyco.re/9228525). 2014/15. Office for National Statistics (UK).

Figure 19.28 Average household market and disposable income of households with primary earners in different age groups.

HOW ECONOMISTS LEARN FROM FACTS

What is the best way to give money to the poor? Randomize and find out.

Most countries adopt some policies to raise the living standards of the poor. But what is the best way to do this? If governments would like to transfer funds to individuals or families, should it go to the very poor, or only those who are working, or only those attempting to find work? Should the transfer be given to just the poor, or everyone?

The questions are controversial, and the answers will depend on more than economics. But economists have been using experiments to illuminate at least the costs and benefits of different mechanisms.

Economists have explored the effects of simply giving away cash to the poor, without requiring that they work or make any repayment. In theory, cash payments that one receives whether or not one is employed should have little impact on labour supply. Experiments have found that cash grants are a remarkably cost-effective way of reducing poverty on many dimensions, from increasing consumption to decreasing stress levels. These results have led policymakers to rethink their programs, for example, by comparing the anti-poverty effect of a dollar spent on, say, job training programs, with the effect of simply giving that dollar away.

Some have proposed to expand the cash payment to everyone, not just the poor, in what has been called Unconditional Basic Income Grants (UBI or BIG). Some Silicon Valley groups are funding initial experiments in these more universal cash grants in Oakland, California, randomizing access to cash. Some of them believe that technology is accelerating at such a rate, reducing labour demand to such an extent that universal income grants are going to be needed to keep the vast bulk of humanity from destitute unemployment.

Another proposal in Finland randomly selects betwen 2,000 and 3,000 people to receive monthly lump-sum payments of $600 to see if basic income grants can lower poverty as well as simplify the administration of programs to help the poor. Experimenting with a policy before adopting it wholesale is allowing economists to study some of the effects of particular policies, as well as letting policymakers use evidence to decide whether or not to adopt a policy.

policy might mean that in absolute terms (in units of currency), the richer households are receiving more.

Consider Bruno, the landlord, and Angela, the farmer. Suppose that the outcome of their bargaining is that Bruno's income is three times as large as Angela's, with Bruno receiving 3,000 pesos per year and Angela receiving 1,000. Suppose also that Angela has two children and Bruno three, all of whom go to publicly funded schools, and that the government spends 200 pesos per year per child. This means that Angela receives in-kind transfers worth 400 pesos per year and Bruno 600. For Angela this implies an increase in her final income of 40%. For Bruno, it is an increase of only 20%. So the transfer is progressive, and the Gini coefficient for final income will decline.

If it seems odd that the Gini will decline even if Bruno receives more than Angela, the explanation is that the Gini coefficient depends on *relative incomes*, or the ratios of incomes between households. Bruno's market income is three times Angela's market income. A policy that reduces that ratio will reduce the Gini coefficient. In the second case above, Bruno's final income was 3,600 pesos while Angela's was 1,400, which gives a ratio of 2.57 compared to 3 for market income. Even though Bruno received more in absolute terms, relative inequality between them declined, so the Gini coefficient declined.

Primary schooling is usually very progressive. A case of education expenditure that can be regressive is publicly funded university education. This is because children from richer families are much more likely to go to university. So if Bruno's and Angela's children were all of university age, but Bruno's children were attending university while Angela's were working, then public university spending would be regressive: Angela's family would receive nothing, while Bruno's would receive something.

When it comes to taxes, an analogous principle applies. A tax is progressive if richer households pay a larger share of their incomes than poorer households, and regressive if poorer households pay a larger share of their incomes than richer households. So if Bruno paid 300 pesos in tax and Angela paid 150 pesos, then the tax would be regressive, even though Bruno is paying more in absolute terms: Bruno's tax is 10% of his income while Angela's is 15% of hers. Again, this is explained by the effect on the ratio of their incomes. Their after-tax incomes of 2,700 and 850 have a ratio of 3.18, which is higher (more unequal) than the ratio of their market incomes.

Taxes and expenditures can be analysed separately, but it is important to remember that expenditures are only possible because taxes pay for them. When a government spends money on public schools that benefit some households, they are financed by taxes that are paid by all households. This is why fiscal policy is redistributive: all households both give and receive, but some give more than they receive, and vice versa for others. The net effect is to transfer income from some households to other households.

Figures 19.29a and b show the distribution of taxes and public spending in Mexico. Figure 19.29a gives the figures in absolute terms while Figure 19.29b gives them as a percentage of market income. People in the bottom decile each received total benefits worth Mex$6,682 (Mexican pesos) on average per year, compared with Mex$5,557 received by those in the top decile. As Figure 19.29b shows, when represented as a share of market income, these transfers increase the lower the decile, with the bottom decile receiving benefits worth 135% of their market income and the top decile receiving only 13%. Therefore the transfers are progressive, reducing inequality.

For taxes, on average those in the bottom decile paid Mex$594 each, compared with Mex$25,902 for those in the top decile. But since the market incomes of the top decile were 40 times as high as those of the bottom decile, for both groups these taxes represented 12% of income, indicating that taxes are neither regressive nor progressive.

Figure 19.29a shows that the net effect of taxes and transfers is that the lower the decile, the more they receive—with deciles 9 and 10 being net contributors, rather than beneficiaries. This implies that the overall fiscal system is progressive, reducing the Gini coefficient. It also means that fiscal policy effectively redistributes income from the top two deciles (mainly the top decile) to the bottom eight deciles. However, the benefits to deciles 1 through 8 are larger than the cost to deciles 9 and 10. This is partly because the Mexican government also receives revenues from the production of oil.

These oil revenues are distributed, but are not *re*distributed—they represent income the government receives without taxing households and businesses.

Figure 19.29b shows clearly that expenditures are more progressive than taxes: while richer households tend to pay a slightly larger share of income in taxes than poorer households, public expenditures are a much larger share of income for poorer households than richer households.

Calculations by John Scott using the Encuesta Permanente de Hogares, Mexico.

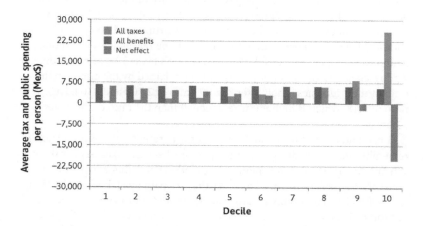

Figure 19.29a Distribution of taxation and public spending (average pesos per person). Deciles of households ordered by per capita net market income, Mexico 2014.

Based on calculations by John Scott using the Encuesta Permanente de Hogares, Mexico.

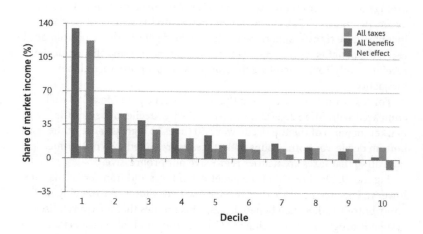

Figure 19.29b Distribution of taxation and public spending as a share of market income. Deciles of households ordered by per capita net market income, Mexico 2014.

EXERCISE 19.10 REGRESSIVE AND PROGRESSIVE TAXES

1. A poll tax is a tax where everyone pays the same absolute amount to the government. Is it progressive, regressive, or distributionally neutral?
2. A basic income is a benefit where everyone receives the same absolute amount from the government. Is it progressive, regressive, or distributionally neutral?
3. Suppose you learn that the richest 10% of people pay 30% of income tax. Does it mean that the tax system is progressive?
4. Some governments of developing countries give scholarships for some of their best students to go to graduate school abroad. If there are no eligibility restrictions, is this policy likely to be progressive or regressive? What might justify this policy?

19.11 EQUALITY AND ECONOMIC PERFORMANCE

The success of Operation Barga in raising productivity in farming (Unit 5), of Oportunidades in Mexico, and of pensions in South Africa in raising school achievement and child health may help explain the fact that more equal countries do as well as (or better than) unequal countries, in terms of standard economic performance.

We saw in Figure 17.15 (page 765) that the low levels of inequality, the enhanced power of trade unions, and the growth of pro-poor tax and transfer policies during the golden age of capitalism were associated with the most rapid growth of income per capita in modern history. Investment, too, occurred at levels not seen before, raising the capital stock at an unprecedented rate of growth.

Earlier in this unit (Figure 19.3) (page 849) we showed the centuries-long U-turn of top incomes in many countries including the US and the UK. By this measure, late twentieth-century inequality had risen to levels not experienced since before the Great Depression. But this U-turn pattern is far from universal, as Figure 19.4 (page 849) showed.

Most of the countries in Figure 19.4—where the U-turn towards greater inequality did not occur or was far less pronounced—are high performers. These countries achieved both rapid growth in income per capita and modest levels of inequality of disposable income, as you can see in Figure 19.30a. In this case, we measure inequality in income after taxes and transfers (disposable income) because this is the best available measure of inequality available across all countries. The conclusion from Figure 19.30a is that countries differ a lot in how equal their living standards are, and that the growth in productivity (GDP per capita) seems unrelated to the level of equality.

There have also been high and low performers among the catch-up countries. Figure 19.30b shows that South Korea and Taiwan were able to achieve high growth with relatively low inequality over the past 30 years, whereas the performance of Latin American economies along both of these dimensions was typically much worse.

Figures 19.30a and 19.30b are initially surprising because economists have often claimed that high taxes and transfers depress incentives for people to work hard and take the kinds of risk necessary for innovation to occur. Explanations of why egalitarian countries such as Japan, South Korea, and Taiwan in Asia, and Nordic and other northern European countries have done so well economically include:

- *High levels of cooperation and trust*: An economy based on services such as the production of knowledge and care of others cannot perform well if people are entirely self-interested. Cooperation and trust are essential for much of the modern economy, but they are difficult to sustain among people paid vastly different sums of money. Societies that are more equal create more trust among citizens and therefore enjoy better economic performance.
- *Policies that enhance the endowments of the poor*: High-quality health services and education contribute to the more productive use of an economy's resources. This is also true of policies that raise the value of the endowments of the poor, as illustrated by the land reform (Operation Barga) in West Bengal.

Chen Wang and Koen Caminada. 2011. 'Leiden Budget Incidence Fiscal Redistribution Dataset.' Version 1. Leiden Department of Economics Research.

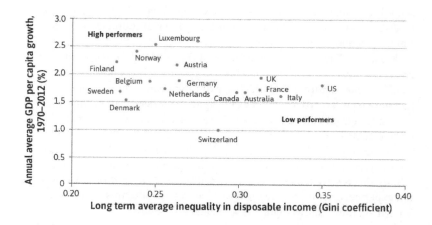

Figure 19.30a The cost of inequality: Inequality and growth in living standards among rich countries.

Chen Wang and Koen Caminada. 2011. 'Leiden Budget Incidence Fiscal Redistribution Dataset' (http://tinyco.re/9338721). Version 1. Leiden Department of Economics Research; OECD; International Monetary Fund. 2014. 'World Economic Outlook Database: October 2014' (http://tinyco.re/8219227).

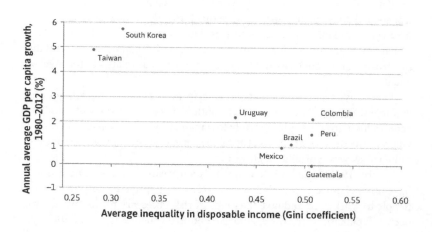

Figure 19.30b The cost of inequality: Inequality and growth in living standards among catch-up countries.

- *Less use of guard labour*: The construction of secure environments for the rich, such as gated communities, and other guarding activities that protect the assets of and provide security to the wealthy divert resources that could be used for productive investment.

Figure 19.30c illustrates this last point: the US, Italy, and the UK are countries with highly unequal disposable incomes that hire three times as many guards (public and private security personnel, excluding armed forces) than do the more equal nations of Finland, Denmark, and Sweden. An unequal society may expend a lot of resources on protecting property rights and enforcing the rule of law.

Samuel Bowles and Arjun Jayadev. 2014. 'One Nation under Guard' (http://tinyco.re/6662441). *New York Times*. Updated 15 February 2014.

Arjun Jayadev and Samuel Bowles. 2006. 'Guard Labor' (http://tinyco.re/4636800). *Journal of Development Economics* 79 (2): pp. 328–48.

EXERCISE 19.11 THE U-TURN COUNTRIES

Look again at the difference between the U-turn countries in Figure 19.3 (page 849), which showed a trend towards greater equality in the first three quarters of the twentieth century followed by an increase in inequality since about 1980, and the countries in Figure 19.4 (page 849), in which inequality did not increase significantly, or at all.

Make a list of possible explanations as to why countries in the two groups took such different courses since 1980, making sure to check (using the Internet or other sources) that any technological or institutional changes you refer to are historically accurate.

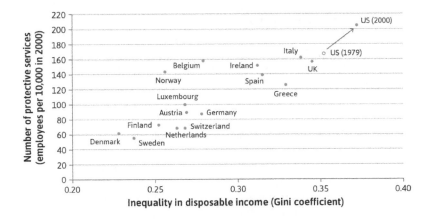

Arjun Jayadev and Samuel Bowles. 2006. 'Guard Labor'. *Journal of Development Economics* 79 (2): pp. 328–48.

Figure 19.30c The cost of inequality: Economic disparity and the fraction of workers employed as guards.

EXERCISE 19.12 HIGH AND LOW PERFORMERS

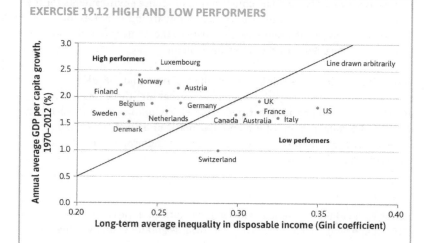

Inequality and economic performance: High and low performers.

Above, we have arbitrarily drawn a line on Figure 19.30a (page 896) to distinguish high from low performers. But what counts as 'high' performance depends on your preferences.

1. Sketch your indifference curves in the space given by Figure 19.30a, according to your preferences for inequality and growth. (Hint: is the slope of the indifference curve positive or negative?)
2. Use your indifference curves to rank the countries in Figure 19.30a, from the most to the least preferable.

QUESTION 19.10 CHOOSE THE CORRECT ANSWER(S)
Which of the following statements is correct regarding policies on inequality?

☐ Japan has a more equal society compared to the US due to its large equalizing effect of taxes and transfers.
☐ Providing high-quality education to citizens is a way of raising the endowments of less well off people.
☐ An increase in the minimum wage increases unemployment, leading to higher inequality unambiguously.
☐ Non-compete contracts mean that workers can demand higher wages, leading to reduced inequality.

19.12 CONCLUSION

As you have seen in this unit, income inequality among the world's households is falling fast, mostly because of the rapid increases in average income in two large and historically poor countries: China and India.

The most recent worldwide Gini coefficient for household income is 0.62. How unequal does that mean that people really are? We know that, for example, the average income of the top 1% in the world is 27 times the income of the poorest half of the people in the world.

But another way to see these differences, represented by a Gini coefficient of 0.62, is the following thought experiment. If you were to randomly pick pairs of households from all over the world and compare their income—you might get one family from Indonesia, one from Norway, one from Brazil, one from India, and two from China (that would not be a surprising outcome, likely even if you were randomly picking families)—you would find that the richer of the two families, on average, had 4.2 times the income of the poorer. The very rich are very few, so when we include them it would not change this average inequality between households.

But are we even that different? Do you think that the income earner (or earners) in the richer of the two families would on average be 4.2 times stronger, smarter, more hard-working or creative? This shows us that the economy produces inequalities, even among people who may not be very different. It rewards some with large incomes, and others with barely enough to survive.

Many of these income differences—seen as rewards for hard work, risk-taking, or creativity for example—are considered by most people to be entirely fair, or at least necessary to provide incentives for a well-working economy. Other income differences—the effects of discrimination, coercion, or accidents of birth for example, are regarded by many as unfair.

Economics can help to address the problem of unfair inequality by clarifying the causes of economic inequality and designing policies that can ensure more just outcomes, as has been done in many countries.

Concepts introduced in Unit 19

Before you move on, review these definitions:

- Gini coefficient
- Market income, disposable income, final income
- Lorenz curve
- Endowment
- Technology
- Institution
- Labour market segmentation
- Predistribution and redistribution policies
- Progressive and regressive policies
- Categorical inequality
- Intergenerational elasticity
- Inequality aversion
- Minimum wage

19.13 REFERENCES

Acemoglu, Daron, and James A. Robinson. 2012. *Why Nations Fail: The Origins of Power, Prosperity and Poverty*, 1st ed. New York, NY: Crown Publishers.

Alvaredo, Facundo, Anthony B. Atkinson, Thomas Piketty, Emmanuel Saez, and Gabriel Zucman. 2016. 'The World Wealth and Income Database (WID)' (http://tinyco.re/5262390).

Atkinson, Anthony B., and Thomas Piketty, eds. 2007. *Top Incomes over the Twentieth Century: A Contrast between Continental European and English-Speaking Countries*. Oxford: Oxford University Press.

Bessen, James. 2015. *Learning by Doing: The Real Connection between Innovation, Wages, and Wealth*. New Haven, CT: Yale University Press.

Bowles, Samuel, and Arjun Jayadev. 2014. 'One Nation under Guard' (http://tinyco.re/6662441). *The New York Times*. Updated 15 February 2014.

Bowles, Samuel, and Herbert Gintis. 2002. 'The Inheritance of Inequality' (http://tinyco.re/8562867). *Journal of Economic Perspectives* 16 (3): pp. 3–30.

Clark, Gregory. 2015. *The Son Also Rises: Surnames and the History of Social Mobility*. Princeton, NJ: Princeton University Press.

Daly, Mary C., and Leila Bengali. 2014. 'Is It Still Worth Going to College?' (http://tinyco.re/5624488). Federal Reserve Bank of San Francisco. Updated 5 May 2014.

Deaton, Angus. 2013. *The Great Escape: Health, Wealth, and the Origins of Inequality*. Princeton, NJ: Princeton University Press.

Diamond, Jared. 1999. *Guns, Germs, and Steel: The Fates of Human Societies*. New York, NY: Norton, W. W. & Company.

Dube, Arindrajit, T. William Lester, and Michael Reich. 2010. 'Minimum Wage Effects across State Borders: Estimates Using Contiguous Counties' (http://tinyco.re/5393066). *Review of Economics and Statistics* 92 (4): pp. 945–64.

Flannery, Kent, and Joyce Marcus. 2014. *The Creation of Inequality: How Our Prehistoric Ancestors Set the Stage for Monarchy, Slavery, and Empire*. Cambridge, MA: Harvard University Press.

Heckman, James. 2013. *Giving Kids a Fair Chance: A Strategy That Works*. Cambridge, MA: MIT Press.

Jayadev, Arjun, and Samuel Bowles. 2006. 'Guard Labor' (http://tinyco.re/4636800). *Journal of Development Economics* 79 (2): pp. 328–48.

Milanovic, Branko. 2007. *Worlds Apart: Measuring International and Global Inequality*. Princeton, NJ: Princeton University Press.

Milanovic, Branko. 2012. *The Haves and the Have-Nots: A Brief and Idiosyncratic History of Global Inequality*. New York, NY: Basic Books.

Norton, Michael I., and Daniel Ariely. 2011. 'Building a Better America–One Wealth Quintile at a Time' (http://tinyco.re/3629531). *Perspectives on Psychological Science* 6 (1): pp. 9–12.

Piketty, Thomas. 2014. *Capital in the Twenty-First Century*. Cambridge, MA: Harvard University Press.

Rawls, John. (1971) 2009. *A Theory of Justice*. Cambridge, MA: Belknap Press of Harvard University Press.

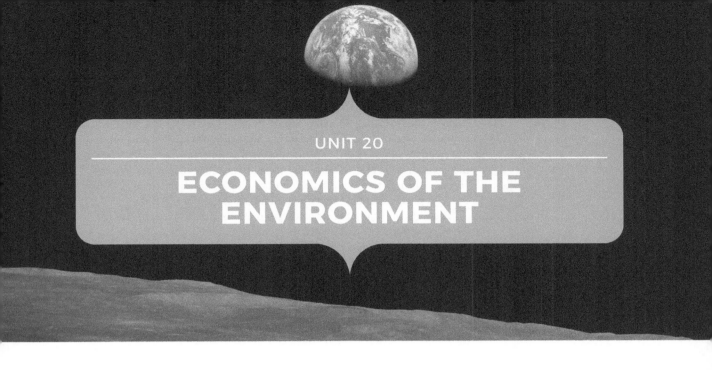

ECONOMICS OF THE ENVIRONMENT

HOW ECONOMIC ACTIVITY AFFECTS THE FRAGILE
BIOSPHERE OF OUR PLANET, AND HOW THE
RESULTING ENVIRONMENTAL PROBLEMS CAN BE
ADDRESSED

- Production and distribution of goods and services unavoidably alter the
  biosphere.
- Climate change resulting from economic activity is a major threat to
  future human wellbeing, and it illustrates many of the challenges of
  designing and implementing appropriate environmental policies.
- Well-designed environmental policies implement the least-cost ways of
  reducing environmental damages and balance the cost of reducing
  environmental damage against the benefits.
- Some policies use taxes or subsidies to alter prices so that people
  internalize the external environmental effects of their production and
  consumption decisions; other policies directly prohibit or limit the use
  of environmentally damaging materials and practices.
- Some environmental systems exhibit processes of degradation, in which
  substantial and hard to reverse environmental damage occurs abruptly.
  Prudent policies avoid triggering such processes.
- Evaluating environmental policies raises challenging questions about
  how to value our natural surroundings and the wellbeing of future
  generations.

In 1980, one of the most famous bets in science history took place. Paul
Ehrlich, a biologist, predicted that rapidly increasing population would
make mineral resources scarcer. Julian Simon, an economist, thought that
humanity would never run out of minerals because higher prices would
stimulate the search for new reserves, and ways of economizing on the use
of resources. Ehrlich bet Simon that the price of a basket of five
commodities—copper, chromium, nickel, tin, and tungsten—would
increase in real terms over the decade, reflecting increased scarcity.

inflation-adjusted price Price that takes into account the change in the overall price level.

On 29 September 1980, they bought $200 of each of the five commodities (a total wager of $1,000). If prices of these resources went up faster than inflation over the next 10 years, Simon would pay Ehrlich the difference between the **inflation-adjusted prices** and $1,000. If real prices fell, Ehrlich would pay Simon the difference. During that time, the global population increased by 846 million (19%). Also during that time, income per person increased by $753 (15%, adjusted for inflation in 2005 dollars). Yet, in those 10 years, the inflation-adjusted prices of the commodities fell from $1,000 to $423.93. Ehrlich lost the bet and sent Simon a cheque for $576.07.

The Ehrlich-Simon bet was motivated by the question of whether the world was 'running out' of natural resources, but an interval of 10 years is unlikely to tell us much about the long-run scarcity of raw materials. The basic framework of supply and demand (see Units 8 and 11) tells us why. Commodities such as copper or chromium generally have inelastic (steep) short-run demand and supply curves because there are few substitutes for these resources. This means that relatively small demand or supply shocks generate large and sudden changes in the market-clearing price, similar to the market for crude oil that you encountered in Unit 11.

But what should happen to the price and availability of copper or chromium in the *long* run?

As the price of copper rises, producers have an incentive to invest in new technologies that will make its extraction cheaper. Consumers will substitute away from copper to other raw materials. Both of these forces push prices down.

As prices of copper begin to fall, firms cut down on new extraction investments and consumers demand more copper. This pushes the prices back up. The presence of market prices for raw materials therefore ensures that despite increases in population and affluence, we do not 'run out of resources'. The ratio of known reserves to production does not fall far.

The World Bank. 2015. 'Commodity Price Data.'

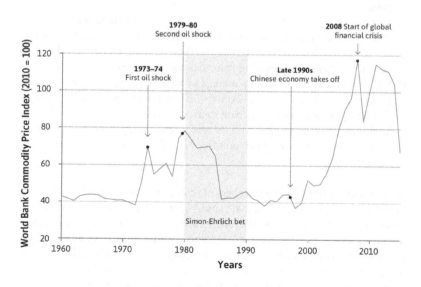

Figure 20.1 Global commodity prices (1960–2015).

Over the last 200 years, prices for many mineral resources have not changed much, although extraction has increased dramatically. Although prices fluctuate from year to year, the overall trend is flat. This indicates that the supply of many raw materials in the earth's crust—**natural resources**—is quite vast.

The transformation of living standards since the Industrial Revolution has been possible because of the combination of human ingenuity and available resources in the form of air, water, soil, metals, hydrocarbons like coal and oil, fish stocks, and so on. These were all once abundant and free, apart from the costs of extraction. Some, like hydrocarbons and mineral resources, are still abundant. Others, like unpolluted air, biodiversity (including coral reefs and many land and marine species), forests (due to deforestation and desertification), and clean water, are becoming scarce.

But the absence of prices is not the only reason why managing renewable natural resources is so hard. In some cases, the fragility of our environment under pressure from the growth of economic activity can lead not only to progressive degradation, but also to accelerating, self-reinforcing collapse. An example is the Grand Banks cod fishery, in the north of the Atlantic Ocean. In the eighteenth and nineteenth centuries, legendary schooners such as the Bluenose (Figure 20.2) raced back to port to sell their catch to be the first on the market, and to offer fresh fish. By the late twentieth century, the Grand Banks had sustained the livelihoods of the US and Canadian fishing communities for 300 years.

Then suddenly, the fishing industry in the Grand Banks died and, along with it, many of the old fishing towns. Figure 20.3 gives the quantity of cod caught over 163 years, showing a gradual upward trend and a pronounced spike coinciding with the introduction of industrial fishing less than 50 years before the eventual disappearance of cod from the Grand Banks. You learned some reasons why an open-access resource is likely to be overexploited in Units 4 Unit 12, and it appears that in this case the cod was greatly overfished. North Atlantic fisheries are now recovering after gov-

resources (natural) The estimated total amount of a substance in the earth's crust. *See also: reserves (natural resource).*

Figure 20.2 The Grand Banks fishing schooner, The Bluenose.

ernments imposed restrictions, but we still do not know if the cod will come back in their previous numbers.

Rapid changes like the Grand Banks cod disappearance are referred to as ecosystem collapse, and result from environmental vicious circles. In the Amazon, for example, change may become self-reinforcing due to the **positive feedback processes** illustrated in Figure 20.4. Past a certain level of deforestation, the process becomes self-sustaining even without further expansion of farming.

Similarly, the process of global warming can be self-reinforcing due, for example, to its impact on Arctic ice cover, as we will see later in Section 20.8.

The depletion of commodities and global warming are two aspects of environmental degradation. But we will see that there is also an important difference between the two: commodities are priced and traded, and so

> **positive feedback (process)** A
> process whereby some initial
> change sets in motion a process
> that magnifies the initial change.
> *See also: negative feedback
> (process).*

Millennium Ecosystem Assessment. 2005. *Ecosystems and Human Well-Being: Synthesis.* Washington, DC: Island Press.

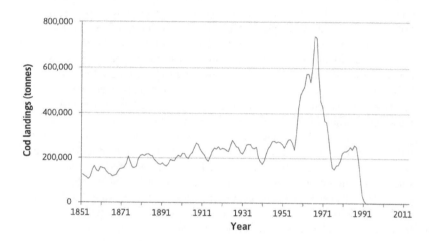

Figure 20.3 The amount of cod caught in the Grand Banks (North Atlantic) fisheries (1851–2014).

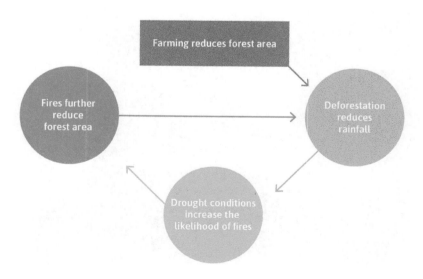

Figure 20.4 Positive feedback processes and deforestation in the Amazon.

over-use of some resources may self-correct as prices of scarce commodites rise. Negative external environmental effects are usually only corrected through coordinated policy or political action, which is harder to achieve. This action has often been too little or too late, as we will see.

In the rest of this unit, we will show that environmental problems are as diverse as nature itself, and that understanding the economics of the environment will require you to employ not only the tools you have learned already, but also to study the interaction of physical and biological processes with human economic activity.

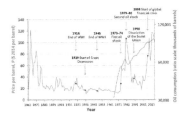

Look back at Figure 11.7 showing world oil prices and global oil consumption to answer Question 20.1.

QUESTION 20.1 CHOOSE THE CORRECT ANSWER(S)

Figure 11.7 (page 469) shows the world oil price (in 2014 prices) and global oil consumption.

You also have the additional information that the world reserves of oil more than doubled to 1.7 trillion barrels between 1981 and 2014. More than 1 trillion barrels were extracted and consumed in the same period. Based on this information, which of the following statements is correct?

☐ Both the 1970s and the 2000s oil price hikes were due to the demand curve shifting to the right.

☐ The sharp fall in the oil price after the global financial crisis of 2008 was due to the supply curve shifting to the right.

☐ Paul Ehrlich's forecast, that the increases in demand due to population growth and growing affluence would outstrip supply, was correct in the period 1981–2014.

☐ Julian Simon's forecast, that the discovery of technologies to find new resources and extract them more efficiently would outstrip increases in demand, was correct in the period 1981–2014.

20.1 RECAP: EXTERNAL EFFECTS, INCOMPLETE CONTRACTS, AND MISSING MARKETS

The study of environmental economics began in Unit 1 of this course, where we saw that economic activity (the production and distribution of goods and services) takes place within the biological and physical system. As we saw in Figure 1.5 and Figure 1.12, the economy is embedded within society, but also within the ecosystem. Resources flow from nature into the human economy. Waste, such as carbon dioxide (CO_2) emissions, or toxic sewage produced by firms and households, flows back into nature—mainly into the atmosphere and the ocean. Scientific evidence suggests that the planet has a limited capacity to absorb the pollutants that the human economy generates. In this unit, we investigate the nature of the global ecosystem, which provides the resources that feed economic processes and the sinks where we dispose of our wastes.

In Unit 4, we introduced environmental problems at a local level, among people who were similar in most respects. Anil and Bala were neighbouring landowners with a pest management problem. They could choose between an environmentally damaging pesticide and benign pest management systems. The outcome was inefficient and environmentally destructive because they could not make a binding agreement (a complete and enforceable contract) in advance about how they would act. In Unit 4, we also discovered that contributing to sustaining the quality of the environment is, to some extent, a public good, and that there are strong self-interested motives to free ride on the activities of others. So, while everyone would benefit if we all contributed to protecting the environment, we often do not do our part.

When small numbers of individuals interact, however, we saw that informal agreements and social norms (a concern for the others' wellbeing, for example) might be sufficient to address environmental problems. Examples found in real life include irrigation systems and the management of common land.

In Unit 12, we expanded the scope of environmental problems to include two groups of people pursuing different livelihoods. We considered a hypothetical pesticide called Weevokil (based, again, on real-world cases) and its effects on fishing and the jobs of workers who produce bananas. In this case, there was a missing market—the plantation owners did not need to buy the right to pollute the fisheries, because they could do it for free. This is another case of an incomplete contract.

In cases like this, taxes can increase the polluter's marginal private cost of production so that it equals the marginal social cost, resulting in the socially optimal level of production (and pollution). We canvassed a variety of solutions to the environmental problem (the external effects of the pesticide on the downstream fisheries), including bargaining between the organizations of fishermen and the plantation owners, and legislation (in the real-world case that inspired our Weevokil model, the government eventually banned the chemical).

Figure 20.5 reproduces a segment of Figure 12.8 that summarizes the nature of market failures in interactions between economic actors and the environment, and lists some possible remedies.

In this unit, we also consider the problem of climate change. Like the market failures above, climate change arises due to missing markets. However, unlike local environmental issues, climate change is global in scope. It involves people with vastly differing interests, ranging from those whose

Decision	How it affects others	Cost or benefit	Market failure (misallocation of resources)	Possible remedies	Terms applied to this type of market failure
A firm uses a pesticide that runs off into waterways	Downstream damage	Private benefit, external cost	Overuse of pesticide and overproduction of the crop for which it is used	Taxes, quotas, bans, bargaining, common ownership of all affected assets	Negative external effect, environmental spillover
You take an international flight	Increase in global carbon emissions	Private benefit, external cost	Overuse of air travel	Taxes, quotas	Public bad, negative external effect

Figure 20.5 External environmental effects.

entire nation may be submerged by rising sea levels to those who profit from the production and use of the carbon-based energy that contributes to global climate change. We will see that many of the concepts developed already, such as feasible sets and indifference curves, apply in these cases as well.

The problem of climate change combines missing markets, uncertainty about its effect on the economy, the possibility of positive feedbacks and environmental tipping points, the need for international cooperation, and intergenerational issues. It is the greatest challenge of our time, and we need to use our entire toolkit (and more) to see how we can address it.

QUESTION 20.2 CHOOSE THE CORRECT ANSWER(S)
Refer to Figure 20.5 (page 906).

Based on this information, which of the following statements is correct?

☐ Bargaining between affected parties is always effective in reducing the inefficiencies caused by externalities.
☐ The market price of pesticides is unlikely to reflect the full social cost of their use.
☐ All externalities result in the good producing the external effect being overused.
☐ Reducing air travel is an unfortunate and inefficient by-product of taxing flights.

20.2 CLIMATE CHANGE

Many scientists now see climate change as the greatest threat to future human wellbeing. We focus on climate change because of its importance as an environmental problem, and because it illustrates the difficulties of designing and implementing adequate environmental policies. This problem tests our framework of efficiency and fairness to the limit, because of five features that climate change shares with other environmental problems:

- *Stabilizing yearly emissions is not sufficient:* Climate is affected by the total amount of **greenhouse gases** in the atmosphere. This is increasing due to the annual flow of emissions. But merely stabilizing emissions at current levels will not be enough, because the stock of greenhouses gases would then continue to increase.
- *Irreversibility of climate change:* Increases in the amount of CO_2 in the atmosphere are partially irreversible, which means that our current actions have long-lasting effects on future generations.
- *The worst-case scenario:* Experts are uncertain about the scale, timing, and global pattern of the effects of climate change, but most agree that climate change could be catastrophic. Therefore, the *most likely* scenario should not be the only guide to policy. We need to take into account a range of possible scenarios, including some very unlikely but disastrous ones.
- *A global problem requiring international cooperation:* The contributions to climate change come from all parts of the world, and its effects will be felt by all of nearly 200 autonomous nations. It will be solved only by a

greenhouse gas Gases—mainly water vapour, carbon dioxide, methane and ozone—released in the earth's atmosphere that lead to increases in atmospheric temperature and changes in climate.

high level of cooperation between the largest and most powerful nations, at a minimum, on a scale without historical precedent.

- *Conflicts of interest:* The impacts of climate change differ among people according to their economic circumstances, both across the globe and within countries. Future generations will experience the effects of today's emissions, but also the actions we take to reduce them. It is unclear how to balance the competing interests of individuals in different economic circumstances, and the interests of current and future generations.

Climate change and economic activity

Figure 20.6 shows the data on the stock of CO_2 (in parts per million) using the right-hand scale, and global temperature (as the deviation from the average over the period 1961–1990) using the left-hand scale, for the period since 1750.

Burning fossil fuels for power generation and industrial use leads to emissions of CO_2 into the atmosphere. These activities, together with CO_2 emissions from land-use changes, generate greenhouse gases equivalent to around 36 billion tonnes of CO_2 each year. Concentrations of CO_2 in the atmosphere have increased from 280 parts per million in 1800 to 400 parts per million, currently rising at 2–3 parts per million each year. CO_2 allows incoming sunlight to pass through it, but traps reflected heat on the earth, leading to increases in atmospheric temperatures and changes in climate. Some CO_2 also gets absorbed into the oceans. This increases the acidity of the oceans, killing marine life.

Figure 20.6 illustrates a key fact of climate science: that global warming is an effect of the amount of CO_2 and other greenhouse gases in the atmosphere. To use the language of Unit 10, where we discussed income (a flow) and wealth (a stock), climate change is caused by the stock of atmospheric greenhouse gases, not by the flow of our annual emissions. It's what's in the tub that matters. Figure 20.7 presents this new use of the bathtub model to illustrate the problem.

Years 1010–1975: David M. Etheridge, L. Paul Steele, Roger J. Francey, and Ray L. Langenfelds. 2012. 'Historical Record from the Law Dome DE08, DE08-2, and DSS Ice Cores'. Division of Atmospheric Research, CSIRO, Aspendale, Victoria, Australia. Years 1976–2010: Data from Mauna Loa observatory; Tom A. Boden, Gregg Marland, and Robert J. Andres. 2010. 'Global, Regional and National Fossil-Fuel CO_2 Emissions'. Carbon Dioxide Information Analysis Center (CDIAC) Datasets. Note: This data is the same as in Figures 1.6a and 1.6b. Temperature is average northern hemisphere temperature.

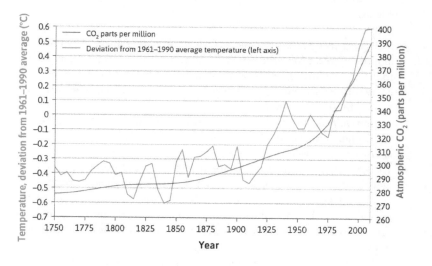

Figure 20.6 Global atmospheric concentration of carbon dioxide and global temperatures (1750–2010).

The increase in CO_2 in the atmosphere is occurring because the processes reducing the stock (natural decay of the CO_2 and absorption of CO_2 by forests) are far less than the new emissions that we add annually. Moreover, deforestation in the Amazon, Indonesia and elsewhere is reducing the CO_2 'outflows' while also adding to CO_2 emissions. These forests are often replaced by agricultural activities that produce further greenhouse gas emissions in the form of methane releases from livestock and nitrous oxide releases from fertilizer overuse.

The natural decay of CO_2 is extraordinarily slow. Of the carbon dioxide that humans have put in the atmosphere since the mass burning of coal that started in the Industrial Revolution, two-thirds will still be there a hundred years from now. More than a third of it will still be 'in the tub' a thousand years from now. The natural processes that stabilized greenhouse gases in the atmosphere in pre-industrial times have been entirely overwhelmed by human economic activity. And the imbalance is accelerating.

It is estimated that we can emit only a further 1 to 1.5 trillion tonnes of CO_2 into the atmosphere to give reasonable odds of limiting the increase in temperature to 2°C above pre-industrial levels. Should we manage to achieve this limit on emissions, there is still a probability of around 1% that temperature increases would be more than 6°C, causing a global economic catastrophe. If we exceed the limit and temperature rises to 3.4°C above pre-industrial levels, the probability of a climate-induced economic catastrophe would rise to 10%.

Figure 20.8 shows the relationship between estimated temperature increases and CO_2 emitted. It also shows the amount of CO_2 that would be emitted if we:

- burnt the fossil fuels that can be economically extracted at current prices and technology (**reserves**)
- burnt *all* fossil fuels in the earth's crust (**resources**)

Figure 20.8 indicates that keeping the warming to 2°C implies that the majority of fossil fuel reserves and resources should remain in the ground.

Martin Weitzman argues there is a non-trivial risk of a catastrophe from climate change in an *EconTalk* podcast (http://tinyco.re/ 7088528).

Gernot Wagner and Martin L. Weitzman. 2015. *Climate Shock: The Economic Consequences of a Hotter Planet.* Princeton, NJ: Princeton University Press.

reserves (natural resource) The amount of a natural resource that is economically feasible to extract given existing technologies. *See also: resources (natural).*

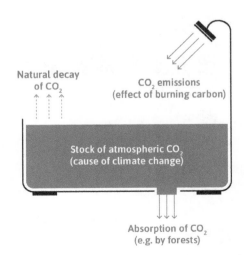

Figure 20.7 Another bathtub model: The stock of atmospheric CO_2.

EXERCISE 20.1 ASSESSING THE ECONOMIC IMPACTS OF GLOBAL WARMING

In 1896, Swedish scientist Svante Arrhenius estimated the impact of doubling CO_2 concentrations in the atmosphere, and later suggested that 'the colder regions of the earth' might want to burn more coal so as to enjoy a 'better climate'.

In the next century, entire countries may disappear as the level of the oceans rise in response to the melting of the West Antarctic and Greenland ice sheets.

1. Find out what you can about which regions, industries, occupations, firms, or cities are likely to be:
   (a) most positively affected by climate change
   (b) most negatively affected by climate change
2. What are the main reasons why the effects of climate change differ across these groups?

Calculations by Alexander Otto of the Environmental Change Institute, University of Oxford, based on: Aurora Energy Research. 2014. 'Carbon Content of Global Reserves and Resources'; Bundesanstalt für Geowissenschaften und Rohstoffe (The Federal Institute for Geosciences and Natural Resources). 2012. *Energy Study 2012*; IPCC. 2013 *Climate Change 2013: The Physical Science Basis. Contribution of Working Group I to the Fifth Assessment Report of the Intergovernmental Panel on Climate Change.* Cambridge: Cambridge University Press; Cameron Hepburn, Eric Beinhocker, J. Doyne Farmer, and Alexander Teytelboym. 2014. 'Resilient and Inclusive Prosperity within Planetary Boundaries'. *China & World Economy* 22 (5): pp. 76–92.

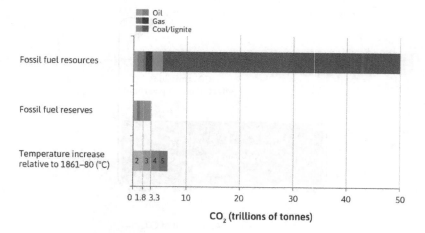

Figure 20.8 Carbon dioxide contained in fossil fuel reserves and resources, relative to the atmospheric capacity of the earth.

EXERCISE 20.2 CLIMATE CHANGE CAUSES AND EVIDENCE

Use information from the National Aeronautics and Space Administration web page on climate change (http://tinyco.re/5897476), and the latest report of the Intergovernmental Panel on Climate Change (http://tinyco.re/9013146) to answer the following questions:

1. Explain what climate scientists believe to be the main causes of climate change.
2. What evidence is there to indicate that climate change is already occurring?
3. Name and explain three potential consequences of climate change in the future.
4. Discuss why the three consequences you have listed may lead to disagreements and conflicts of interest about climate policy. (Hint: You may find it useful to draw on your answers to Exercise 20.1 about the winners and losers from climate change.)

QUESTION 20.3 CHOOSE THE CORRECT ANSWER(S)

Figure 20.8 (page 910) shows the temperature increase arising from the CO_2 emitted, generated at different levels of use of fossil fuel reserves (which can be technically and economically extracted) and resources (estimated total amounts) in the earth's crust. For example, it states that a further 1 to 1.5 trillion tonnes of CO_2 emissions would be likely to lead to a 2°C increase in temperature, compared to the pre-industrial average.

You are also given that 36 billion tonnes of CO_2 are generated each year currently. Based on this information, which of the following statements is correct?

☐ The figure suggests that the world should stop using coal immediately.
☐ Using up all the reserves but none of the resources should keep the temperature from rising more than 2°C.
☐ Limiting further CO_2 emissions to 1 to 1.5 trillion tonnes will ensure that the temperature will not rise more than 2°C.
☐ Stabilizing the emission rate at the current level will not be enough to prevent the possibility of a climate-induced economic catastrophe.

20.3 THE ABATEMENT OF ENVIRONMENTAL DAMAGES: COST-BENEFIT ANALYSIS

Like other environmental problems, climate change can be addressed by environmental damage **abatement policies** such as:

abatement policy A policy designed to reduce environmental damages. *See also: abatement.*

- discovering and adopting technologies that are less polluting
- choosing to consume fewer or less environmentally damaging goods
- banning or limiting the use of environmentally harmful substances or activities

However, the economic costs of immediately eliminating *all* CO_2 emissions would surely exceed the environmental benefits. But what level of environmental abatement should be adopted instead?

This is in part a question about the facts: What is the trade-off between the benefits of producing and consuming more, and the enjoyment of a less-degraded environment? It is also an ethical question: how should we value environmental quality? How should we trade off consumption now, with environmental quality enjoyed both by current and future generations?

If we ask citizens about their views of proposed environmental policies, we expect their responses will differ, partly because a deteriorating environment affects different people in different ways. Your point of view may depend on whether you work outdoors (you will benefit more from a less polluted local environment) or in fossil fuel production (you may lose your job if the higher abatement costs levied on your firm causes it to shut down). It may depend on whether you have no choice but to live near a source of air pollution, or are wealthy enough to have a second home in the countryside.

Your opinion about how much we should spend today to protect future environments would no doubt differ from the values of those who make up the distant future generations that would be affected by our choices, if we could ask them. People's views are strongly influenced by their self-interest but, as you would expect from the behavioural experiments in Unit 4, not totally so. We worry about the effect on others, even complete strangers.

For simplicity, we begin by setting aside these differences and consider a population composed of identical individuals. We ignore future generations, or optimistically assume that we will all live forever. We will begin by also assuming that everyone enjoys (or suffers from) the same level of environmental quality. Later in this unit we will look at what changes when we do not make these assumptions.

We will also start off with what we call the 'ideal policymaker' who seeks to serve the citizens' interests.

How can economics help the policymaker determine the level of environmental quality that we would like to enjoy, knowing that people may have to consume less so they can enjoy a better environment? The first thing to think about is the actions that we can take and their consequences: the feasible set of outcomes.

To do this, we need to consider the ways that the resources of the society could be diverted from their current uses to reduce the environmentally degrading effects of economic activity. The nation may adopt policies to limit environmental damage. We refer to such policies as **abatement policies**, since they abate (reduce) pollution and environmental damage. The amount of reduction in emissions caused by these policies is referred to as the quantity of abatement. Abatement policies include taxes on emissions of pollutants, and incentives to use fuel-efficient cars.

In the rest of this section, we use a specific example to illustrate the general approach to environmental cost-benefit analysis. The specific case is the choice of global policies that reduce greenhouse gas emissions. Keep in mind that we are assuming that the policymakers throughout the world are able to implement these policies.

Abatement costs and the feasible set

To get some idea of how economists assess abatement policy options, we look at the estimated cost of reduction of global greenhouse gas emissions in Figure 20.9, which shows the relationship between potential abatement and the cost of abatement per tonne. It is the marginal cost curve for the good, which we refer to as the **global greenhouse gas abatement cost curve**. These estimates were made by the consultancy firm McKinsey (http://tinyco.re/6905614).

Each bar represents a change that could reduce carbon emissions. The height shows the cost of using the technology to reduce carbon emissions, in terms of euros per tonne of reduced CO_2 emissions. The width shows the reduction of CO_2 emissions, compared to the level without policy intervention. Therefore, for each method, a short bar means that there is a lot of abatement per euro spent. A wider bar means that this method has a higher potential to abate emissions.

Note that in this figure we have only included policies which *have* a cost. There are many other policies that are win-win, because they both reduce carbon emissions and save money, such as fitting insulation in older houses. The full range of policies can be seen in Figure 20.26 (page 956); the costly ones are in Figure 20.9. We discuss the implications of win-win policies in Section 20.10. You may wish to read that section now before working through the rest of the unit.

In Figure 20.9, we order the policies from those with the least cost per tonne of CO_2 abated on the left to the highest cost per tonne abated on the right. By this measure, abating carbon emissions through changes in agriculture is the most efficient method, if we disregard the win-win policies. Nuclear, wind, and solar photovoltaics are all moderately efficient. At the time these estimates were produced, retrofitting gas-fired power plants for carbon capture and storage is the highest-cost policy per tonne of CO_2 abated. Together, the bars form a marginal cost curve, showing the cost of an additional tonne of abatement at any given level of abatement, assuming that we adopt the most efficient technologies first.

The science in this field is young, and technologies are continuously developing. As knowledge advances, the estimated abatement cost curve will change—indeed, it is likely to have changed already from the data shown here, which was published in 2013. For instance, rapid reductions in costs of solar power are likely to increase the efficiency of solar abatement, and therefore reduce the height of the bars associated with solar energy (see Figure 20.19a).

But even focusing on only the most efficient bars, implementing any of these abatement policies would divert resources from the production of other goods and services: the opportunity cost of an improved environment would be reduced consumption.

We can use data from the marginal cost curve for abatement (as in Figure 20.9) to estimate how much abatement we get for any level of expenditure, assuming we implement the most efficient methods first.

global greenhouse gas abatement cost curve This shows the total cost of abating greenhouse gas emissions using abatement policies ranked from the most cost-effective to the least. *See also: abatement policy*.

The measure of potential abatement, gigatonnes (10^9 tonnes) of carbon dioxide equivalent (GtCO2e), is a unit used by the UN climate change scientific panel, the IPCC, to measure the effect of a technology or process on global warming. It expresses how much warming a given type of greenhouse gas would cause by using the equivalent amount of CO_2 emissions that would have the same effect.

These calculations are given in Figure 20.10. We would start by implementing the cheap and effective measures, such as land management and conversion policies. Having exhausted these policies, the curve becomes flatter at higher levels of expenditure, where we would be devoting more resources to less efficient methods such as carbon capture and storage (CCS) modifications to power stations. For more detail on the calculations of marginal abatement costs, see the Einstein at the end of this section.

The curve in the figure, called the least-cost abatement curve, gives all the combinations of expenditures and resulting abatement when the lowest-cost changes are introduced first and the higher-cost ones are introduced later.

Using figures like 20.10, we can establish all of the possible combinations of consumption and abatement that are feasible. The available abatement technology is shown by the shaded set of points in Figure 20.11. In this figure, the horizontal axis measures the expenditure on abatement. The vertical axis measures environmental quality by the amount of abatement achieved. The zero point on the vertical axis is a situation in which no abatement occurs.

The shaded area is the feasible set of abatement expenditures and environmental outcomes. Points like A in the interior of the set are inefficient abatement policies. At A, we can see that there are alternative measures that would achieve the same level of abatement (25 gigatonnes) at lower cost (€400 billion rather than €600 billion). Similarly, for an expenditure of €600 billion, the choice of the most cost-effective abatement techniques would deliver 30 tonnes of CO_2 abatement and therefore higher environmental quality than at point A. Economists say that a point like A is **dominated** by points A′ and A″ and all the points in between. This means that at any of these other points there could be lower abatement costs and

dominated We describe an outcome in this way if more of something that is positively valued can be attained without less of anything else that is positively valued. In short: an outcome is dominated if there is a win-win alternative.

McKinsey & Company. 2013. *Pathways to a Low-Carbon Economy: Version 2 of the Global Greenhouse Gas Abatement Cost Curve*. McKinsey & Company.

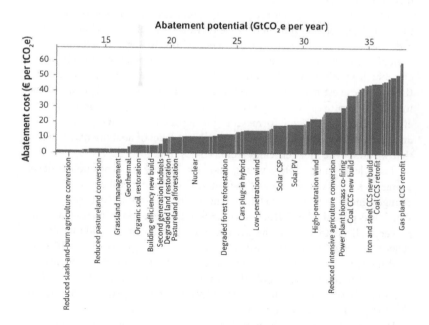

Figure 20.9 The cost of potential global greenhouse abatement in 2030 (compared with business as usual), using different policies.

the same level of abatement (A′), or greater abatement at the same cost (A″).

How would an inefficient point like A in Figure 20.11 occur? In Figure 20.10, the policies were ordered so that the first expenditures on abatement are devoted to the most effective abatement policy. After exhausting the potential of each policy we moved to the next most effective policy.

To highlight the difference between an efficient and an inefficient abatement policy, Figure 20.12 shows the abatement options based on the data in

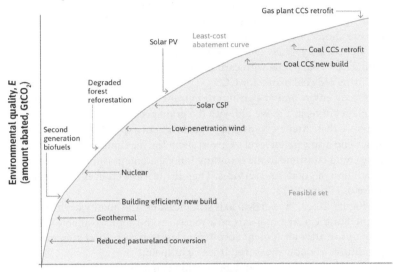

McKinsey & Company. 2013. *Pathways to a Low-Carbon Economy: Version 2 of the Global Greenhouse Gas Abatement Cost Curve*. McKinsey & Company.

Figure 20.10 The least-cost abatement curve: How total abatement (at least cost) depends on total abatement expenditures.

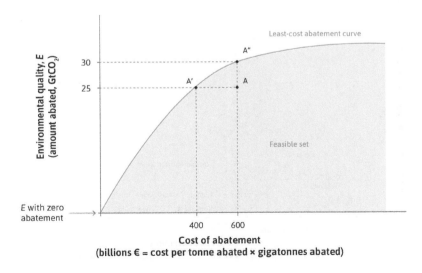

Figure 20.11 The least-cost abatement curve: The trade-off between total cost of abatement and amount of abatement.

Figure 20.9, but with more costly policies adopted first. If a society has committed to spend €8.37 billion on abatement, and spends it all on coal carbon capture, nuclear, and other less effective options, then the least-cost abatement curve would be as shown in Figure 20.12.

We can see that if €8.37 billion were spent on abatement, the level of abatement would be 4.94 gigatonnes of CO_2, rather than the abatement of 11.2 gigatonnes that would have occurred if the society implemented least-cost policies, as shown in Figure 20.10.

Figures 20.10 and 20.12 send a clear message about priorities. If we have a limited amount to spend on abatement, and abatement technology does not change, focus on reducing pastureland conversion. According to Figure 20.10, we should also adopt nuclear power (assuming that waste storage and other security issues can be addressed), solar, and wind power before building new coal plants with carbon capture and storage (CCS), or retrofitting old coal plants for CCS.

To study environment-consumption trade-offs, we invert the least-cost abatement curve, just as we did with the grain production function in Unit 3. Suppose that, after a given level of government expenditure on other policies and also a given level of investment, the maximum amount that people could consume in the economy if no abatement is implemented is €500 billion of goods and services. Then the feasible choices are the shaded portion of Figure 20.13.

In Figure 20.13, the vertical axis still measures the quality of the environment, but the horizontal axis now measures the goods available for consumption after abatement costs (from left to right). So, abatement expenditures are now measured from right to left.

The abatement choice problem now looks familiar. The policymaker wishes to select a point among the alternatives on the feasible frontier.

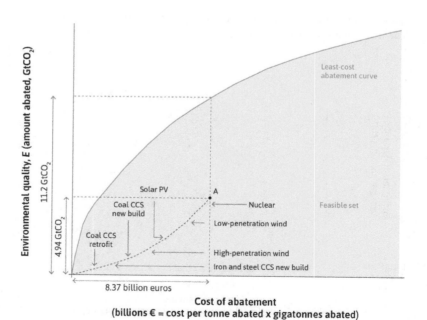

Figure 20.12 An abatement cost curve in which more costly technologies are adopted first.

Recall from the earlier units that the slope of the feasible frontier, also known as the marginal rate of transformation (MRT), is how much of the quantity on the vertical axis you would get by giving up one unit of the quantity on the horizontal axis. In the consumption-environment feasible frontier, this is the marginal rate of transformation of foregone consumption into environmental quality:

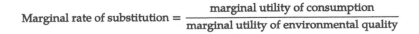

$$\text{Marginal rate of transformation} = \frac{\text{increase in environmental quality}}{\text{decrease in consumption}}$$

The steeper the feasible frontier (the greater the slope), the smaller the opportunity cost, in terms of foregone consumption, of further environmental improvements.

Environment-consumption indifference curves

Which point on the feasible set will the policymaker choose? The answer can be found by studying the policymaker's environment-consumption indifference curves in Figure 20.14, which show how much consumption citizens are willing to trade in exchange for better environmental quality.

We can write the slope of the indifference curve, the marginal rate of substitution (MRS) as:

$$\text{Marginal rate of substitution} = \frac{\text{marginal utility of consumption}}{\text{marginal utility of environmental quality}}$$

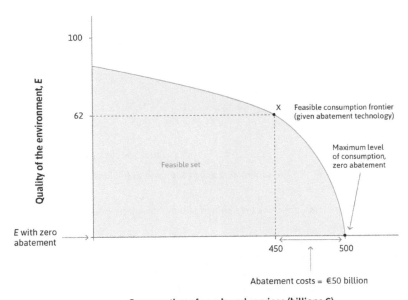

Figure 20.13 Feasible consumption and environmental quality.

1. If no abatement policies are adopted
If abatement costs are zero, the nation can have €500 billion of consumption.

2. €50 billion of abatement costs
The nation is at point X after spending this amount.

The policymaker's MRS will be high (a steep indifference curve) if consumption is valued highly by the citizens (a large marginal utility of consumption), and if citizens do not place a high value on additional abatement to improve environmental quality (marginal utility of abatement is low). Conversely, if the citizens value additional environmental quality highly relative to consumption, the MRS will be less steep.

In Figure 20.14, the indifference curves are straight lines because we have assumed for simplicity that the marginal utility of consumption and the marginal utility of environmental quality are both constant. That means they do not depend on the quantity of consumption or on the amount of abatement.

To think about how citizens' preferences affect the optimal policy chosen, we suppose that the policymaker takes account of the preferences of all of the citizens, counting them equally. This means that if citizens decide to value environmental quality more, then the indifference curves of the policymaker will be flatter to reflect this.

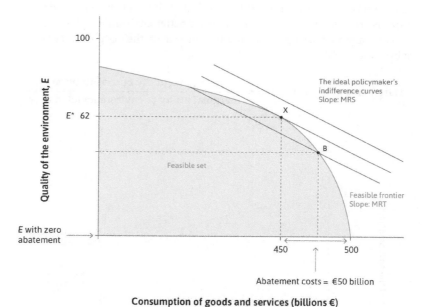

Figure 20.14 The ideal policymaker's choice of the abatement level.

1. Allocating €50 billion to abatement
Point X is the level of environmental protection that the policymaker would wish to implement, with environmental quality at E^*.

2. Allocating less than €50 billion to abatement
At B, the MRS is less than the MRT (the slope of the feasible set at B), so the policymaker would be better off by switching more resources from consumption into improving environmental quality. Spending more on abatement shifts the policymaker onto higher indifference curves until point X is reached.

Cost-benefit analysis: The ideal policymaker chooses an abatement level

Our policymaker uses two principles to make a decision about the level of abatement:

- *She considers only abatement policies on the frontier of the feasible set*: This eliminates higher-cost abatement policies that are inside the shaded area.
- *She chooses the combination of environmental quality and consumption that puts her on the highest possible indifference curve.*

To satisfy both conditions, she finds the point on the feasible frontier that equates the MRT (the slope of the feasible frontier) with the MRS (the slope of her highest possible indifference curve).

We can see from Figure 20.14 that point X is the level of environmental protection that the policymaker will wish to implement. The *benefit* indicated by the environmental quality index of 62 is achieved at a *cost* of reducing consumption by €50 billion and allocating it to abatement.

What would produce a different choice of abatement level?

- *Different values*: If the citizens cared less about the environment, then the indifference curves would be steeper than those in Figure 20.14, and the policymaker would choose a point like B, with higher consumption and lower abatement.
- *Different costs of abatement*: If abatement became cheaper than shown in Figure 20.14, then the feasible set would be steeper at each level of abatement. This would expand the production frontier upwards, implying that the policymaker would choose a higher level of abatement and lower consumption.

EXERCISE 20.3 CHOOSING ABATEMENT STRATEGIES

Look at the high-cost abatement strategies that we use to illustrate an inefficient abatement policy in Figure 20.12 (page 916). Can you think of reasons why these policies might be introduced instead of the more cost-effective ones?

EXERCISE 20.4 OPTIMISTIC AND PESSIMISTIC POLICIES

In Figure 20.14 (page 918), we described how a policymaker representing a uniform group of identical citizens chooses the optimal amount of abatement.

1. Draw the indifference curves of the policymaker if she were to represent two different groups of citizens (again, we assume that all citizens in each group are identical, and the marginal utility of consumption and environmental quality are both constant). In the first group, citizens care more about environmental quality than consumption, and in the other group, citizens care more about consumption of goods and services. Explain why the optimal level of abatement costs will differ across groups.
2. Now consider the example in the text of the abatement of global greenhouse gases. What are the main simplifications in the model that might lead the policy maker who uses this model to ignore important aspects of the problem of global greenhouse gas abatement?

In reality, there is uncertainty about the effectiveness of abatement expenditure and hence how costly abatement of environmental damage will be.

3. On a new diagram, draw the feasible consumption frontier based on an optimistic assessment of the costs of abatement.
4. Now draw the feasible consumption frontier based on a pessimistic assessment of the costs of abatement on the same diagram.
5. By adding the policymaker's indifference curves to your diagram in each case (assuming all citizens are identical), show how actual environmental quality chosen by the policymaker will differ, even if preferences are the same, depending on whether costs of abatement are assessed optimistically or pessimistically.

QUESTION 20.4 CHOOSE THE CORRECT ANSWER(S)

Figure 20.9 (page 914) shows a global greenhouse gas abatement curve, defined as the abatement in 2030 compared with 'business as usual', produced by McKinsey in 2015. The width of each bar indicates potential abatement measured in gigatonnes of CO_2, while the height indicates the cost of abatement per tonne.

Based on this information, which of the following statements is correct?

☐ Solar energy produces more abatement per euro spent than nuclear power.
☐ Nuclear energy has a higher potential to abate emissions than reforestation of degraded forests.
☐ Geothermal technology has a very low abatement potential and therefore should never be adopted.
☐ Solar energy should be preferred to nuclear power in the abatement of greenhouse gas emissions.

QUESTION 20.5 CHOOSE THE CORRECT ANSWER(S)
Figure 20.11 (page 915) shows the graph of the amount abated against its total cost, under different abatement policies.

Based on this information, which of the following statements are correct?

☐ Point A is not a feasible option.
☐ Point A′ is dominated by point A″.
☐ The fact that the slope of the curve is monotonically diminishing implies that the technologies are adopted in increasing order of their cost.
☐ It is possible to attain a higher curve by modifying the order in which the technologies are adopted.

EINSTEIN

Marginal abatement costs and the total productivity of abatement expenditures

How do we construct the line segments that define the boundary of the feasible set in Figure 20.10 from the data in Figure 20.9?

Let the height of the first bar (the most cost-effective abatement expenditure) in Figure 20.8 be y and the width of that bar be x. Then, in Figure 20.10:

- the initial slope of the curve is $1/y$
- the horizontal axis value of the first point is xy
- this point's vertical axis value is x

The other line segments making up the curve in Figure 20.9 are constructed in the same way.

20.4 CONFLICTS OF INTEREST: BARGAINING OVER WAGES, POLLUTION, AND JOBS

Conflicts of interest arise because environmental quality is never the same for everyone. Some people benefit or suffer more than others, depending on their location and income, as we saw in the banana pesticide case studied in Unit 12.

Here are two examples of how costs and benefits are not equally shared. In 2008 and 2009, two oil spills in the Niger River delta destroyed fisheries. The spills resulted from the oil extraction activities of the Anglo-Dutch company, Royal Dutch Shell. Lawyers for the Ogoni people, who suffered these external effects, brought a lawsuit against the Nigerian subsidiary of Shell in the British courts. In 2015, Shell settled out of court and paid £3,525 per person, of which £2,200 was paid to each individual, and the rest to support community public goods. This award amounted to more than most Ogoni people would earn in a year. Lawyers representing the community helped to set up bank accounts for the 15,600 beneficiaries.

The transfers may have compensated the Ogoni in part for the loss of a healthy environment, restoration of which the UN Environment Programme has estimated will cost $1 billion and take 30 years. For Royal Dutch Shell, the settlement at least partially internalizes the negative external effects of their activities, and might lead the company's owners (and others extracting oil in the delta) to consider a change in their behaviour.

In 1974 a giant lead, silver, and zinc smelter owned by the Bunker Hill Company was the only major employer in the town of Kellogg, in the American state of Idaho, employing 2,300 people. Many children in the town developed flu-like symptoms. Doctors discovered that they were the result of high lead levels in their blood—high enough to impair cognitive and social development of children.

Three of the children of Bill Yoss, a welder at the smelter, had been found to have dangerously high levels of lead poisoning. 'I don't know where we'll end up,' he told a *People* reporter, 'We may pull out of the state.'

The company refused to release its own tests of the smelter's lead emission levels. Unless the state's emissions regulations were relaxed, it said, the smelter would shut down, which it did, in 1981. Former employees looked for work elsewhere. The value of the homes and businesses in the town fell to a third of its earlier level. The local schools, which were supported by property taxes, did not have the funding to cope with those who remained.

We model this problem by considering a hypothetical town, Brownsville, with a single business that employs the entire labour force but whose toxic emissions are a threat to the health of the citizens. The firm can vary the level of emissions that it imposes on the town, but the costs of implementing emissions capture and storage means lost profits. The single owner of the firm (who bears the costs of reducing the level of emissions) lives far enough away that the level of emissions he selects does not affect the quality of his environment. Therefore citizens and the business will have a conflict of interest over the level of emissions in the town, and also over the wages paid. You can think of the citizens as valuing 'environmental quality', which decreases when emissions increase and can be measured by an air quality index.

The citizens of the town have some bargaining power because each is free to leave Brownsville and seek employment elsewhere. So the business must offer them a package of environmental quality and wages that is at least as desirable as their reservation option, which is what they might expect to receive if they left Brownsville. We call this limit on what the business must offer the citizens the 'leave town condition'.

The business owner has bargaining power, too, because the wage and environment package that he offers must result in profits high enough that the firm does not simply shut down or relocate (we call this the firm's 'shutdown condition'). The citizens cannot demand more than this wage, or they would be unemployed (remember there are no other firms in Brownsville). Thus the firm's reservation option places limits on the bargain that the citizens can strike with the firm.

We represent the relationship between the business and the citizens in Figure 20.15. The wage paid to the employees of the firm is on the horizontal axis. The level of environmental quality experienced by the citizens is on the vertical axis. We make the following assumptions:

- *Citizens are identical and so experience the same environmental quality.*
- *The owner is unaffected by the level of pollution*: For him, the environmental external effects resulting from his decision about emissions are borne by others. Pollution for him is a private 'good', and he does not consume any of it.

Work through the analysis in Figure 20.15 to see how the choices of the citizens and businesses are modelled.

You may recall that this figure is very similar to Figure 5.8, in which Angela the farmer and Bruno the landowner were bargaining over the amount of grain Angela would transfer to Bruno. As in that problem, the study of a bargaining problem is easier if the slope of the indifference curves remains unchanged at a given wage as utility increases.

Here, the conflict is about the amount of emissions that the townspeople will suffer. The firm's profits depend on the emissions, and profits are greater if it can dispose of more toxic materials freely.

The position of the citizens' reservation indifference curve depends on what they would expect to get in some other location. If they could find a

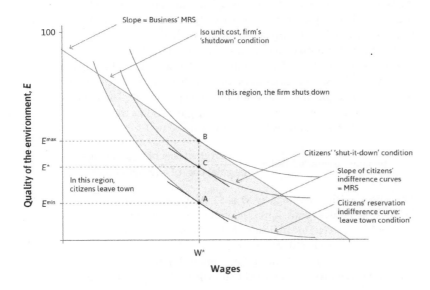

Figure 20.15 Conflicts of interest over wages and abatement.

1. The representative citizen's reservation indifference curve is the 'leave town condition'
This gives all the combinations of wages and environmental quality that would be just barely sufficient to induce a representative citizen to stay.

2. The firm's 'shutdown condition'
This shows the combinations of wages and environmental quality offered by the firm that would just barely keep the firm in Brownsville.

3. Infeasible options
The portions of the figure above the firm's shutdown condition and below the citizen's leave town condition are infeasible.

4. The citizens have power, point B
Suppose the citizens could impose a legally enforceable level of environmental quality in the town and set their own wages. Consistent with the firm remaining in town, the citizens set wages at w^* and quality of the environment at E^{max}.

5. A take-it-or-leave-it ultimatum, point A
On the other hand, if the firm could announce a take-it-or-leave-it ultimatum, it would minimize costs whilst ensuring the citizens do not choose to leave town at E^{min}.

6. The difference between E^{max} and E^{min}
This is a measure of the extent of mutual gains the citizens and the business may enjoy. Any outcome in the shaded area is preferred by both parties to their outside option, but only the points between A and B, such as C, are Pareto efficient.

high-paying job in a non-toxic community, the curve would be higher and to the right of the one that is shown. Its slope, the marginal rate of substitution, is the citizens' marginal utility of higher wages, divided by the marginal utility of environmental quality.

$$\text{citizens' MRS} = \frac{\text{marginal utility of wages}}{\text{marginal utility of environmental quality}}$$

We assume that the citizens' marginal valuation of improvements in the environment is constant, but (in contrast to the model in Section 20.3) they have diminishing marginal utility of receiving higher wages. At high wages (and very poor environmental quality) on the far right of the reservation indifference curve, the MRS is small (the curve is almost flat) because citizens would not care much about wages (as they are already getting paid a high wage) but they are very concerned about the poor environment. At low wages the curve is steep, because they place a high value on wage increases.

The firm's shutdown condition shows the combinations of wages and environmental quality offered by the firm that would barely keep the firm in Brownsville. All of the points on this line have the same cost of producing a unit of output and, as a result, the same profit rate. The firm's profits are increasing as you move towards the origin. It is like the isocost curve in Unit 2, and the isocost lines for effort in Unit 6.

$$\text{business owner's MRS} = \frac{\text{marginal cost of higher wages}}{\text{marginal cost of environmental quality}}$$

The cost of raising the wage by \$1 is \$1. Assume the cost incurred by the owner if he reduces emissions is p per unit of abatement, so the owner's MRS $= 1/p$. A steep line indicates that p is small—avoiding emissions and thereby allowing a healthier environment is cheap.

The firm faces a trade-off. If it is at point B in the figure, it pays wages and produces emissions at a level that makes it barely profitable enough to stay in business. Therefore, if it offers a higher-quality environment to the citizens, it can only do this by offering a lower wage. The opportunity cost of one unit of a better environment is p in reduced wages.

Any combination of wages and environmental quality in the shaded portion of the figure is a feasible outcome of this conflict. Any combination on the vertical line between A and B is a Pareto-efficient outcome. We cannot say which feasible outcome will occur, though, unless we know more about the bargaining power of the citizens and the firm.

The firm has all the bargaining power

If the firm could simply announce a take-it-or-leave-it ultimatum, then it would choose point A in Figure 20.15. The firm's costs will then be well below the shutdown level of costs because they will be freely emitting toxic materials, which reduce the citizen's environmental quality from $E^{\max}$, the least emissions (and highest quality environment) consistent with the firm staying in business, to $E^{\min}$. This difference ($E^{\max} - E^{\min}$) shows up as cost reductions, and hence as additional profits, in the firm's accounts. It also shows up as exposure to health hazards in the medical records of the people who live in the town.

The firm's chosen point, A, is on the citizens' reservation indifference curve where the vertical distance between the firm's shutdown condition and the citizens' leave town condition is the greatest. This will occur when:

$$\text{business' MRS} = \frac{1}{p}$$

$$= \frac{\text{marginal utility of wages}}{\text{marginal utility of environmental quality}}$$

$$= \text{citizens' MRS}$$

Citizens have all the bargaining power

If the bargaining power had been reversed, then the citizens would choose to impose E^{max} and wages w^*. This ensures that the citizens are on their highest possible indifference curve, while also satisfying the firm's shutdown condition. Again, at this point the MRS of the business is equal to the MRS of the citizens.

Dividing the mutual gains

The difference between E^{max} and E^{min} measures the extent of mutual gains the townspeople and the business may enjoy. Any outcome between A and B on the figure is preferable to the next best alternative for the business (shut down) and the citizens (leave town). You can think of the mutual gains as a pie that the citizens and the business owner will divide. How the pie is divided up between the two parties depends, as we have seen in Units 4 and 5, on their relative bargaining power.

A point such as C in Figure 20.15 might be possible if the citizens, acting jointly through their town council, imposed a legal minimal level of environmental quality and wages for the business to continue to operate. Acting together, the citizens would have more bargaining power than if they used the threat to leave town as individuals: they could require that the business at least meet the citizens' 'shut-it-down condition' shown in Figure 20.15.

Bargaining power in this case would be affected not only by the two parties' reservation options but also by:

- *Enforcement capacity:* The town government may not have enforcement capacities to impose an emissions limit on the firm.
- *Verifiable information:* The citizens may not have sufficient information about the levels and dangers of emissions to win a case in court. If so, the firm would not comply with an agreed-upon emissions level such as at C in Figure 20.15.
- *Citizen consensus:* If the town's citizens were not in agreement about the dangers of the emissions, the elected officials of the town who legislate an emissions limit might not be re-elected.
- *Lobbying:* The firm may be able to convince the citizens that their health concerns were misplaced, or had little to do with the firm's emissions.
- *Legal recourse:* The firm may be legally entitled to emit any level of emissions that it finds profitable (perhaps subject to having purchased permits allowing it to do this).

So far we have focused on the question of how much abatement there should be. Now we consider a second question: How should the desired level of abatement be accomplished?

Consider a town with a single business that employs the entire labour force, whose toxic emissions are a threat to the health of the citizens. Figure 20.15 (page 923) shows the business' 'shutdown' curve (the combination of wages and environmental quality offered by the firm that would just about keep the firm operating) and the citizens' indifference curves for the quality of environment and their wage income. The citizens' reservation indifference curve is also shown.

Based on this information, which of the following statements is correct?

☐ All points below the citizens' reservation indifference curve and above the business' 'shutdown' curve are infeasible.
☐ If the business has all the bargaining power, then point B is chosen.
☐ If the citizens have all the bargaining power, then they will choose the point with the highest possible wage.
☐ Point C is the only Pareto-efficient choice.

20.5 CAP AND TRADE ENVIRONMENTAL POLICIES

price-based environmental policy A policy that uses a tax or subsidy to affect prices, with the goal of internalizing the external effects on the environment of an individual's choices.

quantity-based environmental policy Policies that implement environmental objectives by using bans, caps, and regulations.

cap and trade A policy through which a limited number of permits to pollute are issued, and can be bought and sold on a market. It combines a quantity-based limit on emissions, and a price-based approach that places a cost on environmentally damaging decisions.

In Unit 12, we saw possible remedies for the market failure that arose from the negative external effects of pesticide use. The range of remedies included private bargaining between the pesticide users and the fishing community whose livelihoods were threatened, taxes to make the pesticides (or the bananas produced using them) more expensive, ownership of all affected assets by a single business or other decision-making entity, and quotas or outright bans on the use of the pesticide. Some of these policies would have made it more expensive to harm the environment so as to provide incentives for greener economic decision making (**price-based policies**). Others would have made it illegal (**quantity-based policies**).

A policy called **cap and trade** is a policy that combines a legal limit on the amount of emissions with an incentive-based approach to assigning the abatement required to meet this legal limit among firms and other actors.

Here is the idea:

- *The government or governments set the total level of abatement required:* This is called the 'cap' and it constitutes the 'quantity' side of the policy.
- *The government creates permits:* The number of permits issued limits total emissions to the size of the cap.
- *The government allocates permits:* They can be given to the firms operating in industries emitting the pollutant, or they can be auctioned to polluting firms by the government.
- *The permits are traded:* For some firms, polluting is very profitable and abatement costly. They will buy permits from other firms. Firms that produce little pollution or have low costs of abatement may have excess permits, which they can sell. Trade occurs until the gains from trade are eliminated.
- *The firms submit permits to government to cover their emissions:* For each tonne of emissions produced, firms are required to provide one permit to the government. Ideally, government monitoring ensures that firms cannot cheat, and any firms caught violating the law are penalized with large fines.

Cap and trade policies are a way of implementing some desired level of emissions (or, equivalently, the total level of abatement required, E^*) as the ideal policymaker did in Figure 20.13.

The desired level, however decided, is shown by the length of the horizontal axis in Figure 20.16. The question addressed by cap and trade is: given that firms vary in their production technologies, how will the total amount of required abatement be divided among them? The objective of a scheme for trading permits is that the abatement should be done by the firms for which this is least costly because this saves scarce resources that can be used elsewhere.

To see how this works, go through the analysis in Figure 20.16, which shows the case where the number of permits is initially divided equally between two firms with different costs of abatement.

There are many ways in which the permits might be traded once they are issued. One is the auction-type market studied in Unit 11, in which we saw (from an experiment) that the traders quickly converged to trading at a price like P^*, which is the market-clearing price. The trading of permits achieves the desired level of abatement at the lowest resource cost to the economy. P^* is the permit price and is equal to the marginal cost of abatement in the economy.

Cap and trade: Examples of emissions trading

One of the earliest cases of successful emissions trading was the sulphur dioxide (SO_2) cap and trade scheme in the US, implemented in the 1990s and intended to reduce acid rain. By 2007, annual SO_2 emissions had declined by 43% from 1990 levels, despite electricity generation from coal-fired power plants increasing more than 26% during the same period.

The European Union Emissions Trading Scheme (EU ETS), launched in 2005, is the largest CO_2 cap and trade scheme in the world, and now covers 11,000 polluting installations across the EU. National governments auction 57% of permits in the EU ETS, and the overall emission cap (that is, the amount E^* in Figure 20.16) is tightened every year. Some of the auction proceeds are used to fund low-carbon energy innovation. Similar carbon trading schemes exist in other countries and regions.

The EU ETS has been less successful than the US SO_2 scheme. Some analysts think this is due largely to the fact that the permitted level of emissions was too high (too large a cap). After the financial crisis in Europe, lower aggregate demand caused the demand for electric power to shrink and with it, firms' profit-maximizing emissions levels. With demand exceeding supply, the price of permits fell dramatically, providing little incentive for firms to undertake abatement expenditures. These effects are shown in Figure 20.17.

This highlights a drawback of cap and trade. The price signal is not necessarily a reliable guide for future abatement investment decisions. In Germany, for example, the fall in permit prices led to several high-emitting coal power plants reopening, because dirty technology was profitable again.

But emissions trading schemes do not need to leave the market entirely free. The UK, for example, uses a carbon price floor, which sets a minimum price for British participants in the Emissions Trading Scheme. They do this to avoid the 'virtually free pollution' outcome that occurs when the permit price crashes.

The estimated total external cost of a tonne of carbon dioxide emissions differs depending on how we value future generations, as we shall see in

Section 20.9. A low-end estimate in 2017 dollars is about $40 per tonne of CO_2 emissions, and it is rising fast because the greater the amount of CO_2 in the atmosphere, the higher the marginal effect on climate of adding more. The recent price of a permit on the European Union Emissions Trading Scheme (shown in Figure 20.17) is less than a fifth of this cost, so the permit plan is inducing decision-makers to internalize only a small fraction of the negative external effects.

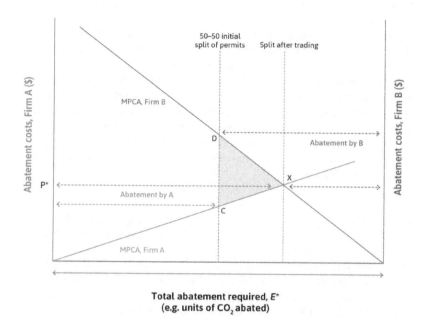

Figure 20.16 Cap and trade: Buying and selling permits to pollute.

1. The marginal private cost of abatement (MPCA) of firm A
This is shown in red and measured in the usual way from the left-hand axis. It rises as its cost of abatement increases. Firm A uses a relatively low-emissions technology to produce its product.

2. The marginal cost of abatement (MPCA) of firm B
This is shown in blue and measured from the right-hand axis, so it rises from the right origin as B engages in more abatement. Firm B uses a more emissions-intensive technology to produce its product, and therefore its marginal cost of abatement is higher than for Firm A.

3. Permits split 50–50
Let's see what happens if the permits to pollute are initially split 50–50 between the two firms.

4. Permits split 50–50: The possibility of gains from trading permits.
Firm B has a higher MPCA. If it can buy a permit to pollute more from Firm A for a price less than its marginal cost, it will purchase the permit, rather than abate. This creates the possibility of gains from the trade in permits.

5. Firm B will buy permits from A: How many?
How many permits will they exchange? As long as MCPA of firm B exceeds the MPCA of Firm A, both benefit by A selling permits to B. If the market is competitive, we expect trading until the MPCA is equalized across all firms.

6. The gains from trade
The shaded triangle shows the gains from trade created by the market for permits. P^* is the permit price and is equal to the marginal cost of abatement in the economy. The green area above the red dashed line is the share of the gains from trade that Firm B receives, while the area below is Firm A's share of the gains from trade.

Ideally, a tax on fossil fuels could entirely offset these external effects, with the added advantage that businesses and others would then face less uncertainty about the cost of burning carbon. A tax on carbon would raise the cost of emitting carbon in exactly the same way as having to pay for an emissions permit would do. In fact, the effect on costs would be identical if the market-determined cost of the permit were to be the same as the tax rate per tonne of emissions set by the government. The effect of the increase in costs would be higher prices of emissions-intensive goods and hence, *ceteris paribus*, demand for such goods would fall. Both the cap and trade and a carbon tax are said to be a way to 'put a price on' the external effects of carbon emissions.

How high should the price of carbon emissions be?

Given that producers and users of fossil fuels are usually heavily subsidized (at very different rates from country to country) the tax or the cost of a permit would have to exceed $40. On average around the world, fossil fuel subsidies are about $15 per tonne, so an optimal tax would be $55 per tonne (to internalize the external costs and to offset the subsidy). A simpler policy would be to eliminate the subsidies and set the carbon tax at our best estimate of the external cost of burning carbon.

The pros and cons of these two policies:

- a cap and trade permit based system with a sufficiently low cap
- a carbon tax at a sufficiently high rate to offset the external costs (and subsidies, if these remain)

These have been actively debated among environmental economists, with no clear consensus other than that either is preferable to the policies being pursued in most countries. Cap and trade, however, has been more popular, perhaps because it has the advantage of flexiblity. The ability to set the carbon price, but then to control the way in which permits are allocated and traded, gives the policymaker two 'levers'. In contrast, a single tax may be politically unpopular for a policymaker to implement.

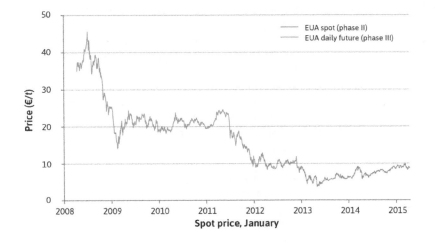

Data provided by SendeCO$_2$ based on prices from Bloomberg Business.

Figure 20.17 Permit prices in the European Union Emissions Trading Scheme (EU ETS).

EXERCISE 20.5 ASSESSING CAP AND TRADE POLICIES

1. Explain why the green area in Figure 20.16 (page 928) represents the total gains from trade. Hint: think about the first permit that Firm B buys from Firm A. How much is the most that Firm B would have been willing to pay? How much was the least that Firm A would have been willing to accept in order to part with the permit?

2. How would you explain the way a cap and trade policy works to someone who has not studied economics? How would you respond to their concerns that the policy is likely to be ineffective or unfair? Many newspapers and blogs publish 'op-eds', that is, opinion editorials from the public. A common length limit is 600 words. Find some op-eds on climate policy, and having looked at how they are written, draft your answer to this question in the form of an op-ed.

EXERCISE 20.6 A SUCCESSFUL TRADABLE EMISSIONS PERMIT PROGRAM

The cap and trade sulphur dioxide permit program in the US successfully reduced emissions. The program costs were approximately one-fiftieth of the estimated benefits.

Read Robert Stavins and colleagues' views on the US sulphur dioxide cap and trade program at VOXeu.org (http://tinyco.re/7237191).

1. In the view of the authors, why are cap and trade systems such powerful tools to achieve reductions in emissions?

Also read 'The SO$_2$ Allowance Trading System' (http://tinyco.re/6011888) by Richard Schmalensee and Robert Stavins of the MIT Center for Energy and Environmental Policy Research.

2. Summarize the evolution of permit prices using Figure 2 in the article.
3. How well can the price movements in permit prices be explained by the analysis in Figure 20.16 (page 928)?

Look again at Hayek's explanation of prices as messages (Unit 11), and the analyses of asset price bubbles (Unit 11) and housing bubbles (Unit 17).

4. Could we use similar reasoning to explain price movements in Figure 2 of the paper by Schmalensee and Stavins?

EXERCISE 20.7 WOULD A CARBON TAX REDUCE EMISSIONS MORE THAN REGULATION?

In 2017, economists Martin Feldstein and Greg Mankiw (respectively economic advisors to US Presidents Ronald Reagan and George W. Bush), together with Ted Halstead, a climate campaigner, suggested in the op-ed 'A Conservative Case for Climate Action' (http://tinyco.re/8116600) that an ideal climate policy in the US should consist of three parts:

- A single carbon tax should replace all regulations that are aimed at reducing carbon emissions.
- Revenues collected from the tax should be refunded to American taxpayers in quarterly paychecks ('carbon dividend').
- American firms that export to countries without carbon taxes should not pay a carbon tax, while importers should face an import tax on the carbon contents of their products (a 'carbon border adjustment').

1. Explain the economic reasoning behind each part of the proposal.
2. Why do the economists think replacing regulations with a single carbon tax would be more efficient?
3. Some environmental groups oppose the carbon dividend. They argue that the money could be better spent (http://tinyco.re/8646263). Do you agree? What should carbon revenues be spent on? Do you think citizens are more likely to support a carbon tax if there is a carbon dividend?
4. Why do the economists think a border carbon adjustment is necessary? What would be the effect of a domestic carbon tax without a border carbon adjustment? What incentives does it create for American companies and for foreign companies? Is it fair on firms from developing countries (who often generate a lot of electricity from high emissions coal) who export their products to the US?
5. Do you support the proposal by Feldstein, Mankiw, and Halstead. Explain why or why not. What changes would you make?

20.6 THE MEASUREMENT CHALLENGES OF ENVIRONMENTAL POLICY

To implement environmental policies using the framework we have provided, we need to measure the value of abatement.

Placing a value on the benefits of abatement is challenging because we are dealing with missing markets for environmental quality and uncertain long-term impacts. What is the value of preserving a rainforest, saving a threatened species, creating better air, or less noise? To answer these questions, different methods are used depending on whether the environmental issue in question is affecting environmental wellbeing, health, consumption, or future assets.

We examine two methods of measuring the benefits of abatement: **hedonic pricing** and **contingent valuation**.

Contingent valuation

Among the easiest and most widely used methods of valuing the benefits of abatement is simply to ask people. For example, after the 1989 Exxon Valdez oil spill in Alaska, which released 11 million gallons (42 million litres) of crude oil into beautiful Prince William Sound, the court used contingent valuation to assess the value of the losses (such as the value of natural beauty) caused by the spill. They did this in a survey by asking respondents how much they would be willing to pay to prevent a new spill. The study estimated the lost value in 1990 to be at least $2.8 billion. Exxon eventually paid $1 billion in damages in a settlement with the governments of Alaska and the US.

Researchers used contingent valuation techniques (http://tinyco.re/9038928) to get a quantitative estimate of the value of elephant conservation in Sri Lanka. Farmers were killing elephants to protect crops and homes. The researchers wanted to know how much Sri Lankans would be willing to pay to the farmers as compensation for the damages caused by the elephants, if the farmers stopped killing them.

Contingent evaluation is called a *stated* preference approach because it is survey-based and accepts the respondents' statements of their values as indicative of their true preferences. This is not the case for hedonic pricing.

Hedonic pricing

Hedonic pricing is called a *revealed* preference approach because it uses people's economic behaviour (not their statements) to reveal what their preferences are. Laboratory experiments are a similar method of studying revealed preferences, as we saw in Unit 4. But lab experiments are not very useful in valuing the environment.

For example, how much do you value having your residence being free of the sound of aircraft flying overhead? Economists observe that houses under aircraft flight paths are sold for less than equivalent houses in quieter locations. By comparing data on house prices, we can calculate the amount people are prepared to pay to avoid the noise pollution.

This technique was used in the UK to set the tax for landfill waste. The marginal benefits of abatement were estimated in a study that used data on more than half a million housing transactions over the period 1991–2000. By controlling for a large number of factors that can account for the variation in house prices, the researchers then tested whether any of the variation left unexplained could be accounted for by the proximity of the house to a landfill site. The researchers found that being within a quarter of

hedonic pricing A method used to infer the economic value of unpriced environmental or perceptual qualities that affect the price of a marketed good. It allows a researcher to put a price on hard-to-quantify characteristics. Estimations are based on people's revealed preferences, that is, the price they pay for one thing compared to another.
contingent valuation A survey-based technique used to assess the value of non-market resources. *Also known as: stated-preference model.*

Stephen Smith. 2011. *Environmental Economics: A Very Short Introduction*. Oxford: Oxford University Press.

a mile (400 metres) of a working landfill site reduced house prices by 7%. They calculated that the marginal benefit from reducing the proximity to a landfill site was £2.86 per tonne of waste (in 2003 prices).

Hedonic pricing and contingent valuation give us a way to measure the way people value a particular change in the environment given their experience of this change. Green growth accounting gives us a way to estimate the value of conserving environmental resources for society as a whole, today and in the future. Below, you will learn about how some economists are placing a monetary value on society's use of natural assets.

HOW ECONOMISTS LEARN FROM FACTS

Natural capital and green growth

Recall that **depreciation** refers to the wearing out or using up of the physical capital goods used in production. In the green growth accounting framework, the environment is similarly considered as an asset that can be used up. The environment is part of what society needs to produce goods and services. Thus, environmental degradation reduces the assets of the society in much the same way as the wear and tear or obsolescence of machines used in production.

Remember that income is the most a person, or a nation, could consume without reducing its capacity to produce in the future. This was the message of the bathtub in Unit 10. Income is the flow of water into the tub minus the amount of evaporation that is reducing the total amount of water in the tub. Income according to this definition is gross income minus depreciation.

Although environmental degradation is not measured in conventional national accounts, it should be, because using up our natural capital is no different from the wear and tear on the machines and other equipment we use.

The World Bank estimates that in low-income countries, natural capital comprises 36% of wealth, so using some of this up and not counting the loss overstates how fast income is really growing. By how much though? In order to take natural capital loss into account, we must figure out how much it will cost (per year) to replace the lost natural capital and then subtract it from the annual GDP figure (remember that the most common measure of income, GDP, does not even take account of the depreciation of capital goods because of difficulties with measurement).

If you make this accounting adjustment (also known as a **green adjustment**), 'success stories' of economic growth look less impressive. When Indonesian government policy generated a timber boom between 1979 and 1982, Robert Repetto and his colleagues from the World Resources Institute estimated that the country used up more than $2 billion of potential forest revenues. They showed that, after considering deforestation, oil depletion, and soil erosion, Indonesia's true average annual rate of growth of income (net of used up natural capital)—originally reported as 7.1% from 1971 to 1984—was in reality only 4%. A similar exercise was carried out for Sweden between 1993 and 1997, where the loss of natural assets was estimated to be around 1% of GDP per year.

depreciation The loss in value of a form of wealth that occurs either through use (wear and tear) or the passage of time (obsolescence).

green adjustment Accounting adjustment made to conventional measures of national income to include the value of natural capital.

WHEN ECONOMISTS DISAGREE

Willingness to pay versus the right to a livable environment

The Constitution of the Republic South Africa asserts the citizen's 'right to an environment which is not detrimental to his or her health or wellbeing'. The Supreme Court of India ruled that the 'right to life' guaranteed by the Constitution of India 'includes the right to enjoyment of pollution-free water and air ...' Similar rights are granted in at least 13 other constitutions, including those of Portugal, Turkey, Chile, and South Korea. Use the Constitute Project website (http://tinyco.re/9458720) to check the constitution of your country, or any other in which you are interested, to see if you can find these guarantees.

Political movements opposing the privatization of water supply have used similar language. Access to clean water, they argue, is a human right. When a feature of the environment such as proximity to a landfill, noise pollution, or toxic emissions from a smelter is valued in monetary terms using the methods described above, this ignores the principle advanced by many that people have a right to an environment free of these hazards.

But in response, others ask: why should the quality of the environment that you experience be any different from the quality of the car that you drive or the food that you eat? You get what you pay for, and if you are unwilling to pay, then why should the policymaker worry about your values? If you believe this, the benefits of abatement policies can be measured by the citizens' willingness to pay (WTP) for the improved environment that the abatement will allow.

The WTP measure is criticized by some economists and citizens because it implies that people with hardly any money place a limited value on the environment, just as they have a limited willingness to pay for anything else. They do not lack the will, but they lack the way. Therefore using WTP as the method of estimating the benefits of abatement—for example, when either contingent valuation or hedonic pricing is used—means that policies that improve environmental hazards that mostly affect the poor, like ensuring safe drinking water in urban areas, will be valued less than policies that raise the environmental quality experienced by rich people, like pristine rivers, lakes, and oceans to enjoy while boating.

Also, this value may depend on how the question that determines the stated preference is asked. If, instead of our WTP for preservation of the environment, we are asked what compensation we are willing to accept (WTA) for the same proposed reduction in the quality of the same environment, empirical evidence is that the result would be a higher number.

If a safe environment is a right, an economist would term it a **merit good**, which you may recall from Unit 12. It is like the right to vote, or legal representation in court, or an adequate education: a good that should be available to all citizens irrespective of their ability to pay.

The advantage of the approach based on willingness to pay is that it makes use of information on how people value the environment. This should be relevant to how much we invest in environmental quality. Defining the environment as a right has the advantage that it does not give priority to the preferences of those with higher incomes in shaping environmental policy.

merit goods Goods and services that should be available to everyone, independently of their ability to pay.

EXERCISE 20.8 WEALTH AND NATURAL CAPITAL
Download the World Bank data in 'The Changing Wealth of Nations' dataset (http://tinyco.re/8096132).

1. Using the total wealth data, calculate the change in natural capital between 1995 and 2000 and between 2000 and 2005 in absolute terms for three high income, middle income, and low income countries. Summarize and interpret your results.

Go to the World Bank's open data website (http://tinyco.re/8085370). Find and download GDP (in constant prices) for your chosen countries for 1995, 2000, and 2005.

2. Calculate the change in GDP between these periods in absolute terms. Draw a scatter plot with the percentage change in GDP on the vertical axis and the percentage change in natural capital on the horizontal axis. Does it look like there is a relationship between these two variables? Suggest explanations for any relationship you find.

QUESTION 20.7 CHOOSE THE CORRECT ANSWER(S)
Which of the following statements is correct regarding valuation of the benefits of abatement?

☐ An estimation of a nation's GDP currently includes the depletion of the nation's natural resources as a negative adjustment.
☐ In the hedonic pricing method, the cost of noise pollution near an airport is estimated by a survey of how much the residents are willing to pay to reduce the noise.
☐ In the contingent valuation method, the pollution due to landfill waste is estimated using the differences in the house prices according to the proximity to a landfill site.
☐ Asking citizens for their willingness to pay for a 'greener' environment may result in policies that mostly affect the poor being valued less than those that raise the environmental quality experienced by the rich.

20.7 DYNAMIC ENVIRONMENTAL POLICIES: FUTURE TECHNOLOGIES AND LIFESTYLES

The trade-offs given by the feasible sets and indifference curves we have used in our analysis will change as people adopt new values and lifestyles and develop new technologies, and as our impact on the environment intensifies.

Prices, quantities and green innovation

Improvements in technology can enlarge the feasible set. Some improvements may make abatement more efficient, lowering the opportunity cost of an improved environment. Others may improve methods of producing goods, reducing the environmental costs of consumption as a result. Figure 20.18 illustrates the effect of a technological improvement, which improves the marginal rate of transformation of foregone consumption into abatement (otherwise known as the **marginal productivity of abatement expenditure**), and hence into an improvement in environmental quality. By increasing the marginal productivity of abatement expenditure, it makes the feasible frontier steeper.

In Unit 2, you learned how the rents from innovation drive progress and the improvement of productivity. If the right incentives exist to create innovation rents, we would expect technological breakthroughs that can deliver substitutes for some resources that would otherwise be used up, or that need to stay in the ground if climate change is to be safely limited. One such case is the technological progress achieved in solar energy.

Subsidies to firms producing the panels and other equipment has helped fund research and development in these new sources of electricity. Subsidies to those installing solar panels have increased demand. The growth of demand has in turn led to a sharp decrease in the price of solar panels thanks to **learning by doing** in the production process, which makes production cheaper and cheaper.

The idea that environmental regulation can create greater efficiency and be an incentive to innovation is known as the 'Porter Hypothesis', because it

> **marginal productivity of abatement expenditures** The marginal rate of transformation (MRT) of abatement costs into improved environment. It is the slope of the feasible frontier. *See also: marginal rate of transformation, feasible frontier.*

> Michael E. Porter and Claas van der Linde. 1995. 'Toward a New Conception of the Environment-Competitiveness Relationship'. *Journal of Economic Perspectives* 9 (4): pp. 97–118.

> **learning by doing** This occurs when the output per unit of inputs increases with greater experience in producing a good or service.

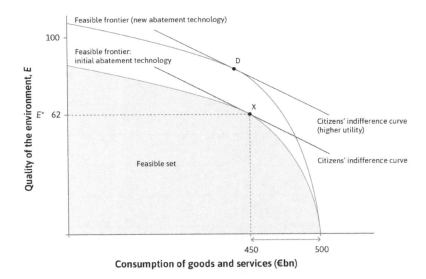

Figure 20.18 The abatement technology changes.

was first argued by Michael Porter, an economist, in 1995. He argued that the costs of regulation led firms to look for cleaner, more efficent technologies. The benefits of these technologies compensate both the costs of regulation, and the costs of innovation.

Figures 20.19a and b show the dramatic improvement in photovoltaic cell efficiency over the last few decades, which has led to a reduction in the cost of producing solar electricity.

In the US, many renewable energy technologies can already compete with fossil fuel generation without the need for subsidies, in terms of the total cost per unit of electricity generated, as shown in Figure 20.19b. However, since we can only generate wind power when the wind blows and solar power when the sun shines, renewable energy generation can be less reliable than fossil fuel generation. Fossil fuel generation may therefore be preferred in the absence of subsidies, even though the unit costs for solar power are lower.

To illustrate how a tax can create innovation rents by changing relative prices and promote innovation by the private sector, we apply a model introduced in Unit 2. Imagine a textile producer called Olympiad Industries (a hypothetical business), located in a country where the supply of electricity is intermittent, and so like most firms in the country it owns a coal-fired power generator. Burning fossil fuel generates greenhouse gases but the alternative (solar power) is more expensive. While the firm has installed some solar panels, it relies primarily on coal for electricity generation.

Figure 20.20 illustrates the cost comparison. You will be familiar with the model: it is the one in Unit 2 in which we explained how relatively high wages in England made the introduction of a labour-saving innovation (the spinning jenny) profitable. The difference is that we are not considering an innovation that saves labour but instead saves environmental resources, many of which (unlike labour in England in the eighteenth century) have no price.

In this figure, we study the effects of a tax on carbon-based energy sources on a firm's choice of technology. Prior to the tax, the coal-intensive

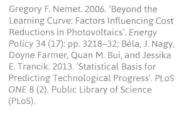

Gregory F. Nemet. 2006. 'Beyond the Learning Curve: Factors Influencing Cost Reductions in Photovoltaics'. *Energy Policy* 34 (17): pp. 3218–32; Béla, J. Nagy, Doyne Farmer, Quan M. Bui, and Jessika E. Trancik. 2013. 'Statistical Basis for Predicting Technological Progress'. *PLoS ONE* 8 (2). Public Library of Science (PLoS).

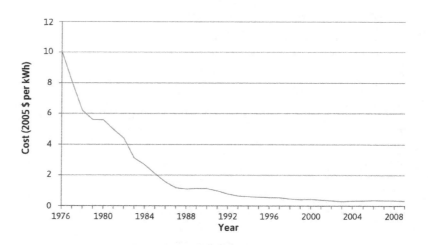

Figure 20.19a Cost of generating electricity (new capacity) using photovoltaic cells in the US (1976–2009).

technology was the cost-minimizing way to produce. Hence there was no incentive for a firm to develop and use renewable energy sources, and as a result, there were no profits to gain from developing the alternative to coal. After the tax, the firm would save the equivalent of a tonne of coal per unit of output by developing and using the solar technology.

The comparison of costs gives the owner of Olympiad a reason to adopt solar technology. Here the tax has changed the message sent by prices. It now says that you can make a profit by using renewable sources of energy. It also says that sticking with coal may mean being undercut by your competitors, if they switch to the lower-cost technology.

Environmental policy and long-term changes in lifestyles

In the long run, in addition to the role of policy in green innovation, how much we value the goods that contribute to our wellbeing can also change. Recall our discussion of social preferences from Unit 4. We saw that individual behaviours can be motivated by a desire to contribute to the common good. Below, you see how economists apply this general idea of pro-social preferences to evaluate the potential contribution of such preferences to environmental conservation.

We saw above that environmental behaviours can arise because of pro-social preferences. But they can also arise because of changes in lifestyles. The example of the Netherlands will illustrate this point.

In Figure 3.1, you saw that production workers in the Netherlands worked fewer than half as many hours in the year 2000 as they had in 1900. In 2000 they enjoyed a lot more free time and consumed less than half as many goods and services as they would have done had they continued working more than 3,000 hours a year, as they did in 1900. If they still worked long hours and used all these earnings for consumption, their adverse impact on the environment would be larger.

Look ahead to Figure 20.25a, which shows the CO_2 emissions and GDP per capita for a wide range of countries. As a thought experiment, imagine that the Netherlands were twice as rich as it is in that graph. What would be the environmental impact in terms of CO_2 emissions? In that figure the

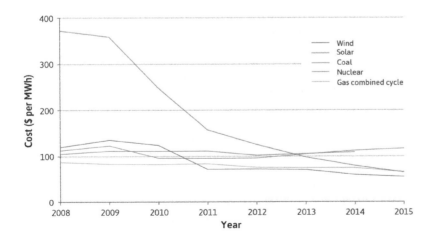

Lazard. 2015. 'Levelized Cost of Energy Analysis 9.0'. Lazard.com. Updated November 17 2015.

Figure 20.19b Cost of generating electricity (new capacity) from different sources in the US (2008–2015).

Netherlands is slightly below the 'predicted' line so if we assume that this was also true of our hypothetical workaholic Dutch nation, we can determine the level of CO_2 emissions using the line of best fit. Instead of emitting 11 tonnes of CO_2 per capita per year, they would be emitting more than 20 tonnes. This would make the Netherlands among the top polluters in the world.

The Netherlands experienced an unusually large fall in its work hours (Figure 3.1 shows that work hours in France and the US fell, but not on the same scale as the Dutch). But even for these and other countries, if free time had not expanded at the opportunity cost of less consumption, the impact on global climate change would have been worse.

A lifestyle that is rich in free time, and less rich than it could be in goods and services produced in the economy, is a 'greener' lifestyle. Environmental policies can contribute to people adopting this lifestyle.

To see how, imagine that Omar is considering how far to travel by air for his holiday. Omar has enough income to fly anywhere, but he knows that burning aviation fuel is a major source of greenhouse gases. He would also

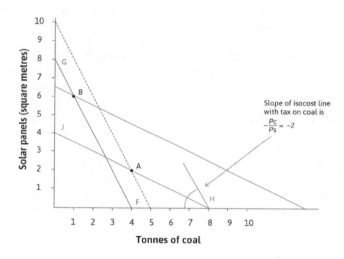

Figure 20.20 Olympiad Industries' choice of technology: The effect of an environmental tax on firm behaviour.

1. Technologies A and B
Both technologies produce 100 metres of textiles: A is coal-intensive and B is solar-intensive. The new technology, B, uses almost entirely solar power with just a bit of coal use for periods of the year when solar power is unreliable.

2. The firm's isocost line
The isocost line shows all of the possible combinations of solar and coal (sufficient to produce 100 metres of textiles) that have the same cost. If the isocost is HJ, firms use technology A, because B costs more (it lies outside the line HJ). The flat slope of the isocost line says that coal is a bargain.

3. Taxing fossil fuels
A tax per kilowatt-hour on the use of coal for energy-generation is introduced. This means that for the same cost as 4 tonnes of coal, the firm could now be using 8 solar panels.

4. The new isocost line
The solar-intensive technology B is on the blue isocost line and is now cheaper than the status quo A-technology.

HOW ECONOMISTS LEARN FROM FACTS

Social preferences and environmental sustainability

Do the kinds of altruistic and reciprocal **social preferences** that we studied in Unit 4 motivate people to act in ways that will sustain the environment? This is not an easy question to answer because people are naturally happy to attribute their environmentally friendly actions to their green values, even if the latter were not really the reason for the action.

But two experimental studies suggest that social preferences do support green actions.

In the northeastern region of Brazil, shrimp are caught in large plastic bucket-like contraptions; the fishermen cut holes in the bottoms of the traps to allow the immature shrimp to escape, thereby preserving the stock for future catches. The fishermen thus face a real-world social dilemma like the ones we studied in Unit 4: the expected income of each would be greater if he were to cut smaller holes in his traps (increasing his own catch) while others cut larger holes in theirs (preserving future stocks).

In prisoners' dilemma terms, small trap holes are a form of defection that maximizes the individual's material payoff irrespective of what others do (it is the dominant strategy). But a shrimper might resist the temptation to defect if he were both public spirited toward the other fishermen and sufficiently patient to value the future opportunities that they all would lose if he were to use traps with smaller holes.

Experimental economists Ernst Fehr and Andreas Leibbrandt implemented both a public good experimental game and an experimental measure of impatience with the shrimpers. Like the experiments in Unit 4, both were played anonymously and the payoffs were real. Those who did not contribute in the public goods game went home with more money than the cooperative types who contributed.

The researchers found that the shrimpers with both greater patience and greater cooperativeness in the experimental game punched significantly larger holes in their traps, thereby protecting future stocks for the entire community. The effects, controlling for a large number of other possible influences on hole size, were substantial.

Additional evidence that social preferences can support green outcomes comes from a set of experiments and field studies with 49 groups of herders of the Bale Oromo people in Ethiopia, who were engaged in forest-commons management. Devesh Rustagi and his co-authors implemented public-goods experiments with a total of 679 herders, and also studied the success of the herders' cooperative forest projects.

The most common behavioural type in the experiments, constituting just over a third of the subjects, were 'conditional cooperators', who reciprocated higher contributions by others by contributing more to the public good themselves. Controlling for a large number of other influences on the success of the forest projects, the authors found that groups with a larger number of conditional cooperators were more successful (planted more new trees) than those with fewer conditional cooperators.

This was in part because members of groups with more conditional cooperators spent significantly more time monitoring others' use of the

social preferences Preferences that place a value on what happens to other people, and on acting morally, even if it results in lower payoffs for the individual.

Ernst Fehr and Andreas Leibbrandt. 2011. 'A Field Study on Cooperativeness and Impatience in the Tragedy of the Commons'. *Journal of Public Economics* 95 (9–10): pp. 1144–55.

Devesh Rustagi, Stefanie Engel, and Michael Kosfeld. 2010. 'Conditional Cooperation and Costly Monitoring Explain Success in Forest Commons Management'. *Science* 330: pp. 961–65.

forest. As with the Brazilian shrimpers, differences in the fraction of conditional cooperators in a group were associated with substantial increases in trees planted or time spent monitoring others.

This does not mean that generous, cooperative, and reciprocal preferences are sufficient to address problems of environmental sustainability. But it does show that these social preferences can help.

like to have more free time, but realizes that a shorter working week would mean he has less money for his next holiday.

We represent the trade-offs affecting his choice in Figure 20.21. On the horizontal axis we measure hours of free time per year. On the vertical axis we indicate his kilometres of air travel during the year. The red line gives the total amount of air travel that he can afford for each choice of free time. The red line is therefore his feasible air travel/free time frontier.

The feasible frontier is constructed as follows. Suppose Omar makes $50 an hour after taxes and that he is free to set his own hours of work. He spends $90,000 on things other than air travel and to earn this amount, he must work 1,800 hours during the year. So, from the 8,760 hours in the year that he could give to work (as in Unit 3), he chooses to work 1,800 hours. Thus he has 6,960 hours of free time if he takes no air travel at all: this is the horizontal axis intercept of the frontier. How much air travel will he choose if $1 buys 4 km of air travel?

Omar's preferences for free time and air travel are given by the indifference curves shown. The slope of the indifference curve indicates how much he values free time relative to air travel, that is, his MRS of free time for air travel.

Work through the analysis in Figure 20.21 to follow Omar's decision making.

Omar flies less. There are two reasons for the change:

income effect The effect that the additional income would have if there were no change in the price or opportunity cost.

substitution effect The effect that is only due to changes in the price or opportunity cost, given the new level of utility.

- The **income effect**: Omar's choices are now more limited than before because the price of something that he consumes has gone up. His real income has fallen.
- The **substitution effect**: The tax has increased the relative price of air travel, leading Omar to substitute to other ways of having a good life, by consuming other goods (not shown in the figure), working less, or both.

EXERCISE 20.9 IMPROVEMENTS IN TECHNOLOGY

1. Redraw Figure 20.18 (page 935) to show an improvement in the technology for producing consumption goods, instead of an improvement in abatement technology.
2. Based on your diagram, explain what happens to the feasible frontier and the optimal choice of environmental quality and consumption, assuming nothing else changes.

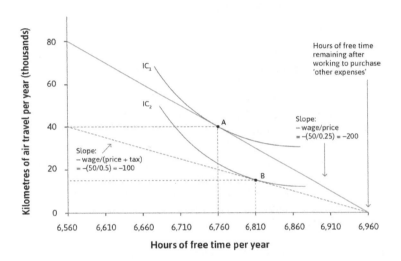

Figure 20.21 Omar's choice: The effect of an environmental tax on choices of air travel and free time.

1. The feasible frontier
The marginal rate of transformation of foregone free time into air travel is the slope of the feasible frontier. By giving up an hour of free time, Omar can work for an additional hour and earn $50. Each dollar gets him 4 km of air travel, so the MRT is 200. Giving up an hour of free time gets him 200 km of feasible air travel.

2. The highest indifference curve that Omar can reach
This is point A. It results from his choosing to work 200 extra hours so he has 6,760 hours of free time and 40,000 km of air travel.

3. The private cost of travel
To Omar, the private cost of 1 km of air travel is $0.25.

4. A fuel tax
Consider a tax levied on aviation fuel, so that the price of air travel rises. As a result, a dollar spent on a ticket now purchases only 2 km of air travel. This tax could force airlines and consumers to account for the negative environmental effects of air travel.

5. Omar's choice
Omar chooses the point on the new dashed feasible frontier that is on the highest indifference curve, which is now point B.

EXERCISE 20.10 THE PRICE ELASTICITY OF DEMAND

A study of vehicle use and gasoline prices in California (http://tinyco.re/ 8928260) estimated that the short-run price elasticity of demand for the number of miles a car is driven is –0.22. Suppose the price of gas is now $3 per gallon and a proposed tax would raise the price to $4 per gallon.

1. For someone who drives 200 miles per week, what is the predicted reduction in the miles driven if the tax is implemented?

The same study found that people with higher incomes responded more to gas price changes than people with lower incomes.

2. Can you think of reasons why this may be the case?
3. Sketch two demand curves reflecting the difference in price responsiveness among different income groups: one for high-income people and one for low-income people. Show why the tax will impose a larger cost on the low-income group.

QUESTION 20.8 CHOOSE THE CORRECT ANSWER(S)

In Figure 20.20 (page 938), points A and B are the two technologies available to a firm in its production. Specifically, technology A uses 4 tonnes of coal and 2 m² of solar panel to produce 100 metres of textiles, while technology B uses 1 tonne of coal and 6 m² of solar panel for the same output.

Initially, the price of 1 tonne of coal is half that of the price of using 1 m² of solar panel. In its latest budget statement, the government proposes a tax on the use of coal such that the price ratio increases from 1/2 to 2. Based on this information, which of the following statements is correct?

☐ At the original prices, the firm's isocost line is given by FG.
☐ At the original prices, the firm chooses technology B as it is on a higher isocost line than A.
☐ After the implementation of the tax, the slope of the firm's isocost line steepens from –1/2 to –2.
☐ After the implementation of the tax, the firm chooses technology A as it is on a lower isocost line than B.

QUESTION 20.9 CHOOSE THE CORRECT ANSWER(S)
The following diagram shows a consumer's choice of the amount of air travel per year, using indifference curves between hours of free time per year and kilometres of air travel. The consumer cannot afford air travel when he chooses 6,960 hours of free time. The consumer's after-tax hourly wage is $50.

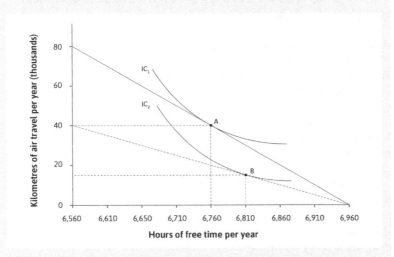

Initially, the cost of a 1 km of air travel is $0.25. In its latest budget statement, the government proposes a fuel tax such that the cost of 1 km of air travel doubles to $0.50. Based on this information, which of the following statements is correct?

- ☐ The marginal rate of transformation between kilometres of air travel and free time rises from 100 to 200 as a result of the fuel tax.
- ☐ The substitution effect of the tax means that the consumer substitutes out of air travel into consumption of other goods by working more.
- ☐ The income effect of the tax means that the consumer will unambiguously consume more free hours.
- ☐ If the fuel tax reflects the social cost of the consumer's air travel, then the socially optimal level of travelling is 15,000 km per year.

20.8 ENVIRONMENTAL DYNAMICS

Equilibrium is a fundamental concept of economics. It is essential to the way we predict the prices of goods using the model of supply and demand, or the level of unemployment using the model of the labour market. But for practical purposes we need to know more than simply the equilibrium of a model. In Units 16 and 18, for example, you learned that it may take a very long time for the labour market to move from one equilibrium to another, so what happens along the way is important.

And as the examples of the Grand Banks fisheries collapse or the threats to the Amazon rainforest described at the beginning of the unit showed, there may be more than one equilibrium. A healthy sustainable environment could be an equilibrium—think of Grand Banks cod fishing in the 100 years prior to 1950. And another could be the same geographical location devoid of cod, an example of environmental collapse. We sometimes refer to the process of getting to the second equilibrium as a vicious cycle, and environmental sustainability as a virtuous cycle.

The passage from one of these equilibria to another—called a **disequilibrium process**—can be rapid, because it is propelled by positive feedback processes, which you studied in Unit 17 in the case of housing markets. Just as in the case of a house price bubble, the reduction in fish stocks in the Grand Banks became self-reinforcing.

Here we study these disequilibrium processes. We explain why, when they are present and when we lack important pieces of information about what kinds of human actions will set off a collapse, we need a different approach to policymaking, one that stresses the need to avoid a cataclysmic environmental collapse.

The dynamics of the biosphere

Long before human economic and other activity began to have a substantial effect, the natural environment was constantly changing as a result of the chemical and physical processes that make up the biosphere.

Over tens of thousands of years, an ice age would give way to a period of warming in which glaciers and sea ice covers retreated towards the poles, to be followed by a new period of cold temperatures with the advance of the ice sheets into what are now temperate climates. On shorter time scales, clouds of dust sent up by massive volcanic eruptions blocked out the sun, as occurred during the 'little ice age' 500 years ago (you can see the drop in average temperature around the middle of the fifteenth century in Figure 1.6b).

Climate today is heavily influenced by human economic activity, but it is a process with its own dynamics of change. A challenge to environmental policymaking is that some natural processes themselves set in motion positive feedback processes so that small initial changes can lead to much larger effects, resulting in faster and greater deterioration than anticipated.

Like the Grand Banks fisheries and the Amazon rainforest, many freshwater systems, such as lakes and rivers, are subject to similar vicious circles of deterioration and collapse.

Where positive feedbacks are important there may be some level of environmental deterioration called a **tipping point**, which if passed, sets in motion a process leading to abrupt and hard-to-reverse destruction of an environmental resource. When this is the case, environmental policy must go beyond balancing the costs and benefits of the abatement of environmental damage. Instead, policymakers must devise measures to ensure that a tipping point—especially if it is uncertain—for a critical resource is not passed. In this context, a **prudential policy** would seek to avoid the risk that the given situation may itself be radically and irreversibly degraded.

Environmental equilibria

To understand the idea of planetary boundaries and environmental collapse, we will use the example of Arctic sea ice. This is an example of an environmental system that may have already passed a tipping point due to global climate change. Figure 20.22 shows that for the past 50 years, the extent of the sea ice at the end of summer has been declining at an increasing rate. The insert in the figure illustrates the change in the last few decades.

First, consider the vicious cycle. Open sea surface area is darker than ice so more open sea surface area leads the earth's surface to reflect less radiation. It therefore absorbs more radiation and warms up. The resulting

disequilibrium process An economic variable may change either because the things that determine the equilibrium value of that variable have changed (an equilibrium process), or because the system is not in equilibrium so that there exist forces for change that are internal to the model in question (a disequilibrium process). The latter process applies when the economy moves towards a stable equilibrium (which itself is not moving) or away from a tipping point (an unstable equilibrium).

tipping point An unstable equilibrium at the boundary between two regions characterized by distinct movements in some variable. If the variable takes a value on one side, the variable moves in one direction; on the other, it moves in the other direction. See also: asset price bubble.

prudential policy A policy that places a very high value on reducing the likelihood of a disastrous outcome, even if this is costly in terms of other objectives foregone. Such an approach is often advocated where there is great uncertainty about the conditions under which a disastrous outcome would occur.

higher winter and spring surface temperatures in turn cause less ice in the summer. The virtuous cycle is just the opposite: when there is extensive summer ice, the radiation is reflected rather than absorbed and the temperatures stay low, maintaining the ice which reflects the radiation, keeping temperatures low, and so on.

'Extensive summer sea ice' and 'no summer sea ice' are the stable equilibria of the Arctic sea ice ecology. Each of these states is reinforced by the positive feedback loop shown in Figure 20.23. You may want to compare this positive feedback process to the one causing housing price bubbles and busts discussed in Unit 17.

What happens 'in between' these two stable equilibria? We analyse this using the model introduced in Unit 17 for the housing market. You will note the similarity between Figure 20.23 and Figure 17.18 of boom and bust in a housing market. But now, instead of the house price this year and next on the axes, the horizontal axis is the extent of sea ice today (called E_t to refer to the environment this year). The vertical axis is sea ice next year. This figure shows how the extent of sea ice today maps to the extent of sea ice tomorrow.

The 45-degree line depicts an unchanging environment, since along that line any value of sea ice this period on the horizontal axis is the same next period (on the vertical axis). The S-shaped line is the 'environmental dynamics curve' or EDC for short. Just as in Unit 17, points at which the EDC crosses the 45-degree line are equilibria. This is because the amount of sea ice this year is the same as next year (remember an equilibrium is something stationary, that is, unchanging from year to year). Two of the equilibria are stable: each equilibrium is stabilized by self-reinforcing feed-

> **ENVIRONMENTAL TIPPING POINT**
> - On one side of an environmental **tipping point**, processes of environmental degradation are self-limiting.
> - On the other side, positive feedbacks lead to self-reinforcing, runaway environmental degradation.

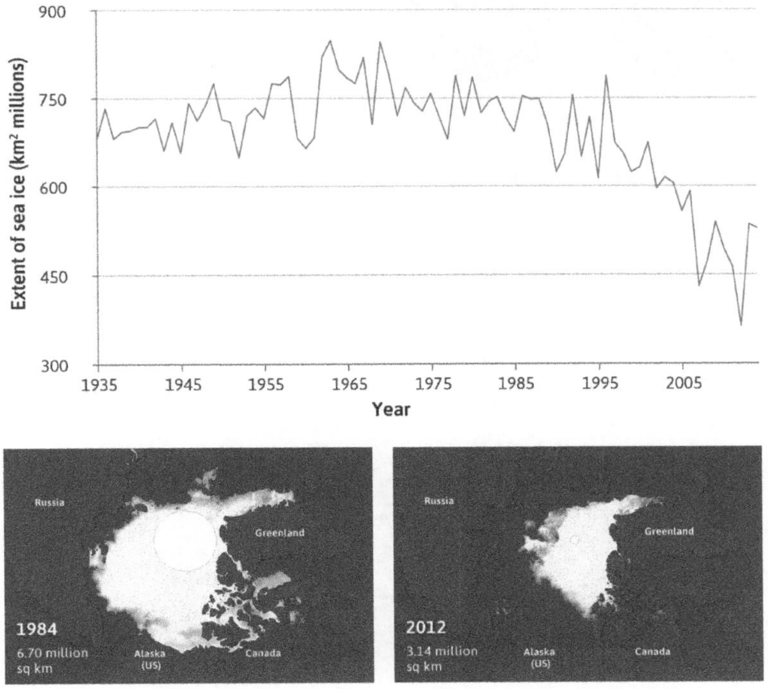

Miguel Ángel Cea Pirón and Juan Antonio Cano Pasalodos. 2016. 'Nueva serie de extensión del hielo marino ártico en septiembre entre 1935 y 2014'. *Revista de Climatología*, Vol. 16 (2016): pp. 1–19.

Figure 20.22 Arctic sea ice coverage (1935–2014).

back processes shown in the upper panel. You can refer back to Figures 11.18 and 11.19 for the adjustment processes around a stable and an unstable equilibrium. Point A is the unstable equilibrium or tipping point. Any slight change in sea ice at the unstable equilibrium leads in the direction of either B or C.

At any point in between the two stable equilibria at B and C, from year to year the sea ice cover will either be increasing towards the virtuous equilibrium at B or disappearing towards the no-sea-ice equilibrium at C. For example, beginning with a sea ice extent of E_0, the EDC shows the (higher) level the following year and the arrow indicates the adjustment to the equilibrium at point B.

This occurs as follows: from an initial level of E_0 with a cold climate and Arctic summer ice, the sea ice next year would be more than this year as shown, since the EDC is above the 45-degree line. When there is a lot of ice, the feedback in the direction of maintaining the ice cover is strong, and we tend to stay there even when variations in temperatures (due to seasons or decadal variation in ocean currents) cause temporary warming and temporary reductions in sea ice. The extent of the ice means that the system 'rebounds' towards the high equilibrium.

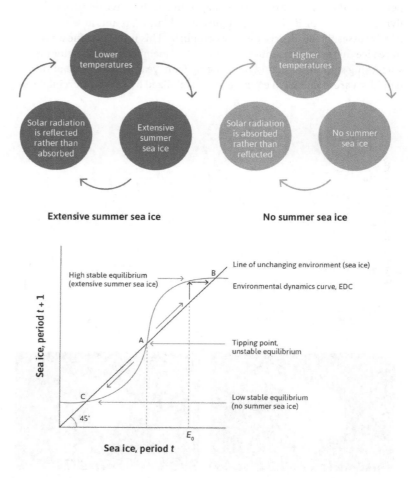

Figure 20.23 The environmental dynamics curve and the environmental tipping point.

Planetary boundaries

As we have seen, the two stable equilibria are separated by an unstable equilibrium at A. So a reduction in sea ice below the tipping point will be amplified, rather than dampened. At that point, the feedback becomes stronger in the direction of reducing the ice cover and bringing the system to the no-Arctic-summer-ice state. The capacity of the system to recover would have been pushed beyond its limits.

What is the role of climate change in all that? We shall see that to analyse this we need to explain why the S-shaped environmental dynamics curve can shift down. If it shifts, the system will not stabilize around the high-summer-ice equilibrium at B.

A warming climate does two things, one of which is gradual, the other cataclysmic. First, starting from the high equilibrium, a warming climate brings the system closer to a tipping point, illustrated by a downward shift in the S-shaped curve. Second, it may change the system such that at some point, the equilibrium with extensive summer sea ice disappears.

To understand these effects, take a look at Figure 20.24. A warmer climate means that for any amount of sea ice this year, the amount that will be there next year is less. This is not a movement along the EDC but instead a downward shift of the whole curve. As a result, less ice forms in the winter and the whole system is more vulnerable to the increase in temperature and open surface area in the summer.

In Figure 20.24, the shift down in the EDC has moved the 'high' equilibrium downwards, so there will be less sea ice from year to year. Notice too that the warmer climate has also shifted the tipping point upwards to Z

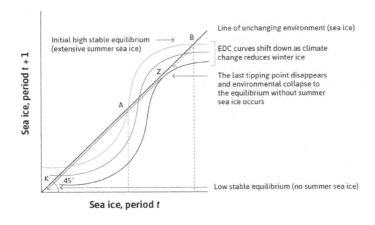

Figure 20.24 Climate change and irreversible loss of summer Arctic sea ice.

1. Initial high stable equilibrium
The environment starts at equilibrium point B.

2. Global warming lowers the EDC curve
A warmer climate means that for any amount of sea ice this year, the amount that will be there next year is less. The whole curve shifts downward.

3. System collapse to ice-free summers
Beyond a certain amount of winter warming, the EDC shifts down so much that there is no longer a high stable equilibrium. The last tipping point, Z, disappears and the system is permanently locked in the no-sea-ice stable state at K.

from its initial position at A, which widens the 'danger zone' of environmental collapse.

Is this what has been happening over the last century? From Figure 20.22, it appears that until the late 1960s, the Arctic sea ice was approaching a high equilibrium (like B). Thereafter, the extent of sea ice declined at first gradually, illustrated in Figure 20.24 by the movement from B downwards towards Z. But then Figure 20.22 shows that from the mid-1980s, the reduction in sea ice was much more rapid, as would occur if the last tipping point had been passed and the system was in freefall towards no summer sea ice at all (point K).

Combining the model and the available evidence, the change from the Arctic with extensive summer ice to the Arctic with no-summer-ice equilibria appears to be underway. Scientists are unsure how reversible this loss of the Arctic summer ice is even if we reverse global warming. We may have crossed a point of no return. The lack of Arctic sea ice—if that is what is in store—will add to the already powerful forces creating a warmer climate.

The sea ice might be restored eventually by a new ice age of sharply colder climate. Given the pattern of climate change over the past 800,000 years, this might be expected 50,000 years from now.

Prudential policies to address tipping points

The aim of policies to slow global warming would be to keep the EDC within the set of feasible environmental equilibria shown by the green dashed line between B and Z. In the presence of tipping points, prudential policies should reduce the risk that a tipping point will be crossed.

The need to be prudent arises not just because there is a tipping point but also because of the uncertainty about how close we are to the last tipping point. Prudent policy means seeking to avoid cataclysmic risks even if their likelihood is extremely small. The closer we are to a tipping point, the higher the chance of unknowingly crossing it and finding it impossible to reverse the degradation and avoid a catastrophic outcome.

Planetary boundaries are defined for critical environmental variables (such as temperature and **biodiversity loss**), and give levels of these variables that scientists think will keep us sufficiently far away from problematic tipping points to be within a 'safe operating space'. Respecting planetary boundaries is a prudential policy.

The value of prudence has implications for which kinds of policies are most appropriate. To see this, suppose there is no uncertainty about either:

* *The state of the environment*: How close to a tipping point the ecosystem was, for example.
* *The effect of tax incentives*: What will the effect be on carbon emissions?

Given this level of certainty, a tax on carbon emissions or a cap and trade policy could obtain the same outcome. Cap and trade would impose the desired level of abatement and the carbon tax would set the right price for carbon emissions, also leading to the desired level of abatement. In both cases, the policymaker must decide on the desired level of abatement before selecting the most appropriate policy.

However, we are often highly uncertain about both the state of the environment and the effectiveness of tax or subsidy policies. In these cases, cap and trade is more prudent because it can guarantee a particular level of emissions (the cap), which can be set sufficiently far away from the possible thresholds.

biodiversity loss (rate of)
Proportion of species that become extinct every year.

EXERCISE 20.11 REPRESENTING REGIME SHIFTS

The Regime Shifts DataBase (http://tinyco.re/3834638) documents different types of regime shifts (another word for tipping point) that we have evidence for in human-dominated ecological systems. Choose one from the database and describe the situation in your own words, including the types of equilibria and their characteristics, and how the system transitions from one equilibrium to another. Draw a diagram similar to Figure 20.23 (page 946) to represent it, and explain the feedback loops that are involved.

EXERCISE 20.12 SELF-REINFORCING PROCESSES

Self-reinforcing processes, such as the ones described above, do not happen only in nature. In Unit 17, for example, we discussed how increases in house prices can reinforce a boom and become self-sustaining, leading to a housing price bubble.

Explain the ways in which the cumulative self-reinforcing processes described by environmental scientists are similar to (or different from) processes that occur in a housing or stock price bubble.

20.9 WHY IS ADDRESSING CLIMATE CHANGE SO DIFFICULT?

While scientists agree that climate change is occurring and that our economic activity is contributing to it, there are large gaps in scientific understanding of the processes involved and the costs of containing them.

Moreover, as we have seen in Sections 20.3 and 20.4, conflicts of interest over the extent and methods of abatement make it difficult for national governments to adopt broadly supported strategies for mitigating environmental degradation. These conflicts include disagreements about what climate science has shown. In 2015 in the US, 64% of Democratic Party supporters were of the opinion that global warming is both occurring and a result of human activity, but the similar fraction among Republicans was 23%.

Also, owners and employees of companies producing or using fossil fuels anticipate income losses as the result of policies to reduce emissions, and spend heavily to influence public opinion on environmental questions. You can read about the impact of this spending in a *New York Times* article on lead poisoning (http://tinyco.re/6681574) and examine a list of chemical industry lobbying expenditure for 2015 on OpenSecrets.org (http://tinyco.re/8516286).

Lack of adequate information and conflicts of interest are impediments to good public policy in many other areas, but climate change poses two unusual challenges: the problem cannot be solved by national governments acting alone, and those affected by our choices today include generations in the distant future.

International cooperation

Using the tools of game theory in Unit 4, we saw that avoiding the **tragedy of the commons** that affects the supply of public goods depends on the rules of the game (the institutions). Where there are repeated interactions of the players and there

tragedy of the commons A social dilemma in which self-interested individuals acting independently deplete a common resource, lowering the payoffs of all. *See also: social dilemma.*

dominant strategy equilibrium An outcome of a game in which every player plays his or her dominant strategy.

are opportunities to punish those who do not contribute to the public good, the socially optimal outcome can be sustained. The presence of sustainable water-use systems or fish stocks in several continents shows that the tragedy of the commons is avoidable.

In the case of climate change, game theory helps us understand the obstacles to its solution. Recall the way we modelled the climate change game as a prisoners' dilemma in which two countries (the US and China) can either restrict carbon emissions or continue with business as usual (see Figure 4.17). Complete self-interest makes the business as usual scenario the **dominant strategy equilibrium**.

To understand how an international agreement might be negotiated to avoid the business as usual outcome, we introduced inequality aversion and reciprocity. If citizens of the US and China give some weight to the wellbeing of citizens in the other country or experience less wellbeing when inequality rises, and if they are willing to implement costly measures as long as this is also done in the other country, then an outcome where both countries restrict emissions is possible.

Our hypothetical model of climate change negotiations between China and the US gave rise to two Nash equilibria if citizens had both inequality aversion and reciprocity. It is also not completely unrealistic: after intense negotiations following failed talks and a non-binding agreement in Copenhagen in 2009, all countries committed to eventual emission cuts at the United Nations Conference on Climate Change in Paris in December 2015, with the goal of stabilizing global temperatures at 2°C above pre-industrial levels. Virtually all countries also submitted their individual plans for cutting emissions, but these plans are not yet consistent with this temperature stabilization goal.

Unrepresented generations

Our economic activity today will affect climate changes in the distant future, so we are essentially creating consequences that others will bear. This is just an extreme form of external effects that we have studied throughout the course. It is extreme not only in its potential consequences, but also in that those who will suffer the consequences are future generations.

In many countries, public policies have been adopted to address other kinds of environmental external effects, such as local pollution, under pressure from voters bearing the costs of these effects. If you look ahead at Figure 20.25b, you will notice that many of the stars (well above the line) on the Environmental Performance Index are, and have long been, electoral democracies. This is not the case for most of the low performers.

But the future generations that will bear the consequences of our decisions are unrepresented in the policymaking process today. The only way the wellbeing of these unrepresented generations will be taken into account at the environmental bargaining tables around the world is the fact that most people care about, and would like to behave ethically toward, others, as we have seen in Unit 4.

These social preferences underlie the debates among economists about how much we should value the future benefits and costs of the climate change decisions that we make today.

In considering alternative environmental policies, how much we value the wellbeing of future generations is commonly measured by an interest rate, which is literally the rate at which we **discount future generations'**

costs or benefits. There are, however, debates about how this **discounting** process should be done.

WHEN ECONOMISTS DISAGREE

The discounting dilemma: How should we account for future costs and benefits?

When considering policies, economists seek to compare the benefits and costs of alternative approaches. Doing this presents especially great challenges when the policy problem is climate change. The reason is that the costs will be borne by the present generation but the benefits of a successful abatement policy will be enjoyed by people in the future, many of whom are not yet alive.

Put yourself in the shoes of the impartial policymaker we studied earlier and ask yourself: are there any reasons why, in summing up the benefits and costs of an abatement policy, I should value the benefits expected to be received by future generations any less than the benefits and costs that will be borne by people today? Two reasons come to mind:

- *Technological progress*: The people in the future may have either greater or lesser needs than we do today. For example, as a result of continuing improvements in technology, they may be richer (either in goods or free time) than we are today, so it might seem fair that we should not value the benefits they will receive from our policies as highly as we value the costs that we will bear as a result.
- *Extinction of the human species*: There is a small possibility that future generations will not exist because humanity becomes extinct.

These are good reasons why we might discount the benefits received by future generations. Notice that neither of these reasons for discounting is related to **pure impatience**.

This was the approach adopted in the 2006 *Stern Review on the Economics of Climate Change* (read the executive summary on the WWF website (http://tinyco.re/8438738)). Nicholas Stern, an economist, selected a discount rate to take account of the likelihood that people in the future would be richer. Based on an estimate of future productivity increases, Stern discounted the benefits to future generations by 1.3% per annum. To this he added a 0.1% per annum discount rate to account for the risk that in any future year there might no longer be surviving generations. Based on this assessment, Stern advocated policies that would have implemented substantial abatement investments today in order to protect the environment of the future.

Several economists, including William Nordhaus, criticized the *Stern Review* for its low discount rate. Nordhaus wrote that Stern's choice of discount rate 'magnifies impacts in the distant future'. He concluded that, with a higher discount rate, 'the Review's dramatic results disappear'.

Nordhaus advocated the use of a discount rate of 4.3%, which gave vastly different implications. Discounting at this rate means that a $100 benefit occurring 100 years from now is worth $1.48 today, while under Stern's 1.4% rate it would be worth $24.90. This means a policymaker

discounting future generations' costs and benefits A measure of how we currently value the costs and benefits experienced by people who will live in the future. Note that this is not a measure of individual impatience about one's own future benefits and costs.

discount rate A measure of the person's impatience: how much the person values an additional unit of consumption now relative to an additional unit of consumption later. It is the slope of the person's indifference curve for consumption now and consumption later, minus one. *Also known as: subjective discount rate.*

pure impatience This is a characteristic of a person who values an additional unit of consumption now over an additional unit later, when the amount of consumption is the same now and later. It arises when a person is impatient to consume more now because she places less value on consumption in the future for reasons of myopia, weakness of will, or for other reasons.

William D. Nordhaus. 2007. 'A Review of the Stern Review on the Economics of Climate Change.' *Journal of Economic Literature* 45 (3): pp. 686–702.

using Nordhaus' discount rate would approve of a project that would save future generations $100 in environmental damages only if it cost less than $1.48 today. A policymaker using Stern's 1.4% would approve the project only if it cost less than $24.90.

Not surprisingly, then, Nordhaus' recommendations for climate change abatement were far less extensive and less costly than those that Stern proposed. When comparing the use of cap and trade with a carbon tax in Section 20.5, we referred to $40 per tonne as a low-end estimate of the external cost of carbon emissions. This is comparable to the carbon price of $35 per tonne in 2015 proposed by Nordhaus to deter the use of fossil fuels. Stern recommended a price of $360.

Why did the two economists differ by so much? They agreed on the need to discount for the likelihood that future generations would be better off. But Nordhaus had an additional reason to discount future benefits: impatience.

Reasoning as we did in Unit 10 for Julia's and Marco's consumption now or later, Nordhaus used estimates based on market interest rates as measures of how people today value future versus present consumption. Using this method, he came up with a discount rate of 3% to measure the way people discount future benefits and costs that they themselves may experience. Nordhaus included this in his discount rate, which is why Nordhaus' discount rate (4.3%) is so much higher than Stern's (1.4%).

Critics of Nordhaus pointed out that in evaluating the claims that future generations should have on our concern, a psychological fact like our own impatience is not a reason to discount the needs and aspirations of other people in future generations.

Stern's approach counts all generations as equally worthy of our concern for their wellbeing. Nordhaus, in contrast, takes the current generation's point of view and counts future generations as less worthy of our concern than the current generation, much in the way that, for reasons of impatience, we typically value current consumption more highly than our own future consumption.

Is the debate resolved? The discounting question ultimately requires adjudicating between the competing claims of different individuals at different points of time. This involves questions of ethics on which economists will continue to disagree.

Frank Ackerman. 2007. 'Debating climate economics: the Stern Review vs. its critics' (http://tinyco.re/6591851). Report to Friends of the Earth, July 2007.

EXERCISE 20.13 SIMULATING DIFFERENT DISCOUNT RATES

Download the simple discount rate simulation spreadsheet from our CORE website (http://tinyco.re/4973495). The simulator allows you to calculate the present value of receiving $1 in one, 10, 50, and 100 years from now for four discount rates.

In the spreadsheet, the first three discount rates are fixed: zero, Stern's suggestion, and the alternative suggested by Nordhaus.

1. Explain the effect of different discount rates on the present value of receiving $1 in the future.

The fourth rate is your choice: use the slider in the table to choose a discount rate you think is appropriate for the evaluation of the benefits and costs of climate change policy in the distant future.

2. Justify your choice. Is it closer to the Nordhaus or Stern proposal? Or is it higher than or lower than both?

3. Try to find out what discount rate your government (or another government of your choice) uses to evaluate public investment projects. Do you think it is appropriate?

QUESTION 20.10 CHOOSE THE CORRECT ANSWER(S)

The following table shows the present values of a $1 payment in the future, discounted at different rates. For example, $1 paid in 10 years' time is worth $0.82 today when discounted at 2% annually.

Discount rate (%)	Years in the future				
	0	1	10	50	100
0.0%	$1.00	$1.00	$1.00	$1.00	$1.00
1.0%	$1.00	$0.99	$0.90	$0.61	$0.37
2.0%	$1.00	$0.98	$0.82	$0.37	$0.14
5.0%	$1.00	$0.95	$0.61	$0.09	$0.01

Based on this information, which of the following statements are correct?

☐ The divergence of the discounting effect between different discount rates is larger the longer the time to payment.
☐ Doubling the time to payment leads to halving of the present value.
☐ Doubling the discount rate leads to halving of the present value.
☐ A discount rate of 0% means that payments are worth the same today and at all points in future.

20.10 POLICY CHOICES MATTER

Differences between countries

Environmental policies make a difference. We can see that countries vary greatly in the global environmental damage they inflict and in their success at managing environmental quality in their country. Figure 20.25a shows CO_2 emissions per capita for each country in 2010 alongside income per capita. Richer countries produce more CO_2 per capita than poorer ones. This is to be expected because greater income per capita is the result of a higher level of production of goods and services per capita, with associated impacts on the biosphere. This is shown by the upward-sloped line that indicates the relationship between the two variables.

But notice, too, that among countries at approximately the same level of per capita income, some emit much more than others. Compare the high emissions levels in the US, Canada, and Australia with the lower emissions levels of France, Sweden, and Germany, countries at approximately the same level of per capita income. Another way to read the graph is horizontally: Norway has the same emissions level that would be predicted (by the line) for a country $20,000 poorer in per capita income. Russia pollutes as much as would be expected from a country $20,000 richer.

Measured by its direct emissions, Singapore is a high-performing outlier. It is a high-income city-state with an effective public transport network and a commercial rather than industrial economic base, resulting in limited levels of pollution. In addition to public transportation, the government has adopted other effective environmental policies. For example, if you want to use a car in Singapore, you are first required to purchase a permit for a car at an auction, and then pay the congestion charge (a tax) every time you drive into the city.

Though richer countries emit more CO_2 per capita, they have also adopted more effective policies to manage their own environmental resources, such as forests, soil, biodiversity, and water. Figure 20.25b plots the Environmental Performance Index (EPI) against GDP per capita. The EPI is a broad index of country-level environmental health and ecosystem vitality, including the state of wastewater treatment, fisheries, and forests. It brings together 20 different country-level indicators including trends in carbon emissions, fish stocks, changes in forest cover, quality of wastewater treatment, access to sanitation, air pollution, and child mortality. In this case, a curved rather than straight line fits the data better, indicating that differences in per capita income are associated with major differences in the EPI for very poor countries, but not as major for the richer countries, on average.

As in Figure 20.25a, Russia underperforms, with the Environmental Performance Index expected of a country half as rich. Germany, Sweden, and Switzerland are high performers. Notice that Australia, which is an

The World Bank. 2015. 'World Development Indicators.' Note: Three small very high-income countries (Kuwait, Luxembourg, and Qatar) are not shown.

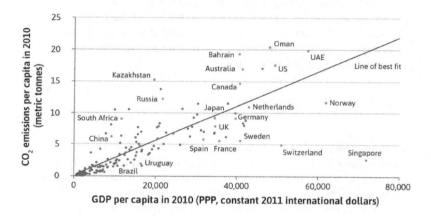

Figure 20.25a Carbon dioxide emissions are higher in richer countries ...

Development indicators; EPI. 2014. 'Environmental Protection Index 2014.' Yale Center for Environmental Law & Policy (YCELP) and the Center for International Earth Science Information Network.

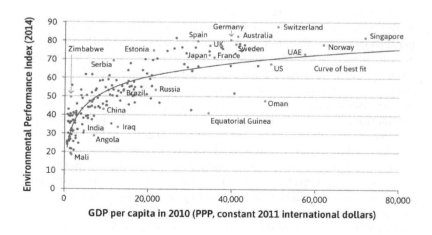

Figure 20.25b ... but so is the quality of their local environment.

unusually big emitter of CO_2 (Figure 20.25a), is a top performer on the national environmental amenities measured by the EPI. A good part of the environmental damage done by economic activity in Australia is thus imposed as a cost on those outside the country.

The message of Figure 20.25b is similar to the previous one. Countries, even at similar levels of income per capita, differ greatly in their environmental performance. Compare Switzerland with the US or Spain with Russia, for example. Both India and China are substantially below the line. These country differences suggest the importance of the kinds of policies that are adopted and enforced.

Lessons from the existence of win-win policies

We have introduced many difficult trade-offs confronting environmental policies, for example, between our consumption now and our environmental quality now. But we have also uncovered some evidence of win-win opportunities.

In Figure 20.26, we look again at the estimates of the marginal abatement costs that we previously saw in Figure 20.9. The global abatement cost curve is displayed vertically in Figure 20.26. In Figure 20.9, we only included measures that are costly and would have to be promoted as an objective of government policy. In Figure 20.26, when the monetary benefit is greater than the cost, the bar extends to the left of the vertical axis. When cost is greater, it extends to the right.

All of the actions to the left of the vertical axis in Figure 20.26 would not only accomplish significant abatement, but would also be privately beneficial in the sense that they result in monetary benefits greater than the costs. These are win-win actions because they improve the environment, and their cost savings also allow greater consumption.

Replacing incandescent light bulbs with LED bulbs in our houses is one of these win-win opportunities. It is the most cost-saving policy of all but it is a narrow bar, meaning it does not have a big abatement potential. Fuel-efficient vehicles, insulation in houses and offices, and other technologies with bars to the left of the axis are also cost-saving. Note that if we were only to adopt cost-saving policies between now and 2030, we would still achieve more than a quarter of the total potential abatement shown in the figure.

We can represent the unrealized abatement potential of these changes in the feasible set figure. The dashed line in Figure 20.27 is the feasible frontier that we have been using thus far, which ignored the win-win opportunities shown on the left side of Figure 20.26. The solid feasible frontier takes account of the possible use of these win-win options.

Start at point C on the horizontal axis in Figure 20.27. The evidence from Figure 20.26 is that implementing the measures (starting at the top of Figure 20.26, with replacement of incandescent bulbs by LEDs) will generate abatement benefits and at the same time allow for higher consumption of other goods and services.

This produces the positively sloped part of the feasible frontier, with both environmental quality and consumption rising from C to D. Once all the win-win measures have been introduced, at D, it begins to be costly to achieve further abatement and the feasible frontier is negatively sloped, as we saw when we analysed the implications of Figure 20.9.

The unrealized abatement potential of changes, that would save money for the individuals or firms implementing them, suggests that implementation by market incentives may be slow and incomplete. The fact that environmental benefits could be generated by economic decisions that would provide monetary benefits (not costs) to the decision-maker means mutual gains are feasible but are not being realized. Thus, Figure 20.27 provides another piece of evidence that contemporary economies are often not even close to being Pareto efficient.

These factors point to a primary advantage of policies to make some environmentally harmful practices illegal rather than simply making them more expensive. In those cases where the government has the necessary

McKinsey & Company. 2013. 'Pathways to a Low-Carbon Economy: Version 2 of the Global Greenhouse Gas Abatement Cost Curve.' McKinsey & Company.

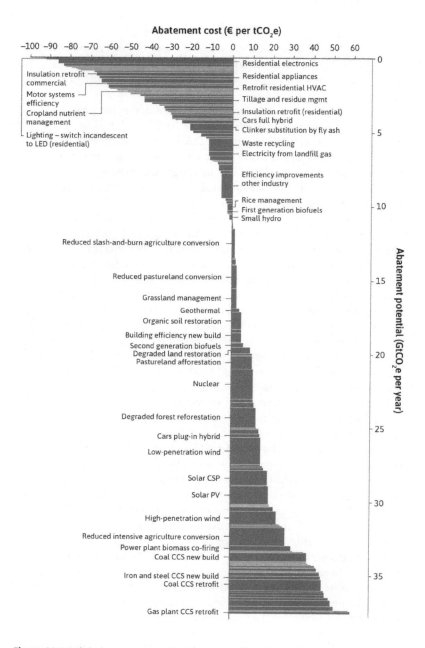

Figure 20.26 Global greenhouse gas abatement curve: Abatement in 2030, compared with business as usual.

information and enforcement capacities, implementation can be rapid and complete. An example is the dramatic reduction in the use of lead in petrol in many countries around the world, following a ban. But as we will see in Unit 22, governments often lack the information and administrative capabilities to design and implement effective policies of this kind.

Is 'make the polluter pay' fair?

Think about the **polluter pays principle**. This principle can be interpreted as an application of the basic economics of environmental policies. Environmental external effects often impose costs on others, and making the polluter pay for these external effects is a way to internalize (and therefore eliminate) them.

This could be accomplished by taxing the polluting activity so as to equate the marginal private cost with the marginal social cost. This may be an efficient way to abate the pollution. But as we saw in Unit 12, the same abatement could be accomplished by providing the firm with a subsidy for the use of an alternative technology that resulted in a lower level of pollution.

The firm's view of these two policies may be that the tax is the stick and the subsidy the carrot. The tax, which reflects the polluter pays principle, lowers the profits of the firm. A subsidy raises the firm's profits. Whether the carrot or the stick is the right policy depends on the feasibility and cost

> **polluter pays principle** A guide to environmental policy according to which those who impose negative environmental effects on others should be made to pay for the damages they impose, through taxation or other means.

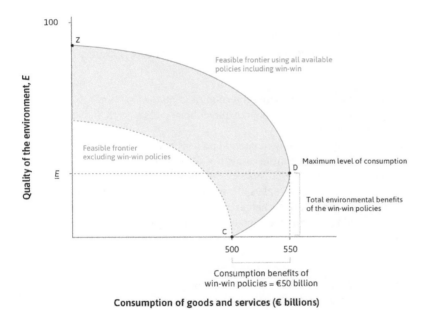

Figure 20.27 Is there always a trade-off between consumption and environmental quality?

1. Unrealized potential
We use the feasible set figure to represent the unrealized abatement potential.

2. Win-win actions
Moving from C to D takes the quality of the environment up to $\underline{E}$. Consumption rises because costs (for example for lighting) fall.

3. Implementing abatement along the feasible frontier
Moving from D to Z takes the quality of the environment above $\underline{E}$, but at the cost of lower consumption.

of implementing the subsidy compared to the tax, and whether raising or lowering the income of the target of the policy is desired on fairness grounds.

Seen in this light, the polluter pays principle is not always a good guide to the best policy. Think of a large city in a low-income country in which much of the cooking is still done over wood fires, generating high levels of airborne particulate matter and causing asthma and other respiratory illnesses:

- *Fairness:* It is mostly poor families who lack the income or access to electricity that would allow them to cook and heat their homes with fewer external environmental effects. In this case, many would object to making the polluters pay on the grounds of fairness, and instead favour subsidizing kerosene or providing a better electricity supply.
- *Effectiveness:* Subsidizing kerosene is likely to be cost-effective in reducing smog, compared to tracking down and extracting payments from hundreds of thousands of people who are polluting the city's air with wood fires.

This example is helpful because it shows not only the value of considering fairness as well as efficiency, but also the importance of being clear about which objective we are pursuing when we design policies.

EXERCISE 20.14 HIGH AND LOW PERFORMERS
Consider the labelled countries above the best-fit curve in Figure 20.25b (page 954) and those below it.

1. What characteristics about the countries and the way they are governed do you think might explain their status as high and low performers respectively?
2. Find out about the environmental policies and political systems of one or more of these countries using the World Bank Development Indicators (http://tinyco.re/8871968), the Freedom in The World 2016 data (http://tinyco.re/6239533), and your own research. What information from these sources helps you to explain the differences between high and low performers, and how does it help?

QUESTION 20.11 CHOOSE THE CORRECT ANSWER(S)
Figure 20.27 (page 929) is the diagram of the amount abated for the total cost of abatement using different abatement policies.

Based on this information, which of the following statements is correct?

☐ The points between C and D represent the more costly policies being adopted first.
☐ D should always be the optimal policy choice.
☐ The optimal policy choice can be a point on the segment CD.
☐ The optimal policy choice will have the quality of the environment higher than E.

20.11 CONCLUSION

For 100,000 years or more, humans—like other animals—lived in ways that modified the biosphere but did not substantially and irreversibly degrade its capacity to support life on the planet. Starting 200 years ago, humans learned how to use the energy available from nature (burning carbon) to transform how we produced goods and services, radically increasing the productivity of our labour.

The capitalist economy provided both the carrots and the sticks that made the technological revolution profitable to private firms and hence a permanent feature of our lives. The result was a sustained increase in the output of goods and services per person.

In many countries, the extension of the vote to people who worked as employees, and their organization into trade unions and political parties enhanced the bargaining power and the wages of workers (Figure 2.19). The increasing costs of hiring labour provided ongoing incentives for owners of firms to seek innovations that would use less labour, replacing human labour with machinery and the non-human energy of coal and other fuels that powered them.

In many countries, this process of increased productivity and bargaining power of labour resulted in growing living standards for workers. But the replacement of human labour by non-human energy to power the machines also led to an impoverishment of nature.

A degraded and threatened environment cannot be reversed, however, by the same mechanism that created this affluence. When it came to developing an economically equitable society, workers were their own advocates, and their success in pursuing their private interests of seeking a higher living standard led to wage increases and a pattern of technological change in which less labour was used in production.

You could imagine that a similar process would raise the price of using our natural environment, leading to nature-saving technical change, just as higher wages led to labour-saving innovations. But the biosphere does not have the vote. Political organizations of soon-to-be-extinct animals will not be formed. Future generations of our own species and non-human elements of the contemporary and future biosphere are not capable of advocating for saving nature in the same way that workers indirectly advocated for saving labour, that is, by raising its price.

Public policies to impose prices on the use of nature sufficient to deter the degrading external effects of the production of goods and services today will be propelled not by the silent voices of the biosphere and generations unborn, but by people today, concerned not only about their private interests, but about the preservation of a flourishing biosphere in the future.

Economists along with other scholars can clarify the costs and benefits of alternative environmental policies and practices and help to inform public debate on these policies.

Concepts introduced in Unit 20
Before you move on, review these definitions:

- Abatement
- Abatement policies
- Natural resources and reserves
- Global greenhouse gas abatement cost curve
- Marginal productivity of abatement expenditures
- Price- and quantity-based environmental policies
- Cap and trade
- Contingent valuation
- Hedonic pricing
- Discounting future generations' costs and benefits
- The polluter pays principle
- Tipping point, disequilibrium process
- Prudential policy

20.12 REFERENCES

Ackerman, Frank. 2007. 'Debating climate economics: the Stern Review vs. its critics' (http://tinyco.re/6591851). Report to Friends of the Earth, July 2007.

EconTalk. 2015. 'Martin Weitzman on Climate Change' (http://tinyco.re/7088528). Library of Economics and Liberty. Updated 1 June 2015.

Fehr, Ernest and Andreas Leibbrandt. 2011. 'A Field Study on Cooperativeness and Impatience in the Tragedy of the Commons'. *Journal of Public Economics* 95 (9–10): pp. 1144–55.

Freedom House. 2016. 'Freedom in the World 2015' (http://tinyco.re/6239533).

Nordhaus, William D. 2007. 'A Review of the Stern Review on the Economics of Climate Change' (http://tinyco.re/9892599). *Journal of Economic Literature* 45 (3): pp. 686–702.

OpenSecrets.org. 2015. 'Lobbying Spending Database Chemical & Related Manufacturing' (http://tinyco.re/8516286).

Porter, Michael E., and Claas van der Linde. 1995. 'Toward a New Conception of the Environment-Competitiveness Relationship' (http://tinyco.re/9888498). *Journal of Economic Perspectives* 9 (4): pp. 97–118.

Rustagi, Devesh, Stefanie Engel, and Michael Kosfeld. 2010. 'Conditional Cooperation and Costly Monitoring Explain Success in Forest Commons Management' (http://tinyco.re/3733299). *Science* 330: pp. 961–65.

Schmalensee, Richard, and Robert N. Stavins. 2013. 'The SO2 Allowance Trading System: The Ironic History of a Grand Policy Experiment' (http://tinyco.re/6011888). *Journal of Economic Perspectives* 27 (1): pp. 103–22.

Smith, Stephen. 2011. *Environmental Economics: A Very Short Introduction* (http://tinyco.re/9038928). Oxford: Oxford University Press.

Stavins, Robert N., Gabriel Chan, Robert Stowe, and Richard Sweeney. 2012. 'The US Sulphur Dioxide Cap and Trade Programme and Lessons for Climate Policy' (http://tinyco.re/7237191). *VoxEU.org*. Updated 12 August 2012.

Stern, Nicholas. 2007. *The Economics of Climate Change: The Stern Review* (http://tinyco.re/5785938). Cambridge: Cambridge University Press.

Wagner, Gernot, and Martin L. Weitzman. 2015. *Climate Shock: The Economic Consequences of a Hotter Planet* (http://tinyco.re/6928664). Princeton, NJ: Princeton University Press.

Wilkins, Barbara. 1974. 'Lead Poisoning Threatens the Children of an Idaho Town' (http://tinyco.re/5420273). *People.com*.

World Bank, The. 2011. 'The Changing Wealth of Nations' (http://tinyco.re/8096132).

World Bank, The. 2015. 'Commodity Price Data' (http://tinyco.re/9946436).

World Bank, The. 2015. 'World Development Indicators' (http://tinyco.re/8871968).

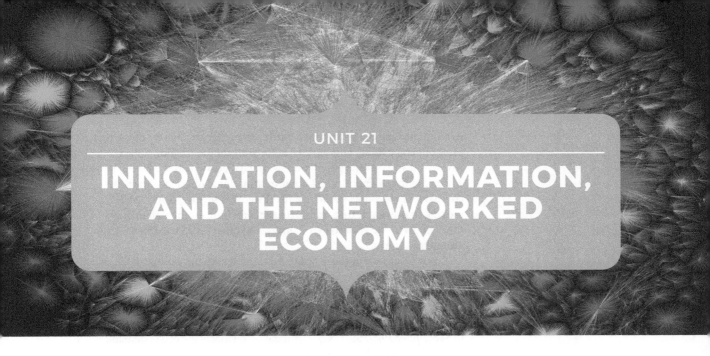

INNOVATIONS THAT ENHANCE OUR WELLBEING ARE A HALLMARK OF CAPITALISM. MAKING THE MOST OF HUMAN CREATIVITY AND INVENTIVENESS IS A PUBLIC POLICY CHALLENGE

- Innovation depends on many factors: the state of knowledge, individual creativity, public policy, economic institutions, and social norms.
- Individuals or companies who introduce socially beneficial innovations are rewarded with profits above the opportunity cost of capital, referred to as innovation rents.
- Innovation rents are eventually competed away by imitators who spread the new knowledge by using it.
- The production and use of new knowledge is unusual in three ways: knowledge is a non-rival good, producing new knowledge is initially costly, but once produced it can be distributed and used for free, and innovations generally become more useful as more people use them.
- Innovating firms often have little immediate competition and can profit by setting prices far above the marginal costs of production, which disadvantages consumers.
- But innovating firms still cannot capture all of the benefits their innovations generate, so may invest too little in innovation.
- Public policy therefore seeks to spread socially beneficial innovations, while at the same time providing adequate rewards for those producing innovations.
- Given this trade-off, intellectual property rights can be either 'too strong', preventing new innovations from spreading, or 'too weak', providing innovation rents that are too small to sufficiently reward innovators.
- Digital technologies support 'two-sided markets' like Facebook, eBay, and Airbnb, which match individuals who can mutually benefit from exchanges.

- These technologies have altered the nature of economic competition, but exhibit many of the same market failures observed in the production of knowledge.

Around the turn of the present century, South Africa had one of the highest rates of people living with HIV in the world: about 5 million South Africans, 1 in 10 of the population, were HIV positive. But in 1998, Bristol-Myers Squibb, Merck, and 37 other multinational pharmaceutical companies brought a lawsuit against the government of South Africa, seeking to prevent it from importing generic (non-brand name) drugs, other inexpensive antiretroviral drugs, and other AIDS treatments from around the world.

Street protests erupted in South Africa, and both the European Union and the World Health Organization announced their support for the South African government's position. Al Gore, then US vice president, who had represented the interests of pharmaceutical companies in negotiations with South Africa, was confronted by AIDS activists chanting, 'Gore's greed kills!' In September 1999, the US government—previously the drug companies' strongest ally—said that it would not impose sanctions on poor countries that are affected by the HIV epidemic, even if US patent laws were broken, so long as the countries abided by international treaties governing intellectual property. The pharmaceutical giants pushed back, engaging an army of intellectual property rights lawyers to promote their case. They closed factories in South Africa and cancelled planned investments.

But three years later, with millions of dollars spent on litigation and with the even greater cost to their reputations, the companies backed down (even paying the South African government's legal fees). Jean-Pierre Garnier, the chief executive officer of GlaxoSmithKline, telephoned Kofi Annan, secretary general of the United Nations, to ask him to help make a deal with President Thabo Mbeki of South Africa. 'We're not insensitive to public opinion. That is a factor in our decision-making,' Garnier later explained.

It was too late: the damage had already been done. 'This has been a public relations disaster for the companies,' commented Hemant Shah, an industry analyst. 'The probability of any drug company suing a developing country on a life-saving medicine is now extremely low based on what they learned in South Africa.'

Of course, pharmaceutical company owners cannot sell an AIDS treatment at less than what it cost them to manufacture it and still stay in business. Moreover, few of the industry's research projects lead to a marketable product (research in 2016 estimated the industry's success rate as just over 4%). The sales of a successful product must therefore cover the costs of many failed projects because, of course, it is impossible to predict which research projects will succeed.

In this instance, the drug companies went to court in South Africa to protect their patents. In the pharmaceutical industry, the patent system gives the innovating company a time-limited monopoly that allows the company to charge a price much higher than the cost of producing the drug (sometimes by a factor of 10) during the years of patent protection. The prospect of high profits provides an incentive for companies to invest in risky research and development.

By creating a government-imposed monopoly, patent protection often conflicts with the equally important objective of making goods and services available at their marginal cost (recall from Unit 7 that a monopolist will set

Swarns Rachel L. 2001. 'Drug Makers Drop South Africa Suit over AIDS Medicine'. *New York Times*. Updated 20 April 2001.

Sarah Boseley. 2016. 'Big Pharma's Worst Nightmare'. *The Guardian*, Updated 5 February 2016.

a price above the marginal cost). The high price—sufficient to cover the cost of research and development, including investments on failed projects—means that many of those who could benefit from access to the drug will not get it. This is an example of the deadweight efficiency losses resulting from monopoly pricing studied in Unit 7.

Conflicts between competing objectives—in this case, the production of new knowledge on the one hand and its rapid diffusion on the other—are unavoidable in the economy, and are particularly difficult to resolve when they concern innovation, as we will see.

But sometimes, new technologies allow for win-win outcomes.

Recall the problem of the fishermen and fish buyers of Kerala that we described at the beginning of Unit 11. On returning to port to sell their daily catch of sardines to fish dealers, fishermen often found that there was excess supply in the market. The result was higher prices for the consumer, on average, and lower incomes for the fishermen.

When the fishermen got mobile phones, they would phone the many coastal fish markets from out at sea, and pick the one where the prices that day were highest. The mobile phone made it possible to implement the **law of one price** in Keralan fish markets, to the benefit of fishermen and consumers. It was not entirely win-win, however. The mobile phones greatly increased the competition among the dealers who were the intermediaries between fishermen and buyers, because a fisherman could bargain for higher prices before choosing which market to enter. The dealers were the losers from this innovation.

But the mobile phone had much weaker effects in other parts of the world, such as Uttar Pradesh and Rajasthan in India, where the lack of roads and storage facilities prevented farmers from profiting from information on price differences. A small farmer in Allahabad remarked that price information that he could get on his phone was not worth much to him because there were 'no roads to go there'. In this case the innovation was of little use, because of a lack of public investment in the necessary infrastructure.

Similarly, when mobile phones came to Niger, in West Africa, farmers lacked the means to transport their cowpeas and other crops to alternative markets, and so traders who transported the goods took much of the benefit. The fishermen did not face this problem because the boats used to catch the fish were also a means of transport, allowing them to choose among markets.

In this unit, we will show how economic concepts can make sense of the South African government's policies to make AIDS treatments more widely available, the conflict that the policies caused, and the contrasting impact of the mobile phone on fishermen in Kerala and farmers in other Indian states.

To understand innovation, you will have to forget about the image of an eccentric inventor, working alone, creating a 'better mousetrap,' and getting rich as a reward for the public benefit of his inspiration. Innovation is not a one-off event set off by a spark of genius. Instead:

- *Innovation is a process*: It is a fundamental source of change in our life that itself is constantly undergoing change.
- *Innovation is also systemic*: It connects networks of users, private firms, individuals, and government bodies.

We discuss innovation as a process and as a system in the next two sections.

'To Do with the Price of Fish'. *The Economist*. Updated 10 May 2007.

Robert Jensen. 2007. 'The Digital Provide: Information (Technology), Market Performance, and Welfare in the South Indian Fisheries Sector'. *The Quarterly Journal of Economics* 122 (3): pp. 879–924.

law of one price Holds when a good is traded at the same price across all buyers and sellers. If a good were sold at different prices in different places, a trader could buy it cheaply in one place and sell it at a higher price in another. *See also: arbitrage.*

F. M. Scherer, an economist who specializes in the effects of technological change, explains how patents support innovation in pharmaceuticals. http://tinyco.re/8674643

innovation The process of invention and diffusion considered as a whole.

invention The development of new methods of production and new products.

diffusion The spread of the invention throughout the economy. See also: diffusion gap.

process innovation An innovation that allows a good or service to be produced at lower cost than its competitors.

product innovation An innovation that produces a new good or service at a cost that will attract buyers.

innovation rents Profits in excess of the opportunity cost of capital that an innovator gets by introducing a new technology, organizational form, or marketing strategy. Also known as: Schumpeterian rents.

Peter A. Hall, and David Soskice. 2001. *Varieties of Capitalism: The Institutional Foundations of Comparative Advantage.* New York, NY: Oxford University Press.

Stephen Witt. 2015. *How Music Got Free: The End of an Industry, the Turn of the Century, and the Patient Zero of Piracy.* New York, NY: Viking.

21.1 THE INNOVATION PROCESS: INVENTION AND DIFFUSION

We begin with a few new terms. We use the word **innovation** to refer to both the development of new methods of production and new products (**invention**) and the spread of the invention throughout the economy (**diffusion**). An innovating firm can produce a good or service at a cost lower than its competitors, or a new good at a cost that will attract buyers. The first is called a **process innovation** and the second is called a **product innovation**.

Invention and innovation

The descriptive term *invention* is sometimes reserved for major breakthroughs, but we use it to refer to:

Radical innovation

Radical innovation introduces a brand new technology or idea that had not been previously available. The invention of incandescent lighting (producing light by running electricity through a filament) was a major advance over light made by burning oil or kerosene. The MP3 format allowed music to be compressed in a manner that enabled easy storage on hard drives and transmission over the Internet, offering a vastly different way to store music than CD or vinyl.

Incremental innovation

This improves an existing product or process cumulatively. After Edison and Swan patented their designs for the incandescent electric light bulb in 1880 and started working together in 1883, all subsequent improvements in the filament that generates the light were incremental innovations in lighting. You have already learned about the incremental improvement of the spinning jenny, one of the major inventions of the Industrial Revolution, which began with just eight spindles and eventually operated hundreds.

Many of the concepts that are useful for the study of innovation have already been introduced in earlier units. They are listed in Figure 21.1, and you will encounter them again throughout this unit. Before going on, make sure you understand these concepts.

Recall from Unit 2 that at the going price, a company introducing a successful invention makes profits in excess of the profits that other firms make, termed **innovation rents**. In Figure 21.2, the research, development, and implementation costs of undertaking an innovation are shown along with the temporary innovation rents (profits above the opportunity cost of capital) from a successful invention.

Diffusion

The prospect of these innovation rents then induces others to try to copy the invention. If they are successful, the temporary rents of the innovator are eventually entirely competed away. The result of this copying process is that eventually the initial innovator will again earn profits that just cover the opportunity cost of capital, so economic profit returns to zero.

Latecomers are also eventually pushed to adopt the innovation, because the falling prices that result when the new methods become widely adopted typically mean that sticking with the old technology is a recipe for bankruptcy. A firm that does not innovate will make negative economic profits, meaning that its revenues fail to cover the opportunity cost of capital. This carrot-and-stick combination of the promise of rents from successful innovation and the threat of bankruptcy if firms fail to keep up with innovators has proved a powerful force in reducing the amount of labour required to produce goods and services, thereby raising our living standards.

Although there have been inventions throughout human history, the acceleration of the innovation process started in England around 1750 (as we saw in Unit 2) with some key new technologies introduced in textiles, energy, and transportation. It did not end with the Industrial Revolution. Important new technologies with applications to many industries such as the steam engine, electricity, and transportation (canals, railroads, automobiles, airplanes) are called **general-purpose technologies**.

William Nordhaus, an economist whose analysis of the discount rate applied to environmental problems you read about in Unit 20, has estimated the speed of computation using an index that has a value of 1 for the speed of

> **general-purpose technologies**
> Technological advances that can be applied to many sectors, and spawn further innovations. Information and communications technology (ICT), and electricity are two common examples.

Concepts	Previously in Units
Innovation rents	1, 2
External effects and public goods	4, 12
Strategic interactions	4, 5, 6
Property rights, including IPR	1, 2, 5, 12
Economies of scale	7
Complements and substitutes	7, 16
Mutual gains and conflicts over their distribution	5
Creative destruction	2, 16
Institutions and social norms	4, 5, 16

Figure 21.1 Concepts relevant to innovation that you have studied.

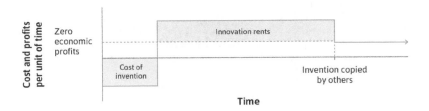

Figure 21.2 The costs and rents associated with innovations.

a computation done by hand (like dividing one number by another). For example, in 1920 a Japanese abacus master could perform computations 4.5 times faster than a mathematically competent person could do the same calculation by hand. This difference had probably been constant for many centuries, because the abacus is an ancient computational device.

But sometime around 1940, computational speed takes off. The IBM 1130 introduced in 1965 was 4,520 times faster than hand computation (and as you can see, it was below the line of best fit through the data points from 1920).

The most recent entry in Figure 21.3, the SiCortex supercomputer, performs more than 1 billion computations per second. It is more than a quadrillion (count the zeros) times faster than you, and it is well above a line of best fit through the data points from 1920, so there is no indication that the process is slowing down.

But as the 'When economists disagree' box shows, engineers and economists disagree over whether improvements in computation or any other technology will continue at the pace given in Nordhaus's chart, or instead will return to the modest pace of improvement that prevailed over most of human history.

The stepped line in Figure 21.2 illustrated a simple theory of innovation and diffusion of technical progress. It clarifies how innovation rents, costs of innovation, and the copying of innovations are interrelated from the standpoint of a firm or individual that wants to develop a new product or process.

To understand this process, we need to know how inventions actually happen, how the costs and rents are decided, and when the process of copying takes place. To do this, we have to go beyond the point of view of the single firm in Figure 21.2 and think of innovation as the product of interactions among firms, the government, educational institutions, and many other players in the **innovation system**.

innovation system The relationships among private firms, governments, educational institutions, individual scientists, and other actors involved in the invention, modification, and diffusion of new technologies, and the way that these social interactions are governed by a combination of laws, policies, knowledge, and social norms in force.

David C. Mowery and Timothy Simcoe. 2002. 'Is the Internet a US Invention? An Economic and Technological History of Computer Networking'. *Research Policy* 31 (8–9): pp. 1369–87.

William D. Nordhaus. 2007. 'Two Centuries of Productivity Growth in Computing'. *The Journal of Economic History* 67 (01), Index updated to 2010.

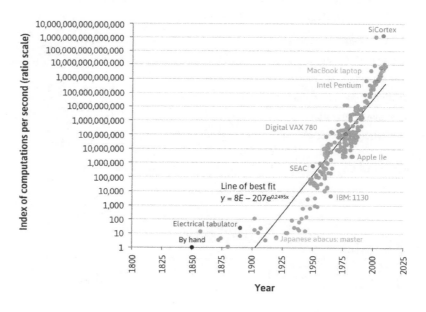

Figure 21.3 Innovation in computing power: Index of computing speed. Particular examples are shown in colour and labelled.

WHEN ECONOMISTS DISAGREE

The end of the permanent technological revolution?

We began Unit 1 with the Industrial Revolution, the capitalist revolution, and history's hockey sticks of rapid technological progress. In Unit 2, we explained how these advances translated into improvements in wellbeing. And we have just seen the dramatic (and possibly even accelerating) rate of technical advance in computation.

In Unit 16, we studied the long-run trend for the economy to produce more services relative to goods. If service productivity grows more slowly than manufacturing productivity, the shift from goods to services reduces overall productivity growth in the economy.

Will this limit the ability of technological progress to increase labour productivity at the rate that has occurred since the Industrial Revolution, and especially during the golden age of capitalism? It seems appropriate to begin this unit with the disagreement among economists about whether the 'permanent' technological revolution is ending.

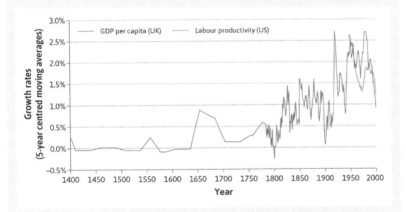

Jutta Bolt and Jan Juiten van Zanden. 2013. 'The First Update of the Maddison Project Re-Estimating Growth Before 1820'. Maddison-Project Working Paper WP-4, January; Stephen Broadberry. 2013. 'Accounting for the Great Divergence'. London School of Economics and Political Science. The Conference Board. 2015. Total Economy Database.

Figure 21.4 The growth rate of productivity over the long run (1400–2013).

Figure 21.4 shows the best available data on the advance of productivity of labour in the UK since 1400, and also for the US for the period in which the US has been the global technology leader. Robert Gordon, an economist who specializes in productivity and growth, has written extensively about productivity growth and its effects, particularly in the first chapter of his book *The Rise and Fall of American Growth* (http://tinyco.re/5970404). He points to the downturn in the productivity growth rate series at the end of the period in the chart.

Gordon believes that the rapid growth era from the first half of the twentieth century is long gone, and slower growth lies ahead of us. In contrast, Erik Brynjolfsson and Andrew McAfee, both economists, advance the view that digital technology is opening up a 'second machine age'. In a video broadcast by Swiss National Television (http://tinyco.re/4612085) and its second part (http://tinyco.re/3087136), they explain their points of view.

EXERCISE 21.2 THE PERMANENT TECHNOLOGICAL REVOLUTION
Use all the sources above, as well as Thomas Edsall's *New York Times* article 'Boom or Gloom' (http://tinyco.re/5275846) and Lee Koromvokis' PBS Newshour article 'Are the best days of the U.S. economy over?' (http://tinyco.re/1182018), to answer the following questions:

1. According to Gordon, Brynjolfsson, and McAfee, which other factors, apart from technological innovation, affect the rate of GDP per capita growth? Why might it take a long time for today's innovations to affect the economy's growth rate?
2. How well do you think GDP per capita growth measures the effect of innovation? Suggest alternative ways to measure the effects of innovation.
3. According to Brynjolfsson and McAfee, how will technological progress affect inequality? Use the data and models from Units 16 and 19 to discuss whether you agree with Brynjolfsson and McAfee's analysis of the relationship between technological progress and inequality.
4. In this unit, we discuss how policies and institutions can help the process of innovation. How can policies and institutions also help the economy adjust to the effects of innovation?

QUESTION 21.1 CHOOSE THE CORRECT ANSWER(S)
Which of the following statements regarding innovation is correct?

☐ An innovation is the development of new methods of production and new products. The spread of these is not innovation.
☐ A product innovation is when a firm produces a good or service at cost lower than its competitors.
☐ A process innovation is when a firm produces a new good at a cost that will attract buyers.
☐ Innovation comprises of both invention and diffusion.

21.2 INNOVATION SYSTEMS

Jerome S. Engel. 2015. 'Global Clusters of Innovation: Lessons from Silicon Valley'. *California Management Review* 57 (2). University of California Press: pp. 36–65.

Innovative activities are not spread evenly across the globe or even across a country. Think of the area now known as Silicon Valley in California, once a sleepy farming area centred on Santa Clara Valley. Silicon Valley got its nickname when high-growth firms in computing and semiconductor design moved in, later joined by innovators in biotech. In 2010, in a single US postal area (ZIP code 95054) in the centre of Silicon Valley, 20,000 patents were registered. Patent attorneys cluster in this part of Santa Clara. If this small area of 16.2 km² were a country, it would have ranked 17th in the world in patents in 2010.

The outpouring of patents from Silicon Valley is a measure of its output of what is termed **codified knowledge**, meaning knowledge that can be written down. But much of the knowledge produced cannot be written down, or at least not exactly. This non-codifiable knowledge is termed **tacit knowledge**.

The difference between codified and tacit knowledge can be illustrated this way. A recipe for a cake can be written down, as it is codified knowledge, but being able to read the recipe and follow it exactly does not get you a reputation for being an outstanding cook; on the other hand, the tacit knowledge of an exceptional chef is not something that you can easily write in a book.

The importance of tacit knowledge is demonstrated in the destruction and re-emergence of the German chemical industry. After the First World War and again after the Second World War, German chemical companies had their factories in Germany disassembled and their facilities in the US and UK expropriated. All that remained were key personnel.

Had all of the necessary knowledge to build a modern chemical industry been codified, there is no particular reason why Germany should have resumed its leadership in this field. Any country with a large scientific and engineering labour force could have created the industry using the available codified knowledge, more or less like the cook following a recipe. But using their know-how and experience (the tacit knowledge), German companies nevertheless managed to resume dominant positions in some markets.

Silicon Valley is as famous for its tacit knowledge as it is for its patented codified knowledge. The extraordinary concentration of innovative businesses in Silicon Valley reflects the importance of external effects and public goods in the production and application of new technologies. The two words 'Silicon Valley' no longer just refer to a place. They now represent a particular way that innovation gets done. Silicon Valley has become associated with an innovation system.

As well as the legal institutions that protect codifiable knowledge and that govern how easily holders of tacit knowledge can move between firms, an innovation system includes financial institutions such as venture capital funds, banks, or technology-oriented firms that will finance projects that seek to commercialize innovations.

Different countries provide quite different innovation systems that often co-evolve with industries in which they specialize. For example, radical innovation is more prevalent in the US, where labour can move easily between firms and venture capital is well developed, and incremental innovation is more prevalent in Germany, where ties of workers to firms are stronger and finance for innovation comes from retained profits and banks rather than from venture capital.

Even within the US, Silicon Valley was unusual. During the 1960s, Silicon Valley was a minor player in technology compared to the Route 128 concentration near Boston, Massachusetts, which benefited from proximity to Harvard and MIT. But Route 128 differed from Silicon Valley in important ways, including the use of **non-compete contracts** that prohibited anyone leaving one firm from taking up employment with a competing firm, as a way of protecting information that a firm produced:

- *The state of Massachusetts enforced non-compete contracts*: This limited inter-firm mobility and the information-sharing that resulted from it.
- *The state of California took the opposite position*: It outlawed non-compete contracts, saying that: 'Every contract by which anyone is restrained from engaging in a lawful profession, trade, or business of any kind is … void.' The resulting circulation of engineers among firms in Silicon Valley promoted the rapid diffusion of new knowledge among firms.

codified knowledge Knowledge that can be written down in a form that would allow it to be understood by others and reproduced, such as the chemical formula for a drug. *See also: tacit knowledge.*

tacit knowledge Knowledge made up of the judgments, know-how, and other skills of those participating in the innovation process. The type of knowledge that cannot be accurately written down. *See also: codified knowledge.*

non-compete contract A contract of employment containing a provision or agreement by which the worker cannot leave to work for a competitor. This may reduce the reservation option of the worker, lowering the wage that the employer needs to pay.

AnnaLee Saxenian. 1996. *Regional Advantage: Culture and Competition in Silicon Valley and Route 128*. Cambridge, MA: Harvard University Press.

Michele Boldrin and David K. Levine. 2008. *Against Intellectual Monopoly*. New York, NY: Cambridge University Press.

The Silicon Valley innovation system

Why is innovation concentrated in Silicon Valley? Institutions and incentives reinforce each other to produce a radical innovation cluster. The Silicon Valley model is one of highly mobile entrepreneurs, investors, and employees linked within a small geographical area, with support from government and educational institutions.

The Silicon Valley system consists of:

1. *Innovating firms:* Most innovation takes place in firms specializing in producing new methods or products (start-ups) rather than in existing firms that produce goods and services.
2. *Other innovating institutions:* In a partnership that began early in the 1900s, two universities, one public (University of California at Berkeley) and the other private (Stanford University) work closely with firms to commercialize innovations. An industrial park was set up in 1951 at Stanford with major corporations like General Electric, IBM, and Hewlett Packard. University, government, and private R&D labs are co-located in the Valley, even including the R&D centre of Walmart, the retail giant.
3. *Government:* Military research in electronics and high-energy physics was funded at the universities and in private firms in the area, starting in the run-up to the Second World War. During the Cold War (from the end of the Second World War until the 1990s), this continued with Lockheed Missiles and Space the largest employer in the Valley. A change in the law in 1980, called the Bayh-Dole Act, enabled universities to gain ownership of their output and commercialize it even if the federal government had helped fund it. This brought private investors into the network.
4. *Social norms:* A social norm for high-risk, high-return behaviour, which some say has its origins in the speculators who flooded into California to mine for gold in the nineteenth century, sustains a culture of serial entrepreneurship. Failed innovators can start again with a new idea. High firm failure rates and other reasons for employee mobility across firms distribute the tacit knowledge acquired in one firm to other firms. Some have concluded that this unintentional sharing of information among firms was key to Silicon Valley's success.
5. *Finance:* Entrepreneurs at an early stage will pitch their project to venture capital (VC) investors. When the VCs decide to invest and take a substantial ownership stake, usually for a period of 12 to 18 months, it creates strong incentives for the startup to grow rapidly and, if successful, means the VC investor can exit with a high rate of profit. The funding model for startups is a rapid-paced cycle of pitching a new business idea to investors, which is based on the commercialization of an invention, followed by recruiting key employees (often with earnings linked to the value of the firm when it is sold), market growth, and seeking more cash. Founders, investors, and employees all understand that failure is likely. Funders still benefit, because the few successful ventures produce large returns that compensate for many losses.

The German innovation system

Innovation in the US is concentrated in industries whose patents heavily cite scientific articles. This is one indicator of radical innovation. By contrast, the very successful export industries of Germany rely on incremental innovation, where patents are much less intensive in scientific citations and tacit knowledge tends to be more important. Networks are also crucial to the

German innovation system but they work differently from those in Silicon Valley. Like Silicon Valley, innovation is concentrated geographically, with centres around Munich and Stuttgart in southwest Germany.

The German system consists of:

1. *Innovating firms:* Incremental innovation takes place in medium-size and large long-lived companies in Germany, and relies on long-term relationships between employers and workers, between firms and banks, and among firms linked through production relationships and ownership and control ties. To succeed in introducing new technology, firms face many coordination problems, which can be solved through cooperative and competitive relationships with employees, other firms, and banks.

2. *Government:* The government supports the training of highly skilled workers through a government-subsidized apprenticeship system, which is supervised by industry associations. This system reduces training costs for firms and ensures high quality training. Apprentices contribute by accepting low training wages. Large firms are required to have elected bodies to represent workers in negotiations with managers. They help to devise ways to exploit all possible mutual gains and to distribute these gains in a way acceptable to all.

3. *Innovators:* Skilled workers are needed for the successful introduction of process and product innovations. To make this possible, young people need to be assured of long-term, high-wage employment before they are willing to commit to multi-year apprenticeships. Similarly, workers engaging in innovation that could result in job cuts need to be assured that they will not lose their jobs. The vocational training scheme addresses these issues in a number of ways. As discussed above, the government sponsors and subsidizes high-quality apprenticeships. Training schemes are also certified. This assures trainees that their skills are valuable outside the firm, improving their reservation position should their job end, and helping to ensure high wages as long as the job continues.

4. *Social norms:* Incremental innovation (for example, in the automobile industry) requires industry-wide standards to make technology transfer easier. Long-term relationships and cross-ownership among firms are essential for facilitating technology transfer, because long-term employment contracts mean that the Silicon Valley-style technology transfer that occurs when workers move from one firm to another is much less common. Similarly, the assurance that firms' highly trained workers will not be poached is not achieved through laws but by norms that are widely respected by the otherwise highly competitive firms.

5. *Finance:* The system of ownership of large German firms differs sharply from that of US or UK firms. Takeovers are easier in the US or the UK, and allow for rapid changes in the use of the assets of a firm. Because ownership of firms is much more concentrated in Germany, it is virtually impossible for a hostile takeover—that is, one opposed by the management—to occur. Therefore, long-run inter-firm collaboration over technology development is possible, and industry-wide standards are easier to set. The financing of innovation in Germany comes from retained profits (profits not distributed to shareholders) and bank loans. Long-term finance provides reassurance for trainees who invest in acquiring company-specific skills, as well as for other companies investing in related technology developments.

Read the introduction to: Peter A Hall and David Soskice. 2001. *Varieties of Capitalism: The Institutional Foundations of Comparative Advantage.* New York, NY: Oxford University Press.

Figure 21.5 compares the two systems. Both are successful, but in different ways. Silicon Valley-based firms dominate important digital technologies (ICT) associated with the latest general-purpose technology, while the German firms making up its distinctive innovation system have managed to sustain a much higher level of well-paid industrial jobs in the face of global competition, compared to the US or any other country outside of East Asia.

The economics of innovation systems

Successful innovation can contribute to rising living standards by expanding the set of products available to consumers, and by reducing the prices of existing products. However, many societies struggle to innovate.

Compare the amount of innovation in capitalist economies to the amount in centrally planned economies of the Soviet Union and its allies during the twentieth century. In a list of 111 major non-military product and process innovations between 1917 and 1998, only one—synthetic rubber—came from Soviet bloc countries. Scholars have suggested that an important factor contributing to the collapse of the Soviet planned economies was the Communist Party's failure to deliver innovation in consumer goods, which eroded the legitimacy of its rule.

The successful capitalist innovation systems in Silicon Valley and Germany have two things in common:

János Kornai. 2013. *Dynamism, Rivalry, and the Surplus Economy: Two Essays on the Nature of Capitalism*. Oxford: Oxford University Press.

- *The innovation system is not based on individual creativity:* A single firm or an inventor relies on the relationships among all of the actors—owners, employees, governments, and sources of finance. Regions without these support networks are less successful at innovation.
- *There is a helping hand as well as an 'invisible hand':* Successful innovation systems involve profit-seeking competition among individuals and firms, but the government also plays an essential role—military contracts in Silicon Valley and worker training in Germany, for example.

In the next three sections, we explore three aspects of invention and diffusion that make the innovation process a challenge to public policy, and why it has proven so difficult for other localities to copy the Silicon Valley or German innovation systems.

	Silicon Valley	German innovation system
Innovation	Radical codified, especially in ICT	Incremental tacit, especially in capital goods and transport equipment
Innovating firms	Entrepreneurial innovation specialists	Established industrial and other firms
Government	Military contracts, higher education	Subsidies for training workers
Innovators	Engineers, scientists, universities	Skilled workers and engineers
Social norms	Competitive; risk-taking	Cooperative; risk-pooling
Finance	Venture capital	Bank loans, retained earnings
Property rights	Patents of more importance	Non-patent forms of protection of more importance

Figure 21.5 Two innovation systems: Silicon Valley and Germany.

These aspects are:

- *External effects* and the problem of coordination among innovators*: A firm's successful invention almost always has either positive or negative effects on the value of other firms' investments in the innovation process. Owners of a firm who are concerned solely about their profits will fail to take into account these external effects.
- *Public goods*: Innovation can be seen as the production of new knowledge by the use of a combination of old knowledge and creativity. The fact that most forms of knowledge are non-rival—making it available to an additional user does not mean that some current user will be deprived of its use—makes the innovation process one that uses public goods to produce other public goods.
- *Economies of scale* and *winner-take-all competition*: Big is beautiful when it comes to the knowledge-based economy. Average costs fall as more units of a good or service are provided, and this means that firms entering a market first often can take the entire market, at least temporarily.

Recall from Unit 12 that these three characteristics are all sources of market failure. Simply letting market competition regulate the process of innovation will generally not result in an efficient outcome. These same three aspects of the innovation process also pose challenges to governments that seek to address these market failures. This is because governments may lack the necessary information (or the motivation) to develop appropriate policies.

We begin with a model of the problem of external effects and the problem of coordination among innovators, simplified to just two firms considering investing in innovations, and a government that may assist in the innovation process.

external effect A positive or negative effect of a production, consumption, or other economic decision on another person or people that is not specified as a benefit or liability in a contract. It is called an external effect because the effect in question is outside the contract. *Also known as: externality. See also: incomplete contract, market failure, external benefit, external cost.*

public good A good for which use by one person does not reduce its availability to others. *Also known as: non-rival good. See also: non-excludable public good, artificially scarce good.*

economies of scale These occur when doubling all of the inputs to a production process more than doubles the output. The shape of a firm's long-run average cost curve depends both on returns to scale in production and the effect of scale on the prices it pays for its inputs. *Also known as: increasing returns to scale. See also: diseconomies of scale.*

EXERCISE 21.3 COMPARING INNOVATION SYSTEMS
In this unit, we compared the Silicon Valley and German innovation systems.

Which of these two systems do you think would be more likely to be introduced and succeed in the country or region in which you are now living? Why or why not? (If you are in Germany, would the Silicon Valley system work where you are? If you are in California, would the German system work there?)

QUESTION 21.2 CHOOSE THE CORRECT ANSWER(S)
Which of the following statements is correct regarding the Silicon Valley and German innovation systems?

☐ The Silicon Valley innovation system is considered much more successful than the German innovation system.

☐ Both Silicon Valley and German innovation systems rely on universities to provide highly skilled, and therefore highly paid, graduates.

☐ The successes of Silicon Valley and German innovation systems are both due to the relationships among all of the actors (owners, employees, governments and financiers) that promote innovation.

☐ Both Silicon Valley and German innovation systems benefit from a high level of financing from venture capitalists, whose high tolerance for business failure sustain a culture of entrepreneurship.

21.3 EXTERNAL EFFECTS: COMPLEMENTS, SUBSTITUTES, AND COORDINATION

Innovations considered by a firm will typically either increase or decrease other firms' profit levels, and affect those firms' choices about innovation. Think about just two firms, each considering innovations that are either:

complements Two goods for which an increase in the price of one leads to a decrease in the quantity demanded of the other. *See also: substitutes.*

substitutes Two goods for which an increase in the price of one leads to an increase in the quantity demanded of the other. *See also: complements.*

- *Complements*: The value of one innovation is greater in the presence of the other. Tin cans were invented to store food in 1810 by Peter Durand, a British merchant, and the first canning factory began production in 1813. But the cans were very difficult to open and not widely used in the home until 1858, when Ezra Warner invented a simple can opener.
- *Substitutes*: The two innovations are valuable alone, but less valuable when some other innovation has already occurred. A good example is the video format war during the 1980s between two competing standards, VHS and Betamax. Videos made using one format could not be played on machines designed to play the other. Either Sony Betamax or JVC's rival VHS would have been a perfectly good single format for home video recording, but the introduction of both led to a costly rivalry.

In the absence of explicit government policies or private means of coordination among firms, the challenges posed by complementary innovations and substitute innovations are quite different:

- *When potential innovations are complements:* Innovations sometimes do not occur even when it would have been socially beneficial, and profitable to the firms, if they had both occurred.
- *When potential innovations are substitutes:* Both innovations sometimes occur, when having only one or the other would be more socially beneficial and profitable to the firms involved. Competition between substitutes may impose a high cost on both innovators.

We can use game theory to understand how two potential innovating firms interact strategically, and show why these contrasting problems arise and why they may be difficult to solve. (You may wish to review the introduction to game theory in Unit 4.)

Innovations that are complements

Here we have two hypothetical firms, Plugcar, which is considering developing a novel electric car, and Netflex, which is weighing up the likely profits and costs of investing in a mobile network of battery exchanges. As above, the presence of Netflex makes Plugcar more valuable and vice versa, so they are complements. They will make their decisions (Innovate or Do not innovate) independently, but they know the profits and losses that will result in each of the four possible outcomes. They are given in the payoff matrix below. The row player is Plugcar, and its payoffs come first in each cell; the column player is Netflex, its payoffs are second in each cell. Positive numbers are profits for the company, while negative numbers are losses.

Imagine that you are Plugcar. If you do not innovate you will get zero, whatever Netflex does. If you knew that Netflex was not going to introduce its product, then you surely would not develop the Plugcar. What if Netflex does introduce its product? If you innovate you will get profits of 1. But you also stand to incur losses of 0.5 if Netflex does not innovate.

Unless you are pretty sure that Netflex is going to innovate, you may decide that you have better uses for your funds. If Netflex reasoned the same way, then neither firm might innovate even though they both would have profited from doing so.

Innovations that are substitutes

When two innovations are substitutes we have the opposite problem. A good example is the video format war during the 1980s between two competing standards, VHS (for 'video home system' developed by Victor Company of Japan (JVC)) and Sony's Betamax format. As discussed above, videos using one format could not be played on machines designed to play the other, so both companies had an interest in making their format the most widely accepted.

We consider two hypothetical firms based on the Sony-JVC case. Here is the payoff matrix facing them. JVC is the row player, and Sony is the column player. As before, the first entry in each cell is the payoff of the row player.

If Sony is sure that JVC will innovate, then it will face a costly battle with big losses if JVC wins. The payoffs in the upper left-hand cell are negative for both firms, because the costs of developing the new product and competing for market share do not offset the uncertain prospect of profits

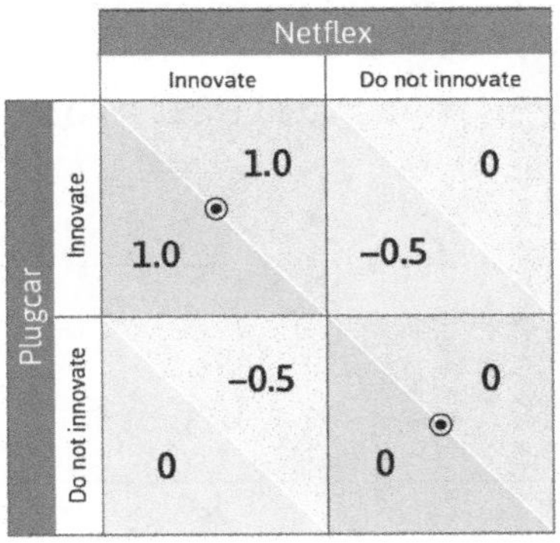

Figure 21.6 The decision to innovate when products are complements.

1. Begin with the row player

Begin with the row player and ask: 'What would be the best response to the column player's decision to innovate?'

2. The best response

The best response would be Innovate, since the payoff is 1 rather than 0. Place a dot in the top left-hand cell.

3. The row player's response

Then ask what the row player's best response would be to the column player's choice of Do not innovate: the answer is Do not innovate. Place a dot in the bottom right-hand cell.

4. The column player's reasoning

Now turn to the column player. What would be the best response to the row player's strategy of Innovate? The answer is Innovate. Place an open circle in the top left-hand cell—there will now be a dot inside a circle.

5. The column player's response

Do the same for the column player's response to row player's strategy of Do not innovate. There is now a dot inside a circle.

6. Finding the Nash equilibria

Wherever there is a dot inside a circle in a cell, this is a Nash equilibrium because it shows that each player is playing the best response to what the other does.

should they win. Of course, if Sony knew that JVC was not going to invest, or if it was sure it would win a not-very-costly battle with its product should both invest, then Sony would definitely invest and enjoy the winner-take-all profits, while inflicting losses on JVC.

The result is that there is sometimes too little innovation for the good of society when ideas are complementary, and too much when the innovations are substitutes.

The role of public policy

Complements

If the payoffs in the matrix were known to everyone, then a wise government would know that the top left (Innovate, Innovate) in Figure 21.6 is the best outcome for society. It could, in the case of complementary innovations, provide both firms with sufficient subsidies so that both would find it profitable to make the investment regardless of what the other firm did. Or, more reasonably, it could help the two firms to cooperate in the innovation process, promising not to prosecute them for any anti-competitive practices if coordinated decision making is prohibited by antitrust or other law.

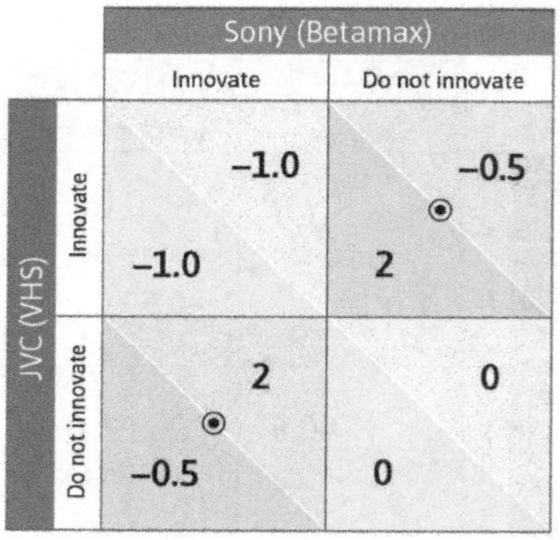

		Sony (Betamax)	
		Innovate	Do not innovate
JVC (VHS)	**Innovate**	−1.0 −1.0	−0.5 ⊙ 2
	Do not innovate	2 ⊙ −0.5	0 0

Figure 21.7 The decision to innovate when products are substitutes.

1. Begin with the row player
Begin with the row player and ask: 'What would be the best response to the column player's decision to innovate?'

2. The best response
The best response would be Do not innovate, since the payoff is −0.5 rather than −1.0. Place a dot in the bottom left-hand cell.

3. The row player's response
Then ask what the row player's best response would be to the column player's choice of Do not innovate: the answer is Innovate. Place a dot in the top right-hand cell.

4. The column player's reasoning
Now turn to the column player. What would be the best response to the row player's strategy of Innovate? The answer is Do not innovate. Place an open circle in the bottom left-hand cell—there will now be a dot inside a circle.

5. The column player's response
Do the same for the column player's response to row player's strategy of Do not innovate. There is now a dot inside a circle.

6. Finding the Nash equilibria
Wherever there is a dot inside a circle in a cell, this is a Nash equilibrium because it shows that each player is playing the best response to what the other does.

But using public policy to avoid an unfavourable outcome is a greater challenge than our simple model would suggest. There are likely to be more than two potential innovators, and hence many proposed designs for electric cars and for recharging systems. The government would have to choose the cooperating firms, and the terms under which the cooperation would occur. In this case, companies have incentives to spend resources to influence government decisions (lobbying). As we shall see in Unit 22, there are many reasons why governments may fail to achieve the socially beneficial outcome in cases like this.

Private exchanges might have a role to play here. If the firms themselves have better information than the government, they might engage in private agreements. This is the equivalent to the bargaining among private economic bodies that occurred in Unit 12 as an alternative to government regulation of the use of chemical weedkillers.

Finally, firms with promising complementary innovations might agree to merge so that, as a single company, the problem of coordinating their innovation decisions would be internal to the firm.

Substitutes and standards

The substitutes in Figure 21.7 present similar challenges for government policy. There may be a great many competing substitute innovations. Sony's Betamax and JVC's VHS were not the only entrants in the early stages of the formatting wars. Governments may also lack the relevant information, or may be under the influence of one of the contestants.

As we will see later, sometimes one competitor's technology wins over the other. Eventually, Betamax, for example, died out and VHS became the universal home videotape standard. Sometimes, companies in an industry apply the same standards, because consistency increases the size of the market and benefits all firms. An example is the way the shipping industry implemented the standard for the size of containers they carry, which allowed trucks and ports to become more efficient, and therefore achieve economies of scale.

Often, however, public sector agencies play an important role in encouraging agreement among all the firms in an industry about technical standards. These are usually international bodies, like the International Telecommunications Union or the European Commission. The EU, for example, helped mobile phone companies to agree on the GSM standard for phone handsets and networks, which enabled all the manufacturers and operators to benefit from a rapidly growing European mobile market, and enabled consumers to benefit from the ease of calling other networks and declining prices.

EXERCISE 21.4 COMPLEMENTS

1. List some pairs of innovations that are complements, and some that are substitutes.
2. In the game in Figure 21.6 (page 977), what probability of one firm choosing 'Innovate' would make it profitable for the other firm to choose 'Innovate'? Explain your answer. (Hint: Compare the expected payoffs of choosing either option, given that the probability of the other firm choosing 'Innovate' is x. What range of probabilities would give a higher expected payoff from choosing 'Innovate'?)

EXERCISE 21.5 SUBSTITUTES AND COMPLEMENTS

1. Go back to Figure 4.16a (page 174) and consider the game between Bettina and Astrid, in which they choose whether to use two different programming languages, C++ and Java. Describe the similarities and differences in the strategies, payoffs, and optimal outcome of Figure 4.16 and the Sony-JVC game depicted here.
2. In Figure 21.7 (page 978), for innovating to be profitable, with what probability should the other firm choose 'Do not innovate'?

Now suppose that decisions in Figures 21.6 (page 977) and 21.7 are made sequentially rather than simultaneously. In the case of substitutes (Sony and JVC), imagine that JVC developed its product and put it on the market (or at least convinced Sony that it would definitely do this). In the case of complements (Plugcar and Netflex), assume that Plugcar could convince Netflex that it will definitely bring the new electric car to the market.

3. Explain what the outcome in those cases would be if the two firms made their decisions sequentially rather than simultaneously.

QUESTION 21.3 CHOOSE THE CORRECT ANSWER(S)

The following matrix shows the payoffs for two firms according to whether they innovate or not. The first number is the payoff for firm A while the second number is for firm B.

		Firm B	
		Innovate	Do not innovate
Firm A	Innovate	−1.0 / −2.0	1.5 / −1.0
	Do not innovate	−0.5 / 2.5	0 / 0

Based on this information, which of the following statements is correct?

☐ In this game, the two innovations are complements.
☐ There are two Nash equilibria in this game: (Innovate, Innovate) and (Do not innovate, Do not innovate).
☐ Firm B will definitely choose to innovate because of the potentially high profits from innovation.
☐ Firm A will choose to innovate if the probability of Firm B investing is 75% or less.

21.4 ECONOMIES OF SCALE AND WINNER-TAKE-ALL COMPETITION

Innovation involves developing new knowledge, and putting it to use. Recall that knowledge is unusual in two ways. It is a public good (what one consumes does not subtract from what is available to others) and its production and use are characterized by extraordinary increasing returns to scale. We discussed knowledge as a public good in Unit 12. In this section, we discuss the two ways in which knowledge-intensive innovation creates economies of scale.

The supply side: First copy costs and economies of scale in production

The first copy of new knowledge is costly to produce, but virtually costless to make available to others. Because **first copy costs** are large relative to the costs (variable or marginal) of making additional goods available, information production and distribution is different from any other part of the economy.

first copy costs The fixed costs of the production of a knowledge-intensive good or service.

- *Thriller, by Michael Jackson*: This is the best-selling music album in history. It cost $750,000 to produce in 1982 (about twice that amount in 2015 dollars). The marginal cost of producing additional copies is less than $1 for a CD, and almost nothing if it is a download. A CD sells for about $10, and a download for the same amount. The first copy cost of even a modest production by a new band will be at least $10,000, with marginal costs of around $1 for each CD, and zero for a download.
- *Textbooks*: To develop a new high-quality textbook in the US costs between $1 million and $2 million, to compensate the writers, designers, editors, and others for their work. This is the first copy cost. The cost of producing and distributing the physical books (printing, warehousing, and delivery included) for a successful text are approximately $12 per book. This is its marginal cost. Students all over the world know that introductory course textbooks typically sell for ten times this amount.
- *Star Wars: The Force Awakens*: the production budget for this film, released in 2015, was $200 million. The development cost for the computer game *Star Wars: The Old Republic* (2011) was between $150 million and $200 million. These figures do not include the marketing and promotion costs, such as advertising, that should be included in the first copy cost, and may be bigger than the production costs. Now that movies are distributed digitally to cinemas, making a film available costs virtually nothing. The marginal costs for movies or games sold on DVD are around the same as for a CD, and when they are sold as digital downloads, they are zero.
- *New drugs*: The average first copy cost of a new drug according to a study in the US in 2003 was $403 million. This fact explains the difference in price between drugs that are still under patent, giving the producer a temporary monopoly, and the prices that users pay once the patent has expired so that other producers compete with the originator of the drug. For instance, Omeprazole, a very widely prescribed dyspepsia drug, was patented and launched in 1989, sold under the brand name Prilosec. In the US the patent expired in 2001, and by 2003, 28 tablets of brand-name Prilosec sold for $124, while the equivalent packet of generic Omeprazole cost only $24.

Marc Rysman. 2009. 'The Economics of Two-Sided Markets'. *Journal of Economic Perspectives* 23 (3): pp. 125–43.

In Unit 7 we studied how a firm sets prices, and how it decides how much to produce. In Figure 21.8, we show a set of cost curves for a firm producing a knowledge-intensive good. The numbers are hypothetical, and they understate the true size of the first copy cost relative to marginal cost. Even so, the vertical axis is still not drawn to scale so we can read the figure.

- *Total cost*: The curve starts at the first copy cost, and then rises very little with increased production.
- *Marginal cost (MC)*: The curve is low and constant.
- *Average cost (AC)*: The curve (including economic profits and the first copy costs) falls as quantity increases, as the cost of the first copy is spread over larger units of output.
- *MC < AC*: No matter how many units are produced, the marginal cost will always be less than the average.

A firm producing a knowledge-intensive good that wants to make economic profits will have to cover its first copy cost. To do so, the price will have to be at least as high as the average cost curve and therefore higher than marginal cost.

This means the production of knowledge-intensive goods cannot be described by the competitive markets of Unit 8 in which price equals marginal cost (P = MC), but instead by the model of price-setting firms in Unit 7. In Unit 7, we assumed that P > MC because of limited competition. Here it is an unavoidable consequence of first copy costs, and no matter how many competitors there are, price cannot be competed all the way down to marginal cost.

Earlier in this unit (and in Units 1 and 2), we explain that in the absence of intellectual property rights, competition from followers would eventually eliminate the innovation rents made by first adopters of an

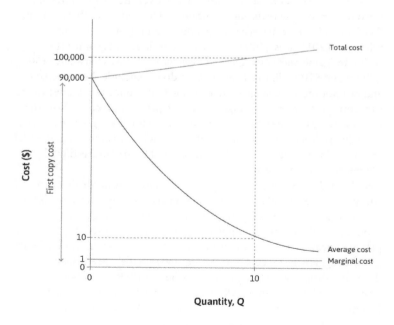

Figure 21.8 A knowledge-intensive good: Marginal, average, and first copy costs.

improved technology or new product. This is how the diffusion of a new technology happens, and results in lower prices. The same process will take place where first copy costs are important. Other firms will copy the innovator until the economic profits (rents) are eliminated, so that the price being charged offsets the average cost of production, including the first copy cost and the opportunity cost of the capital goods used. But in this situation, the price being charged must be greater than the average cost (due to the first copy costs, as shown in Figure 21.8). Figure 21.9 below illustrates these cases.

The demand side: Economies of scale through network effects

The value of many forms of knowledge increases when more people use it. Because the benefits to users increase as the network of users grows, demand-side increasing returns are sometimes called **network external effects**. The external effect is that when one more person joins the network, all others benefit.

> **network external effects** An external effect of one person's action on another, occuring because the two are connected in a network. *See also: external effect.*

Languages are a good example. Today, more than one billion people are learning English, which is more than three times as many people who speak English as their first language. The demand for English is not due to the intrinsic superiority of the language or because it is easy to learn (as many of you will know), but simply because so many other people, in many parts of the world, speak it. There are many more people who speak Mandarin (Chinese) and Spanish as a first language, and almost as many Hindi and Arabic speakers, but none of these languages is as useful to communicate globally as is English.

Having a particular games console is better when lots of people have the same one, because developers will produce more games for it. A credit card is more useful when many people have the same card, because lots of shops will accept it as payment.

But have you ever wondered who bought the first telephone, and what they intended to do with it? Or what you could do with the first fax machine?

The technology behind the fax, a device to send images of documents over a telephone line, was first patented by Alexander Bain in 1843—although his image-sending innovation had to use the telegraph, because nobody had invented a telephone yet. A commercial service that could transmit handwritten signatures using the telegraph was available in the 1860s. But the fax remained a niche product until 120 years later when it became so popular that, within the space of 10 years, almost every office installed its own fax machine.

This tells us the first thing we need to know about demand-side economies of scale: there is little incentive to be the first to adopt a technology with this characteristic.

	Restricted entry (IPR or other)	Unrestricted entry
Declining average costs	Economic profits $P > AC > MC$	No economic profits $P = AC > MC$
Non-declining average costs	Economic profits $P > MC \gtreqless AC$	No economic profits $P = MC = AC$

Figure 21.9 The average cost curve, economic profits, and competition.

The second thing we need to know is that, if two versions of this type of technology are competing, the one that gains a larger number of adopters at the outset will have an advantage, even if the other one is cheaper or better. To see this, let's take another look at the video format war between Sony and JVC.

Sony's Betamax format was superior to JVC's VHS for its picture and sound quality. But in the early 1980s, Sony made a strategic error by limiting the recording time to 60 minutes. If customers wanted to use their new Sony Betamax to record a feature film, they needed to change the tape in the middle of the recording. By the time Sony had extended its recording length to 120 minutes, there were so many more VHS users that the Betamax format all but disappeared.

The video formatting war, and its outcome, is an example of **winner-take-all competition**, in which economies of scale in production or distribution give the firm with the largest share of the market a commanding competitive edge. Winner-take-all competition does not necessarily select the best.

To see how this works, Figure 21.10 depicts competition based on the Sony and JVC case. The length of the horizontal axis is the number of people purchasing either Sony's Betamax or JVC's VHS. We assume that the price of the two products is identical.

To simplify our example, assume that the value of using the product for a new user is approximately the number of individuals currently using the product, n, multiplied by an index for the quality of the product, q. The net benefit of purchasing a good is then equal to the benefit from using the good, qn, minus the price that the consumer pays, p. Our simplifying assumptions then allow us to write the net value of buying the product as $\Pi = qn - p$. Higher quality products have a higher value of q, so consumers faced with two products with the same number of users and same price will prefer the higher quality good.

The number of individuals buying Betamax is measured from the left to the right, starting at zero and extending potentially all the way to the entire market. The blue line shows the net benefits of using Betamax for consumers. Its equation is $\Pi^B = q^B n^B - p$, where the superscript 'B' is for Betamax. If everyone buys Betamax, the value to each purchaser is shown in the figure, Π^{Bmax}, which is equal to $q^B n^{total} - p$. If no one else buys Betamax, the value to that first purchaser is negative and equal to the price paid, shown by the intercept on the left-hand vertical axis below the horizontal axis.

In the same figure, the net value of JVC's product VHS is given by the red line whose equation is $\Pi^V = q^V n^V - p$ (where the superscript 'V' stands for VHS). Because there are only two firms competing, the number buying VHS is just the total size of the market, minus the number buying Betamax.

Let's assume that the Betamax format is higher quality. Within our model, this means that $q^B > q^V$. This implies that if everyone bought Betamax, the net value would be greater than if everyone bought VHS format, that is $\Pi^{Bmax} > \Pi^{Vmax}$. In Figure 21.10, this is illustrated by the fact that the height of the blue Betamax line where it intersects the right-hand axis (everyone using Betamax) is above the intercept of the red VHS line with the left-hand axis (everyone using VHS).

The first thing to notice is that if at a particular moment everyone is buying VHS (point B), then a new buyer will certainly prefer VHS to Betamax. To see this in the diagram, look at the left-hand side and consider a new buyer. For this person, the value of VHS is high (the intercept with the left-hand axis), whereas the value of Betamax is negative. This is because the new user would have to pay the price of the Betamax recorder, but would not get any benefits because there are no other users, and therefore no video content is provided. This is true even though we have assumed that Betamax costs the same as VHS, and that Betamax is the better quality video cassette.

The second lesson from the figure is that even if many consumers (but fewer than 4,000) were buying Betamax, the new consumer would still prefer VHS (the red line is still above the blue line at that point). For Betamax to break the VHS monopoly, it would have to get at least 4,000 buyers. Then Betamax rather than VHS would offer higher value, and could eventually take the entire market (at point A).

So the winner need not be the better alternative. This is sometimes called **lock-in**.

But this is not the whole story. The history of innovation in the knowledge economy is full of more complicated stories, in which changes are constantly occurring for many reasons.

> **lock-in** A consequence of the network external effects that create winner-take-all competition. The competitive process results in an outcome that is difficult to change, even if users of the technology consider an alternative innovation superior.

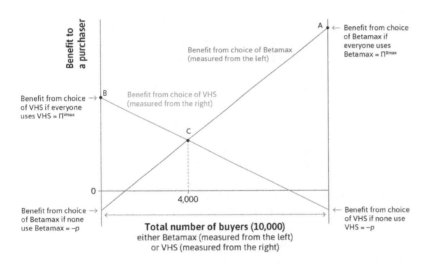

Figure 21.10 The net value of becoming part of a network.

1. The net benefit of Betamax
The net benefit to a consumer of Betamax is given by the blue line, reading from left to right.

2. If everyone buys Betamax
The net benefit to each purchaser is shown in the figure by Π^{Bmax}, which is equal to $q^B n^{total} - p$. This is the case where Betamax is the winning format and takes all of the market, shown by point A.

3. If nobody buys Betamax
The net benefit to a purchaser would be negative and equal to the price paid for it.

4. The net benefit of VHS
The red line gives the net benefit to a consumer of the VHS format. The VHS format is the winner and takes all the market at point B.

5. For Betamax to break a VHS monopoly
For the net benefit of Betamax to be greater than the net benefit of VHS, it would require at least 4,000 buyers to purchase a Betamax recorder, shown in the diagram as all the outcomes to the right of point C.

For example:

- *Browser wars:* When the Internet became popular, the market for Internet browsers was dominated by a product called Netscape Navigator. It was displaced by Microsoft Internet Explorer in the 'browser wars' of the early 2000s. Internet Explorer, in turn, was later challenged by Mozilla Firefox and Google Chrome.
- *Smartphones:* At the beginning of 2009, Android smartphones had a market share of 1.6%, Apple's iPhones had 10.5%, and the market was dominated by a technology called Symbian, with 48.8% share. At the beginning of 2016, 84.1% of smartphones sold were based on Android, Apple's smartphones had a share of 14.8%, and Symbian smartphones were no longer being manufactured.
- *Social networks:* In June 2006, 80% of people who used a social network used a site called MySpace. By May 2009, more people used Facebook than MySpace.

QUESTION 21.4 CHOOSE THE CORRECT ANSWER(S)
Figure 21.8 (page 982) shows the cost curves for a firm producing a knowledge-intensive good.

The marginal cost is constant at $1 for all output Q. Based on this information, which of the following statements is correct?

☐ With positive first copy cost and constant marginal cost, the firm's average cost will always be above its marginal cost.
☐ The firm's average costs will eventually start increasing, at which point the firm's production no longer benefits from economies of scale.
☐ The government should encourage competition to drive the price down to $p = \$1$.
☐ A small-scale car valeting business is a good example of a firm with the cost structure shown in the graph.

21.5 MATCHING (TWO-SIDED) MARKETS

A market is a way of putting together people who might benefit from exchanging a good or service. Often these are potential buyers and sellers of the same commodity, such as milk, and the sides of this market are farmers supplying milk and consumers demanding it. In common usage, a market may also refer to a place such as the Fulton Fish Market that we described in Unit 8, or a place where those selling fresh vegetables, cheese, and baked goods congregate, knowing that they will encounter potential customers. In these markets, buyers do not care about who produced the fish or the milk that they buy, and sellers are similarly not concerned about who is buying, as long as someone buys their products.

Matching (two-sided) markets

People also use the term market to describe a different kind of connection, in which the people on each side of the market care whom they are matched with on the other side. This is what people have in mind when they speak about the 'marriage market', for example. Most of us do not get married in the way that we get a carton of milk in the grocery market. The marriage market is about getting married to a person with the combination of characteristics that you find most desirable in a spouse. Markets like these are called **matching markets** or **two-sided markets**.

In our 'Economist in action' video, Alvin Roth, an economist who specializes in how markets are designed (and who won the Nobel Prize for his work on the subject in 2012), explains how matching markets function.

We have recently seen a proliferation of online platforms that connect individuals in two groups, starting with the launch of consumer-to-consumer trader eBay in 1995. These platforms make up a general-purpose technology that allows the participants to benefit from being networked together, and so are examples of two-sided markets.

Another example is Airbnb, a service that connects travellers looking for short-term apartment rentals with owners seeking to make money by making their home available while they are not living in it. Airbnb is a platform that puts the group of apartment seekers in touch with the group of apartment owners who would like to offer their apartments for rent. Tinder does the same thing for people who want to find a date for the evening. A service called JOE Network puts employers in contact with people who have recently been awarded PhDs in economics.

The CORE Project is itself a matching market, as it provides a digital platform for researchers, teachers and students in economics to connect in ways that are mutually beneficial, although it is not really a market as the services of the researchers of providing the content in the ebook and the ebook itself are provided without pay.

These matching platforms have become an important topic in economics because of the magnitude of the network connections that are now possible. But while connections on this scale are now technically feasible, there is no mechanism that will reliably bring two-sided markets into existence even if they create gains for the participants on both sides.

At an early stage, these markets—meaning the creation of the platform, or the marketplace, or whatever it is that connects people—face a chicken-and-egg problem. Think about Airbnb: it makes money by charging a commission on each deal that is struck. Unless there are a large number of apartment seekers consulting its website, there is no reason for an apartment owner seeking a rental to offer an apartment for rent. Without apartments to rent, Airbnb will not be able to make money, so there would be no incentive to create the platform in the first place.

A model of a two-sided matching market

In economics, these two activities—seeking an apartment by going to Airbnb's web page, and posting one's apartment on it—are termed **strategic complements**. This term means that the more of the first (seeking) that occurs, the more benefit there is to someone who does the second (posting); also, the more posting there is, then the more benefit there is to seeking. This is closely related to the network externalities typical of a new innovation that we discussed in the previous section, where the benefit to using Betamax increased with the number of individuals using that video format. However, in this case, the external benefit depends on how many members of the *opposite* group are on the platform, rather than just how many people are using the platform in total.

Figure 21.11a illustrates the chicken-and-egg problem. We begin with the number of apartments posted on Airbnb. People post their apartment because they believe that many apartment seekers will see the posting and

Alvin Roth explains how matching markets work. http://tinyco.re/8435358

Marc Rysman. 2009. 'The Economics of Two-Sided Markets'. *Journal of Economic Perspectives* 23 (3): pp. 125–43.

Alvin Roth. 1996. 'Matching (Two-Sided Matching)'. Stanford University.

eventually rent the apartment. If there are few people logging onto the Airbnb site (seeking), then few apartment owners will think it's worth their effort to post their apartment on the site.

The 'posters' curve shows hypothetically how many apartments would be posted in response to each possible number of apartment seekers who consult the site. As illustrated in the figure, unless more than 500 apartment seekers are going to the site, no apartment owner will post their home for rent. To see this, look at where the curve labelled 'posters' intercepts the horizontal axis. As the number of apartment seekers (those 'demanding' apartments) viewing the site rises beyond 500, an increasing number of owners will post their information. But there is a limit to how many people will want to rent out their home temporarily, so the 'posters' curve flattens out as we move to the right.

The situation is similar for those seeking to rent an apartment. The number of people checking the Airbnb site depends on how many apartments are posted there. As long as more than a minimum number of apartments are posted on the site (from the figure, more than 200), then some people will look for an apartment there. This is the intercept of the 'seeker's' curve with the vertical axis. The 'seekers' curve shows that the more apartments are posted, the more people will look.

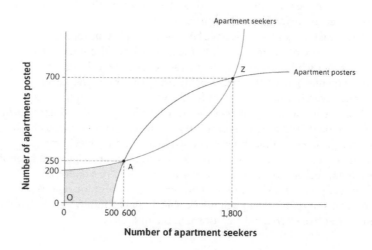

Figure 21.11a A two-sided matching market: The case of Airbnb.

1. The number of apartment seekers checking the Airbnb site
This depends on the number of those posting an apartment.

2. The number of apartments posted by owners
This depends on the number of apartment seekers checking the Airbnb site.

3. Point Z
At Z, the two curves intersect. This point is a Nash equilibrium.

4. If no apartment seekers are consulting the site
No owners will post their apartment. Nobody doing anything is therefore another Nash equilibrium, as shown by O.

5. Point A
At A, the curves also intersect, but the point is not a Nash equilibrium.

To see how the Airbnb market works, think about point Z in the figure. Z is a mutually consistent outcome in that:

- There are 700 apartments posted, so there will be 1,800 apartment seekers.
- Since there are 1,800 apartment seekers, there will be 700 apartments posted.

This means that the behaviours of the posters and the seekers is mutually consistent at point Z, and so point Z is a Nash equilibrium. If the market is at point Z, with 700 apartments posted and 1,800 apartment seekers, neither the apartment posters or seekers will want to change their behaviour.

But notice that there are two other points that also have this mutual consistency property:

- *There is a Nash equilibrium in which there is no Airbnb*: At point O, nobody is posting an apartment on Airbnb so there is no incentive for anyone to look at the site, and because nobody is looking at the site there is no incentive for anyone to post their apartment there. This is the chicken-and-egg problem.
- *Point A is a mutually consistent outcome, with 250 apartments posted and 600 people seeking apartments*: It is unlikely to last, however, for reasons discussed below.

To see what happens in the latter case, suppose that the number of apartment seekers unexpectedly dropped from 600 to 450. The best response for the 250 apartment owners who had previously posted their homes would then be to completely pull out of the market. If all the apartment posters drop out of the market, the remaining 450 seekers will also eventually drop out. So, if we enter the blue zone, a 'vicious cycle' of both posters and seekers abandoning the market will ensue and the result will be no market at all, which is depicted on the diagram as point O.

This process of adjustment away from an equilibrium is similar to the example you studied in Unit 11, about house prices and the value of durable assets. Because a small move away from point A leads to a cumulative process leading further away from A, we say that point A is **unstable**. A situation like point A is sometimes described as a **tipping point**.

Given the chicken-and-egg problem, how could Airbnb ever come into existence? Point Z is a Nash equilibrium, but how could the market ever get there?

If a sufficient number of seekers (greater than 600) somehow showed up on the site then more than 250 owners would post their apartments on the site. Or if by chance 300 owners posted their apartments, then more than 600 seekers would be motivated to check out the Airbnb site.

Figure 21.11b shows that in these cases, a virtuous cycle of both seekers and posters entering the market will take place and the number of both will grow until there are 700 posters and 1,800 seekers.

The figure explains why we might end up either with no market at all, or with a functioning market that matches some of the 1,800 seekers with the 700 posters. To see that the second is preferable to the first, think about a particular transaction: all of those posting and seeking are doing so voluntarily, so they must all see a personal benefit in doing it. When one of

unstable equilibrium An equilibrium such that, if a shock disturbs the equilibrium, there is a subsequent tendency to move even further away from the equilibrium.

tipping point An unstable equilibrium at the boundary between two regions characterized by distinct movements in some variable. If the variable takes a value on one side, the variable moves in one direction; on the other, it moves in the other direction. *See also: asset price bubble.*

the seekers is paired with a poster, both seeker and renter benefit (otherwise they would not agree). This is true for every market participant. So, having the market must be better than not having it.

The figure also shows that the market can come into existence and persist *if* we somehow started out with more than 600 seekers and or 250 posters. But that is a big *if*.

Market failures in matching markets

The economic policy challenge is to find a way to ensure that someone will create the platforms that produce benefits for participants that are sufficient to justify the cost. This is sometimes done by the public sector playing a role in creating the platform, as it did in the case of the Internet, or physical marketplaces in cities and towns. But in many cases (such as Airbnb, Tinder, and many other private platforms), the existence of a two-sided market is the haphazard result of a forward-looking individual having both the idea and the resources to launch a large, risky project.

For example, to solve the chicken-and-egg startup problem in the Airbnb market, the originator of the platform could have paid the first 250 posters to post their apartments, giving them an incentive to post on the website even when nobody was consulting the site. That could have kicked off the virtuous cycle of additional seekers and posters joining the market.

A common strategy for solving the chicken-and-egg problem is for companies to charge low or zero prices to one group of users, which then attracts the other group. For example, Adobe lets you download its PDF

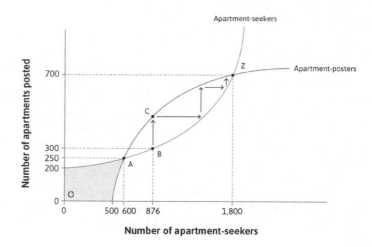

Figure 21.11b A two-sided matching market: The case of Airbnb.

1. Many people seeking apartments
Consider the case where there are 876 seekers but only 300 posters, at point B.

2. New posters join the market
This encourages new posters to list their site (point C) ...

3. New seekers respond
This in turn attracts new apartment seekers.

4. A stable equilibrium
The upward spiral leads to point Z, which is a stable Nash equilibrium.

5. A better outcome
Comparing the three equilibria, point Z is the preferred one, better than no market, and better than the unstable equilibrium at point A.

reader for no cost. If many people read documents as PDFs, it incentivizes document creators to pay for Adobe Acrobat, the software used to create PDF files.

While some two-sided markets, such as Wikipedia, are not designed to be money-makers, most are. And some of those who succeeded in creating widely used platforms have gained extraordinary wealth. In 2017, Facebook was valued at $245 billion and Mark Zuckerberg, who founded the company, owned 28.4% of it.

These innovation rents, unlike those associated with a new technical innovation like the spinning jenny studied in Unit 2, may not be competed away because would-be competitors face the very same chicken-and-egg problem that the successful innovators solved.

The problem is similar to the example of the strategic interaction between Plugcar and Netflex discussed earlier in this unit. There are probably many potentially mutually beneficial two-sided markets that do not exist (or do not exist yet) because of this chicken-and-egg problem. For instance, there has been little new competition in the credit card industry. It would be difficult to persuade merchants to accept a new type of card if not many shoppers carried it, and it would be difficult to encourage shoppers to carry a card that not many merchants would accept.

A catalogue of policies

The last three sections have introduced three reasons why market competition for profits cannot create an efficient innovation process by itself: external (network) effects, public goods and economies of scale. Public policies can encourage useful innovations and accelerate their diffusion to all users who may benefit. We have already mentioned the possible coordinating role of government-set standards.

In the next three sections we study two other types of policies:

- *Intellectual property rights:* These policies support innovation rents accruing to successful innovators.
- *Subsidizing innovation*: These policies either directly or indirectly provide basic research and low-cost dissemination of information.

EXERCISE 21.6 UNDERSTANDING MATCHING MARKETS

Watch the 'Economist in action' video of Alvin Roth (page 987). Based on the video, answer the following questions:

1. How are matching markets different from commodity markets?
2. Even if a market might be Pareto-improving, why might it not exist? Outline how the New England program helped to resolve a 'repugnant markets' problem.
3. What are some aspects of the relationship between buyers and sellers that could be a source of market failure in matching markets?

EXERCISE 21.7 WHY DO CURVES IN THE MATCHING MARKETS MODEL SLOPE UPWARDS?

Explain why both curves in the matching markets model, shown in Figure 21.11a (page 988), are upward sloping. (Hint: Remember that posting (supplying) apartments and seeking (demanding) apartments are strategic complements.)

EXERCISE 21.8 MISMATCHED POSTERS AND SEEKERS IN A MATCHING MARKET MODEL

Imagine that for some reason there were 1,850 seekers and 750 posters in the matching markets model in Figure 21.11a (page 988). Locate this point in the figure. How would posters respond to the number of seekers? How would seekers respond to the number of posters? Which point would the market move to, and why?

EXERCISE 21.9 CHICKEN-AND-EGG

Platforms such as Airbnb, Uber, YouTube, and eBay have successfully overcome the chicken-and-egg problem mentioned above.

1. Pick one of the platforms mentioned above. What are the gains that this platform offers, and which other markets have they disrupted?
2. What factors made it possible for this platform to disrupt existing markets?

QUESTION 21.5 CHOOSE THE CORRECT ANSWER(S)

Figure 21.11a (page 988) shows a hypothetical market for Airbnb, a service that connects travellers looking for short-term apartment rentals with owners looking to rent out their home while they are away.

Based on this information, which of the following statements is correct?

☐ There will be no posting of apartments when the number of seekers is below 200, while there will be no seeking when the number of apartments posted is below 500.
☐ There are three stable Nash equilibria.
☐ As long as there are more than 200 seekers and 500 apartments posted, there will always be a positive number of matches.
☐ An initial number of 2,000 seekers and 800 posters would result in an equilibrium of 1,800 seekers and 700 apartments posted.

21.6 INTELLECTUAL PROPERTY RIGHTS

Patent protection may be unnecessary for an innovator if secrecy is possible, or social norms prevent copying. The formula for Coca-Cola has famously remained a secret for 100 years. The company claims it is known by only two executives at any time, who never travel on the same aeroplane. A chef's signature dish is not a secret, but social norms among chefs would make the costs of copying a recipe without permission extraordinarily high. Comedians rarely steal each other's jokes for the same reason.

In other cases, an innovation may be known, but barriers to copying can be built into the product itself. Digital watermarking technology allowed some music distributors (briefly) to make recorded music that could not be copied. Seed companies successfully accomplished the same thing by introducing hybrid corn and other varieties that do not reproduce well.

Firms can also rely on superior capabilities that are complementary to a technological product to protect their innovation rents. Such capabilities could be a superior sales force, the ability to bring products to market more quickly, or exclusive contracts with input suppliers.

Secrecy, barriers to copying, or complementary capabilities may not be effective against rivals who manage to invent the same product independently, or who reverse-engineer it by starting with the finished product and working out how it was made.

Where a novel idea is both codifiable (it can be written down) and non-excludable (imitation cannot be prevented), governments have created laws protecting intellectual property rights. There are many kinds of intellectual property, but the most commonly used are **patents**, **trademarks**, and **copyright**. What they have in common is that they give the holder of the right exclusive use of the thing covered by the right for some designated period of time. In economic terms, the holder of the intellectual property right is made a temporary monopolist.

Intellectual property rights

Codifiable and non-excludable ideas can be protected by the following forms of intellectual property rights in the following ways:

Patents

Patents require the innovator to disclose their idea in a patent application, which is examined by a patent office and subsequently published. If the examiners are convinced the idea is sufficiently new and inventive, they will grant the innovator a **patent**. In most cases, a patent gives the innovator the right to take any imitator to court for 20 years: this can be extended to 25 years in the case of pharmaceutical patents. Some countries vary the length of patent protection.

Trademarks

A **trademark** gives the owner of a logo, a name, or a registered design the right to exclude others from using it to identify their products. Trademarks can be extended indefinitely. Patents and trademarks are generally registered at a dedicated office.

Copyright

Copyright gives the author of an intellectual work such as a book, an opera, or software code the right to exclude others from reproducing, adapting, and selling it. Copyright is generally not registered. The author

patent A right of exclusive ownership of an idea or invention, which lasts for a specified length of time. During this time it effectively allows the owner to be a monopolist or exclusive user.
trademark A logo, a name, or a registered design typically associated with the right to exclude others from using it to identify their products.
copyright Ownership rights over the use and distribution of an original work.

must make a claim if he or she believes it has been violated. Copyright terms are far longer than those for patents, and have been progressively extended. Copyright applies for a minimum of 25 years and in the US currently for 70 years after the death of the creator. Long copyright terms are controversial, because often the benefits go to people who did not create the work.

How intellectual property rights affect innovation

Until recently, it had been thought that patents encourage the development and use of innovations. Now economists and historians are taking a second look at whether intellectual property rights promote or actually destroy innovation. The answer depends on which of two opposite effects is more important:

- *Creating a monopoly*: This has a beneficial effect for the holder of the intellectual property rights, and creates economic profits (**innovation rents**) which stimulate research and development.
- *Impeding innovation and diffusion of new ideas*: These rights limit the ability of others to copy the innovation.

An important historical case is the steam engine, which was so important to the Industrial Revolution. There were several types of steam engine invented during the eighteenth century, but the most successful type was patented in 1769 by James Watt. He was an engineer, and did nothing to commercialize his innovation. In fact, he did not begin production in earnest until six years after he invented it.

The commercial value of the patent was an afterthought for Watt. The businessman Matthew Boulton bought a share in the patent, and persuaded Watt to move to Birmingham (one of the centres of the Industrial Revolution) to develop the new engine he had invented. Boulton also campaigned successfully to extend the period of the patent from 14 to 31 years.

Afterwards, Watt and Boulton used the courts vigorously to prevent any other steam engines from being sold, even if they were different to Watt's design. Among these was Jonathan Hornblower's rival invention, which was more efficient that the Watt design. Watt and Boulton challenged Hornblower's patent, eventually winning the case in 1799.

Another superior invention, created by an employee, was blocked when Watt and Boulton succeeded in broadening their patent to cover the new design, even though they had not had any part in its development. Ironically, Watt knew how to make his machine more efficient, but he couldn't make the improvement. Someone else held the patent.

Under the Watt-Boulton patent, the UK added about 750 horsepower of steam engines per year. In the 30 years after it expired, more than 4,000 horsepower a year of steam engines were installed in England. Fuel efficiency, which had barely improved while the patent was in force, increased by a factor of five between 1810 and 1835.

There is no doubt that patent protection is essential to the process of new knowledge creation in some industries. When the patent on a pharmaceutical blockbuster drug (a drug with annual sales of more than $1 billion in the US) expires, firms specializing in copying drug formulations and selling generic versions of the drug can enter the market, and the drug's price decreases as it is exposed to price competition. The patent owner's profits decrease significantly. Rapid falls in profits demonstrate that the

monopolies created by patents can be immensely valuable for the patent owner, but costly for users of the patented innovation.

When the DVD was introduced, it became apparent that the technology would allow consumers to not just own, but also to copy music and films from these disks in high quality. This posed a significant dilemma for the music and film industries that was addressed through new laws making it illegal to subvert digital rights management (DRM) technology, which the film companies used to stop people copying the content without permission. These same laws are now often used when users share content that is copyright protected over the Internet. Today DRM technology helps to protect the companies we now call content providers, who use the Internet as a distribution device—think of a television company that streams sports events live to computers and phones.

Figure 21.12 is a schematic representation of the innovation process. Arrows represent inputs, pointing towards the aspect of innovation that they affect. The figure highlights how the creation of new knowledge always builds on existing knowledge. For instance, Hornblower built on the existing Watt-Boulton design to improve efficiency. As was the case in the early days of the Industrial Revolution, existing patents restrict the ability to build on existing knowledge, and can therefore have a negative effect on innovation. On the other hand, by securing innovation rents for creators, they encourage innovation.

When Petra Moser, an economic historian, studied the number and quality of technical inventions shown at mid-nineteenth century technology expositions, she found that countries with patent systems were no more inventive than countries without patents. Patents did, however, affect the kinds of inventive activities in which countries excelled.

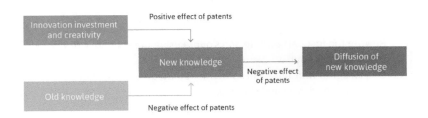

Figure 21.12 Patents and the production of new knowledge.

1. Old knowledge helps make new knowledge
Patents slow down this process. As Watt and Boulton found out, patents can impede the use of some aspects of old knowledge that are covered by patents.

2. Patents encourage innovation
The creation of new knowledge gives successful inventors recognition and innovation rents. Watt did not invent the steam engine to profit from the patent he would receive, but other innovators are strongly motivated by the prospect of commercializing their inventions.

3. Patents slow diffusion
Patents prevent other innovators from realizing the full benefits of new knowledge after it has been created. Watt and Boulton managed to use patents to stop rival inventors from creating their own, perhaps better, steam engines.

WHEN ECONOMISTS DISAGREE

Intellectual property rights: Dynamo or drag?

Recall that in one of our 'Economist in action' videos (page 966), F. M. Scherer argues that patents incentivize R&D in pharmaceutical companies (unlike in many other sectors, he says), so that they continue to develop new blockbuster drugs.

Petra Moser explains that copyright protection for nineteenth-century Italian operas led to more and better operas being written. But she also presents evidence suggesting that intellectual property rights may do more harm than good for the innovation process if they are too broad or too long term.

Petra Moser. 2013. 'Patents and Innovation: Evidence from Economic History'. *Journal of Economic Perspectives* 27 (1): pp. 23–44.

Petra Moser. 2015. 'Intellectual Property Rights and Artistic Creativity'. *VoxEU.org*. Updated November 4 2015.

EXERCISE 21.10 THOMAS JEFFERSON

Thomas Jefferson (1743–1826), America's third president, noted the peculiar and wonderful nature of an idea:

> Its peculiar character ... is that no one possesses the less, because every other possesses the whole of it. He who receives an idea from me, receives instruction himself without lessening mine; as he who lights his taper [candle] at mine, receives light without darkening me. ('Thomas Jefferson to Isaac McPherson', *Writings*, 1813)

Jefferson went on to say something that even then was controversial:

> It would be curious, then, if an idea, the fugitive fermentation of an individual brain could ... be claimed in exclusive and stable property.

To him, granting to an individual the exclusive right to own and exclude others from the use of an idea just did not make sense, any more than it would make sense for a person to refuse to tell someone what time of day it was.

1. Rewrite the first part of Jefferson's quote using the economic terms you learned in this course.
2. Do you agree with Jefferson's statement that ideas should not be 'claimed in exclusive and stable property'? Why, or why not?

Petra Moser discusses copyright protection for nineteenth century Italian operas. http://tinyco.re/ 3460846

EXERCISE 21.11 HOW COPYRIGHT IMPROVED ITALIAN OPERA, AND HOW SUCH PROTECTION SHOULD BE LIMITED

Watch our 'Economist in action' video, in which Petra Moser discusses copyright protection for nineteenth-century Italian operas.

1. Outline Petra Moser's research question, and her approach to answering it.
2. What were Petra Moser's findings about patents and copyrights?
3. What factors should governments consider when determining the effective time period of IPR protection laws such as patents and copyrights?

EXERCISE 21.12 INTELLECTUAL PROPERTY RIGHTS

Why does an extension of copyright terms (for example, an extension of the life of the protection) not change incentives to improve intellectual works (texts and operas) as much as the introduction of copyright itself? In your answer, consider who benefits from extended copyright terms.

QUESTION 21.6 CHOOSE THE CORRECT ANSWER(S)

Which of the following statements is correct regarding laws protecting intellectual property rights?

☐ A patent is a non-registered right that gives the producer of an intellectual work (such as a book or software code) the right to exclude others from reproducing, adapting and selling it.

☐ Copyright is granted if a work is found to be sufficiently new and inventive after an examination by the copyright office.

☐ Trademarks give the owners of a registered design the right to exclude others from using it.

☐ Economists agree that patents, copyright, and trademarks all promote innovation unambiguously.

21.7 OPTIMAL PATENTS: BALANCING THE OBJECTIVES OF INVENTION AND DIFFUSION

Patents confront us with an economic problem: how best to balance the competing objectives of making good use of existing knowledge, devoting sufficient economic resources and creativity to producing new knowledge, and diffusing the new knowledge that is created. An 'optimal patent' is one that best advances the use of knowledge in the economy. Currently, agreements administered by the World Trade Organization, which regulates international trade, may prevent countries from choosing patent length, but given complete freedom of choice, how could a policymaker decide the optimal patent length?

In Figure 21.13, we look first at the decision of an innovator in the upper panel. Work through the analysis in Figure 21.13 to understand the timing of costs and benefits of innovation and who receives them.

In the lower panel of Figure 21.13, we include the benefits to others in the economy that arise from the innovation. The term 'patent cliff' is from the point of view of the innovator, and refers to the significant decrease in profits when the patent expires. But in the lower panel we see the opposite effect—the benefits of the innovation shoot up when the patent expires, because the innovation is now free to diffuse throughout the economy.

This demonstrates the trade-off. Without the innovation, there are no benefits to others and the likelihood of the innovation increases with longer patents. However, for any given innovation, the benefits are reduced by the duration of the patent. Earlier imitation of the innovation brings benefits to the economy, shown by the dashed rectangle in the lower panel.

From this, we can see that a long patent emphasizes the benefits of rapid innovation, and a short patent emphasizes the benefits of rapid imitation. But we can't decide by looking at Figure 21.13 how long the optimal patent should be.

> **isototal benefits curve** The combinations of the probability of innovation and the total benefits to society from a firm's innovation that yield the same total benefits.

The trade-off between the benefits of diffusion and of invention

Figure 21.14 shows how we can represent the benefits of innovation to society as a whole. On the horizontal axis are shown the total benefits to others in the economy if the firm innovates. This is called B. On the vertical axis we estimate the probability of innovation, called p^I. The downward-sloping curves are indifference curves called **isototal benefits curves**. The total benefits to others from innovation are:

$$\text{total benefits to others} = \text{probability of innovation}$$
$$\times \text{benefits to others if firm innovates}$$
$$= p^I B$$

Feasible invention and diffusion

What are the constraints? What limits the total benefits that will occur if the innovation takes place? This will depend on the length of the patent, because a longer period of patent protection is thought at least initially to increase the probability of innovation, p^I, but to reduce the amount of total benefits for others, B, if the innovation occurs because of the delay in copying.

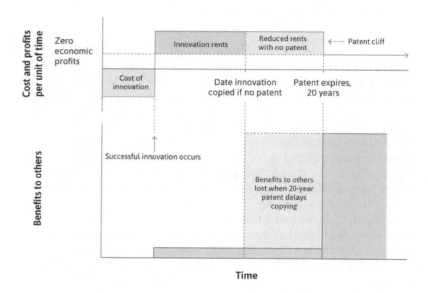

Figure 21.13 Costs and rents associated with innovation for the inventor and others.

1. The innovator incurs costs
The costs of innovation are shown by the red rectangle.

2. The innovation is successful
The firm makes innovation rents above economic profits. This is the rectangle above the dotted zero economic profits line.

3. A patent
The firm benefits from innovation rents for the life of the patent.

4. The benefits to others in the economy
The lower panel shows the benefits that arise from the innovation. If the innovation did not exist, there would be no benefits to others.

5. A patent
The patent reduces benefits to others, because it delays copying and diffusion.

Even when there is no patent, innovation can occur, as shown on the vertical axis of Figure 21.15. In these cases the innovator could capture innovation rents just by being the first in the market, because it takes competitors some time to catch up.

Figure 21.15 shows that as the duration of patents increases (moving to the right along the horizontal axis), so does the probability of innovation because innovation rents are protected for a longer period of time. Beyond a particular length of patent protection, however, the probability of innovation begins to decline because long-term patents will prevent other potential innovators from using protected knowledge or processes to develop an idea.

We can show the feasible set in Figure 21.16, which presents the trade-off between a higher probability of innovation and the total benefits to others if the firm innovates.

Each point on the feasible set is the result of a given patent length, starting at the left-hand side with a patent that never expires. As we move to the right, the duration of a patent declines. There are increasing benefits to others. Initially this increases both the benefits to others should the innovation occur, and (as we saw in Figure 21.15) the probability of innovation. This gives the positively sloped section of the feasible set. However, as we have also seen, at some point there will be a trade-off: a further reduction in patent duration will decrease the probability of innovation, even though it expands the total benefits that would result should the innovation occur. This explains the downward-sloping portion of the frontier of the feasible set.

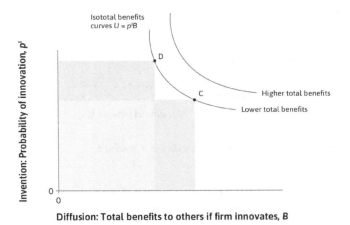

Figure 21.14 Isototal benefits curves: The trade-off between the benefits of invention and diffusion.

1. The isototal benefits curve
The downward-sloping curve is an indifference curve, called an isototal benefits curve. Along the curve the total benefits arising from an innovation are equal to $p^I B$ and remain constant.

2. Rectangles that touch the curve
Any rectangle with a corner on the curve has the same area as any other. Points C and D illustrate this.

3. A preferable curve
The higher isototal benefits curve is preferable to the curve through C and D.

Optimal patent duration

If we now put the feasible set together with the isototal benefits curves, we can determine the length of the patent that maximizes the expected benefits consistent with the constraints imposed by the trade-off between the incentive for innovation and stimulating diffusion. The highest attainable level of total benefits is shown by the tangency of the isototal benefits curve with the feasible set. This is point A in Figure 21.17.

This outcome on its own is not a policy, but it allows us to determine one. We can now go back to Figure 21.15 and ask what patent duration would a policymaker set so that the innovating firm will choose society's optimal probability of innovation, p^*? Figure 21.18 shows the answer.

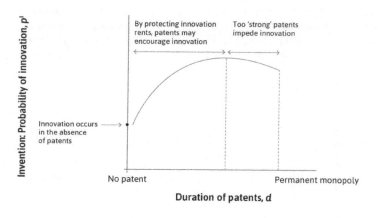

Figure 21.15 Patent duration and probability of innovation.

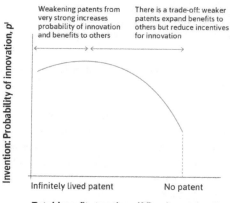

Figure 21.16 The feasible set: Innovation probability and benefits to others.

EXERCISE 21.13 OPTIMAL PATENTS

1. Consider two contrasting technologies. For one, the government would optimally choose a short patent duration. For the other, it would choose a longer patent duration. In each case, draw the feasible set and label the optimal point, as in Figure 21.17. Assume the same isototal benefits curves.

2. The length of patents and copyrights has increased steadily since the Industrial Revolution. Explain why this may have happened, and discuss whether this could be a good or a bad thing.

3. How should patent offices react if firms seek to cement patent monopolies by patenting improved versions of the original technology at a later date? (This is a process known as 'evergreening'—it's described in the *Journal of Health Economics* (http://tinyco.re/4728486) by C. Scott Hemphill and Bhaven N. Sampat.)

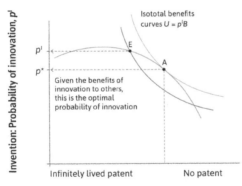

Figure 21.17 The optimal probability of innovation for society.

1. Maximizing expected benefits to society
Combining the feasible set with the isototal benefits curves, we can determine the length of the patent that maximizes the expected benefits to society as a whole.

2. The highest attainable level of total benefits
This is shown by the tangency of the isototal benefits curve with the feasible set at point A.

3. The optimal probability of innovation
From the perspective of society as a whole, the optimal probability of innovation is p^*.

4. Higher probability of innovation but lower benefits to society
At E, with a longer patent than the optimal one at A, innovation is more likely but because of less diffusion, its benefits to society as a whole are lower as shown by the lower isototal benefits curve.

QUESTION 21.7 CHOOSE THE CORRECT ANSWER(S)
Figure 21.13 (page 998) depicts the costs and rents associated with innovation for the inventor and others.

Based on this diagram, which of the following statements is correct?

- ☐ When there is no patent, the innovation is copied immediately.
- ☐ At the point that the patent expires, the patent owner 'falls off a patent cliff' where they lose innovation rents.
- ☐ There is zero benefit to others from the innovation during the patent period.
- ☐ The innovator's benefit from the patent outweighs the lost benefits to the others.

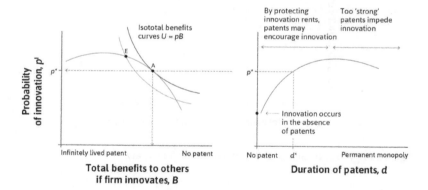

Figure 21.18 The optimal patent duration.

1. The optimal probability of innovation
Given the benefits of innovation to others, we established in Figure 21.17 that p^* is the optimal probability of innovation. This can tell us what the duration of the patents should be.

2. The optimal duration of patents
If we know p^*, we can use Figure 21.15 (the right-hand figure here) to determine the optimal duration of patents, d^*.

3. What if there were no patents?
We can see that innovation will still occur, but below the optimal level for society.

QUESTION 21.8 CHOOSE THE CORRECT ANSWER(S)

The following diagram depicts the probability of innovation as the duration of patents is increased.

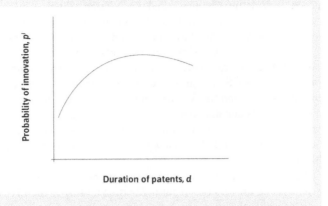

Based on this information, which of the following statements is correct?

☐ There is no innovation in the absence of patents.
☐ Longer patent duration will always lead to an increase in the probability of innovation.
☐ The downward sloping part of the graph demonstrates the trade-off between greater incentive to innovate from higher innovation rent income and the disincentive for potential innovators from using patented knowledge.
☐ The optimal duration of patents is where the probability of innovation is maximized.

21.8 PUBLIC FUNDING OF BASIC RESEARCH, EDUCATION, AND INFORMATION INFRASTRUCTURE

The pros and cons of various kinds of intellectual property rights are just a part of the problem of designing an effective innovation system. Another important element is the role of the government. Recall, for example, from the introduction of this unit, that in some cases the expected beneficial effects on markets from the spread of mobile phones did not materialize because necessary public infrastructure—mostly roads and means of transport—were lacking. Governmental provision of goods and services, such as the roads that would have allowed Indian farmers to benefit from their new access to price information, are essential to successful diffusion of the benefits of innovation. As we shall see, the origins of the computer, and by extension, the entire information revolution makes the essential role of government clear in the innovation process itself.

Adequate public policies concerning innovation can help in two main ways:

- *Increasing the pace of innovation:* This occurs through such interventions as the support of basic research and communications infrastructure, setting standards, as well as the design of patents, copyright, and trademarks.
- *Influencing the direction of innovation:* This tilts the process towards the production of novel ideas and applications with environmental, learning, medical, or other socially valued applications.

Government-funded research

The roots of the IT revolution can be traced to the building of the first electronic programmable computers after the Second World War, although as with any technology, some elements are older. Charles Babbage first proposed a calculating machine called the Difference Engine, in a learned paper published in 1822 (and was funded by the British government to develop it), and his ideas helped Ada Lovelace develop the first computer program.

The British and American governments' efforts during and after the Second World War pioneered programmable electronic computing in practice. In the US, the early focus was on supporting the development of missile systems and the Manhattan Project to develop the atomic bomb. These projects demanded huge numbers of rapid calculations in ballistics and predicting atomic reactions. US government money supported private entities such as Bell Labs in New Jersey, as well as federal research facilities like Los Alamos.

There was a close partnership between the private sector, government agencies and universities, resulting in the building of the ENIAC machine in 1946 under the auspices of the US Army. It was the first electronic computer, although it could not store programs. Other innovations followed swiftly, such as the development of the transistor by William Shockley at Bell Labs in 1948, as well as the creation of new companies such as Fairchild Semiconductor. American government support for the industry has continued through research funding, including, famously, the creation of the Internet (in 1969) in a project financed by the Defense Advance Research Projects Agency, or DARPA.

In the UK, early progress in computing was focused on the efforts at Bletchley Park, where the mathematician Alan Turing worked, to crack Germany's Enigma code. The Colossus machine developed there remained a secret until the 1970s, but Bletchley Park scientists and engineers went on to build in 1948 the world's first postwar stored-program computer with a memory, called Baby, at the University of Manchester, another publicly funded institution. The commercial development of computers followed swiftly, by companies such as Ferranti.

This pattern of government funding of early-stage research, either through government agencies including the military or through universities, followed by commercial applications is common. As well as the computer and electronics industries, the Internet, and the World Wide Web (created by Tim Berners-Lee at the CERN research laboratory funded by a consortium of governments), the modern pharmaceuticals and biotech sectors, and commercial applications of new materials, such as graphene, all have roots in publicly financed basic research and early-stage development. Touch screens and the computer mouse were also the result of US government-funded research.

The MP3 format was created by a small group of researchers at a public research lab in Germany, belonging to the Fraunhofer Gesellschaft. Their patent allows shrinking the size of audio files by a factor of 12, while maintaining sound quality. This innovation made music sharing via the Internet possible and contributed to major upheaval in the global music industry. Commercial firms did not initially adopt it as a standard, and it became widely diffused because the creators responded by distributing encoding software to users for a low price and did not pursue hackers who then made it available for free.

Mariana Mazzucato, an economist who specializes in the causes and impacts of innovation, uses the example of some of the basic digital innova-

William H. Janeway. 2012. *Doing Capitalism in the Innovation Economy: Markets, Speculation and the State*. Cambridge: Cambridge University Press.

tions such as the Internet, GPS and touch screens to argue (http://tinyco.re/2203568) that the government has an essential role in funding research and start-up technology companies. She sees the government's role not just as filling in activities the market will not undertake, perhaps because the returns are too far in the future and uncertain, but also as shaping what kind of activities the private sector will do. In her view, strategic investment by the US government helps explain why American companies dominate high-tech industries including digital and biotechnology.

Competitions and prizes

A quite different policy for the support of innovation is to award a prize for the successful development of a solution to a problem that will meet some specifications. The prize-winner is rewarded for the cost of development, rather than with a monopoly over the novel idea or method, and the innovation then goes immediately into the public domain.

For example, in the aftermath of the Deepwater Horizon oil rig disaster, the XPrize Foundation offered $1 million to any team who could significantly improve current technology for the clean-up of oil spills. Within a year, a team had devised a method that quadrupled the industry-standard recovery rate.

A more famous example is the invention by watchmaker John Harrison of the marine chronometer, a device that for the first time allowed the (reasonably) accurate measurement of a vessel's longitude at sea. Harrison started work on his chronometer in 1730 in response to an offer made in 1714 by the British government of a cash prize (about £2.5 million in 2014 prices) for the invention of a device to measure longitude. Harrison's approach to the challenge was to build an accurate clock small enough to be seaborne in order that the Greenwich time at which the sun reached its zenith could be determined. This would allow the ship's position west of Greenwich to be calculated. The problem had attracted some of the best minds of the time, including Isaac Newton's. Harrison produced many versions, each better than the last, but argued with the government about whether he deserved the prize money. The argument arose because Harrison's solution to the problem was rather different from that expected by the government. He was awarded a series of smaller sums over the years.

Another example of where competitions work well is the creation of prizes for the successful development of drugs for neglected diseases. These drugs treat illnesses that are common in parts of the world in which there is little pharmaceutical innovation because the private market for them is limited by the low incomes of those afflicted with the diseases.

Michael Kremer and Rachel Glennerster. 2004. *Strong Medicine: Creating Incentives for Pharmaceutical Research on Neglected Diseases*. Princeton, NJ: Princeton University Press.

Today, the Longitude Prize (http://tinyco.re/2341984) is funded by the UK government. Unusually the Longitude Committee, which will award the prize, asked the general public to choose from six challenges, which they could direct the prize money towards.

The public selected the problem of resistance to antibiotics, which we noted in Unit 12, a choice that many experts would support. This is interesting because many people are skeptical that government agencies are good at picking where R&D investments should be directed, in spite of the history of rather good investment decisions in technologies during and after the Second World War.

If you believe that the general public are better than governments at identifying pressing problems, then the Longitude Committee have solved this problem neatly by letting us choose.

MARIANA**MAZZUCATO**

In this video, Mazzucato suggests that governments should start to take investment stakes in technology companies, so that they will earn a return on the funds they invest in research. http://tinyco.re/2203568

EXERCISE 21.14 GOVERNMENT-FUNDED RESEARCH

1. What are the arguments for and against direct government investment in the commercial application of new technologies?
2. Describe ways in which governments could pick technologies in which to invest, so that the process would be more transparent to taxpayers.
3. Do you think it would be sensible to involve taxpayers in the choices about which technologies in which to invest? Explain your answer.
4. Which kind of technologies do you think governments should spend more on and which technologies should governments leave to the private sector? Explain your answer.

QUESTION 21.9 CHOOSE THE CORRECT ANSWER(S)

Which of the following policies promote efficient innovation processes?

- ☐ prizes for successful innovation to resolve the coordination problem in the innovation of substitute goods
- ☐ subsidizing the supply of inputs to innovation, such as public infrastructure, research and education, to alleviate the coordination problem of complementary innovations
- ☐ establishing a patent system to address high first copy costs of knowledge-intensive innovations
- ☐ promoting low-cost dissemination of information

QUESTION 21.10 CHOOSE THE CORRECT ANSWER(S)

Which of the following statements are correct regarding public policies for innovation?

- ☐ The government should not invest in innovations whose returns are too far in the future and uncertain.
- ☐ By taking equity stakes in innovation companies, the government would enhance its ability to enforce competition policy.
- ☐ The government could support innovation by setting up a scheme that awards a prize for successful development of a solution to a specific problem.
- ☐ The government can fund early-stage research, through government agencies such as the military or universities, that can then be used for commercial applications.

21.9 CONCLUSION

The UK and the Netherlands, birthplaces of capitalism and the Industrial Revolution, were not unique in the intelligence and creativity of their peoples. China, arguably, had proven to be an equally, if not more inventive society, in earlier years having first developed paper, printing, gunpowder, the compass, and literally hundreds of other important innovations. Other countries, notably Japan, were adept at the adaptation and spread of novel methods and ideas. But the combined pull of innovation rents and the push of competition to survive that was characteristic of the innovation and diffusion process under capitalism made it a uniquely dynamic economic system that transformed the British and Dutch economies.

Public policy also played an important part. For innovators to take the risk of introducing a new product or production process, it is crucial that their innovation rents not be seized by the government or others. This requires that property rights be protected by a well-functioning legal system as was the case in the UK, the Netherlands, and other countries that experienced the kink in the hockey stick of per capita income early.

More recently, Silicon Valley, the German innovation system, and other successful examples of innovation have been assisted by governments that provide complementary inputs such as physical infrastructure, basic research and public education, guaranteed markets (like those for military goods), and allow the innovator only a temporary monopoly so that competition eventually will reduce prices.

David S. Landes. 2000. *Revolution in Time*. Cambridge, MA: Harvard University Press.

In a nutshell, it is this combination of private incentives and supportive public policy that explains why capitalism can be such a dynamic economic system. Among the consequences in many countries are the increased living standards as measured by income per capita (documented in Unit 1), as well as the reduction in working hours seen in Unit 3.

But remember that Joseph Schumpeter, the economist who contributed most to our current understanding of innovation (and who you encountered in Unit 16) called the process of technological change 'creative destruction'.

In this unit, we have stressed the creative part: the development of new processes and products that allow us to produce our livelihoods with progressively less time at work. But in Unit 16 we studied the ways in which the process of technological change also puts people out of work and devalues once respected and well-paid skills. And in Unit 20, you saw that the expansion of production and the substitution of fossil-fuel-based energy for human and other animal energy made possible by technological change has posed challenges to our environment, even as improved technologies hold out the hope that under the right policies, these challenges may be addressed.

Economists can help to design these policies and to evaluate the benefits and costs of ways of promoting beneficial innovations and also addressing the 'destructive' aspect of new technologies.

> *Concepts introduced in Unit 21*
> Before you move on, review these definitions:
>
> - Process innovation and product innovation
> - Radical innovation and incremental innovation
> - Innovations as substitutes or complements
> - Codified knowledge and tacit knowledge
> - Invention and diffusion
> - Innovation systems (Silicon Valley and Germany)
> - First copy costs
> - Winner-take-all competition
> - Patents, copyrights, trademarks
> - Demand-side economies of scale and network external effects
> - Matching (two-sided) markets
> - Optimal patent duration

21.10 REFERENCES

Boldrin, Michele, and David K. Levine. 2008. *Against Intellectual Monopoly*. New York, NY: Cambridge University Press.

Boseley, Sarah. 2016. 'Big Pharma's Worst Nightmare' (http://tinyco.re/5692579). *The Guardian*, Updated 5 February 2016.

DiMasi, Joseph A., Ronald W. Hansen, and Henry G. Grabowski. 2003. 'The Price of Innovation: New Estimates of Drug Development Costs'. *Journal of Health Economics* 22 (2): pp. 151–85.

Edsall, Thomas B. 2016. 'Boom or Gloom?' (http://tinyco.re/5275846). *New York Times*. Updated 27 January 2016.

Engel, Jerome S. 2015. 'Global Clusters of Innovation: Lessons from Silicon Valley.' *California Management Review* 57 (2): pp. 36–65. University of California Press.

Gordon, Robert J. 2016. *The Rise and Fall of American Growth: The US Standard of Living since the Civil War*. Princeton, NJ: Princeton University Press.

Hall, Peter A., and David Soskice. 2001. *Varieties of Capitalism: The Institutional Foundations of Comparative Advantage*. New York, NY: Oxford University Press.

Hemphill, C. Scott, and Bhaven N. Sampat. 2012. 'Evergreening, Patent Challenges, and Effective Market Life in Pharmaceuticals' (http://tinyco.re/4728486). *Journal of Health Economics* 31 (2): pp. 327–39.

Janeway, William H. 2012. *Doing Capitalism in the Innovation Economy: Markets, Speculation and the State*. Cambridge: Cambridge University Press.

Jensen, Robert. 2007. 'The Digital Provide: Information (Technology), Market Performance, and Welfare in the South Indian Fisheries Sector.' *The Quarterly Journal of Economics* 122 (3): pp. 879–924.

Kornai, János. 2013. *Dynamism, Rivalry, and the Surplus Economy: Two Essays on the Nature of Capitalism*. Oxford: Oxford University Press.

Koromvokis, Lee. 2016. 'Are the Best Days of the US Economy Over?' (http://tinyco.re/1182018). PBS NewsHour. 28 January 2016.

Kremer, Michael, and Rachel Glennerster. 2004. *Strong Medicine: Creating Incentives for Pharmaceutical Research on Neglected Diseases* (http://tinyco.re/7475598). Princeton, NJ: Princeton University Press.

Landes, David S. 2000. *Revolution in Time*. Cambridge, MA: Harvard University Press.

Mazzucato, Mariana. 2013. 'Government – investor, risk-taker, innovator' (http://tinyco.re/2203568).

Moser, Petra. 2013. 'Patents and Innovation: Evidence from Economic History' (http://tinyco.re/7074474). *Journal of Economic Perspectives* 27 (1): pp. 23–44.

Moser, Petra. 2015. 'Intellectual Property Rights and Artistic Creativity' (http://tinyco.re/2212476). *Voxeu.org*. Updated 4 November 2015.

Mowery, David C., and Timothy Simcoe. 2002. 'Is the Internet a US Invention?—an Economic and Technological History of Computer Networking'. *Research Policy* 31 (8–9): pp. 1369–87.

Roth, Alvin. 1996. 'Matching (Two-Sided Matching)' (http://tinyco.re/9329190). Stanford University.

Rysman, Marc. 2009. 'The Economics of Two-Sided Markets' (http://tinyco.re/4978467). *Journal of Economic Perspectives* 23 (3): pp. 125–43.

Saxenian, AnnaLee. 1996. *Regional Advantage: Culture and Competition in Silicon Valley and Route 128*. Cambridge, MA: Harvard University Press.

Swarns, Rachel L. 2001. 'Drug Makers Drop South Africa Suit over AIDS Medicine' (http://tinyco.re/4752443). *New York Times*. Updated 20 April 2001.

The Economist. 2007. 'To Do with the Price of Fish' (http://tinyco.re/6300967). Updated 10 May 2007.

Witt, Stephen. 2015. *How Music Got Free: The End of an Industry, the Turn of the Century, and the Patient Zero of Piracy*. New York, NY: Viking.

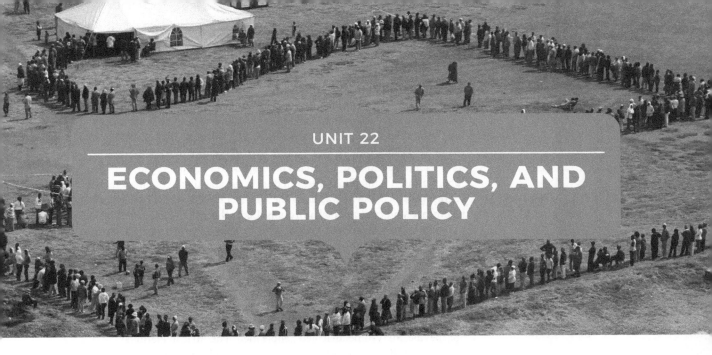

UNIT 22
ECONOMICS, POLITICS, AND PUBLIC POLICY

AS AN ECONOMIC ACTOR, A DEMOCRATIC GOVERNMENT IN A CAPITALIST ECONOMY CAN PROMOTE IMPROVED LIVING STANDARDS, WITH GAINS FAIRLY SHARED. OFTEN, THOUGH, THIS DOES NOT HAPPEN

- In this unit, we look at how institutions and policies are chosen. Why are some institutions and policies adopted, and not others?
- Like firms and families, the government of a nation is an important economic actor whose actions can be understood by studying the preferences of government leaders, and the constraints under which they operate.
- A government is distinct from other actors in society in that it can require citizens to abide by its decisions, using force if necessary (for example, police powers).
- Governments also have obligations that they owe to their citizens as a matter of right. As a result, they use tax funds to provide goods and services (such as police protection or basic schooling), which are usually free of charge.
- Ideally, democracy empowers citizens by extending voting rights in competitive elections to everyone, and limits what governments can do by ensuring individual rights of speech and association.
- Ideally, governments should adopt policies to ensure that possibilities for mutual gains (for example through exchange) are realized, and that economic outcomes are fair.
- Even in a democracy, inefficient or unfair economic outcomes occur because there are limits to what public policy can accomplish. Even when public policies are economically feasible, they may still not be implemented because powerful groups oppose them, or governments do not have the capacity to implement them.

The year that he became deputy president of South Africa, Cyril Ramaphosa was ranked the 29th-richest person in Africa. During his twenties and thirties Ramaphosa was a militant trade unionist who became general secretary of the National Union of Mineworkers and was deeply involved in the anti-apartheid movement. He probably did not anticipate that by 2012 he would be worth more than $700 million.

 Born in 1952 in Soweto, then a poor black township outside Johannesburg, Ramaphosa grew up during the apartheid system of racial segregation. Because he was black, he was excluded from the best schools, healthcare, and even public bathrooms. Like others in the majority black population, he had no right to vote. The per capita income of black African families in the late 1980s was around 11% of that of white families. It had been stuck at this level for at least 50 years.

Resistance to the apartheid regime, together with the international support it generated, was one of the major social movements of the late twentieth century. But within South Africa it was brutally repressed from the beginning. In 1960, police fired on protesters against apartheid at Sharpeville. Sixty-nine unarmed people died. The African National Congress (ANC) was banned. Four years later Nelson Mandela, one of the leaders of the ANC, was imprisoned for life.

Ramaphosa was part of the next generation of anti-apartheid activists. As general secretary of the National Union of Mineworkers he was part of a wave of strikes and community protests in the mid- and late 1980s that convinced many white business owners that apartheid had to go. Eventually the government conceded defeat, releasing Mandela from prison.

Figure 22.1 shows how the size of the South African public old age pension received by different groups changed over the last 50 years. It tells a dramatic story of apartheid and its demise. Under apartheid, the government awarded different pensions to each of the 'racial' groups making up the population. In 1975, for example, the pension received by a white person was more than seven times that received by a black African person. The gradual equalization of the pension was dramatically achieved at the beginning of 1993 even before the first democratic election, with the abolition of all race-based distinctions in pension policy.

In 1994, South Africa's first democratic election made Mandela president. Ramaphosa was elected to parliament.

The transition to a democratic political system led to economic gains for the black population. For the first time, black workers were able to work in skilled jobs, which raised their wages. Schooling and healthcare were desegregated. Piped water and electricity became available to many more families.

But the transition to democratic rule did not narrow the gap between rich and poor. The Gini coefficient for income stood at 0.66 the year before the first democratic election, the highest of any major country in the world at the time. Fifteen years later (in 2008), it had risen to 0.70.

Though by most measures economic disparities between the major population groups had declined, inequalities within the groups dramatically increased. This was especially true among black Africans, with a new class of the very rich pulling away from the rest.

Murray Leibbrandt, Ingrid Woolard, Arden Finn, and Jonathan Argent. 2010. 'Trends in South African Income Distribution and Poverty since the Fall of Apartheid'. OECD Social, Employment and Migration Working Papers, No. 101. Paris: OECD Publishing.

Cyril Ramaphosa's life story, and South Africa's recent history, show some of the many ways that political power affects the economy and how the economy shapes political power. The economic inequality between blacks and whites was a consequence of political institutions that prevented black South Africans from voting and restricted their political activities. These undemocratic measures united the opposition to apartheid from trade unions, neighbourhood organizations and students, the ANC, and other opposition parties, and finally brought **democracy** to South Africa. Yet after more than 20 years of democracy, no party other than the ANC has governed the country, and South Africa remains one of the world's most unequal countries. The arrival of democracy, the abolition of apartheid, and the change in distribution of political power, did not lead to the reduction in inequality that might have been expected.

The government and the public policies it adopts have played a role in every unit in *The Economy*. But until now we have not asked why some policies are adopted and some are not, and how these policies change as the distribution of power changes, as it did so dramatically in South Africa over Cyril Ramaphosa's lifetime.

This unit will first consider the nature of the government as an economic actor: what the government wants, how it achieves its goals, and how its actions are constrained. We will then consider democratic institutions in more depth. We will develop a model for how parties in a democracy choose their policies, and consider how differences between democratic institutions can affect political outcomes. Finally, we will explain how economic, administrative, and political barriers can prevent efficient and fair policies, even in highly democratic countries.

democracy A political system, that ideally gives equal political power to all citizens, defined by individual rights such as freedom of speech, assembly, and the press; fair elections in which virtually all adults are eligible to vote; and in which the government leaves office if it loses.

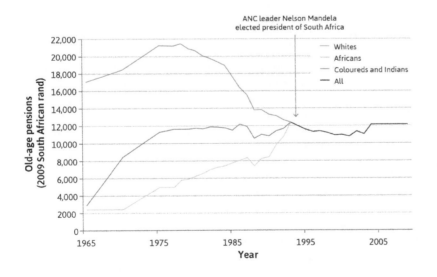

Murray Leibbrandt, Ingrid Woolard, Arden Finn, and Jonathan Argent. 2010. 'Trends in South African Income Distribution and Poverty since the Fall of Apartheid', OECD Social, Employment and Migration Working Papers, No. 101, OECD Publishing, Paris. Note: The names of the population groups are the official South African census terms. 'Coloured' is the South African term meaning people of mixed European, Asian and African origin.

Figure 22.1 Apartheid and its demise: The value of South Africa's old age pension.

Angus Deaton. 2013. *The Great Escape: health, wealth, and the origins of inequality*. Princeton: Princeton University Press.

22.1 THE GOVERNMENT AS AN ECONOMIC ACTOR

A government allows people to do things together that they could not do individually, notably going to war. But governments also engage in activities that vastly improve living standards and the quality of life for their citizens. Examples include:

- *Poverty*: Fifty years ago, even in rich countries, many retired or elderly people were trapped in poverty. For example, in 1966, 28.5% of US citizens aged 65 and over were classed as 'poor'. Government transfers in many countries have virtually eliminated serious economic deprivation among the elderly. In 2012 just 9.1% of elderly people in the US were poor.
- *Economic security*: The increased size of government spending, as well as the policy lessons from the Great Depression and the golden age of capitalism, have reduced economic insecurity by making the business cycle less volatile.
- *Increased life expectancy and the dramatic reduction in child mortality in many countries*: When these occurred in the late nineteenth and early twentieth century, they were not primarily the result of advances in medicine, most of which came later. They followed government policies that improved sanitation and water supply.

Like firms and families, the government is an economic actor. Its taxes, spending, laws, wars, and other activities are as much a part of economic life as the investment, savings, buying, and selling activities of families and firms.

Coercion and providing public services

Peter Lindert. 2004. *Growing Public: Social Spending and Economic Growth since the Eighteenth Century*. Cambridge: Cambridge University Press.

Jon Bakija, Lane Kenworthy, Peter Lindert, and Jeff Madrick. 2016. *How Big Should Our Government Be?* Berkeley: University of California Press.

The government is an actor that dwarfs families and most firms. The US government, federal and local, employs almost 10 times as many people as the country's largest firm, Walmart. However, governments were not always economic actors on this large a scale. In Figure 22.2 we show the total tax revenues collected by the government of the UK as a fraction of gross domestic product—a measure of the size of the government relative to the size of the economy—over more than 500 years. The figure rises from about 3% in the period prior to 1650 to 10 times that amount after the Second World War.

Not only is the government a much bigger economic actor than any family or firm, it is also unique among actors in any society. Within a given territory, it can dictate what people must do or not do and can use force and restraints on an individual's freedom to achieve that end. Because citizens generally see the use of the government's coercive powers to maintain order, regulate the economy and deliver services as legitimate—meaning that they accept the government's authority—most citizens comply with government-made laws. One application of government's coercive power is the collection of taxes, which can be used to fund government operations.

government Within a given territory, the only body that can dictate what people must do or not do, and can legitimately use force and restraints on an individual's freedom to achieve that end. *Also known as: state.*

To distinguish governments from private economic actors like firms, families, individuals, trade unions, and professional organizations, we define the **government** as the only body in a geographical territory (the nation) that can legitimately use force and the threat of force on citizens of that nation. Governments routinely do things—locking people up, for example—which, if done by a private individual, would be considered wrong.

To see why the government's monopoly on the use of force is important, return to Bruno and Angela, whom you met in Unit 5.

Initially, Bruno was heavily armed and Angela was at his mercy. Bruno was not a government official. He was acting only as a private citizen. He used the threat of force to control the labour of others and to enjoy the fruits of their labour. As an economic actor, the only constraint Bruno faced was biological. He could not force Angela to work under conditions that would result in her death, not because that would have been murder, but because it would have deprived Bruno of 'his' worker.

Then we introduced a government that imposed laws on both Angela and Bruno, disarming Bruno. If he wanted Angela to work for him, he now had to make her an offer that she would accept without threat of harm from him. The government, in other words, came to monopolize the use of force. It used its force to protect Bruno's private ownership of the land, which is why Angela could not simply farm the land herself, keeping all of the crops that she produced.

In the next stage of the story, the government became democratic, and as there were many more 'Angelas' than 'Brunos' in the population, Angela improved her economic position.

Beyond its legitimate use of coercive powers, a second feature of the government, one that also distinguishes it from firms and other private economic entities, is that it has obligations to its citizens based on civil and human rights. To advance and protect these rights, governments use tax funds to provide services such as national defence, police protection, and schooling. These services are often provided without restrictions to those who use them, and without charging a price.

People differ greatly in their income and wealth, and therefore in the taxes they pay, but because they are citizens, they are equally entitled to many of the services of the government. This is the cause of many debates about the appropriate 'size' of the government: people with less income and wealth benefit from many government services but, as we saw in Unit 19,

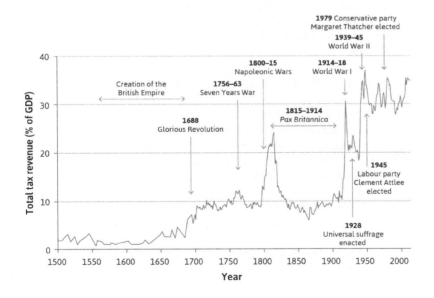

UK Public Revenue; Patrick K. O'Brien and Philip A. Hunt. 1993. 'The rise of a fiscal state in England, 1485-1815'. *Historical Research* 66 (160): pp.129–76. Note: *Pax Britannica* refers to the century between the end of the Napoleonic Wars and the beginning of the First World War, in which (compared to earlier or subsequent periods) Europe and most of the world was relatively peaceful, with the UK the militarily dominant nation. The Glorious Revolution deposed King James II in 1688 and increased the independent power of parliament.

Figure 22.2 The growth of government in the UK (1500–2015).

people with more wealth and income pay more (in absolute terms) of the taxes that finance these services.

The tax, transfer, and expenditure systems of democratic governments typically redistribute income from those with higher to those with lower incomes, as shown in Figure 5.16 for a large sample of countries, and in more detail for the case of Mexico in Figure 19.29a. At the same time, ecologically and socially damaging practices are often used by those with higher incomes to increase their income further, at the expense of the poor.

Part of the solution

Jean Tirole, an economist who specializes in the role of intervention and regulation, describes the way that governments can intervene in his Nobel prize lecture (http://tinyco.re/4684631).

In Figures 12.8 and 12.9, we looked at a variety of decisions made by private actors in the economy that affect others by imposing an uncompensated external cost or benefit. We also examined possible remedies for these market failures, often through government intervention. We also saw that governments adopt policies to correct the unfairness that sometimes results from private economic interactions. Governments may adopt the twin objectives that we have used in this course:

- ensuring that the mutual gains possible through our economic interactions are as large as possible and are fully realized
- sharing these gains in a fair manner

Examples of policies to address market failures and unfairness include:

- *Competition policies*: To reduce the price-setting powers of monopolies.
- *Environmental policies*: To reduce emissions of pollutants.
- *Subsidies*: For R&D.
- *Policies that establish the expectation that aggregate demand will be relatively stable*: So that firms will invest.
- *Public provision of healthcare or compulsory insurance.*
- *Providing information*: To allow people to make better decisions, such as the risks associated with financial products, children's toys, and foods.
- *Central bank policies*: That require commercial banks to minimize their risk exposure by restricting the leverage of their balance sheets.
- *Minimum wage laws*: That prohibit contracts that pay below a stated minimum.

Governments pursue these objectives by some combination of four means:

- *Incentives:* Taxes, subsidies, and other expenditures alter the costs and benefits of activities that have external effects, which would lead to market failures or unfair outcomes if left unaccounted for.
- *Regulation:* Direct regulation of economic activities such as the degree of competition, including mandatory universal participation in social and medical insurance, and regulation of aggregate demand.
- *Persuasion or information:* Altering available information and people's expectations about what others will do (for example, their belief that their property is secure or that other firms will invest) so as to allow people to coordinate their actions in a desirable way.
- *Public provision:* In-kind provision or through monetary transfers, including merit goods such as basic education, legal representation in court proceedings, and income transfers to alter the distribution of living standards.

Figure 22.3 brings together many of the examples of policies studied in earlier units. In each case, the policy targets a particular market failure or perceived unfairness. We identify the objective of the policy and the instrument used. The further readings to be found in the units and videos shed light on the extent to which the policy objectives were achieved.

Whilst such policies have been effective in addressing concerns of inefficiency and unfairness in some countries, in Section 22.9 we discuss why market failures and economic outcomes viewed as unfair by many citizens can still persist in democracies.

Part of the problem

To accomplish these valuable policies, governments must have extraordinary powers to acquire information and to compel compliance. This creates a dilemma. For the government to be a successful problem-solver, it must also be powerful enough to potentially be a problem itself. Examples from history, and today's news, show governments using their monopoly on the use of force to silence opposition and to acquire huge personal wealth for their officials and leaders.

Before the French Revolution, Louis XIV of France, called the 'Sun King' by his subjects, claimed '*L'etat, c'est moi*' (I am the state). The word 'state' is sometimes used—as the Sun King did here—to mean 'government in general', distinguishing it from any particular body such as the government of France. In neighbouring Britain, at almost the same time, William Pitt had a different view of his King, declaring that 'The poorest man may in his cottage bid defiance to all the forces of the Crown,' as we saw in Exercise 1.6 (page 23).

Well-governed societies have devised ways to limit the damage that the use of government powers can inflict without undermining the government's capacity to solve society's problems. These have generally included a combination of:

- *Democratic elections*: To allow citizens to dismiss a government that is using its powers for its own benefit, or the interests of some other small group.
- *Institutional checks and balances*: Plus constitutional restrictions on what the government can do.

The second point is why Pitt could observe that while the farmer may have difficulty keeping rain out of his cottage, he could confidently exclude the King of England.

In a capitalist economy, barring exceptional circumstances, the government cannot seize what you own, which limits its capacity to enrich itself at your expense. This is an essential limit on arbitrary government powers. An example of a special case would be if you owned a piece of land that was the only possible site for a bridge that was needed to solve a traffic problem. Most governments would have the right to acquire the land at what is independently judged to be a fair price, even if you were unwilling to sell. This power to take private property for public use has many names. For example it is known as the 'right of eminent domain' in the US or a 'compulsory purchase order' in the UK.

Even with well-designed limits on government powers, and provision for exceptions allowing governments to better serve the public, we will see that governments, like markets, sometimes fail.

Policy	Unit	Market failure or unfairness	Policy objective	Type of policy instrument	Example referred to in the text
Tax on sugary drinks	7	Too much sugar consumption; negative external effects from health consequences	Reduce sugar consumption	Incentives; information	Denmark; France
Progressive structure of taxes; monetary and in-kind transfers	19	Unfair inequality of market incomes	Reduce unfair inequality of final incomes	Incentives; public provision	Mexico; South Africa; Brazil; EU
Reduce tariffs	18	Too few imports are purchased ($P > MC$)	Exploit all possible gains from trade	Incentives	Globalizations I and II; (Dani Rodrik video (http://tinyco.re/8475334))
R&D subsidies	12, 21	Too little R&D	Increase R&D	Incentives	Germany
Cap and trade or carbon tax	20	Too much CO_2 emissions (common-pool resource)	Reduce CO_2 emissions	Regulation (cap); incentives (trade)	EU and US (cap and trade)
Ban on CFCs	4	Emissions damaging ozone layer (common-pool resource)	Eliminate use	Regulation	Montreal Protocol 1989
Patent protection but limited in length	21	Too little R&D	Encourage R&D but ensure timely diffusion	Regulation (monopoly on innovation); incentives (for R&D)	Copyright on 19th century operas; US pharmaceutical patents; (Petra Moser video (http://tinyco.re/3460846); (F. M. Scherer video (http://tinyco.re/8674643))
Competition policy to address monopoly	7	Too low a quantity is sold ($P > MC$); monopoly favours owners over consumers	Bring price closer to MC	Regulation	European Commission (Volvo/Scania); US Department of Justice (Microsoft)
Land tenure reform	5	Poverty among share-croppers; unfair distribution of the crop	Raise farmers' income as higher share of harvest goes to farmer	Regulation	Operation Barga; West Bengal
Minimum wage	19	Incomes at the bottom of the income distribution are too low	Reduce poverty	Regulation	US state legislation (Arin Dube video (http://tinyco.re/3737648))
Eliminate ethnic, gender, or racial discrimination in labour markets	19	Unfair inequalities in labour earnings	Raise incomes of targeted groups	Regulation; information	South Africa

Policy	Unit	Market failure or unfairness	Policy objective	Type of policy instrument	Example referred to in the text
Mandatory purchase of health insurance or public provision	12, 19	Adverse selection: Too little insurance offered; premiums too high for high-risk people	Improve access to health care	Regulation; public provision	UK; US; Finland
Capital requirements on banks	17	Excessively risky lending with external costs for others (for example taxpayers)	Reduce risk to the financial system and to government finance	Incentives; regulation	Comparison between pre- and post-global financial crisis regulation (Joseph Stiglitz video (http://tinyco.re/3866047); Anat Admati video (http://tinyco.re/8573554))
Inflation-targeting monetary policy	15, 17	Unemployment higher than the inflation-stabilizing rate	Keep unemployment close to the labour market Nash equilibrium	Incentives; persuasion	Bank of England, Federal Reserve, and other central banks during the great moderation
Labour market reforms (active labour market policy, shorter-duration unemployment benefits)	16	Unemployment too high	Improve matching between vacancies and unemployed	Incentives; regulation; information	Hartz reforms in Germany
Aggregate demand management policy	14, 17	Coordination failure among firms about expected demand	Stabilize aggregate demand	Persuasion; public provision	Comparison between Great Depression and post-Second World War policy regimes (Barry Eichengreen video (http://tinyco.re/6433456))
International cooperation	14	Coordination failure among countries about fiscal stimulus	Prevent collapse in aggregate demand	Persuasion	2009 London G20 Summit
International cooperation	20	Coordination failure among countries about climate change mitigation	Reduce CO_2 emissions	Persuasion	2015 Paris Climate Agreement
R&D public funding	21	Too little R&D	Increase publicly funded R&D (university and other)	Public provision	US military and higher education; UK government; CERN consortium
Early childhood intervention in education	19	Non-level playing field for children	Increases opportunities for poorer children to attain more advanced schooling	Public provision	Interventions in US (James Heckman video (http://tinyco.re/3964341))

Figure 22.3 Economic policies aimed at mitigating market failures or addressing unfairness, discussed in earlier units.

natural monopoly A production process in which the long-run average cost curve is sufficiently downward-sloping to make it impossible to sustain competition among firms in this market.

To see why neither markets nor governments may provide ideal solutions to economic problems, think about the case of a **natural monopoly** that we studied in Units 7 and 12. An example would be the provision of tap water in a city, or electricity transmission over a national network. In these cases, economies of scale means that the most efficient solution would be to have a single entity—a private firm or the government—provide the service.

If it was privately owned as a monopoly, we know that the firm would face a downward-sloping demand curve, which would limit the price at which it could sell its goods. The monopoly firm would both seek to reduce costs and restrict output so that it could charge a higher price. The result would be a price above the marginal cost of production, which would mean that some consumers who value the service at more than its marginal cost would not consume it.

Would the government do a better job?

Ideally a government-owned natural monopoly would set the price equal to the marginal cost and finance the fixed costs through well-designed taxation. But the government may have little incentive to reduce costs. The publicly owned water or electricity supply company may be under pressure to overstaff the company with well-paying jobs for politically connected individuals. As a result, the costs may be higher than they otherwise would be. Wealthy individuals or firms may lobby the government-owned monopoly to provide its services on favourable terms to special-interest groups.

economic accountability Accountability achieved by economic processes, notably competition among firms or other entities in which failure to take account of those affected will result in losses in profits or in business failure. *See also: accountability, political accountability.*

political accountability Accountability achieved by political processes such as elections, oversight by an elected government, or consultation with affected citizens. *See also: accountability, economic accountability.*

market failure When markets allocate resources in a Pareto-inefficient way.

government failure A failure of political accountability. (This term is widely used in a variety of ways, none of them strictly analogous to market failure, for which the criterion is simply Pareto inefficiency).

This case illustrates both the similarities and differences between the **economic accountability** provided by the market and the **political accountability** provided by a democratic form of government. Both the monopoly firm and the government may act to further their own interests at the expense of the consumer or taxpayer, but they would both operate within constraints. The monopoly firm would not be free to charge whatever price it wished. Its profits were limited by the demand curve. The government would not be free to inflate the costs of provision by only hiring or catering to 'friends of the government', because it may suffer an election defeat.

These two cases—private or government ownership of a natural monopoly—illustrate the problem of **market failure** (the monopoly charging more than the marginal cost) and what is sometimes called **government failure** (the failure to minimize the cost of providing the service), and the problem of adopting policies in a real world in which neither issue can be avoided entirely.

Which works better? There is no general answer to this question. And there are many choices besides private ownership or government ownership, including:

- private ownership under public regulation
- public ownership with competition among private firms for the time-limited right to produce and price the service

Andrei Shleifer. 1998. 'State versus private ownership'. *Journal of Economic Perspectives* 12 (4): pp. 133–150.

Viewing the government as an economic actor that pursues its objectives, but is constrained by what is feasible, helps us clarify which factors can influence a government to be more of a problem-solver, and less of a problem.

EXERCISE 22.1 BUILDING SELF-CONTROL INTO GOVERNMENT
James Madison, a leading figure in the debates about the US Constitution after the formerly British colonies in the United States of America won its war of independence, wrote in 1788:

> In framing a government which is to be administered by men over men, the great difficulty lies in this: you must first enable the government to control the governed; and in the next place oblige it to control itself.

How does democracy (including the rule of law) address Madison's concerns to oblige the government to 'control itself'?

Alexander Hamilton, James Madison and John Jay (1961). *The Federalist*. Middletown, Ct., Wesleyan University Press.

EXERCISE 22.2 THE RELATIONSHIP BETWEEN ECONOMIC DEVELOPMENT AND SIZE OF GOVERNMENT
Use Figure 22.2 (page 1015) to help you answer the following questions:

1. Why was *Pax Britannica* a period of smaller government?
2. Compare Figure 22.2 (page 1015) with Figure 1.1a (page 2). Why do you think that the growth of the size of government coincides with both the emergence of capitalism as an economic system in the seventeenth and eighteenth century, and the increase in output per capita?
3. Compare two 'peacetime' periods—*Pax Britannica*, and the period since the end of the Second World War. Why do you think the size of government was so much larger in the second?

22.2 GOVERNMENT ACTING AS A MONOPOLIST

As mentioned in the previous section, governments have the power to solve problems, but also cause them. Heads of governments and their associates often misuse their power for personal gain:

* *France*: The 'Sun King' Louis XIV ruled France from 1643 to 1715. Between 1661 and 1710 he constructed a luxurious palace and grounds for himself at the Palace of Versailles, which is now one of the top tourist attractions of the world.
* *Ivory Coast*: As president from 1960 to 1993, Felix Houphouet Boigny accumulated a fortune estimated to be between $7 and $11 billion, much of it held in Swiss bank accounts. He once asked, 'Is there any serious man on earth not stocking parts of his fortune in Switzerland?'
* *Romania*: Nicolae Ceausescu, the head of state under Communist Party rule for over two decades, amassed extraordinary wealth, the most visible parts of which were more than a dozen palaces that had bathrooms with gold-tiled baths and solid-gold toilet paper holders.
* *Russia*: Personal connections with President Vladimir Putin have allowed a class of business people called *oligarchs* to obtain hundreds of millions of roubles worth of assets.

Other governments, even undemocratic ones like the ones just mentioned, sometimes provide valuable public services and rule without extravagant personal gain.

Preferences and feasible sets

To understand why governments do what they do, we first model the government as a single individual, and use the usual concepts:

- his preferences
- the constraints which determine which actions and outcomes are feasible for him

We consider the government as a single actor, but in fact it is made up of a large number of actors. And just as managers and owners of firms have a wide variety of motivations, so do those in government. The following motives are common among those in leadership roles in government:

- *Benevolence*: To improve the wellbeing of citizens.
- *Nepotism*: To give special importance to a particular group, such as the region from which government leader comes, or a particular religion.
- *Self-interest*: Using the power of the government position for personal enrichment.

To begin, we model the government as a 'political monopolist', which means there is no competition from elections that could remove it from power. We call this the 'government as monopolist' model, and a government like this is referred to as a dictatorship. Even in the absence of elections, the dictator faces a feasibility constraint: his powers are not unlimited, because if he takes too much from the population, he may be removed from office by an uprising of citizens.

Depending on its preferences and the constraints it faces, the government may use the tax revenues it collects for a variety of purposes, which may include:

- *The provision of services to virtually all citizens*: These include schooling and health.
- *The delivery of government services or other benefits to a narrowly targeted group*: These might be well-paying jobs, or special reductions in tax obligations.
- *Granting substantial incomes to themselves*: Or other economic benefits, to themselves or their families.

A rent-seeking dictator

As with all models, we simplify greatly so as to focus on the most important aspects of the problem:

- the 'dictator' is entirely selfish
- he decides on a tax that he will collect from the citizens …
- … and keeps the tax revenue, apart from his spending on a public service (such as basic health services or schooling) for the citizens …
- … whom he provides for because if he keeps too much, a popular uprising may remove him from office

While simple, this model captures some key realities:

- The Romanian people revolted against Nicolae Ceausescu in 1989 after he had been in office for 29 years. The armed forces joined the revolt, and he and his wife were executed.
- Louis XVI of France was removed from power in a revolution in 1789, during which thousands of armed men and women besieged the Palace of Versailles. He was executed by guillotine in 1793.

The costs of the public service include what the dictator would earn as a normal civilian. The amount the dictator receives (taxes in excess of the costs of the public service) is called a **political rent**:

- *It is a rent*: This is what the dictator gets above and beyond his next best alternative (namely, working as an ordinary civilian).
- *The rents are political*: They exist as a consequence of the political institutions in force. The dictator receives an income above his reservation income because he occupies a position of power in government.

These rents are an example of persistent (or stationary) rents (as in Figure 11.23). Unlike the stationary rents that encourage workers to work hard and well, or the dynamic rents received by successful innovators, these rents do not play a useful role in the economy. They are simply a reward for having power.

Rent-seeking by the dictator (activities to enlarge or to perpetuate these high incomes) often involves using the economy's resources to police the population in order to keep the dictator in power, rather than to produce goods and services. These are similar to some of the rent-seeking activities of a profit-maximizing firm—advertising or lobbying the government to gain a tax break, for example—but are different from other rent-seeking activities such as innovation, which often creates substantial economic benefits.

To simplify the dictator's decision-making problem, we assume that the dictator does not choose the public service to supply—the public service is taken as given. The dictator only chooses how much to collect in taxes.

Even a dictator faces constraints on what he can do

As in Unit 5, when Bruno was using his coercive powers to exploit Angela, the dictator will not want to collect so much in taxes that the citizens would lack the strength and ability to produce. But the dictator will face an additional constraint: if the taxes are too high, the citizens will try to remove him from power, by revolting or engaging in other forms of civil unrest.

We assume there are two reasons for removing the dictator:

- *Performance-related reasons*: He collects too much tax, for example.
- *Reasons unrelated to performance*: The dictator has no control over these.

The dictator wants to maximize the total political rent that he can expect to get over his period in office, not the rent he can get in any particular year. So he has to think about how long he is likely to last. Of course, this is impossible to predict, but he will reasonably expect that if he is providing a given amount of the public service, then the lower the taxes he imposes, the longer his duration in office will be.

political rent A payment or other benefit in excess of the individual's next best alternative (reservation position) that exists as a result of the individual's political position. The reservation position in this case refers to the individual's situation were he or she to lack a privileged political position. *See also: economic rent.*

Figure 22.4 illustrates how a forward-looking dictator would evaluate two possible levels of taxation. With the higher tax, the dictator gets a larger rent per year but for a shorter time in office, because the likelihood of being removed is greater.

Assuming the private sector does not also provide this service to the public, you can think about the government as a monopolist providing the public service at a 'price' (the tax), which citizens are legally obliged to pay. The dictator faces a constraint similar to a demand curve. Just as the amount a monopolistic firm is able to sell is inversely related to the price that it sets, the duration of the government's time in office is inversely related to the tax rate it sets.

Figure 22.5 shows how the tax rate imposed by the dictator affects the expected duration of the government, defined as the number of years he may expect to stay in office following this year.

What is the longest time (D^{max}) that the dictator could expect to remain in office? To figure this out, imagine that our dictator suddenly lost interest in money and simply wanted to remain in office as long as possible. What would he do?

He cannot reduce the probability that he will be removed for reasons unrelated to his performance. But he can reduce the 'performance-related' probability of being removed by only collecting enough taxes to meet the production costs of the public service. In Figure 22.5, D^{max} is therefore where the duration curve meets the cost line. It is the expected duration when only considering factors unrelated to the dictator's performance. Any tax rate above the cost of production will reduce the expected duration below D^{max}, as shown by the downward slope of the duration curve.

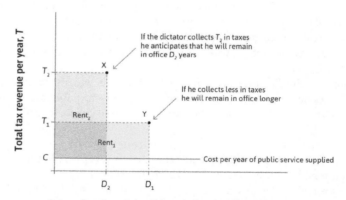

Figure 22.4 The forward-looking dictator contemplates the total political rent he will get with two different levels of annual taxation.

1. Higher tax

If the dictator collects T_2 in taxes, he anticipates that he will remain in office for D_2 years. His total political rent is $(T_2 - C)D_2$, where C is the cost of supplying the public good.

2. Lower tax

If he collects less in taxes, he will expect to remain in office longer. His total political rent is $(T_1 - C)D_1$.

The duration curve goes through points X and Y in Figure 22.4 and does not go below the cost line because if it did, the dictator would be paying out of his own pocket toward the cost of the public service. A dictator in a country with a stronger rule of law—and therefore a lower likelihood of a coup unrelated to performance—would face a duration curve that meets the cost line to the right of the one shown.

The duration curve is the feasible frontier for the dictator. Points in the feasible set above the cost curve result in positive rents for him. The curve represents a familiar trade-off:

- *Higher taxes*: More rents in the short run at the cost of a greater likelihood of an early dismissal from office. A shorter duration in office is the opportunity cost of higher rents per year.
- *Lower taxes*: The dictator earns rents for longer, but at a lower level per year. Lower rents per year is the opportunity cost of a longer duration in office.

The dictator chooses a tax to maximize his total rents

How does a dictator facing a duration curve decide the tax rate to impose on the citizens? The answer is similar to the way that a monopolistic firm decides on the price to charge for its product. This can be seen in Figure 22.6.

The dictator will find the tax that maximizes his total expected political rent, which as in Figure 22.6 will be

$$\text{Expected rent} = \text{rent per year} \times \text{expected duration (in years)}$$
$$= (T - C)D$$

This is analogous to the profit-maximizing firm that chooses the price that allows it to get the highest expected profits equal to $(P - C)Q$, where P is the price charged by the firm and Q is the quantity sold.

Leibniz: Expected duration of the dictator or governing elite (http://tinyco.re/L220201)

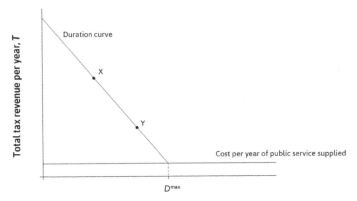

Figure 22.5 The duration curve: The dictator sets the tax given the cost of the public service.

Convexity means that for a given value of D, moving upwards in the figure (increasing T) makes the curves steeper, while for a given T, moving to the right (increasing D) makes the curves flatter.

Just as we used the firm's isoprofit curves to determine the price it would charge in order to maximize profits, we can now use the dictator's isorent curves shown in the figure to determine the tax rate it will impose on the citizens. The shape of the isorent curves is similar to the isoprofit curves:

- Higher isorent curves are further from the origin.
- The absolute value of their slope is $(T - C)/D$.
- They are 'bowed inward' (convex) towards the origin, as shown in the figure.
- The 'no rent' isorent curve is the horizontal cost line (its slope is zero).

Now suppose the dictator is considering setting a modest tax and expecting a long tenure in office, indicated by point A. Because the isorent curve is flatter than the duration curve at this point, we can see that he would do better by raising the tax and bearing the opportunity cost associated with doing so (a shorter expected stay in office).

Continuing this reasoning, we can see that the tax rate indicated by point F on the duration curve gets the dictator a large surplus per year, but not enough to offset the short duration of his government. A lower tax rate would increase his expected rent.

Leibniz: How the monopolist sets the rent-maximizing level of taxes (http://tinyco.re/L220202)

To maximize his political rent, the dictator will select point B, imposing the tax T^* and expecting to stay in office for D^* years, making a total rent of $(T^* - C)D^*$. At this point, the slope of the highest isorent curve is equal to the slope of the feasible frontier (the duration curve):

$$\text{Slope of the duration curve} = \text{MRT}$$
$$= \text{MRS}$$
$$= \text{slope of the highest feasible isorent curve}$$

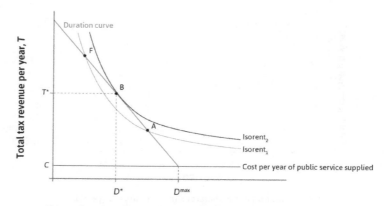

Figure 22.6 The dictator chooses a tax level to maximize his political rents.

QUESTION 22.1 CHOOSE THE CORRECT ANSWER(S)
Consider Figure 22.6 (page 1026). Which of the following statements is true?

- ☐ A self-interested dictator will maximize the annual tax revenue they collect.
- ☐ Moving from A to B in the diagram is a Pareto improvement, improving outcomes for both citizens and the dictator.
- ☐ At T^*, an increase in the tax rate will increase total expected rent.
- ☐ Dictators use some tax revenues to provide essential public services.

22.3 POLITICAL COMPETITION AFFECTS HOW THE GOVERNMENT WILL ACT

Just as competition disciplines firms in the economy by limiting the profits they can get by setting too high a price, competition to win elections is the way that a democracy disciplines its politicians to provide the services desired by the public at a reasonable cost (in terms of taxes). Below we give some evidence of this from the US.

There is also evidence from other countries that the prospect of being removed from office affects what politicians do. The introduction of village-level elections in China led to increased provision of local public services such as health services and schooling, and arguably a reduction in corruption.

Even in undemocratic settings, the threat of losing office can discipline politicians. In China, provincial governors and Communist Party secretaries are not subject to review by voters but instead by higher officials in the central government. Governors and party secretaries are frequently promoted and almost as frequently fired. The records of all terminations over the period 1975–1998 show that those whose provinces experienced rapid economic growth were promoted, while those whose provinces lagged behind in growth were dismissed.

Monica Martinez-Bravo, Gerard P. i Miquel, Nancy Qian, and Yang Yao. 2014. 'Political reform in China: the effect of local elections.' NBER working paper, 18101.

HOW ECONOMISTS LEARN FROM FACTS

Does electoral competition affect policy?

Think of a politician as wanting to stay in office and knowing that she must satisfy a majority of voters when seeking re-election. But she also has her own objectives: to advance a particular project that she favours, or to maintain good relations with wealthy individuals who will support her political campaigns or employ her when her political career is over. Does the threat of 'give the voters what they want or get thrown out' lead her to emphasize the public's interests, instead of her own?

Just comparing the policies adopted by politicians in districts that are non-competitive (for example, there will be no other candidate for the seat) with those who face electoral competition will not answer the question. The reason is that competitive and non-competitive political districts, and the politicians who represent them, are different in so many ways that the comparison would mix the effects of political competition with the effects of these other differences.

Economists Tim Besley and Anne Case devised an ingenious way to answer the question (http://tinyco.re/2599264). Some state governors in the US are limited to two four-year terms of office. This means that at the end of their first term they will face electoral competition when they ask voters to re-elect them. During their second term, the prospect of political competition does not affect them, because they are not allowed to stand for re-election.

Considered as an experiment, the 'treatment' is the prospect of electoral competition, the governors in the first term are the 'treatment group' and the same governors in the second term are the 'control group'. As in any good experiment, other important influences are held constant. We are measuring the same individuals, in the same districts, under a treatment and a control condition.

They found that during their first terms (the treatment period), Republican and Democratic governors implemented virtually identical levels of total taxation per capita. But during their second terms (the control period), Democratic Party governors, who tend to favour more public expenditures and taxation, implemented much higher levels of taxation than Republicans did. And Republican governors, when not facing political competition, implemented much lower levels of the state minimum wage.

Whether Democrat or Republican, governors faced with electoral competition in their first term implemented very similar policies to those favoured by the 'swing' voters who tend to change who they vote for, and so tend to decide many elections—lower taxes and higher minimum wages. But they diverged according to their own political preferences or economic interests when electoral competition was removed.

Political competition as a constraint

Next, we introduce political competition to the model to see how it affects the government's choice of tax level. The government leadership is no longer represented by a dictator, but instead by what we call a **governing elite**, that is the top government officials and legislative leaders, unified by a common interest such as membership in a particular party. Unlike a dictator, the elite can only be removed from office by losing an election, and not by a citizen uprising or some other non-electoral means.

governing elite Top government officials such as the president, cabinet officials, and legislative leaders, unified by a common interest such as membership in a particular party.

When we speak of its removal from power or the duration of its time in office, we do not mean the removal of an individual (as might have been the case with a dictator), but rather the entire group and its affiliation with a political party. In the US, for example, the Republican Party governing elite was removed from office in 2008, when President Obama was elected. The Democratic Party governing elite associated with President Obama was removed from office when President Trump was elected eight years later.

In the model, there are now two ways that a governing elite can be removed from office, both of which occur through elections (although, of course, reality is more complex):

- *Performance-related reasons*: It collects too much tax, for example.
- *Reasons unrelated to performance*: Even governing elites that serve the interests of their citizens often lose elections.

Figure 22.7 illustrates a few of examples of governing elites' duration in office and the reasons that they eventually left office. The longest continuous rule by a governing elite was the government of the Mexican Institutional Revolutionary Party (PRI), which governed Mexico from the time of the Mexican revolution in the early twentieth century right into the twenty-first century. The longest rule by an individual at the head of a governing elite was by Fidel Castro (49 years) in Cuba, who was then succeeded by his brother Raul. The shortest period in office in this table is the elected government of Gough Whitlam in Australia, which was removed by the Governor General (not an elected official) following a parliamentary impasse over the budget.

The key idea in our model is that political competition makes the likelihood of losing an election more dependent on the government's performance. This means that it makes the duration curve flatter. In other words, an increase in taxes by the government will have a larger effect on the elite's expected duration in office than it would if there was no political competition.

The response of expected duration to the change in taxes is:

$$\Delta D / \Delta T = -\text{change in duration associated with a change in taxes}$$

This is the inverse of the slope of the duration curve. If we have weak political competition, the duration curve is steep, just as a steep (inelastic) demand curve indicates weak competition in a market for goods or services.

The flatter, more competitive, duration curve that you see in Figure 22.8 shows a situation in which raising taxes above the cost of providing the public services is associated with a reduction in the current governing elite's period in power.

The model helps show why governing elites, and the wealthy and powerful members of society who are allied to these elites, have so often resisted democracy, and attempted to limit the political rights of the less

Governing elite	Country	Rule	Came to power by	Left power by
Congress Party	India	1947–1977	Election (end of colonial rule)	Election
Communist Party	Cuba	1959–	Revolution	Still in power as of 2017
Social Democratic Party	Sweden	1932–1976	Election	Election
Second Republic	Spain	1931–1939	Election	Military coup civil war
Francisco Franco	Spain	1939–1975	Military coup, civil war	Natural death; return to democracy
Institutional Revolutionary Party	Mexico	1929–2000	Election	Election
Democratic Party	US	1933–1953	Election	Election
Sandinista Party	Nicaragua	1979–1990	Revolution	Election
African National Congress	South Africa	1994–	Non-violent revolution & election	Still in power as of 2017
Australian Labor Party	Australia	1972–1975	Election	Dismissed by (unelected) executive

Figure 22.7 Examples of governing elites, their period of rule, and reasons for their end.

well off. In Figure 22.9, voting is initially restricted to the wealthy and as a result, the elite faces little political competition (the duration curve is steep), and maximizes its rents at point B. But now suppose that everyone has the right to vote and that opposition political parties are allowed to challenge the elite. This increase in political competition is represented by the flatter duration curve, indicating that the feasible set of the elite has shrunk. It now chooses point G, and collects lower taxes per year.

Notice that, in the figure, the governing elite in a more competitive political system implements lower taxes but has the same expected duration as the elite in the less competitive system (with higher taxes). But this need not be the case. Generally, the duration could be longer or shorter if conditions become more competitive.

You are already familiar with the reason why the expected duration might not change after increase in political competition. There are two offsetting effects:

- *Raising taxes bears a heavier risk of the governing elite being dismissed*: We can see the duration curve is flatter. This is the **substitution effect**: leading the governing elite to choose a higher expected duration and lower rent per year.
- *The governing elite has lost some of its power*: The inward shift of the duration curve means that it will now receive lower rents whatever it does. This is the **income effect** that results in the governing elite choosing a lower expected duration, and lower tax rate.

substitution effect The effect that is only due to changes in the price or opportunity cost, given the new level of utility.
income effect The effect that the additional income would have if there were no change in the price or opportunity cost.

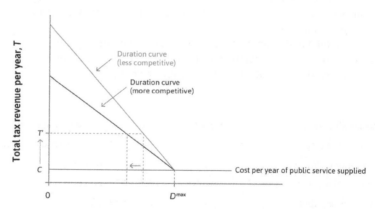

Figure 22.8 The feasible set for taxes and government duration in a relatively uncompetitive and competitive political system.

1. A dictatorship
In a dictatorship, the duration curve is steep.

2. A flatter curve
The more competitive duration curve (darker) is flatter.

3. A rise in taxes
Raising taxes to T' above the cost of providing the public services is associated with a more substantial reduction in the current government's expected lifetime when political competition is stronger.

In the case we have shown, the substitution effect happens to exactly offset the income effect.

> **EXERCISE 22.3 COMPARING DURATION CURVES FOR GOVERNMENTS AND MONOPOLISTIC FIRMS**
> How is the duration curve in Figure 22.8 (page 1030) similar to and different from the demand curve faced by a monopolistic firm that you studied in Unit 7?

> **EXERCISE 22.4 INCOME AND SUBSTITUTION EFFECTS**
> Applying what you learned about income and substitution effects and how they can be analysed in a diagram with indifference curves and feasible frontiers (from Unit 3), redraw Figure 22.9 to show the decomposition of the final choice after increased competition into the income effect (reduction in duration, D) and the substitution effect (increase in D).

Leibniz: The income and substitution effect of an increase in political competition
(http://tinyco.re/L220301)

22.4 WHY AN ERSTWHILE DICTATOR MIGHT SUBMIT TO POLITICAL COMPETITION

We have now seen two versions of the 'government as monopolist' model: one in which the 'government' is a dictator who may be overthrown, as Louis XVI and Nicolae Ceausescu were, and the other in which the governing elite is subject to electoral competition, with the possibility that another political party may defeat it in an election and become the new governing elite.

Over the course of the past 200 years, many countries have seen an increase in the degree of political competition so that the 'political competition' version of the 'government as a monopoly' model applies more often than the 'dictator' version.

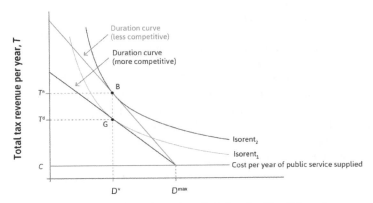

Figure 22.9 Choice of taxes under less and more competitive conditions.

Read more on South Africa's and El Salvador's transitions to democracy in this book: Elisabeth Jean Wood. 2000. *Forging Democracy from Below: Insurgent Transitions in South Africa and El Salvador.* Cambridge: Cambridge University Press.

This has happened in many cases because governing elites have found it in their interest to concede to a more competitive political system, or even introduce one on their own initiative:

- *South Africa*: You already read that the population of European origin (those who were both business and governing elites) responded to waves of industrial strikes, community protests, and student stay-away-from-school demonstrations by extending the vote to all adult South Africans, irrespective of race.
- *El Salvador*: After 10 years of civil war, and faced with an armed insurrection that they could not defeat, the economic, political, and military elites of El Salvador conceded to the demands of their opponents that the country should adopt a democratic political system.
- *The US*: At the time of adoption of the US Constitution in the late eighteenth century, James Madison, the author of *The Tenth Federalist Paper*, thought that the only way to ensure stability was to increase democracy. He persuaded his fellow wealthy landowners (and slave owners) to take a chance on democracy for this reason. The result was the ratification of the US Constitution in 1788, which despite its recognition of slavery as a legal institution, is considered to be a landmark on the long journey to a full democracy.

Faced with unrest, one way the governing elite in an undemocratic political system could increase the stability of the system would be to use the coercive powers of the government to imprison and intimidate opponents who would expose the extent of the government's political rents. Nevertheless, there are limits to the effectiveness of these 'police state' strategies, as illustrated by the white governing elite under apartheid in South Africa, who attempted to do this, and failed. The elite of the Communist Party of the German Democratic Republic (East Germany) also discovered the limits to its ability to impose stability by force. Popular demonstrations and challenges to the government were successful, in part because the police and armed forces eventually could not be counted on to defend the incumbent government.

An alternative way to ensure stability is to introduce changes in the political system that make it more democratic, providing the dissatisfied with legal means to seek a change in government.

A greater degree of democracy will 'flatten' the duration curve, thereby reducing the size of the elite's feasible set, as we showed in Figure 22.9. If greater democracy also increased the stability of the political system however to the extent shown in Figure 22.10, it might allow the elite an even greater expected rent at the point A'. This would be possible because the increased expected duration of the government, due to increased stability, would more than offset the reduced taxes that could be imposed due to the increased power of the citizens to dismiss the government for excessive rent-taking. In Figure 22.10, the greater expected rent at A' is shown by the larger area of $(T^{**} - C)D^{**}$ as compared with $(T^* - C)D^*$.

EXERCISE 22.5 EFFECTS OF COST-SAVING IMPROVEMENTS TO PUBLIC SERVICES

Suppose the elite can introduce a policy that will provide the same level of public services at a lower cost. This would be called an increase in the effectiveness of the government. An example might be that the government could adopt teaching methods that are more effective, or find ways to motivate teachers to improve their teaching. Or the government could require that the construction firms that build public infrastructure, such as roads, compete with each other rather than colluding in setting high prices.

1. Which curves in the diagram will this change alter? Draw a figure depicting this new situation. Hint: The (absolute value of the) slope of the isorent curves is $(T – C)/D$.
2. Explain why the governing elite would want to introduce these policies.
3. Can you say if the elite will levy the same level of taxes, higher taxes, or lower taxes?
4. Can you think of reasons why these policies might not be introduced?

QUESTION 22.2 CHOOSE THE CORRECT ANSWER(S)

Consider Figure 22.10. Which of the following statements is true?

☐ Moving from A to A′ in the diagram is a Pareto improvement, improving outcomes for both citizens and the governing elite.
☐ Increased competition will always improve outcomes for the governing elite.
☐ Increased competition would make the elite worse off if they did not reduce tax rates in response.
☐ The 'substitution' effect will cause elite that is facing greater competition to charge higher tax rates.

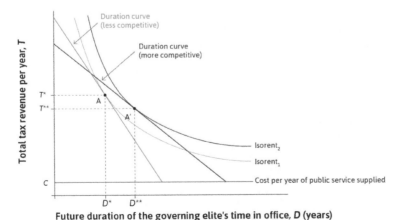

Figure 22.10 Effect of greater stability and competition: A case where the elite gains.

22.5 DEMOCRACY AS A POLITICAL INSTITUTION

We have seen that like firms, the government (treated in the model as if it were a single person) is an important economic actor. As an actor, the government imposes laws, fights wars, collects taxes, and provides public services such as the rule of law, stable currency, roads, healthcare, and schools. But, like firms, the government is also a stage. On the stage of government, politicians, political parties, soldiers, citizens, and bureaucrats interact according to the informal and formal rules that constitute political institutions.

The **political institutions** of a country are the rules of the game that determine who has power and how it is exercised in a society. Democracy is a political institution, which means it is a set of rules that determine

- who makes up the government
- the powers they can use when governing

Political institutions differ from country to country and over time. But major categories of political institutions include democracy and dictatorship.

The key value motivating democracy is political equality. Citizens should have substantially equal opportunities to be able to express their views in ways that can shape the policies and other activities of the government.

Democracy is sometimes advocated as a means to 'let the people rule', or in Abraham Lincoln's words, a 'government of the people, by the people and for the people.' But who 'the people' are and what 'the people' want is difficult to determine. Kenneth Arrow is the economist who contributed most to our understanding of the problems that elections sometimes encounter in selecting between different courses of action.

In Unit 1 we explained that we use the word **democracy** to refer to a form of government in which three political institutions exist:

- *Rule of law*: All individuals are bound by the same laws, and nobody—not even the most powerful government official—is 'above the law'.
- *Civil liberties*: The members of a society are guaranteed rights of free speech, assembly, and the press.
- *Inclusive, fair, and decisive elections*: Fair elections in which no major population group is excluded from voting, and after which the losing party leaves office.

Ideally, in a democracy those who have power are elected in an inclusive and open competitive process, and the rule of law and civil liberties limits the things they can do with that power.

Democracy has been advocated as a good political system on two quite different grounds:

- *Democracy in its own right*: As a political system consistent with individual dignity and freedom.
- *Democracy as a way of addressing national problems*: As a system that works better than other methods.

Here we focus on the consequences of democracy for addressing problems (the second point), not on its intrinsic merits (the first point).

No existing government fulfils the democratic ideal of political equality, where each citizen has equal influence over an outcome. Similarly, no gov-

political institutions The rules of the game that determine who has power and how it is exercised in a society.

GREAT ECONOMISTS

Kenneth Arrow

Kenneth Arrow (1921–2017) was born in New York City to Romanian-American parents. His essay 'A cautious case for socialism' explains how the Great Depression and the Second World War influenced his ideas, especially those of 'freedom and avoidance of war'.

A good summary of Kenneth Arrow's explanation of the problems of using voting to determine which action is preferred, and his broader contributions to economics and social science, are in Steven Durlauf's essay 'Kenneth Arrow and the golden age of economic theory'.

In addition to his work on voting systems, he was among the first to demonstrate that there were conditions under which something like Adam Smith's 'invisible hand' would work. Characteristically scholarly and detached from ideological rhetoric, he later wrote:

> There is by now a long and … imposing line of economists from Adam Smith to the present who have sought to show that a decentralized economy motivated by self interest and guided by price signals would be compatible with a coherent disposition of economic resources that could be regarded … as superior to a large class of possible alternative dispositions. … It is important to know not only whether it *is* true but whether it *could be* true. (original emphasis) (*General Competitive Analysis*, 1971)

Arrow was a pioneer in the study of many of the themes in *The Economy*, including asymmetric information and the economics of knowledge, and helped broaden the scope of economics to include insights from other disciplines. A year before his death, Arrow co-taught a course about inequality at Stanford University using an early draft of Unit 19 of this book, which was revised in light of his comments.

Kenneth J. Arrow .1978. 'A cautious case for socialism' (http://tinyco.re/3618241). *Dissent* 25 (4): pp. 472–480

Steven Durlauf. 2017. 'Kenneth Arrow and the golden age of economic theory' (http://tinyco.re/9029504). *VoxEU.org*. Updated 8 April 2017.

ernment today can be said to perfectly match the three political institutions that define democracy.

Think about inclusive elections. Some population groups—those convicted of major crimes, for example—are excluded from voting in many countries, but we still consider the country's political system as democratic. However, exclusion of a major population group—women, for example, as was common in recent history—is a sufficiently serious violation of the 'inclusive elections' criterion to disqualify a country from the club of democratic nations. Some examples include:

- *West Bengal*: To see how important restricting the right to vote can be, recall that in Unit 5, we examined the implementation of a land reform in West Bengal called Operation Barga and used the Lorenz curve to illustrate the effect of the reform in Figure 5.18. We can now see how inclusive elections could affect the likelihood that reforms like this take place. In the hypothetical case that only landowners have the vote, then if they vote in their own economic interests, they would not support a party pledged to implement such a reform (recall that in the example shown in Figure 5.18, the landowners' share of the crop fell from 50% to 25% following the reform). Since the landowners make up only 10% of the population, if there was universal suffrage, the result would be different. The farmers making up the majority of the electorate would vote for a party proposing the land reform. In real life, the political party that introduced the reforms in West Bengal went on to win elections and, as a result, control of the state government for three decades.

Thomas Fujiwara. 2015. 'Voting technology, political responsiveness and infant health: Evidence from Brazil'. *Econometrica* 83 (2): pp. 423–464.

- *The US*: The Voting Rights Act of 1965 secured the vote for large numbers of effectively disenfranchised African American citizens. The result was a substantial shift in educational spending in districts with large numbers of previously excluded black voters.
- *Brazil*: In Brazil, before the mid-1990s, casting a valid ballot required that voters could read and write reasonably well (which perhaps a quarter of the population could not). Around 11% of ballots cast were declared invalid due to communication barriers, most of them cast by poor voters. New electronic voting introduced in 1996 used pictures of candidates, an interface similar to phone keypads or ATM screens, and prompted the voter through the process step by step. The effect was to increase the number of valid votes made by the poor. The resulting change in the nature of the electorate led elected political leaders to prioritize the kinds of spending predominantly benefiting the less well off. Expenditure on public health, for example, increased by more than a third.

As we will see in the following sections, how a government actually works is not determined solely by the presence or absence of civil liberties, the rule of law, and inclusive fair elections.

22.6 POLITICAL PREFERENCES AND ELECTORAL COMPETITION: THE MEDIAN VOTER MODEL

One of the puzzles of politics is that in two-party electoral systems, parties often offer programs that are remarkably similar. It provokes the criticism that democracy doesn't offer a real choice. Here are some examples:

- *What size should the government be?*: Substantial differences in party objectives and political values—about the appropriate size of the government, for example—have divided Britain's Labour and Conservative Parties since the end of the Second World War. But look again at Figure 22.2, showing the size of the UK government. The big change was an increase during the Second World War. Since then, one can detect the ups and downs of spending in the Labour and Conservative years, but the size of the government has not changed much.
- *What should the government do?*: In the Indian state of Kerala, for the past half-century the elected state government has alternated between the centrist Congress Party (and its allies) and the Communist Party (and its allies). Since the first elected Communist-led government, power has changed hands seven times. In this time, the fundamental priorities of the government have changed little, affirming a strong emphasis on education, health, and other public services.

To understand why political parties sometimes adopt 'lookalike' policies, we borrow a model from economics. Just as firms compete for purchases from customers, in democracies, political parties compete for votes from citizens by offering party platforms, which consist of policies that they say they will enact if elected. We will consider a simple majority-rule system in which the party or candidate with the most votes wins.

The median voter and party platforms in an ideal democracy

Imagine a situation in which there are only two parties, one of which represents the 'left' of politics (favouring higher taxes and government spending, for example) and the other the 'right' (favouring lower taxes and government spending). If the parties care only about winning an election, in what conditions will they offer distinctive platforms tailored to their respective core supporters? And if they offer similar programs, at which point on the political spectrum will that be?

We can provide some answers to these questions using a model developed by Harold Hotelling, an economist. He had imagined the location of stores along a railway line. In his article, Hotelling also applies his model of competition to the political platforms of the Democratic and Republican Parties in the US.

We will apply Hotelling's model to ice creams. Imagine a stretch of beach along which bathers are spread evenly. They can purchase ice cream from one or more mobile ice cream stands. Initially we assume that every bather will buy one ice cream, and that all ice creams cost the same. If there is more than one vendor, they will purchase the ice cream from the vendor located closest to them.

Understanding where the ice cream sellers choose to locate on the beach (to the right, to the left, in the middle) will help us understand where political parties would locate along the high tax (left) to low tax (right) continuum. This is called the **median voter model**.

To begin, a single vendor, April, is at the beach. She has the entire market to herself so it doesn't matter where she is located. Suppose she is at a location shown by A_0 in Figure 22.11, on the left of the beach.

Along comes Bob, a second seller who is identical in economic respects to April. Where will he locate in order to maximize his sales, and hence his profits? He might reason that the market to the right of April is larger than the market to the left, so he will locate in the middle of the stretch of beach to the right of April, at point B_0. He would then get all of the bathers to his right and as well as of those to his left who are closer to him than to April.

But Bob would immediately see that he could expand sales by shifting to the left, towards April. While the customers to his right will now have to walk farther to get ice cream, they would certainly not switch to April who is even farther away. He will therefore be able to gain a few customers to his left, who were previously closest to April but are now closest to him, while losing none of those customers to his right.

How far would he go?

He will end up standing just to the right of April, so that he gets all of the sales along the longer stretch of beach to the right. Could Bob or April make more profits by changing their location? In other words, is this a **Nash equilibrium**?

It is not.

April, understanding the profit-maximizing logic that Bob has just acted on, will shift immediately to the right-hand side of Bob, to A_1. Then she will

Harold Hotelling. 1929. 'Stability in Competition'. *Economic Journal* 39, pp. 41–57.

median voter model An economic model of the location of businesses applied to the positions taken in electoral platforms when two parties compete that provides conditions under which, in order to maximize the number of votes they will receive, the parties will adopt positions that appeal to the median voter. *See also: median voter.*

Nash equilibrium A set of strategies, one for each player in the game, such that each player's strategy is a best response to the strategies chosen by everyone else.

get the larger market. But then Bob will do the same, and they will keep leap-frogging over each other until they are back-to-back in the middle of the beach.

At this point, neither has an incentive to move as they have divided the customers exactly in half. Both locating halfway along the beach is a Nash equilibrium under the rules of the game. The bathers located near to the centre of the beach benefit from this. Their trip to the ice cream stand is shorter than those on the extreme left or right of the beach.

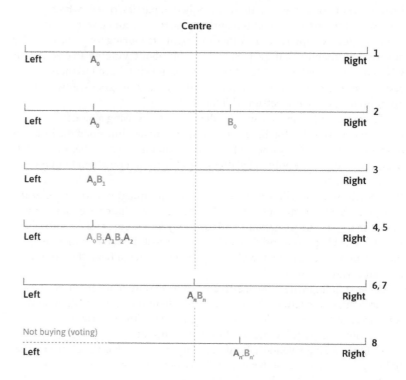

Figure 22.11 Ice cream sellers at the beach: The median voter model of electoral competition and party platforms.

1. A single vendor
A single vendor, April, arrives at the beach and locates her ice cream stand at A_0.

2. A second seller
A second seller, Bob, arrives and sets up at B_0, midway between April and the right-hand end of the beach.

3. Bob shifts to the left
Bob realizes he could expand his sales by shifting to the left towards April, to point B_1.

4. April responds …
Because her customer base has shrunk, she shifts immediately to the right-hand side of Bob, B_1.

5. … and Bob responds again …
But then Bob will do the same.

6. The two sellers keep leap-frogging
They will keep leap-frogging over each other until they are 'back-to-back' in the middle of the beach.

7. The middle of the beach
At this point, neither has an incentive to move as they have divided the customers exactly in half. This is a Nash equilibrium under the rules of the game we have set out.

8. A parallel with politics
Imagine that the bathers on the far-left part of the beach are not going to buy ice cream under any condition (they are like the citizens who do not vote). Then April and Bob will locate in the centre of those who *do* vote at points $A_{n'}$ and $B_{n'}$.

To return to politics, we can think of voters as arranged along a left-to-right spectrum much as the customers are arranged on a beach. If there are two parties competing for votes, and voters will always vote for whichever party offers policies that are closest to their views, the model tells us that the only Nash equilibrium would be for both parties to propose policies in the middle of the left-right spectrum.

On this basis, we would expect to see that voters in the middle of the left-right political spectrum would be offered two party platforms very much to their liking. Those more distant from the centre would have to choose between two platforms. One would be a little better than the other, but they wouldn't like either platform very much.

The citizen in the centre—called the **median voter**—has two advantages. First, she gets to choose between two platforms very close to her preferences.

Second, she is a 'swing voter'. To understand why this is the case, consider a family on the far right of the beach. If the family choose to move slightly to the left, would this affect the Nash equilibrium position of the ice cream stands? Provided that half of the customers are to Bob's right and half are to his left, he would gain nothing by relocating, because half the customers would still be closest to him, and half would still be closest to April. By contrast, if a family who were previously slightly to Bob's right moved to the left, they would be likely to end up closer to April than to Bob. April would now have more customers than Bob, and Bob would want to relocate to the left.

In politics, when swing voters change their political preferences just a little, by moving to the other side of the parties in the centre, the parties in the centre move too. Changes in the political preferences of other voters make a difference too, but someone distant from the centre does not make a difference to party platforms unless he changes his preferences by enough to cross the centre to the 'other side'.

median voter model An economic model of the location of businesses applied to the positions taken in electoral platforms when two parties compete that provides conditions under which, in order to maximize the number of votes they will receive, the parties will adopt positions that appeal to the median voter. *See also: median voter.*

EXERCISE 22.6 ROCK-PAPER-SCISSORS POLITICS
Suppose that April and Bob are happily selling ice cream on the beach, standing side by side, with April getting all of the customers to the left and Bob getting all of those to the right. They will remain there because this is a Nash equilibrium. But now, along comes Caitlin, a third ice cream vendor.

1. Where will she stand?
2. What will happen next? And then?
3. Will this process ever end?
4. Is there a Nash equilibrium?
5. In the 'Rock-Paper-Scissors' game, the best response to Rock is Paper, the best response to Paper is Scissors, and the best response to Scissors is Rock. How is the situation of 'Caitlin-April-Bob-on-the-beach' similar to 'Rock-Paper-Scissors'?

22.7 A MORE REALISTIC MODEL OF ELECTORAL COMPETITION

The median voter model of ice cream sellers on the beach as an illustration of political competition predicts similar party platforms that reflect the median citizen's preferences. This presents a very limited view of the competitive process. Not surprisingly, we see that parties often do not all move toward the centre, or offer identical platforms. For example, two-candidate elections in the US in 2016 and France in 2017 occurred between a nationalist, anti-immigration candidate (Donald Trump and Marine Le Pen) and a candidate who was in favour of global trade and supported tolerance to 'outsiders' (Hillary Clinton and Emmanuel Macron).

Recall that the model of perfect competition among firms that you studied in Unit 8 ignores many of the ways that firms actually compete (for example, advertising, innovation, or lobbying the government for favourable legislation). Similarly, the median voter model leaves a lot out. Four facts will lead us to quite different conclusions from the median voter model:

- *Not everyone votes*: If neither party's platform is attractive to a voter, they may abstain, and in many countries the least well off—those who would benefit from greater public expenditure—are less likely to vote.
- *Winning votes is not the only reason a party or candidate chooses a platform*: It may win financial contributions from citizens, or persuade volunteers to work for the campaign.
- *The leaders of political parties care about other things*: Getting elected isn't the only reason they are in politics.
- *Voters are not evenly distributed*: The political spectrum is not like the beach.

In our beach example from Figure 22.11, we looked at what would happen if the bathers on the furthest left of the beach were not going to buy ice cream under any circumstances (they are like the citizens who do not vote). Then April and Bob would locate in the centre of those who *do* vote, namely at points $A_{n'}$ and $B_{n'}$ to the right of the centre in the figure. If this is the way politics works, then the platforms are similar, but the advantaged voter is now not the median citizen but a voter to the right of centre.

Next, suppose that not all families will buy exactly one ice cream. Some families will buy lots of ice cream, whereas others will buy less. Where would April and Bob stand if bathers wanted to buy lots of ice cream at one end of the beach, but not the other?

Both April and Bob would locate side-by-side as before, but nearer to these ice-cream-loving families. In politics, this means that parties would move their platforms toward voters who could contribute to their election campaign. These contributions could be money, or time spent campaigning. This would lead them to locate further right, if those voters were prepared to make contributions to the party's election funding.

The same would occur if dissatisfied citizens at one end of the political spectrum were more likely to engage in other political activities—demonstrating, or criticizing the party platforms. The desire to attract, or perhaps silence, these 'alienated' voters would be another magnet pulling the platforms of both parties in their direction.

But when these things happen, both parties still have similar platforms. Now suppose there is one more condition. Instead of bathers uniformly spread along our beach, there are few in the centre and most are in two groups. One is on the left, and the other on the right. To make sure as many bathers don't have to walk too far and so are more likely to buy an ice cream, then April and Bob would choose to move away from the centre to be closer to the distant potential buyers on the left or right.

Politics is very different from selling ice cream for another reason. As well as wanting to win elections, party leaders typically do care about the platform. They would be willing to risk losing voters at one end of the political continuum to take a position more in line with their personal values.

The 'bathers on the beach' model, when amended to take account of:

- the problem of voter abstention
- the importance of money and political activities beyond voting
- the fact that voters may not be evenly distributed along the political continuum
- the fact that party leaderships care about the content of their platforms

helps us understand which political platforms will be Nash equilibria in the process of political competition by means of elections.

There is, however, another important difference between elections and ice creams. April and Bob split the market and both survive, one perhaps taking slightly more of the market. In a majoritarian political system, if both parties offer similar platforms, the party that gets just one vote more than the other forms the government. The winner appoints all of the government ministers, for example, not just 51% of them.

Accountability through political and economic competition: Summing up

At the beginning of this unit we considered how a natural monopoly might be run if it were in private or government hands, contrasting two ways that power in the hands of the monopolist or the government official can be made accountable. The key idea is that customers facing a monopoly are not powerless. They have the option to buy less, or even not at all. Citizens facing a government-owned firm similarly have ways of fighting back against inadequate service, by seeking to replace the government in an election.

The models we have studied have clarfied the similarities and differences between the profit-maximizing behaviour of a monopoly firm and the political-rent-maximizing behaviour of a governing elite. These are summarized in Figure 22.12, along with the ways in which each provides some combination of what Albert Hirschman called 'exit' and 'voice' as a way to make power accountable to those affected.

In the table, we represent 'ideal democracy' in the 'government as monopolist model' with a situation where the duration curve is flat (similar to the firm in a perfectly competitive market facing a flat demand curve). This means that any governing elite that sought to skim off any rents at all would be removed from office at the end of the year, just as any firm charging a higher price than the competing firms would lose all of its customers at once, and go out of business.

GREAT ECONOMISTS

Albert O. Hirschman

Albert Hirschman (1915–2012) lived an extraordinary life. Born in Berlin in 1915, he fled to Paris in 1933 after Adolf Hitler won power in Germany, and joined the French Resistance in 1939, helping many artists and intellectuals to escape from the Nazis. He migrated to the US in 1941.

Given this history, it's hardly surprising that Hirschman's career as an economist did not follow a conventional path. He crossed disciplinary boundaries with ease, grappled with questions that lay well outside the professional mainstream, and developed ideas that were imaginative, profound, and enduring.

Among Hirschman's many influential contributions, he is best known for the thesis laid out in his 1970 book *Exit, Voice and Loyalty*. He was concerned with how the performance of entities such as firms and governments could be improved.

He identified two forces—exit and voice—that could serve to alert an organization that it was facing decline and provide incentives for recovery. 'Exit' refers to the departure of a firm's customers to a competitor. And 'voice' refers to protest, the tendency of disappointed customers to 'kick up a fuss'. When a company performs poorly or unethically, shareholders can sell their shares (exit) or campaign for a change of management (voice).

Hirschman observed that economists had traditionally extolled the virtues of exit (competition), while neglecting the operation of voice. They favoured exit-based policies, for example those that made it easier for parents to choose which school their children attended so that schools would have to compete to enroll students.

He considered this an omission, because voice could allow a lapse to be reversed at little cost (parents could usefully seek changes in school policies, in this example), while exit might waste physical capital and human capabilities. Also, exit is not an option in some case, for example tax administration, so the free exercise of voice is critical to good performance.

After making this distinction, Hirschman explored how exit and voice interact. If exit was too readily available, voice would have little time to act. A repairable lapse could end up being fatal to an organization. This effect would be even stronger if those most sensitive to performance decline were also the fastest to exit. As he put it, the 'rapid exit of the highly quality conscious customers … paralyzes voice by depriving it of its principal agents.'

The fact that easy exit undermines voice has some paradoxical implications. A monopolistic firm might welcome a modest amount of competition, allowing it to get rid of its more 'troublesome' customers. A national railway system might perform better if roads were poor, so that

Albert O. Hirschman. 1970. *Exit, voice, and loyalty: Responses to decline in firms, organizations, and states.* Cambridge, MA: Harvard University Press.

angry customers could not easily exit, and would work to improve it instead. And the availability of private school options might result in worse public school performance if the most quality-conscious parents took their children out of the system.

The interplay between exit and voice works through a third factor, which Hirschman called *loyalty*. Attachment to an organization is a psychological barrier to desertion. By slowing exit, loyalty can create the space needed for voice to do its work. But loyalty can hinder performance too if it becomes blind allegiance, because that stifles both exit and voice. Organizations may promote loyalty for precisely this reason. But if they are too effective repressing exit and voice, they would 'deprive themselves of both recuperation mechanisms'.

Hirschman was deeply critical of the claim that, in a two-party system, both parties would adopt similar platforms that reflected the preferences of the median voter. This claim relies on reasoning that accounts for exit and neglects voice. Voters on the extreme fringes of a political party had no viable exit option, Hirschman agreed, but he rejected the implication that such a voter was powerless:

> True, he cannot exit … but just because of that he … will be maximally motivated to bring all sorts of potential influence into play so as to keep … the party from doing things that are highly obnoxious to him … "[T]hose who have nowhere else to go" are not powerless but influential.

Albert Hirschman loved to play with language. English was the fourth language in which he gained fluency (after German, French, and Italian) but he still managed to coin the most wonderful expressions. He invented palindromes (words like 'eve' that read the same backwards as forwards) as a hobby, and presented a collection of these—using the title *Senile Lines* by *Dr. Awkward*—to his daughter Katya as a birthday gift. The right to 'life, liberty and the pursuit of happiness' in the US Declaration of Independence was his inspiration for the memorable phrase 'the happiness of pursuit', by which he meant the joy of engaging in collective action. Hirschman's own playful exercise of voice was itself a demonstration that people often act not simply to *get* something, but also to *be* someone.

For further reading on Albert Hirschman, see these blogs by Rajiv Sethi:

- Rajiv Sethi. 2010. 'The Astonishing Voice of Albert Hirschman' (http://tinyco.re/2899363). Updated April 7 2010.
- Rajiv Sethi. 2011. 'The Self-Subversion of Albert Hirschman' (http://tinyco.re/2163474). Updated April 7 2011.
- Rajiv Sethi. 2013. 'Albert Hirschman and the Happiness of Pursuit' (http://tinyco.re/5203731). 24 Updated March 2013.

EXERCISE 22.7 NASH EQUILIBRIA IN THE MEDIAN VOTER MODEL

Would locating at the middle of the beach still be a Nash equilibrium in the following cases? In each case, explain the political analogy to the ice cream seller example.

1. Suppose people will not walk very far to get their ice cream.
2. Suppose instead of being spread evenly along the beach, there was a concentration of bathers at each end.
3. Suppose the bathers are evenly spread along the beach, but those at the left end of the beach will not walk very far to purchase ice cream, while those at the right end of the beach will surely purchase a cone, no matter what the distance.

QUESTION 22.3 CHOOSE THE CORRECT ANSWER(S)
Consider Figure 22.11 (page 1038). Which of the following statements are true?

☐ When April is positioned at A_0 and Bob is at B_0, April will attract more customers than Bob.
☐ When April is positioned at A_1 and Bob is at B_1, April will attract more customers than Bob.
☐ The Nash equilibrium would change if all of the customers to the far right of the beach moved halfway towards B_n.
☐ Beachgoers that never buy ice cream have no effect on the position of the stalls.

22.8 THE ADVANCE OF DEMOCRACY

Social unrest and universal suffrage

By extending the model of the government as monopolist to include political competition, we have a framework for understanding the emergence of representative institutions and eventually universal suffrage, as described at the beginning of this unit. Governments survived if they provided citizens with essential public services at reasonable tax rates, rather than through palace intrigues or the threat of force.

For example, in the US, the school committee in the textile city of Lowell, Massachusetts advocated an expansion of free public education in its 1846 Annual Report with these words: 'Let then the influence of our Common Schools become universal; for they are … our surest safety against internal commotions.'

Fear of instability that prompted some of the wealthy in the US and elsewhere to advocate greater democracy also helped spread democracy (in Figure 22.13). As you saw in Figure 19.2, inequality grew in the years following the capitalist revolution in the countries for which we have data. During this period, farmers, industrial workers, and the poor demanded greater political equality—and especially the right to vote—as a means of gaining a larger share of the output and wealth of the rapidly growing eco-

Varieties of political and economic competition	Demand/duration curve	Accountability (exit/voice)	Price/tax and cost	Profits/rents	Comment
Limited political competition (dictator)	Steep	None	$T > C$	Political rents > 0	'Govt. as monopolist'
Limited economic competition (monopoly)	Steep	Limited exit	$P > MC$	Economic profits > 0	Unit 7
Ideal democracy (competition among parties)	Flat	Voice and exit	$T = C$	Political rents $= 0$	Section 22.3
'Perfect competition' among firms	Flat	Exit	$P = MC$	Economic profits $= 0$	Units 8 & 11

Figure 22.12 Comparison between models of monopolistic and competitive firms and governments. Notation: T = total taxes raised in a year; C = cost of providing the public good for a year; P = price of the good; MC = marginal cost of the good.

nomies. In 1848 there were attempted revolutions against the monarchy in Sicily, France, Germany, Italy, and the Austrian Empire. At the same time, Karl Marx was writing *The Communist Manifesto*. One of the revolutionary leaders, James Bronterre O'Brien, told the people:

> Knaves will tell you that it is because you have no property, you are unrepresented. I tell you on the contrary, it is because you are unrepresented that you have no property …

Alfred Plummer. 1971. *Bronterre: A Political Biography of Bronterre O'Brien, 1804–1864.* Toronto: University of Toronto Press.

Gaining political power according to O'Brien was the route to gaining a larger slice of the economic pie, not the other way around.

In the late nineteenth and early twentieth century the wealthy in many countries concluded that extending democracy might be prudent, much as the leaders of the South African government were to conclude a century later.

Figure 22.13 shows that democracy, as defined by all three of the characteristics (rule of law, civil liberties, and inclusive fair elections), is a recent arrival in human history.

The first democratic nation was New Zealand, which became fully democratic just before the turn of the twentieth century, although it remained a British colony until 1907. At that time elections were held in many countries but women, those without property, or other disadvantaged groups were denied the right to vote.

South Africa, Mexico and some of the countries once ruled by the Communist Party (Poland, for example) are relatively recent additions to the club of democratic nations. Switzerland is also a recent addition. By the time that Swiss women finally won the right to vote in 1971, the prime ministers of Sri Lanka, India, and Israel were all women. Universal male suffrage in Switzerland had been granted 90 years earlier. If universal male suffrage were considered sufficient for an 'inclusive' election, then Switzerland and France (1848) would have been the first democracies, but

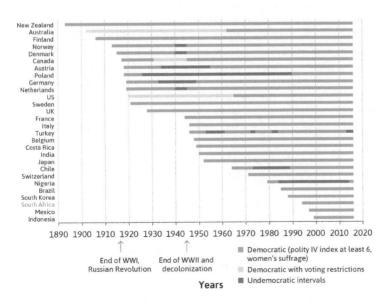

Center for Systemic Peace. 2016. Polity IV annual time series ; Inter-parliamentary union. 2016. 'Women's Suffrage'. Initial periods of democracy of less than five years are not shown in the chart.

Figure 22.13 The advance of democracy in the world.

the exclusion of major population groups means that elections are not inclusive, and so they fail our test.

Excluding women from voting makes a difference in the policies that elected governemnts adopt. The feature in the next section, 'Women's suffrage and the reduction in child mortality in the US', shows that excluding women from the vote had significant effects on government policies, and also on the wellbeing of citizens.

The US enfranchised women in 1920 but had denied the vote to black people in many states before 1965. We indicate the complicated status of the US using a light green bar. We have done the same for Australia, where indigenous Australians were denied the right to vote before 1962, and for Canada, which restricted the voting rights of Native Americans for a brief period.

The world's most populous democracy (by far) is India, since it gained independence from the UK in 1947. The most populous country that is not a democracy is (also by far) China.

Notice in the figure the two waves of countries that became democratic. The first wave occurred at the time of the First World War and the Russian Revolution, which tripled the number of democracies in the world in less than 10 years. The First World War provided much of the impetus for the spread of democracy during this first wave.

If you look at the figure, you will see that the US was not democratic at this time, because the right to vote was restricted to men. The other winning countries in the First World War (France and the UK) were not democracies either at the time. In both countries, women and those without property were denied the right to vote.

A second wave of democracies emerged after the Second World War. Many former colonies, including India and Indonesia, became democratic at this time.

The extension of suffrage in the early years of the twentieth century made many countries in northern Europe and New Zealand into democracies. In those countries, the rule of law and civil liberties—the other two criteria for a democratic political system—had been in force long before the introduction of universal suffrage.

After the Second World War, most countries had already granted the right to vote to virtually all adults (though in Saudi Arabia, for example, women gained voting rights only in 2015). Today, countries judged to be undemocratic (such as Russia) often do not fail our test because of restrictions on the electorate. They are not democracies because the rule of law and civil liberties are inadequate.

The blue patches in the bars show that there have been some interruptions in democracy, including the period of dictatorship in Chile following the military overthrow of the democratic government, and the period of Fascist rule in Germany between 1933 and 1945, but most countries that have become democratic have continued to be democracies.

All the countries in the figure can be decribed as democratic because they are sufficiently close to the criteria we have laid out. But in some cases, there is a large difference between our three criteria of rule of law, civil liberties, and inclusive fair elections, and how the system functions in practice. In the US for example:

- In 2000 and 2016, the winner of the presidential election received fewer votes than his opponent.

- Private contributions from wealthy individuals and groups play a major part in the financing of political campaigns (see the feature 'Does money talk?' in Section 22.14 to see how this may undermine the democratic value of political equality).

As we have seen, before the twentieth century a major activity of governments was defence (in some cases, predation on other nations), and raising the taxation to support it. But well before that time, some ruling institutions came to understand that they would benefit from providing conditions for the growth of the economy—building canals, roads and schools in the nineteenth century, for example. Economic development could be an asset either by creating a larger tax base, a more scientifically oriented cadre of citizens, or by building financial institutions that could loan money to the government.

During the twentieth century large-scale production in firms was easy for the govenment to see, and happened in one place. This made taxation and regulation of firms easier, and governments could also use the accounting books and payroll records of firms to find out who was paid what. This meant that taxing individuals became easier too. Governments in many countries deducted tax directly from the pay of their citizens, and many workers were taxed explicitly for 'social security', that is, to fund pensions and sometimes healthcare.

Changes in the structure of the economy also made it easier for governments to levy taxes, not on a specific good such salt or imports, but on consumption in general and ultimately on value added in production. These broad-based taxes play an important role in the public finances of advanced economies. With the extension of voting rights to virtually all adults, governments became accountable to their citizens for delivering services.

This historical processes of transition from political monopoly to political competition have produced most of the modern governments in the world, with their distinctive patterns of spending.

Figure 22.14 shows how the democratic governments of the US, South Korea, and Finland spend their money.

The size of the government of Finland's expenditure is 57.5% of its GDP, which is the largest among the three countries. For the US, it is 38.8%. Note: this does not mean that the US spends less than Finland in absolute terms, just that government expenditure is a smaller fraction of the country's GDP. Expenditure by South Korea's government is 31.8% of its GDP.

This is what the categories mean:

- *Public services*: These include funds for running parliament, congress, local councils, also foreign aid and public debt transactions.
- *Military*: As previously stated, one of the motivations for government has been for protection or to wage war.
- *Economic affairs*: This includes expenditures on infrastructure such as roads, bridges, and the Internet.
- *Public order and safety*: This includes police, fire, prison services, and law courts.
- *Social protection*: We discussed the **social insurance** spending that a government might make in Unit 19, and those are labelled 'Social protection' in the figure.

SPENDING PRIORITIES IN A DEMOCRACY

Joseph Schumpeter (see Section 2.5) once wrote that the public budget is the 'skeleton of the state stripped of all misleading ideologies'. He argued that the way in which a government spends its money reveals its true priorities, much in the way that an individual's spending pattern is a lens through which to study his or her preferences.

Joseph Schumpeter. 1918. 'The crisis of the tax state.' Reproduced in Swedberg R. (ed.) 1991. *Joseph A. Schumpeter, The Economics and Sociology of Capitalism*. Princeton University Press.

The 2010 *Mirrlees Review* (http://tinyco.re/6726989) offered proposals for a comprehensive reform of the UK's tax and transfer system, addressing the scope for better addressing market failures and unfairness.

social insurance Expenditure by the government, financed by taxation, which provides protection against various economic risks (for example, loss of income due to sickness, or unemployment) and enables people to smooth incomes throughout their lifetime. *See also: co-insurance*.

- *Schooling*: All governments are responsible for at least some education provision.
- *Health*: This includes medical equipment, hospital and outpatient services, and public health.

There are many reasons why governments differ in their spending patterns. One reason is that political institutions differ, even among democracies.

EXERCISE 22.8 PAST INFLUENCES ON CURRENT GOVERNMENT SPENDING PATTERNS

1. How would you characterize the two biggest differences in the pattern of spending between the three pairs of countries (the US vs South Korea, the US vs Finland, and Finland vs South Korea)?
2. Can you think of differences in the countries and their histories that might account for these differences? You will need to do some research to support your claims.

OECD. 2015. 'Government at a Glance'. This dataset takes data from OECD National Accounts Statistics and from Eurostat government finance statistics.

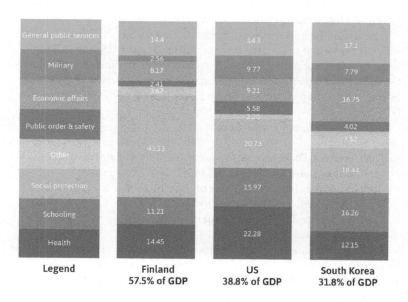

Figure 22.14 Patterns of public expenditure in Finland, the US, and South Korea (2013).

EXERCISE 22.9 COMPARING GOVERNMENT EXPENDITURES

Go to the source of Figure 22.14, OECD statistics (http://tinyco.re/2331814), and see if you can find different countries for each of the following criteria (for the year 2015, or the most recent year available).

1. General government expenditure (as a percentage of GDP) is greater than South Korea's, but less than Finland's.
2. Government expenditure on health (as a percentage of GDP) is greater than the US's.
3. Government expenditure on social protection (as a percentage of GDP) is greater than Finland's.
4. Government expenditure on defence (as a percentage of GDP) is greater than South Korea's.

22.9 VARIETIES OF DEMOCRACY

In Unit 1, we defined capitalism as an economic system and pointed to the important differences among capitalist economies, in terms of the extent of government involvement and the degree of inequality in the economy. Democracy as a set of political institutions (a political system) comes in many varieties, too.

Accountability and transfers of power

The conditions under which one government leaves office and is replaced by another illustrate the varieties of democracy. There are two principles that are essential to democratic government:

- *Democratic accountability*: A governing party that is not serving the interests of a majority of its citizens will lose an election and must leave office. **Democratic accountability** ensures that citizens, through their right to vote, can remove government that they think is performing poorly and replace it with one more to their liking.
- *No non-electoral transfer of power*: Removal from office is (with rare exceptions) the result of losing an election rather than a military coup, assassination, breakdown of social order, or impasse in the process of government.

democratic accountability Political accountability by means of elections and other democratic processes. *See also: accountability, political accountability.*

You have already seen these two principles in the model of the government presented earlier in this unit. In the model, democratic accountability was represented by a flatter duration curve, as there was a greater likelihood that the government would be dismissed if it were collecting large political rents.

Countries differ considerably along these two dimensions (Figure 22.15). Many conform closely to both. Some barely conform to either and their status as a democracy is contested.

- *Singapore*: An example of extraordinary political stability where the likelihood of transfer of power by any means other than an election appears very small. Yet in more than 50 years there has not been a single electoral transfer of power. The same political party has ruled over the city-state since 1959. This remarkable political durability is undoubtedly in part due to the fact that living standards in Singapore have increased rapidly. But if citizens were to seek a transfer of power to a different party, the lack of press freedom, and other undemocratic practices of the ruling party, would make it difficult to do so.

- *Italy*: Without question a democratic nation, Italy struggles to meet the second principle. Governments that disappoint voters are regularly replaced. But governments are also replaced as a result of parliamentary disputes and the intervention of the president, who can dissolve the parliament.

- *Pakistan*: An example of a country in which democracy is not strong in either dimension. The governments of Pakistan have been notoriously unresponsive to the concerns of the electorate, and non-electoral transfers of power in Pakistan have included three successful military takeovers.

		Democratic accountability	
		Strong	Weak
Transfers of power	By elections only	Germany	Singapore
	Also by non-electoral means	Italy	Pakistan

Figure 22.15 Democratic accountability and transfers of power.

EXERCISE 22.10 HOW DEMOCRACY HELPS PROTECT THE GOVERNED

In 1943 there was a famine in West Bengal, India, while the country was under colonial rule from the UK. At least 2 million people died as a result. Amartya Sen, an economist who won the Nobel Prize, said that: 'No famine has taken place in the history of the world in a functioning democracy.'

1. What defining features of a democracy might account for this?

2. How would colonial rule by a foreign power differ from democracy?

3. How might these differences help explain why the 1943 famine occurred, and why no famine has occurred since the transition from colonial to democratic rule?

4. Read this article (http://tinyco.re/2624341), and re-read the introduction to Unit 2 about the Irish famine. Explain how economic thinking at the time may have contributed to the limited response of the British colonial government to famine during that period.

22.10 DEMOCRACY MAKES A DIFFERENCE

Our model of the government also allows us to understand the impact of one of the major developments in twentieth-century economics and politics: the extension of voting rights to virtually all adults. In consequence, governments have increasingly devoted tax revenues to public services and other expenditures that differentially helped the poor. As we saw in Unit 19, the result has been that people have acquired more of their wellbeing by right, as a citizen, rather than purchasing it as a marketed good or service.

The growth of various forms of social insurance is a big part of the two steps up in the size of the government that you saw in the UK in Figure 22.2, the first taking place after the extension of the suffrage in 1928, and the second in the aftermath of the Second World War.

Friedrich Hayek (page 457) warned in his book *Road to Serfdom* that the growing size of government would undermine democracy and the rule of law, pointing to the experience of Germany under fascism and Russia under communism. This does not appear to be the case in general: the countries ranked highest on measures of rule of law—Norway, Finland, Sweden, Denmark, and the Netherlands—all are notable for their high levels of government tax revenues as a fraction of GDP. The US and the UK, with a smaller government, are ranked lower.

But this correlation does not show that a larger government promotes the rule of law and democracy. The most that can be said is that longstanding democracy, rule of law, and a large government (relative to the size of the economy) can coexist.

Friedrich A. Hayek. 1994. *The Road to Serfdom*. Chicago: University of Chicago Press. A condensed version is also available (http://tinyco.re/6168556).

Daniel Kaufmann, Aart Kraay, Massimo Mastruzzi. 2011. 'The worldwide governance indicators: methodology and analytical issues'. *Hague Journal on the Rule of Law* 3 (2): pp. 220–246.

Freedom House. 2016. 'Freedom in the World 2016. Anxious Dictators, Wavering Democracies: Global Freedom under Pressure'. Washington, DC.

HOW ECONOMISTS LEARN FROM FACTS

Women's suffrage and the reduction in child mortality in the US

Recall James Bronterre O'Brien who, when campaigning against property ownership as a requirement for voting in nineteenth century Britain, wrote: 'Because you are unrepresented … you have no property'.

But does getting the right to vote increase the wealth and wellbeing of groups previously excluded from voting?

This is not a simple question to answer. Consider South Africa. Throughout its history prior to 1994, people of non-European origin were denied the right to vote, but they were also discriminated against by employers, landlords, schools, and medical institutions. Were the racial disparities in wealth, health, and other dimensions of wellbeing in that country a result of race restrictions on democratic political rights?

In behavioural experiments and in other evidence, women on average place a higher value on child welfare and public services. In that case, we would expect that public policy would change when women got the vote.

A natural experiment to assess the importance of voting rights is women's suffrage in the US, because voting laws differ by state. As a result, women gained the right to vote at different times, starting from 1869 in Wyoming. In 1920, an amendment to the US Constitution granted the vote to women in all states. Grant Miller used information on when women got the right to vote to do a before-after comparison on actions taken by elected officials, public expenditures related to child health, and health outcomes for children.

Miller chose to focus on child healthcare policies because women had campaigned to expand health services for children, and it is reasonable

Grant Miller. 2008. 'Women's suffrage, political responsiveness, and child survival in American history'. *The Quarterly Journal of Economics* 123 (3): pp. 1287–1327.

to say that women's preferences differed from men's on these issues. But during the nineteenth century and before, those justifying voting restrictions claimed that women had a kind of 'virtual representation' through their husbands or fathers. Even the household servants of the rich were said to be virtually represented by their employers.

The logic of the natural experiment is shown below, with each of the arrows representing possible causes that Miller explored:

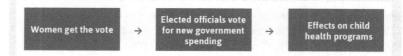

Here is what Miller found:

- Looking state-by-state at the date women got the right to vote, enfranchisement had no apparent effects on state public spending in other areas, but it boosted social service spending by 24%. At the federal government level, within a year of the passage of the Nineteenth Amendment, the US Congress voted a substantial increase in public health spending, especially aimed at children. A historian of the legislation concluded that 'the principal force moving Congress was fear of being punished at the polls ... by women voters.'
- The deaths of children under the age of nine fell by somewhere between 8% and 15%, primarily as a result of drops in the kinds of diseases related to the public programs that had been adopted, especially large-scale door-to-door hygiene campaigns. To put these numbers in perspective, in 1900 one in five children did not live to the age of five. The passage of healthcare programs prevented an estimated 20,000 child deaths per year.

These effects were possible because of the nineteenth-century revolution in scientific knowledge of bacteria and disease, advances that had yet to be brought to the public in improved health. Women's suffrage helped to do this.

Miller's research shows that a big change in public policy resulted when women in the US were directly represented. This is why for Switzerland, where men got the right to vote earlier than any other nation, we nonetheless dated democracy from 1971, the time that women got the vote (Figure 22.10), because who can vote matters.

Adam Przeworski and Fernando Limongi. 1993. 'Political regimes and economic growth'. *The Journal of Economic Perspectives* 7 (3) pp. 51–69.

Other than an increase in the size of government, are there other effects of the advance of democracy on the functioning of the economy? The experience of many countries suggests a positive answer. For example, the golden age of capitalism (the three decades following the Second World War) was the first period in which all of the major economies were governed by democracies.

While it seems reasonable that democracy was partly behind these success stories, for example through greater political stability, it is impossible to establish democracy as the only or main cause. Too many other things changed at the same time that might account for the economic changes.

The countries that took the lead in advancing political equality have a different balance now between work time and free time, as Figure 22.16 shows. This is not surprising, given that the reduction in working hours over the past 100 years was not simply a matter of individuals choosing shorter workdays. As we saw in Unit 3, it was also the result of political parties (especially after the extension of the vote to workers) seeking legislation to limit the number of hours a person could be asked to work without additional pay.

But the countries with the fewest work hours in 2014 and the highest number of years of democracy (Denmark, Sweden, and the Netherlands) had *longer* work hours at the time they became democracies than the average of other countries for which we have data. This is evidence to support the case that democracy had an effect on work hours.

Figure 22.17 shows that countries that were the first to give the vote to all—Finland, Norway, Sweden, Denmark, and the Netherlands—today have more equal disposable incomes than countries with a shorter experience of this kind of political equality. In many cases, reduced inequality in disposable income was the result of government programs that benefited poorer voters (women and workers, for example) who had previously been excluded from voting (as we have seen in Figures 19.1 and 5.16).

Penn World Tables.

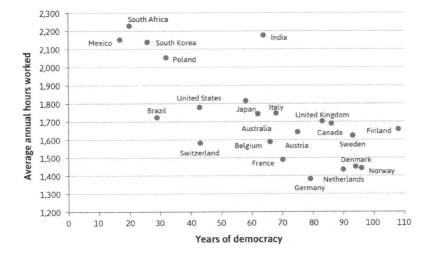

Figure 22.16 The duration of democracy and working hours (2014).

Cross National Data Center. LIS Database. Household market (labour and capital) income and disposable income are equivalized and top- and bottom-coded.

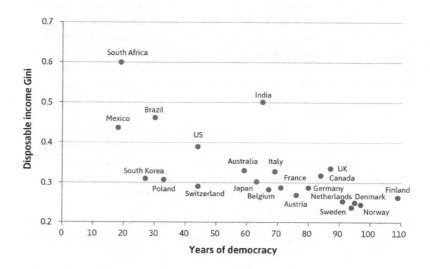

Figure 22.17 The duration of democracy and inequality in disposable income (2015).

EXERCISE 22.11 WORK TIMES AND INEQUALITY IN LESS DEMOCRATIC DEMOCRACIES

1. Redraw Figure 22.16 and 22.17 using a different definition of democracy, over the same period as in Figure 22.13 (1890–2015). For example, allow a country to be 'democratic' even if women and some ethnic minorities were excluded from voting (you already know that this will affect the duration of democracy of Australia, US, Canada, Switzerland, and France). You can download the Polity IV dataset (http://tinyco.re/3970843) that was used to create Figure 22.13, and consider a polity score of 6 or above as democratic. The data on working hours and inequality are shown below.

Country	Average hours worked (2014)	Disposable income Gini
Australia	1,803	0.330
Denmark	1,438	0.247
Germany	1,371	0.287
Netherlands	1,420	0.254
US	1,765	0.390
Sweden	1,609	0.236
UK	1,675	0.335
France	1,474	0.288

Country	Average hours worked (2014)	Disposable income Gini
Italy	1,734	0.327
Belgium	1,575	0.282
Canada	1,688	0.317
Switzerland	1,568	0.291
Finland	1,643	0.262
Norway	1,427	0.244
Austria	1,629	0.268
Brazil	1,711	0.462
South Korea	2,124	0.310
India	2,162	0.502
Japan	1,729	0.302
Poland	2,039	0.307
South Africa	2,215	0.605
Mexico	2,137	0.437

2. Would you reach a different conclusion about how democracy is statistically related to the following, under this alternative, less strict, definition of democracy?
   (a) work time
   (b) inequality

22.11 A PUZZLE: THE PERSISTENCE OF UNFAIRNESS AND MARKET FAILURES IN DEMOCRACIES

Contemporary South Africa is just one example of a society in which there are opportunities for mutual gain that are not exploited—for example, More than one-quarter of the labour force are unemployed. And it is widely held—even by many well-off South Africans—that the distribution of the economy's burdens and benefits is still grossly unfair.

The previous units have shown similar cases in which economic outcomes are Pareto inefficient, so potential mutual gains remain unrealized, as the summary table in Figure 12.8 (page 524) showed. Figure 22.3 (page 1018) listed policies aimed at addressing inefficiency and perceived unfairness. And we know that citizens in many countries think the distribution of wealth or income is unfair.

This is a puzzle. If government action could realize potential gains, and the citizens in a democracy would prefer that it did, why do these inefficiencies persist in a democratic society with a capitalist economy? The short answer is that just as markets fail, so too do governments.

Government failure

Fixing some problem of Pareto inefficiency or perceived unfairness will happen only if:

- *It is economically feasible*: The policy to fix the problem, if implemented, must work.
- *It is administratively feasible*: The government must have the capacity to implement the policy.
- *Special interests allow it*: Those who control government policy must want to see the policy implemented.

Economic infeasibility

Given people's preferences and the information available to private economic actors, there may not be a feasible set of policies that would sustain an efficient and fair outcome. For a policy to have **economic feasibility**, it must be a Nash equilibrium, which means no actor can improve its position by changing its behaviour.

For example, a government that tried to enforce perfect competition in every industry would fail. Since firms are free to advertise, and to differentiate their products, it is impossible for the policymaker to legislate that demand curves be horizontal. We have also seen that no macroeconomic policy can entirely eliminate unemployment, given that the threat of unemployment motivates people to work hard and well.

Administrative infeasibility

Even if there is an economically feasible policy that would address a problem if it were adopted and implemented, this may be impossible in practice due to the limited information and capabilities of government officials, which means it lacks **administrative feasibility**. By failing to understand the incentives of the relevant economic actors or other aspects of the problem, policies adopted by the government may be ill-suited to the objectives of all the actors. So governments may lack the capacity to collect tax revenue efficiently and honestly, to enforce its policies through the judiciary (including anti-monopoly policy), and to deliver public services such as schooling and health.

economically feasible Policies for which the desired outcomes are a Nash equilibrium, so that once implemented private economic actors will not undo the desired effects.

administratively feasible Policies for which the government has sufficient information and staff for implementation.

1055

Special interests

Even if a policy is economically feasible (a Nash equilibrium) and could be implemented administratively, the government may choose not to adopt it because of opposition by groups (including members of the government itself) that would be harmed by the change, which would be the case if certain groups benefit from the unfairness or the inefficiency.

In the next three sections, we will consider in turn how economic infeasibility, administrative infeasibility, and special interests can prevent fair and efficient policies from being introduced.

22.12 ECONOMIC INFEASIBILITY

Many important economic actions cannot be simply enforced by the government. The government can use its powers of tax collection to provide for schools and order that all children must attend those schools until age 16. But it cannot mandate that students study hard and learn a lot, or that teachers teach effectively.

As we saw in Section 22.1, the government uses regulation and public provision, but can also provide incentives and information that are intended to lead people to act in a way consistent with its objectives. For example, the central bank can lower the interest rate at which it lends to commercial banks, with the intention of inducing them to lend to households and businesses at a lower rate, and, in this way, to stimulate spending. Or the government can impose a tax on fuel to alter the opportunity cost of driving, providing people with their own reasons to drive less.

Two examples of important but 'difficult to command' economic activities are investing and working hard. Governments do not have the information or the legal authority to command wealthy individuals to use their financial resources to invest in infrastructure (other than in exceptional circumstances such as wartime), or workers to work hard and well.

How policies work by shifting the Nash equilibrium

Understanding how private actors respond to public policy is essential when addressing social and economic problems. For example, the government official who imposes a tax on sugary drinks in order to reduce obesity does not control the responses of consumers. An economically feasible outcome of the tax must be based on how consumers respond if it costs more to have another soda drink. The policy needs, for example, to take account of consumers who switch from sugary drinks to other sources of sugar that have not been taxed. Economic research surveyed in Section 7.9 (page 303) gives the policymaker some guidelines about how successful the policy might be in controlling diabetes through its effect on relative prices.

To be economically feasible, the intended outcome of the policy must be a Nash equilibrium, that is, all individuals affected are doing the best they can do, given how all other actors are acting in response to the policy. Many of the models economists use include the ***ceteris paribus*** condition, which means other things being equal. But as economists like to point out, in many important applications of economic theory, '*ceteris* ain't *paribus*'. All other things aren't ever equal before and after the policy is implemented. Checking whether a policy is economically feasible means relaxing the *ceteris paribus* condition to consider the full set of strategies available to actors under the new circumstances.

To understand the ways that economic feasibility constrains policymakers, consider the case of the proposal to introduce an unemployment

ceteris paribus Economists often simplify analysis by setting aside things that are thought to be of less importance to the question of interest. The literal meaning of the expression is 'other things equal'. In an economic model it means an analysis 'holds other things constant'.

benefit financed by a tax on profits. The aim of the policy is to improve the standard of living of the unemployed without increasing the unemployment rate.

Unintended consequences

We begin by identifying the Nash equilibrium in the initial situation before the policy is introduced. In Figure 22.18a, the economy is at the point marked N, where the wage- and price-setting curves intersect. As we confirmed in Unit 9 (Section 9.6), this is a Nash equilibrium because neither a worker (employed or unemployed) nor a firm could be better off by setting a different wage or price, offering to work at a different wage, or hiring a different number of workers.

First, we look at the short-run impact of the policy using Figure 22.18a.

- *Initial situation:* The Nash equilibrium is at point N.
- *Voters demand a new policy:* The workers—employed and unemployed— vote to elect a government that wishes to introduce an unemployment benefit that workers will receive when out of work, financed by a tax on profits.
- *Short-run impact:* This raises the reservation option of employed workers, shifting up the wage-setting curve, so that employers now have to pay more to induce workers to work hard and well. This is shown by point C.

The policy has its intended effect: the unemployed receive a higher income, and employed workers' wages have risen too, seemingly an unexpected feature of the policy. However, this unintended effect, raising wages, takes the economy away from its initial Nash Equilibrium. We will see how the long-run effects can differ from the short-run effects.

Using the analysis in Figure 22.18a, follow through the logic of the model as the actors respond to the policy.

What is the long-run impact of the policy? In the labour market diagram, we see that there is:

- *A new Nash equilibrium:* The unemployment benefit has shifted the wage-setting curve upwards. In the short-term, the labour market shifts to point C. But the tax which finances the more generous benefits has shifted the price-setting curve downwards, so in order to ensure the required profit margin for firms, the real wage must be lower.
- *Firms reduce employment, or shut down:* Some firms paying the new higher wage will be making insufficient profits to motivate further investment and so they will cut back employment; other firms will fail or move pro- duction to other countries.
- *Long-run impact:* These changes will push the economy towards point N', where (as intended) the unemployed will now receive higher income when out of work, but fewer workers are employed and the employed workers receive a lower wage.

The policy objective—raise the living standards of the unemployed without increasing unemployment—was economically infeasible.

Yet we have seen in Unit 16, Figure 16.16 (page 728) that countries with more generous unemployment benefits do not necessarily have higher unemployment rates. This suggests that these countries were able to achieve a Nash equilibrium outcome different from either N or N'. Figure 22.18b shows how this may have happened—there is a third Nash equilibrium at N″ where a new higher price-setting curve intersects the post reform wage-setting curve.

The Swedish approach had its origins in the 'solidarity wage policy', devised in 1951 by Gösta Rehn and Rudolph Meidner, two economists who worked at the research institute of the Trade Union Confederation in Sweden.

They reasoned that workers and employers have a common interest in rapid productivity growth, and that workers could enjoy higher wages without the profits of firms being reduced if more of the economy's output was produced by high-productivity firms rather than in firms with low productivity.

The solidarity wage policy in Sweden was actually three linked policies:

- *Equal wages for equal work*: This means that the wage for each job was set at the national level by negotiations between the employers' association and the union. This had the effect of compressing wage differences among workers doing similar jobs. The lowest-productivity firms had survived by paying lower wages to equivalent workers than other firms paid. Under the new policy, they could not pay the negotiated wage and still remain profitable, and so had to exit the industry. Higher-productivity firms survived and took over the market share of the failed firms.

In our 'Economist in action' video, John van Reenen uses the game of cricket to explain how the economy's average productivity is affected by the survival of low productivity firms. http://tinyco.re/4455896

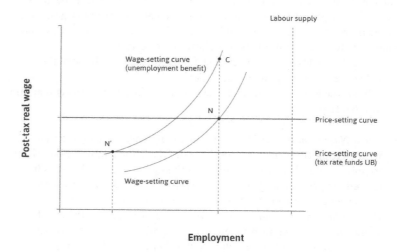

Figure 22.18a Introducing an unemployment benefit: Short- and long-run effects.

1. The status quo
The Nash equilibrium is at point N. The new government introduces an unemployment benefit that workers will receive when out of work, financed by a tax on profits.

2. The unintended consequence
This raises the reservation option of employed workers, so that employers now have to pay more to induce workers to work hard and well. This is shown by point C.

3. The result
The tax on profits shifts the price-setting curve downwards. The new Nash equilibrium is at N', with higher unemployment and a lower real wage.

- *Unemployment benefits*: These were generous but time-limited. See Unit 16 for more detail on how this policy works.
- *Active labour market policy*: Retaining and mobility allowances to displaced workers, for example, aimed to improve matching them with vacancies. It protected workers rather than jobs. Again, you can find more detail on this type of policy in Unit 16.

The tax-financed increase in unemployment benefits alone would likely have pushed the price-setting curve downwards, as in the example above. But the solidarity wage policy also forced low-productivity firms out of the market. The remaining firms had higher productivity and could therefore maintain their profit margins at lower prices, pushing the price-setting curve upwards. Retraining and mobility allowances ensured that these high-productivity firms had access to a well-trained workforce, allowing them to cut costs and prices even further. Figure 22.18b shows how this combination of policies resulted in a new equilibrium with higher real wages at N″, and without the rise in unemployment at N′.

This is an example of how a democratic political environment with large nationally oriented trade unions and a responsive government could sustain low levels of inequality (shown in Figure 22.17), while raising average living standards.

Economic feasibility: An example from Chile

The previous analysis using the labour market model is a simplification. But it helps us understand real economic forces operating in the world. Chile is one example.

In 1970, the socialist Salvador Allende was elected president of Chile in a surprise victory, on a platform promising greater public services and nationalization of many of the privately held firms in the country.

The reaction of the wealthy is seen in the stock market prices, shown in Figure 22.19. A stock (or share) is a share in the ownership of a company,

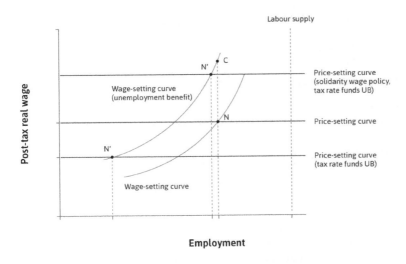

Figure 22.18b Combining the introduction of an unemployment benefit with a solidarity wage policy.

and its price (as you know from Unit 11) measures how much it is worth to own part of that company and as a result receive a share of its profits, and benefit in the future from selling it to another person.

Share prices rise when, taking everything into account, owners or potential buyers of shares think that the company will be more profitable in the future. When a socialist president was elected in Chile, wealthy people were worried about higher taxes, policies favouring their employees that would mean paying them higher wages, and the possibility that the government or even workers might expropriate (take over the ownership of) the firm's assets.

These worries created a limit to the policies that would prove economically feasible for the Allende government. If the wealthy thought that the firms they owned would be less profitable in the future, they would have no incentive to invest in increasing the assets of the firm. Rather than invest in these firms, the wealthy might then invest in another country (known as capital flight), in housing, or in other Chilean assets more likely to be valuable in the future.

As you can see from Figure 22.19, stock prices plummeted straight after Allende's election day. We will pick up the Chile story a bit later, seeing that political interests as well as economic infeasibility can limit what a democratically elected government can do.

Proprietary data from the Santiago stock market. Time zero is the first trading day on the Santiago stock market following the election. Daniele Girardi and Samuel Bowles. 2017. 'Institutional Shocks and Economic Outcomes: Allende's Election, Pinochet's Coup and the Santiago Stock Market'. Santa Fe Institute working paper.

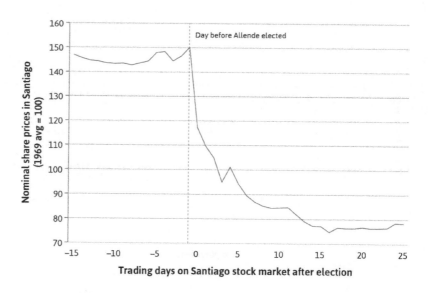

Figure 22.19 Stock market prices in Chile: The election of a socialist president, 1970.

EXERCISE 22.12 ECONOMIES SUCCEED WHEN NATIONAL POLICIES ALIGN WITH INDIVIDUAL IMPULSES

In 1759, Adam Smith wrote in *The Theory of Moral Sentiments*:

> The man ... enamored of his own ideal plan of government, ... seems to imagine that he can arrange the different members of a great society with as much ease as the hand arranges the different pieces upon a chess-board. ... but in the great chess-board of human society, every single piece has a principle of motion of its own, altogether different from that which the legislature might choose to impress upon it. If those two principles coincide and act in the same direction, the game of human society will go on easily and harmoniously, and is very likely to be happy and successful. If they are opposite or different, the game will go on miserably, and the society must be at all times in the highest degree of discord.

1. In your own words, explain Smith's idea of the economic feasibility of government policies.
2. Using what you have learned about the constraints faced by the Central Bank as a policymaker, give an example that illustrates Smith's point.

QUESTION 22.4 CHOOSE THE CORRECT ANSWER(S)

Look again at Figure 22.18a (page 1058). Which of the following statements are true?

☐ The upward shift in the wage-setting curve would have caused real wages to increase if taxes on firms had not also been increased.
☐ Policies that shift the wage-setting curve without also changing the price-setting curve cannot increase real wages in equilibrium.
☐ The long-run impact of financing an increase in unemployment benefit by a tax on profits is the opposite of the short-run impact.
☐ Increasing unemployment benefits made all workers worse off.

22.13 ADMINISTRATIVE INFEASIBILITY

Limited information

Remember that many market failures arise because of **asymmetric information**—the lender does not know how the borrower will use the funds, the employer does not know how hard the employee will work, the insurance company does not know if the person purchasing life insurance is terminally ill, and so on. The limited information available to the principal in these three cases (the lender, the employer, the insurer) made it impossible for them to write a complete contract with the agent (the borrower, the employee, the insured). A complete contract would have 'internalized' the external effects that are the source of the market failure, ensuring that the agent bore all of the costs and enjoyed all of the benefits of his or her actions.

The same is true of environmental market failures. If the citizen suffering from a respiratory illness could bring a lawsuit against the polluting firm that caused it, and secure compensation for the costs of his illness, then this might 'internalize' the external costs of the polluter's

asymmetric information Information that is relevant to the parties in an economic interaction, but is known by some but not by others. *See also: adverse selection, moral hazard.*

actions, leading to more effective abatement efforts. But in most cases, this cannot be done because the citizen does not have the necessary information about who is polluting, and also would not be able to pay the legal and other expenses of pursuing the case.

But this information is not available to the government either, limiting its ability to design policies that address environmental market failures. As we saw in Unit 20, governments often do not know how much citizens value environmental quality, or how effective environmental policies will be in ensuring a sustainable environment. As we also saw, it's hard for the government to find out this information.

Limited information is not the only factor limiting the administrative feasibility of policies.

Limited capacities

Taxes, as we have seen, can change the way that private actors behave. For example, imposing a tax that raises the price of fuel reduces car journeys and the associated environmental damages. But, to levy taxes effectively and collect the revenue, governments need revenue officers who are competent, not corrupt, with sufficient resources to find and punish tax evaders, and with enough legitimacy that most people pay their taxes. Where this is not the case, sellers would continue selling fuel at a lower price, driving their law-abiding competitors out of business.

Administrative capacity is required for many different kinds of taxes, from trade tariffs enforced at the border, to payroll taxes levied on wages, and to corporate income taxes charged on legally incorporated economic entities. The use of accounting books in large firms makes it easier to audit firms and accurately assess their tax bill. But this also depends on the technology and institutions available. International flows of difficult-to-track financial obligations makes illegal tax evasion, and legal tax avoidance (for example by moving profits to international tax havens), a problem for governments who want to collect tax. This lowers their **fiscal capacity**.

Lack of administrative capacity affects all aspects of government, not just taxes. An educational reform, for example, requiring teachers to abandon rote learning methods and engage in more active student-centered learning may simply be impossible to implement given the skills of the current teaching force.

Administrative infeasibility: An application from Nigeria

A lack of information about the progress of infrastructure projects funded by the government, and a poorly functioning and corrupt administration, resulted in poor outcomes in Nigeria.

In 2006–07, the public sector was given funding and made responsible for implementing 4,700 small-scale infrastructure projects like installing water wells, constructing dams, and building health centres. Just 31% of the projects were completed and 38% were not even started. For example, the funding was paid for 1,348 water wells, but 846 were never completed, leaving hundreds of thousands of people without improved access to water.

Economists Imran Rasul and Daniel Rogger wanted to find out why some organizations succeeded in completing projects on schedule and budget and others did not. They were able to do their research because the Nigerian government had collected information from independent teams of engineers about the quantity and quality of completed projects. Accurate

fiscal capacity The ability of a government to impose and collect substantial taxes from a population at low administrative and other costs. One measure of this is the amount collected divided by the cost of administering the tax system.

Timothy Besley and Torsten Persson. 2014. 'Why do developing countries tax so little?'. *The Journal of Economic Perspectives* 28 (4): pp. 99–120.

Imran Rasul and Daniel Rogger. 2016. 'Management of bureaucrats and public service delivery: Evidence from the Nigerian civil service.' *The Economic Journal*.

information of this kind from independent observers on the quantity and quality of public services is very rare for a low-income country.

Rasul and Rogger found that 'getting things done' by public sector organizations is affected by how the organizations are managed. They were surprised to discover that using performance incentives, with which managers were rewarded for good performance as measured by the organization (not by independent assessors), was correlated with lower completion rates. In organizations where officials had greater autonomy in making decisions—not in response to performance incentives—outcomes were better.

While financial incentives can play a positive role in motivating government officials, the Nigerian case shows that, if it is difficult to collect and verify information, trying to attach simple performance incentives to complex tasks may backfire. If there is poor information, then it may be better to give organizations greater autonomy. In this case, officials given automony observed social norms of responsibility, and completion rates were higher.

22.14 SPECIAL INTERESTS

In a democracy, it is often said that ideally the government is the servant of the people. In economic terms, government officials are the agents and the citizens are the principals.

But this immediately raises two questions:

- *Why would the agent (the elected official) do what the principals (the citizens) desire?* As in any **principal-agent relationship** the agent has his or her own objectives, and they differ from the principal's objectives. Our model of the government as a monopolist illustrated how the government need not serve the interests of the people in an undemocratic society. We saw that the problem does not disappear in a democracy.
- *Who are 'the people'?* In economic terms, who is (or are) the principal(s)? Until now the principal has been the lender or the employer, which we could simplify by representing as a single individual. But there are many citizen-principals and they have differing priorities for what the government should do, whether the question is abatement of pollution, school improvement, policies to boost innovation, tax-funded transfers to the poor, and so on.

> **principal-agent relationship** This relationship exists when one party (the principal) would like another party (the agent) to act in some way, or have some attribute that is in the interest of the principal, and that cannot be enforced or guaranteed in a binding contract. *See also: incomplete contract. Also known as: principal-agent problem.*

Democratic accountability of elected officials

Think about the first problem—motivating the elected official to do what the citizens prefer—as a principal-agent problem, like the employer trying to motivate a worker to contribute to the profits of the firm. What are the possible solutions when the manager tries to motivate workers? The manager could:

- *Pay the agent an economic rent*: She will fear losing it if she does an unsatisfactory job.
- *Monitor the work activity of the employee*: To detect signs of inadequate work.
- *Replace the worker by another worker*: If the work is found to be unsatisfactory.

In a democracy, elected officials are held accountable to the electorate by a similar set of strategies:

- *Give the official a sufficient salary, prestige, and other amenities of office*: The offical would then like to keep the job.
- *Monitor the activities of the government*: To determine the quality of the government's performance using legal principles of transparency and judicial review, along with a free press and free speech.
- *Hold periodic elections*: A government that has not performed well in the citizens' eyes is replaced by a different set of political leaders.

This is how democracies solve the principal-agent problem of making elected officials accountable to the public. But it comes with a downside: the fact that officials, like employees, are subject to periodic review gives them an incentive to undertake projects whose objectives will become visible before the next election. This is called **short-termism**.

Governments, for example, sometimes introduce expansionary fiscal policies (cutting taxes or expanding spending) in the run-up to elections, so that disposable incomes will be rising and unemployment falling when people vote. Attempts to push employment above the long-run sustainable level (recall the labour market model) will eventually lead to unsustainable inflationary pressures. But these unwanted consequences would occur only after the election.

Because future elections are an incentive for short-term thinking by political leaders, a partial solution is to remove some policymaking from the hands of elected officials. This is the argument for an independent (not elected) judicial system, and for the political autonomy of the central bank.

For example, the governors of the US Federal Reserve system are appointed by the president for 14-year terms which are staggered, so that it is unlikely that a president will appoint many of them while in office. Figure 15.18 (page 683) shows when central banks across countries in the world adopted inflation-targeting. This was a signal of a greater degree of autonomy of central bank decision making. Also in the US, presidential appointments to the Supreme Court are for life.

Policymaking in a democracy is also sometimes biased in favour of smaller groups. Here is the reason. Consider a policy, such as a reduction in tariffs on imports of clothing, which will make less-expensive clothing available to the population but reduce the employment and income of workers in the domestic clothing industry. Suppose that it will confer a total of €1 million of costs on the 500 clothing workers and at the same time will confer €2 million of benefits on 2 million consumers of clothing.

Now consider the challenges facing those seeking to organize campaigns against and for the policy:

- Each worker in the domestic indstry would lose €2,000 a year if the legislation were passed, so most would support the 'anti-import' cause, and be against the tariff reduction.
- Each consumer would benefit by €1 if the legislation were passed, so few people would be willing even to send an email to their legislator.

> **short-termism** This subjective term refers to the case when the person making a judgement places too much weight on costs, benefits, and other things occurring in the near future than would be appropriate.

'All animals are equal. But some are more equal than others.'
This quote is from George Orwell's 1945 book *Animal Farm*, which was a satirical critique of Joseph Stalin's dictatorship of the Soviet Union. But it also applies to how democracies work in practice. All citizens are legally equal in their rights, but some have much more power to influence government policy than others.

This concerns the second question at the beginning of this section: when persuading elected officials to favour one policy over another, citizens are far from equal. Wealthy citizens in particular may have a disproportionate voice in a democracy because:

- *Wealthy citizens invest*: Their decisions about investment (the case of Chile, for example) may determine the fate of a government.
- *Wealthy citizens donate to politicians*: Their contributions to electoral campaigns (in countries where this is allowed), or even direct personal payments, may influence either who is elected or what the elected officials do once in office.
- *Wealthy citizens control communications*: Some own and direct newspapers and TV stations.
- *Wealthy citizens employ lobbyists*: They, or the firms they own, employ professionals—often former politicians—to influence elected officials.

The result is that economic inequality feeds political inequality, which in turn feeds economic inequality.

For example, the relationship between economic inequality and political inequality affects gender outcomes. In many countries, women participate much less in political life and leadership than men. In India, the reservation of positions for women to head village councils has been shown to increase public spending on the public services that women prefer, like wells, so that they do not have to carry water so far. It also reduces receipts of bribes by those in power and was found to transform stereotypes. Men in villages that were randomly reserved for women leaders subconsciously perceived women more positively as leaders, as compared with viewing them solely in domestic roles.

Kenneth Scheve and Daniel Stasavage. 2010. 'The conscription of wealth: mass warfare and the demand for progressive taxation'. *International Organization* 64 (04): pp. 529–561.

Kenneth Scheve and Daniel Stasavage. 2012. 'Democracy, war, and wealth: lessons from two centuries of inheritance taxation'. *American Political Science Review* 106 (01): pp. 81–102.

Kenneth Scheve and Daniel Stasavage. 2016. *Taxing the rich: A history of fiscal fairness in the United States and Europe.* Princeton University Press.

Jacob S. Hacker and Paul Pierson. 2010. 'Winner-take-all politics: Public policy, political organization, and the precipitous rise of top incomes in the United States'. *Politics & Society* 38 (2): pp. 152–204.

For evidence on how political contributions (as well as special interests) influenced US housing market policy prior to the crisis, read: Atif Mian, Amir Sufi, and Francesco Trebbi. 2013. 'The Political Economy of the Subprime Mortgage Credit Expansion'. *Quarterly Journal of Political Science* 8: pp. 373–408.

HOW ECONOMISTS (AND POLITICAL SCIENTISTS) LEARN FROM FACTS

Does money talk?

In the US, people often say 'money talks'. Many are concerned that it talks particularly loudly when it comes to politics.

To some, it is obvious that when a candidate for political office receives a large contribution for his electoral campaign from a business, or a trade union with an economic interest at stake, the candidate will be more likely to take the side of the contributor when it comes to using political power to influence policy.

We know the election campaigns for the US congress in 2012 spent on average $8.5 million per congressional seat, as a paper on procuring access to congressional representatives relates. But did the winners provide favours for the donors that would not have occurred without the donors' contributions?

In our 'Economist in action' video, Esther Duflo explains what happened when it was mandated that randomly selected villages elect a woman to head their local council. http://tinyco.re/94993365

We might ask if the members of congress who received contributions from those with investments in the oil industry tended to favour the interests of those firms afterwards. Or did those receiving funds from trade union members support an agenda that favoured the union's interests? The answer in both cases would be that they did.

But this does not demonstrate that donor contributions purchased influence over the legislator. Remember causation can work both ways: those with oil wealth are likely to donate to candidates who already favour that industry's interests. Trade union members will donate money to those who already support the interests of trade unions. Simply showing a correlation between the source of the funding and the policies supported by the legislator does not show that the contributions *caused* the legislator to act differently.

Political scientists Joshua Kalla and David Brockman designed a clever experiment to see if the donation caused the congress member to behave in the donor's interest. They reasoned that citizens could influence legislators by meeting with them and expressing their views. Members of Congress are busy people, so gaining access to them for a meeting is something that groups compete for.

They wanted to find out if those who gave money to a congress member were more likely to be granted a meeting. With the cooperation of a (real) interest group Credo Action, they contacted 191 members of congress to ask for a meeting. All of the constituents making this request had contributed some funds to the member's campaign. The control group, randomly chosen, and half of the total sample, said only that they were residents of the member's district. The treatment group also identified themselves as donors. All callers in both groups read from a script, so the requests for a meeting were otherwise identical.

Among those not identified as donors, 2.4% gained a meeting with either the congress member or the chief of staff. For those identified as donors, 12.5% got a meeting.

The authors concluded:

> The vast majority of Americans who cannot afford to contribute to campaigns in meaningful amounts are at a disadvantage when attempting to express their concerns to policy makers.

Joshua L. Kalla and David E. Broockman. (2015). 'Campaign contributions facilitate access to congressional officials: A randomized field experiment'. *American Journal of Political Science* 60 (3): pp. 1–14.

Adam Bonica, Nolan McCarty, Keith T. Poole, and Howard Rosenthal. 2013. 'Why hasn't democracy slowed rising inequality?' *The Journal of Economic Perspectives* 27 (3): pp. 103–123.

Martin Gilens and Benjamin I. Page. 2014. 'Testing theories of American politics: Elites, interest groups, and average citizens'. *Perspectives on politics* 12 (03): pp. 564–581.

Special interests: The story of Chile continued

What happened after the election of Allende in Chile in 1970 tells a story not only of economic limits to feasible policies, but also of political limits.

Amid faltering economic performance, due in part to potential investors holding back on investment in Chile, opposition to Allende mounted, some of it supported in secret by the US government. In 1973, the Chilean armed forces attacked the presidential palace, defeating troops loyal to Allende. They took over the government, ending democracy and replacing Allende with the unelected General Augusto Pinochet.

The wealthy anticipated that Pinochet would introduce pro-business policies, so stock prices rose again (Figure 22.20a). The Pinochet dictatorship would remain until a constitutional referendum in 1988 demanded a return to democracy, which the armed forces respected.

Once again, a sharp change in behaviour of the wealthy is recorded in the stock market prices on the day following the referendum.

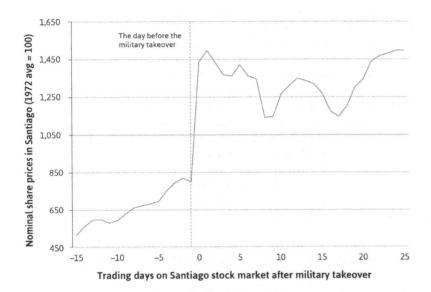

Time zero is the first trading day on the Santiago stock market following the military takeover.

Figure 22.20a Stock market prices in Chile: The military overthrow of the socialist government, 1973.

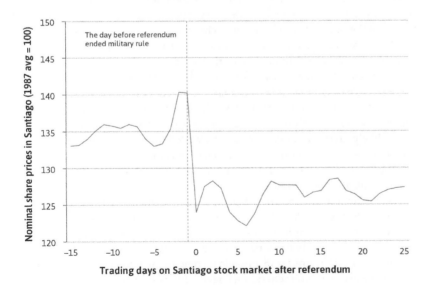

Time zero is the first trading day on the Santiago stock market following the referendum.

Figure 22.20b Stock market prices in Chile: The 1988 referendum, ending military rule.

Allende's economic program was infeasible for two reasons:

- *It was economically infeasible*: He could not force private firms to invest in Chile, and without their investment the economy would stagnate or even shrink.
- *It was politically infeasible*: Though democratically elected he did not control the Chilean armed forces which, with the support of businesses and the US Central Intelligence Agency, turned against him.

22.15 POLICY MATTERS AND ECONOMICS WORKS

In this unit, you have learned that Adam Smith's reasoning about the men on the chessboard can now be expressed in economic terms by saying that, for a policy to improve an outcome, it must change the current Nash equilibrium to a different and preferable one (economic feasibility). And it also must be favoured by a governing elite with the authority and capacity to implement it (political and administrative feasibility).

The limits posed by special interests, as well as economic and administrative feasibility, explain why governments often do not successfully address the problems of market failure and unfairness that we have encountered throughout this course. Looking at the different economies of the world, however, you see substantial differences in the extent to which these problems are effectively addressed. As a result, the limits posed by economic, political, and administrative feasibility differ substantially among countries.

To see this, return to the problem of climate change and Figure 20.25a (page 954). Sweden, Australia and the US have roughly the same per capita income. If they all faced similar constraints of economic, policy, and political feasibility in adopting policies to limit greenhouse gas impacts on climate, then we would expect to see their similarity in income matched by similarity in CO_2 emissions per capita.

But this is not at all what we see in the figure. The US and Australia emit about three times as much per capita as Sweden. It seems likely that what is economically feasible may not differ very much in these three countries, as all share the same knowledge about technologies, and their citizens are likely to respond in similar ways to incentives to adopt cleaner energy sources. The government information and capacities in the three countries are also similar: all have well-informed and capable governments.

Although carbon dioxide emissions are affected by industrial structure and trade specialization, they are also affected by what is desired by the elites, who have political influence. Policies to address climate change are more likely to have political support in Sweden than in Australia and the US. One reason for this difference is the importance in US and Australian politics of lobbies representing the natural resource industries, including the gas, oil, and coal producers.

A similar contrast appears when we look at inequality, shown in Figure 19.30. Germany and the US have both experienced about the same rate of growth in GDP per capita over the past four decades, but they differ markedly in inequality of living standards, as can be seen by the much higher Gini coefficient for disposable income in the US. The comparison for the measure of intergenerational inequality is similar. Denmark, Sweden, and Finland are more equal by this measure than even Germany.

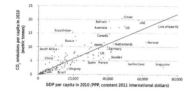

As we saw in Figure 20.25a (page 954), countries with similar per capita income do not necessarily have similar levels of CO_2 emissions per capita.

Many things could account for these differences. They are, at least in part, due to the greater political influence in Germany than in the US, of those who value sustaining a higher living standard for the least well-off.

What can we learn from these comparisons?

One lesson, if we wish to address problems like climate change and unfair inequalities in living standards, is that for most countries it is possible to do a lot more than is currently being done. The fundamental forces contributing to inequality in the high-income countries—new technologies and growing imports (from China, for example) that make the skills of low-paid workers redundant—do not differ much among the high-income countries in Figure 19.30. The differences appear to be a matter of choices among the similar set of policies that are economically and administratively feasible, some countries opting for policies that sustain high levels of inequality, and others pursuing the goal of greater equality.

We also have a lot to learn from the top performers in these and similar figures, by studying the policies and institutions that appear to account for their success in addressing market failures and unfairness.

Not all policies and institutions that are effective in one country can be transferred to another. The comparison between the innovation systems in Silicon Valley and in Germany in Section 21.2 (page 970) shows how different combinations of innovating firms, government policies, financial institutions, and social norms in these two regions produce effective solutions to the market failures associated with knowledge production. Neither would be easily adopted in the other country, or in a country like Brazil or Portugal.

Some countries have school systems that teach much more effectively than others. Because educational policies differ greatly among countries, we can get some idea of the importance of good policy by looking at differences among nations in performance on a mathematics test administered to 15-year-old students around the world.

Let's compare two countries that are ethnically diverse and have about the same per capita income: the US and Singapore. The average maths score in Singapore was 20% higher than in the US. Even more striking, the student whose score placed him or her in the middle of the US students (the student with the median score) would have been in the bottom quarter of Singapore's students. A similar comparison would place the median American student in the bottom quarter of Japanese students, and just above the bottom quarter of Finland's students.

Economic research has explored the question of how schooling and preschool experience affects inequality. A leader in this research is James Heckman, who was the subject of one of our 'Economist in action' videos. You may also want to read his book *Giving kids a fair chance*.

His book begins by noting that:

The accident of birth is a principal source of inequality in America today. American society is dividing into skilled and unskilled ... birth is becoming fate.

Heckman's 'strategy that works' is based on the following logic. 'Both cognitive and socio-emotional skills develop in early childhood and their development depends on family environment.' Growing up poor deprives children of opportunities to develop these skills, and 'family environments in the US have deteriorated'.

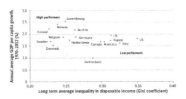

As we saw in Figure 19.30a (page 896), high income countries with a similar growth in GDP per capita do not necessarily have similar levels of inequality.

You can access the data from this test at the OECD's Programme for International Student Assessment (http://tinyco.re/1018246).

James Heckman explores the question of how schooling and preschool experience affects inequality. http://tinyco.re/3964341

James Heckman. 2013. 'Giving Kids a Fair Chance: A Strategy That Works'. Cambridge, MA: MIT Press.

In response, Heckman advocates 'early interventions' such as enriched preschool environments and home visits by professionals to assist parents, which his research shows can 'produce positive and lasting effects on children in disadvantaged families.'

Policies of the kind advocated by Heckman are being implemented in countries including Colombia, Jamaica, Chile, and in the state of Orissa in India. Teams of economists and experts in child development are rigorously evaluating them for their longer-term effects and to assess the feasibility of scaling them up from small pilot interventions. (http://tinyco.re/2744426)

So we know that the kids of poor parents often grow up to be poor. We now also know that this has little to do with genetics, and more to do with the socio-emotional behaviour associated with growing up poor. We now know of, and govenments can implement, effective policy remedies to break this cycle of poverty.

22.16 CONCLUSION

Harold Lasswell, a prominent mid-twentieth-century American political scientist, is best known for his book *Politics: Who gets what, when and how* (http://tinyco.re/2227728). The title captures a basic point of this unit, though we will go beyond Lasswell's title. Politics is all about:

* who gets what
* who gets to be what
* who gets to do what

Daron Acemoglu and James A. Robinson. 2013. 'Economics versus politics: Pitfalls of policy advice'. *The Journal of Economic Perspectives* 27 (2): pp. 173–192.

The reason is that political processes determine the rules of the game—the basic institutions that govern how we interact in the economy and other arenas of our society.

But politics is not simply about dividing up a pie, with the powerful getting the larger slice and the struggle for power sometimes resulting in a smaller pie. Well-designed government policies are also able to increase the size of the pie, improving living standards for the vast majority of people. Examples that you have already seen include the economic policies of the government of China, which since the 1980s resulted in the most rapid eradication of large-scale poverty ever witnessed in human history. Another example was the clean water and sanitation policies that were behind the global reduction in child mortality.

Economics is an essential tool to understanding how government policies can both increase the size of the pie and ensure its fair division. *The Economy* has given you a way of understanding the manner in which we interact with each other, and with our natural environments in producing our livelihoods. Our economy is all about people and what we do as buyers and sellers, borrowers and lenders, employees and employers, voters and government officials. We learn a lot about this economy by seeing actors as doing the best that they can under a given set of circumstances, while also seeking to change their circumstances, often through political movements and governments.

Economics can help to adequately address the problems of inefficiency and unfairness in our economies, by designing policies that are both economically and administratively feasible. Economics can also play a role in making good policies politically possible: economic reasoning can have a powerful effect on public understanding of what can be done in the economy, and even on what ought to be done.

The capitalist revolution with which we began in Unit 1 and the democratic revolutions—extending the vote to all adults—with which we have concluded here have together produced the distinctive economic and political system under which most readers of *The Economy* now live. Capitalism and democracy continue to change, and to change the world.

Economics will help you understand how capitalism and democracy together are changing your circumstances, and how you—with others—in turn might participate in this process of change.

Concepts introduced in Unit 22
Before you move on, review these definitions:

- Government, governing elite
- Economic accountability, political accountability, democratic accountability
- Political rents
- Political institutions
- Median voter model
- Short-termism
- Economic feasibility, administrative feasibility

22.17 REFERENCES

Acemoglu, Daron, and James A. Robinson. 2013. 'Economics versus politics: Pitfalls of policy advice' (http://tinyco.re/5915146). *The Journal of Economic Perspectives* 27 (2): pp. 173–192.

Arrow, Kenneth. J. 1978. 'A cautious case for socialism' (http://tinyco.re/3618241). *Dissent* 25 (4): pp. 472–480.

Arrow, Kenneth J., and F. H. Hahn. 1991. 'General Competitive Analysis', eds. C. J. Bliss and M. D. Intriligator. *Advanced Textbooks in Economics* Vol. 12. San Francisco: Holden-Day.

Bakija, Jon, Lane Kenworthy, Peter Lindert, and Jeff Madrick. 2016. *How Big Should Our Government Be?* Berkeley: University of California Press.

Besley, Timothy, and Anne Case. 1995. 'Does electoral accountability affect economic policy choices? Evidence from gubernatorial term limits' (http://tinyco.re/2599264). *The Quarterly Journal of Economics* 110 (3): pp. 769–798.

Besley, Timothy, and Torsten Persson. 2014. 'Why do developing countries tax so little?' (http://tinyco.re/3513621). *The Journal of Economic Perspectives* 28 (4): pp. 99–120.

Bonica, Adam, Nolan McCarty, Keith T. Poole, and Howard Rosenthal. 2013. Why hasn't democracy slowed rising inequality? (http://tinyco.re/7031342). *The Journal of Economic Perspectives* 27 (3): pp. 103–123.

Deaton, Angus. 2013. *The Great Escape: Health, Wealth, and the Origins of Inequality*. Princeton, NJ: Princeton University Press.

Durlauf, Steven. 2017. 'Kenneth Arrow and the golden age of economic theory' (http://tinyco.re/9029504). *VoxEU.org*. Updated 8 April 2017.

Freedom House. 2016. 'Freedom in the World 2016. Anxious Dictators, Wavering Democracies: Global Freedom under Pressure' (http://tinyco.re/9817968). Washington, DC.

Fujiwara, Thomas. 2015. 'Voting technology, political responsiveness and infant health: Evidence from Brazil' (http://tinyco.re/3783631). *Econometrica* 83 (2): pp. 423–464.

Gilens, Martin, Benjamin I. Page. 2014. 'Testing theories of American politics: Elites, interest groups, and average citizens' (http://tinyco.re/7911085). *Perspectives on politics* 12 (03): pp. 564–581.

Girardi, Daniele and Samuel Bowles. 2017. 'Institutional Shocks and Economic Outcomes: Allende's Election, Pinochet's Coup and the Santiago Stock Market'. Santa Fe Institute working paper.

Hamilton, Alexander, James Madison, and John Jay. 1961. *The Federalist*. Middletown, Ct. Wesleyan University Press.

Hayek, Friedrich A. 1994. *The Road to Serfdom* (http://tinyco.re/0683881). Chicago, Il: University of Chicago Press.

Heckman, James. 2013. *Giving Kids a Fair Chance: A Strategy That Works*. Cambridge, MA: MIT Press.

Hirschman, Albert O. 1970. *Exit, voice, and loyalty: Responses to decline in firms, organizations, and states*. Cambridge, Mass: Harvard University Press.

Hotelling, Harold. 1929. 'Stability in Competition'. *The Economic Journal* 39: pp. 41–57.

Kalla, Joshua L., and David E. Broockman. 2015. 'Campaign contributions facilitate access to congressional officials: A randomized field experiment' (http://tinyco.re/5765353). *American Journal of Political Science* 60 (3): pp. 1–14.

Kaufmann, Daniel, Aart Kraay, and Massimo Mastruzzi. 2011. 'The worldwide governance indicators: methodology and analytical issues' (http://tinyco.re/7305592). *Hague Journal on the Rule of Law* 3 (2): pp. 220–246.

Lasswell, Harold D. 1936. *Politics; who gets what, when and how* (http://tinyco.re/2227728). New York: Whittlesey House.

Leibbrandt, Murray, Ingrid Woolard, Arden Finn, Jonathan Argent. 2010. 'Trends in South African Income Distribution and Poverty since the Fall of Apartheid' (http://tinyco.re/8617393). OECD Social, Employment and Migration Working Papers, No. 101. Paris: OECD Publishing.

Lindert, Peter. 2004. *Growing Public: Social Spending and Economic Growth since the 18th Century*. Cambridge: Cambridge University Press.

Martinez-Bravo, Monica, Gerard Padró i Miquel, Nancy Qian, and Yang Yao. 2014. 'Political reform in China: the effect of local elections' (http://tinyco.re/4667186). NBER working paper, 18101.

Mian, Atif, Amir Sufi, and Francesco Trebbi. 2013. 'The Political Economy of the Subprime Mortgage Credit Expansion' (http://tinyco.re/4522161). *Quarterly Journal of Political Science* 8: pp. 373–408.

Miller, Grant. 2008. 'Women's suffrage, political responsiveness, and child survival in American history' (http://tinyco.re/5731666). *The Quarterly Journal of Economics* 123 (3): pp. 1287–1327.

Nuffield Foundation, The. 2010. 'Mirrlees Review of tax system recommends radical changes' (http://tinyco.re/6726989). Updated 10 November 2010.

O'Brien, Patrick K., and Philip A. Hunt. 1993. 'The rise of a fiscal state in England, 1485–1815'. *Historical Research* 66 (160): pp.129–76.

OECD. 2015. Programme for International Student Assessment (http://tinyco.re/1018246).

Plummer, Alfred. 1971. *Bronterre: A Political Biography of Bronterre O'Brien, 1804–1864*. Toronto: University of Toronto Press.

Przeworski, Adam, Fernando Limongi. 1993. 'Political regimes and economic growth' (http://tinyco.re/6669217). *The Journal of Economic Perspectives* 7 (3): pp. 51–69.

Rasul, Imran, Daniel Rogger. 2016. 'Management of bureaucrats and public service delivery: Evidence from the Nigerian civil service' (http://tinyco.re/9848716). *The Economic Journal*.

Scheve, Kenneth, and David Stasavage. 2010. 'The conscription of wealth: mass warfare and the demand for progressive taxation'. *International Organization* 64 (04): pp. 529–561.

Scheve, Kenneth, and David Stasavage. 2012. 'Democracy, war, and wealth: lessons from two centuries of inheritance taxation' (http://tinyco.re/9000452). *American Political Science Review* 106 (01): pp. 81–102.

Scheve, Kenneth, and David Stasavage. 2016. *Taxing the rich: A history of fiscal fairness in the United States and Europe*. Princeton University Press.

Sethi, Rajiv. 2010. 'The Astonishing Voice of Albert Hirschman' (http://tinyco.re/2899363). *Rajiv Sethi Blog*. Updated 7 April 2010.

Sethi, Rajiv. 2011. 'The Self-Subversion of Albert Hirschman' (http://tinyco.re/2163474). *Rajiv Sethi Blog*. Updated 7 April 2011.

Sethi, Rajiv. 2013. 'Albert Hirschman and the Happiness of Pursuit' (http://tinyco.re/5203731). *Rajiv Sethi Blog*. Updated 24 March 2013.

Shleifer, Andrei. 1998. 'State versus private ownership' (http://tinyco.re/4317440). *Journal of Economic Perspectives* 12 (4): pp. 133–150.

Smith, Adam. 1759. *The Theory of Moral Sentiments* (http://tinyco.re/6582039). London: Printed for A. Millar, and A. Kincaid and J. Bell.

Swedberg, Richard. 1991. *Joseph A. Schumpeter, The Economics and Sociology of Capitalism*. Princeton, NJ: Princeton University Press.

The Economist. 1999. 'The grabbing hand' (http://tinyco.re/8993136). Updated 11 February 1999.

Tirole, Jean. 2017. 'Jean Tirole – Prize Lecture: Market Failures and Public Policy' (http://tinyco.re/4684631). Nobel Media AB 2014, 11 May.

Wood, Elisabeth Jean. 2000. *Forging Democracy from Below: Insurgent Transitions in South Africa and El Salvador*. Cambridge: Cambridge University Press.

LOOKING FORWARD TO ECONOMICS AFTER CORE

If you have just completed your first course in economics you may be asking: what's next? If you're a student, we will explain how *The Economy* relates to the other approaches you will encounter. If you're an instructor, and you want to place CORE's approach to economics in context, this section will also be useful.

The Economy has been an introduction to what we consider is the best of what economists know at this time. Or, perhaps, we should say what we *think we know*. As has always been the case, economics is constantly changing.

In 1848, John Stuart Mill published *Principles of Political Economy*, the first great textbook in economics. It was the core text in the English-speaking world until it was displaced by Alfred Marshall's *Principles of Economics* 42 years later. Mill's readers may have been reassured when they read:

> Happily, there is nothing in the laws of value [microeconomics] which remains for the present writer or any future writer to clear up; the theory of the subject is complete.

No economics textbook writer today could realistically make the same claim. Our understanding of the economy is constantly in flux. You will have seen an example in Unit 17, in the lessons about the macroeconomy that the Great Depression, the end of the golden age of capitalism, and the financial crisis of 2008 taught us.

Three great thinkers, whose key ideas were formed early in the period covered by Unit 17, transformed how we now understand the economy. (You have encountered all three in the 'Great economists'

features). In 1936, during the Great Depression, John Maynard Keynes introduced the idea of aggregate demand and its determinants to explain why a capitalist economy might experience persistent high levels of unemployment. Just 12 years later, aggregate demand became a core concept in an introduction to economics written by Paul Samuelson that would in turn displace the certainties of Marshall's *Principles*, and would become the standard for what every aspiring economist ought to know.

A second great economist, Friedrich Hayek, introduced the idea of the market as an information-processing system. His most famous article, published in 1945, argued that economic systems and organizations should be evaluated on how well they made use of the economically relevant information that was necessarily available to some, but not to others. Hayek stressed that governments could not access all the information necessary to centrally plan an economy. His main ideas—that information is incomplete and asymmetric—became the foundation of the theories of incomplete contracts in labour and credit markets that you have studied.

A third great contributor to economics of the mid-twentieth century was John Nash, a mathematician. Drawing on ideas of John von Neumann and Oskar Morgenstern, Nash pioneered the development of game theory to model strategic interactions among economic or political actors. His work provided a new lens for the study of economic situations. In many situations, Nash argued, people will take account of the likely responses of others to the actions that they take, rather than interacting with a fixed set of prices (as a price-taker). The Nash equilibrium provides a way of studying outcomes that we find in real economies, because they represent the joint outcome of large numbers of people doing the best they can, given what others are doing.

We have been inspired by, and learned from, these three great thinkers. But, as you have read, we have not swallowed whole the thinking of any of them. You have seen models and evidence that question Keynes' optimism that a government's demand-management policies would substantially eliminate involuntary unemployment in the long run. Problems of market failure and economic instability provide reasons to reject Hayek's argument that governments should limit their activities to enforcing property rights and the other fundamental rules that permit markets to function. Finally, the insights of Nash-inspired modelling of interactions among individuals who are apparently able to calculate the highly complex consequences of their own actions, but who are also incapable of cooperating amongst each other to arrive at solutions to their problems, has been questioned by modern behavioural experiments and research on human cognitive capacities.

Nevertheless, the contributions of Keynes, Hayek, and Nash—aggregate demand, the economics of information, and strategic interactions modelled by game theory—have become foundations of modern economic thinking. Before the end of the twentieth century, all three innovations had become the standard content of postgraduate economic courses. You will see the pervasive influence of all of them in advanced textbooks such as *Microeconomic Theory* by Andreu Mas-Colell, Michael Whinston, and Jerry Green, or *Advanced Macroeconomics* by David Romer.

But while aggregate demand was almost immediately introduced as a core topic of introductory economics, asymmetric information and game theory are typically introduced right at the end of the introductory course, if at all. Understandably, students therefore see these approaches simply as extensions of the standard models of Alfred Marshall or Leon Walras (two more of CORE's 'Great economists'). This is not the case. These theories challenge two of the foundational concepts of the standard model—namely price-taking behaviour is the norm in a competitive economy, and complete contracts, which have been made possible by complete information.

Remarkably, most of your fellow students who have used standard introductory textbooks and courses don't know this fundamentally important piece of information, because they haven't been told it.

Just as Samuelson popularized the concept of aggregate demand in an introductory text, CORE has taken information economics and strategic social interaction and made these concepts part of the foundation of an economic paradigm that introductory students can learn. (A scientific paradigm is a set of concepts that are basic to how a group of scholars understand the world as embodied in the introductory textbooks that are widely accepted in the field. Previous paradigms are exemplified by the successive contributions of Mill, Marshall and Samuelson.)

We have also integrated more recent developments in the discipline from the fields of behavioural economics, economic dynamics, and institutional economics. In Figure A, we contrast the Samuelsonian paradigm (it is still the basis of most introductory texts) with what you have just studied in this book. We consider the benchmark Walrasian model codified by Samuelson as in the left column to be the standard case that most students are taught, from which 'deviations' are studied. The most obvious example of this is the idea that price-taking markets are the standard case, with monopolistic competition being an extension.

The right-hand column provides a very different vision of the economy. For example, having studied CORE you may have a different view of competition. Hayek pointed out that assuming a state of equilibrium among price-taking traders effectively shuts down any serious analysis of competition, which he defines, following Samuel Johnson, as 'the action of endeavouring to gain what another endeavours to gain at the same time.'

He continued as follows:

Now, how many of the devices adopted in ordinary life to that end would still be open to a seller in a market in which so-called 'perfect competition' prevails? I believe that the answer is exactly none. Advertising, undercutting, and improving ('differentiating') the goods or services produced are all excluded by definition—'perfect' competition means indeed the absence of all competitive activities.

To study the process of competition CORE replaced the passive price-taker of perfectly competitive equilibrium with the 'perfect competitor'. This active competitor exploits available (but incomplete) information to appropriate any possible rents that may exist when an economy is not in equilibrium. Under some conditions this drives the dynamic process to a Pareto-efficient equilibrium, even when there are impediments to competition.

This is not simply a question of taste. These concepts are essential if we want to try to answer the questions that students all over the world have told us should be the focus of economics.

Topics	Samuelsonian benchmark as taught in introductory economics	Contemporary economics and CORE's benchmark (unit numbers in *The Economy*)
People	are far-sighted and self-interested	are also cognitively limited (for example, they have weakness of will) and have motives other than self-interest, such as social norms of fairness and reciprocity (4, 13)
Interactions	are among price-takers in competitive markets	include price-makers and interest rate and wage-setters, strategic interactions, and non-market interactions (6, 7, 9, 10, 11)
Information	is complete	is usually incomplete, asymmetric, and non-verifiable (6, 9, 10–12, 21)
Contracts	are complete and enforceable at zero cost	are incomplete for effort and diligence in labour and credit markets, and for other external effects such as traffic congestion or knowledge (6, 9, 10, 12)
Institutions	include markets, private property, and governments	also include informal rules (norms), firms, unions, and banks (5–7, 9–11, 22)
History	is largely ignored	provides data about alternative rules of the game and the process of change (most units)
Differences among people	are confined to preference and budget constraint differences among buyers and sellers	also include asymmetric positions, for example as employers or employees, and as lenders or borrowers (6, 9, 10, 12)
Power	is market power and political power	includes also a principal's power over an agent in labour, credit, and other markets (5, 6, 9, 10, 12)
Economic rents	create inefficiencies through 'rent-seeking'	are also endemic in a well-functioning private economy, creating the incentive to innovate, or to work hard (2, 6–12, 21)
Stability and instability	The economy is self-stabilizing.	Stability and instability are both characteristics of the economy. (11, 13–15, 17, 20)
Evaluation	is confined to the presence of unexploited mutual gains (Pareto-inefficiency)	also includes fairness (4, 5, 19, 22)

Figure A Contrasting the Samuelsonian paradigm with CORE's *The Economy*.

The left-hand column of the table in Figure C shows some of the most important problems that students and others tell us that economics should be about; the right-hand column shows some of the concepts essential to understanding these problems.

This is work in progress. The emerging paradigm that you have studied is not fully developed, and not as simple as the Walrasian benchmark. But to create the Samuelsonian paradigm, economics teaching has made simplifications that we all know are often so much at variance with the real world that the resulting model is inappropriate.

For example, assume that complete information and its corollary complete contracts are usual. Another mid-twentieth century economist, Abba Lerner, explained the success of the Walrasian benchmark:

Figure B The word cloud in the preface made from responses of students at Humboldt University, which is dominated by inequality, is typical. Students globally have also told us they are interested in innovation, environmental problems, unemployment and instability.

> An economic transaction is a solved political problem ... Economics has gained the title Queen of the Social Sciences by choosing solved political problems as its domain.

The conflict of interests that exists in every transaction, he argued, is resolved in a contract that would be enforced by the courts, not by the parties to the transaction. 'The solution is essentially the transformation of the conflict from a political problem to an economic transaction,' he wrote.

In a world that ran according to the Walrasian competitive model, based on complete contracts, there would be no role for politics: if the contract was really complete there would be nothing for the exercise of power to be about. If the worker did not work as hard as she had agreed to work, then she simply would not be paid. The employer would have no need to exercise power over the employee, for example by threatening to sack her. The contract would be sufficient in itself to guarantee the outcome needed for the firm to make profits. This aspect of the Walrasian model was what motivated Samuelson's remark that 'In a perfectly competitive market, it really doesn't matter who hires whom, so have labour hire capital.'

The assumption of a complete employment contract also meant that the employer had no need to be concerned about the prospective employee's preferences, for example her work ethic or her desire to send instant messages to her friends while she was working. A result of these and other assumptions of the benchmark

Walrasian model incorporated in the Samuelsonian paradigm was that Lerner's 'Queen of the Social Sciences' could reign alone. Economics could successfully ignore a host of other important insights:

- legal scholars who have studied contracts in the real world, and the challenges of enforcing them
- psychologists and sociologists who seek to understand the motivations and thought processes of real people
- philosophers and ordinary citizens who are animated by economic justice, individual freedom and dignity
- political scientists who consider the top-down structure of a firm as partly a system of power
- historians, anthropologists and archaeologists who study the variety of institutions governing our economic lives, which have shaped our development since pre-history
- biologists and ecologists and others who see the economy as a part of the biosphere with unavoidable 'external' effects on the way it functions, and its sustainability

CORE has drawn (and will continue to draw) on these and other insights from the other disciplines in order to understand how prices, wages, and interest rates are determined, how the aggregate economy functions, and other central questions of economics. Instead of seeing all economic activity through the lens of a single model of competitive markets with complete contracts, CORE has invited you to see the economy the way research economists see it, as a diverse combination of institutions and behaviours that is best studied by judiciously choosing among factually tested models.

If you continue to study economics you will discover this paradigm, and continue to see how it differs from the Samuelsonian and other paradigms. You are fortunate, because you will be able to apply the concepts, facts, and capacities that you have already learned. Eventually you will discover how economics continues to change in response to a changing world, and how this understanding of economics creates the policies that can change the world.

Problems in the world	Essential concepts
Wealth creation, innovation and growth	Schumpeterian (innovation) rents, disequilibrium
Environmental sustainability	Non-market social interactions, other-regarding preferences
Inequality	Rents, bargaining power, institutions, fairness
Unemployment and fluctuations	Incomplete contracts in labour and credit markets
Instability	Prices as information and the dynamics of price setting

Figure C Important problems that students and others tell us that economics should be about.

GLOSSARY

abatement policy A policy designed to reduce environmental damages. *See also: abatement.*

abatement Practices to limit or reverse environmental damages. *See also: abatement policy.*

absolute advantage A person or country has this in the production of a good if the inputs it uses to produce this good are less than in some other person or country. *See also: comparative advantage.*

accountability The obligation of a decision-maker (or body) to be responsive to the needs and wishes of people affected by his, her or its decisions.

acyclical No tendency to move either in the same or opposite direction to aggregate output and employment over the business cycle.

adjustment gap The lag between some outside change in labour market conditions and the movement of the economy to the neighbourhood of the new equilibrium.

administratively feasible Policies for which the government has sufficient information and staff for implementation.

adverse selection The problem faced by parties to an exchange in which the terms offered by one party will cause some exchange partners to drop out. An example is the problem of asymmetric information in insurance: if the price is sufficiently high, the only people who will seek to purchase medical insurance are people who know they are ill (but the insurer does not). This

will lead to further price increases to cover costs. Also referred to as the 'hidden attributes' problem (the state of already being ill is the hidden attribute), to distinguish it from the 'hidden actions' problem of moral hazard. *See also: incomplete contract, moral hazard, asymmetric information.*

aggregate demand The total of the components of spending in the economy, added to get GDP: $Y = C + I + G + X - M$. It is the total amount of demand for (or expenditure on) goods and services produced in the economy. *See also: consumption, investment, government spending, exports, imports.*

aggregate output The total output in an economy, across all sectors and regions.

allocation A description of who does what, the consequences of their actions, and who gets what as a result.

altruism The willingness to bear a cost in order to benefit somebody else.

antitrust policy Government policy and laws to limit monopoly power and prevent cartels. *Also known as: competition policy.*

arbitrage The practice of buying a good at a low price in a market to sell it at a higher price in another. Traders engaging in arbitrage take advantage of the price difference for the same good between two countries or regions. As long as the trade costs are lower than the price gap, they make a profit. *See also: price gap.*

artificially scarce good A public good that it is possible to exclude some people from enjoying. *Also known as: club good.*

asset price bubble Sustained and significant rise in the price of an asset fuelled by expectations of future price increases.

asset Anything of value that is owned. *See also: balance sheet, liability.*

asymmetric information Information that is relevant to the parties in an economic interaction, but is known by some but not by others. *See also: adverse selection, moral hazard.*

austerity A policy where a government tries to improve its budgetary position in a recession by increasing its saving. *See also: paradox of thrift.*

automatic stabilizers Characteristics of the tax and transfer system in an economy that have the effect of offsetting an expansion or contraction of the economy. An example is the unemployment benefits system.

automation The use of machines that are substitutes for labour.

autonomous consumption Consumption that is independent of current income.

autonomous demand Components of aggregate demand that are independent of current income.

average cost The total cost of the firms's output divided by the total number of units of output.

average product Total output divided by a particular input, for example per worker (divided by the number of workers) or per worker per hour (total output divided by the total number of hours of labour put in).

balance of payments (BP) This records the sources and uses of foreign exchange. This account records all payment transactions between the home country and the rest of the world, and is divided into two parts: the current account and the capital and financial account. *Also known as: balance of payments account.*

balance sheet A record of the assets, liabilities, and net worth of an economic actor such as a household, bank, firm, or government.

bank bailout The government buys an equity stake in a bank or some other intervention to prevent it from failing.

bank money Money in the form of bank deposits created by commercial banks when they extend credit to firms and households.

bank run A situation in which depositors withdraw funds from a bank because they fear that it may go bankrupt and not honour its liabilities (that is, not repay the funds owed to depositors).

bank A firm that creates money in the form of bank deposits in the process of supplying credit.

bargaining gap The difference between the real wage that firms wish to offer in order to provide workers with incentives to work, and the real wage that allows firms the markup that maximizes profits given the degree of competition.

bargaining power The extent of a person's advantage in securing a larger share of the economic rents made possible by an interaction.

base money Cash and the balances held by commercial banks in their accounts at the central bank, known as reserves. *Also known as: legal tender, high-powered money.*

best response In game theory, the strategy that will give a player the highest payoff, given the strategies that the other players select.

Beveridge curve The inverse relationship between the unemployment rate and the job vacancy rate (each expressed as a fraction of the labour force). Named after the British economist of the same name.

biodiversity loss (rate of) Proportion of species that become extinct every year.

biological survival constraint This shows all the points that are 'biologically feasible'. *See also: biologically feasibile.*

biologically feasible An allocation that is capable of sustaining the survival of those involved is biologically feasible.

bond A type of financial asset for which the issuer promises to pay a given amount over time to the holder. *Also known as: corporate bonds.*

Bretton Woods system An international monetary system of fixed but adjustable exchange rates, established at the end of the Second World War. It replaced the gold standard that was abandoned during the Great Depression.

broad money The stock of money in circulation, which is the sum of base money (excluding legal tender held by banks) and bank money. *See also: legal tender, bank money.*

budget constraint An equation that represents all combinations of goods and services that one could acquire that exactly exhaust one's budgetary resources.

business cycle Alternating periods of faster and slower (or even negative) growth rates. The economy goes from boom to recession and back to boom. *See also: short-run equilibrium.*

cap and trade A policy through which a limited number of permits to pollute are issued, and can be bought and sold on a market. It combines a quantity-based limit on emissions, and a price-based approach that places a cost on environmentally damaging decisions.

capacity-constrained A situation in which a firm has more orders for its output than it can fill. *See also: low capacity utilization.*

capacity utilization rate A measure of the extent to which a firm, industry, or entire economy is producing as much as the stock of its capital goods and current knowledge would allow.

capital goods The equipment, buildings, raw materials, and other inputs used in producing goods and services, including where applicable any patents or other intellectual property that is used.

capital intensity (of production) The amount of capital goods per worker.

capital-intensive Making greater use of capital goods (for example machinery and equipment) as compared with labour and other inputs. *See also: labour-intensive.*

capital productivity Output per unit of capital good. *See also: labour productivity.*

capitalism An economic system in which private property, markets, and firms play an important role.

capitalist revolution Rapid improvements in technology combined with the emergence of a new economic system.

cartel A group of firms that collude in order to increase their joint profits.

catch-up growth The process by which many (but far from all) economies in the world close the gap between the world leader and their own economy.

categorical inequality Inequality between particular social groups (identified, for instance, by a category such as race, nation, caste, gender or religion). *Also known as: group inequality.*

causality A direction from cause to effect, establishing that a change in one variable produces a change in another. While a cor-relation is simply an assessment that two things have moved together, causation implies a mechanism accounting for the association, and is therefore a more restrictive concept. *See also: natural experiment, correlation.*

central bank The only bank that can create a country's legal tender. Usually part of the government. Commercial banks have accounts at this bank, holding legal tender.

ceteris paribus Economists often simplify analysis by setting aside things that are thought to be of less importance to the question of interest. The literal meaning of the expression is 'other things equal'. In an economic model it means an analysis 'holds other things constant'.

club good *See: artificially scarce good, public good.*

co-insurance A means of pooling savings across households in order for a household to be able to maintain consumption when it experiences a temporary fall in income or the need for greater expenditure.

codified knowledge Knowledge that can be written down in a form that would allow it to be understood by others and reproduced, such as the chemical formula for a drug. *See also: tacit knowledge.*

collateral An asset that a borrower pledges to a lender as a security for a loan. If the borrower is not able to make the loan payments as promised, the lender becomes the owner of the asset.

collateralized debt obligation (CDO) A structured financial instrument (a derivative) consisting of a bond or note backed by a pool of fixed-income assets. The collapse in the value of the instruments of this type that were backed by subprime mortgage loans was a major factor in the financial crisis of 2007–2008.

commodities Physical goods traded in a manner similar to stocks. They include metals such as gold and silver, and agricultural products such as coffee and sugar, oil and gas. Sometimes more generally used to mean anything produced for sale.

common currency area A group of countries that use the same currency. This means there is just one monetary policy for the group. *Also known as: currency union.*

common-pool resource A rival good that one cannot prevent others from enjoying. *Also known as: common property resource.*

comparative advantage A person or country has comparative advantage in the production of a particular good, if the cost of producing an additional unit of that good relative to the cost of producing another good is lower than another person or country's cost to produce the same two goods. *See also: absolute advantage.*

competition policy Government policy and laws to limit monopoly power and prevent cartels. *Also known as: antitrust policy.*

competitive equilibrium A market outcome in which all buyers and sellers are price-takers, and at the prevailing market price, the quantity supplied is equal to the quantity demanded.

complements Two goods for which an increase in the price of one leads to a decrease in the quantity demanded of the other. *See also: substitutes.*

concave function A function of two variables for which the line segment between any two points on the function lies entirely below the curve representing the function (the function is convex when the line segment lies above the function).

conspicuous consumption The purchase of goods or services to publicly display one's social and economic status.

constant prices Prices corrected for increases in prices (inflation) or decreases in prices (deflation) so that a unit of currency represents the same buying power in different periods of time. *See also: purchasing power parity.*

constant returns to scale These occur when doubling all of the inputs to a production process doubles the output. The shape of a firm's long-run average cost curve depends both on returns to scale in production and the effect of scale on the prices it pays for its inputs. *See also: increasing returns to scale, decreasing returns to scale.*

constrained choice problem This problem is about how we can do the best for ourselves, given our preferences and constraints, and when the things we value are scarce. *See also: constrained optimization problem.*

constrained optimization problem Problems in which a decision-maker chooses the values of one or more variables to achieve an objective (such as maximizing profit) subject to a constraint that determines the feasible set (such as the demand curve).

consumer durables Consumer goods with a life expectancy of more than three years such as home furniture, cars, and fridges.

consumer price index (CPI) A measure of the general level of prices that consumers have to pay for goods and services, including consumption taxes.

consumer surplus The consumer's willingness to pay for a good minus the price at which the consumer bought the good, summed across all units sold.

consumption (C) Expenditure on consumer goods including both short-lived goods and services and long-lived goods, which are called consumer durables.

consumption function (aggregate) An equation that shows how consumption spending in the economy as a whole depends on other variables. For example, in the multiplier model, the other variables are current disposable income and autonomous consumption. *See also: disposable income, autonomous consumption.*

consumption good A good or service that satisfies the needs of consumers over a short period.

contingent valuation A survey-based technique used to assess the value of non-market resources. *Also known as: stated-preference model.*

contract A legal document or understanding that specifies a set of actions that parties to the contract must undertake.

cooperation Participating in a common project that is intended to produce mutual benefits.

cooperative firm A firm that is mostly or entirely owned by its workers, who hire and fire the managers.

coordination game A game in which there are two Nash equilibria, of which one may be Pareto superior to the other. *Also known as: assurance game.*

copyright Ownership rights over the use and distribution of an original work.

correlation coefficient A measure of how closely associated two variables are and whether they tend to take similar or dissimilar values, ranging from a value of 1 indicating that the variables take similar values ('are positively correlated') to −1 indicating that the variables take dissimilar variables ('negative' or 'inverse' correlation). A value of 1 or −1 indicates that knowing the value of one of the variables would allow you to perfectly predict the value of the other. A value of 0 indicates that knowing one of the variables provides no information about the value of the other. *See also: correlation, causality.*

correlation A statistical association in which knowing the value of one variable provides information on the likely value of the other, for example high values of one variable being commonly observed along with high values of the other variable. It can be positive or negative (it is negative when high values of one variable are observed with low values of the other). It does not mean that there is a causal relationship between the variables. *See also: causality, correlation coefficient.*

costs of entry Startup costs that would be incurred when a seller enters a market or an industry. These would usually include the cost of acquiring and equipping new premises, research and development, the necessary patents, and the cost of finding and hiring staff.

countercyclical Tending to move in the opposite direction to aggregate output and employment over the business cycle.

creative destruction Joseph Schumpeter's name for the process by which old technologies and the firms that do not adapt are swept away by the new, because they cannot compete in the market. In his view, the failure of unprofitable firms is creative because it releases labour and capital goods for use in new combinations.

credit-constrained A description of individuals who are able to borrow only on unfavourable terms. *See also: credit-excluded.*

credit-excluded A description of individuals who are unable to borrow on any terms. *See also: credit-constrained.*

credit ratings agency A firm which collects information to calculate the credit-worthiness of individuals or companies, and sells the resulting rating for a fee to interested parties.

credit rationing The process by which those with less wealth borrow on unfavourable terms, compared to those with more wealth.

crowding out There are two quite distinct uses of the term. One is the observed negative effect when economic incentives displace people's ethical or other-regarding motivations. In studies of individual behaviour, incentives may have a crowding out effect on social preferences. A second use of the term is to refer to the effect of an increase in government spending in reducing private spending, as would be expected for example in an economy working at full capacity utilization, or when a fiscal expansion is associated with a rise in the interest rate.

current account (CA) The sum of all payments made to a country minus all payments made by the country. *See also: current account deficit, current account surplus.*

current account deficit The excess of the value of a country's imports over the combined value of its exports plus its net earnings from assets abroad. *See also: current account, current account surplus.*

current account surplus The excess of the combined value of its exports and net earnings from assets abroad over the value of its imports. *See also: current account, current account deficit.*

cyclical unemployment The increase in unemployment above equilibrium unemployment caused by a fall in aggregate demand associated with the business cycle. *Also known as: demand-deficient unemployment. See also: equilibrium unemployment.*

deadweight loss A loss of total surplus relative to a Pareto-efficient allocation.

decreasing returns to scale These occur when doubling all of the inputs to a production process less than doubles the output. *Also known as: diseconomies of scale. See also: increasing returns to scale.*

default risk The risk that credit given as loans will not be repaid.

deflation A decrease in the general price level. *See also: inflation.*

demand curve The curve that gives the quantity consumers will buy at each possible price.

demand shock An unexpected change in aggregate demand, such as a rise or fall in autonomous consumption, investment, or exports. *See also: supply shock.*

demand side (aggregate economy) How spending decisions generate demand for goods and services, and as a result, employment and output. It uses the multiplier model. *See also: supply side (aggregate economy).*

demand side The side of a market on which those participating are offering money in return for some other good or service (for example, those purchasing bread). *See also: supply side.*

democracy A political system, that ideally gives equal political power to all citizens, defined by individual rights such as freedom of speech, assembly, and the press; fair elections in which virtually all adults are eligible to vote; and in which the government leaves office if it loses.

democratic accountability Political accountability by means of elections and other democratic processes. *See also: accountability, political accountability.*

demographic transition A slowdown in population growth as a fall in death rate is more than balanced by a fall in birth rates.

depreciation The loss in value of a form of wealth that occurs either through use (wear and tear) or the passage of time (obsolescence).

derivative A financial instrument in the form of a contract that can be traded, whose value is based on the performance of underlying assets such as shares, bonds or real estate. *See also: collateralized debt obligation.*

developmental state A government that takes a leading role in promoting the process of economic development through its public investments, subsidies of particular industries, education and other public policies.

differentiated product A product produced by a single firm that has some unique characteristics compared to similar products of other firms.

diffusion gap The lag between the first introduction of an innovation and its general use. *See also: diffusion.*

diffusion The spread of the invention throughout the economy. *See also: diffusion gap.*

diminishing average product of labour A situation in which, as more labour is used in a given production process, the average product of labour typically falls.

diminishing marginal product A property of some production functions according to which each additional unit of input results in a smaller increment in total output than did the previous unit.

diminishing marginal returns to consumption The value to the individual of an additional unit of consumption declines, the more consumption the individual has. *Also known as: diminishing marginal utility.*

diminishing marginal utility A property of some utility functions according to which each additional unit of a given variable results in a smaller increment to total utility than did the previous additional unit. *Also* *known as: diminishing marginal returns to consumption.*

diminishing returns A situation in which the use of an additional unit of a factor of production results in a smaller increase in output than the previous increase. *Also known as: diminishing marginal returns in production*

discount rate A measure of the person's impatience: how much the person values an additional unit of consumption now relative to an additional unit of consumption later. It is the slope of the person's indifference curve for consumption now and consumption later, minus one. *Also known as: subjective discount rate.*

discounting future generations' costs and benefits A measure of how we currently value the costs and benefits experienced by people who will live in the future. Note that this is not a measure of individual impatience about one's own future benefits and costs.

diseconomies of scale These occur when doubling all of the inputs to a production process less than doubles the output. *Also known as: decreasing returns to scale. See also: economies of scale.*

disequilibrium process An economic variable may change either because the things that determine the equilibrium value of that variable have changed (an equilibrium process), or because the system is not in equilibrium so that there exist forces for change that are internal to the model in question (a disequilibrium process). The latter process applies when the economy moves towards a stable equilibrium (which itself is not moving) or away from a tipping point (an unstable equilibrium).

disequilibrium rent The economic rent that arises when a market is not in equilibrium, for example when there is excess demand or excess supply in a market for some good or service. In contrast, rents that arise in equilibrium are called equilibrium rents.

disinflation A decrease in the rate of inflation. *See also: inflation, deflation.*

disposable income Income available after paying taxes and receiving transfers from the government.

distributionally neutral A policy that is neither progressive or regressive so that it does not alter the distribution of income. *See also: progressive (policy), regressive (policy).*

division of labour The specialization of producers to carry out different tasks in the production process. *Also known as: specialization.*

dominant strategy equilibrium An outcome of a game in which every player plays his or her dominant strategy.

dominant strategy Action that yields the highest payoff for a player, no matter what the other players do.

dominant technology A technology that produces the same amount at lower cost than alternative technologies irrespective of the prices of inputs. It is capable of producing the same amount of output as the alternative technology with less of at least one input, and not more of any input.

dominated We describe an outcome in this way if more of something that is positively valued can be attained without less of anything else that is positively valued. In short: an outcome is dominated if there is a win-win alternative.

earnings Wages, salaries, and other income from labour.

economic accountability Accountability achieved by economic processes, notably competition among firms or other entities in which failure to take account of those affected will result in losses in profits or in business failure. *See also: accountability, political accountability.*

economic cost The out-of-pocket cost of an action, plus the opportunity cost.

economic profit A firm's revenue minus its total costs (including the opportunity cost of capital).

economic rent A payment or other benefit received above and beyond what the individual would have received in his or her next best alternative (or reservation option). *See also: reservation option.*

economic system The institutions that organize the production and distribution of goods and services in an entire economy.

economically feasible Policies for which the desired outcomes are a Nash equilibrium, so

that once implemented private economic actors will not undo the desired effects.

economics The study of how people interact with each other and with their natural surroundings in providing their livelihoods, and how this changes over time.

economies of agglomeration The advantages that firms may enjoy when they are located close to other firms in the same or related industries. *See also: economies of scale.*

economies of scale These occur when doubling all of the inputs to a production process more than doubles the output. The shape of a firm's long-run average cost curve depends both on returns to scale in production and the effect of scale on the prices it pays for its inputs. *Also known as: increasing returns to scale. See also: diseconomies of scale.*

economies of scope Cost savings that occur when two or more products are produced jointly by a single firm, rather being produced in separate firms.

effective tax rate on profits This is calculated by taking the before-tax profit rate, subtracting the after-tax profit rate, and dividing the result by the before-tax profit rate. This fraction is usually multiplied by 100 and reported as a percentage.

efficiency wages The payment an employer makes that is higher than an employee's reservation wage, so as to motivate the employee to provide more effort on the job than he or she would otherwise choose to make. *See also: labour discipline model, employment rent.*

employment protection legislation Laws making job dismissal more costly (or impossible) for employers.

employment rate The ratio of the number of employed to the population of working age. *See also: population of working age.*

employment rent The economic rent a worker receives when the net value of her job exceeds the net value of her next best alternative (that is, being unemployed). *Also known as: cost of job loss.*

endogenous Produced by the workings of a model rather than coming from outside the model. *See also: exogenous*

endowment The facts about an individual that may affect his or her income, such as the physical wealth a person has, either land, housing, or a portfolio of shares (stocks). Also includes level and quality of schooling, special training, the computer languages in which the individual can work, work experience in internships, citizenship, whether the individual has a visa (or green card) allowing employment in a particular labour market, the nationality and gender of the individual, and even the person's race or social class background. *See also: human capital.*

entrepreneur A person who creates or is an early adopter of new technologies, organizational forms, and other opportunities.

environment-consumption indifference curve A curve on which all points are combinations of environmental quality and consumption that are equally valued by an individual or policymaker. The slope of the indifference curve is the ratio of the marginal disutility of lost consumption due to the cost of abating and of the marginal utility of environmental quality (a public good shared by all).

equilibrium (of a market) A state of a market in which there is no tendency for the quantities bought and sold, or the market price, to change, unless there is some change in the underlying costs, preferences, or other determinants of the behaviour of market actors.

equilibrium rent Rent in a market that is in equilibrium. *Also known as: stationary or persistent rents.*

equilibrium unemployment The number of people seeking work but without jobs, which is determined by the intersection of the wage-setting and price-setting curves. This is the Nash equilibrium of the labour market where neither employers nor workers could do better by changing their behaviour. *See also: involuntary unemployment, cyclical unemployment, wage-setting curve, price-setting curve, inflation-stabilizing rate of unemployment.*

equilibrium A model outcome that is self-perpetuating. In this case, something of interest does not change unless an outside or external force is introduced that alters the model's description of the situation.

equity An individual's own investment in a project. This is recorded in an individual's or firm's balance sheet as net worth. *See also: net worth. An entirely different use of the term is synonymous with fairness.*

evolutionary economics An approach that studies the process of economic change, including technological innovation, the diffusion of new social norms, and the development of novel institutions.

excess demand A situation in which the quantity of a good demanded is greater than the quantity supplied at the current price. *See also: excess supply.*

excess supply A situation in which the quantity of a good supplied is greater than the quantity demanded at the current price. *See also: excess demand.*

exchange rate The number of units of home currency that can be exchanged for one unit of foreign currency. For example, the number of Australian dollars (AUD) needed to buy one US dollar (USD) is defined as number of AUD per USD. An increase in this rate is a depreciation of the AUD and a decrease is an appreciation of the AUD.

exogenous shock A sharp change in external conditions affecting a model.

exogenous Coming from outside the model rather than being produced by the workings of the model itself. *See also: endogenous.*

expected inflation The opinion that wage- and price-setters form about the level of inflation in the next period. *See also: inflation.*

exports (X) Goods and services produced in a particular country and sold to households, firms and governments in other countries.

expropriation risk The probability that an asset will be taken from its owner by the government or some other actor.

external benefit A positive external effect: that is, a positive effect of a production, consumption, or other economic decision on another person or people that is not specified as a benefit in a contract. *Also known as: external economy. See also: external effect.*

external cost A negative external effect: that is, the negative effect of production, consumption, or other economic decisions on another person or party, which is not specified as a liability in a contract. *Also*

known as: external diseconomy. See also: external effect.

external diseconomy A negative effect of a production, consumption, or other economic decision, that is not specified as a liability in a contract. *Also known as: external cost, negative externality. See also: external effect.*

external economy A positive effect of a production, consumption, or other economic decision, that is not specified as a benefit in a contract. *Also known as: external benefit, positive externality. See also: external effect.*

external effect A positive or negative effect of a production, consumption, or other economic decision on another person or people that is not specified as a benefit or liability in a contract. It is called an external effect because the effect in question is outside the contract. *Also known as: externality. See also: incomplete contract, market failure, external benefit, external cost.*

factors of production The labour, machinery and equipment (usually referred to as capital), land, and other inputs to a production process.

fairness A way to evaluate an allocation based on one's conception of justice.

fallacy of composition Mistaken inference that what is true of the parts (for example a household) must be true of the whole (in this case the economy as a whole). *See also: paradox of thrift.*

feasible frontier The curve made of points that defines the maximum feasible quantity of one good for a given quantity of the other. *See also: feasible set.*

feasible set All of the combinations of the things under consideration that a decision-maker could choose given the economic, physical or other constraints that he faces. *See also: feasible frontier.*

final income A measure of the value of goods and services a household can consume from its disposable income. This is equal to disposable income minus VAT paid, plus the value of public services received.

financial accelerator The mechanism through which firms' and households' ability to borrow increases when the value of the collateral they have pledged to the lender (often a bank) goes up.

financial deregulation Policies allowing banks and other financial institutions greater freedom in the types of financial assets they can sell, as well as other practices.

fire sale The sale of something at a very low price because of the seller's urgent need for money.

firm-specific asset Something that a person owns or can do that has more value in the individual's current firm than in their next best alternative.

firm A business organization which pays wages and salaries to employ people, and purchases inputs, to produce and market goods and services with the intention of making a profit.

first copy costs The fixed costs of the production of a knowledge-intensive good or service.

fiscal capacity The ability of a government to impose and collect substantial taxes from a population at low administrative and other costs. One measure of this is the amount collected divided by the cost of administering the tax system.

fiscal multiplier The total (direct and indirect) change in output caused by an initial change in government spending. *See also: fiscal stimulus, fiscal policy, aggregate demand.*

fiscal policy Changes in taxes or government spending in order to stabilize the economy. *See also: fiscal stimulus, fiscal multiplier, aggregate demand.*

fiscal stimulus The use by the government of fiscal policy (via a combination of tax cuts and spending increases) with the intention of increasing aggregate demand. *See also: fiscal multiplier, fiscal, policy, aggregate demand.*

Fisher equation The relation that gives the real interest rate as the difference between the nominal interest rate and expected inflation: real interest rate = nominal interest rate – expected inflation.

fixed costs Costs of production that do not vary with the number of units produced.

flow A quantity measured per unit of time, such as annual income or hourly wage.

foreign direct investment (FDI) Ownership and substantial control over assets in a foreign country. *See also: foreign portfolio investment.*

foreign portfolio investment The acquisition of bonds or shares in a foreign country where the holdings of the foreign assets are not sufficiently great to give the owner substantial control over the owned entity. Foreign direct investment (FDI), by contrast, entails ownership and substantial control over the owned assets. *See also: foreign direct investment.*

free ride Benefiting from the contributions of others to some cooperative project without contributing oneself.

fundamental value of a share The share price based on anticipated future earnings and the level of systematic risk, which can be interpreted as a measure of the benefit today of holding the asset now and in the future.

fundamental value *See: fundamental value of a share.*

gains from exchange The benefits that each party gains from a transaction compared to how they would have fared without the exchange. *Also known as: gains from trade. See also: economic rent.*

game theory A branch of mathematics that studies strategic interactions, meaning situations in which each actor knows that the benefits they receive depend on the actions taken by all. *See also: game.*

game A model of strategic interaction that describes the players, the feasible strategies, the information that the players have, and their payoffs. *See also: game theory.*

GDP deflator A measure of the level of prices for domestically produced output. This is the ratio of nominal (or current price) GDP to real (or constant price) GDP.

general-purpose technologies Technological advances that can be applied to many sectors, and spawn further innovations. Information and communications technology (ICT), and electricity are two common examples.

Gini coefficient A measure of inequality of any quantity such as income or wealth, varying from a value of zero (if there is no inequality) to one (if a single individual receives all of it).

global financial crisis This began in 2007 with the collapse of house prices in the US, leading to the fall in prices of assets based on subprime mortgages and to widespread uncertainty about the solvency of banks in the US and Europe, which had borrowed to purchase such assets. The ramifications were felt around the world, as global trade was cut back sharply. Goverments and central banks responded aggressively with stabilization policies.

global greenhouse gas abatement cost curve This shows the total cost of abating greenhouse gas emissions using abatement policies ranked from the most cost-effective to the least. *See also: abatement policy.*

Globalization I and II Two separate periods of increasing global economic integration: the first extended from before 1870 until the outbreak of the First World War in 1914, and the second extended from the end of the Second World War into the twenty-first century. *See also: globalization.*

globalization A process by which the economies of the world become increasingly integrated by the freer flow across national boundaries of goods, investment, finance, and to a lesser extent, labour. The term is sometimes applied more broadly to include ideas, culture, and even the spread of epidemic diseases.

gold standard The system of fixed exchange rates, abandoned in the Great Depression, by which the value of a currency was defined in terms of gold, for which the currency could be exchanged. *See also: Great Depression.*

golden age (of capitalism) The period of high productivity growth, high employment, and low and stable inflation extending from the end of the Second World War to the early 1970s.

goods market equilibrium The point at which output equals the aggregate demand for goods produced in the home economy. The economy will continue producing at this output level unless something changes spending behaviour. *See also: aggregate demand.*

governing elite Top government officials such as the president, cabinet officials, and legislative leaders, unified by a common interest such as membership in a particular party.

government bond A financial instrument issued by governments that promises to pay flows of money at specific intervals.

government budget balance The difference between government tax revenue and government spending (including government purchases of goods and services, investment spending, and spending on transfers such as pensions and unemployment benefits). *See also: government budget deficit, government budget surplus.*

government budget deficit When the government budget balance is negative. *See also: government budget balance, government budget surplus.*

government budget surplus When the government budget balance is positive. *See also: government budget balance, government budget deficit.*

government debt The sum of all the bonds the government has sold over the years to finance its deficits, minus the ones that have matured.

government failure A failure of political accountability. (This term is widely used in a variety of ways, none of them strictly analogous to market failure, for which the criterion is simply Pareto inefficiency).

government spending (G) Expenditure by the government to purchase goods and services. When used as a component of aggregate demand, this does not include spending on transfers such as pensions and unemployment benefits. *See also: government transfers*

government transfers Spending by the government in the form of payments to households or individuals. Unemployment benefits and pensions are examples. Transfers are not included in government spending (G) in the national accounts. *See also: government spending (G)*

government Within a given territory, the only body that can dictate what people must do or not do, and can legitimately use force and restraints on an individual's freedom to achieve that end. *Also known as: state.*

Great Depression The period of a sharp fall in output and employment in many countries in the 1930s.

great moderation Period of low volatility in aggregate output in advanced economies between the 1980s and the 2008 financial crisis. The name was suggested by James Stock and Mark Watson, the economists, and

popularized by Ben Bernanke, then chairman of the Federal Reserve.

great recession The prolonged recession that followed the global financial crisis of 2008.

green adjustment Accounting adjustment made to conventional measures of national income to include the value of natural capital.

greenhouse gas Gases—mainly water vapour, carbon dioxide, methane and ozone—released in the earth's atmosphere that lead to increases in atmospheric temperature and changes in climate.

gross domestic product (GDP) A measure of the market value of the output of the economy in a given period.

gross income Income net of taxes paid. Includes depreciation. *See also: income, net income.*

gross unemployment benefit replacement rate The proportion of a worker's previous gross (pre-tax) wage that is received (gross of taxation) when unemployed.

hedge finance Financing used by firms to fulfil contractual payment obligations using cashflow. Term coined by Hyman Minsky in his Financial Instability Hypothesis. *See also: speculative finance.*

hedonic pricing A method used to infer the economic value of unpriced environmental or perceptual qualities that affect the price of a marketed good. It allows a researcher to put a price on hard-to-quantify characteristics. Estimations are based on people's revealed preferences, that is, the price they pay for one thing compared to another.

hidden actions (problem of) This occurs when some action taken by one party to an exchange is not known or cannot be verified by the other. For example, the employer cannot know (or cannot verify) how hard the worker she has employed is actually working. *Also known as: moral hazard. See also: hidden attributes (problem of).*

hidden attributes (problem of) This occurs when some attribute of the person engaging in an exchange (or the product or service being provided) is not known to the other parties. An example is that the individual purchasing health insurance knows her own

health status, but the insurance company does not. *Also known as: adverse selection. See also: hidden actions (problem of).*

human capital The stock of knowledge, skills, behavioural attributes, and personal characteristics that determine the labour productivity or labour earnings of an individual. Investment in this through education, training, and socialization can increase the stock, and such investment is one of the sources of economic growth. Part of an individual's endowments. *See also: endowment.*

hyperglobalization An extreme (and so far hypothetical) type of globalization in which there is virtually no barrier to the free flows of goods, services, and capital. *See also: globalization.*

idiosyncratic risk A risk that only affects a small number of assets at one time. Traders can almost eliminate their exposure to such risks by holding a diverse portfolio of assets affected by different risks. *Also known as: diversifiable risk.*

impatience Any preference to move consumption from the future to the present. This preference may be derived either from pure impatience or diminishing marginal returns to consumption.

imports (M) Goods and services produced in other countries and purchased by domestic households, firms, and the government.

in-kind transfers Public expenditure in the form of free or subsidized services for households rather than in the form of cash transfers.

inactive population People in the population of working age who are neither employed nor actively looking for paid work. Those working in the home raising children, for example, are not considered as being in the labour force and therefore are classified this way.

incentive Economic reward or punishment, which influences the benefits and costs of alternative courses of action.

inclusive trade union A union, representing many firms and sectors, which takes into account the consequences of wage increases for job creation in the entire economy in the long run.

income effect The effect that the additional income would have if there were no change in the price or opportunity cost.

income elasticity of demand The percentage change in demand that would occur in response to a 1% increase in the individual's income.

income The amount of profit, interest, rent, labour earnings, and other payments (including transfers from the government) received, net of taxes paid, measured over a period of time such as a year. The maximum amount that you could consume and leave your wealth unchanged. *Also known as: disposable income. See also: pre-tax income.*

incomplete contract A contract that does not specify, in an enforceable way, every aspect of the exchange that affects the interests of parties to the exchange (or of others).

increasing returns to scale These occur when doubling all of the inputs to a production process more than doubles the output. The shape of a firm's long-run average cost curve depends both on returns to scale in production and the effect of scale on the prices it pays for its inputs. *Also known as: economies of scale. See also: decreasing returns to scale, constant returns to scale.*

incremental innovation Innovation that improves an existing product or process cumulatively.

index A measure of the amount of something in one period of time, compared to the amount of the same thing in a different period of time, called the reference period or base period. It is common to set its value at 100 in the reference period.

indifference curve A curve of the points which indicate the combinations of goods that provide a given level of utility to the individual.

Industrial Revolution A wave of technological advances and organizational changes starting in Britain in the eighteenth century, which transformed an agrarian and craft-based economy into a commercial and industrial economy.

industry Goods-producing business activity: agriculture, mining, manufacturing, and construction. Manufacturing is the most important component.

inequality aversion A dislike of outcomes in which some individuals receive more than others.

infant industry A relatively new industrial sector in a country that has relatively high costs, because its recent establishment means that it has few benefits from learning by doing, its small size deprives it of economies of scale, or a lack of similar firms means that it does not benefit from economies of agglomeration. Temporary tariff protection of this sector or other support may increase productivity in an economy in the long run.

inflation-adjusted price Price that takes into account the change in the overall price level.

inflation-stabilizing rate of unemployment The unemployment rate (at labour market equilibrium) at which inflation is constant. Originally known as the 'natural rate' of unemployment. *Also known as: non-accelerating rate of unemployment, stable inflation rate of unemployment. See also: equilibrium unemployment.*

inflation targeting Monetary policy regime where the central bank changes interest rates to influence aggregate demand in order to keep the economy close to an inflation target, which is normally specified by the government.

inflation An increase in the general price level in the economy. Usually measured over a year. *See also: deflation, disinflation.*

innovation rents Profits in excess of the opportunity cost of capital that an innovator gets by introducing a new technology, organizational form, or marketing strategy. *Also known as: Schumpeterian rents.*

innovation system The relationships among private firms, governments, educational institutions, individual scientists, and other actors involved in the invention, modification, and diffusion of new technologies, and the way that these social interactions are governed by a combination of laws, policies, knowledge, and social norms in force.

innovation The process of invention and diffusion considered as a whole.

insolvent An entity is this if the value of its assets is less than the value of its liabilities. *See also: solvent.*

institution The laws and social customs governing the way people interact in society.

intellectual property rights Patents, trademarks, and copyrights. *See also: patent, trademark, copyright.*

interest rate (short-term) The price of borrowing base money.

interest rate The price of bringing some buying power forward in time. *See also: nominal interest rate, real interest rate.*

intergenerational elasticity When comparing parents and grown offspring, the percentage difference in the second generation's status that is associated with a 1% difference in the adult generation's status. *See also: intergenerational inequality, intergenerational mobility, intergenerational transmission of economic differences.*

intergenerational inequality The extent to which differences in parental generations are passed on to the next generation, as measured by the intergenerational elasticity or the intergenerational correlation. *See also: intergenerational elasticity, intergenerational mobility, intergenerational transmission of economic differences.*

intergenerational mobility Changes in the relative economic or social status between parents and children. Upward mobility occurs when the status of a child surpasses that of the parents. Downward mobility is the converse. A widely used measure of intergenerational mobility is the correlation between the positions of parents and children (for example, in their years of schooling or income). Another is the intergenerational elasticity. *See also: intergenerational elasticity, intergenerational transmission of economic differences.*

intergenerational transmission of economic differences The processes by which the economic status of the adult sons and daughters comes to resemble the economic status of the parents. *See also: intergenerational elasticity, intergenerational mobility.*

invention The development of new methods of production and new products.

inventory Goods held by a firm prior to sale or use, including raw materials, and partially-finished or finished goods intended for sale.

investment function (aggregate) An equation that shows how investment spending in the economy as a whole depends on other variables, namely, the interest rate and profit expectations. *See also: interest rate, profit.*

investment (I) Expenditure on newly produced capital goods (machinery and equipment) and buildings, including new housing.

irrational exuberance A process by which assets become overvalued. The expression was first used by Alan Greenspan, then chairman of the US Federal Reserve Board, in 1996. It was popularized as an economic concept by the economist Robert Shiller.

isocost line A line that represents all combinations that cost a given total amount.

isoprofit curve A curve on which all points yield the same profit.

isototal benefits curve The combinations of the probability of innovation and the total benefits to society from a firm's innovation that yield the same total benefits.

Joule A unit of energy or work, originally defined as the amount of energy necessary to lift a small apple vertically 1 metre.

labour discipline model A model that explains how employers set wages so that employees receive an economic rent (called employment rent), which provides workers an incentive to work hard in order to avoid job termination. *See also: employment rent, efficiency wages.*

labour force The number of people in the population of working age who are, or wish to be, in work outside the household. They are either employed (including self-employed) or unemployed. *See also: unemployment rate, employment rate, participation rate.*

labour-intensive Making greater use of labour as an input in production as compared with machines and other inputs. *See also: capital-intensive.*

labour market equilibrium The combination of the real wage and the level of employment determined by the intersection of the wage-setting and the price-setting curves. This is the Nash equilibrium of the labour market because neither employers nor workers could do better by changing their behaviour.

See also: equilibrium unemployment, inflation-stabilizing rate of unemployment.

labour market matching The way in which employers looking for additional employees (that is, with vacancies) meet people seeking a new job.

labour market In this market, employers offer wages to individuals who may agree to work under their direction. Economists say that employers are on the demand side of this market, while employees are on the supply side. *See also: labour force.*

labour productivity Total output divided by the number of hours or some other measure of labour input.

law of one price Holds when a good is traded at the same price across all buyers and sellers. If a good were sold at different prices in different places, a trader could buy it cheaply in one place and sell it at a higher price in another. *See also: arbitrage.*

learning by doing This occurs when the output per unit of inputs increases with greater experience in producing a good or service.

lending rate (bank) The average interest rate charged by commercial banks to firms and households. This rate will typically be above the policy interest rate: the difference is the markup or spread on commercial lending. *Also known as: market interest rate. See also: interest rate, policy rate.*

Leontief paradox The unexpected finding by Wassily Leontief that exports from the US were labour-intensive and its imports capital-intensive, a result that contradicts what the economic theories predicted: namely that a country abundant in capital (like the US) would export goods that used a large quantity of capital in their production.

leverage ratio (for banks or households) The value of assets divided by the equity stake in those assets.

leverage ratio (for non-bank companies) The value of total liabilities divided by total assets.

leverage *See: leverage ratio.*

liability Anything of value that is owed. *See also: balance sheet, asset.*

limit order An announced price and quantity combination for an asset, either to be sold or bought.

linear regression line The best-fitting line through a set of data.

liquid *See: liquidity.*

liquidity risk The risk that an asset cannot be exchanged for cash rapidly enough to prevent a financial loss.

liquidity Ease of buying or selling a financial asset at a predictable price.

lock-in A consequence of the network external effects that create winner-take-all competition. The competitive process results in an outcome that is difficult to change, even if users of the technology consider an alternative innovation superior.

logarithmic scale A way of measuring a quantity based on the logarithm function, $f(x) = \log(x)$. The logarithm function converts a ratio to a difference: $\log(a/b) = \log a - \log b$. This is very useful for working with growth rates. For instance, if national income doubles from 50 to 100 in a poor country and from 1,000 to 2,000 in a rich country, the absolute difference in the first case is 50 and in the second 1,000, but $\log(100) - \log(50) = 0.693$, and $\log(2,000) - \log(1,000) = 0.693$. The ratio in each case is 2 and $\log(2) = 0.693$.

long-run equilibrium An equilibrium that is achieved when variables that were held constant in the short run (for example, the number of firms in a market) are allowed to adjust, as people have time to respond the situation.

long run (model) The term does not refer to a period of time, but instead to what is exogenous. A long-run cost curve, for example, refers to costs when the firm can fully adjust all of the inputs including its capital goods; but technology and the economy's institutions are exogenous. *See also: technology, institutions, short run (model), medium run (model).*

Lorenz curve A graphical representation of inequality of some quantity such as wealth or income. Individuals are arranged in ascending order by how much of this quantity they have, and the cumulative share of the total is then plotted against the cumulative share of the population. For complete equality of income, for example, it would be a straight line with a slope of one. The extent to which the curve falls below this perfect equality line is a measure of inequality. *See also: Gini coefficient.*

low capacity utilization When a firm or economy could increase output by increasing employment utilizing the existing capital goods.

marginal cost The effect on total cost of producing one additional unit of output. It corresponds to the slope of the total cost function at each point.

marginal external cost (MEC) The cost of producing an additional unit of a good that is incurred by anyone other than the producer of the good. *See also: marginal private cost, marginal social cost.*

marginal private benefit (MPB) The benefit (in terms of profit, or utility) of producing or consuming an additional unit of a good for the individual who decides to produce or consume it, not taking into account any benefit received by others.

marginal private cost (MPC) The cost for the producer of producing an additional unit of a good, not taking into account any costs its production imposes on others. *See also: marginal external cost, marginal social cost.*

marginal product The additional amount of output that is produced if a particular input was increased by one unit, while holding all other inputs constant.

marginal productivity of abatement expenditures The marginal rate of transformation (MRT) of abatement costs into improved environment. It is the slope of the feasible frontier. *See also: marginal rate of transformation, feasible frontier.*

marginal propensity to consume (MPC) The change in consumption when disposable income changes by one unit.

marginal propensity to import The change in total imports associated with a change in total income.

marginal rate of substitution (MRS) The trade-off that a person is willing to make between two goods. At any point, this is the slope of the indifference curve. *See also: marginal rate of transformation.*

marginal rate of transformation (MRT) The quantity of some good that must be sacrificed to acquire one additional unit of another good. At any point, it is the slope of

the feasible frontier. *See also: marginal rate of substitution.*

marginal revenue The increase in revenue obtained by increasing the quantity from Q to $Q + 1$.

marginal social benefit (MSB) The benefit (in terms of utility) of producing or consuming an additional unit of a good, taking into account both the benefit to the individual who decides to produce or consume it, and the benefit to anyone else affected by the decision.

marginal social cost (MSC) The cost of producing an additional unit of a good, taking into account both the cost for the producer and the costs incurred by others affected by the good's production. Marginal social cost is the sum of the marginal private cost and the marginal external cost.

marginal utility The additional utility resulting from a one-unit increase of a given variable.

market capitalization rate The rate of return that is just high enough to induce investors to hold shares in a particular company. This will be high if the company is subject to a high level of systematic risk.

market-clearing price At this price there is no excess supply or excess demand. *See also: equilibrium.*

market failure When markets allocate resources in a Pareto-inefficient way.

market power An attribute of a firm that can sell its product at a range of feasible prices, so that it can benefit by acting as a price-setter (rather than a price-taker).

market A market is a way of connecting people who may mutually benefit by exchanging goods or services through a process of buying and selling.

matching market A market that matches members of two distinct groups of people. Each person in the market would benefit from being connected to the right member of the other group. *Also known as: two-sided market.*

maturity transformation The practice of borrowing money short-term and lending it long-term. For example, a bank accepts deposits, which it promises to repay at short notice or no notice, and makes long-term

loans (which can be repaid over many years). *Also known as: liquidity transformation*

median voter model An economic model of the location of businesses applied to the positions taken in electoral platforms when two parties compete that provides conditions under which, in order to maximize the number of votes they will receive, the parties will adopt positions that appeal to the median voter. *See also: median voter.*

median voter If voters can be lined up along a single more-versus-less dimension (such as preferring higher or lower taxes, more or less environmental protection), the median voter is the one 'in the middle'—that is (if there is an odd number of voters in total), with an equal number preferring more and preferring less than what he or she does. *See also: median voter model.*

medium run (model) The term does not refer to a period of time, but instead to what is exogenous. In this case capital stock, technology, and institutions are exogenous. Output, employment, prices, and wages are endogenous. *See also: capital, technology, institutions, short run (model), long run (model).*

menu costs The resources used in setting and changing prices.

merchandise trade Trade in tangible products that are physically shipped across borders.

merit goods Goods and services that should be available to everyone, independently of their ability to pay.

minimum acceptable offer In the ultimatum game, the smallest offer by the Proposer that will not be rejected by the Responder. Generally applied in bargaining situations to mean the least favourable offer that would be accepted.

missing market A market in which there is some kind of exchange that, if implemented, would be mutually beneficial. This does not occur due to asymmetric or non-verifiable information.

momentum trading Share trading strategy based on the idea that new information is not incorporated into prices instantly, so that prices exhibit positive correlation over short periods.

monetary policy Central bank (or government) actions aimed at influencing economic activity through changing interest rates or the prices of financial assets. *See also: quantitative easing.*

money wage The amount of money an employer pays to a worker. *Also known as: nominal wage.*

money A medium of exchange consisting of bank notes and bank deposits, or anything else that can be used to purchase goods and services, and is accepted as payment because others can use it for the same purpose.

monopolized market Market in which a single firm produces all the goods that are sold.

monopoly power The power that a firm has to control its own price. The fewer close substitutes for the product are available, the greater the firm's price-setting power. *See also: monopoly.*

monopoly rents A form of economic profits, which arise due to restricted competition in selling a firm's product. *See also: economic profits.*

monopoly A firm that is the only seller of a product without close substitutes. Also refers to a market with only one seller. *See also: monopoly power, natural monopoly.*

moral hazard This term originated in the insurance industry to express the problem that insurers face, namely, the person with home insurance may take less care to avoid fires or other damages to his home, thereby increasing the risk above what it would be in absence of insurance. This term now refers to any situation in which one party to an interaction is deciding on an action that affects the profits or wellbeing of the other but which the affected party cannot control by means of a contract, often because the affected party does not have adequate information on the action. It is also referred to as the 'hidden actions' problem. *See also: hidden actions (problems of), incomplete contract, too big to fail.*

mortgage-backed security (MBS) A financial asset that uses mortgages as collateral. Investors receive payments derived from the interest and principal of the underlying mortgages. *See also: collateral.*

mortgage (or mortgage loan) A loan contracted by households and businesses to purchase a property without paying the total

value at one time. Over a period of many years, the borrower repays the loan, plus interest. The debt is secured by the property itself, referred to as collateral. *See also: collateral.*

multiplier model A model of aggregate demand that includes the multiplier process. *See also: fiscal multiplier, multiplier process.*

multiplier process A mechanism through which the direct and indirect effect of a change in autonomous spending affects aggregate output. *See also: fiscal multiplier, multiplier model.*

multiplier *See: fiscal multiplier.*

Nash equilibrium A set of strategies, one for each player in the game, such that each player's strategy is a best response to the strategies chosen by everyone else.

national accounts The system used for measuring overall output and expenditure in a country.

natural experiment An empirical study exploiting naturally occurring statistical controls in which researchers do not have the ability to assign participants to treatment and control groups, as is the case in conventional experiments. Instead, differences in law, policy, weather, or other events can offer the opportunity to analyse populations as if they had been part of an experiment. The validity of such studies depends on the premise that the assignment of subjects to the naturally occurring treatment and control groups can be plausibly argued to be random.

natural logarithm *See: logarithmic scale.*

natural monopoly A production process in which the long-run average cost curve is sufficiently downward-sloping to make it impossible to sustain competition among firms in this market.

negative feedback (process) A process whereby some initial change sets in motion a process that dampens the initial change. *See also: positive feedback (process).*

net capital flows The borrowing and lending tracked by the current account. *See also: current account, current account deficit, current account surplus.*

net income Gross income minus depreciation. *See also: income, gross income, depreciation.*

net present value The present value of a stream of future income minus the associated costs (whether the costs are in the present or the future). *See also: present value.*

net worth Assets less liabilities. *See also: balance sheet, equity.*

network economies of scale These exist when an increase in the number of users of an output of a firm implies an increase in the value of the output to each of them, because they are connected to each other.

network external effects An external effect of one person's action on another, occuring because the two are connected in a network. *See also: external effect.*

New Deal US President Franklin Roosevelt's program, begun in 1933, of emergency public works and relief programs to employ millions of people. It established the basic structures for modern state social welfare programs, labour policies, and regulation.

nominal interest rate The interest rate uncorrected for inflation. It is the interest rate quoted by high-street banks. *See also: real interest rate, interest rate.*

nominal wage The actual amount received in payment for work, in a particular currency. *Also known as: money wage. See also: real wage.*

non-compete contract A contract of employment containing a provision or agreement by which the worker cannot leave to work for a competitor. This may reduce the reservation option of the worker, lowering the wage that the employer needs to pay.

non-excludable public good A public good for which it is impossible to exclude anyone from having access. *See also: artificially scarce good.*

non-rival good A good that, if available to anyone, is available to everyone at no additional cost. *See also: rival good, non-excludable public good.*

normal profits Corresponds to zero economic profit and means that the rate of profit is equal to the opportunity cost of capital. *See also: economic profit, opportunity cost of capital.*

offshoring The relocation of part of a firm's activities outside of the national boundaries in which it operates. It can take place within a multinational company or may involve outsourcing production to other firms.

Okun's coefficient The change in the unemployment rate in percentage points predicted to be associated with a 1% change in the growth rate of GDP. *See also: Okun's law.*

Okun's law The empirical regularity that changes in the rate of growth of GDP are negatively correlated with the rate of unemployment. *See also: Okun's coefficient.*

oligopoly A market with a small number of sellers, giving each seller some market power.

opportunity cost of capital The amount of income an investor could have received by investing the unit of capital elsewhere.

opportunity cost When taking an action implies forgoing the next best alternative action, this is the net benefit of the foregone alternative.

order book A record of limit orders placed by buyers and sellers, but not yet fulfilled.

ownership The right to use and exclude others from the use of something, and the right to sell the thing that is owned.

paradox of thrift If a single individual consumes less, her savings will increase; but if everyone consumes less, the result may be lower rather than higher savings overall. The attempt to increase saving is thwarted if an increase in the saving rate is unmatched by an increase in investment (or other source of aggregate demand such as government spending on goods and services). The outcome is a reduction in aggregate demand and lower output so that actual levels of saving do not increase.

Pareto criterion According to the Pareto criterion, a desirable attribute of an allocation is that it be Pareto-efficient. *See also: Pareto dominant.*

Pareto dominant Allocation A Pareto-dominates allocation B if at least one party would be better off with A than B, and nobody would be worse off. *See also: Pareto efficient.*

Pareto efficiency curve The set of all allocations that are Pareto efficient. Often referred to as the contract curve, even in social interactions in which there is no contract,

which is why we avoid the term. *See also: Pareto efficient.*

Pareto efficient An allocation with the property that there is no alternative technically feasible allocation in which at least one person would be better off, and nobody worse off.

Pareto improvement A change that benefits at least one person without making anyone else worse off. *See also: Pareto dominant.*

participation rate The ratio of the number of people in the labour force to the population of working age. *See also: labour force, population of working age.*

patent A right of exclusive ownership of an idea or invention, which lasts for a specified length of time. During this time it effectively allows the owner to be a monopolist or exclusive user.

payoff The benefit to each player associated with the joint actions of all the players.

perfectly competitive equilibrium Such an equilibrium occurs in a model in which all buyers and sellers are price-takers. In this equilibrium, all transactions take place at a single price. This is known as the law of one price. At that price, the amount supplied equals the amount demanded: the market clears. No buyer or seller can benefit by altering the price they are demanding or offering. They are both price-takers. All potential gains from trade are realized. *See also: law of one price.*

performance-related pay A pay which varies, at least partially, with a worker's performance. *See also: piece-rate work.*

Phillips curve An inverse relationship between the rate of inflation and the rate of unemployment.

piece-rate work A type of employment in which the worker is paid a fixed amount for each unit of the product made.

Pigouvian subsidy A government subsidy to encourage an economic activity that has positive external effects. (For example, subsidizing basic research.)

Pigouvian tax A tax levied on activities that generate negative external effects so as to correct an inefficient market outcome. *See also: external effect, Pigouvian subsidy.*

policy (interest) rate The interest rate set by the central bank, which applies to banks that

borrow base money from each other, and from the central bank. *Also known as: base rate, official rate. See also: real interest rate, nominal interest rate.*

political accountability Accountability achieved by political processes such as elections, oversight by an elected government, or consultation with affected citizens. *See also: accountability, economic accountability.*

political institutions The rules of the game that determine who has power and how it is exercised in a society.

political rent A payment or other benefit in excess of the individual's next best alternative (reservation position) that exists as a result of the individual's political position. The reservation position in this case refers to the individual's situation were he or she to lack a privileged political position. *See also: economic rent.*

political system A political system determines how governments will be selected, and how those governments will make and implement decisions that affect all or most members of a population.

polluter pays principle A guide to environmental policy according to which those who impose negative environmental effects on others should be made to pay for the damages they impose, through taxation or other means.

population of working age A statistical convention, which in many countries is all people aged between 15 and 64 years.

positive feedback (process) A process whereby some initial change sets in motion a process that magnifies the initial change. *See also: negative feedback (process).*

postwar accord An informal agreement (taking different forms in different countries) among employers, governments, and trade unions that created the conditions for rapid economic growth in advanced economies from the late 1940s to the early 1970s. Trade unions accepted the basic institutions of the capitalist economy and did not resist technological change in return for low unemployment, tolerance of unions and other rights, and a rise in real incomes that matched rises in productivity.

1091

power The ability to do (and get) the things one wants in opposition to the intentions of others, ordinarily by imposing or threatening sanctions.

precautionary saving An increase in saving to restore wealth to its target level. *See also: target wealth.*

predistribution policy Government actions that affect the endowments people have and their value, including the distribution of market income and the distribution of privately held wealth. Examples include education, minimum wage, and anti-discrimination policies. *See also: redistribution policy.*

preferences A description of the benefit or cost we associate with each possible outcome.

present value The value today of a stream of future income or other benefits, when these are discounted using an interest rate or the person's own discount rate. *See also: net present value.*

price-based environmental policy A policy that uses a tax or subsidy to affect prices, with the goal of internalizing the external effects on the environment of an individual's choices.

price discrimination A selling strategy in which different prices are set for different buyers or groups of buyers, or prices vary depending on the number of units purchased.

price elasticity of demand The percentage change in demand that would occur in response to a 1% increase in price. We express this as a positive number. Demand is elastic if this is greater than 1, and inelastic if less than 1.

price gap A difference in the price of a good in the exporting country and the importing country. It includes transportation costs and trade taxes. When global markets are in competitive equilibrium, these differences will be entirely due to trade costs. *See also: arbitrage.*

price markup The price minus the marginal cost divided by the price. It is inversely proportional to the elasticity of demand for this good.

price-setting curve The curve that gives the real wage paid when firms choose their profit-maximizing price.

price-taker Characteristic of producers and consumers who cannot benefit by offering or asking any price other than the market price in the equilibrium of a competitive market. They have no power to influence the market price.

primary deficit The government deficit (its revenue minus its expenditure) excluding interest payments on its debt. *See also: government debt.*

primary labour market A market in which workers are typically represented by trade unions, and enjoy high wages and job security. *See also: secondary labour market, segmented labour market.*

principal-agent relationship This relationship exists when one party (the principal) would like another party (the agent) to act in some way, or have some attribute that is in the interest of the principal, and that cannot be enforced or guaranteed in a binding contract. *See also: incomplete contract. Also known as: principal-agent problem.*

prisoners' dilemma A game in which the payoffs in the dominant strategy equilibrium are lower for each player, and also lower in total, than if neither player played the dominant strategy.

private good A good that is both rival, and from which others can be excluded.

private property The right and expectation that one can enjoy one's possessions in ways of one's own choosing, exclude others from their use, and dispose of them by gift or sale to others who then become their owners.

procedural judgements of fairness An evaluation of an outcome based on how the allocation came about, and not on the characteristics of the outcome itself, (for example, how unequal it is). *See also: substantive judgements of fairness.*

process innovation An innovation that allows a good or service to be produced at lower cost than its competitors.

procyclical Tending to move in the same direction as aggregate output and employment over the business cycle. *See also: countercyclical.*

producer surplus The price at which a firm sells a good minus the minimum price at which it would have been willing to sell the good, summed across all units sold.

product innovation An innovation that produces a new good or service at a cost that will attract buyers.

production function A graphical or mathematical expression describing the amount of output that can be produced by any given amount or combination of input(s). The function describes differing technologies capable of producing the same thing.

profit margin The difference between the price and the marginal cost.

progressive (policy) An expenditure or transfer that increases the incomes of poorer households by more than richer households, in percentage terms. *See also: regressive (policy).*

property rights Legal protection of ownership, including the right to exclude others and to benefit from or sell the thing owned.

protectionist policy Measures taken by a government to limit trade; in particular, to reduce the amount of imports in the economy. These are designed to protect local industries from external competition. They can take different forms, such as taxes on imported goods or import quotas.

prudential policy A policy that places a very high value on reducing the likelihood of a disastrous outcome, even if this is costly in terms of other objectives foregone. Such an approach is often advocated where there is great uncertainty about the conditions under which a disastrous outcome would occur.

public bad The negative equivalent of a public good. It is non-rival in the sense that a given individual's consumption of the public bad does not diminish others' consumption of it.

public good A good for which use by one person does not reduce its availability to others. *Also known as: non-rival good. See also: non-excludable public good, artificially scarce good.*

purchasing power parity (PPP) A statistical correction allowing comparisons of the amount of goods people can buy in different countries that have different currencies. *See also: constant prices.*

pure impatience This is a characteristic of a person who values an additional unit of consumption now over an additional unit later, when the amount of consumption is the same now and later. It arises when a person is impatient to consume more now because she places less value on consumption in the future for reasons of myopia, weakness of will, or for other reasons.

quantitative easing (QE) Central bank purchases of financial assets aimed at reducing interest rates on those assets when conventional monetary policy is ineffective because the policy interest rate is at the zero lower bound. *See also: zero lower bound.*

quantity-based environmental policy Policies that implement environmental objectives by using bans, caps, and regulations.

quota A limit imposed by the government on the volume of imports allowed to enter the economy during a specific period of time.

race to the bottom Self-destructive competition between national or regional governments, resulting in lower wages and less regulation to attract foreign investment in a globalized economy.

radical innovation Innovations based on a broad range of knowledge from different sectors, recombining this to create new and very different products.

rationed goods Goods that are allocated to buyers by a process other than price (such as queueing, or a lottery).

real interest rate The interest rate corrected for inflation (that is, the nominal interest rate minus the rate of inflation). It represents how many goods in the future one gets for the goods not consumed now. *See also: nominal interest rate, interest rate.*

real wage The nominal wage, adjusted to take account of changes in prices between different time periods. It measures the amount of goods and services the worker can buy. *See also: nominal wage.*

recession The US National Bureau of Economic Research defines it as a period when output is declining. It is over once the economy begins to grow again. An alternative

definition is a period when the level of output is below its normal level, even if the economy is growing. It is not over until output has grown enough to get back to normal. The latter definition has the problem that the 'normal' level is subjective.

reciprocity A preference to be kind or to help others who are kind and helpful, and to withhold help and kindness from people who are not helpful or kind.

redistribution policy Taxes, monetary, and in-kind transfers of the government that result in a distribution of final income that differs from the distribution of market income. *See also: predistribution policy.*

regressive (policy) An expenditure or transfer that increases the incomes of richer households by more than poorer households, in percentage terms. *See also: progressive (policy).*

relative price The price of one good or service compared to another (usually expressed as a ratio).

remittances Money sent home by international migrant workers to their families or others in the migrants' home country. In countries which either supply or receive large numbers of migrant workers, this is an important international capital flow.

rent ceiling The maximum legal price a landlord can charge for a rent.

repeated game A game in which the same interaction (same payoffs, players, feasible actions) may be occur more than once.

research and development Expenditures by a private or public entity to create new methods of production, products, or other economically relevant new knowledge.

reservation indifference curve A curve that indicates allocations (combinations) that are as highly valued as one's reservation option.

reservation option A person's next best alternative among all options in a particular transaction. *Also known as: fallback option. See also: reservation price.*

reservation price The lowest price at which someone is willing to sell a good (keeping the good is the potential seller's reservation option). *See also: reservation option.*

reservation wage What an employee would get in alternative employment, or from an unemployment benefit or other support,

were he or she not employed in his or her current job.

reserves (natural resource) The amount of a natural resource that is economically feasible to extract given existing technologies. *See also: resources (natural).*

residual claimant The person who receives the income left over from a firm or other project after the payment of all contractual costs (for example the cost of hiring workers and paying taxes).

resources (natural) The estimated total amount of a substance in the earth's crust. *See also: reserves (natural resource).*

revealed preference A way of studying preferences by reverse engineering the motives of an individual (her preferences) from observations about her or his actions.

reverse causality A two-way causal relationship in which A affects B and B also affects A.

rival good A good which, if consumed by one person, is not available to another. *See also: non-rival good.*

saving When consumption expenditure is less than net income, saving takes place and wealth rises. *See also: wealth.*

scarcity A good that is valued, and for which there is an opportunity cost of acquiring more.

Schumpeterian rents Profits in excess of the opportunity cost of capital that an innovator gets by introducing a new technology, organizational form or marketing strategy. *Also known as: innovation rents.*

secondary labour market Workers typically on short-term contracts with limited wages and job security. This might be due to their age, or because they are discriminated against by race or ethnic group. *See also: primary labour market, segmented labour market.*

segmented labour market A labour market whose distinct segments function as separate labour markets with limited mobility of workers from one segment to the other (including for reasons of racial, language, or other forms of discrimination). *See also: primary labour market, secondary labour market.*

self-insurance Saving by a household in order to be able to maintain its consumption when there is a temporary fall in income or need for greater expenditure.

separation of ownership and control The attribute of some firms by which managers are a separate group from the owners.

sequential game A game in which all players do not choose their strategies at the same time, and players that choose later can see the strategies already chosen by the other players, for example the ultimatum game. *See also: simultaneous game.*

share A part of the assets of a firm that may be traded. It gives the holder a right to receive a proportion of a firm's profit and to benefit when the firm's assets become more valuable. *Also known as: common stock.*

shock An exogenous change in some of the fundamental data used in a model.

short-run equilibrium An equilibrium that will prevail while certain variables (for example, the number of firms in a market) remain constant, but where we expect these variables to change when people have time to respond to the situation.

short run (model) The term does not refer to a period of time, but instead to what is exogenous: prices, wages, the capital stock, technology, institutions. *See also: price, wages, capital, technology, institutions, medium run (model), long run (model).*

short selling The sale of an asset borrowed by the seller, with the intention of buying it back at a lower price. This strategy is adopted by investors expecting the value of an asset to decrease. *Also known as: shorting.*

short side (of a market) The side (either supply or demand) on which the number of desired transactions is least (for example, employers are on the short side of the labour market, because typically there are more workers seeking work than there are jobs being offered). The opposite of short side is the long side. *See also: supply side, demand side.*

short-termism This subjective term refers to the case when the person making a judgement places too much weight on costs, benefits, and other things occurring in the near future than would be appropriate.

simultaneous game A game in which players choose strategies simultaneously, for

example the prisoners' dilemma. *See also: sequential game.*

social dilemma A situation in which actions taken independently by individuals in pursuit of their own private objectives result in an outcome which is inferior to some other feasible outcome that could have occurred if people had acted together, rather than as individuals.

social insurance Expenditure by the government, financed by taxation, which provides protection against various economic risks (for example, loss of income due to sickness, or unemployment) and enables people to smooth incomes throughout their lifetime. *See also: co-insurance.*

social interactions Situations in which the actions taken by each person affect other people's outcomes as well as their own.

social norm An understanding that is common to most members of a society about what people should do in a given situation when their actions affect others.

social preferences Preferences that place a value on what happens to other people, and on acting morally, even if it results in lower payoffs for the individual.

solvent A firm or individual for which net worth is positive or zero. For example, a bank for this assets are more than its liabilities (what it owes). *See also: insolvent.*

sovereign debt crisis A situation in which government bonds come to be considered so risky that the government may not be able to continue to borrow. If so, the government cannot spend more than the tax revenue they receive.

specialization This takes place when a country or some other entity produces a more narrow range of goods and services than it consumes, acquiring the goods and services that it does not produce by trade.

speculation Buying and selling assets in order to profit from an anticipated change in their price.

speculative finance A strategy used by firms to meet payment commitments on liabilities using cash flow, although the firm cannot repay the principal in this way. Firms in this position need to 'roll over' their liabilities, usually by issuing new debt to meet commitments on maturing debt. Term

coined by Hyman Minsky in his Financial Instability Hypothesis. *See also: hedge finance.*

stable equilibrium An equilibrium in which there is a tendency for the equilibrium to be restored after it is disturbed by a small shock.

stagflation Persistent high inflation combined with high unemployment in a country's economy.

stationary state In the absence of technological progress, the marginal contribution of additional capital goods to increased production would eventually become so small that the process of growth could cease. John Stuart Mill welcomed this prospect as 'a very considerable improvement on our present condition'.

statutory minimum wage A minimum level of pay laid down by law, for workers in general or of some specified type. The intention of a minimum wage is to guarantee living standards for the low-paid. Many countries, including the UK and the US, enforce this with legislation. *Also known as: minimum wage.*

stock exchange A financial marketplace where shares (or stocks) and other financial assets are traded. It has a list of companies whose shares are traded there.

stock A quantity measured at a point in time. It's units do not depend on time. *See also: flow.*

strategic complements For two activities A and B: the more that A is performed, the greater the benefits of performing B, and the more that B is performed the greater the benefits of performing A.

strategic interaction A social interaction in which the participants are aware of the ways that their actions affect others (and the ways that the actions of others affect them).

strategic substitutes For two activities A and B: the more that A is performed, the less the benefits of performing B, and the more that B is performed the less the benefits of performing A.

strategy An action (or a course of action) that a person may take when that person is aware of the mutual dependence of the results for herself and for others. The outcomes depend not only on that person's actions, but also on the actions of others.

subprime borrower An individual with a low credit rating and a high risk of default. *See also: subprime mortgage.*

subprime mortgage A residential mortgage issued to a high-risk borrower, for example, a borrower with a history of bankruptcy and delayed repayments. *See also: subprime borrower.*

subsistence level The level of living standards (measured by consumption or income) such that the population will not grow or decline.

substantive judgements of fairness Judgements based on the characteristics of the allocation itself, not how it was determined. *See also: procedural judgements of fairness.*

substitutes Two goods for which an increase in the price of one leads to an increase in the quantity demanded of the other. *See also: complements.*

substitution effect The effect that is only due to changes in the price or opportunity cost, given the new level of utility.

supply curve The curve that shows the number of units of output that would be produced at any given price. For a market, it shows the total quantity that all firms together would produce at any given price.

supply shock An unexpected change on the supply side of the economy, such as a rise or fall in oil prices or an improvement in technology. *See also: wage-setting curve, price-setting curve, Phillips curve.*

supply side (aggregate economy) How labour and capital are used to produce goods and services. It uses the labour market model (also referred to as the wage-setting curve and price-setting curve model). *See also: demand side (aggregate economy).*

supply-side policies A set of economic policies designed to improve the functioning of the economy by increasing productivity and international competitiveness, and by reducing profits after taxes and costs of production. Policies include cutting taxes on profits, tightening conditions for the receipt of unemployment benefits, changing legislation to make it easier to fire workers, and the reform of competition policy to reduce monopoly power. *Also known as: supply-side reforms.*

supply-side problem *See: supply side.*

supply side The side of a market on which those participating are offering something in return for money (for example, those selling bread). *See also: demand side.*

surplus, joint The sum of the economic rents of all involved in an interaction. *Also known as: total gains from exchange or trade.*

systematic risk A risk that affects all assets in the market, so that it is not possible for investors to reduce their exposure to the risk by holding a combination of different assets. *Also known as: undiversifiable risk.*

systemic risk A risk that threatens the financial system itself.

tacit knowledge Knowledge made up of the judgments, know-how, and other skills of those participating in the innovation process. The type of knowledge that cannot be accurately written down. *See also: codified knowledge.*

tangency When two curves share one point in common but do not cross. The tangent to a curve at a given point is a straight line that touches the curve at that point but does not cross it.

target wealth The level of wealth that a household aims to hold, based on its economic goals (or preferences) and expectations. We assume that households try to maintain this level of wealth in the face of changes in their economic situation, as long as it is possible to do so.

tariff A tax on a good imported into a country.

tax incidence The effect of a tax on the welfare of buyers, sellers, or both.

Taylorism Innovation in management that seeks to reduce labour costs, for example by dividing skilled jobs into separate less-skilled tasks so as to lower wages.

technically feasible An allocation within the limits set by technology and biology.

technological progress A change in technology that reduces the amount of resources (labour, machines, land, energy, time) required to produce a given amount of the output.

technology A process taking a set of materials and other inputs, including the work of people and machines, to produce an output.

tipping point (environmental) A state of the environment beyond which some process (typically a degradation) becomes self-reinforcing, because of positive feedback processes. On one side, processes of environmental degradation are self-limiting. On the other side, positive feedbacks lead to self-reinforcing, runaway environmental degradation. *See also: positive feedback (process).*

tipping point An unstable equilibrium at the boundary between two regions characterized by distinct movements in some variable. If the variable takes a value on one side, the variable moves in one direction; on the other, it moves in the other direction. *See also: asset price bubble.*

too big to fail Said to be a characteristic of large banks, whose central importance in the economy ensures they will be saved by the government if they are in financial difficulty. The bank thus does not bear all the costs of its activities and is therefore likely to take bigger risks. *See also: moral hazard.*

total surplus The total gains from trade received by all parties involved in the exchange. It is measured as the sum of the consumer and producer surpluses.

trade balance Value of exports minus the value of imports. *Also known as: net exports. See also: trade deficit, trade surplus.*

trade costs The transport costs, tariffs or other factors incurred in trading between markets in two countries that mean that, for affected goods, the law of one price will not hold across each market. *See also: law of one price.*

trade deficit A country's negative trade balance (it imports more than it exports). *See also: trade surplus, trade balance.*

trade surplus A country's positive trade balance (it exports more than it imports). *See also: trade deficit, trade balance.*

trade union An organization consisting predominantly of employees, the principal activities of which include the negotiation of rates of pay and conditions of employment for its members.

trademark A logo, a name, or a registered design typically associated with the right to exclude others from using it to identify their products.

tragedy of the commons A social dilemma in which self-interested individuals acting independently deplete a common resource, lowering the payoffs of all. *See also: social dilemma.*

transaction costs Costs that impede the bargaining process or the agreement of a contract. They include costs of acquiring information about the good to be traded, and costs of enforcing a contract.

trilemma of the world economy The likely impossibility that any country, in a globalized world, can simultaneously maintain deep market integration (across borders), national sovereignty, and democratic governance. First suggested by Dani Rodrik, an economist.

unemployment benefit A government transfer received by an unemployed person. *Also known as: unemployment insurance*

unemployment, involuntary The state of being out of work, but preferring to have a job at the wages and working conditions that otherwise identical employed workers have. *See also: unemployment.*

unemployment rate The ratio of the number of the unemployed to the total labour force. (Note that the employment rate and unemployment rate do not sum to 100%, as they have different denominators.) *See also: labour force, employment rate.*

unemployment A situation in which a person who is able and willing to work is not employed.

unstable equilibrium An equilibrium such that, if a shock disturbs the equilibrium, there is a subsequent tendency to move even further away from the equilibrium.

utility A numerical indicator of the value that one places on an outcome, such that higher valued outcomes will be chosen over lower valued ones when both are feasible.

value added For a production process this is the value of output minus the value of all inputs (called intermediate goods). The capital goods and labour used in production are not intermediate goods. The value added is equal to profits before taxes plus wages.

verifiable information Information that can be used to enforce a contract.

wage inflation An increase in the nominal wage. Usually measured over a year. *See also: nominal wage.*

wage labour contract *See: wage labour, contract.*

wage labour A system in which producers are paid for the time they work for their employers.

wage-price spiral This occurs if an initial increase in wages in the economy is followed by an increase in the price level, which is followed by an increase in wages and so on. It can also begin with an initial increase in the price level.

wage-setting curve The curve that gives the real wage necessary at each level of economy-wide employment to provide workers with incentives to work hard and well.

weakness of will The inability to commit to a course of action (dieting or foregoing some other present pleasure, for example) that one will regret later. It differs from impatience, which may also lead a person to favour pleasures in the present, but not necessarily act in a way that one regrets.

wealth Stock of things owned or value of that stock. It includes the market value of a home, car, any land, buildings, machinery or other capital goods that a person may own, and any financial assets such as shares or bonds. Debts are subtracted—for example, the mortgage owed to the bank. Debts owed to the person are added.

welfare state A set of government policies designed to provide improvements in the welfare of citizens by assisting with income smoothing (for example, unemployment benefits and pensions).

willingness to accept (WTA) The reservation price of a potential seller, who will be willing to sell a unit only for a price at least this high. *See also: willingness to pay.*

willingness to pay (WTP) An indicator of how much a person values a good, measured by the maximum amount he or she would pay to acquire a unit of the good. *See also: willingness to accept.*

winner-take-all competition Firms entering a market first can often dominate the entire market, at least temporarily.

worker's best response function (to wage) The optimal amount of work that a worker chooses to perform for each wage that the employer may offer.

yield The implied rate of return that the buyer gets on their money when they buy a bond at its market price.

zero economic profit A rate of profit equal to the opportunity cost of capital. *See also: normal profits, opportunity cost of capital.*

zero lower bound This refers to the fact that the nominal interest rate cannot be negative, thus setting a floor on the nominal interest rate that can be set by the central bank at zero. *See also: quantitative easing.*

zero sum game A game in which the payoff gains and losses of the individuals sum to zero, for all combinations of strategies they might pursue.

BIBLIOGRAPHY

Acconcia, Antonio, Giancarlo Corsetti, and Saverio Simonelli. 2014. 'Mafia and Public Spending: Evidence on the Fiscal Multiplier from a Quasi-Experiment'. *American Economic Review* 104 (7) (July): pp. 2185–2209.

Acemoglu, Daron, and James A. Robinson. 2012. *Why Nations Fail: The Origins of Power, Prosperity and Poverty*, 1st ed. New York, NY: Crown Publishers.

Acemoglu, Daron, and James A. Robinson. 2013. 'Economics versus politics: Pitfalls of policy advice' (http://tinyco.re/5915146). *The Journal of Economic Perspectives* 27 (2): pp. 173–192.

Acemoglu, Daron, Simon Johnson, and James A. Robinson. 2005. 'Institutions as a Fundamental Cause of Long-Run Growth' (http://tinyco.re/2662186). In *Handbook of Economic Growth, Volume 1A.*, eds. Philippe Aghion and Steven N. Durlauf. North Holland.

Ackerman, Frank. 2007. 'Debating climate economics: the Stern Review vs. its critics' (http://tinyco.re/6591851). Report to Friends of the Earth, July 2007.

Aesop. 'Belling the Cat'. In *Fables*, retold by Joseph Jacobs. XVII, (1). The Harvard Classics. New York: P. F. Collier & Son, 1909–14; Bartleby.com (http://tinyco.re/6827567), 2001.

Akerlof, George A., and Robert J. Shiller. 2015. *Phishing for Phools: The Economics of Manipulation and Deception*. Princeton, NJ: Princeton University Press.

Aleem, Irfan. 1990. 'Imperfect information, screening, and the costs of informal lending: A study of a rural credit market in Pakistan' (http://tinyco.re/4382174). *The World Bank Economic Review* 4 (3): pp. 329–349.

Allen, Robert C. 2009. 'The Industrial Revolution in Miniature: The Spinning Jenny in Britain, France, and India'. *The Journal of Economic History* 69 (04) (November): p. 901.

Allen, Robert C. 2011. *Global Economic History: A Very Short Introduction*. New York, NY: Oxford University Press.

Almunia, Miguel, Agustín Bénétrix, Barry Eichengreen, Kevin H. O'Rourke, and Gisela Rua. 2010. 'From Great Depression to Great Credit Crisis: Similarities, Differences and Lessons' (http://tinyco.re/9513563). *Economic Policy* 25 (62) (April): pp. 219–265.

Alvaredo, Facundo, Anthony B. Atkinson, Thomas Piketty, Emmanuel Saez, and Gabriel Zucman. 2016. 'The World Wealth and Income Database (WID)' (http://tinyco.re/5262390).

Andersen, Torben M., Bengt Holmström, Seppo Honkapohja, Sixten Korkman, Hans Tson Söderström, and Juhana Vartiainen. 2007. *The Nordic Model: Embracing Globalization and Sharing Risks* (http://tinyco.re/2490148). Helsinki: Taloustierto Oy.

Arnott, Richard. 1995. 'Time for Revisionism on Rent Control?' (http://tinyco.re/7410213). *Journal of Economic Perspectives* 9 (1) (February): pp. 99–120.

Arrow, Kenneth. J. 1978. 'A cautious case for socialism' (http://tinyco.re/3618241). *Dissent* 25 (4): pp. 472–480.

Arrow, Kenneth J., and F. H. Hahn. 1991. 'General Competitive Analysis', eds. C. J. Bliss and M. D. Intriligator. *Advanced Textbooks in Economics* Vol. 12. San Francisco: Holden-Day.

Atkinson, Anthony B., and Thomas Piketty, eds. 2007. *Top Incomes over the Twentieth Century: A Contrast between Continental European and English-Speaking Countries*. Oxford: Oxford University Press.

Auerbach, Alan, and Yuriy Gorodnichenko. 2015. 'How Powerful Are Fiscal Multipliers in Recessions?' (http://tinyco.re/3018428). *NBER Reporter 2015 Research Summary*.

Augustine, Dolores. 2013. 'Innovation and Ideology: Werner Hartmann and the Failure of the East German Electronics Industry'. In *The East German Economy, 1945–2010: Falling behind or Catching Up?* by German Historical Institute, eds. Hartmut Berghoff and Uta Andrea Balbier. Cambridge: Cambridge University Press.

Ausubel, Lawrence M. 1991. 'The Failure of Competition in the Credit Card Market'. *American Economic Review* 81 (1): pp. 50–81.

Autor, David, and Gordon Hanson. *NBER Reporter 2014 Number 2: Research Summary. Labor Market Adjustment to International Trade* (http://tinyco.re/2846538).

Bakija, Jon, Lane Kenworthy, Peter Lindert, and Jeff Madrick. 2016. *How Big Should Our Government Be?* Berkeley: University of California Press.

Ball, Philip. 2002. 'Blackouts Inherent in Power Grid' (http://tinyco.re/9262695). *Nature News*. Updated 8 November 2002.

Ball, Philip. 2004. 'Power Blackouts Likely' (http://tinyco.re/7102799). *Nature News*. 20 January 2004.

Banerjee, Abhijit V., Paul J. Gertler, and Maitreesh Ghatak. 2002. 'Empowerment and Efficiency: Tenancy Reform in West Bengal' (http://tinyco.re/9394444). *Journal of Political Economy* 110 (2): pp. 239–280.

Barro, Robert J. 2009. 'Government Spending Is No Free Lunch' (http://tinyco.re/3208655). *Wall Street Journal*.

Basker, Emek. 2007. 'The Causes and Consequences of Wal-Mart's Growth' (http://tinyco.re/6525636). *Journal of Economic Perspectives* 21 (3): pp. 177–198.

Bentolila, Samuel, Tito Boeri, and Pierre Cahuc. 2010. 'Ending the Scourge of Dual Markets in Europe' (http://tinyco.re/2724010). *VoxEU.org*. Updated 12 July 2010.

Berger, Helge, and Mark Spoerer. 2001. 'Economic Crises and the European Revolutions of 1848'. *The Journal of Economic History* 61 (2): pp. 293–326.

Berghoff, Hartmut, and Uta Andrea Balbier. 2013. 'From Centrally Planned Economy to Capitalist Avant-Garde? The Creation, Collapse, and Transformation of a Socialist Economy'. In *The East German Economy, 1945–2010 Falling behind or Catching Up?* by German Historical Institute, eds. Hartmut Berghoff and Uta Andrea Balbier. Cambridge: Cambridge University Press.

Besley, Timothy, and Anne Case. 1995. 'Does electoral accountability affect economic policy choices? Evidence from gubernatorial term limits' (http://tinyco.re/2599264). *The Quarterly Journal of Economics* 110 (3): pp. 769–798.

Besley, Timothy, and Torsten Persson. 2014. 'Why do developing countries tax so little?' (http://tinyco.re/3513621). *The Journal of Economic Perspectives* 28 (4): pp. 99–120.

Bessen, James. 2015. *Learning by Doing: The Real Connection between Innovation, Wages, and Wealth*. New Haven, CT: Yale University Press.

Bewley, T. 2007. 'Fairness, Reciprocity and Wage Rigidity'. *Behavioral Economics and its Applications*, eds. Peter Diamond and Hannu Vartiainen, pp. 157–188. Princeton, NJ: Princeton University Press.

Bewley, Truman F. 1999. *Why Wages Don't Fall during a Recession*. Cambridge, MA: Harvard University Press.

Blanchard, Olivier. 2012. 'Lessons from Latvia' (http://tinyco.re/8173211). *IMFdirect – The IMF Blog*. Updated 11 June 2012.

Blanchard, Olivier, and Justin Wolfers. 2000. 'The Role of Shocks and Institutions in the Rise of European Unemployment: The Aggregate Evidence'. *The Economic Journal* 110 (462): pp. 1–33.

Blanchflower, David G., and Andrew J. Oswald. 1995. 'An Introduction to the Wage Curve' (http://tinyco.re/2712192). *Journal of Economic Perspectives* 9 (3): pp. 153–167.

Boldrin, Michele, and David K. Levine. 2008. *Against Intellectual Monopoly*. New York, NY: Cambridge University Press.

Bonica, Adam, Nolan McCarty, Keith T. Poole, and Howard Rosenthal. 2013. Why hasn't democracy slowed rising inequality? (http://tinyco.re/7031342). *The Journal of Economic Perspectives* 27 (3): pp. 103–123.

Boseley, Sarah. 2016. 'Big Pharma's Worst Nightmare' (http://tinyco.re/5692579). *The Guardian*, Updated 5 February 2016.

Bosvieux, Jean, and Oliver Waine. 2012. 'Rent Control: A Miracle Solution to the Housing Crisis?' (http://tinyco.re/0599316). *Metropolitics*. Updated 21 November 2012.

Bowles, Samuel. 2006. *Microeconomics: Behavior, institutions, and evolution (the roundtable series in behavioral economics)*. Princeton, NJ: Princeton University Press.

Bowles, Samuel. 2016. *The Moral Economy: Why Good Incentives Are No Substitute for Good Citizens*. New Haven, CT: Yale University Press.

Bowles, Samuel, and Arjun Jayadev. 2014. 'One Nation under Guard' (http://tinyco.re/6662441). *The New York Times*. Updated 15 February 2014.

Bowles, Samuel, and Herbert Gintis. 2002. 'The Inheritance of Inequality' (http://tinyco.re/8562867). *Journal of Economic Perspectives* 16 (3): pp. 3–30.

Braverman, Harry, and Paul M. Sweezy. 1975. *Labor and Monopoly Capital: The Degradation of Work in the Twentieth Century*, 2nd ed. New York, NY: Monthly Review Press.

Brunnermeier, Markus. 2009. 'Lucas Roundtable: Mind the frictions' (http://tinyco.re/0136751). *The Economist*. Updated 6 August 2009.

Burda, Michael, and Jennifer Hunt. 2011. 'The German Labour-Market Miracle' (http://tinyco.re/2090811). *VoxEU.org*. Updated 2 November 2011.

Camerer, Colin, and Ernst Fehr. 2004. 'Measuring Social Norms and Preferences Using Experimental Games: A Guide for Social Scientists'. In *Foundations of Human Sociality: Economic Experiments and Ethnographic Evidence from Fifteen Small-Scale Societies*, eds. Joseph Henrich, Robert Boyd, Samuel Bowles, Colin Camerer, and Herbert Gintis. Oxford: Oxford University Press.

Campbell, C. M., and K. S. Kamlani. 1997. 'The Reasons For Wage Rigidity: Evidence From a Survey of Firms'. *The Quarterly Journal of Economics* 112 (3) (August): pp. 759–789.

Carlin, Wendy and David Soskice. 2015. *Macroeconomics: Institutions, Instability, and the Financial System*. Oxford: Oxford University Press.

Cassidy, John. 2010. 'Interview with Eugene Fama' (http://tinyco.re/4647447). *The New Yorker*. Updated 13 January 2010.

Clark, Andrew E., and Andrew J. Oswald. 2002. 'A Simple Statistical Method for Measuring How Life Events Affect Happiness' (http://tinyco.re/7872100). *International Journal of Epidemiology* 31 (6): pp. 1139–1144.

Clark, Gregory. 2007. *A Farewell to Alms: A Brief Economic History of the World*. Princeton, NJ: Princeton University Press.

Clark, Gregory. 2015. *The Son Also Rises: Surnames and the History of Social Mobility*. Princeton, NJ: Princeton University Press.

Coase, Ronald H. 1937. 'The Nature of the Firm' (http://tinyco.re/8128486). *Economica* 4 (16): pp. 386–405.

Coase, Ronald H. 1992. 'The Institutional Structure of Production' (http://tinyco.re/1636715). *American Economic Review* 82 (4): pp. 713–19.

Collins, Daryl, Jonathan Morduch, Stuart Rutherford, and Orlanda Ruthven. 2009. *Portfolios of the Poor* (http://tinyco.re/8070650). Princeton: Princeton University Press.

Couch, Kenneth A., and Dana W. Placzek. 2010. 'Earnings Losses of Displaced Workers Revisited'. *American Economic Review* 100 (1): pp. 572–589.

Council of Economic Advisers Issue Brief. 2016. *Labor Market Monopsony: Trends, Consequences, and Policy Responses* (http://tinyco.re/7588734).

Cournot, Augustin, and Irving Fischer. 1971. *Researches into the Mathematical Principles of the Theory of Wealth*. New York, NY: A. M. Kelley.

Coyle, Diane. 2014. *GDP: A Brief but Affectionate History*. Princeton, NJ: Princeton University Press.

Crockett, Andrew. 2000. 'Marrying the Micro- and Macro-Prudential Dimensions of Financial Stability' (http://tinyco.re/5128318). Speech to International Conference of Banking Supervisors, Basel, 20–21 September.

Daly, Mary C., and Leila Bengali. 2014. 'Is It Still Worth Going to College?' (http://tinyco.re/5624488). Federal Reserve Bank of San Francisco. Updated 5 May 2014.

Dauth, Wolfgang, Sebastian Findeisen, and Jens Südekum. 2017. *Sectoral employment trends in Germany: The effect of globalisation on their micro anatomy* (http://tinyco.re/2554801). *VoxEU.org*. Updated 26 January 2017.

Davis, Mike. 2000. *Late Victorian holocausts: El Niño famines and the Making of the Third World*. London: Verso Books.

Deaton, Angus. 2013. *The Great Escape: Health, Wealth, and the Origins of Inequality*. Princeton, NJ: Princeton University Press.

DeLong, Bradford. 2015. 'Draft for Rethinking Macroeconomics Conference Fiscal Policy Panel' (http://tinyco.re/4631043). *Washington Center for Equitable Growth*. Updated 5 April 2015.

Diamond, Jared. 1999. *Guns, Germs, and Steel: The Fates of Human Societies*. New York, NY: Norton, W. W. & Company.

Diamond, Jared, and James Robinson. 2014. *Natural Experiments of History*. Cambridge, MA: Belknap Press of Harvard University Press.

DiMasi, Joseph A., Ronald W. Hansen, and Henry G. Grabowski. 2003. 'The Price of Innovation: New Estimates of Drug Development Costs'. *Journal of Health Economics* 22 (2): pp. 151–85.

Dube, Arindrajit, T. William Lester, and Michael Reich. 2010. 'Minimum Wage Effects across State Borders: Estimates Using Contiguous Counties' (http://tinyco.re/5393066). *Review of Economics and Statistics* 92 (4): pp. 945–64.

Durante, Ruben. 2010. 'Risk, Cooperation and the Economic Origins of Social Trust: An Empirical Investigation' (http://tinyco.re/7674543). Sciences Po Working Paper.

Durlauf, Steven. 2017. 'Kenneth Arrow and the golden age of economic theory' (http://tinyco.re/9029504). *VoxEU.org*. Updated 8 April 2017.

EconTalk. 2015. 'Martin Weitzman on Climate Change' (http://tinyco.re/7088528). Library of Economics and Liberty. Updated 1 June 2015.

EconTalk. 2016. 'David Autor on Trade, China, and U.S. Labor Markets' (http://tinyco.re/2829759). Library of Economics and Liberty. Updated 26 December 2016.

Edgeworth, Francis Ysidro. 2003. *Mathematical Psychics and Further Papers on Political Economy*. Oxford: Oxford University Press.

Edsall, Thomas B. 2016. 'Boom or Gloom?' (http://tinyco.re/5275846). *New York Times*. Updated 27 January 2016.

Ehrenreich, Barbara. 2011. *Nickel and Dimed: On (Not) Getting By in America*. New York, NY: St. Martin's Press.

Eichengreen, Barry, and Kevin O'Rourke. 2010. 'What Do the New Data Tell Us?' (http://tinyco.re/9442518). *VoxEU.org*. Updated 8 March 2010.

Eisen, Michael. 2011. 'Amazon's $23,698,655.93 book about flies' (http://tinyco.re/0044329). *It is NOT junk*. Updated 22 April 2011.

Ellison, Glenn, and Sara Fisher Ellison. 2005. 'Lessons About Markets from the Internet' (http://tinyco.re/4419622). *Journal of Economic Perspectives* 19 (2) (June): p. 139.

Engel, Jerome S. 2015. 'Global Clusters of Innovation: Lessons from Silicon Valley.' *California Management Review* 57 (2): pp. 36–65. University of California Press.

Eurostat. 2015. 'Quality of Life Indicators—Measuring Quality of Life' (http://tinyco.re/8771109). Updated 5 November 2015.

Fafchamps, Marcel, and Bart Minten. 1999. 'Relationships and Traders in Madagascar'. *Journal of Development Studies* 35 (6) (August): pp. 1–35.

Falk, Armin, and James J. Heckman. 2009. 'Lab Experiments Are a Major Source of Knowledge in the Social Sciences'. *Science* 326 (5952): pp. 535–538.

Fehr, Ernest and Andreas Leibbrandt. 2011. 'A Field Study on Cooperativeness and Impatience in the Tragedy of the Commons'. *Journal of Public Economics* 95 (9–10): pp. 1144–55.

Flannery, Kent, and Joyce Marcus. 2014. *The Creation of Inequality: How Our Prehistoric Ancestors Set the Stage for Monarchy, Slavery, and Empire*. Cambridge, MA: Harvard University Press.

Fletcher, James. 2014. 'Spurious Correlations: Margarine Linked to Divorce?' (http://tinyco.re/6825314). *BBC News*.

Fogel, Robert William. 2000. *The Fourth Great Awakening and the Future of Egalitarianism*. Chicago: University of Chicago Press.

Freedom House. 2016. 'Freedom in the World 2016. Anxious Dictators, Wavering Democracies: Global Freedom under Pressure' (http://tinyco.re/9817968). Washington, DC.

Freeman, Sunny. 2015. 'What Canada can learn from Sweden's unionized retail workers' (http://tinyco.re/0808135). *Huffington Post Canada Business*. Updated 19 March 2015.

Friedman, Milton. 1953. *Essays in Positive Economics*. Chicago: University of Chicago Press.

Friedman, Milton. 1968. 'The Role of Monetary Policy' (http://tinyco.re/4959694). *The American Economic Review* 58 (1): pp. 1–17.

Fujiwara, Thomas. 2015. 'Voting technology, political responsiveness and infant health: Evidence from Brazil' (http://tinyco.re/3783631). *Econometrica* 83 (2): pp. 423–464.

Gilbert, Richard J., and Michael L. Katz. 2001. 'An Economist's Guide to US v. Microsoft' (http://tinyco.re/7683758). *Journal of Economic Perspectives* 15 (2): pp. 25–44.

Gilens, Martin, Benjamin I. Page. 2014. 'Testing theories of American politics: Elites, interest groups, and average citizens' (http://tinyco.re/7911085). *Perspectives on politics* 12 (03): pp. 564–581.

Girardi, Daniele and Samuel Bowles. 2017. 'Institutional Shocks and Economic Outcomes: Allende's Election, Pinochet's Coup and the Santiago Stock Market'. Santa Fe Institute working paper.

Gordon, Robert J. 2016. *The Rise and Fall of American Growth: The US Standard of Living since the Civil War*. Princeton, NJ: Princeton University Press.

Graddy, Kathryn. 1995. 'Testing for Imperfect Competition at the Fulton Fish Market' (http://tinyco.re/8279962). *The RAND Journal of Economics* 26 (1): pp. 75–92.

Graddy, Kathryn. 2006. 'Markets: The Fulton Fish Market' (http://tinyco.re/4300778). *Journal of Economic Perspectives* 20 (2): pp. 207–220.

Graeber, David. 2012. 'The Myth of Barter' (http://tinyco.re/6552964). In *Debt: The First 5,000 years*. Brooklyn, NY: Melville House Publishing.

Gross, David, and Nicholas Souleles. 2002. 'Do Liquidity Constraints and Interest Rates Matter for Consumer Behavior? Evidence from Credit Card Data'. *The Quarterly Journal of Economics* 117 (1) (February): pp. 149–185.

Habakkuk, John. 1967. *American and British Technology in the Nineteenth Century: The Search for Labour Saving Inventions*. United Kingdom: Cambridge University Press.

Hall, Peter A., and David Soskice. 2001. *Varieties of Capitalism: The Institutional Foundations of Comparative Advantage*. New York, NY: Oxford University Press.

Hamilton, Alexander, James Madison, and John Jay. 1961. *The Federalist*. Middletown, Ct. Wesleyan University Press.

Hansmann, Henry. 2000. *The Ownership of Enterprise*. Cambridge, MA: Belknap Press.

Hardin, Garrett. 1968. 'The Tragedy of the Commons' (http://tinyco.re/4834967). *Science* 162 (3859): pp. 1243–1248.

Harding, Matthew, and Michael Lovenheim. 2013. 'The Effect of Prices on Nutrition: Comparing the Impact of Product- and Nutrient-Specific Taxes' (http://tinyco.re/9374751). SIEPR Discussion Paper No. 13-023.

Harford, Tim. 2010. 'Stimulus Spending Might Not Be As Stimulating As We Think' (http://tinyco.re/8583440). Undercover Economist Blog, *The Financial Times*.

Harford, Tim. 2012. 'Still Think You Can Beat the Market?' (http://tinyco.re/7063932). *The Undercover Economist*. Updated 24 November 2012.

Harford, Tim. 2015. 'The rewards for working hard are too big for Keynes's vision' (http://tinyco.re/5829245). *The Undercover Economist*. First published by *The Financial Times*. Updated 3 August 2015.

Hayek, Friedrich A. 1994. *The Road to Serfdom* (http://tinyco.re/0683881). Chicago, Il: University of Chicago Press.

Heckman, James. 2013. *Giving Kids a Fair Chance: A Strategy That Works*. Cambridge, MA: MIT Press.

Helper, Susan, Morris Kleiner, and Yingchun Wang. 2010. 'Analyzing Compensation Methods in Manufacturing: Piece Rates, Time Rates, or Gain-Sharing?' (http://tinyco.re/4437027). NBER Working Papers No. 16540, National Bureau of Economic Research, Inc.

Hemphill, C. Scott, and Bhaven N. Sampat. 2012. 'Evergreening, Patent Challenges, and Effective Market Life in Pharmaceuticals' (http://tinyco.re/4728486). *Journal of Health Economics* 31 (2): pp. 327–39.

Henrich, Joseph, Richard McElreath, Abigail Barr, Jean Ensminger, Clark Barrett, Alexander Bolyanatz, Juan Camilo Cardenas, Michael Gurven, Edwins Gwako, Natalie Henrich, Carolyn Lesorogol, Frank Marlowe, David Tracer, and John Ziker. 2006. 'Costly Punishment Across Human Societies' (http://tinyco.re/2043845). *Science* 312 (5781): pp. 1767–1770.

Henrich, Joseph, Robert Boyd, Samuel Bowles, Colin Camerer, and Herbert Gintis (editors). 2004. *Foundations of Human Sociality: Economic Experiments and Ethnographic Evidence from Fifteen Small-Scale Societies*. Oxford: Oxford University Press.

Hirsch, Barry T. 2008. 'Sluggish institutions in a dynamic world: Can unions and industrial competition coexist?'. *Journal of Economic Perspectives* 22 (1) (February): pp. 153–176.

Hirschman, Albert O. 1970. *Exit, voice, and loyalty: Responses to decline in firms, organizations, and states*. Cambridge, Mass: Harvard University Press.

Hobsbawm, Eric, and George Rudé. 1969. *Captain Swing*. London: Lawrence and Wishart.

Hotelling, Harold. 1929. 'Stability in Competition'. *The Economic Journal* 39: pp. 41–57.

Howell, David R., Dean Baker, Andrew Glyn, and John Schmitt. 2007. 'Are Protective Labor Market Institutions at the Root of Unemployment? A Critical Review of the Evidence' (http://tinyco.re/2000761). *Capitalism and Society* 2 (1).

International Monetary Fund. 2012. *World Economic Outlook October: Coping with High Debt and Sluggish Growth* (http://tinyco.re/5970823).

IPCC. 2014. 'Climate Change 2014: Synthesis Report'. Contribution of Working Groups I, II and III to the Fifth Assessment Report of the Intergovernmental Panel on Climate Change. Geneva, Switzerland: IPCC.

Jacobson, Louis, Robert J. Lalonde, and Daniel G. Sullivan. 1993. 'Earnings Losses of Displaced Workers'. *The American Economic Review* 83 (4): pp. 685–709.

Janeway, William H. 2012. *Doing Capitalism in the Innovation Economy: Markets, Speculation and the State*. Cambridge: Cambridge University Press.

Jappelli, Tullio, and Luigi Pistaferri. 2010. 'The Consumption Response to Income Changes' (http://tinyco.re/3409802). *VoxEU.org*.

Jayadev, Arjun, and Samuel Bowles. 2006. 'Guard Labor' (http://tinyco.re/4636800). *Journal of Development Economics* 79 (2): pp. 328–48.

Jensen, Jørgen Dejgård, and Sinne Smed. 2013. 'The Danish tax on saturated fat: Short run effects on consumption, substitution patterns and consumer prices of fats'. *Food Policy* 42: pp. 18–31.

Jensen, Robert. 2007. 'The Digital Provide: Information (Technology), Market Performance, and Welfare in the South Indian Fisheries Sector.' *The Quarterly Journal of Economics* 122 (3): pp. 879–924.

Kalla, Joshua L., and David E. Broockman. 2015. 'Campaign contributions facilitate access to congressional officials: A randomized field experiment' (http://tinyco.re/5765353). *American Journal of Political Science* 60 (3): pp. 1–14.

Kaufmann, Daniel, Aart Kraay, and Massimo Mastruzzi. 2011. 'The worldwide governance indicators: methodology and analytical issues' (http://tinyco.re/7305592). *Hague Journal on the Rule of Law* 3 (2): pp. 220–246.

Kay, John. 'The Structure of Strategy' (reprinted from *Business Strategy Review* 1993) (http://tinyco.re/7663497).

Keynes, John Maynard. 1923. *A Tract on Monetary Reform*. London, Macmillan and Co.

Keynes, John Maynard. 1936. *The General Theory of Employment, Interest and Money* (http://tinyco.re/6855346). London: Palgrave Macmillan.

Keynes, John Maynard. 1963. 'Economic Possibilities for our Grandchildren'. In *Essays in Persuasion*, New York, NY: W. W. Norton & Co.

Keynes, John Maynard. 2004. *The End of Laissez-Faire*. Amherst, NY: Prometheus Books.

Keynes, John Maynard. 2005. *The Economic Consequences of Peace*. New York, NY: Cosimo Classics.

Kindleberger, Charles P. 2005. *Manias, Panics, and Crashes: A History of Financial Crises (Wiley Investment Classics)* (http://tinyco.re/6810098). Hoboken, NJ: Wiley, John & Sons.

Kletzer, Lori G. 1998. 'Job Displacement' (http://tinyco.re/8577746). *Journal of Economic Perspectives* 12 (1): pp. 115–136.

Kornai, János. 2013. *Dynamism, Rivalry, and the Surplus Economy: Two Essays on the Nature of Capitalism*. Oxford: Oxford University Press.

Koromvokis, Lee. 2016. 'Are the Best Days of the US Economy Over?' (http://tinyco.re/1182018). PBS NewsHour. 28 January 2016.

Koshal, Rajindar K., and Manjulika Koshal. 1999. 'Economies of Scale and Scope in Higher Education: A Case of Comprehensive Universities' (http://tinyco.re/8137580). *Economics of Education Review* 18 (2): pp. 269–277.

Krajewski, Markus. 2014. 'The Great Lightbulb Conspiracy' (http://tinyco.re/3479245). *IEEE Spectrum*. Updated 24 September 2014.

Kremer, Michael, and Rachel Glennerster. 2004. *Strong Medicine: Creating Incentives for Pharmaceutical Research on Neglected Diseases* (http://tinyco.re/7475598). Princeton, NJ: Princeton University Press.

Kroszner, Randall S., and Louis Putterman (editors). 2009. *The Economic Nature of the Firm: A Reader*, 3rd ed. Cambridge: Cambridge University Press.

Krueger, Alan B., and Alexandre Mas. 2004. 'Strikes, Scabs, and Tread Separations: Labor Strife and the Production of Defective Bridgestone/Firestone Tires'. *Journal of Political Economy* 112 (2): pp. 253–289.

Krugman, Paul. 1987. 'Is Free Trade Passé?' *Journal of Economic Perspectives* 1 (2): pp. 131–44.

Krugman, Paul. 2009. 'The Increasing Returns Revolution in Trade and Geography'. In *The Nobel Prizes 2008*, ed. Karl Grandin. Stockholm: The Nobel Foundation.

Krugman, Paul. 2009. 'War and Non-Remembrance'. (http://tinyco.re/8410113). Paul Krugman – *New York Times* Blog.

Krugman, Paul. 2012. 'A Tragic Vindication' (http://tinyco.re/6611089). Paul Krugman – *New York Times* Blog.

Landes, David S. 1990. 'Why are We So Rich and They So Poor?' (http://tinyco.re/5958995). *American Economic Review* 80 (May): pp. 1–13.

Landes, David S. 2000. *Revolution in Time*. Cambridge, MA: Harvard University Press.

Landes, David S. 2003. *The Unbound Prometheus: Technological Change and Industrial Development in Western Europe from 1750 to the Present*. Cambridge, UK: Cambridge University Press.

Landes, David S. 2006. 'Why Europe and the West? Why not China?'. *Journal of Economic Perspectives* 20 (2) (June): pp. 3–22.

Lasswell, Harold D. 1936. *Politics; who gets what, when and how* (http://tinyco.re/2227728). New York: Whittlesey House.

Lazear, Edward P., Kathryn L. Shaw, and Christopher Stanton. 2016. 'Making Do with Less: Working Harder during Recessions'. *Journal of Labor Economics* 34 (S1 Part 2): pp. 333–360.

Leduc, Sylvain, and Daniel Wilson. 2015. 'Are State Governments Roadblocks to Federal Stimulus? Evidence on the Flypaper Effect of Highway Grants in the 2009 Recovery Act' (http://tinyco.re/3885744). Federal Reserve Bank of San Francisco Working Paper 2013–16 (September).

Lee, James, and Wang Feng. 1999. 'Malthusian models and Chinese realities: The Chinese demographic system 1700–2000'. *Population and Development Review* 25 (1) (March): pp. 33–65.

Leeson, Peter T. 2007. 'An–arrgh–chy: The Law and Economics of Pirate Organization'. *Journal of Political Economy* 115 (6): pp. 1049–94.

Leibbrandt, Murray, Ingrid Woolard, Arden Finn, Jonathan Argent. 2010. 'Trends in South African Income Distribution and Poverty since the Fall of Apartheid' (http://tinyco.re/8617393). OECD Social, Employment and Migration Working Papers, No. 101. Paris: OECD Publishing.

Levitt, Steven D., and John A. List. 2007. 'What Do Laboratory Experiments Measuring Social Preferences Reveal About the Real World?' (http://tinyco.re/9601240). *Journal of Economic Perspectives* 21 (2): pp. 153–174.

Lindert, Peter. 2004. *Growing Public: Social Spending and Economic Growth since the 18th Century.* Cambridge: Cambridge University Press.

Lorenz, Max O. 1905. 'Methods of Measuring the Concentration of Wealth' (http://tinyco.re/0786587). *Publications of the American Statistical Association* 9 (70).

Lucas, Robert. 2009. 'In defence of the dismal science' (http://tinyco.re/6052194). *The Economist.* Updated 6 August 2009.

Malkiel, Burton G. 2003. 'The Efficient Market Hypothesis and Its Critics' (http://tinyco.re/4628706). *Journal of Economic Perspectives* 17 (1) (March): pp. 59–82.

Malthus, Thomas R. 1798. *An Essay on the Principle of Population.* London: J. Johnson, in St. Paul's Church-yard. Library of Economics and Liberty (http://tinyco.re/8473883).

Malthus, Thomas R. 1830. *A Summary View on the Principle of Population.* London: J. Murray

Marshall, Alfred. 1920. *Principles of Economics* (http://tinyco.re/0560708), 8th ed. London: MacMillan & Co.

Martin, Felix. 2013. *Money: The Unauthorised Biography.* London: The Bodley Head.

Martinez-Bravo, Monica, Gerard Padró i Miquel, Nancy Qian, and Yang Yao. 2014. 'Political reform in China: the effect of local elections' (http://tinyco.re/4667186). NBER working paper, 18101.

Marx, Karl. 1906. *Capital: A Critique of Political Economy* (http://tinyco.re/9166776). New York, NY: Random House.

Marx, Karl. 2010. *The Communist Manifesto* (http://tinyco.re/0155765). London: Arcturus Publishing.

Mazzucato, Mariana. 2013. 'Government – investor, risk-taker, innovator' (http://tinyco.re/2203568).

McNeill, William Hardy H. 1976. *Plagues and Peoples.* Garden City, NY: Anchor Press.

Mencken, H. L. 2006. *A Little Book in C Major.* New York, NY: Kessinger Publishing.

Mian, Atif, Amir Sufi, and Francesco Trebbi. 2013. 'The Political Economy of the Subprime Mortgage Credit Expansion' (http://tinyco.re/4522161). *Quarterly Journal of Political Science* 8: pp. 373–408.

Micklethwait, John, and Adrian Wooldridge. 2003. *The Company: A Short History of a Revolutionary Idea.* New York, NY: Modern Library.

Milanovic, Branko. 2007. *Worlds Apart: Measuring International and Global Inequality.* Princeton, NJ: Princeton University Press.

Milanovic, Branko. 2012. *The Haves and the Have-Nots: A Brief and Idiosyncratic History of Global Inequality.* New York, NY: Basic Books.

Mill, John Stuart. 1994. *Principles of Political Economy* (http://tinyco.re/9348882). New York: Oxford University Press.

Mill, John Stuart. 2002. *On Liberty* (http://tinyco.re/6454781). Mineola, NY: Dover Publications.

Miller, Grant. 2008. 'Women's suffrage, political responsiveness, and child survival in American history' (http://tinyco.re/5731666). *The Quarterly Journal of Economics* 123 (3): pp. 1287–1327.

Miller, R. G., and S. R. Sorrell. 2013. 'The Future of Oil Supply' (http://tinyco.re/6167443). *Philosophical Transactions of the Royal Society A: Mathematical, Physical and Engineering Sciences* 372 (2006) (December).

Minsky, Hyman P. 1975. *John Maynard Keynes* (http://tinyco.re/9354915). New York, NY: McGraw-Hill.

Minsky, Hyman P. 1982. *Can 'It' Happen Again? Essays on Instability and Finance.* Armonk, NY: M. E. Sharpe.

Mokyr, Joel. 2004. *The Gifts of Athena: Historical Origins of the Knowledge Economy*, 5th ed. Princeton, NJ: Princeton University Press.

Morduch, Jonathan. 1999. 'The Microfinance Promise' (http://tinyco.re/7650659). *Journal of Economic Literature* 37 (4) (December): pp. 1569–1614.

Moser, Petra. 2013. 'Patents and Innovation: Evidence from Economic History' (http://tinyco.re/7074474). *Journal of Economic Perspectives* 27 (1): pp. 23–44.

Moser, Petra. 2015. 'Intellectual Property Rights and Artistic Creativity' (http://tinyco.re/2212476). *Voxeu.org.* Updated 4 November 2015.

Mowery, David C., and Timothy Simcoe. 2002. 'Is the Internet a US Invention?—an Economic and Technological History of Computer Networking'. *Research Policy* 31 (8–9): pp. 1369–87.

Murphy, Antoin E. 1978. 'Money in an Economy Without Banks: The Case of Ireland'. *The Manchester School* 46 (1) (March): pp. 41–50.

Naef, Michael, and Jürgen Schupp. 2009. 'Measuring Trust: Experiments and Surveys in Contrast and Combination' (http://tinyco.re/3956674). IZA discussion Paper No. 4087.

Nasar, Sylvia. 2011. *A Beautiful Mind: The Life of Mathematical Genius and Novel Laureate John Nash*. New York, NY: Simon & Schuster.

Nelson, Richard R., and Gavin Wright. 1992. 'The Rise and Fall of American Technological Leadership: The Postwar Era in Historical Perspective' (http://tinyco.re/2811203). *Journal of Economic Literature* 30 (4) (December): pp. 1931–1964.

Nickell, Stephen, and Jan van Ours. 2000. 'The Netherlands and the United Kingdom: A European Unemployment Miracle?'. *Economic Policy* 15 (30) (April): pp. 136–180.

Nordhaus, William D. 2007. 'A Review of the Stern Review on the Economics of Climate Change' (http://tinyco.re/9892599). *Journal of Economic Literature* 45 (3): pp. 686–702.

North, Douglass C. 1990. *Institutions, Institutional Change and Economic Performance*. Cambridge: Cambridge University Press.

Norton, Michael I., and Daniel Ariely. 2011. 'Building a Better America–One Wealth Quintile at a Time' (http://tinyco.re/3629531). *Perspectives on Psychological Science* 6 (1): pp. 9–12.

Nuffield Foundation, The. 2010. 'Mirrlees Review of tax system recommends radical changes' (http://tinyco.re/6726989). Updated 10 November 2010.

O'Brien, Patrick K., and Philip A. Hunt. 1993. 'The rise of a fiscal state in England, 1485–1815'. *Historical Research* 66 (160): pp.129–76.

O'Reilly, Tim, and Eric S. Raymond. 2001. *The Cathedral & the Bazaar: Musings on Linux and Open Source by an Accidental Revolutionary*. Sebastopol, CA: O'Reilly.

OECD. 2010. *Employment Outlook 2010: Moving Beyond the Jobs Crisis* (http://tinyco.re/5607435).

OECD. 2015. Programme for International Student Assessment (http://tinyco.re/1018246).

OpenSecrets.org. 2015. 'Lobbying Spending Database Chemical & Related Manufacturing' (http://tinyco.re/8516286).

Ostrom, Elinor. 2000. 'Collective Action and the Evolution of Social Norms' (http://tinyco.re/0059239). *Journal of Economic Perspectives* 14 (3): pp. 137–58.

Ostrom, Elinor. 2008. 'The Challenge of Common-Pool Resources' (http://tinyco.re/0296632). *Environment: Science and Policy for Sustainable Development* 50 (4): pp. 8–21.

Ostrom, Elinor, James Walker, and Roy Gardner. 1992. 'Covenants With and Without a Sword: Self-Governance is Possible' (http://tinyco.re/3121233). *The American Political Science Review* 86 (2).

Owen, Nick A., Oliver R. Inderwildi, and David A. King. 2010. 'The Status of Conventional World Oil Reserves—Hype or Cause for Concern?' (http://tinyco.re/9394545). *Energy Policy* 38 (8) (August): pp. 4743–4749.

Pareto, Vilfredo. 2014. *Manual of political economy: a variorum translation and critical edition*. Oxford, New York, NY: Oxford University Press.

Pencavel, John. 2002. *Worker Participation: Lessons from the Worker Co-ops of the Pacific Northwest*. New York, NY: Russell Sage Foundation Publications.

Phillips, A W. 1958. 'The Relation Between Unemployment and the Rate of Change of Money Wage Rates in the United Kingdom, 1861–1957' (http://tinyco.re/5934214). *Economica* 25 (100): p. 283.

Pigou, Arthur. 1912. *Wealth and Welfare* (http://tinyco.re/2519065). London: Macmillan & Co.

Pigou, Arthur. (1920) 1932. *The Economics of Welfare* (http://tinyco.re/2042156). London: Macmillan & Co.

Piketty, Thomas. 2014. *Capital in the Twenty-First Century*. Cambridge, MA: Harvard University Press.

Plant, E. Ashby, K. Anders Ericsson, Len Hill, and Kia Asberg. 2005. 'Why study time does not predict grade point average across college students: Implications of deliberate practice for academic performance'. *Contemporary Educational Psychology* 30 (1): pp. 96–116.

Plummer, Alfred. 1971. *Bronterre: A Political Biography of Bronterre O'Brien, 1804–1864*. Toronto: University of Toronto Press.

Pomeranz, Kenneth L. 2000. *The Great Divergence: Europe, China, and the Making of the Modern World Economy*. Princeton, NJ: Princeton University Press.

Porter, Michael E., and Claas van der Linde. 1995. 'Toward a New Conception of the Environment-Competitiveness Relationship' (http://tinyco.re/9888498). *Journal of Economic Perspectives* 9 (4): pp. 97–118.

Portes, Jonathan. 2012. 'What Explains Poor Growth in the UK? The IMF Thinks It's Fiscal Policy' (http://tinyco.re/8763401). *National Institute of Economic and Social Research Blog*. Updated 9 October 2012.

Przeworski, Adam, Fernando Limongi. 1993. 'Political regimes and economic growth' (http://tinyco.re/6669217). *The Journal of Economic Perspectives* 7 (3): pp. 51–69.

Rasul, Imran, Daniel Rogger. 2016. 'Management of bureaucrats and public service delivery: Evidence from the Nigerian civil service' (http://tinyco.re/9848716). *The Economic Journal*.

Rawls, John. (1971) 2009. *A Theory of Justice*. Cambridge, MA: Belknap Press of Harvard University Press.

Raychaudhuri, Ajitava. 2004. *Lessons from the Land Reform Movement in West Bengal, India* (http://tinyco.re/0335719). Washington, DC: World Bank.

Reinhart, Carmen M., and Kenneth S. Rogoff. 2009. *This Time Is Different: Eight Centuries of Financial Folly*. Princeton, NJ: Princeton University Press.

Reyes, Jose Daniel, and Julia Oliver. 2013. 'Quinoa: The Little Cereal That Could' (http://tinyco.re/9266629). *The Trade Post*. 22 November 2013.

Ricardo, David. 1815. *An Essay on Profits*. London: John Murray.

Ricardo, David. 1817. *On The Principles of Political Economy and Taxation* (http://tinyco.re/2109109). London: John Murray.

Rifkin, Jeremy. 1996. *The End of Work: The Decline of the Global Labor Force and the Dawn of the Post-Market Era*. New York, NY: G. P. Putnam's Sons.

Robbins, Lionel. 1984. *An Essay on the Nature and Significance of Economic Science*. New York: New York University Press.

Robison, Jennifer. 2011. 'Happiness Is Love – and $75,000' (http://tinyco.re/6313076). *Gallup Business Journal*. Updated 17 November 2011.

Rodrik, Dani. 2012. *The Globalization Paradox: Democracy and the Future of the World Economy*. United States: W. W. Norton & Company.

Romer, Christina D. 1993. 'The Nation in Depression'. (http://tinyco.re/4965855). *Journal of Economic Perspectives* 7 (2) (May): pp. 19–39.

Roth, Alvin. 1996. 'Matching (Two-Sided Matching)' (http://tinyco.re/9329190). Stanford University.

Roth, Alvin E. 2007. 'Chapter 1: Repugnance as a Constraint on Markets' (http://tinyco.re/2118641). *Journal of Economic Perspectives* 21 (3): pp. 37–58.

Rustagi, Devesh, Stefanie Engel, and Michael Kosfeld. 2010. 'Conditional Cooperation and Costly Monitoring Explain Success in Forest Commons Management' (http://tinyco.re/3733299). *Science* 330: pp. 961–65.

Rysman, Marc. 2009. 'The Economics of Two-Sided Markets' (http://tinyco.re/4978467). *Journal of Economic Perspectives* 23 (3): pp. 125–43.

Sandel, Michael. 2009. *Justice*. London: Penguin.

Saxenian, AnnaLee. 1996. *Regional Advantage: Culture and Competition in Silicon Valley and Route 128*. Cambridge, MA: Harvard University Press.

Scheve, Kenneth, and David Stasavage. 2010. 'The conscription of wealth: mass warfare and the demand for progressive taxation'. *International Organization* 64 (04): pp. 529–561.

Scheve, Kenneth, and David Stasavage. 2012. 'Democracy, war, and wealth: lessons from two centuries of inheritance taxation' (http://tinyco.re/9000452). *American Political Science Review* 106 (01): pp. 81–102.

Scheve, Kenneth, and David Stasavage. 2016. *Taxing the rich: A history of fiscal fairness in the United States and Europe*. Princeton University Press.

Schmalensee, Richard, and Robert N. Stavins. 2013. 'The SO2 Allowance Trading System: The Ironic History of a Grand Policy Experiment' (http://tinyco.re/6011888). *Journal of Economic Perspectives* 27 (1): pp. 103–22.

Schor, Juliet B. 1992. *The Overworked American: The Unexpected Decline Of Leisure*. New York, NY: Basic Books.

Schumacher, Ernst F. 1973. *Small Is Beautiful: Economics as If People Mattered* (http://tinyco.re/3749799). New York, NY: HarperCollins.

Schumpeter, Joseph A. 1949. 'Science and Ideology' (http://tinyco.re/4561610). *The American Economic Review* 39 (March): pp. 345–59.

Schumpeter, Joseph A. 1962. *Capitalism, Socialism, and Democracy*. New York: Harper & Brothers.

Schumpeter, Joseph A. 1997. *Ten Great Economists*. London: Routledge.

Seabright, Paul. 2010. 'Chapter 1: Who's in Charge?'. In *The Company of Strangers: A Natural History of Economic Life* (http://tinyco.re/2891054). Princeton, NJ, United States: Princeton University Press.

Seabright, Paul. 2010. *The Company of Strangers: A Natural History of Economic Life* (Revised Edition). Princeton, NJ: Princeton University Press.

Sethi, Rajiv. 2010. 'The Astonishing Voice of Albert Hirschman' (http://tinyco.re/2899363). *Rajiv Sethi Blog*. Updated 7 April 2010.

Sethi, Rajiv. 2011. 'The Self-Subversion of Albert Hirschman' (http://tinyco.re/2163474). *Rajiv Sethi Blog*. Updated 7 April 2011.

Sethi, Rajiv. 2013. 'Albert Hirschman and the Happiness of Pursuit' (http://tinyco.re/5203731). *Rajiv Sethi Blog*. Updated 24 March 2013.

Shiller, Robert. 2009. 'Animal Spirits' (http://tinyco.re/9820978). *VoxEU.org podcast*. Updated 14 August 2009.

Shiller, Robert. 2010. 'Stimulus, Without More Debt' (http://tinyco.re/9857908). *The New York Times*. Updated 25 December 2010.

Shiller, Robert J. 2003. 'From Efficient Markets Theory to Behavioral Finance' (http://tinyco.re/3989503). *Journal of Economic Perspectives* 17 (1) (March): pp. 83–104.

Shiller, Robert J. 2015. 'The Stock Market in Historical Perspective' (http://tinyco.re/4263463). In *Irrational Exuberance*. Princeton, NJ: Princeton University Press.

Shin, Hyun Song. 2009. 'Discussion of "The Leverage Cycle" by John Geanakoplos' (http://tinyco.re/7184580). Discussion prepared for the 2009 NBER Macro Annual.

Shleifer, Andrei. 1998. 'State versus private ownership' (http://tinyco.re/4317440). *Journal of Economic Perspectives* 12 (4): pp. 133–150.

Shum, Matthew. 2004. 'Does Advertising Overcome Brand Loyalty? Evidence from the Breakfast-Cereals Market'. (http://tinyco.re/3909324). *Journal of Economics & Management Strategy* 13 (2): pp. 241–272.

Silver-Greenberg, Jessica. 2014. 'New York Prosecutors Charge Payday Loan Firms with Usury' (http://tinyco.re/8917188). DealBook.

Simon, Herbert A. 1951. 'A Formal Theory of the Employment Relationship' (http://tinyco.re/0460792). *Econometrica* 19 (3).

Simon, Herbert A. 1991. 'Organizations and Markets' (http://tinyco.re/2460377). *Journal of Economic Perspectives* 5 (2): pp. 25–44.

Singer, Natasha. 2014. 'In the Sharing Economy, Workers Find Both Freedom and Uncertainty' (http://tinyco.re/2844216). *The New York Times*. Updated 16 August 2014.

Skidelsky, Robert. 2012. 'Robert Skidelsky—portrait: Joseph Schumpeter' (http://tinyco.re/8488199). Updated 1 December 2007.

Smith, Adam. 1759. *The Theory of Moral Sentiments* (http://tinyco.re/6582039). London: Printed for A. Millar, and A. Kincaid and J. Bell.

Smith, Adam. (1776) 2003. *An Inquiry into the Nature and Causes of the Wealth of Nations* (http://tinyco.re/9804148). New York, NY: Random House Publishing Group.

Smith, Noah. 2013. 'Why the Multiplier Doesn't Matter' (http://tinyco.re/7260376). *Noahpinion*. Updated 7 January 2013.

Smith, Stephen. 2011. *Environmental Economics: A Very Short Introduction* (http://tinyco.re/9038928). Oxford: Oxford University Press.

Spaliara, Marina-Eliza. 2009. 'Do Financial Factors Affect the Capital–labour Ratio? Evidence from UK Firm-level Data'. *Journal of Banking & Finance* 33 (10) (October): pp. 1932–1947.

Statista. 2011. 'Willingness to pay for a flight in space' (http://tinyco.re/7817145). Updated 20 October 2011.

Stavins, Robert N., Gabriel Chan, Robert Stowe, and Richard Sweeney. 2012. 'The US Sulphur Dioxide Cap and Trade Programme and Lessons for Climate Policy' (http://tinyco.re/7237191). *VoxEU.org*. Updated 12 August 2012.

Sterk, Vincent. 2015. 'Home Equity, Mobility, and Macroeconomic Fluctuations' (http://tinyco.re/2186300). *Journal of Monetary Economics* 74 (September): pp. 16–32.

Stern, Nicholas. 2007. *The Economics of Climate Change: The Stern Review* (http://tinyco.re/5785938). Cambridge: Cambridge University Press.

Stigler, George J. 1987. *The Theory of Price*. New York, NY: Collier Macmillan.

Stucke, Maurice. 2013. 'Is Competition Always Good?' (http://tinyco.re/8720076). *OUPblog*. Updated 25 March 2013.

Sutcliffe, Robert B. 2001. *100 Ways of Seeing an Unequal World*. London: Zed Books.

Swarns, Rachel L. 2001. 'Drug Makers Drop South Africa Suit over AIDS Medicine' (http://tinyco.re/4752443). *New York Times*. Updated 20 April 2001.

Swedberg, Richard. 1991. *Joseph A. Schumpeter, The Economics and Sociology of Capitalism*. Princeton, NJ: Princeton University Press.

The Economist. 1999. 'The grabbing hand' (http://tinyco.re/8993136). Updated 11 February 1999.

The Economist. 2001. 'Is Santa a Deadweight Loss?' (http://tinyco.re/7728778). Updated 20 December 2001.

The Economist. 2003. 'Bush's Push' (http://tinyco.re/1194788). Updated 6 January 2003.

The Economist. 2007. 'To Do with the Price of Fish' (http://tinyco.re/6300967). Updated 10 May 2007.

The Economist. 2008. 'Economies of Scale and Scope' (http://tinyco.re/7593630). Updated 20 October 2008.

The Economist. 2009. 'A Load to Bear' (http://tinyco.re/9740912). Updated 26 November 2009.

The Economist. 2009. 'Smooth Operators' (http://tinyco.re/7009658). Updated 14 May 2009.

The Economist. 2012. 'New Cradles to Graves' (http://tinyco.re/8856321). Updated 8 September 2012.

The Economist. 2012. 'The Fear Factor' (http://tinyco.re/6787148). Updated 2 June 2012.

The Economist. 2013. 'Controlling Interest' (http://tinyco.re/7889919). Updated 21 September 2013.

The Economist. 2013. 'In Dollars They Trust' (http://tinyco.re/3392021). Updated 27 April 2013.

The Economist. 2014. 'Keynes and Hayek: Prophets for Today' (http://tinyco.re/0417474). Updated 14 March 2014.

Tirole, Jean. 2017. 'Jean Tirole – Prize Lecture: Market Failures and Public Policy' (http://tinyco.re/4684631). Nobel Media AB 2014, 11 May.

Toynbee, Polly. 2003. *Hard Work: Life in Low-pay Britain*. London: Bloomsbury Publishing.

Veblen, Thorstein. 2007. *The Theory of the Leisure Class*. Oxford: Oxford University Press.

Vickers, John. 1996. 'Market Power and Inefficiency: A Contracts Perspective'. *Oxford Review of Economic Policy* 12 (4): pp. 11–26.

Wagner, Gernot, and Martin L. Weitzman. 2015. *Climate Shock: The Economic Consequences of a Hotter Planet* (http://tinyco.re/6928664). Princeton, NJ: Princeton University Press.

Waldfogel, Joel. 1993. 'The Deadweight Loss of Christmas' (http://tinyco.re/0182759). *American Economic Review* 83 (5).

Walras, Leon. (1874) 2014. *Elements of Theoretical Economics: Or the Theory of Social Wealth*. Cambridge: Cambridge University Press.

Walton, David. 2006. 'Has Oil Lost the Capacity to Shock?' (http://tinyco.re/8182920). *Oxonomics* 1 (1): pp. 9–12.

Walzer, Michael. 1983. *Spheres of Justice: A Defense of Pluralism and Equality*. New York, NY: Basic Books.

Webb, Baumslag, and Robert Read. 2017. *How Should Regulators deal with Uncertainty? Insights from the Precautionary Principle* (http://tinyco.re/7250222). Bank Underground.

Whaples, Robert. 2001. 'Hours of work in U.S. History' (http://tinyco.re/1660378). EH.Net Encyclopedia.

Wiggins, Rosalind, Thomas Piontek, and Andrew Metrick. 2014. 'The Lehman Brothers Bankruptcy A: Overview' (http://tinyco.re/8750749). Yale Program on Financial Stability Case Study 2014-3A-V1.

Wilkins, Barbara. 1974. 'Lead Poisoning Threatens the Children of an Idaho Town' (http://tinyco.re/5420273). *People.com*.

Williamson, Oliver E. 1985. *The Economic Institutions of Capitalism*. New York, NY: Collier Macmillan.

Witt, Stephen. 2015. *How Music Got Free: The End of an Industry, the Turn of the Century, and the Patient Zero of Piracy*. New York, NY: Viking.

Wood, Elisabeth Jean. 2000. *Forging Democracy from Below: Insurgent Transitions in South Africa and El Salvador*. Cambridge: Cambridge University Press.

Wooldridge, Adrian. 2013. *Northern Lights* (http://tinyco.re/2892712). Updated 2 February 2013.

World Bank, The. 1993. *The East Asian miracle: Economic growth and public policy* (http://tinyco.re/3040506). New York, NY: Oxford University Press.

World Bank, The. 2011. 'The Changing Wealth of Nations' (http://tinyco.re/8096132).

World Bank, The. 2015. 'Commodity Price Data' (http://tinyco.re/9946436).

World Bank, The. 2015. 'World Development Indicators' (http://tinyco.re/8871968).

Wren-Lewis, Simon. 2012. 'Multiplier theory: One is the Magic Number' (http://tinyco.re/7820994). *Mainly Macro*. Updated 24 August 2014.

COPYRIGHT ACKNOWLEDGEMENTS

INDEX